EVERY VOTE EQUAL:

A State-Based Plan for Electing the President by National Popular Vote

John R. Koza
Barry F. Fadem
Mark Grueskin
Michael S. Mandell
Robert Richie
Joseph F. Zimmerman

FOREWORDS BY

John B. Anderson	Birch Bayh	John Buchanan
Tom Campbell	Gregory G. Aghazarian	Saul Anuzis
Laura Brod	James L. Brulte	B. Thomas Golisano
Joseph Griffo	Ray Haynes	Robert A. Holmes
Dean Murray	Thomas L. Pearce	Christopher Pearson
	Jake Garn	

NATIONAL POPULAR VOTE PRESS
www.NationalPopularVote.com
Fourth Edition—First Printing

First edition—First Printing (February 6, 2006)
First edition—Second Printing (February 17, 2006)
First edition—Third Printing (March 6, 2006)
First edition—Fourth Printing (March 13, 2006)
First edition—Fifth Printing (April 5, 2006)
First edition—Sixth Printing (May 8, 2006)
First edition—Seventh Printing (July 6, 2006)
First edition—Eighth Printing (December 20, 2006)
Second Edition—First Printing (December 20, 2008)
Third Edition — First Printing (January 5, 2011)
Fourth Edition — First Printing (February 15, 2013)

ISBN-13: 978-0-9790107-3-6

National Popular Vote Press
Post Office Box 1441
Los Altos, California 94023 USA
www.every-vote-equal.com
www.NationalPopularVote.com
Phone: 650-472-1587
Email: info@NationalPopularVote.com

Don Dunwell 4/13

CHAPTER-LEVEL TABLE OF CONTENTS

A detailed table of contents follows.

DETAILED TABLE OF CONTENTS

BIOGRAPHIES

GREGORY G. AGHAZARIAN served in the California State Assembly from 2002 to 2008. He was named Assembly Republican Caucus Chairman in 2006.

JOHN B. ANDERSON served in Congress as a Republican Representative from Illinois from 1961 to 1981. He was Chairman of the House Republican Conference for 10 years. In 1980, he ran for President as an Independent and won 6.6% of the national vote. He is a professor of law at Nova Southeastern University and is the Chair Emeritus of the Board of Directors of FairVote (formerly the Center for Voting and Democracy) in Washington, D.C.

SAUL ANUZIS is former Chairman of the Michigan Republican Party and a member of the Republican National Committee.

BIRCH BAYH was a member of the Indiana House of Representatives from 1955 to 1963, its Speaker from 1961 to 1962, and a United States Senator from Indiana from 1963 to 1980. He is currently a partner in the law firm of Venable LLP in Washington, D.C. Senator Bayh authored two amendments to the U.S. Constitution—the 25th Amendment on presidential and vice-presidential succession, and the 26th Amendment lowering the voting age to 18. He also sponsored and led the efforts to adopt a federal constitutional amendment on direct nationwide election of the President in the 1960s and 1970s.

LAURA BROD is an elected member of the University of Minnesota Board of Regents. She served in the Minnesota House of Representatives from 2003 to 2010 as Assistant Majority Leader and Assistant Minority Leader during her time in office. She was the ranking member of the House Tax Committee. During her time in the State Legislature, she served as a board member of the Council of State Governments, Executive Board Member of the Midwest Legislative Conference, an Aspen-Rodel Fellow, and was the Public Sector Minnesota Chair for the American Legislative Exchange Council.

JAMES L. BRULTE represented California's 31st senate district from 1996 to 2004 and served as the Senate Republican Leader from 2000 to 2004. He was previously the Republican Leader of the California State Assembly from 1992 to 1996.

JOHN BUCHANAN is an ordained Baptist minister who has served churches in Virginia, Tennessee, Alabama, and Washington, D.C. A life-long Republican, he was Alabama Republican State Finance Director and Jefferson County Chairman prior to his service for sixteen years as the first Republican to represent Birmingham in the Congress in the city's history. A legislative consultant and public interest advocate, he has served as Chairman of the Council for the Advancement of Citizenship and as National Vice Chairman of the Republican Mainstream Committee. He was Chairman of the Board of Managers of the Nexus Group.

TOM CAMPBELL earned his bachelor's and master's degrees in economics simultaneously at the University of Chicago, a law degree from Harvard University, and a Ph.D. in economics from the University of Chicago. In Washington, he served as law clerk to U.S. Supreme Court Justice Byron White, a White House Fellow in the Office of the Chief of Staff, and Executive Assistant to the U.S. Deputy Attorney General. He was a law professor at Stanford University Law School for 19 years, beginning in 1983. He was elected as a California state senator once and elected five times to represent the Silicon Valley area of California in the U.S. House of Representatives. Campbell served as Director of the California Department of Finance under Governor Arnold Schwarzenegger. He was the Bank of America Dean and Professor at the Haas School of Business at the University of California Berkeley. He is currently the Kennedy Chair in Law and Dean of the Chapman University School of Law. His book, *Separation of Powers in Practice*, published by Stanford University Press in 2004, examines the constitutionally defined roles and powers of the judicial, legislative, and executive branches of government, in the context of some of America's most contentious policy issues.

BARRY F. FADEM is a partner in the law firm of Fadem & Associates in Lafayette, California. He specializes in all aspects of campaign and election law, and provides expert consultation in the area of initiatives and referendums. He is President of National Popular Vote.

JAKE GARN served as U.S. Senator representing Utah from 1974 to 1993. Garn became the first sitting member of the United States Congress to fly in space when he flew aboard the Space Shuttle Discovery as a Payload Specialist during NASA mission STS-51-D on April 12–19, 1985.

B. THOMAS GOLISANO is an American businessman and philanthropist. He is the founder and Chairman of Paychex, the second-largest payroll processor in the United States. He is also the founder of the B. Thomas Golisano Foundation, an organization dedicated to serving those with developmental disabilities. He is Chairman of Support Popular Vote.

JOSEPH GRIFFO is a New York State Senator (Republican) representing parts of Lewis, Oneida, and St. Lawrence counties since 2007. He was Oneida County Executive from 2003 through 2006 and Mayor of Rome, New York, from 1992 through 2003.

MARK GRUESKIN is a partner in the Denver law firm of Heizer Paul Grueskin LLP. His practice focuses on public policy matters and constitutional law. *Campaigns & Elections* magazine has called him "Colorado's best election lawyer, bar none." Formerly, he served as legal counsel to Colorado Governor Richard Lamm.

RAY HAYNES was first elected to the California State Assembly in 1992. He served in the California State Senate from 1994 to 2002, including as Senate Republican Whip. In 2000, he served as National Chairman of the American Legislative Exchange Council (ALEC). Haynes was again elected to the Assembly in 2002. He is a graduate of the University of Southern California Law School.

ROBERT A. "BOB" HOLMES, PH.D. (Columbia University) is Emeritus Distinguished Professor of Political Science (Atlanta University), former Director of the Southern Center for Studies in Public Policy, and a retired Democratic State Representative (after 34 years of service) in the Georgia General Assembly. He has served as Co-Chair of the Georgia Commission to Revise the State Election Code, an expert witness on voting rights and reapportionment and redistricting cases in several southern region federal district court cases for the ACLU Voting Rights Project and the Southern Poverty Law Center, and an international election observer on election teams in Africa. Dr. Holmes is the author or editor of more than 25 books and more than 60 book chapters and journal articles. His most recent publication is *Maynard Jackson: A Biography*.

DR. JOHN R. KOZA, originator of the plan described in this book, received his Ph.D. in computer science from the University of Michigan in 1972. He published a board game involving Electoral College strategy in 1966. From 1973 through 1987, he was co-founder, chairman, and CEO of Scientific Games, Inc., where he co-invented the rub-off instant lottery ticket used by state lotteries. In the 1980s, he and attorney Barry Fadem (see above) were active in promoting the adoption of lotteries by various states through the citizen-initiative process and legislative action. He taught a course on genetic algorithms and genetic programming between 1988 and 2003 at Stanford University, where he has been consulting professor in the Department of Computer Science, Department of Electrical Engineering, and Department of Medicine. He is Chair of National Popular Vote.

MICHAEL S. MANDELL was an associate with the law firm of Perkins Coie Brown & Bain in Phoenix and the general counsel to the Arizona State Senate. Currently he is Vice President and General Counsel at Husk Partners and Chairman of the Board of Directors at Bank 1440. He received his J.D. with honors from Arizona State University, where he was an editor of the *Arizona State Law Journal*.

DEAN MURRAY (Republican, Conservative Party) is a member of the New York State Assembly for the third district. He was a Tea Party organizer before being elected to the Assembly in February 2010. He was described by Fox News as the first Tea Party candidate elected to office in the United States.

THOMAS L. PEARCE served as a Republican Michigan state Representative from 2005–2010. During his time in the Michigan House, he was appointed Dean of the Republican Caucus. He has led several faith-based initiatives in Lansing. Prior to serving in the House, he was the executive director of the North Kent Service Center and served as director of development at Mel Trotter Ministries.

CHRISTOPHER PEARSON is a state Representative from Burlington, Vermont. He was first appointed to the House of Representatives in 2006. He was elected to the House in 2006 and 2010. Prior to serving in the statehouse, he was the director of the Presidential Election Reform program at FairVote. He began working in politics as a campaign and Congressional aide for then-Congressman Bernard Sanders (I-VT).

ROBERT RICHIE has, since its founding in 1992, been the executive director of FairVote (formerly the Center for Voting and Democracy), a nonprofit organization dedicated to advancing fair elections. His political writings have appeared in many newspapers and in eight books, including the feature essay in *Whose Votes Count*. He has been a guest on C-SPAN, NBC News, National Public Radio, CNN, FOX, and MSNBC. Richie has addressed numerous events, including the annual conventions of the National Association of Counties, and National Conference of State Legislatures, and has drafted several pieces of federal and state legislation.

JOSEPH F. ZIMMERMAN is a Professor of Political Science at the State University of New York at Albany. He has authored *Interstate Cooperation: Compacts and Administrative Agreements* (2012), *Interstate Relations: The Neglected Dimension of Federalism* (1996), *Contemporary American Federalism: The Growth of National Power* (1992), *The Initiative: Citizen Law-Making* (1997), *The Referendum: The People Decide Public Policy* (1997), *The Recall: Tribunal of the People* (1997), *Interstate Economic Relations* (2004), *Interstate Disputes: The Supreme Court's Original Jurisdiction* (2006), *Horizontal Federalism: Interstate Relations* (2011), and *Interstate Water Compacts: Intergovernmental Efforts to Manage America's Water Resources* (2012).

ACKNOWLEDGMENTS

The authors are especially grateful to Paul F. Eckstein of Perkins Coie Brown & Bain in Phoenix for his invaluable advice in the early stages of formulation of their proposal.

Vermont State Representative Chris Pearson made numerous valuable contributions to this book, including researching items.

David Johnstone did legal research for this book and was extremely helpful in this edition and previous editions.

The authors appreciate legal comments from

- Catherine Carroll,
- Edward DuMont,
- Kevin O. Faley,
- Tom Goldstein,
- Martin S. Lederman,
- Spencer Overton,
- Jamin Raskin,
- Leonard Shambon,
- Sonja Starr,
- Laurence H. Tribe, and
- Eugene Volokh.

In addition, the authors gratefully acknowledge the following people who were helpful in preparation of this book:

- Richard Winger, editor of *Ballot Access News*,
- David Andre,
- Christie Carter at the Vermont State Archives,
- Susan Cumberpatch,
- Scott Drexel,
- Neil Erikson at the Nebraska Secretary of State's office,
- Susan Evoy,
- Deb Fadem,
- Kate Gottfredson,
- Mollie Hailey,
- Terri Hudoba,
- Adam Johnson,
- Natalie Marie Koss,

- Alex Michael,
- Bob Michaud, Reference Librarian, Maine State Law and Legislative Reference Library,
- John Mountjoy, Director, National Center for Interstate Compacts at The Council of State Governments,
- William Mydlowec,
- Elisabeth Higgins Null,
- Ryan O'Donnell,
- Pat Rosenstiel,
- Timothy Sahd of the *Cook Political Report* in Washington, D.C.,
- Ernie Sowada and Amy Bunk of the Office of the Federal Register at the National Archives and Records Administration,
- Matthew J. Streeter,
- Neal Suidan,
- Barbara Wardenburg of the League of Women Voters of Mountain View, California, and
- Natalie Young-Lee.

Typesetting for this book was done by BookMatters of Berkeley, California, under the direction of David Peattie.

Yale University Press is gratefully acknowledged for permission to use figure 2.13 from *The People's President: The Electoral College in American History and Direct-Vote Alternative* by Neal R. Peirce and as the copyright owner of that figure.

The Herb Block Foundation is gratefully acknowledged for permission to use the copyrighted Herb Block cartoons shown in figure 1.1 and figure 1.7.

Professor Brendan Doherty of the United States Naval Academy is gratefully acknowledged for permission to include data on presidential travel found in table 1.20.

David Leip's *Atlas of U.S. Presidential Elections* was the source for appendices CC, DD, and EE.

Professor J. Richard Gott III is gratefully acknowledged for permission to use his topologically accurate proportional electoral map in figure 1.6.

FOREWORD

By John B. Anderson

I believe the occupant of the nation's highest office should be determined by a nation-wide popular vote by legally registered voters.

The current system of allocating electoral votes on a statewide winner-take-all basis divides us on regional lines, undercuts accountability, dampens voter participation, and can trump the national popular vote. The system is not based on majority rule, and it fails to provide political equality.

The anti-democratic nature of the Electoral College is deeply grounded in our history. The Framers distrusted democracy and saw the Electoral College as a deliberative body that would pick the best candidate. However, the lofty view of the Founding Fathers was based on a wildly mistaken understanding of the way our political system would evolve.

Many believe that the Electoral College was included in the Constitution to satisfy the last-ditch efforts of the "states' righters" of 1787 to preserve as much of the Articles of Confederation as possible. This group was intent on denying direct popular election of the President and preserving the power of the states. Just as they had succeeded in establishing a provision allowing state legislatures to elect the members of the U.S. Senate, they wanted the primary power to elect a President to be lodged in the states—not in a mass electorate of individual voters.

The initial impact was to give slave states additional weight. The infamous constitutional provision counting slaves as three-fifths of a person for the purpose of apportioning Representatives in Congress (and apportioning electoral votes) was designed to favor Southern states. Slaves could not vote, but they could give their owners extra power in both congressional and presidential elections. It is no accident that slave-owning Virginians served as President for 32 of the nation's first 36 years.

The rule for apportioning electoral votes according to the number of each state's members of Congress is anti-democratic because it makes electoral power in the presidential race dependent on the population of a state, rather than on its number of voters. For this reason, there is no national incentive to spur turnout in a state and expand the franchise.

Majority rule and political equality are fundamental tenets of democracy. The power of one's vote should be equal, no matter where one lives. Candidates for our most important national office should have incentives to speak to everyone. In the past century, we have amended the Constitution to elect Senators directly, to guarantee women's right to vote, and to lower the voting age to 18. We have passed the Voting

Rights Act to provide access to the ballot regardless of race or ethnicity. The Electoral College has escaped the move to greater democracy only because of institutional inertia and misguided, parochial considerations.

A large majority of Americans have consistently supported direct election of the President for many years, and it is time to listen to them. This book describes the "Agreement Among the States to Elect the President by National Popular Vote," an innovative approach that is a politically practical way to achieve the goal of nationwide popular election of the President. It has my enthusiastic support.

FOREWORD

By Birch Bayh

On January 10, 1977, I introduced Senate Joint Resolution 1 entitled "a proposed Amendment to the Constitution to abolish the Electoral College and provide for direct election of the President and Vice President of the United States." As Chairman of the Senate Subcommittee on Constitutional Amendments, I held five days of hearings on this and related proposals that year, receiving testimony from 38 witnesses and hundreds of pages of additional statements and academic studies. This series of hearings was not the first time the Subcommittee on Constitutional Amendments undertook a review of the workings and implications of the Electoral College. In fact, my Subcommittee held its first hearing on the process of electing the President on February 28, 1966, and had amassed a record on the need for electoral reform of nearly 2,600 pages prior to the 1977 hearings.

At the end of this process, I was even more firmly convinced that the Electoral College had outlived whatever positive role it once played as a choice of convenience and compromise. The President and Vice President should be chosen by the same method every other elective office in this country is filled—by citizen voters of the United States in a system that counts each vote equally. In 1979 we came close to getting S.J. Res. 1 through the Senate but in the end we could not get enough votes to end the filibuster blocking the Resolution. Our effort, like many before it, was relegated to the Congressional history books.

Unfortunately, Congress has continued to block this basic reform that has long-standing, overwhelming public support. Gallup polls have shown strong public support for nationwide popular election of the President for over five decades.[1] Numerous other polls have confirmed a high level of public support for this reform. Polls consistently show 60–80% of Americans believe they should be able to cast votes in the direct election of the President. That is why I unequivocally support this new strategy to provide for the direct election of the President and Vice President. This new approach is consistent with the Constitution but does not rely on the arduous process of a Constitutional Amendment.

Today, more than ever, the Electoral College system is a disservice to the voters. With the number of battleground states steadily shrinking, we see candidates and their campaigns focused on fewer and fewer states. While running for the nation's

---

[1] Gallup News Service. 2000. Americans have historically favored changing the way Presidents are elected: Historical polling data show a majority favored abolishing the Electoral College system more than 50 years ago. November 10, 2000.

highest office, candidates in 2004 completely ignored three-quarters of the states, including California, Texas, and New York, our three most populous states. Why should our national leaders be elected by only reaching out to one-fourth of our states? It seems inherently illogical, and it is.

Opponents of direct election often point to the wisdom of the Founding Fathers in drafting the Constitution. No question, the Founders had incredible wisdom and foresight, but they were dealing with a much different society and the Electoral College was designed for the realities of the 18th century. The landmass of the country was huge; travel and communication were arduous and primitive; and education was limited at best. Lack of information about possible presidential candidates among the general public was a very real consideration. Also, there were issues involving slavery. At the time, 90% of the slave population lived in the South. Since the slaves could not vote, without the weighted vote of the Electoral College, the South faced electoral domination from Northern states. While not the first choice of any Founder, the Electoral College system solved these tricky considerations with a compromise that allowed them to complete the monumental task of creating our country's Constitution.

However, it soon became apparent that the Electoral College process devised by the Founders was flawed. In 1804, the initial Electoral College system was changed through the adoption of the 12th Amendment. Additional weaknesses became apparent. In the 1800s, there were three instances when the popular vote winner lost the Presidency. In 1824, John Quincy Adams was a minority vote winner over Andrew Jackson, as were Rutherford B. Hayes over Samuel J. Tilden (1876), and Benjamin Harrison over Grover Cleveland (1888). This anomaly is not that rare in the Electoral College system. In fact, a small shift of votes in one or two states would have thrown the election to the second-place vote winner five additional times in the last 60 years.

For example, in 1976, Jimmy Carter won a nationwide popular vote victory by 1.7 million votes. However, a change of only 25,579 votes in the states of Ohio and Mississippi would have reelected President Gerald Ford in the Electoral College. With a switch of 18,488 votes in the states of Ohio and Hawaii, the Electoral College normally would have produced a Ford victory. However, because a renegade elector from Washington state cast his vote for non-candidate Ronald Reagan, the final electoral vote count would have been Carter–268, Ford–269, and Reagan–1. Under this scenario, with no candidate receiving the necessary 270 electoral votes, the President would have been chosen by the House of Representatives.

In recent history, we all remember the 2000 election, which awarded the Presidency to the candidate who came in second in the popular vote. In 2004, President Bush defeated Senator Kerry by more than 3 million votes nationwide. However, it is easy to overlook that a change of fewer than 60,000 votes would have put Ohio in the Kerry column under the Electoral College system and would have elected him President.

In the final analysis, the most compelling reason for directly electing our President and Vice President is one of principle. In the United States, every vote must count equally. One person, one vote is more than a clever phrase, it's the cornerstone of justice and equality. We can and must see that our electoral system awards victory to the candidates chosen by the most voters. In this day and age of computers, television, rapidly available news, and a nationwide public school system, we don't need nameless electors to cast our votes for president. The voters should cast them directly themselves. Direct election is the only system that counts every vote equally and where the voters cast their ballots directly for the candidates of their choice. It has the additional virtue of operating in the way most Americans think the electoral process operates—and is expected to operate.

It is heartening to see the *Every Vote Equal* strategy described in this book that will correct the flawed system we maintain for electing our top two leaders. Our federation of states must band together to solve this long-standing, vexatious problem. Since Congress has repeatedly refused to act, it's refreshing to know states have the ability under the Constitution to step up and create the sensible solution Americans have long been supporting. I hope you will join me in supporting this important effort.

The election of President of the United States should not be a contest between red states and blue states. The President should be chosen by a majority of our citizens, wherever they may live. Direct popular election would substitute clarity for confusion, decisiveness for danger, and popular choice for political chance.

FOREWORD
By John Buchanan

The founder of my party, Abraham Lincoln, described the American political system as "Government of the people, by the people, for the people." Yet in the first presidential election of the 21st century, once again the presidential candidate who won the popular vote lost the election, and the will of the people who cared enough to be present and voting was frustrated rather than fulfilled. In the next election the then incumbent President won the popular vote, but a change in the electoral vote of a single state could have cost him the election.

Denying the American people the right to determine by their votes who the President and Vice President shall be is a flaw in our system, and one that needs fixing. It is time for "the world's greatest democracy" to in fact become one at the highest level of elective office, as is already the case at all other levels.

As a member of Congress I voted in support of the direct election of the president and nearly saw the system change during my tenure. At the time it was a controversial idea, but not overburdened by the partisan bickering so much as regional concerns. Many of my colleagues in Southern states, for example, believed the Electoral College system, as it stood, benefited their state.

Today, any discussions, although there have been too few, seem to give rise to partisan concerns. Yet this is not, nor should it be, either a regional or a partisan matter. We should rather be guided by patriotism and principle to do what is right for our country and for the American people as a whole. When we look at the method by which we elect the president, we should have a system that is fair, guarantees votes are counted equally, puts residents of each state on an equal footing, and promotes vote-seeking across the nation.

Today, the Electoral College system means that campaigns are focused on dangerously few states. In 2004, over two-thirds of the country was completely neglected during the one nationwide political contest. Candidates spend more and more money to reach fewer and fewer voters. In the close states that do get attention, under the winner-take-all system of allotting electoral votes practiced by most states, all who end up on the losing end of even a 50.1% to 49.9% statewide vote are denied the right for their votes to count toward the election of the candidate of their choice at the national level in a national election. Hence, too many people in too many places have no meaningful role in the election process.

In 1969, I was one of 337 members of the U.S. House of Representatives who passed an amendment for direct election of the president. We had overwhelming support and outside help from the U.S. Chamber of Commerce, the American Bar Association, and others who agreed this was a needed change to our system. Unfortunately the effort went down in the Senate. Yet from that time to the present, a large majority of the American people has continued to support the direct election of the president.

Since 1969 Congress has not taken meaningful action to address this issue. While doing away with the Electoral College would be my preference, that requires a Constitutional amendment. Yet the states themselves have the power to achieve the result of the popular election of the President and Vice President without such an amendment. The time has come for them to act.

The strength of our country and its democracy lies in the public. The people have supported the direct election of the president for over 50 years. In this book, Dr. Koza suggests a way for states to come together and make it happen. If every vote counts equally, if every voter has an equal say in the election of the president and can cast a meaningful vote, then we can better address issues of confidence in our political system, and in fact fully become a true democracy.

I strongly support and applaud any good-faith effort to make the direct election of the president a reality and commend to you the intriguing approach offered in the "Agreement Among the States to Elect the President by National Popular Vote" described in this book.

I want your vote and my vote to count in the most important elections of all. It can happen. It should happen. If enough of us care enough, it will be done.

FOREWORD
By Tom Campbell

California has 35,893,799 residents. Wyoming has 506,520 residents. California casts 55 electoral votes for President. Wyoming casts 3. The result: A Wyoming voter is worth four times a California voter in selecting America's President. If a Third World country, coming into democratic principles out of tyranny, announced a scheme with some citizens worth four times as much as others in their governance, it would be told to try again. Indeed, America would tell it to try again!

No Californian should accept the present way we elect Presidents. No American should accept it.

The ingenious approach put forward in this book provides, for the first time, a solution that is achievable. It does not rely on unrealistic assumptions. It can be implemented, if the very people who are relatively disenfranchised in our country will only be awakened to how to do it.

FOREWORD

By Gregory G. Aghazarian

Every four years a presidential election takes place. Our votes are cast. Our votes are counted. But, do they count?

The truth of the matter is that we, the people, do not directly elect the President. The Electoral College elects the President. Every four years, each state appoints electors who in turn elect a president. Under the U.S. Constitution, each state legislature has the complete and total power as to how it appoints its electors (Article II, section 1, clause 2). The current practice in 48 states is to appoint electors, winner-take-all, based on the outcome of each state's popular vote. This sounds simple enough, but the problem is that the current practice ensures that a large majority of Americans have no say in choosing their chief executive.

Most states are solidly "red" or "blue." This means that no matter how much money or time a presidential candidate spends in states like Texas and Wyoming or New York and Vermont, the result is a foregone conclusion. Consequently, no money or time is spent in these states. Instead, virtually everything goes into a small group of "battleground" states. In 2008, two-thirds of the collective presidential campaigns' time and money was dedicated to just 6 states, with 98% going to only 15 states. Over two-thirds of us just had to sit back and watch.

The real problem with the current winner-take-all practice is that it encourages the wholesale dismissal of the hopes, dreams and aspirations of over 200 million Americans. Issues that are vital to states like Montana and California are routinely disregarded. Under the current system, they do not matter. Issues that are vital to states like Ohio and Pennsylvania are overemphasized. Under the current system, they do matter. It is difficult to imagine that the Founding Fathers intended the disenfranchisement of so many states and the empowerment of so few in their quest to form a more perfect union.

There is a better way. *Every Vote Equal* eloquently lays out the blueprint for a truly democratic and efficient way to elect the President of the United States. Through detailed historic, legal and statistical analysis, this book sets forth a comprehensive and compelling case for each state, pursuant to its constitutional powers, to appoint its electors based on the outcome of the national popular vote. The winner of the election would be the candidate who gets the most popular votes in all 50 states plus the District of Columbia. Every state would matter, because every vote would matter. No longer would the issues of a small handful of states dominate presidential elections. Candidates for President would need to be in tune and in touch with all Americans regardless of their address.

The time has come for a national popular vote system.

FOREWORD
By Saul Anuzis

As former chairman of the Michigan Republican Party, I am asking you to consider a bipartisan, truly representative, and more fair process to elect the President of the United States. Our President.

It is the National Popular Vote bill, which would guarantee the presidency to the candidate who receives the most popular votes in all 50 states, and I support it.

This bill has passed multiple chambers around the country in a bipartisan manner. As someone who has run twice for Chairman of the Republican National Committee and is an active "movement conservative," I'm oftentimes challenged about the fact that I'm supporting something that's not blatantly partisan.

Good public policy is good politics, and sometimes good public policy can be bipartisan.

The National Popular Vote plan does not abolish the Electoral College. Instead, it uses the state's existing authority to change how the Electoral College is chosen. The change would be from the current state-by-state approach to a national popular vote approach that would guarantee the presidency to the candidate who receives the most popular votes in all 50 states and the District of Columbia.

The shortcomings of the current system stem from the winner-take-all rule (that is, awarding all of a state's electoral votes to the candidate who receives the most popular votes in each state).

Because of the winner-take-all rule, a candidate can win the presidency without winning the most popular votes nationwide. This has occurred in four of the nation's 56 presidential elections. As an example, a shift of fewer than 60,000 votes in Ohio in 2004 would have defeated President Bush despite his nationwide lead of over 3 million votes.

This is a state-rights issue and we, the people, have the right to decide how and who is elected president.

The U.S. Constitution gives the states exclusive and plenary control over the manner of awarding their electoral votes. The winner-take-all rule is not in the Constitution. It was not the Founders' choice and was used by only three states in the nation's first presidential election in 1789. Maine and Nebraska award electoral votes by congressional district—a reminder that an amendment to the Constitution is not required to change the way the president is elected.

Under the National Popular Vote bill, all the electoral votes from the enacting states would be awarded to the presidential candidate who receives the most popular votes in all 50 states. The bill would take effect only when enacted by states possessing a majority of the electoral votes—that is, enough electoral votes to elect a president (270 of 538). As of the end of 2012, the National Popular Vote Bill has been passed by 31 legislative chambers in 21 states. The most recent poll of Michigan voters found that 73% of our citizens support this concept. A 2007 national poll showed 72% supported it.

The National Popular Vote bill has passed in states having almost half of the electoral votes necessary to bring this into effect. This proposal would guarantee that every vote matters, that every state is relevant. Every community would have the same value to every candidate for president in every election.

This is a serious proposal that deserves serious consideration and debate. The "knee-jerk" reaction against this bill and the ease with which some can "demonize" this issue without serious study or consideration is frustrating. I encourage everyone who cares about our country to read about the "myths," study and understand the intent of our Founding Fathers, and then make a decision as to whether or not this proposal deserves your support.

FOREWORD

By Laura Brod

Like many conservatives, I view most "election reforms" through a skeptical eye. I share a reverence for the Constitution and our founding documents. I believe that the Founders not only got it right, but that they were visionary and creative in their approach.

In all truthfulness, when I first saw the National Popular Vote Plan, I defaulted to a "No" position on the concept. But I was curious enough to read the legislation, re-read the Constitution, and re-read some relevant Federalist Papers. After evaluating the pros and cons of the current winner-take-all approach and coming to a better understanding of the states' exclusive right to award electors, I moved toward a position of support of both the concept and the legislation.

The concept has too often been referred to by opponents as a "partisan" or even "liberal" effort to eliminate the Electoral College in an attempt to tarnish the issue and scare away those of us on the right side of the political spectrum. But this description could not be further from the truth.

The National Popular Vote bill is not a Democratic bill or Republican bill. It is not even a liberal or conservative bill. The National Popular Vote bill is a bill for Americans interested in both preserving our Electoral College and reforming the shortcomings of our current state-by-state "winner-take-all" system that awards all the electors of one state to the candidate who wins in that particular state. In particular, the "winner-take-all" system has led to a concentration of campaign efforts and policy attention in a few states at the expense of many states. The idea that presidential candidates and campaigns should seek votes from a broad swath of our country—rather than only focusing on what might move a few voters in the few battleground states—is actually quite nonpartisan and has appeal across the political spectrum.

The National Popular Vote plan rightfully utilizes the states' rights, as explicitly spelled out in Section 1, Article II of the United States Constitution. The Founders specifically gave authority to the states to award their electoral votes as they see fit and to achieve the best influence of the citizens of their state. This is an important states' right designed by the Founders as one of the checks and balances within our republican form of government. It is this state power that the National Popular Vote Plan recognizes and this is a right that I support.

The National Popular Vote legislation is not the legislation of the past that many remember. This proposal does *not* abolish the Electoral College that is crucial to the stability of our republic. It preserves the Electoral College while at the same time preserving each state's power to award its electors.

The National Popular Vote compact is an agreement among states that changes how the states award their own electoral votes.

I am one of a growing number of conservatives who support the National Popular Vote legislation because, contrary to what some folks suggest in rhetorical opposition, the many conservative supporters of the idea know that the National Popular Vote plan is not in conflict with the Constitution and is certainly not an end run around the Constitution. In actuality, the legislation is an exercise of power by the states that is explicitly granted by the Constitution.

Legislators across this great country—in red states and blue states, large states and small states—are supporting the National Popular Vote Plan because they are bound by one thing: the fact that their states are "fly-over" states. The great majority of states are effectively ignored in presidential elections. Legislators know this is not good for their state, their citizens, or their entire slate of candidates down the ballot. In fact, that is not good for our country generally. Policies important to the citizens of "flyover" states are not as highly prioritized as policies important to "battleground" states when it comes to governing.

Right now, battleground states enjoy political influence that is less related to the number of their electoral votes and more related to the closeness of the elections. In order to win electoral votes, candidates care what voters in the few battleground states think and want far more than they do voters in the many fly-over states. The hunt for electoral votes leads to an elevation of the importance and perceived immediacy of political and policy issues connected to battleground states. Meanwhile, policy issues more broadly appealing to citizens throughout the country get set aside. Why should the status of the economy or a volatile local issue in a battleground state have the potential to determine the presidency for the entire country? Why should issues important to the few battleground states get addressed, while other issues important to the many fly-over states are ignored?

Reforming our state-based system of elections through an agreement of the states for a National Popular Vote keeps the stability of our republican form of government by preserving our Electoral College, keeps the checks and balances in place to ensure the protection against so-called mob rule, ensures that voters in every state matter in every election, and keeps the states' rights intended by the Founders securely intact.

The National Popular vote plan being discussed by legislatures across the country does exactly that.

FOREWORD

By James L. Brulte

California voters recently joined other states in stripping the state legislature of its power to draw legislative and congressional districts and allowing a citizen's commission to redraw these lines. Voters did this in part because they knew that with politicians creating safe legislative seats, competition would be diminished, and as a result politicians of both major parties could ignore their communities with impunity. Unfortunately, our nation's Electoral College provides on the national level what many citizens are trying to eliminate on our state level.

Most states in the union are not in play in presidential elections. California, for example, has not voted for a Republican nominee for President since George H. W. Bush carried the state in 1988. Texas has been reliably Republican since 1980. In fact only 16 states have been considered swing states in recent presidential elections, while the remainder are relegated to spectator status.

While this might be fine for the partisans who actually run presidential elections (shrinking the number of states in which their candidates need to compete), it is not good for the citizens of most of the states in the nation.

For example, in 2008, after both parties chose their presidential candidates, all 300 of the campaign events with major-party nominees took place in just 19 states. And from September 24, two days before the first general election debate until election day, 99.74% of all advertising took place in just 18 states.

While this might be great for the states involved, the rest of the nation suffers as candidates of both major political parties ignore them during the general election. Why is this a problem? Because during the course of campaigns, political candidates are educated about local, regional, and state issues and they take this knowledge with them once they are elected. And with a nation as large and diverse as ours, it is critical that presidential candidates be educated about all our states, not just the lucky 16 swing states.

Fortunately, our Founding Fathers anticipated the dynamic nature of our country and provided for each state to choose how its presidential electors are chosen. The National Popular Vote provides the necessary incentives to encourage presidential candidates of both major parties to campaign in every state in the union. This is better than the current approach for electing the President. It is better for the candidates, it is better for the citizens of the individual states, and it is better for the nation as a whole.

FOREWORD

By B. Thomas Golisano

Seventy-five percent of voters polled in the United States think the way we elect our President should be changed.

Under our current system, a candidate can win the White House without receiving the most votes nationwide. This has actually happened a number of times in our history, and it is likely to happen again.

The current system awards all the state's electoral votes to the candidate who gets the most votes in that particular state. This is called the "winner-take-all" rule. By the way, this method of awarding electoral votes is not a part of the U.S. Constitution. It is strictly a matter of state laws that were adopted on a piecemeal, state-by-state basis.

Unfortunately the winner-take-all rule creates a problem where the candidate with the most votes can actually lose the election. Would you call that democratic?

We can easily change to a system where the candidate with the most votes always wins.

In fact, the process is already under way. Once states representing a majority of electoral votes approve, the process will change, and the President will be elected by the national popular vote.

In fact, nine states have already approved this legislation, called the National Popular Vote bill. We are already at a half of the votes needed to approve the bill. In 2010, the New York State Senate voted 52 to 7 to go to the National Popular Vote. Republicans supported the change 22 to 5, Democrats 30 to 2. Talk about nonpartisanship.

There are some other very important reasons for this bill to be passed.

Have you noticed how the media categorizes our states into two groups: Battleground and fly-over states? A battleground state is a state where the vote for candidates is undecided. The state could go either way. A fly-over state is a state where the outcome is a foregone conclusion for one candidate or the other.

Unless you live in one of the few battleground states, your particular vote doesn't matter. The presidential candidates don't need to consider your issues as they "fly over" your state on the way to the few states that swing presidential elections.

In 2008, candidates concentrated 98% of their ad money and visits in just 15 states.

In summary we have the option to guarantee that the choice of the American people wins the election. Every American's vote should count. Candidates will pay attention to the needs and concerns of all 50 states, not just a few battleground states. And we can do this while preserving the states' power over how we pick our President.

The President we choose represents this entire nation. We should all count when making that choice. This is the world's greatest democracy. Our presidential election should truly be democratic. Please join me and 75% of Americans in supporting the National Popular Vote bill because it's the right thing to do.

FOREWORD
By Joseph Griffo

Presidential elections should be a time when the entire nation is galvanized into action through a vibrant democracy because every citizen has a voice in setting the nation's direction for the next four years.

Sadly, that is not the reality. By October, 12 to 15 swing states are all that matters in presidential campaigns. Much of the nation is shunted into red or blue piles. We in New York know how it feels to be treated as if we were politically irrelevant: my entire state and its voters are ignored by one party and taken for granted by the other. That's not the democracy I want to leave as my legacy to the future. I want to help create a vibrant new democracy that sparks activism instead of abetting apathy.

The National Popular Vote bill detailed in *Every Vote Equal* will ensure that the voice of the people is heard at every level of government. Isn't that what common sense tells us should happen in the first place?

The current system does not serve the people. According to research by National Popular Vote, presidential candidates concentrate over two-thirds of their advertising money and campaign visits in just six very close states, and over 98% of their advertising money in just 15 battleground states. Something is wrong with this picture.

Elections are the cornerstone of our democracy. There is nothing more important in the American system of government than elections that attract voters to examine the challenges of our time. And elections must deal with all the people and all the issues, not just those important to a small handful of states.

The current system of electing a President effectively disenfranchises millions of Americans because they live in states where one candidate or the other has a safe majority. At a time when America needs its citizens to be involved in government, we need to ensure that every vote counts and that the popular vote is the true measure of victory.

For these reasons and more I am proud to be the lead sponsor of the National Popular Vote bill in the New York Senate. We passed the bill in 2010 by a vote of 52–7, but the Assembly didn't get the bill through in 2010. I will continue to push this legislation until New York is on board with the effort. The American people support the principle of a popular vote for President, and I believe New York and the country will be well served once we make this reform a reality.

FOREWORD

By Ray Haynes

Elected officials know how to get elected to office. They know how to raise the necessary resources to get their message out to the voters. They know where to find the people who will work on their campaigns. They know what messages to communicate to voters, and how to communicate those messages. They know the rules that determine what they must do to get elected. The "science" of getting elected requires those who pursue public office to know the rules of elections, discover how voters vote, where their likely voters are located, what messages will persuade these voters to vote, and how best to communicate those messages to voters. It requires them to know where to find the money to communicate those messages, where to find the people who will help communicate those messages, and where those messages can be most effectively communicated to maximize the chances of getting elected.

The art of politics is marshaling the resources available, and using the knowledge obtained, and the rules of the election, to maximize the opportunity for getting elected. Elected officials, and those who help them get elected, spend a lot of time and effort attempting to get elected. They have limited resources (reports to the contrary notwithstanding). Therefore, no one can expect them to spend time or money in places where the expenditure of financial, public relations, or operational resources will not affect the outcome of an election. They work within the rules provided to communicate with the voters whose votes will make a difference in the election in the most effective way.

In most elections, a candidate runs in one district, or state, and if he or she gets the most votes in that district or state, he or she wins. People understand that process. Since the United States Constitution awards presidential electors on the basis of the congressional representation in each state, and since most states award their electors to the winner of the popular vote in that state, presidential candidates end up running 50 separate elections in the 50 different states. The goal? Win enough states to get 270 electoral votes for president. In my opinion, our Founding Fathers could have set up any number of ways to choose the president. They chose this one, and I see no reason to change it. The Electoral College (and its allocation of presidential electors to the states based on the number of its congressional representatives) has worked quite well for over 200 years.

These rules, however, have led to elections that a lot of people don't understand. Why do candidates spend a lot of time in Ohio, Florida, New Mexico, Wisconsin, Missouri, Pennsylvania, or a few other states, and virtually no time in most of the other states? Why are the citizens of some states virtually pummeled with political advertisements, while others are literally ignored? The reason is, of course, the rules of the game. A candidate can spend millions in California and New York, and not change the electoral outcome, and thousands in New Mexico and become President. We cannot expect our presidential candidates to do things that will not change the outcome of an election, and quite frankly, spending money in some states will not change a single electoral vote.

The good news is our Constitution grants the states the right to award those electors on any basis the state chooses. While the rules each state has adopted up to this point have skewed the allocation of political resources up to this time, there is no reason that the states cannot change those rules, without changing the Constitution, in order to encourage presidential candidates to run a more national campaign. I believe we should be circumspect in changing the Constitution. Elected officials and voters in the various states should not, however, be afraid of changing the rules of elections in ways the Constitution allows, in order to correct perceived problems in the electoral process.

The National Popular Vote proposal does just that. The proposal does not change the Constitution, or the method of awarding electors to the various states. If it did, I personally would have found it problematic. It respects the Electoral-College system as established in the Constitution, and the role of the various states in the awarding of their presidential electors. It preserves the fundamental framework provided by the United States Constitution in the election of the President.

It also changes the rules by which the states award their electors, by going to each of those states, and convincing the elected officials and the voters in those states, to award their electors to the candidate that wins the popular vote in all 50 states. It changes the rules by which the electors are awarded to the candidates, and therefore, it will change the decisions a candidate makes when trying to allocate resources in that candidate's campaign.

How will the National Popular Vote proposal affect a candidate's decisions?

First, it will require the candidate to campaign in more places, and in more states. No longer will 10, 12, or 15 states determine the outcome of a presidential campaign. Candidates will allocate their resources to change the minds of voters in more places, because now the votes of each voter in each state could change the outcome in the national election. Today, presidential candidates spend millions to pick up a thousand votes in Florida, Pennsylvania, or Ohio. Under National Popular Vote, that money may get spent to change the minds of voters in Washington State, or Georgia, or Texas, or New York, because those votes will now affect the awarding of electoral votes. Since the states will now agree to award their electors to the candidate that receives the most votes in all 50 states, candidates will devote their resources to receiving the most votes nationwide, and not just the most votes in Missouri or Wisconsin.

Second, it will add more legitimacy to the outcome of the presidential election. People still don't really understand how someone can win an election without winning the most votes. No other election in the country works that way. Governors, Senators, and state legislators throughout the country win office by winning the most votes. People understand that, and do not question that outcome. The National Popular Vote proposal coincides with the beliefs of most voters on how elections should be decided.

Finally, it preserves the Electoral-College system, and the flexibility that comes with a true federalist proposal. Our federal system has set up a workable framework for elections and governance, granting the states a substantial amount of power to organize their elections and their internal rules in the ways that make sense to the various states. The National Popular Vote proposal respects that process. It sets up a system that makes sense, but allows for changes from the states if the states find that the changes the proposal has implemented are not working. It avoids the inflexibility that a constitutional amendment would impose, and protects the rights and powers of the individual states. It is the blending of common sense and constitutional flexibility that I believe our Founding Fathers contemplated when they drafted the Electoral-College framework.

I support this concept because it will change the rules, and therefore the behavior of the candidates, in ways that will add legitimacy to the election of our President. It preserves the rights of states, and the integrity of the framework established by our Founding Fathers. Finally, it maintains a level of flexibility that allows the states to rethink the process should the individual states discover that the process is not working as they thought it would. The National Popular Vote proposal is in keeping with the best political traditions of our country, innovation in elections and governance with a strong respect for the constitutional framework which established this country. I believe it is a proposal we all can, and should, support, and I intend to do what I can to persuade elected officials and voters of the wisdom of this approach.

FOREWORD

By Dr. Robert A. "Bob" Holmes

The struggle to achieve voting fairness and political equality has continued since the founding of the United States in 1789. Many voting-rights issues were first discussed and resolved in the states many years before they were finally applied nationwide, such as granting former slaves and women the right to vote. The states are continuing to serve as "laboratories" for developing new and creative solutions to make this nation a more democratic system of government. The National Popular Vote legislation is another opportunity for states to take a leadership role in changing the current archaic and undemocratic method used to elect the President of the United States.

Perhaps the most important issue of voting inequality in the nation today is the method used to choose the President, particularly the awarding of states' Electoral-College votes using the winner-take-all method. Article II, Section 1 of the U.S. Constitution gives the 50 states the exclusive authority to decide how to allocate their electoral votes in presidential elections. Originally, the Electoral College was created to allow a group of "chosen wise men" whose numbers were determined by the size of the congressional delegation from the various states to meet after the general election at their state capitals to vote for the candidate whom they believed should be President. While competing political parties have come and gone, and there have been changes in the methods for choosing members of the Electoral College, the allocation of these Electoral-College votes among the candidates has remained a plenary power of the 50 individual state legislatures. Forty-eight states and the District of Columbia use the winner-take-all method while two states, Maine and Nebraska, assign their votes based on congressional districts. Under the current system, four of the 56 presidential elections (1 of each 14) have been "won" by the candidate who finished second in terms of the total national popular vote of the electorate. Further, a change of less than 1% in one or two states would have led to the same results in five of the last 12 presidential elections.

In fact, two of the first three elections in the 21st century provide good examples of a major flaw in the current system. In the 2000 contest, Democratic presidential candidate Al Gore won 537,000 more votes than his Republican opponent George Bush, but the latter became President. Then in the 2004 election, President Bush won more than 3 million more popular votes than Democrat John Kerry, but Kerry would have won the Presidency if he had received only 60,000 more votes in Ohio.

The winner-take-all rule (used in 48 states and Washington, D.C.) awards all of the Electoral-College votes to the candidate who receives the most popular votes in the state (or the District of Columbia). This method of awarding electoral votes is the primary culprit of undemocratic outcomes in presidential elections.

A second major problem of the current system is that both major party candidates regularly ignore about 35 of the 50 states in their campaigns because the polls show they are either far ahead in some states or way behind their opponent. Thus, neither candidate has any incentive to campaign in states that are reliably Republican (red) or Democrat (blue) in voting for presidential candidates. Therefore, candidates spend 98% of their financial resources and campaign activities in only 15 states that are considered competitive battlegrounds (which, in practice, means less than a 5% difference in the polls between candidates). And even worse, persons who vote for the losing candidate in their state have their votes awarded to the winning candidate who receives all of the Electoral-College votes in the state!

The current system of electing the President is similar to the method used to elect the Governor of Georgia until 1962. Georgia used the county "unit system" and allocated units (similar to electoral votes) to each county based on their population. The largest counties (including Fulton with 300,000) had a maximum of six units to vote for Governor, whereas the smallest counties (some having only 2,000 residents) were guaranteed a minimum of one unit. Thus, six of the smallest counties (with a combined total of less than 20,000 people) had more voting power than one county with more than 300,000 people.

Fortunately, the U.S. Supreme Court declared the county unit system used to elect the Governor of Georgia unconstitutional because it violated the political equality doctrine of "one person, one vote." Yet in the 21st century, the President of the United States is still elected by an Electoral-College vote system that is clearly inequitable. It is important to know that none of the more than 200 nations in the world uses such an anti-democratic method to elect their head of state.

The national popular vote method of electing the President provides a new innovative and creative method that will produce much-needed reform that will guarantee that all future Presidents will be chosen based on the candidate receiving the most national popular votes cast in the 50 states and the District of Columbia.

Recent polls taken between 2008 and 2010 in 32 states show that the American electorate overwhelmingly supports the idea of the direct election of the President by a national electorate, not 51 separate political jurisdictions. In every one of the 32 states where polls were conducted, there was a minimum of 67% who favored the new system over the current method. Also, the actions of many state legislators have already resulted in eight states and the District of Columbia enacting the National Popular Vote bill (half of the electoral votes required). The bill has been approved by 31 legislative bodies in 21 states.

Under the national popular vote method, all of the Electoral-College votes of states that enact legislation to join the interstate compact would agree to cast their Electoral-College votes for the candidate who receives the most national popular votes.

The compact would be activated when the number of states that adopt the legislation constitute a majority (270) of the Electoral-College votes (538) required to elect the President.

The public and their elected state legislators understand that the new method would make every vote equal in each state and would likely achieve two other democratic outcomes: (1) cause all presidential candidates to campaign in all of the states just as they do to win their party's nomination, and (2) generate greater voter interest and turnout in Presidential elections because election data show that fewer people turn out in solid red and blue states compared to competitive states. For example, when North Carolina and Virginia (which had been red states for 50 years) became competitive in the 2008 election, voter turnout increased by 8% and 10%, respectively.

Under a national popular vote, candidates would have to pay attention and respond to the policy priorities and concerns of voters in the 50 states, not just 15 states.

Many organizations that have for decades been at the forefront of electoral reform in this nation have recently endorsed the national popular vote legislation because they recognize that the current system of electing the President is the antithesis of the fundamental democratic principles of "one person, one vote" and "every vote equal." Among these organizations are: the American Civil Liberties Union, Common Cause, FairVote, Demos, The League of Women Voters, the National Association for the Advancement of Colored People, the National Black Caucus of State Legislators, the National Coalition on Black Civic Participation, and many others. Their support resolutions passed at their national conventions included phrases stating the justification for their support, such as: "It would effectively ensure that no future President would be elected without having received the most popular votes" and "It would guarantee that each American vote in this process would count equally."

The National Popular Vote legislation is the most significant proposed election reform in this nation since the Voting Rights Act of 1965 because it will ensure that the principle that every vote should be equal will apply in the election of the President of the United States. This excellent treatise provides a detailed historical, legal, and political analysis of attempts at presidential election reform and also effectively answers the questions and criticisms (myths) made by opponents. More important, it provides the best solution to democratize the process of electing the President. In sum, it is an idea whose time has come, and I urge the reader to contact their state legislators and get involved in their state to ensure that this great idea reaches fruition.

FOREWORD
By Dean Murray

Playwright Tom Stoppard once said, "It's not the voting that's democracy, it's the counting." That's the case when it comes to electing a President in our country—thanks to the Electoral College.

In school, we were all taught about the democratic principal of "one man, one vote." That's the case in every election we have here in New York—for school boards, state legislators, and even our governor and U.S. Senators. The only exception to this, however, is for our President.

When it comes to presidential elections, New York is usually completely ignored by candidates from both parties—except for fundraising stops in New York City and the Hamptons. Why? For the simple reason that rarely, if ever, is the Empire State considered a "battleground" or "swing" state.

The Tea Party is the most powerful movement to hit this country in years. We have successfully transformed politics as usual and given voice to the concerns and issues of ordinary taxpayers and working people.

However, the long-term impact of the Tea Party is threatened by a presidential election process that systematically silences voters throughout the country.

The 2012 presidential election will leave fully two-thirds of the voters in the country wondering what is happening. When the general election campaign rolls around in the summer and fall of 2012, the presidential candidates, whoever they are, will ignore voters as they focus their campaigns exclusively on the swing states. Whether you align yourself with the Tea Party, Republicans, Democrats, Libertarians, or Greens, whether you are conservative, liberal, or moderate, the candidates and the campaign will pass you by unless you live in one of a handful of states.

In both 2004 and 2008, candidates spent 98% of their resources in just 15 closely divided battleground states. They concentrated over two-thirds of their resources in just six states. Simply put, the millions and millions of dollars spent advertising and polling and visiting and organizing in this small group of states means that their votes are more important than those of us who live in fly-over country.

This marginalization of the majority of our country is why I support and have sponsored the National Popular Vote legislation in New York. This proposal, once enacted, will guarantee the Presidency to the candidate receiving the most popular votes in all 50 states.

A vote should be a vote regardless of where it was cast. A voter in Ohio shouldn't be more important than a voter in Kansas. Miami shouldn't trump Main Street. Every voter should be heard, and every vote should count equally.

America can make this happen.

The National Popular Vote bill preserves the Electoral College and the intent of the Constitution. It recognizes that it is the exclusive right of the states, not Congress, the President, or anyone else, to decide how to award their electoral votes. The Constitution makes this perfectly clear under Article II, Section 1.

The current system that allows vast areas of the country to be completely disregarded during the general election was not one that was envisioned by the Founding Fathers. Forty-eight of the 50 states use the winner-take-all rule for allocating their electoral votes (as opposed to just three states in the first election). Under this rule, the candidate who wins the most popular votes in a given state receives all the electoral votes. As a result, the overwhelming majority of Americans are rendered irrelevant when electing their President because they live in a "safe state" where the Republican or Democrat candidate for President is comfortably ahead or hopelessly behind.

The National Popular Vote bill would take effect only when enacted by states possessing a majority of the electoral votes—that is, enough electoral votes to elect a president. When the bill is in effect, all the electoral votes from the states that enacted the bill would be awarded, as a bloc, to the presidential candidate who receives the most popular votes in all 50 states.

A national popular vote based on the candidate receiving the most votes in the country would encourage candidates to court voters of every party, in every state, and to reach out across our great nation. Candidates would be forced to listen to the concerns of Americans everywhere, not just where it counts politically under today's system.

The Tea Party movement is about many things. Perhaps the most important is that our voices and our values be heard by our government.

President Dwight D. Eisenhower said, "The future of this republic is in the hands of the American voter." The best way to make that happen in the long term is to make every vote count. A national popular vote for President, where every vote counts and every vote counts equally, ensures that no one will be marginalized or overlooked in the future.

FOREWORD

By Thomas L. Pearce

In 2008, the state of Michigan had 17 electoral votes. As a state with nearly twice the population of the average state, not to mention twice the problems, Michigan should have had a strong voice in the presidential election. You would have expected both candidates to fight long and hard for our vote.

Not so. In fact, John McCain pulled out of Michigan four weeks before the election, ceding Michigan's electoral votes to Barack Obama. As a Republican I was disappointed, of course. But as a citizen of this great state, I was outraged.

Of course, Michigan was the victim of a policy that actually rewards presidential candidates for ignoring the majority of states. The winner-take-all system of awarding electoral votes treats election results in more than thirty states as a foregone conclusion.

The result? No campaign stops, no campaign dollars, and no incentive to represent the needs of Michigan voters at a national level.

If every single voter in Michigan had cast his or her vote for Barack Obama, the outcome would have been exactly the same. The winner-take-all system of awarding electoral votes effectively disenfranchises every voter beyond those needed to establish a plurality. In 2008, the people of Michigan spoke, and nobody listened.

When I think of blue states or red states, Michigan doesn't exactly come to mind. Our presidential vote totals are typically close. We recently flipped the state House, and the Governor's office. Michigan isn't a one-party state like Utah or Massachusetts. Even moderate states like Michigan are being cast aside as the list of battleground states continues to shorten.

This is a high-school civics lesson gone wrong.

We see the impact of this political calculus at a national level. Compare the response to hurricane Katrina (in Louisiana, a "safe" state) to the federal response to hurricanes in Florida (a "swing" state) under Presidents of both parties. President Obama only became angry about the BP oil spill once it reached Florida's shores.

Thankfully, hurricanes and oil spills aren't a problem here in Michigan. We have an equally urgent disaster, however, in the form of unemployment. Our people need jobs, and deserve respect from the executive branch in accordance with our population. This is no time to be taken for granted.

Fortunately, the U.S. Constitution gives the states the means to remedy the shortcomings of the present system, and restore a voice to voters in states like Michigan. The winner-take-all rule, which may have once made sense, can be continued or discontinued at our, or any, state's discretion. It is not mentioned anywhere in the Constitution, much less mandated.

The National Popular Vote compact leverages the power accorded to the states by the Constitution to ensure that every vote counts equally. Under this system, states agree to award their electoral votes to the candidate who wins the most votes in all 50 states. This would give Michigan a voice commensurate with its population.

When states like Michigan are getting lost in our electoral system, it's time for a change. The National Popular Vote initiative is long overdue, and it has my full support.

FOREWORD

By Christopher Pearson

By the time I became familiar with the National Popular Vote bill I already liked the idea of a popular vote for president. There is something so basic about one person, one vote. I didn't need much convincing.

As I learned more about this proposal for state action I began to appreciate how far-reaching the impacts of this bill would be. Living in Vermont, we are all familiar with the organized treks of campaign volunteers to the swing state of New Hampshire. This occurs at the time of the New Hampshire primary and then, because New Hampshire has been a battleground state for several cycles, the trek occurs again in the fall campaign. As somebody who has worked on Vermont campaigns, it is frustrating to lose good volunteers to our neighbor to the east.

There is nothing special about New Hampshire's voters. They just happen to be evenly divided. They aren't solid blue or solid red. The end result in New Hampshire is up for grabs, and so the candidates and their teams do everything they can to get the four electoral votes New Hampshire offers. Candidates do next to nothing to earn the three votes we hold here in Vermont.

Our three electoral votes get completely taken for granted because we are a reliably blue state. Thirty-four other states are similarly reliable for one party or the other. Examining election results makes it obvious that more and more Americans are effectively left out of our process. This isn't some fluke of the last few cycles—it's a trend that's been continuing for 50 years. It's obvious to most Americans that our electoral system is broken.

Vermont isn't ignored because we're a small state. And we don't get any meaningful bonus because we're little, despite what we learned in high-school civics. The bottom line is candidates either care about earning your votes or they don't. Because we're a safe "blue" state, Democrats running for the White House know they have us, and Republicans know they couldn't possibly win us. Therefore, nobody polls us, nobody visits us, and campaigns are organized to get our people on the phone to Ohio or knock on the doors in New Hampshire.

But the impact of National Popular Vote goes way beyond the basic fairness of every vote counting equally; that only scratches the surface.

Does anybody really believe a sitting president doesn't consider his re-election when his administration hands out stimulus money? Or makes trade policy? Or energy policy? Is it a coincidence that President Bush, a free trader, put a tariff on steel—an industry that just happens to be important in Pennsylvania? I doubt it.

A close examination of everything from policy decisions to travel schedules of a president reveals a strong bias to the states that happen to be up for grabs in the Electoral College. While most states wrestle with budget deficits and soaring costs I hope you might take a bit of time and right a fundamental flaw in American politics. The impact will be far-reaching and positive for generations to come.

FOREWORD

By Jake Garn

The National Popular Vote plan would guarantee the Presidency to the candidate who receives the most popular votes in all 50 states and the District of Columbia.

The National Popular Vote bill preserves the Electoral College. It would change state law to ensure that Utah voters will matter in every presidential election, and that the candidate with the most votes wins.

Article II, Section 1 of the U.S. Constitution gives the states exclusive control over the manner of awarding their electoral votes: "Each State shall appoint, in such Manner as the Legislature thereof may direct, a Number of Electors. . . ." The winner-take-all rule is not in the U.S. Constitution. It was not the Founders' choice (having been used by only three states in the nation's first presidential election in 1789). Maine and Nebraska currently award electoral votes by district—a reminder that a constitutional amendment is not required to change the method of electing the President.

The shortcomings of the current system stem from state winner-take-all statutes that award all of a state's electoral votes to the candidate who receives the most popular votes in each state.

Because of these state-level winner-take-all statutes, presidential candidates have no reason to poll, visit, advertise, or organize in states where they are comfortably ahead or hopelessly behind. In 2008, candidates concentrated over two-thirds of their post-convention general election campaign visits and ad money in just six states and 98% in just 15 states. States that reliably vote for one party, such as Utah, are thus ignored by presidential campaigns.

Another shortcoming of the winner-take-all rule is that a candidate can win the Presidency without winning the most popular votes nationwide. This has occurred in 4 of the nation's 57 presidential elections—1 in 14 times. A shift of 60,000 votes in Ohio in 2004 would have defeated Bush despite his nationwide lead of over 3,000,000 votes.

I think it is time we do something to fix this problem and I feel that the National Popular Vote plan is exactly the solution.

WHAT PEOPLE ARE SAYING ABOUT NATIONAL POPULAR VOTE

"innovative new proposal . . . Legislatures across the country should get behind it"

—New York Times—*March 14, 2006*

"The Sun-Times News Group backs the concept and applauds the National Popular Vote group for thinking outside the box"

—Chicago Sun Times *Editorial*—*March 1, 2006*

"an inventive proposal"

—*Neal Peirce*—Houston Chronicle—*March 5, 2006*

"a brilliant idea"

—*Andrew Gumbel*—LA CityBeat—*March 9, 2006*

"the Legislature [should] do the right thing and endorse the new compact."

—Minneapolis Star-Tribune—*March 27, 2006*

"This book describes the 'Agreement among the States to Elect the President by National Popular Vote'—an innovative approach that is a politically practical way to achieve the goal of nationwide popular election of the President. It has my enthusiastic support."

—*John B. Anderson (R–Illinois and Independent presidential candidate)*

"The President and Vice President should be chosen by the same method every other elective office in this country is filled—by citizen voters of the United States in a system that counts each vote equally. . . . I unequivocally support this new strategy to provide for the direct election of the President and Vice President. This new approach is consistent with the Constitution . . . It's refreshing to know states have the ability under the Constitution to step up and create the sensible solution Americans have long been supporting."

—*Birch Bayh (D–Indiana)*

"The people have supported the direct election of the president for over 50 years. In this book, Dr. Koza suggests a way for states to come together and make it happen. . . . I strongly support and applaud any good-faith effort to make the direct election of the President a reality and commend to you the intriguing approach offered in the 'Agreement among the States to Elect the President by National Popular Vote' described in this book.'"

—*John Buchanan (R–Alabama)*

"The ingenious approach put forward in this book provides, for the first time, a solution that is achievable. It does not rely on unrealistic assumptions. It can be implemented, if the very people who are relatively disenfranchised in our country will only be awakened to how to do it."

—*Tom Campbell (R–California and Dean of the Chapman University School of Law)*

"What makes the National Popular Vote plan particularly promising is how neatly it fits in with American traditions. A century ago it was states that first established women's suffrage and direct election of U.S. Senators. Under the U.S. Constitution it is states that have the power to fix our broken presidential election system. This book provides the roadmap."

—*Chellie Pingree (D–Maine and formerly President of Common Cause)*

1 | Introduction

In elections for President and Vice President of the United States, every vote should be equal. The presidential candidate who receives the most popular votes throughout the United States should win the Presidency. Every voter in every state should be politically relevant in every election.

The current system for electing the President and Vice President does not satisfy the three principles above. This book presents a politically practical way—based on powers specifically delegated to the states by the U.S. Constitution—by which presidential elections can be brought into conformity with these three principles.

Figure 1.1 Herb Block cartoon of October 7, 1948[1]

---

[1] The Herb Block Foundation is gratefully acknowledged for permission to use the copyrighted Herb Block cartoon in Figure 1.1.

This chapter

- describes what the U.S. Constitution says—and, more important, *does not say*—about how presidential elections are to be run (section 1.1),
- highlights three significant shortcomings of the current system for electing the President and identifies their common cause, namely state-by-state winner-take-all statutes (section 1.2),
- identifies nationwide popular election as a remedy for the current system's three shortcomings (section 1.3),
- notes the fortuitous convergence of factors favoring reform at the present time (section 1.4),
- provides a roadmap to the remainder of this book (section 1.5), and
- identifies additional sources of information (section 1.6).

1.1 WHAT THE U.S. CONSTITUTION SAYS—AND DOES NOT SAY—ABOUT PRESIDENTIAL ELECTIONS

The politically most important aspects of the system for electing the President of the United States are not established by the U.S. Constitution. Instead, the Constitution delegates the power to make those decisions to the states.

The Constitution specifies that the President and Vice President are to be chosen every four years by a small group of people (currently 538[2]) who are individually referred to as "presidential electors." The presidential electors are collectively referred to as the "Electoral College" (although this term does not appear in the Constitution).

The U.S. Constitution delegates the power to choose the method of appointing presidential electors to the states. Section 1 of Article II states:

> "The executive Power shall be vested in a President of the United States of America. He shall hold his Office during the Term of four Years, and, together with the Vice President, chosen for the same Term, be elected, as follows:
>
> "**Each State shall appoint, in such Manner as the Legislature thereof may direct, a Number of Electors**, equal to the whole Number of Senators and Representatives to which the State may be entitled in the Congress: but no Senator or Representative, or Person holding an Office of Trust or Profit under the United States, shall be appointed an Elector."[3] [Emphasis added]

---

[2] The total of 538 electoral votes corresponds to the 435 U.S. Representatives from the 50 states *plus* the 100 U.S. Senators from the 50 states *plus* the three electoral votes that the District of Columbia received as a result of the 23rd Amendment to the Constitution (ratified in 1961). Every 10 years, the 435 U.S. Representatives are reapportioned among the states in accordance with the latest federal census, thereby automatically reapportioning the electoral votes among the states. The number of U.S. Representatives (currently 435) is set by federal statute.

[3] U.S. Constitution, Article II, section 1, clauses 1 and 2.

The U.S. Constitution also contains procedural and administrative provisions concerning various aspects of presidential elections,[4] including

- the establishment of the date for appointing presidential electors and the meeting date for the Electoral College,[5]
- the majority required in the Electoral College to elect the President and Vice President,[6]
- the conduct of the "contingent election" in the event that no candidate receives the required majority in the Electoral College,[7]
- the procedure by which presidential electors cast their votes,[8] and
- the procedures for communicating each state's votes to Congress and the procedures by which Congress counts the electoral votes.[9]

The U.S. Constitution is silent about the two politically most important aspects of modern-day presidential elections, namely

- whether voters have any direct voice in electing presidential electors, and
- whether votes for the office of presidential elector should be counted using the winner-take-all rule (that is, all of a state's electoral votes are awarded to the presidential candidate who receives the most popular votes in each separate state).

---

[4] For the reader's convenience, appendix A contains all the provisions of the U.S. Constitution relating to presidential elections. Appendix B contains the federal statutes governing presidential elections.

[5] Article II, section 1, clause 4 of the U.S. Constitution states, "The Congress may determine the Time of chusing the Electors, and the Day on which they shall give their Votes; which Day shall be the same throughout the United States."

[6] In order to be elected, a presidential candidate must win the votes of an absolute majority of the presidential electors who have been "appointed" (See U.S. Constitution, Article II, section 1, clause 3 and the 12th Amendment). Assuming that all states appoint their presidential electors, that requirement currently means winning 270 of the 538 electoral votes. In 1789, New York failed to appoint its electors for the nation's first presidential election because of a disagreement between the two houses of the legislature as to procedure (joint convention versus concurrent resolution) by which the legislature would appoint the state's presidential electors. During the Civil War, the 11 Southern states failed to appoint their electors for the 1864 election because they claimed to be outside of the Union.

[7] According to Article II, section 1, clause 3 of the U.S. Constitution (restated in the 12th Amendment), if no presidential candidate receives an absolute majority of the electors "appointed," the U.S. House of Representatives chooses the President in a "contingent election" (with each state casting one vote regardless of the size of its congressional delegation). In the contingent election for President under the original Constitution, the House had to choose among the top five candidates, but under the 12th Amendment, the House chooses among the top three. Under the original Constitution, the second-place candidate (even if he lacked an absolute majority, as John Adams did in 1789) became Vice President, with the U.S. Senate breaking a tie for second place. Under the 12th Amendment, if no vice-presidential candidate receives an absolute majority of the electors "appointed," the U.S. Senate chooses the Vice President between the top two candidates (with each Senator casting one vote).

[8] Under the original Constitution, each presidential elector cast two votes, with the leading candidate becoming President, and the second-place candidate becoming Vice President. The 12th Amendment to the Constitution (ratified in 1804) changed this procedure so that each presidential elector casts a separate vote for President and Vice President.

[9] The 12th Amendment (ratified in 1804) modified and restated certain aspects of the casting, recording, and counting of electoral votes.

Specifically, the U.S. Constitution says nothing about issues such as:

(1) **Who Votes for Presidential Electors?**

- Should the nation's voters have a direct voice in choosing the presidential electors (as they did in only six states in the nation's first presidential election in 1789)?
- Or should the state legislature appoint the presidential electors (as they did in three states in 1789)?
- Or should the governor and his cabinet appoint the state's presidential electors (as was the case in New Jersey in 1789)?

(2) **What Is the Method for Counting the Votes Cast for Presidential Electors?**

- If the nation's voters are permitted to vote directly for the presidential electors, are their votes counted on a statewide winner-take-all basis (as they were in only three states in 1789)?
- Should the voters choose presidential electors from specially created presidential-elector districts (as was the case in Virginia in 1789)?
- Or from each state's congressional districts?
- Or from regional multi-member districts?
- Or should they be elected in proportion to the statewide division of the popular vote?
- Is an absolute majority of the popular vote necessary to choose presidential electors (and, if so, what happens if a candidate receives only a plurality)?
- If the legislature is to appoint the presidential electors, should it meet in a joint convention of its two houses, or should the appointment require approval of each house separately (a concurrent resolution)?

The U.S. Constitution's 17-word delegation of power to the states does not provide any guidance concerning these politically important questions. It simply states:

> "Each State shall appoint, **in such Manner as the Legislature thereof may direct**, a Number of Electors . . . . "[10] [Emphasis added]

The Constitution's delegation of power to the states concerning the conduct of presidential elections differs significantly from the Constitution's delegation of power to the states concerning the conduct of congressional elections.

> "The Times, Places and Manner of holding Elections for Senators and Representatives, shall be prescribed in each State by the Legislature thereof; **but the Congress may at any time by Law make or alter such Regulations**. . . . "[11] [Emphasis added]

---

[10] U.S. Constitution, Article II, section 1, clause 2.

[11] U.S. Constitution, Article I, section 4, clause 1.

State power over congressional elections is subject to congressional veto, whereas state power over presidential elections is complete (plenary).

The U.S. Supreme Court has characterized state power concerning the choice of manner of appointing presidential electors as "exclusive" and "plenary." As the Court wrote in the 1892 case of *McPherson v. Blacker*—the leading case on the manner of appointing presidential electors:

> "[F]rom the formation of the government until now the practical construction of the clause has conceded **plenary** power to the state legislatures in the matter of the appointment of electors."[12,13]

> "In short, the appointment and mode of appointment of electors belong **exclusively** to the states under the constitution of the United States."[14] [Emphasis added]

In the only decision on this subject at the state level, the Maine Supreme Judicial Court wrote in a 1919 case involving a state statute entitled "An act granting to women the right to vote for presidential electors":

> "[E]ach state is thereby clothed with the **absolute power to appoint electors in such manner as it may see fit, without any interference or control on the part of the federal government**, except, of course, in case of attempted discrimination as to race, color, or previous condition of servitude. . . . "[15] [Emphasis added]

Over the years, the states have used the Constitution's built-in flexibility concerning presidential elections in a remarkable variety of ways. Many of the most familiar features of present-day presidential elections (notably, voting by the people and the state-by-state winner-take-all rule) did not come into widespread use until decades after the Founders died.

(1) **Who Votes for Presidential Electors?** In the nation's first presidential election in 1789, only six states permitted the voters to elect the state's presidential electors. In many states, there was no election for President at all. In New Jersey, the Governor and his Council appointed the state's presidential electors. In many states, the legislature appointed the presi-

---

[12] *McPherson v. Blacker.* 146 U.S. 1 at 36. 1892.

[13] In the 2000 case of *Bush v. Gore*, the U.S. Supreme Court wrote, "The individual citizen has no federal constitutional right to vote for electors for the President of the United States unless and until the state legislature chooses a statewide election as the means to implement its power to appoint members of the Electoral College. U.S. Const., Art. II, §1. This is the source for the statement in *McPherson v. Blacker*, 146 U.S. 1, 35 (1892), that the State legislature's power to select the manner for appointing electors is plenary; it may, if it so chooses, select the electors itself, which indeed was the manner used by State legislatures in several States for many years after the Framing of our Constitution. Id., at 28–33." (531 U.S. 98. 2000).

[14] *McPherson v. Blacker.* 146 U.S. 1 at 29. 1892.

[15] In re *Opinion of the Justices*, 107 A. 705. 1919.

dential electors. In the nation's second presidential election in 1792, the Vermont Governor and his Council and the state House of Representatives appointed the presidential electors.[16] Over a period of decades, the state legislatures gradually empowered their voters to vote directly for presidential electors. By 1836, the voters elected the presidential electors in all states except South Carolina. Between 1836 and 1876, there was never more than one state in any given presidential election where the voters did not elect the state's presidential electors. No state legislature has appointed presidential electors since Colorado did so in 1876.[17]

(2) **What Is the Method for Counting the Votes Cast for Presidential Electors?** In 1789, only three states awarded their electoral votes using a method that resembles the system that is now used by 48 states, namely the statewide "winner-take-all" rule (also called the "unit rule" or "general ticket"). In 1789, Virginia elected presidential electors in specially created presidential elector districts, thereby creating the possibility that minority sentiment within the state could win some of the state's electoral votes. At various times in other states, voters elected presidential electors from congressional districts, by county, or from multi-member regional districts. Several states occasionally used indirect methods. In 1828, some of New York's presidential electors were chosen by other presidential electors.[18] In Tennessee in 1796, a miniature state-level Electoral College chose the state's national members of the Electoral College.[19] Today, the voters in Maine and Nebraska elect presidential electors by congressional district.

Neither popular voting for presidential electors nor the state-by-state winner-take-all rule came into existence by amending the U.S. Constitution. Instead, these now-familiar features came into existence on a piecemeal basis as a result of states using the flexibility that the Founders built into the Constitution. In particular, the winner-take-all rule was created by state law and, therefore, may be repealed by state law.

The politics behind the adoption by the states of the winner-take-all rule is instructive. As the U.S. Supreme Court noted in its historical review of presidential elections in *McPherson v. Blacker*, many of the Founding Fathers considered the district system (such as that used by Virginia in the nation's first presidential election in 1789) to be "the most equitable."[20]

---

[16] There was no Vermont Senate until 1836.

[17] Section 2.2 provides additional details on the history of methods of selecting presidential electors.

[18] In 1828, the New York legislature created an indirect system in which the state's two senatorial presidential electors were elected by the presidential electors chosen by the voters from each of the state's congressional districts. See section 2.2.4.

[19] As detailed in section 2.2.2, in 1796 in Tennessee, specific citizens from various groups of counties were named in a state law, and those specifically named individuals then chose the state's presidential electors.

[20] *McPherson v. Blacker*, 146 U.S. 1 at 29. 1892.

The three states that used the winner-take-all rule in the nation's first presidential election in 1789 had abandoned it by 1800.[21]

However, a counter-trend developed in favor of the winner-take-all rule.

As early as the nation's first competitive presidential election (1796), it had become clear to political observers that the district system divided a state's electoral votes and thereby diminished the influence of the state's dominant political party. As historian Noble Cunningham wrote:

> "The presidential election of 1796 had been extremely close, and in examining the results of that contest Republican Party managers had been struck by the fact that **Adams' 3-vote margin of victory in the Electoral College could be attributed to 1 vote from Pennsylvania, 1 from Virginia, and 1 from North Carolina**. In each of these states, the Republicans had won an impressive victory, amassing in the three states a total of 45 electoral votes. The loss of 3 votes in these strongly Jeffersonian states was due to the district method of electing presidential electors. **In looking for ways to improve their chances for victory in the next presidential election, Republican managers thus turned their attention to state election laws.**"[22] [Emphasis added]

In 1798, Virginia Republicans became further alarmed by the fact that the Federalists won eight of Virginia's 19 congressional races.[23]

On January 12, 1800, Thomas Jefferson (the losing Republican[24] candidate from the 1796 presidential election) wrote James Monroe (then a member of the legislature in Jefferson's home state of Virginia):

> "On the subject of an election by a general ticket [the statewide winner-take-all rule], or by districts, most persons here seem to have made up their minds. All agree that an **election by districts would be best, if it could be general; but while 10 states chuse either by their legislatures or by a general ticket, it is folly & worse than folly** for the other 6. not to do it."[25,26] [Emphasis added; spelling and punctuation per original]

---

[21] Maryland, Pennsylvania, and New Hampshire.

[22] Cunningham, Noble E., Jr. 2002. In Schlesinger, Arthur M., Jr. and Israel, Fred L. (editors). *History of American Presidential Elections 1878–2001*. Philadelphia, PA: Chelsea House Publishers. Pages 104–105. See section 2.2.2 for additional details on the 1796 election.

[23] Ferling, John. 2004. *Adams vs. Jefferson: The Tumultuous Election of 1800*. Oxford, UK: Oxford University Press. Page 156.

[24] Jeffersonians were known as "Republicans" or "Democratic-Republicans," and eventually "Democrats."

[25] The January 12, 1800, letter is discussed in greater detail and quoted in its entirety in section 2.2.3. Ford, Paul Leicester. 1905. *The Works of Thomas Jefferson*. New York: G. P. Putnam's Sons. 9:90.

[26] In an August 23, 1823, letter from James Madison to George Hay, Madison referred to the winner-take-all rule as "the only expedient for baffling the policy of the particular States which had set the example." Madison wrote, "I agree entirely with you in thinking that the election of Presidential Electors by districts, is an amendment very proper to be brought forward at the same time with that relating to the eventual choice of

The result, as described by Cunningham was that:

> "In January 1800, the Republican-controlled legislature of Virginia passed an act providing for the election of presidential electors on a **general ticket instead of by districts** as in previous elections. By changing the election law, Republicans in Virginia, confident of carrying a majority of the popular vote throughout the state but fearful of losing one or two districts to the Federalists, ensured the entire electoral vote of the Union's largest state for the Republican candidate."[27] [Emphasis added]

This politically motivated change ensured Jefferson 100% of his home state's electoral votes in the 1800 election.

Of course, the Republicans were not the only politicians who had a keen eye for political advantage. The Federalists unexpectedly lost control of the New York legislature in April 1800. Under New York's existing law, the legislature had empowered itself to appoint all of the state's presidential electors. The loss of control of the legislature meant that the Federalists would lose all 12 of New York's electoral votes when the new legislature was scheduled to meet later in the year to choose the state's presidential electors.[28] As John Ferling wrote in *Adams vs. Jefferson: The Tumultuous Election of 1800*:

> "Jarred by the specter of defeat in the autumn [Federalist Alexander] Hamilton importuned Governor John Jay to call a special session of the Federalist-dominated New York legislature so that it might act before the newly elected assemblymen took their seats [on July 1]. Hamilton's plan was for the outgoing assembly to enact legislation providing for the popular election—in districts—of the state's presidential electors, a ploy virtually guaranteed to ensure that the Federalists would capture nine or ten of the twelve electoral college slots."[29]

As Alexander Hamilton put it in his letter to Governor John Jay on May 7, 1800:

> "The moral certainty therefore is, that there will be an anti-federal majority in the ensuing legislature; and the very high probability is, that this will

President by the H. of Reps. The district mode was mostly, if not exclusively in view when the Constitution was framed and adopted; & was exchanged for the general ticket & the legislative election, as the only expedient for baffling the policy of the particular States which had set the example." From Kurland, Philip B., and Lehner, Edward. *The Founder's Constitution*. Published on the web at http://press-pubs.uchicago.edu/founders/documents/a2_1_2-3s10.html.

[27] Cunningham, Noble E., Jr. 2002. In Schlesinger, Arthur M., Jr. and Israel, Fred L. (editors). *History of American Presidential Elections 1878–2001*. Philadelphia, PA: Chelsea House Publishers. Page 105.

[28] Weisberger, Bernard A. 2001. *America Afire: Jefferson, Adams, and the First Contested Election*. New York, NY: William Morrow. Page 238.

[29] Ferling, John. 2004. *Adams vs. Jefferson: The Tumultuous Election of 1800*. Oxford, UK: Oxford University Press. Page 131.

bring Jefferson into the chief magistracy, unless it be prevented by the measure which I now submit to your consideration, namely, the immediate calling together of the existing legislature.

"**I am aware that there are weighty objections to the measure**; but the reasons for it appear to me to outweigh the objections. And in times like these in which we live, **it will not do to be over-scrupulous**. It is easy to sacrifice the substantial interests of society by a strict adherence to ordinary rules.

"In observing this, I shall not be supposed to mean that anything ought to be done which integrity will forbid; but merely that the **scruples of delicacy and propriety**, as relative to a common course of things, **ought to yield to the extraordinary nature of the crisis**. They ought not to hinder the taking of a legal and constitutional step to prevent an atheist in religion, and a fanatic in politics, from getting possession of the helm of State."[30] [Emphasis added]

Hamilton did not get his way. Governor Jay (a former Chief Justice of the United States) wrote the following notation on Hamilton's letter:

"Proposing a measure for party purposes which it would not become me to adopt."[31]

Ironically, *prior* to the April 1800 legislative elections, New York Republicans—believing that the district system would be advantageous for them—had unsuccessfully urged the Federalist-controlled legislature to switch from legislative appointment of presidential electors to popular election using districts. As it turned out, a shift of only five electoral votes from Jefferson to Adams in the 1800 election would have resulted in Adams' re-election. Had the Federalists agreed to the Republican's earlier proposal, "an atheist in religion, and a fanatic in politics" (namely Thomas Jefferson) would not have won all 12 of New York's electoral votes (and, ultimately, the presidency) in the 1800 election.

Over a period of years, the states—one by one—gravitated to the statewide winner-take-all rule to avoid the "folly" of fragmenting their electoral votes. The compelling reason for this change was that the political party that controlled the governorship and legislature in a particular state was generally confident of winning the statewide vote for President (but almost never confident of winning every single dis-

---

[30] The complete letter can be found in *Brief of F.A. Baker for Plaintiffs in Error* in *McPherson v. Blacker.* 1892. Pages 30–31. See also Cunningham, Noble E., Jr. 1957. *Jeffersonian Republicans: The Formation of Party Organizations.* Chapel Hill, NC: University of North Carolina Press. Page 185. See also Weisberger, Bernard A. 2001. *America Afire: Jefferson, Adams, and the First Contested Election.* William Morrow. Page 239.

[31] *Brief of F.A. Baker for Plaintiffs in Error* in *McPherson v. Blacker.* 1892. Page 31.

trict within the state). As more and more states adopted the winner-take-all rule, the winner-take-all rule seemed to make more and more sense to the remaining states.

As James Madison wrote to George Hay in 1823:

> "The district mode was mostly, if not exclusively in view when the Constitution was framed and adopted; & **was exchanged for the general ticket** & the legislative election, **as the only expedient for baffling the policy of the particular States which had set the example**."[32] [Emphasis added]

It can be seen, in retrospect, that the emergence of national political parties in 1796, in conjunction with the Constitution's 17-word delegation of power to the states, made it almost inevitable that the statewide winner-take-all rule would become the predominant method of choosing presidential electors.

Thus, by 1836, all but one state had adopted the concept of popular election of presidential electors using the statewide winner-take-all rule.[33]

All the states used the statewide winner-take-all rule in the lengthy period between 1868 and 1968 with three isolated exceptions (namely legislative appointment in Florida in 1868 and Colorado in 1876 and district-level elections in Michigan in 1892).

Maine (in 1969) and Nebraska (in 1992) broke this pattern and adopted laws that awarded one electoral vote to the presidential candidate carrying each congressional district (and two electoral votes to the candidate carrying the state). In the 11 presidential elections in which the congressional-district approach has been used in Maine, the presidential candidate carrying the state also carried both of the state's two districts. In the six elections in which the congressional-district approach has been used in Nebraska, there has been one occasion where one of Nebraska's three districts was won by a candidate who did not carry the state (namely, Barack Obama in 2008).

The present-day state laws in Maine and Nebraska are reminders of the flexibility that the Founders built into the U.S. Constitution. These laws are reminders that the manner of awarding electoral votes is strictly a matter of state law. They are also reminders that a federal constitutional amendment is not necessary to change the way states award their electoral votes. Most importantly, they are reminders that the winner-take-all rule may be repealed by any state in the same manner as it was originally enacted, namely by passage of a different state law.

1.2 SHORTCOMINGS OF THE CURRENT SYSTEM

The current system for electing the President and Vice President of the United States has three major shortcomings:

---

[32] Letter from James Madison to George Hay on August 23, 1823. http://press-pubs.uchicago.edu/founders/documents/a2_1_2-3s10.html.

[33] The South Carolina legislature continued to elect the state's presidential electors until 1860. See chapter 2 for a detailed history of the proliferation of the statewide winner-take-all rule.

- **Voters Are Effectively Disenfranchised in Four-Fifths of the States in Presidential Elections**. One of the consequences of the statewide winner-take-all rule (i.e., awarding all of a state's electoral votes to the presidential candidate who receives the most popular votes in each separate state) is that presidential candidates do not campaign in states in which they are comfortably ahead or hopelessly behind. Presidential candidates ignore such states because they do not receive additional or fewer electoral votes based on the margin by which they win or lose those states. The result is that presidential candidates concentrate their public appearances, organizational efforts, advertising, polling, and policy attention on states where the outcome of the popular vote is not a foregone conclusion. In practical political terms, a vote matters in presidential politics only if it is cast in a closely divided battleground state. To put it another way, the value of a vote in presidential elections depends on whether *other* voters in the voter's state happen to be closely divided. Between 1988 and 2008, about two-thirds of the states were ignored by presidential campaigns. Four-fifths of the states were ignored in 2012. Twelve of the 13 least-populous states are spectator states,[34] including six that have regularly gone Republican (Alaska, Idaho, Montana, Wyoming, North Dakota, and South Dakota) and six that have regularly gone Democratic (Hawaii, Vermont, Maine, Rhode Island, Delaware, and the District of Columbia).[35]

- **The Current System Does Not Reliably Reflect the Nationwide Popular Vote**. The statewide winner-take-all rule makes it possible for a candidate to win the presidency without winning the most popular votes nationwide. This has occurred in four of the nation's 56 presidential elections—1 in 14 (as detailed in section 1.2.2). In the past six decades, there have been six presidential elections in which a shift of a relatively small number of votes in one or two states would have elected (and, of course, in 2000, did elect) a presidential candidate who lost the popular vote nationwide.

- **Not Every Vote Is Equal.** The statewide winner-take-all rule creates variations of 1,000-to-1 and more in the weight of a vote (as detailed in section 1.2.3).

---

[34] The non-battleground states are sometimes called "spectator" states, "fly-over" states, "wall flower" states, "dark" states (in reference to the absence of TV advertising), "orphan" states, or simply "dead" states.

[35] There are 13 states with just one or two U.S. House members (and hence three or four electoral votes). Of the 13 least populous states, only New Hampshire has been a closely divided battleground state in recent presidential elections (having gone Republican in 1988 and 2000, and Democratic in 1996, 2004, 2008, and 2012). The small states tend to be noncompetitive because they are apt to be one-party states in terms of presidential elections.

1.2.1 VOTERS IN FOUR-FIFTHS OF THE STATES ARE EFFECTIVELY DISENFRANCHISED

Most people who follow politics are aware of the fact that presidential campaigns are concentrated in a handful of closely divided battleground states; however, many people are not aware of the extreme degree of this concentration.

Although there is no precise definition of a "battleground" state, these states can be readily identified in practice by simply observing where presidential candidates campaign, where they spend their money (on advertising and organizational activities), and where they closely watch public opinion (through polls, focus groups, and other means).

Presidential candidates pay almost no attention to the concerns of voters in states that are not closely divided. In fact, they do not even bother to poll public opinion in spectator states. As Charlie Cook reported in 2004:

> "Senior Bush campaign strategist Matthew Dowd pointed out yesterday that the Bush campaign hadn't taken a national poll in almost two years; instead, it has been polling 18 battleground states."[36,37]

2004 Presidential Election

One way to identify battleground states is to "follow the money."

In 2004, 99% of the $237,423,744 reported advertising money in the last month of the campaign was spent in only 17 states.

Table 1.1 lists the 17 states in order of per capita spending.[38]

The nine states where spending exceeded $2.00 per capita correspond to the top-tier battleground states and account for seven-eighths (87%) of the $237,423,744.

Five states (Florida, Iowa, Ohio, Pennsylvania, and Wisconsin) account for almost three quarters (72%) of the money.

A mere 1% of the money was spent in the remaining states and the District of Columbia. Nothing at all was spent in 23 states.

Advertising expenditures were similarly concentrated during the earlier part of the presidential campaign period.[39]

Candidate travel is another way to identify battleground states. The major-party presidential or vice-presidential candidates appeared at 307 campaign events in the

---

[36] Cook, Charlie. 2004. Convention dispatches—As the nation goes, so do swing states. *Charlie Cook's Political Report*. August 31, 2004.

[37] Kerry similarly pursued an 18-state strategy in 2004.

[38] The period covered was October 2 to November 4, 2004. See FairVote. 2005. *Who Picks the President?* Takoma Park, MD: The Center for Voting and Democracy. http://www.fairvote.org/whopicks. See also http://www.cnn.com/ELECTION/2004/special/president/campaign.ads/.

[39] An article by Chuck Todd in the *New York Times* (November 3, 2004) reported that five states accounted for 66% of the TV ad spending over the entire campaign period ($380 million of the $575 million spent).

Table 1.1 THE 17 STATES RECEIVING 99% OF THE ADVERTISING MONEY AT THE HEIGHT OF THE 2004 PRESIDENTIAL CAMPAIGN

PER CAPITA AD SPENDING	STATE	AD SPENDING
$4.45	New Mexico	$8,096,270
$4.30	Nevada	$8,596,795
$4.16	Ohio	$47,258,386
$4.02	Florida	$64,280,557
$3.73	New Hampshire	$4,608,200
$3.22	Iowa	$9,412,462
$3.00	Pennsylvania	$36,813,492
$2.70	Wisconsin	$14,468,062
$2.18	Minnesota	$10,734,683
$1.70	Maine	$2,171,101
$1.63	Colorado	$7,015,486
$1.36	Michigan	$13,518,566
$1.22	West Virginia	$2,213,110
$0.67	Oregon	$2,280,367
$0.42	Missouri	$2,361,944
$0.32	Hawaii	$388,095
$0.20	Washington	$1,198,882
	Total	**$235,416,458**

last month of the 2004 campaign. These 307 events were concentrated in 27 states.[40] If one excludes from consideration the six states receiving only one visit,[41] the home states of the four candidates,[42] and the District of Columbia (where all four candidates had day jobs),[43] all the remaining events (92% of the 307) were concentrated in just 16 states (as shown in table 1.2). Two-thirds of the events (200 of 307) were concentrated in Florida, Ohio, Iowa, Wisconsin, and Pennsylvania—the same five states that accounted for three quarters of the money. In general, campaign events and campaign spending are closely correlated in presidential campaigns.

Table 1.2 shows that 35 (over two-thirds) of the 51 jurisdictions entitled to vote in

---

[40] For simplicity, we frequently refer to the District of Columbia as a "state" in this book. The 23rd Amendment provides that the District of Columbia's three electoral votes "shall be considered, for the purposes of the election of President and Vice President, to be electors appointed by a state."

[41] Hawaii, Kansas, Maine, Maryland, West Virginia, and New York.

[42] There were four events in Texas (Bush's home state) and Massachusetts (Kerry), three in Wyoming (Cheney), and two in North Carolina (Edwards). None of these states was considered to be "in play" in the 2004 presidential election.

[43] There were six events in the District of Columbia.

Table 1.2 THE 16 STATES RECEIVING 92% OF
         THE CANDIDATE VISITS AT THE HEIGHT
         OF THE 2004 PRESIDENTIAL CAMPAIGN

STATE	CAMPAIGN EVENTS
Florida	61
Ohio	48
Iowa	37
Wisconsin	31
Pennsylvania	23
Michigan	19
Minnesota	14
Colorado	10
Nevada	7
New Hampshire	6
New Mexico	6
Oregon	5
Missouri	5
Arizona	4
New Jersey	4
California	2
Total	**282**

presidential elections (that is, the 50 states and the District of Columbia) cumulatively received only 8% of the campaign events. Over half received no campaign events at all.

Not surprisingly, this concentration of polling, advertising, and travel corresponds closely to the states where the presidential election was expected to be close. Table 1.3 shows the 19 states in which the two-party vote for President was between 46% and 54% in the 2000 presidential election, starting with the least Democratic state.[44]

Table 1.4 and figure 1.2 show the 16 states in which the two-party vote for President was between 46% and 54% in the 2004 presidential election, starting with the least Democratic state.

The 16 states in table 1.4 and figure 1.2 together represent 182 electoral votes—34% of the total (538).

To put it another way, states possessing the remaining 356 electoral votes (66% of the total) received little or no attention in the presidential election.

---

[44] Not all of the states in the tables are full-fledged battleground states. The 2004 Kerry campaign made efforts to pick up three states that Bush had carried in 2000 (Missouri, Colorado, and Nevada), and the 2004 Bush campaign made similar efforts to reverse the Democratic outcome in 2000 in Delaware, Washington, New Jersey, and Oregon. Nonetheless, as the 2004 campaign progressed, it became apparent that none of these states would actually change hands. By the end of the campaign, there were only a few top-tier battleground states.

Table 1.3 NINETEEN CLOSE STATES IN THE
2000 PRESIDENTIAL ELECTION

STATE	ELECTORAL VOTES	DEMOCRATIC PERCENTAGE
Louisiana	9	46.06%
Arizona	8	46.72%
West Virginia	5	46.76%
Arkansas	6	47.20%
Tennessee	11	48.04%
Nevada	4	48.14%
Ohio	21	48.18%
Missouri	11	48.29%
New Hampshire	4	49.33%
Florida	25	50.00%
New Mexico	5	50.03%
Wisconsin	11	50.12%
Iowa	7	50.16%
Oregon	7	50.24%
Minnesota	10	51.29%
Pennsylvania	23	52.15%
Michigan	18	52.63%
Maine	4	52.75%
Washington	11	52.94%
Total	**200**	

The "Electoral College scorecard" periodically published by the *Cook Political Report* provides another way to view presidential races and, in particular, to identify top-tier battleground states and second-tier battleground states.

On July 6, 2004, Charlie Cook listed the following 33 jurisdictions as being safe for one candidate or another. These 33 jurisdictions had 347 electoral votes (64% of the 538 electoral votes). That is, starting right at the beginning of the presidential contest, two-thirds of the states were safe for one candidate or another. Approximately two-thirds of the population of the United States lived in those states.

- **Solid Kerry:** States with 92 electoral votes were rated as "solid Kerry"—Connecticut, the District of Columbia, Hawaii, Illinois, Maryland, Massachusetts, New York, and Rhode Island.
- **Likely Kerry:** 73 electoral votes were rated as "likely Kerry"—California, New Jersey, and Vermont.
- **Likely Bush:** 72 electoral votes were rated as "likely Bush"—Arizona, Arkansas, Georgia, Kentucky, Louisiana, Tennessee, and Virginia.

Table 1.4 SIXTEEN CLOSE STATES IN THE 2004 PRESIDENTIAL ELECTION

STATE	ELECTORAL VOTES	DEMOCRATIC PERCENTAGE
Missouri	11	46.33%
Colorado	9	47.35%
Florida	27	47.47%
Nevada	5	48.67%
Ohio	20	48.75%
New Mexico	5	49.42%
Iowa	7	49.54%
Wisconsin	10	50.20%
New Hampshire	4	50.68%
Pennsylvania	21	51.13%
Michigan	17	51.73%
Minnesota	10	51.76%
Oregon	7	51.97%
New Jersey	15	53.13%
Washington	11	53.60%
Delaware	3	53.82%
Total	**182**	

Figure 1.2 Sixteen close states in the 2004 presidential election

- **Solid Bush:** 110 electoral votes were rated as "solid Bush"—Alabama, Alaska, Idaho, Indiana, Kansas, Mississippi, Montana, Nebraska, North Dakota, Oklahoma, South Carolina, South Dakota, Texas, Utah, and Wyoming.

It was no surprise that, in November 2004, all 33 of these safe jurisdictions voted precisely as predicted in July.

Table 1.5 shows the remaining 18 states. The *Cook Political Report* listed five of these states as "lean Kerry," 10 as "toss-up," and three as "lean Bush."

The 2004 presidential campaign then played out in these 18 battleground states. There were no surprises in November 2004 in any of the eight states (with 71 electoral votes) that Cook listed as "leaning" to one candidate or the other in table 1.5. All five of the states that Cook listed as "lean Kerry" in July 2004 ended up voting for Kerry in November. Similarly, all three states that Cook listed as "lean Bush" ended up voting for Bush. In other words, the net effect of the campaign in the eight "leaning" states (which were, in effect, "second-tier" battleground states) was to solidify and consolidate initial expectations. In November, the 10 "toss up" states (the "first tier" battleground states) decided the election.

As the 2004 campaign progressed, Cook's assessment changed slightly from month to month. Cook's August 16, 2004 scorecard (table 1.6) showed 17 battleground states. The states of Delaware and Washington were deemed safer for Kerry and therefore do not appear in this table. Arizona was deemed less safe for Bush and appeared in the "lean Bush" column. The 10 core battleground states remained the same as the previous (July 6) scorecard.

The September 10, 2004 scorecard (table 1.7) contained the same 17 battleground states as the previous (August 16) table. The only change was that Missouri moved from "toss up" to "lean Bush."

The number of battleground states decreased by three in Cook's September 27, 2004 scorecard (table 1.8) because Arizona, Missouri, and North Carolina appeared safe for Bush by that point in the campaign. Bush, in fact, carried all three in November. Colorado and West Virginia were moved from "lean Bush" to "toss up."

In Cook's October 4, 2004, scorecard (table 1.9), there were 15 battleground states because Washington was considered less safe for Kerry than in the previous (September 27) scorecard.

In the actual election in November, Kerry won all four of "lean Kerry" states as well as four of the 11 "toss up" states (Minnesota, New Hampshire, Pennsylvania, and Wisconsin). Bush won seven of the 11 remaining "toss up" states (Colorado, Florida, Iowa, Nevada, New Mexico, Ohio, and West Virginia). Thus, President Bush won re-election with a total of 286 electoral votes (16 more than the 270 needed for election).

The 41 jurisdictions that the *Cook Political Report* considered "solid," "likely" or "leaning" to one candidate or other on its original July 6, 2004, scorecard ended up voting for the expected candidate.

Table 1.5 COOK'S 18 BATTLEGROUND STATES AS OF JULY 6, 2004

LEAN KERRY	TOSS UP	LEAN BUSH
Delaware	Florida	Colorado
Maine	Iowa	North Carolina
Michigan	Minnesota	West Virginia
Oregon	Missouri	
Washington	Nevada	
	New Hampshire	
	New Mexico	
	Ohio	
	Pennsylvania	
	Wisconsin	
42 electoral votes	**120 electoral votes**	**29 electoral votes**

Table 1.6 COOK'S 17 BATTLEGROUND STATES AS OF AUGUST 16, 2004

LEAN KERRY	TOSS UP	LEAN BUSH
Maine	Florida	Arizona
Michigan	Iowa	Colorado
Oregon	Minnesota	North Carolina
	Missouri	West Virginia
	Nevada	
	New Hampshire	
	New Mexico	
	Ohio	
	Pennsylvania	
	Wisconsin	
28 electoral votes	**120 electoral votes**	**29 electoral votes**

Table 1.7 COOK'S 17 BATTLEGROUND STATES AS OF SEPTEMBER 10, 2004

LEAN KERRY	TOSS UP	LEAN BUSH
Maine	Florida	Arizona
Michigan	Iowa	Colorado
Oregon	Minnesota	Missouri
	Nevada	North Carolina
	New Hampshire	West Virginia
	New Mexico	
	Ohio	
	Pennsylvania	
	Wisconsin	
28 electoral votes	**109 electoral votes**	**50 electoral votes**

Table 1.8 COOK'S 14 BATTLEGROUND STATES AS OF SEPTEMBER 27, 2004

LEAN KERRY	TOSS UP	LEAN BUSH
Maine	Colorado	
Michigan	Florida	
Oregon	Iowa	
	Minnesota	
	Nevada	
	New Hampshire	
	New Mexico	
	Ohio	
	Pennsylvania	
	West Virginia	
	Wisconsin	
28 electoral votes	**123 electoral votes**	**0 electoral votes**

Table 1.9 COOK'S 15 BATTLEGROUND STATES AS OF OCTOBER 4, 2004

LEAN KERRY	TOSS UP	LEAN BUSH
Maine	Colorado	
Michigan	Florida	
Oregon	Iowa	
Washington	Minnesota	
	Nevada	
	New Hampshire	
	New Mexico	
	Ohio	
	Pennsylvania	
	West Virginia	
	Wisconsin	
39 electoral votes	**123 electoral votes**	**0 electoral votes**

In short, the outcome of the 2004 presidential campaign was decided by a small number of battleground states (essentially the "first-tier" battleground states).

The Electoral College map for 2004 was strikingly similar to that in 2000. Only three states changed hands between 2000 and 2004. Kerry won New Hampshire in 2004, whereas Bush won it in 2000. Bush won New Mexico and Iowa in 2004, whereas Gore won those states in 2000.

In fact, the electoral map has changed very little in the five presidential elections between 1992 and 2008. In all five elections:

- 19 states with 242 electoral votes have voted Democratic and
- 13 states with 102 electoral votes have voted Republican.

A total of 41 states voted for the same party in four of the five elections. These 41 states possess approximately two-thirds (64%) of the electoral votes.

Forty-one states voted for the same party between 2000 and 2012.

Thirty-two states voted for the same party between 1992 and 2012 (table 9.41).

2008 Presidential Election

The degree of concentration on battleground states intensified in the 2008 presidential election.

As Professor George Edwards pointed out in his book *Why the Electoral College Is Bad for America*:

> **"Barack Obama campaigned in only fourteen states**, representing only 33-percent of the American people, during the entire general election."[45] [Emphasis added]

In that same post-convention period, John McCain campaigned in only 19 states.

Table 1.10 shows the states in which the presidential and vice-presidential candidates held their 300 post-convention general election campaign events in 2008. This table is based on the *Washington Post* campaign tracker and covers the period from September 5, 2008, to November 4.[46] The table is sorted according to the number of campaign events (with Ohio's 62 events at the top). The same information is presented in table 9.1, where it is sorted according to each jurisdiction's number of electoral votes. As can be seen from the table, only 19 states received any attention in the post-convention period.

Fourteen states received seven or more of the 300 post-convention general election campaign events in 2008.

- Ohio—62 events,
- Florida—46 events,
- Pennsylvania—40 events,
- Virginia—23 events,
- Missouri—21 events,
- Colorado—20 events,
- North Carolina—15 events,
- Nevada—12 events,
- New Hampshire—12 events,
- Michigan—10 events,[47]
- Indiana—9 events,

---

[45] Edwards, George C., III. 2011. *Why the Electoral College Is Bad for America*. New Haven, CT: Yale University Press. Second edition. Pages 3–5.

[46] This count is based on *public* campaign events (e.g., rallies, speeches, town hall meetings). It does not include private fund-raisers, private meetings (e.g., Palin's meetings with world leaders in New York), non-campaign events (e.g., the Al Smith Dinner in New York City or the Clinton Global Initiative dinner), televised national debates (e.g., flying into Mississippi, New York, Tennessee, and Missouri just to participate in a debate), or interviews in television studios (e.g., flying into New York City to do an interview). A "visit" to a state may consist of one or more individual events held at different places and times within the state. A joint appearance of a presidential and vice-presidential candidate is counted as one event.

[47] On October 2, 2010, the McCain campaign abruptly pulled out of Michigan after it concluded that McCain could not win Michigan. Thus, Michigan appears on this list even though it was a "jilted battleground" state.

Table 1.10 POST-CONVENTION CAMPAIGN EVENTS IN 2008

ELECTORAL VOTES	STATE	CAMPAIGN EVENTS
20	Ohio	62
27	Florida	46
21	Pennsylvania	40
13	Virginia	23
11	Missouri	21
9	Colorado	20
15	North Carolina	15
4	New Hampshire	12
5	Nevada	12
17	Michigan	10
11	Indiana	9
5	New Mexico	8
10	Wisconsin	8
7	Iowa	7
4	Maine	2
10	Minnesota	2
3	D.C.	1
5	West Virginia	1
11	Tennessee	1
3	Wyoming	0
3	Vermont	0
3	North Dakota	0
3	Alaska	0
3	South Dakota	0
3	Delaware	0
3	Montana	0
4	Rhode Island	0
4	Hawaii	0
4	Idaho	0
5	Nebraska	0
5	Utah	0
6	Kansas	0
6	Arkansas	0
6	Mississippi	0
7	Connecticut	0
7	Oklahoma	0
7	Oregon	0
8	Kentucky	0
9	Louisiana	0
8	South Carolina	0
9	Alabama	0
10	Maryland	0
12	Massachusetts	0
10	Arizona	0
11	Washington	0
15	New Jersey	0
15	Georgia	0
21	Illinois	0
31	New York	0
34	Texas	0
55	California	0
538	**Total**	**300**

- New Mexico—8 events,
- Wisconsin—8 events, and
- Iowa—7 events.

These 14 closely divided battleground states accounted for 97.7% of the 300 post-convention campaign events in the 2008 general election campaign for President (that is, 293 of the 300 events).[48]

Half of the 300 post-convention campaign events (148 of 300) were in just three states—Ohio (62 events), Florida (46 events), and Pennsylvania (40 events).

Ninety-eight percent of the 300 post-convention campaign events occurred in just 15 states. That is, under the current system, two-thirds of the states were irrelevant spectators in the 2008 presidential election.

The size of a state is not the determining factor for political relevance in presidential elections. There are small, medium, and large battleground states. The spectator states include small, medium, and large states.

Although some people mistakenly think that the current system of electing the President benefits small states, the reality is that campaign events were held in only seven of the 25 least populous states. This is shown in table 1.10 but even more dramatically in table 9.7 (which presents the very same information sorted by state size).

In fact, 39 of the 43 events held in the 25 least populous states took place in just four of these states, namely

- New Hampshire (12 events),
- New Mexico (8 events),
- Nevada (12 events), and
- Iowa (7 events).

The 25 least populous states (with a combined total of 155 electoral votes) received only 43 post-convention campaign events. In contrast, Ohio (with only 20 electoral votes) received 62 of the 300 post-convention campaign events.

In short, a state's size has nothing to do with whether a state receives attention. The controlling factor is whether the state is a closely divided battleground state.

As a general rule, the money that presidential candidates spend in the various states closely parallels the distribution of campaign events.

Table 1.11 shows the states ranked in order of their peak-season candidate advertising expenses (using data compiled by CNN) covering the period from September 24, 2008 (two days before the first debate), to Election Day (using data from the Federal Elections Commission records compiled by FairVote).[49] Column 3 shows the percentage of total national peak-season candidate advertising expenses for each state.

---

[48] The remaining seven of the 300 post-convention events (representing 2% of the events) occurred in five additional places, namely Maine (two events), Minnesota (two events), the District of Columbia (one event), Tennessee (one event), and West Virginia (one event).

[49] http://www.fairvote.org/following-the-money-campaign-donations-and-spending-in-the-2008-presidential-race.

Table 1.11 CAMPAIGN ADVERTISING SPENDING FOR THE 2008 ELECTION

STATE	ADVERTISING EXPENDITURES	PERCENT OF ADVERTISING
Florida	$29,249,985	18.18%
Pennsylvania	$24,903,675	15.48%
Ohio	$16,845,415	10.47%
Virginia	$16,634,262	10.34%
North Carolina	$9,556,598	5.94%
Indiana	$8,964,817	5.57%
Wisconsin	$8,936,200	5.56%
Missouri	$7,970,313	4.95%
Colorado	$7,944,875	4.94%
Nevada	$7,108,542	4.42%
Michigan	$5,780,198	3.59%
Minnesota	$4,262,784	2.65%
Iowa	$3,713,223	2.31%
New Mexico	$3,134,146	1.95%
New Hampshire	$2,924,839	1.82%
Montana	$971,040	0.60%
Maine	$832,204	0.52%
West Virginia	$733,025	0.46%
Georgia	$177,805	0.11%
Arizona	$75,042	0.05%
Illinois	$53,896	0.03%
California	$28,288	0.02%
North Dakota	$18,365	0.01%
Tennessee	$9,955	0.01%
Washington	$5,062	0%
Texas	$4,641	0%
Oklahoma	$4,170	0%
Kansas	$3,141	0%
Oregon	$2,754	0%
Louisiana	$2,279	0%
New York	$2,235	0%
Arkansas	$1,897	0%
Mississippi	$1,731	0%
Alabama	$1,385	0%
South Dakota	$980	0%
South Carolina	$910	0%
Nebraska	$807	0%
Kentucky	$635	0%
Idaho	$368	0%
Alaska	$310	0%
Utah	$66	0%
Massachusetts	$20	0%
D.C.	$0	0%
Maryland	$0	0%
New Jersey	$0	0%
Connecticut	$0	0%
Hawaii	$0	0%
Vermont	$0	0%
Rhode Island	$0	0%
Delaware	$0	0%
Wyoming	$0	0%
Total	**$160,862,883**	**100.00%**

Note that an alternative way of looking at the data in column 2 of this table is available in table 9.2, where the states are ranked in order of campaign contributions.

Table 1.11 shows that 99.75% of all advertising spending was in just 18 states. As can be seen, this allocation closely parallels the allocation of all 300 post-convention campaign events (in just 19 states).

The table also shows that 32 states received a combined total of *one quarter of one percent* (1/4%) of the advertising money.

2012 Presidential Election

The number of battleground states has been declining for many decades, as detailed in FairVote's 2008 report entitled *The Shrinking Battleground*.[50] The shrinkage accelerated in the 2012 presidential election.

A mere four weeks after the November 2010 congressional elections, a televised debate on C-SPAN among candidates for the chairmanship of the Republican National Committee focused on the question of how the party would conduct the presidential campaign in the 14 states that were expected to matter in 2012.[51]

On January 3, 2011—almost two years before the November 2012 election—the *Cook Political Report* issued its first Electoral College scorecard for 2012. The January 3, 2011, scorecard (table 1.12) listed 13 battleground states—four Democratic-leaning states, seven toss-up states, and two Republican-leaning states.

In other words, as early as January 2011, it appeared that the 2012 election would exhibit a dramatic decline in the number of battleground states from 2000, 2004, and 2008.

On June 2, 2011, Cook issued a scorecard (table 1.13) that again had 13 battleground states (five Democratic-leaning states, six toss-up states, and two Republican-leaning states).

On September 15, 2011, Cook issued a scorecard with 13 battleground states—two Democratic-leaning states, 10 toss-up states, and one Republican-leaning state.

On February 3, February 6, and February 23, Cook issued scorecards with 13, 14, and 14 battleground states, respectively.

On April 24, 2012, the *Cook Political Report* issued a scorecard (table 1.14) with 14 battleground states—five Democratic-leaning states, seven toss-up states, and two Republican-leaning states.

On May 10, 2012, Cook's scorecard (table 1.15) showed 13 battleground states—four Democratic-leaning states, seven toss-up states, and two Republican-leaning states.

Six of the toss-up states in May 2012 were among the seven states that appeared on Cook's scorecard 15 months earlier—Colorado, Florida, Iowa, Nevada, Ohio, and

---

[50] FairVote. 2005. *The Shrinking Battleground: The 2008 Presidential Election and Beyond.* Takoma Park, MD: The Center for Voting and Democracy. http://www.fairvote.org/shrinking.

[51] Freedomworks debate on December 1, 2010, available at http://www.freedomworks.org/rnc.

Table 1.12 COOK'S 13 BATTLEGROUND STATES AS OF JANUARY 3, 2011

LEAN DEMOCRATIC	TOSS UP	LEAN REPUBLICAN
Michigan	Colorado	Missouri
Minnesota	Florida	Virginia
New Hampshire	Iowa	
New Mexico	Nevada	
	Ohio	
	Pennsylvania	
	Wisconsin	
35 electoral votes	**98 electoral votes**	**23 electoral votes**

Table 1.13 COOK'S 13 BATTLEGROUND STATES AS OF JUNE 2, 2011

LEAN DEMOCRATIC	TOSS UP	LEAN REPUBLICAN
Michigan	Colorado	Missouri
Minnesota	Florida	North Carolina
New Hampshire	Iowa	
Pennsylvania	Nevada	
Wisconsin	Ohio	
	Virginia	
60 electoral votes	**81 electoral votes**	**25 electoral votes**

Table 1.14 COOK'S 14 BATTLEGROUND STATES AS OF APRIL 24, 2012

LEAN DEMOCRATIC	TOSS UP	LEAN REPUBLICAN
Maine	Colorado	New Hampshire
Michigan	Florida	North Carolina
Minnesota	Iowa	
New Mexico	Nevada	
Wisconsin	Ohio	
	Pennsylvania	
	Virginia	
45 electoral votes	**101 electoral votes**	**19 electoral votes**

Table 1.15 COOK'S 13 BATTLEGROUND STATES AS OF MAY 10, 2012

LEAN DEMOCRATIC	TOSS UP	LEAN REPUBLICAN
Maine	Colorado	New Hampshire
Michigan	Florida	North Carolina
New Mexico	Iowa	
Wisconsin	Nevada	
	Ohio	
	Pennsylvania	
	Virginia	
35 electoral votes	**101 electoral votes**	**19 electoral votes**

Pennsylvania. Virginia was listed as the seventh toss-up state in May 2012 (having been classified as a Republican-leaning state 15 months earlier).

As former Massachusetts Governor Mitt Romney emerged in April 2012 as the presumptive Republican nominee, he said:

> "I hope that we're able to resolve our nomination process as soon as possible, of course, **because I'd like to focus time and attention on those key battleground states.**"[52] [Emphasis added]

On June 6, 2012 (five months before Election Day), the *New York Times* reported on the vigorous early campaign in nine battleground states (Florida, Ohio, Virginia, North Carolina, Iowa, Pennsylvania, Colorado, Nevada, and New Hampshire). The article noted that the number of battleground states was considerably smaller than in 2000, 2004, and 2008.

> **"The presidential campaigns and their allies are zeroing in mainly on nine swing states**, bombarding them with commercials in the earliest concentration of advertising in modern politics.

> **"With so many resources focused on persuading an ever-shrinking pool of swing voters . . . , the 2012 election is likely to go down in history as the one in which the most money was spent reaching the fewest people.**

> "Already, ads about President Obama or Mitt Romney have been run nearly 6,000 times in and around Las Vegas since April 11. . . . And the $5 million spent by both sides during that eight-week stretch translates into the highest rate of spending per electoral vote anywhere by far. Underscoring the state's importance this year, Mr. Obama campaigned in Las Vegas on Thursday; Mr. Romney visited last week for a rally and a fund-raiser.

> "All this effort is to reach just 1.4 million registered voters, a sign of how tight this election is expected to be. And it points to how **the country's growing partisan divide has redrawn the political geography, with fewer states than ever not firmly designated 'red' or 'blue.'"**

> **"'It is unusual that so few states are in play from an advertising standpoint,'** said Will Feltus, senior vice president of National Media, which researches and plans advertising placement."

> "But **no recent general election advertising strategy has covered so little ground so early. In the spring of 2000, George W. Bush and Al Gore fought an air war in close to 20 states. In early 2004, there**

---

[52] Davis, Julie Hirschfeld, and McCormick, John. Romney charges Obama with harming U.S. economy. *POTUS News.* April 5, 2012. http://potusnews.net/2012/04/romney-charges-obama-with-harming-us-economy/.

**were the 'Swing Seventeen.' And in 2008, the Obama campaign in-
cluded 18 states in its June advertising offensive**, its first of the general election."[53] [Emphasis added]

Figure 1.3 shows the nine battleground states as of June 2012 (Florida, Ohio, Virginia, North Carolina, Iowa, Pennsylvania, Colorado, Nevada, and New Hampshire).

Table 1.16 shows the advertising spending expenditures (in millions of dollars)
by supporters of Obama and Romney from April 10 to June 28, 2012, as reported in
the *New York Times*[54] using data compiled by the Campaign Media Analysis Group
(CMAG) at Kantar Media. The CMAG data start on April 10 because:

> "April 10 is considered by many to be the unofficial start of the general elec-
> tion. It was the day former Sen. Rick Santorum of Pennsylvania suspended
> his presidential campaign. Santorum was former Massachusetts Gov. Mitt
> Romney's main rival for the Republican presidential nomination, and when
> he left the race, Romney became the presumptive GOP nominee.[55]

The money was spent in the nine battleground states shown in figure 1.3 and two
other states (Michigan and Wisconsin). Romney was advertising in Michigan and Wisconsin, but Obama was not.

In an article entitled "Modern Elections Decided by a Few States," the *Columbus
Dispatch* newspaper in Ohio said:

> "For President Barack Obama, today it's visits to Ohio and Virginia. And it's
> no coincidence that likely Republican presidential nominee Mitt Romney
> just visited those two states, and is returning to Ohio on Monday.
>
> "You'd better get used to that kind of schedule. Much like the 2000 and 2004
> presidential elections, **this year's contest is not about the millions of
> voters in all 50 states. Instead, the outcome will be decided by a
> slice of swing voters in Ohio and a handful of other states.**
>
> "'It's a small number of people in a small number of states,' said Merle Black,
> a professor of political science at Emory University in Atlanta.
>
> "That helps explain . . . why both candidates will spend so much time in
> Florida, Arizona, Colorado, New Hampshire, North Carolina and Virginia.
>
> "**The shrinking pool of competitive states is symbolic of the deep
> ideological divide among voters.** Unlike the 1960 presidential election,
> when the margin of victory in 17 states was 3 percentage points or less,

[53] Peters, Jeremy W. Campaigns blitz 9 swing states in a battle of ads. *New York Times*. June 8, 2012.

[54] Who's running the ads, and where. *New York Times*. June 30, 2012. http://www.nytimes.com/interactive/
2012/06/30/us/election-news/who-s-running-the-ads-and-where.html?ref=politics.

[55] Steinhauser, Paul. Nevada number one in ad spending per electoral vote. *CNN Politics*. July 4, 2012.

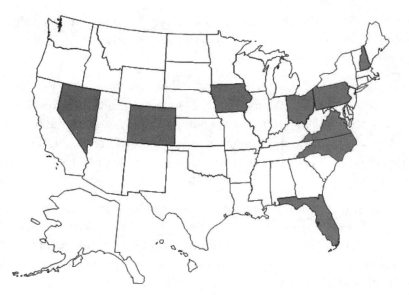

Figure 1.3 Nine battleground states in June 2012

Table 1.16 ADVERTISING SPENDING FROM APRIL 10 TO
JUNE 28, 2012 (IN MILLIONS)

STATE	OBAMA	ROMNEY	TOTAL
Florida	10.0	9.0	19.0
Ohio	8.6	8.8	17.4
North Carolina	3.8	6.4	10.2
Pennsylvania	4.2	4.5	8.7
Nevada	4.4	4.1	8.5
Virginia	3.9	4.1	8.0
Iowa	3.1	4.5	7.6
Colorado	4.8	2.6	7.4
New Hampshire	0.8	0.8	1.6
Michigan	0.0	3.3	3.3
Wisconsin	0.0	0.7	0.7
Total	**43.6**	**48.8**	**92.4**

today's electoral map shows that California, New York, New Jersey and
Illinois are solidly Democratic, while Texas and most southern states are
securely Republican.

"Gone are the days when John F. Kennedy campaigned in 45 states and
Richard Nixon appeared in all 50 in the 1960 race. They maintained such a
grueling pace because half the states—ranging from New York to Ohio to
Texas to California—were up for grabs.

"In contrast, when Republican George W. Bush won the presidency in 2000 by five electoral votes over Democrat Al Gore, only seven states were decided by margins of 3 percentage points or less. . . .

"'**You have your battleground states and your flyover states**,' said David Leland, former chairman of the Ohio Democratic Party."[56] [Emphasis added]

Mitt Romney's "Every Town Counts" bus tour in June 2012 illustrates two important aspects of presidential campaigns.

The "Every Town Counts" tour started with campaigning in the battleground state of New Hampshire. It then quickly drove through several non-battleground northeastern states where, manifestly, every town did *not* count. The bus then stopped for campaigning in the battleground states of Pennsylvania and Ohio. The tour went on to Iowa (again speeding through other non-battleground states where no town counted). The first part of the tour illustrated the fact that presidential campaigns simply do not pay attention to any states other than battleground states.

As reported in an article entitled "Romney Bus Tour Will Hit Swing States" in *Politico*:

"Romney's tour is launching as polls set the stage for an aggressive fight in swing states, with big ad buys from outside groups and heavy investments by both campaigns.

"A number of **the states Romney will visit were identified by Romney pollster Neil Newhouse of Public Opinion Strategies as among the seven key states the campaign needs to pick up to hit 270 electoral votes**."[57] [Emphasis added]

The Romney bus tour (figure 1.4) also included Michigan and Wisconsin. This part of the tour illustrated a second aspect of modern-day presidential campaigns, namely an attempt by one campaign to expand the playing field to states in which the opposition is leading (but not spending advertising money). Romney's efforts to put Michigan and Wisconsin into play involved spending advertising money in those states (as shown in the bottom two rows of table 1.16).[58]

Meanwhile, the July 5, 2012, Cook scorecard (table 1.17) reflected the ongoing shrinkage in the number of battleground states. There were 14 on April 24, 2012, and 13 on May 10, 2012. On July 5, there were only 11—three Democratic-leaning states, seven toss-up states, and one Republican-leaning state.

The focus on just a handful of closely divided battleground states continued in

---

[56] Torry, Jack. Modern elections decided by a few states: That's why Obama visits OSU today to start campaign. *Columbus Dispatch*. May 5, 2012.

[57] Summers, Juana. Romney bus tour will hit swing states. *Politico*. June 12, 2012.

[58] Obama also conducted a two-state bus tour in June 2012 (to Ohio and Pennsylvania).

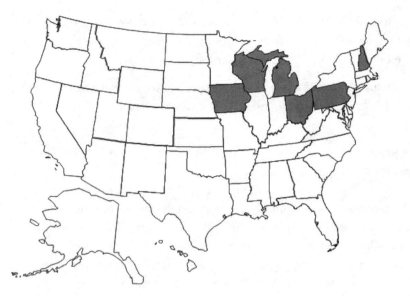

Figure 1.4 The six states visited by the "Every Town Counts" bus tour in June 2012

Table 1.17 COOK'S 11 BATTLEGROUND STATES AS OF JULY 5, 2012

LEAN DEMOCRATIC	TOSS UP	LEAN REPUBLICAN
Michigan	Colorado	North Carolina
Pennsylvania	Florida	
Wisconsin	Iowa	
	Nevada	
	New Hampshire	
	Ohio	
	Virginia	
35 electoral votes	**101 electoral votes**	**19 electoral votes**

July 2012, as reported by the *Washington Post* in an article entitled "Campaign Ads Flood into Swing States for a Summertime Blitz."

> "Voters in swing states . . . will be deluged with tens of millions of dollars in political ads over the next month as part of an intensifying broadcast war through the Olympic Games.

> "In addition to spots from President Obama and Republican challenger Mitt Romney, many ads will be aired by independent nonprofit groups that are not required to reveal who is funding them. . . .

> "Crossroad GPS, a conservative nonprofit group co-founded by former George W. Bush adviser Karl Rove, announced Friday that it was purchasing $25 million worth of anti-Obama ads in swing states. . . . The campaign starts Tuesday and will run through early August in **nine swing states:**

Colorado, Florida, Iowa, Michigan, North Carolina, New Hampshire, Nevada, Ohio and Virginia."[59] [Emphasis added]

The existence of the new "Swing States Poll" conducted by *USA Today* is a recognition of the role of the battleground states created by state winner-take-all statutes. A July 8, 2012, article in *USA Today* states:

"**When it comes to campaign ads in the presidential race, there are two Americas.**

"**'In a swing state, you're part of the presidential campaign,**' says political scientist Darrell West, author of *Air Wars*. '**Everywhere else, you're outside.**' . . .

"The swing states survey focuses on a dozen states that aren't firmly aligned with either Democrats or Republicans. That puts them in a position to tip the outcome in the Electoral College. The states: Colorado, Florida, Iowa, Michigan, Nevada, New Hampshire, New Mexico, North Carolina, Ohio, Pennsylvania, Virginia and Wisconsin."[60]

Political strategist Karl Rove predicted on May 23 that the 2012 election would come down to essentially six states.

"Mr. Romney needs 270 votes in the Electoral College. A '3-2-1' strategy will get him there. . . .

"None of Mr. McCain's states appear in real jeopardy for the GOP this year. . . .

"After this initial hurdle, Mr. Romney's victory road starts with '3'—as in Indiana, North Carolina and Virginia, a trio of historically Republican states. In 2008, Mr. Obama won by narrow margins in Indiana (barely 1%) and North Carolina (0.32%). . . .

"Next up is '2'—as in Florida and Ohio. They flipped from Republican in 2004 to Democratic in 2008. Both were close—a 2.8% margin for Mr. Obama in the former and 4.6% in the latter. . . .

"Which brings us to '1.' Mr. Romney then needs one more state—any state— and the White House is his."[61]

The *Cook Political Report* adjusted their Electoral-College scorecard as a result of Governor Romney's selection of Congressman Paul Ryan of Wisconsin as the Republi-

---

[59] Eggen, Dan. Campaign ads flood into swing states for a summertime blitz. *Washington Post*. June 6, 2012.
[60] Page, Susan. Swing states poll: Amid barrage of ads, Obama has edge. *USA Today*. July 8, 2012.
[61] Rove, Karl. Romney's Roads to the White House: A 3-2-1 strategy can get him to the magic 270 electoral votes. *Wall Street Journal*. May 23, 2012.

Table 1.18 COOK'S NINE BATTLEGROUND STATES AS OF OCTOBER 18, 2012

LEAN DEMOCRATIC	TOSS UP	LEAN REPUBLICAN
Ohio	Colorado	Florida
Wisconsin	Iowa	North Carolina
	Nevada	Virginia
	New Hampshire	
28 electoral votes	**25 electoral votes**	**57 electoral votes**

can vice-presidential nominee. The August 28, 2012, Cook scorecard moved Wisconsin from the "lean Democratic" to the "toss-up" category; however, this reclassification did not increase the number of battleground states.

The October 28, 2012, Cook scorecard (table 1.18) reduced the number of battleground states from 11 to nine. The scorecard removed Michigan and Pennsylvania from the "lean Democratic" category and placed them in the safer "likely Democratic" category (not shown in the table here). The scorecard also moved Ohio and Wisconsin from "toss up" to "lean Democratic." President Obama's poor performance in the first presidential debate in early October resulted in Florida, Virginia, and North Carolina being moved from "toss-up" to "lean Republican." The nine battleground states in this scorecard consisted of two Democratic-leaning states, four toss-up states, and three Republican-leaning states.

The presidential and vice-presidential candidates conducted 253 general-election campaign events after being nominated.

Table 1.19 shows the distribution of the 253 post-convention general-election campaign events in 2012. This table is based on CNN's "On the Trail" campaign tracker and covers the period from September 7, 2012 (the day after the Democratic National Convention) to November 6 (Election Day).[62,63] The data was compiled by FairVote.[64] The table is sorted according to the total number of campaign events per state (column 2). Columns 3, 4, 5, and 6 show the number of events by President Barack Obama, Vice President Joe Biden, Governor Mitt Romney, and Congressman Paul Ryan, respectively.

---

[62] This count is based on *public* campaign events (e.g., rallies, speeches, town hall meetings). It does not include private fund-raisers, private meetings, non-campaign events (e.g., the Al Smith Dinner in New York City, the Clinton Global Initiative dinner), televised national debates (e.g., flying into a state just to participate in the debate), or interviews in television studios (e.g., flying into New York to do an interview). A "visit" to a state may consist of one or more individual events held at different places and times within the state. A joint appearance of a presidential and vice-presidential candidate is counted as one event. Additional information is available at http://www.fairvote.org/presidential-tracker.

[63] For the reader's convenience, this same data is also presented in table 9.8 where is it sorted by state size.

[64] The FairVote tally excluded two events listed by CNN. In Kentucky, the Ryan family had breakfast at a diner on the morning after the vice-presidential debate. The event did not appear to be large enough, organized enough, or public enough to warrant being counted as a campaign event. See video at http://www.cbsnews.com/video/watch/?id=50133025n&tag=mg%3Bpolitics. In Minnesota, Congressman Ryan flew into Minneapolis on his way to the storm relief events in Wisconsin on October 30. The Minnesota press made it seem that Ryan was campaigning there, but Ryan barely stopped to talk to reporters before heading to Wisconsin. He ate at a St. Paul restaurant later that night.

As can be seen from table 1.19:

- In 2012, President Obama conducted post-convention campaign events in just eight states after being nominated, and Governor Romney did so in only 10 states. In comparison, in 2008, Obama conducted post-convention events in 14 states, and McCain did so in 19 states.
- Four out of five states (and four out of five Americans) were ignored by the candidates in the post-convention campaign period in 2012. That is, no post-convention campaign event was conducted in 39 jurisdictions (38 states and the District of Columbia) involving a major-party presidential or vice-presidential candidate.
- Ohio received 73 of the 253 post-convention campaign events (29%).
- Over two-thirds (69%) of the post-convention campaign events were conducted in just four states (Ohio, Florida, Virginia, and Iowa).
- Only one of the 13 smallest states (New Hampshire) received any post-convention campaign events.
- Only three of the 25 smallest states (i.e., those with seven or fewer electoral votes) received any post-convention campaign events (New Hampshire, Iowa, and Nevada).
- Post-convention campaign events were conducted in only 12 states, and two of them (Michigan and Minnesota) received one event each (out of the 253 events).
- The presidential campaign was fully joined in only eight states in the sense that only eight states received campaign events from Obama, Romney, Biden, and Ryan.

Figure 1.5 shows the same information as table 1.19 concerning the states in which the presidential and vice-presidential candidates conducted their 253 post-convention general-election campaign events in 2012.

The irrelevance of voters in non-battleground states was made clear by a *Washington Post* article entitled "Networks, AP Cancel Exit Polls in 19 States."

"Breaking from two decades of tradition, this year's election exit poll is set to include surveys of voters in 31 states, not all 50 as it has for the past five presidential elections. . . .

"Dan Merkle, director of elections for ABC News, and a member of the consortium that runs the exit poll, confirmed the shift Thursday. The aim, he said, 'is to still deliver a quality product in **the most important states.**' . . .

"**All 19 of the states with no exit polls are classified as either "solid Obama" or "solid Romney."** [65] [Emphasis added]

[65] Cohen, Jon and Clement, Scott. Networks, AP cancel exit polls in 19 states. *Washington Post*. October 4, 2012. http://www.washingtonpost.com/blogs/the-fix/wp/2012/10/04/networks-ap-cancel-exit-polls-in-19-states/.

Table 1.19 POST-CONVENTION CAMPAIGN EVENTS IN 2012

STATE	TOTAL	OBAMA	BIDEN	ROMNEY	RYAN
Ohio	73	15	13	27	18
Florida	40	9	8	15	8
Virginia	36	6	4	17	9
Iowa	27	5	6	7	9
Colorado	23	5	3	6	9
Wisconsin	18	5	6	1	6
Nevada	13	4	2	3	4
New Hampshire	13	4	4	3	2
Pennsylvania	5			3	2
North Carolina	3		2	1	
Michigan	1				1
Minnesota	1				1
Alabama					
Alaska					
Arizona					
Arkansas					
California					
Connecticut					
Delaware					
D.C.					
Georgia					
Hawaii					
Idaho					
Illinois					
Indiana					
Kansas					
Kentucky					
Louisiana					
Maine					
Maryland					
Massachusetts					
Mississippi					
Missouri					
Montana					
Nebraska					
New Jersey					
New Mexico					
New York					
North Dakota					
Oklahoma					
Oregon					
Rhode Island					
South Carolina					
South Dakota					
Tennessee					
Texas					
Utah					
Vermont					
Washington					
West Virginia					
Wyoming					
Total	**253**	**53**	**48**	**83**	**69**

Figure 1.5 Post-convention campaign events in 2012

USA Today reported:

"Exit polls—surveys of people who have already voted—have been narrowed this year to focus on battleground states. . . .

"'What we did was just what every journalistic organization does: **We focused our resources on where the story is. The story appears to be in those states that are competitive**,' says Sheldon Gawiser, NBC's director of elections and head of the National Election Pool, a consortium of ABC, CBS, NBC, CNN, Fox News and the Associated Press."[66] [Emphasis added]

On Election Day (November 6, 2012), President Obama ended up with a total of 332 electoral votes to Governor Romney's 206. Obama's nationwide lead was almost five million votes.[67]

Obama won eight of the nine battleground states identified by the *Cook Political Report* in its October 18, 2012 electoral scorecard (table 1.18)—that is, all except North Carolina.

Figure 1.6 shows the results of the 2012 presidential election on a proportional map. The darker gray states voted for President Barack Obama and the lighter gray states voted for Governor Mitt Romney. In this figure, the size of each state is proportional to the state's number of electoral votes. The advantage of a proportional map is that it more accurately shows the distribution of the nation's population (and the distribution of popular support) than the more familiar geographic map. This proportional

---

[66] Moore, Martha T. and Korte, Gregory. Exit polling goes the way of changing media trends. *USA Today*. November 5, 2012. http://www.usatoday.com/story/news/politics/2012/11/05/exit-polls-networks-election-day/1680839/.

[67] See appendix HH for the two-party results of the 2012 election. Table 9.43 presents the presidential vote for Barack Obama (Democrat), Mitt Romney (Republican), Gary Johnson (Libertarian), Jill Stein (Green), and the other 22 minor-party and independent candidates that were on the ballot in 2012 in at least one state.

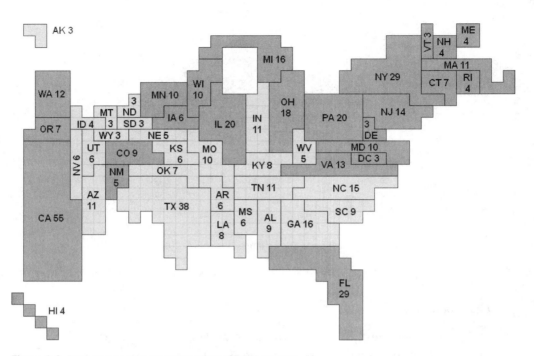

Figure 1.6 Proportional map showing results of 2012 election

map (created by Princeton Astrophysics Professor J. Richard Gott III)[68] is topologically accurate in the sense that geographically adjacent states are adjacent in this map. See figure 9.4 for a presentation of the results of the 2012 election on a geographic map.

Thirty-two states voted for the same party in all six presidential elections between 1992 and 2012. These 32 states (shown in table 9.41) possess about two-thirds (64%) of the 538 votes in the Electoral College. Of these 32 states, 19 states (possessing 242 electoral votes based on the 2010 census) voted Democratic in all six presidential elections between 1992 and 2012. Thirteen states (possessing 102 electoral votes) voted Republican in all six elections.

The fact that four out of five states and four out of five Americans, were ignored by the 2012 presidential campaign rekindled proposals to modify the manner by which states award their electoral votes.

> In December 2012, legislators in Pennsylvania, Michigan, Wisconsin, and Virginia announced that they would introduce legislation in 2013 to divide their state's electoral votes by congressional district (as discussed in greater detail in section 9.23.1).

---

[68] Professor J. Richard Gott III is gratefully acknowledged for permission to use his topologically accurate proportional electoral map. Professor Gott collaborated with Wesley N. Colley (a senior research scientist at the Center for Modeling, Simulation and Analysis at the University of Alabama in Huntsville) in publishing an electoral scoreboard based on Gott and Colley's method of median poll statistics at http://www.colleyrankings.com/election2012/.

Also, Pennsylvania Senate Majority Leader Dominic Pileggi (R) announced in December 2012 that he planned to introduce legislation to award 18 of Pennsylvania's 20 electoral votes proportionally and two electoral votes to the statewide winner (as discussed in greater detail in section 9.23.2).

In 2012, voter turnout was 11% higher in the battleground states than in the remainder of the country.

Professor Michael P. McDonald of George Mason University computed voter turnout for each state and the nation as a whole.[69]

Based on the 130,234,600 ballots that were counted in the November 2012 elections, the national turnout rate was 59.4%.

Voter turnout in the nine battleground states identified by the *Cook Political Report* in its October 18, 2012 electoral scorecard (table 1.18) was as follows:

- 71.1% in Colorado,
- 63.6% in Florida,
- 70.2% in Iowa,
- 57.2% in Nevada,
- 70.9% in New Hampshire,
- 65.2% in North Carolina
- 65.2% in Ohio
- 66.9% in Virginia, and
- 72.5% in Wisconsin.

The average voter turnout in the nine battleground states was 67.0%—11% higher than the 59.4% rate for the nation as a whole).

The absence of a meaningful presidential campaign in most states diminishes voter turnout in the ignored states. A 2005 Brookings Institution report entitled *Thinking About Political Polarization* pointed out:

> "The electoral college can depress voter participation in much of the nation. Overall, the percentage of voters who participated in last fall's election was almost 5 percent higher than the turnout in 2000. Yet, most of the increase was limited to the battleground states. Because the electoral college has effectively narrowed elections like the last one to a quadrennial contest for the votes of a relatively small number of states, people elsewhere are likely to feel that their votes don't matter."[70],[71]

---

[69] The figures are from the web page entitled "2012 General Election Turnout Rates" found at http://elections.gmu.edu/Turnout_2012G.html on December 31, 2012. The voter turnout figures are those for the number of ballots that were counted, except for Wisconsin where the highest office turnout rate was used.

[70] Nivola, Pietro S. 2005. *Thinking about Political Polarization*. Washington, DC: The Brookings Institution. Policy Brief 139. January 2005.

[71] Voter turnout is adversely affected in non-battleground states because voters of both parties in such states realize that their votes do not matter in presidential elections. As reported by the Committee for the Study of the American Electorate, "Turnout in battleground states increased by 6.3 percentage points, while turnout in the other states (and the District of Columbia) increased by only 3.8 percentage points." See

Diminished voter turnout in presidential races in non-battleground states weakens down-ballot candidates, thereby making the state even less competitive in the future.

Governance—not just electioneering—is affected by the winner-take-all rule.

While governing, every sitting President is either anticipating his own run for re-election (during his first term) or contemplating the election of his preferred successor (in his second term).

As former Illinois Governor Jim Edgar (R) pointed out:

> **"People who are in elected office remember what they learned when they were campaigning."**[72]

Edgar continued:

> "After serving in government, I learned first-hand how important it is for the candidate to know the district, or the state, or the nation they're running in. And know all of it, not just parts of it. And it's even more important after the election . . . .

> **"When you're governing,** when you're doing your duty, **you remember particularly where you campaigned. You remember who you met during the campaign. You remember the issues that were raised. It's just human nature. You're going to remember that, because that was very important to you during the campaign."**[73] [Emphasis added]

However, in present-day presidential campaigns, candidates do not campaign throughout the entire United States. As Scott Wilson reported in the *Washington Post*:

> "During his first five months in office, **public policy and electoral politics have come together seamlessly in his domestic travel itinerary.** On nearly every trip he has taken, **Obama has followed the timeworn path of presidential travel—go where the votes matter most.** . . .

> "Of the 16 states Obama has visited, nine shifted from the Republican to Democratic column in 2008. Five of the states are among the six that posted the narrowest margins of victory for either Obama or Sen. John McCain (R-Ariz.), and are likely to remain the most closely divided through the coming campaign cycles."[74] [Emphasis added]

November 4, 2004, report from the Committee for the Study of the American Electorate entitled "President Bush, mobilization drives propel turnout to post-1968 high."

[72] Press conference at the National Press Club in Washington, D.C. May 12, 2011. http://www.nationalpopular vote.com/pages/misc/hl_20110514_thompson-culver-edgar.php

[73] Press conference at the National Press Club in Washington, D.C. May 12, 2011. http://www.nationalpopular vote.com/pages/misc/hl_20110514_thompson-culver-edgar.php

[74] Wilson, Scott. Obama's travel mixes policy, politics: States with close electoral results getting most of his visits. *Washington Post.* June 21, 2009.

In the 2012 book *The Rise of the President's Permanent Campaign*,[75] Professor Brendan Doherty of the United States Naval Academy has tracked presidential travels during the year *before* the re-election campaigns of Presidents Bill Clinton (1995), George W. Bush (2003), and Barack Obama (2011). Table 1.20 shows the distribution of presidential travel by state during the year before re-election campaigns.[76]

Table 1.21 shows the relationship between 2011 presidential travel and state population. Column 2 shows the state's 2010 population, and column 4 shows each state's percentage share of the population of the 50 states. Note that the District of Columbia is not included in this table because Professor Doherty did not count events in the District by a sitting President as "travel." Column 3 is the number of presidential visits for 2011 (that is, the same information as in column 4 of table 1.20). Column 5 shows each state's percentage share of the 104 visits.

Column 6 of table 1.21 shows the index of 2011 presidential travel in relation to state population. The index is computed by dividing column 5 by column 3 and multiplying by 100. An index above 100 means that a state received proportionately more visits than its share of the nation's population. Conversely, an index below 100 indicates that a state received proportionately fewer visits. Table 1.19 is sorted by the index (column 6), thereby placing the states receiving more attention at the top of this table.

For example, Hawaii's percentage share of the nation's population is 0.44% (as shown in column 4 of the first row of table 1.21). Hawaii's four visits during 2011 represent a 3.85%-share of the 104 total visits. This 3.85% is 8.7 times Hawaii's share of the nation's population. Thus, Hawaii's index is 870. The explanation for Hawaii's high index is that President Obama often vacations there.

Table 1.19 shows that

- 19 states received no visits in 2011 even though these states represent one in six Americans.[77]

- Eight of the nine closely divided battleground states where $100,000,000 was spent by June 2012 by Obama and Romney supporters (as reported in the June 8, 2012, *New York Times* article discussed earlier in this section) had indices above 100. These states were Virginia, Iowa, New Hampshire, Nevada, Pennsylvania, Colorado, North Carolina, and Ohio.

- Two additional states with indices above 100 (Michigan and Minnesota) appeared on Cook's scorecards (shown earlier in this section) as "lean Democratic" during 2011.

---

[75] Doherty, Brendan J. 2012. *The Rise of the President's Permanent Campaign*. Lawrence, KS: University Press of Kansas.

[76] The authors gratefully acknowledge Professor Brendan Doherty of the United States Naval Academy for permission to include data on presidential travel found in the table.

[77] In fact, seven states did not receive any visits in 1995, 2003, and 2011, namely Alabama, Idaho, Louisiana, North Dakota, Rhode Island, South Dakota, and Utah). Eight additional states did not receive any visits in two of those three years, namely Maine, Mississippi, Montana, Nebraska, New Mexico, Oklahoma, and South Carolina. Arkansas would also be on that list except for the fact that President Bill Clinton's home state was Arkansas (and hence received nine of Clinton's visits in 1995).

Table 1.20 PRESIDENTIAL TRAVEL DURING THE YEAR BEFORE RE-ELECTION

STATE	CLINTON 1995	BUSH 2003	OBAMA 2011
Alabama	0	1	1
Alaska	0	0	0
Arizona	0	2	1
Arkansas	9	2	0
California	13	8	8
Colorado	3	2	3
Connecticut	2	2	1
Delaware	0	0	1
Florida	3	5	4
Georgia	3	3	0
Hawaii	4	1	4
Idaho	0	0	0
Illinois	4	3	4
Indiana	0	2	1
Iowa	4	0	3
Kansas	0	0	1
Kentucky	0	2	1
Louisiana	0	0	0
Maine	0	1	0
Maryland	NA	NA	6
Massachusetts	2	0	4
Michigan	1	5	4
Minnesota	1	2	2
Mississippi	0	2	0
Missouri	0	5	2
Montana	2	0	0
Nebraska	0	1	0
Nevada	0	1	2
New Hampshire	1	1	1
New Jersey	2	2	1
New Mexico	0	2	0
New York	4	3	12
North Carolina	1	3	5
North Dakota	0	0	0
Ohio	2	5	4
Oklahoma	1	0	0
Oregon	1	1	1
Pennsylvania	3	6	8
Rhode Island	0	0	0
South Carolina	0	2	0
South Dakota	0	0	0
Tennessee	1	2	1
Texas	3	8	2
Utah	0	0	0
Vermont	1	0	0
Virginia	NA	NA	14
Washington	0	1	1
West Virginia	0	1	0
Wisconsin	0	1	1
Wyoming	3	0	0
Total	**74**	**88**	**104**

- New York and Massachusetts are non-battleground states, but major sources of campaign funds (as shown in table 1.11).
- Three non-battleground states with indices above 100 (Alaska, Delaware, and Kansas) appeared in the top part of the table by virtue of a single visit and are thus statistical anomalies.

Maryland's appearance in table 1.21, in relation to Virginia's, is especially noteworthy. Both Maryland and Virginia are near Washington, D.C. Neither state received any attention in presidential campaigns for decades prior to 2008—the year in which Virginia suddenly emerged as a closely divided battleground state. As Paul West pointed out in the "Maryland Politics" section of the *Baltimore Sun*:

> "**Recent presidents have divided their time more or less evenly between Maryland and Virginia**. But Obama, by a lopsided margin, is favoring the commonwealth on the other side of the Potomac."

The article continued:

> "Obama has shown Virginia far more love than Maryland since taking office.
>
> "**Presidents of both parties frequently use the neighboring states as sites for their public events**. Since many Americans revile the capital city, it is often necessary to escape to a more suitable 'real world' locale. Next-door Maryland and Virginia are obvious choices, since they are only a quick trip away (time is a president's scarcest resource).
>
> "Today, for example, the White House announced that Obama plans to deliver a national back-to-school address next Tuesday from a high school in northern Virginia. . . .
>
> "**There isn't much mystery in Obama's apparent preference for Virginia over Maryland.** . . .
>
> "**Obama has concentrated his domestic travels on key electoral states—favoring those that will matter in 2012, while largely ignoring states that are either out of reach (such as those in the Deep South) or are safely Democratic.** . . . "[78] [Emphasis added]

Cabinet travel exhibits a similar pattern.

> "A half-dozen Cabinet members have made more than 85 trips this year to electoral battlegrounds such as Colorado, Florida, Nevada, North Carolina, Ohio and Pennsylvania, according to a *Politico* review of public speeches

[78] West, Paul. Maryland politics: Obama favoring purple Virginia over blue Maryland by 8-1 margin. *Baltimore Sun*. September 2, 2009.

Table 1.21 INDEX OF 2011 PRESIDENTIAL TRAVEL IN RELATION TO POPULATION

STATE	POPULATION	OBAMA 2011	SHARE OF POPULATION	SHARE OF VISITS	INDEX
Hawaii	1,366,862	4	0.44%	3.85%	870
Virginia	8,037,736	14	2.60%	13.46%	518
Alaska	721,523	1	0.23%	0.96%	412
Delaware	900,877	1	0.29%	0.96%	330
Maryland	5,789,929	6	1.87%	5.77%	308
Iowa	3,053,787	3	0.99%	2.88%	292
New Hampshire	1,321,445	1	0.43%	0.96%	225
Nevada	2,709,432	2	0.88%	1.92%	219
Pennsylvania	12,734,905	8	4.12%	7.69%	187
New York	19,421,055	12	6.28%	11.54%	184
Massachusetts	6,559,644	4	2.12%	3.85%	181
Colorado	5,044,930	3	1.63%	2.88%	177
North Carolina	9,565,781	5	3.09%	4.81%	155
Michigan	9,911,626	4	3.21%	3.85%	120
Minnesota	5,314,879	2	1.72%	1.92%	112
Kansas	2,863,813	1	0.93%	0.96%	104
Ohio	11,568,495	4	3.74%	3.85%	103
Missouri	6,011,478	2	1.94%	1.92%	99
Illinois	12,864,380	4	4.16%	3.85%	92
Connecticut	3,581,628	1	1.16%	0.96%	83
Oregon	3,848,606	1	1.24%	0.96%	77
Kentucky	4,350,606	1	1.41%	0.96%	68
California	37,341,989	8	12.08%	7.69%	64
Florida	18,900,773	4	6.11%	3.85%	63
Wisconsin	5,698,230	1	1.84%	0.96%	52
Tennessee	6,375,431	1	2.06%	0.96%	47
Arizona	6,412,700	1	2.07%	0.96%	46
Indiana	6,501,582	1	2.10%	0.96%	46
Washington	6,753,369	1	2.18%	0.96%	44
New Jersey	8,807,501	1	2.85%	0.96%	34
Texas	25,268,418	2	8.17%	1.92%	24
Alabama	4,802,982	0	1.55%	-	-
Arkansas	2,926,229	0	0.95%	-	-
Georgia	9,727,566	0	3.15%	-	-
Idaho	1,573,499	0	0.51%	-	-
Louisiana	4,553,962	0	1.47%	-	-
Maine	1,333,074	0	0.43%	-	-
Mississippi	2,978,240	0	0.96%	-	-
Montana	994,416	0	0.32%	-	-
Nebraska	1,831,825	0	0.59%	-	-
New Mexico	2,067,273	0	0.67%	-	-
North Dakota	675,905	0	0.22%	-	-
Oklahoma	3,764,882	0	1.22%	-	-
Rhode Island	1,055,247	0	0.34%	-	-
South Carolina	4,645,975	0	1.50%	-	-
South Dakota	819,761	0	0.27%	-	-
Utah	2,770,765	0	0.90%	-	-
Vermont	630,337	0	0.20%	-	-
West Virginia	1,859,815	0	0.60%	-	-
Wyoming	568,300	0	0.18%	-	-
Total	**309,183,463**	**104**	**100.00%**	**100.00%**	

and news clippings. Those **swing-state visits represent roughly half of all travel for those six Cabinet officials this year.**"[79] [Emphasis added]

The pattern of presidential interviews with local news stations shows a similar pattern:

"Mr. Obama also has granted about 50 interviews [in 2011] with local news outlets, the majority from swing states."[80]

Professor Andrew Reeves examined presidential disaster declarations, which allow Presidents to unilaterally authorize potentially billions of dollars to specific constituencies. He reported in a 2011 paper:

"In an analysis extending from 1981 to 2004, I find that a state's electoral competitiveness influences whether they receive a disaster declaration from the president. **A highly competitive state can expect to receive twice as many presidential disaster declarations as an uncompetitive state**. This relationship has existed since the passage of the 1988 Stafford Act, which expanded the disaster declaration powers of the president. Additionally, I find that **these decisions have the intended electoral benefits—voters react and reward presidents for presidential disaster declarations. A president can expect over a one point increase in a statewide contest in return for a single presidential disaster declaration**."[81] [Emphasis added]

Dana Ross of Durham, North Carolina, noted a pattern in federal exemptions from the No Child Left Behind law:

"The purple state balance of the Obama administration's exemptions appears to be based on a '**no swing state left behind**' calculation."[82] [Emphasis added]

The executive branch has sole discretionary authority over the distribution of billions of dollars of discretionary grants.

In a study entitled *The Politics of Federal Grants: Presidential Influence over the Distribution of Federal Funds*, Dr. John Hudak of the Brookings Institution observed:

"Because of the institutional design of the Electoral College, presidents do not face a national electorate, but instead a series of sub-national, state-

[79] Samuelsohn, Darren. Obama's cabinet members mix policy, politics. *Politico*. June 7, 2012.

[80] Weisman, Daniel, and Lee, Carol E. Obama swing-state visits surpass presidential record. *Wall Street Journal*. November 28, 2011.

[81] Reeves, Andrew. 2011. Political disaster: unilateral powers, electoral incentives, and presidential disaster declarations. *Journal of Politics*. 73(4):1142–1151.

[82] Ross, Dana. President Obama's 'No swing state left behind' policy. *Wall Street Journal On-Line*. June 5, 2012.

level electorates. Moreover, only a handful of states [are] competitive in presidential elections, reducing a huge national electoral to a much smaller set of competitive races. . . . The small size of the truly competitive presidential electorate makes an electoral strategy that utilizes the distribution of government funds a feasible and appealing tactic."[83]

Using a recently available database that permits the study of all federal grants by state between 1996 and 2008, Hudak concluded:

"The President and his subordinates strategically direct federal funding toward electorally competitive states. . . .

"The executive branch delivers more money and grants to swing states than all other states.

"Further, the proximity of a presidential election enhances this swing state bias in the distribution of funds."

"Swing states are more likely to be benefactors of federal money than states that the president (or his party) has no chance of winning.…

"Through the strategic use of discretion, presidents influence the distribution of federal funds, essentially using them as a campaign resource.

"Presidents strategically time grant allocation announcements in order to reap the maximum benefits in terms of credit claiming."[84]

In his study, Hudak defined "core" states, "lost cause" states, and "swing" states as follows:

"Core states are those in which the incumbent party received more than 55% of the vote in the previous election.

"Lost cause states are those in which the incumbent party received less than 45% of the vote.

"Swing states are those which were decided by 10% or less in the previous election."[85]

Hudak reached the following conclusion regarding federal discretionary grants controlled by the executive branch:

---

[83] Hudak, John Joseph. 2011. *The Politics of Federal Grants: Presidential Influence over the Distribution of Federal Funds.* Center for the Study of Democratic Institutions. Working Paper # 01-2011. Pages 10–11. http://www.vanderbilt.edu/political-science/graduate/CSDI-WP-01-2011.pdf.

[84] *Ibid.* Pages 1–5.

[85] *Ibid.* Page 11.

"Swing states receive between 7.3% and 7.6% more grants than do other states. . . .

"Swing states see a benefit of 5.7% more grant dollars than other states."[86]

In summary:

"Presidents use their discretionary control over huge sums of federal grant dollars to target funds to swing states. . . .

"Federal grants function as an incumbent-controlled pool of campaign funds that presidents are able to allocate strategically."[87]

Additional details are found in Hudak's 2012 study.[88]

In the same vein, Professor Kevin Stack of Vanderbilt University and Dr. John Hudak presented a tentative study in August 2012 revealing a similar relationship between the location of Superfund enforcement actions and a state's battleground status.[89]

In September 2011, a bill was introduced in the Pennsylvania state legislature to award Pennsylvania's electoral votes by congressional district (as Maine and Nebraska currently do). The approach proposed in the bill would replace Pennsylvania's current state statute allocating all 20 of its electoral votes to the candidate who receives the most votes statewide. The effect of the proposed bill would be to divide Pennsylvania's electoral votes between the parties.

State Senator Daylin Leach (a leading Democratic opponent of the bill) said on the *PBS News Hour* on September 28, 2011:

"Pennsylvania is a battleground state, it gets a ton of attention, a ton of resources. **The day this bill passes we become irrelevant to electoral campaigns**. . . . We become Utah on the day this bill passes."[90] [Emphasis added]

In a September 27, 2011, article entitled "Specter Bluntly Says Electoral Change Will Cut Fed Funding for PA," former U.S. Senator Arlen Specter (who was a Republican until 2009) said:

"I think it'd be very bad for Pennsylvania because we wouldn't attract attention from Washington on important funding projects for the state."

[86] *Ibid.* Pages 21–22.

[87] *Ibid.* Page 28.

[88] Hudak, John Joseph. 2012. *The Politics of Federal Grants: Presidential Influence over the Distribution of Federal Funds.* PhD dissertation. Nashville, TN: Vanderbilt University. May 2012.

[89] Hudak, John Joseph and Stack, Kevin M. *The President and the Politics of Agency Enforcement: The Case of Superfund.* Conference draft. August 19, 2012.

[90] *PBS News Hour.* September 28, 2011.

"**Under the current electoral system, Obama has good reason to give us the money to carry Pennsylvania. Because Presidents think that way. It affects their decisions.**"

"**In 2004, when I ran with Bush, he was running for re-election and so was I. The President came to Pennsylvania 44 times, and he was looking for items the state needed to help him win the state.**"

"That has been the tradition with the Presidents I served with and it helped us get federal funding throughout the state. It has worked pretty well for us for 30 years, I can tell you."

"**It's undesirable to change the system so Presidents won't be asking us always for what we need, what they can do for us.**"

"For 30 years, that system has worked pretty well for us, and **it's undesirable to alter a system that is not broken.**"[91] [Emphasis added]

Former Pennsylvania Governor Ed Rendell (D) said on September 17, 2011:

"**Why would you pay any attention to Pennsylvania? Why would you care, day in and day out, about doing things for Pennsylvania?** . . . We're sacrificing tremendous clout that we presently have."[92] [Emphasis added]

On September 13, Rendell said that presidential elections are decided by

"basically Pennsylvania, Michigan, Ohio and Florida . . . . "

"That gives us tremendous clout when the governor of Pennsylvania asks the president or Congress for something, such as disaster recovery aid, Rendell said. If the disaster's cost is close to what qualifies the state for federal aid, its electoral votes tip the balance in its favor."[93]

Rob Gleason, the Republican State Chairman, said on September 17, 2011:

"We would no longer be a battleground state with all the benefits that come with that."[94]

In summary, political influence in presidential elections is today concentrated in a scattered handful of battleground states, while the vast majority of states (small and large) are politically irrelevant.

---

[91] DeCoursey, Peter L. Specter bluntly says electoral change will cut fed funding for PA. *Pennsylvania Capitol Wire*. September 27, 2011.

[92] *Chron.com*. September 17, 2011.

[93] Wereschagin, Mike, and Bumsted, Brad. GOP plan could jeopardize Pennsylvania's political clout. *Pittsburgh Tribune-Review*. September 13, 2011.

[94] *PoliticsPA*. September 17, 2011.

As former Illinois Governor Jim Edgar (R) said:

"We need a President who is a President for all the nation—not just the battleground states."[95]

As former White House Press Secretary Ari Fleischer said in 2009 about the current state-by-state winner-take-all system:

"If people don't like it, they can move from a safe state to a swing state and see their president more."[96] [Emphasis added]

In chapter 6 of this book, the authors show that the American people have an alternative to moving their families to another state in order to obtain a permanent and equal voice in presidential elections, namely a national popular vote for President.

1.2.2 THE CURRENT SYSTEM DOES NOT ACCURATELY REFLECT THE NATIONWIDE POPULAR VOTE

One of the other consequences of the statewide winner-take-all rule (i.e., awarding all of a state's electoral votes to the presidential candidate who receives the most popular votes in each separate state) is that it is possible for a candidate to win the Presidency without winning the most popular votes nationwide.

Of the 56 presidential elections between 1789 and 2008, there have been four elections in which the candidate with the most popular votes nationwide did not win the Presidency (table 1.22).[97] The rate of such occurrences is one in 14, or 7%.[98]

There have been six presidential elections since World War II in which a shift of a relatively small number of votes in one or two states would have elected (and, of course, in 2000, did elect) a presidential candidate who lost the popular vote nationwide. In 1976, for example, Jimmy Carter led Gerald Ford by 1,682,970 votes nationwide; however, a shift of 3,687 votes in Hawaii and 5,559 votes in Ohio would have elected Ford. As shown in table 1.23, there has been about one such "near miss" election each decade.[99]

In 2004, President George W. Bush had a nationwide lead of 3,012,171 popular votes; however, the outcome of the election remained in doubt on election night because it was not initially clear which candidate was going to win Ohio's 20 electoral votes. In the end, Bush received 118,785 more popular votes than Kerry in Ohio,[100] thus

---

[95] Press conference at the National Press Club in Washington, DC, May 12, 2011. http://www.nationalpopular vote.com/pages/misc/hl_20110514_thompson-culver-edgar.php

[96] *Washington Post.* June 21, 2009.

[97] Congressional Quarterly. 2002. *Presidential Elections 1789–2002.* Washington, DC: CQ Press.

[98] A 2012 analysis used the mathematical technique of principal components analysis to arrive at an estimate of 5% for the likelihood of a modern presidential election in which the winner of the national popular vote is not also the winner in the Electoral College. See Neubauer, Michael; Schilling, Mark; and Zeitlin, Joel. *Exploring Unpopular Presidential Elections.* June 12, 2012. Cornell University Library. arXiv:1206.2683v1.

[99] Ibid.

[100] Ohio Certificate of Ascertainment, December 6, 2004.

Table 1.22 PRESIDENTIAL ELECTIONS IN WHICH THE CANDIDATE WITH THE MOST
POPULAR VOTES DID NOT WIN THE PRESIDENCY

YEAR	CANDIDATE WITH THE MOST POPULAR VOTES NATIONWIDE	CANDIDATE WITH THE MOST ELECTORAL VOTES	POPULAR VOTES FOR THE CANDIDATE WITH THE MOST POPULAR VOTES	POPULAR VOTES FOR THE CANDIDATE WHO PLACED SECOND IN THE POPULAR VOTE	POPULAR VOTE DIFFERENCE
1824	Andrew Jackson	John Q. Adams	151,271	113,122	38,149
1876	Samuel J. Tilden	Rutherford B. Hayes	4,288,191	4,033,497	254,694
1888	Grover Cleveland	Benjamin Harrison	5,539,118	5,449,825	89,293
2000	Al Gore	George W. Bush	50,992,335	50,455,156	537,179

winning all of the state's 20 electoral votes and ensuring his re-election. However, if 59,393 Bush voters in Ohio had shifted to Kerry in 2004, Kerry would have ended up with 272 electoral votes (two more than the 270 required to be elected). The 59,393 voters in Ohio were decisive, whereas Bush's nationwide lead of more than three million votes was irrelevant.[101] The illusion of closeness in 2004 resulted from the statewide winner-take-all system—not because the election was genuinely close on the basis of the nationwide popular vote.

In his 2011 book *Why the Electoral College Is Bad for America*, Professor George Edwards argues that a fair accounting of the popular vote cast in Alabama in 1960 would make Richard Nixon—not John F. Kennedy—the winner of the nationwide popular vote in 1960. Under this method of accounting, there would have been five (instead of four) out of 56 presidential elections in which the candidate winning the Electoral College did not win the nationwide popular vote.

The issue arises because neither Nixon's name nor Kennedy's name actually appeared on the ballot in Alabama in 1960 (figure 2.13). Instead, only the names of 11 candidates from each party for the position of presidential electors appeared on the ballot. Each party's group of 11 candidates for the position of presidential elector were arranged in columns headed only by the political party's name, but not the name of the party's presidential candidate. In the primary election that chose the Democratic nominees for the 11 positions, only five of the Democratic nominees were publicly pledged to their party's national nominee (John F. Kennedy). Six of the elector candidates were unpledged and made it clear that they opposed the national party. All 11 candidates in the Democratic column were elected as presidential electors. The six unpledged Democratic electors ultimately voted for Harry F. Byrd in the Electoral College. A reason-

[101] Ohio was not the only key state in the Electoral College in 2004. A shift of 6,743 votes in Iowa (with seven electoral votes), 4,295 in New Mexico (with five electoral votes), and 10,784 in Nevada (with five electoral votes) would have given George W. Bush and John Kerry each 269 electoral votes. If this shift of 21,822 popular votes had occurred, the presidential election would have been thrown into the House of Representatives (with each state casting one vote and states with an equal division casting no vote), and the vice-presidential election would have been thrown into the Senate (with each Senator having one vote).

Table 1.23 SIX "NEAR MISS" PRESIDENTIAL ELECTIONS SINCE WORLD WAR II

YEAR	POPULAR VOTE WINNER	ELECTORAL VOTE WINNER	NATIONWIDE POPULAR VOTE LEAD	ELECTORAL VOTES RECEIVED BY NATIONWIDE POPULAR VOTE WINNER	ELECTORAL VOTES RECEIVED BY ELECTORAL VOTE WINNER	POPULAR VOTE SHIFT THAT WOULD HAVE CHANGED THE OUTCOME
2004	Bush	Bush	3,319,608	286	286	59,393 in Ohio
2000	Gore	Bush	537,179	267	271	269 in Florida
1976	Carter	Carter	1,682,970	297	297	5,559 in Ohio and 3,687 in Hawaii
1968	Nixon	Nixon	510,645	301	301	10,245 in Missouri and 67,481 in Illinois
1960	Kennedy	Kennedy	114,673	303	303	4,430 in Illinois and 4,782 in South Carolina
1948	Truman	Truman	2,135,570	303	303	3,554 in Ohio and 8,933 in California

able argument can thus be made to proportionally allocate only five-elevenths of the Democratic Party's popular margin in Alabama over the Republican Party to Kennedy. This method of accounting would put Nixon ahead of Kennedy in the nationwide total popular vote. Nixon, however, never publicly argued for this interpretation or claimed to have won the national popular vote in 1960.[102]

About half of American presidential elections have been landslides (that is, elections with a margin of 10% or more). If one considers only non-landslide presidential elections, the four "wrong winner" elections represent one in seven of the non-landslide elections (14%). Thus, it should not be surprising that one of the seven non-landslide elections between 1988 and 2012—namely the 2000 election—was a "wrong winner" election.

Given the relative closeness of all seven presidential elections between 1988 and 2012, and given today's closely divided political environment, problems with the operation of the state-by-state winner-take-all rule can be expected in the future.

The 1991 book *Wrong Winner: The Coming Debacle in the Electoral College* by David Abbott and James P. Levine[103] predicted that emerging political and demographic trends would lead to an increasing number of elections in which the candidate with the most popular votes nationwide would not win a majority in the Electoral College.

Matthew Dowd discussed the possibility of a "wrong winner" election in 2004:

"In 2004, during my tenure as chief strategist for the Bush–Cheney re-election campaign, I did some scenario planning on possible outcomes in a

---

[102] Edwards, George C., III. 2011. *Why the Electoral College Is Bad for America.* New Haven, CT: Yale University Press. Second edition. Pages 67–69.

[103] Abbott, David W., and Levine, James P. 1991. *Wrong Winner: The Coming Debacle in the Electoral College.* Westport, CT: Praeger.

very close election. I had expected that election to be decided by 3 percentage points or less . . . .

"One scenario I raised as a real possibility internally was that George Bush could win the popular vote but lose the electoral college (the exact opposite of what happened in 2000). And this scenario would have come to pass if the Bush margin in Ohio had changed by 120,000 votes. John Kerry would have won the electoral college, 271 to 266, while Bush would have won the popular vote by approximately 3 million votes. . . .

"Subtract 2.2 percent from the margin in each state in 2004 and Bush would have still barely won the popular vote (but by a bigger margin than Gore won the popular vote in 2000), but lost the electoral college to Kerry, 283 to 254, because Ohio, Iowa and New Mexico would have switched from Bush to Kerry."[104] [Emphasis added]

Applying the same methodology to the situation in 2012, Dowd said the following on June 6, 2012, about the possibility of a "wrong winner" election in 2012:

"So let's do some similar scenario planning for 2012, when another tight election is expected. It is also expected to be decided by less than 3 percentage points, just like 2004. . . .

"In a very tight race this November, . . . Romney could win the popular vote by more than 1 million votes and lose the electoral college to Obama by a margin of 272 to 266. . . .

"Let me show you how I arrived at this scenario. Obama won the popular vote by a national percentage of just over 7 points in 2008. If we subtract 8 points from the margin in every state, Romney would have a little less than a 1-point victory nationally (which gives you the 1 million vote margin for him in the popular vote).

"And as we subtract 8 points from every state's margin, what happens to the electoral college? It gets much, much closer, but Obama still wins it by six electoral votes. So in one very possible scenario, Obama can lose the popular vote and still be reelected because he barely carries the electoral college.

"Obviously, much can change over the coming weeks and months, and there are a variety of possibilities. The economy could get worse and Romney wins by a bigger margin and carries the electoral college. The economy could improve and Obama gets reelected comfortably in both the popular

---

[104] Dowd, Matthew. How Obama could lose the popular vote and win the election. *Huffington Post*. June 6, 2012.

vote and the electoral college. Or it's a close election, and as is traditionally the case, the popular vote and electoral college are in sync.

"But keep in mind that in the very tight elections since 2000, we have been increasingly faced with a divergence of the popular vote and the electoral college. **This happened in 2000, it could have easily have happened in 2004, and it could definitely happen in 2012.** But interestingly, if there is a divergence in 2012, it is likely to benefit President Obama and not Mitt Romney."[105] [Emphasis added]

Albert Hunt commented on Dowd's analysis on July 8, 2012:

"If the race is decided by two percentage points or . . . less than that, the president has a slight advantage with the map."[106]

1.2.3 NOT EVERY VOTE IS EQUAL

There are numerous examples of large disparities in the value of votes under the state-wide winner-take-all system.

For example, Gore won five electoral votes by carrying New Mexico by only 365 popular votes in the 2000 presidential election, whereas Bush won five electoral votes by carrying Utah by 312,043 popular votes—an 855-to-1 disparity in the importance of a vote.

In 2000, George W. Bush received 2,912,790 popular votes in Florida, whereas Al Gore received 2,912,353—a difference of 537 popular votes. Meanwhile, Gore had a nationwide lead of 537,179 popular votes. Gore's shortfall of 537 votes in Florida was less than a thousandth of Gore's nationwide lead of 537,179 votes. However, under the winner-take-all rule in effect in Florida, Bush's 537-vote lead in Florida entitled him to all of Florida's 25 electoral votes, thereby giving him the Presidency.[107]

Large differences in the value of a vote in various states have the additional negative side effect of increasing the likelihood of contested presidential elections and re-counts. Because the statewide winner-take-all system divides the nation's 130,000,000 popular votes into 51 separate pools, it regularly manufactures artificial crises even when the nationwide popular vote is not particularly close. There are fewer opportunities for razor-thin outcomes when there is a single large pool of votes than when there are 51 separate smaller pools.

The 2000 presidential election is remembered as having been close because George W. Bush's popular vote in Florida was a mere 537 more than Gore's statewide

---

[105] Dowd, Matthew. How Obama could lose the popular vote and win the election. *Huffington Post*. June 6, 2012.

[106] Hunt, Albert R. Electoral map doesn't always lead straight to White House. *Bloomberg View*. July 8, 2012.

[107] George W. Bush received 271 electoral votes when the Electoral College met in December 2000—one more than the minimum required for election.

Figure 1.7 Herb Block cartoon of September 15, 1970[108]

total. There was, however, nothing particularly close about the 2000 election on the basis of the nationwide popular vote. Al Gore's nationwide lead of 537,179 popular votes was larger than, for example, Nixon's lead of 510,314 in 1968 and Kennedy's lead of 118,574 in 1960.[108] The closeness of the 2000 presidential election was an artificial crisis caused by the statewide winner-take-all system.

In the controversial 1876 presidential election, Democrat Samuel J. Tilden received 4,288,191 popular votes—254,694 more than the 4,033,497 popular votes received by Rutherford B. Hayes. Tilden's lead of 3.05% was substantial. It was, for example, greater than George W. Bush's popular vote lead of 2.8% in 2004. The 1876 election is remembered as having been close because Hayes's one-vote lead in the Electoral College resulted from his winning several states by extremely narrow margins:

---

[108] Congressional Quarterly. 2002. *Presidential Elections 1789–2002*. Washington, DC: CQ Press. Pages 146 and 148.

[109] The Herb Block Foundation is gratefully acknowledged for permission to use the copyrighted Herb Block cartoon in figure1.7.

- 889 votes in South Carolina,
- 922 votes in Florida,
- 1,050 votes in Oregon,
- 1,075 votes in Nevada, and
- 2,798 votes in California.[110]

The closeness of the electoral-vote count in the 1876 election was an artificial crisis created by the statewide winner-take-all system—it was not due to the closeness of the nationwide popular vote for President.

The six problematic presidential elections in the past six decades (table 1.23) are reminders that the operation of the winner-take-all system in 51 separate jurisdictions makes razor-thin margins more likely. This, in turn, makes electoral mischief and fraud more rewarding. As Senator Birch Bayh said in a Senate speech in 1979:

> "[O]ne of the things we can do to limit fraud is to limit the benefits to be gained by fraud.

> "Under a direct popular vote system, one fraudulent vote wins one vote in the return. In the electoral college system, one fraudulent vote could mean 45 electoral votes, 28 electoral votes."[111]

1.3 NATIONWIDE POPULAR ELECTION AS A REMEDY FOR THE SHORTCOMINGS OF THE CURRENT SYSTEM

Nationwide popular election of the President is the only system that

- makes *every* voter in *every* state relevant in *every* presidential election,
- guarantees that the candidate with the most popular votes in the entire country wins the Presidency, and
- makes every vote equal.

The authors of this book believe that George W. Bush's lead of over 3,000,000 popular votes in 2004 should alone have guaranteed him the Presidency in 2004—regardless of which candidate ended up carrying Ohio. Similarly, Al Gore's nationwide lead of 537,179 should alone have been sufficient to elect him as President in 2000—regardless of whether one candidate or the other carried Florida by 537 votes.

1.4 FORTUITOUS CONVERGENCE OF FACTORS FAVORING REFORM AT THE PRESENT TIME

A fortuitous convergence of factors currently exists favoring reform of the current system of electing the President.

First, the public has come to realize that voters are effectively disenfranchised

---

[110] Congressional Quarterly. 2002. *Presidential Elections 1789–2002*. Washington, DC: CQ Press. Page 125.
[111] *Congressional Record*. March 14, 1979. Page 5000.

in presidential elections in about four-fifths of the states. Because of the closeness of the seven presidential elections between 1988 and 2012 and today's closely divided political environment, the media has spotlighted the notion of reliably "red" states and reliably "blue" states and the operation of the state-by-state winner-take-all rule. In particular, the public has become more aware that presidential elections are contested in only a handful of battleground states. In addition, the six problematic presidential elections in the past six decades (table 1.23) have further focused public attention on the mechanics of the Electoral College.

Second, neither major political party gains a partisan advantage from the small states. The small states have been equally divided between the major political parties in the seven most recent presidential elections (1988 through 2012).

- Six of the 13 small states (Alaska, Idaho, Montana, North Dakota, South Dakota, and Wyoming) have regularly given their combined 19 electoral votes to the Republican presidential candidate. The only exception was when Clinton carried Montana in 1992 (undoubtedly because of Ross Perot's presence on the ballot).

- Six other small jurisdictions (Delaware, the District of Columbia, Hawaii, Maine, Rhode Island, and Vermont) have regularly given their combined 21 electoral votes to the Democratic presidential candidate. The only exceptions were that George H. W. Bush carried Vermont, Maine, and Delaware in 1988.

- Only one of the 13 smallest states (New Hampshire) is a closely divided battleground state. New Hampshire supported the Democrat in 1992 and 1996, the Republican in 1988 and 2000, and the Democrat in 2004, 2008, and 2012.

As it happens, the small states are disadvantaged by the statewide winner-take-all rule to a considerably greater degree than the other states. Specifically, 92% (12 of the 13) of the smallest states are routinely ignored by presidential campaigns.

The 13 smallest states have a combined population of 11,448,957.[112] Coincidentally, Ohio has almost the same population (11,353,140) as the 13 smallest states combined. Excluding the one competitive small state (New Hampshire) from consideration, the Constitution gives 40 electoral votes to the 12 noncompetitive small states—16 electoral votes warranted by population and 24 because of the two electoral-vote bonus per state). The Constitution gives Ohio only 20 electoral votes—half as many as the 12 noncompetitive small states. If it were true that the two-vote bonus enhanced the influence of small states, the 12 small states should exert considerably more influence than Ohio in presidential elections. This is not, of course, the case. The battleground state of Ohio (with its "mere" 20 electoral votes) is very important in presidential elections, whereas the 12 noncompetitive small states (with their total of 40 electoral votes) are politically irrelevant. Table 1.2 (on 2004 campaign events) dramatically shows the irrelevance of the 12 noncompetitive small states in presidential elections. Table 1.1

---

[112] Unless otherwise stated, population figures in this book refer to the 2000 federal census.

shows that almost none of the $237,423,744 in advertising expenditures was spent in the 12 noncompetitive small states. The 11 million people in Ohio are politically important, whereas the 11 million people in the 12 small noncompetitive states are not.

It is true that the Founding Fathers intended, as part of the political compromise that led to the Constitution, to confer a certain amount of extra influence on the less populous states by giving every state a bonus of two electoral votes corresponding to its two U.S. Senators. The additional influence intended for the small states was not large, but neither was it negligible. At the present time, the 13 smallest states (i.e., those with three or four electoral votes) collectively possess about 4% of the nation's population but have 8% of the electoral votes (44 of 538). The Founders' intended allocation of additional political influence to the small states was not achieved because the political effect of the arithmetic bonus provided by the Constitution was trumped by the influence-cancelling effect of the state-by-state winner-take-all rule. Because of the winner-take-all rule, political power in presidential elections resides in the scattered collection of states where the popular vote happens to be closely divided—that is, the battleground states. Because small states have an unusually high probability of being one-party states in presidential elections, 12 of the 13 (92%) least populous states are non-battleground states.

In short, the two-vote bonus established by the Constitution to enhance the influence of the small states exists today in *form*; however, the nearly unanimous use by the states of the winner-take-all rule robs the electoral votes of the small states of any political *substance*. If, hypothetically, the Constitution had given each state a bonus of *four* electoral votes (instead of just two), the 12 noncompetitive small states would then collectively have 64 electoral votes (16 warranted by population plus 48 bonus electoral votes). Even then, these states still would not have any meaningful influence in presidential elections. A competitive state, such as Ohio with only 20 electoral votes, would remain far more important in terms of practical politics than the 12 noncompetitive small states. Political power in a system based on the statewide winner-take-all rule comes from being a closely divided battleground state—not from mathematical bonuses.

The Founding Fathers also intended that the Constitution's formula for allocating electoral votes would give the most populous states a large amount of influence in presidential elections.[113] A glance at table 1.1, table 1.2, and figure 1.2 demonstrates that the Founders did not achieve this objective. If size mattered, the nation's most populous states would be at center stage in presidential elections. But this is not the case. The political reality is that six of the 12 largest states (California, Texas, New York, Illinois, Georgia, and New Jersey) suffer from the same spectator status as the 12 noncompetitive small states—none has mattered in recent presidential elections.

---

[113] Out of the present-day 538 electoral votes, 435 are allocated according to population because they correspond to the 435 members of the House of Representatives. That is, about 81% of the 538 electoral votes are allocated according to population.

The Founders' intended allocation of political influence to the large states was not achieved because it was trumped by the widespread adoption of the winner-take-all rule by the states. If, hypothetically, each of these six large spectator states were to suddenly acquire an extra 10 electoral votes each, they still would not matter in presidential elections. Presidential candidates would continue to take the noncompetitive states for granted and concentrate on the closely divided battleground states.

Civics books often recite the argument that a vote in a small state is worth more than a vote in a large state because of the bonus of two electoral votes that each state receives in the Electoral College. The argument is that a Wyoming vote is worth 3.74 times that of a California vote because one electoral vote corresponds to 164,594 people in Wyoming, compared to 615,848 people in California.[114] This argument is arithmetically correct, but it does not reflect political reality. A vote in a small spectator state such as Wyoming and a vote in a large spectator state such as California simply do not matter because everyone knows which candidate will win the electoral votes from those states. From the perspective of presidential candidates operating under the winner-take-all system, a vote in Wyoming is equal to a vote in California in presidential elections—*both are equally worthless.*

Third, as discussed in detail in chapter 9, there is no fact-based argument in favor of the position that either political party gains a partisan advantage from a national popular vote for President.

Fourth, there has been long-standing support for nationwide popular election among the public and from members of Congress in both political parties from small, medium, and large states in all parts of the country. As shown in appendix S of this book, there has been at least one U.S. Senator or U.S. Representative in each of the 50 states over the past 40 years who has either sponsored a bill for nationwide popular election or voted for nationwide popular election of the President in a roll-call vote in Congress.

1.5 ROADMAP OF THIS BOOK

Chapter 2 of this book describes the current system of electing the President, including the federal constitutional and statutory provisions that govern presidential elections (section 2.1). Section 2.2 reviews the history of the various methods that the states have used over the years to elect their presidential electors, and section 2.3 discusses present-day methods.

The chapter also discusses the certification of the popular vote for President by the states (section 2.4), the meeting of the Electoral College in mid-December (section 2.5), the certification of the votes cast by the presidential electors (section 2.6), and the counting of the electoral votes in Congress (section 2.7). The chapter also covers write-in voting for President (section 2.8), voting for individual presidential electors

---

[114] Wyoming has a population of 493,782 (according to the 2000 federal census) and has three electoral votes (one warranted by population plus its two-vote bonus). California (with a population of 33,871,648) has 55 electoral votes (53 warranted by population plus its two-vote bonus). Thus, one electoral vote corresponds to 164,594 people in Wyoming, compared to 615,848 people in California.

(section 2.9), fusion voting in presidential races (section 2.10), unpledged presidential electors (section 2.11), and faithless presidential electors (section 2.12).

Chapter 2 identifies five salient features of present-day presidential elections that did not exist or that were not prominent at the time of ratification of the U.S. Constitution, namely

- popular voting for presidential electors,
- the nondeliberative nature of the Electoral College,
- the statewide winner-take-all rule,
- nomination of presidential candidates by political parties, and
- the short presidential ballot.

As chapter 2 demonstrates, these present-day features of the system evolved over a period of many decades as a result of the piecemeal passage of laws by individual states and the emergence of political parties. As summarized in section 2.13, these features are not contained in the U.S. Constitution or any federal law. None reflects a consensus of the Founding Fathers. None came into being because of the adoption of any federal constitutional amendment. Instead, these features came into existence because the states used the built-in flexibility of the Constitution to make them part of our present-day political landscape.

Chapter 3 starts by reviewing the history of problematic presidential elections (section 3.1). It then examines the three most prominent approaches to presidential election reform that have been proposed in the form of a federal constitutional amendment, including

- fractional proportional allocation of electoral votes (section 3.2),
- district allocation of electoral votes (section 3.3), and
- nationwide popular election (section 3.4).

Each of these three proposed approaches is examined in light of three criteria:

- whether the proposed approach accurately reflects the nationwide popular vote;
- whether the proposed approach makes every state competitive; and
- whether every vote is equal.

Chapter 4 examines the two most prominent approaches to presidential election reform that can be enacted at the state level (i.e., without a federal constitutional amendment and without action by Congress), namely

- the whole-number proportional approach (section 4.1), and
- the congressional-district approach (section 4.2).

Again, each proposed approach is examined in light of the above three criteria.

Chapter 5 provides background on interstate compacts—a contractual arrangement authorized in the Constitution by which states can act in concert to address an issue that cannot be readily solved by unilateral action. The chapter begins with the constitutional basis for interstate compacts, starting with the Articles of Confederation (section 5.1), the legal standing of compacts (section 5.2), and the history of compacts (section

5.3). The chapter then covers the wide variety of subjects addressed by compacts (section 5.4), the variety of parties that may participate in compacts (section 5.5), the procedures for drafting, negotiating, and formulating compacts (section 5.6), the methods by which a state may adopt an interstate compact (section 5.7), and the contingent nature of compacts (section 5.8). Section 5.9 discusses congressional involvement in interstate compacts and the process of congressional consent; section 5.10 discusses the effect of congressional consent; section 5.11 gives examples of compacts that are contingent on the enactment of federal legislation; and section 5.12 gives examples of compacts that do not require congressional consent. Section 5.13 discusses enforcement of compacts; section 5.14 discusses amendments to compacts; section 5.15 discusses the duration of compacts and the process of terminating and withdrawing from compacts; section 5.16 discusses administration of compacts; and section 5.17 discusses the style of drafting compacts. Section 5.18 compares treaties and compacts; section 5.19 compares uniform state laws and compacts; and section 5.20 compares federal multi-state commissions and compacts. The future of interstate compacts is discussed in section 5.21.

Chapter 6 presents the authors' proposal to reform the presidential election process—an interstate compact entitled the "Agreement Among the States to Elect the President by National Popular Vote" (generally called the "National Popular Vote" compact). The compact is a proposed state law that would not become operative when a particular state enacts it. Instead, the compact would govern presidential elections only after it is enacted by states collectively possessing a majority of the electoral votes (i.e., 270 of the 538 electoral votes).

The National Popular Vote compact would not change any state's internal procedures for conducting or counting its presidential vote. The compact would not reduce state control over elections. After the people cast their ballots on Election Day in early November of presidential election years, the popular vote counts from all 50 states and the District of Columbia would be added together to determine the national grand total for each presidential slate. At the present time, the Electoral College reflects the voters' state-by-state choices for President or, in the cases of Maine and Nebraska, the voters' district-wide choices. The compact would change the Electoral College from an institution that reflects the voters' state-by-state choices (or district-wide choices) into a body that reflects the voters' nationwide choice. To accomplish this, the National Popular Vote compact specifies that each member state will award all of its electoral votes to the presidential candidate who received the largest total number of popular votes in all 50 states and the District of Columbia. Because the compact would become effective only when it encompasses states collectively possessing a majority of the electoral votes, the presidential candidate receiving the most popular votes in all 50 states and the District of Columbia would be guaranteed enough electoral votes (that is, at least 270 of the 538 electoral votes) in the Electoral College to be elected.

Membership in the National Popular Vote compact is *not* required for all the popular votes of a state to count. Every state's popular vote is included on equal footing in the nationwide total regardless of whether the state has enacted the compact. Note also that the political complexion of the states belonging to the compact does not affect the outcome produced by the compact. The presidential candidate receiving the most popular votes in all 50 states and the District of Columbia is guaranteed enough electoral votes (that is, at least 270 of the 538) to be elected regardless of which states happen to belong to the compact.

Chapter 7 outlines the strategy for enacting the National Popular Vote compact, including a discussion of the roles of public opinion (section 7.1), the state legislatures (section 7.2), the citizen-initiative process (section 7.3), and Congress (section 7.4).

Chapter 8 discusses the possible role of the citizen-initiative process in enacting the National Popular Vote compact. Section 8.1 describes the citizen-initiative process (and the related protest-referendum processes). Section 8.2 discusses the question of whether the citizen-initiative process may be used to enact interstate compacts in general. Section 8.3 discusses whether the citizen-initiative process may be used to enact a state law concerning the manner of choosing presidential electors (such as the National Popular Vote compact).

Chapter 9 contains responses to myths about the National Popular Vote compact. Chapter 10 is the epilogue.

1.6 SOURCES OF ADDITIONAL INFORMATION

There is a large body of literature analyzing the arguments for and against the current electoral system and possible alternatives.

The congressional hearings held in 1967,[115] 1969,[116,117,118] 1975,[119] 1977,[120] 1979,[121]

---

[115] U.S. Senate Committee on the Judiciary. 1967. *Election of the President: Hearings on S.J. Res. 4, 7, 11, 12, 28, 58, 62, 138 and 139, 89th Congress; and S.J. Res. 2, 3, 6, 7, 12, 15, 21, 25, 55, 84, and 86.* 89th Congress, 2nd Session and 90th Congress, 1st Session. February 28–August 23, 1967. Washington, DC: U.S. Government Printing Office.

[116] U.S. House of Representatives Committee on the Judiciary. 1969. *Electoral College Reform: Hearings on H.J. Res. 179, H.J. Res. 181, and Similar Proposals to Amend the Constitution Relating to Electoral College Reform.* 91st Congress, 1st Session. February 5, 6, 19, 20, 26, and 27; March 5, 6, 12, and 13, 1969. Washington, DC: U.S. Government Printing Office.

[117] U.S. Senate Committee on the Judiciary. 1969. *Electing the President: Hearings on S.J. Res. 1, S.J. Res. 2, S.J. Res. 4, S.J. Res. 12, S.J. Res. 18, S.J. Res. 20, S.J. Res. 25, S.J. Res. 30, S.J. Res. 31, S.J. Res. 33, S.J. Res. 71, and S.J. Res. 72 to Amend the Constitution Relating to Electoral College Reform.* 91st Congress, 1st Session. January 23–24, March 10, 11, 12, 13, 20, 21, April 30, May 1–2, 1969. Washington, DC: U.S. Government Printing Office.

[118] U.S. Senate Committee on the Judiciary. 1969. *Direct Popular Election of the President: Report, with Additional Minority, Individual, and Separate Views on H.J. Res. 681, Proposing an Amendment to the Constitution of the United States Relating to the Election of the President and Vice President.* 91st Congress, 1st Session. Washington, DC: U.S. Government Printing Office.

[119] U.S. Senate Committee on the Judiciary. 1975. *Direct Popular Election of the President: Report (to Accompany S.J. Res. 1).* 94th Congress, 1st Session. Washington, DC: U.S. Government Printing Office.

[120] U.S. Senate Committee on the Judiciary. 1977. *The Electoral College and Direct Election: Hearings on the Electoral College and Direct Election of the President and Vice President (S.J. Res. 1, 8, and 18): Supplement.* 95th Congress, 1st Session. July 20, 22, and 28, and August 2, 1977. Washington, DC: U.S. Government Printing Office.

[121] U.S. Senate Committee on the Judiciary. 1979. *Direct Popular Election of the President and Vice President of the United States: Hearings on S.J. Res. 28, Joint Resolution Proposing an Amendment to the*

1993,[122] and 1999[123] contain detailed discussions of the current system and its alternatives from various experts, members of the public, organizations, and public officials.

Books on reforming the method of electing the President include:

- *Wrong Winner: The Coming Debacle in the Electoral College* by David Abbott and James P. Levine (1991),[124]
- *Taming the Electoral College* by Robert W. Bennett (2006),[125]
- *Choice of the People? Debating the Electoral College* by Judith A. Best (1996),[126]
- *The Case against Direct Election of the President: A Defense of the Electoral College* by Judith Vairo Best (1975),[127]
- *Electoral College Reform: Challenges and Possibilities*, a collection of articles edited by Gary Bugh (2010),[128]
- *Why the Electoral College Is Bad for America* by George C. Edwards III (2011, second edition),[129]
- *The Importance of the Electoral College* by George Grant (2004),[130]
- *Securing Democracy: Why We Have an Electoral College*, a collection of articles edited by Gary L. Gregg II (2001),[131]
- *The Electoral College and the Constitution: The Case for Preserving Federalism* by Robert M. Hardaway (1994),[132]

Constitution to Provide for the Direct Popular Election of the President and Vice President of the United States. 96th Congress, 1st Session. March 27 and 30, April 3 and 9, 1979. Washington, DC: U.S. Government Printing Office.

[122] U.S. Senate Committee on the Judiciary. 1993. *The Electoral College and Direct Election of the President: Hearing on S.J. Res. 297, S.J. Res. 302, and S.J. Res. 312, Measures Proposing Amendments to the Constitution Relating to the Direct Election of the President and Vice President of the United States*. 102nd Congress, 2nd Session. July 22, 1992. Washington, DC: U.S. Government Printing Office.

[123] U.S. House Committee on the Judiciary. 1999. *Proposals for Electoral College Reform: Hearing on H.J. Res. 28 and H.J. Res. 43*. 105th Congress, 1st Session. September 4, 1997. Washington, DC: U.S. Government Printing Office.

[124] Abbott, David W., and Levine, James P. 1991. *Wrong Winner: The Coming Debacle in the Electoral College*. Westport, CT: Praeger.

[125] Bennett, Robert W. 2006. *Taming the Electoral College*. Stanford, CA: Stanford University Press.

[126] Best, Judith A. 1996. *Choice of the People? Debating the Electoral College*. Lanham, MD: Rowman & Littlefield.

[127] Best, Judith Vairo. 1975. *The Case against Direct Election of the President: A Defense of the Electoral College*. Ithaca, NY: Cornell University Press.

[128] Bugh, Gary (editor). 2010. *Electoral College Reform: Challenges and Possibilities*. Burlington, VT: Ashgate.

[129] Edwards, George C., III. 2011. *Why the Electoral College Is Bad for America*. New Haven, CT: Yale University Press. Second edition.

[130] Grant, George. 2004. *The Importance of the Electoral College*. San Antonio, TX: Vision Forum Ministries.

[131] Gregg, Gary L., II (editor). 2001. *Securing Democracy: Why We Have an Electoral College*. Wilmington, DE: ISI Books.

[132] Hardaway, Robert M. 1994. *The Electoral College and the Constitution: The Case for Preserving Federalism*. Westport, CT: Praeger.

- *The Electoral College* by Suzanne LeVert (2004),[133]
- *The Politics of Electoral College Reform* by Lawrence D. Longley and Alan G. Braun (1972),[134]
- *The People's President: The Electoral College in American History and Direct-Vote Alternative* by Neal R. Peirce (1968),[135]
- *Enlightened Democracy: The Case for the Electoral College* by Tara Ross (2004),[136]
- *Choosing a President*, a collection of articles edited by Paul D. Schumaker and Burdett A. Loomis (2002),[137]
- *History of American Presidential Elections 1878–2001*, an 11-volume collection of articles edited by Arthur M. Schlesinger, Jr., and Fred L. Israel (2002),[138]
- *A History of the Presidency from 1788 to 1897*[139] and *A History of the Presidency from 1897 to 1916* by Edward Stanwood (1924),[140] and
- *The Electoral College* by Lucius Wilmerding (1958).[141]

Among books that have come out since the 2000 presidential election, the 2004 book *Enlightened Democracy: The Case for the Electoral College*[142] contains some of the clearest arguments supporting the existing system. On the other side of the argument, the 2004 book (and its 2011 second edition) *Why the Electoral College Is Bad for America*[143] is noteworthy because it closely examines and analyzes many of the most commonly invoked arguments in favor of the existing system—such as protection of federalism and protection of state interests.

---

[133] LeVert, Suzanne. 2004. *The Electoral College*. New York, NY: Franklin Watts.

[134] Longley, Lawrence D., and Braun, Alan G. 1972. *The Politics of Electoral College Reform*. New Haven, CT: Yale University Press.

[135] Peirce, Neal R. 1968. *The People's President: The Electoral College in American History and Direct-Vote Alternative*. New York, NY: Simon & Schuster.

[136] Ross, Tara. 2004. *Enlightened Democracy: The Case for the Electoral College*. Los Angeles, CA: World Ahead Publishing Company.

[137] Schumaker, Paul D., and Loomis, Burdett A. (editors). 2002. *Choosing a President*. New York, NY: Chatham House Publishers.

[138] Schlesinger, Arthur M., Jr. and Israel, Fred L. (editors). 2002. *History of American Presidential Elections 1878–2001*. Philadelphia, PA: Chelsea House Publishers. 11 volumes.

[139] Stanwood, Edward. 1924. *A History of the Presidency from 1788 to 1897*. Boston, MA: Houghton Mifflin Company.

[140] Stanwood, Edward. 1916. *A History of the Presidency from 1897 to 1916*. Boston, MA: Houghton Mifflin Company.

[141] Wilmerding, Lucius, Jr. 1958. *The Electoral College*. Boston, MA: Beacon Press.

[142] Ross, Tara. 2004. *Enlightened Democracy: The Case for the Electoral College*. Los Angeles, CA: World Ahead Publishing Company.

[143] Edwards, George C., III. 2011. *Why the Electoral College Is Bad for America*. New Haven, CT: Yale University Press. Second edition.

FairVote (formerly the Center for Voting and Democracy) published two insightful reports on presidential elections:

- *The Shrinking Battleground: The 2008 Presidential Election and Beyond*[144] and
- *Who Picks the President?*[145]

This book's bibliography contains numerous additional references to books about particular problematic elections (e.g., 1800, 1876, and 2000) as well as the history and operation of the present system over the years.

---

[144] FairVote. 2005. *The Shrinking Battleground: The 2008 Presidential Election and Beyond.* Takoma Park, MD: The Center for Voting and Democracy. www.fairvote.org/shrinking.

[145] FairVote. 2005. *Who Picks the President?* Takoma Park, MD: The Center for Voting and Democracy. www.fairvote.org/whopicks.

2 | How the Electoral College Works

The current system for electing the President and Vice President of the United States is governed by a combination of federal and state statutory provisions and constitutional provisions. This chapter discusses the:

- federal constitutional and federal statutory provisions governing presidential elections (section 2.1),
- history of various methods for appointing presidential electors (section 2.2),
- current state laws governing the election of presidential electors (section 2.3),
- certification of the popular vote by the states (section 2.4),
- meeting of the Electoral College (section 2.5),
- certification of the votes cast by a state's presidential electors (section 2.6),
- counting of the electoral votes in Congress (section 2.7),
- write-in votes for president (section 2.8),
- state laws permitting a voter to cast separate votes for individual candidates for the position of presidential elector (section 2.9),
- fusion voting (section 2.10),
- unpledged electors (section 2.11),
- faithless presidential electors (section 2.12), and
- five major changes in the manner of appointing presidential electors that have been implemented without a federal constitutional amendment (section 2.13).

2.1 FEDERAL CONSTITUTIONAL AND STATUTORY PROVISIONS

The President and Vice President of the United States are not elected directly by the voters. Instead, the President and Vice President are elected by a group of 538 people who are known individually as "presidential electors" and collectively as the "Electoral College."

The U.S. Constitution provides:

"The executive Power shall be vested in a President of the United States of America. He shall hold his Office during the Term of four Years, and, together with the Vice President, chosen for the same Term, be elected, as follows:

"**Each State shall appoint, in such Manner as the Legislature thereof may direct, a Number of Electors**, equal to the whole Number of Senators and Representatives to which the State may be entitled in the Congress. . . . "[1] [Emphasis added]

Presidential electors are elected by each state and the District of Columbia on the Tuesday after the first Monday in November in presidential election years.

The presidential electors meet to cast their votes for President and Vice President in 51 separate meetings held around the country in mid-December.

The number of presidential electors depends on the size of the U.S. House of Representatives and the U.S. Senate. The number of seats in the House is set by federal statute, and there are currently 435 U.S. Representatives. There are, in addition, two Senators from each state. Consequently, the 50 states together currently have 535 electoral votes. The District of Columbia acquired three electoral votes as a result of the ratification of the 23rd Amendment to the U.S. Constitution in 1961. Thus, in total, there are currently 538 electoral votes.

In order to be elected, the Constitution requires that a presidential or vice-presidential candidate win the votes of a majority of the presidential electors who have been "appointed." Assuming that all states appoint their presidential electors,[2] that requirement currently means winning 270 of the 538 electoral votes.

After each decennial federal census, the 435 seats in the United States House of Representatives are reapportioned among the 50 states. The 2010 census determined the apportionment of electoral votes that will apply to the 2012, 2016, and 2020 presidential elections.

Table 2.1 shows the distribution of electoral votes among the 51 jurisdictions that appoint presidential electors for the period between 1992 and 2020. Because each state has two Senators and at least one Representative, no state has fewer than three electoral votes. Column 2 shows the number of electoral votes for the 1992, 1996, and 2000 presidential elections. Column 3 shows the numbers for the 2004 and 2008 elections. Column 4 shows the number for the 2012, 2016, and 2020 elections. The average number of electoral votes for the 51 jurisdictions is 10.5, and the median number is 8.

The U.S. Constitution provides (Article II, section 1, clause 4):

"The Congress may determine the Time of chusing the Electors, and the Day on which they shall give their Votes; which Day shall be the same throughout the United States." [Spelling as per original]

Federal election law establishes the date for choosing presidential electors. In 2012, the designated date was Tuesday, November 6.

---

[1] U.S. Constitution. Article II, section 1, clauses 1 and 2.

[2] On rare occasions, states have failed to appoint presidential electors. For example, in the nation's first presidential election in 1789, New York failed to appoint its electors because of a disagreement between the State Senate and Assembly on the manner of appointing presidential electors. During the Civil War, the 11 Southern states failed to appoint electors for the 1864 election.

Table 2.1 DISTRIBUTION OF ELECTORAL VOTES 1992-2020

STATE	1992-2000	2004-2008	2012-2020
Alabama	9	9	9
Alaska	3	3	3
Arizona	8	10	11
Arkansas	6	6	6
California	54	55	55
Colorado	8	9	9
Connecticut	8	7	7
Delaware	3	3	3
D.C.	3	3	3
Florida	25	27	29
Georgia	13	15	16
Hawaii	4	4	4
Idaho	4	4	4
Illinois	22	21	20
Indiana	12	11	11
Iowa	7	7	6
Kansas	6	6	6
Kentucky	8	8	8
Louisiana	9	9	8
Maine	4	4	4
Maryland	10	10	10
Massachusetts	12	12	11
Michigan	18	17	16
Minnesota	10	10	10
Mississippi	7	6	6
Missouri	11	11	10
Montana	3	3	3
Nebraska	5	5	5
Nevada	4	5	6
New Hampshire	4	4	4
New Jersey	15	15	14
New Mexico	5	5	5
New York	33	31	29
North Carolina	14	15	15
North Dakota	3	3	3
Ohio	21	20	18
Oklahoma	8	7	7
Oregon	7	7	7
Pennsylvania	23	21	20
Rhode Island	4	4	4
South Carolina	8	8	9
South Dakota	3	3	3
Tennessee	11	11	11
Texas	32	34	38
Utah	5	5	6
Vermont	3	3	3
Virginia	13	13	13
Washington	11	11	12
West Virginia	5	5	5
Wisconsin	11	10	10
Wyoming	3	3	3
Total	**538**	**538**	**538**

"The electors of President and Vice President shall be appointed, in each State, on the **Tuesday next after the first Monday in November**, in every fourth year succeeding every election of a President and Vice President."[3] [Emphasis added]

Similarly, the date for the meeting of the Electoral College is established by federal law. In 2012, the designated day for the meeting of the Electoral College was Monday, December 17.

"The electors of President and Vice President of each State shall meet and give their votes on the **first Monday after the second Wednesday in December** next following their appointment at such place in each State as the legislature of such State shall direct."[4] [Emphasis added]

The above statute was enacted in 1934 after the 20th Amendment (ratified in 1933) changed the date for the presidential inauguration from March 4 to January 20.

The Electoral College meeting in mid-December is governed by the 12th Amendment to the U.S. Constitution which provides (in part):

"The Electors shall meet in their respective states, and vote by ballot for President and Vice-President, one of whom, at least, shall not be an inhabitant of the same state with themselves; they shall name in their ballots the person voted for as President, and in distinct ballots the person voted for as Vice-President, and they shall make distinct lists of all persons voted for as President, and of all persons voted for as Vice-President, and of the number of votes for each, which lists they shall sign and certify, and transmit sealed to the seat of the government of the United States, directed to the President of the Senate."

For the reader's convenience, appendix A contains the provisions of the U.S. Constitution relating to presidential elections, and appendix B contains the relevant provisions of federal law.

The voters who have the qualifications to vote for the lower house of their state legislature have the right, under the Constitution, to vote for U.S. Representatives.[5] The 17th Amendment (ratified in 1913) gave the voters the right to directly elect U.S. Senators (who, under the original Constitution, had been elected by state legislatures).

The voters, however, have no federal constitutional right to vote for President or Vice President or for presidential electors. Instead, the Constitution provides:

---

[3] United States Code. Title 3, chapter 1, section 1.

[4] United States Code. Title 3, chapter 1, section 7.

[5] At the time of ratification of the Constitution, the qualifications to vote for the lower house of the state legislature varied considerably from state to state. Many states had highly restrictive property or wealth qualifications. See Table A.3 (page 314) in Keyssar, Alexander. 2000. *The Right to Vote: The Contested History of Democracy in the United States*. New York, NY: Basic Books.

"Each State shall **appoint, in such Manner as the Legislature thereof may direct,** a Number of Electors, equal to the whole Number of Senators and Representatives to which the State may be entitled in the Congress. . . . "[6] [Emphasis added]

As the Court wrote in the 1892 case of *McPherson v. Blacker*—the leading case on the manner of appointing presidential electors:

"**The constitution does not provide that the appointment of electors shall be by popular vote**, nor that the electors shall be voted for upon a general ticket [i.e., the winner-take-all rule], nor that the majority of those who exercise the elective franchise can alone choose the electors. . . . "[7]

"In short, the appointment and mode of appointment of electors belong exclusively to the states under the constitution of the United States."[8] [Emphasis added]

The full text of the Court's decision in *McPherson v. Blacker* can be found in appendix O.

In 2000, the U.S. Supreme Court in *Bush v. Gore* reiterated the principle that the people have no federal constitutional right to vote for President.

"**The individual citizen has no federal constitutional right to vote for electors for the President of the United States** unless and until the state legislature chooses a statewide election as the means to implement its power to appoint members of the Electoral College. U.S. Const., Art. II, §1. **This is the source for the statement in** *McPherson v. Blacker*, 146 U.S. 1, 35 (1892), that the State legislature's power to select the manner for appointing electors is plenary; it may, if it so chooses, select the electors itself, which indeed was the manner used by State legislatures in several States for many years after the Framing of our Constitution. *Id.*, at 28–33. . . . "[9] [Emphasis added]

2.2 HISTORY OF METHODS OF SELECTING PRESIDENTIAL ELECTORS

In 1787, the Constitutional Convention considered a variety of methods for electing the President and Vice President, including election by

- state governors,
- Congress,
- state legislatures,

---

[6] U.S. Constitution. Article II, section 1, clause 2.
[7] *McPherson v. Blacker*. 146 U.S. 1 at 27. 1892.
[8] Ibid. at 35.
[9] *Bush v. Gore*. 531 U.S. 98. 2000.

- nationwide popular vote, and
- electors.

The delegates debated the method of electing the President on 22 separate days and held 30 votes on the topic.[10],[11] As described in George Edwards's book *Why the Electoral College Is Bad for America*:

> "The delegates were obviously perplexed about how to select the president, and their confusion is reflected in their voting. On July 17, for example, the delegates voted for selection of the president by the national legislature. Two days later they voted for selection by electors chosen by state legislatures. Five days after that, they again voted for selection by the national legislature, a position they rejected the next day and then adopted again the day after that. Then, just when it appeared that the delegates had reached a consensus, they again turned the question over to a committee. This committee changed the convention's course once more and recommended selection of the president by electors. . . . "[12]

In the end, the 1787 Constitutional Convention never agreed on a method for choosing the presidential electors. The matter was simply turned over to the state legislatures.

The U.S. Constitution gives the states considerably more discretion in choosing the manner of appointing their presidential electors than it does in choosing the manner of electing U.S. Representatives and Senators. The states' power to choose the manner of conducting congressional elections is subject to congressional oversight. Article I, section 4, clause 1 of the U.S. Constitution provides:

> "The Times, Places and Manner of holding Elections for Senators and Representatives, shall be prescribed in each State by the Legislature thereof; **but the Congress may at any time by Law make or alter such Regulations**, except as to the Places of chusing Senators." [Emphasis added]

In contrast, Article II, section 1, clause 2 of the U.S. Constitution gives Congress no comparable oversight power concerning a state's choice of the manner of appointing its presidential electors.

> "Each State shall appoint, **in such Manner as the Legislature thereof may direct**, a Number of Electors, equal to the whole Number of Sena-

---

[10] Peirce, Neal R. 1968. *The People's President: The Electoral College in American History and Direct-Vote Alternative.* New York, NY: Simon & Schuster. Pages 28–57.

[11] Longley, Lawrence D., and Braun, Alan G. 1972. *The Politics of Electoral College Reform.* New Haven, CT: Yale University Press. Pages 22–41.

[12] Edwards, George C., III. 2004. *Why the Electoral College Is Bad for America.* New Haven, CT: Yale University Press. Pages 79–80.

tors and Representatives to which the State may be entitled in the Congress. . . . " [Emphasis added]

As the U.S. Supreme Court wrote in *McPherson v. Blacker*:

> "In short, the appointment and mode of appointment of electors belong **exclusively** to the states under the constitution of the United States."[13] [Emphasis added]

That is, the states have plenary authority in choosing the manner of appointing their presidential electors.

Of course, plenary authority is not unfettered power. State power in this area is limited by numerous general constitutional limitations on the exercise of governmental power, such as the Equal Protection clause of the 14th Amendment, the 15th Amendment (outlawing the denial of vote based on race, color, or previous condition of servitude), the 20th Amendment (women's suffrage), the 24th Amendment (outlawing poll taxes), and the 26th Amendment (establishing the right to vote for 18-year-olds).

In addition, the U.S. Supreme Court noted in *McPherson v. Blacker* that a state legislature's choices over the manner of appointing the state's presidential electors may be limited by its state constitution.[14] Colorado is the only state to have an explicit state-constitutional limitation on the state legislature's choices. In the section of the Colorado Constitution containing the "schedule" governing the transition from territorial status to statehood, the Colorado Constitution specified that the legislature could appoint presidential electors in 1876; however,

> "after the year eighteen hundred and seventy-six the electors of the electoral college shall be chosen by direct vote of the people."[15]

As it happens, the Colorado legislature's direct appointment of presidential electors in 1876 was the last occasion in the United States when the voters were not allowed to vote directly for presidential electors.

2.2.1 THE FIRST AND SECOND PRESIDENTIAL ELECTIONS

In the nation's first presidential election in 1789 and second election in 1792, the states employed a wide variety of methods for choosing presidential electors, including

- appointment of the state's presidential electors by the Governor and his Council,
- appointment by both houses of the state legislature,

---

[13] *McPherson v. Blacker.* 146 U.S. 1 at 35. 1892.

[14] *McPherson v. Blacker.* 146 U.S. 1 at 27. 1892.

[15] Section 20 of the article of the Colorado Constitution governing the transition from territorial status to statehood.

- popular election using special single-member presidential-elector districts,
- popular election using counties as presidential-elector districts,
- popular election using congressional districts,
- popular election using multi-member regional districts,
- combinations of popular election and legislative choice,
- appointment of the state's presidential electors by the Governor and his Council combined with the state legislature, and
- statewide popular election.

In New Jersey in 1789, the state legislature passed a law authorizing the Governor and his Council to appoint all of the state's presidential electors.[16]

In four of the 10 states that participated in the first presidential election (Connecticut, Georgia, New Jersey, and South Carolina), the state legislatures designated themselves as the appointing authority for all of the state's presidential electors. That is, the voters had no direct involvement in choosing presidential electors in those states.

Note that the appointment of presidential electors by a state legislature did not seem as odd in 1789 as it would today. In 1789, the state legislatures had the power to appoint United States Senators[17] and, in all but two states, the state's governor.[18] Moreover, the state legislatures appointed the delegates to the 1787 Constitutional Convention.

In four of the 10 states that participated in the first presidential election, the voters chose all of the presidential electors.

In New Hampshire, Pennsylvania, and Maryland, all of the state's presidential electors were elected on the basis of a version of the statewide winner-take-all rule (sometimes called the "general ticket system" or the "unit rule").

The version of the winner-take-all rule used in 1789 in New Hampshire and Pennsylvania differed from today's version in two respects.

First, the names of the presidential and vice-presidential candidates did not appear on the ballot in the early years of the Republic. Instead, the voter cast votes for individual candidates for the position of presidential elector. For example, a voter in

---

[16] An Act for carrying into effect, on the part of the state of New Jersey, the Constitution of the United States. November 21, 1788. *Acts of the General Assembly of the State of New Jersey.* Page 481. See also DenBoer, Gordon; Brown, Lucy Trumbull; and Hagermann, Charles D. (editors). 1986. *The Documentary History of the First Federal Elections 1788–1790.* Madison, WI: University of Wisconsin Press. Volume 3. Page 29. Interestingly, the U.S. Supreme Court's opinion in the 1892 case of *McPherson v. Blacker* contains an error concerning New Jersey. In its historical review of methods used to appoint presidential electors in 1789, the Court (incorrectly) stated, "At the first presidential election, the appointment of electors was made by the legislatures of Connecticut, Delaware, Georgia, New Jersey, and South Carolina." 146 U.S. 1 at 29. The source of this misinformation about New Jersey appears to be page 19 of the plaintiff's brief in the 1892 case. *Brief of F.A. Baker for Plaintiffs in Error* in *McPherson v. Blacker.* 1892.

[17] The ratification of the 17th Amendment in 1913 permitted the voters to directly elect U.S. Senators.

[18] State constitutions were changed over the years so that, today, the voters directly elect all state governors.

New Hampshire (which had five electoral votes in 1789) could vote for five individual presidential-elector candidates.

Second, the version of the winner-take-all rule used in New Hampshire in 1789 differed from the present-day system in that an absolute majority of the popular vote was necessary to elect a presidential elector (with the legislature intervening and making the selection in the absence of an absolute majority). Today, a plurality of voters is sufficient to elect all of a state's presidential electors in all 48 states that use the winner-take-all system.

Maryland added a regional twist to its version of the winner-take-all rule. All of the state's voters were permitted to vote for three electors from the Eastern Shore and five from the Western Shore. This approach enabled a statewide majority to control all of the state's electoral votes on a winner-take-all basis while ensuring a regional distribution of presidential electors.

In Virginia (which, at the time, had 10 congressional districts and hence 12 electoral votes), the state was divided into 12 presidential-elector districts. Each voter cast a vote for an elector for his district.

Delaware has three counties and had three electoral votes in 1789 (as it does today). One presidential elector was elected from each county.[19]

Massachusetts used a combination system in 1789. In each of the state's eight congressional districts, the voters cast ballots in a popular election for their choice for the district's presidential elector. However, the actual appointment of the presidential elector for each district was then made by the state legislature from between the two elector candidates receiving the most popular votes in each district. The state legislature also chose the state's two senatorial electors. Thus, a majority of the legislature[20] effectively exercised the power to choose all 10 of the state's district electors. The practical role of the voters was simply to nominate candidates for consideration by the legislature.

In New York, the legislature could not agree on a method for choosing presidential electors. Both houses of the legislature agreed that the legislature—not the voters—would choose the state's presidential electors. However, the Senate and Assembly deadlocked over the question of whether the legislature would choose the presidential

---

[19] DenBoer, Gordon; Brown, Lucy Trumbull; and Hagermann, Charles D. (editors). 1984. *The Documentary History of the First Federal Elections 1788–1790.* Madison, WI: University of Wisconsin Press. Volume 2. Page 83. The election returns shown on page 83 of *The Documentary History* indicate that the candidate receiving the most votes in each county was elected as presidential elector. This appears to be accordance with a legislative acted passed on October 28, 1788. Interestingly, the U.S. Supreme Court decision in the 1892 case of *McPherson v. Blacker* contains an error concerning Delaware. In its historical review of the election laws of 1789, the Court (incorrectly) stated, "At the first presidential election, the appointment of electors was made by the legislatures of Connecticut, Delaware, Georgia, New Jersey, and South Carolina." 146 U.S. 1 at 29. This source of this misinformation appears to be page 19 of the plaintiff's brief in the 1892 case. *Brief of F.A. Baker for Plaintiffs in Error* in *McPherson v. Blacker.* 1892.

[20] Sitting in a joint convention of both houses.

electors in a joint session (consisting of all the state Senators and all the state Assembly-men) or by means of a concurrent resolution (containing the names of the presidential electors) that had to be separately approved by both the Senate and Assembly.[21] As a result of this unresolved dispute over the relative power of the Senate and Assembly, New York was unable to cast its votes in the Electoral College in the first presidential election.

Rhode Island and North Carolina did not participate in the nation's first presidential election in 1789, because they had not ratified the Constitution in time to participate.

George Washington received a vote from all of the 69 presidential electors who voted in the Electoral College in 1789.[22] John Adams was elected Vice President in 1789.

Vermont became a state in time to participate in the 1792 presidential election. Vermont passed legislation authorizing the state's presidential electors to be appointed by a "Grand Committee" consisting of the Governor and his Council and the state House of Representatives (the state being unicameral at the time).[23]

Kentucky became a state in time for the 1792 election and permitted its voters to elect presidential electors by district.

By 1792, New York had resolved the dispute that had prevented it from appointing any presidential electors in 1789. A law was passed authorizing the legislature to appoint presidential electors in the same manner as it appointed the state's United States Senators.[24]

In 1792, the Massachusetts legislature loosened its grip on the choice of presidential electors. The state was divided into four regional multi-member districts for the purpose of electing the state's 16 electors.[25] The 1792 plan in Massachusetts permitted the voters to directly elect all of the state's presidential electors (except that if a candidate were to fail to receive a majority of the popular votes cast in a particular district, the legislature would make the choice).

In 1792, the Delaware legislature took the power to elect the state's presidential electors from the voters and vested it in itself. The legislatures of Rhode Island and North Carolina chose presidential electors in 1792.

In 1792 (as in 1789), George Washington again received a vote from all of the presidential electors who voted.

---

[21] The issue of whether to use a joint session (versus a concurrent resolution) also vexed state legislative elections of U.S. Senators for many decades, with the result that U.S. Senate seats would often remain unfilled for years because of a partisan division between the two houses of the state legislature.

[22] In addition to the missing electoral votes from New York (and the non-ratifying states of Rhode Island and North Carolina), two presidential electors from Maryland and two from Virginia failed to vote in the Electoral College in 1789.

[23] An Act directing the mode of appointing electors to elect a president and vice president of the United States. Passed November 3, 1791. *Laws of 1791*. Page 43.

[24] An Act for appointing electors in this state for the election of a president and vice president of the United States of America. Passed April 12, 1792. *Laws of New York*. Pages 378–379.

[25] As a consequence of the 1790 federal census, Massachusetts became entitled to choose 16 presidential electors in the 1792 presidential election (as compared to 10 in the 1789 election).

2.2.2 THE NATION'S FIRST COMPETITIVE ELECTION (1796)

In the early years of the republic, Thomas Jefferson led the opposition to the policies of the ruling Federalist Party.

George Washington's decision not to run for a third term in 1796 opened the way for a contested presidential election between the country's two emerging political parties.

In the summer of 1796, the Federalist members of Congress caucused and nominated John Adams of Massachusetts and Thomas Pinckney of South Carolina as their party's candidates. Meanwhile, the Republican caucus (sometimes also called the "Democratic-Republicans" and later called the "Democrats") voted to support the candidacies of Thomas Jefferson of Virginia and Aaron Burr of New York.[26,27,28]

For the 1796 election, Massachusetts abandoned the multi-member districts used in 1792 and switched to a system in which the voters elected the presidential electors by congressional district (with the legislature intervening if the leading candidate were to fail to receive an absolute majority of the popular votes cast in his district). The state legislature appointed the state's two senatorial electors.

Maryland switched from popular election of presidential electors using the winner-take-all rule to popular election by districts for the 1796 election.

Georgia switched from legislative appointment to statewide popular election.

Thus, the number of states that used the statewide winner-take-all system remained at three for the 1796 election.

The system used by the newly admitted state of Tennessee in 1796 (and also in 1800) was perhaps the most unusual system ever used by a state. A state-level Electoral College chose Tennessee's members of the national Electoral College. The legislative act establishing this system asserted that this multi-layered method had the advantage that presidential electors could

"be elected with as little trouble to the citizens as possible."[29]

To that end, the Tennessee legislature specifically named, in its statute, certain prominent local persons from Washington, Sullivan, Green, and Hawkins Counties to meet and select one presidential elector from their part of the state. Then, it named another group of individuals from Knox, Jefferson, Sevier, and Blount Counties to select their area's presidential elector. Finally, it named yet another group from Davidson, Sumner, and Tennessee Counties to select a presidential elector from their district. The three presidential electors would then meet and vote for President and Vice President.

The Founding Fathers anticipated that the Electoral College would act as a deliber-

[26] Peirce, Neal R. 1968. *The People's President: The Electoral College in American History and Direct-Vote Alternative.* New York, NY: Simon & Schuster. Pages 63–64.

[27] Grant, George. 2004. *The Importance of the Electoral College.* San Antonio, TX: Vision Forum Ministries. Pages 23–26.

[28] The congressional caucus was replaced by the national nominating convention during the 1820s.

[29] Laws Tenn. 1794, 1803, p. 209; Acts 2d Sess. 1st Gen. Assem. Tenn. c. 4.

ative body in which the presidential electors would exercise independent and detached judgment in order to select the best persons to serve as President and Vice President.

As John Jay (the presumed author of *Federalist No. 64*) wrote in 1788:

> "As the **select assemblies for choosing the President** . . . will in general be **composed of the most enlightened and respectable citizens**, there is reason to presume that their attention and their votes will be directed to those men only who have become the most distinguished by their abilities and virtues." [Emphasis added]

As Alexander Hamilton (the presumed author of *Federalist No. 68*) wrote in 1788:

> "[T]he immediate election should be made by men most capable of analyzing the qualities adapted to the station, and **acting under circumstances favorable to deliberation**, and to a **judicious combination** of all the reasons and inducements which were proper to govern their choice. **A small number of persons**, selected by their fellow-citizens from the general mass, will be most likely to possess **the information and discernment requisite to such complicated investigations**." [Emphasis added]

The Electoral College actually acted in a reasonably deliberative manner in the 1789 election. Under the original Constitution, each presidential elector had two votes. As previously mentioned, all 69 presidential electors voted for George Washington (making his election unanimous). However, the electors scattered their second votes among 11 candidates for Vice President.[30] Moreover, in six of the 10 states that participated in the election, the presidential electors split their votes among two or more candidates. Moreover, they did not vote in lockstep at the state level but instead exhibited a degree of independent and deliberative judgment in casting their votes.[31] The votes were cast as follows:

- Connecticut
    John Adams—5
    Samuel Huntington—2
- Georgia
    John Milton—2
    James Armstrong–1
    Edward Telfair—1
    Benjamin Lincoln—1

---

[30] Stanwood, Edward. 1924. *A History of the Presidency from 1788 to 1897*. Boston, MA: Houghton Mifflin Company. Page 27.

[31] In contrast, presidential electors split their votes in only two of the 15 states participating in the 1792 election. In that election, only two of the 132 electors deviated from the choice made by the rest of their state's delegation (one in Pennsylvania and one in South Carolina). Stanwood, Edward. 1924. *A History of the Presidency from 1788 to 1897*. Boston, MA: Houghton Mifflin Company. Page 29.

- New Jersey
  - John Jay—5
  - John Adams—1
- Pennsylvania
  - John Adams—8
  - John Hancock—2
- South Carolina
  - John Rutledge—6
  - John Hancock—1
- Virginia
  - John Adams—5
  - John Jay—1
  - John Hancock—1
  - George Clinton—3

In the remaining four states, the presidential electors voted in lockstep for one candidate:

- Delaware—John Jay—3
- New Hampshire—John Adams—5
- Maryland—Robert H. Harrison—6
- Massachusetts—John Adams—10

John Adams was thus elected as the nation's first Vice President with 34 of 69 electoral votes.[32]

The Founding Fathers' lofty expectations that the Electoral College would be a deliberative body were dashed by the political realities of the nation's first competitive presidential election.[33]

In 1796, both political parties nominated candidates for President and Vice President on a centralized basis (the party's caucus in Congress). Both parties then campaigned throughout the country for their centrally designated nominees. The necessary consequence of the emergence of centrally designated nominees was that presidential electors would be expected to cast their votes in the Electoral College for the party's nominees.

As the Supreme Court observed in *McPherson v. Blacker*:

---

[32] John Adams was elected Vice President in 1789 without receiving an absolute majority of the presidential electors "appointed." His 34 electoral votes (out of 69) were sufficient for election at the time because the original Constitution (Article II, section 1, clause 3) required an absolute majority of the presidential electors "appointed" to elect the President, but required only the second largest number of votes to elect the Vice President. Under the 12th Amendment (ratified in 1804), an absolute majority of the presidential electors "appointed" is required to elect both the President and Vice President.

[33] White, Theodore H. 1969. *The Making of the President 1968*. New York, NY: Atheneum Publishers. Page 471.

"Doubtless **it was supposed that the electors would exercise a reasonable independence and fair judgment in the selection of the chief executive**, but experience soon demonstrated that, **whether chosen by the legislatures or by popular suffrage on general ticket or in districts, they were so chosen simply to register the will of the appointing power** in respect of a particular candidate. In relation, then, to the independence of the electors, the original expectation may be said to have been frustrated."[34] [Emphasis added]

Table 2.2 shows the distribution, by state, of the 71 electoral votes received by John Adams and the 68 electoral votes received by Thomas Jefferson in the nation's first contested presidential election in 1796.[35,36]

Despite the distinguished qualifications of both Adams and Jefferson, there was no hint of independent judgment by any of the presidential electors chosen by the legislatures of the nine states in which presidential electors were chosen by the state legislature.[37] As table 2.2 demonstrates, all 66 presidential electors from these nine states voted in lockstep for Jefferson or Adams in accordance with "the will of the appointing power"—that is, the will of the legislative majority.

In the one state (New Hampshire) in which the voters elected the state's presidential electors in a statewide popular election in 1796, all of the state's presidential electors voted for Adams. That is, the voters were "the appointing power" at the state level in New Hampshire, and the winning electors faithfully did the bidding of the statewide majority.

All of the presidential electors in Massachusetts voted for their home state candidate, Adams. All four presidential electors in Kentucky voted for Jefferson.

In three states (Virginia, North Carolina, and Maryland), the electoral votes were fragmented because the presidential electors were elected from districts. Although Thomas Jefferson was very popular in all three states, one elector from Virginia, one from North Carolina, and four electors from Maryland voted differently from the statewide majority. These presidential electors were not demonstrating independence or detached judgment—they were merely voting in accordance with "the will of the appointing power"—that is, the voters of their respective districts.

---

[34] *McPherson v. Blacker.* 146 U.S. 1 at 36. 1892.

[35] Congressional Quarterly. 2002. *Presidential Elections 1789–2002.* Washington, DC: CQ Press. Page 176.

[36] The table simplifies the results of the 1796 election by presenting only the number of electoral votes received by Adams and Jefferson. Thirteen different people received electoral votes in the 1796 election. Under the original Constitution, each presidential elector cast two votes. The candidate with the most electoral votes (provided that it was a majority of the electors appointed) became President. The second-ranking candidate (if he received a majority of the electors appointed) became Vice President.

[37] This count (nine) treats Tennessee as a state in which the legislature, in effect, chose the state's presidential electors. When Tennessee's three presidential electors cast their votes in the Electoral College in 1796, they unanimously supported Thomas Jefferson—the candidate who was popular with a majority of the Tennessee legislature.

Table 2.2 **ELECTORAL VOTES FOR ADAMS AND JEFFERSON IN THE NATION'S FIRST COMPETITIVE PRESIDENTIAL ELECTION (1796)**

STATE	ELECTORAL VOTES	ADAMS	JEFFERSON	METHOD OF CHOOSING PRESIDENTIAL ELECTORS
Connecticut	9	9		Legislature
Delaware	3	3		Legislature
Georgia	4		4	Legislature
Kentucky	4		4	Popular voting in elector districts
Maryland	11	7	4	Popular voting in districts
Massachusetts	16	16		Popular voting in congressional districts (with the legislature choosing the two senatorial electors)
New Hampshire	6	6		Popular voting statewide
New Jersey	7	7		Legislature
New York	12	12		Legislature
North Carolina	12	1	11	Popular voting in elector districts
Pennsylvania	15	1	14	Popular voting statewide
Rhode Island	4	4		Legislature
South Carolina	8		8	Legislature
Tennessee	3		3	Presidential electors chosen by county electors chosen by the state legislature
Vermont	4	4		Legislature
Virginia	21	1	20	Popular voting in 21 elector districts
Total	**139**	**71**	**68**	

Although Pennsylvania employed the winner-take-all system in 1796, its electoral votes were divided for a different reason. Voters were required to cast separate votes for the 15 individual positions of presidential elector. As Edward Stanwood reported in *A History of the Presidency from 1788 to 1897*:

> "In Pennsylvania, the vote was extremely close. There were . . . two tickets, each bearing fifteen names. The highest number polled by any candidate for elector was 12,306; the lowest of the thirty had 12,071. Thus 235 votes only represented the greatest difference; and two of the Federalist electors were chosen."[38]

The result of this close election was that 13 Jeffersonians and two Federalists were chosen as presidential electors from Pennsylvania in 1796. When the Electoral College met, 14 of the 15 electors slavishly voted, as expected, for their own party's designated nominee for President.

---

[38] Stanwood, Edward. 1924. *A History of the Presidency from 1788 to 1897*. Boston, MA: Houghton Mifflin Company. Page 48.

One of the two Federalist electors, Samuel Miles did not vote as expected. Instead, he cast his vote in the Electoral College for Thomas Jefferson—instead of John Adams.[39] In the December 15, 1796, issue of *United States Gazette*, a Federalist supporter complained:

> "What, do I chuse Samuel Miles to determine for me whether John Adams or Thomas Jefferson is the fittest man to be President of the United States? No, **I chuse him to act, not to think**." [Emphasis as per original; spelling as per original].[40]

The expectation that presidential electors should "act" and not "think" has remained strong ever since 1796. Of the 22,991 electoral votes cast for President in the 57 presidential elections between 1789 and 2012, only 17 were cast in an unfaithful way. Moreover, among these 17 cases, the vote of Samuel Miles for Thomas Jefferson in 1796 remains the only instance when the elector might have thought, at the time he voted, that his vote might affect the national outcome.[41]

In summary, because of the emergence of political parties and centralized nomination of presidential and vice-presidential candidates in 1796, the Electoral College has not acted as the deliberative body envisioned by the nation's Founding Fathers. As early as 1796, the Electoral College simply became a rubberstamp for affirming "the will of the appointing power" of each separate entity that selected electors. Since 1796, the Electoral College has had the form, but not the substance, of the deliberative body envisioned by the Founders.

2.2.3 THE SECOND COMPETITIVE ELECTION (1800)

Thomas Jefferson lost the presidency in the nation's first competitive election (1796) by a mere three electoral votes (table 2.2).

As Noble E. Cunningham wrote in *History of American Presidential Elections 1878–2001*:

> "The presidential election of 1796 had been extremely close, and in examining the results of that contest Republican Party managers had been struck by the fact that Adams' 3-vote margin of victory in the electoral college could be attributed to 1 vote from Pennsylvania, 1 from Virginia, and 1 from North Carolina. In each of these states, the Republicans had won an impressive victory, amassing in the three states a total of 45 electoral votes. The loss of 3 votes in these strongly Jeffersonian states was due to the

---

[39] Peirce, Neal R. 1968. *The People's President: The Electoral College in American History and Direct-Vote Alternative*. New York, NY: Simon & Schuster. Page 64.

[40] This piece was signed "CANDOUR."

[41] All but two of the 17 instances of deviant electoral votes for President were "grand-standing" votes (that is, votes cast after the presidential elector knew that his vote would not affect the national outcome). One electoral vote (in Minnesota in 2004) was cast by accident. See section 2.12 for additional details.

district method of electing presidential electors. **In looking for ways to improve their chances for victory in the next presidential election, Republican managers thus turned their attention to state election laws.** No uniform system of selection of presidential electors prevailed. In some states electors were chosen by the state legislature; in others they were elected on a general ticket throughout the state; in still others they were elected in districts. This meant that the party that controlled the state legislature was in a position to enact the system of selection that promised the greatest partisan advantage. Thus, in January 1800 the Republican-controlled legislature of Virginia passed an act providing for the election of presidential electors on a general ticket instead of districts as in previous elections. By changing the election law, Republicans in Virginia, confident of carrying a majority of the popular vote throughout the state but fearful of losing one or two districts to the Federalists ensured the entire electoral vote of the Union's largest state for the Republican candidate."[42,43] [Emphasis added]

Vice President Thomas Jefferson (soon to be a candidate for President in the 1800 election) summed up the reasons for Virginia's switch from the district system to the statewide winner-take-all system in a January 12, 1800, letter to James Monroe (then a member of the Virginia legislature):

"On the subject of an election by a general ticket, or by districts, most persons here seem to have made up their minds. **All agree that an election by districts would be best, if it could be general; but while 10 states chuse either by their legislatures or by a general ticket, it is folly & worse than folly** for the other 6. not to do it. In these 10. states the minority is entirely unrepresented; & their majorities not only have the weight of their whole state in their scale, but have the benefit of so much of our minorities as can succeed at a district election. This is, in fact, ensuring to our minorities the appointment of the government. To state it in another form; it is merely a question whether we will divide the U S into 16. or 137. districts. The latter being more chequered, & representing the people in smaller sections, would be more likely to be an exact representation of their diversified sentiments. But a representation of a part by great, & a part

---

[42] Cunningham, Noble E., Jr. In Schlesinger, Arthur M., Jr. and Israel, Fred L. (editors). 2002. *History of American Presidential Elections 1878–2001*. Philadelphia, PA: Chelsea House Publishers. Pages 104–105. The quotation from Cunningham contains a small error. Pennsylvania did not use a district system in 1796. The split vote in Pennsylvania resulted from the closeness of the statewide popular vote, as explained in section 2.2.2.

[43] Although the thrust of Cunningham's analysis is correct, Cunningham incorrectly attributes Jefferson's lost electoral vote in Pennsylvania to the use of the district system. As pointed out in section 2.2.2, the closeness of the Pennsylvania *statewide* vote permitted the Federalists to elect two of their elector candidates. One of the two Federalist electors defected to Jefferson, but one loyally voted for Adams.

by small sections, would give a result very different from what would be the sentiment of the whole people of the U S, were they assembled together."[44] [Emphasis added; spelling and punctuation as per original]

Thus, in 1800, Virginia ended its "folly" and adopted the statewide winner-take-all system to replace the district system used in the state in the first three presidential elections.[45] As a result of this change in Virginia's election law, Jefferson received all of Virginia's electoral votes in the 1800 election.[46]

Meanwhile, Virginia's "folly" of dividing its electoral votes did not go unnoticed by the Federalist Party in Massachusetts. In the 1796 election, Adams had succeeded in winning all his home state's electoral votes. The Jeffersonians, however, were making such significant inroads into Massachusetts that the Federalist-controlled legislature feared that the Jeffersonians might win as many as two districts in Massachusetts in the upcoming 1800 election.[47] Thus, the Massachusetts legislature eliminated the district system and, just to be safe, also eliminated the voters from the process. That is, the Massachusetts legislature decided to choose all of the state's presidential electors themselves for the 1800 election.[48]

---

[44] Ford, Paul Leicester. 1905. *The Works of Thomas Jefferson*. New York, NY: G.P. Putnam's Sons. 9:90.

[45] In 1892, the U.S. Supreme Court commented on the "folly" of dividing a state's electoral votes by saying, "The district system was largely considered the most equitable, and Madison wrote that it was that system which was contemplated by the framers of the constitution, although it was soon seen that its adoption by some states might place them at a disadvantage by a division of their strength, and that a uniform rule was preferable." *McPherson v. Blacker*. 146 U.S. 1 at 29. 1892.

[46] The remainder of Thomas Jefferson's January 12, 1800, letter to James Monroe is interesting in that it discusses the political calculations in the decisions by the New York and New Jersey legislatures not to permit the voters to participate in choosing the state's president electors. The letter continues, "I have today had a conversation with 113 [Aaron Burr] who has taken a flying trip here from N Y. He says, they have really now a majority in the H of R, but for want of some skilful person to rally round, they are disjointed, & will lose every question. In the Senate there is a majority of 8. or 9. against us. But in the new election which is to come on in April, three or 4. in the Senate will be changed in our favor; & in the H of R the county elections will still be better than the last; but still all will depend on the city election, which is of 12. members. At present there would be no doubt of our carrying our ticket there; nor does there seem to be time for any events arising to change that disposition. There is therefore the best prospect possible of a great & decided majority on a joint vote of the two houses. They are so confident of this, that the republican party there will not consent to elect either by districts or a general ticket. They chuse to do it by their legislature. I am told the republicans of N J are equally confident, & equally anxious against an election either by districts or a general ticket. The contest in this State will end in a separation of the present legislature without passing any election law, (& their former one is expired), and in depending on the new one, which will be elected Oct 14. in which the republican majority will be more decided in the Representatives, & instead of a majority of 5. against us in the Senate, will be of 1. for us. They will, from the necessity of the case, chuse the electors themselves. Perhaps it will be thought I ought in delicacy to be silent on this subject. But you, who know me, know that my private gratifications would be most indulged by that issue, which should leave me most at home. If anything supersedes this propensity, it is merely the desire to see this government brought back to it's republican principles. Consider this as written to mr. Madison as much as yourself; & communicate it, if you think it will do any good, to those possessing our joint confidence, or any others where it may be useful & safe. Health & affectionate salutations."

[47] Cunningham, Noble E., Jr. In Schlesinger, Arthur M., Jr. and Israel, Fred L. (editors). 2002. *History of American Presidential Elections 1878–2001*. Philadelphia, PA: Chelsea House Publishers. Page 105.

[48] Congressional Quarterly. 2002. *Presidential Elections 1789–2002*. Washington, DC: CQ Press.

Similarly, the Federalist-controlled New Hampshire legislature feared losing the statewide vote to the Jeffersonians under the state's existing statewide winner-take-all popular election system and decided to choose all of the state's presidential electors themselves.

Cunningham describes election law politics in New York and Pennsylvania in 1800 as follows:

> "In New York, Republicans introduced a measure to move from legislative choice to election by districts, but the proposal was defeated by the Federalists, an outcome that ultimately worked to the advantage of the Republicans when they won control of the legislature in the state elections of 1800. In Pennsylvania, a Republican House of Representatives and a Federalist Senate produced a deadlock over the system to be used to select electors, and the vote of that state was eventually cast by the legislature in a compromise division of the 15 electoral votes, eight Republican and seven Federalist electors being named." [49],[50]

The Pennsylvania legislature permitted its voters to elect all of the state's presidential electors in 1789, 1792, and 1796 using the statewide winner-take-all rule; however, it did not implement this policy decision by means of permanent legislation. When it came time to appoint presidential electors for the 1800 election, the Federalists and the Republicans each controlled one house of the legislature. Faced with the possibility of not being able to appoint any presidential electors in 1800, the divided legislature agreed on a compromise. The compromise involved having the legislature appoint the presidential electors with an 8–7 division between the parties.

Georgia switched from the winner-take-all rule (first used in 1796) to legislative appointment for the 1800 election.

Thus, all four states that used the winner-take-all rule prior to 1800 had abandoned it by the time of the 1800 election (Maryland abandoning it in 1796 and New Hampshire, Pennsylvania, and Georgia abandoning it in 1800).

For the 1800 election, Rhode Island switched from legislative appointment to the winner-take-all rule.

Thus, only one state (Rhode Island) used the winner-take-all rule for the 1800 election.

---

[49] Cunningham, Noble E., Jr. In Schlesinger, Arthur M., Jr. and Israel, Fred L. (editors). 2002. *History of American Presidential Elections 1878–2001.* Philadelphia, PA: Chelsea House Publishers. Pages 105.

[50] It is interesting to note that, by the time of the nation's second competitive presidential election (1800), both of the states (Pennsylvania and New Hampshire) in which presidential electors were elected in a statewide popular vote in 1796 had switched to a system of legislative election of the state's presidential electors. That is, no state used a statewide popular vote system in the 1800 presidential election.

2.2.4 THE EMERGENCE OF THE CURRENT SYSTEM

The method of choosing presidential electors varied from state to state and from election to election over the next several decades.

Chief Justice Melville Fuller of the U.S. Supreme Court recounted the history of methods used to appoint presidential electors between 1804 and 1828 in his opinion in *McPherson v. Blacker*:

> "[W]hile most of the states adopted the general ticket system, the district method obtained in Kentucky until 1824; in Tennessee and Maryland until 1832; in Indiana in 1824 and 1828; in Illinois in 1820 and 1824; and in Maine in 1820, 1824, and 1828. Massachusetts used the general ticket system in 1804, . . . chose electors by joint ballot of the legislature in 1808 and in 1816, . . . used the district system again in 1812 and 1820, . . . and returned to the general ticket system in 1824. . . . In New York, the electors were elected in 1828 by districts, the district electors choosing the electors at large. . . .
> The appointment of electors by the legislature, instead of by popular vote, was made use of by North Carolina, Vermont, and New Jersey in 1812."[51]

By 1824, presidential electors were chosen by popular vote (either by districts or statewide) in 18 of the 24 states. State legislatures chose presidential electors in Delaware, Georgia, Louisiana, New York, South Carolina, and Vermont.

By 1832, the voters, rather than the state legislatures, chose presidential electors in 22 of the 23 states, with South Carolina being the only exception.

By 1832, Maryland was the only state where presidential electors were elected by district. Maryland changed to the statewide winner-take-all system in 1836.

Thus, in 1836, presidential electors were elected on a statewide basis in all of the states (that is, either by the people or, in the case of South Carolina, by the legislature).

As previously noted, the Founding Fathers did not advocate the use by the states of a statewide winner-take-all system to allocate their electoral votes. Nonetheless, because the state legislatures possessed the exclusive power to choose the manner of appointing their presidential electors, it was probably inevitable, in retrospect, that they would realize the disadvantage of dividing their electoral votes and, therefore, adopt the unit rule.

Thus, the Constitution's grant of the power to the states to choose the manner of allocating their electoral votes resulted in the emergence throughout the country of a system that the Founding Fathers never envisioned. Instead of being a deliberative body, the Electoral College, in practice, was composed of presidential electors who voted in lockstep to rubberstamp the choices that had been previously made by extra-constitutional bodies (namely, the nominating caucuses of the political parties).

This fundamental change in the system for electing the President did not come

---

[51] *McPherson v. Blacker*. 146 U.S. 1 at 32. 1892.

about from a federal constitutional amendment but instead from the use by the states of a power that Article II of the U.S. Constitution specifically granted to them. As Stanwood noted in *A History of the Presidency from 1788 to 1897,*

> "the [statewide] method of choosing electors had now become uniform throughout the country, **without the interposition of an amendment to the Constitution.**"[52] [Emphasis added]

The South Carolina legislature last chose presidential electors in 1860. Since the Civil War, there have been only two instances when presidential electors have been chosen by a state legislature. In 1868, the Florida legislature did so because Reconstruction was not complete in the state in time for the presidential election. In 1876, Colorado did so because it was admitted as a new state shortly before the presidential election.

By 1876, the principle that the people should elect presidential electors was so well established that the Colorado Constitution specifically addressed the exceptional nature of the appointment of the state's presidential electors by the legislature:

> "**Presidential electors, 1876.** The general assembly shall, at their first session, immediately after the organization of the two houses and after the canvass of the votes for officers of the executive department, and before proceeding to other business, provide by act or joint resolution for the appointment by said general assembly of electors in the electoral college, and such joint resolution or the bill for such enactment may be passed without being printed or referred to any committee, or read on more than one day in either house, and shall take effect immediately after the concurrence of the two houses therein, and the approval of the governor thereto shall not be necessary."[53]

The next section of the Colorado Constitution then mandated an immediate transition from legislative appointment to popular election of presidential electors by providing that after 1876:

> "[T]he electors of the electoral college shall be chosen by direct vote of the people."[54]

The inclusion of the above section in the Colorado Constitution was a congressional condition for Colorado's admission to the Union.

---

[52] Stanwood, Edward. 1924. *A History of the Presidency from 1788 to 1897.* Boston, MA: Houghton Mifflin Company. Page 165. See also Busch, Andrew E. 2001. The development and democratization of the electoral college. In Gregg, Gary L. II (editor). 2001. *Securing Democracy: Why We Have an Electoral College.* Wilmington, DE: ISI Books. Pages 27–42.

[53] Section 19 of the article of the Colorado Constitution governing the transition from territorial status to statehood.

[54] Section 20 of the article of the Colorado Constitution governing the transition from territorial status to statehood.

2.2.5 DEVELOPMENTS SINCE 1876

Since 1876, the norm has been that a state's voters directly elect presidential electors in a statewide popular election under the winner-take-all system (with only three exceptions, as described below).

The first exception arose as a consequence of the controversial 1888 presidential election. In that election, President Grover Cleveland received 5,539,118 popular votes in his re-election campaign, whereas Republican challenger Benjamin Harrison received only 5,449,825 popular votes.[55] Despite Cleveland's margin of 89,293 popular votes, Harrison won an overwhelming majority of the electoral votes (233 to Cleveland's 168) and was elected President. In the 1890 mid-term elections, the Democrats won political control of the then-usually-Republican state of Michigan. Under the Democrats, Michigan switched from the statewide winner-take-all system (then prevailing in all the states) to an arrangement in which one presidential elector was elected from each of Michigan's 12 congressional districts; one additional presidential elector was elected from a specially created eastern district (consisting of the first, second, sixth, seventh, eighth, and 10th congressional districts); and the state's remaining presidential elector was elected from a western district (consisting of the state's other six congressional districts). The Republicans contested the constitutionality of the change to the district system before the U.S. Supreme Court in the 1892 case of *McPherson v. Blacker* (appendix O). In that case, the Court upheld Michigan's right to use the district method of allocating its electoral votes. As a result, in the 1892 presidential election, Democrat Grover Cleveland received five electoral votes from Michigan, and Republican Benjamin Harrison received the other nine. When the Republicans regained political control of the state government in Michigan, they promptly restored the statewide winner-take-all system. In the 1896 election, McKinley (the Republican nominee) received 100% of Michigan's electoral votes.

The second exception arose in 1969 when Maine adopted a system in which the state's two senatorial presidential electors are awarded to the presidential slate winning the statewide vote, and one additional presidential elector is awarded to the presidential slate carrying each of the state's two congressional districts. This system remains in effect.

The third exception arose in 1992 when Nebraska adopted Maine's system of district and statewide electors. Nebraska law provides:

> "Receipt by the presidential electors of a party or a group of petitioners of the highest number of votes statewide shall constitute election of the two at-large presidential electors of that party or group of petitioners. Receipt by the presidential electors of a party or a group of petitioners of the highest number of votes in a congressional district shall constitute election

---

[55] Congressional Quarterly. 2002. *Presidential Elections 1789–2002*. Washington, DC: CQ Press. Page 128.

of the congressional district presidential elector of that party or group of petitioners."[56]

Until 2008, the district system used in Maine and Nebraska did not result in a political division of either state's presidential electors. However, in 2008, Barack Obama carried Nebraska's 2nd congressional district and thereby won one of Nebraska's five electoral votes.

After the 2008 presidential election, Nebraska's Republican Governor Heineman urged that the state abolish the district system and re-adopt the winner-take-all rule. The legislature did not, however, act on the governor's recommendation.[57]

2.2.6 THE SHORT PRESIDENTIAL BALLOT

Until the middle of the 20th century, voters generally cast separate votes for individual candidates for the position of presidential elector. In other words, in a state with 20 electoral votes using the statewide winner-take-all rule, the voter was entitled to cast 20 separate votes.

Inevitably, some voters would accidentally invalidate their ballot by voting for more than 20 candidates—something that was especially easy to do on the paper ballots that were in general use at the time. Other voters would accidentally vote for fewer than 20 electors (thereby diminishing the value of their franchise). Still other voters would mistakenly vote for just one presidential elector (thereby drastically diminishing the value of their vote). A small number of voters intentionally split their ticket and voted for presidential electors from opposing parties (perhaps because they liked or disliked individual candidates for the position of presidential elector).

One result of these long "bed sheet" ballots was that a state's electoral vote would occasionally split between two political parties when the election was close in a particular state. For example, the Federalists elected two presidential electors in Pennsylvania in 1796. In 1916, Woodrow Wilson received one of West Virginia's electoral votes, while Charles Evans Hughes received seven. In 1912, Wilson received two of California's electoral votes, with Theodore Roosevelt receiving 11. The statewide winner came up short by one electoral vote in California in 1880, in Ohio and Oregon in 1892, in California and Kentucky in 1896, and in Maryland in 1904.[58]

The *short ballot* was developed to simplify voting for President. It enables a voter to cast a single vote for a presidential slate composed of a named candidate for Presi-

---

[56] Nebraska election law. Section 32.1038.

[57] See section 7.1 for a poll of Nebraska voters on the subject of the district system, the winner-take-all rule, and the national popular vote approach.

[58] Congressional Quarterly. 2002. *Presidential Elections 1789–2002*. Washington, DC: CQ Press. Pages 158–159.

PRESIDENTIAL ELECTORS

OFFICIAL BALLOT

Town of

WINDSOR

for the

General Election November 3, 1964

Electors of President and Vice-President of the United States

To vote a straight party ticket, make a cross (X) in the square at the head of the party column of your choice.
If you desire to vote for a person whose name is not on the ballot, fill in the name of the candidate of your choice in the blank space provided therefor.

If you do not wish to vote for every person in a party column, make a cross (X) opposite the name of each candidate of your Choice; or you may make a cross (X) in the square at the head of the party column of your choice which shall count as a vote for every name in that column, except for any name through which you may draw a line, and except for any name representing a candidate for an office to fill which you have otherwise voted in the manner heretofore prescribed.

REPUBLICAN PARTY	DEMOCRATIC PARTY
For President	*For President*
BARRY M. GOLDWATER of Arizona	**LYNDON B. JOHNSON of Texas**
For Vice-President	*For Vice-President*
WILLIAM E. MILLER of New York	**HUBERT H. HUMPHREY of Minnesota**
☐	☐

For Electors of President and Vice-President of the United States	Vote for THREE	For Electors of President and Vice-President of the United States	Vote for THREE
MABEL STAFFORD, Republican, South Wallingford		MARGARET M. FARMER, Democratic, Burlington	
LEE EMERSON, Republican, Barton		PETER J. HINCKS, Democratic, Middlebury	
OLIN GAY, Republican, Springfield		HAROLD RAYNOLDS, Democratic, Springfield	

Figure 2.1 Presidential ballot in Vermont in 1964

dent and a named candidate for Vice President. By 1940, 15 states had adopted the short ballot. The number increased to 26 states by 1948 and to 36 by 1966.[59]

The presidential ballot in Ohio in 1948 was particularly confusing. Ohio employed the short ballot for established political parties. The newly formed Progressive Party (supporting Henry Wallace for President) failed to qualify in Ohio as a regular party in time for the 1948 presidential election. Consequently, the individual names of the Progressive Party's 25 candidates for the position of presidential elector appeared on the ballot. In the confusion caused by this hybrid system, an estimated 100,000 ballots

---

[59] Peirce, Neal R. 1968. *The People's President: The Electoral College in American History and Direct-Vote Alternative.* New York, NY: Simon & Schuster. Page 120.

were invalidated because voters mistakenly voted for some individual presidential electors while simultaneously also voting for either Democrat Harry Truman or Republican Thomas Dewey. Truman carried Ohio by 7,107 votes.

Vermont used a combination of the short presidential ballot and the traditional long ballot until 1980. Figure 2.1 shows a 1964 sample presidential ballot in Vermont. As can be seen, the voter had the option of casting a vote for all three of a party's presidential electors; voting for one, two, or three individual presidential-elector candidates on the ballot; or voting for one, two, or three write-in candidates for the position of presidential elector.

Since 1980, all states have employed the short presidential ballot.

Nonetheless, it is still possible today, under some circumstances in some states, to cast write-in votes for individual presidential electors (section 2.8), to cast votes for unpledged presidential electors (section 2.11), and, on an exceptional basis, to cast separate votes for individual candidates for the position of presidential elector (section 2.9).

2.3 CURRENT METHODS OF ELECTING PRESIDENTIAL ELECTORS

As stated previously, the people have no federal constitutional right to vote for President or Vice President of the United States. In Colorado, the people have a state constitutional right to vote for presidential electors. In all the other states, the people have acquired the presidential vote by means of state law.

In this book, we will frequently refer to the laws of Minnesota to illustrate the way in which states implement the process of electing the President and Vice President.

As a convenience for the reader, appendix D contains the provisions of Minnesota election law that are relevant to presidential elections.

Section 208.02 of Minnesota election law gives the people of Minnesota the right to vote for presidential electors.

> "Presidential electors shall be chosen at the state general election held in the year preceding the expiration of the term of the president of the United States."

In Minnesota, the presidential ballot is prepared and printed by county auditors in accordance with state law. Accordingly, when a voter walked into a polling place in Hennepin County, Minnesota, on November 2, 2004, he or she received a "short presidential ballot" resembling the sample ballot shown in figure 2.2, containing nine presidential slates, including the Republican slate consisting of George W. Bush for President and Dick Cheney for Vice President, and the Democratic slate consisting of John F. Kerry and John Edwards.

As demonstrated by figure 2.2, Minnesota's presidential ballot is entirely silent as to the existence of the Electoral College or the fact that the state has 10 electoral votes. The ballot simply reads,

> "U.S. President and Vice President—Vote for one team."

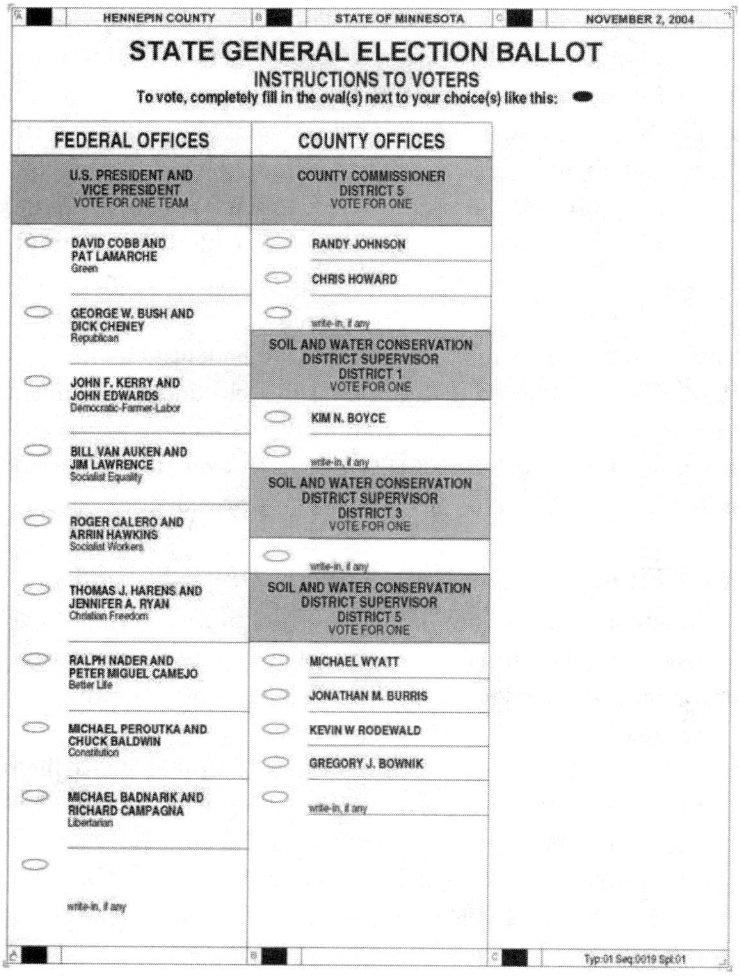
HENNEPIN COUNTY | STATE OF MINNESOTA | NOVEMBER 2, 2004

STATE GENERAL ELECTION BALLOT

INSTRUCTIONS TO VOTERS

To vote, completely fill in the oval(s) next to your choice(s) like this:

FEDERAL OFFICES	COUNTY OFFICES
U.S. PRESIDENT AND VICE PRESIDENT VOTE FOR ONE TEAM	COUNTY COMMISSIONER DISTRICT 5 VOTE FOR ONE
DAVID COBB AND PAT LAMARCHE Green	RANDY JOHNSON
	CHRIS HOWARD
GEORGE W. BUSH AND DICK CHENEY Republican	write-in, if any
	SOIL AND WATER CONSERVATION DISTRICT SUPERVISOR DISTRICT 1 VOTE FOR ONE
JOHN F. KERRY AND JOHN EDWARDS Democratic-Farmer-Labor	KIM N. BOYCE
BILL VAN AUKEN AND JIM LAWRENCE Socialist Equality	write-in, if any
	SOIL AND WATER CONSERVATION DISTRICT SUPERVISOR DISTRICT 3 VOTE FOR ONE
ROGER CALERO AND ARRIN HAWKINS Socialist Workers	write-in, if any
THOMAS J. HARENS AND JENNIFER A. RYAN Christian Freedom	SOIL AND WATER CONSERVATION DISTRICT SUPERVISOR DISTRICT 5 VOTE FOR ONE
RALPH NADER AND PETER MIGUEL CAMEJO Better Life	MICHAEL WYATT
	JONATHAN M. BURRIS
MICHAEL PEROUTKA AND CHUCK BALDWIN Constitution	KEVIN W RODEWALD
	GREGORY J. BOWNIK
MICHAEL BADNARIK AND RICHARD CAMPAGNA Libertarian	write-in, if any
write-in, if any	

Typ:01 Seq:0019 Spl:01

Figure 2.2 Presidential ballot in Minnesota in 2004

The linkage between a vote cast for a presidential slate on Minnesota's ballot and the state's 10 presidential electors is established by state law.

> "When Presidential electors are to be voted for, a vote cast for the party candidates for president and vice-president **shall be deemed** a vote for that party's electors as filed with the secretary of state."[60] [Emphasis added]

Thus, a voter filling in the oval next to the names of George W. Bush and Dick Cheney on November 2, 2004, was directly casting a vote not for Bush and Cheney, but instead for a slate of 10 Republican candidates for the position of presidential elector who, if elected on November 2, 2004, were expected to meet on December 13, 2004, and vote for Bush and Cheney in the Electoral College.

Minnesota law outlines the procedure by which the Minnesota Secretary of State

[60] Minnesota election law. Section 208.04, subdivision 1.

becomes officially informed of the names of the persons running for President and Vice President and the names of the candidates for the position of presidential elector:

> "Presidential electors for the major political parties of this state shall be nominated by delegate conventions called and held under the supervision of the respective state central committees of the parties of this state. On or before primary election day **the chair of the major political party shall certify to the secretary of state the names of the persons nominated as Presidential electors and the names of the party candidates for president and vice-president.**"[61] [Emphasis added]

Thus, it is the state chair of each major political party in Minnesota who officially informs the Minnesota Secretary of State as to the name of the person nominated for President by the party's national convention, the name of the person nominated for Vice President by the party's national convention, and the names of the 10 persons nominated by the party's state convention for the position of presidential elector.

Twenty-nine states follow Minnesota's approach of nominating elector candidates at state party conventions. In six other states and the District of Columbia, the state (or district) party committee nominates the party's presidential electors. In several states, a party's nominees for presidential elector are selected in a primary election. Many of the remaining states (e.g., California) permit each political party in the state to choose its method for itself. In Pennsylvania, each party's presidential nominee directly nominates the elector candidates who will run under his name in the state.[62]

Minnesota law also provides the procedure by which the county auditors become officially notified of the names of the persons running for President and Vice President:

> "The secretary of state shall certify the names of all duly nominated Presidential and Vice-Presidential candidates to the county auditors of the counties of the state."[63]

Laws in the other states and the District of Columbia operate in a broadly similar way to accomplish the above objectives.

Today, there is nothing on the ballot in 34 states to indicate the existence of the Electoral College or presidential electors.

Ballots in five states (Arizona, Idaho, North Dakota, Oklahoma, and South Dakota) explicitly list the names of all of the candidates for the position of presidential elector associated with each presidential slate. For example, the 2004 presidential ballot in North Dakota (figure 2.3) made it clear that a vote for "Bush–Republican" is, in fact, a vote for the Republican Party's three presidential-elector candidates, namely Betsy Dalrymple, Evan Lips, and Ben Clayburgh.

---

[61] Minnesota election law. Section 208.03.

[62] Berns, Walter (editor). 1992. *After the People Vote: A Guide to the Electoral College*. Washington, DC: The AEI Press. Page 11. See section 2.12 for Pennsylvania law.

[63] Minnesota election law. Section 208.04, subdivision 1.

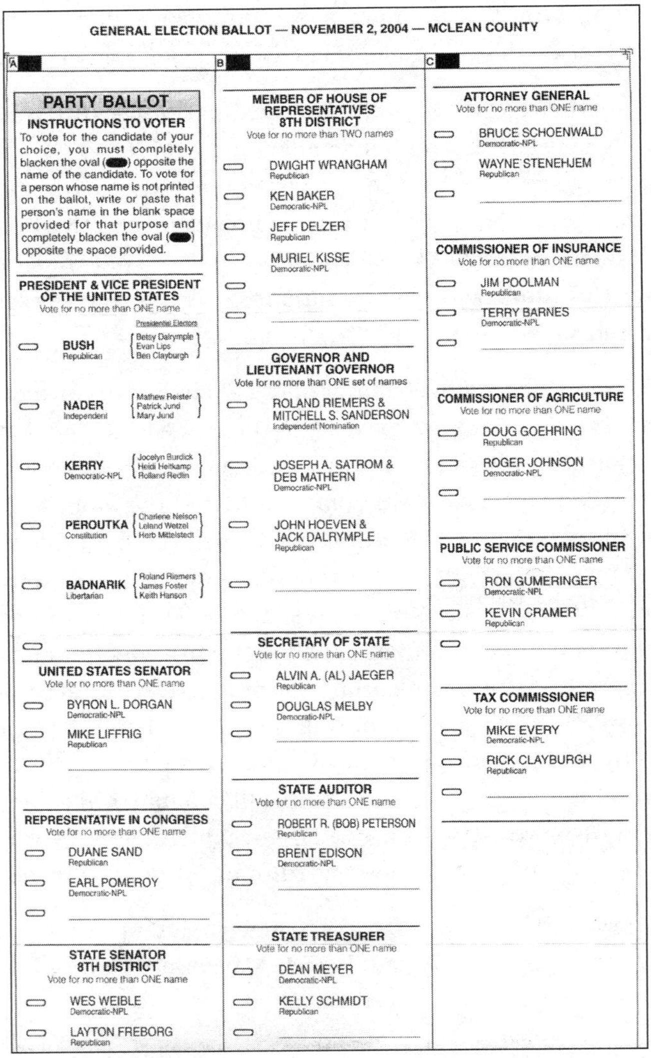

Figure 2.3 Presidential ballot in North Dakota in 2004

Curiously, in North Dakota, the name of the candidate for Vice President does not appear on the ballot even though the ballot is headed by the words "President & Vice President of the United States—Vote for no more than one team."[64]

Ballots in 12 additional states (Colorado, Connecticut, Kansas, Massachusetts, Michigan, Mississippi, New Jersey, New York, Oregon, Pennsylvania, Rhode Island, and Tennessee) and the District of Columbia mention that the voter is voting for presidential electors but do not include the names of the individual candidates for the position of presidential elector.

---

[64] The names of vice-presidential candidates do not appear on the ballot in Arizona or North Dakota.

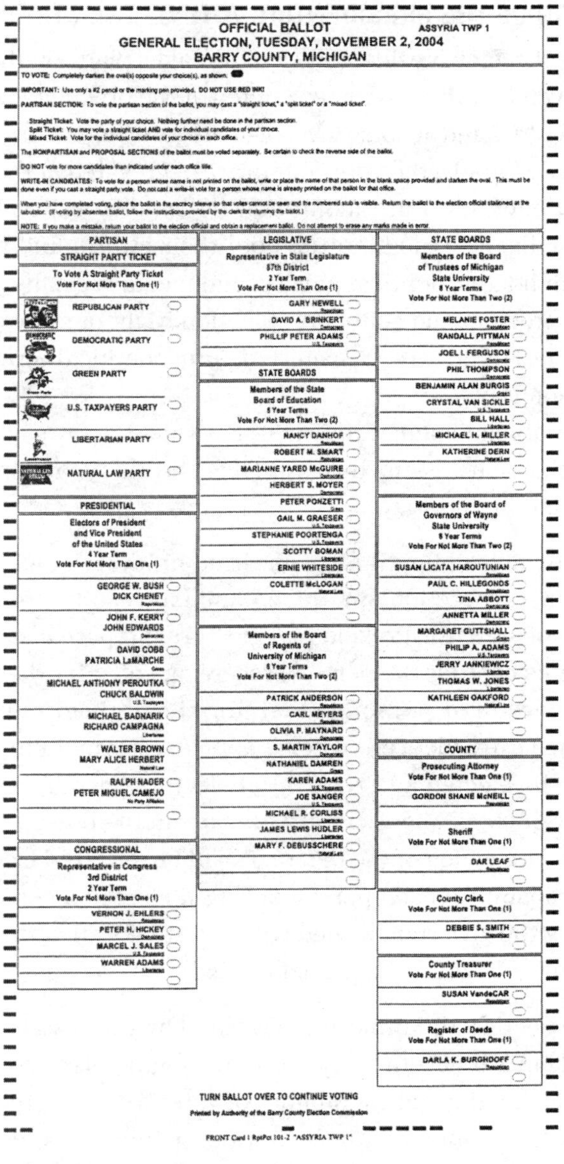

Figure 2.4 Presidential ballot in Michigan in 2004

Oregon's presidential ballot is unusually explicit and informs the voter:

"Your vote for the candidates for United States President and Vice President shall be a vote for the electors supporting those candidates."

Figure 2.4 shows a 2004 presidential ballot from Michigan.[65] It refers to "Presidential: Electors of President and Vice President of the United States—4 Year Term."

---

[65] The Michigan ballot in figure 2.4 and the ballots of a number of other states provide the voter with the option of casting a "straight party" vote.

2.4 CERTIFICATION OF THE PRESIDENTIAL VOTE BY THE STATES

After the popular voting for presidential electors takes place on the Tuesday after the first Monday in November, the votes are counted at the precinct level. The vote counts are then typically aggregated at some level of local government (e.g., city, town, village, township, or county). Finally, the vote counts are aggregated at the statewide level.

Vote counts at each level are monitored by candidates, political parties, civic groups, and the media. The media often pool their efforts and have a joint reporting system. The candidates, political parties, and media typically have unofficial vote counts from every precinct and county on Election Night or shortly thereafter.

The official vote counts are transmitted from the local level to the state level shortly after Election Day.

In terms of the official count, Minnesota law (and the laws of many other states) specifies that the state canvassing board shall ascertain the number of votes cast for each presidential slate in the state.

> "The state canvassing board at its meeting on the second Tuesday after each state general election shall open and canvass the returns made to the secretary of state for Presidential electors, prepare a statement of the number of votes cast for the persons receiving votes for these offices, and **declare the person or persons receiving the highest number of votes for each office duly elected**. When it appears that more than the number of persons to be elected as Presidential electors have the highest and an equal number of votes, the secretary of state, in the presence of the board shall decide by lot which of the persons shall be declared elected. The governor shall transmit to each person declared elected a certificate of election, signed by the governor, sealed with the state seal, and countersigned by the secretary of state."[66] [Emphasis added]

It is the above section of Minnesota election law that establishes the statewide winner-take-all rule in Minnesota by means of the highlighted words "declare the person or persons receiving the highest number of votes for each office duly elected."

Minnesota law (in common with the laws of many states) calls for the use of a lottery in the event of a statewide tie vote for presidential electors. In some states (including Maine and Michigan), the state legislature is empowered to break a tie among presidential electors. For example, Maine law provides:

> "If there is a tie vote for presidential electors, the Governor shall convene the Legislature by proclamation. The Legislature by joint ballot of the members assembled in convention shall determine which are elected."[67]

---

[66] Minnesota election law. Section 208.05.
[67] Maine 21-A M.R.S, section 732. The State of Maine claims a copyright in its codified statutes. All copyrights and other rights to statutory text are reserved by the State of Maine.

Although elections are primarily controlled by state law, various federal laws also govern presidential elections. For example, federal law requires each state to create seven "Certificates of Ascertainment" certifying the number of votes cast for each presidential slate. One of these certificates is sent to the Archivist of the United States in Washington, D.C., and six are supplied to the presidential electors for their use during their meeting in mid-December. Title 3, chapter 1, section 6 of the United States Code specifies:

> "It shall be the duty of the executive of each State, as soon as practicable after the conclusion of the appointment of the electors in such State by the final ascertainment, under and in pursuance of the laws of such State providing for such ascertainment, to communicate by registered mail under the seal of the State to the Archivist of the United States a certificate of such ascertainment of the electors appointed, **setting forth the names of such electors and the canvass** or other ascertainment under the laws of such State of **the number of votes** given or cast for each person for whose appointment any and all votes have been given or cast; and it shall also thereupon be the duty of the executive of each State to deliver to the electors of such State, on or before the day on which they are required by section 7 of this title to meet, six duplicate-originals of the same certificate under the seal of the State. . . . " [Emphasis added]

Figures 2.5, 2.6, and 2.7 show the first three pages of Minnesota's 2004 Certificate of Ascertainment (with all eight pages being shown in appendix E). Minnesota's Certificate of Ascertainment is signed by the Governor and Secretary of State, bears the state seal, and was issued on November 30, 2004 (four weeks after the voting by the people on November 2).

The second page of Minnesota's Certificate of Ascertainment (figure 2.6) shows that 1,445,014 popular votes were cast for each of the 10 presidential electors associated with the presidential slate consisting of John Kerry for President and John Edwards for Vice President of the Minnesota Democratic-Farmer-Labor Party. All 10 elector candidates received the identical number of votes because Minnesota law (in common with the laws of many other states) specifies that a vote cast for the Kerry–Edwards presidential state "shall be deemed" to be a vote for each of the 10 presidential electors associated with that slate.[68]

Similarly, the third page of Minnesota's Certificate of Ascertainment (figure 2.7) shows that 1,346,695 popular votes were cast for presidential electors associated with the presidential slate consisting of George W. Bush and Dick Cheney of the Republican Party.[69]

---

[68] Minnesota election law. Section 208.04, subdivision 1.

[69] Minnesota's 2004 Certificate of Ascertainment goes on to report the votes cast for candidates of the Better Life Party, Libertarian Party, Green Party, Constitution Party, Christian Freedom Party, Socialist Equity Party, and Socialist Workers Party.

Figure 2.5 First page of Minnesota's 2004 Certificate of Ascertainment

The Certificate of Ascertainment reflects Minnesota's use of the winner-take-all system of awarding electoral votes. In particular, the second page (figure 2.6) of the certificate states that the 10 presidential electors associated with the presidential slate consisting of John Kerry for President and John Edwards for Vice President of the Minnesota Democratic-Farmer-Labor Party

> "received the greatest number of votes for the office of Electors of President and Vice President of the United States and are duly elected to fill such office."

In the two states that use the district system (Maine and Nebraska), the Certificate of Ascertainment shows the statewide vote (which decides the state's two

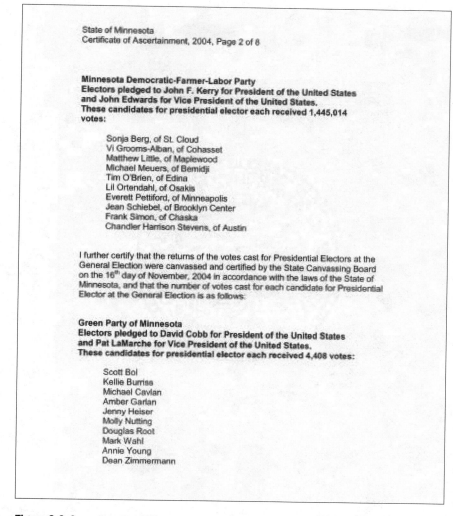

State of Minnesota
Certificate of Ascertainment, 2004, Page 2 of 8

Minnesota Democratic-Farmer-Labor Party
Electors pledged to John F. Kerry for President of the United States
and John Edwards for Vice President of the United States.
These candidates for presidential elector each received 1,445,014
votes:

Sonja Berg, of St. Cloud
Vi Grooms-Alban, of Cohasset
Matthew Little, of Maplewood
Michael Meuers, of Bemidji
Tim O'Brien, of Edina
Lil Ortendahl, of Osakis
Everett Pettiford, of Minneapolis
Jean Schiebel, of Brooklyn Center
Frank Simon, of Chaska
Chandler Harrison Stevens, of Austin

I further certify that the returns of the votes cast for Presidential Electors at the
General Election were canvassed and certified by the State Canvassing Board
on the 16th day of November, 2004 in accordance with the laws of the State of
Minnesota, and that the number of votes cast for each candidate for Presidential
Elector at the General Election is as follows:

Green Party of Minnesota
Electors pledged to David Cobb for President of the United States
and Pat LaMarche for Vice President of the United States.
These candidates for presidential elector each received 4,408 votes:

Scott Bol
Kellie Burriss
Michael Cavlan
Amber Garlan
Jenny Heiser
Molly Nutting
Douglas Root
Mark Wahl
Annie Young
Dean Zimmermann

Figure 2.6 Second page of Minnesota's 2004 Certificate of Ascertainment showing that the Kerry–Edwards slate received 1,445,014 popular votes and carried the state

senatorial electors) as well as the district vote (which decides the presidential elector for each congressional district). Maine's 2004 Certificate of Ascertainment is shown in appendix F, and Nebraska's 2004 Certificate of Ascertainment is shown in appendix G.

Controversies about voting for President generally focus on the steps leading up to the issuance of the Certificate of Ascertainment in the contested state. Title 3, chapter 1, section 5 of the United States Code creates a "safe harbor" date six days before the scheduled meeting of the Electoral College for reaching a "final determination of any controversy" concerning the November voting for presidential electors. Title 3, chapter 1, section 5 of the United States Code states:

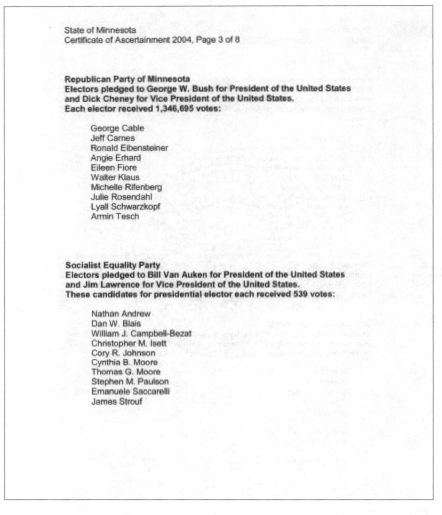

State of Minnesota
Certificate of Ascertainment 2004, Page 3 of 8

Republican Party of Minnesota
Electors pledged to George W. Bush for President of the United States
and Dick Cheney for Vice President of the United States.
Each elector received 1,346,695 votes:

George Cable
Jeff Carnes
Ronald Eibensteiner
Angie Erhard
Eileen Fiore
Walter Klaus
Michelle Rifenberg
Julie Rosendahl
Lyall Schwarzkopf
Armin Tesch

Socialist Equality Party
Electors pledged to Bill Van Auken for President of the United States
and Jim Lawrence for Vice President of the United States.
These candidates for presidential elector each received 539 votes:

Nathan Andrew
Dan W. Blais
William J. Campbell-Bezat
Christopher M. Isett
Cory R. Johnson
Cynthia B. Moore
Thomas G. Moore
Stephen M. Paulson
Emanuele Saccarelli
James Strouf

Figure 2.7 Third page of Minnesota's 2004 Certificate of Ascertainment showing that the Bush–Cheney slate received 1,346,695 popular votes

"If any State shall have provided, by laws enacted prior to the day fixed for the appointment of the electors, for its final determination of any controversy or contest concerning the appointment of all or any of the electors of such State, by judicial or other methods or procedures, and such determination shall have been made at least six days before the time fixed for the meeting of the electors, such determination made pursuant to such law so existing on said day, and made at least six days prior to said time of meeting of the electors, shall be conclusive, and shall govern in the counting of the electoral votes as provided in the Constitution, and as hereinafter regulated, so far as the ascertainment of the electors appointed by such State is concerned."

This "safe harbor" date played a central role in the decision of the U.S. Supreme Court in *Bush v. Gore*[70] concerning the disputed counting of the popular votes in Florida in the 2000 presidential election.

The federally established "safe harbor" date for the November 6, 2012, presidential election is Monday December 10, 2012 (with December 17, 2012, being the date for the meeting of the Electoral College).

Many states finalize their Certificate of Ascertainment in late November. Maine's 2004 Certificate of Ascertainment (shown in appendix F) was issued on November 23, 2004. Almost all states have a law setting a specific deadline for finalizing the canvassing of their statewide elections (sometimes with a special earlier deadline for presidential electors). Appendix T lists these deadlines.

The federal "safe harbor" date established by Title 3, chapter 1, section 5 of the United States Code is generally regarded as the deadline for each state to finalize its Certificate of Ascertainment. For example, New York's 2004 Certificate of Ascertainment (shown in appendix H) was issued on December 6, 2004 (i.e., six days before the scheduled December 13 meeting of the Electoral College). Ohio also finalized its Certificate of Ascertainment on December 6, 2004.[71]

2.5 MEETING OF THE ELECTORAL COLLEGE

The U.S. Constitution (Article II, section 1, clause 4) grants Congress the power to choose the time for choosing presidential electors (what we call "Election Day") and the day that the Electoral College must meet:

> "The Congress may determine the Time of chusing the Electors, and the Day on which they shall give their Votes; **which Day shall be the same throughout the United States**." [Spelling as per original] [Emphasis added]

Given the slow communications of the pre-telegraph era, this provision of the Constitution effectively prevented the electors from knowing, with certainty, how the electors in other states were voting.[72]

Federal law specifies that presidential electors shall be appointed on the Tuesday after the first Monday in November.[73]

Federal law specifies one particular day for the meeting of the Electoral College.

> "The electors of President and Vice President of each State shall meet and give their votes on the **first Monday after the second Wednesday in**

---

[70] *Bush v. Gore.* 531 U.S. 98. 2000.

[71] Appendix J shows the date on which each state's Certificate of Ascertainment was finalized in 2000 and 2004.

[72] The Meeting Clause of the 12th Amendment (ratified in 1804) specifies that the meeting of the presidential electors must be physically conducted in each state ("The Electors shall meet in their respective states . . . ").

[73] United States Code, Title 3, section 1.

December next following their appointment at such place in each State as the legislature of such State shall direct."[74] [Emphasis added]

State law, in turn, specifies the place and time of the meeting of the Electoral College. These meetings are typically held at the State Capitol. For example, Minnesota law provides:

> "The Presidential electors, before 12:00 [P.] M. on the day before that fixed by congress for the electors to vote for president and vice-president of the United States, shall notify the governor that they are at the state capitol and ready at the proper time to fulfill their duties as electors. The governor shall deliver to the electors present a certificate of the names of all the electors. If any elector named therein fails to appear before 9:00 A. M. on the day, and at the place, fixed for voting for president and vice-president of the United States, the electors present shall, in the presence of the governor, immediately elect by ballot a person to fill the vacancy. If more than the number of persons required have the highest and an equal number of votes, the governor, in the presence of the electors attending, shall decide by lot which of those persons shall be elected."[75]

2.6 CERTIFICATION OF VOTES OF THE PRESIDENTIAL ELECTORS

Federal law requires that each state's presidential electors sign six separate Certificates of Vote reporting the outcome of their voting for President and Vice President. Of the seven Certificates of Ascertainment created by each state, one is sent to the National Archivist in Washington, D.C., and six are given to the presidential electors for use at their meeting. At the Electoral College meeting, the electors attach one Certificate of Ascertainment to each of the six required "Certificates of Vote."

> "The electors shall make and sign six certificates of all the votes given by them, each of which certificates shall contain two distinct lists, one of the votes for President and the other of the votes for Vice President, and shall annex to each of the certificates one of the lists of the electors which shall have been furnished to them by direction of the executive of the State."[76]

In addition, federal law[77] specifies that one of these sets of documents be sent to the President of the U.S. Senate in Washington, D.C.; two be sent to the Secretary of State of the United States; two be sent to the Archivist of the United States in Washington, D.C.; and one be sent to the federal district court in the judicial district in which

---

[74] United States Code. Title 3, chapter 1, section 7.

[75] Minnesota election law. Section 208.06.

[76] United States Code. Title 3, chapter 1, section 9.

[77] United States Code. Title 3, chapter 1, section 11.

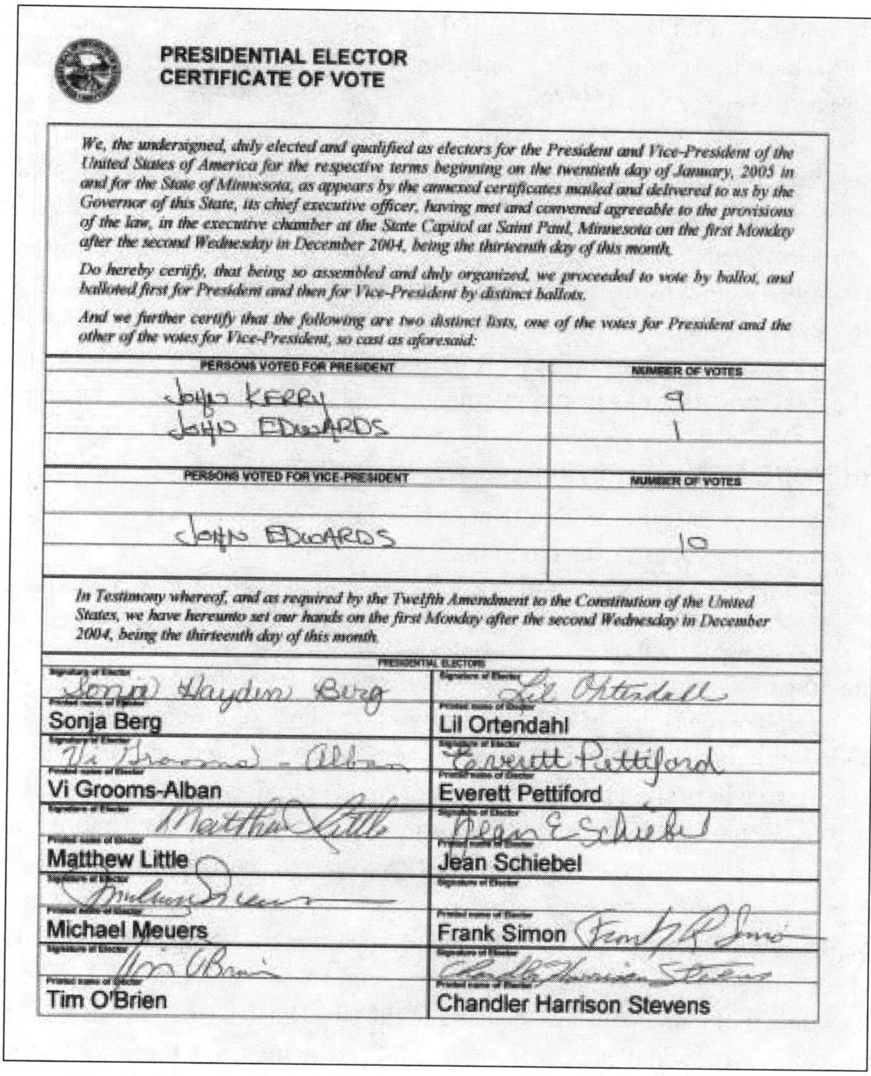

PRESIDENTIAL ELECTOR CERTIFICATE OF VOTE

We, the undersigned, duly elected and qualified as electors for the President and Vice-President of the United States of America for the respective terms beginning on the twentieth day of January, 2005 in and for the State of Minnesota, as appears by the annexed certificates mailed and delivered to us by the Governor of this State, its chief executive officer, having met and convened agreeable to the provisions of the law, in the executive chamber at the State Capitol at Saint Paul, Minnesota on the first Monday after the second Wednesday in December 2004, being the thirteenth day of this month,

Do hereby certify, that being so assembled and duly organized, we proceeded to vote by ballot, and balloted first for President and then for Vice-President by distinct ballots.

And we further certify that the following are two distinct lists, one of the votes for President and the other of the votes for Vice-President, so cast as aforesaid:

PERSONS VOTED FOR PRESIDENT	NUMBER OF VOTES
JOHN KERRY	9
JOHN EDWARDS	1

PERSONS VOTED FOR VICE-PRESIDENT	NUMBER OF VOTES
JOHN EDWARDS	10

In Testimony whereof, and as required by the Twelfth Amendment to the Constitution of the United States, we have hereunto set our hands on the first Monday after the second Wednesday in December 2004, being the thirteenth day of this month.

PRESIDENTIAL ELECTORS

Sonja Berg	Lil Ortendahl
Vi Grooms-Alban	Everett Pettiford
Matthew Little	Jean Schiebel
Michael Meuers	Frank Simon
Tim O'Brien	Chandler Harrison Stevens

Figure 2.8 Minnesota 2004 Certificate of Vote

the electors assemble. In the event that no certificates are received from a particular state by the fourth Wednesday in December, federal law[78] establishes procedures for sending a special messenger to the local federal district court in order to obtain the missing certificates.

In Minnesota in 2004, the Kerry–Edwards presidential slate received the most votes in the statewide popular election held on November 2, 2004. Thus, all 10 Democratic-Farmer-Labor Party presidential electors were elected. Figure 2.8 shows Minnesota's 2004 Certificate of Vote.

[78] United States Code. Title 3, chapter 1, sections 13 and 14.

In Minnesota in 2004, the presidential electors voted by secret ballot. In accordance with the 12th Amendment, each presidential elector cast one vote for President and a separate vote for Vice President.

As can be seen in figure 2.8, all 10 of Minnesota's Democratic presidential electors voted, as expected, for John Edwards for Vice President. However, unexpectedly, one of the 10 electors also voted for John Edwards for President. That vote was apparently accidental because, after the votes were counted, all 10 electors said that they had intended to vote for John Kerry for President. The result of this error was that John Kerry officially received only 251 electoral votes for President in 2004 (with John Edwards receiving one electoral vote for President). The vote for Edwards for President in Minnesota in 2004 was, as far as is known, the only electoral vote ever cast by accident.[79]

2.7 COUNTING OF THE ELECTORAL VOTES IN CONGRESS

Under the terms of the 20th Amendment (ratified in 1933), the newly elected Congress convenes on January 3 after the election.

The electoral votes are counted in a joint session of Congress on January 6.

"Congress shall be in session on the sixth day of January succeeding every meeting of the electors. The Senate and House of Representatives shall meet in the Hall of the House of Representatives at the hour of 1 o'clock in the afternoon on that day, and the President of the Senate shall be their presiding officer. Two tellers shall be previously appointed on the part of the Senate and two on the part of the House of Representatives, to whom shall be handed, as they are opened by the President of the Senate, all the certificates and papers purporting to be certificates of the electoral votes, which certificates and papers shall be opened, presented, and acted upon in the alphabetical order of the States, beginning with the letter A; and said tellers, having then read the same in the presence and hearing of the two Houses, shall make a list of the votes as they shall appear from the said certificates; and the votes having been ascertained and counted according to the rules in this subchapter provided, the result of the same shall be delivered to the President of the Senate, who shall thereupon announce the state of the vote, which announcement shall be deemed a sufficient declaration of the persons, if any, elected President and Vice President of the United States, and, together with a list of the votes, be entered on the Journals of the two Houses."[80]

The 12th Amendment to the Constitution governs the counting of the electoral votes by Congress. In order to be elected President, a candidate must receive "a majority of the whole number of Electors appointed." Assuming that all 538 electors are

---

[79] See section 2.12 for a discussion of the related issue of faithless electors.
[80] United States Code. Title 3, chapter 1, section 15.

appointed, 270 electoral votes are currently necessary for election. The 12th Amendment states in part:

> "[T]he President of the Senate shall, in the presence of the Senate and House of Representatives, open all the certificates and the votes shall then be counted;—The person having the greatest number of votes for President, shall be the President, if such number be a majority of the whole number of Electors appointed. . . . "

In the event that no candidate for President receives the required majority, the 12th Amendment (appendix A) provides a procedure for a "contingent election" in which the House of Representatives chooses the President (with each state having one vote). The 12th Amendment also provides for a contingent election in the event that no candidate receives the required majority for Vice President. In a contingent election for Vice President, each Senator has one vote.

The President and Vice President are inaugurated on January 20 in accordance with the terms of the 20th Amendment (ratified in 1933). Prior to the 20th Amendment, the inauguration date was March 4.

2.8 WRITE-IN VOTES FOR PRESIDENT

Write-in votes for the offices of President and Vice President are inherently more complex than those for any other office because the voters are not voting directly for candidates to fill the office of President and Vice President, but instead, for candidates to fill the position of presidential elector.

Minnesota law permits a voter to cast presidential write-in votes in two ways.

- **Advance Filing of Write-Ins:** Under this approach, supporters of a write-in presidential slate may file a slate of presidential electors prior to Election Day. Such advance filing makes write-in voting more convenient because it enables the voter to write in the name of a presidential slate (just two names), without having to write in the names of 10 (in the case of Minnesota) individual candidates for the position of presidential elector.
- **Election-Day Write-Ins:** Under this approach, there is no advance filing, and the voter must write in the names of up to 10 individual presidential electors.

Minnesota law implements the method of advance filing of write-ins as follows:

> "(a) A candidate for state or federal office who wants write-in votes for the candidate to be counted must file a written request with the filing office for the office sought no later than the fifth day before the general election. The filing officer shall provide copies of the form to make the request.

> "(b) A candidate for president of the United States who files a request under this subdivision must include the name of a candidate for vice-president of

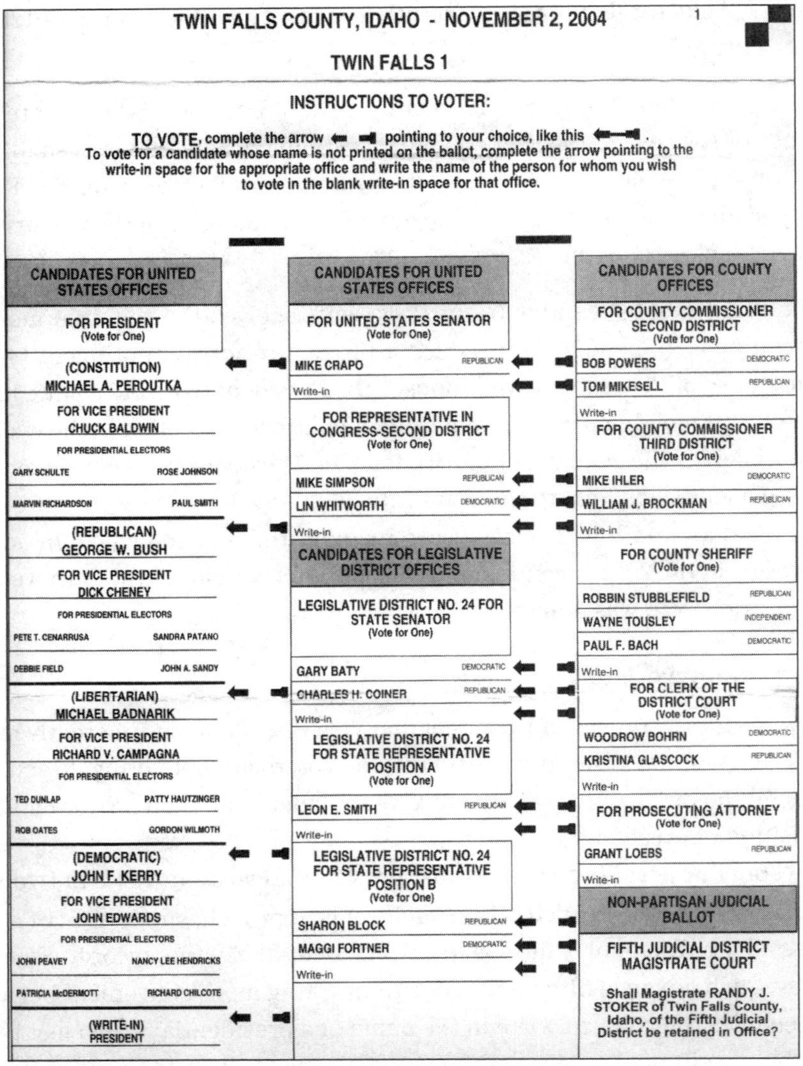

TWIN FALLS COUNTY, IDAHO - NOVEMBER 2, 2004 1

TWIN FALLS 1

INSTRUCTIONS TO VOTER:

TO VOTE, complete the arrow pointing to your choice, like this.
To vote for a candidate whose name is not printed on the ballot, complete the arrow pointing to the write-in space for the appropriate office and write the name of the person for whom you wish to vote in the blank write-in space for that office.

CANDIDATES FOR UNITED STATES OFFICES

FOR PRESIDENT
(Vote for One)

(CONSTITUTION)
MICHAEL A. PEROUTKA
FOR VICE PRESIDENT
CHUCK BALDWIN
FOR PRESIDENTIAL ELECTORS
GARY SCHULTE ROSE JOHNSON
MARVIN RICHARDSON PAUL SMITH

(REPUBLICAN)
GEORGE W. BUSH
FOR VICE PRESIDENT
DICK CHENEY
FOR PRESIDENTIAL ELECTORS
PETE T. CENARRUSA SANDRA PATANO
DEBBIE FIELD JOHN A. SANDY

(LIBERTARIAN)
MICHAEL BADNARIK
FOR VICE PRESIDENT
RICHARD V. CAMPAGNA
FOR PRESIDENTIAL ELECTORS
TED DUNLAP PATTY HAUTZINGER
ROB OATES GORDON WILMOTH

(DEMOCRATIC)
JOHN F. KERRY
FOR VICE PRESIDENT
JOHN EDWARDS
FOR PRESIDENTIAL ELECTORS
JOHN PEAVEY NANCY LEE HENDRICKS
PATRICIA McDERMOTT RICHARD CHILCOTE

(WRITE-IN)
PRESIDENT

CANDIDATES FOR UNITED STATES OFFICES

FOR UNITED STATES SENATOR
(Vote for One)
MIKE CRAPO REPUBLICAN
Write-in

FOR REPRESENTATIVE IN CONGRESS-SECOND DISTRICT
(Vote for One)
MIKE SIMPSON REPUBLICAN
LIN WHITWORTH DEMOCRATIC
Write-in

CANDIDATES FOR LEGISLATIVE DISTRICT OFFICES

LEGISLATIVE DISTRICT NO. 24 FOR STATE SENATOR
(Vote for One)
GARY BATY DEMOCRATIC
CHARLES H. COINER REPUBLICAN
Write-in

LEGISLATIVE DISTRICT NO. 24 FOR STATE REPRESENTATIVE POSITION A
(Vote for One)
LEON E. SMITH REPUBLICAN
Write-in

LEGISLATIVE DISTRICT NO. 24 FOR STATE REPRESENTATIVE POSITION B
(Vote for One)
SHARON BLOCK REPUBLICAN
MAGGI FORTNER DEMOCRATIC
Write-in

CANDIDATES FOR COUNTY OFFICES

FOR COUNTY COMMISSIONER SECOND DISTRICT
(Vote for One)
BOB POWERS DEMOCRATIC
TOM MIKESELL REPUBLICAN
Write-in

FOR COUNTY COMMISSIONER THIRD DISTRICT
(Vote for One)
MIKE IHLER DEMOCRATIC
WILLIAM J. BROCKMAN REPUBLICAN
Write-in

FOR COUNTY SHERIFF
(Vote for One)
ROBBIN STUBBLEFIELD REPUBLICAN
WAYNE TOUSLEY INDEPENDENT
PAUL F. BACH DEMOCRATIC
Write-in

FOR CLERK OF THE DISTRICT COURT
(Vote for One)
WOODROW BOHRN DEMOCRATIC
KRISTINA GLASCOCK REPUBLICAN
Write-in

FOR PROSECUTING ATTORNEY
(Vote for One)
GRANT LOEBS REPUBLICAN
Write-in

NON-PARTISAN JUDICIAL BALLOT

FIFTH JUDICIAL DISTRICT MAGISTRATE COURT

Shall Magistrate RANDY J. STOKER of Twin Falls County, Idaho, of the Fifth Judicial District be retained in Office?

Figure 2.9 Presidential ballot in Idaho in 2004

the United States. The request must also include the name of at least one candidate for Presidential elector. The total number of names of candidates for Presidential elector on the request may not exceed the total number of electoral votes to be cast by Minnesota in the presidential election."[81]

Minnesota's 2004 Certificate of Ascertainment (appendix E) shows that 1, 1, 2, 2, and 4 votes were cast for the presidential electors associated with the five officially declared write-in slates in the presidential election in Minnesota in 2004.

Many other states permit advance filing of write-ins in a similar manner.

[81] Minnesota election law. Section 204B.09, subdivision 3.

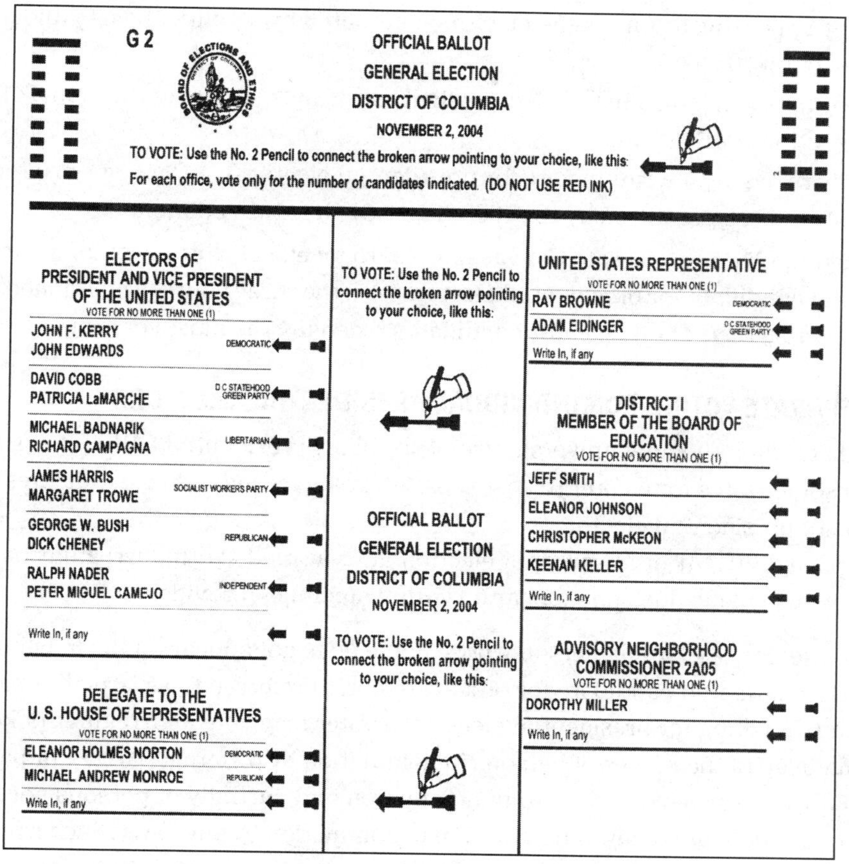
G 2

BOARD OF ELECTIONS AND ETHICS

OFFICIAL BALLOT
GENERAL ELECTION
DISTRICT OF COLUMBIA
NOVEMBER 2, 2004

TO VOTE: Use the No. 2 Pencil to connect the broken arrow pointing to your choice, like this:
For each office, vote only for the number of candidates indicated. (DO NOT USE RED INK)

ELECTORS OF PRESIDENT AND VICE PRESIDENT OF THE UNITED STATES
VOTE FOR NO MORE THAN ONE (1)

JOHN F. KERRY / JOHN EDWARDS — DEMOCRATIC
DAVID COBB / PATRICIA LaMARCHE — D C STATEHOOD GREEN PARTY
MICHAEL BADNARIK / RICHARD CAMPAGNA — LIBERTARIAN
JAMES HARRIS / MARGARET TROWE — SOCIALIST WORKERS PARTY
GEORGE W. BUSH / DICK CHENEY — REPUBLICAN
RALPH NADER / PETER MIGUEL CAMEJO — INDEPENDENT
Write In, if any

DELEGATE TO THE U. S. HOUSE OF REPRESENTATIVES
VOTE FOR NO MORE THAN ONE (1)

ELEANOR HOLMES NORTON — DEMOCRATIC
MICHAEL ANDREW MONROE — REPUBLICAN
Write In, if any

TO VOTE: Use the No. 2 Pencil to connect the broken arrow pointing to your choice, like this:

OFFICIAL BALLOT
GENERAL ELECTION
DISTRICT OF COLUMBIA
NOVEMBER 2, 2004

TO VOTE: Use the No. 2 Pencil to connect the broken arrow pointing to your choice, like this:

UNITED STATES REPRESENTATIVE
VOTE FOR NO MORE THAN ONE (1)

RAY BROWNE — DEMOCRATIC
ADAM EIDINGER — D C STATEHOOD GREEN PARTY
Write In, if any

DISTRICT I MEMBER OF THE BOARD OF EDUCATION
VOTE FOR NO MORE THAN ONE (1)

JEFF SMITH
ELEANOR JOHNSON
CHRISTOPHER McKEON
KEENAN KELLER
Write In, if any

ADVISORY NEIGHBORHOOD COMMISSIONER 2A05
VOTE FOR NO MORE THAN ONE (1)

DOROTHY MILLER
Write In, if any

Figure 2.10 Presidential ballot in the District of Columbia in 2004

Election-Day write-ins (without advance filing) are permitted in fewer states. This option is allowed in Minnesota as the consequence of a 1968 opinion of the Minnesota Attorney General.[82] That ruling declared that a presidential write-in vote may be cast in Minnesota by writing between one and 10 names of persons for the position of presidential elector. The Minnesota Attorney General also ruled that a pre-printed sticker containing the names of between 1 and 10 presidential electors could be employed in Minnesota. Given the small amount of space available for a write-in for president on Minnesota's ballot (figure 2.2), a pre-printed sticker is the most practical way to cast such a vote.

A similar small space (figure 2.9) is provided on the ballot for presidential write-ins in Idaho (which has four electoral votes) and the District of Columbia (figure 2.10).

In Minnesota, it is possible for an individual candidate for the position of presidential elector in Minnesota to receive votes in three separate ways:

[82] Op. Atty. Gen., 28c–5. October 5, 1968. The question of Election-Day write-ins arose from those desiring to vote for Eugene McCarthy instead of Hubert Humphrey.

- by appearing as one of the electors nominated by a political party under section 208.03;
- by appearing on a list of electors filed in advance under subdivision 3 of section 204B.09; and
- by receiving a write-in vote for presidential elector (e.g., on a pre-printed sticker) as permitted by the 1968 Attorney General's opinion.

When the Minnesota State Canvassing Board meets, all votes cast for a particular individual candidate for presidential elector, from the three sources mentioned above, are added together. The 10 elector candidates receiving the most votes are elected.

2.9 SEPARATE VOTING FOR INDIVIDUAL PRESIDENTIAL ELECTORS

Notwithstanding the now-universal use of the short presidential ballot, it is still possible in some states for a voter to cast separate votes for individual candidates for the position of presidential elector.

Section 23.15.431 of Mississippi election law, entitled "Voting irregular ballot for person whose name does not appear on voting machine," provides:

> "Ballots voted for any person whose name does not appear on the machine as a nominated candidate for office, are herein referred to as irregular ballots. In voting for presidential electors, a voter may vote an irregular ticket made up of the names of persons in nomination by different parties, or partially of names of persons so in nomination and partially of persons not in nomination, or wholly of persons not in nomination by any party. Such irregular ballots shall be deposited, written or affixed in or upon the receptacle or device provided on the machine for that purpose. With that exception, no irregular ballot shall be voted for any person for any office whose name appears on the machine as a nominated candidate for that office; any irregular ballot so voted shall not be counted. An irregular ballot must be cast in its appropriate place on the machine, or it shall be void and not counted."[83]

In addition, Mississippi election law concerning "Electronic Voting Systems" provides:

> "No electronic voting system, consisting of a marking or voting device in combination with automatic tabulating equipment, shall be acquired or used in accordance with Sections 23.15.461 though 23.15.485 unless it shall . . .

> "(c) Permit each voter, at presidential elections, by one (1) mark or punch to vote for the candidates of that party for President, Vice-President, and their presidential electors, or to vote individually for the electors of his choice when permitted by law."[84]

---

[83] Mississippi election law. Section 23.15.431.

[84] Mississippi election law. Section 23.15.465. Similar statutory provisions are applicable to other voting systems that may be used in Mississippi (e.g., optical mark-reading equipment).

Although Mississippi law permits such "irregular" voting, Mississippi's 2004 Certificate of Ascertainment (appendix I) and the state's 2000 Certificate indicate that no such votes were actually cast in the state in either the 2004 or 2000 presidential elections.

2.10 FUSION VOTING IN NEW YORK

Fusion voting is a major aspect of partisan politics in the state of New York. In New York, candidates for political office may appear on the ballot in the general election as nominees of more than one political party. For example, George Pataki has run for Governor as the candidate of both the Republican Party and the Conservative Party. That is, Pataki's name appeared more than once on the same ballot. Under New York election law, the votes that a candidate receives on each ballot line are added together in a process called *fusion*.

One of the political effects of fusion is that it enables a minor party to make a nominee of a major political party aware that he or she would not have won without the minor party's support.

New York is not the only state that currently allows fusion voting. For example, fusion voting is currently permitted under Vermont election law.

Fusion voting played an important role in Minnesota politics prior to the merger that resulted in the formation of that state's present-day Democratic-Farmer-Labor Party.

Figure 2.11 shows the 2004 New York presidential ballot. As can be seen, the Bush–Cheney presidential slate ran with the support of both the Republican Party and the Conservative Party, and the Kerry–Edwards slate ran with the support of both the Democratic Party and the Working Families Party.

When fusion voting is applied to presidential races, the question arises as to how to handle the presidential electors. New York law permits two parties to nominate a common slate of presidential electors. For example, the Republican and Conservative parties nominated the same slate of presidential electors for the 2004 presidential election. Similarly, the Democratic Party and Working Families Party nominated the same slate of presidential electors.

Figure 2.12 shows the third page of New York's 2004 Certificate of Ascertainment indicating that the Bush–Cheney presidential slate received 2,806,993 votes on the Republican Party line and an additional 155,574 votes on the Conservative Party line, for a grand total of 2,962,567 votes.

Similarly, the fourth page of New York's 2004 Certificate of Ascertainment (appendix H) shows that the Kerry–Edwards slate received 4,180,755 votes on the Democratic Party line and an additional 133,525 votes on the Working Families Party line, for a grand total of 4,314,280 votes.

The second page of New York's 2004 Certificate of Ascertainment states that the 31 presidential electors shared by the Democratic Party and the Working Families Party (i.e., the Kerry–Edwards electors)

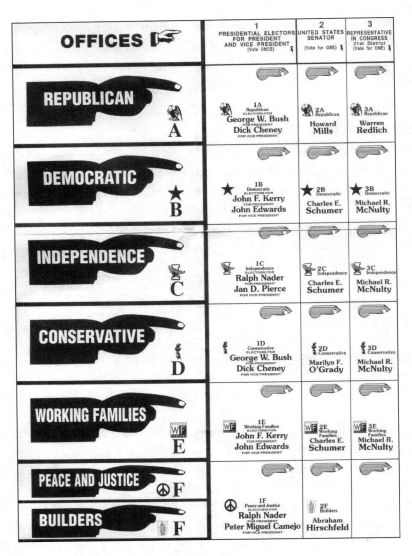

Figure 2.11 2004 New York presidential ballot

"were, by the greatest number of votes given at said election, duly elected elector of President and Vice-President of the United States."

New York's 2004 presidential ballot (figure 2.11) shows that the election is conducted on the basis of distinct presidential *slates*. Ralph Nader appeared on the ballot in New York as the presidential nominee of both the Independence Party and the Peace and Justice Party. Nader, however, ran with Jan D. Pierce for Vice President on the Independence Party line but with Peter Miguel Camejo for Vice President on the Peace and Justice Party line. Thus, there were two different "Nader" presidential slates in New York in 2004, each with a different slate of presidential electors.

STATE OF NEW YORK, ss:

Statement of the whole number of votes cast for all the candidates for the office of ELECTOR OF PRESIDENT and VICE-PRESIDENT at a General Election held in said State on the Second day of November, 2004.

The whole number of votes given for the office of ELECTOR OF PRESIDENT and VICE-PRESIDENT was **7,448,266** of which

		REPUBLICAN	CONSERVATIVE	TOTAL
George E. Pataki	received	2,806,993	155,574	2,962,567
Alexander F. Treadwell	received	2,806,993	155,574	2,962,567
Joseph Bruno	received	2,806,993	155,574	2,962,567
Charles Nesbitt	received	2,806,993	155,574	2,962,567
Mary Donohue	received	2,806,993	155,574	2,962,567
Rudolph Giuliani	received	2,806,993	155,574	2,962,567
Charles Gargano	received	2,806,993	155,574	2,962,567
Joseph Mondello	received	2,806,993	155,574	2,962,567
J. Patrick Barrett	received	2,806,993	155,574	2,962,567
John F. Nolan	received	2,806,993	155,574	2,962,567
Robert Davis	received	2,806,993	155,574	2,962,567
Peter J. Savago	received	2,806,993	155,574	2,962,567
Maggie Brooks	received	2,806,993	155,574	2,962,567
Catherine Blaney	received	2,806,993	155,574	2,962,567
Howard Mills	received	2,806,993	155,574	2,962,567
John Cahill	received	2,806,993	155,574	2,962,567
Rita DiMartino	received	2,806,993	155,574	2,962,567
Libby Pataki	received	2,806,993	155,574	2,962,567
Stephen Minarik	received	2,806,993	155,574	2,962,567
Raymond Meier	received	2,806,993	155,574	2,962,567
Thomas M. Reynolds	received	2,806,993	155,574	2,962,567
Adam Stoll	received	2,806,993	155,574	2,962,567
Herman Badillo	received	2,806,993	155,574	2,962,567
Jane Forbes Clark	received	2,806,993	155,574	2,962,567
James Garner	received	2,806,993	155,574	2,962,567
Shawn Marie Levine	received	2,806,993	155,574	2,962,567
Viola J. Hunter	received	2,806,993	155,574	2,962,567
Laura Schreiner	received	2,806,993	155,574	2,962,567
Carmen Gomez Goldberg	received	2,806,993	155,574	2,962,567
Bernadette Castro	received	2,806,993	155,574	2,962,567
Cathy Jimino	received	2,806,993	155,574	2,962,567

Figure 2.12 Third page of New York's 2004 Certificate of Ascertainment

The Nader–Pierce presidential slate received 84,247 votes on the Independence Party line (shown on the fifth page of the Certificate of Ascertainment in appendix H). The Nader–Camejo presidential slate received 15,626 votes on the Peace and Justice Party line (shown on the sixth page of the Certificate of Ascertainment in appendix H). Because there were two distinct presidential slates (with different candidates for Vice President) and two distinct slates of presidential electors, there was no fusion of votes between the Independence Party and the Peace and Justice Party.

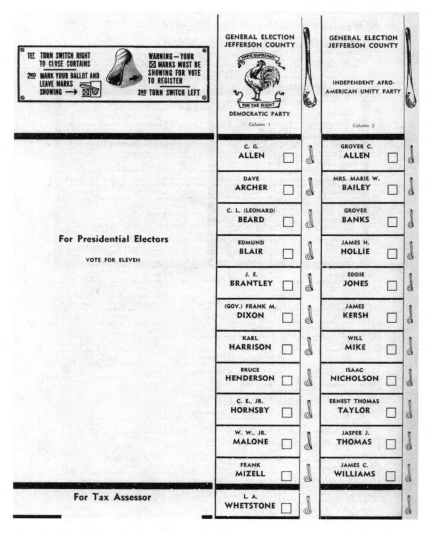

Figure 2.13a 1960 Alabama presidential ballot

2.11 UNPLEDGED PRESIDENTIAL ELECTORS

Unpledged electors were a prominent feature of presidential voting in various Southern states immediately before and after passage of the civil rights legislation of the mid-1960s.

In 1960, for example, the names of no presidential or vice-presidential candidate appeared on the ballot. Instead, Alabama's presidential ballot (figure 2.13) contained 11 separate lines. Each line contained the names of five candidates for the position of presidential elector (each nominated by one of the five political parties on the ballot). There was a separate lever for each of the 55 candidates.[85] The 11 electors of the Ala-

---

[85] The 1960 Alabama presidential ballot is shown in appendix K of Peirce, Neal R. 1968. *The People's President: The Electoral College in American History and Direct-Vote Alternative.* New York, NY: Simon & Schuster. The 1960 Alabama presidential ballot is reprinted as figure 2.13 in this book with the permission of Yale University Press.

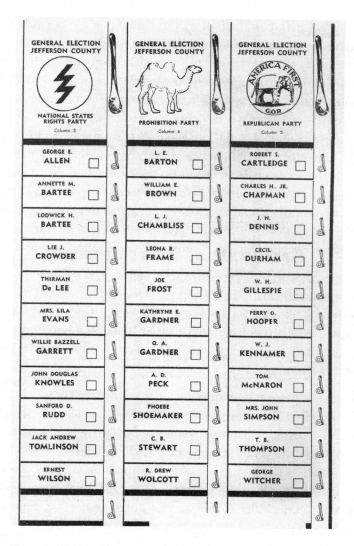

Figure 2.13b 1960 Alabama presidential ballot (cont.)

bama Democratic Party appeared under the party's rooster logo and the slogan "White Supremacy—For the Right." Similarly, there were lists of 11 elector candidates for the Alabama Republican Party and 11 elector candidates for each of three other political parties on the ballot in Alabama that year. The 11 Democratic candidates were elected on Election Day in November 1960. When the Electoral College met in mid-December, John F. Kennedy received the votes of five of the 11 presidential electors, and Harry F. Byrd of Virginia received six electoral votes.

In his 2011 book *Why the Electoral College Is Bad for America*, Professor George Edwards argues that a fair accounting of the popular vote cast in Alabama in 1960 would have made Richard Nixon—not John F. Kennedy—the winner of the nation-wide popular vote in 1960.[86] This accounting issue arises because neither presidential

---

[86] Pages 67–69.

candidate's name appeared on the ballot in Alabama (shown in figure 2.13). Instead, only the names of 11 candidates for the position of presidential electors appeared on the ballot. These names were arranged in columns headed only by the political party's name, but not the name of the presidential candidate nominated by that party's national convention. In the primary election that chose the Democratic nominees for the 11 candidates for the position of presidential elector, only five of the winning Democratic nominees were publicly pledged to their party's national nominee (John F. Kennedy). Six were unpledged and made it clear that they opposed the national party. An argument can therefore be made to proportionally allocate only five-elevenths of the Democratic Party's popular margin in Alabama over the Republican Party to Kennedy. This method of accounting would have put Nixon ahead of Kennedy in the nationwide popular vote. Nixon, however, never publicly argued for this interpretation.

Current Mississippi law provides for unpledged presidential electors:

"(1) When presidential electors are to be chosen, the Secretary of State of Mississippi shall certify to the circuit clerks of the several counties the names of all candidates for President and Vice-President who are nominated by any national convention or other like assembly of any political party or by written petition signed by at least one thousand (1,000) qualified voters of this state.

"(2) The certificate of nomination by a political party convention must be signed by the presiding officer and secretary of the convention and by the chairman of the state executive committee of the political party making the nomination. Any nominating petition, to be valid, must contain the signatures as well as the addresses of the petitioners. Such certificates and petitions must be filed with the State Board of Election Commissioners by filing the same in the office of the Secretary of State not less than sixty (60) days previous to the day of the election.

"(3) Each certificate of nomination and nominating petition must be accompanied by a list of the names and addresses of persons, who shall be qualified voters of this state, equal in number to the number of presidential electors to be chosen. Each person so listed shall execute the following statement which shall be attached to the certificate or petition when the same is filed with the State Board of Election Commissioners:

'I do hereby consent and do hereby agree to serve as elector for President and Vice-President of the United States, if elected to that position, and do hereby agree that, if so elected, I shall cast my ballot as such for _____ for President and _____ for Vice-President of the United States'

(inserting in said blank spaces the respective names of the persons named as nominees for said respective offices in the certificate to which this statement is attached).

"(4) The State Board of Election Commissioners and any other official charged with the preparation of official ballots shall place on such official ballots the words

'PRESIDENTIAL ELECTORS FOR (here insert the name of the candidate for President, the word 'AND' and the name of the candidate for Vice-President)'

in lieu of placing the names of such presidential electors on such official ballots, and a vote cast therefore shall be counted and shall be in all respects effective as a vote for each of the presidential electors representing such candidates for President and Vice-President of the United States. In the case of unpledged electors, the State Board of Election Commissioners and any other official charged with the preparation of official ballots shall place on such official ballots the words 'UNPLEDGED ELECTOR(S) (here insert the name(s) of individual unpledged elector(s) if placed upon the ballot based upon a petition granted in the manner provided by law stating the individual name(s) of the elector(s) rather than a slate of electors).'"[87]

2.12 FAITHLESS PRESIDENTIAL ELECTORS

Political parties and formal national nominations for President and Vice President emerged at the time of the nation's first competitive presidential election (1796).

Since then, the vast majority of electoral votes have been cast faithfully—that is, for the presidential candidate nominated by the same political party that nominated the presidential elector. The reason is that candidates for the position of presidential electors are nominated by each political party, and parties only generally nominate people who are known to be loyal party members.

U.S. Supreme Court Justice Robert H. Jackson summarized the history of presidential electors as follows in the 1952 case of *Ray v. Blair*:

"No one faithful to our history can deny that the plan originally contemplated, what is implicit in its text, that electors would be free agents, to exercise an independent and nonpartisan judgment as to the men best qualified for the Nation's highest offices. . . .

"This arrangement miscarried. Electors, although often personally eminent, independent, and respectable, officially become voluntary party lackeys and intellectual nonentities to whose memory we might justly paraphrase a tuneful satire:

'They always voted at their party's call
'And never thought of thinking for themselves at all'"[88]

---

[87] Mississippi election law. Section 23.15.785.
[88] *Ray v. Blair* 343 U.S. 214 at 232. 1952.

Among the 22,991 electoral votes cast in the 57 presidential elections between 1789 and 2012, there have been 17 cases when a presidential elector has cast a vote for President in a deviant way.[89,90,91]

- In 1796, Samuel Miles was one of the two Federalist presidential electors chosen in Pennsylvania; however, he voted for Thomas Jefferson (the Republican candidate) instead of for Federalist John Adams (section 2.2.2).

- In the 1808 presidential election, James Madison was the prohibitive favorite and secured 122 of the 176 electoral votes. George Clinton was a Founding Father, New York's first governor, and the then-sitting Vice President (under Jefferson). Clinton had not been nominated for President by either major party in 1808 and was poised to become the first Vice President not to rise eventually to the Presidency. In an apparent gesture of respect to Clinton, six of New York's 19 presidential electors voted for Clinton instead of Madison.

- In the uncontested presidential election of 1820, there was another gesture of respect in the Electoral College. A New Hampshire Democratic-Republican presidential elector who had been expected to vote for James Monroe voted for John Quincy Adams, thereby preventing Monroe from duplicating George Washington's 1789 and 1792 unanimous votes in the Electoral College.

- In 1948, a Truman elector (Preston Parks) in Tennessee voted for Strom Thurmond, the Dixiecrat presidential nominee.

- In 1956, a Stevenson elector (W. F. Turner) in Alabama voted for Walter B. Jones, a local judge.

- Nixon lost one electoral vote on each of the three occasions (1960, 1968, and 1972) when he ran for President. In 1960, an Oklahoma Republican elector (Henry D. Irwin) voted for United States Senator Harry F. Byrd (a Democrat). In 1968, a North Carolina Republican elector (Lloyd W. Bailey) voted for Governor George Wallace (that year's nominee of the American Independent Party). In 1972, a Virginia Republican elector (Roger L. MacBride) voted for John Hospers (a Libertarian).

- In 1976, one Ford elector from the state of Washington voted for Ronald Reagan for President (who had lost the presidential nomination to Ford at the closely divided 1976 Republican nominating convention).

- In 1988, a Democratic elector (Margaret Leach) from West Virginia voted for Lloyd Bentsen for President and Michael Dukakis for Vice President,

[89] Congressional Quarterly. 2002. *Presidential Elections 1789–2002*. Washington, DC: CQ Press. Page 159.
[90] Peirce, Neal R. 1968. *The People's President: The Electoral College in American History and Direct-Vote Alternative*. New York, NY: Simon & Schuster. Pages 122–127.
[91] Edwards, George C., III. 2004. *Why the Electoral College Is Bad for America*. New Haven, CT: Yale University Press. Pages 21–27.

saying that she thought that the Democratic ticket would have been better in opposite order.

- In 2000, a Democratic presidential elector from the District of Columbia (Barbara Lett-Simmons) did not vote for Al Gore, as a protest against the District's lack of representation in Congress.

- In 2004, an unknown Democratic presidential elector from Minnesota voted, in an apparent accident, for John Edwards for both President and Vice President (section 2.6). Afterwards, all 10 of the Democratic presidential electors said that they intended to vote for Kerry for President.

These 17 cases can be divided into three categories:

- **Clear Case of a Faithless Elector:** In 1796, Samuel Miles cast his electoral vote in an unexpected way in an election in which the overall electoral vote was very close (71 for Adams and 68 for Jefferson). Given the fact that this was the first presidential election in which political parties made formal national nominations for President, and the slow communications of the day, Miles might have had reason to believe, at the time he voted, that his vote might affect the outcome of the election in the Electoral College (section 2.2.2).

- **Grand-Standing Votes:** There have been 15 cases of presidential electors who cast a deviant vote; however, these electors knew, at the time they voted, that their vote would not affect the outcome of the election in the Electoral College. These cases include several instances where the deviant votes were a gesture of respect.

- **Accidental Vote:** In 2004 in Minnesota, there was one accidentally miscast electoral vote for President (section 2.6).

Thus, after 56 presidential elections, the vote of Samuel Miles in 1796 was the only case when an electoral vote was cast in an unfaithful way by a presidential elector who might have thought, at the time he voted, that his vote might affect the outcome.

Table 2.3 shows the number of presidential electors voting in the nation's 57 presidential elections between 1789 and 2012 (a total of 22,991 electoral votes), the number of electoral votes that were cast as expected for President, and the 17 electoral votes that were cast for President in a deviant way (that is, one clear faithless elector, 15 grand-standing votes, and one accidental vote).[92,93]

Deviant electoral votes were cast on two other occasions.

---

[92] Congressional Quarterly. 2002. *Presidential Elections 1789–2002*. Washington, DC: CQ Press. Page 159.

[93] There were, arguably, three additional faithless electors in the 1796 presidential election. As *Congressional Quarterly* notes, "Some historians and political scientists claim that three Democratic-Republican electors voted for Adams. However, the fluidity of political party lines at that early date, and the well-known personal friendship between Adams and at least one of the electors, makes the claim of their being 'faithless electors' one of continuing controversy." See Congressional Quarterly. 1979. *Presidential Elections Since 1789*. Second edition. Washington, DC: CQ Press. Page 7.

Table 2.3 FAITHLESS ELECTORS FOR PRESIDENT

ELECTION	ELECTORS VOTING	CAST AS EXPECTED	CLEAR FAITHLESS ELECTOR	GRAND-STANDING VOTE	ACCIDENTAL VOTE
1789	69	69			
1792	132	132			
1796	138	138			
1800	138	137	1		
1804	176	176			
1808	175	169		6	
1812	218	218			
1816	221	221			
1820	232	231		1	
1824	261	261			
1828	261	261			
1832	288	288			
1836	294	294			
1840	294	294			
1844	275	275			
1848	290	290			
1852	296	296			
1856	296	296			
1860	303	303			
1864	234	234			
1868	294	294			
1872	366	366			
1876	369	369			
1880	369	369			
1884	401	401			
1888	401	401			
1892	444	444			
1896	447	447			
1900	447	447			
1904	476	476			
1908	483	483			
1912	531	531			
1916	531	531			
1920	531	531			
1924	531	531			
1928	531	531			
1932	531	531			

Table 2.3 *(continued)*

ELECTION	ELECTORS VOTING	CAST AS EXPECTED	CLEAR FAITHLESS ELECTOR	GRAND-STANDING VOTE	ACCIDENTAL VOTE
1936	531	531			
1940	531	531			
1944	531	531			
1948	531	530		1	
1952	531	531			
1956	531	530		1	
1960	537	536		1	
1964	538	538			
1968	538	537		1	
1972	538	537		1	
1976	538	537		1	
1980	538	538			
1984	538	538			
1988	538	537		1	
1992	538	538			
1996	538	538			
2000	538	537		1	
2004	538	537			1
2008	538	538			
2012	538	538			
Total	**22,991**	**22,974**	**1**	**15**	**1**

In the 1872 election, a number of electoral votes for President were cast in an un-expected (but not "unfaithful") way. The Democratic candidate, Horace Greeley, died shortly after Election Day, but before the Electoral College met. Greeley had won 63 electoral votes, and Grant had won 286. Greeley's 63 presidential electors split their support among four other persons.

In the 1836 election, 23 Democratic presidential electors from Virginia did not vote for the Democratic Party's vice-presidential nominee. Richard M. Johnson of Kentucky was nominated by more than a two-to-one margin at the party's second national convention held in Baltimore in 1835. Before the voting, the Virginia delegation, referring to Johnson, announced that they would not support any candidate who did not support the party's principles. After Johnson was nominated, the Virginia delegation reiterated their position that they would not support Johnson. In the 1836 election, the Democratic ticket won Virginia (and won nationally). In the Electoral College, all 23 of Virginia's presidential electors duly voted for their party's nominee for President (Martin Van Buren); however, they then all voted for William Smith for Vice President, instead of Johnson. As a result, Johnson did not receive an absolute majority of the electoral votes, and the election of the Vice President was thrown into the U.S. Senate.[94] Johnson won by a party-line vote of 33 to 16 in the Senate.[95] Given the fact that the Virginia Democratic Party announced their vigorous opposition to Johnson at the convention (both before and after Johnson's nomination), it is difficult to characterize the pre-announced votes of the 23 Democratic presidential electors as being unexpected, much less "faithless." Moreover, given the level of Johnson's support in the Senate, the 23 anti-Johnson presidential electors almost certainly realized that their deviant votes were not going to prevent Johnson from becoming Vice President (and hence these votes can be categorized as "grand-standing" votes).

In 2004, Richie Robb, one of the Republican nominees for the position of presidential elector from West Virginia, threatened, prior to Election Day, to not vote for George W. Bush in the Electoral College. However, Robb ultimately voted for Bush when the Electoral College met on December 13, 2004. In any case, Robb's vote could not have affected the outcome because George W. Bush won the Presidency in 2004 with 16 more than the required majority of 270.

The laws of most states (including Minnesota) do not specify the way that a presidential elector should vote. However, many states have attempted to address the problem of potential faithless electors.

Nineteen states have laws that assert that a presidential elector is obligated to vote for the nominee of his or her party, but these laws contain no provision for enforcement.[96,97] For example, Maine law provides:

> "The presidential electors at large shall cast their ballots for the presidential and vice-presidential candidates who received the largest number of votes in the State. The presidential electors of each congressional district shall cast their ballots for the presidential and vice-presidential candidates who received the largest number of votes in each respective congressional district."[98]

Five states (New Mexico, North Carolina, Oklahoma, South Carolina, and Washington) have laws imposing penalties of up to $1,000 on faithless electors. However, these laws provide no mechanism for reversing a vote that has already been faithlessly cast.

---

[94] Stanwood, Edward. 1924. *A History of the Presidency from 1788 to 1897*. Boston, MA: Houghton Mifflin Company. Pages 182–188.

[95] Sibley, Joel H. 2002. Election of 1836. In Schlesinger, Arthur M., Jr. and Israel, Fred L. (editors). *History of American Presidential Elections 1878–2001*. Philadelphia, PA: Chelsea House Publishers. Volume 2. Page 600.

[96] Berns, Walter (editor). *After the People Vote: A Guide to the Electoral College*. Washington, DC: The AEI Press. Pages 10–13 and 86–88.

[97] Concerning pledges by presidential electors, see *Ray v. Blair*. 343 U.S. 214. 1952.

[98] Maine 21-A M.R.S. section 805.

Pennsylvania, North Carolina, and Montana arguably have the most effective laws for ensuring that presidential electors vote in the intended way.

Pennsylvania election law (section 2878) addresses the problem of potential faithless electors proactively by providing that each party's presidential nominee shall have the power to nominate the entire slate of candidates for the position of presidential elector in Pennsylvania:

> "The nominee of each political party for the office of President of the United States shall, within thirty days after his nomination by the National convention of such party, nominate as many persons to be the candidates of his party for the position of presidential elector as the State is then entitled to. If for any reason the nominee of any political party for President of the United States fails or is unable to make the said nominations within the time herein provided, then the nominee for such party for the office of Vice-President of the United States shall, as soon as may be possible after the expiration of thirty days, make the nominations. The names of such nominees, with their residences and post office addresses, shall be certified immediately to the Secretary of the Commonwealth by the nominee for the office of President or Vice-President, as the case may be, making the nominations. Vacancies existing after the date of nomination of presidential electors shall be filled by the nominee for the office of President or Vice-President making the original nomination. Nominations made to fill vacancies shall be certified to the Secretary of the Commonwealth in the manner herein provided for in the case of original nominations."

North Carolina's election law specifies that failure to vote as pledged
- constitutes resignation from the office of elector,
- cancels the vote cast by the faithless elector, and
- provides for another person to be appointed to cast the vote by the remaining electors.[99]

North Carolina law (section 163-212) provides:

> "Any presidential elector having previously signified his consent to serve as such, who fails to attend and vote for the candidate of the political party which nominated such elector, for President and Vice-President of the United States at the time and place directed in G.S. 163-210 (except in case of sickness or other unavoidable accident) shall forfeit and pay to the State five hundred dollars ($500.00), to be recovered by the Attorney General in the Superior Court of Wake County. In addition to such forfeiture, refusal or failure to vote for the candidates of the political party which nominated

---

[99] Berns, Walter (editor). *After the People Vote: A Guide to the Electoral College.* Washington, DC: The AEI Press. Pages 12 and 87–88.

such elector shall constitute a resignation from the office of elector, his vote shall not be recorded, and the remaining electors shall forthwith fill such vacancy as hereinbefore provided."

At its 119th annual meeting in 2010, the Uniform Law Commission (also known as the National Conference of Commissioners on Uniform State Laws or NCCUSL) approved a "Uniform Faithful Presidential Electors Act" and recommended it for enactment in all the states.[100]

The Conference, formed in 1892, is a nongovernmental body that has produced more than 200 recommended uniform state laws. The Conference is most widely known for its work on the Uniform Commercial Code.

The Uniform Faithful Presidential Electors Act has several of the features of North Carolina's current law. The Act provides a statutory remedy in the event a presidential elector fails to vote in accordance with the voters of his or her state. The Act has a state-administered pledge of faithfulness, with any attempt by an elector to submit a vote in violation of that pledge, effectively constituting resignation from the office of elector. The proposed uniform law calls for the election of both electors and alternate electors. The Act provides a mechanism for filling a vacancy created for that reason or any other.

As of mid-2012, the Uniform Faithful Presidential Electors Act has been enacted by Montana.

The Uniform Faithful Presidential Electors Act has also been introduced in the legislatures of Minnesota, Nebraska, and North Carolina. The National Popular Vote organization has endorsed this proposed uniform law.

In summary, faithless electors are a historical curiosity associated with the Electoral College, but they never have had any practical effect on any presidential election.[101]

2.13 FIVE MAJOR CHANGES IN THE PRESIDENTIAL ELECTION SYSTEM THAT HAVE BEEN IMPLEMENTED WITHOUT A FEDERAL CONSTITUTIONAL AMENDMENT

Five of the most salient features of the present-day system of electing the President and Vice President of the United States are:

- popular voting for president,
- the statewide winner-take-all rule,
- nomination of candidates by nationwide political parties,
- the nondeliberative nature of the Electoral College since 1796, and
- the short presidential ballot.

---

[100] http://nccusl.org/Act.aspx?title=Faithful%20Presidential%20Electors%20Act.

[101] Edwards, George C., III. 2004. *Why the Electoral College Is Bad for America*. New Haven, CT: Yale University Press. Pages 25–27.

Although some people today mistakenly believe that the current system of electing the President and Vice President of the United States was designed by the Founding Fathers and embodied in the U.S. Constitution, none of the above five features reflected a consensus of the Founding Fathers or is mentioned in the original U.S. Constitution. None of these features was implemented by means of a federal constitutional amendment. None was the creation of federal legislation.

Instead, three of these five features came into being by the piecemeal enactment of state laws over a period of years, and two resulted from actions taken by non-government entities—namely the political parties that emerged at the time of the nation's first competitive presidential election (1796).

- **Popular Vote:** As recounted in section 2.2, there was no agreement among the Founding Fathers as to whether the voters should be directly involved in the process of choosing presidential electors. Some favored permitting the voters to directly select presidential electors, while others did not. The Constitution left the manner of choosing presidential electors to the states. In fact, the voters were allowed to choose presidential electors in only six states in the nation's first presidential election (1789). However, state laws changed over the years. By 1824, voters were allowed to choose presidential electors in three-quarters of the states, and by 1832, voters were able to choose presidential electors in all but one state.[102] Since 1876, all presidential electors have been elected directly by the voters. In short, direct popular voting for presidential electors became the norm by virtue of the piecemeal enactment of state laws—not because the Founders advocated popular voting, not because the original Constitution required it, and not because of any federal constitutional amendment. The states used the built-in flexibility of the Constitution to change the system.

- **Statewide Winner-Take-All Rule:** The Founding Fathers certainly did not advocate that presidential electors be chosen by the people on a statewide winner-take-all basis. The winner-take-all rule was not debated at the Constitutional Convention. It was not mentioned in the *Federalist Papers*. The winner-take-all approach was used by only three of the states participating in the nation's first presidential election in 1789. Some states elected presidential electors by districts in the early years of the Republic. However, those states soon came to realize what Thomas Jefferson called the "folly"[103] of diminishing their influence by fragmenting their electoral votes, and the states gravitated toward the winner-take-all rule. It was not

---

[102] The South Carolina legislature chose presidential electors up to 1860. There were two isolated instances of the election of presidential electors by the state legislature since 1860, namely Florida in 1868 and Colorado in 1876.

[103] Letter from Thomas Jefferson to James Monroe on January 12, 1800. Ford, Paul Leicester. 1905. *The Works of Thomas Jefferson.* New York: G. P. Putnam's Sons. 9:90.

until the 11th presidential election (1828) that the winner-take-all rule was used by a majority of the states. Since 1836, the presidential slate receiving the most popular votes in each separate state has won all of a state's presidential electors—with only occasional and isolated exceptions.[104] The statewide winner-take-all rule emerged over a period of years because of the piecemeal enactment of state laws—not because the Founders advocated the winner-take-all rule, not because the original Constitution required it, and not because of any federal constitutional amendment.

- **Nomination of Presidential Candidates by Political Parties:** Since the nation's first competitive presidential election (1796), candidates for President and Vice President have been nominated on a nationwide basis by a central body of a political party (e.g., by the congressional caucus of each party starting in 1796 and by national conventions of each party starting in the 1820s). This feature of the present-day system of electing the President emerged because of the actions taken by nongovernment entities—namely the political parties. This change did not come about because the Founders wanted it, because the original Constitution mentioned it or required it, or because of any federal constitutional amendment.

- **Nondeliberative Nature of the Electoral College Since 1796:** The Founding Fathers intended that the Electoral College would act as a deliberative body in which the presidential electors would exercise independent judgment as to the best persons to serve as President and Vice President. However, starting in 1796, political parties began nominating presidential and vice-presidential candidates on a centralized basis and began actively campaigning for their nominees throughout the country. As a result, presidential electors necessarily became rubber stamps for the choices made by the parties. "[W]hether chosen by the legislatures or by popular suffrage on general ticket or in districts, [the presidential electors] were so chosen simply to register the will of the appointing power."[105] Thus, starting in 1796, presidential electors have been expected to vote for the candidates nominated by their party—that is, "to act, not to think."[106] Moreover, this expectation has been achieved with remarkable fidelity. Of the 22,991 electoral votes cast for President in the 57 presidential elections between 1789 and 2012, the vote of Samuel Miles for Thomas Jefferson in 1796 was the only instance when a presidential elector might have thought, at the time he voted, that his vote might affect the national outcome for

---

[104] The three exceptions since 1836 include the present-day district system in Maine (since 1969), the present-day district system in Nebraska (since 1992), and the one-time use of a district system by Michigan in 1892.

[105] *McPherson v. Blacker.* 146 U.S. 1 at 36. 1892.

[106] *United States Gazette.* December 15, 1796. Item signed "CANDOUR."

President.[107] The change in character of the Electoral College from the deliberative body envisioned by the Founding Fathers to a rubber stamp came about because of the emergence of political parties. This change did not come into being because the Founders wanted it, because the original Constitution mentioned it or required it, or because of any federal constitutional amendment.

- **Short Presidential Ballot**: The universal adoption of the short presidential ballot has almost entirely eliminated presidential electors from the public's consciousness. Since 1980, voters have generally not cast separate votes for individual candidates for the position of presidential elector, but instead have cast a single vote for a presidential slate consisting of a candidate for President and a candidate for Vice President. Moreover, in all but a few states, the names of the presidential electors have disappeared from the ballot. The short presidential ballot emerged over a period of years because of the piecemeal enactment of laws by the individual states—not because the Founders advocated it, not because the original Constitution mentioned it or required it, and not because of any federal constitutional amendment.

In short, the flexibility built into the U.S. Constitution permitted the development of a system for electing the President and Vice President that is very different from the one that the Founding Fathers envisioned.

---

[107] As discussed in greater detail in section 2.12, 15 of the other instances of deviant electors are considered to have been grand-standing votes, and one electoral vote (in 2004 in Minnesota) was cast by accident.

3 | Three Previously Proposed Federal Constitutional Amendments

In this chapter, we first present a brief history of troublesome presidential elections.

We then examine the three most prominent approaches to presidential election reform that have been proposed in the form of federal constitutional amendments.

The next chapter (chapter 4) will analyze two approaches that can be enacted entirely at the state level (without a federal constitutional amendment and without action by Congress). Later, chapter 6 will discuss another approach not requiring a federal constitutional amendment, namely the National Popular Vote interstate compact.

The three most discussed proposals involving a federal constitutional amendment are:

- **Fractional Proportional Allocation of Electoral Votes,** in which a state's electoral votes are divided proportionally according to the percentage—*carried out to three decimal places*—of votes received by each presidential slate in that state (section 3.2);
- **District Allocation of Electoral Votes,** in which the voters select one presidential elector for each congressional district and two presidential electors statewide (section 3.3); and
- **Direct Nationwide Popular Election,** in which all the popular votes are added together on a nationwide basis (section 3.4).[1]

The chapter analyzes how each of the above approaches would operate in terms of the following three criteria:

- **Accuracy:** Would the method accurately reflect the nationwide popular vote?
- **Making Every Vote Politically Relevant**: Would the method improve upon the current situation in which two-thirds of the states and two-thirds of the people of the United States are ignored by presidential campaigns?
- **Making Every Vote Equal:** Would the method make every vote equal?

---

[1] There are numerous variations on each of the three approaches presented in this chapter. The differences include the extent to which the proposal empowers Congress to adopt uniform federal laws governing particular aspects of presidential elections, whether the casting of electoral votes is made automatic (i.e., the office of presidential elector is eliminated), the percentage of the vote required to trigger a contingent election, and the procedures for a contingent election (e.g., separate voting by the two houses of Congress, voting in a joint session of Congress, or a nationwide popular run-off election).

3.1 BRIEF HISTORY OF TROUBLESOME PRESIDENTIAL ELECTIONS

Interest in reforming the current system of electing the President has peaked following each troublesome presidential election. Thus, before proceeding, we review some of the troublesome elections.

Under the original Constitution, each presidential elector cast two votes. The candidate with the most electoral votes (provided that the candidate had an absolute majority of the electoral votes) became President, and the second-place candidate became Vice President (regardless of whether that candidate had an absolute majority). In the nation's first two presidential elections (1789 and 1792), George Washington received a vote from each presidential elector who voted and was thus elected unanimously.

The problems inherent with giving each presidential elector two votes surfaced as soon as political parties formed.

In 1796, the Federalist members of Congress caucused and nominated Vice President John Adams of Massachusetts for President and Thomas Pinckney of South Carolina for Vice President. Meanwhile, their opponents in Congress (called the "Republicans" or "Democratic Republicans," and later the "Democrats") caucused and nominated Thomas Jefferson of Virginia for President and Aaron Burr of New York for Vice President.

As John Ferling wrote in *Adams vs. Jefferson: The Tumultuous Election of 1800*:

> "The election was overshadowed by the Constitutional Convention's ill-advised notion that electors were to 'vote by ballot for two persons' for the presidency. The electoral college system was a calamity waiting to happen."[2]

The Federalists were strongest in the north, and the Republicans were strongest in the south. Each party had a nominee from both regions. However, Federalist nominee Thomas Pinckney was expected to be able to win electoral votes from his home state of South Carolina (where the legislature appointed the presidential electors), whereas Republican nominee Aaron Burr was not expected to be able to win similar support in the New York legislature.

Given that the election was expected to be close in the Electoral College and that each presidential elector cast two votes in the Electoral College—not differentiated as to whether for President or Vice President—the Federalist Party faced the excruciating dilemma of whether to give its wholehearted support to its own nominees. If 100% of the Federalist presidential electors had cast one of their two votes for Adams and their other vote for Thomas Pinckney, and if Thomas Pinckney had then won the expected additional bloc of electoral votes from South Carolina, Thomas Pinckney

---

[2] Ferling, John. 2004. *Adams vs. Jefferson: The Tumultuous Election of 1800*. Oxford, UK: Oxford University Press. Page 887.

would have ended up with more electoral votes than the person (Vice President John Adams) most Federalists wanted to become President. Federalist Thomas Pinckney (instead of Federalist John Adams) would end up as President. As presidential historian Edward Stanwood reports,

> "No less than eighteen [Federalist] electors in New England resolved that Pinckney's vote should not exceed Adam's and withheld their votes from the [Federalist] candidate for Vice president, and scattered them upon others."[3]

This strategic voting by Federalist presidential electors succeeded in ensuring the Presidency to John Adams; however, it simultaneously enabled Republican Thomas Jefferson to end up with the second-highest number of electoral votes. Under the original Constitution, the candidate with the second highest number of electoral votes (regardless of whether it was an absolute majority) became Vice President. Thus, Federalist John Adams was elected President, and his chief critic (Jefferson) became Vice President.[4,5,6]

The problems inherent with giving each presidential elector two undifferentiated votes surfaced again in the nation's second competitive presidential election (1800). Thomas Jefferson and Aaron Burr again were the nominees of the Republican Party. The Republicans won an absolute majority in the Electoral College in 1800. All of the Republican presidential electors loyally voted for both of their party's nominees— thereby avoiding the scattering of electoral votes that had elected the opposing party's nominee in 1796. However, the result of this lockstep loyalty was that Jefferson and Burr each received an equal number of votes in the Electoral College.

Under the Constitution, ties in the Electoral College were to be resolved by a "contingent election" in which the U.S. House of Representatives elects the President and the U.S. Senate elects the Vice President. In the House, each state is entitled to cast one vote for President (with equally divided states being unable to cast a vote). In the Senate, each Senator is entitled to cast one vote for Vice President.

In the contingent election in the House, Republican nominee Thomas Jefferson ran against Republican nominee Aaron Burr.

---

[3] Stanwood, Edward. 1924. *A History of the Presidency from 1788 to 1897*. Boston, MA: Houghton Mifflin Company. Page 49.

[4] Peirce, Neal R. 1968. *The People's President: The Electoral College in American History and Direct-Vote Alternative*. New York, NY: Simon and Schuster. Pages 63–64.

[5] Stanwood, Edward. 1924. *A History of the Presidency from 1788 to 1897*. Boston, MA: Houghton Mifflin Company. Pages 49–53. There is considerable historical controversy concerning Alexander Hamilton's possible motives and role in the "strategic voting" by Federalist presidential electors in the 1796 election. The main point, for the purposes of this chapter, is that the original Constitution's provision for double voting by presidential electors was unworkable in the context of political parties and in the context of a competitive presidential election.

[6] John Adams received 71 electoral votes to Jefferson's 68. Adams received an absolute majority (71 out of 138) of the electoral votes. Jefferson received the second highest number of electoral votes but not an absolute majority.

Neither party controlled a majority of the state delegations in the House.

After a prolonged and bitter dispute involving 36 ballots in the House of Representatives, Thomas Jefferson emerged as President.[7,8,9]

Given the demonstrated problems associated with giving each presidential elector two undifferentiated votes in the Electoral College, Congress passed the 12th Amendment specifying that each presidential elector would cast separate votes for President and Vice President. Separate voting enables the winning political party to elect both of its nominees to national office. The states quickly ratified the amendment, and the new procedure was in effect in time for the 1804 election.[10] The 12th Amendment can be viewed as formalizing the central role of political parties in presidential elections and recognizing that the Electoral College was not a deliberative body.

In 1824, there was a four-way race for President. The election was again thrown into the U.S. House and Senate. The House elected John Quincy Adams as President—rejecting Andrew Jackson, the candidate who had received the most popular votes. This controversial election spotlighted various undemocratic practices, including the continued selection of presidential electors by the state legislatures in about a quarter of the states.[11] Within two presidential elections, the laws of all but one of these states (South Carolina) were changed to empower the voters to choose the state's presidential electors directly.

In 1876, Democrat Samuel J. Tilden received 254,694 more popular votes than the 4,033,497 votes received by Rutherford B. Hayes; however, Hayes led by one electoral vote by virtue of carrying a number of states by extremely small margins (e.g., South Carolina by 889 votes, Florida by 922 votes, Oregon by 1,050 votes, Nevada by 1,075 votes, and California by 2,798 votes).[12] Conflicting returns were submitted from three Southern states that still had Reconstruction governments (South Carolina, Florida, and Louisiana). A 15-member electoral commission eventually awarded the presidency to Hayes.[13,14,15] The contested Tilden-Hayes 1876 election led to the passage of

---

[7] Dunn, Susan. 2004. *Jefferson's Second Revolution: The Elections Crisis of 1800 and the Triumph of Republicanism.* Boston, MA: Houghton Mifflin Company.

[8] Weisberger, Bernard A. 2001. *America Afire: Jefferson, Adams, and the First Contested Election.* William Morrow.

[9] Ferling, John. 2004. *Adams vs. Jefferson: The Tumultuous Election of 1800.* Oxford, UK: Oxford University Press.

[10] Kuroda, Tadahisa. 1994. *The Origins of the Twelfth Amendment: The Electoral College in the Early Republic, 1787–1804.* Westport, CT: Greenwood Press.

[11] Hopkins, James F. 2002. In Schlesinger, Arthur M., Jr., and Israel, Fred L. (editors). *History of American Presidential Elections 1878–2001.* Philadelphia, PA: Chelsea House Publishers. Volume 1. Pages 349–381.

[12] Congressional Quarterly. 2002. *Presidential Elections 1789–2002.* Washington, DC: CQ Press. Page 125.

[13] Morris, Roy B. 2003. *Fraud of the Century: Rutherford B. Hayes, Samuel Tilden, and the Stolen Election of 1876.* Waterville, ME: Thorndike Press.

[14] Robinson, Lloyd. 1996. *The Stolen Election: Hayes versus Tilden—1876.* New York, NY: Tom Doherty Associates Books.

[15] Rehnquist, William H. 2004. *Centennial Crisis: The Disputed Election of 1876.* New York, NY: Alfred A. Knopf.

federal legislation (the "Electoral Vote Act") governing the procedures for certifying state election results and resolving disputed elections. The federal election laws resulting from the 1876 election evolved into what is now Title 3 of the United States Code (found in appendix B).

In the 1888 election, President Grover Cleveland received 5,539,118 popular votes to Benjamin Harrison's 5,449,825. However, Harrison won in the Electoral College by a substantial 233–168 margin, despite Cleveland's 89,293-vote lead in the popular vote.

In the 1890 mid-term elections, the Democrats won political control of Michigan (then a regularly Republican state). In reaction to the 1888 election, the Democrats passed a law switching Michigan from the statewide winner-take-all system to one in which one presidential elector was to be elected from each of the state's congressional districts and in which the state's two senatorial electors were to be elected from two special districts, each comprising half of the state's congressional districts. Republicans contested the constitutionality of Michigan's change from the statewide winner-take-all system to the district system. In the 1892 case of *McPherson v. Blacker* (discussed in chapter 2), the U.S. Supreme Court upheld Michigan's right to change its law concerning the method of choosing its presidential electors.

The 1968 presidential election was held in the midst of continuing controversy over recently passed civil rights laws, urban rioting, and the war in Vietnam. Governor George Wallace of Alabama ran for President against Richard Nixon and Hubert Humphrey.[16] Wallace hoped to win enough electoral votes to prevent either major-party nominee from winning a majority of the electoral votes. His primary goal was not to throw the election into the Congress. Instead, he planned to negotiate with one of the major-party candidates before the meeting of the Electoral College in mid-December to extract policy concessions on civil rights and cabinet positions. To aid in his anticipated negotiations, Wallace obtained affidavits (secret at the time) from each of his presidential electors committing them to vote in the Electoral College for Wallace or "for whomsoever he may direct."[17]

In the 1968 election, Wallace won 45 electoral votes by carrying Alabama, Arkansas, Georgia, Louisiana, and Mississippi. Richard Nixon ended up with 43.4% of the popular vote (compared to Hubert Humphrey's 42.7%) as well as a majority of the electoral votes. Although Nixon was elected President by a majority of the Electoral College, a shift of only 10,245 popular votes in Missouri and 67,481 popular votes in Illinois would have left Nixon without a majority of the electoral votes (while still leading Humphrey by more than 300,000 popular votes on a nationwide basis).

Faithless presidential electors emerged as an irritant in presidential politics in several Southern states during the period immediately before and after passage of

---

[16] Longley, Lawrence D., and Braun, Alan G. 1972. *The Politics of Electoral College Reform.* New Haven, CT: Yale University Press. Pages 7–21.

[17] Congressional Quarterly. 1979. *Presidential Elections Since 1789.* Second edition. Washington, DC: CQ Press. Page 8.

the civil rights legislation of the mid-1960s. In the 1968 presidential election, George Wallace received one electoral vote from a faithless Republican presidential elector from North Carolina. In fact, Nixon suffered the loss of one electoral vote because of a faithless Republican elector on each of the three occasions when he ran for President.

Thus, shortly after taking office as President in 1969, Nixon sent a message to Congress saying:

> "I have in the past supported the proportional plan. But I am not wedded to the details of this plan or any other specific plan. I will support any plan that moves toward . . . the abolition of individual electors . . . allocation of presidential candidates of the electoral vote of each state and the District of Columbia in a manner that may more closely approximate the popular vote than does the present system . . . making a 40 percent electoral vote plurality sufficient to choose a President."[18]

President Nixon's message ignited a flurry of activity in the 91st Congress. Members of Congress stepped forth and introduced bills to implement each of the three most prominent approaches.

- **Senator Howard Cannon (D–Nevada)** introduced a proposed constitutional amendment for a fractional proportional allocation of each state's electoral votes (section 3.2).
- **Senator Karl Mundt (R–South Dakota)** introduced a proposed constitutional amendment for electing presidential electors by congressional district (section 3.3).
- **Representative Emmanuel Celler (D–New York) and Senator Birch Bayh (D–Indiana)** introduced constitutional amendments for nationwide popular election of the president (section 3.4).

After considerable debate on the three approaches, Celler's proposed constitutional amendment (House Joint Resolution 681 of the 91st Congress) passed in the House of Representatives by a 338–70 vote in 1969. Celler's constitutional amendment satisfied all three of the criteria in Nixon's message to Congress. As a result of the strong bipartisan vote in the House, President Nixon urged the Senate to adopt Celler's proposed amendment. Celler's proposal was, however, filibustered, and it died in the Senate.[19]

Interest in electoral reform was rekindled after the 1976 presidential elections. A shift of 3,687 popular votes in Hawaii and 5,559 popular votes in Ohio would have elected Gerald Ford, even though Jimmy Carter led Ford by 1,682,970 popular votes nationwide.

President Carter, President Ford (the losing presidential candidate in 1976), and Senator Robert Dole (the losing vice-presidential candidate in 1976 and the Republican

---

[18] February 20, 1969.

[19] Congressional Quarterly. 2002. *Presidential Elections 1789–2002*. Washington, DC: CQ Press. Page 169.

presidential nominee in 1996) publicly supported nationwide popular election of the President. In 1979, a majority (but not two-thirds) of the Senate voted in favor of a proposed constitutional amendment (Senate Joint Resolution 28) sponsored by Senator Birch Bayh that closely resembled the bill that had passed in the House in 1969.

In 1992, there was a flurry of proposals for reforming the method of electing the President as a result of the candidacy of third-party candidate Ross Perot. A June 1992 nationwide poll showed that Perot had 39% support, incumbent President George H. W. Bush had 31%, and Bill Clinton had 25%. Such a division of the popular vote, if it had persisted until Election Day, would have either elected Perot outright or thrown the presidential election into the House of Representatives.[20]

The 2000 election resulted in the election of a President who had not received the most popular votes nationwide. After the 2000 election, former Presidents Jimmy Carter and Gerald Ford created a bipartisan commission to make recommendations for improving the nation's electoral system. Many of the reforms proposed by the Carter-Ford Commission became part of the Help America Vote Act (HAVA) of 2002.

In 2004, if 59,393 Ohio voters had voted for John Kerry instead of George W. Bush, Kerry would have been elected President despite Bush's lead of over 3,000,000 votes in the nationwide popular vote. After the 2004 election, former President Jimmy Carter and former Secretary of State James Baker formed another bipartisan commission to make additional recommendations concerning election administration and to review the implementation of HAVA in light of the nation's experience in the 2004 election.

Potential problems with the current statewide winner-take-all system appear to be becoming increasingly common.[21] As shown in table 1.3, there have been six presidential elections—1948, 1960, 1968, 1976, 2000, and 2004—in the past six decades in which the shift of a relatively small number of votes in one or two states would have elected a presidential candidate who had not received the most popular votes nationwide.

Meanwhile, the 2004 presidential election made it clear that the number of closely divided battleground states was steadily decreasing from year to year. Although voter turnout increased in the battleground states in 2004, turnout decreased in spectator states.[22]

On February 23, 2006, the National Popular Vote organization held its first press conference in which it announced its state-based proposal to reform the Electoral College (described in chapter 6) and released the first edition of this book.

We now discuss the three most discussed proposals involving a federal constitutional amendment.

---

[20] The 1992 poll was cited in Stanley, Timothy. Why Romney is stronger than he seems. *CNN Election Center.* April 10, 2012.

[21] Abbott, David W., and Levine, James P. 1991. *Wrong Winner: The Coming Debacle in the Electoral College.* Westport, CT: Praeger.

[22] Committee for the Study of the American Electorate (2004). *President Bush, Mobilization Drives Propel Turnout to Post-1968 High.* November 4, 2004.

3.2 FRACTIONAL PROPORTIONAL ALLOCATION OF ELECTORAL VOTES

In the fractional proportional approach (Senator Cannon's proposal), a state's electoral votes are divided proportionally—*carried out to three decimal places*—according to the percentage of votes received in the state by each presidential slate.

Before proceeding, it should be noted that the "fractional proportional" approach discussed in this section differs significantly from the "whole-number proportional" approach (discussed in section 4.1). In the whole-number proportional approach, the office of presidential elector is not abolished and, therefore, the states continue to choose presidential electors. Because presidential electors each have one indivisible vote, it is not possible to divide a state's electoral votes in a fine-grained manner (e.g., to three decimal places, as specified in Senator Cannon's proposed constitutional amendment). Instead, under the whole-number proportional approach, a state's electoral votes must necessarily be rounded off to the nearest whole number. In a nation in which the average state has only 11 electoral votes and the median state has only 7 electoral votes, this rounding-off to the nearest whole number would have a number of unexpected and counter-intuitive effects (as discussed in detail in section 4.1).

Senator Howard Cannon (D–Nevada) introduced the following proposed federal constitutional amendment (Senate Joint Resolution 33 in the 91st Congress) to implement the fractional proportional approach:

> *"Resolved by the Senate and House of Representatives of the United States of America in Congress assembled (two-thirds of each House concurring therein),*

> That the following article is proposed as an amendment to the Constitution of the United States, which shall be valid to all intents and purposes as part of the Constitution if ratified by the legislatures of three-fourths of the several States:

>> 'Article—
>> 'SECTION 1. The Executive power shall be vested in a President of the United States of America. He shall hold his office during the term of four years, and, together with the Vice President, chosen for the same term, be elected as provided in this article. No person constitutionally ineligible for the office of President shall be eligible for the office of Vice President.

>> 'SECTION 2. The President and Vice President shall be elected by the people of the several States and the District of Columbia. The electors in each State shall have the qualifications requisite for electors of the most numerous branch of the State legislature, except that the legislature of any State may prescribe lesser qualifications with respect to residence therein. The electors of the District of Columbia shall have such qualifications as the Congress may prescribe. The places and manner of

holding such election in each State shall be prescribed by the legislature thereof, but the Congress may at any time by law make or alter such regulations. The place and manner of holding such election in the District of Columbia shall be prescribed by the Congress. The Congress shall determine the time of such election, which shall be the same throughout the United States. Until otherwise determined by the Congress, such election shall be held on the Tuesday next after the first Monday in November of the year preceding the year in which the regular term of the President is to begin.

'SECTION 3. Each state shall be entitled to a number of electoral votes equal to the whole number of Senators and Representatives to which each State may be entitled in the Congress. The District of Columbia shall be entitled to a number of electoral votes equal to the whole number of Senators and Representatives in Congress to which such District would be entitled if it were a State, but in no event more than the least populous State.

'SECTION 4. Within forty-five days after such election, or at such time as Congress shall direct, the official custodian of the election returns of each State and the District of Columbia shall make distinct lists of all persons for whom votes were cast for President and the number of votes cast for each person, and the total vote cast by the electors of the State of the District for all persons for President, which lists he shall sign and certify and transmit sealed to the seat of Government of the United States, directed to the President of the Senate. On the 6th day of January following the election, unless the Congress by law appoints a different day not earlier than the 4th day of January and not later than the 10th day of January, the President of the Senate shall, in the presence of the Senate and House of Representatives, open all certificates and the votes shall then be counted. Each person for whom votes were cast shall be credited with such proportion of the electoral votes thereof as he received of the total vote cast by the electors therein for President. In making the computation, fractional numbers less than one one-thousandth shall be disregarded. The person having the greatest aggregate number of electoral votes of the States and the District of Columbia for President shall be President, if such number be at least 40 per centum of the whole number of such electoral votes, or if two persons have received an identical number of such electoral votes which is at least 40 per centum of the whole number of electoral votes, then from the persons having the two greatest number of such electoral votes for President, the Senate and the House of Representatives sitting in joint session shall choose immediately, by ballot, the President. A majority of the votes of the combined membership of the Senate and House of Representatives shall be necessary for a choice.

'SECTION 5. The Vice President shall be likewise elected, at the same time, in the same manner, and subject to the same provisions as the President.

'SECTION 6. The Congress may by law provide for the case of the death of any of the persons from whom the Senate and the House of Representatives may choose a President whenever the right of choice shall have devolved upon them, and for the case of death of any of the persons from whom the Senate and the House of Representatives may choose a Vice President whenever the right of choice shall have devolved upon them. The Congress shall have power to enforce this article by appropriate legislation.

'SECTION 7. The following provisions of the Constitution are hereby repealed: paragraphs 1, 2, 3, and 4 of section 1, Article II; the twelfth article of amendment; section 4 of the twentieth article of amendment; and the twenty-third article of amendment.

'SECTION 8. This article shall take effect on the 1st day of February following its ratification, except that this article shall be inoperative unless it shall have been ratified as an amendment to the Constitution by the legislatures of three-fourths of the States within seven years from the date of its submission to the States by the Congress.'"

The remainder of this section analyzes how Senator Howard Cannon's proposed fractional proportional approach would operate in terms of the following criteria:

- **Accuracy:** Would the method accurately reflect the nationwide popular vote?
- **Making Every Vote Politically Relevant**: Would the method improve upon the current situation in which two-thirds of the states and two-thirds of the people of the United States are ignored by presidential campaigns?
- **Equality:** Would every vote be equal?

In a landslide election, almost any of the commonly discussed electoral systems will result in the election of the candidate who receives the most popular votes nationwide. Thus, the test of accuracy of an electoral system is how it works in a close election. We start our analysis of the fractional proportional approach with data from the very closest recent presidential election, namely the 2000 election.

Table 3.1 shows how the fractional proportional approach would have operated in the 2000 presidential election. Column 2 shows each state's electoral votes (EV) in 2000. Columns 3, 4, and 5 show, for each state, the number of popular votes received by the three leading candidates in that race, namely Al Gore, George W. Bush, and Ralph Nader. Column 6 shows, for each state, the number of electoral votes that Gore would have received under the fractional proportional approach (expressed as a fraction with three decimal places of precision, as specified by Senator Cannon's proposal). This number of electoral votes is obtained by dividing Gore's popular vote in the state by the total popular vote received by Gore, Bush, and Nader together, and then multiplying this quotient by the number of electoral votes possessed by the state. Columns 7 and 8 show the same information for Bush and Nader. For each state, the number of electoral votes for the three presidential candidates (columns 6, 7, and 8) adds up to the number of electoral votes possessed by the state (column 2). As can be seen from the bottom line of the table, Al Gore would have received 259.969 electoral votes; George W. Bush would have received 260.323 electoral votes; and Ralph Nader would have received 17.707 electoral votes if the 2000 presidential election had been run under the fractional proportional approach.[23]

For comparison, appendix CC shows, by state, the number of electoral votes won by Bush (271) and Gore (267).

Concerning the accurate reflection of the nationwide popular vote, table 3.1 shows that, if the fractional proportional approach had been in use throughout the country in the 2000 presidential election, it would *not* have awarded the most electoral votes to the candidate receiving the most popular votes nationwide. Gore would have received 0.354 fewer electoral votes than George W. Bush even though Gore led by 537,179 popular votes nationwide. Because Bush would have received "the greatest aggregate number of electoral votes" and such number would have been "at least 40 per centum of the whole number of such electoral votes," Bush would have been elected under the terms of the constitutional amendment proposed by Senator Cannon in 1969 (Senate Joint Resolution 33).

Under a variant of Senator Cannon's proposed fractional proportional approach, no electoral votes would be awarded to a presidential slate receiving less than a specified "cut-off" percentage (e.g., 5%) of a state's popular vote (or the national popular vote). Table 3.2 shows how the fractional proportional approach would have operated in the 2000 presidential election if only the two major political parties are considered. Column 2 shows Gore's popular vote percentage for each state. Columns 3 and 4 show, for each state, the electoral votes (rounded off to three decimal places) that Gore and Bush, respectively, would have received under the fractional proportional approach with a cut-off.

Table 3.2 shows that, if the fractional proportional approach had been used in the

---

[23] In this book, all hypothetical analyses of the results of using an alternative electoral system are necessarily based on the actual election returns using the *current* electoral system, even though the authors recognize that the campaign would have been conducted differently if an alternative electoral system had been in effect.

Table 3.1 2000 ELECTION UNDER THE FRACTIONAL PROPORTIONAL APPROACH (TOP THREE PARTIES)

STATE	EV	GORE	BUSH	NADER	GORE-EV	BUSH-EV	NADER-EV
Alabama	9	692,611	941,173	18,323	3.773	5.127	0.100
Alaska	3	79,004	167,398	28,747	0.861	1.825	0.313
Arizona	8	685,341	781,652	45,645	3.625	4.134	0.241
Arkansas	6	422,768	472,940	13,421	2.790	3.121	0.089
California	54	5,861,203	4,567,429	418,707	29.178	22.737	2.084
Colorado	8	738,227	883,748	91,434	3.447	4.126	0.427
Connecticut	8	816,015	561,094	64,452	4.529	3.114	0.358
Delaware	3	180,068	137,288	8,307	1.659	1.265	0.077
DC	3	171,923	18,073	10,576	2.571	0.270	0.158
Florida	25	2,912,253	2,912,790	97,488	12.293	12.295	0.412
Georgia	13	1,116,230	1,419,720	134,322	5.434	6.912	0.654
Hawaii	4	205,286	137,845	21,623	2.251	1.512	0.237
Idaho	4	138,637	336,937	122,922	0.927	2.252	0.822
Illinois	22	2,589,026	2,019,421	103,759	12.087	9.428	0.484
Indiana	12	901,980	1,245,836	185,312	4.639	6.408	0.953
Iowa	7	638,517	634,373	29,374	3.432	3.410	0.158
Kansas	6	399,276	622,332	36,086	2.265	3.530	0.205
Kentucky	8	638,898	872,492	23,192	3.331	4.548	0.121
Louisiana	9	792,344	927,871	20,473	4.097	4.797	0.106
Maine	4	319,951	286,616	37,127	1.988	1.781	0.231
Maryland	10	1,145,782	813,797	53,768	5.691	4.042	0.267
Massachusetts	12	1,616,487	878,502	173,564	7.269	3.950	0.780
Michigan	18	2,170,418	1,953,139	84,165	9.285	8.355	0.360
Minnesota	10	1,168,266	1,109,659	126,696	4.858	4.615	0.527
Mississippi	7	404,614	572,844	8,122	2.874	4.069	0.058
Missouri	11	1,111,138	1,189,924	38,515	5.224	5.595	0.181
Montana	3	137,126	240,178	24,437	1.024	1.794	0.182
Nebraska	5	231,780	433,862	24,540	1.679	3.143	0.178
Nevada	4	279,978	301,575	15,008	1.877	2.022	0.101
New Hampshire	4	266,348	273,559	22,198	1.895	1.947	0.158
New Jersey	15	1,788,850	1,284,173	94,554	8.471	6.081	0.448
New Mexico	5	286,783	286,417	21,251	2.412	2.409	0.179
New York	33	4,107,697	2,403,374	244,030	20.067	11.741	1.192
North Carolina	14	1,257,692	1,631,163	0	6.095	7.905	0.000
North Dakota	3	95,284	174,852	9,486	1.022	1.876	0.102
Ohio	21	2,186,190	2,351,209	117,857	9.862	10.606	0.532
Oklahoma	8	474,276	744,337	0	3.114	4.886	0.000
Oregon	7	720,342	713,577	77,357	3.337	3.305	0.358
Pennsylvania	23	2,485,967	2,281,127	103,392	11.740	10.772	0.488
Rhode Island	4	249,508	130,555	25,052	2.464	1.289	0.247
South Carolina	8	565,561	785,937	20,200	3.298	4.584	0.118
South Dakota	3	118,804	190,700	0	1.152	1.848	0.000
Tennessee	11	981,720	1,061,949	19,781	5.233	5.661	0.105
Texas	32	2,433,746	3,799,639	137,994	12.223	19.084	0.693
Utah	5	203,053	515,096	35,850	1.347	3.416	0.238
Vermont	3	149,022	119,775	20,374	1.546	1.243	0.211
Virginia	13	1,217,290	1,437,490	59,398	5.830	6.885	0.284
Washington	11	1,247,652	1,108,864	103,002	5.580	4.959	0.461
West Virginia	5	295,497	336,475	10,680	2.299	2.618	0.083
Wisconsin	11	1,242,987	1,237,279	94,070	5.311	5.287	0.402
Wyoming	3	60,481	147,947	46,252	0.712	1.743	0.545
Total	**538**	**50,999,897**	**50,456,002**	**2,882,955**	**259.969**	**260.323**	**17.707**

2000 presidential election (with a cut-off percentage excluding all but the two major-party candidates), it would *not* have awarded the most electoral votes to the candidate receiving the most popular votes nationwide. Even though Al Gore led by 537,179 popular votes nationwide, he would have received only 268.766 electoral votes, whereas George W. Bush would have received 269.234 electoral votes. Since 269.234 is more than half of 538, George W. Bush would have been elected President under this variation of the fractional proportional approach.

Concerning making every vote politically relevant regardless of the state in which it is cast, the fractional proportional approach definitely improves upon the current situation in which about four-fifths of states are ignored by presidential campaigns. A presidential candidate could, for example, earn an additional 0.001 electoral vote by winning a hundred or so additional popular votes in any state under the fractional proportional approach. Thus, no state would be written off, or taken for granted, by any presidential candidate. Every voter in every state would, for all practical purposes, be politically relevant. If the percentage calculation were carried out to a few more decimal places, then it could be said, without qualification, that every vote would matter in every state in every presidential election.

On the other hand, not every vote is equal under the fractional proportional approach. In fact, there are three different substantial inequalities inherent in the fractional proportional approach. These inequalities amount to variations of 3.79-to-1, 1.76-to-1, and 1.27-to-1. In particular, these inequalities are considerably larger than the small variations that are considered to be constitutionally tolerable nowadays when congressional and other types of districts are drawn within states.[24]

The inequalities under the fractional proportional approach arise from the

- two bonus electoral votes that each state receives regardless of its population,
- inequalities in the apportionment of the membership of the House of Representatives among the several states, and
- differences in voter turnout in various states.

First, a vote cast in a large state has less weight than a vote cast in a small state because of the two-vote bonus in the Electoral College (corresponding to each state's two U.S. Senators). For example, in the 2000 presidential election, Wyoming (with a population of 453,588 in 1990) had three electoral votes, whereas California (with a population of 29,760,021 in 1990) had 54 electoral votes. As shown in table 3.3, in the presidential elections of 1992, 1996, and 2000, one electoral vote corresponded to 151,196 people in Wyoming but to 572,308 in California. The last column of this table shows the ratio of California's population per electoral vote to that of Wyoming—a 3.79-to-1 variation.

---

[24] Of course, if the fractional proportional approach were enacted in the form of a federal constitutional amendment, it could not be successfully challenged in court on the grounds that it countenances inequalities that are greater than those constitutionally allowed for election districts for other offices.

Table 3.2 2000 ELECTION UNDER THE FRACTIONAL PROPORTIONAL APPROACH

STATE	GORE PERCENT	GORE EV	BUSH EV
Alabama	42.393058%	3.815	5.185
Alaska	32.063051%	0.962	2.038
Arizona	46.717401%	3.737	4.263
Arkansas	47.199310%	2.832	3.168
California	56.202990%	30.350	23.650
Colorado	45.514080%	3.641	4.359
Connecticut	59.255658%	4.740	3.260
Delaware	56.740065%	1.702	1.298
DC	90.487694%	2.715	0.285
Florida	49.995391%	12.499	12.501
Georgia	44.016246%	5.722	7.278
Hawaii	59.827296%	2.393	1.607
Idaho	29.151510%	1.166	2.834
Illinois	56.180010%	12.360	9.640
Indiana	41.995217%	5.039	6.961
Iowa	50.162779%	3.511	3.489
Kansas	39.083093%	2.345	3.655
Kentucky	42.272213%	3.382	4.618
Louisiana	46.060754%	4.145	4.855
Maine	52.747842%	2.110	1.890
Maryland	58.470825%	5.847	4.153
Massachusetts	64.789344%	7.775	4.225
Michigan	52.634606%	9.474	8.526
Minnesota	51.286412%	5.129	4.871
Mississippi	41.394515%	2.898	4.102
Missouri	48.288051%	5.312	5.688
Montana	36.343638%	1.090	1.910
Nebraska	34.820519%	1.741	3.259
Nevada	48.143162%	1.926	2.074
New Hampshire	49.332200%	1.973	2.027
New Jersey	58.211409%	8.732	6.268
New Mexico	50.031926%	2.502	2.498
New York	63.087885%	20.819	12.181
North Carolina	43.536003%	6.095	7.905
North Dakota	35.272603%	1.058	1.942
Ohio	48.181568%	10.118	10.882
Oklahoma	38.919329%	3.114	4.886
Oregon	50.235892%	3.517	3.483
Pennsylvania	52.148479%	11.994	11.006
Rhode Island	65.649116%	2.626	1.374
South Carolina	41.846973%	3.348	4.652
South Dakota	38.385287%	1.152	1.848
Tennessee	48.037133%	5.284	5.716
Texas	39.043730%	12.494	19.506
Utah	28.274495%	1.414	3.586
Vermont	55.440351%	1.663	1.337
Virginia	45.852764%	5.961	7.039
Washington	52.944771%	5.824	5.176
West Virginia	46.757926%	2.338	2.662
Wisconsin	50.115068%	5.513	5.487
Wyoming	29.017694%	0.871	2.129
Total	**50.268045%**	**268.766**	**269.234**

Table 3.3 DIFFERENCE IN WEIGHT OF A POPULAR VOTE IN THE NATION'S
LARGEST AND SMALLEST STATES

STATE	POPULATION	REPRESENTATIVES	SENATORS	ELECTORAL VOTES	POPULATION CORRESPONDING TO ONE ELECTORAL VOTE	RATIO TO LOWEST
California	29,760,021	52	2	54	572,308	3.79
Wyoming	453,588	1	2	3	151,196	1.00

Second, a vote cast in certain states has less weight than a vote cast in certain other states because of inequalities inherent in the method of apportioning U.S. Representatives among the states. For example, Wyoming (with a population of 453,588 in 1990) and Montana (with a population of 799,065 in 1990) each had one member in the House of Representatives (and hence three electoral votes). As shown in table 3.4, in the presidential elections of 1992, 1996, and 2000, one electoral vote corresponded to 151,196 people in Wyoming but to 266,355 in Montana. The last column of this table shows the ratio of Montana's population per electoral vote to the ratio for Wyoming—a 1.76-to-1 variation. There are numerous other pairs of states with similar variations.[25]

Table 3.4 COMPARISON OF WEIGHT OF A POPULAR VOTE CAST IN
TWO STATES WITH THREE ELECTORAL VOTES

STATE	POPULATION	POPULATION CORRESPONDING TO ONE ELECTORAL VOTE	RATIO TO LOWEST
Montana	799,065	266,355	1.76
Wyoming	453,588	151,196	1.00

Third, voter turnout within a voter's own state changes the weight of a given voter's vote. For example, a vote cast in a state with a low turnout has a greater weight than a vote cast in a state where more total votes are cast. Column 4 of table 3.5 shows the number of popular votes cast in the 2000 presidential election in the four states with five electoral votes (Nebraska, New Mexico, Utah, and West Virginia). As can be seen in column 5 of the table, one electoral vote corresponds to 118,900 popular votes in New Mexico but to 150,800 popular votes in Utah. Column 6 shows the ratio of the number of votes representing one electoral vote in each state to that of the lowest in the table (New Mexico). The greatest variation is between Utah and New Mexico—a 1.27-to-1 variation.

---

[25] These include pairs of states with more than three electoral votes and pairs of states with different numbers of electoral votes.

Table 3 .5 COMPARISON OF WEIGHT OF A POPULAR VOTE CAST IN FOUR STATES WITH
           FIVE ELECTORAL VOTES

STATE	1990 POPULATION	2000 POPULATION	VOTES CAST IN 2000 PRESIDENTIAL ELECTION	POPULAR VOTES CORRESPONDING TO ONE ELECTORAL VOTE	RATIO TO LOWEST
Nebraska	1,578,385	1,711,263	690,182	138,000	1.16
New Mexico	1,515,069	1,819,046	594,451	118,900	1.00
Utah	1,722,850	2,233,169	753,999	150,800	1.27
West Virginia	1,793,477	1,808,344	642,652	128,600	1.08

The total number of votes cast in states with the same number of electoral votes varies for at least two reasons.

- First, the actual population of the state at the moment of the election might have increased or decreased since the last census.
- Second, the number of voters turning out for the particular election depends on the degree of civic participation in the state.

As to the first of these factors, a state's allocation of electoral votes depends on its number of Representatives and Senators. The number of Representatives to which a state is entitled can change every 10 years based on the federal census. For example, the 1992, 1996, and 2000 presidential elections were conducted under the apportionment that resulted from the 1990 census. This means that the 2000 presidential election was conducted using an allocation of electoral votes based on 10-year-old population data. Thus, the weight of a citizen's vote in a rapidly growing state is diminished. Column 2 of table 3.5 shows the population of each state according to the 1990 census. Column 3 shows the population of each state according to the 2000 census. The 2000 census was taken in the spring of 2000 but was not applicable to the 2000 presidential election. These numbers closely approximate each state's population in the 2000 presidential election held a few months later. As can be seen, Utah, a fast-growing state, had 510,319 more people in 2000 than it did in 1990, whereas West Virginia barely grew at all during the 10-year period (only 14,867 more people than in 1990). New Mexico also experienced rapid population growth during the 1990s. Because of the time lag in reallocating electoral votes (a full 10 years in the case of the 2000 election), Utah and New Mexico had the same number of electoral votes in the 2000 presidential election as West Virginia.

Concerning the second of the above factors, voter turnout within a state also affects the relative weight of a vote under the fractional proportional approach. A citizen's vote gets less weight if it happens to be cast in a state with a high degree of civic participation. For example, Utah consistently has high voter turnout in its elections.

In summary, if the fractional proportional approach had been in use throughout the country in the 2000 presidential election,

- it *would not* accurately reflect the nationwide popular vote;
- it *would* improve upon the current situation by virtually making every vote in every state politically relevant in presidential elections, and
- it *would not* make every vote equal.

Senator Cannon's proposed 1969 constitutional amendment operates in substantially the same way as the amendment proposed in 1950 by Massachusetts Senator Henry Cabot Lodge (R) and Texas Representative Ed Gossett (D). The Lodge-Gossett amendment (Senate Joint Resolution 2 of the 81st Congress) passed the U.S. Senate by a 64–27 margin on February 1, 1950, but it died in the House of Representatives.[26,27,28]

The Lodge-Gossett amendment would have retained the distribution of electoral votes among the states based on a state's number of U.S. Senators and Congressmen. It would have made the awarding of electoral votes automatic (that is, the position of presidential elector would have been eliminated). Under the proposed amendment, electoral votes would have been allocated among the candidates in proportion to each candidate's vote in each state, with the calculation carried out to three decimal places. Under the amendment, a plurality would have been sufficient for election. The amendment would have eliminated the "contingent election" for President in the U.S. House of Representatives.[29]

The Lodge-Gossett amendment would not have altered state control over presidential elections.

The Lodge-Gossett amendment provided:

"Resolved by the Senate and House of Representatives of the United States of America in Congress assembled (two-thirds of each House concurring there-in), That an amendment is hereby proposed to the Constitution of the United States which shall be valid to all intents and purposes as part of the Constitution when ratified by three-fourths of the legislatures of the several States. Said amendment shall be as follows:

"ARTICLE —

"Section 1. The executive power shall be vested in a President of the United States of America. He shall hold his office during the term of four years, and together with the Vice-President, chosen for the same term, be elected as herein provided.

---

[26] Bennett, Emmett L. 1950. The reform of presidential elections: The Lodge amendment. *American Bar Association Journal*. Volume 37. February 1951. Page 89ff.

[27] Morley, Felix. 1961. Democracy and the Electoral College. *Modern Age*. Fall 1961. Pages 373–388.

[28] Editorial: Giving the minority vote a voice. *St. Petersburg Times*. August 6, 1951.

[29] Silva, Ruth C. 1950. The Lodge-Gossett resolution: A critical review. *The American Political Science Review*. Volume 44. Number 1. March 1950. Pages 86–99.

"The Electoral College system for electing the President and Vice President of the United States is hereby abolished. The President and Vice President shall be elected by the people of the several States. The electors in each State shall have the qualifications requisite for electors of the most numerous branch of the State legislature. Congress shall determine the time of such election, which shall be the same throughout the United States. Until otherwise determined by the Congress, such election shall be held on the Tuesday next after the first Monday in November of the year preceding the year in which the regular term of the President is to begin. Each State shall be entitled to a number of electoral votes equal to the whole number of Senators and Representatives to which such State may be entitled in the Congress.

"Within forty-five days after such election, or at such time as the Congress shall direct, the official custodian of the election returns of each State shall make distinct lists of all persons for whom votes were cast for President and the number of votes for each, and the total vote of the electors of the State for all persons for President, which lists he shall sign and certify and transmit sealed to the seat of the Government of the United States, directed to the President of the Senate. The President of the Senate shall in the presence of the Senate and House of Representatives open all certificates and the votes shall then be counted. Each person for whom votes were cast for President in each State shall be credited with such proportion of the electoral votes thereof as he received of the total vote of the electors therein for President. In making the computations, fractional numbers less than one one-thousandth shall be disregarded. The person having the greatest number of electoral votes for President shall be President. If two or more persons shall have an equal and the highest number of such votes, then the one for whom the greatest number of popular votes were cast shall be President.

"The Vice-President shall be likewise elected, at the same time and in the same manner and subject to the same provisions, as the President, but no person constitutionally ineligible for the office of President shall be eligible to that of Vice-President of the United States.

"Section 2. Paragraphs 1, 2, and 3 of section 1, article II, of the Constitution and the twelfth article of amendment to the Constitution, are hereby repealed.

"Section 3. This article shall take effect on the tenth day of February following its ratification.

"Section 4. This article shall be inoperative unless it shall have been ratified as an amendment to the Constitution by the legislatures of three-fourths of the States within seven years from the date of the submission hereof to the States by the Congress"

3.3 DISTRICT ALLOCATION OF ELECTORAL VOTES

In the district approach, voters elect two presidential electors statewide and one presidential elector for each district.

Senator Karl Mundt (R–South Dakota) was the leading sponsor of a proposed federal constitutional amendment to implement the district system in 1969. Senate Joint Resolution 12 of the 91st Congress provided (in part):

> *"Resolved by the Senate and House of Representatives of the United States of America in Congress assembled (two-thirds of each House concurring therein),*

> That the following article is proposed as an amendment to the Constitution of the United States, which shall be valid to all intents and purposes as part of the Constitution if ratified by the legislatures of three-fourths of the several States within seven years from the date of its submission by the Congress:

> 'Article—
> 'SECTION 1. Each State shall choose a number of electors of President and Vice President equal to the whole number of Senators and Representatives to which the State may be entitled in the Congress; but no Senator or Representative, or person holding an office of trust or profit under the United States shall be chosen elector.

> 'The electors assigned to each State with its Senators shall be elected by the people thereof. Each of the electors apportioned with its Representatives shall be elected by the people of a single-member electoral district formed by the legislature of the State. Electoral districts within each State shall be of compact and contiguous territory containing substantially equal numbers of inhabitants, and shall not be altered until another census of the United States has been taken. Each candidate for the office of elector of President and Vice President shall file in writing under oath a declaration of the identity of the persons for whom he will vote for President and Vice President, which declaration shall be binding on any successor to his office. In choosing electors the voters in each State have the qualifications requisite for electors of the most numerous branch of the State legislature.

> 'The electors shall meet in their respective States, fill any vacancies in their number as directed by the State legislature, and vote by signed bal-

lot for President and Vice President, one of whom, at least, shall not be an inhabitant of the State with themselves . . . .

"Any vote cast by an elector contrary to the declaration made by him shall be counted as a vote cast in accordance with his declaration.'"

Senate Joint Resolution 12 of the 91st Congress in 1969 was sponsored by the following Senators:

- Boggs (R–Delaware),
- Byrd (D–West Virginia),
- Cotton (R–New Hampshire),
- Curtis (R–Nebraska),
- Dominick (R–Colorado),
- Fong (R–Hawaii),
- Goldwater (R–Arizona),
- Hansen (R–Wyoming),
- Hruska (R–Nebraska),
- Jordan (R–Idaho),
- Miller (R–Iowa),
- Mundt (R–South Dakota),
- Sparkman (D–Alabama),
- Stennis (D–Mississippi),
- Thurmond (R–South Carolina),
- Tower (R–Texas),
- Williams (R–Delaware), and
- Young (R–North Dakota).

The shortcomings of the congressional-district approach are analyzed in detail in section 4.2, where it is demonstrated that

- it *would not* accurately reflect the nationwide popular vote;
- it *would not* improve upon the current situation in which two-thirds of the states and two-thirds of the people of the United States are ignored by presidential campaigns, but, instead, would create a small set of battleground congressional districts (with most districts being written off or taken for granted); and
- it *would not* make every vote equal.

The Mundt proposal was noteworthy in that it retained the office of presidential elector while eliminating the possibility of a faithless presidential elector. First, Mundt's proposed amendment provided that each candidate for presidential elector must take an oath to vote in the Electoral College for particular persons for President and Vice President (and made the original candidate's oath binding on any replacement). Second, Mundt's proposal then stated that regardless of the way the presidential elector actually voted in the Electoral College, his or her vote would "be counted as a vote cast in accordance with his declaration."

3.4 DIRECT NATIONWIDE POPULAR ELECTION

In 1969, the House of Representatives approved, by a bipartisan 338–70 vote, a federal constitutional amendment sponsored by Representative Emmanuel Celler for direct nationwide popular election.

Celler's proposal (House Joint Resolution 681 of the 91st Congress) provided:

"Resolved by the Senate and House of Representatives of the United States of America in Congress assembled (two-thirds of each House concurring therein),

That the following article is proposed as an amendment to the Constitution of the United States, which shall be valid to all intents and purposes as part of the Constitution when ratified by the legislatures of three-fourths of the several States within seven years from the date of its submission by the Congress:

'Article—

'SECTION 1: The people of the several States and the District constituting the seat of government of the United States shall elect the President and Vice President. Each elector shall cast a single vote for two persons who shall have consented to the joining of their names as candidates for the offices of President and Vice President. No candidate shall consent to the joinder of his name with that of more than one other person.

'SECTION 2: The electors of President and Vice President in each State shall have the qualifications requisite for electors of the most numerous branch of the State legislature, except that for electors of President and Vice President, the legislature of any State may prescribe less restrictive residence qualifications and for electors of President and Vice President the Congress may establish uniform residence qualifications.

'SECTION 3: The pair of persons having the greatest number of votes for President and Vice President shall be elected, if such number be at least 40 per centum of the whole number of votes cast for such offices. If no pair of persons has such number, a runoff election shall be held in which the choice of President and Vice President shall be made from the two pairs of persons who received the highest number of votes.

'SECTION 4: The times, places, and manner of holding such elections and entitlement to inclusion on the ballot shall be prescribed in each State by the legislature thereof; but the Congress may at any time by law make or alter such regulations. The days for such elections shall be determined by Congress and shall be uniform throughout the United States. The Congress shall prescribe by law the time, place, and manner in which the results of such elections shall be ascertained and declared.

'SECTION 5: The Congress may by law provide for the case of the death or withdrawal of any candidate for President or Vice President before a

President and Vice President have been elected, and for the case of the death of both the President-elect and Vice-President-elect.

'SECTION 6: The Congress shall have power to enforce this article by appropriate legislation.

'SECTION 7: This article shall take effect one year after the 21st day of January following ratification.'"

When it was first introduced, House Joint Resolution 681 was sponsored by the following Representatives:

- Biester (R–Pennsylvania),
- Cahill (R–New Jersey),
- Celler (D–New York),
- Conyers (D–Michigan),
- Donohue (D–Massachusetts),
- Edwards (D–California),
- Eilberg (D–Pennsylvania),
- Feighan (D–Ohio),
- Fish (R–New York),
- Hungate (D–Missouri),
- Jacobs (D–Indiana),
- Kastenmeier (D–Wisconsin),
- MacGregor (R–Minnesota),
- McClory (R–Illinois),
- McCulloch (R–Ohio),
- Meskill (R–Connecticut),
- Mikva (D–Illinois),
- Railsback (R–Illinois),
- Rodino (D–New Jersey),
- Rogers (D–Colorado),
- Ryan (D–New York),
- Sandman (R–New Jersey),
- Smith (R–New York), and
- St. Onge (D–Connecticut),
- Waldie (D–California).

George Herbert Walker Bush (then a Republican congressman from Texas), like many of his colleagues in Congress, supported all three of the prominent approaches to abolish the present Electoral College system. Bush spoke in favor of nationwide direct popular election (House Joint Resolution 681) on September 18, 1969, saying:

"Frankly I think this legislation has a great deal to commend it. It will correct the wrongs of the present mechanism because by calling for direct election of the President and Vice President it will eliminate the formality of the electoral college and by providing for a runoff in case no candidate receives 40 percent of the vote it eliminates the unrealistic ballot casting in the House of Representatives. Yet, in spite of these drastic reforms, the bill is not, when viewed in the light of current practice, one that will be detrimental to our federal system or one that will change the departmentalized and local nature of voting in this country.

"In electing the President and Vice President, the Constitution establishes the principle that votes are cast by States. This legislation does not tamper with that principle. It only changes the manner in which the States vote.

Instead of voting by intermediaries, the States will certify their popular vote count to the Congress. The states will maintain primary responsibility for the ballot and for the qualifications of voters. In other words, they will still designate the time, place, and manner in which elections will be held. Thus, there is a very good argument to be made that the basic nature of our federal system has not been disturbed.

"On the walls of the Jefferson Memorial are written these words that we might well consider today:

'I am not an advocate for frequent changes in laws and constitutions, but laws and constitutions must go hand in hand with the progress of the human mind as that becomes more developed, more enlightened, as new discoveries are made, new truths discovered, and manners and opinions change. With the change of circumstances institutions must advance also to keep pace with the times.'

"The world has changed a great deal since the 12th amendment was approved, and the system it perpetuates is one fraught with a history of fraud, leaves our country open to constitutional crisis, and is clearly unresponsive to the desires of the American people. I do support the proposal before us today because I believe it combines the best features of our current practice with the desirable goal of a simpler, more direct voting system."[30]

Senator Birch Bayh (D–Indiana) introduced Senate Joint Resolution 1 in the 91st Congress in 1969 (with substantially the same provisions as Representative Celler's House Joint Resolution 681). The sponsors of Senate Joint Resolution 1 included the following Senators:

- George D. Aiken (R–Vermont),
- Birch Bayh (D–Indiana),
- Henry Bellmon (R–Oklahoma),
- Alan Bible (D–Nevada),
- Quentin Burdick (D–North Dakota),
- Robert C. Byrd (D–West Virginia),
- Clifford P. Case (R–New Jersey),
- Frank Church (D–Idaho),
- Marlow Cook (R–Kentucky),
- Alan Cranston (D–California),
- Thomas F. Eagleton (D–Missouri),
- Charles E. Goodell (R–New York),
- Mike Gravel (D–Alaska),
- Fred R. Harris (D–Oklahoma),
- Vance Hartke (D–Indiana),
- Mark O. Hatfield (R–Oregon),
- Daniel K. Inouye (D–Hawaii),
- Henry M. Jackson (D–Washington),
- Jacob K. Javits (R–New York),
- Warren G. Magnuson (D–Washington),
- Mike Mansfield (D–Montana),

---

[30] *Congressional Record.* September 18, 1969. Pages 25,990–25,991.

- Charles McC. Mathias, Jr. (R–Maryland),
- George McGovern (D–South Dakota),
- Thomas J. McIntyre (D–New Hampshire),
- Lee Metcalf (D–Montana),
- Walter F. Mondale (D–Minnesota),
- Joseph M. Montoya (D–New Mexico),
- Edmund S. Muskie (D–Maine),
- Gaylord Nelson (D–Wisconsin),
- Robert W. Packwood (R–Oregon),
- John O. Pastore (D–Rhode Island),
- James B. Pearson (R–Kansas),
- Claiborne Pell (D–Rhode Island),
- William Proxmire (D–Wisconsin),
- Jennings Randolph (D–West Virginia),
- Abraham Ribicoff (D–Connecticut),
- Richard S. Schweiker (R–Pennsylvania),
- Joseph D. Tydings (D–Maryland),
- Harrison A. Williams, Jr. (D–New Jersey), and
- Stephen M. Young (D–Ohio).

After the 338–70 vote in the House of Representatives in favor of House Joint Resolution 681 in 1969, the House bill was filibustered and died in the Senate.

Throughout the 1970s, Senator Bayh repeatedly introduced constitutional amendments for nationwide popular election of the President. For example, the sponsors of Bayh's Senate Joint Resolution 1 in the 95th Congress in 1977 included the following Senators:

- Abourezk (R–South Dakota),
- Anderson (D–Minnesota),
- Baker (R–Tennessee),
- Bartlett (R–Oklahoma),
- Bayh (D–Indiana),
- Bellmon (R–Oklahoma),
- Brooke (R–Massachusetts),
- Chafee (R–Rhode Island),
- Church (D–Idaho),
- Clark (D–Iowa),
- Cranston (D–California),
- Danforth (R–Missouri),
- DeConcini (D–Arizona),
- Dole (R–Kansas),
- Ford (D–Kentucky),
- Garn (R–Utah),
- Glenn (D–Ohio),
- Gravel (D–Alaska),
- Hart (D–Michigan),
- Haskell (D–Colorado),
- Hatfield (R–Oregon),
- Hathaway (D–Maine),
- Huddleston (D–Kentucky),
- Humphrey (D–Minnesota),
- Inouye (D–Hawaii),
- Jackson (D–Washington),
- Javits (R–New York),
- Kennedy (D–Massachusetts),
- Leahy (D–Vermont),
- Magnuson (D–Washington),
- Mathias (R–Maryland),
- Matsunaga (D–Hawaii),
- McIntyre (D–New Hampshire),
- Metzenbaum (D–Ohio),
- Packwood (R–Oregon),
- Randolph (D–West Virginia),
- Ribicoff (D–Connecticut),
- Riegle (D–Michigan),

- Schweiker (R–Pennsylvania),
- Stafford (R–Vermont),
- Stevenson (D–Illinois),
- Williams (D–New Jersey), and
- Zorinsky (D–Nebraska).

The sponsors of Senate Joint Resolution 28[31] in the 96th Congress in 1979 included the following Senators:

- Baker (R–Tennessee),
- Bayh (D–Indiana),
- Bellmon (R–Oklahoma),
- Burdick (D–North Dakota),
- Chafee (R–Rhode Island),
- Cranston (D–California),
- Danforth (R–Missouri),
- DeConcini (D–Arizona),
- Dole (R–Kansas),
- Durenberger (R–Minnesota),
- Ford (D–Kentucky),
- Garn (R–Utah),
- Gravel (D–Alaska),
- Hatfield (R–Oregon),
- Huddleston (D–Kentucky),
- Inouye (D–Hawaii),
- Jackson (D–Washington),
- Javits (R–New York),
- Johnston (D–Louisiana),
- Kennedy (D–Massachusetts),
- Leahy (D–Vermont),
- Levin (D–Michigan),
- Magnuson (D–Washington),
- Mathias (R–Maryland),
- Matsunaga (D–Hawaii),
- Packwood (R–Oregon),
- Pell (D–Rhode Island),
- Proxmire (D–Wisconsin),
- Pryor (D–Arkansas),
- Randolph (D–West Virginia),
- Ribicoff (D–Connecticut),
- Riegle (D–Michigan),
- Stafford (R–Vermont),
- Stevenson (D–Illinois),
- Tsongas (D–Massachusetts),
- Williams (D–New Jersey), and
- Zorinsky (D–Nebraska).

Senator Robert E. Dole of Kansas, the Republican nominee for Vice President in 1976 and later Republican nominee for President in 1996, spoke in the Senate on January 14, 1979, on the subject of nationwide popular election of the President and Vice President, saying:

"That candidates for these two positions should be selected by direct election is an idea which I have long supported. . . .

"The electoral college system was provided for in the Constitution because, at one time, it seemed the most fair way to select the President and Vice President. Alexander Hamilton apparently expressed the prevailing view when he wrote that a small number of persons selected from the general population would most likely have the ability and intelligence to select the

---

[31] Senate Joint Resolution 28 of the 96th Congress in 1979 was substantially the same as Celler's House Joint Resolution 681 that the House of Representatives passed in 1969.

best persons for the job. I have no doubt but that in the 18th century, the electoral college was well suited for our country. However, already by the early 19th century, misgivings were being voiced about the college.

"The skepticism seems to be related to the formation of political party candidates and the difference they made in the selection of the President and Vice President. In the years since then, the electoral college has remained in use. It has served us fairly well—except for three times when it allowed a candidate to gain the Presidency who did not have the most popular votes.

"There have been numerous other elections in which a shift of a few thousand votes would have changed the outcome of the electoral college vote, despite the fact that the would-be winner came in second place in popular votes. Mr. President, I think we are leaving a little too much to chance, and to hope, that we will not witness yet another unrepresentative election."[32]

Senator Dole then specifically addressed the question of the effect of the bonus of two electoral votes that each state receives regardless of its population.

"Many persons have the impression that the electoral college benefits those persons living in small states. I feel that this is somewhat of a misconception. Through my experience with the Republican National Committee and as a Vice Presidential candidate in 1976, it became very clear that the populous states with their large blocks of electoral votes were the crucial states. It was in these states that we focused our efforts.

"Were we to switch to a system of direct election, I think we would see a resulting change in the nature of campaigning. While urban areas will still be important campaigning centers, there will be a new emphasis given to smaller states. **Candidates will soon realize that all votes are important, and votes from small states carry the same import as votes from large states. That to me is one of the major attractions of direct election. Each vote carries equal importance.**

"Direct election would give candidates incentive to campaign in States that are perceived to be single party states. For no longer will minority votes be lost. Their accumulated total will be important, and in some instances perhaps even decisive.

"The objections raised to direct election are varied. When they are analyzed, I think many objections reflect not so much satisfaction with the electoral college, but rather a reluctance to change an established political

---

[32] *Congressional Record.* January 14, 1979. Page 309.

system. While I could never advocate change simply for the sake of changing, neither should we defer action because we fear change.

"In this situation, I think the weaknesses in the current system have been demonstrated, and that the prudent move is to provide for direct election of the President and Vice President.

"I hope that the Senate will be able to move ahead on this resolution. As long as we continue with the electoral college system, we will be placing our trust in an institution which usually works according to design, but which sometimes does not. There are remedies available to us, and I trust the Senate will act to correct this weakness in our political system."[33] [Emphasis added]

In a 1979 Senate speech, Senator Henry Bellmon (R–Oklahoma) described how his views on the Electoral College had changed while he had served as Governor, Senator, national campaign director for Richard Nixon's presidential campaign, and a member of the American Bar Association's commission studying electoral reform.

"While the consideration of the electoral college began—and I am a little embarrassed to admit this—I was convinced, as are many residents of smaller States, that the present system is a considerable advantage to less populous States such as Oklahoma, and that it was to the advantage of the small States for the electoral college concept be preserved.

"I think if any Member of the State has that concept he would be greatly enlightened by the fact that the Members of the Senate from New York are now actively supporting the retention of the electoral college system. . . .

"Mr. President, as the deliberations of the American Bar Association Commission proceeded and as more facts became known, I came to the realization that the present electoral system does not give an advantage to the voters from the less populous States. Rather, it works to the disadvantage of small State voters who are largely ignored in the general election for President.

"It is true that the smaller States which are allowed an elector for each U.S. Senator and for each Congressman do, on the surface, appear to be favored; but, in fact, the system gives the advantage to the voters in the populous States. The reason is simple as I think our friends from New York understand: A small State voter is, in effect, the means whereby a Presidential candidate may receive a half-dozen or so electoral votes. On the other hand, a vote in a large State is the means to 20 or 30 or 40 or more electoral votes.

---

[33] *Congressional Record.* January 14, 1979. Page 309.

Therefore, Presidential candidates structure their campaigns to appeal to the States with large blocs of electors. This gives special and disproportionate importance to the special interest groups which may determine the electoral outcome in those few large States.

"Here, Mr. President, let me say parenthetically that during 1967 and part of 1968 I served as the national campaign director for Richard Nixon, and I know very well as we structured that campaign we did not worry about Alaska, about Wyoming, or about Nevada or about New Mexico or about Oklahoma or Kansas. We worried about New York, California, Pennsylvania, Texas, Michigan, Illinois, all of the populous States, where there are these big blocks of electors that we could appeal to, provided we chose our issues properly and provided we presented the candidates in an attractive way.

"The result, Mr. President, is that the executive branch of our National Government has grown and is continuing to become increasingly oriented toward populous States, to the disadvantage of the smaller, less populous areas. An examination of past campaign platforms and campaign schedules of the major party candidates will bear out this position. Therefore, it is obvious that any political party or any candidate for President or Vice President will spend his efforts primarily in the populous States. The parties draft their platforms with the view in mind of attracting the voters of the populous States and generally relegate the needs of the smaller States to secondary positions.

"This whole situation would change if we go for a direct election and, therefore, **make the voters of one State equally important with the voters of any other State.**"[34] [Emphasis added]

Senator Carl Levin (D–Michigan) spoke in the Senate on June 21, 1979, and said:

"Mr. President, the direct election of the President and the Vice President of the United States is an electoral reform which is long overdue. It is long overdue because of its basic fairness, democratic nature, and its inherent simplicity. There is no principle which is more basic to our concept of democracy than equal treatment under the law. And yet when this Nation goes to the polls every 4 years in the only truly national election that we have, that principle is abrogated. The effect of the electoral college system on our Presidential election is often drastically unequal treatment of individual voters and their votes. The discrepancies are real and widespread, and they defy our basic sense of fairness. . . .

---

[34] *Congressional Record.* July 10, 1979. Page 17748.

"Mr. President, we ask the wrong question when we ask who gains and who loses under the electoral college, and how will this group lose its advantage under direct election? The function of the President is to serve the interests of all persons, all citizens of this country, and, therefore, all citizens should have an equal say as to who the President will be. In the debate over who will gain and who will lose, there is only one real winner in implementing direct election, and that is the American people who will finally be able to participate in a democratic and fair national election where **each vote counts for as much as every other vote**.

"The American people will also win because we have eliminated the threat which the electoral college has always posed—that is the possibility that a candidate who has not won the popular vote will, through the mechanisms of the electoral college, be elevated to the Presidency."[35] [Emphasis added]

In a Senate speech on July 10, 1979, Senator Charles McC. Mathias, Jr. (R–Maryland) listed the faults of the existing system, including the "state-by-state winner-take-all" system and the possibility of electing the second-place candidate, saying:

"Direct election is the most effective method to remedy these faults. As the late Senator Hubert Humphrey noted, only direct election ensures that

'the votes of the American people wherever cast [are] counted directly and equally in determining who shall be President of the United States.'

"Only by direct election can the fundamental principle of equal treatment under the law for all Americans be incorporated into our Presidential selection process."[36] [Emphasis added]

After discussing the ever-present possibility that the presidential candidate receiving the most popular votes nationwide might not win the presidency, Senator David Durenberger (R–Minnesota) said:

"[T]he most damaging effect of the electoral system has already occurred, in **every** State and in **every** Presidential election. For with its 'winner take all' requirement, the electoral college effectively disenfranchises every man and woman supporting the candidate who fails to carry their State. Under that system, votes for the losing candidate have no significance whatsoever in the overall outcome of the election. And for this reason, candidates who either pull far ahead or fall far behind in a State have the incentive to 'write it off'—simply ignore it—in planning their campaign appearances. In

---

[35] *Congressional Record.* June 21, 1979. Page 15095.
[36] *Congressional Record.* July 10, 1979. Page 17751.

contrast, **the proposed amendment would grant every vote the same degree of significance in determining the final outcome**. Candidates would be forced to consider their margins in every State, and the tendency to ignore a 'safe' or 'lost' State would be sharply diminished. By restoring the significance of every vote, Senate Joint Resolution 28 increases the incentive to vote, which in itself is a significant argument for passage."

"Had the Founding Fathers adopted a direct election system, it is inconceivable that anyone would be rising after 200 years to propose replacing that system with the electoral college."[33] [Emphasis added]

Appendix W contains the March 14, 1979, speech of Senator Birch Bayh on his proposed constitutional amendment.

On July 20, 1979, 51 senators voted in favor of Senate Joint Resolution 28 (with one additional senator being announced in favor).

Since 1979, numerous other proposed federal constitutional amendments for nationwide popular election of the President have been introduced. Ross Perot's candidacy in 1992 rekindled interest in reforming the method of electing the President.

In 1992, Senator J. James Exon of Nebraska introduced a proposed federal constitutional amendment. The sponsors included the following Senators:

- Adams (D–Washington),
- Boren (D–Oklahoma),
- Burdick (D–North Dakota),
- Coats (R–Indiana),
- D'Amato (R–New York),
- Dixon (D–Illinois),
- Durenberger (R–Minnesota),
- Exon (D–Nebraska),
- Glenn (D–Ohio),
- Hollings (D–South Carolina),
- Kennedy (D–Massachusetts),
- Lieberman (D–Connecticut),
- Murkowski (R–Alaska), and
- Reid (D–Nevada).

The Exon proposal (Senate Joint Resolution 302) reads as follows:

"Resolved by the Senate and House of Representatives of the United States of America in Congress assembled,

"That the following article is proposed as an amendment to the Constitution of the United States, which shall be valid to all intents and purposes as part of the Constitution when ratified by the legislatures of three-fourths of the several States within seven years from the date of its submission by the Congress:

'Article—
'SECTION 1. The people of the several States and the District constituting the seat of government of the United States shall elect the President

---

[37] *Congressional Record.* July 10, 1979. Pages 17706–17707.

and Vice President. Each elector shall cast a single vote for two persons who shall have consented to the joining of their names as candidates for the offices of President and Vice President.

'SECTION 2. The electors of President and Vice President in each State shall have the qualifications requisite for electors of the most numerous branch of the State legislature, except that for the electors of President and Vice President, any State may prescribe by law less restrictive residence qualifications and for electors of President and Vice President the Congress may by law establish uniform residence qualification.

'SECTION 3. The persons joined as candidates for President and Vice President having the greatest number of votes shall be elected President and Vice President, if such number be at least 50 per centum of the whole number of votes cast and such number be derived from a majority of the number of votes cast in each State comprising at least one-third of the several States. If, after any such election, none of the persons joined as candidates for President and Vice President is elected pursuant to the preceding paragraph, a runoff election shall be held within sixty days in which the choice of President and Vice President shall be made from the two pairs of persons joined as candidates for President and Vice President receiving the greatest number of votes in such runoff election shall be elected President and Vice President.

'SECTION 4. The times, places, and manner of holding such elections and entitlement to inclusion on the ballot shall be prescribed by law in each State; but the Congress may by law make or alter such regulations. The days for such elections shall be determined by Congress and shall be uniform throughout the United States. The Congress shall prescribe by law the times, places, and manner in which the results of such elections shall be ascertained and declared. No such election, other than a runoff election, shall be held later than the first Tuesday after the first Monday in November, and the results thereof shall be declared no later than thirty days after the date on which the election occurs.

'SECTION 5. The Congress may by law provide for the case of the death, inability, or withdrawal of any candidate for President or Vice President before a President and Vice President have been elected, and for the case of the death of either the President-elect or the Vice President-elect.

'SECTION 6. Sections 1 through 4 of this article shall take effect two years after ratification of this article.

'SECTION 7. The Congress shall have power to enforce this article by appropriate legislation.'"

In 2005, Representatives Jesse Jackson Jr. (D–Illinois) and Barney Frank (D–Massachusetts) introduced a federal constitutional amendment for nationwide popular election of the President (House Joint Resolution 36). Like the Exon proposal of 1992, this proposal would have required that a candidate receive "a majority of the votes cast" in order to be elected.

In addition, Senator Dianne Feinstein (D–California) introduced Senate Joint Resolution 11 in March 2005 as follows:

> *"Resolved by the Senate and House of Representatives of the United States of America in Congress assembled (two-thirds of each House concurring therein),*
>
> That the following article is proposed as an amendment to the Constitution of the United States, which shall be valid to all intents and purposes as part of the Constitution when ratified by the legislatures of three-fourths of the several States within seven years after the date of its submission to the States for ratification:
>
> 'Article—
>
> 'SECTION 1. The President and Vice President shall be elected by the people of the several States and the district constituting the seat of government of the United States. The persons having the greatest number of votes for President and Vice President shall be elected.
>
> 'SECTION 2. The voters in each State shall have the qualifications requisite for electors of Representatives in Congress from that State, except that the legislature of any State may prescribe less restrictive qualifications with respect to residence and Congress may establish uniform residence and age qualifications. Congress may establish qualifications for voters in the district constituting the seat of government of the United States.
>
> 'SECTION 3. Congress may determine the time, place, and manner of holding the election, and the entitlement to inclusion on the ballot. Congress shall prescribe by law the time, place, and manner in which the results of the election shall be ascertained and declared.
>
> 'SECTION 4. Each voter shall cast a single vote jointly applicable to President and Vice President in any such election. Names of candidates shall not be joined unless both candidates have consented thereto, and no candidate shall consent to being joined with more than one other person.
>
> 'SECTION 5. Congress may by law provide for the case of the death of any candidate for President or Vice President before the day on which

the President-elect or the Vice President-elect has been chosen, and for the case of a tie in any such election.

'SECTION 6. This article shall take effect one year after the twenty-first day of January following ratification.'"

The Exon proposal of 1992 provided that a run-off election would be held if no presidential slate were to receive at least 50% of the popular vote. In contrast, the constitutional amendment introduced by Senator Feinstein in 2005 (Senate Joint Resolution 11) required only a plurality of the popular votes.

"The persons having the greatest number of votes for President and Vice President shall be elected."

The 2005 Feinstein proposal also differed from the 1992 Exon proposal in that the Feinstein proposal provided that

"Congress may determine the time, place, and manner of holding the election, and the entitlement to inclusion on the ballot . . ."

The Exon proposal provided that

"The times, places, and manner of holding such elections and entitlement to inclusion on the ballot shall be prescribed by law in each State; but the Congress may by law make or alter such regulations."

In 2009, proposed constitutional amendments for direct election of the President were introduced by Senator Bill Nelson of Florida (Senate Joint Resolution 4), Representative Jesse Jackson, Jr. of Illinois (House Joint Resolution 36), and Representative Gene Green (House Joint Resolution 9).

Appendix S shows, state by state, members of Congress who have sponsored proposed constitutional amendments for nationwide popular election of the President in recent years or who voted in favor of constitutional amendments in the 1969 roll call in the House of Representatives or the 1979 roll call in the Senate. As shown in appendix S, there has been at least one supporter in Congress from each of the 50 states.

In summary, in terms of the three criteria mentioned at the beginning of this chapter, nationwide popular voting for President

- *would* accurately reflect the nationwide popular vote;
- *would* improve upon the current situation in which two-thirds of the states and two-thirds of the people of the United States are ignored by presidential campaigns; and
- *would* make every vote equal.

4 | Two Previously Proposed Approaches for State-Level Action

Chapter 3 analyzed the three most prominent proposals for federal constitutional amendments for changing the current system of electing the President.

This chapter analyzes the two most prominent previously proposed approaches to presidential election reform that can be enacted at the state level (i.e., without a federal constitutional amendment and without action by Congress).

Later, chapter 6 will discuss another approach not requiring a federal constitutional amendment, namely the National Popular Vote interstate compact.

The office of presidential elector is established by the Constitution (as discussed in section 2.1) and therefore cannot be changed or eliminated without a federal constitutional amendment. However, the manner of choosing presidential electors is determined on a state-by-state basis by means of state legislation. Section 1 of Article II of the Constitution says:

> "Each State shall appoint, in such Manner **as the Legislature thereof may direct**, a Number of Electors. . . ."[1] [Emphasis added]

As the U.S. Supreme Court stated in *McPherson v. Blacker* in 1892:

> "In short, the appointment and mode of appointment of electors belong **exclusively** to the states under the constitution of the United States."[2] [Emphasis added]

Neither of the two most prominent approaches that can be enacted at the state level abolishes the Electoral College or the office of presidential elector. Both approaches involve appointing presidential electors in a manner that is different from the statewide winner-take-all system (i.e., awarding all of a state's electoral votes to the presidential candidate who receives the most popular votes in each separate state).

These two approaches are the:

- **Whole-Number Proportional Approach,** in which a state's electoral votes are divided proportionally—*rounded off to the nearest whole number*—

---

[1] U.S. Constitution. Article II, section 1, clause 2.
[2] *McPherson v. Blacker.* 146 U.S. 1 at 35. 1892.

according to the percentage of votes received by each presidential slate in the state (section 4.1); and

- **Congressional-District Approach,** in which one presidential elector is elected from each congressional district and two presidential electors are elected statewide (section 4.2).

4.1 WHOLE-NUMBER PROPORTIONAL APPROACH

The whole-number proportional approach was considered by Colorado voters in the November 2, 2004, election. The proposition, called Amendment 36, was placed on the ballot by initiative petition. It was defeated by the voters.

The *whole-number* proportional approach is distinctly different from the *fractional* proportional approach proposed by Senator Cannon (discussed in section 3.2). The two approaches differ in that the whole-number proportional approach (discussed in this chapter) divides a state's electoral votes *to the nearest whole number*, whereas Senator Cannon's fractional proportional approach carries out the division of a state's electoral votes *to three decimal places*. Although this difference may initially appear to be a minor detail, the whole-number proportional approach would operate, as will be seen below, in an unexpected and counter-intuitive way in a nation in which the average number of electoral votes per state is 11 and the median number of electoral votes per state is 7.

The voting in Colorado in the 2004 presidential election can be used to illustrate the difference between the two approaches. George W. Bush received 1,068,233 popular votes (52.6508712%), and John Kerry received 960,666 popular votes (47.3606128%) in Colorado (which has nine electoral votes).

Under Senator Cannon's proposed fractional proportional approach (section 3.2), Bush would have received 4.739 electoral votes, and Kerry would have received 4.261 electoral votes. These fractional numbers from Colorado would be added together with fractional numbers from all the other states (and the District of Columbia) in order to yield a nationwide grand total. Candidates could receive fractional numbers of electoral votes from each state because Cannon's fractional proportional approach was to be implemented by a federal constitutional amendment that would have abolished the office of presidential elector. Fractions (carried out to three decimal places) would be possible because the human presidential electors (each casting one *indivisible* vote) would have been eliminated by Cannon's constitutional amendment.

As discussed in section 3.2, Senator Cannon's proposed federal constitutional amendment implementing the fractional proportional approach would definitely improve upon the current situation in which four-fifths of the states and four-fifths of the people of the United States are ignored by presidential campaigns. A presidential candidate could, for example, earn an additional 0.001 electoral vote by winning a hundred or so additional popular votes in any state. Thus, no state would be written off, or taken for granted, by any presidential candidate. Every voter in every state would, for all practical purposes, be politically relevant.

In contrast, the whole-number proportional approach (i.e., Colorado's Amendment 36) was a *state* constitutional amendment—not a *federal* constitutional amendment. A state may not abolish the office of presidential elector—it may simply change the method by which it allocates its own electoral votes within the Electoral College. Any approach adopted unilaterally in Colorado must necessarily award 0, 1, 2, 3, 4, 5, 6, 7, 8, or 9 presidential electors to one candidate or the other. Only whole numbers—not fractions carried out to several decimal places—are allowed because, absent a *federal* constitutional amendment, Colorado must still choose nine human presidential electors, each casting one *indivisible* vote in the Electoral College.

Based on the fact that George W. Bush received 52.6508712% of the popular vote in the November 2004 voting in Colorado, Bush would have received five of Colorado's nine electoral votes, and John Kerry would have received four under the whole-number proportional approach. In other words, the whole-number proportional approach would have produced a 5–4 division of Colorado's electoral votes, compared to the 9–0 division produced by Colorado's current statewide winner-take-all rule.

The problem with the whole-number proportional approach stems from the fact that there are only 538 electoral votes in the Electoral College (i.e., one for each U.S. Representative and Senator). The average number of electoral votes per state is, therefore, only about 11. Moreover, about three-quarters (36) of the states have a below-average number of electoral votes, and the median number of electoral votes per state is only 7.

The important difference between *whole numbers* and *fractions carried out to three decimal places* arises because the number of electoral votes possessed by a typical state is so small. For example, in an average-sized state with 11 electoral votes, one electoral vote corresponds to a 9.09% share of the state's popular vote under the whole-number proportional approach. In Colorado (a state that is slightly below the average of 11 electoral votes), one electoral vote corresponds to an 11.11% share of the popular vote. In a median-sized state, one electoral vote corresponds to a 14.29% share of the popular vote. In states with only three electoral votes, one electoral vote corresponds to a 33.3% share of the popular vote.

In a typical close presidential election, the campaign shifts only a small percentage of the popular vote in each state. As noted in chapter 1, almost all campaigning in presidential elections typically occurs in states that are divided within the tight range of 46%–54%. In fact, the bulk of campaign activity occurs in states that are even closer than that.

As a matter of practical politics, only one electoral vote would be in play in almost all the states under the whole-number proportional approach. That is, the whole-number proportional approach would be a "winner-take-*one*" system in almost every state.[3] For example, in Colorado, where one electoral vote represents an 11% share of the popular vote, the only likely outcomes would be a 5–4 split or a 4–5 split.

A system that requires a 33% share, a 14% share, an 11% share, or even a 9% share of the popular vote in order to win one electoral vote is fundamentally out of sync with the small-percentage vote shifts that are involved in real-world presidential campaigns.

More importantly, in the vast majority of states, there would be no realistic possibility of shifting 33%, 14%, 11% or even 9% of the popular vote during the presidential campaign, and, hence, those states would be ignored.

Thus, although the whole-number proportional approach might initially seem to offer the possibility of making every voter in every state relevant, it would not do this in practice.

As will be shown in the detailed analysis below, if the whole-number proportional approach were adopted nationwide,

- it would *not* accurately reflect the nationwide popular vote;
- it would *not* improve upon the current situation in which four-fifths of the states and four-fifths of the people of the United States are ignored by presidential campaigns, but, instead, would create a very small set of states in which only one electoral vote is in play (while making most states politically irrelevant); and
- it would *not* make every vote equal.

In a landslide election, almost any of the commonly discussed electoral systems will result in the election of the candidate who receives the most popular votes nationwide. Thus, the test of the accuracy of an electoral system is how it works in a close election. Thus, we start our analysis of the fractional proportional approach with data from the very closest recent presidential election, namely the 2000 election.

Column 2 of table 4.1 shows the number of electoral votes (EV) possessed by each of the 50 states and the District of Columbia in the 2000 presidential election. The table is sorted in order of the number of electoral votes that each state possessed in the 2000 election, with the smallest states listed first. Columns 3 and 4 show the percentage of the two-party popular vote received by Al Gore and George W. Bush, respectively. Columns 5 and 6 show the number of electoral votes[4] received respectively by Al Gore and George W. Bush under the existing statewide winner-take-all system.[5]

---

[3] Under the whole-number proportional approach, New York, Florida, and Texas might be "winner-take-two" states, and California might be a "winner-take-three" state.

[4] Electoral votes are reapportioned among the states as a result of the federal census conducted every 10 years. See table 2.1.

[5] Maine and Nebraska use the congressional-district approach for allocating their electoral votes. However, since the adoption of this system (in 1969 in Maine and in 1992 in Nebraska), the candidate carrying the state has, with one exception, also carried all the districts. The only exception occurred in 2008 when Barack Obama carried Nebraska's 2nd congressional district.

Table 4.1 RESULTS OF 2000 PRESIDENTIAL ELECTION

STATE	EV	GORE	BUSH VOTE	GORE EV	BUSH EV
Alaska	3	32%	68%		3
Delaware	3	57%	43%	3	
District of Columbia	3	90%	10%	3	
Montana	3	36%	64%		3
North Dakota	3	35%	65%		3
South Dakota	3	38%	62%		3
Vermont	3	55%	45%	3	
Wyoming	3	29%	71%		3
Hawaii	4	60%	40%	4	
Idaho	4	29%	71%		4
Maine	4	53%	47%	4	
Nevada	4	48%	52%		4
New Hampshire	4	49%	51%		4
Rhode Island	4	66%	34%	4	
Nebraska	5	35%	65%		5
New Mexico	5	50%	50%	5	
Utah	5	28%	72%		5
West Virginia	5	47%	53%		5
Arkansas	6	47%	53%		6
Kansas	6	39%	61%		6
Iowa	7	50%	50%	7	
Mississippi	7	41%	59%		7
Oregon	7	50%	50%	7	
Arizona	8	47%	53%		8
Colorado	8	46%	54%		8
Connecticut	8	59%	41%	8	
Kentucky	8	42%	58%		8
Oklahoma	8	39%	61%		8
South Carolina	8	42%	58%		8
Alabama	9	42%	58%		9
Louisiana	9	46%	54%		9
Maryland	10	58%	42%	10	
Minnesota	10	51%	49%	10	
Missouri	11	48%	52%		11
Tennessee	11	48%	52%		11
Washington	11	53%	47%	11	
Wisconsin	11	50%	50%	11	
Indiana	12	42%	58%		12
Massachusetts	12	65%	35%	12	
Georgia	13	44%	56%		13
Virginia	13	46%	54%		13
North Carolina	14	44%	56%		14
New Jersey	15	58%	42%	15	
Michigan	18	53%	47%	18	
Ohio	21	48%	52%		21
Illinois	22	56%	44%	22	
Pennsylvania	23	52%	48%	23	
Florida	25	50%	50%		25
Texas	32	39%	61%		32
New York	33	63%	37%	33	
California	54	56%	44%	54	
Total	**538**			**267**	**271**

4.1.1 JURISDICTIONS WITH THREE ELECTORAL VOTES

There were eight jurisdictions with three electoral votes in the 2000 presidential election—Alaska, Delaware, the District of Columbia, Montana, North Dakota, South Dakota, Vermont, and Wyoming (as shown in the top eight rows of table 4.1).[6]

Under the whole-number proportional approach, one electoral vote corresponds to a 33.3% share of the state's popular vote for the states with three electoral votes.

To implement the whole-number proportional approach, the number of popular votes that each presidential slate received statewide is divided by the total number of votes cast statewide in order to obtain that slate's percentage of the statewide popular vote. This percentage is then multiplied by the state's number of electoral votes. The number of electoral votes received by each presidential slate is then rounded off to the nearest whole number.

There are only four possibilities in states with three electoral votes under the whole-number proportional approach:[7]

- If a presidential slate receives less than 16.67% of the popular vote (that is, less than one half of the 33.3% share necessary to win one electoral vote), then it gets no electoral votes.
- If a presidential slate receives between 16.67% and 50.00% of the popular vote, then it gets one electoral vote.
- If a presidential slate receives between 50.01% and 83.33% of the popular vote, then it gets two electoral votes.
- Finally, at the high end of the scale, if a presidential slate receives more than 83.33% of the popular vote, then it gets all three of the state's electoral votes.

Table 4.2 summarizes the number of electoral votes (from zero to three) that a presidential slate receives for various ranges of percentages of the popular vote in the states with three electoral votes. Column 3 shows the *breakpoints* (i.e., 16.67%, 50.00%, and 83.33%) in the ranges of percentages of popular votes. These breakpoints are the spots, along the percentage scale from 0% to 100%, where the number of electoral votes changes. The breakpoints are the critical numbers that would dictate campaign strategy under the whole-number proportional approach.

Figure 4.1 graphically presents the breakpoints (at 16.67%, 50.0%, and 83.33%) for states with three electoral votes. The horizontal line in the figure represents a presidential candidate's percentage share of the popular vote—from 0% to 100%. The vertical tick marks show the breakpoints (16.67%, 50.0%, and 83.33%) for states with three electoral votes. The small numbers (0, 1, 2, or 3) immediately under the horizontal

---

[6] Electoral votes are reapportioned among the states as a result of the federal census conducted every 10 years. See table 2.1. As it happens, the 2010 census did not change the number of electoral votes for any of the eight jurisdictions with three electoral votes.

[7] Under the terms of Amendment 36 in Colorado in 2004, if there are more than two presidential slates on the ballot in a state with three electoral votes and no minor-party slate receives at least 16.66% of the popular vote in the state, it may be necessary to repeat the calculation without the minor parties in order to allocate all of the state's electoral votes.

Table 4.2 **TABLE OF BREAKPOINTS FOR STATES WITH THREE ELECTORAL VOTES**

PERCENT OF POPULAR VOTE	NUMBER OF ELECTORAL VOTES	BREAKPOINT
0.00% to 16.66%	0	16.67%
16.67% to 50.00%	1	50.00%
50.01% to 83.33%	2	83.33%
83.33% to 100.00%	3	NA

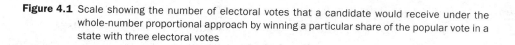

Figure 4.1 Scale showing the number of electoral votes that a candidate would receive under the whole-number proportional approach by winning a particular share of the popular vote in a state with three electoral votes

line show the number of electoral votes that a candidate would receive by winning a particular share of the popular vote. For example, a candidate receiving 58% of the popular vote would get two electoral votes under the whole-number proportional approach in a state with three electoral votes.

Table 4.3 shows the consequences of the whole-number proportional approach in the eight jurisdictions with three electoral votes in the 2000 presidential election. In this table and other tables in this chapter, "WTA" refers to "winner-take-all;" "WNP" refers to "whole-number proportional;" and "EV" refers to "electoral votes."

Table 4.3 **2000 ELECTION UNDER THE WINNER-TAKE-ALL (WTA) AND WHOLE-NUMBER PROPORTIONAL APPROACH (WNP) IN JURISDICTIONS WITH THREE ELECTORAL VOTES**

STATE	GORE VOTE	GORE EV UNDER WTA	BUSH EV UNDER WTA	GORE EV UNDER WNP	BUSH EV UNDER WNP	BREAKPOINT JUST BELOW GORE VOTE	BREAKPOINT JUST ABOVE GORE VOTE	CHANGE NEEDED TO GAIN OR LOSE 1 EV UNDER WNP
AK	32.06%	0	3	1	2	16.67%	50.00%	−15.39%
DE	56.74%	3	0	2	1	50.00%	83.33%	−6.74%
DC	90.49%	3	0	3	0	83.33%	100.00%	−7.16%
MT	36.34%	0	3	1	2	16.67%	50.00%	+13.66%
ND	35.27%	0	3	1	2	16.67%	50.00%	+14.18%
SD	38.39%	0	3	1	2	16.67%	50.00%	+11.61%
VT	55.44%	3	0	2	1	50.00%	83.33%	−5.44%
WY	29.02%	0	3	1	2	16.67%	50.00%	−12.35%
Total		**9**	**15**	**12**	**12**			

Column 2 of table 4.3 shows Al Gore's percentage share of the two-party presidential vote for the 2000 presidential election for the eight jurisdictions with three electoral votes.

Columns 3 and 4 present the respective number of electoral votes that Al Gore and George W. Bush received under the existing winner-take-all system in the 2000 presidential election.

Columns 5 and 6 show the respective number of electoral votes that Gore and Bush would have received if the whole-number proportional approach had been in effect for the 2000 presidential election.

Column 7 of table 4.3 shows the breakpoint (taken from table 4.2) that is just below the percentage that Gore actually received in the 2000 presidential election.

Column 8 shows the breakpoint that is just above the percentage that Gore actually received in the 2000 presidential election.

Column 9 of table 4.3 shows the percentage change in popular votes that Gore would have needed to change his electoral vote count in the state. That is, column 9 shows the difference between the percentage of the vote that Gore actually received (column 2) and the *nearer* of the two breakpoints in columns 7 and 8.

The percentage in column 9 is the most important number in understanding how the whole-number proportional approach would work in practice in a particular state. It shows whether it is likely for a candidate to gain or lose one electoral vote in the state. Unless this percentage is small, it would be very difficult for a candidate to gain or lose one electoral vote in that state in a non-landslide election. In other words, unless the percentage in column 9 is small, candidates will simply write off the state (just as they now write off the vast majority of states under the state-by-state winner-take-all system). Candidates simply do not spend their time, effort, and money in states where they have nothing to lose, and nothing to gain.

In column 9 of table 4.3, an entry with a positive sign, such as +11.61% for South Dakota, means that if Gore had received an additional 11.61% share of the popular vote (i.e., 11.61% added to the 38.39% share of the popular vote that he actually received in South Dakota), he would have gained one electoral vote under the whole-number proportional approach. The reason why Gore would have gained one electoral vote is that he would have risen above the breakpoint of 50.00%—the breakpoint between one and two electoral votes in a state with three electoral votes. Gore would have received one fewer electoral vote (i.e., no electoral votes) in South Dakota under the whole-number proportional approach if his share of the popular vote had dropped below 16.67% (the breakpoint between one and zero electoral votes). This would occur by losing a 21.72% share of the popular vote (i.e., 21.72% subtracted from the 38.39%). Column 9 contains an entry of "+11.61%" because the breakpoint at 50.00% is closer to Gore's actual popular vote (38.39%) than the breakpoint at 16.67%.

Figure 4.2 presents, along a horizontal line, Gore's percentage share (38.39%) of the two-party popular vote in South Dakota in the 2000 presidential election. As in

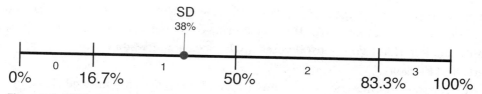

Figure 4.2 2000 presidential vote in South Dakota (with the Democrat receiving 38% of the popular vote)

figure 4.1, the figure contains tick marks along the horizontal line representing the breakpoints of 16.67%, 50.00%, and 83.33% applicable to states with three electoral votes under the whole-number proportional approach. The small numbers (0, 1, 2, or 3) immediately under the horizontal line show the number of electoral votes that a candidate would receive under the whole-number proportional approach by winning a particular share of the popular vote. The figure shows that Gore's vote share in South Dakota was not close to the 16.67% or 50.00% breakpoints.

Because Gore's vote share was so distant from these breakpoints, it is unlikely that a Democratic presidential candidate could gain or lose even a single electoral vote in South Dakota under the whole-number proportional approach in a non-landslide election. In terms of practical politics, figure 4.2 shows that South Dakota would be ignored by both the Democrats and Republicans because there would be no realistic possibility that either party could gain or lose an electoral vote under the whole-number proportional approach in that state. In short, South Dakota would be ignored by both political parties under the whole-number proportional approach for the same reason that it is ignored under the current winner-take-all approach, namely, neither party would have anything to gain or lose by paying attention to South Dakota.

An entry with a negative sign in column 9 of table 4.3, such as −7.16% for the District of Columbia, means that if Gore's share of the popular votes had been 7.16% less than he actually received in the District of Columbia (that is, 7.16% subtracted from the 90.49%), he would have lost one electoral vote under the whole-number proportional approach. The reason why Gore would have lost one electoral vote is that he would have fallen below the breakpoint of 83.33%—the boundary between two and three electoral votes in the District of Columbia.

Table 4.3 shows the division of electoral votes for the eight jurisdictions with three electoral votes in the 2000 presidential election. The Gore–Bush division was 9–15 under the existing statewide winner-take-all system (columns 3 and 4) and would be 12–12 under the whole-number proportional approach (columns 5 and 6).

Overall, table 4.3 shows that the effect of the whole-number proportional approach for awarding electoral votes in the states with three electoral votes is generally to convert the existing statewide winner-take-all system (yielding either three or zero electoral votes to each presidential slate) into a "winner-take-one" system. Indeed, the discussion below will establish, for states of all sizes, that the whole-number proportional approach is, as a practical matter, a "statewide winner-take-one" system (except that two or three electoral votes might occasionally be in play in California and that two electoral votes might occasionally be in play in Texas, New York, and Florida).

Under the existing statewide winner-take-all system, Gore carried three of the eight jurisdictions with three electoral votes and, therefore, received nine of the 24 available electoral votes (column 3 of table 4.3). George W. Bush carried five of the eight jurisdictions and, therefore, received 15 of the 24 (column 4). Under the whole-number proportional approach, the 24 electoral votes available in these eight jurisdictions would have divided 12–12 (columns 5 and 6).

None of the eight jurisdictions with three electoral votes is politically competitive under the existing statewide winner-take-all system. Accordingly, none received any significant attention from any presidential campaign in 2000.

Under the whole-number proportional approach, *all eight jurisdictions would remain politically irrelevant.* The reason that they would remain uncompetitive can be seen from the percentages in column 9 of table 4.3, namely –15.39%, –6.74%, –7.16%, +13.66%, +14.18%, +11.61%, –5.44%, and –12.35%. These percentages (averaging 10.8%) are so large that it is unlikely that a presidential slate could gain or lose even a single electoral vote in a non-landslide election in any of these eight jurisdictions under the whole-number proportional approach.

Figure 4.3 summarizes the information in table 4.3. The figure presents, along a horizontal line, Gore's percentage share of the two-party popular vote in the 2000 presidential election for the eight jurisdictions with three electoral votes (obtained from column 2 of table 4.3). As in figure 4.1, the figure contains tick marks along the horizontal line at 16.67%, 50.00%, and 83.33%, representing the breakpoints applicable to jurisdictions with three electoral votes under the whole-number proportional approach. The small numbers (0, 1, 2, or 3) immediately under the horizontal line show the number of electoral votes that a candidate would receive under the whole-number proportional approach by winning a particular share of the popular vote. Figure 4.3 shows graphically that Gore's share of the vote was not close to 50.00% in any of the eight jurisdictions. Thus, none of the eight is competitive under the existing statewide winner-take-all system. The figure also shows that Gore's vote share was not close to any of the three breakpoints (16.67%, 50.00%, and 83.33%).

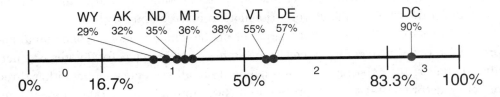

Figure 4.3 2000 presidential vote in jurisdictions with three electoral votes

4.1.2 STATES WITH FOUR ELECTORAL VOTES

There were six states with four electoral votes in the 2000 presidential election—Hawaii, Idaho, Maine, Nevada, New Hampshire, and Rhode Island.[8]

For the states with four electoral votes, one electoral vote corresponds to a 25.0% share of the state's popular vote under the whole-number proportional approach.

Table 4.4 shows the number of electoral votes that a presidential slate would receive for various ranges of percentages of the popular vote in the states with four electoral votes. Column 3 shows the breakpoints that are applicable to states with four electoral votes.

Table 4.6 is constructed in the same manner as table 4.2. The general rule for constructing this table (and table 4.2 and the other similar tables in the section) is that if x is the number of electoral votes,

- $\frac{1}{2x}$ is the breakpoint between 0 and 1 electoral vote (0.1250 when x is 4);

- $\frac{1}{2x} + \frac{1}{x}$ is the breakpoint between 1 and 2 electoral votes (0.3750 when x is 4);

- $\frac{1}{2x} + \frac{2}{x}$ is the breakpoint between 2 and 3 electoral votes (0.6250 when x is 4);

  and

- $\frac{1}{2x} + \frac{3}{x}$ is the breakpoint between 3 and 4 electoral votes (0.8750 when x is 4).

Thus, the breakpoints are 12.50%, 37.50%, 62.50%, and 87.50% for states with four electoral votes.

Table 4.4 TABLE OF BREAKPOINTS FOR STATES WITH FOUR ELECTORAL VOTES

PERCENT OF POPULAR VOTE	NUMBER OF ELECTORAL VOTES	BREAKPOINT
0.00% to 12.50%	0	12.50%
12.51% to 37.50%	1	37.50%
37.51 to 62.50%	2	62.50%
62.51% to 87.50%	3	87.50%
87.51% to 100.00%	4	NA

In table 4.4, there is no breakpoint at 50.00% for the states with four electoral votes under the whole-number proportional approach. In fact, this observation is true for every state with an even number of electoral votes under the whole-number proportional approach. Thus, it no longer would matter which presidential slate carries

---

[8] All of these states, except Nevada, continued to have four electoral votes in the 2004 and 2008 elections and will continue to have four electoral votes in the 2012, 2016, and 2020 elections. Nevada had five electoral votes in the 2004 and 2008 elections and will have six electoral votes in the 2012, 2016, and 2020 elections.

a state with an even number of electoral votes under the whole-number proportional approach. The winner of the state would get no particular reward for carrying a state. This characteristic contrasts with the situation in the states with an odd number of electoral votes (where carrying the state would still matter). In other words, the whole-number proportional approach operates in a manner that is politically different in states with an even number of electoral votes from the manner it does in states with an odd number of electoral votes.

Table 4.5 is constructed in the same manner of table 4.3 and shows the consequences of the whole-number proportional approach in the six states with four electoral votes in the 2000 presidential election.

Table 4.5 shows the division of electoral votes between Gore and Bush for the six states with four electoral votes in the 2000 presidential election. The division was 12–12 under the existing statewide winner-take-all system (columns 4 and 5) and would remain at 12–12 under the whole-number proportional approach (columns 6 and 7).

Table 4.5 2000 ELECTION UNDER THE WINNER-TAKE-ALL (WTA) AND WHOLE-NUMBER PROPORTIONAL APPROACH (WNP) IN STATES WITH FOUR ELECTORAL VOTES

STATE	GORE VOTE	GORE EV UNDER WTA	BUSH EV UNDER WTA	GORE EV UNDER WNP	BUSH EV UNDER WNP	BREAKPOINT JUST BELOW GORE VOTE	BREAKPOINT JUST ABOVE GORE VOTE	CHANGE NEEDED TO GAIN OR LOSE 1 EV UNDER WNP
HI	59.83%	4	0	2	2	37.50%	62.50%	+2.67%
ID	29.15%	0	4	1	3	12.50%	37.50%	+8.35%
ME	52.75%	4	0	2	2	37.50%	62.50%	+9.75%
NV	48.14%	0	4	2	2	37.50%	62.50%	−10.64%
NH	49.33%	0	4	2	2	37.50%	62.50%	−11.83%
RI	65.65%	4	0	3	1	62.50%	87.50%	−3.15%
Total		**12**	**12**	**12**	**12**			

Despite not affecting the overall 12–12 allocation of electoral votes between the presidential candidates, the whole-number proportional approach would have a dramatic effect on four of the states of this group in terms of their competitiveness. As explained below, the whole-number proportional approach would convert three battleground states into noncompetitive spectator states and convert one spectator state into a competitive state.

Figure 4.4 presents, along a horizontal line, Gore's percentage share of the popular vote in the 2000 presidential election for the six states with four electoral votes (from column 2 of table 4.5). The figure contains tick marks along the horizontal line at 12.50%, 37.50%, 62.50%, and 87.50%, representing the breakpoints (from table 4.4) that are applicable to states with four electoral votes under the whole-number proportional approach. The small numbers between zero and four immediately under the horizontal line show the number of electoral votes that a candidate would receive under the whole-number proportional approach by winning a particular share of the popular vote.

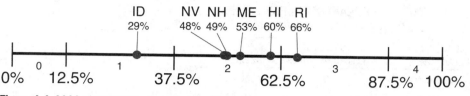

Figure 4.4 2000 presidential vote in states with four electoral votes

New Hampshire (where Gore received 49.33% of the popular vote) and Nevada (where Gore received 48.14%) were competitive under the existing winner-take-all system in 2000. However, both New Hampshire and Nevada would become noncompetitive under the whole-number proportional approach because a candidate gets two electoral votes for receiving anywhere between 37.50% and 62.50% of the popular vote in states with four electoral votes. There is no breakpoint at 50% for states with four electoral votes. The Democratic vote shares in New Hampshire and Nevada (49.33% and 48.14%, respectively) were almost in the middle of the band between 37.50% and 62.50%. Thus, in anything other than a landslide election, both the Democrats and Republicans would be virtually certain to win two electoral votes each in New Hampshire and Nevada. In New Hampshire, for example, it would take a downswing of 11.83% in the share of the Democratic vote (from 49.33%) for the Democratic candidate to lose one electoral vote. It would take an upswing of 13.19% by the Democrat to gain one electoral vote in New Hampshire. Neither is likely to happen in an ordinary election.

Similarly, Maine (where Gore received 52.75% of the popular vote in 2000) would become a distinctly noncompetitive state under the whole-number proportional approach. A candidate would win two electoral votes for receiving anywhere between 37.50% and 62.50% of the popular vote under the whole-number proportional approach.

As will be seen in the sections below relating to other states with an even number of electoral votes, the whole-number proportional approach frequently converts current battleground states into noncompetitive states.

On the other hand, Hawaii (which is a noncompetitive spectator state under the winner-take-all system) would become competitive under the whole-number proportional approach. In Hawaii, a change of +2.67% in 2000 would have resulted in a gain for the Democrats of one electoral vote.

Thus, the overall effect of the whole-number proportional approach in terms of competitiveness is to convert New Hampshire, Nevada, and Maine into noncompetitive spectator states and to convert Hawaii into a competitive state.

4.1.3 STATES WITH FIVE ELECTORAL VOTES

There were four states with five electoral votes in the 2000 presidential election—Nebraska, New Mexico, Utah, and West Virginia. For states with five electoral votes, one electoral vote corresponds to a 20% share of the state's popular vote under the whole-number proportional approach.

Table 4.6 TABLE OF BREAKPOINTS FOR STATES WITH FIVE ELECTORAL VOTES

PERCENT OF POPULAR VOTE	NUMBER OF ELECTORAL VOTES	BREAKPOINT
0.00% to 10.00%	0	10.00%
10.01 to 30.00%	1	30.00%
30.01% to 50.00%	2	50.00%
50.01% to 70.00%	3	70.00%
70.01% to 90.00%	4	90.00%
90.01% to 100.00%	5	NA

Table 4.6 shows the number of electoral votes that a presidential slate would receive for various ranges of percentages of the popular vote in the states with five electoral votes.

Table 4.7 shows the consequences of the whole-number proportional approach in the four states with five electoral votes in the 2000 presidential election.

Table 4.7 2000 ELECTION UNDER THE WINNER-TAKE-ALL (WTA) AND WHOLE-NUMBER PROPORTIONAL APPROACH (WNP) IN STATES WITH FIVE ELECTORAL VOTES

STATE	GORE VOTE	GORE EV UNDER WTA	BUSH EV UNDER WTA	GORE EV UNDER WNP	BUSH EV UNDER WNP	BREAKPOINT JUST BELOW GORE VOTE	BREAKPOINT JUST ABOVE GORE VOTE	CHANGE NEEDED TO GAIN OR LOSE 1 EV UNDER WNP
NE	34.82%	0	5	2	3	30.00%	50.00%	−4.82%
NM	50.03%	5	0	3	2	50.00%	70.00%	−0.03%
UT	28.27%	0	5	1	4	10.00%	30.00%	+1.73%
WV	46.76%	0	5	2	3	30.00%	50.00%	+3.24%
Total		**5**	**15**	**8**	**12**			

Gore received five electoral votes in 2000 from the four states with five electoral votes but would have received eight under the whole-number proportional approach.

Figure 4.5 presents, along a horizontal line, Gore's percentage share (column 2 of table 4.7) of the popular vote in the 2000 presidential election for the four states with five electoral votes. The figure contains tick marks along the horizontal line at 10%, 30%, 50%, 70%, and 90%, representing the breakpoints that are applicable to states with five electoral votes (from table 4.6). The small numbers from zero to five immediately under the horizontal line show the number of electoral votes that a candidate would receive under the whole-number proportional approach by winning a particular share of the popular vote.

As a general rule, states with an odd number of electoral votes always have a breakpoint at 50%. Thus, states that have an odd number of electoral votes and are competitive under the existing statewide winner-take-all system will remain competitive under the whole-number proportional approach. For instance, New Mexico is

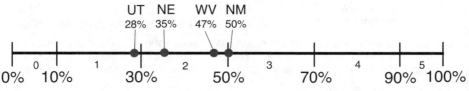

Figure 4.5 2000 presidential vote in states with five electoral votes

competitive under the existing winner-take-all system and would remain so under the whole-number proportional approach.

Utah (with five electoral votes in 2000) is an example of a state that is noncompetitive under the existing statewide winner-take-all system but that becomes competitive under the whole-number proportional approach. In a state with a lopsided partisan balance, the breakpoint at 30.00% can become politically important under the whole-number proportional approach. Specifically, Gore could have gone from one to two electoral votes by increasing his popular vote by 1.73% from 28.27% to 30.00%. Utah is an example of the phenomenon of a noncompetitive spectator state becoming a battleground state because of a breakpoint other than 50.00%.

4.1.4 STATES WITH SIX ELECTORAL VOTES

Arkansas and Kansas each had six electoral votes in the 2000 presidential election. For these states, one electoral vote corresponds to a 16.67% share of the state's popular vote under the whole-number proportional approach. Table 4.8 shows the number of electoral votes that a presidential slate would receive in states with six electoral votes for various ranges of percentages of the popular vote.

Table 4.8 TABLE OF BREAKPOINTS FOR STATES WITH SIX ELECTORAL VOTES

PERCENT OF POPULAR VOTE	NUMBER OF ELECTORAL VOTES	BREAKPOINT
0.00% to 8.33%	0	8.33%
8.34% to 25.00%	1	25.00%
25.01% to 41.66%	2	41.66%
41.67% to 58.33%	3	58.33%
58.34% to 75.00%	4	75.00%
75.00% to 91.66%	5	91.66%
91.67% to 100.00%	6	NA

Table 4.9 shows the consequences of the whole-number proportional approach in the two states with six electoral votes in the 2000 presidential election.

Gore received no electoral votes in 2000 from the two states with six electoral votes, but he would have received five under the whole-number proportional approach.

Table 4.9 2000 ELECTION UNDER THE WINNER-TAKE-ALL (WTA) AND WHOLE-NUMBER PROPORTIONAL APPROACH (WNP) IN STATES WITH SIX ELECTORAL VOTES

STATE	GORE VOTE	GORE EV UNDER WTA	BUSH EV UNDER WTA	GORE EV UNDER WNP	BUSH EV UNDER WNP	BREAKPOINT JUST BELOW GORE VOTE	BREAKPOINT JUST ABOVE GORE VOTE	CHANGE NEEDED TO GAIN OR LOSE 1 EV UNDER WNP
AR	47.20%	0	6	3	3	41.66%	58.33%	−5.54%
KS	39.08%	0	6	2	4	25.00%	41.66%	+2.58%
Total		**0**	**12**	**5**	**7**			

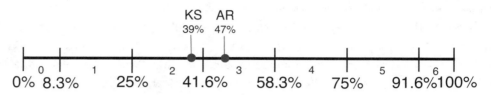

Figure 4.6 2000 presidential vote in states with six electoral votes

Figure 4.6 presents, along a horizontal line, Gore's percentage share of the popular vote in the 2000 presidential election for the two states with six electoral votes.

Using the vote counts from the 2000 presidential election, Arkansas was competitive under the existing winner-take-all system (requiring a change of 2.80% in the popular vote to switch its six electoral votes). The whole-number proportional approach would make Arkansas considerably less competitive because a change of 5.54% in the popular vote would be necessary to affect one electoral vote there. Meanwhile, Kansas (which is noncompetitive under the existing winner-take-all system) would become somewhat more competitive under the whole-number proportional approach.

4.1.5 STATES WITH SEVEN ELECTORAL VOTES

Iowa, Mississippi, and Oregon each had seven electoral votes in the 2000 presidential election. For states with seven electoral votes, one electoral vote corresponds to a 14.29% share of the state's popular vote under the whole-number proportional approach. Table 4.10 shows the number of electoral votes that a presidential slate would receive in states with seven electoral votes for various ranges of percentages of the popular vote.

Table 4.11 shows the consequences of the whole-number proportional approach in the three states with seven electoral votes.

Gore received 14 electoral votes in 2000 from the three states with seven electoral votes, but he would have received 11 under the whole-number proportional approach.

Figure 4.7 presents, along a horizontal line, Gore's percentage share of the popular vote in the 2000 presidential election for the three states with seven electoral votes.

Iowa and Oregon are competitive under the existing winner-take-all system. They would remain so under the whole-number proportional approach because Gore's pop-

Table 4.10 TABLE OF BREAKPOINTS FOR STATES
WITH SEVEN ELECTORAL VOTES

PERCENT OF POPULAR VOTE	NUMBER OF ELECTORAL VOTES	BREAKPOINT
0.00% to 7.14%	0	7.14%
7.15% to 21.43%	1	21.43%
21.44% to 35.71%	2	35.71%
35.72% to 50.00%	3	50.00%
50.01% to 64.28%	4	64.28%
64.29% to 78.57%	5	78.57%
78.58% to 92.86%	6	92.86%
92.87% to 100.00%	7	NA

Table 4.11 2000 ELECTION UNDER THE WINNER-TAKE-ALL (WTA) AND WHOLE-NUMBER
PROPORTIONAL APPROACH (WNP) IN STATES WITH SEVEN ELECTORAL VOTES

STATE	GORE VOTE	GORE EV UNDER WTA	BUSH EV UNDER WTA	GORE EV UNDER WNP	BUSH EV UNDER WNP	BREAKPOINT JUST BELOW GORE VOTE	BREAKPOINT JUST ABOVE GORE VOTE	CHANGE NEEDED TO GAIN OR LOSE 1 EV UNDER WNP
IA	50.16%	7	0	4	3	50.00%	64.28%	−0.16%
MS	41.39%	0	7	3	4	35.71%	50.00%	−5.68%
OR	50.24%	7	0	4	3	50.00%	64.28%	−0.24%
Total		**14**	**7**	**11**	**10**			

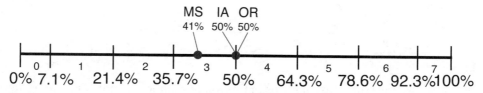

Figure 4.7 2000 presidential vote in states with seven electoral votes

ular vote in those states was near the breakpoint of 50.00%. Mississippi, however,
would have been noncompetitive under both systems.

4.1.6 STATES WITH EIGHT ELECTORAL VOTES

Arizona, Colorado, Connecticut, Kentucky, Oklahoma, and South Carolina each had
eight electoral votes in the 2000 presidential election. For those states, one electoral
vote corresponds to a 12.5% share of the state's popular vote under the whole-number
proportional approach.

Table 4.12 shows the number of electoral votes that a presidential slate would receive in states with eight electoral votes for various ranges of percentages of popular
votes.

Table 4.12 TABLE OF BREAKPOINTS FOR STATES WITH EIGHT ELECTORAL VOTES

PERCENT OF POPULAR VOTE	NUMBER OF ELECTORAL VOTES	BREAKPOINT
0.00% to 6.25%	0	6.25%
6.26% to 18.75%	1	18.75%
18.76% to 31.25%	2	31.25%
31.26% to 43.75%	3	43.75%
43.76% to 56.25%	4	56.25%
56.26% to 68.75%	5	68.75%
68.76% to 81.25%	6	81.25%
81.26% to 93.75%	7	93.75%
93.76% to 100.0%	8	NA

Table 4.13 2000 ELECTION UNDER THE WINNER-TAKE-ALL (WTA) AND WHOLE-NUMBER PROPORTIONAL APPROACH (WNP) IN STATES WITH EIGHT ELECTORAL VOTES

STATE	GORE VOTE	GORE EV UNDER WTA	BUSH EV UNDER WTA	GORE EV UNDER WNP	BUSH EV UNDER WNP	BREAKPOINT JUST BELOW GORE VOTE	BREAKPOINT JUST ABOVE GORE VOTE	CHANGE NEEDED TO GAIN OR LOSE 1 EV UNDER WNP
AZ	46.72%	0	8	4	4	43.75%	56.25%	−2.97%
CO	45.51%	0	8	4	4	43.75%	56.25%	−1.76%
CT	59.26%	8	0	5	3	56.25%	68.75%	−3.01%
KY	42.27%	0	8	3	5	31.25%	43.75%	+1.48%
OK	38.92%	0	8	3	5	31.25%	43.75%	+4.83%
SC	41.85%	0	8	3	5	31.25%	43.75%	+1.90%
Total		**8**	**40**	**22**	**26**			

Table 4.13 shows the consequences of the whole-number proportional approach in the six states with eight electoral votes in the 2000 presidential election.

Among these six states, Gore carried only Connecticut in 2000. His popular vote was in the 40% range in the other five states of this group. Gore, therefore, received only eight electoral votes out of the 48 available from these six states. He would have received 22 under the whole-number proportional approach.

Figure 4.8 presents, along a horizontal line, Gore's percentage share of the popular vote for the six states with eight electoral votes in the 2000 presidential election.

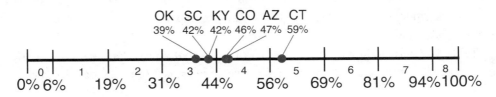

Figure 4.8 2000 presidential vote in states with eight electoral votes

The 2000 Gore presidential vote in Arizona, Colorado, Kentucky, and South Carolina was reasonably close to the 44% breakpoint for states with eight electoral votes. Connecticut was reasonably close to the 56% breakpoint. Thus, these states would become competitive under the whole-number proportional approach.

4.1.7 STATES WITH NINE ELECTORAL VOTES

Alabama and Louisiana each had nine electoral votes in the 2000 presidential election. For these states with nine electoral votes, one electoral vote corresponds to an 11.11% share of the state's popular vote under the whole-number proportional approach.

Table 4.14 shows the consequences of the whole-number proportional approach in these states. The relevant breakpoints for this table are at 38.88% (the boundary between three and four electoral votes) and 50.00% (the boundary between four and five electoral votes).

Table 4.14 2000 ELECTION UNDER THE WINNER-TAKE-ALL (WTA) AND WHOLE-NUMBER PROPORTIONAL APPROACH (WNP) FOR STATES WITH NINE ELECTORAL VOTES

STATE	GORE VOTE	GORE EV UNDER WTA	BUSH EV UNDER WTA	GORE EV UNDER WNP	BUSH EV UNDER WNP	BREAKPOINT JUST BELOW GORE VOTE	BREAKPOINT JUST ABOVE GORE VOTE	CHANGE NEEDED TO GAIN OR LOSE 1 EV UNDER WNP
AL	42.39%	0	9	4	5	38.88%	50.00%	−3.51%
LA	46.06%	0	9	4	5	38.88%	50.00%	+3.94%
Total		**0**	**18**	**8**	**10**			

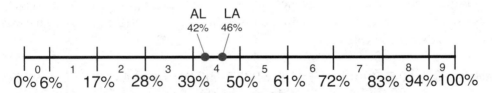

Figure 4.9 2000 presidential vote in states with nine electoral votes

Figure 4.9 presents, along a horizontal line, Gore's percentage share of the popular vote in the 2000 presidential election for the two states with nine electoral votes.

4.1.8 STATES WITH 10 ELECTORAL VOTES

There were two states with 10 electoral votes in the 2000 presidential election—Maryland and Minnesota. For those states, one electoral vote corresponds to a 10% share of the state's popular vote under the whole-number proportional approach.

Table 4.15 shows the consequences of the whole-number proportional approach in these states. The relevant breakpoint for this table is at 55.00% (the boundary between five and six electoral votes).

Table 4.15 2000 ELECTION UNDER THE WINNER-TAKE-ALL (WTA) AND WHOLE-NUMBER
PROPORTIONAL APPROACH (WNP) IN STATES WITH 10 ELECTORAL VOTES

STATE	GORE VOTE	GORE EV UNDER WTA	BUSH EV UNDER WTA	GORE EV UNDER WNP	BUSH EV UNDER WNP	BREAKPOINT JUST BELOW GORE VOTE	BREAKPOINT JUST ABOVE GORE VOTE	CHANGE NEEDED TO GAIN OR LOSE 1 EV UNDER WNP
MD	58.47%	10	0	6	4	55.00%	65.00%	−3.47%
MN	51.29%	10	0	5	5	45.00%	55.00%	+3.71%
Total		20	0	11	9			

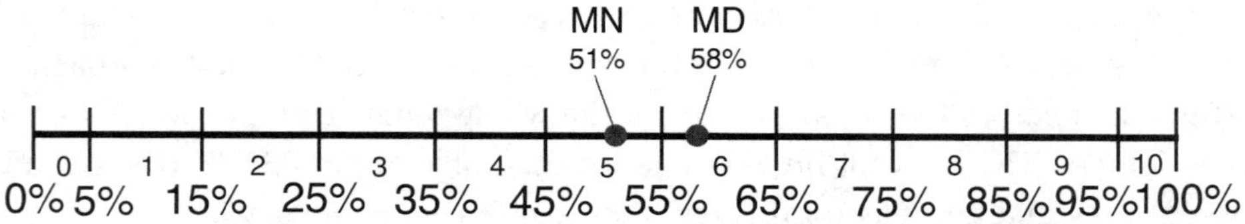

Figure 4.10 2000 presidential vote in states with 10 electoral votes

Figure 4.10 presents, along a horizontal line, Gore's percentage share of the popular vote in the 2000 presidential election for the two states with 10 electoral votes.

4.1.9 STATES WITH 11 ELECTORAL VOTES

There were four states with 11 electoral votes in the 2000 presidential election—Missouri, Tennessee, Washington, and Wisconsin. For states with 11 electoral votes, one electoral vote corresponds to a 9.09% share of the state's popular vote under the whole-number proportional approach.

Table 4.16 shows the consequences of the whole-number proportional approach in these states. The relevant breakpoint for this table is at 50.00% (the boundary between five and six electoral votes).

Table 4.16 2000 ELECTION UNDER THE WINNER-TAKE-ALL (WTA) AND WHOLE-NUMBER
PROPORTIONAL APPROACH (WNP) IN STATES WITH 11 ELECTORAL VOTES

STATE	GORE VOTE	GORE EV UNDER WTA	BUSH EV UNDER WTA	GORE EV UNDER WNP	BUSH EV UNDER WNP	BREAKPOINT JUST BELOW GORE VOTE	BREAKPOINT JUST ABOVE GORE VOTE	CHANGE NEEDED TO GAIN OR LOSE 1 EV UNDER WNP
MO	48.29%	0	11	5	6	40.91%	50.00%	+1.71%
TN	48.04%	0	11	5	6	40.91%	50.00%	+1.96%
WA	52.94%	11	0	6	5	50.00%	59.09%	−2.94%
WI	50.12%	11	0	6	5	50.00%	59.09%	−0.12%
Total		22	22	22	22			

Figure 4.11 presents, along a horizontal line, Gore's percentage share of the popular vote (column 2 of table 4.16) in the 2000 presidential election for the four states with 11 electoral votes.

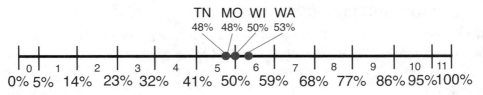

Figure 4.11 2000 presidential vote in states with 11 electoral votes

Because Gore's percentage was reasonably close to 50.00% in all four of the states with 11 electoral votes in 2000 (table 4.16), the whole-number proportional approach would have made no difference in terms of the degree of competitiveness for these particular states.

4.1.10 STATES WITH 12 ELECTORAL VOTES

Indiana and Massachusetts each had 12 electoral votes in the 2000 presidential election. For these two states, one electoral vote corresponds to an 8.33% share of the state's popular vote under the whole-number proportional approach.

Table 4.17 shows the consequences of the whole-number proportional approach in states with 12 electoral votes. The relevant breakpoints for this table are at 45.83% (the boundary between five and six electoral votes) and 62.50% (the boundary between seven and eight electoral votes).

Table 4.17 2000 ELECTION UNDER THE WINNER-TAKE-ALL (WTA) AND WHOLE-NUMBER PROPORTIONAL APPROACH (WNP) IN STATES WITH 12 ELECTORAL VOTES

STATE	GORE VOTE	GORE EV UNDER WTA	BUSH EV UNDER WTA	GORE EV UNDER WNP	BUSH EV UNDER WNP	BREAKPOINT JUST BELOW GORE VOTE	BREAKPOINT JUST ABOVE GORE VOTE	CHANGE NEEDED TO GAIN OR LOSE 1 EV UNDER WNP
IN	42.00%	0	12	5	7	37.50%	45.83%	+3.83%
MA	64.79%	12	0	8	4	62.50%	70.83%	−2.29%
Total		12	12	13	11			

Figure 4.12 presents, along a horizontal line, Gore's percentage share of the popular vote in the 2000 presidential election for the two states with 12 electoral votes.

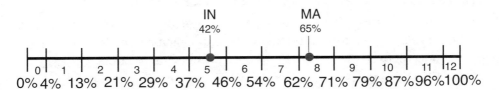

Figure 4.12 2000 presidential vote in states with 12 electoral votes

4.1.11 STATES WITH 13 ELECTORAL VOTES

There were two states with 13 electoral votes in the 2000 presidential election—Georgia and Virginia. For the states with 13 electoral votes, one electoral vote corresponds to a 7.69% share of the state's popular vote under the whole-number proportional approach.

Table 4.18 shows the consequences of the whole-number proportional approach in the states with 13 electoral votes. The relevant breakpoints for this table are at 42.31% (the boundary between five and six electoral votes) and 50.00% (the boundary between six and seven electoral votes).

Table 4.18 2000 ELECTION UNDER THE WINNER-TAKE-ALL (WTA) AND WHOLE-NUMBER PROPORTIONAL APPROACH (WNP) IN STATES WITH 13 ELECTORAL VOTES

STATE	GORE VOTE	GORE EV UNDER WTA	BUSH EV UNDER WTA	GORE EV UNDER WNP	BUSH EV UNDER WNP	BREAKPOINT JUST BELOW GORE VOTE	BREAKPOINT JUST ABOVE GORE VOTE	CHANGE NEEDED TO GAIN OR LOSE 1 EV UNDER WNP
GA	44.02%	0	13	6	7	42.31%	50.00%	−1.71%
VA	45.85%	0	13	6	7	42.31%	50.00%	−3.54%
Total		**0**	**26**	**12**	**14**			

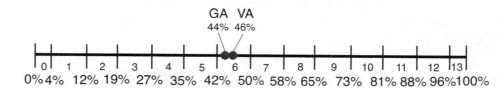

Figure 4.13 2000 presidential vote in states with 13 electoral votes

Figure 4.13 presents, along a horizontal line, Gore's percentage share of the popular vote for the two states with 13 electoral votes in the 2000 presidential election.

Under the whole-number proportional approach, Gore would have received 12 of the 26 electoral votes available from these two states (compared to none under the statewide winner-take-all system).

One of Georgia's electoral votes would have been contested under the whole-number proportional approach.

4.1.12 THE 10 STATES WITH 14 OR MORE ELECTORAL VOTES

The remaining 10 states (North Carolina, New Jersey, Michigan, Ohio, Illinois, Pennsylvania, Florida, Texas, New York, and California) each had a different number of electoral votes (between 14 and 54) in the 2000 presidential election.

Table 4.19 shows the percentage share of the popular vote that corresponds to one electoral vote under the whole-number proportional approach for the 10 states with 14 or more electoral votes in the 2000 election.

Table 4.19 SHARE OF THE POPULAR VOTE CORRESPONDING TO ONE ELECTORAL VOTE FOR THE 10 LARGEST STATES

STATE	ELECTORAL VOTE	SHARE OF POPULAR VOTE CORRESPONDING TO 1 ELECTORAL VOTE
North Carolina	14	7.1%
New Jersey	15	6.7%
Michigan	18	5.6%
Ohio	21	4.8%
Illinois	22	4.5%
Pennsylvania	23	4.4%
Florida	25	4.0%
Texas	32	3.1%
New York	33	3.0%
California	54	1.9%
Total	**254**	

The breakpoints for the 10 states with 14 to 54 electoral votes were different because each of these states had a different number of electoral votes. Table 4.20 shows the consequences of the whole-number proportional approach for these 10 states for the 2000 presidential election.

Table 4.20 2000 ELECTION UNDER THE WINNER-TAKE-ALL (WTA) AND WHOLE-NUMBER PROPORTIONAL APPROACH (WNP) FOR THE 10 STATES WITH 14 OR MORE ELECTORAL VOTES

STATE	GORE VOTE	GORE EV UNDER WTA	BUSH EV UNDER WTA	GORE EV UNDER WNP	BUSH EV UNDER WNP	BREAKPOINT JUST BELOW GORE VOTE	BREAKPOINT JUST ABOVE GORE VOTE	CHANGE NEEDED TO GAIN OR LOSE 1 EV UNDER WNP
NC	43.54%	0	14	6	8	39.28%	46.42%	+2.88%
NJ	58.21%	15	0	9	6	56.66%	63.33%	−1.55%
MI	52.63%	18	0	10	8	47.22%	52.78%	+0.15%
OH	48.18%	0	21	10	11	45.23%	50.00%	+1.82%
IL	56.18%	22	0	12	10	52.27%	56.82%	+0.18%
PA	52.15%	23	0	12	11	50.00%	54.35%	−2.15%
FL	49.99%	0	25	12	13	46.00%	50.00%	+0.01%
TX	39.04%	0	32	12	20	35.94%	39.06%	+0.02%
NY	63.09%	33	0	20	13	62.12%	65.15%	−0.97%
CA	56.20%	54	0	30	24	54.63%	56.48%	+0.28%
Total		**165**	**92**	**133**	**124**			

Figure 4.14 presents, along a horizontal line, Gore's percentage share of the popular vote in the 2000 presidential election in North Carolina (14 electoral votes). As can be seen, the Democrats were within 2.88% of the breakpoint (46.42%) between getting six and seven electoral votes in North Carolina and therefore could have gained one electoral vote in North Carolina under favorable circumstances. This opportunity is, however, not symmetrical. There would have been little likelihood of the Republicans being able to reduce Gore's share of the electoral vote from six to five.

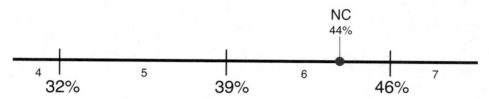

Figure 4.14 2000 presidential vote in North Carolina (14 electoral votes)

Figure 4.15 presents, along a horizontal line, Gore's percentage share of the popular vote in New Jersey (15 electoral votes) in the 2000 presidential election. As can be seen, the Democrats were within 1.55% of the breakpoint between getting nine and eight electoral votes. Thus, the Republicans could have gained one electoral vote in New Jersey under favorable circumstances. This opportunity to affect one electoral vote is not, however, symmetrical. There would have been little likelihood of the Democrats being able to increase their share of the electoral vote from nine to 10.

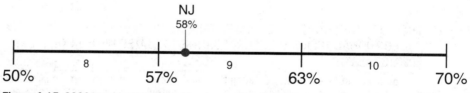

Figure 4.15 2000 presidential vote in New Jersey (15 electoral votes)

Figure 4.16 presents, along a horizontal line, Gore's percentage share of the popular vote in the 2000 presidential election in Michigan (18 electoral votes). The Democrats were within 0.15% of getting 11 (as compared to 10) electoral votes from Michigan. Neither party, however, has any realistic chance of gaining or losing as many as two electoral votes in Michigan in anything other than a landslide election.

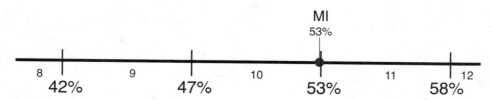

Figure 4.16 2000 presidential vote in Michigan (18 electoral votes)

Figure 4.17 presents, along a horizontal line, Gore's percentage share of the popular vote in the 2000 presidential election in Ohio (which had 21 electoral votes in 2000). The Democrats were within 1.82% of the breakpoint between getting 10 and 11 electoral votes in Ohio and could have gained one electoral vote in the state under favorable circumstances. There would have been little likelihood, however, of the Republicans' decreasing the Democrats' share of the electoral vote in Ohio from 10 to nine.

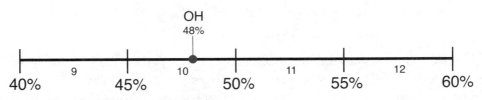

Figure 4.17 2000 presidential vote in Ohio (21 electoral votes)

Figure 4.18 presents, along a horizontal line, Gore's percentage share of the popular vote in the 2000 presidential election in Illinois (which had 22 electoral votes in 2000). The Democrats were within 0.18% of the breakpoint between getting 12 and 13 electoral votes in Illinois.

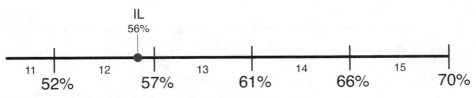

Figure 4.18 2000 presidential vote in Illinois (22 electoral votes)

Figure 4.19 presents, along a horizontal line, Gore's percentage share of the popular vote in the 2000 presidential election in Pennsylvania (23 electoral votes). The Democrats were within 2.15% of the nearest breakpoint, and the Republicans were within 2.20% of the nearest breakpoint. Thus, one electoral vote would potentially be in play for both parties under the whole-number proportional approach.

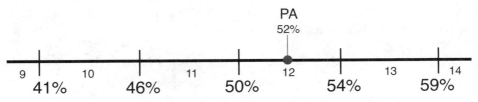

Figure 4.19 2000 presidential vote in Pennsylvania (23 electoral votes)

Figure 4.20 presents, along a horizontal line, Gore's percentage share of the popular vote in the 2000 presidential election in Florida (which had 25 electoral votes in

2000). The Democrats were within +0.01% of the breakpoint between getting 12 and 13 electoral votes in Florida.

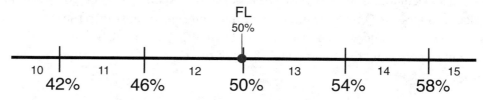

Figure 4.20 2000 presidential vote in Florida (25 electoral votes)

Figure 4.21 presents, along a horizontal line, Gore's percentage share of the popular vote in the 2000 presidential election in Texas (32 electoral votes in 2000). The Democrats were within +0.02% of the breakpoint between getting 12 and 13 electoral votes in Texas. Thus, one electoral vote would have been in play in Texas under the whole-number proportional approach. Two electoral votes might occasionally be in play in Texas because one electoral vote corresponds to a mere 3.33% share of the state's popular vote.

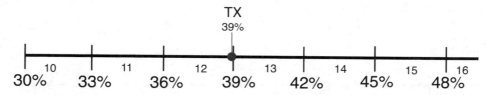
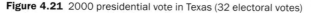

Figure 4.21 2000 presidential vote in Texas (32 electoral votes)

Figure 4.22 presents, along a horizontal line, Gore's percentage share of the popular vote in the 2000 presidential election in New York (which had 33 electoral votes in 2000). The Democrats were within 0.97% of the breakpoint between getting 20 and 19 electoral votes in New York. Thus, the Republicans could possibly have gained one electoral vote in the state. The opportunity is not, however, symmetrical. It is less likely that the Democrats would have been able to increase their share of the electoral vote from 20 to 21. Two electoral votes might occasionally be in play in New York because one electoral vote corresponds to a mere 3.33% share of the state's popular vote under the whole-number proportional approach.

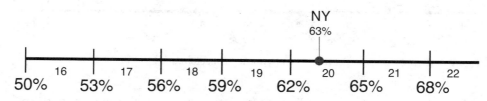
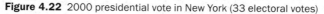

Figure 4.22 2000 presidential vote in New York (33 electoral votes)

Figure 4.23 presents, along a horizontal line, Gore's percentage share of the popular vote in California (which had 54 electoral votes in the 2000 presidential election). The Democrats were within 0.28% of getting 31 (as compared to 30) electoral votes from California. One electoral vote would definitely be in play in California for both parties under the whole-number proportional approach. Moreover, two or three electoral votes might occasionally be in play in California because one electoral vote corresponds to a mere 1.85% share of the state's popular vote. For example, if the Democrats were to increase their share of the popular vote by 2.13% (0.28% plus 1.85%), they would pick up two electoral votes. That is, the whole-number proportional approach could operate as a "statewide winner-take-two" system for the Democrats in California. Note that this opportunity is not symmetric. A change of 3.43% in the popular vote would have been necessary for the Bush campaign to pick up two electoral votes in California.

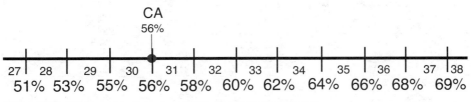

Figure 4.23 2000 presidential vote in California (54 electoral votes)

In summary, table 4.20 shows that all of the 10 most populous states would become competitive (to a limited degree) under the whole-number proportional approach.

In particular, the six biggest states (North Carolina, New Jersey, Illinois, Texas, New York, and California) that were spectator states in 2000 under the winner-take-all system would become competitive under the whole-number proportional approach.

Michigan, Ohio, Pennsylvania, and Florida were battleground states in 2000 under the current winner-take-all system. These four states would remain competitive under the whole-number proportional approach. However, the battle would not be for 18, 21, 23, or 25 electoral votes but, instead, for only one electoral vote in each state.

4.1.13 NATIONWIDE ANALYSIS OF THE WHOLE-NUMBER PROPORTIONAL APPROACH

This section addresses two questions. The first is whether the whole-number proportional approach would, if adopted by every state, more accurately reflect the nationwide popular vote than the existing statewide winner-take-all system. The second question is whether the whole-number proportional approach would, if adopted by every state, improve upon the current situation in which four-fifths of the states and four-fifths of the people of the United States are ignored by presidential campaigns.

Table 4.21 combines the information from 12 of the foregoing tables in order to show the overall consequences of the whole-number proportional approach for all

Table 4.21 2000 ELECTION UNDER WHOLE-NUMBER PROPORTIONAL APPROACH

STATE	GORE VOTE	GORE EV UNDER WTA	BUSH EV UNDER WTA	GORE EV UNDER WNP	BUSH EV UNDER WNP	BREAKPOINT JUST BELOW GORE VOTE	BREAKPOINT JUST ABOVE GORE VOTE	CHANGE NEEDED TO GAIN OR LOSE 1 EV UNDER WNP
ND	35.27%	0	3	1	2	16.67%	50.00%	14.18%
MT	36.34%	0	3	1	2	16.67%	50.00%	13.66%
SD	38.39%	0	3	1	2	16.67%	50.00%	11.61%
ME	52.75%	4	0	2	2	37.50%	62.50%	9.75%
ID	29.15%	0	4	1	3	12.50%	37.50%	8.35%
OK	38.92%	0	8	3	5	31.25%	43.75%	4.83%
LA	46.06%	0	9	4	5	38.88%	50.00%	3.94%
IN	42.00%	0	12	6	6	37.50%	45.83%	3.83%
MN	51.29%	10	0	5	5	45.00%	55.00%	3.71%
WV	46.76%	0	5	2	3	30.00%	50.00%	3.24%
NC	43.54%	0	14	6	8	39.28%	46.42%	2.88%
HI	59.83%	4	0	2	2	37.50%	62.50%	2.67%
KS	39.08%	0	6	2	4	25.00%	41.66%	2.58%
TN	48.04%	0	11	5	6	40.91%	50.00%	1.96%
SC	41.85%	0	8	3	5	31.25%	43.75%	1.90%
OH	48.18%	0	21	10	11	45.23%	50.00%	1.82%
UT	28.27%	0	5	1	4	10.00%	30.00%	1.73%
MO	48.29%	0	11	5	6	40.91%	50.00%	1.71%
KY	42.27%	0	8	3	5	31.25%	43.75%	1.48%
CA	56.20%	54	0	30	24	54.63%	56.48%	0.28%
IL	56.18%	22	0	12	10	52.27%	56.82%	0.18%
MI	52.63%	18	0	10	8	47.22%	52.78%	0.15%
FL	49.99%	0	25	12	13	46.00%	50.00%	0.01%
TX	39.04%	0	32	12	20	35.94%	39.06%	−0.02%
NM	50.03%	5	0	3	2	50.00%	70.00%	−0.03%
WI	50.12%	11	0	6	5	50.00%	59.09%	−0.12%
IA	50.16%	7	0	4	3	50.00%	64.28%	−0.16%
OR	50.24%	7	0	4	3	50.00%	64.28%	−0.24%
NY	63.09%	33	0	20	13	62.12%	65.15%	−0.97%
NJ	58.21%	15	0	9	6	56.66%	63.33%	−1.55%
GA	44.02%	0	13	6	7	42.31%	50.00%	−1.71%
CO	45.51%	0	8	4	4	43.75%	56.25%	−1.76%
PA	52.15%	23	0	12	11	50.00%	54.35%	−2.15%
MA	64.79%	12	0	7	5	62.50%	70.83%	−2.29%
WA	52.94%	11	0	6	5	50.00%	59.09%	−2.94%
AZ	46.72%	0	8	4	4	43.75%	56.25%	−2.97%
CT	59.26%	8	0	5	3	56.25%	68.75%	−3.01%
RI	65.65%	4	0	3	1	62.50%	87.50%	−3.15%
MD	58.47%	10	0	6	4	55.00%	65.00%	−3.47%
AL	42.39%	0	9	4	5	38.88%	50.00%	−3.51%
VA	45.85%	0	13	6	7	42.31%	50.00%	−3.54%
NE	34.82%	0	5	2	3	30.00%	50.00%	−4.82%
VT	55.44%	3	0	2	1	50.00%	83.33%	−5.44%
AR	47.20%	0	6	3	3	41.66%	58.33%	−5.54%
MS	41.39%	0	7	3	4	35.71%	50.00%	−5.68%
DE	56.74%	3	0	2	1	50.00%	83.33%	−6.74%
DC	90.49%	3	0	3	0	83.33%	100.00%	−7.16%
NV	48.14%	0	4	2	2	37.50%	62.50%	−10.64%
NH	49.33%	0	4	2	2	37.50%	62.50%	−11.83%
WY	29.02%	0	3	1	2	16.67%	50.00%	−12.35%
AK	32.06%	0	3	1	2	16.67%	50.00%	−15.39%
Total		**267**	**271**	**269**	**269**			

50 states and the District of Columbia for the 2000 presidential election. Table 4.21 is sorted in descending order according to the percentage change (column 9) in popular votes that Gore would have needed to change his electoral vote count by one electoral vote in each jurisdiction.

Table 4.21 shows that, if the whole-number proportional approach had been in use throughout the country in the 2000 presidential election, it would not have awarded the most electoral votes to the candidate receiving the most popular votes nationwide. Instead, the result would have been a tie of 269–269 in the electoral vote, even though Al Gore led by 537,179 popular votes across the nation.[9] That is, the whole-number proportional approach would not have accurately reflected the nationwide popular vote.

In order to analyze competitiveness, let us try to visualize how each political party might have approached the 2004 presidential election if all states had used the whole-number proportional approach.

The best starting point for planning a strategy in any election is the outcome of the previous election. Thus, under the whole-number proportional approach, the starting point for planning a strategy for the 2004 presidential election would have been the data in table 4.21 (showing both parties tied at 269 electoral votes). The central question for each party's campaign would be about how to win more than 269 electoral votes. Each party's campaign would have been aware that the whole-number proportional approach is predominantly a "statewide winner-take-one" system. Thus, the challenge to each party would be to devise a strategy for accumulating additional electoral votes by targeting particular states.

Landslides take care of themselves. Thus, the planning process for a political campaign inevitably concentrates on what might happen if the upcoming election turns out to be close. Planners for the Bush 2004 campaign would have carefully considered what might happen if they were to improve their nationwide popular vote by various reasonably attainable percentages—1%, 2%, or 3%.

We *now* know that the Republicans increased their share of the two-party popular presidential vote by 1.98% (from 49.72% in 2000 to 51.71% in 2004). Hindsight of this sort is not, however, required for us to know that, at the beginning of the 2004 presidential campaign, it would have been imperative for each campaign to consider small percentage swings such as 1%, 2%, or 3%.

Referring to table 4.21, those involved in planning the Bush 2004 campaign would have immediately identified the nine battleground states where a gain of 2% or less in the popular vote could yield them one additional electoral vote under the whole-

---

[9] If there had been a tie when the electoral votes for the 2000 presidential election were counted on January 6, 2001, the election for President would have been thrown into the House of Representatives (voting on a one-state-one-vote basis). Based on the party alignment of the newly elected House, George W. Bush would have been elected President. However, the newly elected Senate—responsible for electing the new Vice President—was equally divided after the 2000 elections. The U.S. Constitution is not entirely clear as to whether Vice President Gore (whose term of office ran until January 20, 2001) would have been entitled to vote to break the tie in the Senate in order to elect a new Vice President.

number proportional approach. These nine states (shown in table 4.22 and in figure 4.24) would have been the highest-priority "upside" battleground states for Bush in 2004.

Table 4.22 shows that the Bush 2004 campaign could have picked up nine electoral votes in the following way under the whole-number proportional approach:

- **Lowest-Hanging Fruit**: Pick up one electoral vote in Texas by reducing the Democratic share of the vote there by a mere 0.02% (from 39.04% to the breakpoint of 39.02%).

- **Easy Pickings:** Pick up one electoral vote in each of four states by reducing the Democratic share of the vote by 0.03% in New Mexico, 0.16% in Iowa, 0.12% in Wisconsin, and 0.24% in Oregon.

- **1% Neighborhood:** Pick up one electoral vote in New York by reducing the Democratic share of the vote by 0.97% (from 63.09% to the breakpoint of 62.12%).

- **2% Neighborhood:** Pick up one electoral vote by reducing the Democratic share of the vote by 1.55% in New Jersey, 1.71% in Georgia and 1.76% in Colorado.

Similarly, those involved in planning the Kerry 2004 campaign under the whole-number proportional approach would surely have considered the consequences of improving upon Gore's popular vote in 2000 by various attainable small percentages. Referring to table 4.21, planners for the Kerry 2004 campaign surely would have quickly identified the 10 battleground states where a gain of 2% or less could yield them one additional electoral vote. These 10 states (shown in table 4.23 and in figure 4.25) would have been the highest-priority "upside" battleground states for Kerry in 2004.

Table 4.23 shows that the Kerry 2004 campaign could pick up 10 electoral votes in the following way under the whole-number proportional approach:

- **Lowest-Hanging Fruit**: Pick up one electoral vote in Florida by increasing the Democratic share of the vote in Florida by 0.01% (from 49.99% to the breakpoint of 50.00%).

- **Easy Pickings:** Pick up one electoral vote by increasing the Democratic share of the vote by 0.15% in Michigan, 0.18% in Illinois, and 0.28% in California.

- **1% Neighborhood:** Pick up one electoral vote in Kentucky by increasing the Democratic share of the vote by 1.48% (from 42.27% to the breakpoint of 43.75%).

- **2% Neighborhood:** Pick up one electoral vote by increasing the Democratic share of the vote by 1.71% in Missouri, 1.73% in Utah, 1.82% in Ohio, 1.90% in South Carolina, and 1.96% in Tennessee.

Of course, the 10 "upside" states for the Kerry 2004 campaign would have been the same states where the Bush 2004 campaign would have had to play defense under

Table 4.22 THE NINE "UPSIDE" BATTLEGROUND STATES FOR BUSH IN 2004 UNDER THE WHOLE-NUMBER PROPORTIONAL APPROACH

STATE	GORE VOTE	GORE EV UNDER WTA	BUSH EV UNDER WTA	GORE EV UNDER WNP	BUSH EV UNDER WNP	BREAKPOINT JUST BELOW GORE VOTE	BREAKPOINT JUST ABOVE GORE VOTE	CHANGE NEEDED TO GAIN OR LOSE 1 EV UNDER WNP
TX	39.04%	0	32	12	20	35.94%	39.06%	−0.02%
NM	50.03%	5	0	3	2	50.00%	70.00%	−0.03%
WI	50.12%	11	0	6	5	50.00%	59.09%	−0.12%
IA	50.16%	7	0	4	3	50.00%	64.28%	−0.16%
OR	50.24%	7	0	4	3	50.00%	64.28%	−0.24%
NY	63.09%	33	0	20	13	62.12%	65.15%	−0.97%
NJ	58.21%	15	0	9	6	56.66%	63.33%	−1.55%
GA	44.02%	0	13	6	7	42.31%	50.00%	−1.71%
CO	45.51%	0	8	4	4	43.75%	56.25%	−1.76%
Total		**78**	**53**	**68**	**63**			

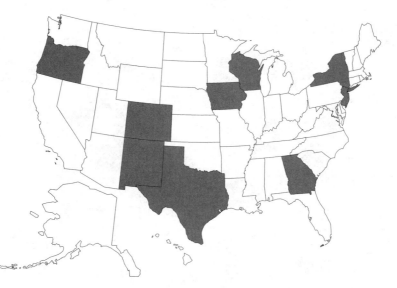

Figure 4.24 The nine "upside" battleground states for Bush in 2004 under the whole-number proportional approach

the whole-number proportional approach. Conversely, the nine "upside" states for the Bush 2004 campaign are the states where Kerry would have been on the defensive.

Of course, those planning a campaign would have, in practice, added or deleted certain states from the above list of 19 battleground states for numerous reasons, including the following:

First, planners of both campaigns would have considered adding or deleting a

Table 4.23 THE 10 "UPSIDE" BATTLEGROUND STATES FOR KERRY IN 2004 UNDER THE WHOLE-NUMBER PROPORTIONAL APPROACH

STATE	GORE VOTE	GORE EV UNDER WTA	BUSH EV UNDER WTA	GORE EV UNDER WNP	BUSH EV UNDER WNP	BREAKPOINT JUST BELOW GORE VOTE	BREAKPOINT JUST ABOVE GORE VOTE	CHANGE NEEDED TO GAIN OR LOSE 1 EV UNDER WNP
TN	48.04%	0	11	5	6	40.91%	50.00%	1.96%
SC	41.85%	0	8	3	5	31.25%	43.75%	1.90%
OH	48.18%	0	21	10	11	45.23%	50.00%	1.82%
UT	28.27%	0	5	1	4	10.00%	30.00%	1.73%
MO	48.29%	0	11	5	6	40.91%	50.00%	1.71%
KY	42.27%	0	8	3	5	31.25%	43.75%	1.48%
CA	56.20%	54	0	30	24	54.63%	56.48%	0.28%
IL	56.18%	22	0	12	10	52.27%	56.82%	0.18%
MI	52.63%	18	0	10	8	47.22%	52.78%	0.15%
FL	49.99%	0	25	12	13	46.00%	50.00%	0.01%
Total		**94**	**89**	**91**	**92**			

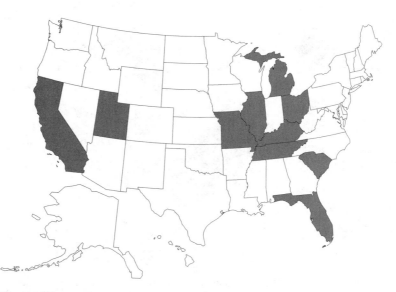

Figure 4.25 The 10 "upside" battleground states for Kerry in 2004 under the whole-number proportional approach

state with various unusual local political factors, such as a noticeable shift in partisan alignment since the last election, significant demographic changes since the last election, the localized impact of a controversial existing or planned government policy, the effect of an unusually popular or unpopular state administration due to scandals or other reasons, the home states of the candidates, or other political considerations.

Second, those involved in planning the Bush 2004 campaign would have given some consideration to the three states where they could have picked up one electoral vote each by reducing the Democratic share of the popular vote by between 2% and 3% (e.g., 2.29% in Massachusetts, 2.94% in Washington, and 2.97% in Arizona). Similarly, planners for the Kerry 2004 campaign would have given some consideration to the four states where they could have picked up one electoral vote each by increasing the Democratic share of the popular vote by between 2% and 3% (e.g., 2.15% in Pennsylvania, 2.29% in Massachusetts, 2.94% in Washington, and 2.97% in Arizona). Both campaigns would have glanced briefly at states where they might conceivably pick up an electoral vote by increasing their popular vote by 4% or more.

Third, the four biggest states are the exceptions to the statement that, except in landslide elections, the whole-number proportional approach is a "winner-take-one" system. In California, one electoral vote corresponds to a 1.85% share of the state's popular vote. If, for example, the 2004 Kerry campaign could have increased the Democratic share of the vote by 2.13% (0.28% plus 1.85%), it would have picked up two electoral votes in California. It would have required a change of 3.43% in the popular vote for the Bush 2004 campaign to have gained two electoral votes in California. Changing three electoral votes would be a possibility in California. Thus, California could be a "winner-take-two" or even a "winner-take-three" state.

In states other than California, the share of popular vote corresponding to one electoral vote is considerably larger than 1.85%. For example, for the two next largest states in the 2004 election (New York and Texas), the shares of popular vote corresponding to one electoral vote were 3.0% and 3.1%, respectively. For the fourth largest state (Florida), the percentage was 4.0%. Changing up to two electoral votes would become a possibility in these states. Thus, they could be "winner-take-two" states.

Notwithstanding the above caveats, the political reality is that campaign strategies in ordinary elections are based on trying to change a reasonably achievable small percentage of the votes—1%, 2%, or 3%. The bottom line is that the number of battleground states under the whole-number proportional approach would approximate the list of 19 states shown in tables 4.22 and 4.23. Something like 32 states would be noncompetitive under the whole-number proportional approach. That is, the whole-number proportional approach would not improve upon the current situation in which most voters of the United States are ignored by presidential campaigns.

Table 4.24 presents the 19 battleground states in 2004 (based on a 2% swing) under the whole-number proportional approach. The states in this table are sorted in order of the absolute value of the percentage change that would have been needed in order to gain or lose one electoral vote under the whole-number proportional approach.

Figure 4.26 summarizes the information in table 4.24. The figure presents, along a horizontal line, Gore's percentage share of the popular vote in the 19 battleground states listed in table 4.24.

Several observations can be made by comparing the 19 battleground states under

Table 4.24 THE 19 BATTLEGROUND STATES IN 2004 UNDER THE WHOLE-NUMBER PROPORTIONAL APPROACH

STATE	CHANGE NEEDED TO GAIN OR LOSE 1 ELECTORAL VOTE UNDER THE WHOLE-NUMBER PROPORTIONAL APPROACH
Florida	0.01%
Texas	−0.02%
New Mexico	−0.03%
Wisconsin	−0.12%
Michigan	0.15%
Iowa	−0.16%
Illinois	0.18%
Oregon	−0.24%
California	0.28%
New York	−0.97%
Kentucky	1.48%
New Jersey	−1.55%
Missouri	1.71%
Georgia	−1.71%
Utah	1.73%
Colorado	−1.76%
Ohio	1.82%
South Carolina	1.90%
Tennessee	1.96%

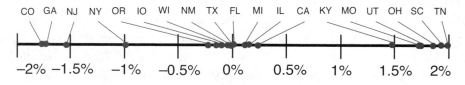

Figure 4.26 The 19 battleground states in 2004 under the whole-number proportional approach

the whole-number proportional approach listed in table 4.24 with the 19 closest states in the 2000 presidential election and the 16 closest states in the 2004 presidential election (section 1.2.1).

First, over half of the 19 battleground states under the whole-number proportional approach in table 4.24 are different from the actual battleground states of the 2004 election. The 19 battleground states under the whole-number proportional approach include states such as Texas, Illinois, California, New York, Kentucky, New Jersey,

Georgia, Utah, South Carolina, and Tennessee. None of these 10 states was a battleground state in the actual 2004 presidential election. Five of the hypothetical newcomers are among the nation's 10 largest states (i.e., states with 14 or more electoral votes). Kentucky, Georgia, Utah, South Carolina, and Tennessee would become newcomers because of the accident of the numerical breakpoints.

Second, the biggest states would be more likely to be battleground states under the whole-number proportional approach (subject to a caveat below concerning the difference between vote percentages and popular votes). The reason is that the share of the popular vote corresponding to one electoral vote is smaller for large states. Eight of the 10 states with 14 or more electoral votes would be among the 19 battleground states under the whole-number proportional approach (table 4.24). Moreover, Pennsylvania and North Carolina would be included on the list of battleground states if the percentage window considered by a particular campaign were widened to 3%. In contrast, six of the nation's 10 largest states (California, Texas, New York, Illinois, New Jersey, and North Carolina) are decidedly noncompetitive under the current statewide winner-take-all system.

Third, five states (Florida, New Mexico, Wisconsin, Iowa, and Oregon) are battleground states under both the existing winner-take-all-system and the whole-number proportional approach. These states are on the list either because the major parties received close to 50% of the vote in those states in 2000 or because these states happen to have had an odd number of electoral votes in 2000 (and hence have a breakpoint at 50.00%). On the other hand, states with an even number of electoral votes that were battlegrounds under the existing statewide winner-take-all system, such as New Hampshire, would not be battlegrounds under the whole-number proportional approach because there is no breakpoint at 50.00%.

It is, of course, difficult to predict exactly how a new system, such as the whole-number proportional approach, would actually work in practice if all the states were to adopt it for a future presidential election. For one thing, the above discussion is based on *percentages* and therefore somewhat overstates the degree of competitiveness of the larger states under the whole-number proportional approach. Almost all of the 19 or so battleground states under the whole-number proportional approach offer a campaign the possibility of winning or losing only one electoral vote. Changing the statewide percentage of the popular vote in a large state is far more costly (in terms of campaigning time, advertising, and organizational efforts) than generating the same percentage change in a small state. Thus, in practice, the largest of the 19 battleground states in table 4.24 would, almost certainly, receive less attention because they would offer far less "bang for the buck" to the campaign managers who are responsible for prudently allocating limited resources. If we were to exclude the 10 largest states (i.e., the states with 14 or more electoral votes), the actual list of battleground states under the whole-number proportional approach might consist of the following 11 states (as shown in figure 4.27):

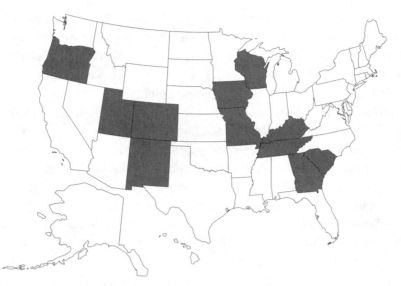

Figure 4.27 The 11 battleground states with greatest "bang for the buck" under the whole-number proportional approach

- New Mexico,
- Iowa,
- Wisconsin,
- Oregon,

- Kentucky,
- Missouri,
- Georgia,
- Utah,

- Colorado,
- South Carolina, and
- Tennessee.

4.1.14 AMENDMENT 36 IN COLORADO IN 2004

The whole-number proportional approach was on the ballot in November 2, 2004, as a proposed amendment to the Colorado state constitution. It received only 35% of the vote. There are three main reasons why the voters defeated Amendment 36 in 2004.

First, Amendment 36 was presented to the voters using the argument that it would take effect immediately and apply to the November 2004 presidential election. That is, the initiative would have applied to the very election in which the voters were deciding the initiative's fate. Many voters said that they would have approved the change for a subsequent election but that they were troubled by changing the rules of the game in the midst of a presidential campaign.[10]

Second, the claimed retroactivity of Amendment 36 interacted with the changing fortunes of the presidential candidates during the campaign. During the summer of 2004, Bush was expected to carry Colorado easily. Given that political expectation,

---

[10] The Colorado amendment would not, as a matter of law, have applied to the 2004 presidential election if it had been adopted by the voters on Election Day in 2004 because of section 5 of title 3 of the United States Code making a state's election results conclusive only if the presidential electors were appointed under laws "enacted prior to the day fixed for the appointment of the electors."

the political effect of Amendment 36 would have been to give four of Colorado's nine electoral votes in 2004 to the candidate who was expected to lose the state (Kerry). Part of the historical context of the 2004 presidential campaign was that Bush received only 271 votes in the Electoral College in 2000 (i.e., one more electoral vote than is necessary to win). Based on the closeness of the 2000 election and the political atmosphere in 2004, it was widely (and correctly) predicted that the vote in the Electoral College was likely to be very close in 2004. Indeed, Bush ultimately received only 16 more electoral votes than he needed in order to win in 2004. Therefore, Amendment 36 was perceived to have a strong possibility of affecting the national outcome of the 2004 presidential election. Thus, from the beginning, there was little Republican support for Amendment 36 because it was perceived to be a partisan effort to take four electoral votes from President Bush. Bill Owens (then Colorado's Republican Governor) made a decision to lead a campaign that spent over a million dollars in opposition to Amendment 36. Then, as Election Day approached, some polls showed Kerry almost tied with Bush in Colorado. At that point, Democrats started believing that the measure could cost Kerry four electoral votes, and the proposition's support from the Democratic side of the aisle evaporated.

Third, if Amendment 36 had been adopted, Colorado would have been the only state in the country dividing its electoral votes proportionally. Everyone agreed that the practical political effect of Amendment 36 would be to convert Colorado from a "winner-take-nine" state into a "winner-take-one" state. Many voters in Colorado felt that Colorado's influence would be greatly reduced if it were the only state in the nation to select its presidential electors proportionally. In his campaign against Amendment 36, Governor Owens argued that it did not make sense for just one state to adopt the whole-number proportional approach. The Governor's argument was, in essence, the same argument that Thomas Jefferson had made in his January 12, 1800, letter to James Monroe concerning the district system that had worked to Jefferson's disadvantage by dividing Virginia's electoral votes in the 1796 presidential election (quoted immediately below in the next section).

4.1.15 PRACTICAL POLITICAL IMPEDIMENT CONCERNING THE WHOLE-NUMBER PROPORTIONAL APPROACH

Whatever the merits of the whole-number proportional approach, there is a prohibitive practical impediment associated with the adoption of this approach on a piecemeal basis by individual states, namely the political disadvantage suffered by the states dividing their electoral vote in a political environment in which most other states retain the winner-take-all rule.

Thomas Jefferson summed up this objection in his January 12, 1800, letter to James Monroe arguing that Virginia should switch from its existing district system[11] to the statewide winner-take-all system. As Jefferson wrote:

---

[11] At the time, Virginia chose its 14 presidential electors from 14 special presidential elector districts.

"All agree that an election by districts would be best, if it could be general; but while 10. states chuse either by their legislatures or by a general ticket, **it is folly & worse than folly** for the other 6. not to do it."[12] [Emphasis added; spelling and punctuation as per original]

The now-prevailing statewide winner-take-all system became entrenched in the political landscape by the 1830s precisely because virtually all political parties came to realize that any fragmentation of a state's electoral votes diminishes the influence of the state's dominant party in comparison to states employing a winner-take-all approach. Once a few states adopt the statewide winner-take-all approach, it is disadvantageous for other states not to do so as well.

Suppose, for the sake of argument, that 50 of the 51 jurisdictions entitled to appoint presidential electors decided to allocate their electoral votes using the whole-number proportional approach. Recall (from table 4.24) that there could be about 19 battleground states under the whole-number proportional approach where one electoral vote would be in play. If even one state with 19 or more electoral votes were to retain the statewide winner-take-all system, then that single state would immediately become (in most cases) the only state that would matter in presidential politics. Indeed, even a single state with 10 or 15 electoral votes would, as a practical matter, become the most important state in an environment in which all the other jurisdictions used the whole-number proportional approach. The same argument would apply *a fortiori* if 49, 48, 47, or 46 jurisdictions were to adopt the whole-number proportional approach.

Moreover, if states were to ever start adopting the whole-number proportional approach on a piecemeal basis, each additional state adopting the approach would increase the influence of the remaining states and thereby would decrease the incentive of the remaining states to adopt it. Thus, a state-by-state process of adopting the whole-number proportional approach would quickly bring itself to a halt, leaving the states that adopted it with only minimal influence in presidential elections.

Of course, the above impediment associated with piecemeal adoption by the states of the whole-number proportional approach would not apply if it were adopted on a uniform national basis in the form of a federal constitutional amendment. A federal constitutional amendment would, if ratified, take effect simultaneously in all 50 states and the District of Columbia.

4.2 CONGRESSIONAL-DISTRICT APPROACH

The congressional-district approach would retain the existing statewide winner-take-all approach for both of the state's senatorial electors; however, it would use a district-level winner-take-all rule for the state's remaining presidential electors.

Of the three approaches described in chapter 3 and the two approaches described

---

[12] The entire letter and citations appear in the text and footnotes of section 2.2.3 of this book.

in this chapter, the congressional-district approach is the only approach that has ever been used.

In recent times, the district approach has been used in Maine since 1969 and in Nebraska since 1992. Maine has only two congressional districts, and Nebraska has only three. In the 10 presidential elections in which the congressional-district approach has been used in Maine and in the five elections in which it has been used in Nebraska, there has been only one occasion where this approach has yielded an electoral vote to a presidential candidate who lost the state. That occasion occurred in 2008 when Barack Obama carried Nebraska's 2nd congressional district and thereby won one electoral vote. Moreover, in most elections, presidential campaigns were not enticed to pay attention to either Maine or Nebraska because no congressional district appeared to be winnable. There has, however, been campaigning in some election years in Maine's 2nd congressional district (the northern part of the state) and, in 2008, in Nebraska's 2nd district (the Omaha area).

In this section, we will analyze two questions. The first is whether the congressional-district approach, if adopted nationwide, would more accurately reflect the nationwide popular vote than the existing statewide winner-take-all system. The second is whether the approach, if adopted nationwide, would improve upon the current situation in which four-fifths of the states and four-fifths of the people of the United States are ignored by presidential campaigns.

As will be seen in the analysis below, if the congressional-district approach were adopted nationwide,

- it would *not* accurately reflect the nationwide popular vote; and
- it would *not* improve upon the current situation in which four-fifths of the states and four-fifths of the people of the United States are ignored by presidential campaigns; and
- it would *not* make every vote equal.

In fact, the congressional-district approach would make all three of the major shortcomings of the current system even worse.

We start our analysis with the closest recent election (the 2000 election).

In the 2000 presidential election:

- George W. Bush carried 228 of the 435 congressional districts, whereas Al Gore carried 207 districts.
- Bush carried 30 states (having 60 senatorial electors), whereas Gore carried 20 states (having 40 senatorial electors).
- Gore carried the District of Columbia, which has three electoral votes.

If the congressional-district approach were applied to the results of the 2000 presidential election,[13] then Bush would have received 288 electoral votes (53.3% of the total

---

[13] Note that we use the actual results of the 2000 presidential election to make this comparison, while recognizing that if the congressional-district approach had been operating in 2000, the campaign would have been conducted differently.

number of electoral votes), and Gore would have received 250 electoral votes (46.5% of the total). That is, the congressional-district approach would have given Bush a 6.8% lead in electoral votes over Gore in 2000.

Gore received 50,992,335 popular votes (50.2% of the two-party popular vote), whereas Bush received 50,455,156 (49.7% of the two-party popular vote). Under the existing statewide winner-take-all system, Bush received 271 electoral votes in 2000 (50.4% of the total number of electoral votes)—a 0.8% lead in electoral votes over Gore.

In summary, the congressional-district approach would have been even less accurate than the existing statewide winner-take-all system in terms of mirroring the nationwide popular vote.

There are three reasons why the congressional-district approach would not, in general, accurately reflect the nationwide popular vote in presidential elections.

First, congressional districts are generally skewed in favor of the Republican Party because the Democrats are more concentrated in those geographic areas where Democrats are in the majority than is the case for the areas where Republicans are in the majority. This is one reason why Bush carried 228 of the 435 congressional districts, whereas Gore carried only 207 districts in 2000, despite the fact that Gore received 537,179 more popular votes nationwide than Bush.

The Republican geographical bias in congressional districts became more pronounced after the 2000 census. The congressional district boundaries that were in place at the time of the 2000 presidential election were, of course, the ones that were adopted in the early 1990s using data from the 1990 federal census. If the results of the 2000 presidential election are viewed from the perspective of the up-to-date congressional districts based on data from the 2000 federal census (i.e., those first used in the 2002 congressional elections), George W. Bush would have carried 241 (55%) of the 435 congressional districts.[14]

In the 2004 presidential election, George W. Bush carried 255 (59%) of the 435 congressional districts, whereas John Kerry carried 180.[15] Bush also carried 31 (61%) of the 51 jurisdictions entitled to appoint presidential electors. If the congressional-district approach had been in place nationwide for the 2004 presidential election, Bush would have won 317 (59%) of the 538 electoral votes in an election in which he received 51.5% of the two-party popular vote.

Second, the congressional-district approach retains the existing statewide winner-take-all approach for 100[16] of the 538 presidential electors (i.e., the two presidential electors to which each state is entitled regardless of its population). That is, the

---

[14] Barone, Michael; Cohen, Michael; and Ujifusa, Grant. 2003. *The 2004 Almanac of American Politics*. Washington, DC: National Journal Group.

[15] America's choice in 2004: Votes by congressional district. *Cook Political Report*. 2005.

[16] This total would be 102 if one were to count the District of Columbia (which has three presidential electors) as a state. The District of Columbia, like the seven states with three electoral votes, employs the winner-take-all rule. The District does not have any voting representation in Congress.

congressional-district approach overlays a "statewide winner-takes-two" system on top of a "district-wide winner-takes-one" system.

The third, and most fundamental, reason why the congressional-district approach does not accurately reflect the nationwide popular vote is simply that it is a *district* system. At the end of the day, the congressional-district approach would merely replace one kind of district (the existing state boundaries) with another (the congressional district boundaries) for 435 of the 538 presidential electors. Whenever a single political office is filled by an electoral process in which the winner-take-all rule is applied to geographic areas that are smaller than the entire jurisdiction encompassed by the office, there will be significant differences in the political value of individual votes. The inequality arises because some geographic areas will be battlegrounds, whereas others will not. Inevitably, candidates will compete vigorously for votes in the closely divided areas, while ignoring the voters in non-competitive areas. In addition, there is always the possibility, in any district system, of electing a candidate who did not receive the most popular votes in the jurisdiction as a whole.

Turning now to competitiveness, table 4.25 lists the 55 congressional districts in which the difference between George W. Bush and Al Gore was 4% or less in the 2000 presidential election.[17] Column 2 shows Bush's percentage of the popular vote for President in the district, and column 3 shows Gore's percentage. Column 4 shows the difference.

Overall, table 4.25 shows that

- in 6.7% of the congressional districts (29 of 435), the difference in the presidential vote was 2% or less;
- in 10.8% of the congressional districts (47 of 435), the difference in the presidential vote was 3% or less; and
- in 12.6% of the congressional districts (55 of 435), the difference in the presidential vote was 4% or less.

In short, the vast majority of congressional districts were non-competitive in terms of the 2000 presidential election.[18]

The same conclusions apply to the 2004 presidential election. Table 4.26 lists the 42 congressional districts in which the difference between George W. Bush and John Kerry was 4% or less in the district in 2004. Note that congressional districts were redrawn and renumbered in most states in 2002 on the basis of the 2000 federal census, so the district numbers in this table generally do not correspond to those found in the previous table.

Overall, table 4.26 shows that the difference in the presidential vote was 4% or less in only 9.6% of the congressional districts (42 of 435). In short, the vast majority of congressional districts were non-competitive in terms of the 2004 presidential candidates.

---

[17] *Cook Political Report.* April 10, 2001.

[18] Of course, the vast majority of congressional districts are also non-competitive in congressional elections.

Table 4.25 THE 55 CLOSEST CONGRESSIONAL DISTRICTS IN THE 2000 PRESIDENTIAL ELECTION

DISTRICT	BUSH	GORE	DIFFERENCE
California–22	49%	45%	4%
Florida–7	51%	47%	4%
Ohio–13	50%	46%	4%
Wisconsin–4	50%	46%	4%
Arizona–5	49%	46%	3%
California–11	50%	47%	3%
California–41	50%	47%	3%
New Hampshire–1	49%	46%	3%
Pennsylvania–4	50%	47%	3%
Pennsylvania–10	50%	47%	3%
Texas–10	46%	43%	3%
California–44	49%	47%	2%
Florida–8	50%	48%	2%
Iowa–4	50%	48%	2%
Minnesota–1	48%	46%	2%
Minnesota–6	48%	46%	2%
Oregon–5	48%	46%	2%
Arkansas–2	49%	48%	1%
Florida–2	49%	48%	1%
Iowa–3	49%	48%	1%
Pennsylvania–21	49%	48%	1%
Tennessee–8	50%	49%	1%
Washington–3	48%	47%	1%
Michigan–10	49%	49%	0%
Michigan–11	49%	49%	0%
New York–24	48%	48%	0%
Texas–27	49%	49%	0%
Virginia–4	49%	49%	0%
California–23	47%	48%	–1%
New Hampshire–2	47%	48%	–1%
Wisconsin–7	47%	48%	–1%
California–20	48%	50%	–2%
California–28	47%	49%	–2%
New Mexico–1	47%	49%	–2%
Pennsylvania–15	47%	49%	–2%
Texas–25	48%	50%	–2%

Table 4.25 *(continued)*

DISTRICT	BUSH	GORE	DIFFERENCE
Virginia–11	47%	49%	–2%
Washington–2	46%	48%	–2%
Washington–8	47%	49%	–2%
Wisconsin–1	47%	49%	–2%
Arkansas–1	47%	50%	–3%
Arkansas–4	47%	50%	–3%
Florida–16	47%	50%	–3%
Michigan–8	47%	50%	–3%
North Carolina–4	48%	51%	–3%
Ohio–1	47%	50%	–3%
Ohio–3	47%	50%	–3%
Pennsylvania–7	47%	50%	–3%
Pennsylvania–8	47%	50%	–3%
Texas–24	48%	51%	–3%
Wisconsin–3	46%	49%	–3%
Florida–5	46%	50%	–4%
Ohio–19	46%	50%	–4%
Pennsylvania–20	47%	51%	–4%
West Virginia–3	47%	51%	–4%

One reason why the congressional-district approach is so much less competitive than the existing statewide winner-take-all approach is that congressional districts are gerrymandered in many states. Gerrymandering is most commonly done to give a partisan advantage to one political party. It is sometimes done to protect congressional incumbents of both parties.

If the presidential election were based on congressional districts, then the incentive for politically motivated districting would be even greater than it is today.

Many current efforts to change the process of congressional districting require districts to be compact in shape and to adhere closely to existing city and county boundaries. Generally, geometrically compact districts that adhere closely to local government boundaries tend to yield non-competitive areas. In most cases, the only way to achieve competitiveness (in the context of the single-member districts) is to intentionally create irregularly shaped districts that make competitiveness the top priority (after population equality, of course). Thus, to the extent that redistricting procedures are changed to favor compact districts adhering to local government boundaries, one can expect to see fewer (not more) competitive districts.

Table 4.26 THE 42 CLOSEST CONGRESSIONAL DISTRICTS IN THE 2004 PRESIDENTIAL ELECTION

DISTRICT	BUSH	KERRY	DIFFERENCE
New York–23	51%	47%	4%
Minnesota–10	51%	47%	4%
Arkansas–4	51%	48%	3%
Arkansas–2	51%	48%	3%
Minnesota–3	51%	48%	3%
New Hampshire–1	51%	48%	3%
Iowa–4	51%	48%	3%
New Jersey–3	51%	49%	2%
Florida–10	51%	49%	2%
Ohio–12	51%	49%	2%
Michigan–9	51%	49%	2%
Ohio–6	51%	49%	2%
Washington–3	50%	48%	2%
Ohio–1	51%	50%	1%
Oregon–5	50%	49%	1%
California–47	50%	49%	1%
New Jersey–2	50%	49%	1%
Virginia–11	50%	49%	1%
Nevada–3	50%	49%	1%
California–18	50%	49%	1%
Ohio–15	50%	50%	0%
Iowa–3	50%	50%	0%
Pennsylvania–15	50%	50%	0%
New York–1	49%	49%	0%
Connecticut–5	49%	49%	0%
Wisconsin–7	50%	49%	–1%
Oregon–4	50%	49%	–1%
Kentucky–3	49%	51%	–2%
California–20	49%	51%	–2%
Pennsylvania–12	49%	51%	–2%
New York–25	48%	50%	–2%
Illinois–17	48%	51%	–3%
Colorado–7	48%	51%	–3%
Washington–8	48%	51%	–3%
Pennsylvania–8	48%	51%	–3%
New Mexico–1	48%	51%	–3%
Wisconsin–3	48%	51%	–3%
Pennsylvania–6	48%	52%	–4%
Florida–22	48%	52%	–4%
Illinois–12	48%	52%	–4%
Tennessee–5	48%	52%	–4%
Washington–2	47%	51%	–4%

Table 4.27 **CONGRESSIONAL DISTRICTS IN THE 10 LARGEST STATES THAT WERE CLOSE IN THE 2004 PRESIDENTIAL ELECTION**

STATE	NUMBER OF CONGRESSIONAL DISTRICTS THAT WERE CLOSE IN THE PRESIDENTIAL RACE
California	7
Pennsylvania	7
Florida	5
Ohio	4
Texas	4
Michigan	3
New York	1
North Carolina	1

Table 4.27 shows that the congressional districts that were close in the presidential race are heavily concentrated in the 10 largest states. Specifically, 58% of the 55 close congressional districts in 2000 (32 of the 55) lie in eight of the 10 largest states. Thus, the congressional-district approach would not only focus presidential campaigns on a tiny fraction of the nation's congressional districts, but it would also concentrate the presidential race on the 10 largest states to a degree that exceeds their share of the nation's population and that exceeds their prominence under the current winner-take-all system. Four of the eight large states in the table were competitive statewide in presidential elections in 2000 and 2004 (i.e., Pennsylvania, Florida, Ohio, and Michigan), whereas four were not (i.e., California, Texas, New York, and North Carolina).

Votes do not have equal weight under the congressional-district approach. In fact, there are five different inequalities inherent in the congressional-district approach, namely

- inequalities resulting from the fact that each state has two statewide (senatorial) presidential electors regardless of its population;
- inequalities stemming from the apportionment of the membership of the House of Representatives among the states;
- inequalities (particularly late in a decade) stemming from the fact that seats in the House of Representatives are only reapportioned once each decade;
- inequalities caused by differences in voter turnout caused by the level of civic participation in the state or the state's rate of population growth; and
- inequalities caused by differences in voter turnout in particular congressional districts.

First, a vote cast in a large state for the two statewide (senatorial) presidential electors has less weight than a vote cast in a small state for its two statewide electors. For example, in the 2000 presidential election, Wyoming had two statewide presidential electors (with a 1990 population of 453,588), whereas California had two statewide presidential electors (with a 1990 population of 29,760,021). As shown in table 4.28 for the presidential elections of 1992, 1996, and 2000, each statewide presidential elector corresponded to 226,794 people in Wyoming but to 14,880,011 people in California. The last column of this table shows the ratio of California's population per electoral vote compared to that of Wyoming—a 65.6-to-1 variation.

Table 4.28 DIFFERENCE IN WEIGHT OF A VOTE CAST FOR THE
TWO STATEWIDE PRESIDENTIAL ELECTORS UNDER
THE CONGRESSIONAL-DISTRICT APPROACH

STATE	POPULATION	POPULATION CORRESPONDING TO EACH STATEWIDE PRESIDENTIAL ELECTOR	RATIO TO LOWEST
California	29,760,021	14,880,011	65.6
Wyoming	453,588	226,794	1.00

Second, a vote cast in certain states has less weight than a vote cast in certain other states because of inequalities in the apportionment of the membership of the House of Representatives among the several states. For example, in the 1990 census, Wyoming had a population of 453,588, and Montana had 799,065; however, both states received one House seat. As shown in table 4.29, in the presidential elections of 1992, 1996, and 2000, each statewide presidential elector corresponded to 226,794 people in Wyoming but to 399,533 in Montana. The last column of this table shows the ratio of Montana's population per electoral vote to that of the lowest in the table (Wyoming)— a 1.76-to-1 variation.

Table 4.29 DIFFERENCE IN WEIGHT OF A VOTE CAST BECAUSE
OF CONGRESSIONAL APPORTIONMENT UNDER
THE CONGRESSIONAL-DISTRICT APPROACH

STATE	POPULATION	POPULATION CORRESPONDING TO EACH STATEWIDE PRESIDENTIAL ELECTOR	RATIO TO LOWEST
Montana	799,065	399,533	1.76
Wyoming	453,588	226,794	1.00

Numerous other such substantial variations could be cited between various pairs of states, including variations between states with differing numbers of electoral votes.

Third, a vote cast in a rapidly growing state has less weight than a vote cast elsewhere. The discrepancy expands in later years of a decade. For example, a rapidly growing state such as Nevada was entitled to four electoral votes as a result of the 1990 census, five as a result of the 2000 census, and six as a result of the 2010 census (as shown in table 2.1). In the 2000 presidential election, Nevada had only four-fifths of the voting power in the Electoral College that its 2000 population justified. Nevada did not receive the benefit in the Electoral College of its increased population until the 2004 election. Similarly, a vote cast in a slowly growing, non-growing, or declining state has relatively greater weight.

Fourth, among states with equal numbers of electoral votes, a vote cast in a state with a lower voter turnout has a greater weight than a vote cast in a state where more votes are cast. See table 3.5.

Fifth, a vote cast in a congressional district where fewer total votes are cast has a greater weight than a vote cast in a congressional district where more total votes are cast. There are many congressional districts (typically those with lopsided majorities in favor of one party) where voter turnout is noticeably lower than that of other districts within the state.

Summarizing the above points, if the congressional-district approach were adopted nationwide,

- it would not accurately reflect the nationwide popular vote;
- it would not improve upon the current situation in which four-fifths of the states and four-fifths of the people of the United States are ignored by presidential campaigns; and
- it would not make every vote equal.

4.2.1 PRACTICAL POLITICAL IMPEDIMENT CONCERNING THE CONGRESSIONAL-DISTRICT APPROACH

Whatever the merits of the congressional-district approach, there is a prohibitive practical impediment associated with the adoption of this approach on a piecemeal basis by individual states.

In his January 12, 1800, letter to James Monroe, Thomas Jefferson argued that Virginia should switch from its then-existing district system to the statewide winner-take-all system because of the political disadvantage suffered by states that divided their electoral votes by districts in a political environment in which other states use the winner-take-all approach:

> "All agree that an election by districts would be best, if it could be general; but while 10. states chuse either by their legislatures or by a general ticket, **it is folly & worse than folly** for the other 6. not to do it."[19] [Emphasis added; spelling and punctuation as per original]

Indeed, the now-prevailing statewide winner-take-all system became entrenched in the political landscape in the 1830s precisely because dividing a state's electoral

---

[19] The entire letter and citations appear in the text and footnotes of section 2.2.3 of this book.

votes diminishes the state's political influence relative to states employing the state-wide winner-take-all approach.

The Florida legislature considered adopting the congressional-district approach in the early 1990s. The proposal failed there largely because of concern that it would reduce the state's political importance in presidential elections. As it happened, George W. Bush carried 13 of Florida's 23 congressional districts in the 2000 presidential election, whereas Gore carried 10. If the congressional-district approach had been used in Florida in the 2000 presidential election (with the electoral system remaining unchanged in all other states), Gore would have been elected President because Bush would have received only 13 of Florida's 25 electoral votes (instead of all 25).

The "folly" of individual states adopting the congressional-district approach on a *piecemeal* basis is shown by the listing of the 55 closest congressional districts in table 4.25. Suppose that 50 of the 51 jurisdictions entitled to appoint presidential electors were to allocate electoral votes by district but that California (with 55 electoral votes in the 2004 presidential election) did not. California would immediately become the only state that would matter in presidential politics. The same thing would happen if two or three medium-sized states were to retain the statewide winner-take-all system while the remaining states decided to employ the congressional-district approach. The congressional-district approach only makes sense if 100% of the states adopt it.

Moreover, if states started adopting the congressional-district approach on a piecemeal basis, each additional state adopting the approach would increase the influence of the remaining states and thereby would increase the disincentive for the remaining states to adopt it. Thus, a state-by-state process adopting the congressional-district approach would bring itself to a halt.

Of course, the above impediment associated with piecemeal adoption of the congressional-district approach would not apply if the system were adopted simultaneously on a nationwide basis as a federal constitutional amendment (such as Senator Mundt's proposed amendment described in section 3.3).

5 | Background on Interstate Compacts

An interstate compact is a contractual agreement between two or more states. This chapter covers the

- constitutional basis for interstate compacts (section 5.1),
- legal standing of compacts (section 5.2),
- history of compacts (section 5.3),
- subjects covered by compacts (section 5.4),
- parties to compacts (section 5.5),
- formulation of compacts (section 5.6),
- methods by which a state enacts a compact (section 5.7),
- contingent nature of compacts (section 5.8),
- congressional consent and involvement in compacts (section 5.9),
- effect of congressional consent (section 5.10),
- compacts that are contingent on enactment of federal legislation at the time Congress grants its consent to the compact (section 5.11),
- compacts that do not require congressional consent (section 5.12),
- enforcement of compacts (section 5.13),
- amendments to compacts (section 5.14),
- duration, termination, and withdrawals from compacts (section 5.15),
- administration of compacts (section 5.16),
- style of compacts (section 5.17),
- comparison of treaties and interstate compacts (section 5.18),
- comparison of uniform state laws and interstate compacts (section 5.19),
- comparison of federal multi-state commissions and interstate compacts (section 5.20),
- future of interstate compacts (section 5.21), and
- proposals for compacts on elections (section 5.22).

5.1 CONSTITUTIONAL BASIS FOR INTERSTATE COMPACTS

Interstate compacts predate the U.S. Constitution. The Articles of Confederation (proposed by the Continental Congress in 1777 and ratified by the states by 1781) provided:

> "No two or more States shall enter into any treaty, confederation or alliance whatever between them, without the consent of the United States in Con-

gress assembled, specifying accurately the purposes for which the same is to be entered into, and how long it shall continue."[1]

The Continental Congress consented to four interstate compacts under the Articles of Confederation. One interstate compact (regulating fishing and navigation) received the consent of the Continental Congress under the Articles of Confederation in 1785 and remained in force until 1958.

The U.S. Constitution was proposed by the Constitutional Convention in 1787 and ratified by the requisite number of states by 1789.

Article I, section 10, clause 3 of the U.S. Constitution provides:

"No state shall, without the consent of Congress, . . . enter into any agreement or compact with another state. . . ."[2]

The terms "compact" and "agreement" are generally used interchangeably. As the U.S. Supreme Court wrote in the 1893 case of *Virginia v. Tennessee*:

"Compacts or agreements . . . we do not perceive any difference in the meaning. . . ."[3]

The Supreme Court also wrote:

"The terms 'agreement' or 'compact,' taken by themselves, are sufficiently comprehensive to embrace all forms of stipulation, written or verbal, and relating to all kinds of subjects. . . ."[4]

The terms "compact" and "agreement" encompass arrangements that are enacted by statutory law as well as those entered into by a state's executive officers and commissions.

5.2 LEGAL STANDING OF INTERSTATE COMPACTS

An interstate compact is, first and foremost, a contract. As the Supreme Court wrote in the 1959 case of *Petty v. Tennessee-Missouri Bridge Commission*:

"A compact is, after all, a contract."[5]

As contracts, compacts enjoy strong protection from the Impairments Clause of the U.S. Constitution. Article I, section 10, clause 1 provides:

"No State shall . . . pass any . . . Law impairing the Obligation of Contracts. . . ."[6]

---

[1] Articles of Confederation. Article VI, clause 2.
[2] See appendix C for full wording of the compacts clause.
[3] *Virginia v. Tennessee.* 148 U.S. 503 at 520. 1893.
[4] Id. at 517–518.
[5] *Petty v. Tennessee-Missouri Bridge Commission.* 359 U.S. 275 at 285. 1959.
[6] See appendix C for the full wording of the Impairments Clause.

The Council of State Governments summarizes the nature of interstate compacts as follows:

"Compacts are agreements between two or more states that bind them to the compacts' provisions, just as a contract binds two or more parties in a business deal. As such, compacts are subject to the substantive principles of contract law and are protected by the constitutional prohibition against laws that impair the obligations of contracts (U.S. Constitution, Article I, Section 10).

"That means that **compacting states are bound to observe the terms of their agreements, even if those terms are inconsistent with other state laws**. In short, compacts between states are somewhat like treaties between nations. Compacts have the force and effect of statutory law (whether enacted by statute or not) and **they take precedence over conflicting state laws, regardless of when those laws are enacted.**

"However, unlike treaties, compacts are not dependent solely upon the good will of the parties. **Once enacted, compacts may not be unilaterally renounced by a member state, except as provided by the compacts themselves.** Moreover, Congress and the courts can compel compliance with the terms of interstate compacts. That's why **compacts are considered the most effective means of ensuring interstate cooperation.**"[7] [Emphasis added]

Once a state enters into an interstate compact, the state—like an individual, corporation, or any other legal entity—is bound by the compact's terms. The contractual obligations undertaken by a state in an interstate compact bind all state officials. In addition, an interstate compact binds the state legislature because a legislature may not enact any law impairing a contract. Thus, after a state enters into an interstate compact, the state is bound by all the terms of the compact until the state withdraws from the compact in accordance with the compact's terms for withdrawal, until the compact is terminated in accordance with the compact's terms for termination, or until the compact ends in accordance with the compact's stated duration.

States generally enter into interstate compacts in order to obtain some benefit that can only be obtained by cooperative and coordinated action with one or more sister states. In most cases, it would make no sense for a state to agree to the terms of a compact unless certain other states simultaneously agreed to abide by the terms of the compact. For example, a state generally would not want to agree to limitations on its use of water in a river basin unless the other states in the basin agreed to limit their

7 Council of State Governments. 2003. *Interstate Compacts and Agencies 2003*. Lexington, KY: The Council of State Governments. Page 6.

water use. When two states are involved in a boundary dispute, neither state would generally want to acknowledge a compromise boundary until the other state accepted the compromise.

When a state enters into an interstate compact (other than a purely advisory compact), it is typically agreeing to a constraint, to one degree or another, on its ability to exercise some power that it otherwise might independently exercise.

5.3 HISTORY OF INTERSTATE COMPACTS

There were four interstate compacts approved under the Articles of Confederation. Three of them were settlements of boundary disputes.

The first regulatory compact was an agreement between Maryland and Virginia concerning fishing and navigation on the Chesapeake Bay and the Potomac River. This compact received the consent of the Continental Congress under the Articles of Confederation in 1785. This compact did not receive the consent of the new Congress established by the U.S. Constitution. It remained in force until it was replaced by the Potomac River Compact (which received congressional consent in 1958).

Prior to 1921, pre-existing agencies of the compacting states administered all interstate compacts.

In their seminal article entitled "The Compact Clause of the Constitution," Felix Frankfurter (subsequently a Justice of the U.S. Supreme Court) and James Landis noted that the vast majority (25 of the 32) of interstate compacts prior to 1921 were for the purpose of resolving boundary disputes.[8]

The modern era of interstate compacts began in 1921 with the Port of New York Authority Compact. The inadequacies of the port of New York became obvious during World War I. After the war, the states of New York and New Jersey decided that efficient operation and development of the port required closer cooperation and coordination between the two states. The result was the Port of New York Authority Compact. This 1921 compact broke new ground by establishing a bi-state governmental entity—the Port Authority. Under the compact, the Port Authority is administered by its own governing body—a commission appointed by the governors of the two states. The compact's intended purposes are summarized in the compact's preamble:

> "Whereas, In the year eighteen hundred and thirty-four the states of New York and New Jersey did enter into an agreement fixing and determining the rights and obligations of the two states in and about the waters between the two states, especially in and about the bay of New York and the Hudson river; and

> "Whereas, Since that time the commerce of the port of New York has greatly developed and increased and the territory in and around the port has become commercially one center or district; and

---

[8] Frankfurter, Felix, and Landis, James. 1925. The compact clause of the constitution—A study in interstate adjustments. 34 *Yale Law Journal* 692–693 and 730–732. May 1925.

"Whereas, It is confidently believed that a better co-ordination of the terminal, transportation and other facilities of commerce in, about and through the port of New York, will result in great economies, benefiting the nation, as well as the states of New York and New Jersey; and

"Whereas, The future development of such terminal, transportation and other facilities of commerce will require the expenditure of large sums of money and the cordial co-operation of the states of New York and New Jersey in the encouragement of the investment of capital, and in the formulation and execution of the necessary physical plans; and

"Whereas, Such result can best be accomplished through the co-operation of the two states by and through a joint or common agency."

After 1921, the number of compacts and the variety of topics covered by compacts increased dramatically. Nowadays, about one half of all interstate compacts establish a commission to administer the subject matter of the compact.[9] Compact commissions are generally composed of a specified number of representatives from each party state. Many modern-day compacts receive annual funding from each member state for the operation of the compact commission and its staff.

5.4 SUBJECT MATTER OF INTERSTATE COMPACTS

There are no constitutional restrictions on the subject matter of interstate compacts other than the implicit limitation that the compact's subject matter must be among the powers that the states are permitted to exercise.

Interstate compacts have been employed for a wide variety of purposes, including those listed below.

An *advisory compact* establishes a commission that is authorized only to conduct studies and to develop recommendations to solve interstate problems. Advisory compacts are the weakest form of interstate compacts.

Examples of *agricultural compacts* include the Compact on Agricultural Grain Marketing and the Northeast Interstate Dairy Compact.

Two states may enter into a *boundary compact*. A freely negotiated settlement of a boundary dispute is often a desirable alternative to a trial in the U.S. Supreme Court to establish the official boundaries between two states. The South Dakota–Nebraska Boundary Compact (which received congressional consent in 1990) settled a dispute arising from the fact that the Missouri River had changed its course with the passage of time.

Many *civil defense compacts* were adopted during the Cold War period. The Emergency Management Assistance Compact (found in appendix N), to which Congress

---

[9] Council of State Governments. 2003. *Interstate Compacts and Agencies 2003*. Lexington, KY: The Council of State Governments.

consented in 1996, is a broad compact that effectively replaces the earlier Civil Defense Compact.

Crime-control and *corrections compacts* are traceable to 1910 when Congress gave its consent in advance to four states—Illinois, Indiana, Michigan, and Wisconsin—to enter into an agreement with respect to the exercise of jurisdiction "over offenses arising out of the violation of the laws" of these states on the waters of Lake Michigan.[10] The Interstate Agreement on Detainers is one of the best-known compacts concerning crime. This agreement facilitates speedy and proper disposition of detainers based on indictments, information, or complaints from the jurisdictions that are parties to the compact. The parties to this compact include 48 states, the District of Columbia, Puerto Rico, the Virgin Islands, and the federal government.

In 2000, Congress gave its consent to Kansas and Missouri to enter into the nation's first *cultural compact*. The compact established a metropolitan cultural district governed by a commission.

The first *education compact* pooled the resources of Southern states by means of the Southern Regional Education Compact. The aim of the compact was to reduce each state's need to maintain expensive post-graduate and professional schools. There are two additional compacts of this nature: the New England Higher Education Compact and the Western Regional Education Compact. The New Hampshire–Vermont Interstate School Compact has been used to establish two interstate school districts, each involving a New Hampshire town and one or more Vermont towns.

Energy Compacts include the Interstate Compact to Conserve Oil and Gas, the Southern States Energy Compact (originally the Southern Interstate Nuclear Compact), the Midwest Energy Compact, and the Western Interstate Energy Compact (originally the Western Interstate Nuclear Compact).

Facilities compacts provide for the joint construction and operation of physical facilities—commonly bridges and tunnels. A compact entered into by Maine and New Hampshire dealt with the construction and maintenance of a single bridge over the Piscataqua River.[11] On the other hand, the Port Authority of New York and New Jersey operates extensive facilities, including the Holland and Lincoln Tunnels, the George Washington Bridge, three airports (Kennedy, LaGuardia, and Newark Liberty), the PATH rail system, ferries, industrial development projects, and marine facilities. The Port Authority's police force alone numbers over 1,600.

The four *fisheries compacts* are the Atlantic States Marine Fisheries Compact of 1942, the Pacific States Marine Fisheries Compact of 1947, the Gulf States Marine Fisheries Compact of 1949, and the Connecticut River Basin Atlantic Salmon Compact of 1983.

Flood-control compacts relate to the construction of projects to prevent flooding. A 1957 compact between Massachusetts and New Hampshire established the Mer-

---

[10] 36 Stat. 882.

[11] 50 Stat. 536.

rimack Valley Flood Control Commission, which determines the annual amount of compensation that Massachusetts must pay New Hampshire for loss of tax revenue resulting from the construction of flood-control projects.

The Interstate Compact on Mental Health and the New England Compact on Radiological Health Protection are examples of *health compacts.*

Congress encouraged the formation of *low-level radioactive waste compacts* to construct regional waste storage facilities as an alternative to the development of individual storage sites in each state. In particular, the federal Low-Level Radioactive Waste Policy Act of 1980[12] (as amended in 1985) encourages the use of interstate compacts to establish and operate regional facilities for management of low-level radioactive waste. A total of 44 states have entered into 10 such compacts. One example is the Southwestern Low-Level Radioactive Waste Disposal Compact in which California agreed to serve, for 35 years, as the host state for the storage of radioactive waste for the states of Arizona, North Dakota, South Dakota, and California (and such other states to which the compact commission might later decide to grant membership).

Because of the politically sensitive subject matter, radioactive-waste compacts generally attract considerable public attention and generate fierce debate in state legislatures. Voters have often become directly involved in radioactive waste compacts by means of the citizen-initiative process, the protest-referendum process, and the legislative referral process.[13]

Marketing and development compacts address a variety of subjects and include the Agricultural Grain Marketing Compact, the Midwest Nuclear Compact promoting the use of nuclear energy, and the Mississippi River Parkway Compact.

The Washington Metropolitan Area Transit Regulation Compact was entered into by the District of Columbia, Maryland, and Virginia and was granted congressional consent in 1960.[14] It is an example of a *metropolitan problems compact.*

The only *military compact* is the National Guard Mutual Assistance Compact. It provides for the sharing of military personnel and equipment among its member states.

There are 12 *motor vehicle compacts*, including ones that relate to driver's licenses, nonresident violators, equipment safety, and uniform vehicle registration prorogation.

Natural resources compacts are designed to settle disputes and to promote the conservation and development of resources. For example, in 1963, Maryland and Virginia established the Potomac River Fisheries Commission to settle a dispute that had originated during the colonial period. Ever since a royal charter made the river a part of Maryland, Maryland oyster fishermen have resented Virginia oyster fisher-

---

[12] 94 Stat. 3347.

[13] See sections 5.7 and 5.13 for discussion of the political controversies, spanning a 20-year period, concerning Nebraska's participation in the Central Interstate Low-Level Radioactive Waste Compact.

[14] 74 Stat. 1031.

men intruding in Maryland's waters. The more recent Connecticut River Basin Atlantic Salmon Restoration Compact involves the return of salmon to the river.[15]

The Columbia River Gorge Compact and the 1900 Palisades Interstate Park Compact are two of the five *parks and recreation compacts*.

Economic interest groups often encourage the establishment of *regulatory compacts*. Such groups typically lobby Congress not to exercise its preemption powers in a particular area by arguing that coordinated action by the states, by means of an interstate compact, is sufficient to solve a problem.

The Interstate Sanitation Compact, entered into by New Jersey and New York in 1935 and by Connecticut in 1941, created a commission with the power to abate and prevent pollution in tidal waters of the New York City metropolitan area. Subsequently, the compact was amended to allow the commission to monitor, but not to regulate, air quality. The commission (renamed the Interstate Environmental Commission) shares concurrent regulatory authority with the environmental protection departments of the member states.

The Atlantic States Marine Fisheries Compact does not grant its commission regulatory enforcement powers; however, the commission obtained indirect regulatory authority by a congressional act. In 1986, the Atlantic Striped Bass Conservation Act was amended to offer each concerned state the choice of complying with the management plan developed by the commission or being subject to a fishing moratorium on striped bass imposed by the U.S. Fish and Wildlife Service in the state's coastal waters.[16]

One of the greatest problems in southwestern states—the shortage of water—led to the filing of numerous lawsuits between states in the U.S. Supreme Court. *River basin* compacts provide an alternative to litigation. The first such compact was the Colorado River Compact apportioning waters of the river among various western states. More recently, various mid-Atlantic states have entered into river basin compacts.

A *service compact* seeks to eliminate social problems by committing each member state to provide services to legal residents of other member states. The Interstate Compact on the Placement of Children in Interstate Adoption, for example, facilitates the adoption of children by qualified foster parents in other compact states if there are too few families willing to adopt children in the home state. This compact has 50 members—49 states and the Virgin Islands.

In 1934, Congress enacted the Crime Control Consent Act authorizing states to enter into crime-control compacts.[17] The Interstate Compact for Supervision of Parolees and Probationers is based on this statute and is the first interstate compact to have been joined by all states. Puerto Rico and the Virgin Islands also are members. The importance of this compact is illustrated by the fact that more than 300,000 people are on parole or probation in states other than those in which they committed their crimes.

---

[15] 97 Stat. 1983.

[16] 100 Stat. 989, 16 U.S.C. §1857.

[17] Crime Control Consent Act of 1934. 48 Stat. 909. 4 U.S.C. §112.

The Interstate Compact on Juveniles and the Interstate Corrections Compact authorize the return of delinquents and convicts, respectively, to their states of domicile to serve their sentences. Supporters of these compacts believe that rehabilitation of delinquents and convicts will be promoted if they are incarcerated in close proximity to their families.

The levying of state income and sales taxes and the growth of interstate commerce has encouraged states to enter into *tax compacts*. The Great Lakes Interstate Sales Compact was the first multi-state compact to focus on enforcement of state sales and use taxes. New Jersey and New York belong to an agreement providing for a mutual exchange of information relative to purchases by residents of the other state from in-state vendors. The states have also entered into numerous administrative agreements concerning taxation.

Twenty-three states and the District of Columbia are parties to the Multistate Tax Compact. Twenty-one additional states are associate members of the compact by virtue of their participation in, and their providing funding for, various programs established by the compact's commission. The impetus for the Multistate Tax Compact was the 1966 decision of the U.S. Supreme Court in *Northwestern States Portland Cement Company v. Minnesota*. The Court ruled that a state may tax the net income of a foreign corporation (i.e., one chartered in a sister state) if the tax is nondiscriminatory and is apportioned equitably on the basis of the corporation's activities with a nexus to the taxing state.[18]

A *federal-interstate compact* is an interstate compact to which the federal government is one of the parties.

Felix Frankfurter and James Landis anticipated the possibility of *federal-interstate compacts* in 1925 and wrote:

> "[T]he combined legislative powers of Congress and of the several states permit a wide range of permutations and combinations for governmental action. Until very recently these potentialities have been left largely unexplored. . . . Creativeness is called for to devise a great variety of legal alternatives to cope with the diverse forms of interstate interests."[19]

Frankfurter and Landis's call for creativity led to the first *federal-interstate compact* in 1961. After a prolonged drought in the 1950s made the careful management of Delaware River waters essential, four states and the federal government entered into the Delaware River Basin Compact. Congress enacted the compact into federal law with a provision that the United States be a member of the compact. That law created a commission with a national co-chairman and a state co-chairman. The commission also has additional members from the national and member state governments.

---

[18] *Northwestern States Portland Cement Company v. Minnesota*. 358 U.S. 450. 1966.

[19] Frankfurter, Felix, and Landis, James. 1925. The compact clause of the constitution—A study in interstate adjustments. 34 *Yale Law Journal* 692–693 and 730–732. May 1925.

Additionally, the federal government, Maryland, New York, and Pennsylvania entered into the Susquehanna River Basin Compact, which became effective in 1971. This is another example of a federal-interstate compact. It is modeled on the Delaware River Basin Compact.

Federal-interstate compacts have also been employed to promote economic development in large regions of the nation. The Appalachian Regional Compact was the first such compact. It was enacted by Congress and 13 states in 1965. This compact has a commission with a state co-chairman appointed by the governors involved and a federal co-chairman appointed by the President with the Senate's advice and consent.[20]

A unique federal-interstate agreement resulted from a 1980 congressional statute granting consent to an agreement entered into by the Bonneville Power Administration, a federal entity, with Idaho, Montana, Oregon, and Washington.[21] The term "interstate compact" does not appear in the act, and the agreement was not negotiated by the member states. Instead, the proposed compact was drafted by the Pacific Northwest Electric Power and Conservation Planning Council, which sent the proposal to the states. If the states had not enacted the proposed compact, a federal council would have been appointed by the U.S. Secretary of the Interior to perform the functions of the proposed federal-interstate council, namely preparing a conservation and electric power plan and implementing a program to protect fish and wildlife. A second unique feature of this legislation was the provision for membership by a federal agency, rather than the federal government.[22]

In 1990, Congress created a similar temporary body—the Northern Forest Lands Council. The Northern Forest Lands Council Act[23] authorized each of the governors of Maine, New Hampshire, New York, and Vermont to appoint four council members charged with developing plans to maintain the "traditional patterns of land ownership and use" of the northern forest. The council was disbanded in 1994.

The National Criminal Prevention and Privacy Compact Act, enacted by Congress in 1998, established what may be termed a federal-interstate compact that

> "organizes an electronic information sharing system among the Federal Government and the States to exchange criminal history records for non-criminal justice purposes authorized by Federal or State law, such as background checks for governmental licensing and employment."[24]

Federal and state law enforcement officers were not involved in the negotiations leading to this compact. The compact is activated when entered into by two or more

[20] Appalachian Regional Development Act of 1966, 79 Stat. 5, 40 U.S.C. app. §1.
[21] Pacific Northwest Electric Power and Conservation Planning Act of 1980. 94 Stat. 2697. 16 U.S.C. §839b.
[22] Olsen, Darryll and Butcher, Walter R. The Regional Power Act: A model for the nation? *Washington State Policy Notes 35*. Winter 1984. Pages 1–6.
[23] Northern Forest Lands Council Act of 1990, 104 Stat. 3359, 16 U.S.C. §2101.
[24] National Crime Prevention and Privacy Compact Act of 1998. 112 Stat. 1874. 42 U.S.C. §14611.

states. Article VI of the compact established a Compact Council with authority to promulgate rules and procedures pertaining to the use of the Interstate Identification Index System for non-criminal justice purposes. The council is composed of 15 members appointed by the Attorney General of the United States, including nine members selected from among the law enforcement officers of member states, two at-large members nominated by the Chairman of the Compact Council, two other at-large members, a member of the FBI's advisory policy board, and an FBI employee appointed by the FBI director. The Director of the FBI designates the federal "Compact Officer."

Indian tribe gaming compacts are a new type of compact. The origin of such compacts is the U.S. Supreme Court's 1987 decision in the case of *Cabazon Band of Mission Indians v. California,* which held that a state may not unduly restrict gaming on Indian lands.[25] This decision led to a sharp increase in gaming on Indian lands. Congress became concerned that tribal governments and their members were not actually profiting from the gaming and that organized crime might acquire a stake in such activity. The Indian Gaming Regulatory Act of 1988[26] therefore authorized tribe–state gaming compacts. The 1988 act established three classes of Indian gaming. Class I gaming—primarily social gaming for small prizes—is regulated totally by Indian tribes. Class II gaming—bingo and bingo-type games and non-banking card games—is regulated by tribes, but is subject to limited oversight by the National Indian Gaming Commission. Class III contains all other types of gaming. Class III gaming is prohibited in the absence of a tribal-state compact approved by the U.S. Secretary of the Interior. The compact device permits states to exercise their reserved powers without the need for direct congressional action.

Appendix M contains a listing of 196 active interstate compacts compiled by the National Center for Interstate Compacts (NCIC) of the Council of State Governments (CSG). The Center has also identified 62 defunct or inactive interstate compacts.[27]

In recent years, groups that advocate that the states exercise their powers more vigorously, such as the Goldwater Institute in Arizona, have drafted model interstate compacts for a variety of novel purposes.[28]

5.5 PARTIES TO INTERSTATE COMPACTS

Although most early interstate compacts usually involved only two states, modern-day interstate compacts frequently involve numerous parties.

The parties to an interstate compact are often determined by geography (e.g., the Colorado River Compact and the Great Lakes Basin Compact). Membership in many

---

[25] *Cabazon Band of Mission Indians v. California.* 480 U.S. 202. 1987.

[26] Indian Gaming Regulatory Act of 1988. 108 Stat. 2467. 25 U.S.C. §2701.

[27] Council of State Governments. 2003. *Interstate Compacts and Agencies 2003.* Lexington, KY: The Council of State Governments.

[28] See http://goldwaterinstitute.org/model-legislation for draft interstate compacts proposed by the Goldwater Institute.

compacts is defined by the activities in which the states engage. For example, the Interstate Oil Compact encompasses the 22 oil-producing states. The Multistate Lottery Agreement operates a quasi-national lotto game in geographically scattered states. In some cases, compacts are open to all states, and actual membership is simply determined by whichever states decide to enact the compact. Examples include the Interstate Compact for Adult Offender Supervision (enacted by 38 states) and the Agreement on Detainers (enacted by 47 states).

Today, there are interstate compacts that include as few as two states and compacts that involve all 50 states. Some interstate compacts include the District of Columbia, the Commonwealth of Puerto Rico, the Virgin Islands, American Samoa, and provinces of Canada. The Interstate Compact for Education, for example, encompasses 48 states, the District of Columbia, American Samoa, Puerto Rico, and the Virgin Islands.

The Northeastern Interstate Forest Fire Compact (1949) became the first interstate compact to include a Canadian province. The Great Lakes Basin Compact (appendix K) includes Ontario and Quebec.

The federal government may be a party to an interstate compact. For example, the membership of the Agreement on Detainers (appendix L) includes 47 states, the District of Columbia, and the federal government as parties.

The Interstate Compact on the Placement of Children and the Interstate Compact on Juveniles are examples of compacts adhered to by all 50 states and the District of Columbia.

States belong to an average of 25.4 interstate compacts.[29] The numbers of compacts entered into range from a low of 16 for Hawaii and Wisconsin to a high of 32 for Colorado and Maryland.

5.6 FORMULATION OF INTERSTATE COMPACTS

Prior to 1930, gubernatorially appointed commissioners negotiated and drafted all interstate compacts. This method is especially appropriate when the contemplated compact requires lengthy negotiations among the prospective parties and frequent consultation with the governors and legislative leaders of the states involved.

Since the 1930s, some interstate compacts (e.g., the Interstate Compact on Parolees and Probationers) have been drafted by non-governmental organizations. Over the years, the National Conference of State Legislatures (NCSL) and the Council of State Governments (CSG) have proposed numerous interstate compacts to the states.[30] The Goldwater Institute has advocated the enactment of interstate compacts for a variety

---

[29] Bowman, Ann O'M. 2004. Trends and issues in interstate cooperation. In *The Book of the States 2004 Edition*. Chicago, IL: The Council of State Governments. Page 36.

[30] Hardy, Paul T. 1982. *Interstate Compacts: The Ties That Bind*. Athens, GA: Institute of Government, University of Georgia.

of purposes.[31] The National Popular Vote interstate compact (described in chapter 6) is another example of a compact drafted by a non-governmental organization.

Compacts have occasionally been initiated by private citizens. As Marian E. Ridgeway describes in *Interstate Compacts: A Question of Federalism*:

> "The Compact on Education is largely the product of the zeal and energy of former governor Terry Sanford of North Carolina, acting on a suggestion of James B. Conant in his [1964 book] *Shaping Education Policy*."[32]

Interstate compacts may also originate in state legislatures. A legislature may unilaterally enact a statute that serves as a prospective compact and an open invitation (an "offer") to other states to join by enacting identical statutes.

In recent years, various industry groups have promoted interstate regulatory compacts in attempts to discourage Congress from exercising its preemptive powers over the subject matter involved. These groups argue that a compact obviates the need for federal regulation and that cooperative action by the states can adequately address the problem at hand.

Representatives of the federal government occasionally participate in the negotiation of interstate compacts. Such federal participation is usually at the invitation of the states themselves. Federal participation is, however, sometimes necessary, given the nature of the compact. For example, federal representatives participated from the beginning in the negotiation of the Potomac River Compact. Both the federal government and the District of Columbia are represented on the commission established by the compact.

In the case of the Colorado River Compact, Congress took the initiative in creating an interstate compact. In 1921, Congress passed legislation[33] calling on the seven western states in the Colorado River basin (Arizona, California, Colorado, Nevada, New Mexico, Utah, and Wyoming) to enter negotiations to resolve their long-standing water dispute and to provide for the use of the water for agriculture and power generation. Under the terms of the federal legislation, the negotiations were headed by Secretary of Commerce Herbert Hoover. These negotiations led to the Colorado River Compact of 1922.[34,35]

There are no constitutional or statutory restrictions on the length of time for the negotiation of interstate compacts.

---

[31] See http://goldwaterinstitute.org/model-legislation for draft interstate compacts proposed by the Goldwater Institute.

[32] Ridgeway, Marian E. 1971. *Interstate Compacts: A Question of Federalism*. Carbondale, IL: Southern Illinois University Press. Page 41.

[33] 42 Stat. 171.

[34] Barton, Weldon V. 1967. *Interstate Compacts in the Political Process*. Chapel Hill, NC: University of North Carolina Press.

[35] Zimmerman, Joseph F. 2012. *Interstate Cooperation: Compacts and Administrative Agreements*. Westport, CT: Praeger. Second edition.

5.7 METHODS BY WHICH A STATE ENACTS AN INTERSTATE COMPACT

A state may enter an interstate compact in several ways.

In certain circumstances, the Governor, the head of an administrative department, or a commission may have sufficient legal authority to enter into a compact on a particular subject on behalf of the state. For example, the Multi-State Lottery Agreement was adopted in many states merely by the action of state lottery commissions.

The focus of this book is, however, on compacts that require explicit legislative action in order to come into effect.

Enactment of an interstate compact by a state legislature is generally accomplished in the same way that ordinary state laws are enacted. Enactment of a state statute typically requires a majority vote of the state legislature and submission of the legislative bill to the state's Governor for approval or disapproval. If the Governor approves a bill that has been passed by the legislature, then the bill becomes law. All Governors have the power to veto legislation passed by their state legislatures. If a Governor vetoes a bill, the bill may nonetheless become law if the legislature overrides the veto in the manner provided by the state's constitution. Overriding a gubernatorial veto typically requires a super-majority (e.g., a two-thirds vote of all houses of the state legislature). See *The Book of the States* for general information about vetoes in particular states.[36] The veto by the Governor of Vermont of the bill enacting the New England Water Pollution Compact is an example of a gubernatorial veto of a legislative bill enacting an interstate compact.

If a state allows the citizen-initiative process, an interstate compact may be enacted in that fashion. Each state constitution specifies the legislature's role, if any, in the initiative process. For example, in some states, the legislature has the option (sometimes the obligation) of voting on an initiative petition before the proposition is submitted to the voters. See *The Initiative: Citizen Law-Making*[37] for additional information on the citizen-initiative process.

The citizen-initiative process may, in general, be used to repeal a state law. Thus, a state law enacting an interstate compact can be subjected to review and possible repeal by the voters. For example, an initiative petition was used in Nebraska in 1988 to force a statewide vote on the question of Nebraska's continued participation in the Central Interstate Low-Level Radioactive Waste Compact. The compact (which had been passed several years earlier by the Nebraska legislature) provided for the building of a nuclear waste site in Nebraska. In the statewide vote on Proposition 402 in 1988, Nebraska voters rejected the opportunity to repeal the state's participation in the compact. The compact nonetheless remained controversial, and, in 1999, the Nebraska legislature enacted a law withdrawing the state from the compact.[38]

---

[36] Council of State Governments. 2005. *The Book of the States*. Lexington, KY: The Council of State Governments. 2005 Edition. Volume 37. Pages 161–162.

[37] Zimmerman, Joseph F. 1999. *The Initiative: Citizen Law-Making*. Westport, CT: Praeger. See pages 24–25 for citations to the constitutional and statutory provisions governing the initiative processes in various states.

[38] See section 5.13 for additional discussion of the controversies surrounding this compact.

The protest-referendum process, if available in a given state, provides another way to subject a law enacted by the legislature (including a law enacting an interstate compact) to review by the voters. The protest-referendum process usually must be invoked within a short and limited time after the law was originally passed by the legislature. See *The Referendum: The People Decide Public Policy*[39] for additional information on the protest-referendum process.

In some cases, the state legislature has itself referred enactment of an interstate compact to the state's voters. For example, the Maine legislature referred the question of enactment of the Texas Low-Level Radioactive Waste Disposal Compact to its voters in 1993. The question on the ballot was:

> "Do you approve of the interstate compact to be made with Texas, Maine and Vermont for the disposal of the State's low-level radioactive waste at a proposed facility in the State of Texas?"

The proposition received 170,411 "yes" votes and 63,672 "no" votes.

The statutory language required to enact an interstate compact at the state level is not complex. For example, the legislation by which the state of Ohio entered into the Great Lakes Basin Compact in 1963 consists of two parts. The first part consists of the following 43-word enacting clause:

> "The 'great lakes basin compact' is hereby ratified, enacted into law, and entered into by this state as a party thereto with any other state or province which, pursuant to Article II of said compact, has legally joined in the compact as follows: . . ."

The second part consists of the text of the compact (placed inside quotation marks). Appendix K contains the entire text of the Ohio legislation.

Statutory language for enacting an interstate compact at the state level may or may not be self-executing. The above Ohio legislation is an example of self-executing legislation—that is, no further action is required by any official or body in Ohio with respect to the process of adopting the compact in Ohio. On the other hand, the statutory language enacting an interstate compact may require that the compact be subsequently executed by the state's Governor, Attorney General, or other official—perhaps at the discretion of the official involved, perhaps after some specified condition is satisfied, or perhaps merely after a certain number of other states have joined the compact. The Interstate Compact for the Supervision of Parolees and Probationers is an example of a non-self-executing compact. That particular compact was enacted in 1936 by the New York Legislature; however, because of the opposition of Governor Herbert H. Lehman, the compact remained unexecuted for eight years.

When the "state" entering into an interstate compact is the District of Columbia, two different procedures have been used.

---

[39] Zimmerman, Joseph F. 1997. *The Referendum: The People Decide Public Policy.* Westport, CT: Praeger.

Prior to 1973, it was customary for Congress to enact interstate compacts on behalf of the District of Columbia.

However, in the District of Columbia Home Rule Act of 1973, Congress delegated its authority to pass laws concerning the District to the District of Columbia Council in all but 10 specifically identified areas listed in section 602(a) of the Act.[40]

None of the 10 specific restrictions in section 602(a) of the Home Rule Act precluded the District of Columbia from entering into interstate compacts. Accordingly, the District of Columbia Council has itself entered into numerous interstate compacts since 1973. For example, the Council entered into the Interstate Parole and Probation Compact[41] in 1976 (three years after enactment of the Home Rule Act). In 2000, the Council entered into the Interstate Compact on Adoption and Medical Assistance.[42] In 2002, the Council entered into the Emergency Management Assistance Compact.[43] In 2010, the District of Columbia Council approved the National Popular Vote compact.

An interstate compact may sometimes be adopted on a temporary basis by executive or administrative action. For example, the Compact for Education stipulates that it may be adopted

> "either by enactment thereof or by adherence thereto by the Governor; provided that in the absence of enactment, adherence by the Governor shall be sufficient to make his state a party only until December 31, 1967."

The governor authorized participation by Kansas in the Interstate Compact for Supervision of Parolees and Probationers for a period of time prior to enactment of the compact by the legislature.

There are no constitutional or statutory restrictions on the length of time that potential parties to an interstate compact may take in deciding whether to join the compact.[44] Indeed, history is replete with examples of long delays prior to the enactment of interstate compacts. In 1955, the Great Lakes Basin Compact (appendix K) was enacted by the state legislatures in Illinois, Indiana, Michigan, Minnesota, and Wisconsin. It was enacted in 1956 by the Pennsylvania General Assembly. However, the New York Legislature did not enact the compact until 1960, and the Ohio General Assembly did not enact the compact until 1963. It took 12 years to gain approval from the California and Nevada legislatures for the California-Nevada Water Apportion-

---

[40] D.C. Code § 1-233.

[41] D.C. Code § 24-452.

[42] Title 4, Chapter 3, D.C. ST § 4-326, June 27, 2000, D.C. Law 13-136, § 406, 47 DCR 2850.

[43] Interestingly, the Council originally entered into this compact on an emergency 90-day temporary basis (by D.C. Council Act 14-0081) under the authority of section 412(a) of the Home Rule Act. The Council subsequently entered into this same compact (by D.C. Council Act A14-0317) under the authority of section 602(c)(1) of the Home Rule Act (providing for the usual 30-day congressional review period).

[44] Of course, a particular compact could explicitly contain a time limitation for its adoption by its prospective members.

ment Interstate Compact. It took five years to secure the necessary enactments of the Atlantic States Marine Fisheries Compact (which became effective in 1942).

5.8 CONTINGENT NATURE OF COMPACTS

As a general rule, a state enters into an interstate compact in order to obtain some benefit that can only be obtained by mutually agreed coordinated action with its sister state(s). In most cases, it would make no sense for a state to agree to the terms of a compact unless certain other states agreed to the compact. Thus, an interstate compact generally does not come into effect until it is approved by a specified number or a specified combination of prospective parties.

A bi-state compact comes into effect when it is adopted by both of the states involved.

A compact involving three or more parties typically contains a specific provision specifying the conditions under which the compact will come into effect. If a compact is silent as to the number of parties necessary to bring it into effect, then, in accordance with standard contract law, it comes into effect only when adopted by all of its named parties. For example, the Tri-State Lotto Compact is an example of a multi-state compact that did not come into effect until it was enacted by all of its prospective parties (Maine, New Hampshire, and Vermont).

The Gulf States Marine Fisheries Compact contemplated participation of five states but required only two states to enact the compact in order to bring it into effect.

> "This compact shall become operative immediately as to those states ratifying it whenever any two or more of the States of Florida, Alabama, Mississippi, Louisiana and Texas have ratified it."

The Multistate Tax Compact is open to all states and provides:

> "This compact shall enter into force when enacted into law by any seven states. Thereafter, this compact shall become effective as to any other state upon its enactment thereof."

The Great Lakes Basin Compact was intended to include eight states but came into effect when four states enacted it.

> "This compact shall enter into force and become effective and binding when it has been enacted by the legislatures of any four of the states of Illinois, Indiana, Michigan, Minnesota, New York, Ohio, Pennsylvania, and Wisconsin and thereafter shall enter into force and become effective and binding as to any other of said states when enacted by the legislature thereof."

The Great Lakes Basin Compact is noteworthy because it permitted two Canadian provinces to join the compact. The Canadian provinces did not, however, count toward the threshold of four states necessary to bring the compact into effect.

"The province of Ontario and the province of Quebec, or either of them, may become states party to this compact by taking such action as their laws and the laws of the government of Canada may prescribe for adherence thereto. For the purpose of this compact the word 'state' shall be construed to include a province of Canada."

The Midwest Interstate Passenger Rail Compact came into effect when it was enacted by three states out of a pool of 12 named prospective members. The membership of this compact may be expanded by action of the commission established by the compact.

"The states of Illinois, Indiana, Iowa, Kansas, Michigan, Minnesota, Missouri, Nebraska, North Dakota, Ohio, South Dakota and Wisconsin are eligible to join this compact. Upon approval of the Commission, according to its bylaws, other states may also be declared eligible to join the compact. As to any eligible party state, this compact shall become effective when its legislature shall have enacted the same into law; provided that it shall not become initially effective until enacted into law by any three (3) party states incorporating the provisions of this compact into the laws of such states. Amendments to the compact shall become effective upon their enactment by the legislatures of all compacting states."[45]

The Central Interstate Low-Level Radioactive Waste Compact named 10 states as eligible for membership. It specified that it would become effective when enacted by any three of the 10 prospective parties. The compact enabled the compact's commission to admit additional states by a unanimous vote.

Sometimes the specific requirements for bringing a compact into effect are of paramount political importance. The original version of the Colorado River Compact was negotiated in 1922 by gubernatorially appointed commissioners from the seven western states involved (Arizona, California, Colorado, Nevada, New Mexico, Utah, and Wyoming). The negotiations were headed by Herbert Hoover, and the compact was signed, amid considerable fanfare, on November 24, 1922, in Santa Fe, New Mexico. The 1922 version provided:

"This compact shall become binding and obligatory when it shall have been approved by the legislatures of each of the signatory states."[46]

The Arizona legislature, however, did not enact a statute approving the 1922 compact. In reaction to Arizona's intransigence, Congress initiated a revised version of the compact—The Boulder Canyon Project Act of 1928. The 1928 version of the compact

---

[45] Midwest Interstate Passenger Rail Compact. Section 1 of Article X.
[46] See http://ssl.csg.org/compactlaws/coloradoriver.html.

specified that the compact would come into effect when enacted by six of the seven western states involved, provided that California was one of the six.[47] As expected, Arizona, the seventh prospective member, held out. In fact, Arizona did not approve of the 1928 version of the compact until 1944.

5.9 CONGRESSIONAL CONSENT AND INVOLVEMENT IN INTERSTATE COMPACTS

Congress may become involved with an interstate compact in a number of different ways:

- explicitly consenting to a compact,
- explicitly consenting to a compact on behalf of the District of Columbia,
- making the federal government a party to a compact,
- providing implied consent to a compact,
- consenting in advance to a broad category of compacts, and
- consenting in advance to a particular compact.

The statutory language necessary for congressional consent to an interstate compact is straight forward.

A joint resolution is generally used if Congress is simply granting its consent to the compact (and not enacting other statutory provisions). For example, House Joint Resolution 193 (Public Law 104–321)[48] of the 104th Congress entitled "Joint Resolution Granting the Consent of Congress to the Emergency Management Assistance Compact" was used to grant consent to the Emergency Management Assistance Compact in 1996. The joint resolution consists of three major parts. In the first part, Congress grants its consent.

> *"Resolved by the Senate and House of Representatives of the United States in Congress assembled,*
>
> "SECTION 1: CONGRESSIONAL CONSENT.
> "The Congress consents to the Emergency Management Assistance Compact entered into by Delaware, Florida, Georgia, Louisiana, Maryland, Mississippi, Missouri, Oklahoma, South Carolina, South Dakota, Tennessee, Virginia and West Virginia. The compact reads substantially as follows . . ."

The second part of this joint resolution consists of the entire wording of the Emergency Management Assistance Compact (which is inserted in the joint resolution inside quotation marks).

The third part of a joint resolution consenting to a compact generally contains several sections that qualify the grant of consent.

---

[47] 45 Stat.1057.

[48] Appendix N contains Public Law 104–321 of 1996 entitled "Joint Resolution Granting the Consent of Congress to the Emergency Management Assistance Compact."

"SECTION 2. RIGHT TO ALTER, AMEND, OR REPEAL.

"The right to alter, amend, or repeal this joint resolution is hereby expressly reserved. The consent granted by this joint resolution shall

(1) not be construed as impairing or in any manner affecting any right or jurisdiction of the United States in and over the subject of the compact;

(2) not be construed as consent to the National Guard Mutual Assistance Compact;

(3) be construed as understanding that the first paragraph of Article II of the compact provides that emergencies will require procedures to provide immediate access to existing resources to make a prompt and effective response;

(4) not be construed as providing authority in Article IIIA.7 that does not otherwise exist for the suspension of statutes or ordinances;

(5) be construed as understanding that Article IIIC does not impose any affirmative obligation to exchange information, plans, and resource records on the United States or any party which has not entered into the compact; and

(6) be construed as understanding that Article XIII does not affect the authority of the President over the National Guard provided by article I of the Constitution and title 10 of the United States Code.

"SECTION 3. CONSTRUCTION AND SEVERABILITY.

"It is intended that the provisions of this compact shall be reasonably and liberally construed to effectuate the purposes thereof. If any part or application of this compact, or legislation enabling the compact, is held invalid, the remainder of the compact or its application to other situations or persons shall not be affected.

"SECTION 4. INCONSISTENCY OF LANGUAGE.

"The validity of this compact shall not be affected by any insubstantial difference in its form or language as adopted by the States."

When the District of Columbia is a party to a compact, Congress may consent to the compact on behalf of the District. When the federal government is a party to a compact, Congress enters into the compact on behalf of the United States. Thus, when Congress acted on the Interstate Agreement on Detainers, it simultaneously consented to the compact on behalf of the District of Columbia, made the federal government a party to the compact, and enacted some additional permanent statutory language (sections 5 and 6). Appendix L contains Public Law 91–538 of 1970 entitled "An Act to enact the Interstate Agreement on Detainers into law." This law begins:

> *"Be it enacted by the Senate and House of Representatives of the United States of America in Congress assembled,*

> "[Sec. 1.] That this Act may be cited as the 'Interstate Agreement on Detainers Act.'

> "Sec. 2. The Interstate Agreement on Detainers is hereby enacted into law and entered into by the United States on its own behalf and on behalf of the District of Columbia with all jurisdictions legally joining in substantially the following form: . . ."

At this point, Public Law 91–538 incorporates the entire Interstate Agreement on Detainers (inside quotation marks).

Public Law 91–538 then concludes with several additional sections:

> "Sec. 3. The term 'Governor' as used in the agreement on detainers shall mean with respect to the United States, the Attorney General, and with respect to the District of Columbia, the Commissioner of the District of Columbia.

> "Sec. 4. The term 'appropriate court' as used in the agreement on detainers shall mean with respect to the United States, the courts of the United States, and with respect to the District of Columbia, the courts of the District of Columbia, in which indictments, informations, or complaints, for which disposition is sought, are pending.

> "Sec. 5. All courts, departments, agencies, officers, and employees of the United States and of the District of Columbia are hereby directed to enforce the agreement on detainers and to cooperate with one another and with all party States in enforcing the agreement and effectuating its purpose.

> "Sec. 6. For the United States, the Attorney General, and for the District of Columbia, the Commissioner of the District of Columbia, shall establish such regulations, prescribe such forms, issue such instructions, and perform such other acts as he deems necessary for carrying out the provisions of this Act.

> "Sec. 7. The right to alter, amend, or repeal this Act is expressly reserved.

> "Sec. 8. This Act shall take effect on the ninetieth day after the date of its enactment."

Congressional consent to an interstate compact need not be explicit. For example, there is nothing in Public Law 91–538 (quoted above) that specifically mentions that Congress is consenting to the Interstate Agreement on Detainers. The reason is that congressional consent is *implied* by its consent to the compact on behalf of the District of Columbia and by its action making the federal government a party to the compact. As the U.S. Supreme Court ruled in the 1893 case of *Virginia v. Tennessee*:

> **"The constitution does not state when the consent of congress shall be given, whether it shall precede or may follow the compact made, or whether it shall be express or may be implied.** In many cases the consent will usually precede the compact or agreement. . . . But where the agreement relates to a matter which could not well be considered until its nature is fully developed, it is not perceived why the consent may not be subsequently given. [Justice] Story says that **the consent may be implied, and is always to be implied when congress adopts the particular act by sanctioning its objects and aiding in enforcing them**; and observes that where a state is admitted into the Union, notoriously upon a compact made between it and the state of which it previously composed a part, there the act of congress admitting such state into the Union is an implied consent to the terms of the compact. Knowledge by congress of the boundaries of a state and of its political subdivisions may reasonably be presumed, as much of its legislation is affected by them, such as relate to the territorial jurisdiction of the courts of the United States, the extent of their collection districts, and of districts in which process, civil and criminal, of their courts may be served and enforced."[49] [Emphasis added]

Congressional consent is given in the same way that Congress enacts any other statute or joint resolution. That is, such legislation requires a majority vote of both houses of Congress and approval of the President. As part of the legislative process, the President may veto such legislation. Congress has the power to override a presidential veto by a two-thirds vote in both houses. For example, in 1941, Franklin D. Roosevelt vetoed the bill granting consent to the Republican River Compact (perhaps preferring a Democratic river); however, two years later he signed a bill consenting to a modified version of the compact. Congress's failure to grant its consent for the Connecticut River and Merrimack River Flood Control Compacts in the 1930s has been attributed to the threat of a presidential veto.

There is no constitutional limitation on the amount of time that Congress may take in considering a compact. Maryland, New York, and Pennsylvania enacted the Susquehanna River Basin Compact in 1967 and 1968, but Congress did not grant its consent until 1970. The Washington Metropolitan Area Transit Regulation Compact was approved by Maryland, Virginia, and the District of Columbia in 1958; however, the compact did not receive the consent of Congress until 1960.

---

[49] *Virginia v. Tennessee*. 148 U.S. 503 at 521. 1893.

Congress is free to grant its unrestricted consent in advance for all compacts pertaining to a particular subject. For example, Congress consented in advance to interstate crime-control compacts in the Crime Control Consent Act of 1934.

> *"Be it enacted by the Senate and House of Representatives of the United States of America in congress assembled,*
>
> "[Sec. 1.] That the consent of Congress is hereby given to any two or more States to enter into agreements or compacts for cooperative effort and mutual assistance in the prevention of crime and in the enforcement of their respective criminal laws and policies, and to establish such agencies, joint or otherwise, as they deem desirable for making effective such agreement and compacts.
>
> "Sec. 2. The right to alter, amend, or repeal this Act is hereby expressly reserved."

In the Weeks Act of 1911, Congress granted unrestricted consent in advance to interstate compacts formed

> "for the purpose of conserving the forests and water supply. . . ."[50]

In the Tobacco Control Act of 1936, Congress authorized tobacco-producing states to enter into interstate compacts

> "to enable growers to receive a fair price for such tobacco."[51]

Another example of congressional consent in advance involved the development and operation of airports.[52]

In 1939, President Franklin D. Roosevelt vetoed a bill that would have granted consent in advance to states to enter into compacts relating to fishing in the Atlantic Ocean because he considered the advance authorization to be overly vague.

On rare occasions, Congress has combined consent and advance permission in the same statute. For example, in 1921, it granted its consent to a Minnesota–South Dakota compact relating to criminal jurisdiction over boundary waters and simultaneously granted its consent in advance for a similar compact among Iowa, Minnesota, Nebraska, North Dakota, South Dakota, and Wisconsin.[53]

In 1951, Congress authorized states to enter into interstate civil defense compacts that, upon enactment, were required to be filed with the U.S. House of Representatives

---

[50] 36 Stat. 961.

[51] 49 Stat. 1239.

[52] 73 Stat. 333.

[53] 41 Stat. 1447.

and Senate. These compacts were all deemed to have the consent of Congress unless disapproved by a concurrent resolution within 60 days of filing.[54]

Generally, a congressional grant of consent to an interstate compact is for an indefinite period of time. However, Congress originally subjected the Interstate Oil and Gas Compact of 1935 and the Atlantic States Marine Fisheries Compact to sunset provisions. Later, Congress removed the time restrictions on its consent.[55] The 10 compacts (involving a total of 44 states) authorized by the Low-Level Radioactive Waste Policy Act of 1980 were each approved for a period of five years.[56]

Of course, Congress is not obligated to renew its consent. The controversial Northeast Interstate Dairy Compact established a commission with authority to fix the price of fluid or drinking milk above the minimum prices set by the New England federal milk-marketing order. This compact was enacted by each state legislature in New England. Congress granted its consent to this particular compact for a limited period of time. In the meantime, the compact attracted considerable opposition from consumer groups and midwestern and western dairy states. Consumer advocates opposed the compact because it would increase the retail price of milk, thereby adversely impacting low-income citizens. Representatives of midwestern and western dairy states argued that their farmers suffered from low milk prices because of the compact. Wisconsin dairy farmers, in particular, argued that the compact prevented them from selling their products in New England. The compact became inactive in 2001 when Congress failed to grant an extension of its consent.

Congress may impose conditions in granting its consent. For example, Congress granted its consent to the Wabash Valley Compact in 1959[57] and the Washington Metropolitan Area Transit Regulation Compact in 1960[58] with the proviso that each compact authority was to publish specified data and information. In addition, Congress has, to date, always reserved its authority over navigable waters. Congress almost always reserves its right to "alter, amend, or repeal" its consent to a compact. The Boulder Canyon Project Act of 1928[59] granted congressional consent to the Colorado River Compact subject to several stipulated conditions, including approval of the modified compact by California and five of the other six states involved (it being understood, at the time, that Arizona was unlikely to join immediately).

In the 1962 case of *Tobin v. United States*, the United States Court of Appeals for the District of Columbia Circuit upheld the authority of Congress to attach conditions to a compact.[60] The U.S. Supreme Court declined to review that decision.

---

[54] 64 Stat. 1249.
[55] 86 Stat. 383 and 64 Stat. 467.
[56] 94 Stat. 3347.
[57] 73 Stat. 694.
[58] 74 Stat. 1031.
[59] 45 Stat. 1057.
[60] *Tobin v. United States*. 306 F.2d 270 at 272–74. 1962.

The Constitution does not detail the specific form or manner by which congressional consent is to be granted. In 1823, the U.S. Supreme Court in *Green v. Biddle* noted this fact in a case involving a congressional statute that granted consent to the admission of Kentucky to the Union and simultaneously referred to the Virginia–Kentucky Interstate Compact of 1789.[61] Kentucky challenged the compact on the ground that Congress had not explicitly consented to the compact. Kentucky's challenge was unsuccessful, and the Supreme Court ruled that Congress's reference to the compact was sufficient.

The Central Interstate Low-Level Radioactive Waste Compact enabled the commission established by the compact to accept additional states as members by a unanimous vote. The compact (which was submitted to Congress for its consent) contained a provision granting advance congressional consent to any additional new states:

> "The consent given to this compact by the Congress shall extend to any future admittance of new party states under subsections B and C of Article VII of the compact."

5.10 EFFECT OF CONGRESSIONAL CONSENT

The question arises as to whether an interstate compact is converted into federal law when Congress grants its consent. This question is important because it may determine which court has the power to interpret the compact and whether the compact is interpreted under state or federal law.

The Supreme Court's answer to this question has changed over the years. In 1938, the Court held in the case of *Hinderlider v. La Plata River and Cherry Creek Ditch Company* that congressional consent does not make a compact the equivalent of a United States statute or treaty.[62]

The Court modified its *Hinderlider* ruling in the 1940 case of *Delaware River Joint Toll Bridge Commission v. Colburn.* The Court expanded the authority of a compact that had been granted consent by Congress and involved

> "a federal 'title, right, privilege, or immunity' which when explicitly identified and claimed in a state court may be reviewed here on *certiorari. . . .*"[63]

In 1874, the Supreme Court held in *Murdock v. City of Memphis* that federal courts are required to apply the interpretation of state law by the highest state court in the state.[64]

In 1981, however, the Court overturned *Murdock* in *Cuyler v. Adams.* The Court held that congressional consent converts an interstate compact into federal law provided that the compact's subject matter was

---

[61] *Green v. Biddle.* 21 U.S. 1. 1823.

[62] *Hinderlider v. La Plata River and Cherry Creek Ditch Company.* 304 U.S. 92. 1938.

[63] *Delaware River Joint Toll Bridge Commission v. Colburn.* 320 U.S. 419. 1940.

[64] *Murdock v. City of Memphis.* 87 U.S. 590. 1874.

"an appropriate subject for congressional legislation."[65]

By overturning *Murdock*, the Court was free to reject the interpretation provided by the Pennsylvania Supreme Court and interpret the statute on its own.[66,67]

The question repeatedly arises as to whether the grant of congressional consent to an interstate compact invalidates other federal statutes containing inconsistent provisions. Courts could interpret congressional consent as repealing, relative to the interstate compact, conflicting federal statutes. The question also arises as to the effect of a new federal statute whose provisions conflict with an interstate compact previously approved by Congress. Apparently, the consent would be repealed relative to the conflicting provisions with the exception of any vested rights protected by the Fifth Amendment to the Constitution.

5.11 COMPACTS CONTINGENT ON ENACTMENT OF FEDERAL LEGISLATION

An interstate compact may contain terms specifying that it is contingent on the enactment of federal legislation at the time Congress grants its consent to the compact.

For example, the Belle Fourche River Compact between South Dakota and Wyoming stipulated that it would not become effective unless congressional consent were accompanied by congressional legislation satisfactorily addressing three enumerated points that the compact's parties desired. The compact provided:

"This compact shall become operative when approved by the legislature of each of the states, and when consented to by the congress of the United States by legislation providing, among other things, that:

"(i) Any beneficial uses hereafter made by the United States, or those acting by or under its authority, within a state, of the waters allocated by this compact, shall be within the allocations hereinabove made for use in that state and shall be taken into account in determining the extent of use within that state;

"(ii) The United States, or those acting by or under its authority, in the exercise of rights or powers arising from whatever jurisdiction the United States has in, over and to the waters of the Belle Fourche River and all its tributaries, shall recognize, to the extent consistent with the best utilization of the waters for multiple purposes, that beneficial use of the waters within the basin is of paramount importance to development of the basin, and no exercise of such power or right thereby that would interfere with the full beneficial use of the waters shall be

[65] *Cuyler v. Adams.* 449 U.S. 433. 1981.

[66] Hardy, Paul T. 1982. *Interstate Compacts: The Ties That Bind.* Athens, GA: Institute of Government, University of Georgia.

[67] Zimmerman, Joseph F. 2012. *Interstate Cooperation: Compacts and Administrative Agreements.* Westport, CT: Praeger. Second edition.

made except upon a determination, giving due consideration to the objectives of this compact and after consultation with all interested federal agencies and the state officials charged with the administration of this compact, that such exercise is in the interest of the best utilization of such waters for multiple purposes;

"(iii) The United States, or those acting by or under its authority, will recognize any established use, for domestic and irrigation purposes, of the apportioned waters which may be impaired by the exercise of federal jurisdiction in, over, and to such waters; provided, that such use is being exercised beneficially, is valid under the laws of the appropriate state and in conformity with this compact at the time of the impairment thereof, and was validly initiated under state law prior to the initiation or authorization of the federal program or project which causes such impairment."

Congress agreed to the states' request in its legislation granting consent to the Belle Fourche River Compact.

Similarly, the Republican River Compact contained a description of congressional legislation desired by the compact's parties. Again, Congress agreed to the states' request at the time of granting its consent to the compact.

5.12 COMPACTS NOT REQUIRING CONGRESSIONAL CONSENT

Two reasons are generally given as to why the U.S. Constitution requires congressional consent for interstate compacts.

First, congressional consent provides a means of protecting the federal government from efforts by the states to encroach upon its delegated powers and federal supremacy.

Second, congressional consent provides a means of safeguarding the interests of states that are not parties to the compact. For example, absent congressional supervision, upstream states in a river basin might enter into a compact to use water to the extreme disadvantage of downstream states that do not belong to the compact.

At first glance, the Constitution seems to be unambiguous as to the necessity for congressional consent to interstate compacts. Article I, section 10, clause 3 provides:

"No state shall, without the consent of Congress, . . . enter into any agreement or compact with another state. . . ."

Since 1893, the Supreme Court has interpreted this clause to allow states to enter into compacts without congressional consent.

In deciding the 1978 case of *U.S. Steel Corporation v. Multistate Tax Commission*,[68] the Court wrote:

---

[68] *U.S. Steel Corporation v. Multistate Tax Commission.* 434 U.S. 452. 1978.

"Read literally, the Compact Clause would require the States to obtain congressional approval before entering into any agreement among themselves, irrespective of form, subject, duration, or interest to the United States. The difficulties with such an interpretation were identified by Mr. Justice Field in his opinion for the Court in *Virginia v. Tennessee*, supra.[69] His conclusion that the Clause could not be read literally was approved in subsequent dicta, . . . but this Court did not have occasion expressly to apply it in a holding until our recent [1976] decision in *New Hampshire v. Maine*."[70,71]

Litigation started in the early 19th century over whether congressional consent to interstate compacts is necessary in all circumstances.

In the 1833 case of *Barron v. Baltimore*, Chief Justice John Marshall wrote:

"If these compacts are with foreign nations, they interfere with the treaty-making power, which is conferred entirely on the general government; if with each other, for political purposes, they can scarcely fail to interfere with the general purpose and intent of the constitution."[72]

In 1845, the New Hampshire Supreme Court in *Dover v. Portsmouth Bridge* dismissed the contention that an 1819 New Hampshire statute and an 1821 Maine statute that authorized construction of a bridge over navigable waters (the Piscataqua River) without congressional consent violated the U.S. Constitution.[73] The court held that there is no constitutional provision precluding each of the two states from granting authority for the erection of a bridge to the middle of the river.

In 1854, the U.S. Supreme Court held in *Florida v. Georgia* that a boundary compact enacted by the two states would be invalid unless Congress were to grant its consent.[74]

The seminal case on the issue of the necessity for congressional consent to interstate compacts is the 1893 case of *Virginia v. Tennessee*.[75] The two states involved never obtained congressional consent for a boundary agreement that they had reached earlier in the 19th century. The U.S. Supreme Court framed the issue in the case as follows:

"Is the agreement, made without the consent of congress, between Virginia and Tennessee, to appoint commissioners to run and mark the boundary line between them, within the prohibition of this clause? The terms 'agreement' or 'compact,' taken by themselves, are sufficiently comprehensive to

---

[69] *Virginia v. Tennessee*. 148 U.S. 503. 1893.

[70] *New Hampshire v. Maine*. 426 U.S. 363. 1976.

[71] *U.S. Steel Corporation v. Multistate Tax Commission*. 434 U.S. 452 at 459. 1978.

[72] *Barron v. Baltimore*. 32 U.S. 243. 1833.

[73] *Dover v. Portsmouth Bridge*. 17 N.H. 200. 1845.

[74] *Florida v. Georgia*. 55 U.S. 478. 1854.

[75] *Virginia v. Tennessee*. 148 U.S. 503. 1893.

embrace all forms of stipulation, written or verbal, and relating to all kinds of subjects; to those to which the United States can have no possible objection or have any interest in interfering with, as well as to those which may tend to increase and build up the political influence of the contracting states, so as to encroach upon or impair the supremacy of the United States, or interfere with their rightful management of particular subjects placed under their entire control."[76]

The Court observed:

"**There are many matters upon which different states may agree that can in no respect concern the United States.** If, for instance, Virginia should come into possession and ownership of a small parcel of land in New York, which the latter state might desire to acquire as a site for a public building, it would hardly be deemed essential for the latter state to obtain the consent of congress before it could make a valid agreement with Virginia for the purchase of the land."[77] [Emphasis added]

The Court continued:

"If Massachusetts, in forwarding its exhibits to the World's Fair at Chicago, should desire to transport them a part of the distance over the Erie canal, it would hardly be deemed essential for that state to obtain the consent of congress before it could contract with New York for the transportation of the exhibits through that state in that way."[78]

Further, the Court stated:

"If the bordering line of two states should cross some malarious and disease-producing district, there could be no possible reason, on any conceivable public grounds, to obtain the consent of congress for the bordering states to agree to unite in draining the district, and thus removing the cause of disease. So, in case of threatened invasion of cholera, plague, or other causes of sickness and death, it would be the height of absurdity to hold that the threatened states could not unite in providing means to prevent and repel the invasion of the pestilence without obtaining the consent of congress, which might not be at the time in session."[79]

Having established that the requirement for congressional consent is not universal, the Court then recast the issue in the case:

---

[76] Id. at 517–518.
[77] Id. at 518.
[78] Id.
[79] Id.

"If, then, the terms 'compact' or 'agreement' in the constitution do not apply to every possible compact or agreement between one state and another, for the validity of which the consent of congress must be obtained, to what compacts or agreements does the constitution apply?"[80]

The Court then answered the question as follows:

"We can only reply by looking at the object of the constitutional provision, and construing the terms 'agreement' and 'compact' by reference to it. It is a familiar rule in the construction of terms to apply to them the meaning naturally attaching to them from their context. '*Noscitur a sociis*' is a rule of construction applicable to all written instruments. Where any particular word is obscure or of doubtful meaning, taken by itself, its obscurity or doubt may be removed by reference to associated words; and the meaning of a term may be enlarged or restrained by reference to the object of the whole clause in which it is used.

"Looking at the clause in which the terms 'compact' or 'agreement' appear, it is evident that **the prohibition is directed to the formation of any combination tending to the increase of political power in the states, which may encroach upon or interfere with the just supremacy of the United States.**"[81] [Emphasis added]

The Court continued:

"[Justice] Story, in his Commentaries, (section 1403) referring to a previous part of the same section of the constitution in which the clause in question appears, observes that its language

'may be more plausibly interpreted from the terms used, 'treaty, alliance, or confederation,' and upon the ground that the sense of each is best known by its association ('*noscitur a sociis*') to apply to treaties of a political character; such as treaties of alliance for purposes of peace and war, and treaties of confederation, in which the parties are leagued for mutual government, political co-operation, and the exercise of political sovereignty, and treaties of cession of sovereignty, or conferring internal political jurisdiction, or external political dependence, or general commercial privileges;'

"and that

'the latter clause, 'compacts and agreement,' might then very properly apply to such as regarded what might be deemed mere private rights of

---

[80] Id.

[81] Id. at 519.

sovereignty; such as questions of boundary, interests in land situate in the territory of each other, and other internal regulations for the mutual comfort and convenience of states bordering on each other.'

"And he [Story] adds:

'In such cases the consent of congress may be properly required, in order to check any infringement of the rights of the national government; and, at the same time, a total prohibition to enter into any compact or agreement might be attended with permanent inconvenience or public mischief.'"[82]

The Court continued:

"Compacts or agreements—and we do not perceive any difference in the meaning, except that the word 'compact' is generally used with reference to more formal and serious engagements than is usually implied in the term 'agreement'—cover all stipulations affecting the conduct or claims of the parties. The mere selection of parties to run and designate the boundary line between two states, or to designate what line should be run, of itself imports no agreement to accept the line run by them, and such action of itself does not come within the prohibition. Nor does a legislative declaration, following such line, that is correct, and shall thereafter be deemed the true and established line, import by itself a contract or agreement with the adjoining state. It is a legislative declaration which the state and individuals affected by the recognized boundary line may invoke against the state as an admission, but not as a compact or agreement. The legislative declaration will take the form of an agreement or compact when it recites some consideration for it from the other party affected by it; for example, as made upon a similar declaration of the border or contracting state. The mutual declarations may then be reasonably treated as made upon mutual considerations. The compact or agreement will then be within the prohibition of the constitution, or without it, according as the establishment of the boundary line **may lead or not to the increase of the political power or influence of the states affected, and thus encroach or not upon the full and free exercise of federal authority.**"[83] [Emphasis added]

The Court continued:

"If the boundary established is so run as to cut off an important and valuable portion of a state, the political power of the state enlarged would be affected by the settlement of the boundary; and to an agreement for the run-

---

[82] Id. at 520–521.

[83] Id.

ning of such a boundary, or rather for its adoption afterwards, the consent of congress may well be required. But the running of a boundary may have no effect upon the political influence of either state; it may simply serve to mark and define that which actually existed before, but was undefined and unmarked. In that case the agreement for the running of the line, or its actual survey, would in no respect displace the relation of either of the states to the general government. There was, therefore, no compact or agreement between the states in this case which required, for its validity, the consent of congress, within the meaning of the constitution, until they had passed upon the report of the commissioners, ratified their action, and mutually declared the boundary established by them to be the true and real boundary between the states. Such ratification was mutually made by each state in consideration of the ratification of the other.

"The constitution does not state when the consent of congress shall be given, whether it shall precede or may follow the compact made, or whether it shall be express or may be implied. In many cases the consent will usually precede the compact or agreement, as where it is to lay a duty of tonnage, to keep troops or ships of war in time of peace, or to engage in war. But where the agreement relates to a matter which could not well be considered until its nature is fully developed, it is not perceived why the consent may not be subsequently given. [Justice] Story says that the consent may be implied, and is always to be implied when congress adopts the particular act by sanctioning its objects and aiding in enforcing them; and observes that where a state is admitted into the Union, notoriously upon a compact made between it and the state of which it previously composed a part, there the act of congress admitting such state into the Union is an implied consent to the terms of the compact. Knowledge by congress of the boundaries of a state and of its political subdivisions may reasonably be presumed, as much of its legislation is affected by them, such as relate to the territorial jurisdiction of the courts of the United States, the extent of their collection districts, and of districts in which process, civil and criminal, of their courts may be served and enforced.

"In the present case the consent of congress could not have preceded the execution of the compact, for until the line was run it could not be known where it would lie, and whether or not it would receive the approval of the states. The preliminary agreement was not to accept a line run, whatever it might be, but to receive from the commissioners designated a report as to the line which might be run and established by them. After its consideration each state was free to take such action as it might judge expedient upon their report. The approval by congress of the compact entered into between the states upon their ratification of the action of their commissioners is fairly implied from its subsequent legislation and proceedings. The line established was treated by that body as the true boundary between the states in the assignment of territory north of it as a portion of districts set apart for judicial and revenue purposes in Virginia, and as included in territory in which federal elections were to be held, and for which appointments were to be made by federal authority in that state, and in the assignment of territory south of it as a portion of districts set apart for judicial and revenue purposes in Tennessee, and as included in territory in which federal elections were to be held, and for which federal appointments were to be made for that state. Such use of the territory on different sides of the boundary designated in a single instance would not, perhaps, be considered as absolute proof of the assent or approval of congress to the boundary line; but the exercise of jurisdiction by congress over the country as a part of Tennessee on one side, and as a part of Virginia on the other, for a long succession of years, without question or dispute from any quarter, furnishes as conclusive proof of assent to it by that body as can usually be obtained from its most formal proceedings."[84]

In summary, despite the absence of congressional consent, the U.S. Supreme Court upheld the interstate compact involved in *Virginia v. Tennessee* because the compact did not

- increase "the political power or influence" of the party states, or
- encroach "upon the full and free exercise of federal authority."

In deciding *Virginia v. Tennessee*, the Court also noted that Congress had relied, over the years, upon the compact's terms for judicial and revenue purposes, thereby implying the grant of consent.

Relying on the seminal 1893 case of *Virginia v. Tennessee*, the legislatures of New York and New Jersey did not submit the Palisades Interstate Park Agreement of 1900 to Congress for its consent.

In the same vein, the legislatures of New Jersey and New York initially had no intention of submitting the 1921 Port of New York Authority Compact to Congress. The compact simply specified that it would become effective

"when signed and sealed by the Commissioners of each State as hereinbefore provided and the Attorney General of the State of New York and the Attorney General of New Jersey. . . ."[85]

As previously mentioned, the Port of New York Authority Compact was the first interstate compact that created a governing commission to carry out the purposes of the compact.

---

[84] Id.
[85] New York Laws of 1921. Chapter 154.

After the newly created Authority's bankers and bond counsels advised the Authority that potential investors might be hesitant to purchase bonds of such an unusual governmental entity in the absence of congressional consent, the two states sought, and quickly obtained, congressional consent for the compact.[86]

In the 1976 case of *New Hampshire v. Maine*, the U.S. Supreme Court reaffirmed the 1893 case of *Virginia v. Tennessee* and decided that an interstate agreement locating an ancient boundary did not require congressional consent.[87]

As a matter of convention, compacts typically do not explicitly mention congressional consent, even when it is the intent of the compacting parties to seek it.

The 1978 case of *U.S. Steel Corporation v. Multistate Tax Commission*[88] is the most important recent case on the issue of whether congressional consent is necessary for interstate compacts. In that case, the U.S. Supreme Court reaffirmed its 1893 holding in *Virginia v. Tennessee*.[89]

The Multistate Tax Compact addresses issues relating to multistate taxpayers and uniformity among state tax systems. Like many compacts, the compact itself is silent as to congressional consent, saying only:

> "This compact shall enter into force when enacted into law by any seven states."[90]

The Multistate Tax Compact was submitted to Congress for its consent. However, the compact languished there because of fierce political opposition from various business interests that were concerned about multi-million-dollar tax audits. The compacting states then decided to proceed with the implementation of the compact without congressional consent. Predictably, the opponents of the compact, led by U.S. Steel, challenged the constitutionality of their action.

In upholding the constitutionality of the Multistate Tax Compact, despite the lack of congressional consent, the Supreme Court noted that the compact did not

> "authorize the member states to exercise any powers they could not exercise in its absence. . . ."[91]

The Court again applied the interpretation of the Compact Clause from its 1893 holding in *Virginia v. Tennessee*, writing that:

---

[86] Zimmerman, Joseph F. 1996. *Interstate Relations: The Neglected Dimension of Federalism.* Westport, CT: Praeger.

[87] *New Hampshire v. Maine.* 426 U.S. 363. 1976.

[88] *U.S. Steel Corporation v. Multistate Tax Commission.* 434 U.S. 454. 1978.

[89] *Virginia v. Tennessee.* 148 U.S. 503. 1893.

[90] Multistate Tax Compact. Section 1 of Article X.

[91] *U.S. Steel Corporation v. Multistate Tax Commission.* 434 U.S. 454 at 473. 1978. Justice Powell wrote the opinion of the Court, joined by Chief Justice Burger and Justices Brennan, Stewart, Marshall, Rehnquist, and Stevens.

"the test is whether the Compact enhances state power *quaod* the National Government."[92]

The dissent of Justice Byron White (joined by Justice Harry Blackmun) in *U.S. Steel Corporation v. Multistate Tax Commission* is noteworthy because it suggests that the Court's majority opinion may have implicitly recognized a second test, namely whether a compact possibly encroaches on non-party states.

"A proper understanding of what would encroach upon federal authority, however, must also incorporate encroachments on the authority and power of non-Compact States."[93]

Thus, in the view of the two dissenters in the 1978 case, it might be necessary to analyze the impact of a disputed compact on both the power of the federal government and the power of non-member states in order to determine whether Congressional consent is required for a particular compact.

As the Supreme Court noted in *U.S. Steel Corporation v. Multistate Tax Commission*:

"most multilateral compacts have been submitted for Congressional approval."[94]

Recognizing the historical precedent of submitting compacts to Congress for approval, we have been unable to locate a single case where a court invalidated a compact for lack of consent on the grounds that it impermissibly encroached on federal supremacy.[95]

In analyzing the diverse range of issues on which courts have allowed states to enter into interstate compacts, it is hard to predict circumstances under which a court will invalidate an interstate compact that has not received congressional approval, except in the rare cases where the compact clearly encroaches on federal supremacy.[96] As Michael S. Greve wrote in 2003:

---

[92] Id. at 473.

[93] Id. at 494.

[94] Id. at 471.

[95] See *Star Scientific, Inc. v. Beales*, 278 F.3d 339 (4th Cir. 2002) involving the Master Settlement Agreement that resolved the lawsuit between states and major companies in the tobacco industry and established an administrative body to determine compliance with the agreement; *McComb v. Wambaugh*, 934 F.2d 474 (3rd Cir. 1991) involving the Interstate Compact on Placement of Children focusing on adoption and foster care of children; *New York v. Trans World Airlines, Inc.*, 728 F.Supp. 162 (S.D.N.Y. 1990) involving a compact among several states to regulate airline advertising; and *Breest v. Moran*, 571 F.Supp. 343 (D.R.I. 1983) involving the New England Interstate Corrections Compact allowing for the transfer of prisoners among detention facilities in the New England states.

[96] Even where encroachment arguably occurs, Congressional consent might not be required. For example, encroachment on federal powers arguably occurred in both the Multistate Tax Compact involved in *U.S. Steel Corporation v. Multistate Tax Commission* (434 U.S. 454, 1978), which sought to short-circuit a federal statutory solution to the allocation of interstate taxes and the compact involved in *Star Scientific*,

"After *U.S. Steel* one can hardly imagine a state compact that would run afoul of the Compact Clause without first, or at least also, running afoul of other independent constitutional obstacles."[97]

In the 1991 case of *McComb v. Wambaugh*, the U.S. Court of Appeals for the Third Circuit held that no encroachment occurs where the subject of the compact concerns

"areas of jurisdiction historically retained by the states."[98]

In *The Law and Use of Interstate Compacts*, Frederick L. Zimmermann[99] and Mitchell Wendell point out:

"Consent bills for interstate compacts dealing with issues in the realm of state activity, law, and administration, with interstate jurisdictional problems and with the settlement of interstate equities, normally serve only to clutter congressional calendars and complicate and obstruct interstate cooperation."[100]

A number of compacts involving states' constitutionally reserved powers have been submitted to Congress for its consent. On one occasion, one house of Congress declined to grant consent on the grounds that congressional consent was unnecessary. The House of Representatives approved a bill granting consent to the Southern Regional Education Compact; however, the Senate did not concur because it concluded that the subject matter of the compact—education—was entirely a state prerogative.[101]

In recent years, groups that advocate that the states exercise their powers more vigorously, such as the Goldwater Institute in Arizona, have drafted a number of model interstate compacts that the Institute maintains do not require congressional consent in order to take effect.[102] Several of these compacts proposed rely on Congress's advance consent to interstate compacts in the field of crime control contained in the Crime Control Consent Act of 1934.

Inc. v. Beales, 278 F.3d 339 (4th Cir. 2002) that resolved the lawsuit between states and major tobacco companies concerning the regulation of national cigarette advertising. Yet, both were held to be valid despite not receiving congressional consent.

[97] Compacts, cartels, and congressional consent. 68 *Mo. L. Rev.* 285 at 308. 2003.

[98] 934 F.2d at 479 (3rd Cir. 1991).

[99] Not to be confused with Joseph F. Zimmerman, co-author of this book.

[100] Zimmermann, Frederick Lloyd, and Wendell, Mitchell. 1976. *The Law and Use of Interstate Compacts.* Lexington, KY: Council of State Governments.

[101] Barton, Weldon V. 1967. *Interstate Compacts in the Political Process.* Chapel Hill, NC: University of North Carolina Press. Pages 132–133.

[102] See http://goldwaterinstitute.org/model-legislation for draft interstate compacts proposed by the Goldwater Institute.

5.13 ENFORCEMENT OF INTERSTATE COMPACTS

The granting of consent suggests that Congress may enforce compact provisions; however, in practice, enforcement of interstate compacts is usually left to the courts.

Party states have, on numerous occasions, filed suits in the U.S. Supreme Court requesting its interpretation of the provisions of interstate compacts. For example, the Court granted a request by Kansas in 2001 to file a bill of complaint in equity against Colorado in an attempt to resolve disputes pertaining to the Arkansas River Compact. In *Kansas v. Colorado,* the Court rejected Colorado's argument that the 11th Amendment barred a damages award for Colorado's violation of the compact because the damages were losses suffered by individual farmers in Kansas and not by the State of Kansas.[103]

An individual or a state may challenge the validity of a compact in state or federal court. Similarly, an individual or a state may bring suit to have provisions of a compact enforced. In general, the 11th Amendment forbids a federal court from considering a suit in law or equity against a state brought by a citizen of a sister state or a foreign nation. Notwithstanding the 11th Amendment, a citizen can challenge a compact or its execution in a state or federal court in a proceeding to prevent a public officer from enforcing a compact. If brought in a state court, the suit can potentially be removed to a United States District Court under provisions of the Removal of Causes Act of 1920 on the ground the state court

> ". . . might conceivably be interested in the outcome of the case. . . ."[104]

Nebraska's participation in the Central Interstate Low-Level Radioactive Waste Compact created controversy over a 20-year period starting in the 1980s. As discussed in section 5.7, an initiative petition was used in Nebraska in 1988 in an unsuccessful attempt to repeal the law authorizing Nebraska's participation in the compact. Then, in 1999, the legislature decided to withdraw from the compact. Nebraska's change of heart proved costly. The Central Interstate Low-Level Radioactive Waste Commission filed a federal lawsuit resulting from Nebraska's withdrawal from the compact and its alleged refusal to meet its contractual obligations to store the radioactive waste. Waste generators and the compact commission's contractor filed a suit in the U.S. District Court for the District of Nebraska, alleging that the state of Nebraska had deliberately delayed review of their license application for eight years and that it had always intended to deny it. The court ruled in 1999 that Nebraska had waived its 11th Amendment immunity when it joined the compact.[105] In 2001, the U.S. Court of Appeals for the Eighth Circuit affirmed the lower court's decision.[106] In 2004, Nebraska agreed to settle the lawsuit for $141,000,000.[107]

---

[103] *Kansas v. Colorado.* 533 U.S. 1. 2001.

[104] 41 Stat. 554.

[105] *Entergy, Arkansas, Incorporated v. Nebraska,* 68 F.Supp.2d 1093 at 1100 (D.Neb.1999).

[106] *Entergy, Arkansas, Incorporated v. Nebraska,* 241 F.3d 979 at 991–992 (8th Cir. 2001).

[107] *Lincoln Journal Star.* July 15, 2005.

5.14 AMENDMENTS TO INTERSTATE COMPACTS

Party states may amend an interstate compact. Proposed amendments to an interstate compact typically follow the same process employed in the enactment of the original compact by each party (e.g., approval of a bill by the legislature and governor). For example, the Tri-States Lotto Compact provides:

> "Amendments and supplements to this compact may be adopted by concurrent legislation of the party states."

In addition, the consent of Congress is necessary for an amendment of an interstate compact if the original compact received congressional consent.

As a matter of practical politics, an objection by a member of Congress who represents an area affected by a compact will often be able to halt congressional consideration of consent. This fact is illustrated by the experience of the New Jersey Legislature and the New York Legislature, which each enacted an amendment to the Port Authority of New York and New Jersey Compact (signed by the two Governors) allowing the Port Authority to initiate industrial development projects. Representative Elizabeth Holtzman of New York placed a hold on the consent bill on the grounds that the Port Authority had failed to solve the port's transportation problems. Holtzman argued that the Port Authority should construct a railroad freight tunnel under the Hudson River to obviate the need of trains to travel 125 miles to the north to a rail bridge over the river. She removed the hold upon reaching an agreement with the Authority. The Port Authority agreed that it would finance an independent study of the economic feasibility of constructing such a tunnel. The study ultimately reached the conclusion that a rail freight tunnel would not be economically viable.

The Constitution (section 10 of Article I) authorizes Congress to revise state statutes levying import and export duties; however, it does not grant similar authority to revise interstate compacts. Congress withdrew its consent to a Kentucky–Pennsylvania Interstate Compact that stipulated that the Ohio River should be kept free of obstructions. In 1855, the U.S. Supreme Court ruled in *Pennsylvania v. Wheeling and Belmont Bridge Company* that the compact was constitutional under the Constitution's Supremacy Clause (Article VI) and that a compact approved by Congress did not restrict Congress's power to regulate an interstate compact.[108] In the 1917 case of *Louisville Bridge Company v. United States*, the Court ruled that Congress may amend a compact even in the absence of a specific provision reserving to Congress the authority to alter, amend, or repeal the compact.[109] A federal statute terminating a compact is not subject to the due process guarantee of the Fifth Amendment to the Constitution on the ground that this constitutional protection extends only to persons.

---

[108] *Pennsylvania v. Wheeling and Belmont Bridge Company.* 50 U.S. 647. 1855.
[109] *Louisville Bridge Company v. United States.* 242 U.S. 409. 1917.

5.15 DURATION, TERMINATION, AND WITHDRAWALS

The duration of an interstate compact, the method of terminating a compact, and the method by which a party may withdraw from a compact are generally specified by the compact itself.

5.15.1 DURATION OF AN INTERSTATE COMPACT

The U.S. Constitution does not address the question of the permissible duration of interstate compacts. The duration of some compacts has been considerable. For example, the 1785 Maryland–Virginia compact regulating fishing and navigation on the Chesapeake Bay and the Potomac was ratified under the Articles of Confederation and remained in effect until 1958 (when it was replaced by the Potomac River Compact).

Some compacts contain a sunset provision specifying the compact's duration. For example, in the Southwestern Low-Level Radioactive Waste Disposal Compact, California agreed to serve for 35 years as the host state for the storage of radioactive waste for the states of Arizona, North Dakota, South Dakota, and California.

5.15.2 TERMINATION OF AN INTERSTATE COMPACT

Many compacts contain a termination provision.

The Colorado River Compact stipulates that termination may be authorized only by a unanimous vote of all party states.

The Central Interstate Low-Level Radioactive Waste Compact permits states to withdraw, but specifies that the compact shall not be terminated until all parties leave the compact.

> "The withdrawal of a party state from this compact under subsection D of Article VII of the compact or the revocation of a state's membership in this compact under subsection E of Article VII of the compact shall not affect the applicability of this compact to the remaining party states.

> "This compact shall be terminated when all party states have withdrawn pursuant to subsection D of Article VII of the compact."

5.15.3 WITHDRAWAL FROM AN INTERSTATE COMPACT

An interstate compact is, first of all, a contract.

States enter into interstate compacts voluntarily. When a state enters into a compact, it becomes a party to that contract. Consequently, the general principles of contract law apply to interstate compacts. In particular, unless a contract provides otherwise, a party may not amend, terminate, or withdraw from a contract without the unanimous consent of the contract's signatories. Specifically, unless a contract provides otherwise, a party cannot unilaterally renounce a contract.

With the exception of compacts that are presumed to be permanent (e.g., boundary settlement compacts), almost all interstate compacts permit a state to withdraw and specify the procedures that a party state must follow in order to withdraw.

If a state originally joined a compact by enacting a statute, withdrawal is usually accomplished by repealing that statute.

A small number of interstate compacts permit any party state to withdraw instantaneously—without any advance notice to the compact's other parties and without any delay. For example, the Boating Offense Compact provides:

> "Any party state may withdraw from this compact by enacting a statute repealing the same."

The Interstate Compact on Licensure of Participants in Horse Racing with Parimutuel Wagering permits instantaneous withdrawal as soon as the Governor of the withdrawing state performs the (modest) task of notifying the other compacting states.

> "Any party state may withdraw from this compact by enacting a statute repealing this compact, but no such withdrawal shall become effective until the head of the executive branch of the withdrawing state has given notice in writing of such withdrawal to the head of the executive branch of all other party states."

In contrast, the majority of interstate compacts impose both a notification requirement for withdrawal and a delay before a withdrawal becomes effective. The length of the delay is typically calibrated based on the nature of the compact. Compacts frequently specify that a withdrawal cannot interrupt, in midstream, any process that began while the withdrawing state was part of the compact. Compacts almost always specify that a withdrawal does not cancel obligations that a withdrawing state incurred while it belonged to the compact.

For example, the compact on the Interstate Taxation of Motor Fuels Consumed by Interstate Buses permits withdrawal after one year's notice.

> "This compact shall enter into force when enacted into law by any 2 states. Thereafter it shall enter into force and become binding upon any state subsequently joining when such state has enacted the compact into law. Withdrawal from the compact shall be by act of the legislature of a party state, but shall not take effect until one year after the governor of the withdrawing state has notified the governor of each other party state, in writing, of the withdrawal."

The Interstate Mining Compact contains similar provisions.

The delay is generally based on the subject matter of the compact. The delay is typically lengthy when the compact's remaining parties may need time to make alternative arrangements or to adjust economically to a withdrawal. For example, the Rhode Island–Massachusetts Interstate Low-Level Radioactive Waste Management Compact requires that a withdrawing state give notice five years in advance.

"Any party state may withdraw from this compact by repealing its authorizing legislation, and such rights of access to regional facilities enjoyed by
generators in that party state shall thereby terminate. However, no such
withdrawal shall take effect until five years after the governor of the withdrawing state has given notice in writing of such withdrawal to the Commission and to the governor of each party state."

Some compacts impose different delays, depending on the withdrawing party's specific obligations under the compact. For example, the Southwestern Low-Level Radioactive Waste Disposal Compact imposes a five-year delay for withdrawal on the state that
receives and stores the radioactive waste (California in this case), but only a two-year
delay on the non-host states (Arizona, North Dakota, and South Dakota). A host state
withdrawal would require that all of the non-host states scramble to find an alternative
place to store their radioactive waste, whereas a withdrawal by a non-host state would
merely necessitate an economic readjustment at the facility operated by the host state.

"A party state, other than the host state, may withdraw from the compact
by repealing the enactment of this compact, but this withdrawal shall not
become effective until two years after the effective date of the repealing
legislation. . . .

"If the host state withdraws from the compact, the withdrawal shall not
become effective until five years after the effective date of the repealing
legislation."

The Texas Low-Level Radioactive Waste Disposal Compact similarly imposes a
longer time delay for withdrawal by hosts than non-hosts.

The Delaware River Basin Compact requires advance notice of at least 20 years
for withdrawal, with such notice being allowed only during a five-year window every
100 years.

"The duration of this compact shall be for an initial period of 100 years from
its effective date, and it shall be continued for additional periods of 100 years
if not later than 20 years nor sooner than 25 years prior to the termination of
the initial period or any succeeding period none of the signatory States, by
authority of an act of its Legislature, notifies the commission of intention to
terminate the compact at the end of the then current 100-year period."

Many compacts provide that a state's withdrawal will not affect any "liability already incurred" or interrupt any legal process that was started while the withdrawing
party was part of the compact. For example, the Multistate Tax Compact provides:

"Any party state may withdraw from this compact by enacting a statute repealing the same. No withdrawal shall affect any liability already incurred
by or chargeable to a party state prior to the time of such withdrawal.

"No proceeding commenced before an arbitration board prior to the withdrawal of a state and to which the withdrawing state or any subdivision thereof is a party shall be discontinued or terminated by the withdrawal, nor shall the board thereby lose jurisdiction over any of the parties to the proceeding necessary to make a binding determination therein."

The Agreement on Detainers provides:

"This agreement shall enter into full force and effect as to a party state when such state has enacted the same into law. A state party to this agreement may withdraw herefrom by enacting a statute repealing the same. However, the withdrawal of any state shall not affect the status of any proceedings already initiated by inmates or by state officers at the time such withdrawal takes effect, nor shall it affect their rights in respect thereof."

The Interstate Compact on the Placement of Children (one of the compacts to which all 50 states and the District of Columbia belong) provides:

"This compact shall be open to joinder by any state, territory or possession of the United States, the District of Columbia, the Commonwealth of Puerto Rico, and, with the consent of Congress, the Government of Canada or any province thereof. It shall become effective with respect to any such jurisdiction when such jurisdiction has enacted the same into law. Withdrawal from this compact shall be by the enactment of a statute repealing the same, but shall not take effect until two years after the effective date of such statute and until written notice of the withdrawal has been given by the withdrawing state to the Governor of each other party jurisdiction. Withdrawal of a party state shall not affect the rights, duties and obligations under this compact of any sending agency therein with respect to a placement made prior to the effective date of withdrawal."

The Interstate Compact on Juveniles (another compact to which all 50 states and the District of Columbia adhere) provides:

"That this compact shall continue in force and remain binding upon each executing state until renounced by it. Renunciation of this compact shall be by the same authority which executed it, by sending six months' notice in writing of its intention to withdraw from the compact to the other states party hereto. The duties and obligations of a renouncing state under Article VII hereof shall continue as to parolees and probationers residing therein at the time of withdrawal until retaken or finally discharged. Supplementary agreements entered into under Article X hereof shall be subject to renunciation as provided by such supplementary agreements, and shall not be subject to the six months' renunciation notice of the present Article."

The Interstate Agreement Creating a Multistate Lottery (MUSL) delays return of the departing lottery's share of the prize reserve fund until the expiration of the period for winners to claim their lotto prizes.

> "That MUSL shall continue in existence until this agreement is revoked by all of the party lotteries. The withdrawal of one or more party lotteries shall not terminate this agreement among the remaining lotteries. . . .

> "A party lottery wishing to withdraw from this agreement shall give the board a six months notice of its intention to withdraw. . . .

> "In the event that a party lottery terminates, voluntarily or involuntarily, or MUSL is terminated by agreement of the parties, the prize reserve fund share of the party lottery or lotteries shall not be returned to the party lottery or lotteries until the later of one year from and after the date of termination or final resolution of any pending unresolved liabilities arising from transactions processed during the tenure of the departing lottery or lotteries. The voluntary or involuntary termination of a party lottery or lotteries does not cancel any obligation to MUSL which the party lottery or lotteries incurred before the withdrawal date."

Many compacts specifically provide that a state's withdrawal will not affect any obligations that the withdrawing state incurred while it was part of the compact. For example, the Multistate Tax Compact provides:

> "No withdrawal shall affect any liability already incurred by or chargeable to a party state prior to the time of such withdrawal."

The Rhode Island–Massachusetts Interstate Low-Level Radioactive Waste Management Compact and Central Interstate Low-Level Radioactive Waste Compact have a similar provision.

Occasionally, a compact permits a member state to withdraw selectively from its obligations under the compact—that is, to withdraw from the compact with respect to some states, but to remain in the compact with respect to other states. For example, the Interpleader Compact provides:

> "This compact shall continue in force and remain binding on a party state until such state shall withdraw therefrom. To be valid and effective, any withdrawal must be preceded by a formal notice in writing of one year from the appropriate authority of that state. Such notice shall be communicated to the same officer or agency in each party state with which the notice of adoption was deposited pursuant to Article VI. In the event that a state wishes to withdraw with respect to one or more states, but wishes to remain a party to this compact with other states party thereto, its notice

of withdrawal shall be communicated only to those states with respect to which withdrawal is contemplated."

Although withdrawals from interstate compacts are relatively rare, they do occur. In 1995, the Virginia General Assembly enacted a statute withdrawing from the Atlantic States Marine Fisheries Compact, complaining that Virginia's fishing quotas were too low. Maryland withdrew from the Interstate Bus Motor Fuel Tax Compact in 1967 and from the National Guard Mutual Assistance Compact in 1981.

States may withdraw from a compact and then rejoin it. For example, Florida withdrew from the Atlantic States Marine Fisheries Compact and then subsequently rejoined the compact.

5.16 ADMINISTRATION OF INTERSTATE COMPACTS

About one half of all modern-day interstate compacts establish a commission to administer the subject matter of the compact. The remaining compacts are generally administered by departments and agencies of the party states.

For example, the Driver License Compact (to which 45 states adhere) requires a party state to report each conviction of a driver from another party state for a motor vehicle violation to the licensing authority of the driver's home state. The compact requires the home state to treat the reported violation as if it had occurred in the home state. The compact also requires the licensing authority of each member state to determine whether an applicant for a driver's license has held or currently holds a license issued by another party state.

Similarly, the Nonresident Violator Compact (enacted by 44 states) ensures that nonresident drivers answer summonses or appearance tickets for moving violations. This compact (like the Driver License Compact) requires each member state to report each conviction of a driver from another party state for a motor vehicle violation to the licensing authority of the driver's home state. This compact is designed to ensure that nonresident motorists are treated in the same manner as resident motorists and that their due process rights are protected. A driver who fails to respond to an appearance ticket or summons will have his or her license suspended by the issuing state.

5.17 STYLE OF INTERSTATE COMPACTS

As a matter of convention, modern interstate compacts are typically organized into articles, with unnumbered sections. After each member state enacts the compact, the various articles of the compact are given numbers and letters in the state's compiled code in accordance with the state's style. Similarly, after Congress consents to a compact, the various articles of the compact may be assigned different letters and numbers. Thus, compacts (and congressional legislation consenting to compacts) typically make reference to enactment of "substantially" the same agreement by other member states.

5.18 COMPARISON OF TREATIES AND COMPACTS

Although interstate compacts bear many similarities to international treaties among nations, they differ in three important respects.

First, Congress may enact a statute that conflicts with an international treaty, whereas a state legislature lacks the authority to enact a statute conflicting with any provision of an interstate compact.

Second, a compact is a contract that is enforceable by courts. In contrast, the procedure for the enforcement of an international treaty is specified within the treaty itself. In practice, many treaties contain no specific provision for enforcement and merely rely on the goodwill of the parties.

Third, under the Constitution, the President is granted the sole authority to negotiate a treaty with another nation. In contrast, no provision in the Constitution stipulates the manner of negotiation of interstate compacts. Moreover, Congress has never enacted any general statute specifying procedures to be followed by a state that is contemplating entry into an interstate compact.

There is no international law provision authorizing citizens of a signatory to a treaty to be involved in its termination. In 1838, the U.S. Supreme Court applied this principle of international law to interstate compacts. The Court ruled, in the case of *Georgetown v. Alexander Canal Company*, that citizens whose rights would be affected adversely by a compact are not parties to a compact and that they consequently can have no direct involvement in a compact's termination.[110]

5.19 COMPARISON OF UNIFORM STATE LAWS AND INTERSTATE COMPACTS

The term "uniform state law" usually refers to a law drafted and recommended by the National Conference of Commissioners on Uniform State Laws (NCCUSL), although the term is occasionally used to refer to laws originating elsewhere.

The Conference is a non-governmental body formed in 1892 upon the recommendation of the American Bar Association. The Conference is most widely known for its work on the Uniform Commercial Code. Since 1892, the Conference has produced more than 200 recommended laws in areas such as commercial law, family and domestic relations law, estates, probate and trusts, real estate, implementation of full faith and credit, interstate enforcement of judgments, and alternative dispute resolution.

Many of the Conference's recommended uniform laws have been adopted by large numbers of states, including the Uniform Anatomical Gift Act, the Uniform Fraudulent Transfer Act, the Uniform Interstate Family Support Act, the Uniform Enforcement of Foreign Judgments Act, and the Uniform Transfers to Minors Act.

There is some resemblance between an interstate compact and a uniform state law. Both, for example, entail enactment of identical statutes by a group of states.

---

[110] *Georgetown v. Alexander Canal Company.* 37 U.S. 91 at 95–96. 1838.

An interstate compact encompassing all 50 states and the District of Columbia and a uniform state law enacted by the same 51 jurisdictions each has the practical effect of establishing national policy. There are, however, a number of important differences.

First, the goal of the Conference in recommending a uniform state law is, almost always, enactment of the identical statute by *all* states. Many interstate compacts are inherently limited to a particular geographic area (e.g., the Port of New York Authority Compact, the Arkansas River Compact, and the Great Lakes Basin Compact) or to scattered states that are engaged in a particular activity (e.g., the Interstate Oil Compact and the Multistate Lottery Agreement).

Second, the effective date of a uniform state law is typically not contingent on identical legislation being passed in any other state. A uniform state law generally takes effect in each state as soon as each state enacts it. That is, a uniform state law stands alone and is not coordinated with the identical laws that other states may, or may not, pass. If it happens that all 50 states enact a particular uniform state law, then the Conference's goal of establishing a uniform policy for the entire country is achieved. If a substantial fraction of the states enact a uniform state law, then the goal of uniformity is partially achieved. If only one state enacts a uniform state law, that particular statute nonetheless serves as the law of that state on the subject matter involved. In contrast, the effective date of an interstate compact is almost always contingent on the enactment by some specified number or some specified combination of states. The reason for this is that states typically enter into interstate compacts in order to obtain some benefit that can be obtained only by cooperative and coordinated action with one or more sister states.

Third, although the goal of the National Conference of Commissioners on Uniform State Laws is that identical laws be adopted in all states, it is very common for individual states to amend the Conference's recommended statute in response to local pressures. If the changes are not major, the Conference's goal of uniformity may nonetheless be substantially (albeit not perfectly) achieved. In contrast, adoption of a compact requires a meeting of the minds. Because an interstate compact is a contract, each party that desires to adhere to an interstate compact must enact identical wording (except for insubstantial differences such as numbering and punctuation). Variations in substance are not allowed.

Fourth, and most importantly, a uniform state law does not establish a contractual relationship among the states involved. When a state enacts a uniform state law, it undertakes no obligations to other states. The enacting state merely seeks the benefits associated with uniform treatment of the subject matter at hand. Each state's legislature may repeal or amend a uniform state law at any time, at its own pleasure and convenience. There is no procedure for withdrawal (or advance notice required prior to withdrawal) in a uniform state law. Indeed, a uniform state law does not create any new legal entity, and therefore there is no legal entity from which to withdraw. In contrast, an interstate compact establishes a contractual relationship among its member states. Once a state enters into a compact, it is legally bound to the compact's terms, including the compact's specified restrictions and procedures for withdrawal and termination.

5.20 COMPARISON OF FEDERAL MULTI-STATE COMMISSIONS AND INTERSTATE COMPACTS

Federal multi-state commissions bear some resemblance to the commissions that are established by some interstate compacts. There are, however, a number of important differences between federally created multi-state commissions and interstate compacts.

In 1879, Congress first recognized the need for a governmental body in a multi-state region by establishing the Mississippi River Commission. The enabling statute directed the Commission to deepen channels; improve navigation safety; prevent destructive floods; and promote commerce, the postal system, and trade. The Commission's original members were three officers of the U.S. Army Corps of Engineers, one member of the U.S. Coast and Geodetic Survey, and three citizen members, including two civil engineers. Commission members are nominated by the President, subject to the Senate's advice and consent.

In a similar vein, the Water Resources Planning Act of 1965 authorizes the President, at the request of the concerned governors, to establish other river basin commissions. Such commissions have been created for the Ohio River and Upper Mississippi River basins.

The best-known multi-state commission—the Tennessee Valley Authority—was created by Congress in 1933. The TVA operates in an area encompassing parts of seven states. Its purposes are to promote agricultural and industrial development, control floods, and improve navigation on the Tennessee River. The President appoints, with the Senate's advice and consent, three TVA commissioners for nine-year terms. The creation of the TVA is credited to populist Senator George Norris of Nebraska, who conducted a crusade for many years against the high rates charged by electric utility companies. Aside from the benefits to the states in the Tennessee Valley, Norris and his supporters argued that the cost of TVA-generated electricity would serve as a yardstick for evaluating the rates charged by private power companies elsewhere in the country.

Although the TVA possesses broad powers to develop the river basin, the authority has largely concentrated its efforts on dams and channels, fertilizer research, and production of electricity. The TVA is generally credited with achieving considerable success in its flood control, land and forest conservation, and river-management activities. At the same time, the TVA has engendered considerable controversy over the years in a number of areas.

There are several differences between federal multi-state commissions and the commissions that are established by interstate compacts.

First, federal multi-state commissions are entirely creatures of the federal government. The states play no official role in enacting the enabling legislation establishing such bodies. In contrast, each state makes its own decision as to whether to enact an interstate compact.

Second, although state officials often provide advice on appointments to federal multi-state commissions, the appointing authority for members of a federal multi-state commission is entirely federal (i.e., the President). In contrast, the members of a commission established by an interstate compact are typically appointed by the states (e.g., by the Governors).

5.21 FUTURE OF INTERSTATE COMPACTS

In recent years, Congress has, with increasing frequency, exercised its preemption powers to remove regulatory authority totally or partially from the states. This tendency is responsible for the decrease in the number of new regulatory compacts since the mid 1960s.[111] For example, the Mid-Atlantic States Air Pollution Control Compact was entered into by Connecticut, New Jersey, and New York; however, Congress did not consent to the compact and instead enacted the Air Quality Act of 1967,[112] preempting state regulatory authority over air pollution abatement.

There are countervailing tendencies. Economic interest groups frequently lobby for the establishment of regulatory compacts among states, arguing that coordinated action by the states is sufficient to solve a particular problem.

It is reasonable to predict that increasing urban sprawl may someday lead to an interstate compact that establishes an "interstate city" encompassing an urban area spread over two or more states. Although no such interstate city has been created to date, the New Hampshire–Vermont Interstate School Compact has been used to establish two interstate school districts, each including a New Hampshire town and one or more Vermont towns. In the same vein, Kansas and Missouri have entered into a compact establishing a metropolitan cultural district governed by a commission. The commission's membership consists of the counties that decide to join the district. Eligible counties include one with a population exceeding 300,000 that is adjacent to the state line, one that contains a part of a city with a population exceeding 400,000, and counties that are contiguous to one of these.[113]

5.22 PROPOSALS FOR INTERSTATE COMPACTS ON ELECTIONS

There have been suggestions, over the years, for using interstate compacts in the field of elections.

---

[111] Zimmerman, Joseph F. 2005. *Congressional Preemption: Regulatory Federalism.* Albany, NY: State University of New York Press.

[112] 81 Stat. 485.

[113] 114 Stat. 909.

The 1970 U.S. Supreme Court case of *Oregon v. Mitchell* was concerned with congressional legislation to bring about uniformity among state durational residency requirements for voters in presidential elections. In his opinion (partially concurring and partially dissenting), Justice Potter Stewart pointed out that if Congress had not acted, the states could have adopted an interstate compact to accomplish the same objective. Justice Stewart observed that a compact involving all the states would, in effect, establish a nationwide policy on residency for election purposes.[114]

In the 1990s, U.S. Senator Charles Schumer of New York proposed a bi-state interstate compact in which New York and Texas would pool their electoral votes in presidential elections. Both states were (and still are) spectator states in presidential elections. Schumer observed that the two states are approximately the same size and that they regularly produce majorities of approximately the same magnitude in favor of each state's respective dominant political party. The Democrats typically carry New York by about 60%, and the Republicans typically carry Texas by about 60%. The purpose of the proposed compact was to create a large super-state (slightly larger than California) that would attract the attention of the presidential candidates during presidential campaigns.

---

[114] *Oregon v. Mitchell.* 400 U.S. 112 at 286–287. 1970.

6 | The Agreement Among the States to Elect the President by National Popular Vote

This chapter

- summarizes the motivation for the authors' proposal to employ an interstate compact to change the system for electing the President and Vice President of the United States (section 6.1),
- presents the text of the authors' proposed National Popular Vote compact—called the "Agreement Among the States to Elect the President by National Popular Vote" (section 6.2),
- explains the proposed National Popular Vote compact on a line-by-line basis (section 6.3),
- mentions federal legislation that might be enacted by Congress in connection with the proposed National Popular Vote compact (section 6.4), and
- discusses previous proposals for multi-state electoral legislation (section 6.5).

6.1 MOTIVATION FOR THE NATIONAL POPULAR VOTE INTERSTATE COMPACT

Chapter 1 of this book made the following points:

- Under state winner-take-all statutes, all of a state's electoral votes are controlled by a plurality of the popular votes in each separate state. Because of these state statutes (that are in use in nearly every state), a person's vote is politically irrelevant unless the voter happens to live in a closely divided battleground state.
- Voters in four-fifths of the states are ignored in presidential elections.
- The existing winner-take-all system divides the nation's 130,000,000 popular votes into 51 separate pools, thereby regularly manufacturing artificial electoral crises even when the nationwide popular vote is not particularly close. In the past six decades, there have been six presidential elections in which a shift of a small number of votes in one or two states would have elected (and in 2000, did elect) a presidential candidate who lost the popular vote nationwide. There have been five litigated state counts among the nation's 56 presidential elections. This frequency of disputes is far higher than the rate for ordinary elections in which the winner is the candidate who receives the most popular votes.

- The existing system has elected a candidate to the Presidency who did not win the nationwide popular vote in four of the nation's 56 presidential elections— a failure rate of one in 14.
- State winner-take-all statutes are the reason why presidential voting does not matter in four-fifths of the states, artificial crises are regularly manufactured, and second-place candidates are sometimes elected to the presidency.

Chapter 2 established the following facts:

- The statewide winner-take-all system is established by state law—not the U.S. Constitution or federal law.
- The U.S. Constitution gives each state the exclusive power to choose the manner of choosing its presidential electors. Unlike the states' power to choose the manner of electing U.S. Representatives and Senators, the states' power to choose the manner of allocating its electoral votes is not subject to congressional oversight. The U.S. Supreme Court has repeatedly ruled that the power of each state to award its electoral votes is an "exclusive" and "plenary" state power.
- The Founding Fathers did not design or advocate the current system of electing the President. Instead, the current system evolved over a period of decades as a result of political considerations. The statewide winner-take-all rule was used by only three states in the nation's first presidential election (1789). Because each state realized that it diminished its voice by dividing its electoral votes, the statewide winner-take-all rule for the popular election of presidential electors gradually became the norm in the first five decades after the Constitution's ratification.
- Because the power to allocate electoral votes is exclusively a state power and the statewide winner-take-all rule is contained only in state statutes, a federal constitutional amendment is not necessary to change existing state winner-take-all statutes. The states already have the constitutional power to change the current system.

Chapter 3 analyzed the three most prominent approaches to presidential election reform that have been proposed in the form of a federal constitutional amendment, namely the fractional proportional allocation of electoral votes, allocation of electoral votes by congressional district, and direct nationwide popular election. Each of these three approaches was analyzed in terms of three criteria:

- **Accuracy**: Would it ensure the election to the presidency of the candidate with the most popular votes nationwide?
- **Competitiveness**: Would it improve upon the current situation in which voters in four-fifths of the states are ignored because they live in noncompetitive states?
- **Equality**: Would every vote be equal?

Chapter 4 analyzed the two most prominent approaches to presidential election reform that can be unilaterally enacted by the states without a federal constitutional amendment and without action by Congress, namely the whole-number proportional approach and the congressional-district approach.

Chapters 3 and 4 reached the conclusion that nationwide popular election of the President is the only approach that satisfies the criteria of accuracy, competitiveness, and equality.

Chapter 5 provided background on interstate compacts and made the following points:

- Interstate compacts are specifically authorized by the U.S. Constitution as a means by which the states may act in concert to address a problem.
- There are several hundred interstate compacts in existence, covering a wide variety of topics.
- An interstate compact may be enacted in the same manner as a state law—that is, by a legislative bill receiving gubernatorial approval (or sufficient legislative support to override a gubernatorial veto) or by the citizen-initiative process (in states having this process).
- Interstate compacts typically address problems that cannot be solved unilaterally, but that can be solved by coordinated action. Accordingly, a compact almost always takes effect on a contingent basis—that is, the compact does not take effect until it is enacted by a specified number or combination of states that are sufficient to achieve the compact's goals.
- There are no constitutional restrictions on the subject matter of interstate compacts (other than the implicit limitation that the compact's subject matter must be among the powers that the states are permitted to exercise).
- An interstate compact has the force and effect of statutory law in the states belonging to the compact. The provisions of an interstate compact bind all state officials with the same force as all other state laws. The provisions of a compact are enforceable in court in the same way that any other state law is enforceable—that is, a court may compel a state official to execute the provisions of a compact (by mandamus), and a court may enjoin a state official from violating a compact's provisions (by injunction).
- An interstate compact is a binding contractual arrangement among states involved. The Impairments Clause of the U.S. Constitution prohibits states from impairing the obligations of any contract, including interstate compacts. Thus, each state belonging to an interstate compact is assured that its sister states will perform their obligations under the compact.
- Because a compact is a contract, the provisions of an interstate compact take precedence over any conflicting law of any state belonging to the compact. As long as a state remains a party to a compact, it may not enact a law in conflict

with its obligations under the compact. That is, the provisions of an interstate compact take precedence over a conflicting law—even if the conflicting law is enacted after the state enters into the compact.

- A state may withdraw from an interstate compact in accordance with the provisions for withdrawal contained in the compact. In fact, a state may withdraw from an interstate compact only under the terms provided for in the compact.

The authors' proposal, namely an interstate compact entitled the "Agreement Among the States to Elect the President by National Popular Vote," would not become effective in any state until it is enacted by states collectively possessing a majority of the electoral votes (that is, 270 of the 538 electoral votes).

The National Popular Vote compact would not change a state's internal procedures for operating a presidential election. After the 50 states and the District of Columbia certify their popular vote counts for President in the usual way, a grand total of popular votes would be calculated by adding up the popular vote count from all 51 jurisdictions.

The Electoral College would remain intact under the National Popular Vote compact. The compact would simply change the Electoral College from an institution that reflects the voters' state-by-state choices (or, in the case of Maine and Nebraska, district-by-district choices) into a body that reflects the voters' nationwide choice. Specifically, the National Popular Vote compact would require that each member state award its electoral votes to the presidential candidate who received the largest number of popular votes in all 50 states and the District of Columbia. Because the compact would become effective only when it encompasses states collectively possessing a majority of the electoral votes, the presidential candidate receiving the most popular votes in all 50 states and the District of Columbia would be guaranteed enough electoral votes in the Electoral College to be elected to the Presidency.

The National Popular Vote compact would reform the Electoral College while retaining our federalist system of state control over elections.

Note that every state's popular vote would be included in the nationwide total regardless of whether it is a member of the compact. Membership in the compact is not required for the popular votes of a state to count. That is, every vote in every state would be equal under the compact.

Note also that the political complexion of the particular states belonging to the compact would not affect the outcome—that is, the presidential candidate receiving the most popular votes in all 50 states and the District of Columbia would be assured sufficient electoral votes to be elected to the presidency.

6.2 TEXT OF THE NATIONAL POPULAR VOTE COMPACT

This section presents the entire text (888 words) of the proposed "Agreement Among the States to Elect the President by National Popular Vote."

Article I—Membership

I–1   Any State of the United States and the District of Columbia may become a member of this agreement by enacting this agreement.

Article II—Right of the People in Member States to Vote for President and Vice President

II–1   Each member state shall conduct a statewide popular election for President and Vice President of the United States.

Article III—Manner of Appointing Presidential Electors in Member States

III–1   Prior to the time set by law for the meeting and voting by the presidential electors, the chief election official of each member state shall determine the number of votes for each presidential slate in each State of the United States and in the District of Columbia in which votes have been cast in a statewide popular election and shall add such votes together to produce a "national popular vote total" for each presidential slate.

III–2   The chief election official of each member state shall designate the presidential slate with the largest national popular vote total as the "national popular vote winner."

III–3   The presidential elector certifying official of each member state shall certify the appointment in that official's own state of the elector slate nominated in that state in association with the national popular vote winner.

III–4   At least six days before the day fixed by law for the meeting and voting by the presidential electors, each member state shall make a final determination of the number of popular votes cast in the state for each presidential slate and shall communicate an official statement of such determination within 24 hours to the chief election official of each other member state.

III–5   The chief election official of each member state shall treat as conclusive an official statement containing the number of popular votes in a state for each presidential slate made by the day established by federal law for making a state's final determination conclusive as to the counting of electoral votes by Congress.

III–6   In event of a tie for the national popular vote winner, the presidential elector certifying official of each member state shall certify the appointment of the elector slate nominated in association with the presidential slate receiving the largest number of popular votes within that official's own state.

III–7   If, for any reason, the number of presidential electors nominated in a member state in association with the national popular vote winner is less than or greater than that state's number of electoral votes, the presidential candidate on the presidential slate that has been designated as the national popular vote winner shall have the power to nominate the presidential electors for that state and that state's presidential elector certifying official shall certify the appointment of such nominees.

III–8   The chief election official of each member state shall immediately release to the public all vote counts or statements of votes as they are determined or obtained.

III–9   This article shall govern the appointment of presidential electors in each member state in any year in which this agreement is, on July 20, in effect in states cumulatively possessing a majority of the electoral votes.

Article IV—Other Provisions

IV–1   This agreement shall take effect when states cumulatively possessing a majority of the electoral votes have enacted this agreement in substantially the same form and the enactments by such states have taken effect in each state.

IV–2   Any member state may withdraw from this agreement, except that a withdrawal occurring six months or less before the end of a President's term shall not become effective until a President or Vice President shall have been qualified to serve the next term.

IV–3   The chief executive of each member state shall promptly notify the chief executive of all other states of when this agreement has been enacted and has taken effect in that official's state, when the state has withdrawn from this agreement, and when this agreement takes effect generally.

IV–4   This agreement shall terminate if the electoral college is abolished.

IV–5   If any provision of this agreement is held invalid, the remaining provisions shall not be affected.

Article V—Definitions	
V–1	For purposes of this agreement, "chief executive" shall mean the Governor of a State of the United States or the Mayor of the District of Columbia;
V–2	"elector slate" shall mean a slate of candidates who have been nominated in a state for the position of presidential elector in association with a presidential slate;
V–3	"chief election official" shall mean the state official or body that is authorized to certify the total number of popular votes for each presidential slate;
V–4	"presidential elector" shall mean an elector for President and Vice President of the United States;
V–5	"presidential elector certifying official" shall mean the state official or body that is authorized to certify the appointment of the state's presidential electors;
V–6	"presidential slate" shall mean a slate of two persons, the first of whom has been nominated as a candidate for President of the United States and the second of whom has been nominated as a candidate for Vice President of the United States, or any legal successors to such persons, regardless of whether both names appear on the ballot presented to the voter in a particular state;
V–7	"state" shall mean a State of the United States and the District of Columbia; and
V–8	"statewide popular election" shall mean a general election in which votes are cast for presidential slates by individual voters and counted on a statewide basis.

6.3 SECTION-BY-SECTION EXPLANATION OF THE NATIONAL POPULAR VOTE COMPACT

6.3.1 EXPLANATION OF ARTICLE I—MEMBERSHIP

Article I of the compact identifies the compact's prospective parties, namely the 51 jurisdictions that are currently entitled to appoint presidential electors under the U.S. Constitution. These 51 jurisdictions include the 50 states and the District of Columbia (which acquired the right to appoint presidential electors under terms of the 23rd Amendment). Elsewhere in the compact, the uncapitalized word "state" (defined in article V of the compact) refers to any of these 51 jurisdictions. The term "member state" refers to a jurisdiction where the compact has been enacted into law and is in effect.

6.3.2 EXPLANATION OF ARTICLE II—RIGHT OF THE PEOPLE IN MEMBER STATES TO VOTE FOR PRESIDENT AND VICE PRESIDENT

Article II of the compact mandates a popular election for President and Vice President in each member state.

> "Each member state shall conduct a statewide popular election for President and Vice President of the United States."

The term "statewide popular election" is defined in article V of the compact as

> "a general election at which votes are cast for presidential slates by individual voters and counted on a statewide basis."

From the perspective of the operation of the compact, this clause guarantees that there will be popular votes for President and Vice President to count in each member state. It fortifies the practice of the states (universal since the 1880 election) to permit the people to vote for President. As discussed in detail in section 2.2, the people of the United States have no federal constitutional right to vote for President and Vice President. The people have acquired the privilege to vote for President and Vice President as a consequence of legislative action by their respective states. Moreover, except in Colorado, the people have no state constitutional right to vote for President and Vice President, and the existing privilege may be withdrawn at any time merely by passage of a state law. Indeed, the voters chose the presidential electors in only six states in the nation's first presidential election (1789). Moreover, state legislatures have occasionally changed the rules for voting for President for purely political reasons. For example, just prior to the 1800 presidential election, the Federalist-controlled legislatures of Massachusetts and New Hampshire—fearing Jeffersonian victories in the popular votes in their states—repealed existing state statutes allowing the people to vote for presidential electors and vested that power in themselves.

Because an interstate compact is a contractual obligation among the member states, the provisions of a compact take precedence over any conflicting law of any member state. This principle applies regardless of when the conflicting law may have been enacted.[1] Thus, once a state enters into an interstate compact and the compact takes effect, the state is bound by the terms of the compact as long as the state remains in the compact. Because a compact is a contract, a state must remain in an interstate compact until the state withdraws from the compact in accordance with the compact's terms for withdrawal. Thus, in reading each provision of a compact, the reader may find it useful to imagine that every section of the compact is preceded by the words

> "Notwithstanding any other provision of law in the member state, whether enacted before or after the effective date of this compact, . . . "

Thus, as long as a state remains in the compact, Article II of the compact establishes the right of the people in each member state to vote for President and Vice President.

In addition, the wording of Article II of the compact requires continued use by member states of another feature of presidential voting that is currently in universal use by the states, namely the "short presidential ballot." Under the short presidential ballot (described in detail in section 2.2.6), the voter is presented with a choice among "presidential slates" containing a specifically named presidential nominee and a specifically named vice-presidential nominee.[2] This clause does not prevent states from

---

[1] Council of State Governments. 2003. *Interstate Compacts and Agencies 2003.* Lexington, KY: The Council of State Governments. Page 6.

[2] This clause does not prevent a presidential candidate from running with more than one vice-presidential nominee. In 2004, for example, there were two different Nader "presidential slates" in New York. Ralph Nader appeared on the ballot in New York as the presidential nominee of the Independence Party with Jan D. Pierce as his vice-presidential nominee. He simultaneously appeared on the New York ballot as the presidential nominee of the Peace and Justice Party with Peter Miguel Camejo as his vice-presidential nominee. There were, necessarily, two different lists of 31 nominees for presidential elector associated with each

displaying the names of candidates for presidential elector on the ballot (as a small number of states currently do). It simply requires that the names of the presidential candidates appear on the ballot. The term "presidential slate" is defined in Article V of the compact as

> "a slate of two persons, the first of whom has been nominated as a candidate for President of the United States and the second of whom has been nominated as a candidate for Vice President of the United States, or any legal successors to such persons. . . . "

The continued use of the short presidential ballot permits the aggregation, from state to state, of the popular votes that have been cast for the various presidential slates. If, for example, the voters in a particular state were to cast separate votes for individual presidential electors (say, as they did in 1964 as shown by the Vermont ballot in figure 2.1 and discussed in section 2.2.6 or as they did in 1960 as shown by the Alabama ballot in figure 2.13 and discussed in section 2.11), the winning presidential electors from that state would each inevitably receive a (slightly) different number of votes. Thus, there would not be any single number available to add into the nationwide tally being accumulated by the presidential slates running in the remainder of the country.

6.3.3 EXPLANATION OF ARTICLE III—MANNER OF APPOINTING PRESIDENTIAL ELECTORS IN MEMBER STATES

Article III of the compact is the heart of the compact. It establishes the mechanics of a nationwide popular election by prescribing the "manner of appointing presidential electors in member states."

The National Popular Vote compact is state legislation that exercises existing state power under Article II, section 1, clause 2 of the U.S. Constitution:

> "**Each State shall appoint, in such Manner as the Legislature thereof may direct, a Number of Electors**, equal to the whole Number of Senators and Representatives to which the State may be entitled in the Congress: but no Senator or Representative, or Person holding an Office of Trust or Profit under the United States, shall be appointed an Elector."[3] [Emphasis added]

The first three clauses of Article III are the main clauses for implementing nationwide popular election of the President and Vice President.

The first clause of Article III of the compact provides:

> "Prior to the time set by law for the meeting and voting by the presidential electors, the chief election official of each member state shall determine

---

of the two Nader "presidential slates" in New York in 2004. Existing New York law treated and counted Nader's Independence Party votes separately from Nader's Peace and Justice Party votes.

[3] U.S. Constitution. Article II, section 1, clauses 1 and 2.

the number of votes for each presidential slate in each State of the United States and in the District of Columbia in which votes have been cast in a statewide popular election and shall add such votes together to produce a 'national popular vote total' for each presidential slate."

The phrase "the time set by law for the meeting and voting by the presidential electors" refers to the federal law (Title 3, chapter 1, section 7 of the United States Code) providing:

"The electors of President and Vice President of each State shall meet and give their votes on the first Monday after the second Wednesday in December next following their appointment at such place in each State as the legislature of such State shall direct."

For example, the federally designated day for the meeting of the Electoral College in 2012 was Monday, December 17, 2012.

The term "chief election official" used throughout the compact is defined in Article V of the compact as

"the state official or body that is authorized to certify the total number of popular votes cast for each presidential slate."

In most states, the "chief election official" is the Secretary of State or the state canvassing board. In Alaska, the Lieutenant Governor is the "chief election official."

The first clause of Article III of the compact requires that the chief election official obtain statements showing the number of popular votes cast for each presidential slate in each state. Then, this clause requires that the popular votes for each presidential slate from all the states be added together to yield a "national popular vote total" for each presidential slate.

Because the purpose of the compact is to achieve a nationwide popular vote for President and Vice President, the popular vote counts from *all* 50 states and the District of Columbia are included in the "national popular vote total" regardless of whether the jurisdiction is a member of the compact. That is, the compact counts the popular votes from member states on an equal footing with those from non-member states. Votes from *all* states and the District of Columbia are treated equally in calculating the "national popular vote total."

Popular votes can, however, only be counted from non-member states if there are popular votes available to count. As previously mentioned, Article II of the compact guarantees that each member state will produce a popular vote count because it requires member states to permit their voters to vote for President and Vice President in a "statewide popular election." Even though all states have permitted their voters to vote for presidential electors in a "statewide popular election" since the 1880 election, non-member states are, of course, not bound by the compact. In the unlikely event that a non-member state were to take the presidential vote away from its own people, there would be no popular vote count available from such a state.

Similarly, in the unlikely event that a non-member state were to remove the names of the presidential nominees and vice-presidential nominees from the ballot and present the voters only with names of candidates for presidential elector (as was the case in 1960 in Alabama as shown by the ballot in figure 2.13 and discussed in section 2.11), there would be no way to associate the vote counts of the various presidential electors with the nationwide tally being accumulated by any regular "presidential slate" running in the rest of the country.

The compact addresses the above two unlikely possibilities by specifying that the popular votes that are to be aggregated to produce the "national popular vote total" are those that are

> ". . . cast for each presidential slate in each State of the United States and in the District of Columbia **in which votes have been cast in a statewide popular election** . . . ." [Emphasis added]

In this way, the first clause of Article III of the compact deals with the unlikely possibility of a "one-state veto" preventing the orderly operation of the compact.

The word "determine" is discussed below in connection with the fourth and fifth clauses of Article III of the compact.

The purpose of the second clause of Article III of the compact is to identify the winner of the presidential election:

> "The chief election official of each member state shall designate the presidential slate with the largest national popular vote total as the 'national popular vote winner.'"

The third clause of Article III of the compact guarantees that the "national popular vote winner" will end up with a majority of the electoral votes in the Electoral College.

> "The presidential elector certifying official of each member state shall certify the appointment in that official's own state of the elector slate nominated in that state in association with the national popular vote winner."

The third clause of Article III of the compact refers to the "presidential elector certifying official" (defined in Article V of the compact) rather than the "chief election official" because these two officials are not necessarily the same in every state.

Because the purpose of the compact is to implement a nationwide popular election of the President and Vice President, it is the *national* vote total—not each state's separate statewide vote count—that would determine the national winner. Under the compact, the Electoral College would reflect the *nationwide* will of the voters—not the voters' separate statewide choices. Thus, if, for example, the Republican presidential slate is the national popular vote winner, the presidential electors nominated by the Republican Party in *all* states belonging to the compact would win election as members of the Electoral College in those states.

For purposes of illustration, suppose that the compact had been in effect in 2004, and that California had been a member of the compact in 2004, and that the Republican Bush–Cheney presidential slate received the most popular votes in all 50 states and the District of Columbia (as indeed was the case in the 2004 presidential election). In that event, the California Secretary of State would have declared the 55 presidential electors who had been nominated by the California Republican Party to be elected as California's members of the Electoral College. Those 55 Republican presidential electors would have gone to Sacramento in mid-December and cast their votes for their own party's nominees, namely George W. Bush and Dick Cheney.

In fact, 55% of California voters favored the Kerry–Edwards slate in 2004. Nonetheless, all 55 Republican candidates for presidential elector (not the 55 Democrats) would have won election as members of the Electoral College in California in 2004 because the specific purpose of the compact is to guarantee the presidency to the presidential slate (Bush–Cheney in the case of 2004) with the most votes nationwide.

Because the compact becomes effective only when it encompasses states collectively possessing a majority of the electoral votes (i.e., 270 or more of the 538 electoral votes), the presidential slate receiving the most popular votes in all 50 states and the District of Columbia is guaranteed at least 270 electoral votes when the Electoral College meets in mid-December. Given the fact that the Bush–Cheney presidential slate received 3,012,171 more popular votes in the 50 States and the District of Columbia in 2004 than the Kerry–Edwards slate, the compact would have guaranteed the Bush–Cheney slate a majority of the electoral votes in the Electoral College. Under the compact, the Bush–Cheney slate would have received a majority of the electoral votes even if 59,393 Bush–Cheney voters in Ohio had shifted to the Kerry–Edwards slate in 2004, thereby giving Kerry–Edwards the most popular votes in Ohio. In contrast, under the current system, if the Kerry–Edwards slate had carried Ohio, the Democrats would have received all of the state's 20 electoral votes and the Kerry–Edwards slate would have been elected to office with 272 electoral votes (to Bush's 266).

The first three clauses of Article III of the compact are the main clauses for implementing nationwide popular election of the President and Vice President. The remaining clauses of Article III of the compact deal with administrative matters, various contingencies, and technical issues.

The fourth clause of Article III of the compact requires the timely issuance by each of the compact's member states of an "official statement" of the state's "final determination" of its presidential vote.

> "At least six days before the day fixed by law for the meeting and voting by the presidential electors, each member state shall make a final determination of the number of popular votes cast in the state for each presidential

slate and shall communicate an official statement of such determination within 24 hours to the chief election official of each other member state."

The particular deadline in this clause corresponds to the deadline contained in the "safe harbor" provision of federal law (section 5 of Title 3, chapter 1 of the United States Code). The phrase "final determination" in this clause corresponds to the term used in the "safe harbor" provision. Section 5 provides:

> "If any State shall have provided, by laws enacted prior to the day fixed for the appointment of the electors, for its **final determination** of any controversy or contest concerning the appointment of all or any of the electors of such State, by judicial or other methods or procedures, and such determination shall have been made at least six days before the time fixed for the meeting of the electors, such determination made pursuant to such law so existing on said day, and made at least six days prior to said time of meeting of the electors, shall be conclusive, and shall govern in the counting of the electoral votes as provided in the Constitution, and as hereinafter regulated, so far as the ascertainment of the electors appointed by such State is concerned." [Emphasis added]

The federally established "safe harbor" date for the November 6, 2012, presidential election was Monday December 10, 2012.

The fourth clause of Article III of the compact, in effect, mandates each member state to comply with the "safe harbor" deadline. As a practical matter, this clause is merely a backstop because most states already have specific state statutory deadlines for certifying the results of presidential elections, and these existing statutory deadlines generally come considerably earlier than the federal "safe harbor" date (appendix T).

The word "communicated" in the fourth clause of Article III of the compact is intended to permit transmission of the "official statement" by secure electronic means that may become available in the future (rather than, say, physical delivery of the official statement by an overnight courier service).

The fourth clause of Article III of the compact is a backstop for section 5 of Title 3, chapter 1 of the United States Code. The U.S. Supreme Court in *Bush v. Gore* effectively treated the "safe harbor" date as a deadline for a state's "final determination" of its presidential election results.[4]

As to the non-compacting states, existing federal law (section 6 of Title 3 of the United States Code) requires that an official count of the popular vote for President from each state be certified and sent to various federal officials in the form of a "certificate of ascertainment."

> "It shall be the duty of the executive of each State, as soon as practicable after the conclusion of the appointment of the electors in such State by the

---

[4] *Bush v. Gore.* 531 U.S. 98. 2000.

final ascertainment, under and in pursuance of the laws of such State providing for such ascertainment, to communicate by registered mail under the seal of the State to the Archivist of the United States **a certificate of such ascertainment** of the electors appointed, setting forth the names of such electors and **the canvass or other ascertainment under the laws of such State of the number of votes given or cast for each person for whose appointment any and all votes have been given or cast.** . . . " [Emphasis added]

Figure 6.1 shows Vermont's 2008 Certificate of Ascertainment. The Certificate reads:

"Pursuant to the laws of the United States, I, James H. Douglas, Governor of the State of Vermont, certify that the following named persons, residing in the towns indicated, received the number of votes indicated for the office of ELECTORS OF PRESIDENT AND VICE PRESIDENT OF THE UNITED STATES. These votes were cast at the election held on Tuesday November 4, 2008."

Vermont's 2008 Certificate of Ascertainment contains the election results for eight political parties and scattered write-ins. The candidates receiving the most votes (219,262) are listed first on the certificate, and they were:

"For President and Vice President of the United States"

"Barack Obama and Joe Biden, Democratic

"Electors of President and Vice President of the United States

"Claire Ayer, Weybridge

"Euan Bear, Bakersfield

"Kevin B. Christie, Hartford

"219,262"

Vermont's 2008 Certificate of Ascertainment similarly presents the number of popular votes received by each of the other candidates.

Appendices E, F, G, H, and I show examples of certificates of ascertainment from Minnesota, Maine, Nebraska, New York, and Mississippi, respectively (each of which has specific features of interest discussed in chapter 2). Figure 9.5 shows Oregon's 2012 certificate of ascertainment. The certificates of ascertainment from all 50 states and the District of Columbia are available online for the 2000, 2004, and 2008 presidential elections.[5]

The certificate of ascertainment is not, of course, the only official document exist-

---

[5] For the 2004 presidential election, see http://www.archives.gov/federal-register/electoral-college/2004/certificates_of_ascertainment.html.

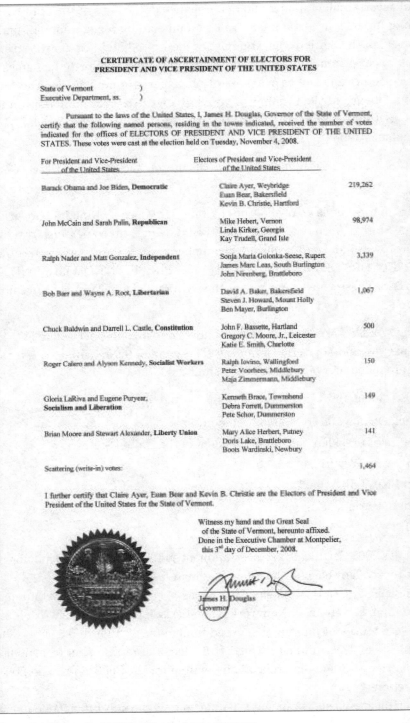

Figure 6.1 Vermont's 2008 Certificate of Ascertainment

ing in a state from which the vote count for presidential elections may be determined. As discussed in chapter 2, the vote counts for all elective offices (including the votes for presidential slates) are already officially recorded and contained in certificates that are created at the local level and then transmitted to the state official or body that is authorized to certify the total number of popular votes for each elective office in the state. Thus, the same information as contained in the Certificate of Ascertainment is available from other sources in the state.

The fifth clause of Article III of the compact provides:

> "The chief election official of each member state shall treat as conclusive an official statement containing the number of popular votes in a state for each presidential slate made by the day established by federal law for making a state's final determination conclusive as to the counting of electoral votes by Congress."

When the joint session of Congress counts the electoral votes on January 6 as provided in Title 3, chapter 1, section 15 of the United States Code, each state's own "final determination" of its vote is considered "conclusive" as to the counting of electoral votes by Congress if it was finalized by the date established in the "safe harbor" provision of federal law (Title 3, chapter 1, section 5). This section makes each state's (and, in particular, each *non-member* state's) final determination of its popular vote similarly "conclusive" when the chief election officials of the compact's member states add up the national popular vote under the terms of the compact. In other words, the chief election officials of the compact's member states are bound to honor each state's "final determination" in the same way that the joint session of Congress is currently bound to honor each state's "final determination."

The sixth clause of Article III of the compact deals with the highly unlikely event of a tie in the national popular vote count:

> "In event of a tie for the national popular vote winner, the presidential elector certifying official of each member state shall certify the appointment of the elector slate nominated in association with the presidential slate receiving the largest number of popular votes within that official's own state."

The purpose of the seventh clause of Article III of the compact is a contingency clause designed to ensure that the presidential slate receiving the most popular votes nationwide gets what it is entitled to—namely, 100% of the electoral votes of each member state.

> "If, for any reason, the number of presidential electors nominated in a member state in association with the national popular vote winner is less than or greater than that state's number of electoral votes, the presidential candidate on the presidential slate that has been designated as the national popular vote winner shall have the power to nominate the presidential

electors for that state and that state's presidential elector certifying official shall certify the appointment of such nominees."

This clause addresses at least six potential situations that might prevent the national popular vote winner from receiving all of the electoral votes from a member state. These situations arise because of gaps and ambiguities in the widely varying language of state election laws concerning presidential elections.

First, the winning presidential slate might not be on the ballot in a particular member state. Generally, serious candidates for President qualify for the ballot in all 50 states. Ross Perot was on the ballot in all 50 states in both 1992 and 1996. John Anderson was on the ballot in all 50 states in 1980. Ralph Nader (who received only about 1/2% of the national popular vote in 2008) was on the ballot in 45 states. As of early July 2012, it was clear that the 2012 nominee of the Green Party (presumptively Jill Stein) will have a place on the ballot in at least 45 states.[6] However, third-party presidential candidates sometimes fail to get on the ballot in a particular state because they fail to comply with the state's ballot-access requirements. In the unlikely event that a third-party presidential candidate were to win the popular vote nationally without having qualified to be on the ballot in a particular state belonging to the compact, there would be no official slate of presidential electors "nominated in association with" the "national popular vote winner" in that particular state. The remedy for this situation (and each of the other situations described below) is to employ the concept behind Pennsylvania's current law for nominating presidential electors (described in section 2.12). Under current Pennsylvania law, each presidential nominee directly nominates the presidential electors who will run in association with the nominee's presidential slate in Pennsylvania.[7] The seventh clause of Article III of the compact gives the unrepresented presidential candidate the power to nominate the presidential electors for the state involved. The state's presidential elector certifying official would then certify the appointment of the candidate's choices for presidential elector.

Second, no presidential electors may be "nominated in association with" the winning presidential slate in a particular member state because of some unforeseen situation that might arise under the language of state election codes. The Republican National Committee scheduled the 2004 Republican National Convention to be held after Alabama's statutory deadline for each political party to provide the name of its presidential and vice-presidential nominees to state officials. The scheduling of the convention created the possibility that there would be no Republican presidential slate

---

[6] Saulny, Susan. Green Party, still the outsider looking in, has a new face this campaign. *New York Times*. July 13, 2012.

[7] The method of direct appointment of presidential electors by the presidential nominee is regularly used in Pennsylvania. Section 2878 of the Pennsylvania election code provides: "The nominee of each political party for the office of President of the United States shall, within thirty days after his nomination by the National convention of such party, nominate as many persons to be the candidates of his party for the office of presidential elector as the State is then entitled to."

on the Alabama ballot in 2004. The problem was satisfactorily resolved when the Alabama legislature agreed to pass special legislation in early 2004 to change the state law. Because the 2012 Republican National Convention is in late August and the 2012 Democratic Convention is in early September, similar special legislation will be required in 2012 in several states. In the unlikely event that a problem of this type could not be satisfactorily addressed by emergency state legislation, the seventh clause of Article III of the compact provides the means to ensure that the presidential candidate who received the most popular votes nationwide receives the electoral votes from all compacting states.

Third, a full slate of eligible presidential electors might not be nominated in association with the winning presidential slate in a particular member state. For example, in 2004, then-Congressman Sherrod Brown was nominated as a Democratic presidential elector in Ohio. Brown was ineligible to be a presidential elector because the U.S. Constitution provides:

> "No Senator or Representative, or Person holding an Office of Trust or Profit under the United States, shall be appointed an Elector."[8]

Although Congressman Brown resigned his nomination as presidential elector and the Ohio Democratic Party nominated a replacement, some contended that Ohio's procedure for filling a vacancy among the list of nominees for presidential elector did not permit naming a replacement in this situation because there had been no legal nomination for the position in the first place, and hence no vacancy to fill. This contention arose because of ambiguous language in Ohio law. This contention remained unresolved because Kerry did not carry Ohio in 2004.

Fourth, the possibility exists that more presidential electors might be nominated in association with a presidential candidate than the state is entitled to send to the Electoral College. Fusion voting (section 2.10) creates the possibility that two or more competing slates of presidential electors could be nominated in association with the same presidential slate.

At the present time, fusion voting is routinely and widely used in only one state— New York. Because fusion voting is so routinely used in New York, the procedures for handling fusion voting in connection with presidential elector slates are a settled issue. In 2004, for example, voters in New York had the opportunity to vote for the Bush–Cheney presidential slate on either the Republican Party line or the Conservative Party line (as shown by the voting machine face in figure 2.11). The political parties sharing a presidential nominee in New York nominate a common slate of presidential electors. Thus, the Republican and Conservative parties nominated the same slate of 31 presidential electors for the 2004 presidential election. The popular votes cast for Bush–Cheney on the Republican and Conservative lines were added together and treated as

---

[8] U.S. Constitution. Article II, section 1, clause 2.

votes for all 31 Republican-Conservative candidates for the position of presidential elector. The popular votes cast for Kerry–Edwards on the Democratic Party line and the Working Families Party line were similarly aggregated and attributed to the common Kerry–Edwards slate of presidential electors. In 2004, the Kerry–Edwards presidential slate received the most popular votes in New York and therefore became entitled to all of New York's 31 electoral votes. The common Kerry–Edwards slate of 31 presidential electors was therefore declared to be elected to the Electoral College in New York. New York's 2004 Certificate of Ascertainment (appendix H) shows this aggregation.

Fusion voting is permissible at the present time under the laws of numerous other states under various circumstances (e.g., Vermont). The laws of states where fusion is not routinely used could lead to situations in which two competing elector slates are nominated under the banner of the same presidential slate.

Fifth, there is another way in which more presidential electors might be nominated in association with a particular presidential candidate than the state is entitled to send to the Electoral College. In states permitting advance filing of presidential write-ins (section 2.8), it is possible that different slates of presidential electors might be filed in association with the same write-in presidential slate. In the unlikely event that such a presidential slate were to win the national popular vote, the winning presidential candidate would have to pare down his group of presidential electors in that state.

Sixth, in some states permitting presidential write-ins, it is possible that an insufficient number of presidential electors may be nominated in association with a particular presidential slate. For example, the Minnesota election code does not specifically require that a full slate of 10 presidential electors be identified at the time of the advance filing of write-in slates (section 2.8). In fact, it requires advance filing of the name of only one presidential elector, even though Minnesota has 10 electoral votes.[9] Moreover, voters in Minnesota may cast write-in votes for President without advance filing.

The eighth clause of Article III of the compact enables the public, the press, and political parties to closely monitor the implementation of the compact within each member state:

> "The chief election official of each member state shall immediately release to the public all vote counts or statements of votes as they are determined or obtained."

The unmodified term "statements" is intended to refer to both "official statements" of a state's "final determination" of its presidential vote (the fourth clause of Article III of the compact) and any intermediate statements that the chief election official may obtain or consider at any time during the process of determining a state's presidential vote. The unmodified term "statement" is also intended to encompass the variety of types of documentation that may arise under the various practices and procedures of the states for officially recording and reporting presidential votes. The Certificate of

---

[9] Minnesota election law. Section 204B.09, subdivision 3.

Ascertainment issued by the state in accordance with federal law,[10] for example, would be considered to be a "statement." However, the Certificate of Ascertainment is not the only "statement" from which a state's presidential vote might be determined.

Because time is severely limited prior to the constitutionally mandated meeting of the Electoral College in mid-December, the term "immediately" is intended to eliminate any delays that might otherwise apply to the release of information by a public official under general public-disclosure laws.

The ninth clause of Article III of the compact provides:

> "This article shall govern the appointment of presidential electors in each member state in any year in which this agreement is, on July 20, in effect in states cumulatively possessing a majority of the electoral votes."

This "governing" clause operates in conjunction with the first clause of Article IV of the compact relating to the date when the compact as a whole first comes into effect:

> "This agreement shall take effect when states cumulatively possessing a majority of the electoral votes have enacted this agreement in substantially the same form and the enactments by such states have taken effect in each state."

The ninth clause of Article III—the "governing" clause—employs the date of July 20 of a presidential election year because the six-month period starting on this date contains the following six important events relating to presidential elections:

- the national nominating conventions,[11]
- the fall general election campaign period,
- Election Day on the Tuesday after the first Monday in November,
- the meeting of the Electoral College on the first Monday after the second Wednesday in December,
- the counting of the electoral votes by Congress on January 6, and
- the scheduled inauguration of the President and Vice President for the new term on January 20.

The ninth clause of Article III of the compact addresses the question of whether Article III governs the conduct of the presidential election in a particular year, whereas the first clause of Article V specifies when the compact as a whole initially comes into effect. The importance of this distinction is that it is theoretically possible that the compact could come into effect by virtue of enactment by states possessing a majority of the votes in the Electoral College (i.e., 270 or more of the 538 electoral votes), but

---

[10] Title 3, chapter 1, section 6 of the United States Code deals with issuance of Certificates of Ascertainment by the states (and is discussed in section 2.4). See appendix A for the provisions of the U.S. Constitution and appendix B for provisions of federal law relating to presidential elections.

[11] All recent national nominating conventions of the major parties have met after July 20.

that, at some future time, the compacting states might no longer possess a majority of the electoral votes. The situation could arise in any of four ways.

First, a future federal census might reduce the number of electoral votes possessed by the compacting states so that they no longer account for a majority of the electoral votes. This could occur if the compacting states happened to lose population relative to the remainder of the country. In that event, the compact provides that the compact as a whole would remain in effect (because the compact would have come into initial effect under the first clause of Article IV of the compact); however, Article III (the operative article in the compact) would then not "govern" the next presidential election. If additional state(s) subsequently enacted the compact— thereby raising the number of electoral votes possessed by the compacting states above 270 by July 20 of a subsequent presidential election year—Article III of the compact would then again govern presidential elections.[12]

As a second example, if one or more states withdrew from the compact and thereby reduced the number of electoral votes possessed by the remaining compacting states below 270 by July 20 of a presidential election year, the compact as a whole would remain in effect, but Article III (the operative article in the compact) would not govern the next presidential election.

As a third example, if a new state were admitted to the Union and if the total number of seats in the U.S. House of Representatives (and hence the total number of electoral votes) were permanently or temporarily adjusted upwards, it is conceivable that the compacting states might no longer possess a majority of the new number of electoral votes. If the newly admitted state and/or some combination of pre-existing state(s) subsequently enacted the compact—thereby raising the number of electoral votes possessed by the compacting states above a majority of the new number of electoral votes—Article III of the compact would again govern.

As a fourth example, if the number of U.S. Representatives (set by federal statute) were changed so that the number of electoral votes possessed by the compacting states no longer accounted for a majority of the new number of electoral votes, Article III of the compact would not govern the next presidential election. Proposals to change the number of members of the House are periodically floated for a variety of reasons. For example, in 2005, Representative Tom Davis (R–Virginia) proposed increasing the number of Representatives from 435 to 437 on a temporary basis in connection with his bill to give the District of Columbia voting representation in Congress.[13]

---

[12] As a practical matter, the scenario can only arise if the number of electoral votes possessed by states belonging to the compact hovers close to 270.

[13] Under the D.C. Fairness in Representation Act (H.R. 2043) introduced May 3, 2005, the size of the House of Representatives would have been increased from 435 to 437 until the 2010 census. Utah is the state that would have become entitled to one of the two additional congressional seats under the 2000 census and under the existing formula for apportioning U.S. Representatives among the states. The District of Columbia would have received the other seat. As a matter of practical politics, the two additional seats would be expected to divide equally among the Democrats and Republicans. The Davis bill provided that the number of seats in the House would revert to 435 after the 2010 census.

As long as the compacting states possess a majority of the electoral votes on July 20 of a presidential election year, Article III of the compact would govern the presidential election. In practice, the question as to whether the compact would govern a particular presidential election would be known long before July 20 of the presidential election year. Changes resulting from the census are no surprise because the census does not affect congressional reapportionment until two years after the census.[14] A new state enters the Union only after a time-consuming process. Enactment of a state law withdrawing from an interstate compact is a time-consuming, multi-step legislative process involving the introduction of a bill, action on the bill in a committee in each house of the state legislature, debate and voting on the bill on the floor of each house, and presentment of the bill to the state's Governor for approval or disapproval.[15] In addition, new state laws generally do not take immediate effect, but instead take effect at a particular future time specified by the state constitution.[16] Moreover, a withdrawal from the compact cannot take effect during the six-month period between July 20 of a presidential election year and the subsequent January 20 inauguration date (as discussed below). Finally, enactment of any federal statutory change in the number of U.S. Representatives is a time-consuming, multi-step legislative process.

6.3.4 EXPLANATION OF ARTICLE IV—ADDITIONAL PROVISIONS

The first clause of Article IV of the compact specifies the time when the compact initially could take effect.

> "This agreement shall take effect when states cumulatively possessing a majority of the electoral votes have enacted this agreement in substantially the same form and the enactments by such states have taken effect in each state."

Note that a state is not counted, for purposes of this clause, until the state statute enacting the compact is "in effect" in the state in accordance with the state's constitutional schedule specifying when state laws take effect.

The same version of a compact must, of course, be enacted by each member state. The phrase "substantially the same form" is found in numerous interstate compacts and is intended to permit minor variations (e.g., differences in punctuation, differences in numbering, or inconsequential typographical errors) that sometimes occur when the same law is enacted by various states.

The second clause of Article IV of the compact permits a state to withdraw from

---

[14] For example, the 2000 federal census did not affect the 2000 presidential election. The results of the 2000 census affected the 2002 congressional election and the 2004 presidential election.

[15] Similarly, the citizen-initiative process is a time-consuming, multi-step process that typically involves an initial filing and review by a designated state official (e.g., the Attorney General), circulation of the petition, and voting in a statewide election (usually a November general election).

[16] In most states, a super-majority vote is necessary to give immediate effect to a legislative bill. The details vary from state to state.

the compact but provides for a "blackout" period (of approximately six months) restricting withdrawals:

> "Any member state may withdraw from this agreement, except that a withdrawal occurring six months or less before the end of a President's term shall not become effective until a President or Vice President shall have been qualified to serve the next term."

The purpose for the delay in the effective date of a withdrawal is to ensure that a withdrawal will not be undertaken—perhaps for partisan political purposes—in the midst of a presidential campaign or in the period between the popular voting in early November and the meeting of the Electoral College in mid-December. This restriction on withdrawals is warranted in light of the subject matter of the compact.[17] The blackout period starts on July 20 of a presidential election year and would normally end on January 20 of the following year (the scheduled inauguration date). Thus, if a statute repealing the compact in a particular state were enacted and came into effect in the midst of the presidential election process, that state's withdrawal from the compact would not take effect until completion of the entire current presidential election cycle. The language used in the compact tracks the wording of the 20th Amendment. The date for the end of the present President's term is fixed by the 20th Amendment as January 20; however, the 20th Amendment recognizes the possibility that a new President might, under certain circumstances, not have been "qualified" by that date. The blackout period in the compact ends when the entire presidential election cycle is completed under the terms of the 20th Amendment.

The third clause of Article IV of the compact concerns the process by which each state notifies all the other states of the status of the compact. Notices are required on three occasions—namely, when the compact has taken effect in a particular state, when the compact has taken effect generally (that is, when it has been enacted and taken effect in states cumulatively possessing a majority of the electoral votes), and when a state's withdrawal has taken effect.

The fourth clause of Article IV provides that the compact would automatically terminate if the Electoral College were to be abolished.

The fifth clause of Article IV is a severability clause.

6.3.5 EXPLANATION OF ARTICLE V—DEFINITIONS

Article V of the compact contains definitions.

There are separate definitions for the "chief election official" and the "presidential elector certifying official" because these terms may refer to a different official or body.

---

[17] Delays in the effective date of withdrawals are commonplace in interstate compacts (and, indeed, in contracts in general). See section 5.15.3 for additional discussion on withdrawals from interstate compacts in general and chapter 9 for additional discussion on withdrawals from the National Popular Vote compact in particular.

The definition of "presidential slate" in Article V of the compact is important because voters cast votes for a team consisting of a presidential and vice-presidential candidate and because the votes for each distinct team are aggregated separately in the national count under the terms of the compact. "Presidential slate" is defined as

> "a slate of two persons, the first of whom has been nominated as a candidate for President of the United States and the second of whom has been nominated as a candidate for Vice President of the United States, or any legal successors to such persons, regardless of whether both names appear on the ballot presented to the voter in a particular state."

The above definition permits the substitution of nominees on a given presidential slate if, for example, a nominee died during the presidential election cycle,[18] resigned from a slate,[19] or became disqualified.[20]

Because ballots in North Dakota and Arizona list only the name of the presidential candidate (see figure 2.3), the definition of "presidential slate" in the compact contains a savings clause for North Dakota and Arizona.

Note that this definition comports with present practice in that it treats a slate as a unit containing two particular candidates in a specified order. As discussed in section 2.10 and shown in figure 2.11, Ralph Nader appeared on the ballot in New York in 2004 as the presidential nominee of both the Independence Party and the Peace and Justice Party. Nader ran with Jan D. Pierce for Vice President on the Independence Party line in New York in 2004, but with Peter Miguel Camejo for Vice President on the Peace and Justice Party line. Thus, there were two different "Nader" presidential slates in New York in 2004. Each "Nader" slate had a different slate of presidential electors in New York in 2004. The votes for these two distinct "presidential slates" were counted separately (as shown on the sixth page of New York's Certificate of Ascertainment in appendix H). There was no fusion of votes between the Independence Party and the Peace and Justice Party in this situation because there were two distinct presidential slates and two distinct slates of presidential electors.

The definition of "statewide popular election" in Article V is important. At the present time, all states conduct a "statewide popular election" for President. However, if a state were to withdraw from its voters the power to vote for President (as Massachusetts and New Hampshire did in the 1800 presidential election, as described in section 2.2.3), there would be no popular votes available to count from that state. If there were no popular vote to count from a particular state, the "national popular vote total" would necessarily not include that state.

---

[18] Horace Greeley, the (losing) Democratic presidential nominee in 1872, died between the time of the November voting and the counting of the electoral votes.

[19] Senator Thomas F. Eagleton of Missouri resigned from the 1972 Democratic presidential slate.

[20] A presidential candidate must be a natural-born citizen.

6.4 POSSIBLE FEDERAL LEGISLATION

The enactment of the "Agreement among the States to Elect the President by National Popular Vote" would provide an excellent opportunity for Congress to review existing federal laws concerning presidential elections.

The proposed "Agreement among the States to Elect the President by National Popular Vote" is intended to be entirely self-executing. To this end, the compact identifies officials in each member state to perform the necessary tasks of obtaining the popular vote counts from all the states, adding up the votes from all the states to yield the "national popular vote total," and designating the "national popular vote winner." These tasks could be simplified by the establishment of an administrative clearinghouse for these functions. The officials of the compacting states might themselves establish such a clearinghouse. Alternatively, such a clearinghouse might be established by federal law.

Numerous problems have been identified concerning the existing schedule of events involving the November general election, the "safe harbor" date, the timing of the meeting of the Electoral College in mid-December, the counting of the votes by Congress in early January, and the presidential inauguration scheduled for January 20.

Leonard M. Shambon, an assistant to the co-chairman of the Ford-Carter Commission on Election Reform in 2001 and a member of the advisory board to the Carter-Baker Commission in 2005, described some of the problems associated with the current schedule in a 2004 article entitled "Electoral-College Reform Requires Change of Timing."[21] Solutions to several of the problems identified in the Shambon article were incorporated in H.R. 1579, introduced by Representative David Price (D–North Carolina) on April 12, 2005.[22] They are discussed further by Suzanne Nelson in an article entitled "Three-Month Period Imperils Presidency."[23]

In addition, Norman Ornstein, a resident scholar at the American Enterprise Institute, described additional potential problems concerning presidential elections in a 2004 article entitled "Want a Scary Scenario for Presidential Chaos? Here Are a Few."[24]

Additional issues have been raised by John C. Fortier, a resident fellow of the American Enterprise Institute, and Norman Ornstein in a 2004 article entitled "If Terrorists Attack Our Presidential Elections"[25] and by Jerry H. Goldfeder, an elections law

---

[21] Shambon, Leonard M. 2004. Electoral-College reform requires change of timing. *Roll Call*. June 15, 2004.

[22] H.R. 1579— To amend Title 3, United States Code, to extend the date provided for the meeting of electors of the President and Vice President in the States and the date provided for the joint session of Congress held for the counting of electoral votes, and for other purposes. Introduced April 12, 2005.

[23] Nelson, Suzanne. Three-month period imperils presidency. *Roll Call*. November 2, 2004.

[24] Ornstein, Norman. 2004. Want a scary scenario for presidential chaos? Here are a few. *Roll Call*. October 21, 2004.

[25] Fortier, John C., and Ornstein, Norman. 2004. If terrorists attack our presidential elections. 3 *Election Law Journal* 4. Pages 597–612.

attorney in New York and Adjunct Professor at Fordham University School of Law, in an article entitled "Could Terrorists Derail a Presidential Election?"[26]

A possible new federal law concerning recounts is contained the discussion of recounts in section 9.15.7.

The enactment of the National Popular Vote compact would provide an excellent opportunity for Congress to address these issues.

6.5 PREVIOUS PROPOSALS FOR MULTI-STATE ELECTORAL LEGISLATION

The "Agreement among the States to Elect the President by National Popular Vote" described in this chapter is a combination of numerous ideas and previous proposals for multi-state electoral legislation.

In *Oregon v. Mitchell*, U.S. Supreme Court Justice Potter Stewart pointed out in 1970 that an interstate compact could be employed by the states for electoral purposes. *Oregon v. Mitchell* concerned congressional legislation establishing uniformity among the states for durational residency requirements for voters in presidential elections. In his opinion (partially concurring and partially dissenting), Justice Potter Stewart observed that if Congress had not enacted federal legislation concerning residency requirements, the states could have adopted an interstate compact to accomplish the same objective.[27]

In the 1990s, U.S. Senator Charles Schumer (D–New York) proposed a bi-state compact in which New York and Texas would pool their electoral votes in presidential elections. Both states were then (and still are) noncompetitive in presidential politics and receive little attention in presidential campaigns except for fund-raising. Schumer observed that the two states had almost the same number of electoral votes (at the time, 33 for New York and 32 for Texas)[28] and the two states regularly produced majorities of approximately the same magnitude in favor of each state's dominant political party. The Democrats typically carry New York by about 60%, and the Republicans typically carry Texas by about 60%. The purpose of Schumer's proposed bi-state compact was to create a presidentially competitive super-state (slightly larger than California) that would attract the attention of the presidential candidates during presidential campaigns.

The 2000 election stimulated discussion by a number of people of ideas about how direct election of the President might be achieved by state-level action.

The earliest (currently known) published discussion along those lines was from Brent White of Seattle on December 30, 2000. In a web posting entitled "Direct Prez Election W/O Amendment," White wrote:

---

[26] Goldfeder, Jerry H. 2005. Could terrorists derail a presidential election? 32 *Fordham Urban Law Journal* 3. May 2005. Pages 523–566.

[27] *Oregon v. Mitchell*. 400 U.S. 112 at 286–287. 1970.

[28] In the 2004 presidential election, New York had 31 electoral votes, and Texas had 34.

"If the goal is to eventually have the president elected directly, then there is a straighter path to get there—one that does not require an amendment to the US Constitution.

"Article II of the Constitution grants each state legislature the power to determine how that state's presidential electors will be allotted. **A state legislature could, if it so chose, award that state's electors to the winner of the national popular vote.**

"If even one state gives its electoral votes to the national popular winner, the voters of every other noncompetitive state would be instantly re-enfranchised, causing an immediate bump in the presidential turnout. . . .

"If several Democratic-leaning and several Republican-leaning states give their electoral votes to the national popular winner, they would form a block that virtually assures victory to the popular winner.

"If states carrying a majority of the Electoral College do this, they will make the popular winner the automatic electoral winner."[29] [Emphasis added]

On December 31, 2000, Tony Anderson Solgard of Minneapolis commented on White's web posting and wrote:

"Brent's proposal . . . would provide a result consistent with the national popular vote. And that is precisely the point: the Presidency is a single-winner office without a need for proportionality in an electoral college.

"The political problem would be the criticism that it gives away the decision of each state's voters to the nation as a whole. And unless all the other states went along with it, you couldn't convince one state to disenfranchise its voters.

"To get around this, **a variation on Brent's idea would be to put a multi-state compact clause into the proposal: when X number of states agree to adopt the same allocation plan, then the law goes into effect.**[30] [Emphasis added]

[29] The list was the full-representation@igc.topica.com list. This December 30, 2000, posting is archived at http://lists.topica.com/lists/full-representation@igc.topica.com/read/message.html?mid=702433464&sort=d&start=800. The authors are grateful to Steve Chessin, President of Californians for Electoral Reform, who remembered and located White's December 30, 2000, web posting after this book was first published in 2006.

[30] See http://lists.topica.com/lists/full-representation@igc.topica.com/read/message.html?mid=702436082&sort=d&start=800. The authors are grateful to Steve Chessin, President of Californians for Electoral Reform, who remembered and located Solgard's December 31, 2000, web posting after this book was first published in 2006. Chessin notes that this posting was made using the e-mail address of Tony Solgard's wife (Karen L. Solgard).

At a January 11–12, 2001, conference and in an April 19, 2001, web posting, Professor Robert W. Bennett, former Dean of the Northwestern University School of Law, made the observation that a federal constitutional amendment was not necessary to achieve the goal of nationwide popular election of the President because the states could use their power under Article II of the U.S. Constitution to allocate their electoral votes based on the nationwide popular vote.[31]

In December 2001, law Professors Akhil Reed Amar and Vikram David Amar cited Professor Bennett's earlier 2001 posting and continued the discussion about the fact that the states could allocate their electoral votes to the nationwide winner of the popular vote.[32,33]

One variation of the proposals made by Professors Robert W. Bennett, Akhil Reed Amar, and Vikram David Amar was based on the (politically implausible) premise that single states would unilaterally enact laws awarding their electoral votes to the nationwide winner without regard to whether other states had enacted similar legislation. Another variation was based on the (politically implausible) assumption that carefully selected pairs of states of equal size and opposite political leanings could be found to enact the proposal.

Initially, it was argued the resulting multi-state arrangement would not constitute an interstate compact, and, as a result, the proposed arrangement would not require congressional consent.[34] Later, the use of an interstate compact was suggested.

In 2002, Bennett expanded his thoughts in subsequent publications suggesting several variations on his basic idea.[35,36]

The authors of this book started developing the National Popular Vote compact

---

[31] Bennett, Robert W. 2001. Popular election of the president without a constitutional amendment. 4 *Green Bag.* Spring 2001. Posted on April 19, 2001. The January 11–12, 2001, presentation was contained in *Conference Report, Election 2000: The Role of the Courts, The Role of the Media, The Roll of the Dice* (Northwestern University).

[32] Amar, Akhil Reed, and Amar, Vikram David. 2001. How to achieve direct national election of the president without amending the constitution: Part three of a three-part series on the 2000 election and the electoral college. *Findlaw's Writ.* December 28, 2001. http://writ.news.findlaw.com/amar/20011228.html.

[33] Amar, Akhil Reed, and Amar, Vikram David. 2001. Rethinking the electoral college debate: The Framers, federalism, and one person, one vote. 114 *Harvard Law Review* 2526 at 2549, n. 112.

[34] The question of whether a given arrangement is an interstate compact is separate from the question of whether the arrangement requires congressional consent. A multi-state arrangement (1) that takes effect in response to an "offer" made by one or more states, (2) that does not take effect without assurance of complementary action by other states (through acceptance of the offer), and (3) that then commits the states to act in concert would almost certainly be regarded by the courts as a contract, and hence an "agreement or compact" as that phrase is used in the U.S. Constitution. However, as discussed in section 5.12, many interstate compacts do not require congressional consent.

[35] Bennett, Robert W. 2002. Popular election of the president without a constitutional amendment. In Jacobson, Arthur J., and Rosenfeld, Michel (editors). *The Longest Night: Polemics and Perspectives on Election 2000.* Berkeley, CA: University of California Press. Pages 391–396.

[36] Bennett, Robert W. 2002. Popular election of the president II: State coordination in popular election of the president without a constitutional amendment. *Green Bag.* Winter 2002.

in 2004 and released the first edition of this book (which contained the compact) at a press conference at the National Press Club in Washington, DC, on February 23, 2006.[37]

Later in 2006, Jennings "Jay" Wilson analyzed the numerous variations proposed by Professors Robert W. Bennett, Akhil Reed Amar, and Vikram David Amar in 2001 and 2002. Wilson's analysis points out the political impracticality of the various proposals made in 2001 and 2002.[38]

These earlier proposals differ from the authors' proposed "Agreement Among the States to Elect the President by National Popular Vote" in several respects.

None of the earlier proposals contained a provision making the effective date of the system contingent on the enactment of identical laws in states that collectively possess a majority of the electoral votes (i.e., 270 of the 538 electoral votes). No single state would ever be likely to unilaterally enact a law awarding its electoral votes to the nationwide winner. For one thing, such an action would give the voters of all the other states a voice in the selection of the state's own presidential electors, while not giving the enacting state the benefit of a voice in the selection of presidential electors in other states. Moreover, enactment of such a law in a single state would encourage the presidential candidates to ignore the enacting state. Such unilateral action would not guarantee achievement of the goal of nationwide popular election of the President.

Moreover, the earlier proposals do not work in an even-handed and nonpartisan way if enacted by states possessing less than a majority of the electoral votes. Suppose, for example, that a group of states that consistently voted Democratic in presidential elections were to participate in an arrangement—without the electoral-majority threshold—to award their electoral votes to the nationwide popular vote winner. Then, if the Republican presidential candidate won the most popular votes nationwide (but did not carry states with a majority of the electoral votes), the participating (Democratic) states would award their electoral votes to the Republican candidate—thereby achieving the desired result of electing the presidential candidate with the most popular votes nationwide. On the other hand, if the Democratic presidential candidate won the most popular votes nationwide (but did not carry states

---

[37] The authors of the National Popular Vote compact became aware (thanks to the research efforts of Steve Chessin, President of Californians for Electoral Reform) of the 2000 web publications by Brent White of Seattle and Tony Anderson Solgard of Minneapolis after the compact was written and after the first edition of this book was released on February 23, 2006. The authors became aware of the 2001 web publications of Professor Bennett and the Amar brothers after the compact was written but just before the first edition of this book in 2006 went to the printer. Accordingly, the first edition of this book in 2006 referenced and discussed only the 2001 web publications by Professor Bennett and the Amar brothers. The earlier 2000 web postings by Brent White and Tony Anderson Solgard are now recognized as the earliest (now known) publications on this topic. John Koza and Barry Fadem had discussed the possibility of state legislation being used to award a state's electoral votes to the national popular vote winner at the time of the 1992 Perot candidacy; however, they had not, at that time, combined that general idea with either the mechanism of an interstate compact or the concept of a compact taking effect when enacted by states possessing a majority of the Electoral College.

[38] Wilson, Jennings Jay. 2006. Bloc voting in the Electoral College: How the ignored states can become relevant and implement popular election along the way. 5 *Election Law Journal* 384.

with a majority of the electoral votes), the similarly situated Democratic presidential candidate would not receive a symmetric benefit. Instead, the Republican candidate would be elected because the Democratic candidate could not receive any additional electoral votes from the group of states involved because the Democratic candidate would already be getting all of the electoral votes from that group of states. In short, a Republican presidential nominee would be the only beneficiary if only Democratic states participated in such an arrangement, and vice versa. In fact, an arrangement without an electoral majority threshold would operate in an even-handed and non-partisan way only in the unlikely event that the participating states were equally divided (in terms of electoral votes) among reliably Republican and reliably Democratic states. In contrast, if the states participating in the arrangement possess a majority of the electoral votes, the system operates in an even-handed and nonpartisan way without regard to the political complexion of the enacting states. With an electoral majority threshold, the political complexion of the enacting states becomes irrelevant.

In his 2006 article, Wilson proposed his own "bloc voting" variation (in which only the popular votes of *only* the enacting states would decide which candidate received the electoral votes of the enacting states).[39] The obvious flaw of this variation is illustrated if one considers a scenario in which one or more Republican-leaning states were to enact the "bloc voting" proposal. If, subsequently, a group of Democratic-leaning states that together generated a larger popular-vote margin than the existing Republican group were to enact Wilson's "bloc voting" proposal, all the electoral votes of the less muscular Republican group would be go to the Democrats. In other words, the Democratic group of states would have commandeered the electoral votes of the Republican states. More important, this would occur irrespective of whether the Democratic presidential candidate received the most popular votes nationwide.

The authors submit that the proposed "Agreement Among the States to Elect the President by National Popular Vote" does not have the above problems of any of the other variations that have been previously discussed. In any event, specific legislative language was never created for any of the other proposals, and none of the other proposals has ever been introduced in any state legislature. Soon after National Popular Vote's initial press conference on February 23, 2006, the National Popular Vote compact had been introduced in all 50 state legislatures. As of mid-2012, 2,110 state legislators have either sponsored the National Popular Vote compact in their state legislatures or cast a recorded vote in favor of it.

---

[39] Wilson, Jennings Jay. 2006. Bloc voting in the Electoral College: How the ignored states can become relevant and implement popular election along the way. 5 *Election Law Journal* 384.

7 | Strategy for Enacting the National Popular Vote Compact

The National Popular Vote compact (described in chapter 6) must be enacted by states possessing a majority of electoral votes (i.e., 270 out of 538) in order to take effect.

This chapter discusses four elements of the strategy to win enactment of the compact by the requisite combination of states, including

- the role of public opinion (section 7.1),
- the role of state legislatures in enacting the compact (section 7.2),
- the role of the citizen-initiative process in enacting the compact in certain states (section 7.3), and
- the role of Congress (section 7.4).

7.1. THE ROLE OF PUBLIC OPINION

The starting point for the strategy to enact the National Popular Vote Compact is public opinion.

Public opinion has supported nationwide popular election of the President for over six decades.

According to a Gallup report entitled "Americans Have Historically Favored Changing Way Presidents Are Elected," the first nationwide poll on the topic of direct election of the President is believed to have been a 1944 Gallup poll that asked:

> "It has been suggested that the electoral vote system be discontinued and Presidents of the United States be elected by total popular vote alone. Do you favor or oppose this proposal?"[1]

In 1977 and 1980, the nationwide Gallup poll asked:

> "Would you approve or disapprove of an amendment to the Constitution which would do away with the Electoral College and base the election of a President on the total vote cast throughout the nation?"[2]

---

[1] Gallup News Service. 2000. *Americans Have Historically Favored Changing Way Presidents Are Elected.* November 10, 2000. Page 1.

[2] *Id.* at 2.

Table 7.1 shows the results for the Gallup nationwide public opinion polls in 1944, 1977, and 1980.[3]

Table 7.1 PUBLIC SUPPORT FOR NATIONWIDE POPULAR ELECTION OF THE PRESIDENT

	APPROVE	DISAPPROVE	NO OPINION
June 22–27, 1944	65%	23%	13%
January 14–17, 1977	73%	15%	12%
November 7–10, 1980	67%	19%	15%

The Gallup News Service has also reported:

"The greatest level of support, 81%, was recorded after the 1968 election when Richard Nixon defeated Hubert Humphrey in another extremely close election."[4]

In 2007, the *Washington Post*, the Kaiser Family Foundation, and Harvard University conducted a nationwide poll that showed 72% support for direct nationwide election of the President.

In 2008, AOL conducted a nationwide online poll of 113,691 people asking:

"How would you prefer the United States elect its President?

The results were:

- National popular vote—74%,
- Electoral College vote—21%, and
- Some other way—5%.

A 2010 nationwide poll prepared for the Aspen Institute by Penn Schoen Berland and released at the Aspen Ideas Festival found that "74 percent agree it is time to abolish the Electoral College and have direct popular vote for the president."[5]

State-level polls have been conducted by a number of groups.

In California in August 2007, Fairbank, Maslin, Maullin & Associates conducted a poll of 800 likely voters in California for the Californians for the Fair Election Reform organization. Voters were asked about a

"proposal [that] would guarantee that the presidential candidate who receives the most popular votes in all 50 states and the District of Columbia

---

[3] Other Gallup polls on this subject are discussed in Carlson, Darren K. 2004. Public flunks electoral college system. November 2, 2004. *Gallup Daily News*. See http://www.gallup.com/poll/13918/Public-Flunks-Electoral-College-System.aspx. Also see Saad, Lydia. 2011. Americans would swap electoral college for popular vote. *Gallup Daily News*. October 24, 2011.

[4] Gallup News Service. 2000. *Americans Have Historically Favored Changing Way Presidents Are Elected.* November 10, 2000. Page 2.

[5] http://www.slideshare.net/PennSchoenBerland/time-aspen-ideas-festival-2011-full-report.

will win the Presidency. Would you generally support or oppose switching to a system in which the Presidency is decided by the actual votes in all 50 states combined?"

The results of this 2007 poll in California were that 69% would support a change to popular vote; 21% would oppose the change; and 9% didn't know.

In California in October 2008, the Public Policy Institute of California (PPIC) conducted a telephone survey of 2,004 Californians asking:

"For future presidential elections, would you support or oppose changing to a system in which the president is elected by direct popular vote, instead of by the Electoral College?"[6]

The results of the 2008 PPIC poll in California were that 70% would support a change to popular vote; 21% would oppose the change; and 10% didn't know.

In New York in October 2008, the Global Strategy Group conducted a poll on the National Popular Vote bill and reported:

"Voters in New York are largely in favor of switching to a system that elects the President of the United States according to vote totals in all 50 states. Two-thirds of voters (66%) currently support the proposal, while just a quarter (26%) is in opposition to it. Support for the proposal is broad across demographics as a majority of each subgroup is in favor of it."

Recent polls conducted by Public Policy Polling for the National Popular Vote organization show high levels of public support for a national popular vote for President in battleground states, small states, Southern, border states, and elsewhere. Detailed reports on the polls, including the cross-tabs, are available at the web site of National Popular Vote.[7] Overall support in the various states was

- Alaska–70%,
- Arizona–67%,
- Arkansas–80%,
- California–70%,
- Colorado–68%,
- Connecticut–74%,
- Delaware–75%,
- District of Columbia–76%,
- Florida–78%,
- Idaho–77%,

---

[6] *PPIC Statewide Survey: Californians and Their Government.* October 2008.

[7] http://www.nationalpopularvote.com/pages/polls.php.

- Iowa–75%,
- Kentucky–80%,
- Maine–77%,
- Massachusetts–73%,
- Michigan–73%,
- Minnesota–75%,
- Mississippi–77%,
- Missouri–70%,
- Montana–72%,
- Nebraska–67%,
- Nevada–72%,
- New Hampshire–69%,
- New Mexico–76%,
- New York–79%,
- North Carolina–74%,
- Ohio–70%,
- Oklahoma–81%,
- Oregon–76%,
- Pennsylvania–78%,
- Rhode Island–74%,
- South Carolina–71%,
- South Dakota–75%,
- Utah–70%,
- Vermont–75%,
- Virginia–74%,
- Washington–77%,
- West Virginia–81%,
- Wisconsin–71%, and
- Wyoming–69%.

The poll in Nebraska is noteworthy because Nebraska awards three of its electoral votes by congressional district (with two being awarded statewide) under a law first used in the 1992 election. In 2008, Barack Obama won Nebraska's 2nd congressional district, thereby winning one of Nebraska's electoral votes.

A survey of 977 Nebraska voters conducted on January 26–27, 2011, contained a comparative question about a national popular vote, Nebraska's current congressional-district approach, and the statewide winner-take-all rule that Nebraska's current governor advocates as a replacement for Nebraska's congressional-district approach.

The first question was:

"How do you think we should elect the President: Should it be the candidate who gets the most votes in all 50 states, or the current Electoral College system?"

The survey showed 67% overall support for a national popular vote for President. On this first question, support for a national popular vote by political affiliation was 78% among Democrats, 62% among Republicans, and 63% among others. By congressional district, support for a national popular vote was 65% in the 1st congressional district, 66% in the 2nd district (which voted for Obama in 2008), and 72% in the 3rd district. By gender, support for a national popular vote was 76% among women and 59% among men. By age, support for a national popular vote was 73% among 18–29-year-olds, 67% among 30–45-year-olds, 65% among 46–65-year-olds, and 69% among those older than 65. By race, support for a national popular vote was 68% among whites and 63% among others.

The second question in the survey presented a three-way choice among various methods of awarding Nebraska's electoral votes,

- 16% favored a statewide winner-take-all system (i.e., awarding all five of Nebraska's electoral votes to the candidate who receives the most votes statewide);
- 27% favored Nebraska's current system of awarding electoral votes by congressional district; and
- 57% favored a national popular vote.

Table 7.2 shows the results of this second question by political affiliation.

Table 7.2 NEBRASKA RESULTS, BY POLITICAL AFFILIATION, ON THREE ALTERNATIVE METHODS OF ELECTING THE PRESIDENT.

METHOD	DEMOCRAT	REPUBLICAN	OTHER
Candidate who gets the most votes in all 50 states	65%	53%	51%
Nebraska's current district system	26%	27%	32%
Statewide winner-take-all system	9%	20%	17%

Table 7.3 shows the results of this second question by congressional district. Note that the 2nd district was the district carried by Obama in 2008.

Table 7.3 NEBRASKA RESULTS, BY POLITICAL AFFILIATION, ON THREE ALTERNATIVE METHODS OF ELECTING THE PRESIDENT.

METHOD	FIRST DISTRICT	SECOND DISTRICT	THIRD DISTRICT
Candidate who gets the most votes in all 50 states	53%	58%	59%
Nebraska's current district system	26%	31%	26%
Statewide winner-take-all system	21%	12%	15%

Another noteworthy survey involved 800 Utah voters conducted on May 19–20, 2009. This survey showed 70% overall support for the idea that the President of the United States should be the candidate who receives the most popular votes in all 50 states. Voters were asked:

> "How do you think we should elect the President: Should it be the candidate who gets the most votes in all 50 states, or the current Electoral College system?"

By political affiliation, support for a national popular vote on the first question was 82% among Democrats, 66% among Republicans, and 75% among others. By gender, support was 78% among women and 60% among men. By age, support was 70% among 18–29-year-olds, 70% among 30–45-year-olds, 70% among 46–65-year-olds, and 68% for those older than 65.

Then, voters were pointedly asked a "push" question that specifically highlighted the fact that Utah's electoral votes would be awarded to the winner of the national popular vote in all 50 states under the National Popular Vote compact.

> "Do you think it more important that a state's electoral votes be cast for the presidential candidate who receives the most popular votes in that state, or is it more important to guarantee that the candidate who receives the most popular votes in all 50 states becomes President?"

Support for a national popular vote did drop in this "push" question, but only from 70% to 66%.

On this second question, the results by political affiliation were as follows: 77% among Democrats, 63% among Republicans, and 62% among others. By gender, support was 72% among women and 58% among men. By age, support was 61% among 18–29-year-olds, 64% among 30–45-year-olds, 68% among 46–65-year-olds, and 66% for those older than 65.[8]

---

[8] The Utah survey (and the others cited in this section) was conducted by Public Policy Polling and had a margin of error of plus or minus 3 1/2%. See http://www.nationalpopularvote.com/pages/polls.

7.2. THE ROLE OF STATE LEGISLATURES

A state legislature enacts an interstate compact in the same way that it enacts an ordinary state statute.

The law-making process at the state level generally entails adoption of a proposed legislative bill by a majority vote of each house of the state legislature. All state Governors currently have veto power over legislative bills (or at least most bills[9]) passed by their legislatures. Thus, bills are presented to the Governor for approval or disapproval.[10] If a Governor vetoes a bill, the legislation may nonetheless become law if the legislature overrides the veto in the manner specified by the state's constitution. Overriding a gubernatorial veto typically requires a super-majority (typically a two-thirds vote, but sometimes only a majority) of both houses of the legislature.[11]

In the District of Columbia, interstate compacts may be enacted by the Council of the District of Columbia. The Mayor has veto power, and the Council has power to override a veto. In addition, all legislation enacted by the Council is subject to congressional review under the District of Columbia Home Rule Act of 1973. Prior to 1973, Congress typically approved interstate compacts on behalf of the District.

On February 23, 2006, the National Popular Vote organization held its first press conference in which it announced its state-based proposal to reform the Electoral College (described in chapter 6) and released the first edition of this book.

The National Popular Vote bill was introduced into all 50 state legislatures shortly thereafter.

As of mid-2012, the National Popular Vote bill has been enacted into law by nine jurisdictions:

- California (55 electoral votes),
- the District of Columbia (3 electoral votes),
- Hawaii (4 electoral votes),
- Illinois (20 electoral votes),
- Maryland (10 electoral votes),
- Massachusetts (11 electoral votes),
- New Jersey (14 electoral votes),
- Vermont (3 electoral votes), and
- Washington state (12 electoral votes).

The nine jurisdictions that have enacted the National Popular Vote compact possess 132 electoral votes—49% of the 270 electoral votes needed to bring the compact into effect.

---

[9] For example, the North Carolina Governor does not have veto power over redistricting bills.

[10] Council of State Governments. 2005. *The Book of the States.* Lexington, KY: The Council of State Governments. 2005 edition. Volume 37. Pages 161–162.

[11] For simplicity, we refer to the two houses of a state legislature, even though Nebraska has a unicameral state legislature.

As of mid-2012, the National Popular Vote bill has been approved by 31 legislative chambers in 21 jurisdictions. In addition to the legislative bodies of the above nine jurisdictions, the bill has been approved by the

- Arkansas House,
- Colorado Senate,
- Colorado House (in different years),
- Connecticut House
- Delaware House,
- Maine Senate,
- Michigan House,
- New Mexico House,
- Nevada Assembly,
- New York Senate,
- North Carolina Senate,
- Oregon House,
- Rhode Island Senate, and
- Rhode Island House.

See appendix Z for a history of the National Popular Vote bill.

7.3. THE ROLE OF THE CITIZEN-INITIATIVE PROCESS

The effort to secure adoption of the National Popular Vote compact could potentially involve the use of the citizen-initiative process.

State statutes are most commonly changed by passing a new law that amends or repeals existing law. State statutes are sometimes altered by passage of an amendment to the state constitution. In certain states, state statutes or state constitutional amendments may be enacted by the citizen-initiative process.

The people in 22 states have reserved to themselves the power to enact state statutes through the citizen-initiative process.

In addition, the people in 19 states have reserved to themselves the power to adopt state constitutional amendments through the citizen-initiative process. These 19 states include two states (Florida and Mississippi) that are not among the just-mentioned 22 states with the statutory initiative process.

Also, the District of Columbia has a citizen-initiative process for statutes.

Thus, a total of 25 jurisdictions permit either statutory or constitutional initiatives.

Table 7.4 shows the 25 jurisdictions that permit either statutory or constitutional initiatives. These 25 jurisdictions collectively possess 260 electoral votes based on the 2000 census. Note that, as of mid-2012, the National Popular Vote compact has been enacted in five of the 25 jurisdictions having the citizen-initiative process (California, the District of Columbia, Illinois, Massachusetts, and Washington state).

Table 7.4 THE 25 JURISDICTIONS WITH THE CITIZEN-INITIATIVE PROCESS

STATE	STATUTORY	CONSTITUTIONAL	ELECTORAL VOTES
Alaska	Yes	No	3
Arizona	Yes	Yes	10
Arkansas	Yes	Yes	6
California	Yes	Yes	55
Colorado	Yes	Yes	9
District of Columbia	Yes	No	3
Florida	No	Yes	27
Idaho	Yes	Very limited	4
Illinois	Advisory only	Very limited	21
Maine	Yes	No	4
Massachusetts	Yes	Yes	12
Michigan	Yes	Yes	17
Mississippi	No	Yes	6
Missouri	Yes	Yes	11
Montana	Yes	Yes	3
Nebraska	Yes	Yes	5
Nevada	Yes	Yes	5
North Dakota	Yes	Yes	3
Ohio	Yes	Yes	20
Oklahoma	Yes	Yes	7
Oregon	Yes	Yes	7
South Dakota	Yes	Yes	3
Utah	Yes	No	5
Washington	Yes	No	11
Wyoming	Yes	No	3
Total			260

The book *The Initiative: Citizen Law-Making*[12] provides details on the constitutional and statutory provisions governing the initiative processes in the various states.

The citizen-initiative process is problematic in several of the 25 jurisdictions listed in table 7.4 for a number of reasons.

For example, in Illinois, the statutory initiative is advisory only. Moreover, the constitutional initiative in Illinois is limited to matters relating to legislative procedure. Fortuitously, the National Popular Vote bill has already been enacted by the Illinois legislature.

---

[12] Zimmerman, Joseph F. 1999. *The Initiative: Citizen Law-Making.* Westport, CT: Praeger. Pages 24–25.

Because there is no statutory initiative in Florida or Mississippi, the constitutional initiative process would have to be invoked in those states in order to adopt the National Popular Vote compact.

In Florida, the initiative process for constitutional amendments is unusually time-consuming and uncertain. The procedure generally includes the circulation of a small petition followed by a preliminary review of the proposition by the Florida Supreme Court. If the Supreme Court approves, then a substantial number of additional signatures are required.

In Mississippi, the initiative process for constitutional amendments is somewhat difficult to use, and, as a result, it has been successfully invoked on only a few occasions.

The first step in invoking the citizen-initiative process in a typical state is to file the wording of the proposed legislation and the wording of the proposed petition with a state official (usually the Attorney General). Ohio, Maine, Massachusetts, Mississippi, Nevada, Florida, and Missouri have deadlines for starting the citizen-initiative process that come unusually early in each two-year election cycle.

There are numerous other difficulties associated with the use of the citizen-initiative process. In some states, there are significant legal limitations (involving both statutory law and case law) concerning the circulation of petitions on private property. In some states (such as Alaska and Arizona), weather conditions shorten the time window during which it is practical to circulate initiative petitions. Signature gathering is difficult in Michigan because of a combination of the weather and relatively tight legal limitations on petition circulation on private property. In some states, election administrators and the courts are not favorably disposed to the citizen-initiative process, and it is common for ballot measures to be disqualified in pre-election or post-election challenges. In some states, state constitutional provisions and existing judicial interpretations do not make it clear whether the citizen-initiative process is co-extensive with the powers of the state legislature.

Notwithstanding the difficulties in invoking the citizen-initiative process, the fact is that, in numerous states (notably many western states), the citizen-initiative process is an accepted part of the overall political process and can be successfully invoked in a relatively routine manner.

Section 8.1 contains additional information about the citizen-initiative process.

7.4. THE ROLE OF CONGRESS

Congress typically does not consider interstate compacts until the compact has been enacted by the requisite combination of states.

Congress has the option of explicitly consenting to a compact (section 5.10). However, as the U.S. Supreme Court wrote in the 1893 case of *Virginia v. Tennessee*,

". . . consent may be implied, and is always to be implied when congress adopts the particular act by sanctioning its objects and aiding in enforcing them . . . ."[13]

Legislation conferring congressional consent on an interstate compact may be adopted by a majority vote of both houses of Congress and approval by the President. The President can veto such legislation. If the President vetoes the bill, the Congress can override the veto by a two-thirds vote of both houses.

The question of whether the National Popular Vote compact requires explicit consent of Congress is discussed in sections 5.9, 5.10, and chapter 9.

In the event that all of the above steps are completed by July 20, 2016, the compact would govern the 2016 presidential election, and the President would, for the first time in American history, be elected by all of the people in an election in which every voter in every state is politically relevant and in which every vote is equal.

If, on the other hand, the compact is not effective by July 20, 2016, the debate on the issue of the nationwide popular election of the President would inevitably become a part of the 2016 campaign. Candidates for Senator, Representative, and President would be asked for their position on the issue. Newspapers and television stations would editorialize on the question of how the President should be elected. The travel, advertising, and "on the ground" activity of the presidential candidates would be scrutinized in terms of whether the candidates are, in fact, ignoring voters in a large number of states. In addition, the citizen-initiative process could be used in the November 2016 elections to further demonstrate voter support for nationwide popular election of the President (and to increase the number of states that have enacted the National Popular Vote compact). The authors of this book believe that a robust debate on the issue will inevitably lead to a nationwide decision to embrace nationwide popular election of the President.

---

[13] *Virginia v. Tennessee.* 148 U.S. 503 at 521. 1893.

8 | The Initiative Process and the National Popular Vote Compact

A state may enact an interstate compact in the same manner that it enacts an ordinary statute.

In certain states, the citizen-initiative process may be used to enact state statutes or constitutional amendments without the involvement of the state legislature.

This chapter

- describes the citizen-initiative process and the related protest-referendum process (section 8.1),
- discusses the question of whether the citizen-initiative process may be used to enact interstate compacts in general (section 8.2), and
- discusses the specific question of whether the citizen-initiative process may be used to enact a state law (such as the National Popular Vote compact) concerning the manner of choosing presidential electors (section 8.3).

8.1. DESCRIPTION OF THE CITIZEN-INITIATIVE PROCESS

The people in 22 states have reserved to themselves the power to enact state statutes through the citizen-initiative process.[1]

In addition, the people in 19 states have reserved to themselves the power to adopt state constitutional amendments through the citizen-initiative process. These 19 states include two states (Florida and Mississippi) that are not among the above-mentioned 22 states with the statutory initiative process.

Also, the District of Columbia has a citizen-initiative process for statutes.

The 25 jurisdictions that permit either statutory or constitutional initiatives are shown in table 7.4.

The initiative process is invoked by filing a petition signed by a constitutionally specified number of voters. The voters then decide whether to enact the proposed law in a statewide vote.[2]

---

[1] Zimmerman, Joseph F. 1999. *The Initiative: Citizen Law-Making*. Westport, CT: Praeger.

[2] In addition, the voters in 19 states may use the citizen-initiative process to propose and enact amendments to the state constitution. These 19 states include two states (Florida and Mississippi) that are not among the group of 22 states with the statutory initiative process. Also, the District of Columbia has a citizen-initiative process for statutes. Thus, there are 25 jurisdictions with the process. See table 7.4 for details.

In many of these same states, the voters have also reserved to themselves an additional power called the *protest-referendum*.[3] This process may be used to temporarily suspend a law enacted by the legislature and subsequently to vote on whether to retain the law in a statewide referendum. The protest-referendum process must be invoked in a strictly limited period of time immediately after the enactment of the statute. After the expiration of that period, the citizen-initiative process (if it exists in that particular state) can be used to enact a law repealing the statute.

The Michigan Constitution (Article II, section 9) provides a good description of both the citizen-initiative process and the protest-referendum process:

> "The people reserve to themselves the power to propose laws and to enact and reject laws, called the initiative, and the power to approve or reject laws enacted by the legislature, called the referendum. The power of initiative extends only to laws which the legislature may enact under this constitution. The power of referendum does not extend to acts making appropriations for state institutions or to meet deficiencies in state funds and must be invoked in the manner prescribed by law within 90 days following the final adjournment of the legislative session at which the law was enacted. To invoke the initiative or referendum, petitions signed by a number of registered electors, not less than eight percent for initiative and five percent for referendum of the total vote cast for all candidates for governor at the last preceding general election at which a governor was elected shall be required.

> "No law as to which the power of referendum properly has been invoked shall be effective thereafter unless approved by a majority of the electors voting thereon at the next general election.

> "Any law proposed by initiative petition shall be either enacted or rejected by the legislature without change or amendment within 40 session days from the time such petition is received by the legislature. If any law proposed by such petition shall be enacted by the legislature it shall be subject to referendum, as hereinafter provided.

> "If the law so proposed is not enacted by the legislature within the 40 days, the state officer authorized by law shall submit such proposed law to the people for approval or rejection at the next general election. The legislature may reject any measure so proposed by initiative petition and propose a different measure upon the same subject by a yea and nay vote upon separate roll calls, and in such event both measures shall be submitted by such state officer to the electors for approval or rejection at the next general election.

---

[3] Zimmerman, Joseph F. 1997. *The Referendum: The People Decide Public Policy.* Westport, CT: Praeger.

"Any law submitted to the people by either initiative or referendum petition and approved by a majority of the votes cast thereon at any election shall take effect 10 days after the date of the official declaration of the vote. No law initiated or adopted by the people shall be subject to the veto power of the governor, and no law adopted by the people at the polls under the initiative provisions of this section shall be amended or repealed, except by a vote of the electors unless otherwise provided in the initiative measure or by three-fourths of the members elected to and serving in each house of the legislature. Laws approved by the people under the referendum provision of this section may be amended by the legislature at any subsequent session thereof. If two or more measures approved by the electors at the same election conflict, that receiving the highest affirmative vote shall prevail."[4]

The Arizona Constitution provides:

"The legislative authority of the state shall be vested in the legislature, consisting of a senate and a house of representatives, but the people reserve the power to propose laws and amendments to the constitution and to enact or reject such laws and amendments at the polls, independently of the legislature; and they also reserve, for use at their own option, the power to approve or reject at the polls any act, or item, section, or part of any act, of the legislature."[5]

The Ohio Constitution provides:

"The legislative power of the state shall be vested in a General Assembly consisting of a Senate and House of Representatives, but the people reserve to themselves the power to propose to the General Assembly laws and amendments to the Constitution, and to adopt or reject the same at the polls on a referendum vote as hereinafter provided."[6]

The origin of the citizen-initiative process is generally attributed to various Swiss cantons in the early 19th century.[7] In 1898, the state constitution of South Dakota was amended to permit the citizen-initiative process. Oregon adopted the process in 1902. In 1904, Oregon voters became the first in the United States to use the citizen-initiative process to enact legislation when they enacted a direct primary statute and a local-option liquor statute.[8]

The initiative process spread rapidly to additional states as part of the Progressive

---

[4] Michigan Constitution. Article II, section 9.

[5] Arizona Constitution. Article I, section 1.

[6] Ohio Constitution. Article II, section 1.

[7] Zimmerman, Joseph F. 1999. *The Initiative: Citizen Law-Making.* Westport, CT: Praeger.

[8] *Id.*

movement in the early decades of the 20th century. Maine adopted the initiative and referendum in 1908. In California, the voters adopted the initiative process in the belief that it would reduce the dominance of the state legislature by the railroads and other corporations and that it would reduce the power of political machines. By 1918, 19 states had adopted the initiative. All were west of the Mississippi River, except for Maine, Massachusetts, and Ohio. The initiative process was included in Alaska's original constitution at the time of that state's admission to the Union in 1959.[9]

Section 7.2 discusses some of the practical and legal difficulties associated with the use of the citizen-initiative process.

8.2. MAY THE CITIZEN-INITIATIVE PROCESS BE USED TO ENACT AN INTERSTATE COMPACT?

The question arises as to whether an interstate compact may be enacted by means of the citizen-initiative process.

The scope of the statutory initiative process and the protest-referendum process varies considerably from state to state. Thus, an examination of the provisions of each state constitution is necessary to answer this question.

There is no provision of any state constitution that specifically singles out interstate compacts as being ineligible for enactment by the voters by means of the citizen-initiative process. Likewise, there is no provision of any state constitution that specifically states that interstate compacts are ineligible for temporary suspension and subsequent repeal by the voters by means of the protest-referendum process.

Having said that, there are significant limitations as to subject matter of the citizen-initiative and protest-referendum processes in about half of the states having these processes.[10] The limitations on the citizen-initiative process are so severe in Illinois that it would not be possible to enact an interstate compact using the initiative process in that state.[11]

In general, the restraints on the protest-referendum process are more severe than those applying to the initiative process.[12] The constitutional limitations on the protest-referendum process typically relate to appropriations, the judiciary, measures involving the support of governmental operations, and emergency measures.[13]

In short, unless an interstate compact deals with a subject that is outside a state's constitutional power, there is no state with the citizen-initiative process (other than Illinois) where an interstate compact could not, in principle, be adopted by the citizen-initiative process.

---

[9] *Id.*

[10] Alaska, California, Illinois, Massachusetts, Michigan, Mississippi, Missouri, Montana, Nebraska, Nevada, North Dakota, Ohio, South Dakota, and Wyoming.

[11] In Illinois, the statutory initiative process is advisory only, and the constitutional initiative process is limited to matters relating to legislative procedure.

[12] Zimmerman, Joseph F. 1997. *The Referendum: The People Decide Public Policy.* Westport, CT: Praeger.

[13] Zimmerman, Joseph F. 1999. *The Initiative: Citizen Law-Making.* Westport, CT: Praeger.

In fact, both the citizen-initiative process and protest-referendum processes have been used in connection with interstate compacts.

In 1988, an initiative petition forced a statewide vote on the question of repealing a law providing for Nebraska's participation in the Central Interstate Low-Level Radioactive Waste Compact (enacted several years earlier by the legislature).[14] In the statewide vote on Proposition 402, voters rejected the initiative proposition to repeal the compact.

In South Dakota in 1984, there was a statewide vote on an initiated law to require the approval of the voters of the state on the state's participation in any nuclear-waste-disposal compact. The measure passed 182,952 to 112,161. In 1985, the South Dakota Supreme Court upheld the referral of the Dakota Interstate Low-Level Radioactive Waste Management Compact to voters.[15]

In addition, legislatures have occasionally referred the enactment of an interstate compact to the state's voters. For example, the Maine legislature referred the question of enactment of the Texas Low-Level Radioactive Waste Disposal Compact to its voters in 1993. The question on the ballot was:

> "Do you approve of the interstate compact to be made with Texas, Maine and Vermont for the disposal of the State's low-level radioactive waste at a proposed facility in the State of Texas?"

The proposition received 170,411 "yes" votes and 63,672 "no" votes.

8.3. MAY THE CITIZEN-INITIATIVE PROCESS BE USED TO ENACT THE NATIONAL POPULAR VOTE COMPACT?

The National Popular Vote compact could be brought into effect solely by the collective action of state legislatures. However, it was suggested in chapter 7 that the citizen-initiative process might be used to enact the compact in certain states.

Article II, section 1, clause 2 of the U.S. Constitution (which we will frequently refer to as "Article II" in the remainder of this section) provides:

> "Each State shall appoint, in such Manner as the **Legislature** thereof may direct, a Number of Electors, equal to the whole Number of Senators and Representatives to which the State may be entitled in the Congress . . . ." [Emphasis added]

The use of the word "legislature" in Article II raises the question of whether the citizen-initiative process may be used to enact legislation specifying the manner of choosing presidential electors.

---

[14] The protest-referendum process is typically available only for a relatively short period after a state legislature enacts a particular law. After expiration of that period, the citizen-initiative process may be used to repeal an existing law.

[15] *Wyatt v. Kundert.* 375 N.W.2d 186 (1985).

An answer to this question requires an examination of the way that the word "legislature" is used in the U.S. Constitution.

The word "legislature" appears in 15 places in the U.S. Constitution—13 of which relate to the powers of state legislatures.[16] As will become clear later in this section, the word "legislature" is used with two distinct meanings in the U.S. Constitution, namely

- **the state's two legislative chambers**—that is, the state house of representatives and the state senate agreeing on a common action—either by sitting together in a joint convention or adopting a concurrent resolution while sitting separately;[17] or
- **the state's law-making process**—that is, the process of enacting a state law.

These 13 occurrences of the word "legislature" appear in the following 11 provisions of the U.S. Constitution:

- electing United States Senators in the state legislature (prior to ratification in 1913 of the 17th Amendment providing for popular election of Senators);
- filling a U.S. Senate vacancy (prior to the 17th Amendment);
- ratifying a proposed federal constitutional amendment;
- making an application to Congress for a federal constitutional convention;
- choosing the manner of electing U.S. Representatives and U.S. Senators;
- choosing the manner of appointing presidential electors;
- choosing the manner of conducting a popular election to fill a U.S. Senate vacancy (under the 17th Amendment);
- empowering the state's Governor to fill a U.S. Senate vacancy temporarily until the voters fill the vacancy in a popular election (under the 17th Amendment);
- consenting to the purchase of enclaves by the federal government for "forts, magazines, arsenals, dock-yards, and other needful buildings;"
- consenting to the formation of new states from territory of existing state(s); and
- requesting federal assistance to quell domestic violence.

Table 8.1 displays these 11 provisions of the U.S. Constitution referring to the powers of the state "legislature."

---

[16] Two of the 15 occurrences of the word "legislature" in the U.S. Constitution are unrelated to the powers of state legislatures and will therefore not be discussed further in this chapter. The first such provision is the requirement in Article I, section 2, clause 1 that voters for U.S. Representatives have "the Qualifications requisite for Electors of the most numerous Branch of the State Legislature." The second is the requirement in Article VI, clause 2 that "Members of the several State Legislatures" take an oath or affirmation to support the U.S. Constitution.

[17] For simplicity, we refer to the "two houses" of a state legislature throughout this discussion, even though Nebraska has a unicameral state legislature.

Table 8.1 PROVISIONS OF THE U.S. CONSTITUTION REFERRING TO POWERS OF THE STATE "LEGISLATURE"

	POWER	PROVISION OF THE U.S. CONSTITUTION
1	**Electing U.S. Senators** (prior to the 17th Amendment)	"The Senate of the United States shall be composed of two Senators from each State, chosen by the **Legislature** thereof, for six Years; and each Senator shall have one Vote."[1] [Emphasis added]
2	**Filling a U.S. Senate vacancy** (prior to the 17th Amendment)	". . . if Vacancies happen by Resignation, or otherwise, during the Recess of the **Legislature** of any State, the Executive thereof may make temporary Appointments until the next Meeting of the **Legislature, which shall then fill such Vacancies.**"[2] [Emphasis added]
3	**Ratifying a proposed federal constitutional amendment**	"The Congress, whenever two thirds of both Houses shall deem it necessary, shall propose Amendments to this Constitution, or, on the Application of the Legislatures of two thirds of the several States, shall call a Convention for proposing Amendments, which, in either Case, shall be valid to all Intents and Purposes, as Part of this Constitution, **when ratified by the Legislatures** of three fourths of the several States, or by Conventions in three fourths thereof, as the one or the other Mode of Ratification may be proposed by the Congress . . . "[3] [Emphasis added]
4	**Making an application to Congress for a federal constitutional convention**	"The Congress, whenever two thirds of both Houses shall deem it necessary, shall propose Amendments to this Constitution, or, **on the Application of the Legislatures** of two thirds of the several States, shall call a Convention for proposing Amendments, which, in either Case, shall be valid to all Intents and Purposes, as Part of this Constitution, when ratified by the Legislatures of three fourths of the several States, or by Conventions in three fourths thereof, as the one or the other Mode of Ratification may be proposed by the Congress . . . "[4] [Emphasis added]
5	**Choosing the manner of electing U.S. Representatives and Senators**	"The Times, Places and Manner of holding Elections for Senators and Representatives, shall be **prescribed in each State by the Legislature thereof**; but the Congress may at any time by Law make or alter such Regulations, except as to the Places of chusing Senators."[5] [Emphasis added]
6	**Choosing the manner of appointing presidential electors**	"Each State shall appoint, in such Manner **as the Legislature thereof may direct**, a Number of Electors, equal to the whole Number of Senators and Representatives to which the State may be entitled in the Congress . . . ."[6] [Emphasis added]
7	**Choosing the manner of conducting a popular election to fill a U.S. Senate vacancy** (under the 17th Amendment)	"When vacancies happen in the representation of any State in the Senate, the executive authority of such State shall issue writs of election to fill such vacancies: Provided, That the legislature of any State may empower the executive thereof to make temporary appointments until the people fill the vacancies by election **as the legislature may direct.**"[7] [Emphasis added]

[1] U.S. Constitution. Article I, section 3, clause 1. Superseded by the 17th Amendment.

[2] U.S. Constitution. Article I, section 3, clause 2. Superseded by the 17th Amendment.

[3] U.S. Constitution. Article V.

[4] U.S. Constitution. Article V.

[5] U.S. Constitution. Article I, section 4, clause 1.

[6] U.S. Constitution. Article II, section 1, clause 2.

[7] U.S. Constitution. 17th Amendment, section 2.

Table 8.1 *(continued)*

	POWER	PROVISION OF THE U.S. CONSTITUTION
8	**Empowering the Governor to fill a U.S. Senate vacancy temporarily until a popular election is held** (under the 17th Amendment)	"When vacancies happen in the representation of any State in the Senate, the executive authority of such State shall issue writs of election to fill such vacancies: Provided, That **the legislature of any State may empower** the executive thereof to make temporary appointments until the people fill the vacancies by election as the legislature may direct."[8] [Emphasis added]
9	**Consenting to the purchase of enclaves by the federal government**	"To exercise exclusive Legislation in all Cases whatsoever, over such District (not exceeding ten Miles square) as may, by Cession of particular States, and the Acceptance of Congress, become the Seat of the Government of the United States, and to exercise like Authority over all Places purchased by the **Consent of the Legislature** of the State in which the Same shall be, for the Erection of Forts, Magazines, Arsenals, dock-Yards, and other needful Buildings."[9] [Emphasis added]
10	**Consenting to the formation of new states from territory of existing state(s)**	"New States may be admitted by the Congress into this Union; but no new State shall be formed or erected within the Jurisdiction of any other State; nor any State be formed by the Junction of two or more States, or Parts of States, without the **Consent of the Legislatures** of the States concerned as well as of the Congress."[10] [Emphasis added]
11	**Requesting federal military assistance to quell domestic violence**	"The United States shall guarantee to every State in this Union a Republican Form of Government, and shall protect each of them against Invasion; and on **Application of the Legislature**, or of the Executive (when the **Legislature** cannot be convened) against domestic Violence."[11] [Emphasis added]

[8] U.S. Constitution. 17th Amendment, section 2.

[9] U.S. Constitution. Article I, section 9, clause 17.

[10] U.S. Constitution. Article IV, section 3, clause 1.

[11] U.S. Constitution. Article IV, section 4.

In the next 11 sections of this chapter, we discuss the meaning of the 13 occurrences of the word "legislature" in these 11 provisions of the U.S. Constitution.

As will be seen, history, practice, and law indicate that the word "legislature" in the U.S. Constitution means "the state's two legislative chambers" when the legislature's action consists of a decision that can be expressed in one or two words—that is, the name of the person being elected to a full-term or to fill a vacancy in the U.S. Senate (prior to ratification of the 17th Amendment), a "yes" response to the yes-or-no question of ratifying a constitutional amendment, or an affirmative decision to apply to Congress for a federal constitutional convention.

In contrast, history, practice, and law indicate that the word "legislature" in the U.S. Constitution means "the state's law-making process" when detailed legislation is required.

8.3.1. ELECTING U.S. SENATORS

Under the original Constitution, each state legislature elected the state's two U.S. Senators. Two methods were commonly used by the states. In some states, the two houses of the state legislature met in a joint convention in which each state representative and each state senator cast one vote in the election for the state's U.S. Senator. In other states, the state house of representatives and the state senate voted separately on a concurrent resolution expressing their choice for the state's U.S. Senator.[18] Regardless of which method was used, the state's Governor was *not* part of the constitutional process of electing U.S. Senators. Neither the decision of a joint convention of the two houses nor the concurrent resolution agreed to by both houses of the legislature was presented to the Governor for approval or disapproval. In other words, the word "legislature" in the U.S. Constitution, in connection with the election of U.S. Senators (the first entry in table 8.1), refers to the state's two legislative chambers—not to the state's usual process for making laws.

8.3.2. FILLING A U.S. SENATE VACANCY

Similarly, under the original Constitution, a vacancy in the U.S. Senate was filled by action of the state's two legislative chambers (either voting in a joint convention or acting separately by concurrent resolution). That is, the word "legislature" in the U.S. Constitution, in connection with the filling of U.S. Senate vacancies (the second entry in table 8.1), refers to the state's two legislative chambers.

8.3.3. RATIFYING A PROPOSED FEDERAL CONSTITUTIONAL AMENDMENT

The meaning of the word "legislature" in connection with the ratification of amendments to the federal Constitution (the third entry in table 8.1) was decided by the U.S. Supreme Court in *Hawke v. Smith* in 1920.[19] Article V of the U.S. Constitution provides that proposed amendments

> ". . . shall be valid to all Intents and Purposes, as Part of this Constitution, when ratified by the **Legislatures** of three fourths of the several States . . . ."
> [Emphasis added]

---

[18] Separate voting for U.S. Senators by the two houses of the state legislature, of course, created the possibility of a deadlock between the two houses. Thus, it became common for U.S. Senate seats to remain vacant for prolonged periods. Article I, section 4, clause 1 of the U.S. Constitution provides that "The Times, Places and Manner of holding Elections for Senators and Representatives, shall be prescribed in each State by the Legislature thereof; but the Congress may at any time by Law make or alter such Regulations, except as to the Places of chusing Senators." In 1866, Congress exercised its power under this constitutional provision to change the "manner" by which state legislatures conducted their Senate elections and to specify the "time" of such elections. Congress required the two houses of each state legislature to meet in a joint convention on a specified day and to meet every day thereafter until a Senator was selected (14 Stat. 243).

[19] *Hawke v. Smith.* 253 U.S. 221. 1920.

Before deciding the specific issue in the *Hawke* case in 1920, the U.S. Supreme Court reviewed its 1798 decision in *Hollingsworth et al. v. Virginia*.[20] The *Hollingsworth* case explored the two distinct meanings of the word "Congress" in the U.S. Constitution (the analog of the issue concerning the two meanings of the word "legislature").

The U.S. Constitution frequently uses the word "Congress" to refer to the national government's law-making process—that is, the process by which the legislative bills are passed by the two houses of Congress and presented to the President for approval or disapproval. The word "Congress" appears with this meaning in numerous places in the Constitution, including

> "The **Congress** shall have Power To lay and collect Taxes, Duties, Imposts and Excises, to pay the Debts and provide for the common Defence and general Welfare of the United States. . . ."[21] [Emphasis added]

The word "Congress" also appears in Article V:

> "The **Congress**, whenever two thirds of both Houses shall deem it necessary, shall propose Amendments to this Constitution. . . ." [Emphasis added]

The *Hollingsworth* case addressed the question of whether the word "Congress" in the U.S. Constitution meant

- **the national government's legislative chambers**—that is, the U.S. House of Representatives and U.S. Senate sitting separately and agreeing to a concurrent resolution, or
- **the national government's law-making process.**

In 1798, the U.S. Supreme Court ruled that when the Congress proposes an amendment to the U.S. Constitution, the resolution of ratification need not be submitted to the President for approval or disapproval. Referring to the 1798 *Hollingsworth* case, the Court noted in the 1920 *Hawke* case:

> "At an early day this court settled that the submission of a constitutional amendment did not require the action of the President. The question arose over the adoption of the Eleventh Amendment. *Hollingsworth et al. v. Virginia*, 3 Dall. 378. In that case it was contended that the amendment had not been proposed in the manner provided in the Constitution as an inspection of the original roll showed that it had never been submitted to the President for his approval in accordance with article 1, section 7, of the Constitution. The Attorney General answered that **the case of amend-**

---

[20] *Hollingsworth et al. v. Virginia.* 3 Dall. 378. 1798.
[21] U.S. Constitution. Article I, section 8, clause 1.

ments is a substantive act, unconnected with the ordinary business of legislation, and not within the policy or terms of the Constitution investing the President with a qualified negative [veto] on the acts and resolutions of Congress. In a footnote to this argument of the Attorney General, Justice Chase said:

> 'There can, surely, be no necessity to answer that argument. **The negative of the President applies only to the ordinary cases of legislation. He has nothing to do with the proposition, or adoption, of amendments to the Constitution.**'

"The court by a unanimous judgment held that the amendment was constitutionally adopted."[22] [Emphasis added]

In other words, the 1798 *Hollingsworth* case concluded that a federal constitutional amendment was *not* the "ordinary business of legislation."

The U.S. Supreme Court then addressed the specific issue in the 1920 *Hawke* case, namely the constitutionality of a 1918 amendment to the Ohio Constitution. This state constitutional amendment extended the protest-referendum process to resolutions of ratification by the Ohio legislature of proposed federal constitutional amendments. Specifically, the 1918 amendment to the Ohio Constitution provided:

> "The people also reserve to themselves the legislative power of the referendum on the action of the General Assembly ratifying any proposed amendment to the Constitution of the United States."

The *Hawke* case arose as a result of the Ohio Legislature's ratification of the 18th Amendment prohibiting the manufacture, sale, and transportation of intoxicating liquors for beverage purposes. On January 7, 1919, the Ohio Legislature passed a concurrent resolution[23] ratifying the Amendment.[24] Ohio's ratification was crucial because the U.S. Secretary of State was in possession of resolutions of ratification from 35 other states, and 36 ratifications were sufficient, at the time, to make a pending amendment part of the U.S. Constitution. A protest-referendum petition was quickly circulated in Ohio. Supporters of the 18th Amendment challenged the petition's validity in state court. The Ohio Supreme Court decided that the legislature's ratification of the 18th Amendment should be temporarily suspended and submitted to the state's vot-

---

[22] *Hawke v. Smith.* 253 U.S. 221 at 229–230. 1920.

[23] A concurrent resolution is a type of resolution that is passed by both houses of the legislature but not submitted to the Governor for approval or disapproval.

[24] The resolution of ratification for the 18th Amendment was adopted by the Ohio Legislature in accordance with the long-standing practice in Ohio (and other states) of not submitting the legislature's resolution to the state's Governor for approval or disapproval.

ers for approval or disapproval in a statewide referendum. The U.S. Supreme Court, however, decided otherwise.

> "The argument to support the power of the state to require the approval by the people of the state of the ratification of amendments to the federal Constitution through the medium of a referendum rests upon the proposition that the federal Constitution requires ratification by the legislative action of the states through the medium provided at the time of the proposed approval of an amendment. This argument is fallacious in this—**ratification by a state of a constitutional amendment is not an act of legislation** within the proper sense of the word. **It is but the expression of the assent of the state to a proposed amendment.**"[25] [Emphasis added]

In short, in connection with ratification of amendments to the U.S. Constitution (the third entry in table 8.1), the word "legislature" in the U.S. Constitution refers to the state's two legislative chambers. Ratification is

- "unconnected with the ordinary business of legislation,"[26] and
- "not an act of legislation."[27]

Appendix U contains the full text of the Supreme Court's 1920 decision in *Hawke v. Smith*.

8.3.4. MAKING AN APPLICATION TO CONGRESS FOR A FEDERAL CONSTITUTIONAL CONVENTION

The word "legislature" appears in the U.S. Constitution in connection with one of the two ways by which amendments to the Constitution may be proposed to the states. Article V provides:

> "The Congress, whenever two thirds of both Houses shall deem it necessary, shall propose Amendments to this Constitution, or, on the **Application of the Legislatures** of two thirds of the several States, shall call a Convention for proposing Amendments . . . ." [Emphasis added]

State legislatures sometimes call on Congress to convene a federal Constitutional Convention. For example, prior to congressional passage of the 17th Amendment, 26 states had petitioned Congress for a federal Constitutional Convention to consider the specific question of the popular election of U.S. Senators. In addition, two additional states had, during the period immediately prior to congressional action on the 17th

---

[25] *Hawke v. Smith.* 253 U.S. 221 at 229–230. 1920.

[26] *Id.* at 230.

[27] *Id.*

Amendment, issued requests for a federal Constitutional Convention without mentioning the topic to be considered by the Convention. Similarly, by the time Congress acted on the 21st Amendment, almost two-thirds of the states had petitioned Congress for a federal Constitutional Convention to repeal the 18th Amendment.

According to Orfield's *The Amending of the Federal Constitution*, when state legislatures apply to Congress for a federal Constitutional Convention, the long-standing practice of the states has been that the action of the legislature is not presented to the state's Governor for approval or disapproval.[28] Instead, the two houses of the state legislature pass a concurrent resolution. Thus, in connection with applications to Congress for a federal Constitutional Convention (the fourth entry in table 8.1), historical practice indicates that the word "legislature" in the U.S. Constitution refers to the state's two legislative chambers.

8.3.5. CHOOSING THE MANNER OF ELECTING U.S. REPRESENTATIVES AND SENATORS

As demonstrated in the previous four sections, judicial precedent and long-standing practice by the states indicate that the word "legislature" in the U.S. Constitution refers, in connection with the first, second, third, and fourth entries in table 8.1, to the state's two legislative chambers—not to the state's Governor or the state's citizen-initiative or protest-referendum processes.

In many other parts of the U.S. Constitution, however, the word "legislature" has a different meaning—namely, the state's law-making process. In these parts of the Constitution, "legislature" includes the state's Governor—an official who is manifestly not part of the state legislature. Moreover, in these parts of the U.S. Constitution, "legislature" may also include the state's voters—who, like the Governor, are plainly not members of the two chambers of the state legislature.

An example of this second meaning of the word "legislature" is found in Article I, section 4, clause 1 of the U.S. Constitution concerning the manner of holding elections for U.S. Representatives and Senators (the fifth entry in table 8.1).

> "The Times, Places and **Manner** of holding Elections for Senators and Representatives, shall be prescribed in each State by the **Legislature** thereof; but the Congress may at any time by Law make or alter such Regulations, except as to the Places of chusing Senators." [Emphasis added]

The U.S. Supreme Court addressed the meaning of "legislature" in Article I, section 4, clause 1 in *Smiley v. Holm* in 1932.[29] The issue in *Smiley* was whether the

---

[28] Orfield, Lester Bernhardt. 1942. *The Amending of the Federal Constitution*. Ann Arbor: The University of Michigan Press.

[29] *Smiley v. Holm*. 285 U.S. 355. 1932.

Minnesota Governor could veto a law passed by the legislature redrawing the state's congressional districts after the 1930 census. In other words, the question in *Smiley* was whether the word "legislature" refers to the state's two legislative chambers or the state's law-making process which, in Minnesota in 1932, included the Governor.

The question of whether the word "legislature" includes a state's Governor depends, in large part, on the answer to the following question:

> "When a state exercises authority pursuant to powers granted to it by the U.S. Constitution in connection with deciding on the manner of electing its U.S. Representatives,
>
> (1) does it derive the power to act solely from the U.S. Constitution, or
>
> (2) does it enact the legislation in accordance with the procedures specified in the state's constitution?"

The 1932 *Smiley* case involving the meaning of the word "legislature" in the U.S. Constitution came to the U.S. Supreme Court over a decade after various cases arising from the adoption of the initiative and referendum processes in the early years of the 20th century. These earlier cases included the 1920 *Hawke* case (discussed above) and the 1916 case of *State of Ohio ex rel. Davis v. Hildebrant* (discussed below). *Smiley* thus provided the Court with the opportunity to put all of these related cases into perspective. The U.S. Supreme Court wrote in *Smiley* in 1932:

> **"[W]henever the term 'legislature' is used in the Constitution, it is necessary to consider the nature of the particular action in view."**[30] [Emphasis added]

Applying this test, the Court found that the term "legislature" in Article I, section 4, clause 1 referred to "making laws"[31] and therefore included the Governor.

> **"[I]t follows, in the absence of an indication of a contrary intent, that the exercise of the authority must be in accordance with the method which the State has prescribed for legislative enactments. We find no suggestion in the Federal constitutional provision of an attempt to endow the legislature of the State with power to enact laws in any manner other than that in which the constitution of the State has provided that laws shall be enacted."**[32] [Emphasis added]

Thus, the word "legislature" in the U.S. Constitution, in connection with the state's deciding on the "manner of holding Elections" for U.S. Representatives" (the fifth entry

---

[30] *Id.* at 366.

[31] *Id.* at 365.

[32] *Id.* at 368.

in table 8.1), refers to the state's process of making laws—not just to the two chambers of the state legislature.

Appendix V contains the full text of the Supreme Court's 1932 decision in *Smiley v. Holm*.

In 1916, the U.S. Supreme Court addressed the specific question of whether the word "legislature" in Article I, section 4, clause 1 of the U.S. Constitution included the voters acting through the processes of direct democracy. The Supreme Court described the origins of *State of Ohio ex rel. Davis v. Hildebrant* as follows:

> "By an amendment to the Constitution of Ohio, adopted September 3d, 1912, the **legislative power was expressly declared to be vested** not only in the senate and house of representatives of the state, constituting the general assembly, but **in the people**, in whom a right was reserved by way of referendum to approve or disapprove by popular vote any law enacted by the general assembly." [33] [Emphasis added]

The Supreme Court continued:

> "In May, 1915, the general assembly of Ohio passed an act redistricting the state for the purpose of congressional elections, by which act twenty-two congressional districts were created, in some respects differing from the previously established districts, and this act, after approval by the governor, was filed in the office of the secretary of state. The requisite number of electors under the referendum provision having petitioned for a submission of the law to a popular vote, such vote was taken and the law was disapproved.
>
> "Thereupon, in the supreme court of the state, the suit before us was begun against state election officers for the purpose of procuring a mandamus, directing them to disregard the vote of the people on the referendum, disapproving the law, and to proceed to discharge their duties as such officers in the next congressional election, upon the assumption that the action by way of referendum was void, and that the law which was disapproved was subsisting and valid." [34]

Summarizing the issue, the Supreme Court wrote:

> "**The right to this relief was based upon the charge that the referendum vote was not and could not be a part of the legislative authority of the state,** and therefore could have no influence on the subject of the law creating congressional districts for the purpose of representation in

---

[33] *State of Ohio ex rel. Davis v. Hildebrant.* 241 U.S. 565 at 566. 1916.
[34] *Id.* at 566–567.

Congress. Indeed, it was in substance charged that both from the point of view of the state Constitution and laws and from that of the Constitution of the United States, especially [clause] 4 of article 1, providing that

> 'the times, places and manner of holding elections for Senators and Representatives, shall be prescribed in each state by the legislature thereof; but the Congress may at any time by law, make or alter such regulations, except as to the places of choosing Senators;'

and also from that of the provisions of the controlling act of Congress of August 8, 1911 (chap. 5, 37 Stat. at L. 13, Comp. Stat. 1913, 15), apportioning representation among the states, the attempt to make the referendum a component part of the legislative authority empowered to deal with the election of members of Congress was absolutely void. **The court below adversely disposed of these contentions, and held that the provisions as to referendum were a part of the legislative power of the state, made so by the Constitution, and that nothing in the act of Congress of 1911, or in the constitutional provision, operated to the contrary**, and that therefore the disapproved law had no existence and was not entitled to be enforced by mandamus."[35] [Emphasis added]

The U.S. Supreme Court then upheld the Ohio Supreme Court and rejected the argument that the word "legislature" in Article I, section 4, clause 1 of the U.S. Constitution excluded the referendum process. The popular vote rejecting Ohio's redistricting statute was allowed to stand.

Additionally, the Court noted:

> "Congress recognize[d] the referendum as part of the legislative authority of a state."[36]

Appendix P contains the full text of the Supreme Court's 1916 decision in *State of Ohio ex rel. Davis v. Hildebrant*.

In 1920, the U.S. Supreme Court distinguished its decision in *Hawke* from its decision in *State of Ohio ex rel. Davis v. Hildebrant* by saying in *Hawke*:

> "But it is said this view runs counter to the decision of this court in *Davis v. Hildebrant* (241 U.S. 565) 36 S. Ct. 708. But that case is inapposite. It dealt with article 1 section 4, of the Constitution, which provides that the times, places, and manners of holding elections for Senators and Representatives in each state shall be determined by the respective Legislatures thereof,

---

[35] *Id.* at 568.

[36] *Id.* at 569.

but that Congress may at any time make or alter such regulations, except as to the place for choosing Senators. As shown in the opinion in that case, Congress had itself recognized the referendum as part of the legislative authority of the state for the purpose stated. It was held, affirming the judgment of the Supreme Court of Ohio, that the referendum provision of the state Constitution, when applied to a law redistricting the state with a view to representation in Congress, was not unconstitutional. **Article 1, section 4, plainly gives authority to the state to legislate within the limitations therein named. Such legislative action is entirely different from the requirement of the Constitution as to the expression of assent or dissent to a proposed amendment to the Constitution. In such expression no legislative action is authorized or required.**"[37] [Emphasis added]

Relying on *Smiley v. Holm*[38] and *State of Ohio ex rel. Davis v. Hildebrant*,[39] the Colorado Supreme Court wrote in *Colorado, ex rel. Salazar v. Davidson* in 2003:

"[T]he United States Supreme Court has interpreted the word 'legislature' in Article I to broadly encompass any means permitted by state law [including] citizen referenda and initiatives, mandatory gubernatorial approval, and any other procedures defined by the state." [40,41]

Chief Justice Rehnquist, joined by Justices Thomas and Scalia, affirmed this view in a dissenting opinion when the U.S. Supreme Court denied review of the *Colorado, ex rel. Salazar v. Davidson* decision. Rehnquist stated that the Court had

"explained that the focus of our inquiry was **not on the 'body' but the function performed** [and that] the function referred to by Article I, §4, was **the lawmaking process**, which is defined by state law."[42] [Emphasis added]

The distinction between "the lawmaking process" and the two chambers of the state legislature is not new. In fact, this distinction has been made since the earliest

---

[37] *Hawke v. Smith.* 253 U.S. 221 at 230–231. 1920.

[38] *Smiley v. Holm.* 285 U.S. 355. 1932.

[39] *State of Ohio ex rel. Davis v. Hildebrant.* 241 U.S. 565. 1916.

[40] *Colorado, ex rel. Salazar v. Davidson.* 79 P.3d 1221, 1232 (Colorado 2003).

[41] In *Cook v. Gralike*, 531 U.S. 510, 526 n.20 (2001), the Court declined to consider whether the Elections Clause of Art. 1, §4, which is a grant of power to "each State by the Legislature thereof," could be invoked concerning a statute adopted by referendum. The Court reaffirmed, however, the notion in *Smiley* that "[w]herever the term 'legislature' is used in the Constitution, it is necessary to consider the nature of the particular action in view." *Id*.

[42] *Colorado General Assembly v. Salazar*, 124 S. Ct. 2228 at 2230. 2004.

days of the U.S. Constitution. When the U.S. Constitution took effect in 1788, two states had the gubernatorial veto.[43],[44]

The provisions of the Massachusetts Constitution at the time when the U.S. Constitution took effect were substantially the same as the procedures for gubernatorial approval, veto, and legislative override found in most state constitutions today (and substantially the same as the procedures for presidential veto in the U.S. constitution).

> "No bill or resolve of the senate or house of representatives shall become a law, and have force as such, until it shall have been laid before the governor for his revisal; and if he, upon such revision, approve thereof, he shall signify his approbation by signing the same. But if he have any objection to the passing of such bill or resolve, he shall return the same, together with his objections thereto, in writing, to the senate or house of representatives, in whichsoever the same shall have originated, who shall enter the objections sent down by the governor, at large, on their records, and proceed to reconsider the said bill or resolve; but if, after such reconsideration, two-thirds of the said senate or house of representatives shall, notwithstanding the said objections, agree to pass the same, it shall, together with the objections, be sent to the other branch of the legislature, where it shall also be reconsidered, and if approved by two-thirds of the members present, shall have the force of law; but in all such cases, the vote of both houses shall be determined by yeas and nays; and the names of the persons voting for or against the said bill or resolve shall be entered upon the public records of the commonwealth."[45]

On November 20, 1788, both chambers of the Massachusetts legislature approved legislation specifying the manner for electing U.S. representatives. This legislation was forwarded to Governor John Hancock, and he approved it.[46]

The New York Constitution required that all bills passed by the legislature be submitted to a Council of Revision composed of the Governor, the Chancellor, and the judges of the state supreme court. A two-thirds vote of both houses of the legislature was necessary to override a veto by the Council. On January 23, 1789, the New York legislature approved legislation specifying the manner for electing U.S.

---

[43] Kole, Edward A. 1999. *The First 13 Constitutions of the First American States.* Haverford, PA: Infinity Publishing.

[44] Kole, Edward A. 1999. *The True Intent of the First American Constitutions of 1776–1791.* Haverford, PA: Infinity Publishing.

[45] Massachusetts Constitution of 1780. Chapter I, Section I, Article II.

[46] Smith, Hayward H. 2001. *Symposium, Law of Presidential Elections: Issues in the Wake of Florida 2000.* History of the Article II independent state legislature doctrine. 29 *Florida State University Law Review* 731–785 at 760. Issue 2.

representatives. The bill was presented to the Council; the Council approved the bill; and the bill became law.

Article I, section 4, clause 1 of the U.S. Constitution covers the manner of electing U.S. Senators as well as the manner of electing U.S. Representatives.

> "The Times, Places and **Manner** of holding Elections for **Senators** and Representatives, shall be prescribed in each State by the **Legislature** thereof . . . ." [Emphasis added]

The two meanings of the word "legislature" in the U.S. Constitution are dramatically illustrated by the actions of the first New York legislature that met under the U.S. Constitution. As mentioned in section 8.3.1, the state's Governor was not part of the constitutional process of electing U.S. Senators under the original Constitution. The two chambers of the state legislature elected the state's U.S. Senators. The Governor of New York was, however, part of the law-making process that decided the *manner* of electing U.S. Senators. For example, in 1789, both houses of the New York legislature passed a bill providing for the manner of electing U.S. Senators. This bill was presented to the Council composed of the Governor, the Chancellor, and judges of the state supreme court. The Council vetoed the bill.[47] That bill did not become law. In short, when a state chose the "manner" of electing its U.S. Senators, the word "legislature" in the U.S. Constitution meant "the lawmaking process" (which included the Governor and Council); however, when the state actually elected its U.S. Senators, the same word "legislature" meant only the two legislative chambers (which did not include the Governor or the Council).

Congressional districting is arguably the most important aspect of the "manner" of electing U.S. Representatives.

In recent years, the voters have used the protest-referendum process not only to review congressional districting plans enacted by state legislatures (leading to the 1916 case of *State of Ohio ex rel. Davis v. Hildebrant*), but also to entirely exclude the state legislature from the process of congressional districting.

For example, in 2000, Arizona voters used the citizen-initiative process to adopt a state constitutional amendment (called "Proposition 106") establishing the Arizona Independent Redistricting Commission to draw the state's congressional and state legislative districts. The petition proposing the state constitutional amendment described the proposal as follows:

> "This citizen-sponsored Arizona Constitutional amendment will create a new 'citizens' independent redistricting commission' to draw new legislative and congressional district boundaries after each U.S. Census. **This**

---

[47] DenBoer, Gordon, Brown, Lucy Trumbull, and Hagermann, Charles D. (editors). 1986. *The Documentary History of the First Federal Elections 1788–1790*. Madison, WI: University of Wisconsin Press. Volume 3.

amendment takes the redistricting power away from the Arizona Legislature and puts it in the hands of a politically neutral commission of citizens who are not active in partisan politics and who will serve without pay to create fair districts that are not "gerrymandered" for any party's or incumbent's advantage."[48] [Emphasis added]

In 2008, California voters established a similar nonpartisan commission using the citizen-initiative process (Proposition 11).

These actions by Arizona and California voters are noteworthy for two reasons.

First, the establishment of a commission was accomplished by a citizen-initiative petition—not the "legislature."

Second, both commissions were established by an amendment to the state constitution, as distinguished from a statutory enactment of "legislation."[49]

In other words, neither the "legislature" nor "legislation" was involved in the decision to exclude the state legislature.

The Arizona Independent Redistricting Commission created the congressional districts that were used throughout the decade following the 2000 census. These districts were generally viewed as favorable to Republicans.

However, Arizona Republicans vigorously objected to the districts created by the commission after the 2010 census. In the period since the 2010 census, the Republicans controlled both the legislature and governorship. During the dispute, the Republicans removed the chair of the commission; however, the Arizona Supreme Court restored the chair to her position. The districts created by the commission took effect for the 2012 elections.

Then, in June 2012, a lawsuit (authorized by both houses of the legislature) was filed in the U.S. District Court in Arizona challenging the constitutionality of the Arizona Independent Redistricting Commission under Article I, section 4, clause 1 of the U.S. Constitution.

The complaint in *Arizona State Legislature v. Arizona Independent Redistricting Commission et. al.* states:

> "Prop. 106 removes entirely from the Legislature the authority to prescribe legislative and congressional district lines and reassigns that authority wholly to the IRC—a new entity created by Prop. 106.

> "Prop. 106 also prescribes the process by which the IRC members are appointed and the process and procedures by which the IRC is to establish legislative and congressional district lines.

---

[48] July 6, 2000, application to Arizona Secretary of State by the "Fair Districts, Fair Elections" organization.

[49] See the discussion of Arkansas's implementation of the 17th Amendment in section 8.3.7.

"Prop. 106 eliminates entirely the Legislature's prescriptive role in congressional redistricting. . . ."[50] [Emphasis added]

The outcome of this June 2012 lawsuit is not known as of the time of this writing.

In summary, present-day practice, practice at the time of ratification of the U.S. Constitution, and existing court decisions consistently support the interpretation that the word "legislature" in Article I, section 4, clause 1 of the U.S. Constitution (the fifth entry in table 8.1) does not refer to the two chambers of the state legislature, but instead refers to the "lawmaking process" that includes

- the state's Governor, an official who is manifestly not a member of the two chambers of the state legislature, and
- in states having the citizen-initiative process and protest-referendum processes, the state's voters, who, like the Governor, are manifestly not members of the two chambers of the state legislature.

8.3.6. CHOOSING THE MANNER OF APPOINTING PRESIDENTIAL ELECTORS

The word "legislature" appears in Article II of the U.S. Constitution (the sixth entry in table 8.1).

"Each State shall appoint, in such Manner **as the Legislature thereof may direct**, a Number of Electors, equal to the whole Number of Senators and Representatives to which the State may be entitled in the Congress. . . ."[51] [Emphasis added]

In *U.S. Term Limits v. Thornton*, the U.S. Supreme Court in 1995 noted the parallelism between the use of the word "legislature" in Article I, section 4, clause 1 (relating to the "manner" of electing U.S. Representatives) and the word "legislature" in Article II. The Court wrote:

". . . the provisions governing elections reveal the Framers' understanding that powers over the election of federal officers had to be delegated to, rather than reserved by, the States. It is surely no coincidence that **the context of federal elections provides one of the few areas in which the Constitution expressly requires action by the States**, namely that

'[t]he Times, Places and **Manner** of holding Elections for Senators and Representatives, shall be prescribed in each State by the **legislature** thereof.' [Art I., §4, cl. 4.]

---

[50] Complaint in *Arizona State Legislature* v. *Arizona Independent Redistricting Commission et al.* Page 5.
[51] U.S. Constitution. Article II, section 1, clause 2.

"This duty parallels the duty under Article II that

'Each State shall appoint, in such **Manner** as the **Legislature** thereof may direct, a Number of Electors.' Art II., §1, cl. 2.

"These Clauses are express delegations of power to the States to act with respect to federal elections."[52] [Emphasis added]

The parallelism noted by the Court supports the power of the people to act legislatively through the citizen-initiative process concerning the manner of electing presidential electors.

The question of whether the word "legislature" includes the state's initiative and referendum processes depends, in large part, on the answer to the following question:

"When a state exercises authority pursuant to powers granted to it by the U.S. Constitution in connection with deciding on the manner of choosing its presidential electors,

(1) does it derive the power to act solely from the U.S. Constitution, or

(2) does it enact the legislation in accordance with the procedures specified in the state's constitution?"

The leading U.S. Supreme Court case interpreting Article II, section 1, clause 2 of the U.S. Constitution is the 1892 case of *McPherson v. Blacker*.[53] In *Blacker*, the U.S. Supreme Court rejected a challenge to Michigan legislation providing for selection of presidential electors by district, as opposed to the statewide winner-take-all method that Michigan had been using prior to 1892 and that had become the national norm. In that case, the Court analyzed the meaning of the word "legislature" as used in Article II and noted that the interpretation of this word was governed by the fundamental law of the state. The U.S. Supreme Court wrote:

"The state does not act by its people in their collective capacity, but through such political agencies as are duly constituted and established. The legislative power is the supreme authority, **except as limited by the constitution of the state**, and the sovereignty of the people is exercised through their representatives in the legislature, **unless by the fundamental law power is elsewhere reposed**. The constitution of the United States frequently refers to the state as a political community, and also in terms to the people of the several states and the citizens of each state. What is forbidden

---

[52] *U.S. Term Limits v. Thornton.* 514 U.S. 779 at 805. 1995.

[53] *McPherson v. Blacker.* 146 U.S. 1. 1892.

or required to be done by a state is forbidden or required of **the legislative power under state constitutions as they exist.**"[54] [Emphasis added]

The possibility that a state's legislative power might be "reposed" in a place other than the state legislature is noteworthy, given that the case was decided when the idea of the citizen-initiative process was an active topic of public debate (just before South Dakota became the first state to adopt the citizen-initiative process in 1898).

Given that the citizen-initiative process is generally considered to be a co-equal grant of authority to that given to the state's legislature, the treatment of the initiative process as a legislative power is consistent with the fundamental law of states that have the initiative process.

There are two cases that have specifically involved the question of whether the word "legislature" in Article II of the U.S. Constitution includes the initiative and referendum processes.[55]

The first case arose as a result of a 1919 law entitled "An act granting to women the right to vote for presidential electors." This law was passed by the two houses of the Maine legislature and presented to the state's Governor. The Governor signed the law. Under the protest-referendum provisions of the Maine Constitution, if a petition protesting a just-enacted law is filed with the signatures of at least 10,000 voters, the new law is temporarily suspended and referred to the voters for their approval or disapproval in a statewide referendum. A petition was circulated and duly filed with the Governor's office concerning this statute. Before proceeding with the referendum, the Governor raised the question of whether the referendum provision of the Maine Constitution applied to legislation involving the manner of appointing the state's presidential electors. Specifically, he propounded the following question to the Justices of the Maine Supreme Judicial Court:

> "Is the effect of the act of the Legislature of Maine of 1919, entitled 'An act granting to women the right to vote for presidential electors,' approved by the Governor on March 28, 1919, suspended by valid written petitions of not less than 10,000 electors, addressed to the Governor and filed in the office of the secretary of state within 90 days after the recess of the Legislature, requesting that it be referred to the people, and should the act be referred to

---

[54] *Id.* at 27.

[55] Court cases specifically interpreting the word "legislature" in Article II in relation to the initiative or referendum process are necessarily rare for several reasons. First, the initiative and referendum processes are only slightly more than 100 years old. Second, the initiative or referendum processes are available in fewer than half of the states. Third, only a handful of the laws that a state enacts in a typical year involve the conduct of elections. Fourth, few new state laws involve the manner of conducting congressional and senatorial elections, and even fewer relate to presidential elections. Fifth, the vast majority of new state laws each year are enacted without the use of either the initiative or referendum processes.

the people as provided in article 4 of the Constitution of Maine, as amended by Amendment 31, adopted September 14, 1908?"

On August 28, 1919, the Maine Supreme Judicial Court unanimously answered this question in the affirmative. Relying extensively on the 1892 decision of the U.S. Supreme Court in *McPherson v. Blacker*,[56] the Maine Supreme Judicial Court wrote:

"The language of section 1, subd. 2, is clear and unambiguous. It admits of no doubt as to where the constitutional power of appointment is vested, namely, in the several states.

'Each state shall appoint in such manner as the Legislature thereof may direct'

are the significant words of the section, and their plain meaning is that **each state is thereby clothed with the absolute power to appoint electors in such manner as it may see fit, without any interference or control on the part of the federal government**, except, of course, in case of attempted discrimination as to race, color, or previous condition of servitude under the fifteenth amendment. The clause,

'in such manner as the Legislature thereof may direct,'

means, simply that **the state shall give expression to its will, as it must, of necessity, through its law-making body, the Legislature**. The will of the state in this respect must be voiced in legislative acts or resolves, which shall prescribe in detail the manner of choosing electors, the qualifications of voters therefor, and the proceedings on the part of the electors when chosen.

"**But these acts and resolves must be passed and become effective in accordance with and in subjection to the Constitution of the state, like all other acts** and resolves having the force of law. **The Legislature was not given in this respect any superiority over or independence from the organic law of the state in force at the time when a given law is passed**. Nor was it designated by the federal Constitution as a mere agency or representative of the people to perform a certain act, as it was under article 5 in ratifying a federal amendment, a point more fully discussed in the answer to the question concerning the federal prohibitory amendment. 107 Atl. 673. **It is simply the ordinary instrumentality of**

---

[56] *McPherson v. Blacker*. 146 U.S. 1. 1892. The *Blacker* case is also discussed in section 2.2.5 and later in this section. The complete opinion of the U.S. Supreme Court in the *Blacker* case is found in appendix O.

the state, the legislative branch of the government, the law-making power, to put into words the will of the state in connection with the choice of presidential electors. The distinction between the function and power of the Legislature in the case under consideration and its function and power as a particular body designated by the federal Constitution to ratify or reject a federal amendment is sharp and clear and must be borne in mind.

"It follows, therefore, that under the provisions of the federal Constitution the state by its legislative direction may establish such a method of choosing its presidential electors as it may see fit, and may change that method from time to time as it may deem advisable; but **the legislative acts both of establishment and of change must always be subject to the provisions of the Constitution of the state in force at the time such acts are passed** and can be valid and effective only when enacted in compliance therewith."[57] [Emphasis added]

The Court continued:

"It is clear that this act, extending this privilege to women, constitutes a change in the method of electing presidential electors. . . .

". . . this state during the century of its existence prior to 1919, had by appropriate legislative act or resolve directed that only male citizens were qualified to vote for presidential electors. By the act of 1919 it has attempted to change that direction, by extending the privilege of suffrage, so far as presidential electors are concerned, to women. Had this act been passed prior to the adoption of the initiative and referendum amendment in 1908, it would have become effective, so far as legal enactment is concerned, without being referred to the people; but now under Amendment 31 such reference must be had, if the necessary steps therefor are taken."

". . . **This is the public statute of a law-making body, and is as fully within the control of the referendum amendment as is any other of the 239 public acts passed at the last session of the Legislature**, excepting, of course, emergency acts. **It is shielded from the jurisdiction of that referendum neither by the state nor by the federal Constitution.** In short, the state, through its Legislature, has taken merely the first step toward effecting a change in the appointment of presidential electors; but, because of the petitions filed, it must await the second step

---

[57] *In re Opinion of the Justices.* 107 A. 705. 1919.

which is the vote of the people. The legislative attempt in this case cannot be fully effective until

'thirty days after the Governor shall have announced by public proclamation that the same has been ratified by a majority of the electors voting thereon at a general or special election.' "[58] [Emphasis added]

Appendix Q contains the entire text of the Court's opinion in *In re Opinion of the Justices.*

When the voters of Maine voted on the suspended law, it was passed by a vote of 88,080 to 30,462.[59]

The second case involving an interpretation of the word "legislature" in Article II of the U.S. Constitution came just prior to the November 2, 2004, presidential election. *Napolitano v. Davidson* involved a federal court challenge to an initiative petition proposing an amendment to the Colorado Constitution to adopt the whole-number proportional approach for choosing the state's presidential electors (section 4.1.14). In that case, a Colorado voter asked that the Colorado Secretary of State be enjoined from holding the election on the proposed amendment. The plaintiff alleged that Amendment 36 violated Article II of the U.S. Constitution in that the voters were attempting to unconstitutionally preempt the role of the "legislature" in connection with the manner of appointing presidential electors.

The Colorado Attorney General defended the Secretary of State. Two representatives of those who had signed initiative petitions to place Amendment 36 on the ballot (the "proponents") were granted the right to intervene in the litigation. Additionally, one Democratic and one Republican candidate for presidential elector in the November 2004 election attempted to intervene.[60]

The Colorado Attorney General unqualifiedly defended the substantive provisions of Amendment 36. In response to the claim that the voters' exercise of the initiative power to allocate presidential electors infringed upon Article II, the Attorney General stated that, when the people of Colorado use the initiative process, they act as the "legislature." Specifically, the State of Colorado took the position that its voters were fully empowered to act, pursuant to Article II, to allocate presidential electors.

---

[58] *Id.*

[59] There was a flurry of activity concerning women's suffrage at the time. The Maine legislature adopted its contested law on women's suffrage in presidential elections on March 28, 1919. Congress proposed the women's suffrage amendment to the U.S. Constitution on June 4, 1919, and sent it to the states for ratification. The Maine Supreme Judicial Court announced its decision on August 28, 1919. The Maine Legislature ratified the proposed federal constitutional amendment on November 5, 1919. Tennessee's ratification on August 18, 1920, brought the 19th Amendment to the U.S. Constitution into effect.

[60] The Elector-Intervenors were permitted to brief each of their legal arguments. After addressing the substance of their arguments, however, Judge Babcock ruled from the bench that their attempted intervention was not authorized, as they lacked standing to participate in the litigation.

"Article II, §1 authorizes each state to act in a lawmaking capacity to select the manner in which it appoints its presidential electors . . . . For example, the lawmaking authority conferred by Article II, §1 encompasses the people's power of referendum when such power is provided by the state constitution. *Cf. Hildebrant*, 241 U.S. at 569.[61] It follows that **the lawmaking authority conferred by Article II, §1 also encompasses the people's power of initiative where the people are empowered by the state constitution to legislate via initiative** . . . .

"**The Proposal (to proportionally allocate presidential electors based on the state's popular vote)** is an initiative by the people of Colorado as authorized by the Colorado Constitution. As such, it **is an exercise of legislative power** for the purpose of appointing presidential electors. **The Proposal, therefore, is authorized by Article II, §1.**"[62] [Emphasis added]

By the time the matter was fully briefed for the court, early voting had commenced in Colorado. Most absentee ballots had been sent to voters. A little more than one week remained until Election Day. On October 26, 2004, Judge Lewis Babcock heard the motions for preliminary injunction, filed by the plaintiff and the elector-intervenors, as well as the motions to dismiss filed by the Colorado Attorney General and the petition's proponents. Judge Babcock denied the former and granted the latter, clearing the way for a vote by the people on Amendment 36 on November 2, 2004.

From the bench, Judge Babcock noted that the matter was not ripe for adjudication, as an actual controversy could be said to exist only if the election were held and a majority of voters approved the proposed change in the method of allocating Colorado's presidential electors. Until that time, any opinion would only be advisory in nature.

Judge Babcock also noted that the issues involved in this case should be resolved in the first instance by the Colorado state courts and, therefore, that it was proper for the federal courts to abstain from intervening in this matter. Indeed, the Colorado challenge to the initiative petition on Amendment 36 was unusual in that it started in federal court. Most challenges to initiative and referendum petitions start in state courts.

In his oral ruling, Judge Babcock noted that the elector-intervenors had argued that Amendment 36 was "patently unconstitutional." The judge expressly stated that this was not the case, but he added that because he did not have to reach the merits

---

[61] Appendix P contains the opinion of the U.S. Supreme Court in the case of *State of Ohio ex rel. Davis v. Hildebrant* cited by the Colorado Attorney General.

[62] The Secretary of State's Combined Motion to Dismiss and Response to Motion for Preliminary Injunction at 21–22, filed in *Napolitano v. Davidson*, Civil Action No. 04–B–2114, D.Colo. (2004).

of the case, his ruling should not be taken as a judicial imprimatur concerning the constitutionality of Amendment 36.

In order to obtain a preliminary injunction, one generally must establish (among other things) that there is a substantial likelihood of prevailing on the merits when the matter goes to trial. This standard generally applies when one seeks to enjoin an election or any part of the election process.[63] The federal district court, in evaluating the motions for preliminary injunction, did not find that either the plaintiff or the elector-intervenors had a substantial likelihood of success on the merits with regard to their argument that Amendment 36 violated Article II.

On November 2, 2004, Amendment 36 was rejected by the voters (section 4.1.14), so none of the legal issues raised by the pre-election lawsuit was subsequently addressed in court. Nonetheless, the voters' right to use the initiative process to change the manner of appointing presidential electors in Colorado was not disturbed by the judiciary.

Long-standing historical practice by the states is consistent with the 1920 decision by the Maine Supreme Judicial Court and the outcome of the 2004 litigation in Colorado concerning the meaning of the word "legislature" in Article II of the U.S. Constitution.

When the U.S. Constitution took effect in 1788, the gubernatorial veto existed in Massachusetts.[64,65]

On November 20, 1788, both chambers of the Massachusetts legislature approved legislation specifying the manner for appointing the state's presidential electors. This legislation was presented to Governor John Hancock—an official who was manifestly not part of the two chambers of the state legislature. Governor Hancock approved the legislation.[66]

In New York, a comprehensive bill was introduced in the Senate on December 13, 1788, for electing presidential electors, U.S. Representatives, and U.S. Senators. The Federalists controlled the state Senate, and the Anti-Federalists controlled the Assembly.

The two houses could not agree on the method by which the legislature would elect presidential electors or U.S. Senators because each house wanted to enhance its own power. The three issues were therefore considered separately.

First, as previously mentioned in section 8.3.5, the legislature passed legislation

---

[63] *Libertarian Party v. Buckley*. 938 F.Supp. 687, 690 (D. Colo. 1997). See also *Chandler v. Miller*. 520 U.S. 305, 311. 1997.

[64] Kole, Edward A. 1999. *The First 13 Constitutions of the First American States*. Haverford, PA: Infinity Publishing.

[65] Kole, Edward A. *The True Intent of the First American Constitutions of 1776–1791*. Haverford, PA: Infinity Publishing.

[66] Smith, Hayward H. 2001. Symposium, law of presidential elections: Issues in the wake of Florida 2000, History of the Article II independent state legislature doctrine, 29 *Florida State University Law Review* 731 at 760.

on January 27, 1789, providing the "manner" of electing U.S. Representatives (including the districts to be used). This bill was submitted to the Council of Revision composed of the Governor, the Chancellor, and the judges of the state supreme court. The Council approved the bill; the bill became law; and the elections of U.S. Representatives were held on March 3, 1789, in accordance with that law.

Second, as previously mentioned in section 8.3.5, the legislature passed a bill in 1789 providing for the manner of electing U.S. Senators. This legislation called for U.S. Senators to be elected by the two houses of the state legislature—without involvement of the Governor (or the Council). This bill specifying the manner of electing U.S. Senators was presented to the Council of Revision. The Council vetoed the bill, and the bill did not become law.

Third, the legislature debated a bill entitled "An act for regulating the manner of appointing electors who are to elect the President, and Vice-President of the United States of America."[67] This legislation specifying the manner of appointing presidential electors was similar to the vetoed bill concerning U.S. Senators. The two chambers of the New York legislature did not reach an agreement on the manner of appointing presidential electors in time for the first presidential election in 1789. Consequently, New York did not appoint any presidential electors in the 1789 presidential election.

Later, on April 12, 1792, a bill was passed by both chambers of the legislature and submitted to the Council in time for the 1792 presidential election. This legislation called for presidential electors to be elected by the two houses of the state legislature—without involvement of the Governor (or the Council). The Council approved this legislation, and New York participated in the 1792 presidential election.[68]

Thus, actual practice in the two states that had the gubernatorial veto at the time when the U.S. Constitution first took effect indicates that, in connection with the state's decision on the manner of appointing presidential electors, the word "legislature" in Article II meant the state's lawmaking process—not just the two chambers of the state legislature.

Present-day practice by the states is consistent with practice from the time when the U.S. Constitution first took effect. Table 8.2 shows the section of each state's current law specifying the manner of appointing presidential electors.[69] In every state, the law was not enacted merely by action of the two chambers of the state legislature but, instead, was presented to the state's Governor for approval or disapproval.

---

[67] DenBoer, Gordon, Brown, Lucy Trumbull, and Hagermann, Charles D. (editors). 1986. *The Documentary History of the First Federal Elections 1788–1790*. Madison, WI: University of Wisconsin Press. Volume 3. Pages 217–435.

[68] An Act for appointing electors in this state for the election of a president and vice president of the United States of America. Passed April 12, 1792. *Laws of New York*. Pages 378–379.

[69] That is, the statewide winner-take-all rule in 48 states and the District of Columbia and the congressional district system in Maine and Nebraska.

Table 8.2 PRESENT-DAY PRACTICE OF THE STATES CONCERNING THE MEANING OF THE WORD "LEGISLATURE" IN CONNECTION WITH STATE LAWS SPECIFYING THE MANNER OF APPOINTING PRESIDENTIAL ELECTORS

STATE	SECTION	WAS THE LEGISLATURE'S BILL PRESENTED TO GOVERNOR?
Alabama	Ala. Code § 17-19-4	Yes
	Ala. Code § 17-19-5	Yes
	Ala. Code § 17-19-6	Yes
Alaska	AK ST § 15.15.450	Yes
Arizona	A.R.S. § 16-650	Yes
Arkansas	Ar. Code § 7-8-304	Yes
California	Cal. Elec. Code § 15505	Yes
Colorado	C.R.S. § 1-11-106	Yes
	Section. 20 of Schedule to Colorado Constitution	No—Provision of 1876 Colorado Constitution
Connecticut	C.G.S. § 9-315	Yes
Delaware	15 Del. C. § 5703	Yes
	15 Del. C. § 5711	Yes
District of Columbia	D.C. Code § 1-1001.10	Yes
Florida	F.S.A. § 9.103.011	Yes
Georgia	Ga. Code Ann., § 21-2-499	Yes
Hawaii	H.R.S. § 2-14-24	Yes
Idaho	ID ST § 34-1215	Yes
Illinois	10 ILCS 5/21-2	Yes
	10 ILCS 5/21-3	Yes
Indiana	IC 3-12-5-7	Yes
Iowa	I.C.A. § 50.45	Yes
Kansas	KS ST § 25-702	Yes
Kentucky	KRS § 118.425	Yes
Louisiana	LSA-R.S. 18:1261	Yes
Maine	21-A M.R.S. § 723	Yes
	21-A M.R.S. § 802	Yes
Maryland	MD Code § 11-601	Yes
Massachusetts	M.G.L.A. 54 § 118	Yes
Michigan	M.C.L.A. 168.42	Yes
Minnesota	M.S.A. § 208.05	Yes
Mississippi	Miss. Code Ann. § 23-15-605	Yes
Missouri	V.A.M.S. 128.070	Yes
Montana	Mt. St. § 13-25-103	Yes
	Mt. St. § 13-1-103	Yes
Nebraska	NE ST § 32-710	Yes
	NE ST § 32-1040	Yes
Nevada	N.R.S. 293.395	Yes
New Hampshire	N.H. Rev. Stat. § 659:81	Yes

Table 8.2 *(continued)*

New Jersey	§ 19:3-26	Yes
New Mexico	N.M.S.A. 1978, § 1-15-14	Yes
New York	§ 12-102	Yes
North Carolina	N.C.G.S.A. § 163-210	Yes
North Dakota	ND ST 16.1-14-01	Yes
Ohio	R.C. § 3505.33	Yes
Oklahoma	26 Okl.St.Ann. § 7-136	Yes
	26 Okl.St.Ann. § 10-103	Yes
Oregon	O.R.S. § 254.065	Yes
Pennsylvania	25 P.S. § 3166	Yes
Rhode Island	§ 17-4-10	Yes
South Carolina	Code 1976 § 7-19-70	Yes
South Dakota	SDCL. § 12-20-35	Yes
Tennessee	T. C. A. § 2-8-110	Yes
Texas	§ 192.005	Yes
Utah	Utah Code 20A-4-304	Yes
	Utah Code 20A-13-302	Yes
Vermont	VT ST T. 17 § 2731	Yes
	VT ST T. 17 § 2592	Yes
Virginia	§ 24.2-675	Yes
	§ 24.2-673	Yes
Washington	Rev. Code Wash. (ARCW) § 29A.56.320[1]	Yes
West Virginia	Article VII, section 3 of West Virginia Constitution[2]	No
Wisconsin	W.S.A. 5.01	Yes
Wyoming	WY ST § 22-17-117	Yes
	WY ST § 22-19-103	

[1] Article III, section 4 of the Washington State Constitution specifies that, in all elections, the candidate "having the highest number of votes shall be declared duly elected."

[2] Article VII, section 3 (ratified November 4, 1902) specifies that, in all elections, the candidate with "the highest number of votes for either of said offices, shall be declared duly elected thereto."

None of the state laws in table 8.2 was enacted by means of the citizen-initiative process; however, there have been numerous initiatives and referenda over the years on provisions of state election laws involving the manner of electing presidential electors.

On February 23, 1917, Maine voted on a "Proposed Constitutional Amendment Granting Suffrage to Women upon Equal Terms with Men." The proposition received 20,604 "yes" vote and 38,838 "no" votes.

In 1919, the Maine Supreme Judicial Court upheld the constitutionality of holding a protest-referendum on a state statute entitled "An act granting to women the right to vote for presidential electors."[70] The voters supported women's suffrage in the 1919 vote.

---

[70] *In re Opinion of the Justices.* 107 Atl. 705. 1919.

In the late 1950s and early 1960s, there was considerable controversy in Michigan (and other states) concerning the coattail effect of votes cast for President on races for lower offices. In particular, Republican county and township officeholders in Michigan sought to eliminate the voter's option to vote for all nominees of one party by casting a single so-called *straight-party* vote. When the Republicans ended 14 years of Democratic control of the Governor's office in 1962, the new Republican Governor and the Republican legislature enacted a statute requiring that voters cast a separate vote for President and a separate vote for each other office on the ballot (the so-called "Massachusetts ballot").[71] A protest-referendum petition was circulated and filed, thereby suspending the statute. The voters rejected the statute in the November 1964 election. Thus, presidential electors remained tethered in Michigan to the party's candidates for other offices (if the voter so desired to cast a straight-party ballot).

Similarly, in 1972, an initiative petition was filed in Maine proposing to change the form of the ballot from party columns to individual offices (the Massachusetts ballot). This proposition passed by a vote of 110,867 to 64,506.

In 1976, an Oklahoma court wrote the following in *McClendon v. Slater* about state legislation concerning the manner of appointing presidential electors:

"It is fundamental that each state and its Legislature, under a Republican form of government possess all power to protect and promote the peace, welfare and safety of its citizens. The only restraints placed thereon are those withdrawn by the United States Constitution and the state's fundamental law. Art. V, ss 1 and 2 express that these reservations or **withdrawals in the people under the Constitution of the State of Oklahoma are two in nature and as explicitly set out in Art. V, s 2 to be the 'initiative' and the 'referendum' processes**. For our purpose, **no other withdrawal or restraint is placed upon the broad fundamental powers of this state's Legislature** by Art. V of the State Constitution."[72] [Emphasis added]

More recently, voters have considered initiatives for instant run-off voting for presidential electors and other offices in Alaska in 2002, requirements for voter identification in Arizona in 2004, and voting by convicted felons in Massachusetts in 2000.

In *Commonwealth ex rel. Dummit v. O'Connell*, the Kentucky Court of Appeals wrote the following in 1944 in connection with a state law permitting soldiers to vote by absentee ballot for U.S. Representatives, U.S. Senators, and presidential electors:

"[T]he legislative process must be completed in the manner prescribed by the State Constitution in order to result in a valid enactment, even though

---

[71] Michigan Public Act 240 of 1964.
[72] *McClendon v. Slater.* 554 P.2d 774, 776 (Ok. 1976).

that enactment be one which the Legislature is authorized by the Federal Constitution to make."[73]

It is important to note that the decision of the U.S. Supreme Court in *Bush v. Gore* in 2000 did nothing to change the meaning of the word "legislature" in the U.S. Constitution in Article II. In that case, the Court settled the dispute over Florida's 2000 presidential vote by halting the manual recount of ballots that the Florida Supreme Court had ordered.

Referring to the 1892 case of *McPherson v. Blacker*, the U.S. Supreme Court wrote in *Bush v. Gore*:[74]

> "The individual citizen has no federal constitutional right to vote for elec-
> tors for the President of the United States unless and until the state legis-
> lature chooses a statewide election as the means to implement its power to
> appoint members of the Electoral College. U.S. Const., Art. II, §1. **This is
> the source for the statement in *McPherson v. Blacker*, 146 U.S. 1, 35
> (1892), that the State legislature's power to select the manner for
> appointing electors is plenary**; it may, if it so chooses, select the electors
> itself, which indeed was the manner used by State legislatures in several
> States for many years after the Framing of our Constitution. Id., at 28–33.
> History has now favored the voter, and in each of the several States the citi-
> zens themselves vote for Presidential electors. When the state legislature
> vests the right to vote for President in its people, the right to vote as the leg-
> islature has prescribed is fundamental; and one source of its fundamental
> nature lies in the equal weight accorded to each vote and the equal dignity
> owed to each voter. The State, of course, after granting the franchise in the
> special context of Article II, can take back the power to appoint electors.
> See Id., at 35."[75] [Emphasis added]

The U.S. Supreme Court did not change the prevailing definition of the word "legis-lature" in *Bush v. Gore* but, instead, identified the source (i.e., *McPherson v. Blacker*) of the undisputed statement that the "legislature" is indeed supreme in matters of choosing the manner of appointing a state's presidential electors. The issues in *Bush v. Gore* did not concern the way that Florida's election code was originally enacted (e.g., whether the election code was presented to the Governor for approval or dis-approval or whether the voters had perhaps enacted the election code through the citizen-initiative process). Indeed, the Florida election code at issue in *Bush v. Gore* was not enacted by the legislature alone but, instead, was enacted by the ordinary

---

[73] *Commonwealth ex rel. Dummit v. O'Connell.* 181 S.W.2d 691, 694 (Ky. Ct. App. 1944).

[74] *McPherson v. Blacker.* 146 U.S. 1 at 27. 1892.

[75] *Bush v. Gore.* 531 U.S. 98 at 104. 2000.

lawmaking process involving presentation of the bill to the Governor for approval or disapproval (as shown in table 8.2).

Rather, *Bush v. Gore* was concerned with the breadth of authority of the Florida Supreme Court to establish a recount process *not found in Florida's pre-existing legislation* after the voters had cast their votes on November 7, 2000. The U.S. Supreme Court specifically identified two issues to be decided in *Bush v. Gore*, namely

(1) "whether the Florida Supreme Court established new standards for resolving Presidential election contests, thereby violating Art. II, §1, cl. 2, of the United States Constitution and failing to comply with 3 U.S.C. §5, . . . "[76] and

(2) "whether the use of standardless manual recounts violates the Equal Protection and Due Process Clauses."[77]

In reaching its decision in *Bush v. Gore*, the Court referred to the "safe harbor" provision (3 U.S.C. §5).

> "If any State shall have provided, **by laws enacted prior to the day fixed for the appointment of the electors**, for its final determination of any controversy or contest concerning the appointment of all or any of the electors of such State, by judicial or other methods or procedures, and such determination shall have been made at least six days before the time fixed for the meeting of the electors, such determination made pursuant to such law so existing on said day, and made at least six days prior to said time of meeting of the electors, shall be conclusive, and shall govern in the counting of the electoral votes as provided in the Constitution, and as hereinafter regulated, so far as the ascertainment of the electors appointed by such State is concerned."[78] [Emphasis added]

The Court ruled (on December 12, 2000) that insufficient time remained to conduct a constitutional recount before the meeting of the Electoral College scheduled for December 18, 2000. Because there was insufficient time for a constitutional recount, Bush's 537-vote plurality that had already been certified under terms of the Florida election code was allowed to stand.[79]

In *Bush v. Gore*, the Supreme Court did not address the issue of whether the Florida voters could substitute themselves for the legislature, through the citizen-initiative process or the protest-referendum process, concerning the manner of

---

[76] *Bush v. Gore*. 531 U.S. 98 at 103. 2000. See Appendix B for the complete wording of the so-called "safe harbor" provision—Title 3, Chapter 1, section 5 of the United States Code.

[77] *Bush v. Gore*. 531 U.S. 98 at 103. 2000.

[78] Title 3, chapter 1, section 5 of the United States Code.

[79] *Bush v. Gore*. 531 U.S. 98 at 110. 2000.

choosing presidential electors in Florida. In fact, the 1892 case (*McPherson v. Blacker*) cited by the Court in *Bush v. Gore* specifically mentioned the possibility that a state's legislative power might be "reposed" in a place other than the state legislature.

> **"The legislative power is the supreme authority, except as limited by the constitution of the state**, and the sovereignty of the people is exercised through their representatives in the legislature, **unless by the fundamental law power is elsewhere reposed**."[80] [Emphasis added]

The citizen-initiative process—representing the authority of the citizens of a state to make their own laws—is consistent with the two exceptions contained in *McPherson v. Blacker*, namely that the legislature's power is supreme "except as limited by the constitution of the state" and except when "power is elsewhere reposed" "by the [state's] fundamental law." Initiatives are limitations on the power of the legislature because they enable the voters to displace the legislature by enacting laws of their own design. The initiative process is established by the state's fundamental law (i.e., constitution). Indeed, initiatives are the obvious alternative place where the state's legislative power might be "elsewhere reposed."

The citizen-initiative process has consistently been viewed as a limitation on the state legislature. For example, in 1964, *Lucas v. Forty-Fourth General Assembly*[81] approved the use of the initiative to "obtain relief against alleged malapportionment" of state legislative seats. In 1975, *Chapman v. Meier*[82] concerned the adoption of an initiative substituting the voters' will for the legislature's unwillingness to act. As a reservation of legislative power by the voters, the initiative process is necessarily an element of the fundamental law. In *Eastlake v. Forest City Enterprises, Inc.*, the U.S. Supreme Court wrote in 1976:

> "Under our constitutional assumptions, all power derives from the people, who can delegate it to representative instruments which they create. See e.g., *The Federalist*, No. 39 (J. Madison). **In establishing legislative bodies, the people can reserve to themselves power to deal directly with matters which might otherwise be assigned to the legislature**."[83,84] [Emphasis added]

In commenting on *Bush v. Gore* in *Breaking the Deadlock*, Judge Richard Posner wrote:

[80] *McPherson v. Blacker*. 146 U.S. 1 at 25. 1892.

[81] *Lucas v. Forty-Fourth General Assembly*. 377 U.S. 713 at 732–733. 1964.

[82] *Chapman v. Meier*. 420 U.S. 1 at 21. 1975.

[83] *Eastlake v. Forest City Enterprises, Inc.* 426 U.S. 668 at 672. 1976.

[84] *Cf. James v. Valtierra*, 401 U.S. 137, 141 (1971) "[p]rovisions for referendums demonstrate devotion to democracy."

"[I]t is important that the approach be understood, and not rejected out of hand as meaning, for example, that the governor of a state cannot veto a proposed law on the appointment of the state's Presidential electors or that the state's supreme court cannot invalidate an election law as unconstitutional. **Article II does not regulate the process by which state legislation is enacted and validated**, any more than it precludes interpretation. **But once the law governing appointment of the state's presidential electors is duly enacted**, upheld, and interpreted, (so far as interpretation is necessary to fill gaps and dispel ambiguities), the legislature has spoken and **the other branches of the state government must back off** . . . ."[85] [Emphasis added]

Bush v. Gore was not about "the process by which state legislation is enacted" but, instead, was about the extent to which the Florida Supreme Court should "back off."

In summary, present-day practice by the states, actual practice by the states at the time that the U.S. Constitution took effect, legal commentary, and court decisions are consistent in supporting the view that the word "legislature" in Article II, section 1, clause 2 of the U.S. Constitution (the sixth entry in table 8.1) means the state's lawmaking process—a process that includes the state's Governor and the state's voters in states having citizen-initiative and protest-referendum procedures.

As Kirby stated in 1962,

"it is safe to assume that state legislatures are limited by constitutional provisions for veto, referendum, and initiative in prescribing the manner of choosing presidential electors."[86]

The wording "as the _____ may direct" also appears in the 23rd Amendment (ratified in 1961) stating:

"The District constituting the seat of government of the United States shall appoint in such manner **as the Congress may direct**: A number of electors of President and Vice President. . . ." [Emphasis added].

In implementing the 23rd Amendment, the congressional legislation establishing the winner-take-all rule for the District of Columbia was presented to the President.

---

[85] Posner, Richard A. 2001. *Breaking the Deadlock: The 2000 Election, the Constitution, and the Courts.* Princeton, NJ: Princeton University Press. Page 111.

[86] Kirby, J. 1962. Limitations on the powers of the state legislatures over presidential elections. 27 *Law and Contemporary Problems* 495 at 504.

8.3.7. CHOOSING THE MANNER OF CONDUCTING A POPULAR ELECTION TO FILL A U.S. SENATE VACANCY

The 17th Amendment (providing for popular election of U.S. Senators) was ratified in 1913—in the midst of the period (1898–1918) when 19 states were adopting the initiative and referendum processes.[87,88] The 17th Amendment provides:

> "When vacancies happen in the representation of any State in the Senate, the executive authority of such State shall issue writs of election to fill such vacancies: Provided, That the legislature of any State may empower the executive thereof to make temporary appointments until the people fill the vacancies by election **as the legislature may direct**." [Emphasis added]

The phrase "as the legislature may direct" in the 17th Amendment parallels the wording of Article II of the U.S. Constitution concerning presidential electors, namely

> "Each State shall appoint, in such Manner **as the Legislature thereof may direct**, a Number of Electors, equal to the whole Number of Senators and Representatives to which the State may be entitled in the Congress . . . ."[89] [Emphasis added]

Moreover, the phrase "as the legislature may direct" in the 17th Amendment and Article II parallels the wording of Article I, section 4, clause 1 of the U.S. Constitution concerning the "manner" of holding elections for U.S. Representatives and Senators, namely

> "The Times, Places and Manner of holding Elections for Senators and Representatives, shall be **prescribed in each State by the Legislature thereof**; but the Congress may at any time by Law make or alter such Regulations, except as to the Places of chusing Senators." [Emphasis added]

The practice of the states in enacting laws to implement the 17th Amendment is shown in table 8.3. This table shows the section of each state's law that specifies the manner of holding the popular election to fill a vacancy in the U.S. Senate under the 17th Amendment and the section that specifies each state's law that specifies whether the Governor is empowered to make temporary appointments to the U.S. Senate prior to the vacancy-filling election. As can be seen, in no state was enactment of the implementing legislation for the 17th Amendment accomplished merely by action of the two chambers of the legislature. Instead, the actual practice of all states has been to treat the word "legislature" in the 17th Amendment to mean the "lawmaking process." The

---

[87] Zimmerman, Joseph F. 1999. *The Initiative: Citizen Law-Making*. Westport, CT: Praeger.

[88] Zimmerman, Joseph F. 1997. *The Referendum: The People Decide Public Policy*. Westport, CT: Praeger.

[89] U.S. Constitution. Article II, section 1, clause 2.

Table 8.3 PRACTICE BY THE STATES CONCERNING THE MEANING OF THE WORD "LEGISLATURE" IN CONNECTION WITH STATE LAWS SPECIFYING THE IMPLEMENTATION OF THE 17TH AMENDMENT

STATE	SECTIONS	WAS THE LEGISLATURE'S BILL PRESENTED TO THE STATE'S GOVERNOR?
Alabama	Ala. Code § 36-9-7	Yes
	Ala. Code § 36-9-8	Yes
Alaska	AK ST § 15.40.140	No—Citizen-initiative process
	AK ST § 15.40.145	
Arizona	A.R.S. § 16-222	Yes
Arkansas	Const. Am. 29, § 1	No—Citizen-initiative process
California	Cal. Elec. Code § 10720	Yes
Colorado	C.R.S.A. § 1-12-201	Yes
Connecticut	C.G.S.A. § 9-211	Yes
Delaware	DE ST TI 15 § 7321	Yes
Florida	F.S.A. § 100.161	Yes
Georgia	Ga. Code Ann., § 21-2-542	Yes
Hawaii	HI ST § 17-1	Yes
Idaho	ID ST § 59-910	Yes
Illinois	10 ILCS 5/25-8	Yes
Indiana	IC 3-13-3-1	Yes
Iowa	I.C.A. § 69.8	Yes
Kansas	KS ST § 25-318	Yes
Kentucky	KRS § 63.200	Yes
Louisiana	LSA-R.S. 18:1278	Yes
Maine	21-A M.R.S.A. § 391	Yes
Maryland	MD Code, Election Law, § 8-602	Yes
Massachusetts	M.G.L.A. 54 § 140	Yes
Michigan	M.C.L.A. 168.105	Yes
Minnesota	M.S.A. § 204D.28	Yes
Mississippi	Miss. Code Ann. § 23-15-855	Yes
Missouri	V.A.M.S. 105.040	Yes
Montana	Mt. St. 13-25-202	Yes
Nebraska	NE ST § 32-565	Yes
Nevada	N.R.S. 304.030	Yes
New Hampshire	N.H. Rev. Stat. § 661:5	Yes
New Jersey	§ 19:3-26	Yes
New Mexico	N.M.S.A. 1978, § 1-15-14	Yes
New York	Mckinney's Consolidated Laws of New York, Chapter 47, Article 3	Yes
North Carolina	N.C.G.S.A. § 163-12	Yes
North Dakota	ND ST 16.1-13-08	Yes
Ohio	R.C. § 3521.02	Yes

Table 8.3 *(continued)*

STATE	SECTIONS	WAS THE LEGISLATURE'S BILL PRESENTED TO THE STATE'S GOVERNOR?
Oklahoma	26 Okl. St.Ann. § 12-101	Yes
Oregon	O.R.S. § 188.120	Yes
Pennsylvania	25 P.S. § 2776	Yes
Rhode Island	§ 17-4-9	Yes
South Carolina	Code 1976 § 7-19-20	Yes
South Dakota	SDCL. § 12-11-4	Yes
	SDCL. § 12-11-5	Yes
Tennessee	T. C. A. § 2-16-101	Yes
Texas	§ 204.001	Yes
	§ 204.002	Yes
	§ 204.003	Yes
	§ 204.004	Yes
Utah	§ 20A-1-502	Yes
Vermont	VT ST T. 17 § 2621	Yes
	VT ST T. 17 § 2622	Yes
Virginia	§ 24.2-207	Yes
Washington	RCW 29A.28.030	Yes
	RCW 29A.28.041	Yes
West Virginia	W. Va. Code, § 3-10-3	Yes
Wisconsin	W.S.A. 17.18	Yes
	W.S.A. 8.50	Yes
Wyoming	WY ST § 22-18-111	Yes

"lawmaking process" concerning the 17th Amendment has involved legislative bills that have been presented to the state's Governor for approval or disapproval and the use of the citizen-initiative process (in the cases of Arkansas in 1938 and Alaska in 2004).

Arkansas's implementation of the 17th Amendment is noteworthy for two reasons.

First, Arkansas's current implementation of the 17th Amendment was put on the ballot (on November 8, 1938) as a result of a citizen-initiative petition—not by the legislature.

Second, Arkansas's implementation of the 17th Amendment was in the form of an amendment to the state constitution as distinguished from a statutory enactment.

In other words, neither the "legislature" nor "legislation" was involved in implementing the 17th Amendment in Arkansas.[90]

The November 2004 elections provided two additional examples of the interpretation given to the word "legislature" by the states in connection with the 17th Amendment.

When U.S. Senator John Kerry was running for President in 2004, the Democratic–controlled legislature in Massachusetts passed a bill changing the procedure for filling

---

[90] See the discussion of the Arizona Independent Redistricting Commission created in the November 2000 election and a similar commission created in California in the 2008 election in section 8.3.5.

U.S. Senate vacancies in Massachusetts. Under the pre-existing Massachusetts law, the Governor had the power to appoint a temporary replacement who would serve until the next general election. In other words, if Democrat Kerry had won the presidency in November 2004, then the Republican Governor of Massachusetts would have been able to appoint a Republican to serve in the then-closely-divided U.S. Senate until November 2006 (almost two full years). Under the bill that the legislature passed, the Senate seat would remain vacant until a special election could be held (between 145 and 160 days after the creation of the vacancy). That is, a special Senate election would have been held in Massachusetts in the spring of 2005 if Kerry had been elected President. The legislative bill was presented to Governor Mitt Romney for his approval or disapproval. Thus, the constitutional phrase "as the Legislature thereof may direct" was interpreted to mean the law-making process. Predictably, the Republican Governor vetoed the bill passed by the Democratic legislature. As it happened, the legislature overrode the Governor's veto, and the bill became law.

The election of U.S. Senator Frank Murkowski as Governor of Alaska in 2002 created a vacancy in the U.S. Senate. Murkowski appointed his daughter Lisa to serve the last two years of his Senate term, thereby focusing public attention on the operation of the 17th Amendment in Alaska. An initiative petition was circulated and filed to require that, in the future, a vacancy in the U.S. Senate would remain vacant until a special election could be called. The Alaska Constitution enables the legislature to keep an initiative proposition off the ballot if the legislature responds to the petition by enacting a "substantially" similar law. The legislature's bill resembled the proposal in the petition in that it required a special election to fill a Senate vacancy; however, the legislature's bill differed from the petition in that it authorized the Governor to appoint a temporary Senator prior to the popular election. This legislature's bill was presented to the Governor for his approval or disapproval, and he signed it. The petition's sponsors protested that the legislature's alternative approach was not substantially the same as the initiative proposition because it gave the Governor's appointee the advantage of incumbency in the special election.

On August 20, 2004, the Alaska Supreme Court decided that the legislature's alternative was not substantially the same as the proposition in the initiative petition.[91] At the same time, the Court refused to consider a pre-election challenge to the use of the citizen-initiative process to change the manner of filling a vacancy in the U.S. Senate on the grounds that the U.S. Constitution required the "legislature" to make the decision. The Alaska Supreme Court allowed the voters to vote on the proposition in the petition in the November 2004 election. The voters then enacted the proposition in the petition (Ballot Measure 4) in the November 2004 election by a margin of 165,017 to 131,821.[92]

---

[91] *State of Alaska et al. v. Trust the People Initiative Committee.* Supreme Court Order No. S–11288.

[92] In the same election, the voters elected Lisa Murkowski to a full six-year term in the Senate by a margin of 149,446 to 139,878.

That is, the phrase "as the Legislature thereof may direct" in the 17th Amendment (the seventh entry in table 8.1) has been interpreted as the state's entire law-making process—not action by the two chambers of state's legislature.

8.3.8. EMPOWERING THE GOVERNOR TO TEMPORARILY FILL A U.S. SENATE VACANCY UNTIL A POPULAR ELECTION IS HELD

The word "legislature" also appears in the 17th Amendment in connection with temporary appointments to the U.S. Senate.

> "When vacancies happen in the representation of any State in the Senate, the executive authority of such State shall issue writs of election to fill such vacancies: Provided, That **the legislature of any State may empower the executive thereof to make temporary appointments until the people fill the vacancies by election** as the legislature may direct." [Emphasis added]

As shown in table 8.3, the word "legislature" in the 17th Amendment (the eighth entry in table 8.1) has meant the state's entire law-making process—not action by the two chambers of a state's legislature.

8.3.9. CONSENTING TO THE FEDERAL PURCHASE OF ENCLAVES

The U.S. Constitution empowers Congress to exercise exclusive

> "... Authority over all Places purchased by the **Consent of the Legislature** of the State in which the Same shall be, for the Erection of Forts, Magazines, Arsenals, dock-Yards, and other needful Buildings."[93] [Emphasis added]

Prior to ratification of the U.S. Constitution, the states had been paying for the operation and maintenance of 13 lighthouses. Moreover, in 1789, several additional lighthouses were under construction. When the first Congress met in 1789, it offered to fund the operation and maintenance of all the lighthouses; however, Congress insisted that the sites become federal enclaves. Accordingly, Congress passed the Lighthouse Act on August 7, 1789, offering permanent funding for lighthouses on the condition that the state "legislatures" consented to the creation of the federal enclaves by August 15, 1790.[94] The Constitution required consent from the state "legislatures" and thus set the stage for a contemporary interpretation of the word "legislature" in the Enclaves Clause of the U.S. Constitution. The question was whether the word "legislature" referred to the two chambers of the state legislature or "the lawmaking process."

At the time when the U.S. Constitution took effect, the gubernatorial veto existed

---

[93] U.S. Constitution. Article I, section 9, clause 17.

[94] Grace, Adam S. 2005. *Federal-State "Negotiations" over Federal Enclaves in the Early Republic: Finding Solutions to Constitutional Problems at the Birth of the Lighthouse System.* Berkeley, CA: Berkeley Electronic Press. Working Paper 509. http://law.bepress.com/expresso/eps/509. Pages 1–11.

in Massachusetts and New York.[95] Both chambers of the legislatures of Massachusetts and New York approved legislation consenting to the cession of their lighthouses. These legislative bills were then presented, respectively, to the Governor of Massachusetts (an official who was manifestly not part of the state legislature) and the New York Council of Revision (a body composed of the Governor and other officials who were manifestly not part of the state legislature). The Massachusetts legislation became law on June 10, 1790,[96] and the New York legislation became law on February 3, 1790.[97] Cession legislation was similarly enacted in New York in connection with the construction of a new lighthouse at Montauk in 1792—with the legislative bill again being presented to the Governor and the Council.[98]

Thus, practice by the states in connection with the ninth entry in table 8.1 has interpreted the word "legislature" to mean the state's law-making process in connection with the consent by a state to the acquisition of enclaves by the federal government (the ninth entry in table 8.1).

8.3.10. CONSENTING TO THE FORMATION OF NEW STATES FROM TERRITORY OF EXISTING STATES

The U.S. Constitution provides:

> ". . . No new State shall be formed or erected within the Jurisdiction of any other State; nor any State be formed by the Junction of two or more States, or Parts of States, without the **Consent of the Legislatures** of the States concerned as well as of the Congress."[99] [Emphasis added]

As of the time of the writing of this edition, the authors believe that this usage of the word "legislature" refers to the state's law-making process in connection with the consent of a state to the formation of a new state from its territory (the 10th entry in table 8.1).

8.3.11. REQUESTING FEDERAL MILITARY ASSISTANCE TO QUELL DOMESTIC VIOLENCE

The U.S. Constitution provides:

> "The United States shall guarantee to every State in this Union a Republican Form of Government, and shall protect each of them against Invasion; and on **Application of the Legislature**, or of the Executive (when the

---

[95] Kole, Edward A. 1999. *The First 13 Constitutions of the First American States.* Haverford, PA: Infinity Publishing.

[96] Ch. 4, 1790 Massachusetts Laws 77.

[97] New York, Ch. 3, February 3, 1790.

[98] New York, Ch. 4, December 18, 1792.

[99] U.S. Constitution. Article IV, section 3, clause 1.

Legislature cannot be convened) against domestic Violence."[100] [Emphasis added]

This provision of the U.S. Constitution (the Guarantee Clause) specifically creates a contrast between the state's "executive" and the "legislature."

The Guarantee Clause has been only rarely invoked. On April 4, 1842, Rhode Island Governor Samuel Ward King requested that President John Tyler provide federal military aid to quell a potential insurrection, known as the Dorr Rebellion, in which an alternative government for Rhode Island was attempting to gain recognition and legitimacy. The Governor's request was not accompanied by any action by the state legislature. President Tyler took no action in response to the Governor's request.[101]

Then, in 1844, the Freeholders' legislature of Rhode Island passed a resolution requesting that President John Tyler provide federal military aid to quell the Dorrites. Again, President Tyler took no action in response to the Legislature's resolution.[102]

The Guarantee Clause of the U.S. Constitution distinguishes the state's "legislature" from the state's Governor. These two requests concerning the Dorr Rebellion in Rhode Island suggest that the word "legislature" in Article IV, section 4 of the U.S. Constitution (the 11th entry in table 8.1) was interpreted, in Rhode Island in the 1840s, to mean the two chambers of the state legislature.

8.3.12. PRE-ELECTION CHALLENGES VERSUS POST-ELECTION LITIGATION

The use of the citizen-initiative process to enact the National Popular Vote compact can be challenged either before or after the statewide vote on the statute proposed by a petition.

Both state and federal courts have been reluctant, as a general principle, to intervene in the citizen-initiative process prior to enactment of a proposition by the voters. In "Pre-Election Judicial Review of Initiatives and Referendums," James Gordon and David Magleby wrote:

> "Most courts will not entertain a challenge to a measure's substantive validity before the election. A minority of courts, however, are willing to conduct such review. Arguably, pre-election review of a measure's substantive validity involves issuing an advisory opinion, violates ripeness requirements and the policy of avoiding unnecessary constitutional questions, and is an unwarranted judicial intrusion into a legislative process." [103]

---

[100] U.S. Constitution. Article IV, section 4.

[101] Wiecek, William M. 1972. *The Guarantee Clause of the U.S. Constitution.* Ithaca, NY: Cornell University Press. Page 105.

[102] Gettleman, Marvin E. 1973. *The Dorr Rebellion: A Study in American Radicalism 1833–1849.* New York: NY: Random House. Page 105.

[103] Gordon, James D., and Magleby, David B. 1989. Pre-Election judicial review of initiatives and referendums. 64 *Notre Dame Law Review* 298–320 at 303.

The numerous practical difficulties with pre-election judicial challenges to ballot propositions partly explain judicial reluctance to such challenges. As Justice William O. Douglas wrote in his concurring opinion in *Ely v. Klahr* in 1971:

> "We are plagued with election cases coming here on the eve of election, with the remaining time so short we do not have the days needed for oral argument and for reflection on the serious problems that are usually presented."[104]

The practical difficulties associated with pre-election challenges have been compounded in recent years by the increasing use of absentee voting and early voting (where walk-in polling places are operated at designated locations, such as government buildings, for several weeks prior to election day).

The general reluctance of courts to prevent a vote on ballot measures proposed by the citizen-initiative process is illustrated by the efforts in the early 1990s to enact state constitutional amendments imposing term limits on members of the U.S. House of Representatives and U.S. Senate. Many questioned whether the proposed state constitutional amendments were consistent with the specific federal constitutional provisions establishing qualifications for these federal offices. Despite pre-election legal challenges to the initiative petitions in some states, in no instance did the courts prevent a vote by the people on the grounds that congressional term limits violated the U.S. Constitution. It was only after these propositions had been enacted by the voters in a number of states that the courts examined the constitutional validity of the ballot propositions. In 1995, the U.S. Supreme Court held that term limits on members of the U.S. House of Representatives and U.S. Senate could not be imposed at the state level.[105]

More recently, the California Supreme Court refused, on July 26, 2005, to remove an initiative proposition from the ballot in California's November 8, 2005, statewide election. The court order stated:

> "The stay issued by the Court of Appeal as part of its July 22, 2005, decision, restraining the Secretary of State from taking any steps, pending the finality of the Court of Appeal's decision, to place Proposition 80 in the ballot pamphlet or on the ballot of the special election to be held on November 8, 2005, is vacated. As the Court of Appeal recognized, California authorities establish that
>
> > 'it is usually more appropriate to review constitutional and other challenges to ballot propositions or initiative measures after an election rather than to disrupt the electoral process by preventing the exercise of

---

[104] *Ely v. Klahr.* 403 U.S. 103 at 120–121. 1971.
[105] *U.S. Term Limits v. Thornton.* 514 U.S. 779. 1995.

the people's franchise, in the absence of some clear showing of invalidity.' (*Brosnahan v. Eu* (1982) 31 Cal.3d 1, 4.)

"Because, unlike the Court of Appeal, at this point we cannot say that it is clear that article XII, section 5, of the California Constitution precludes the enactment of Proposition 80 as an initiative measure, we conclude that the validity of Proposition 80 need not and should not be determined prior to the November 8, 2005 election. Accordingly, the Secretary of State and other public officials are directed to proceed with all the required steps to place Proposition 80 in the ballot pamphlet and on the ballot of the special election to be held on November 8, 2005. After that election, we shall determine whether to retain jurisdiction in this matter and resolve the issues raised in the petition."[106]

8.3.13. CURABILITY OF INVALIDITY OF A PARTICULAR BALLOT MEASURE

Were a court decision to invalidate a particular ballot measure adopting the National Popular Vote Compact on state constitutional grounds applicable to one state or on federal constitutional grounds applicable to all states, the fact would remain that the people would have spoken in favor of nationwide popular election of the President. The favorable public vote would remain as a political fact. In that event, practical political considerations suggest that legislators in any affected state would be willing to correct the technical defect concerning the method of enactment of the compact in their state by re-enacting the compact in the legislature. The National Popular Vote compact is not inherently adverse to the interests of state legislators, and there is no reason that state legislators are, as a group, any less likely to favor the concept of nationwide popular election of the President than the public at large. It should, therefore, be possible to re-enact the compact in the legislatures of many or all states where the voters spoke in favor of the compact. Regardless of the extent to which the citizen-initiative process may be used to spotlight the issue of the nationwide popular election of the President, state legislatures must necessarily provide most of the support needed to bring the National Popular Vote compact into effect.

---

[106] *Independent Energy Producers Association et al., Petitioners, v. Bruce McPherson, as Secretary of State, etc., Respondent; Robert Finkelstein et al., Real Parties in Interest.* Case number S135819. July 26, 2005.

9 | Responses to Myths about the National Popular Vote Compact

This chapter provides responses to 131 myths about the National Popular Vote plan. The 131 myths are organized into 40 groups as follows:

The 131 myths about the National Popular Vote plan discussed in this chapter are organized into 40 groups as follows:

9.1. MYTHS ABOUT THE U.S. CONSTITUTION

9.1.1. MYTH: A federal constitutional amendment is necessary for changing the current method of electing the President.

QUICK ANSWER:

- The U.S. Constitution gives the states the "exclusive" and "plenary" power to choose the method of awarding their electoral votes.
- The shortcomings of the current system of electing the President stem from state winner-take-all statutes that award all of a state's electoral votes to the candidate who receives the most popular votes within each separate state.
- The state-by-state winner-take-all method of awarding electoral votes is not in the U.S. Constitution. It was not debated at the Constitutional Convention. It was not discussed in the *Federalist Papers*.

- The winner-take-all rule was used by only three states in the nation's first presidential election in 1789 (all of which abandoned it by 1800). The Founders were dead for decades before the winner-take-all rule became the predominant method of awarding electoral votes.
- Maine and Nebraska currently award electoral votes by congressional district—a reminder that the method of awarding electoral votes is a state decision.
- The winner-take-all rule is used today in 48 of the 50 states because it was enacted as a state statute in those states, under the same provision of the U.S. Constitution (empowering the states to choose the method of awarding their electoral votes) being used to enact the National Popular Vote plan.
- Winner-take-all statutes may be repealed in the same way they were enacted—namely, through each state's process for enacting and repealing state laws. Therefore, a federal constitutional amendment is not necessary to change the state-by-state winner-take-all method of awarding electoral votes.
- The Constitution's grant of exclusive power to the states to decide how presidential elections are conducted was not a historical accident or mistake, but was intended as a "check and balance" on a sitting President who, in conjunction with a compliant Congress, might manipulate election rules to perpetuate himself in office.

MORE DETAILED ANSWER:

It is important to recognize what the U.S. Constitution says—and does not say—about electing the President.

Article II, section 1, clause 2 of the U.S. Constitution provides:

> "Each State shall appoint, in such Manner **as the Legislature thereof may direct**, a Number of Electors. . . ."[1] [Emphasis added]

These 17 words are the Constitution's delegation of power to the states concerning how they may award their electoral votes.

In 1787, the delegates to the Constitutional Convention debated the method of electing the President on 22 separate days and held 30 separate votes on the topic.

One of the major points of contention at the Convention was whether the people should be allowed to vote for President.

On four separate occasions, the Convention voted (and then reversed its decision) that Congress should choose the President—that is, the people would not be allowed to vote for President. On another occasion, the delegates voted that the state legisla-

---

[1] The complete wording of clause 2 is "Each State shall appoint, in such Manner as the Legislature thereof may direct, a Number of Electors, equal to the whole Number of Senators and Representatives to which the State may be entitled in the Congress: but no Senator or Representative, or Person holding an Office of Trust or Profit under the United States, shall be appointed an Elector."

tures would choose the President. At one point, the delegates considered empowering state Governors to choose the President.[2]

Even when the delegates eventually decided—toward the end of the Constitutional Convention—that the President would be elected by presidential electors (collectively called the "Electoral College"), the Founders were still unable to agree on how the presidential electors would be chosen. They left several politically significant questions undecided, including:

- Should the presidential electors be chosen directly by the people—analogous to the method of electing members of the U.S. House of Representatives?
- Should the presidential electors be chosen by the state legislatures—analogous to the method of appointment of U.S. Senators by state legislatures that was specified in the original Constitution?[3]
- Should the presidential electors be chosen by some other method (perhaps by Governors)?

In the end—unable to agree upon any particular method for selecting presidential electors—the Founding Fathers adopted the language contained in section 1 of Article II, leaving the decision to the states.

The eventual wording in section 1 of Article II ("as the Legislature . . . may direct") is unqualified. It does not encourage, discourage, require, or prohibit the use of any particular method for awarding a state's electoral votes.

If the legislature decides to give the people a vote for President, the Constitution does not specify whether the presidential electors should be elected statewide, in single-member presidential elector districts, in single-member congressional districts, or in multi-member districts.

If the legislature decides against giving the people a vote for President, the Constitution does not specify whether the presidential electors should be appointed by the Governor, the Governor and his cabinet, by the Governor and the lower house of the state legislature, by both houses of the legislature sitting together in a joint convention, or by both houses of the legislature using a concurrent resolution.[4]

Indeed, *all* of the above methods have been used in our country's history.

The most salient feature of our nation's current method of electing the President—the state-by-state winner-take-all method of awarding electoral votes—was never debated at the Constitutional Convention. It was never voted upon at the Constitutional Convention. It appears nowhere in the U.S. Constitution. It was never mentioned in

---

[2] Edwards, George C. III. 2004. *Why the Electoral College Is Bad for America.* New Haven, CT: Yale University Press.

[3] The 17th Amendment (ratified in 1913) provided for popular election of U.S. Senators.

[4] When a concurrent resolution is used, the two houses of the legislature meet separately, and a majority of both houses must agree on a common slate of presidential electors. When both houses of the legislature meet in a joint convention, a majority of the joint convention controls the choice of presidential electors. Use of a concurrent resolution makes the individual members of the smaller body (i.e., the state Senate) relatively more important.

the *Federalist Papers*. It was not until the 11th presidential election (1828) that the winner-take-all rule was used by a majority of the states. Indeed, the Founders were long dead before the winner-take-all rule became the predominant method of awarding electoral votes.

Under the winner-take-all rule (also known as the "unit rule" or "general ticket"), a plurality[5] of a state's voters are empowered to choose all of a state's presidential electors.

When the Founding Fathers returned from the Constitutional Convention in Philadelphia to organize the nation's first presidential election in 1789, only three states chose to employ the winner-take-all method for awarding their electoral votes.[6]

Today, the winner-take-all method of awarding electoral votes is used in 48 of the 50 states and the District of Columbia.[7]

Maine and Nebraska currently elect presidential electors by congressional district (with two electors-at-large).

The U.S. Supreme Court has repeatedly characterized the authority of the states over the manner of awarding their electoral votes as "exclusive" and "plenary."

The leading case on the awarding of electoral votes is the 1892 case of *McPherson v. Blacker*. The U.S. Supreme Court ruled:

> **"The constitution does not provide that the appointment of electors** shall be by popular vote, nor that the electors **shall be voted for upon a general ticket [the winner-take-all rule]** nor that the majority of those who exercise the elective franchise can alone choose the electors. It recognizes that the people act through their representatives in the legislature, and **leaves it to the legislature exclusively to define the method** of effecting the object. The framers of the constitution employed words in their natural sense; and, where they are plain and clear, resort to collateral aids to interpretation is unnecessary, and cannot be indulged in to narrow or enlarge the text. . . .

---

[5] In some early versions of the winner-take-all rule, an absolute majority of the state's voters was required to choose presidential electors.

[6] The three states that used the winner-take-all rule in 1789 were New Hampshire, Pennsylvania, and Maryland. All three states abandoned it by 1800, but later returned to it. In the version of the winner-take-all rule that was used in 1789 (and, indeed, until the middle of the 20th century in most states), each voter was allowed to cast as many votes as the state's number of presidential electors. Voting for individual presidential electors remained in use as late as 1980 in Vermont. During the early 20th century, states started to shift to the so-called "short presidential ballot." The short presidential ballot enables a voter to conveniently vote for an entire slate of presidential electors merely by casting one vote for a named candidate for President and Vice President. Under the short presidential ballot, a vote for the presidential and vice-presidential candidate whose names appear on the ballot is deemed to be a vote for all of the individual presidential electors nominated in association with the named candidates. For example, when a voter cast a vote for McCain–Palin in California in 2008, the voter was deemed to be casting a vote for each of 55 individual candidates for the position of presidential elector nominated by the California Republican Party. See section 2.2.6.

[7] Maine and Nebraska currently choose presidential electors by congressional district (and also choose two presidential electors statewide).

"In short, **the appointment and mode of appointment of electors belong exclusively to the states** under the constitution of the United States."[8] [Emphasis added]

In *Bush v. Gore* in 2000, the Court approvingly referred to the characterization in *McPherson v. Blacker* of the state's power under section 1 of Article II of the Constitution.

> "The individual citizen has no federal constitutional right to vote for electors for the President of the United States unless and until the state legislature chooses a statewide election as the means to implement its power to appoint members of the Electoral College. U.S. Const., Art. II, §1. **This is the source for the statement in** *McPherson* **v.** Blacker, 146 U.S. 1, 35 (1892), that the State legislature's power to select the manner for appointing electors is **plenary**; it may, if it so chooses, select the electors itself, which indeed was the manner used by State legislatures in several States for many years after the Framing of our Constitution. Id., at 28-33. . . .
>
> **"There is no difference between the two sides of the present controversy on these basic propositions."**[9] [Emphasis added]

In short, states may exercise their power to choose the manner of appointing their presidential electors in any way they see fit (provided, of course, that they do not violate any restriction contained elsewhere in the U.S. Constitution).[10,11]

There is good reason to give the states the power to control the conduct of presidential elections. State control over presidential elections thwarts the possibility of an over-reaching President, in conjunction with a compliant Congress, manipulating the rules governing his own re-election. This delegation of control over presidential elections was intended to guard against the establishment of a self-perpetuating President and, in particular, the establishment of a monarchy in the United States. For these good reasons, control over presidential elections is an exclusive state power.

---

[8] *McPherson v. Blacker.* 146 U.S. 1 at 29. 1892.

[9] *Bush v. Gore.* 531 U.S. 98. 2000.

[10] All powers delegated to Congress and the states are subject to general restrictions found elsewhere in the Constitution. For example, in *Bush v. Gore* (531 U.S. 98), the Court observed that "Having once granted the right to vote on equal terms, the State may not, by later arbitrary and disparate treatment, value one person's vote over that of another. See, e.g., *Harper v. Virginia Bd. of Elections*, 383 U.S. 663, 665 (1966) ('[O]nce the franchise is granted to the electorate, lines may not be drawn which are inconsistent with the Equal Protection Clause of the Fourteenth Amendment'). It must be remembered that 'the right of suffrage can be denied by a debasement or dilution of the weight of a citizen's vote just as effectively as by wholly prohibiting the free exercise of the franchise.' *Reynolds v. Sims*, 377 U.S. 533, 555 (1964). There is no difference between the two sides of the present controversy on these basic propositions."

[11] As the U.S. Supreme Court noted in *McPherson v. Blacker*, the state legislature's discretion over the manner of appointing presidential electors may be limited by the state constitution. For example, the Colorado constitution prohibited the state legislature from appointing presidential electors after 1876.

All of the existing winner-take-all statutes are state law. The winner-take-all method of awarding electoral votes was adopted piecemeal on a state-by-state basis. The winner-take-all rule was never the prevailing method of awarding electoral votes during the lifetimes of the Founding Fathers. Instead, winner-take-all statutes became prevalent decades later, in the period prior to the Civil War, with the emergence of strong political parties aiming to maximize their own political power by stifling the state's minority party.

More importantly, existing winner-take-all statutes did not come into use by means of an amendment to the U.S. Constitution. The winner-take-all rule does not have constitutional status. Accordingly, repealing state winner-take-all statutes does not require an amendment to the U.S. Constitution. Winner-take-all statutes may be repealed in the same way they were enacted, namely through each state's process for enacting and repealing state laws.

Indeed, the winner-take-all method of awarding electoral votes has been adopted, and repealed, by various states on numerous occasions over the years.

All three of the states that used the winner-take-all rule in the first presidential election in 1789 abandoned it by 1800.

Massachusetts has used 11 different methods of awarding its electoral votes.

- In 1789, Massachusetts had a two-step system in which the voters cast ballots indicating their preference for presidential elector by district, and the legislature chose from the top two vote-getters in each district (with the legislature choosing the state's remaining two electors).
- In 1792, the voters were allowed to choose presidential electors in four multi-member regional districts (with the legislature choosing the state's remaining two electors).
- In 1796, the voters elected presidential electors by congressional districts (with the legislature choosing only the state's remaining two electors).
- In 1800, the legislature took back the power to pick all of the state's presidential electors (excluding the voters entirely).
- In 1804, the voters were allowed to elect 17 presidential electors by district and two on a statewide basis.
- In 1808, the legislature decided to pick the electors itself.
- In 1812, the voters elected six presidential electors from one district, five electors from another district, four electors from another, three electors from each of two districts, and one elector from a sixth district.
- In 1816, Massachusetts again returned to state legislative choice.
- In 1820, the voters were allowed to elect 13 presidential electors by district and two on a statewide basis.
- Then, in 1824, Massachusetts adopted its 10th method of awarding electoral votes, namely the statewide winner-take-all rule that is in effect today.

- Finally, in 2010, Massachusetts changed its method of appointing its presidential electors by enacting the National Popular Vote interstate compact. This change will go into effect when states possessing a majority of the electoral votes (270 out of 538) enact the same compact.

None of these 11 changes involved an amendment to the U.S. Constitution. These changes were accomplished using the Constitution's built-in method for changing the method of electing the President, namely section 1 of Article II. That constitutional provision gives Massachusetts (and all the other states) exclusive and plenary power to choose the manner of awarding their electoral votes.

In the nation's first presidential election in 1789, the New Jersey legislature passed a law empowering the Governor and his Council to appoint the state's presidential electors.[12] In 1804, the legislature permitted the people to vote for presidential electors under the winner-take-all rule.

Delaware has used three different methods. In 1789, one presidential elector was elected from each of the state's three counties. Then, between 1792 and 1828, the Delaware legislature decided to exclude the voters and appointed all of the state's presidential electors itself. Starting in 1832, Delaware allowed the people to vote for presidential electors under the winner-take-all rule.

The North Carolina legislature has exercised its power to change the method of awarding the state's electoral votes on four occasions. In 1792, the legislature chose the presidential electors. Between 1796 and 1808, the people then voted for electors from presidential-elector districts. Then, the legislature chose the electors in 1812. In 1816, the legislature changed to the statewide winner-take-all rule.[13]

As recently as 1992, Nebraska replaced its winner-take-all statute with a congressional-district system of awarding electoral votes. Maine did so in 1969. After the 2008 presidential election (when Barack Obama won one district-level electoral vote in Nebraska), the Nebraska legislature conducted hearings on the possibility of repealing the congressional-district system and returning to the statewide winner-take-all approach. Within the past decade, a Republican-controlled New York Senate and a Democratic-controlled North Carolina House and Senate passed bills, at various times, switching to the congressional-district system (although none of these bills became law).

In summary, there is nothing in the U.S. Constitution that needs to be amended in order to repeal existing state winner-take-all statutes for awarding a state's electoral votes. The states *already have the power* to make this change.

For additional information, see section 1.1 and chapter 2.

---

[12] DenBoer, Gordon (editor). 1986. *The Documentary History of the First Federal Elections.* Madison, WI: The University of Wisconsin Press. Volume III. Page 29.

[13] Since 2000, both the North Carolina Senate and House have voted, in different years, to change from the statewide winner-take-all rule to a congressional-district system for awarding electoral votes.

9.1.2. MYTH: The traditional and appropriate way of changing the method of electing the President is by means of a federal constitutional amendment.

QUICK ANSWER:

- Nearly all the major reforms in the method of conducting U.S. presidential elections have been initiated at the state level—not by means of an amendment to the U.S. Constitution.
- State-level action is the traditional, appropriate, and most commonly used way of changing the method of electing the President.
- The politically most important characteristics of our nation's current system of electing the President (e.g., permitting the people to vote for President and the winner-take-all rule) were established by state statute—not by federal constitutional amendments.
- The winner-take-all method of awarding electoral votes was not established by a constitutional amendment. It may be repealed by any state in the same manner as it was originally adopted, namely by state statute.
- State action is the right way to change the method of awarding electoral votes because this is the mechanism that is built into the U.S. Constitution (section 1 of Article II).

MORE DETAILED ANSWER:

John Samples has written the following about the National Popular Vote compact:

> "NPV brings about this change without amending the Constitution, thereby undermining the legitimacy of presidential elections."[14]

In fact, nearly all the major reforms in the method of conducting U.S. presidential elections have been initiated at the state level—not by means of an amendment to the U.S. Constitution. State-level action is the traditional, appropriate, and most commonly used way of changing the method of electing the President.

Major changes in the method of electing the President that were implemented entirely at the state level—without a federal constitutional amendment—include:

- permitting the people to vote for President,
- abolition of property qualifications for voting, and
- the winner-take-all rule—the target of the National Popular Vote compact.

Examples of changes that were initiated at the state level and then later adopted at the national level, include:

---

[14] Samples, John. *A Critique of the National Popular Vote Plan for Electing the President*. Cato Institute Policy Analysis No. 622. October 13, 2008. Page 1.

- women's suffrage,
- direct election of U.S. Senators,
- the 18-year-old vote, and
- black suffrage.

Permitting the People to Vote for President

The most significant change that has ever been made in the way the President of the United States is elected was to allow the people to vote for President. This change was implemented by means of state statutes—not a federal constitutional amendment.

There is nothing in the original U.S. Constitution that gave the people the right to vote for President or presidential electors.

As the U.S. Supreme Court stated in the 1892 case of *McPherson v. Blacker*:

> **"The constitution does not provide that the appointment of electors shall be by popular vote**, nor that the electors shall be voted for upon a general ticket, nor that the majority of those who exercise the elective franchise can alone choose the electors. **It recognizes that the people act through their representatives in the legislature, and leaves it to the legislature exclusively to define the method of effecting the object."**[15] [Emphasis added]

As the U.S. Supreme Court wrote in 2000:

> **"The individual citizen has no federal constitutional right to vote for electors for the President of the United States** unless and until the state legislature chooses a statewide election as the means to implement its power to appoint members of the Electoral College."[16] [Emphasis added]

The Founding Fathers were divided as to whether the people should be allowed to vote for President.

The people were permitted to vote for presidential electors in the nation's first presidential election in 1789 in only six states. In some states, the state legislature appointed the presidential electors. In New Jersey, the Governor and his 13-member Legislative Council (Privy Council) appointed the state's presidential electors.[17]

The *Federalist Papers* made it clear that the choice of method for appointing presidential electors is a state power, but skirted the question of exactly what method the states would likely choose.

Federalist No. 45 (presumably written by James Madison) says:

---

[15] *McPherson v. Blacker.* 146 U.S. 1 at 27. 1892.

[16] *Bush v. Gore.* 531 U.S. 98. 2000.

[17] DenBoer, Gordon; Brown, Lucy Trumbull; and Hagermann, Charles D. (editors). 1986. *The Documentary History of the First Federal Elections 1788–1790.* Madison, WI: University of Wisconsin Press. Volume III.

"Without the intervention of the State legislatures, the President of the United States cannot be elected at all. They must in all cases have a great share in his appointment, and will, perhaps, **in most cases, of themselves determine it**." [Emphasis added]

Federalist No. 44 (said to be written by James Madison) says:

"The members and officers of the State governments . . . will have an essential agency in giving effect to the federal Constitution. **The election of the President and Senate will depend, in all cases, on the legislatures of the several States**." [Emphasis added]

Section 1 of Article II of the U.S. Constitution gives the states flexibility in the manner of appointing their presidential electors. In the nation's first presidential election, only six states—New Hampshire, Pennsylvania, Maryland, Delaware, Virginia, and Massachusetts[18]—permitted the people to vote for presidential electors.[19]

In permitting the people to vote for President, the states exercised their role, under the U.S. Constitution, as the "laboratories of democracy."[20]

With the passage of time, more and more states observed that the practice of permitting the people to vote for President did not produce disastrous consequences. Indeed, popular elections became popular.

By 1824, three-quarters of the states had embraced the idea of permitting the people to vote for the state's presidential electors. However, the state-by-state process of empowering the people to vote for President was not completed until the 1880 election—almost a century after the Constitutional Convention.[21]

This fundamental change in the manner of electing the President was not accomplished by means of a federal constitutional amendment. It was instituted through state-by-state changes in state laws.

Today, this feature of presidential elections is so widely regarded as a fixed feature of American politics that virtually no one suggests that the people should not be permitted to vote for President.

Permitting the people to vote for President was not an "end run" around the U.S.

---

[18] In this book, we are somewhat generous in counting Massachusetts among the six states that permitted the people to vote for President in 1789. The legislature appointed the state's presidential electors from the top two candidates from each district. In modern-day terminology, the people "nominated" the candidates for the position of presidential elector, and the legislature "elected" them.

[19] New Hampshire, Pennsylvania, and Maryland used the winner-take-all method, whereas Virginia, Delaware, and Massachusetts used districts to elect presidential electors.

[20] Justice Louis Brandeis wrote in the 1932 case of *New State Ice Co. v. Liebmann* (285 U.S. 262), "It is one of the happy incidents of the federal system that a single courageous state may, if its citizens choose, serve as a laboratory; and try novel social and economic experiments without risk to the rest of the country."

[21] The appointment of presidential electors by the legislature of the newly admitted state of Colorado in 1876 was the last occasion when presidential electors were not chosen by a direct vote of the people.

Constitution but instead, an exercise of a power that the Founding Fathers explicitly assigned to state legislatures in the Constitution.

We have not encountered a single person who argues that state legislatures did anything improper, inappropriate, or unconstitutional when they made this fundamental change in the way the President is elected.

Does John Samples think that permitting the people to vote for President without a federal constitutional amendment "undermine[d] the legitimacy of presidential elections?"

Abolition of Property Qualifications for Voting

When the U.S. Constitution came into effect in 1789, 10 of the 13 states had property qualifications for voting. The requirements varied from state to state. The requirements typically included factors such as ownership of a specific number of acres of land, ownership of assets with a specific value, or specific amounts of income.[22]

In 1789, there were only about 100,000 eligible voters in a nation of over 3,000,000 people.

By 1855, only three of the then-31 states had property qualifications for voting.[23]

Today, there are no property qualifications for voting in any state.

The elimination of property qualifications was not accomplished by means of a federal constitutional amendment. The elimination of property qualifications for voting by the states was not improper, inappropriate, or unconstitutional. It was not an "end run" around the U.S. Constitution. This substantial expansion of the electorate occurred because state legislatures used a power that rightfully belonged to them to change the method of conducting elections.

Women's Suffrage

In several instances, a major reform initiated at the state level led to a subsequent federal constitutional amendment after the reform had become established in a substantial number of states.

For example, women did not have the right to vote when the U.S. Constitution came into effect in 1789 (except in New Jersey, where that right was withdrawn in 1807).

Wyoming gave women the right to vote in 1869.

By the time the 19th Amendment was passed by Congress (50 years later), women already had the vote in 30 of the then-48 states. The main effect of the 19th Amend-

---

[22] In many states, there were different requirements for voting for the lower house of the state legislature than for the upper house.

[23] Keyssar, Alexander. 2000. *The Right to Vote: The Contested History of Democracy in the United States.* New York, NY: Basic Books. Table A.3. Page 314.

ment was to impose women's suffrage on the minority of states (18) that had not already adopted it at the state level.[24]

The decision by 30 separate states to permit women to vote in the 50-year period between 1869 and 1919 was not an "end run" around the U.S. Constitution. We have not encountered a single person who argues that state legislatures did anything improper, inappropriate, or unconstitutional when they made this very substantial expansion of their electorates. Women's suffrage is another example of state legislatures using the authority granted to them by the U.S. Constitution to institute a major change concerning the conduct of elections.

Women's suffrage was achieved because 30 states exercised their power as the "laboratories of democracy" to change the manner of conducting their own elections.[25] The federal constitutional amendment followed.

Direct Election of U.S. Senators

The direct election of U.S. Senators is another example of a major change initiated at the state level (and later enshrined in the Constitution by means of a constitutional amendment).

The original U.S. Constitution was explicit in specifying that U.S. Senators were to be elected by state legislatures.

Support for the direct election of Senators grew throughout the 19th century—particularly after popular voting for presidential electors became the norm during the Jacksonian "era of the common man." The 1858 Lincoln-Douglas debates were public events aimed at influencing the choice for U.S. Senator that was ultimately made by the Illinois state legislature.

Starting with the "Oregon Plan" in 1907, states passed laws establishing "advisory" elections for U.S. Senator. Under the Oregon plan, the people cast their votes for U.S. Senator in a statewide "advisory" election, and the state legislature then dutifully rubberstamped the people's choice by formally electing the winner of the "advisory" election. By the time the 17th Amendment passed the U.S. Senate in 1912, the voters in 29 states were, for all practical purposes, electing U.S. Senators.

18-Year-Old Vote

States took the lead in granting suffrage to 18-year-olds. Citizens under the age of 21 first acquired the right to vote in various states (e.g., Georgia, Kentucky, Alaska,

---

[24] The amendment also served to extend women's suffrage to all offices in those states where women only had the right to vote for certain specified offices (e.g., just President, just local offices). In addition, the constitutional amendment made it more difficult to ever reverse the granting of the vote to women.

[25] The reasons that the 19th Amendment passed Congress in 1919 was that (1) women already constituted half the electorate in 30 states and (2) members of Congress from the remaining states knew that it was only a matter of time before women would obtain the right to vote in the remaining states—with or without a federal constitutional amendment.

Hawaii, and New Hampshire). In 1971, the 26th Amendment extended the 18-year-old vote to all states.

Black Suffrage

States also took the lead in granting suffrage to African Americans. African Americans were given the right to vote in New York in the 1820s and in five states by the 1850s. Black suffrage was later extended to all states by the 15th Amendment (ratified in 1870).

The Winner-Take-All Rule

Finally, it should be noted that one of the politically most important characteristics of our nation's current system of electing the President—the winner-take-all rule—was established by state statute—not a federal constitutional amendment.

Why does John Samples say that repealing the winner-take-all rule without a federal constitutional amendment would "undermin[e] the legitimacy of presidential elections," while not criticizing the original adoption of the winner-take-all rule by the states as illegitimate?

The fact is that state-level action is the traditional, appropriate, and most commonly used way of changing the method of electing the President.

In terms of electing the President, state control is precisely what the Founding Fathers intended, and it is precisely what the U.S. Constitution specifies. The Founding Fathers created an open-ended system with built-in flexibility concerning the manner of electing the President.

Indeed, the 12th Amendment (ratified in 1804) was the only time when a federal constitutional amendment was used to initiate a change in the manner of voting for the President.

In this instance, a constitutional amendment was necessary. The original Constitution specifically provided that each presidential elector would vote for two persons (with the candidate receiving the most votes becoming President and the second-place candidate becoming Vice President). The 12th Amendment changed that procedure and specified that each presidential elector would cast a separate vote for President and a separate vote for Vice President.[26]

---

[26] The 12th Amendment acknowledged the reality of the emergence of political parties. When political parties emerged in the 1796 election, each party centrally nominated its candidate for President and Vice President (through the party's congressional caucus). Once there were national nominees, presidential electors were expected to vote for their party's nominee for President in the Electoral College. The emergence of political parties extinguished the vision of the Founding Fathers that the Electoral College would act as a deliberative body. In the 1800 presidential election, the winning party's electors each dutifully cast one vote for their party's presidential and vice-presidential nominees—thus creating a tie in the Electoral College and throwing the election of the President and Vice President into Congress. The 1800 election made it clear that ties in the Electoral College would be a continuing occurrence if political parties continued to exist. Thus, a constitutional amendment was necessary. See Ferling, John. 2004. *Adams vs. Jefferson: The Tumultuous Election of 1800.* Oxford: Oxford University Press. See also Kuroda, Tadahisa. 1994. *The Origins of the Twelfth Amendment: The Electoral College in the Early Republic, 1787–1804.* Westport, CT: Greenwood Press.

In referring to the National Popular Vote plan, Professor Joseph Pika (author of *The Politics of the Presidency*) pointed out:

> "This effort would represent **amendment-free constitutional reform, the way that most other changes have been made in the selection process since 1804.**"[27] [Emphasis added]

It is worth noting that while the states have exclusive control over the awarding of their electoral votes, the Constitution treats state power over congressional elections differently. Article I, section 4, clause 1 of the U.S. Constitution states:

> "The Times, Places and Manner of holding Elections for Senators and Representatives, shall be prescribed in each State by the Legislature thereof; **but the Congress may at any time by Law make or alter such Regulations**, except as to the Places of chusing Senators." [Emphasis added]

Thus, the U.S. Constitution gives *primary*—but not *exclusive*—control over the manner of electing Congress to the states. In the case of congressional elections, the U.S. Constitution gave Congress the power to review and override state decisions. This override power has been used sparingly over the years.

In contrast, state power to choose the manner of electing the President is "exclusive" and "plenary" (i.e., complete). In particular, Congress does not have the power to override a state's decision concerning the manner of awarding its electoral votes.

9.1.3. MYTH: The Electoral College would be abolished by the National Popular Vote compact.

QUICK ANSWER:

- The National Popular Vote compact would preserve the Electoral College. It would not abolish it. It would not affect the structure of the Electoral College contained in the U.S. Constitution.

- The National Popular Vote plan is based on the power of the states to choose the method of awarding their electoral votes. The compact would replace existing state winner-take-all statutes with a different state statute, namely one that guarantees the Presidency to the candidate who receives the most popular votes in all 50 states and the District of Columbia.

- Under the National Popular Vote plan, the states would retain their exclusive and plenary power to choose the method of awarding their electoral votes, including the option to make other changes in the future.

---

[27] Pika, Joseph. Improving on a doubly indirect selection system. *Delaware On-Line.* September 16, 2008. http://www.delawareonline.com/apps/pbcs.dll/article?AID=/20080916/OPINION09/809160318/1004/OPINION.

MORE DETAILED ANSWER:

The National Popular Vote bill is state legislation—not a federal constitutional amendment. As such, it would not (and indeed could not) change the structure of the Electoral College as specified in the U.S. Constitution.

Instead, the National Popular Vote bill would change the method by which the states award their electoral votes in the Electoral College.

The National Popular Vote bill uses the Constitution's built-in state-based power for changing the method of awarding electoral votes namely, section 1 of Article II of the U.S. Constitution:

> "Each State shall appoint, in such Manner **as the Legislature thereof may direct**, a Number of Electors. . . ."[28] [Emphasis added]

The "manner" of appointment of presidential electors is specified by clause 3 of Article III of the National Popular Vote compact.

> "The presidential elector certifying official of each member state shall certify the appointment in that official's own state of the elector slate nominated in that state in association with the national popular vote winner."

Because the compact only takes effect when enacted by states possessing a majority of the electoral votes (i.e., 270 of 538), the compact guarantees that presidential electors supporting the "national popular vote winner" will have enough votes to choose the President.

The National Popular Vote compact would not abolish the Electoral College. Instead, it would reform the Electoral College so that it reflects the choice of the voters in all 50 states and the District of Columbia.

Under the National Popular Vote plan, the states would retain their exclusive and plenary power to choose the method of awarding their electoral votes, including the option to make other changes in the future.

9.1.4. MYTH: The Founding Fathers designed and favored our nation's current system of electing the President.

QUICK ANSWER:

- The Founding Fathers never decided how presidential electors should be chosen. Instead, they left the matter to the states.
- The Founding Fathers expected that the Electoral College would be a deliberative body. However, presidential electors became a rubberstamp for the candidates nominated by their parties by the time of the nation's first competitive presidential election in 1796.

---

[28] U.S. Constitution. Article II, section 1, clause 2.

- The Electoral College further deviated from the Founders' vision when state winner-take-all statutes became prevalent (long after the Founders were dead).
- The winner-take-all method of awarding electoral votes was not debated (much less voted upon or adopted) at the 1787 Constitutional Convention.
- The winner-take-all rule is not mentioned in the *Federalist Papers*.
- The winner-take-all method was not the choice of the Founders and was, in fact, used by only three states in the nation's first presidential election in 1789 (all of which abandoned it by 1800).
- The electoral system that we have today was not designed, anticipated, or favored by the Founding Fathers. Instead, it is the result of decades of evolutionary change driven primarily by the emergence of political parties and the desire of each state's ruling party not to give any of the state's electoral votes to the minority party.
- The winner-take-all rule came into widespread use because of the pressure created by its use in other states.

MORE DETAILED ANSWER:

The Founding Fathers did not design nor anticipate—much less favor—the most salient feature of our nation's present-day system of electing the President, namely state winner-take-all statutes (i.e., awarding all of a state's electoral votes to the presidential candidate who receives the most popular votes within each separate state).

The Founding Fathers never intended that all of a state's presidential electors would mindlessly vote, in lockstep, for the candidate nominated by an extra-constitutional body (a political party's nominating caucus or convention).

In the debates of the Constitutional Convention and in the *Federalist Papers*, there is no mention of the winner-take-all method of awarding electoral votes. When the Founding Fathers went back to their states in 1789 to organize the nation's first presidential election, only three state legislatures chose to employ the winner-take-all method. Each of these three states repealed it by 1800.

Instead, the Founding Fathers envisioned an Electoral College composed of "wise men" who would act as a deliberative body and exercise independent and detached judgment as to the best person to serve as President.

As John Jay (the presumed author of *Federalist* No. 64) wrote in 1788:

> "As the **select assemblies** for choosing the President . . . will in general be composed of **the most enlightened and respectable citizens**, there is reason to presume that their attention and their votes will be directed to those men only who have become the most distinguished by their abilities and virtues." [Emphasis added]

As Alexander Hamilton (the presumed author of *Federalist No. 68*) wrote in 1788:

"[T]he immediate election should be made by men most capable of analyzing the qualities adapted to the station, and **acting under circumstances favorable to deliberation**, and to a **judicious combination** of all the reasons and inducements which were proper to govern their choice. **A small number of persons**, selected by their fellow-citizens from the general mass, will be most likely to possess **the information and discernment requisite to such complicated investigations**." [Emphasis added]

In this regard, the Electoral College was patterned after ecclesiastical and royal elections. For example, the College of Cardinals in the Roman Catholic Church constitutes the world's oldest and longest-running electoral college. Cardinals (with lifetime appointments) deliberate to choose the Pope. The Holy Roman Emperor was elected by a similar small and distinguished group of "electors." In many kingdoms in Europe, a small group of "electors" would, upon the death of the king, choose the person best suited to be king from a pool consisting of certain members of the royal family or nobility.

The Founding Fathers' expectations that the Electoral College would be a deliberative and contemplative body were dashed by the political realities of the nation's first competitive presidential election in 1796 and the emergence of political parties.

After George Washington declined to run for a third term in 1796, the Federalist and Republican parties nominated candidates for President and Vice President. These nominations were made by each party's congressional caucus. In other words, the nominations were made by extra-constitutional political organizations.

The necessary consequence of national nominees was that each party nominated candidates for the position of presidential elector who made it known that they would serve as willing "rubberstamps" for their party's nominee in the Electoral College.

As the Supreme Court observed in its opinion in the 1892 case of *McPherson v. Blacker*:

> "Doubtless **it was supposed that the electors would exercise a reasonable independence and fair judgment in the selection of the chief executive**, but experience soon demonstrated that, **whether chosen by the legislatures or by popular suffrage on general ticket or in districts, they were so chosen simply to register the will of the appointing power** in respect of a particular candidate. In relation, then, to the independence of the electors, the original expectation may be said to have been frustrated."[29] [Emphasis added]

The centralized nomination by the political parties for President and Vice President in 1796 extinguished the notion that the Electoral College would operate as a deliberative body.

---

[29] *McPherson v. Blacker.* 146 U.S. 1 at 36. 1892.

All but one of the 138 electoral votes cast in the 1796 election were synchronized with "the will of the appointing power."

In the eight states where the state legislature appointed presidential electors in 1796, there was no hint of independent judgment by any of the presidential electors. The votes in the Electoral College coincided with "the will of the appointing power" (whether a Federalist or Jeffersonian state legislature):

- Connecticut—100% for Adams
- Delaware—100% for Adams
- New Jersey—100% for Adams
- New York—100% for Adams
- Rhode Island—100% for Adams
- South Carolina—100% for Jefferson
- Tennessee—100% for Jefferson[30]
- Vermont—100% for Adams

In the eight states where the voters chose the presidential electors in 1796, the votes cast by the presidential electors mirrored (with one exception discussed below) the sentiment of the voters that elected them—whether at the statewide level or the district level.[31]

The one exception was the unexpected vote cast in 1796 by Samuel Miles (a Federalist presidential elector) for Thomas Jefferson.

Public reaction to Miles's unexpected vote cemented the presumption that presidential electors should vote for their party's nominees. As a Federalist supporter notably complained in the December 15, 1796, issue of the *United States Gazette*:

> "What, do I chufe Samuel Miles to determine for me whether John Adams or Thomas Jefferfon is the fittest man to be President of the United States? No, **I chufe him to act, not to think**." [Emphasis added] [Spelling per original]

Of the 22,991 electoral votes cast for President in the nation's 57 presidential elections between 1789 and 2012, the vote of Samuel Miles for Thomas Jefferson in 1796 remains the only instance when the elector may have believed, at the time he cast his vote, that his vote might possibly affect the national outcome.[32]

---

[30] As explained in section 2.2.2, the Tennessee legislature effectively appointed the state's presidential electors.

[31] The winner-take-all rule was used in New Hampshire and Georgia, and the votes cast in the Electoral College were cast unanimously for the statewide preference (Adams and Jefferson, respectively). Multimember regional districts were used in Massachusetts, and the votes cast in the Electoral College mirrored voter sentiment (for Adams) in the four districts. Districts were used in Kentucky, and the votes cast in the Electoral College matched voter sentiment (for Jefferson). Districts were used in Virginia, North Carolina, and Maryland, and the votes cast in the Electoral College (although not unanimous) matched voter sentiment in each district.

[32] Fifteen of the 17 deviating electoral votes for President were "grand-standing" votes (that is, votes cast after the presidential elector knew that his vote would not affect the national outcome). One electoral vote (in Minnesota in 2004) was cast by accident. In addition, 63 electoral votes were cast in an unexpected way in

The expectation that presidential electors should faithfully support the candidates nominated by their party has persisted to this day.[33]

In the 1952 case of *Ray v. Blair*, U.S. Supreme Court Justice Robert H. Jackson summarized the history of presidential electors as follows:

> "No one faithful to our history can deny that the plan originally contemplated, what is implicit in its text, that electors would be free agents, to exercise an independent and nonpartisan judgment as to the men best qualified for the Nation's highest offices. . . .

> "This arrangement miscarried. Electors, although often personally eminent, independent, and respectable, officially become voluntary party lackeys and intellectual nonentities to whose memory we might justly paraphrase a tuneful satire:

> > 'They always voted at their party's call
> > 'And never thought of thinking for themselves at all' "[34]

In short, the Electoral College that we have today was not designed, anticipated, or favored by the Founding Fathers. It is, instead, the product of decades of evolutionary change precipitated by the emergence of political parties and the enactment of winner-take-all statutes by most states. The actions taken by the Founding Fathers in organizing the nation's first presidential election in 1789 (in particular, the fact that only three states used the winner-take-all method in 1789) make it clear that the Founding Fathers never gave their imprimatur to the winner-take-all method.

9.1.5. MYTH: Alexander Hamilton considered our nation's current system of electing the President to be "excellent."

QUICK ANSWER:

- Alexander Hamilton's statement in *Federalist No. 68* saying that the Electoral College is "excellent" is frequently quoted out-of-context in order to suggest that Hamilton (and perhaps the whole Founding Generation) would have favored our current system of electing the President. In fact, Hamilton's statement does not refer to the current state-by-state winner-take-all system but instead, to the Founders' never-achieved vision of a "judicious" and "deliberative" Electoral College.
- Hamilton's statement that the Electoral College is "excellent" was made in the *Federalist Papers* during the debate on ratification of the U.S. Constitution—

---

the 1872 presidential election when the losing Democratic candidate died after Election Day, but before the Electoral College met. For details, see section 2.12.

[33] In 2010, the National Conference of Commissioners on Uniform State Laws drafted a "Uniform Faithful Presidential Electors Act" and recommended it for enactment by all the states.

[34] *Ray v. Blair* 343 U.S. 214 at 232. 1952.

that is, *before* Hamilton or anyone else could see how the Electoral College would operate in practice.

- Hamilton's only known statement on the method by which a state should award its electoral votes is contained in an 1800 letter in which he advocated that New York switch from legislative appointment of presidential electors to popular election using districts. There is no record of Hamilton ever endorsing the currently prevailing system in which states conduct popular elections to award 100% of their electoral votes to the candidate who receives the most popular votes in the state.

- Hamilton was dead for a quarter century before the winner-take-all rule become prevalent in most states (including his own state of New York).

MORE DETAILED ANSWER:

Tara Ross, an opponent of the National Popular Vote plan, has asserted:

> "[The National Popular Vote compact] . . . tears apart a well-established institution that was **admired by the Founding generation** and that has **served America successfully for centuries**. Alexander Hamilton described its reception by the Founding generation, noting that
>
> > 'the mode of appointment of the Chief Magistrate of the United States is almost the only part of the system . . . which has escaped without severe censure. . . . I venture somewhat further, and hesitate not to affirm that **if the manner of it be not perfect, it is at least excellent**.'" [Emphasis added]

Trent England (a lobbyist opposing the National Popular Vote compact and Vice-President of the Evergreen Freedom Foundation of Olympia, Washington) has written:

> "**An 'excellent' system** Alexander Hamilton wrote in *The Federalist* (No. 68) that, if the Electoral College is not perfect, 'it is at least excellent.' **The system probably works even better than the American Founders expected, considering the addition of 37 states . . . since Hamilton's original judgment.**"[35] [Emphasis added]

These out-of-context quotations about the excellence of the Electoral College do not refer to the way that the Electoral College has actually operated "for centuries" or how it operates today.

Instead, as Hamilton made clear a few sentences later in *Federalist* No. 68, he was referring to the Founders' never-achieved vision of a "deliberative" Electoral College:

> "[The] election should be made by **men most capable of analyzing the qualities** adapted to the station, and **acting under circumstances favor-**

---

[35] England, Trent. Op-Ed: Bypass the Electoral College? *Christian Science Monitor.* August 12, 2010.

able to deliberation, and to a **judicious combination** of all the reasons and inducements which were proper to govern their choice. **A small number of persons,** selected by their fellow-citizens from the general mass, will be most **likely to possess the information and discernment requisite to such complicated investigations.**" [Emphasis added]

The practice of presidential electors acting as rubberstamps started at the time of the nation's first competitive election in 1796 (as discussed in greater detail in section 9.1.4). In 1796, political parties started making national nominations for President and Vice President. The obvious and necessary way to ensure the election of a party's national nominees was to nominate presidential electors who could be relied upon to vote in lockstep in the Electoral College for the party's nominees.

Both parties were immediately successful in converting presidential electors into rubberstamps in 1796. All but one presidential elector in 1796 voted for his own party's nominee for President (that is, either John Adams or Thomas Jefferson). The one exception was Samuel Miles (the deviant Federalist elector from Pennsylvania), who unexpectedly cast his vote in the Electoral College for Jefferson—instead of Adams. A Federalist supporter famously complained in the December 15, 1796, issue of the *United States Gazette* that Samuel Miles had voted for Thomas Jefferson, instead of John Adams, by saying,

> "What, do I chufe Samuel Miles to determine for me whether John Adams or Thomas Jefferfon is the fittest man to be President of the United States? No, **I chufe him to act, not to think**." [Emphasis added] [Spelling per original]

Of the 22,991 electoral votes cast for President in the nation's 57 presidential elections (between 1789 and 2012), only 17 were cast in a deviant way.[36] Moreover, the unexpected vote of Samuel Miles in 1796 remains the only instance (among these 17 cases) when the elector might have thought, at the time he voted, that his vote could possibly affect the national outcome.[37]

It should be noted that Hamilton's statement in *Federalist* No. 68 that the Electoral College is "excellent" was made during the debate on ratification of the U.S. Constitution—that is, *before* Hamilton or anyone else could see how the Electoral College would operate in practice.

The fact that "the mode of appointment of the [President] is almost the only part of the system . . . which has escaped without severe censure" during the debate on ratification of the U.S. Constitution reflected the fact that George Washington was universally expected to become President and the fact that designating a deliberative body to choose the President seemed, at the time, to be a reasonable way to fill the office.

---

[36] See section 2.12.

[37] As discussed in greater detail in section 2.12, all but one of the other instances of faithless electors are considered grand-standing votes. One electoral vote (in 2004) was cast by accident.

Hamilton's only known statement on the method by which a state should award its electoral votes is contained in an 1800 letter in which he advocated that New York switch from legislative appointment of presidential electors to popular election using districts.

The Federalists unexpectedly lost control of the New York legislature in the April 1800 legislative elections. Under an existing New York statute, the legislature appointed all of the state's presidential electors. The loss of the legislature meant that the Federalists would lose all of New York's electoral votes when the legislature would meet later in the year to choose the state's presidential electors.[38]

> "Jarred by the specter of defeat in the autumn [Federalist Alexander] Hamilton importuned Governor John Jay to call a special session of the Federalist-dominated New York legislature so that it might act before the newly elected assemblymen took their seats [on July 1]. Hamilton's plan was for the outgoing assembly to enact legislation providing for the popular election—in districts—of the state's presidential electors, a ploy virtually guaranteed to ensure that the Federalists would capture nine or ten of the twelve electoral college slots."[39]

As Alexander Hamilton put it in his letter to Governor John Jay on May 7, 1800:

> "The moral certainty therefore is, that there will be an anti-federal majority in the ensuing legislature; and the very high probability is, that this will bring Jefferson into the chief magistracy, unless it be prevented by the measure which I now submit to your consideration, namely, the immediate calling together of the existing legislature.

> "**I am aware that there are weighty objections to the measure**; but the reasons for it appear to me to outweigh the objections. And in times like these in which we live, **it will not do to be over-scrupulous**. It is easy to sacrifice the substantial interests of society by a strict adherence to ordinary rules.

> "In observing this, I shall not be supposed to mean that anything ought to be done which integrity will forbid; but merely that the **scruples of delicacy and propriety**, as relative to a common course of things, **ought to yield to the extraordinary nature of the crisis**. They ought not to hinder the taking of a legal and constitutional step to prevent an atheist in religion, and a fanatic in politics, from getting possession of the helm of State."[40] [Emphasis added]

---

[38] Weisberger, Bernard A. 2001. *America Afire: Jefferson, Adams, and the First Contested Election.* William Morrow. Page 238.

[39] Ferling, John. 2004. *Adams vs. Jefferson: The Tumultuous Election of 1800.* Oxford, UK: Oxford University Press. Page 131.

[40] The complete letter can be found in *Brief of F.A. Baker for Plaintiffs in Error* in *McPherson v. Blacker.* 1892. Pages 30–31. See also Cunningham, Noble E., Jr. 1957. *Jeffersonian Republicans: The Formation of Party*

Governor Jay (a former Chief Justice of the United States) rejected Hamilton's proposal and wrote on the letter:

> "Proposing a measure for party purposes which it would not become me to adopt."[41]

There is no record of Hamilton ever endorsing the currently prevailing system in which states conduct popular elections to award 100% of their electoral votes to the candidate who receives the most popular votes in the state.

Alexander Hamilton died in 1804. Hamilton's home state of New York did not adopt the winner-take-all rule until 1832. It was not until 1832 that the winner-take-all rule became predominant throughout the country.

In short, Alexander Hamilton, the other Founding Fathers, and the rest of the Founding Generation were dead for decades before the state-by-state winner-take-all rule became the predominant method for awarding electoral votes.[42]

9.1.6. MYTH: The National Popular Vote compact should be rejected because a proposal for direct election of the President was rejected by the 1787 Constitutional Convention.

QUICK ANSWER:

- The 1787 Constitutional Convention voted against several methods for selecting the President, including having state legislatures choose the President, having Governors make the choice, election of the President by presidential electors chosen by districts, and nationwide popular election.

- The wording that actually ended up in the Constitution does not prohibit the use of any of the methods that were debated and rejected, as evidenced by the fact that three of the methods rejected by the Constitutional Convention were used in the nation's first presidential election in 1789, namely election of presidential electors by district, appointment by legislatures, and gubernatorial appointment.

MORE DETAILED ANSWER:

In referring to supporters of the National Popular Vote plan, John Samples of the Cato Institute wrote:

> "They suggest that the power to appoint electors is unconstrained by the Constitution. It is accurate that the Constitution does not explicitly con-

---

Organizations. Chapel Hill, NC: University of North Carolina Press. Page 185. See also Weisberger, Bernard A. 2001. *America Afire: Jefferson, Adams, and the First Contested Election*. William Morrow. Page 239.

[41] Brief of F.A. Baker for Plaintiffs in Error in *McPherson v. Blacker*. 1892. Page 31.

[42] After 1832 (and until 1992), there was never more than one state, in any one presidential election, that did not employ the winner-take-all rule to award all of its electoral votes to the candidate who received the most popular votes in the state.

strain the power of state legislatures in allocating electors. But **a brief consideration of the history of the drafting of this part of the Constitution suggests some implicit constraints on state choices**.

"The Framers considered several ways of electing a president. . . . On July 17, 1787, the delegates from nine states voted against direct election of the president; the representatives of one state, Pennsylvania, voted for it."[43]

. . .

"NPV offers a way to institute a means of electing the president that was rejected by the Framers of the Constitution."[44] [Emphasis added]

Professor Norman Williams of Willamette University has stated:

"The Framers expressly and overwhelmingly rejected vesting the selection of the President directly in the people. Despite their republican instincts, the delegates believed that the people would be unable to identify worthy candidates, most of whom (in the framers' expectations) would be unknown to the people at large. In a predominantly rural nation lacking a developed system of public education and a nationwide system of transportation or communication, theirs was not a trifling concern."[45]

Prior to arriving at the eventual wording of section 1 of Article II, the 1787 Constitutional Convention debated the method of choosing the President on 22 separate days and took 30 (mostly contradictory) votes on the matter.[46]

The methods that were rejected included:

- electing presidential electors by districts,
- having state legislatures choose the President,
- having Governors choose the President,
- nationwide direct election, and
- having Congress choose the President.

If John Samples and Norman Williams were correct in asserting that it is unconstitutional for a state to use a method of choosing presidential electors that was rejected by the Constitutional Convention, then George Washington, John Adams, Thomas Jefferson, James Madison, and James Monroe were all elected unconstitutionally. Indeed,

---

[43] Samples, John. *A Critique of the National Popular Vote Plan for Electing the President.* Cato Institute Policy Analysis No. 622. October 13, 2008. Page 8.

[44] Samples, John. *A Critique of the National Popular Vote Plan for Electing the President.* Cato Institute Policy Analysis No. 622. October 13, 2008. Page 13.

[45] Williams, Norman. Why the National Popular Vote compact is unconstitutional. *Brigham Young University Law Review.* November 19, 2012. Page 138. http://papers.ssrn.com/sol3/papers.cfm?abstract_id=2188020.

[46] Edwards, George C. III. 2004. *Why the Electoral College Is Bad for America.* New Haven, CT: Yale University Press.

a *majority* of the presidential electors in the nation's *first nine presidential elections* (1789–1820) were chosen using methods rejected by the Constitutional Convention.

On June 2, 1787, the Convention voted against a motion by James Wilson of Pennsylvania specifying that the voters would elect presidential electors by district.[47] Madison reported:

> "Mr. Wilson made the following motion, to be substituted for the mode proposed by Mr. Randolph's resolution,
>
> > 'that the Executive Magistracy shall be elected in the following manner: **That the States be divided into ___ districts: & that the persons qualified to vote in each district for members of the first branch of the national Legislature elect ___ members for their respective districts to be electors of the Executive magistracy**, that the said Electors of the Executive magistracy meet at ___ and they or any ___ of them so met shall proceed to elect by ballot, but not out of their own body [the] person in whom the Executive authority of the national Government shall be vested.'" [Emphasis added]

Despite the Constitutional Convention's rejection of the district system, Virginia and Delaware implemented Wilson's rejected plan and authorized their voters to elect their state's presidential electors by district in the nation's first presidential election in 1789. Moreover, in the nine presidential elections between 1789 and 1820 (when James Monroe was elected), the voters in a total of eight states (including Massachusetts, Maryland, North Carolina, Kentucky, Illinois, and Maine) elected presidential electors by district on one or more occasions.

Moreover, if John Samples and Norman Williams were correct in asserting that section 1 of Article II precludes states from using a method of choosing presidential electors that was rejected by the Constitutional Convention, Maine and Nebraska's *current* district method would be unconstitutional.

Of course, the U.S. Supreme Court upheld Michigan's 1892 law specifying that the voters elect the state's presidential electors by congressional district in *McPherson v. Blacker*.[48]

On July 24, 1787, the Constitutional Convention rejected selection of the President by state legislatures. Nonetheless, in 1789, Connecticut, South Carolina, and Georgia chose to appoint their presidential electors in the state legislature. In the nine presidential elections between 1789 and 1820, the legislatures of a total of 15 states (including New Hampshire, Massachusetts, Rhode Island, New York, New Jersey, Pennsylva-

---

[47] Madison Debates. Yale Law School. *The Avalon Project: Documents in Law, History, and Diplomacy.* On June 2, 1787, http://avalon.law.yale.edu/18th_century/debates_602.asp.

[48] *McPherson v. Blacker*, 146 U.S. 1. 1892.

nia, Delaware, South Carolina, Kentucky, Louisiana, Indiana, Alabama, and Missouri) appointed their state's presidential electors on one or more occasions.[49]

On June 15, 1787, the Constitutional Convention voted against selection of the President by state Governors. Nonetheless, New Jersey's presidential electors were appointed by the Governor and his Council in the nation's first presidential election in 1789.[50] In 1792, Vermont combined two methods that were rejected by the Constitutional Convention. Its presidential electors were appointed by a "Grand Committee" consisting of the Governor and his Council along with the state House of Representatives (the only house Vermont had at the time).[51]

In summary, the course of conduct of the Founding Generation immediately after ratification of the Constitution indicates that no one interpreted section 1 of Article II as precluding the states from using methods of choosing presidential electors that were rejected at some point during the Constitutional Convention.

9.1.7. MYTH: The National Popular Vote compact should be rejected because of implied restrictions on a state's choices for appointing presidential electors and because only the Founders' "failure of imagination" prevented them from explicitly prohibiting the National Popular Vote compact.

QUICK ANSWER:

- Section 1 of Article II of the U.S. Constitution does not prohibit, require, encourage, or discourage the use of any particular method for awarding a state's electoral votes. The wording "as the Legislature . . . may direct" permits the states to exercise their power to choose the manner of appointing their presidential electors in any way they see fit—subject only to the implicit limitation on all grants of power in the Constitution, namely that the states not violate any specific restriction on state action contained elsewhere in the Constitution.

- The U.S. Supreme Court rejected the urging of (the losing) attorney in *McPherson v. Blacker* that it ignore the wording of the section 1 of Article II

---

[49] In *Bush v. Gore* in 2000, the U.S. Supreme Court agreed that state legislators could appoint presidential electors. 531 U.S. 98.

[50] An Act for carrying into effect, on the part of the state of New Jersey, the Constitution of the United States. November 21, 1788. *Acts of the General Assembly of the State of New Jersey.* Page 481. See also DenBoer, Gordon; Brown, Lucy Trumbull; and Hagermann, Charles D. (editors). 1986. *The Documentary History of the First Federal Elections 1788–1790.* Madison, WI: University of Wisconsin Press. Volume III. Page 29. Interestingly, the U.S. Supreme Court's opinion in the 1892 case of *McPherson v. Blacker* contains an error concerning New Jersey. In its historical review of methods used to appoint presidential electors in 1789, the Court (incorrectly) stated, "At the first presidential election, the appointment of electors was made by the legislatures of Connecticut, Delaware, Georgia, New Jersey, and South Carolina." 146 U.S. 1 at 29. The source of this misinformation about New Jersey appears to be page 19 of the plaintiff's brief in the 1892 case. *Brief of F.A. Baker for Plaintiffs in Error* in *McPherson v. Blacker.* 1892.

[51] An Act Directing the Mode of Appointing Electors to Elect a President and Vice President of the United States. Passed November 3, 1791. *Laws of 1791.* Page 43.

and judicially manufacture restrictions on the power of the states to choose the manner of appointing their presidential electors.

- In deciding *McPherson v. Blacker*, the U.S. Supreme Court rejected the argument that the widespread use of the winner-take-all rule, over an extended period of time, extinguished the power of the states to adopt different methods of appointing their presidential electors (that is, the non-use argument).

- The 10th Amendment independently addresses the question of whether the states are prohibited from exercising a particular power when the Constitution contains no specific prohibition against it and, therefore, the question of whether there are unstated implicit restrictions on the allowable methods for appointing presidential electors.

MORE DETAILED ANSWER:

In referring to supporters of the National Popular Vote plan, John Samples of the Cato Institute wrote:

> "They suggest that the power to appoint electors is unconstrained by the Constitution. It is accurate that the Constitution does not explicitly constrain the power of state legislatures in allocating electors. But a brief consideration of the history of the drafting of this part of the Constitution suggests **some implicit constraints on state choices**."[52] [Emphasis added]

Throughout her book *Enlightened Democracy: The Case for the Electoral College*, Tara Ross, an opponent of the National Popular Vote compact, generally describes the Founding Fathers in glowing terms.

> "The Electoral College is . . . **a carefully considered and thought-out solution**."[53] [Emphasis added]

Ross repeatedly refers to the

> "**finely wrought procedures** found in the Constitution." [Emphasis added]

Ross reminds us that:

> "The Founders spent months debating the appropriate presidential election process for the new American nation."[54]

---

[52] Samples, John. *A Critique of the National Popular Vote Plan for Electing the President.* Cato Institute Policy Analysis No. 622. October 13, 2008. Page 8.

[53] Ross, Tara. 2004. *Enlightened Democracy: The Case for the Electoral College.* Los Angeles, CA: World Ahead Publishing Company. Page 51.

[54] Ross, Tara. 2010. Federalism & Separation of Powers: Legal and Logistical Ramifications of the National Popular Vote Plan. *Engage.* Volume 11. Number 2. September 2010. Pages 37–44.

Then, after extolling the Founders' work product and wisdom, Ross writes:

"The [U.S. Supreme] Court has held that 'the State legislature's power to select the manner for appointing electors is plenary.' . . .

"Is this power of state legislators completely unrestricted? If it is, then Rhode Island could decide to allocate its electors to the winner of the Vermont election. In a more extreme move, New York could allocate its electors to the United Nations. **Florida could decide that Fidel Castro always appoints its electors.** . . .

"NPV is the opposite of what the Founders wanted, but failure of imagination prevented the Founders from explicitly prohibiting this particular manner of allocating electors."[55] [Emphasis added]

A glance at the U.S. Constitution shows that the Founders displayed no shortage of legal talent and certainly did not suffer from any "failure of imagination" in crafting restrictions on the exercise of power when they thought that restrictions were advisable. Section 8 of Article I provides:

"The Congress shall have Power To lay and collect Taxes, Duties, Imposts and Excises . . . **but all Duties, Imposts and Excises shall be uniform throughout the United States**." [Emphasis added]

Section 10 of Article I provides:

"No State shall . . . make any Thing **but gold and silver Coin** a Tender in Payment of Debts." [Emphasis added]

The Founders even limited the scope of future constitutional amendments in Article V with two specific restrictions:

"No Amendment which may be made prior to the Year One thousand eight hundred and eight shall in any Manner affect the first[56] and fourth[57] Clauses in the Ninth Section of the first Article; and that no State, without its Consent, shall be deprived of its equal Suffrage in the Senate." [Emphasis added]

---

[55] Ross, Tara. 2010. Federalism & Separation of Powers: Legal and Logistical Ramifications of the National Popular Vote Plan. *Engage.* Volume 11. Number 2. September 2010. Pages 37–44.

[56] Clause 1 of section 9 of Article I states, "The Migration or Importation of such Persons as any of the States now existing shall think proper to admit, shall not be prohibited by the Congress prior to the Year one thousand eight hundred and eight, but a Tax or duty may be imposed on such Importation, not exceeding ten dollars for each Person."

[57] Clause 4 of section 9 of Article I of the Constitution states "No Capitation, or other direct, Tax shall be laid, unless in Proportion to the Census or Enumeration herein before directed to be taken."

There are numerous additional examples of carefully crafted restrictions placed on grants of power throughout the Constitution.

Even section 1 of Article II itself contains a restriction on the power of the states to appoint their presidential electors.

> "Each State shall appoint, in such Manner as the Legislature thereof may direct, a Number of Electors, equal to the whole Number of Senators and Representatives to which the State may be entitled in the Congress: **but no Senator or Representative, or Person holding an Office of Trust or Profit under the United States, shall be appointed an Elector.**"
> [Emphasis added]

Tellingly, section 1 of Article II contains *no other restriction* on the manner by which the states exercise their power.

Ross' "failure of imagination" argument echoes the argument made in 1892 before the U.S. Supreme Court by the losing attorney in *McPherson v. Blacker*.

Referring to Great Britain (the villainous 1890's analog of Fidel Castro in present-day American politics), attorney F. A. Baker argued:

> "The crown in England is hereditary, the succession being regulated by act of parliament.
>
> "Would it be competent for a State legislature to pass a similar act, and provide that A. B. and his heirs at law forever, or some one or more of them, should appoint the presidential electors of that State?"[58]

In its unanimous ruling in *McPherson v. Blacker*, the U.S. Supreme Court answered Baker's argument about unstated constitutional restrictions on the power of the states to award their electoral votes:

> "The constitution does not provide that the appointment of electors shall be by popular vote, nor that the electors shall be voted for upon a general ticket, **nor that the majority of those who exercise the elective franchise can alone choose the electors**. It recognizes that the people act through their representatives in the legislature, and **leaves it to the legislature exclusively to define the method** of effecting the object. The framers of the constitution employed words in their natural sense; and, where they are plain and clear, **resort to collateral aids to interpretation is unnecessary, and cannot be indulged in to narrow or enlarge the text.**"[59] [Emphasis added]

---

[58] Brief of F.A. Baker for Plaintiffs in Error in *McPherson v. Blacker*. 1892. Page 73.

[59] *McPherson v. Blacker*. 146 U.S. 1 at 27. 1892.

The U.S. Supreme Court recognized in *McPherson v. Blacker* that there are limitations on a state's power under section 1 of Article II. For example, a state's constitution may constrain a state's power to choose the method of appointing presidential electors.

> "The state does not act by its people in their collective capacity, but through such political agencies as are duly constituted and established. The legislative power is the supreme authority, **except as limited by the constitution of the state**, and the sovereignty of the people is exercised through their representatives in the legislature, unless by the fundamental law power is elsewhere reposed. The constitution of the United States frequently refers to the state as a political community, and also in terms to the people of the several states and the citizens of each state. **What is forbidden or required to be done by a state is forbidden or required of the legislative power under state constitutions as they exist.** The clause under consideration does not read that the people or the citizens shall appoint, but that "each state shall;" and if the words, 'in such manner as the legislature thereof may direct,' had been omitted, it would seem that the legislative power of appointment could not have been successfully questioned **in the absence of any provision in the state constitution in that regard**. Hence the insertion of those words, while operating as a limitation upon the state in respect of any attempt to circumscribe the legislative power, cannot be held to operate as a limitation on that power itself."[60] [Emphasis added]

The Court continued:

> "In short, the appointment and mode of appointment of electors belong **exclusively** to the states under the constitution of the United States"[61] [Emphasis added]

The losing attorney in *McPherson v. Blacker* (F.A. Baker) urged the Court to judicially manufacture restrictions that do not actually appear in the Constitution and to adopt a "more elastic system of government."

> "There is no rule of constitutional interpretation, or of judicial duty, which requires the court . . . to adhere to the obsolete design of the constitution."[62]

In his plea to the U.S. Supreme Court to engage in judicial activism, Baker bemoaned his client's earlier loss at the Michigan Supreme Court:

---

[60] *McPherson v. Blacker*. 146 U.S. 1 at 25. 1892.

[61] *Id.* at 29.

[62] Brief of F.A. Baker for Plaintiffs in Error in *McPherson v. Blacker*. 1892. Page 80.

"There can be no such thing as an absolutely rigid constitution. It is an impossibility, although the supreme court in Michigan in its wisdom most solemnly declares, that it will recognize no other.[63]"

Baker also argued that the widespread use of state winner-take-all statutes, over an extended period of time, extinguished the power of the states to adopt different methods of appointing their presidential electors (that is, the non-use argument).

"There is no rule of constitutional interpretation, or of judicial duty, which requires the court . . . to **disregard the plan of the electoral college as it actually exists, after a century of practical experience and development**."[64] [Emphasis added]

In 2012, Professor Norman Williams of Willamette University echoed the non-use argument made by (losing) attorney Baker in the 1892 case of *McPherson v. Blacker* by saying that the states are limited today to choices of methods for appointing presidential electors that have been used in the past. Tellingly, while remaking Baker's non-use argument, Williams concedes that the Constitution does not actually "express" the limitation for which he is arguing.

"The framers had created a presidential election system . . . [in which] the choice of President would be made not by an undifferentiated mass of people nationwide, but by **electors accountable to the people of their individual states. To be sure, the framers did not make these expectations express.** The notion that any state would appoint its electors in accordance with the wishes, even in part, of voters in other states was **beyond the imagination of any at the time.** Nevertheless, **if any doubt about this expectation exists, it is negated by actual experience.** As Part III will show, the actual practice of the states in the wake of the Constitutional Convention—a practice that has continued to this day— demonstrates the universal understanding among the states, both then and now, that presidential electors from each state are to be selected in accordance with the will of the voters in each state, not the entire national populace.[65] . . .

"**History illuminates and informs the scope of state power under Article II. Throughout the nation's history, states have used one of four processes for selecting their presidential electors:** (1) legislative

---

[63] *Id.* at 80.

[64] Brief of F.A. Baker for Plaintiffs in Error in *McPherson v. Blacker.* 1892. Page 80.

[65] Williams, Norman. Why the National Popular Vote Compact is unconstitutional. *Brigham Young University Law Review.* November 19, 2012. Pages 139–140. http://papers.ssrn.com/sol3/papers.cfm?abstract _id=2188020.

appointment, (2) popular election in which all electors are selected on the basis of the statewide vote (an at-large or winner-take-all system), (3) popular election by district, or (4) a combination of the latter two electoral systems—a hybrid process in which some electors are elected on the basis of the statewide vote and some on the basis of a district vote. **Critically, under all four systems, each state's electors are selected in accordance with the wishes of the people of the state, not the nation generally.**

"**Not once between 1880 and today,** a period in which every state in the union has conducted a statewide popular election for its electors, **has any state selected its electors based on the votes of individuals in other states**. Rather, as the framers expected, states have selected their electors based on the will of state voters, not the nation at large."[66] [Emphasis added]

The U.S. Supreme Court rejected the non-use argument in its ruling in *McPherson v. Blacker*:

"The question before us is not one of policy, but of power . . .. **The prescription of the written law cannot be overthrown because the states have laterally exercised, in a particular way, a power which they might have exercised in some other way.**"[67] [Emphasis added]

If it were the case that the states were precluded from using any method of awarding electoral votes that was not specifically "imagined" by the Founders, then the winner-take-all method would itself be unconstitutional. No historian, or anyone else of whom we are aware, has ever argued that the Founders expected, or wanted, 100% of a state's presidential electors to vote slavishly, in lockstep, for a choice for President made by an extra-constitutional meeting (namely, a political party's national nominating caucus or convention).

The winner-take-all rule was never debated or voted upon by the 1787 Constitutional Convention.

It is not mentioned in the *Federalist Papers*.

It was used by only three states in the nation's first presidential election in 1789 (and was abandoned by all three by 1800).

The Founders were dead for decades by the time the winner-take-all rule came into widespread use.

It was not until the 11th presidential election (1828) that the winner-take-all rule was used by a majority of the states.

---

[66] Williams, Norman. Why the National Popular Vote Compact is unconstitutional. *Brigham Young University Law Review*. November 19, 2012. Page 151. http://papers.ssrn.com/sol3/papers.cfm?abstract_id=2188020.

[67] *McPherson v. Blacker*. 146 U.S. 1 at 36. 1892.

There is virtually unanimous agreement among historians that the Founding Fathers intended that the Electoral College would operate as a deliberative body and did not anticipate the emergence of political parties.

The Constitutional Convention never agreed on any particular method for choosing the President. On August 31, 1787, the Convention assigned the question of electing the President to a special Committee of Eleven. On September 4, the Committee of Eleven returned with a recommendation that the President be chosen by presidential electors (an element of Wilson's rejected motion of June 2, 1787); however, the Committee *could not agree on any particular method for choosing the presidential electors*. The result was that section 1 of Article II empowered the states to decide how to choose their presidential electors.

> "Each State shall appoint, in such Manner **as the Legislature thereof may direct**, a Number of Electors . . . ."[68] [Emphasis added]

Section 1 of Article II of the U.S. Constitution does not prohibit, require, encourage, or discourage the use of any particular method for awarding a state's electoral votes. The wording "as the Legislature . . . may direct" permits the states to exercise their power to choose the manner of appointing their presidential electors in any way they see fit—subject only to the implicit limitation on all grants of power in the Constitution, namely that the states not violate any specific restriction on state action contained elsewhere in the Constitution.[69]

The report of the U.S. Senate Committee on Privileges and Elections in 1876 reviewed the history of the appointment of presidential electors by state legislatures and Governors:

> "The appointment of these electors is thus placed absolutely and wholly with the Legislatures of the several states. **They may be chosen by the Legislature**, or the Legislature may provide that they shall be elected by the people of the State at large, or in districts, as are members of Congress, which was the case formerly in many States, and **it is no doubt competent for the Legislature to authorize the governor, or the Supreme Court of the State, or any other agent of its will, to appoint these electors.**"[70] [Emphasis added]

---

[68] U.S. Constitution. Article II, section 1, clause 2.

[69] Among the specific restrictions on the states concerning the manner of appointing their presidential electors are those contained in the 14th Amendment (equal protection), 15th Amendment (prohibiting denial of the vote on account of "race, color, or previous condition of servitude"), the 19th Amendment (woman's suffrage), the 24th amendment (prohibiting poll taxes), and the 26th Amendment (18-year-old vote). The Constitution's explicit prohibition against *ex post facto* laws and the Impairments Clause also operate as restraints on section 1 of Article II.

[70] Senate Report 395. Forty-Third Congress.

The 10th Amendment independently addresses the question of whether the states are prohibited from exercising a particular power when the Constitution contains no specific prohibition against it and, therefore, the question of whether there are implicit restrictions on the allowable methods for appointing presidential electors.

> **"The powers** not delegated to the United States by the Constitution, **nor prohibited by it to the States, are reserved to the States** respectively, or to the people." [Emphasis added]

Section 1 of Article II contains only one restriction on state choices on the manner of appointing their presidential electors, namely that no state may appoint a member of Congress or federal appointees as presidential elector.[71]

The 10th Amendment was ratified in 1791 (that is, *after* ratification of the original Constitution) and thus takes precedence over the original Constitution. Even if there were implicit restrictions in the original 1787 Constitution on state choices on the manner of appointing their presidential electors (perhaps in the form of penumbral emanations emitted by section 1 of Article II), such implicit restrictions were extinguished in 1791 by the 10th Amendment.

9.1.8. MYTH: Federalism would be undermined by a national popular vote.

QUICK ANSWER:

- Federalism concerns the distribution of power between state governments and the national government.
- The power of state governments relative to the federal government is not increased or decreased based on whether presidential electors are elected along state boundary lines (as is the case under the current state-by-state winner-take-all system), along congressional district boundary lines (as is currently the case in Nebraska and Maine), or national lines (as would be the case under the National Popular Vote plan).
- There is no connection between the way power is—or should be—distributed between the state and federal governments and the boundary lines used to tally votes for presidential electors.

---

[71] The original Constitution contains few specific restrictions on state action that bear on the appointment of presidential electors. Thus, under Article II, section 1, clause 1, a state legislature may, for example, pass a law making it a crime to commit fraud in a presidential election. However, a state legislature certainly may not pass an *ex post facto* (retroactive) law making it a crime to commit fraud in a presidential election. Similarly, a state legislature may not pass a law imposing criminal penalties on specifically named persons who may have committed fraudulent acts in connection with a presidential election (that is, a bill of attainder). Also, the Constitution's explicit prohibition against a "law impairing the obligation of contract" operates as a restraint on the delegation of power contained in section 1 of Article II. Of course, various later amendments restrict state choices, including the 14th Amendment (equal protection), 15th Amendment (prohibiting denial of the vote on account of "race, color, or previous condition of servitude"), the 19th Amendment (woman's suffrage), the 24th amendment (prohibiting poll taxes), and the 26th Amendment (18-year-old vote).

- The National Popular Vote approach preserves the power of the states to conduct elections—an important element of federalism.

MORE DETAILED ANSWER:

Federalism concerns the distribution of power between state governments and the national government.

Avid supporters of federalism are typically ardent about preserving and enhancing the power of state government in relation to the power of the national government.

John Samples of the Cato Institute argues that a national popular vote would "weaken federalism."

> "Anti-federalists feared the new Constitution would centralize power and threaten liberty. . . .

> "The founders sought to fashion institutional compromises that responded to the concerns of the states and yet created a more workable government than had existed under the Articles of Confederation. . . .

> "The national government would [be] part of a larger design of checks and balances that would temper and restrain political power." . . .

> "The realization of **the NPV plan would continue [the] trend toward nationalization and centralized power.**"[72] [Emphasis added]

UCLA Professor Daniel H. Lowenstein has argued:

> "Against all the pressures of nationalization, **it is important to maintain the states as strong and vital elements of our system.**"[73] [Emphasis added]

The power of state governments relative to the federal government is not increased or decreased based on whether presidential electors are elected along state boundary lines (as is the case under the current state-by-state winner-take-all system), along congressional district boundary lines (as is currently the case in Nebraska and Maine), or along national lines (as would be the case under the National Popular Vote plan).

The balance of power between the state and federal levels of government is controlled by the U.S. Constitution, state constitutions, and various federal and state laws.

The National Popular Vote plan does not affect the amount of power that state governments possess relative to the federal government.

When the Founding Fathers from Virginia, Delaware, and Massachusetts returned from the 1787 Constitutional Convention and organized the first presidential

---

[72] Samples, John. *A Critique of the National Popular Vote Plan for Electing the President.* Cato Institute Policy Analysis No. 622. October 13, 2008.

[73] Debate entitled "Should We Dispense with the Electoral College?" sponsored by PENNumbra (University of Pennsylvania Law Review) available at http://www.pennumbra.com/debates/pdfs/electoral_college.pdf.

election in their respective states in 1789, they certainly did not reduce the powers of their state governments relative to the federal government when they chose to elect their state's presidential electors by district (rather than the statewide winner-take-all method).

Similarly, the powers of the state governments of Virginia, Massachusetts, and North Carolina were not enhanced relative to the federal government when those states subsequently decided to change (in the early 1800s) to the winner-take-all rule.

Surely, no one would argue that Nebraska and Maine undermined federalism when they decided (in 1992 and 1969, respectively) to award their electoral votes by congressional district (instead of using the statewide winner-take-all method).

The National Popular Vote compact preserves the power of the states to conduct elections—an important element of federalism. It also preserves the power of the states to make future changes in the method of electing the President.

Adoption of the National Popular Vote compact is an exercise of federalism. It constitutes action by state governments to solve a recognized problem. It is an exercise of a power explicitly granted to the states by the U.S. Constitution.

As then-Congressman George H.W. Bush said on September 18, 1969, in support of direct popular election of the President:

> "This legislation has a great deal to commend it. It will correct the wrongs of the present mechanism . . . by calling for direct election of the President and Vice President. . . . Yet, in spite of these drastic reforms, the bill is **not . . . detrimental to our federal system or one that will change the departmentalized and local nature of voting in this country**.

> "In electing the President and Vice President, the Constitution establishes the principle that votes are cast by States. This legislation does not tamper with that principle. It only changes the manner in which the States vote. Instead of voting by intermediaries, the States will certify their popular vote count to the Congress. **The states will maintain primary responsibility for the ballot and for the qualifications of voters.** In other words, they will still designate the time, place, and manner in which elections will be held. Thus, there is a very good argument to be made that **the basic nature of our federal system has not been disturbed**.[74] [Emphasis added]

In short, there is no connection between the way power is—or should be—distributed between the state and federal governments and the boundary lines used to tally votes for presidential electors.

---

[74] *Congressional Record.* September 18, 1969. Pages 25,990–25,991.

9.1.9. MYTH: A national popular vote is contrary to the concept that the United States is a republic, not a democracy.

QUICK ANSWER:

- In a republic (as the term is defined in the *Federalist Papers* and used in the U.S. Constitution), citizens do not rule directly but instead, elect officeholders to represent them and conduct the business of government in the period between elections. Therefore, the United States is currently a republic—not a democracy—and it will remain a republic, with or without the National Popular Vote approach to appointing presidential electors.
- The division of power between the citizenry and elected officeholders to whom governmental power is delegated is not affected by the boundaries of the regions used to tally popular votes in choosing presidential electors.
- Popular election of the chief executive does not determine whether a government is a republic or democracy.

MORE DETAILED ANSWER:

Writing in the *Patriot Action Network*, Brad Zinn refers to former U.S. Senator Fred Thompson (R–Tennessee) and 2008 presidential candidate as follows:

> "Sen. Fred Thompson supports the National Popular Vote Compact, which effectively guts the Electoral College, and ends the Republic as we know it."

> "**With this National Popular Vote method, we will no longer be a Republic, but a democracy**. A democracy is the one thing that the Founding Fathers feared more than anything else. Every democracy in the history of the world has devolved into tyranny. Democracy is two wolves and a sheep voting on what's for dinner. The Founding Fathers knew this and made every effort to prevent the U.S. from slipping into the abyss. As Franklin said, 'This is a Republic, if you can keep it.' **The National Popular Vote Compact will end the Republic**."[75] [Emphasis added]

In *Federalist No. 10*, James Madison—frequently called the "Father of the Constitution"—said that the

> "difference between a democracy and a republic are: first, **the delegation of the government, in the latter, to a small number of citizens elected by the rest**; secondly, the greater number of citizens, and greater sphere of country, over which the latter may be extended."[76] [Emphasis added]

---

[75] Zinn, Brad. Does Fred Thompson really understand the Constitution? *Patriot Action Network*. July 19, 2012. http://resistance.ning.com/forum/topics/does-fred-thompson-really-understand-the-constitution?page =1&commentId=2600775%3AComment%3A5855088&x=1#2600775Comment5855088.

[76] Publius. The utility of the union as a safeguard against domestic faction and insurrection (continued). *Daily Advertiser.* November 22, 1787. *Federalist No. 10*.

In *Federalist No. 14*, Madison distinguished between a republic and a democracy by saying:

> "The true distinction between these forms was also adverted to on a former occasion. It is, that **in a democracy, the people meet and exercise the government in person; in a republic, they assemble and administer it by their representatives and agents**. A democracy, consequently, will be confined to a small spot. A republic may be extended over a large region."[77] [Emphasis added]

In a republic, the citizens do not rule directly, but instead elect officeholders to represent them and to conduct the business of government in the period between elections.

In the United States, legislation is approved by officeholders who serve for a term of two years (in the U.S. House of Representatives), six years (in the U.S. Senate), and four years (the President). Laws are executed and administered by an officeholder (the President) who serves for a term of four years.

The United States has a "republican form of government" because of this existing division of power between the citizenry and the elected officials who act on behalf of the citizenry between elections. Therefore, the United States *is*, at the present time, a republic—not a democracy.

Today, examples of direct democracy in the United States are—to use Madison's wording in *Federalist No. 14*—limited to "small spots," such as town meetings in New Hampshire.

Popular election of the chief executive does not determine whether a government is a republic or democracy. The division of power between the citizenry and elected officeholders to whom governmental power is delegated is not affected by the boundaries of the regions used to tally popular votes in choosing presidential electors. The United States is neither less nor more a "republic" if its chief executive is elected under the state-by-state winner-take-all method (i.e., awarding all of a state's electoral votes to the candidate who receives the most popular votes in each separate state), under a district system (such as used by Maine and Nebraska), or under the proposed national popular vote system (in which the winner would be the candidate receiving the most popular votes in all 50 states and the District of Columbia).

The United States *is* currently a republic under current state winner-take-all statutes, and it would remain so under the National Popular Vote compact.

The meaning of the phrase "republican form of government" can be ascertained by examining the single place in the U.S. Constitution where these words appear, namely the Guarantee Clause:

---

[77] Publius. Objections to the proposed constitution from extent of territory answered. *New York Packet.* November 30, 1787. *Federalist No. 14.*

"The United States shall guarantee to every State in this Union a **Republican Form of Government**."[78] [Emphasis added]

At the time of the Constitutional Convention in 1787, Connecticut, Massachusetts, New Hampshire, and Rhode Island conducted popular elections for Governor.[79]

If popular election of a state's chief executive were a violation of the Guarantee Clause, then these four states would have been in violation of the Guarantee Clause starting from the moment that the writing of the Constitution was finished in 1787.[80]

It seems unlikely that the delegates from these four states would have voted for the Constitution at the 1787 Constitutional Convention if they believed that their own states lacked a "republican form of government" at the time.

It would seem even more unlikely that these four states would have ratified the Constitution if they believed that they were in violation of the Guarantee Clause.

Moreover, in the first few decades after ratification of the Constitution, the remaining original states (as well as additional states that were admitted to the Union) adopted the practice of directly electing their chief executive. No one has ever argued that these states denied their citizens a "republican form of government" because they directly elected their chief executives. No one has ever argued that the federal government should have invoked the Guarantee Clause and intervened (militarily or otherwise) to prevent these states from electing their chief executives by popular vote.

In short, popular election of the chief executive has nothing to do with the question of whether a particular government is a republic or democracy. Direct popular election of the chief executive is not incompatible with a "republican form of government."

As Senator Fred Thompson said (quoted by Zinn):

"The National Popular Vote approach offers the states a way to deal with this issue in a way that is **totally consistent with our constitutional principles**." [Emphasis added]

9.1.10. MYTH: The Guarantee Clause of the Constitution precludes the National Popular Vote compact.

QUICK ANSWER:

- The argument that the National Popular Vote compact violates the Guarantee Clause is based on an interpretation of the clause that is not supported by the clause's language or any judicial precedent.
- Moreover, even if the Guarantee Clause were applied to the national government, direct popular election of the chief executive is not incompatible with "a republican form of government" or the concept of a "compound republic."

---

[78] U.S. Constitution. Article IV, section 4, clause 1.

[79] Dubin, Michael J. 2003. *United States Gubernatorial Elections 1776–1860*. Jefferson, NC: McFarland & Company. Page xx.

[80] Vermont was not one of the 13 original states that ratified the Constitution.

MORE DETAILED ANSWER:

The Guarantee Clause of the U.S. Constitution states:

> "The United States shall guarantee **to every State in this Union** a Republican Form of Government."[81] [Emphasis added]

Kristin Feeley has argued that the National Popular Vote compact would violate the Guarantee Clause.[82]

Feeley's claim requires

(1) extending the interpretation of the words "every State in this Union" to include the national government, and

(2) arguing that direct popular election of the President is incompatible with the concept of a "republican form of government" and incompatible with the concept of a "compound republic."

In her review of Guarantee Clause jurisprudence, Feeley found no judicial precedent (or even a dissenting opinion) that has ever applied the guarantee of the Guarantee Clause to the national government. In other words, the Guarantee Clause has never been interpreted to say:

> "**The United States** shall guarantee **the United States** a Republican Form of Government." [Emphasis added]

Assume, for the sake of argument, that the Guarantee Clause were interpreted to apply to the national government. Based on that assumption, Feeley then argues:

> "The Guarantee Clause provides for a compound republican government at the national level. . . . NPV legislation violates the Guarantee Clause by **blurring important state lines in our compound republic**." [Emphasis added]

There is nothing about direct popular election of the President that is incompatible with the concept of a "republican form of government" or a "compound republic."

As to the definition of a "republic," James Madison—frequently called the "Father of the Constitution"—wrote in *Federalist No. 10* that the

> "difference between a democracy and a republic are: first, **the delegation of the government, in the latter, to a small number of citizens elected by the rest** . . . "[83] [Emphasis added]

In *Federalist No. 14*, Madison wrote:

---

[81] U.S. Constitution. Article IV, section 4, clause 1.

[82] Feeley, Kristin. 2009. Guaranteeing a federally elected president. 103 *Northwestern University Law Review* 1427–1460.

[83] Publius. The utility of the union as a safeguard against domestic faction and insurrection (continued). *Daily Advertiser.* November 22, 1787. *Federalist No. 10.*

"The true distinction between these forms was also adverted to on a former occasion. It is, that **in a democracy, the people meet and exercise the government in person; in a republic, they assemble and administer it by their representatives and agents.**"[84] [Emphasis added]

In short, the definition of a "republic" is based on whether elected officeholders *exercise governmental power* (as opposed to the people directly exercising governmental power). The National Popular Vote compact would do nothing to change the fact that the people delegate power to elected officeholders who, in turn, run the government.

The term "compound republic" appears twice in the *Federalist Papers*.[85]

James Madison's *Federalist No. 51* is entitled "The Structure of the Government Must Furnish the Proper Checks and Balances Between the Different Departments." It distinguishes between a simple "republic" (where the separation of powers among different departments of government works to protect the rights of the people) and a "compound republic" (where there are two distinct levels of government).

"In a single republic, all the power surrendered by the people is submitted to the administration of a single government; and the usurpations are guarded against by a division of the government into distinct and separate departments. **In the compound republic of America, the power surrendered by the people is first divided between two distinct governments**, and then the portion allotted to each subdivided among distinct and separate departments. Hence a double security arises to the rights of the people. **The different governments will control each other**, at the same time that each will be controlled by itself."[86] [Emphasis added]

In *Federalist No. 62*, Madison refers to:

"a compound republic, partaking both of the national and federal character"[87]

In short, the definition of a "compound republic" is based on there being *two* distinct layers of government (state and federal), each of which is a republic. The definition of a "compound republic" is not based on the boundaries of the regions used to count popular votes in electing the head of *one of the three* "departments" (branches)

---

[84] Publius. Objections to the proposed constitution from extent of territory answered. *New York Packet*. November 30, 1787. *Federalist No. 14*.

[85] Brown, Adam. Do we live in a "compound Constitutional Republic" or something else? *Utah Data Points*. July 11, 2011. http://utahdatapoints.com/2011/07/do-we-live-in-a-compound-constitutional-republic-or-something-else/.

[86] Publius. The structure of the government must furnish the proper checks and balances between the different departments. *Independent Journal*. February 6, 1788. *Federalist No. 51*.

[87] Publius. *Federalist No. 62*. The Senate. *Independent Journal*. February 27, 1788. *Federalist No. 62*.

of government (i.e., the executive branch) of *one of the two* distinct layers of government (i.e., the federal government).

The National Popular Vote compact would do nothing to affect the existence of the *two* distinct layers of government implied by the term "compound republic."

In short, even if a court were to apply the Guarantee Clause to the national government, there is nothing in the National Popular Vote compact that would affect the fact that the United States has a "republican form of government" and that the United States is a "compound republic."[88]

9.1.11. MYTH: The Meeting Clause of the 12th Amendment precludes the National Popular Vote compact.

QUICK ANSWER:

* The Meeting Clause of the 12th Amendment requires that the physical location of the meeting of presidential electors be inside each separate state, but does not restrict the manner by which states choose their presidential electors.
* The National Popular Vote compact would not affect the meeting place for presidential electors.

MORE DETAILED ANSWER:

The Meeting Clause of the 12th Amendment (ratified in 1804) specifies that the meeting of the presidential electors must be physically conducted in each state.

The 12th Amendment states:

> "**The Electors shall meet in their respective states**, and vote by ballot for President and Vice-President, one of whom, at least, shall not be an inhabitant of the same state with themselves; they shall name in their ballots the person voted for as President, and in distinct ballots the person voted for as Vice-President, and they shall make distinct lists of all persons voted for as President . . . ."[89] [Emphasis added]

Congress has implemented the Meeting Clause of the 12th Amendment by enacting section 7 of chapter 1 of Title 3 of the United States Code:

> "The electors of President and Vice President of each State shall meet and give their votes on the first Monday after the second Wednesday in December next following their appointment **at such place in each State as the legislature of such State shall direct**." [Emphasis added]

---

[88] We also refer the reader to the discussion in section 9.1.9 of whether direct popular election of governors was viewed as incompatible with a "republican Form of Government" at the time of drafting of Constitution and immediately thereafter.

[89] The full text of the 12th Amendment is available in appendix A.

Individual states, in turn, have further implemented the Meeting Clause of the 12th Amendment and section 7 of the United States Code.

For example, current Alaska law provides that Alaska's presidential electors shall meet at the offices of the Director of the Division of Elections located in Juneau:

> "The electors shall meet at the office of the director or other place designated by the director at 11:00 o'clock in the morning on the first Monday after the second Wednesday in December following their election. If Congress fixes a different day for the meeting, the electors shall meet on the day designated by the Act of Congress."[90]

The 12th Amendment does not address the method of choosing presidential electors.

The National Popular Vote compact would not affect the meeting place for presidential electors.

The National Popular Vote compact does not violate the Meeting Clause of the 12th Amendment.

9.1.12. MYTH: The National Popular Vote compact would contradict the 12th Amendment.

QUICK ANSWER:
- The National Popular Vote compact does not contradict anything in the 12th Amendment of the U.S. Constitution.
- The 12th Amendment does not address the manner by which states choose their presidential electors.

MORE DETAILED ANSWER:
Hans von Spakovsky has stated:

> "Without question, the NPV deprives non-participating states of their right under Article V to participate **in deciding whether the Twelfth Amendment, which governs the Electoral College, should be changed.**"[91] [Emphasis added]

The full text of the 12th Amendment to the U.S. Constitution is as follows:

> "The Electors shall meet in their respective states, and vote by ballot for President and Vice-President, one of whom, at least, shall not be an inhabitant of the same state with themselves; they shall name in their ballots the

---

[90] Section 15.30.070.

[91] Von Spakovsky, Hans. *Destroying the Electoral College: The Anti-Federalist National Popular Vote Scheme.* Legal memo. October 27, 2011. http://www.heritage.org/research/reports/2011/10/destroying-the-electoral-college-the-anti-federalist-national-popular-vote-scheme.

person voted for as President, and in distinct ballots the person voted for as Vice-President, and they shall make distinct lists of all persons voted for as President, and of all persons voted for as Vice-President, and of the number of votes for each, which lists they shall sign and certify, and transmit sealed to the seat of the government of the United States, directed to the President of the Senate; The President of the Senate shall, in the presence of the Senate and House of Representatives, open all the certificates and the votes shall then be counted;--The person having the greatest number of votes for President, shall be the President, if such number be a majority of the whole number of Electors appointed; and if no person have such majority, then from the persons having the highest numbers not exceeding three on the list of those voted for as President, the House of Representatives shall choose immediately, by ballot, the President. But in choosing the President, the votes shall be taken by states, the representation from each state having one vote; a quorum for this purpose shall consist of a member or members from two-thirds of the states, and a majority of all the states shall be necessary to a choice. And if the House of Representatives shall not choose a President whenever the right of choice shall devolve upon them, before the fourth day of March next following, then the Vice-President shall act as President, as in the case of the death or other constitutional disability of the President. The person having the greatest number of votes as Vice-President, shall be the Vice-President, if such number be a majority of the whole number of Electors appointed, and if no person have a majority, then from the two highest numbers on the list, the Senate shall choose the Vice-President; a quorum for the purpose shall consist of two-thirds of the whole number of Senators, and a majority of the whole number shall be necessary to a choice. But no person constitutionally ineligible to the office of President shall be eligible to that of Vice-President of the United States."

What part of the 12th Amendment does Hans Von Spakovsky believe "without question" is changed by the National Popular Vote compact? As can be seen from the above quotation of the full text of the 12th Amendment, there is nothing in it that addresses the manner by which states choose their presidential electors.

9.1.13. MYTH: The National Popular Vote compact would encroach on federal sovereignty.

QUICK ANSWER:

- The U.S. Supreme Court has repeatedly stated that the power to choose the method of awarding a state's electoral votes is an "exclusive" and "plenary" state power.

- The National Popular Vote compact would not encroach on federal sovereignty, because the power to choose the method of awarding a state's electoral votes is an exclusive state power.

MORE DETAILED ANSWER:

Tara Ross, an opponent of the National Popular Vote plan, asserts:

> "If ever a compact encroached on federal . . . sovereignty, this is it."[92]

In fact, the U.S. Constitution gives the federal government *no role* in choosing the manner by which states award their electoral votes:

> "**Each State** shall appoint, in such Manner **as the Legislature thereof may direct**, a Number of Electors . . . ."[93] [Emphasis added]

As the U.S. Supreme Court ruled in the 1892 case of *McPherson v. Blacker*:

> "The constitution does not provide that the appointment of electors shall be by popular vote, nor that the electors shall be voted for upon a general ticket [the winner-take-all rule] nor that the majority of those who exercise the elective franchise can alone choose the electors. It recognizes that **the people act through their representatives in the legislature, and leaves it to the legislature exclusively to define the method of effecting the object.** . . .

> "In short, **the appointment and mode of appointment of electors belong exclusively to the states** under the constitution of the United States."[94] [Emphasis added]

In *Bush v. Gore* in 2000, the Court approvingly referred to *McPherson v. Blacker* and called section 1 of Article II of the Constitution:

> "The source for the statement in McPherson v. **Blacker** . . . that the State legislature's power to select the manner for appointing electors is **plenary**."[95] [Emphasis added]

As a point of comparison, the U.S. Constitution gives the states considerably more discretion in choosing the manner of appointing their presidential electors than it does in choosing the manner of electing members of Congress. The states' power to choose

---

[92] Ross, Tara. 2010. Federalism & Separation of Powers: Legal and Logistical Ramifications of the National Popular Vote Plan. *Engage.* Volume 11. Number 2. September 2010. Page 41.

[93] U.S. Constitution. Article II, section 1, clause 2.

[94] *McPherson v. Blacker.* 146 U.S. 1 at 29. 1892.

[95] *Bush v. Gore.* 531 U.S. 98. 2000.

the manner of conducting congressional elections is subject to congressional review and veto. Article I, section 4, clause 1 of the U.S. Constitution provides:

> "The Times, Places and Manner of holding Elections for Senators and Representatives, shall be prescribed in each State by the Legislature thereof; **but the Congress may at any time by Law make or alter such Regulations**, except as to the Places of chusing Senators." [Emphasis added]

The National Popular Vote compact would not encroach on federal sovereignty because it involves an exercise of the "exclusive" power of the states to choose the method for appointing their presidential electors.

9.1.14. MYTH: The National Popular Vote compact would encroach on state sovereignty.

QUICK ANSWER:
- The National Popular Vote compact is an exercise by states of state sovereignty—not an encroachment.
- The U.S. Supreme Court has repeatedly ruled that the power to choose the method of awarding a state's electoral votes is an "exclusive" and "plenary" state power.
- A state cannot encroach on state sovereignty when a state exercises one of its own "exclusive" and "plenary" powers.

MORE DETAILED ANSWER:

Tara Ross, an opponent of the National Popular Vote plan, asserts:

> "If ever a compact encroached on . . . state sovereignty, this is it."[96]

The U.S. Supreme Court ruled in the 1892 case of *McPherson v. Blacker* that the choice of method for appointing a state's presidential electors is an "exclusive" and "plenary" state power (quoted in section 9.1.13). Moreover, the U.S. Supreme Court approvingly referred to *McPherson v. Blacker* as recently as the 2000 case of *Bush v. Gore*.

How is it possible for a state to "encroach" on state sovereignty when the state is exercising one of its own "exclusive" and "plenary" powers?

The 10th Amendment independently addresses the question of whether the states are prohibited from exercising a particular power when the Constitution contains no specific prohibition against it and, therefore, the question of whether there are unstated, implicit restrictions on the allowable methods for appointing presidential electors.

---

[96] Ross, Tara. 2010. Federalism & Separation of Powers: Legal and Logistical Ramifications of the National Popular Vote Plan. *Engage.* Volume 11. Number 2. September 2010. Page 41.

"The powers not delegated to the United States by the Constitution, **nor prohibited by it to the States, are reserved to the States** respectively, or to the people." [Emphasis added]

Section 1 of Article II contains only one restriction on state choices on the manner of appointing their presidential electors, namely that no state may appoint a member of Congress or federal appointees as presidential elector.[97]

The 10th Amendment was ratified in 1791 (that is, after ratification of the original Constitution) and thus takes precedence over the original 1787 Constitution. Even if there were implied restrictions on state choices on the manner of appointing their presidential electors (perhaps from penumbral emanations emitted by section 1 of Article II), such implicit restrictions were extinguished by the 10th Amendment in 1791.

Moreover, states that choose to enter the National Popular Vote compact retain the power to review their decision and withdraw from the compact at future times. Like virtually every other interstate compact (except for boundary-settlement contracts, which are intended to be permanent), the National Popular Vote compact permits a state to withdraw.[98]

In short, the National Popular Vote compact would be an exercise of state sovereignty—not an encroachment on it.

9.1.15. MYTH: Section 2 of the 14th Amendment precludes the National Popular Vote compact.

QUICK ANSWER:

- The U.S. Supreme Court has considered, and rejected, the argument that section 2 of the 14th Amendment made the statewide winner-take-all method of awarding electoral votes the only constitutional method of appointment of presidential electors.

---

[97] The original Constitution contains few specific restrictions on state action that bear on the appointment of presidential electors. Thus, under Article II, section 1, clause 1, a state legislature may, for example, pass a law making it a crime to commit fraud in a presidential election. However, a state legislature certainly may not pass an *ex post facto* (retroactive) law making it a crime to commit fraud in a presidential election. Similarly, a state legislature may not pass a law imposing criminal penalties on specifically named persons who may have committed fraudulent acts in connection with a presidential election (that is, a bill of attainder). Also, the Constitution's explicit prohibition against a "law impairing the obligation of contract" operates as a restraint on the delegation of power contained in section 1 of Article II. Of course, various later amendments restrict state choices, including the 14th Amendment (equal protection), 15th Amendment (prohibiting denial of the vote on account of "race, color, or previous condition of servitude"), the 19th Amendment (woman's suffrage), the 24th amendment (prohibiting poll taxes), and the 26th Amendment (18-year-old vote).

[98] In particular, clause 2 of Article IV of the National Popular Vote compact would permit a state to withdraw from the compact by simply repealing the statute under which it entered the compact. The effective date of the withdrawal is immediate during 3½ years of every four-year presidential election cycle. The withdrawal is subject to a delay until after Inauguration Day if the withdrawal occurs during a blackout period running between July 20 of a presidential election year and the following January 20 (Inauguration Day).

MORE DETAILED ANSWER:

Section 2 of the 14th Amendment reads:

> "Representatives shall be apportioned among the several States according to their respective numbers, counting the whole number of persons in each State, excluding Indians not taxed. **But when the right to vote at any election for the choice of electors for President and Vice President of the United States**, Representatives in Congress, the Executive and Judicial officers of a State, or the members of the Legislature thereof, **is denied** to any of the male inhabitants of such State, being twenty-one years of age, and citizens of the United States, **or in any way abridged**, except for participation in rebellion, or other crime, **the basis of representation therein shall be reduced** in the proportion which the number of such male citizens shall bear to the whole number of male citizens twenty-one years of age in such State. [Emphasis added]

Section 2 of the 14th Amendment *does not mandate* the states to use any particular method for choosing their presidential electors. Instead, *it provides a remedy* if a state denies or abridges any person's right to vote. The remedy is in the form of reduced congressional representation.

The National Popular Vote compact would not deny or abridge any person's right to vote for presidential electors. Under the National Popular Vote compact, the opportunity of voters to vote for their "choice of electors for President and Vice President of the United States" would neither be denied nor abridged. Therefore, the criterion of section 2 would not be satisfied, and the remedy (namely, reduced congressional representation) would not apply.

Section 2 of the 14th Amendment does not give the voters the right to vote for President, nor does it require that the state-by-state winner-take-all rule be used to appoint presidential electors.

The losing attorney (F.A. Baker) in the 1892 case of *McPherson v. Blacker* strenuously argued before the U.S. Supreme Court that section 2 of the 14th Amendment limited the states in their choice of manner of electing presidential electors.

> "The electoral system as it actually exists is recognized by the 14th and 15th amendments, and by necessary implication, **the general ticket method [i.e., the winner-take-all rule] for choosing presidential electors is made permanent, and the only constitutional method of appointment**.[99]" [Emphasis added]

As pointed out in the brief[100] of the winning attorney (Otto Kirchner) in *McPherson v. Blacker*, one (of the many) deficiencies in Baker's interpretation of section 2 of the

---

[99] Brief of F.A. Baker for Plaintiffs in Error in *McPherson v. Blacker*. 1892. Page 64.
[100] Brief of Otto Kirchner for Defendants in Error in *McPherson v. Blacker*. 1892.

14th Amendment is that "judicial officers of a state" are also mentioned in section 2 of the 14th Amendment. Judges were not elected by the people in many states at the time of formulation, debate, and ratification of the 14th Amendment.

Even more pertinently, the history of the 14th Amendment shows that it was never intended to limit the states in their choice of method of appointing presidential electors. The 14th Amendment was ratified in 1867. *Immediately before, during,* and *after* the period of the Amendment's formulation, debate, and ratification, some state legislatures appointed presidential electors without a vote by the people (e.g., South Carolina in 1860, Florida in 1868, and Colorado in 1876).

In addition, the congressional act providing for Colorado's statehood in 1876 included a specific acknowledgement of the fact that the Colorado legislature would appoint the state's presidential electors for the 1876 election.

If Baker's interpretation of the 14th Amendment had any validity, the appointment of presidential electors by the Florida legislature in 1868 and by the Colorado legislature in 1876 would have been unconstitutional. However, no contemporary argued that these actions by the state legislatures were unconstitutional under the 14th Amendment.

If contemporaries thought the 14th Amendment mandated popular election of presidential electors, that legal argument would certainly have been vigorously advanced during the contentious dispute over the 1876 presidential election. If the Colorado legislature's appointment of the state's three presidential electors (favoring Republican Rutherford B. Hayes) in 1876 had been found to be unconstitutional, Tilden would have had the "majority of the whole number of Electors *appointed*"[101] and, therefore, would have become President—even after losing the contested electoral votes of Louisiana, Florida, and South Carolina in the Electoral Commission. However, contemporaries favoring Tilden never raised this argument.

The history and practices used to choose presidential electors were exhaustively reviewed during the dispute over the 1876 election. The report of the Senate Committee on Privileges and Elections reviewed the history concerning the appointment of presidential electors and stated:

> **"The appointment of these electors is thus placed absolutely and wholly with the Legislatures of the several states**. They may be chosen by the Legislature, or the Legislature may provide that they shall be elected by the people of the State at large, or in districts, as are members of Congress, which was the case formerly in many States, and **it is no doubt competent for the Legislature to authorize the governor, or the Supreme Court of the State, or any other agent of its will, to appoint these electors**."[102] [Emphasis added]

---

[101] The Constitution does not require an absolute majority of the electoral votes to become President but only an absolute majority of the electoral votes "appointed." There have been occasional cases when a state failed to appoint its presidential electors. For example, New York did not in 1789 because the legislature could not agree on how to appoint them. Notably, the Southern states did not appoint presidential electors in 1864.

[102] Senate Report 395. Forty-Third Congress.

In any event, the U.S. Supreme Court was not moved by Baker's argument that section 2 of the 14th Amendment requires the states to use the statewide winner-take-all rule. The Court unanimously ruled in *McPherson v. Blacker* that:

> **"The constitution does not provide that the appointment of electors shall be by popular vote, nor that the electors shall be voted for upon a general ticket [i.e., the 'winner-take-all' rule],** nor that the majority of those who exercise the elective franchise can alone choose the electors."[103] [Emphasis added]

In 2000, the U.S. Supreme Court wrote:

> **"The individual citizen has no federal constitutional right to vote for electors for the President of the United States unless and until the state legislature chooses a statewide election as the means to implement its power to appoint members of the Electoral College.** U.S. Const., Art. II, §1.

> "This is the source for the statement in *McPherson* v. *Blacker* . . . that the State legislature's power to select the manner for appointing electors is plenary." . . .

> "There is no difference between the two sides of the present controversy on these basic propositions."[104] [Emphasis added]

Far from denying or abridging "the right to vote at any election for the choice of electors for President and Vice President of the United States," the National Popular Vote compact would reinforce the people's vote for President in compacting states. Article II of the compact states:

> "Each member state shall conduct a statewide popular election for President and Vice President of the United States."[105]

9.1.16. MYTH: The Privileges and Immunities Clause of the 14th Amendment precludes the National Popular Vote compact.

QUICK ANSWER:
- The National Popular Vote compact would not abridge any protection that citizens currently enjoy relative to abridgments of their rights by the federal government.

---

[103] *McPherson v. Blacker.* 146 U.S. 1 at 27. 1892.

[104] *Bush v. Gore.* 531 U.S. 98. 2000.

[105] The term "statewide popular election" is defined in article V of the compact as "a general election at which votes are cast for presidential slates by individual voters and counted on a statewide basis."

MORE DETAILED ANSWER:

The Privileges and Immunities Clause of the 14th Amendment (ratified in 1867) reads:

> "No State shall make or enforce any law which shall abridge the privileges or immunities of citizens of the United States."

The Privileges and Immunities Clause gives each citizen the same protection against abridgments by state governments as each citizen already possesses, by virtue of national citizenship, relative to abridgments by the federal government.

The National Popular Vote compact would not deny or abridge any constitutional privilege or immunity currently possessed by citizens of the United States.

In particular, as discussed in section 9.1.15, there is no federal right to vote for President conferred by section 2 of the 14th Amendment. Moreover, even if there were a federal right to vote for President, the National Popular Vote compact would do nothing to abridge it.

9.1.17. MYTH: The Due Process Clause of the 14th Amendment precludes the National Popular Vote compact.

QUICK ANSWER:

- The National Popular Vote compact would not deprive any person of life, liberty, or property.

MORE DETAILED ANSWER:

The Due Process Clause of the 14th Amendment provides:

> " . . . nor shall any State deprive any person of life, liberty, or property, without due process of law . . ."

The National Popular Vote compact would not deny any person of life, liberty, or property in any way.

9.1.18. MYTH: The Equal Protection Clause of the 14th Amendment precludes the National Popular Vote compact.

QUICK ANSWER:

- The U.S. Constitution does not require that the election laws of all 50 states be identical. In fact, the Constitution virtually guarantees that election procedures will *not* be identical from state to state because it gives the states control over elections. Thus, differences in election laws are inherent under the federalist system established by the U.S. Constitution.
- The Equal Protection Clause of the 14th Amendment states, "No state shall . . . deny *to any person within its jurisdiction* the equal protection of the laws."

- The Equal Protection Clause does not prevent a state from appointing presidential electors in the manner specified by the National Popular Vote compact because all voters within the jurisdiction of each state are treated equally.

MORE DETAILED ANSWER:

The U.S. Constitution does not require that the election laws of all 50 states be identical. In fact, the Constitution virtually guarantees that election procedures will *not* be identical from state to state because it gives the states control over elections. Thus, differences in election laws are inherent under the federalist system established by the U.S. Constitution.

There are numerous differences in the ways that the states conduct elections.

For example, some states (e.g., Kentucky and Indiana) close their polling places at 6:00 P.M., while others keep their polls open later into the evening. Some states provide numerous opportunities for early voting, while other states are more restrictive.

Some states permit previously incarcerated felons to vote after they serve their prison term, whereas others restore voting rights after passage of a certain amount of time, and other states never restore voting rights.

Some states (e.g., Oregon and Washington) conduct their elections entirely by mail, while other states conduct voting at traditional polling places.

Some states require photo identification at the polls, while others do not.

Professor Norman R. Williams of Willamette University has written the following concerning the National Popular Vote compact:

> "Aggregating votes from each of the fifty states and District of Columbia raises severe problems under the Equal Protection Clause of the Fourteenth Amendment. . . .
>
> "Once the relevant voting community is expanded to include the entire nation, however—as the NPVC seeks to do—**it is hard to see how the disparate voting qualifications and systems in each state would be constitutionally tolerable**. . . .
>
> "The Court in *Bush v. Gore* did require the deployment of a uniform statewide standard for evaluating and tabulating votes for presidential electors, as well as a system of training election personnel to ensure such uniformity. **If the differences in voting standards between Palm Beach and Miami-Dade counties violated the Equal Protection Clause, so too must the differences between states** that count mismarked ballots as valid, such as Massachusetts, and those states, such as California, that typically do not."[106] [Emphasis added]

---

[106] Williams, Norman R. Reforming the Electoral College: Federalism, majoritarianism, and the perils of subconstitutional change. 100 *Georgetown Law Journal* 173. November 2011.

The actual wording of the Equal Protection Clause of the 14th Amendment does not, however, support Williams' contention that "so too must the differences *between* states." The U.S. Constitution provides:

> "No state shall . . . deny **to any person within its jurisdiction** the equal protection of the laws"[107] [Emphasis added]

Voters in Palm Beach and Miami-Dade counties are *within* the jurisdiction of the state of Florida. Consequently, Florida must provide uniformity to them because they are "within its jurisdiction."

The Equal Protection Clause does not, however, impose any obligation on any state concerning a "person" in another state who is not "within its [the first state's] jurisdiction."

Florida state universities do not charge students from Palm Beach County a higher tuition rate than those from Miami-Dade County, nor do they charge black Floridians a different tuition rate than white Floridians. However, Florida state universities do charge different tuition rates to out-of-state students.

Vikram David Amar responded to Williams' contention concerning *interstate* non-uniformity by saying:

> "*Bush v. Gore* (which itself crafted newfangled equal protection doctrine) was concerned with **intrastate—not interstate—non-uniformity**. Under the NPVC, it is hard to see how variations among states results in any one state denying equal protection of the laws 'to any person within its jurisdiction,' insofar as **all persons within each state's jurisdiction (i.e., voters in the state) are being dealt with similarly**. **No single state is treating any people who reside in any state differently than the other folks who live in that state**."[108] [Emphasis added]

Jennings Jay Wilson observed:

> "There is **no legal precedent for inter-state equal protection claims**. Successful equal protection claims have always been brought by citizens being disadvantaged vis-à-vis other citizens of their own state."[109] [Emphasis added]

---

[107] U.S. Constitution. 14th Amendment. Section 1.

[108] Amar, Vikram David. 2011. Response: The case for reforming presidential elections by sub-constitutional means: The Electoral College, the National Popular Vote compact, and congressional power. 100 *Georgetown Law Journal* 237 at 250.

[109] Wilson, Jennings Jay. 2006. Bloc voting in the Electoral College: How the ignored states can become relevant and implement popular election along the way. 5 *Election Law Journal* 384 at 387.

Indeed, the U.S. Supreme Court has previously considered, and rejected, claims that the 14th Amendment applies to interstate differences in connection with the appointment of presidential electors.

In 1968, the constitutionality of the statewide winner-take-all rule was challenged in *Williams v. Virginia State Board of Elections*. In that case, a federal court in Virginia considered and rejected an interstate equal protection claim as well as a claim based on the one-person-one-vote principle. The full opinion may be found in appendix FF.

The plaintiffs in *Williams v. Virginia State Board of Elections* argued that the state of Virginia violated the rights of Virginia voters to equal treatment under the Equal Protection Clause (and, therefore, that Virginia's winner-take-all statute was unconstitutional) because Virginia's statute limited Virginia voters to influencing the selection of only 12 presidential electors, whereas New York's voters influenced the selection of 43 presidential electors.

The federal court described the plaintiff's interstate equal protection argument as follows:

> "Presidential electors provided for in Article II of the Constitution of the United States cannot be selected, plaintiffs charge, by a statewide general election as directed by the Virginia statute. Under it *all* of the State's electors are collectively chosen in the Presidential election by the greatest number of votes cast throughout the entire State. . . .

> "Unfairness is imputed to the plan because it gives the choice of *all* of the electors to the statewide plurality of those voting in the election—"winner take all"—and accords no representation among the electors to the minority of the voters. **An additional prejudice is found in the result of the system as between voters in different States. We must reject these contentions."** . . .

> **"Plaintiffs' proposition is advanced on three counts:**

>> (1) the intendment of Article II, Section 1, providing for the appointment of electors is that they be chosen in the same manner as Senators and Representatives, that is two at large and the remainder by Congressional or other equal districts;

>> (2) **the general ticket method violates the 'one-person, one-vote' principle of the Equal Protection Clause of the Fourteenth Amendment, i.e., the weight of each citizen's vote must be substantially equal to that of every other citizen.** *Gray v. Sanders*, 372 U.S. 368, 381, 83 S.Ct. 801, 9 L.Ed. 2d 821 (1963); *Wesberry v. Sanders*, 376 U.S. 1, 18, 84 S.Ct. 526, 11 L.Ed.2d 481 (1964); and

(3) **the general ticket system gives a citizen in a State having a larger number of electors than Virginia the opportunity to effectuate by his vote the selection of more electors than can the Virginian.**[110] [Emphasis added] [Italics in original]

The federal court made the following ruling concerning the argument that Virginia's statewide winner-take-all statute violates the Equal Protection clause and one-person-one-vote principle:

> "**It is difficult to equate the deprivations imposed by the unit rule with the denial of privileges outlawed by the one-person, one-vote doctrine or banned by Constitutional mandates of protection. In the selection of electors the rule does not in any way denigrate the power of one citizen's ballot and heighten the influence of another's vote.** Admittedly, once the electoral slate is chosen, it speaks only for the element with the largest number of votes. This in a sense is discrimination against the minority voters, but in a democratic society the majority must rule, unless the discrimination is invidious. No such evil has been made manifest here. **Every citizen is offered equal suffrage and no deprivation of the franchise is suffered by anyone.**" [Emphasis added]

The federal court said the following in connection with "interstate inequality of voters":

> "**Further instances of inequality in the ballot's worth between them as Virginia citizens, plaintiffs continue, and citizens of other States, exists as a result of the assignment of electors among the States. To illustrate, New York is apportioned 43 electors and the citizen there, in the general system plan, participates in the selection of 43 electors while his Virginia compatriot has a part in choosing only 12.** His ballot, if creating a plurality for his preference, wins the whole number of 43 electors while the Virginian in the same circumstances could acquire only 12. . . .

> "Disparities of this sort are to be found throughout the United States wherever there is a State numerical difference in electors. **But plainly this unevenness is directly traceable to the Constitution's presidential electoral scheme** and to the permissible unit system.

> "For these reasons the injustice cannot be corrected by suit, especially one

---

[110] *Williams v. Virginia State Board of Elections*, 288 F. Supp. 622. Dist. Court, E.D. Virginia (1968). This decision was affirmed by U.S. Supreme Court at 393 U.S. 320 (1969) (per curiam). The opinion of the federal court in Virginia is found in appendix FF.

in which but a single State is impleaded. Litigation of the common national problem by a joinder of all the States was evidently unacceptable to the Supreme Court. *State of Delaware v. State of New York*, supra, 385 U.S. 895, 87 S.Ct. 198. Readily recognizing these impediments, **plaintiffs point to the district selection of electors as a solution, or at least an amelioration, of this interstate inequality of voters**. However, to repeat, this method cannot be forced upon the State legislatures, for the Constitution gives them the choice, and use of the unit method of tallying is not unlawful." [Emphasis added]

The U.S. Supreme Court affirmed the decision of the Virginia federal court in a *per curiam* decision in 1969.

Tara Ross has made an argument similar to Professor Williams' concerning interstate equal protection.

"NPV claims that its change to a direct election system is needed in order to guarantee 'every vote equal.' Oddly, its proposal guarantees the exact opposite. It would cram voters from across the country into one election pool, despite the fact that different election laws apply to different voters. *Voters would not be more equal.* They would be more unequal. **Lawsuits claiming Equal Protection would certain follow.**

"Consider the issue of early voters. Voters in Alaska have one set of laws regarding early voting. Other states might have provisions regarding when early voting starts, how long it lasts, or who may early vote and how they may early vote. These differences in laws do not matter when Alaskans are participating in their own election only with Alaskans—all voters are treated equitably with other members of the same election pool. However, if NPV throws Alaskans into another, national electorate, then the difference in laws begin to create many inequities. **Some voters in this election pool, for instance, may have more time to vote than Alaskan voters.** Or maybe others have an easier time registering to early vote. **Alaskans are not treated equitably with other members of the national election pool if they must abide by a more restrictive—or even a less restrictive!—set of election laws.**"[111] [Italics in original] [Emphasis added]

There is nothing incompatible between the concept of a national popular vote for President and the inevitable differences in election laws resulting from state control over elections. That was certainly the overwhelming mainstream view when the U.S. House of Representatives passed a constitutional amendment in 1969 for a na-

---

[111] Ross, Tara. 2012. Enlightened Democracy: The Case for the Electoral College. Los Angeles, CA: World Ahead Publishing Company. Second edition. Pages 177–178.

tional popular vote by a 338–70 margin. The 1969 amendment was endorsed by Richard Nixon, Gerald Ford, and Jimmy Carter. It was endorsed by various members of Congress who later ran for Vice President or President, including then-Congressman George H.W. Bush, then-Senator Bob Dole, and then-Senator Walter Mondale. The American Bar Association also endorsed it.

The amendment proposed in 1969 provided that, once a person's vote has been cast under each state's existing (admittedly differing) policies, the popular-vote tallies from each state would be comingled and added together to obtain the nationwide total for each candidate.

The National Popular Vote compact employs the same process, namely once a person's vote has been cast under each state's existing (admittedly differing) policies, the popular-vote tallies from each state would be comingled and added together to obtain the nationwide total for each candidate.

In fact, the *current* state-by-state system of electing the President employs the same process of comingling and adding. Under the current state-by-state system of electing the President, the *electoral vote counts* from all 50 states are comingled and added together—despite the fact that the electoral-vote counts reported by the states are each profoundly affected by differing state policies concerning the hours of voting, voter registration procedures, policies concerning ex-felon voting, the ease of advance voting, the interpretation of mismarked ballots, voter photo identification requirements, and so forth.

The 2000 Certificate of Ascertainment from the state of Florida reported 2,912,790 popular votes for George W. Bush and 2,912,253 popular votes for Al Gore and a 25–0 allocation of electoral votes between Bush and Gore. When Florida's 25–0 allocation of electoral votes was added together with the allocations of electoral votes from other states, Florida's 25–0 allocation decided the outcome of the national election.

The procedures governing presidential elections in closely divided battleground states (e.g., Florida and Ohio) can affect, and indeed have decisively affected, the ultimate outcome of national elections. Thus, everyone in the United States is affected by (and has an "interest" in) every state's allocation of its electoral votes because the Presidency is determined by these state-by-state allocations of electoral votes.

In the same way, the numerical division of the *popular* vote reported on the Certificate of Ascertainment from Florida and every other state would decide the national outcome of some future election conducted under the National Popular Vote compact.

Let us analyze Ross' argument in connection with the closely divided battleground state of Virginia (with no early voting in 2012) and the battleground state of Ohio (with early voting in 2012).[112]

---

[112] States vary considerably in their policies concerning early voting, absentee voting, and mail voting as shown in a summary chart prepared by the National Conference of State Legislatures at http://www.ncsl.org/legislatures-elections/elections/absentee-and-early-voting.aspx.

Ross would argue that votes cast by Virginia citizens are diminished in comparison to votes cast by Ohio citizens because when the (diminished) Virginia votes are comingled and added together with the Ohio votes, the votes of one state "are not treated equitably with other members of the national election pool." Ross would argue that the comingling and adding together of *popular* votes under the National Popular Vote compact violates the Equal Protection Clause of the 14th Amendment. However, this same comingling and adding together happened in 2012 (and all previous presidential elections) under the *current* system in connection with *electoral votes*. The votes cast from the state having less convenient early voting are comingled and added together with electoral votes of other states with more convenient early voting.

If there were a possibility of successful litigation against the National Popular Vote compact on the basis of Ross' doctrine of "interstate inequality" under the 14th Amendment, then the possibility of successful litigation would exist today with respect to the adding together and comingling of *electoral votes* under *the current system*.

Let's assume that, as a result of a close statewide popular vote, Ohio reported an 18–0 division of its electoral votes in favor of Barack Obama on its 2012 Certificate of Ascertainment and that those 18 votes decided the Presidency. There would be no possibility today of successful 14th-Amendment litigation initiated by disgruntled Republicans from Virginia (where there is no early voting) arguing that Virginia voters were devalued and that their party lost the White House because Ohio's early voting benefited the Democrats. The state of Ohio definitely has obligations to "any person in its jurisdiction" to ensure that all of Ohio's voters were treated in the same way, but it has no obligation to disgruntled Virginia Republicans to treat its voters the same way that Virginia does.

If there were such a thing as a doctrine of "interstate inequality" under the 14th Amendment, the courts would quickly use it to declare existing winner-take-all statutes unconstitutional. The argument that was unsuccessfully made in 1968 in *William v. Virginia State Board of Elections* (discussed above) would immediately become a winning legal argument. Moreover, there would suddenly be a legal basis for challenging the numerous other "interstate inequalities" created by the winner-take-all rule. For example, Al Gore won five electoral votes by virtue of his margin of 365 popular votes in New Mexico in 2000, whereas George W. Bush won five electoral votes by virtue of his margin of 312,043 popular votes in Utah—an 855-to-1 disparity in the value of a vote.

The only way to achieve totally uniform national rules governing elections would be to amend the U.S. Constitution to eliminate state control of elections and establish uniform federal election rules. Elimination of state control of elections was not seen as a politically realistic possibility when Congress considered the proposed 1969 federal constitutional amendment.

As then-Congressman George H.W. Bush said on September 18, 1969, in support of a constitutional amendment for direct popular election of the President in which the states would have continued to conduct elections under differing state election laws:

"This legislation has a great deal to commend it. It will correct the wrongs of the present mechanism . . . by calling for direct election of the President and Vice President. . . . Yet, in spite of these drastic reforms, the bill is **not . . . detrimental to our federal system or one that will change the departmentalized and local nature of voting in this country.**

"In electing the President and Vice President, the Constitution establishes the principle that votes are cast by States. This legislation does not tamper with that principle. It only changes the manner in which the States vote. Instead of voting by intermediaries, the States will certify their popular vote count to the Congress. **The states will maintain primary responsibility for the ballot and for the qualifications of voters. In other words, they will still designate the time, place, and manner in which elections will be held.** Thus, there is a very good argument to be made that **the basic nature of our federal system has not been disturbed.**[113] [Emphasis added]

9.1.19. MYTH: The National Popular Vote compact impermissibly delegates a state's sovereign power.

QUICK ANSWER:

- Except for purely advisory compacts, the purpose of almost all interstate compacts is to shift a part of a state's authority to another state or states.
- No court has invalidated an interstate compact on the grounds that the compact impermissibly has delegated a state's sovereign power.

MORE DETAILED ANSWER:

No court has invalidated an interstate compact on the grounds that the compact impermissibly delegated a state's sovereign power.

Indeed, except for purely advisory compacts, the purpose of almost all interstate compacts is, as Marian Ridgeway put it in *Interstate Compacts: A Question of Federalism*:

"[to] shift a part of a state's authority to another state or states."[114]

As summarized in *Hellmuth and Associates v. Washington Metropolitan Area Transit Authority:*

"Upon entering into an interstate compact, a state effectively surrenders a portion of its sovereignty; the compact governs the relations

---

[113] *Congressional Record.* September 18, 1969. Pages 25,990–25,991.

[114] Ridgeway, Marian E. 1971. *Interstate Compacts: A Question of Federalism.* Carbondale, IL: Southern Illinois University Press. Page 300.

of the parties with respect to the subject matter of the agreement and is superior to both prior and subsequent law. Further, when enacted, a compact constitutes not only law, but a contract which may not be amended, modified, or otherwise altered without the consent of all parties."[115] [Emphasis added]

The question arises as to whether the National Popular Vote compact would be an impermissible delegation of a state's sovereign power. In particular, the following question might be raised:

"May a state delegate, under the auspices of an interstate compact, the choice of its presidential electors to the collective choice of the voters of a group of states?"

This inquiry requires an examination of whether the appointment of a state's presidential electors is one of the state's sovereign powers and, if so, whether that power can be shared with voters throughout the United States.

A state's "sovereign powers" may be delegated by an interstate compact

The sovereign authority of a state is not easily defined. The federal courts have not defined sovereignty, although they have attempted to describe it on various occasions. In *Hinderlider v. La Plata River & Cherry Creek Ditch Co.* in 1938, the U.S. Supreme Court traced the history of compacts during the colonial period and immediately thereafter and viewed compacts as a corollary to the ability of independent nations to enter into treaties with one another.

"The compact—the legislative means [for resolving conflicting claims]—adapts to our Union of sovereign States the age-old treaty making power of sovereign nations."[116]

In the 1992 case of *Texas Learning Technology Group v. Commissioner of Internal Revenue*, the U.S. Court of Appeals for the Fifth Circuit wrote:

"The power to tax, the power of eminent domain, and the police power are the generally acknowledged sovereign powers."[117]

The appropriation power is another example of a power that is viewed as fundamental to a state.

The filling of public positions that are central to the operation of state government

---

[115] *Hellmuth and Associates v. Washington Metropolitan Area Transit Authority* (414 F.Supp. 408 at 409). 1976.

[116] *Hinderlider v. La Plata River & Cherry Creek Ditch Co.* 304 U.S. 92 at 104. 1938.

[117] *Texas Learning Technology Group v. Commissioner of Internal Revenue.* 958 F.2d 122 at 124 (5th Cir. 1992).

(including legislative, executive, or judicial positions and the position of delegate to a state constitutional convention) is regarded as a sovereign state power.[118,119]

The historical practice of the states, the long history of approvals of interstate compacts by Congress, and court decisions all support the view that a state's sovereign powers may be granted to a group of states acting through an interstate compact. For example, New York and New Jersey delegated certain sovereign powers to the Port Authority of New York and New Jersey, including the power of eminent domain and the power to exempt property from taxation. New York and New Jersey granted the power to tax to the commission created by the 1953 New York–New Jersey Waterfront Compact. Such delegation was upheld in 1944 in *Commissioner of Internal Revenue v. Shamberg's Estate.*[120]

The Ohio River Valley Water Sanitation Compact provided:

> "The signatory states agree to appropriate for the salaries, office and other administrative expenses, their proper proportion of the annual budget as determined by the Commission and approved by the governors of the signatory states. . . ."

In *West Virginia ex rel. Dyer v. Sims* (discussed at greater length in section 8.6.2), the U.S. Supreme Court upheld the delegation of West Virginia's appropriation power and wrote in 1950:

> "The issue before us is whether the West Virginia Legislature had authority, under her Constitution, to enter into a compact which involves delegation of power to an interstate agency and an agreement to appropriate funds for the administrative expenses of the agency.

> "That a legislature may delegate to an administrative body the power to make rules and decide particular cases is one of the axioms of modern government. The West Virginia court does not challenge the general proposition but objects to the delegation here involved because it is to a body outside the State and because its Legislature may not be free, at any time, to withdraw the power delegated. . . . **What is involved is the conventional grant of legislative power. We find nothing in that to indicate that West Virginia may not solve a problem such as the control of river**

---

[118] See, e.g., *Kingston Associates Inc. v. LaGuardia*, 281 N.Y.S. 390, 398 (S.Ct. 1935) (the exercise of public offices within the legislative, executive, or judicial branches of government); *People v. Brady*, 135 N.E. 87, 89 (Ill. 1922) (same); *People v. Hardin*, 356 N.E.2d 4 (Ill. 1976) (the power to appoint officials to commissions or agencies within the three branches of state government); *State v. Schorr*, 65 A.2d 810, 813 (Del. 1948) (same); and *Forty-Second Legislative Assembly v. Lennon*, 481 P.2d 330, 330 (Mont. 1971) (the role of a delegate to a state constitutional convention).

[119] Engdahl, D. E. 1965. *Characterization of Interstate Arrangements: When Is a Compact Not a Compact?* 64 *Michigan Law Review* 63 at 64–66.

[120] *Commissioner of Internal Revenue v. Shamberg's Estate* 144 F.2d 998 at 1005–1006. (2nd Cir. 1944).

pollution by compact and by the delegation, if such it be, necessary to effectuate such solution by compact. . . . Here, the State has bound itself to control pollution by the more effective means of an agreement with other States. **The Compact involves a reasonable and carefully limited delegation of power to an interstate agency.**"[121] [Emphasis added]

In the 1970 U.S. Supreme Court case of *Oregon v. Mitchell*, Justice Potter Stewart (concurring in part and dissenting in part) pointed out that if Congress had not acted to bring about uniformity among state durational residency requirements for voters casting ballots in presidential elections, then the states could have adopted an interstate compact to do so.[122] The right to vote for a presidential elector is not beyond the reach of an interstate compact.

In short, there is nothing about the nature of an interstate compact that fundamentally prevents the delegation of a state's sovereign power to a group of compacting states.

As Ridgeway wrote:

"If the state chooses to inaugurate some new pattern of local government [by means of an interstate compact] that is not in conflict with the state's constitution, it can do so, as long as the people lose none of their **ultimate power to control the state itself**."[123] [Emphasis added]

This statement reflects various court decisions that emphasize the ability of a sovereign entity to operate independently of any other.[124]

The U.S. Supreme Court has recognized, in the 1892 case of *McPherson v. Blacker*, that a state's constitution may limit the power to choose the method of appointing presidential electors.

"The state does not act by its people in their collective capacity, but through such political agencies as are duly constituted and established. The legislative power is the supreme authority, except as limited by the constitution of the state, and the sovereignty of the people is exercised through their representatives in the legislature, unless by the fundamental law power is elsewhere reposed. The constitution of the United States frequently refers to the state as a political community, and also in terms to the people of the several states and the citizens of each state. **What is forbidden or required to be done by a state is forbidden or required of the legisla-**

---

[121] *West Virginia ex rel. Dyer v. Sims.* 341 U.S. 22 at 30–31. 1950.

[122] *Oregon v. Mitchell.* 400 U.S. 112 at 286–287.

[123] Ridgeway, Marian E. 1971. *Interstate Compacts: A Question of Federalism.* Carbondale, IL: Southern Illinois University Press.

[124] See, for example, the 1793 case of *Chisholm v. Georgia* for a discussion of the historic origins of state sovereignty.

tive power under state constitutions as they exist. The clause under consideration does not read that the people or the citizens shall appoint, but that 'each state shall;' and if the words, 'in such manner as the legislature thereof may direct,' had been omitted, it would seem that the legislative power of appointment could not have been successfully questioned **in the absence of any provision in the state constitution in that regard**. Hence the insertion of those words, while operating as a limitation upon the state in respect of any attempt to circumscribe the legislative power, cannot be held to operate as a limitation on that power itself."[125] [Emphasis added]

The U.S. Supreme Court rejected a specific argument about what constitutes an appointment by the state:

"The manner of the appointment of electors directed by the act of Michigan is the election of an elector and an alternate elector in each of the twelve congressional districts into which the state of Michigan is divided, and of an elector and an alternate elector at large in each of two districts defined by the act. It is insisted that it was not competent for the legislature to direct this manner of appointment, because the state is to appoint as a body politic and corporate, and so must act as a unit, and cannot delegate the authority to subdivisions created for the purpose; and **it is argued that the appointment of electors by districts is not an appointment by the state, because all its citizens otherwise qualified are not permitted to vote for all the presidential electors.**"[126] [Emphasis added]

The Court answered this argument by ruling:

"The constitution does not provide that the appointment of electors shall be by popular vote, nor that the electors shall be voted for upon a general ticket, **nor that the majority of those who exercise the elective franchise can alone choose the electors.** It recognizes that the people act through their representatives in the legislature, and leaves it to the legislature exclusively to define the method of effecting the object.[127] [Emphasis added]

The National Popular Vote compact does not delegate a sovereign state power

There is no authority from any court regarding whether presidential electors exercise a sovereign power of their state. Given the temporary nature of the function of presi-

---

[125] *McPherson v. Blacker.* 146 U.S. 1 at 25. 1892.

[126] *McPherson v. Blacker.* 146 U.S. 1 at 24–25. 1892.

[127] *McPherson v. Blacker.* 146 U.S. 1 at 27. 1892.

dential electors, it is doubtful that a court would rule that presidential electors exercise inherent governmental authority. In contrast to members of the legislative, executive, or judicial branches of state government or members of a state constitutional convention, the function that presidential electors perform is not one that addresses the sovereign governance of the state. Instead, presidential electors decide the identity of the chief executive of the federal government. That is, the selection of electors is not a manifestation of the way in which the state itself is governed.

If the power to determine a state's electors is deemed not to be a sovereign power of the state, then the ability to delegate it is unquestioned. No court has invalidated an interstate compact for delegating a power that is not central to the organic ability of a state to operate independently as a political and legal entity, no matter how broad the delegation. In *Hinderlider v. La Plata River & Cherry Creek Ditch Co.*, the U.S. Supreme Court ruled that a compact to administer an interstate stream was

> "binding upon the citizens of each State and all water claimants, even where the State had granted the water rights before it entered into the compact."[128]

Given the states' exclusive role under the Constitution to determine the manner of appointing its presidential electors,[129] if the determination of a state's electors is a sovereign power and its delegation would shift political power to the group of compacting states, the National Popular Vote compact will not be deemed to compromise federal supremacy.[130] The fact of the delegation would not, in and of itself, violate the U.S. Constitution.

9.1.20. MYTH: Court decisions in the line item veto case and term limit case imply the unconstitutionality of the National Popular Vote plan.

QUICK ANSWER:
- The National Popular Vote compact would not evade any "requirement" of the Constitution (mentioned in the 1995 term limits case).
- The 1995 term limits case was concerned with state legislation that attempted to contravene the "requirements" of a specific clause of the U.S. Constitution, whereas the National Popular Vote compact represents the exercise of a state power that is explicitly (and exclusively) granted to the states by the U.S. Constitution.
- The method of enactment by the states would not evade any "finely wrought procedure" of the U.S. Constitution (mentioned in the 1998 line item veto case).
- The 1998 line item veto case was concerned with federal legislation that attempted to establish a "procedure" that contravened the "finely wrought

---

[128] *Hinderlider v. La Plata River & Cherry Creek Ditch Company.* 304 U.S. 92 at 106. 1938.

[129] *McPherson v. Blacker.* 146 U.S. 1. 1892.

[130] See *Northeast Bancorp, Inc. v. Board of Governors of the Federal Reserve System.* 472 U.S. 159 at 176. 1985.

procedure" contained in the U.S. Constitution, whereas the National Popular Vote compact represents the use by the states of a "finely wrought procedure" explicitly contained in the Constitution.

MORE DETAILED ANSWER:

Tara Ross, an opponent of the National Popular Vote plan, has argued that the decisions of the U.S. Supreme Court in *U.S. Term Limits, Inc. v. Thornton* (the 1995 term limits case) and *Clinton v. City of New York* (the 1998 line item veto case) imply that the National Popular Vote plan would be unconstitutional.

Term Limits Case

The 1995 case of *U.S. Term Limits, Inc. v. Thornton* involved the Qualifications Clause of the U.S. Constitution that establishes three requirements for serving in the U.S. House of Representatives.

> "No Person shall be a Representative who shall not have attained to the Age of twenty five Years, and been seven Years a Citizen of the United States, and who shall not, when elected, be an Inhabitant of that State in which he shall be chosen."[131]

In the mid-1990s, numerous states passed statutes or state constitutional amendments to prevent members of Congress from serving more than a specified number of terms in office (typically by denying long-serving incumbents access to the ballot).

The U.S. Supreme Court ruled that states cannot impose requirements on prospective members of Congress that were stricter than those specified by the Qualifications Clause of the U.S. Constitution.

Ross argues that the Court's decision in *U.S. Term Limits, Inc. v. Thornton* bears on the National Popular Vote compact.

> "In two notable cases, the Court struck down statutes that were said to upset the compromises struck and the delicate balances achieved during the Constitutional Convention. . . .

> "The Court would find support for such a holding in *U.S. Term Limits*. That case held that the Qualifications Clauses of the Constitution prevented an individual state from attempting to impose term limits on its own senators and congressmen.

> "Justice Stevens' majority opinion seemed wary of statutes that attempt to evade the Constitution's **requirements**. Stevens wrote that a state provision

> > 'with the avowed purpose and obvious effect of evading the **require-ments** of the Qualifications Clauses . . . cannot stand. To argue other-

---

[131] U.S. Constitution. Article I, section. 2. clause 2.

wise is to suggest that the Framers spent significant time and energy in debating and crafting Clauses that could be easily evaded.' [Emphasis added]

"Allowing such action, he [Justice Stevens] concluded:

'trivializes the basic principles of our democracy that underlie those Clauses. Petitioners' argument treats the Qualifications Clauses not as the embodiment of a grand principle, but rather as empty formalism.

'It is inconceivable that guaranties embedded in the Constitution of the United States may thus be manipulated out of existence.'"[132]

The clause of the U.S. Constitution at issue in the National Popular Vote bill is Article II, section 1, clause 1 providing:

"Each State shall appoint, in such Manner as the Legislature thereof may direct, a Number of Electors, equal to the whole Number of Senators and Representatives to which the State may be entitled in the Congress: but no Senator or Representative, or Person holding an Office of Trust or Profit under the United States, shall be appointed an Elector." [Emphasis added]

The National Popular Vote compact is state legislation that directs the appointment of 100% of a state's presidential electors from the political party associated with the presidential candidate who receives the most popular votes in all 50 states and the District of Columbia.

The compact would replace state winner-take-all statutes that direct the appointment of 100% of a state's presidential electors from the political party associated with the presidential candidate who receives the most popular votes in each separate state.

The authors of this book agree with the U.S. Supreme Court's ruling in *U.S. Term Limits* against a state statute with the

"avowed purpose and obvious effect of evading the **requirements** of the Qualifications Clause." [Emphasis added]

What "requirement" of Article II, section 1, clause 1 would be evaded by the National Popular Vote compact?

There certainly is no "requirement" in Article II, section 1, clause 1 mandating that 100% of a state's presidential electors must vote in lockstep or that they must vote in accordance with the dictates of an extra-constitutional body such as the nominating caucus or convention of a political party.

Indeed, the Founding Fathers envisioned the Electoral College to be a *deliberative* body whose members would exercise individual judgment in picking the President. As Alexander Hamilton (the presumed author of *Federalist No. 68*) wrote in 1788:

---

[132] *U.S. Term Limits, Inc. v. Thornton*, 514 U.S. 779 at 831. 1995.

"[T]he immediate election should be made by men most capable of analyzing the qualities adapted to the station, and **acting under circumstances favorable to deliberation**, and to a **judicious combination** of all the reasons and inducements which were proper to govern their choice. **A small number of persons**, selected by their fellow-citizens from the general mass, will be most likely to possess **the information and discernment requisite to such complicated investigations**." [Emphasis added]

Moreover, there is no "requirement" in Article II, section 1, clause 1 that states appoint 100% of their presidential electors from just one political party—whether it be the party that carried the state, the party that carried the entire nation, or the party that carried particular districts within the state.

The U.S. Supreme Court ruled in the 1892 case of *McPherson v. Blacker*:

"**The constitution does not provide that the appointment of electors** shall be by popular vote, nor that the electors **shall be voted for upon a general ticket [the winner-take-all rule]** nor that the majority of those who exercise the elective franchise can alone choose the electors. It recognizes that the people act through their representatives in the legislature, and **leaves it to the legislature exclusively to define the method** of effecting the object. The framers of the constitution employed words in their natural sense; and, where they are plain and clear, resort to collateral aids to interpretation is unnecessary, and cannot be indulged in to narrow or enlarge the text. . . .

"In short, **the appointment and mode of appointment of electors belong exclusively to the states** under the constitution of the United States."[133] [Emphasis added]

In fact, Article II, section 1, clause 1 *contains only one "requirement,"* namely that presidential electors not hold federal office. The National Popular Vote compact certainly does not have the "avowed purpose and obvious effect of evading" that "requirement."

Aside from that single "requirement" in Article II, section 1, clause 1, the exercise of any legislative power is indisputably also subject to all the other specific "requirements" in the U.S. Constitution that may apply to the exercise of legislative power.

Five specific restrictions on a state's power under section 1 of Article II are those contained in

- the 14th Amendment (equal protection),
- 15th Amendment (prohibiting denial of the vote on account of "race, color, or previous condition of servitude"),

---

[133] *McPherson v. Blacker.* 146 U.S. 1 at 29. 1892.

- the 19th Amendment (woman's suffrage),
- the 24th amendment (prohibiting poll taxes), and
- the 26th Amendment (18-year-old vote).

Three additional specific restrictions on a state's power under section 1 of Article II are contained in Article I, section 10, clause 1 of the U.S. Constitution:

> **"No State shall** enter into any Treaty, Alliance, or Confederation; grant Letters of Marque and Reprisal; coin Money; emit Bills of Credit; make any Thing but gold and silver Coin a Tender in Payment of Debts; **pass any Bill of Attainder, ex post facto Law, or Law impairing the Obligation of Contracts**, or grant any Title of Nobility." [Emphasis added]

Thus, under Article II, section 1, clause 1, a state legislature may, for example, pass a law making it a crime to commit fraud in a presidential election. However, a state legislature may not pass an *ex post facto* (retroactive) law making it a crime to commit fraud in a *previous* presidential election.

Similarly, a state legislature may not pass a law imposing criminal penalties on specifically named persons whom the legislature believes may have committed fraudulent acts in connection with a presidential election (that is, a bill of attainder).

Also, the Constitution's explicit prohibition against a "law impairing the obligation of contract" operates as a restraint on the delegation of power contained in section 1 of Article II.

However, after reviewing all nine of the above generic restraints on legislative action, we do not find any specific "requirement" of the U.S. Constitution that would be evaded by the National Popular Vote compact.

U.S. Term Limits was concerned with state legislation that attempted to contravene the "requirements" of a specific clause of the U.S. Constitution, whereas the National Popular Vote compact represents the exercise of a state power that is explicitly (and exclusively) granted to the states by the U.S. Constitution.

Line Item Veto Case

The second case cited by Tara Ross is the 1998 case of *Clinton v. City of New York*. That case involved the Presentment Clause of the U.S. Constitution (establishing the specific steps necessary to enact a federal law).

> "Every Bill which shall have passed the House of Representatives and the Senate, shall, before it become a Law, be presented to the President of the United States; If he approve he shall sign it, but if not he shall return it, with his Objections to that House in which it shall have originated, who shall enter the Objections at large on their Journal, and proceed to reconsider it. If after such Reconsideration two thirds of that House shall agree to pass the Bill, it shall be sent, together with the Objections, to the other House,

by which it shall likewise be reconsidered, and if approved by two thirds of that House, it shall become a Law. But in all such Cases the Votes of both Houses shall be determined by yeas and Nays, and the Names of the Persons voting for and against the Bill shall be entered on the Journal of each House respectively. If any Bill shall not be returned by the President within ten Days (Sundays excepted) after it shall have been presented to him, the Same shall be a Law, in like Manner as if he had signed it, unless the Congress by their Adjournment prevent its Return, in which Case it shall not be a Law."[134]

The Line Item Veto Act of 1996 gave the President the power to unilaterally amend or repeal *parts* of statutes that had been duly enacted into law in accordance with the Presentment Clause.

Tara Ross described the U.S. Supreme Court's rejection of the line item veto by saying:

"The 1998 case of *Clinton v. New York* invalidated the federal Line Item Veto Act. Writing for the majority, Justice Stevens emphasized the

'great debates and compromises that produced the Constitution itself,'

"and he found that the Act could not stand because it disrupted

'the 'finely wrought' **procedure** that the Framers designed.'[135] [Emphasis added]

"The Constitution was the product of much give and take among the delegates."

Ross then asserted:

"The Court could reasonably determine that NPV . . . disrupts the 'finely wrought' **procedures** found in the Constitution." [Emphasis added]

The authors of this book agree with the U.S. Supreme Court's ruling in *Clinton v. City of New York* against a statute that attempted to change "procedures" that resulted from careful deliberation by the Founding Fathers and that are laid out in explicit detail in the U.S. Constitution.

The delegates to the 1787 Constitutional Convention debated the method of electing the President on 22 separate days and held 30 votes on the topic.[136] The Convention considered a variety of methods for selecting the President, including

[134] U.S. Constitution. Article I, section 7, clause 2.

[135] *Clinton v. City of New York.* 524 U.S. 417. 1998.

[136] Edwards, George C., III. 2004. *Why the Electoral College Is Bad for America.* New Haven, CT: Yale University Press. Pages 79–80.

- election of presidential electors by districts,
- having state legislatures choose the President,
- having Governors choose the President,
- nationwide direct election, and
- having Congress choose the President.

The Convention never established any of the above methods for selecting the President as the uniform nationwide method for electing the President. Instead, the Convention decided that the President would be elected by presidential electors and then established a "procedure" by which state governments could choose a method for appointing their presidential electors, namely by enacting state laws.

There is evidence that the Convention acted carefully in crafting the "procedure" by which states would choose the manner of appointing their presidential electors. For example, the Convention decided that the states would not be subject to congressional review or veto in choosing the method of choosing their presidential electors, whereas the states would be subject to such review and veto imposed in connection with choosing the method of conducting congressional elections (Article I, section 4, clause 1). This decision reflected the Convention's concern that a sitting President might (in conjunction with a compliant national legislature) manipulate the rules governing his own re-election.

The "procedure" eventually crafted by the Constitutional Convention empowering state legislatures to decide on the method of appointing their presidential electors was explicitly stated in Article II, section 1, clause 1 and provided:

> "Each State shall appoint, in such Manner **as the Legislature thereof may direct**, a Number of Electors . . . " [Emphasis added]

Note that Article II, section 1, clause 1 permits a legislature to choose its method of appointing its presidential electors by passage of state legislation—*without a federal constitutional amendment and without congressional oversight.*

We believe that the Founders' lengthy consideration of Article II, section 1, clause 1 qualifies this constitutional provision as "the product of much give and take among the delegates" and as a "finely wrought procedure."

State winner-take-all statutes were used by only three states in the nation's first presidential election in 1789. The winner-take-all rule became widespread—*without a federal constitutional amendment*—by the 1830's through enactment of state legislation authorized using the "finely wrought procedure" of Article II, section 1, clause 1. The winner-take-all rule specifies that 100% of a state's presidential electors be appointed on the basis of the overall *intra-state* popular vote. The National Popular Vote compact specifies that 100% of an enacting state's presidential electors be appointed on the basis of the overal *interstate* popular vote.

Why does Tara Ross think that the "finely wrought procedure" used to originally enact state winner-take-all statutes would no longer qualify as a "finely wrought procedure" if the states chose to use it to repeal these same state statutes?

The 1998 line item veto case was concerned with federal legislation that attempted to establish a "procedure" that contravened the "finely wrought procedure" contained in the U.S. Constitution, whereas the National Popular Vote compact represents the use by the states of a "finely wrought procedure" explicitly contained in the Constitution.

9.1.21. MYTH: Respect for the Constitution demands that we go through the formal constitutional amendment process.

QUICK ANSWER:

- The Constitution contains a built-in provision for changing the method of awarding a state's electoral votes.
- One does not show respect for the Constitution by unnecessarily and gratuitously amending it.
- The method that is built into the Constitution should be pursued before a constitutional amendment is considered. Amending the Constitution should be the last resort.
- One does not show respect for the Founding Fathers and the Constitution by ignoring the procedures that the Constitution provides. Section 1 of Article II specifically empowers the states to change the method of awarding their electoral votes.
- One does not show respect for the judgment of the Founding Fathers by passing a constitutional amendment that eliminates the states' existing power to make future changes in the method of electing the President.

MORE DETAILED ANSWER:

Tara Ross, an opponent of the National Popular Vote plan, has argued:

> "Even assuming that the Electoral College should be eliminated, respect for the Constitution demands that we go through the formal amendment process."[137]

The National Popular Vote bill does not eliminate the Electoral College. It replaces state winner-take-all statutes (enacted on a piecemeal basis by the states over a period of decades after the 1787 Constitutional Convention) with a system that guarantees the Presidency to the candidate who receives the most popular votes in all 50 states and the District of Columbia.

---

[137] Ross, Tara. 2010. The Electoral College Takes Another Hit. September 22, 2010. http://www.nationalreview.com/corner/247368/electoral-college-takes-another-hit-tara-ross

The Founding Fathers did not anticipate—much less favor—the current winner-take-all method of awarding electoral votes (as discussed in detail in section 9.1.4).

The winner-take-all method is not in the U.S. Constitution and was never ratified as a federal constitutional amendment.

The winner-take-all method may be modified or replaced in the same manner it was originally adopted namely, passage of state-level legislation under the authority of section 1 of Article II.

> "Each State shall appoint, in such Manner **as the Legislature thereof may direct**, a Number of Electors. . . ."[138] [Emphasis added]

One does not show respect for the Founding Fathers by ignoring the specific method they built into the U.S. Constitution for changing the method of electing the President—that is, state-level action under section 1 of Article II. The Founding Fathers gave the states exclusive and plenary control over the manner of awarding their electoral votes.

There is nothing in the Constitution that needs to be amended in order for states to switch from their current practice of awarding their electoral votes to the candidate who receives the most popular votes inside their individual states (the winner-take-all method) to a system in which they award their electoral votes to the candidate who receives the most popular votes in all 50 states and the District of Columbia (the National Popular Vote plan).

One does not show respect for the Constitution by unnecessarily amending it. Before contemplating a change in the U.S. Constitution, states should be given the chance to exercise the specific authority that the Founding Fathers gave to the states in the Constitution to change the electoral system.

The method that is built into the Constitution should be attempted first. Amending the Constitution should be the last resort.

Moreover, one does not show respect for the judgment of the Founding Fathers by passing a constitutional amendment that removes the states' existing power to make changes in the method of electing the President.

9.1.22. MYTH: The most democratic approach for making a change in the manner of electing the President is a federal constitutional amendment.

QUICK ANSWER:
- A federal constitutional amendment favored by states representing 97% of the nation's population can be blocked by states representing only 3% of the population.

---

[138] U.S. Constitution. Article II, section 1, clause 2.

MORE DETAILED ANSWER:

In her book *Enlightened Democracy: The Case for the Electoral College*, Tara Ross characterizes a federal constitutional amendment as being a fairer and more democratic means for replacing state winner-take-all statutes with the National Popular Vote compact because it turns the question of how to elect the President over to "the people."

A federal constitutional amendment must be ratified by 38 of the 50 states. An amendment favored by states representing 97% of the nation's population can be blocked by the 13 smallest states (representing only 3% of the population).

Given that the state-by-state winner-take-all rule is not part of the U.S. Constitution, it is difficult to see why the repeal of the winner-take-all rule would require a constitutional amendment—much less why the constitutional-amendment procedure should be considered to be a more democratic way to repeal the winner-take-all rule than the method of its original adoption.

9.1.23. MYTH: "Eleven colluding states" are trying to impose a national popular vote on the country.

QUICK ANSWER:

- The theoretical possibility that the 11 biggest states (which possess a majority of the electoral votes) would get together to adopt the National Popular Vote compact is as unlikely as the possibility that these same 11 politically disparate states would get together and choose the President in a presidential election under the current system.
- The predicted collusion among the nation's 11 biggest states has already been demonstrated to be false by the actual history of adoption by the states of the National Popular Vote compact. As of 2012, the compact has been enacted by nine jurisdictions, including three small states, three medium-sized states, and three big states.

MORE DETAILED ANSWER:

Tara Ross, an opponent of the National Popular Vote plan, has criticized the compact on the grounds that "11 colluding states" could, if they acted in concert, impose a national popular vote on the country.

The 11 biggest states do, indeed, contain a bare majority of the electoral votes (270 of 538 according to the 2010 census). Theoretically, these same 11 states could, under the current system of electing the President, get together and impose their choice for President on the country in every presidential election.

In reality, the 11 biggest states have little in common with one another politically, and they rarely act in concert on any issue.

In 2000 and 2004, five of the 11 biggest states (Texas, Florida, Ohio, Georgia, and

North Carolina) voted Republican, and six (California, New York, Illinois, Pennsylvania, Michigan, and New Jersey) voted Democratic.

These disparate 11 states are no more likely to get together on enactment of the National Popular Vote compact than they are to get together on their choice of a President or the level of taxation.

Tara Ross' hypothesized scenario of "collusion" among the nation's 11 biggest states has already been demonstrated to be false by the actual history of adoption by the states of the National Popular Vote compact.

As of 2012, the National Popular Vote compact has been enacted by nine jurisdictions possessing a total of 132 electoral votes—49% of the 270 electoral votes needed to activate the compact. These nine jurisdictions include a mixture of small, medium, and big states.

- **Small states**
  - the District of Columbia (3 electoral votes)
  - Hawaii (4 electoral votes)
  - Vermont (3 electoral votes)
- **Medium-sized states**
  - Maryland (10 electoral votes)
  - Massachusetts (11 electoral votes)
  - Washington state (12 electoral votes)
- **Big states**
  - California (55 electoral votes)
  - Illinois (20 electoral votes)
  - New Jersey (14 electoral votes).

Ross' concern about the 11 biggest states is apparently premised on the incorrect belief that support for the National Popular Vote plan is limited to large states. In fact, the National Popular Vote plan has considerable support in small states. As of 2012, the National Popular Vote compact has been approved by a total of nine legislative chambers in small states. In addition to the five legislative chambers in Hawaii, Vermont, and the District of Columbia, the National Popular Vote compact has been approved by the Maine Senate, Delaware House, and both houses in Rhode Island.

Public opinion polls show a high level of support for a nationwide popular election for President in small states such as

- Alaska (70%),
- Delaware (75%),
- District of Columbia (76%),
- Idaho (77%),
- Maine (77%),
- Montana (72%),
- New Hampshire (69%),

- Rhode Island (74%),
- South Dakota (75%),
- Vermont (75%), and
- Wyoming (69%).[139]

In fact, public support for a national popular vote runs slightly higher than the national average in most of the small states. The reason may be that small states are the most disadvantaged group of states under the current system (as discussed in section 9.4.1).

9.1.24. MYTH: A federal constitutional amendment is the superior way to change the system.

QUICK ANSWER:

- State-level action is preferable to a federal constitutional amendment because it is far easier to amend state legislation than to amend or repeal a constitutional amendment if some adjustment becomes advisable.
- State-level action is preferable to a federal constitutional amendment because it leaves existing untouched state control of presidential elections.
- Under the National Popular Vote plan, states would retain their exclusive and plenary power to choose the method of awarding their electoral votes, including the option to make other changes in the future.
- The U.S. Constitution contains a built-in mechanism for changing the winner-take-all method of awarding electoral votes, namely state legislation. This is, of course, the method originally used to adopt the winner-take-all rule (which did not become the prevailing method until decades after ratification of the Constitution). State action is the right way to make this change because it is the way specified in the Constitution.
- Building support from the bottom-up is more likely to yield success than a top-down approach involving a constitutional amendment.

MORE DETAILED ANSWER:

State action to change the winner-take-all method of awarding electoral votes is preferable to a federal constitutional amendment for several reasons.

First, it is far easier to amend or repeal state legislation than to amend or repeal a constitutional amendment if some adjustment becomes advisable. It is inconsistent for opponents of the National Popular Vote compact to argue that nationwide election of the President will usher in numerous adverse consequences, but that the change should be implemented in a manner (namely a federal constitutional amendment) that is not easily amended or repealed.

---

[139] These polls (and many others) are available on National Popular Vote's web site at http://www.national popularvote.com/pages/polls.

Second, the National Popular Vote compact leaves untouched existing state control over presidential elections. Many of the constitutional amendments concerning the Electoral College that have been introduced and debated in Congress over the years would have reduced or eliminated state control over presidential elections. The Constitution's delegation of power over presidential elections (section 1 of Article II) is not a historical accident or mistake, but was intended as a "check and balance" on a sitting President who, with a compliant Congress, might be inclined to manipulate election rules to perpetuate himself in office.[140] The Founders dispersed the power to control presidential elections among the states, knowing that no single "faction" would simultaneously be in power in all the states.

Third, under the National Popular Vote approach, states would retain their exclusive and plenary power to choose the method of awarding their electoral votes, including the option to make other changes in the future. A federal constitutional amendment would eliminate this state power.

Fourth, state action is the right way to make the change. The U.S. Constitution provides a built-in mechanism for changing the method of electing the President. Section 1 of Article II permits the states to choose the manner of awarding their electoral votes. The right way to make a change is the way already contained in the Constitution.

Fifth, passing a constitutional amendment requires an enormous head of steam at the front-end of the process (i.e., getting a two-thirds vote in both houses of Congress). Only 17 constitutional amendments have been ratified since passage of the Bill of Rights. The last time Congress successfully launched a federal constitutional amendment (voting by 18-year-olds) was in 1971. The last constitutional amendment to be ratified was the 27th Amendment in 1992.[141] In contrast, state action permits support to bubble up from the people through the state legislative process. The genius of the U.S. Constitution is that it provides a way for both the central government and state governments to initiate change. Building support from the bottom-up is more likely to yield success than a top-down approach.

Debates over the process to be employed to achieve a particular election reform have frequently delayed achievement of that objective. The passage of women's suffrage, for example, was delayed by decades as a result of a long-running argument within the women's suffrage movement over whether to pursue changes at the state level versus a federal constitutional amendment. Women's suffrage was first adopted by individual states using the state's power, under the U.S. Constitution, to conduct elections. It was 50 years between the time when Wyoming permitted women to vote (1869) and the passage of the 19th Amendment by Congress (1919). By the time Con-

---

[140] In October 2008, the Mayor of New York City, in conjunction with the City Council, amended the City's term-limits law to permit the Mayor to run for a third term.

[141] The 27th Amendment provides, "No law varying the compensation for the services of the Senators and Representatives shall take effect until an election of Representatives shall have intervened."

gress finally passed the 19th Amendment, women had already won the right to vote in 30 of the then-48 states.

9.1.25. MYTH: It is inappropriate for state legislatures to consider changing the method of electing the President.

QUICK ANSWER:

- The U.S. Constitution specifically gives state legislatures exclusive control over the awarding of electoral votes.

MORE DETAILED ANSWER:

The Founding Fathers specifically gave state legislatures the exclusive power to choose the manner of awarding their state's electoral votes. Article II of the U.S. Constitution provides:

> "Each State shall appoint, in such Manner **as the Legislature thereof may direct**, a Number of Electors. . . ."[142] [Emphasis added]

The Founding Fathers had good reason to give states the power to control the conduct of presidential elections. They specifically wanted to thwart the possibility that a sitting President, in conjunction with a possibly compliant Congress, could manipulate the manner of conducting presidential elections in a politically advantageous way.

The U.S. Constitution also gives states the primary power over the manner of conducting congressional elections.[143]

Control over elections is a state power under the U.S. Constitution.

For additional information, see section 1.1 and chapter 2.

9.1.26. MYTH: The National Popular Vote compact is unconstitutional because it would prevent a tie in the Electoral College and thereby deprive the U.S. House of Representatives of its rightful opportunity to choose the President.

QUICK ANSWER:

- Most historians do not subscribe to the view that the Founding Fathers expected the U.S. House of Representatives to routinely choose the President, and most Americans today would oppose that practice.
- If it were unconstitutional for a statute to have the effect, as a matter of practical politics, of preventing a tie in the Electoral College (thereby depriving the U.S. House of Representatives of the opportunity to choose the

---

[142] U.S. Constitution. Article II, section 1, clause 2.

[143] U.S. Constitution. Article I, section 4, clause 1. State power over congressional elections in Article I (unlike state power over presidential elections in Article II) is subject to oversight by Congress.

President), then the federal statutes establishing the size of the U.S. House of Representatives created a constitutionally impermissible structure for the House for about half of American history.

MORE DETAILED ANSWER:

In a 2007 article in the *Akron Law Review*, Adam Schleifer stated:

> "The Framers assumed that the election of the President would often require resort to the House of Representatives; in the absence of a stable two-party system, it did not seem inevitable that all presidential elections would result in a majority vote total for any single candidate. Under the [National Popular Vote] plan, there could never be a situation where the House selected the President, as the electoral vote is guaranteed to constitute a majority of the total as a precondition of enactment of [the National Popular Vote plan]."[144]

Tara Ross, an opponent of the National Popular Vote plan, has stated:

> "**NPV affects the balance of power between federal and state governments** because the House's role in presidential elections will be effectively removed."[145] [Emphasis added]

It is true that the National Popular Vote compact would guarantee an absolute majority of the electoral votes (at least 270 out of 538) to the presidential candidate who receives the most popular votes in all 50 states and the District of Columbia.

Most people would consider the elimination of the possibility that the House of Representatives might elect the President as a highly desirable collateral benefit of the National Popular Vote plan.

Nonetheless, let us consider the argument made by Schleifer and Ross in detail.

A candidate can fail to win an absolute majority in the Electoral College either because of a tie in the Electoral College (which occurred in 1800) or because of a fragmenting of votes among numerous candidates. As Alexander Hamilton (the presumed author of *Federalist* No. 68) noted in 1788:

> "A majority of the votes might not always happen to centre in one man, and as it might be unsafe to permit less than a majority to be conclusive, it is provided that . . . the House of Representatives shall [elect the President]."

In the 1824 election, four candidates received substantial numbers of electoral votes (99, 84, 41, and 37) and, as a result, no presidential candidate received an absolute majority in the Electoral College.

---

[144] Schleifer, Adam. 2007. Interstate agreement for electoral reform. 40 *Akron Law Review* 717 at 739–40.

[145] Ross, Tara. 2010. Federalism & Separation of Powers: Legal and Logistical Ramifications of the National Popular Vote Plan. *Engage.* Volume 11. Number 2. September 2010. Pages 37–44.

In the context of present-day two-party politics, each presidential election presents numerous scenarios for a 269–269 tie in the Electoral College. A recent example is Dan Amira's article entitled "16 Plausible Ways the Electoral College Could Tie in 2012."[146]

In the event that no candidate wins an absolute majority in the Electoral College, the U.S. Constitution provides for a "contingent election" in which the Congress chooses the President and Vice President. The procedures for the contingent election were specified in Article II of the original Constitution. They were revised (and restated) by the 12th Amendment.

In the contingent election, the U.S. House of Representatives would choose the President (with each state having one vote), and the U.S. Senate would choose the Vice President (with each Senator having one vote).

Under the 12th Amendment, the House must make its choice from among the three presidential candidates who received the most electoral votes. The Senate must make its choice from between the two vice-presidential candidates with the most electoral votes.

In a contingent election, if there is no absolute majority in a state's delegation in the House, the state loses its vote for President. Regardless of how many delegations lose their vote in this way, an absolute majority of the states (currently 26 of 50) is necessary to elect a President. Given that many states have divided congressional delegations, the possibility exists that no presidential candidate could amass an absolute majority. If the House is unable to make a choice, the Vice President chosen by the Senate becomes the acting President. Because the Senate is limited to choosing between the two vice-presidential candidates with the most electoral votes, the candidates who competed for the Presidency are precluded from being chosen as the acting President by the Senate.

These choices are made by the newly elected U.S. House of Representatives and Senate in January.

It is, of course, possible that the House and Senate would be controlled by different political parties at the time of the contingent election.

Some have argued that the Founding Fathers did not intend or expect that the Electoral College would elect the President in most elections. Instead, it has been suggested that the Founders anticipated that, after George Washington, no candidate would win a majority of the Electoral College, and the choice for President would routinely devolve on the U.S. House of Representatives. Under this "designed to fail" interpretation of the Constitution's history, the Electoral College would ordinarily serve as a body that would, in effect, merely nominate candidates for President, and the U.S. House of Representatives would ordinarily make the final decision. Gary Gregg II dis-

[146] Amira, Dan. 2010. 16 Plausible ways the electoral college could tie in 2012. *New York.* December 23, 2010.

cusses this "designed to fail" interpretation of the method of electing the President in his article entitled "The Origins and Meaning of the Electoral College."[147]

Based on the "designed to fail" interpretation, it is then argued that the National Popular Vote compact is unconstitutional because the compact would have the almost-certain practical political effect of depriving the U.S. House of Representatives of its rightful constitutional opportunity to choose the President by preventing a tie in the Electoral College and guaranteeing an absolute majority of the electoral votes to the candidate receiving the most popular votes in all 50 states and the District of Columbia.

Gary Gregg II of the University of Louisville, a strong supporter of the current system of electing the President and editor of a book defending the current system, has dismissed this interpretation of the Constitution by writing:

> "Some interpreters have claimed that the system of presidential election outlined in Article II of the Constitution was designed as a type of grand political shell game. On paper it would seem the president would be elected by a select group close to the people in the states, but in reality, the argument goes, it was established to routinely fail and send the actual selection of the president to the House . . . "

> "If one looks closely at the debates during the Constitutional Convention and the votes of the men who drafted the Constitution, one can see quite clearly that there is little evidence for the thesis that the Electoral College was a jerry-rigged system designed to regularly "fail" and send the ultimate decision to Congress."[148]

Prior to 1961, the number of votes in the Electoral College was the sum of the number of members of the U.S. House of Representatives and the U.S. Senate. After ratification of the 23rd Amendment giving the District of Columbia three electoral votes in 1961, the number of votes in the Electoral College has been three more than the sum of the number of members of the U.S. House of Representatives and the U.S. Senate.

The size of the U.S. Senate is twice the number of states (and hence, always an even number).

Prior to ratification of the 23rd Amendment giving the District of Columbia three electoral votes in 1961, the size of the Electoral College was an odd number or an even number, depending on whether the size of the House of Representatives was odd or even, respectively. Since 1961, the size of the Electoral College has been odd or even, depending on whether the size of the House of Representatives was even or

[147] Gregg, Gary L. II 2008. The origins and meaning of the Electoral College. In Gregg, Gary L. II (editor). *Securing Democracy: Why We Have an Electoral College.* Wilmington, DE: ISI Books. Pages 1–26.

[148] Gregg, Gary L. II 2008. The origins and meaning of the Electoral College. In Gregg, Gary L. II (editor). *Securing Democracy: Why We Have an Electoral College.* Wilmington, DE: ISI Books. Pages 7–9.

odd, respectively. The size of the House has been an odd number (435) since 1961, and therefore the size of the Electoral College has been an even number (538) since 1961.

The original size of the U.S. House of Representatives was established in the U.S. Constitution for the nation's first election (at 65 members). Since the 1790 census, the size of the House has been set by federal statute. The statute has been changed on numerous occasions.

It is difficult to sustain the argument that preserving the opportunity for the U.S. House of Representatives to choose the President was ever a significant guiding factor (much less a constitutional imperative) in the choice of the size of the House. In the time between ratification of the 12th Amendment and 2012, the size of the House has been such as to make the size of the Electoral College an even number in only about half of the years in which presidential elections were held.

The Solicitor General's brief to the U.S. Supreme Court in 2010 in the case of *John Tyler Clemons et al. v. United States Department of Commerce* traces the history of the various statutes that set the size of the U.S. House of Representatives.

The (ultimately unsuccessful) plaintiff in that case argued that the present-day size of the U.S. House of Representatives is unconstitutionally small because it creates unconstitutionally large differences in the number of people represented by congressmen from different states.[149]

The Solicitor General's brief shows that Congress did not view protection of its own prerogative to elect the President and Vice President as a factor in setting the size of the House.

> "After each decennial census from 1790 to 1910, Congress reconsidered the number of Representatives, enacting new apportionment legislation 'within two years after the taking of the census.' H.R. Rep. No. 2010, 70th Cong., 2d Sess. 1 (1929) (1929 House Report). Until 1850, Congress first determined the number of persons that would be represented by each Representative, then divided that number into the population of each State, assigned the resulting number of Representatives (less any fractional remainder) to each State, **and summed those numbers to arrive at the overall size of the House of Representatives**. See *United States Dep't of Commerce v. Montana*, 503 U.S. 442, 449-451 (1992). Although Congress repeatedly increased the number of persons represented by each Member of the House, the size of the House continued to grow steadily, rising from 105 Members in 1790 to 243 Members by 1850." [Emphasis added]

If Congress thought that the opportunity to break a tie in the Electoral College was a constitutional imperative—or even a worthy secondary objective—Congress

---

[149] The lower courts rejected the argument advanced by Clemons, and the U.S. Supreme Court declined to hear the case.

could have easily accommodated that factor when it periodically adjusted the size of the House.

If it were unconstitutional to enact an electoral arrangement that has the almost-certain practical effect of depriving the U.S. House of Representatives of the opportunity to occasionally choose the President, then the House has operated with a constitutionally impermissible structure for about half of American history.

The contingent election procedure exists in order to resolve a deadlock if one should arise in the Electoral College. The existence of a contingent procedure does not create a constitutional imperative that other statutes be fashioned so as to guarantee that the contingent procedure will be invoked.

If the U.S. House of Representatives were intended to be a routine part of the procedure for electing the President, the Founding Fathers could have easily specified that the size of the House always be chosen so as to result in an even-numbered size of the Electoral College.

Moreover, if it were important to protect the opportunity of the U.S. House of Representatives to play a routine part in most presidential elections, the country had two convenient opportunities shortly after ratification of the original Constitution to increase the likelihood of House participation.

The first Congress in 1789 debated the issue of the size of the House of Representatives and approved a constitutional amendment on that topic.[150] That particular constitutional amendment (part of a package of 12 amendments that included the 10 amendments that are now called "the Bill of Rights") was never ratified by the states. The amendment proposed in 1791 did not require that the size of the House (and hence the Electoral College) be an even number.

Second, the 1800 presidential election (which produced a tie in the Electoral College) led to a significant reexamination of the procedure of electing the President. Congress then approved, and the states ratified, the 12th Amendment in time for the 1804 election. Congress could easily have included, in the amendment, a requirement that the size of the U.S. House of Representatives always be an even number.[151] [152] [153]

In addition, the Congress had a convenient opportunity when it drafted the 23rd Amendment (giving the District of Columbia three electoral votes) to increase the likelihood of House participation by requiring that the size of the House always be chosen (odd or even) so as to ensure that the size of the Electoral College be an even number.

---

[150] Res. 3, 1st Cong., 1st Sess., Art. I, 1 Stat. 97.

[151] Dunn, Susan. 2004. *Jefferson's Second Revolution: The Elections Crisis of 1800 and the Triumph of Republicanism*. Boston, MA: Houghton Mifflin.

[152] Ferling, John. 2004. *Adams vs. Jefferson: The Tumultuous Election of 1800*. Oxford, UK: Oxford University Press.

[153] Kuroda, Tadahisa. 1994. *The Origins of the Twelfth Amendment: The Electoral College in the Early Republic, 1787–1804*. Westport, CT: Greenwood Press.

9.1.27. MYTH: The National Popular Vote bill is unconstitutional because it circumvents the Constitution's amendment procedures.

QUICK ANSWER:

- Observing that a statute was enacted without employing the Constitution's amendment procedure merely establishes that the legislative body involved believed that a constitutional amendment was not necessary and it had authority to enact that statute.

- Making the observation that a statute was enacted without employing the Constitution's amendment procedure cannot serve as a substitute for a *specific* legal argument as to why the statute in question violates the Constitution.

MORE DETAILED ANSWER:

John Samples of the Cato Institute argues that the National Popular Vote compact

"circumvent[s] the Constitution's amendment procedures."[154]

It is a truism that *every* statute enacted by *every* state legislature circumvents the Constitution's amendment procedures.

If a piece of legislation is a valid exercise of a state legislature's power, then there is no reason for it to be enacted using the Constitution's amendment procedures.

If the piece of legislation is not a valid exercise of powers granted by the Constitution (that is, if it is unconstitutional), then everyone would agree that the Constitution's amendment procedure is the only way to enact the policy involved.

Observing that a statute was enacted without employing the Constitution's amendment procedure cannot serve as a substitute for a *specific* legal argument as to why the statute violates the Constitution.

The fact that a legislative body decided to implement a particular policy by means of a statute is evidence that the legislative body believed that it had authority to enact that statute and that it believed that it was not necessary to implement the policy by means of a constitutional amendment.

The state legislatures that have enacted the National Popular Vote compact believed that section 1 of Article II of the U.S. Constitution provided them with authority to act:

"Each State shall appoint, in such Manner **as the Legislature thereof may direct**, a Number of Electors. . . ."[155] [Emphasis added]

---

[154] Samples, John. *A Critique of the National Popular Vote Plan for Electing the President.* Cato Institute Policy Analysis No. 622. October 13, 2008.

[155] U.S. Constitution. Article II, section 1, clause 2.

That belief is supported by the decision of the U.S. Supreme Court in the leading case on the awarding of electoral votes:

> "**The constitution does not provide that the appointment of electors** shall be by popular vote, nor that the electors **shall be voted for upon a general ticket [the winner-take-all rule]** nor that the majority of those who exercise the elective franchise can alone choose the electors. It recognizes that the people act through their representatives in the legislature, and **leaves it to the legislature exclusively to define the method** of effecting the object. The framers of the constitution employed words in their natural sense; and, where they are plain and clear, resort to collateral aids to interpretation is unnecessary, and cannot be indulged in to narrow or enlarge the text. . . .

> "In short, **the appointment and mode of appointment of electors belong exclusively to the states** under the constitution of the United States."[156] [Emphasis added]

Ultimately, John Sample's argument attempts to use his own desired conclusion (namely that the National Popular Vote compact is unconstitutional) as the justification for his claim that the compact is unconstitutional (and, therefore, requires a constitutional amendment).

9.2. MYTHS THAT CANDIDATES REACH OUT TO ALL THE STATES UNDER THE CURRENT SYSTEM

9.2.1. MYTH: The current system ensures that presidential candidates reach out to all states.

QUICK ANSWER:
- Far from ensuring that presidential candidates reach out to all states, the current state-by-state winner-take-all method of electing the President resulted in four out of five states being ignored in the 2012 general-election campaign for President.
- In 2012, Obama conducted campaign events in just eight states after being nominated, and Romney did so in only 10 states.
- In 2012, only 12 states received even one post-convention campaign event involving a presidential or vice-presidential candidate.
- Two thirds of the presidential and vice-presidential post-convention campaign events were conducted in just four states in 2012 (Ohio, Florida, Virginia, and Iowa).

---

[156] *McPherson v. Blacker.* 146 U.S. 1 at 29. 1892.

- Only three of the 25 smallest states received any attention in the post-convention campaign period in 2012.
- The South is largely ignored in presidential elections because of the state-by-state winner-take-all system.
- Advertising spending was also heavily concentrated in the 12 states where the presidential and vice-presidential candidates held post-convention general-election campaign events in 2012.
- Campaign field offices were also heavily concentrated in the 12 states where the presidential and vice-presidential candidates held post-convention general-election campaign events in 2012.
- The number of battleground states has been consistently shrinking in recent decades.

MORE DETAILED ANSWER:

Tara Ross, an opponent of the National Popular Vote plan, has asserted in testimony at various state legislative hearings:

> "Ultimately, **the Electoral College ensures that the political parties must reach out to all the states.**"[157] [Emphasis added]

> "[Under the current system] candidates can't win unless they build **nationwide support.**"[158] [Emphasis added]

Nothing could be further from the truth.

Because of state winner-take-all statutes (i.e., awarding all of a state's electoral votes to the candidate who receives the most popular votes in each separate state), four out of five states and four out of five Americans were systematically ignored in the general-election campaign for President in 2012.

The reason that four out of five states are ignored is that presidential candidates have no incentive to visit, advertise in, organize in, poll in, or pay attention to the voters in states where they are comfortably ahead or hopelessly behind.

There is simply no benefit to a presidential candidate to spend his limited campaigning time and money visiting, advertising in, and building a grassroots organization in a state in order to win that state with, say, 58% of a state's popular vote as compared to, say, 55%. Similarly, it does not help a presidential candidate to lose a state with 45% of a state's popular vote as compared to, say, 42%.

Because of this political reality, candidates understandably concentrate their attention on a small handful of closely divided battleground states.

As a general rule, a state needs to be approximately in the 46%–54% range (and

---

[157] Oral and written testimony presented by Tara Ross at the Nevada Senate Committee on Legislative Operations and Elections on May 7, 2009.

[158] Written testimony submitted by Tara Ross to the Delaware Senate in June 2010.

preferably closer) to be worthy of attention in the general-election campaign for President.[159] Because most political polls have a margin of error of plus or minus 3% or 4%, another way to state this informal rule-of-thumb is to say that battleground states are those where the difference between the candidates is inside the margin of error of a typical political poll.

2004 Presidential Campaign

In 2004, the presidential candidates concentrated two-thirds of their campaign events and money in the post-convention general election campaign in just five states, 80% in just nine states, and 99% in just 16 states. That's hardly "reach[ing] out to all the states."

2008 Presidential Campaign

In the spring of 2008—even before the nominating process was completed—the major political parties acknowledged that there would be only about 14 battleground states in 2008.[160]

In the 2008 post-convention general election campaign, candidates concentrated over two-thirds of their campaign events and ad money in just six states, and 98% in 15 states.[161] All of the campaign events occurred in just 19 states.

Table 9.1 shows the states in which the presidential and vice-presidential candidates held their 300 post-convention general election campaign events in 2008. The table is sorted according to Obama's percentage of the two-party vote in order to highlight the fact that the states that received campaign events are those where the two-party vote was close (that is, the states where Obama's percentage of the two-party vote was near 50%).[162] The data comes from the *Washington Post* campaign tracker and was compiled by FairVote. The data cover the period from September 5 to November 4, 2008.[163]

Referring to the 2008 election, Professor George C. Edwards III pointed out in his book *Why the Electoral College Is Bad for America*:

---

[159] Virtually all of the states that were considered "battleground states" in 2008 (e.g., the states in table 9.1 that received campaign events and the states in table 9.2 that received substantial amounts of advertising money) lie in this range. This same pattern persisted in 2012 and applied to 2004 and 2000.

[160] Already, Obama and McCain Map Fall Strategies. *New York Times*. May 11, 2008.

[161] http://fairvote.org/tracker/?page=27&pressmode=showspecific&showarticle=230.

[162] For the reader's convenience, this same data are sorted according to the number of campaign events in table 1.10 and sorted by state size in table 9.7.

[163] This table is based on *public* campaign events (e.g., rallies, speeches, town hall meetings). It does not include private fund-raisers, private meetings (e.g., Palin's meetings with world leaders in New York), non-campaign events (e.g., the Al Smith Dinner in New York City or the Clinton Global Initiative dinner), televised national debates (e.g., flying into Mississippi, New York, Tennessee, and Missouri for the sole purpose of participating in the debate), or interviews in television studios (e.g., flying into New York City to do an interview). A "visit" to a state may consist of one or more individual events held at different places and times within the state. A joint appearance of a presidential and vice-presidential candidate is counted as one event.

Table 9.1 POST-CONVENTION CAMPAIGN EVENTS IN 2008

OBAMA PERCENT	STATE	CAMPAIGN EVENTS
33.4%	Wyoming	
34.4%	Oklahoma	
35.5%	Utah	
37.0%	Idaho	
38.9%	Alaska	
39.1%	Alabama	
39.8%	Arkansas	
40.5%	Louisiana	
41.8%	Kentucky	
42.4%	Tennessee	1
42.4%	Kansas	
42.4%	Nebraska	
43.3%	West Virginia	1
43.4%	Mississippi	
44.1%	Texas	
45.5%	South Carolina	
45.6%	North Dakota	
45.7%	Arizona	
45.7%	South Dakota	
47.4%	Georgia	
48.8%	Montana	
49.9%	Missouri	21
50.2%	North Carolina	15
50.5%	Indiana	9
51.4%	Florida	46
52.3%	Ohio	62
53.2%	Virginia	23
54.6%	Colorado	20
54.8%	Iowa	7
54.9%	New Hampshire	12
55.2%	Minnesota	2
55.2%	Pennsylvania	40
56.4%	Nevada	12
57.1%	Wisconsin	8
57.7%	New Mexico	8
57.9%	New Jersey	
58.4%	Michigan	10
58.4%	Oregon	
58.8%	Washington	
58.8%	Maine	2
61.3%	Connecticut	
62.3%	California	
62.6%	Delaware	
62.7%	Illinois	
62.9%	Maryland	
63.2%	Massachusetts	
63.6%	New York	
64.2%	Rhode Island	
68.9%	Vermont	
73.0%	Hawaii	
93.4%	D. C.	1
	Total	**300**

"Barack Obama campaigned in only fourteen states, representing only 33 percent of the American people, during the entire general election."[164] [Emphasis added]

Senator John McCain campaigned in only 19 states in the post-convention period. As table 9.1 shows, only 14 states received seven or more of the 300 post-convention general election campaign events in 2008.

- Ohio—62 events,
- Florida—46 events,
- Pennsylvania—40 events,
- Virginia—23 events,
- Missouri—21 events,
- Colorado—20 events,
- North Carolina—15 events,
- Nevada—12 events,
- New Hampshire—12 events,
- Michigan—10 events,[165]
- Indiana—9 events,
- New Mexico—8 events,
- Wisconsin—8 events, and
- Iowa—7 events.

These 14 closely divided battleground states accounted for 97.7% of the 300 post-convention campaign events in the 2008 general election campaign (that is, 293 of the 300 events).[166]

Moreover, half of these 300 post-convention campaign events in 2008 (148 of 300) were in Ohio (62 events), Florida (46 events), and Pennsylvania (40 events).

Defenders of the current state-by-state winner-take-all system not only incorrectly assert that it "ensures that the political parties must reach out to all the states," but they also incorrectly assert that the current system forces candidates to pay attention to small states. Their claim about small states is not supported by the facts.

Campaign events were held in only seven of the 25 smallest states in 2008. Moreover, the vast majority of the events held in the 25 smallest states (39 of 43) occurred in just four states, namely

---

[164] Edwards, George C., III. 2011. *Why the Electoral College Is Bad for America.* New Haven, CT: Yale University Press. Second edition. Pages 3–5.

[165] On October 2, 2010, the McCain campaign abruptly pulled out of Michigan after it concluded that McCain could not win Michigan. Thus, Michigan appears on this list even though it was a "jilted battleground" state.

[166] The remaining six of the 300 post-convention events (representing 2% of the events) occurred in five additional places, namely Maine (2 events), Minnesota (2 events), the District of Columbia (1 event), Tennessee (1 event), and West Virginia (1 event).

- New Hampshire (12 events),
- New Mexico (8 events),
- Nevada (12 events), and
- Iowa (7 events).

The 25 smallest states together (with 115 electoral votes in 2008) received 43 post-convention campaign events. In contrast, Ohio (with only 20 electoral votes in 2008) received 62 of the 300 post-convention campaign events. The fact that small states are ignored by the current system of electing the President is made clear by table 9.7 in which the data from table 9.1 are sorted according to each state's number of electoral votes.

The South is also largely ignored by presidential campaigns. In an article entitled "The Electoral College is stacked against the South" in *Southern Political Report*, Professor John A. Tures summarized the political effect on the South of the current state-by-state winner-take-all system:

"The South is largely disenfranchised by the Electoral College."[167]

As one might expect, the money that presidential candidates spend in the various states generally parallels the distribution of campaign events.

Table 9.2 shows the states ranked in order of their total contributions (column 2) to the 2008 presidential campaign (using data from Federal Elections Commission records compiled by FairVote).[168] Column 3 shows the percentage of total national donations for each state. Column 4 shows the peak-season candidate advertising expenses (using data compiled by CNN) covering the period from September 24, 2008 (two days before the first presidential debate) to Election Day. Column 5 shows the percentage of total national peak-season candidate advertising expenses for each state.[169]

Table 9.2 shows that:

- 99.75% of all advertising spending was in just 18 states in 2008. This allocation substantially parallels the allocation of the 300 post-convention campaign events to just 19 states, and
- 32 states received a *combined* total of only ¼% of the advertising money in 2008.

Table 9.2 also shows that the 18 net "importers" of campaign money received 99.75% of all advertising money (while providing only 27.70% of all donations). The top six "exporting" states (California, New York, Illinois, Texas, Virginia, and the District of Columbia) made 60% of the donations, but received only 0.06% of the advertising

---

[167] Tures, John A. 2009. The Electoral College is stacked against the South. *Southern Political Report*. November 30, 2009.

[168] http://www.fairvote.org/following-the-money-campaign-donations-and-spending-in-the-2008-presidential -race.

[169] An alternative way of looking at these data is available in table 1.11 where the states are ranked in order of the data in column 4.

Table 9.2 CAMPAIGN DONATIONS AND ADVERTISING SPENDING FOR 2008

STATE	DONATIONS	PERCENT OF DONATIONS	AD SPENDING	PERCENT OF ADVERTISING
California	$151,127,483	17.76%	$28,288	0.02%
New York	$89,538,628	10.52%	$2,235	—
Illinois	$50,900,675	5.98%	$53,896	0.03%
Texas	$46,327,287	5.44%	$4,641	—
Virginia	$44,845,304	5.27%	$16,634,262	10.34%
D.C.	$44,275,246	5.20%	$0	—
Florida	$41,770,516	4.91%	$29,249,985	18.18%
Massachusetts	$36,230,225	4.26%	$20	—
Maryland	$28,723,600	3.37%	$0	—
Washington	$24,666,430	2.90%	$5,062	—
Pennsylvania	$23,929,821	2.81%	$24,903,675	15.48%
New Jersey	$22,756,469	2.67%	$0	—
Colorado	$18,800,854	2.21%	$7,944,875	4.94%
Connecticut	$16,526,530	1.94%	$0	—
Georgia	$16,507,714	1.94%	$177,805	0.11%
Ohio	$15,984,435	1.88%	$16,845,415	10.47%
Arizona	$15,334,618	1.80%	$75,042	0.05%
Michigan	$15,007,118	1.76%	$5,780,198	3.59%
North Carolina	$14,337,669	1.68%	$9,556,598	5.94%
Minnesota	$10,894,627	1.28%	$4,262,784	2.65%
Oregon	$10,155,182	1.19%	$2,754	—
Missouri	$9,997,747	1.17%	$7,970,313	4.95%
Wisconsin	$8,133,046	0.96%	$8,936,200	5.56%
Tennessee	$7,934,886	0.93%	$9,955	0.01%
New Mexico	$6,418,313	0.75%	$3,134,146	1.95%
Indiana	$6,225,848	0.73%	$8,964,817	5.57%
South Carolina	$5,744,471	0.67%	$910	—
Nevada	$5,273,523	0.62%	$7,108,542	4.42%
Hawaii	$5,045,151	0.59%	$0	—
Oklahoma	$4,359,169	0.51%	$4,170	—
Kentucky	$4,338,611	0.51%	$635	—
Alabama	$4,333,420	0.51%	$1,385	—
Louisiana	$4,330,756	0.51%	$2,279	—
New Hampshire	$4,045,877	0.48%	$2,924,839	1.82%
Iowa	$3,649,836	0.43%	$3,713,223	2.31%
Maine	$3,344,447	0.39%	$832,204	0.52%
Kansas	$3,333,235	0.39%	$3,141	—
Utah	$3,287,184	0.39%	$66	—
Vermont	$2,852,896	0.34%	$0	—
Arkansas	$2,446,323	0.29%	$1,897	—
Mississippi	$2,400,625	0.28%	$1,731	—
Rhode Island	$2,343,926	0.28%	$0	—
Montana	$1,882,200	0.22%	$971,040	0.60%
Nebraska	$1,867,197	0.22%	$807	—
Delaware	$1,745,123	0.21%	$0	—
Alaska	$1,611,031	0.19%	$310	—
Idaho	$1,610,072	0.19%	$368	—
Wyoming	$1,488,479	0.17%	$0	—
West Virginia	$1,236,993	0.15%	$733,025	0.46%
South Dakota	$758,626	0.09%	$980	—
North Dakota	$442,998	0.05%	$18,365	0.01%
Total	**$851,122,440**	**100.00%**	**$160,862,883**	**100.00%**

money. For example, California donors contributed \$151,127,483 (about one-sixth of the national total), but California received a mere \$28,288 in advertising. New York donors contributed \$89,538,628 (about one-tenth of the national total), while New York received only \$2,235 in advertising.

2012 Presidential Campaign

The number of battleground states has been declining for many decades, as detailed in FairVote's 2005 report entitled *The Shrinking Battleground*.[170] This shrinkage continued into the 2012 presidential election.

A mere four weeks after the November 2010 congressional elections, a televised debate on C-SPAN among candidates for the chairmanship of the Republican National Committee focused on the question of how the party would conduct the 2012 presidential campaign in the 14 states that were expected to matter.[171]

Five and a half months before Election Day in 2012, Governor Mitt Romney acknowledged that the number of battleground states in 2012 would be even smaller than in 2008. In the now-famous May 17, 2012, *Mother Jones* video (made at the same fund-raising dinner in Boca Raton, Florida, containing Romney's comments about "the 47%"), Romney said:

"All the money will be spent in 10 states."

On June 6, 2012 (five months before Election Day), the *New York Times* reported that the 2012 presidential campaign was effectively being conducted in nine battleground states (Florida, Ohio, Virginia, North Carolina, Iowa, Pennsylvania, Colorado, Nevada, and New Hampshire). The article noted that the number of battleground states was considerably smaller than in 2000, 2004, and 2008.[172]

Table 9.3 shows the states in which the presidential and vice-presidential candidates held their 253 post-convention general-election campaign events in 2012. This table is based on CNN's "On the Trail" campaign tracker and covers the period from September 7, 2012 (the day after the Democratic National Convention) to November 6 (Election Day).[173] The data was compiled by FairVote. The table is sorted according to column 2 (showing the total number of campaign events per state).[174] Columns 3,

---

[170] FairVote. 2005. *The Shrinking Battleground: The 2008 Presidential Election and Beyond.* Takoma Park, MD: The Center for Voting and Democracy. http://archive.fairvote.org/?page=1555.

[171] Freedomworks debate on December 1, 2010, available at http://www.freedomworks.org/rnc.

[172] Peters, Jeremy W. Campaigns Blitz 9 Swing States in a Battle of Ads. *New York Times.* June 8, 2012.

[173] This count is based on *public* campaign events (e.g., rallies, speeches, town hall meetings). It does not include private fund-raisers, private meetings, non-campaign events (e.g., the Al Smith Dinner in New York City, the Clinton Global Initiative dinner), televised national debates (e.g., flying into a state just to participate in the debate), or interviews in television studios (e.g., flying into New York to do an interview). A "visit" to a state may consist of one or more individual events held at different places and times within the state. A joint appearance of a presidential and vice-presidential candidate is counted as one event. Additional information is available at http://www.fairvote.org/presidential-tracker.

[174] For the reader's convenience, the same information is also presented in table 9.8 where is it sorted by state size.

Table 9.3 POST-CONVENTION CAMPAIGN EVENTS IN 2012

STATE	TOTAL	OBAMA	BIDEN	ROMNEY	RYAN
Ohio	73	15	13	27	18
Florida	40	9	8	15	8
Virginia	36	6	4	17	9
Iowa	27	5	6	7	9
Colorado	23	5	3	6	9
Wisconsin	18	5	6	1	6
Nevada	13	4	2	3	4
New Hampshire	13	4	4	3	2
Pennsylvania	5			3	2
North Carolina	3		2	1	
Michigan	1				1
Minnesota	1				1
Alabama					
Alaska					
Arizona					
Arkansas					
California					
Connecticut					
Delaware					
D.C.					
Georgia					
Hawaii					
Idaho					
Illinois					
Indiana					
Kansas					
Kentucky					
Louisiana					
Maine					
Maryland					
Massachusetts					
Mississippi					
Missouri					
Montana					
Nebraska					
New Jersey					
New Mexico					
New York					
North Dakota					
Oklahoma					
Oregon					
Rhode Island					
South Carolina					
South Dakota					
Tennessee					
Texas					
Utah					
Vermont					
Washington					
West Virginia					
Wyoming					
Total	**253**	**53**	**48**	**83**	**69**

4, 5, and 6 show the number of events by President Barack Obama, Vice President Joe Biden, Governor Mitt Romney, and Congressman Paul Ryan, respectively.

As can be seen from table 9.3:

- In 2012, President Obama conducted post-convention campaign events in just eight states after being nominated, and Governor Romney did so in only 10 states. In comparison, in 2008, Obama conducted post-convention events in 14 states, and McCain did so in 19 states.
- Four out of five states (and four out of five Americans) were ignored by the candidates in the post-convention campaign period in 2012.
- Ohio received 73 of the 253 post-convention campaign events (29%).
- Over two-thirds (69%) of the post-convention campaign events were conducted in just four states (Ohio, Florida, Virginia, and Iowa).
- Only one of the 13 smallest states (i.e., those with three or four electoral votes) received any post-convention campaign events (New Hampshire).
- Only three of the 25 smallest states (i.e., those with seven or fewer electoral votes) received any post-convention campaign events (New Hampshire, Iowa, and Nevada).
- In 2012, only 12 states received at least one post-convention campaign event involving a presidential or vice-presidential candidate.
- The battle was fully joined in only eight states. That is, only eight states received campaign events from all four major-party candidates (i.e., Obama, Romney, Biden, and Ryan).

Figure 9.1 is a graphical representation of the same information as table 9.3 concerning the states in which the presidential and vice-presidential candidates held their 253 post-convention general-election campaign events in 2012.

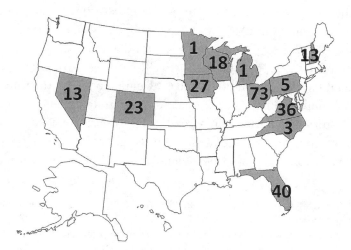

Figure 9.1 Post-convention campaign events in 2012

The top eight battleground states shown in table 9.3 accounted for 96% of the 253 campaign events. They had a combined population of 56,334,828 out of the total U.S. population of 309,785,186 (according to the 2010 census). That is, these eight states had 18.1% of the nation's population.

North Carolina was generally regarded as the ninth significant battleground state in 2012. It was sixth in terms of advertising spending (table 9.4) but tenth in terms of campaign events in table 9.3. These nine states had a combined population of 65,900,609—that is, 21.3% of the nation's population.

Thus, in round numbers, the 2012 presidential campaign ignored about four out of five Americans.

Although defenders of the current state-by-state winner-take-all system often incorrectly assert that the current system forces candidates to pay attention to small states, that claim is not supported by the facts.

Campaign events were held in only three of the 25 smallest states in 2012, namely

- Iowa (27 events),
- Nevada (13 events), and
- New Hampshire (13 events).

The 25 smallest states together (possessing 116 electoral votes in 2012) received 53 of the 253 post-convention campaign events. In contrast, Ohio (with only 18 electoral votes in 2012) received 73 of the 253 post-convention campaign events.[175]

The advertising money that was spent in the various states was just as skewed as the distribution of campaign events.

Table 9.4 shows the advertising spending by the presidential campaign organizations and their supportive outside groups (e.g., super-PACs, 501(c)4 corporations) for each of the 12 states (shown in table 9.3) where at least one of the four candidates of the major parties (Obama, Romney, Biden, and Ryan) conducted at least one campaign event. The table is arranged in descending order according to the total advertising spending by state (shown in column 2). Column 3 shows each state's percentage of the total of $939,370,708 for the 12 states. Column 4 shows the total for the Obama campaign (Obama for America) and supportive Democratic groups (Priorities USA Action and Planned Parenthood Action Fund).[176] Column 5 shows the total for the Romney campaign (Romney for President) and supportive Republican groups (American Crossroads, Restore Our Future, Crossroads GPS, Americans for Prosperity, Republican National Committee, Americans for Job Security, American Future Fund, and Concerned Women for America). These data were compiled by *National Journal*.[177]

---

[175] These facts are highlighted in table 9.3 in which the data from table 9.8 are sorted according to each state's number of electoral votes.

[176] Note that the Democratic National Committee did not run any advertising for the 2012 Obama campaign.

[177] Bell, Peter and Wilson, Reid. Ad Spending in presidential battleground states. *National Journal*. November 4, 2012. http://www.nationaljournal.com/hotline/ad-spending-in-presidential-battleground-states-20120620. This web site also details the spending by each individual group.

Table 9.4 POST-CONVENTION ADVERTISING SPENDING IN 12 STATES IN 2012

STATE	TOTAL	PERCENTAGE OF TOTAL	DEMOCRATIC	REPUBLICAN
Ohio	$192,275,664	20.5%	$91,675,838	$100,599,826
Florida	$182,040,734	19.4%	$77,705,000	$104,335,734
Virginia	$149,217,380	15.9%	$66,767,983	$82,449,397
Colorado	$79,830,466	8.5%	$38,347,150	$41,483,316
Iowa	$71,150,666	7.6%	$28,586,032	$42,564,634
North Carolina	$69,374,780	7.4%	$24,184,071	$45,190,709
Nevada	$58,276,511	6.2%	$25,831,984	$32,444,527
Wisconsin	$45,784,603	4.9%	$14,749,375	$31,035,228
New Hampshire	$43,540,413	4.6%	$21,456,476	$22,083,937
Pennsylvania	$28,089,978	3.0%	$10,896,718	$17,193,260
Michigan	$17,483,109	1.9%	$461,008	$17,022,101
Minnesota	$1,499,045	0.2%	–	$1,499,045
Total	**$939,370,708**	**100.0%**	**$400,661,635**	**$538,709,073**

The data cover the period between September 4, 2012 (the middle of the Democratic National Convention) and November 4, 2012 (two days before Election Day).[178]

The battle for the White House was not meaningfully joined in the three states in table 9.4 with the lowest non-zero advertising expenditures, namely Minnesota, Michigan, and Pennsylvania.

In Minnesota, Democrats spent nothing in pursuit of the state's 10 electoral votes, while Republicans spent a mere 5% of what they spent trying to win the 10 electoral votes in neighboring Wisconsin. Moreover, neither Obama, Romney nor Biden conducted any post-convention events in the state (as shown in table 9.3).

In Michigan, Democrats spent next to nothing ($461,008) in pursuit of the state's 16 electoral votes, while Republican spent (mostly at the last minute) a mere one-sixth of what they spent trying to win Ohio's 18 electoral votes. Congressman Ryan conducted one post-convention event in Michigan (as shown in table 9.3).

Although Pennsylvania was a major battleground state in 2008 (receiving 40 of the 300 post-convention campaign events), the battle was never meaningfully joined in Pennsylvania in 2012. Neither Obama nor Biden conducted any post-convention events in Pennsylvania (as shown in table 9.3). The three last-minute events by Romney and the two last-minute events by Ryan were a token effort (a tiny fraction of the 253 post-

---

[178] The cost per electoral vote of reaching voters in battleground states varies considerably from state to state. Television advertising is highly inefficient for many battleground states. For example, reaching voters in the populous southern part of the battleground state of New Hampshire (with four electoral votes) is highly inefficient because it requires advertising on premium-priced metropolitan Boston TV stations (that primarily reaches politically irrelevant voters in Massachusetts and Rhode Island). Similarly, reaching the northern part of the battleground state of Virginia requires advertising on pricey metropolitan Washington stations (that reaches many politically irrelevant voters in Maryland and the District of Columbia). In contrast, television advertising in the states of Florida, Colorado, and Nevada is more efficient in that it is seen mostly by voters living inside those battleground states.

Table 9.5 LOCATION OF 690 OF OBAMA'S 790 CAMPAIGN OFFICES IN 2012

STATE	OBAMA OFFICES
Colorado	62
Florida	104
Iowa	67
Michigan	28
Minnesota	12
Nevada	26
New Hampshire	22
North Carolina	54
Ohio	131
Pennsylvania	54
Virginia	61
Wisconsin	69
Total	**690**

Table 9.6 LOCATION OF 262 OF ROMNEY'S 284 CAMPAIGN OFFICES IN 2012

STATE	ROMNEY OFFICES
Colorado	13
Florida	48
Iowa	14
Michigan	24
Minnesota	0
Nevada	12
New Hampshire	9
North Carolina	24
Ohio	40
Pennsylvania	25
Virginia	29
Wisconsin	24
Total	**262**

convention campaign events). The spending in pursuit of Pennsylvania's 20 electoral votes (mostly last-minute) was less than one-sixth of what was spent in pursuit of Ohio's 18 electoral votes.

Overall, 98% of the $939,370,708 spent on advertising in the 12 states in 2012 shown in table 9.4 was concentrated in just 10 states, and 95% was spent in just nine states.

The location of field offices confirms the degree to which presidential campaigns concentrated their efforts on the closely divided battleground states.

As discussed in a report entitled "Tracking Presidential Campaign Field Operations" by Andrea Levien of Fair Vote,[179] President Obama's field operation had a total of 790 campaign offices, with at least one in every state. However, there was only one Obama office in 25 states.

Governor Romney's field operation had a total of 284 offices; however, all were located in just 16 states. That is, 34 states had no Romney office.

Table 9.5 shows that 87% of Obama's campaign offices (690 of 790) were in the 12 states where either President Obama, Vice President Biden, Governor Romney, or Congressman Ryan conducted at least one campaign event (shown in table 9.3)

Table 9.6 shows that 92% of Romney's campaign offices (262 of 284) were in the 12 states where either President Obama, Vice President Biden, Governor Romney, or Congressman Ryan conducted at least one campaign event (shown in table 9.3).

In summary, about 90% of all campaign offices were concentrated in 12 states in 2012.

[179] Levien, Andrea. Tracking presidential campaign field operations. Fair Vote report. November 14, 2012. http://www.fairvote.org/tracking-presidential-campaign-field-operations/.

Campaigns Solicit Votes Based on Issues of Concern to Battleground States

The practical political effect of presidential candidates ignoring four out of five states and four out of five voters is that they pay inordinate attention to the issues of concern to the voters living in closely divided battleground states.

Candidates direct their campaign appeals to the issues of concern to the voters of the closely divided battleground states.

For example, an article entitled "Romney Campaign Releases 15 New Commercials in Eight States" illustrates how presidential campaigns solicit votes based on particular issues relevant to voters in particular battleground states:

> "All 15 spots begin identically—with convention footage of Romney's acceptance speech. . . .
>
> **"From there, it starts getting less generic**. . . .
>
> "[The] Florida [ad discusses] . . . the importance of residential real estate to the state's economy. . . .
>
> "A Virginia commercial [deals with] residential real estate . . .
>
> "One of [the] commercials . . . deals with losses resulting from defense-budget cuts and sequestrations, is running in Colorado, Florida, North Carolina, Ohio and Virginia. . . .
>
> "Another [commercial] discussing how government overregulation kills small-business jobs runs in Colorado and Iowa. . . .
>
> "[Another commercial] about government regulatory, trade and tax policies . . . killing manufacturing jobs, runs in North Carolina and Ohio. . . .
>
> "[There is] a New Hampshire commercial about high taxes and energy costs. . . .
>
> "[There is] a Virginia :30 [30-second ad] about how tax cuts can help the lives of middle-class families."[180] [Emphasis added]

A 2012 *Washington Post* article entitled "Obama Showering Ohio with Attention and Money" reported:

> "After President Obama pledged in March to create up to 15 manufacturing centers nationwide, the first federal grant went to a place at the heart of his affections: Ohio.

---

[180] Goldman, Bruce. Romney campaign releases 15 new commercials in eight states. *Examiner.* September 7, 2012.

"When the Obama administration awarded tax credits to promote clean energy, the $125 million taken home by Ohio companies was nearly four times the average that went to other states.

"And **when a Cleveland dairy owner wanted to make more ricotta cheese, he won what was then the largest loan in the history of the U.S. Small Business Administration**.

"'**One of the tastiest investments the government has ever made,' the president joked** as he mentioned the dairy and other businesses his administration has helped in the state."[181] [Emphasis added]

The same article also noted:

"Either Obama or Vice President Biden has popped up in the Buckeye State every three weeks on average since they took office."

Not only do presidential candidates pay inordinate attention to the issues of concern to voters in the closely divided battleground states, they simply do not care about issues of concern to voters in non-battleground states. Because of the state-by-state winner-take-all method of awarding electoral votes, candidates do not even bother to conduct public opinion polls in the remaining states, because issues concerning voters in the non-battleground states are simply not relevant to winning the White House.

As Charlie Cook reported in 2004:

"Senior Bush campaign strategist Matthew Dowd pointed out yesterday that **the Bush campaign hadn't taken a national poll in almost two years; instead, it has been polling 18 battleground states**." [182,183] [Emphasis added]

If candidates (and sitting Presidents contemplating re-election) are not even aware of the issues that concern voters in four out of five states, they are making policy based on the desires of a few at the expense of the many.

As Former White House Press Secretary Ari Fleischer said in 2009:

"**If people don't like it, they can move from a safe state to a swing state** and see their president more."[184] [Emphasis added]

---

[181] Markon, Jerry and Crites, Alice. Obama showering Ohio with attention and money. *Washington Post.* September 25, 2012.

[182] Cook, Charlie. 2004. Convention dispatches—As the nation goes, so do swing states. *Charlie Cook's Political Report.* August 31, 2004.

[183] John Kerry's 2004 campaign similarly concentrated on a small handful of states in the general election campaign.

[184] *Washington Post.* June 21, 2009.

State winner-take-all statutes are the reason why four out of five states and four out of five Americans are ignored in presidential elections. Under the current state-by-state winner-take-all system, voters in non-battleground states receive no attention from either political party because neither party has anything to gain or lose in the state.

The time that candidates spend in various states, as well as the amount of money that they spend, indicates the value that candidates place on the issues of concern to the voters of those states. Policy issues important to voters in the battleground states are more important to a presidential campaign than policy issues important to the voters in the 40-or-so spectator states. When a sitting President is governing (and contemplating his own re-election or the election of his preferred successor), policy issues important to voters in the battleground states are more important than policy issues important to voters in spectator states.

As former Illinois Governor Jim Edgar has said:

> **"People who are in elected office remember what they learned when they were campaigning**. It's important that the candidates campaign in all states, not just the swing states." [Emphasis added]

Consider the reliably Republican state of Idaho as an example of a spectator state. Given George W. Bush's 68% margin of victory in 2004, no amount of campaigning will alter the fact that the Republican nominee for President is virtually certain to win Idaho's four electoral votes in the foreseeable future under the current system. Therefore, the Republican candidate for President risks nothing by ignoring Idaho voters, Idaho issues, and Idaho values. Similarly, the Democratic candidate has nothing to gain in Idaho and can simply write it off. The fact that Idaho is not a battleground state means that Idaho issues are irrelevant to *both* parties.

Under a national popular vote, every vote in Idaho would matter to both the Democratic and Republican nominee in every election. A vote in Idaho would become as valuable as a vote anywhere else in the country. It would be foolish for a Republican nominee to take Idaho voters for granted, because he or she would want to expand his margin of victory or, failing that, at least maintain his party's historically large margin in the state. Similarly, it would be folly for the Democratic nominee to ignore Idaho voters, because he or she would want to decrease the magnitude of his loss or, at a minimum, limit his loss to his party's historical level. Idaho's reliably large Republican margin would no longer be wasted, and the votes of Idaho Democrats would no longer be counted as if they had voted for the Republican presidential candidate. Idaho voters are ignored because the state-by-state winner-take-all rule makes it pointless for either party's presidential candidates to pay any attention to the state.

Note that Idaho is not ignored in presidential elections because it is small—it is ignored because it is not a closely divided battleground state. In 2012, the battleground state of New Hampshire (with the same four electoral votes as Idaho) received 13 of the 253 campaign events in the post-convention general election campaign, while all 12 of the other smallest states (including Idaho) received no attention at all.

If every vote was politically relevant in a presidential campaign, one would reasonably expect each of the 13 smallest states (that is, those with three or four electoral votes) to receive approximately one of the 13 campaign events that are currently conducted in New Hampshire. That is, it would be reasonable to expect each of the six Republican-leaning small states (Alaska, Idaho, Montana, Wyoming, North Dakota, and South Dakota) and each of the seven Democratic-leaning small states (Hawaii, Vermont, Maine, Rhode Island, Delaware, the District of Columbia, and New Hampshire) would receive one of these 13 campaign events.

9.2.2. MYTH: A national popular vote will simply make a different group of states irrelevant in presidential elections.

QUICK ANSWER:

- Candidates must solicit every potential voter in an election in which the winner is the candidate who receives the most popular votes. Every vote, regardless of location, would matter equally under a national popular vote.
- The best indicator of how campaigns would be run under a national popular vote is the way campaigns are conducted today for offices where the winner is the candidate who receives the most votes. Serious candidates for Governor solicit voters throughout their entire state. No serious candidate ignores any part of a state if he or she is running in an election where the winner is the candidate who receives the most votes in the entire state. Inside battleground states, presidential candidates solicit voters throughout the entire state.
- When it is suggested that a national popular vote would make any state irrelevant in presidential elections, the obvious question is "Which state would that be?" Which 40 states would a presidential candidate totally ignore under a national popular vote? Which 240,000,000 Americans would a presidential candidate totally ignore in an election in which the winner is the candidate who receives the most popular votes?

MORE DETAILED ANSWER:

Four out of five states and four out of five Americans are ignored in present-day presidential elections conducted under the state-by-state winner-take-all method of awarding electoral votes.

John Samples, an opponent of the National Popular Vote plan, states:

> "Many states now ignored by candidates will continue to be ignored under NPV."[185]

---

[185] Samples, John. *A Critique of the National Popular Vote Plan for Electing the President.* Cato Institute Policy Analysis No. 622. October 13, 2008. Page 1.

We do not have to speculate on how a campaign would be conducted in an election in which the winner is the candidate who receives the most popular votes, because there is ample evidence available to answer this question. We *know*, from actual experience, how elections are conducted for every other office in the United States.

Serious candidates for Governor or U.S. Senator pay attention to their *entire* constituency. The reason is that every vote is equally important in winning an election in which the winner is the candidate who receives the most popular votes. Focus, for a moment, on a state's congressional districts (remembering that congressional districts within a state contain virtually identical numbers of people). Serious candidates for Governor do not limit their campaigns to just one out of five of their state's congressional districts while totally ignoring four-fifths of the state. Taking Massachusetts as a specific example, it would be inconceivable for a serious candidate for Governor to campaign only in the 1st and 2nd congressional districts, while totally ignoring the 3rd, 4th, 5th, 6th, 7th, 8th, 9th, and 10th districts.

The same principle applies today in present-day presidential races *inside* each closely divided battleground state. Inside a battleground state, every vote is equal. Every vote helps a candidate get closer to winning the most votes in the state and thereby capturing all of the state's electoral votes. Inside Ohio, for example, presidential candidates campaign throughout the state. Presidential candidates seek votes in Cleveland and Columbus as well as suburbs, exurbs, small towns, and rural areas. None of Ohio's 16 congressional districts is ignored. Every method of communication (including television, radio, newspapers, magazines, direct mail, billboards, telephone, and the Internet) is used to reach *every* voter in Ohio. It would be politically preposterous to suggest that any presidential candidate would campaign in only certain parts of Ohio, to the exclusion of other parts. Every vote inside Ohio matters.

As David J. Owsiany of the Buckeye Institute wrote in the *Columbus Dispatch*:

> "In a swing state such as Ohio, the candidates will visit every area of the state, not just the big cities, because they know winning the popular vote in Ohio—regardless of the margin—means the candidate will get all 18 of the Buckeye State's electoral votes."[186]

Similarly, the same is true *inside* Florida in present-day presidential elections. It would be preposterous to suggest that any presidential candidate would ignore any part of Florida because the winner of all of Florida's 29 electoral votes is the candidate who receives the most votes in the state as a whole.

An NPR story entitled "Ads Slice Up Swing States With Growing Precision" reported on presidential campaigning in Colorado's small media markets:

> "Republicans outnumber Democrats in El Paso County more than 2 to 1. Barack Obama lost this part of Colorado to John McCain by 19 points in 2008.

---

[186] Owsiany, David J. Electoral College helps to make sure that president represents entire nation. *Columbus Dispatch*. September 22, 2012.

"'It's not a matter of just winning; it's winning by how much,' says Rich Beeson, a fifth-generation Coloradan and political director for the Romney campaign.

"Presidential campaigns know exactly the margin of victory or defeat that they have to hit in each town in order to carry an entire state. Democratic media strategist Tad Devine says campaigns set extremely specific goals based on hard data. . . .

"Although no one suggests that President Obama will win Colorado Springs, whether he loses it by 15 or 25 points could determine whether he carries Colorado.

"Beeson of the Romney campaign says smaller cities are vital to this chess game, especially since they're cheaper to advertise in.

"'A lot of secondary markets are very key to the overall map, whether it's a Charlottesville in Virginia or a Colorado Springs in Colorado,' he says. 'You can't ever cede the ground to anyone.'"[187] [Emphasis added]

When it is suggested that a national popular vote will make a different group of states irrelevant in presidential elections, the obvious question is "Which states would that be?" Which 40 states would a presidential candidate totally ignore? "Which 240,000,000 Americans (four-fifths of the total U.S. population of 309,000,000) would a presidential candidate totally ignore?

The question answers itself.

Under the National Popular Vote plan, the winner would be the candidate who receives the most popular votes in the entire country. *Every* voter in *every* state would be politically relevant in *every* presidential election.

9.2.3. MYTH: The disproportionate attention received by battleground states is not a problem because spectator states frequently become battleground states and vice versa.

QUICK ANSWER:
- Although spectator states do occasionally become battleground states, and vice versa, a state's political complexion generally changes very slowly.
- A person can easily live out most or all of his or her life without ever being politically relevant in a general-election presidential campaign. In contrast, a person's vote for Governor, U.S. Senator, or any other elective office is politically relevant in *every* election—not just once or twice in a lifetime.

---

[187] Shapiro, Ari. Ads slice up swing states with growing precision. *NPR*. September 24, 2012. http://www.npr.org/2012/09/24/161616073/ads-slice-up-swing-states-with-growing-precision.

- Thirty-two states have voted for the same political party in the six presidential elections between 1992 and 2012—19 states possessing 242 electoral votes voted Democratic and 13 states possessing 102 electoral votes voted Republican.

MORE DETAILED ANSWER:

Opponents of the National Popular Vote plan often argue that the current system forces presidential candidates to pay attention to all the states. For example, Tara Ross has asserted in testimony at various state legislative hearings:

> "Ultimately, **the Electoral College ensures that the political parties must reach out to all the states.**"[188] [Emphasis added]

> "[Under the current system] candidates can't win unless they build **nation-wide support**."[189] [Emphasis added]

When facts are presented that contradict this manifestly incorrect claim (as they are in section 9.2.1), these same opponents then retreat to the argument that the disproportionate attention received by battleground states is not a problem because spectator states sometimes become battleground states and vice versa.

For example, Tara Ross, has argued that

> "safe states and swing states—they change all the time." . . .

> "California, used to vote Republican. Now they vote Democrat."[190]

Although it is true that spectator states do occasionally become battleground states (and vice versa), the rate of change in a state's political complexion is generally rather slow.

A person can easily live out most or all of his or her entire life without ever having a meaningful vote in a general-election presidential campaign. The year 2012 is the 100th anniversary of the last time the popular-vote margin in Utah and Nebraska was less than 6%.

Moreover, battleground status is generally fleeting. Battleground status typically occurs during the relatively brief period when a state is in the process of switching its allegiance from one political party to another. In most cases, a state is a battleground state for one or two (and occasionally three) consecutive presidential elections.

New Mexico voted Republican in presidential elections for decades prior to 2000. Between 2000 and 2008, New Mexico was a closely divided battleground state and con-

---

[188] Oral and written testimony presented by Tara Ross at the Nevada Senate Committee on Legislative Operations and Elections on May 7, 2009.

[189] Written testimony submitted by Tara Ross to the Delaware Senate in June 2010.

[190] Debate at the Dole Institute in Lawrence, Kansas, between Tara Ross and John Koza on November 7, 2011. Time stamp 16:30.

sequently received considerable attention. However, New Mexico was totally ignored in the 2012 presidential campaign (receiving not a single post-convention campaign event).

After decades of voting solidly Republican in presidential elections, Virginia and North Carolina suddenly emerged as battleground states in 2008 (and they remained so in 2012).

California voted Republican in all six presidential elections between 1968 and 1988. During this period, California was meaningfully contested only in 1976 (when Ford won by 1.7%) and 1988 (when George H.W. Bush won by 3.5%). However, between 1992 and 2012, California has consistently voted Democratic in all six presidential elections.

Missouri was a battleground state in 2000 and 2008, but ignored in 2004. Moreover, Missouri was totally ignored in 2012.

Ohio was ignored ("dark" in the parlance of campaign consultants) as recently as the 2000 election. Al Gore and George W. Bush both stopped campaigning there shortly after being nominated.

In 2012, Pennsylvania was not a battleground state, even though it enjoyed battleground status in several previous elections. Pennsylvania received 40 of the 300 post-convention campaign events in 2008, but only a token (last-minute) five of 253 in 2012. Neither President Obama nor Vice President Biden campaigned there after being nominated.

Battleground status is so fleeting that a state can find itself jilted in the middle of the post-convention campaign. On October 2, 2008, the McCain campaign (quite reasonably) decided it could not win Michigan and abruptly pulled out of the state. Michigan was not a battleground state in 2012. It received only one of the 253 post-convention campaign events (from Congressman Ryan).

Despite isolated examples of states whose battleground status has changed, the overall picture is one of great stability and only gradual change.

Table 9.41 shows that 32 states voted for the same political party in all six presidential elections between 1992 and 2012. These 32 states possess about two-thirds (64%) of the 538 votes in the Electoral College. Of these 32 states, 19 states (possessing 242 electoral votes after the 2010 census) voted Democratic in all six presidential elections, and 13 states (possessing 102 electoral votes after the 2010 census) voted Republican in all six presidential elections.

In presidential elections, the importance of a vote depends on whether other voters in the voter's state favor one candidate by 54% or so. Unless the voter happens to live in a state where opinion is closely divided (that is, between 46% and 54%), a person's vote is politically irrelevant in presidential elections.

If the 2016 presidential election is conducted under the state-by-state winner-take-all rule and is reasonably close, it is likely that all (or almost all) of the 32 states that have voted for the same party in the past six presidential elections will support that same party.[191]

---

[191] Nine of the states in table 9.41 that voted Democratic once or twice between 1992 and 2012 (Arkansas, Kentucky, Louisiana, Missouri, Tennessee, West Virginia, Arizona, Georgia, and Montana) did so during the

When a voter votes for Governor, U.S. Senator, or any other office in the United States, *every* vote in *every* precinct (and town and county) is equally relevant in *every* election. A person's vote in a particular county is not ignored in an election for Governor simply because more than 54% of the voter's neighbors in that county favor a particular candidate.

A nationwide vote for President would guarantee that *every* vote in *every* state would be equally relevant in *every* presidential election.

9.3. MYTH THAT "WRONG WINNER" ELECTIONS ARE RARE

9.3.1. MYTH: "Wrong winner" elections are rare, and therefore not a problem.

QUICK ANSWER:

- Far from being rare, there have been four elections out of the nation's 57 presidential elections in which a candidate has won the Presidency without winning the most popular votes nationwide—a failure rate of 1 in 14.
- The failure rate is 1 in 7 among non-landslide presidential elections (i.e., elections where the nationwide margin is less than 10%).
- The country has experienced a string of seven consecutive non-landslide elections since 1988. Because we appear to be in an era of non-landslide presidential elections, additional "wrong winner" elections can be expected in the future.

MORE DETAILED ANSWER:

There have been four "wrong winner" elections out of the nation's 57 presidential elections between 1789 and 2012—a failure rate of 1 in 14.

Moreover, about half of American presidential elections are popular-vote landslides (i.e., those in which the winner's nationwide margin is greater than 10%). Among the *non*-landslide elections, the failure rate for the current system is 1 in 7.

Although landslide presidential elections were common for much of the 20th century, the nation currently appears to be in an era of consecutive non-landslide presidential elections (1988, 1992, 1996, 2000, 2004, 2008, and 2012).

Therefore, it should not be surprising that there has been one "wrong winner" election in the recent string of seven non-landslide presidential elections between 1988 and 2012.

If the country continues to experience non-landslide presidential elections, we can expect additional "wrong winner" elections in the future.

An article on July 24, 2012, by Nate Silver in the *New York Times*, entitled "State

---

Clinton years. Since then, these nine states have consistently voted Republican in presidential elections between 2000 and 2012. Thus, there are 41 states that have voted for the same party between 2000 and 2012.

and National Polls Tell Different Tales About State of Campaign"[192] makes the point that the national popular vote often disagrees with the candidates' status in the closely divided battleground states. The article pointed out that President Obama had a nationwide lead of 1.3% in the *Real Clear Politics* average of national polls at the time. However, at the same moment, Obama led by a mean of 3.5% in the *Real Clear Politics* averages for 10 battleground states (Ohio, Virginia, Florida, Pennsylvania, Colorado, Iowa, Nevada, Michigan, New Hampshire and Wisconsin) that were considered (at the time) to be most likely to determine the outcome of the 2012 election. Thus, on July 24 (when both party's nominees were known), the Republicans were within 1.3% of winning the national popular vote, but considerably farther away from winning the states necessary to elect Mitt Romney as President. See tables 9.42 and 9.43 in Section 9.31.9 for additional discussion.

In an October 31, 2012, article in the *New York Times*, Nate Silver observed:

> "Mitt Romney and President Obama remain roughly tied in national polls, while state polls are suggestive of a lead for Mr. Obama in the Electoral College."[193]

The precariousness of the current state-by-state winner-take-all system is further highlighted by the fact that a shift of a handful of votes in one or two states would have elected the second-place candidate in five of the 13 presidential elections since World War II.

For example, in 1976, Jimmy Carter led Gerald Ford by 1,682,970 votes nationwide; however, a shift of 3,687 votes in Hawaii and 5,559 votes in Ohio would have elected Ford.

In 2004, President George W. Bush was ahead by over 3,000,000 popular votes nationwide on Election Night; however, the outcome of the election remained in doubt until the next day because it was not clear which candidate would win Ohio's 20 electoral votes. In the end, Bush received 118,785 more popular votes than John Kerry in Ohio—thus winning all of Ohio's 20 electoral votes and ensuring his re-election. However, if 59,393 voters in Ohio had switched from Bush to Kerry, Kerry would have become President despite Bush's lead of over 3,000,000 popular votes nationwide.

In 2012, a shift of 214,390 popular votes in four states would have elected Mitt Romney, despite President Obama's nationwide lead of 4,966,945 votes. The four states involved are Florida (29 electoral votes), Ohio (18), New Hampshire (4), and Virginia (13). They cumulatively possess 64 electoral votes. A shift of 64 electoral votes would have given Mitt Romney the 270 electoral votes needed for election.

Other examples are presented in section 1.2.2.

---

[192] Silver, Nate. State and national polls tell different tales about state of campaign. FiveThirtyEight column in *New York Times*. July 24, 2012.

[193] Silver, Nate. What state polls suggest about the national popular vote. FiveThirtyEight column in *New York Times*. October 31, 2012.

9.4. MYTHS ABOUT THE SMALL STATES

9.4.1. MYTH: The small states would be disadvantaged by a national popular vote.

QUICK ANSWER:

- The small states (the 13 states with only three or four electoral votes) are the most disadvantaged and ignored group of states under the current state-by-state winner-take-all method of awarding electoral votes. The reason is that political power in presidential elections comes from being a closely divided battleground state, and almost all of the small states are non-competitive states in presidential elections.

- The small states are not ignored because of their low population, but because they are not closely divided battleground states. The 12 small non-battleground states have about the same population (12 million) as the closely divided battleground state of Ohio. The 12 small states have 40 electoral votes—more than twice Ohio's 18 electoral votes. However, Ohio received 73 of 253 post-convention campaign events in 2012, while the 12 small non-battleground states received none.

- The current state-by-state winner-take-all system actually shifts power from voters in the small and medium-sized states to voters in a handful of big states that happen to be closely divided battleground states in presidential elections.

- The fact that the small states are disadvantaged by the current state-by-state winner-take-all system has long been recognized by prominent officials from those states. In 1966, Delaware led a group of 12 predominantly small states in suing New York (then a closely divided battleground state) in the U.S. Supreme Court in an effort to get state winner-take-all statutes declared unconstitutional.

- Under the current state-by-state winner-take-all system, a vote for President in Wyoming is equal to a vote in California—both are politically irrelevant.

MORE DETAILED ANSWER:

Tara Ross, an opponent of the National Popular Vote plan, writes:

> "NPV will lessen the need of presidential candidates to obtain the support of voters in rural areas and in small states."[194]

A brochure published in 2010 by the Evergreen Freedom Foundation of Olympia, Washington states:

---

[194] Written testimony submitted by Tara Ross to the Delaware Senate in June 2010.

"The seven smallest states (Alaska, Delaware, Montana, North Dakota, South Dakota, Vermont, and Wyoming) and the District of Columbia each have three electoral votes. **A national popular vote would render all low-population states almost permanently irrelevant in presidential political strategy.**"[195] [Emphasis added]

Ross has also stated:

"Minority political interests, particularly the **small states, are protected** [by the current system]."[196] [Emphasis added]

"Ultimately, **the Electoral College ensures that the political parties must reach out to all the states**."[197] [Emphasis added]

Professor Robert Hardaway of the University of Denver Sturm College of Law has said:

"If we had National Popular Vote, you take a state like Alaska, which has a very low population. If it was a national popular vote no presidential candidate would be interested in going up there, because the population is so low. But, as you pointed out, if they have 3 electoral votes, that's the compromise that brought this nation together, that's a lot of votes, that's a lot of electoral votes compared to the population, so you'll see presidential candidates visiting some of those outlying areas."[198]

Referring to the National Popular Vote plan, Senator Mitch McConnell said:

"If the only vote total that counted was just running up the score, query, when would be the next time if you had a state with one congressmen or 2 congressmen and you had a tiny population, when would be the next time you would see or hear from any candidate for president?"[199]

Professor Walter E. Williams of George Mason University says:

"Were it not for the Electoral College, presidential candidates could safely ignore less populous states."[200]

---

[195] Evergreen Freedom Foundation. 2010. Brochure. Olympia, Washington.

[196] Oral and written testimony presented by Tara Ross at the Nevada Senate Committee on Legislative Operations and Elections on May 7, 2009.

[197] *Id.*

[198] Debate at the Larimer County, Colorado, League of Women Voters on June 28, 2012 with Robert Hardaway of the University of Denver Sturm College of Law, Professor Robert Hoffert of Colorado State University, Elena Nunez of Colorado Common Cause, and Patrick Rosenstiel of Ainsley-Shea. 18:00 minute mark. http://www.youtube.com/watch?v=U_yCSqgm_dY.

[199] McConnell, Mitch. The Electoral College and National Popular Vote Plan. December 7, 2011. Washington, DC. 19:36 minute mark.

[200] Williams, Walter E. In defense of the Electoral College. *Gaston Gazette.* November 21, 2012.

Gary Gregg II, a strong supporter of the current system of electing the President and editor of a book defending the current system, says that a national popular vote for President:

"would mean ignoring every rural and small-state voter in our country."[201]

The facts directly contradict all of the above statements.

Far from being "protected," the small states are the most disadvantaged and ignored group of states under the current system of electing the President.

Table 9.7 shows the states in which the presidential and vice-presidential candidates held their 300 post-convention general election campaign events in 2008. The table is organized according to each state's number of electoral votes.[202] The data come from the *Washington Post* campaign tracker. The data cover the period from September 5, to November 4, 2008.[203]

Table 9.7 shows that, with the exception of New Hampshire (the sole battleground state among the 13 smallest states), the 13 smallest states (those with three or four electoral votes) received hardly any attention in the 2008 campaign.

Table 9.8 shows the states in which the presidential and vice-presidential candidates held their 253 post-convention general-election campaign events in 2012. This table is based on CNN's "On the Trail" campaign tracker and covers the period from September 7, 2012 (the day after the Democratic National Convention) to November 6 (Election Day).[204,205] The data was compiled by FairVote. The table is sorted according to a state's number of electoral votes.

As can be seen from table 9.3, only three of the 25 smallest states received any campaign events in 2012, namely:

---

[201] Gregg, Gary. Keep Electoral College for fair presidential votes. *Politico*. December 5, 2012.

[202] For the reader's convenience, the same information is presented in table 1.10 (where it is sorted according to the number of post-convention campaign events in 2008) and in table 9.1 (where it is sorted according to Obama's percentage of the two-party vote in 2008).

[203] This count is based on *public* campaign events (e.g., rallies, speeches, town hall meetings). It does not include private fund-raisers, private meetings (e.g., Palin's meetings with world leaders in New York), non-campaign events (e.g., the Al Smith Dinner in New York City or the Clinton Global Initiative dinner), tele-vised national debates (e.g., flying into Mississippi, New York, Tennessee, and Missouri just to participate in the debate), or interviews in television studios (e.g., flying into New York City to do an interview). A "visit" to a state may consist of one or more individual events held at different places and times within the state. A joint appearance of a presidential and vice-presidential candidate is counted as one event.

[204] This count is based on *public* campaign events (e.g., rallies, speeches, town hall meetings). It does not include private fund-raisers, private meetings, non-campaign events (e.g., the Al Smith Dinner in New York City, the Clinton Global Initiative dinner), televised national debates (e.g., flying into a state just to participate in the debate), or interviews in television studios (e.g., flying into New York to do an interview). A "visit" to a state may consist of one or more individual events held at different places and times within the state. A joint appearance of a presidential and vice-presidential candidate is counted as one event. Additional information is available at http://www.fairvote.org/presidential-tracker.

[205] For the reader's convenience, the same information (including breakdowns for Obama, Biden, Romney, and Ryan) is presented in table 9.3 and table 1.10 where it is sorted according to the number of post-convention campaign events.

Table 9.7 POST-CONVENTION CAMPAIGN EVENTS IN 2008

ELECTORAL VOTES	STATE	CAMPAIGN EVENTS
3	Wyoming	
3	District of Columbia	1
3	Vermont	
3	North Dakota	
3	Alaska	
3	South Dakota	
3	Delaware	
3	Montana	
4	Rhode Island	
4	Hawaii	
4	New Hampshire	12
4	Maine	2
4	Idaho	
5	Nebraska	
5	West Virginia	1
5	New Mexico	8
5	Nevada	12
5	Utah	
6	Kansas	
6	Arkansas	
6	Mississippi	
7	Iowa	7
7	Connecticut	
7	Oklahoma	
7	Oregon	
8	Kentucky	
9	Louisiana	
8	South Carolina	
9	Alabama	
9	Colorado	20
10	Minnesota	2
10	Wisconsin	8
10	Maryland	
11	Missouri	21
11	Tennessee	1
11	Indiana	9
11	Arizona	
11	Washington	
12	Massachusetts	
13	Virginia	23
15	New Jersey	
15	North Carolina	15
15	Georgia	
17	Michigan	10
20	Ohio	62
21	Pennsylvania	40
21	Illinois	
27	Florida	46
31	New York	
34	Texas	
55	California	
538	**Total**	**300**

- New Hampshire (4 electoral votes),
- Nevada (6 electoral votes), and
- Iowa (6 electoral votes).

The 25 smallest states (possessing 116 electoral votes in 2012) received 53 of the 253 post-convention campaign events. In contrast, Ohio (with only 18 electoral votes in 2012) received 73 of the 253 post-convention campaign events.

Although the small states theoretically benefit from receiving two extra electoral votes (corresponding to their two U.S. Senators), this "bonus" does not, in practice, translate into political influence. Political power in presidential elections comes from being a closely divided battleground state—not from the two-vote bonus conferred on all states in the Electoral College.

Under the winner-take-all rule (i.e., awarding all of a state's electoral votes to the candidate who receives the most popular votes in each separate state), candidates have no reason to visit, advertise, build a grassroots organization, poll, or pay attention to the concerns of voters in states where they are comfortably ahead or hopelessly behind. Instead, candidates concentrate their attention on a small handful of closely divided battleground states.

The small states are the most disadvantaged and ignored group of states under the current state-by-state winner-take-all system because all but one of them are reliably Democratic or Republican in presidential races. Consequently, presidential candidates have nothing to lose by ignoring and nothing to gain by soliciting votes in the small states. Under the current system, the small states are not ignored because they are small, but because they are not closely divided battleground states.

In the last seven presidential elections (1988 through 2012), six of the 13 small states (i.e., those with three or four electoral votes) have regularly gone Republican:

- Alaska,
- Idaho,
- Montana,
- North Dakota,
- South Dakota, and
- Wyoming.

Six others have regularly gone Democratic:

- Delaware,
- District of Columbia,
- Hawaii,
- Maine,
- Rhode Island, and
- Vermont.

Table 9.8 POST-CONVENTION CAMPAIGN EVENTS IN 2012 (BY STATE SIZE)

ELECTORAL VOTES	STATE	TOTAL
3	Alaska	
3	Delaware	
3	D.C.	
3	Montana	
3	North Dakota	
3	South Dakota	
3	Vermont	
3	Wyoming	
4	New Hampshire	13
4	Hawaii	
4	Idaho	
4	Maine	
4	Rhode Island	
5	Nebraska	
5	New Mexico	
5	West Virginia	
6	Iowa	27
6	Nevada	13
6	Arkansas	
6	Kansas	
6	Mississippi	
6	Utah	
7	Connecticut	
7	Oklahoma	
7	Oregon	
8	Kentucky	
8	Louisiana	
9	Colorado	23
9	Alabama	
9	South Carolina	
10	Wisconsin	18
10	Minnesota	1
10	Maryland	
10	Missouri	
11	Arizona	
11	Indiana	
11	Massachusetts	
11	Tennessee	
12	Washington	
13	Virginia	36
14	New Jersey	
15	North Carolina	3
16	Michigan	1
16	Georgia	
18	Ohio	73
20	Pennsylvania	5
20	Illinois	
29	Florida	40
29	New York	
38	Texas	
55	California	
538	**Total**	**253**

The exceptions to this currently prevailing 6–6 split were minor and occurred years ago.[206]

New Hampshire has been the only closely divided battleground state among the 13 small states in the last seven presidential elections (1988 through 2012).[207]

The 12 small non-battleground states (named above) have a combined population of 11.5 million. Coincidentally, Ohio has almost the same number of people as these 12 small states. Because of the bonus of two electoral votes that every state receives, the 12 small non-battleground states have 40 electoral votes, whereas Ohio has less than half as many (18 after the 2010 census).

However, political power does not arise from the number of electoral votes that a state possesses, but instead, from whether the state is a closely divided battleground state.

In 2008, there were 62 post-convention campaign events in the closely divided battleground state of Ohio (out of a nationwide total of 300 events), whereas the 12 small non-battleground states received only three (and all three of these events were "exceptions that prove the rule").[208]

In 2012, there were 73 post-convention campaign events (out of 253) in the closely divided battleground state of Ohio, whereas the 12 non-battleground small states each received none.

In short, in 2012, the 11.5 million people in the 12 small non-battleground states received no campaign events, advertising, polling, or policy consideration by presidential candidates because the outcome of the presidential race in those states was a foregone conclusion. In contrast, the state-by-state winner-take-all rule makes the same number of people in Ohio the center of attention.

Note that the 12 small non-battleground states are not ignored because they are small. They are ignored because they are not closely divided politically.

Indeed, presidential candidates pay considerable attention to New Hampshire (with four electoral votes) because it is a closely divided battleground state. As a re-

---

[206] There were only four exceptions to this 6–6 split in the 60 state-level presidential elections conducted in these 12 states between 1988 and 2012. In 1992, Bill Clinton carried Montana (presumably due to Ross Perot's presence on the ballot). In 1988, George H.W. Bush carried Delaware, Maine, and Vermont. Since then, these states have become reliably Democratic in presidential elections.

[207] New Hampshire went Republican in 1988, Democratic in 1992 and 1996, Republican in 2000, and Democratic in 2004, 2008, and 2012.

[208] The two campaign events in Maine in 2008 were the "exceptions that prove the rule." Maine awards two of its electoral votes by congressional district. The two events in Maine in 2008 were in the state's 2nd congressional district. That particular district was closely divided—that is, it was a "battleground district." When there is even one electoral vote to be won or lost, candidates pay attention. The presidential candidates ignored Maine's other congressional district because it was reliably Democratic. Therefore, neither party had anything to gain by paying any attention to it. The third campaign event in a small jurisdiction in 2008 was another "exception that proves the rule." This event occurred in the District of Columbia (which occasionally receives campaign events because it is convenient to the candidates).

sult, New Hampshire received 12 of the 300 post-convention campaign events in 2008 and 13 of the 253 events in 2012.[209]

Meanwhile, the voters of the 12 other small states were ignored because the political division of their voters was outside the 46%–54% range that determines (more or less) whether presidential candidates consider a state to be worth contesting.[210]

A national popular vote would make a voter in each of the 12 small non-battleground states as important as a voter in battleground states such as New Hampshire. In fact, the National Popular Vote plan would make every vote in every state politically relevant in every presidential election.

Under the current state-by-state winner-take-all system, New Hampshire received 13 of the 253 campaign events in 2012, while the 12 other smallest states each received none. Under the National Popular Vote plan, it would be inconceivable that presidential candidates would campaign in only one small state, while ignoring the 12 other small states. Most likely, *each* of the 13 smallest states would *each* receive one campaign event under a nationwide vote for President.

Most of the states with five or six electoral votes are similarly non-competitive in presidential elections (and therefore disadvantaged in the same way as almost all of the 13 small states).

The fact that the small states are disadvantaged by the current state-by-state winner-take-all system has long been recognized by prominent officials from those states.

In a 1979 Senate speech, U.S. Senator Henry Bellmon (R–Oklahoma) described how his views on the Electoral College had changed as a result of serving as national campaign director for Richard Nixon and a member of the American Bar Association's commission studying electoral reform.

> "While the consideration of the electoral college began—and I am a little embarrassed to admit this—I was convinced, as are many residents of smaller States, that the present system is a considerable advantage to less-populous States such as Oklahoma. . . . As the deliberations of the American Bar Association Commission proceeded and as more facts became known, **I came to the realization that the present electoral system does not give an advantage to the voters from the less-populous States. Rather, it works to the disadvantage of small State voters who are largely ignored in the general election for President.**"[211] [Emphasis added]

---

[209] It should be noted that it is only since 1992 that New Hampshire has been a closely divided battleground state in the post-convention campaign period. Prior to 1992, New Hampshire received virtually no attention in general election campaigns because it reliably voted Republican in presidential elections.

[210] See table 1.2.

[211] *Congressional Record.* July 10, 1979. Page 17748.

Senator Robert E. Dole of Kansas, the Republican nominee for President in 1996 and Republican nominee for Vice President in 1976, stated in a 1979 floor speech:

"Many persons have the impression that the electoral college benefits those persons living in small states. I feel that this is somewhat of a misconception. Through my experience with the Republican National Committee and as a Vice Presidential candidate in 1976, it became very clear that the populous states with their large blocks of electoral votes were the crucial states. It was in these states that we focused our efforts.

"Were we to switch to a system of direct election, I think we would see a resulting change in the nature of campaigning. While urban areas will still be important campaigning centers, there will be a new emphasis given to smaller states. **Candidates will soon realize that all votes are important, and votes from small states carry the same import as votes from large states. That to me is one of the major attractions of direct election. Each vote carries equal importance.**

"Direct election would give candidates incentive to campaign in States that are perceived to be single party states."[212] [Emphasis added]

Because so few of the small states are closely divided battleground states in presidential elections, the current state-by-state winner-take-all system actually shifts power from voters in the small and medium-sized states to voters in a handful of big states that happen to be battleground states in presidential elections.

The fact that the small states are disadvantaged by the current state-by-state winner-take-all system has long been recognized by prominent officials from those states.

In 1966, the state of Delaware led a group of 12 predominantly small states (including North Dakota, South Dakota, Wyoming, Utah, Arkansas, Kansas, Oklahoma, Iowa, Kentucky, Florida, and Pennsylvania) in suing New York (then a closely divided battleground state) in the U.S. Supreme Court in an effort to get state winner-take-all statutes declared unconstitutional.[213]

David P. Buckson (Republican Attorney General of Delaware at the time) led the effort. Delaware's brief in *State of Delaware v. State of New York*[214] stated:

"The state unit-vote system [the 'winner-take-all' rule] **debases the national voting rights and political status of Plaintiff's citizens and those of other small states** by discriminating against them in favor of citizens of the larger states. A citizen of a small state is in a position to influ-

---

[212] *Congressional Record.* January 14, 1979. Page 309.

[213] *State of Delaware v. State of New York*, 385 U.S. 895, 87 S.Ct. 198, 17 L.Ed.2d 129 (1966).

[214] In the 1960s, New York was a battleground state and also the state with the most electoral votes (43).

ence fewer electoral votes than a citizen of a larger state, and therefore his popular vote is less sought after by major candidates. **He receives less attention in campaign efforts and in consideration of his interests.**"[215] [Emphasis added]

In their brief, Delaware and the other plaintiffs stated:

"This is an original action by the State of Delaware as *parens patriae* for its citizens, against the State of New York, all other states, and the District of Columbia under authority of Article III, Section 2 of the United States Constitution and 28 U.S. Code sec. 1251. The suit challenges the constitutionality of the respective state statutes employing the 'general ticket' or 'state unit-vote' system, by which the total number of presidential electoral votes of a state is arbitrarily misappropriated for the candidate receiving a bare plurality of the total number of citizens' votes cast within the state.

"The Complaint alleges that, although the states, pursuant to Article II, Section 1, Par. 2 of the Constitution, have some discretion as to the manner of appointment of presidential electors, they are nevertheless bound by constitutional limitations of due process and equal protections of the laws and by the intention of the Constitution that all states' electors would have equal weight. Further, general use of the state unit system by the states is a collective unconstitutional abridgment of all citizens' reserved political rights to associate meaningfully across state lines in national elections."

The plaintiff's brief argued that the votes of the citizens of Delaware and the other plaintiff states are

"diluted, debased, and misappropriated through the state unit system."

The U.S. Supreme Court declined to hear the case (presumably because of the well-established constitutional provision that the manner of awarding electoral votes is exclusively a state decision). Ironically, the defendant (New York) is no longer an influential closely divided battleground state (as it was in the 1960s). Today, New York suffers the very same disadvantage as the plaintiff states because it, too, has become politically non-competitive in presidential elections. Today, a vote in New York in a presidential election is equal to a vote in Delaware—both are equally irrelevant.

The Electoral College is not the bulwark of influence for the small states in the U.S. Constitution. The bulwark of influence for the small states is the equal representation of the states in the U.S. Senate. The 13 small states (with 3% of the nation's population)

---

[215] Delaware's brief, New York's brief, and Delaware's argument in its request for a re-hearing in the 1966 case of *State of Delaware v. State of New York* may be found at http://www.nationalpopularvote.com/pages/misc/de_lawsuit.php.

have 25% of the votes in the U.S. Senate—a very significant source of political clout. However, the 13 small states (i.e., those with three or four electoral votes) have only 26 extra votes in the Electoral College by virtue of the two-vote bonus—not a large number in relation to the overall total of 538 electoral votes. Although the 13 small states cast 3% of the nation's popular vote while possessing 6% of the electoral votes, the extra 3% is a minor numerical factor in the context of a presidential election. More importantly, this small theoretical advantage is negated by the fact that the small states are equally divided between the two major political parties and because the one-party character of 12 of the 13 small states makes them irrelevant to presidential campaigns.

The states that are important in the presidential election can usually be identified very early in each election cycle—even before the party nominations are settled. In the spring of 2008, both major political parties acknowledged that there would be 14 battleground states (involving only 166 of the nation's 538 electoral votes) in the 2008 presidential election.[216] In other words, two-thirds of the states were acknowledged to be irrelevant even before the national nominating conventions were held. New Hampshire (with 4 electoral votes) was the only small state that was identified as being a battleground state. The net result is that the current system shifts power from voters in the small states to voters in a handful of closely divided battleground states (almost all of which are big states).

A mere four weeks after the November 2010 congressional elections, a debate was televised on C-SPAN among candidates for chair of the Republican National Committee. The debate touched on the question of how the party would conduct the presidential campaign in the 14 states that were expected to matter in 2012.[217] Thus, two years before the 2012 presidential election, 36 states had been written off.

Tara Ross claims that

> "NPV will lessen the need of presidential candidates to obtain the support of voters in rural areas and in small states."[218]

The political reality is that the National Popular Vote plan cannot possibly "lessen the need" of candidates to win the support of small states because candidates have *no need* whatsoever to solicit the support of the small states under the current state-by-state winner-take-all system. In fact, it is the winner-take-all rule that renders the small states "almost permanently irrelevant in presidential political strategy."[219]

In fact, a national popular vote is the *only* way to give voters in the nation's small states a voice in presidential elections. For example, proposals to award electoral votes by congressional district or proportionally (section 9.23) would have no meaningful effect in states with only three or four electoral votes. Under a national popular

---

[216] Already, Obama and McCain Map Fall Strategies. *New York Times.* May 11, 2008.

[217] Freedomworks debate on December 1, 2010, available at http://www.freedomworks.org/rnc.

[218] Written testimony submitted by Tara Ross to the Delaware Senate in June 2010.

[219] See section 9.31.10 for a discussion of rural states..

vote, a voter in a reliably one-party small state would become as important as a voter anywhere else in the country.

9.4.2. MYTH: Thirty-one states would lose power under a national popular vote.

QUICK ANSWER:

- Morton Blackwell's calculation purportedly showing that 31 states would "lose power" under a national popular vote is based on a politically irrelevant calculation comparing each state's percentage of the nation's 132 million voters with its percentage of the 538 electoral votes.

- This arithmetic calculation gives the impression that the 31 smallest states have clout in presidential elections because their percentage of the 538 electoral votes is larger than their percentage of the nation's voters (because of each state's two senatorial presidential electors). However, this calculation ignores the political reality that clout in presidential elections comes from being a closely divided battleground state.

- Under the current state-by-state winner-take-all method for awarding electoral votes, the political reality is that a vote for President in most below-average-sized states is politically irrelevant.

MORE DETAILED ANSWER:

Morton C. Blackwell (who hails from the battleground state of Virginia) stated in a 2011 article entitled "National Popular Vote Plan Would Hurt Most States" that

> "31 states would lose power in presidential elections under [the National Popular Vote] plan."[220]

Blackwell bases this statement upon an arithmetic calculation that compares each state's percentage of the nation's 132 million voters to its percentage of the 538 electoral votes.

For example, Wyoming's three electoral votes is 0.56% of the 538 votes in the Electoral College. The 256,035 popular votes cast in Wyoming in 2008 were 0.19% of the nation's 132 million voters—a much smaller percentage than 0.56%. The difference between 0.56% and 0.19% is 0.37%, and this 0.37% difference represents a loss of 66% from the original 0.56%.

Blackwell then interprets this 0.37% drop as meaning that Wyoming would "lose power."

As Blackwell says:

---

[220] Blackwell, Morton C. National Popular Vote plan would hurt most states. June 25, 2011. http://www.western journal.com/national-popular-vote-plan-would-hurt-most-states/.

"If NPV had been in effect in 2008, Delaware would have lost 44% of its power. Rhode Island would have lost 51.49% of its power. Wyoming's power would have dropped by 65.48%. The pattern is the same for all the smaller-population states.

"Gainers under NPV would be the larger states."

Table 9.7 shows that 33 states have fewer electoral votes than 11—the number of electoral votes possessed by the average-sized state. For each of these 33 states, the state's percentage of the 538 electoral votes is (because of each state's two senatorial electoral votes) larger than the state's percentage of the nation's population.

A calculation similar to Blackwell's creates the impression that these states would "lose power" under a national popular vote; however, this arithmetic calculation ignores the political reality (as explained in detail in section 9.4.1) that political clout in presidential elections comes from being a closely divided battleground state—not from a state's number of electoral votes.

As can be seen from a glance at table 9.7, most of the 33 below-average-sized states are ignored under the current state-by-state winner-take-all system because they are not battleground states. Only 10 of these below-average-sized states received any of the 300 post-convention campaign events in 2008. These 10 states together received 72 of the 300 post-convention events. Moreover, six states received 67 of these 72 events:

- New Hampshire–12
- New Mexico–8
- Nevada–12
- Iowa–7
- Colorado–20
- Wisconsin–8.

Twenty-three of the 33 below-average-sized states received no campaign events. Yet, Blackwell claims that the below-average-sized states somehow benefit from the current state-by-state winner-take-all system.

In summary, far from having enhanced influence under the current system, most below-average-sized states have no clout in presidential elections because they are not battleground states.

9.4.3. MYTH: The small states are so small that they will not attract any attention under any system.

QUICK ANSWER:

- The small states (those with three or four electoral votes) are not ignored because they are small, but because almost all of them are non-competitive one-party states in presidential elections. The battleground state of New Hampshire received 13 of the 253 post-convention campaign events in 2012, while the 12 other small non-battleground states received none.

- Serious candidates for office solicit every vote *that matters*. Every vote in every state would matter in every presidential election under the National Popular Vote plan.

- Under a national popular vote, a voter in a small state would become as important as any other voter in the United States.

- The 13 small states together have approximately the same population as Ohio, and no one would suggest that Ohio would be ignored in a national popular vote for President.

- In most cases, small states offer presidential candidates the attraction of considerably lower per-impression media costs.

MORE DETAILED ANSWER:

Some argue that the small states have so few people that they will not attract any attention from presidential candidates under any system. However, the fact is that serious candidates for office solicit every voter *that matters* regardless of location.

Table 9.9 addresses the argument that small states are too small to attract the attention of presidential candidates. For the 13 small states (i.e., those with three or four electoral votes), the table shows the distribution of presidential and vice-presidential campaign events during the post-convention general election campaign for 2008.

The table shows that the determinant of whether a state receives attention is whether it is a closely divided battleground state—not its size.

Because it was a closely divided battleground state, New Hampshire received 12 of the 300 post-convention general election campaign events in 2008 and 13 of the 253 post-convention events in 2012.

Because Maine awards electoral votes by congressional district, and its 2nd congressional district is a closely divided district, Maine's 2nd district received two post-convention campaign events in 2008.

Aside from one campaign event in the District of Columbia, all of the other small states received no attention whatsoever.

Wyoming, Vermont, North Dakota, Alaska, South Dakota, Delaware, Montana, Rhode Island, Hawaii, and Idaho were all ignored not because they were small, but because presidential candidates had nothing to gain by paying any attention to them under the state-by-state winner-take-all system.

The fact that serious candidates solicit every voter *that matters* was also demonstrated in 2008 by Nebraska's 2nd congressional district (the Omaha area). Even though each congressional district in the country contains only 1/4% of the country's population, the Obama campaign operated three separate campaign offices staffed by 16 people there. The Campaign Media Analysis Group at Kantar Media reported that $887,433 in ads were run in the Omaha media market in 2008.[221] The reason for this

---

[221] The 2008 ad spending figure was reported in Steinhauser, Paul. Nevada number one in ad spending per electoral vote. *CNN Politics*. July 4, 2012.

Table 9.9 CAMPAIGN EVENTS IN THE
13 SMALLEST STATES IN 2008

STATE	CAMPAIGN EVENTS
Wyoming	–
District of Columbia	1
Vermont	–
North Dakota	–
Alaska	–
South Dakota	–
Delaware	–
Montana	–
Rhode Island	–
Hawaii	–
New Hampshire	**12**
Maine	2
Idaho	–

activity in the Omaha area was that Nebraska awards electoral votes by congressional district. Both parties paid attention to the 2nd district because it was a closely divided battleground district where one electoral vote was at stake. The outcome in 2008 was that Barack Obama carried the 2nd district by 3,378 votes and thus won one electoral vote from Nebraska.

The fact that serious candidates solicit every voter *that matters* was also demonstrated by the fact that Mitt Romney opened a campaign office in Omaha in July 2012 in order to compete in Nebraska's 2nd district[222] and that the Obama campaign was also active in the Omaha area.[223]

One Nebraska state senator whose district lies partially in the 2nd congressional district reported a heavy concentration of lawn signs, mailers, precinct walking, telephone calls to voters, and other campaign activity related to the 2008 presidential race in the portion of his state senate district that was inside the 2nd congressional district, but no such activity in the remainder of his state senate district. Indeed, neither the Obama nor the McCain campaigns paid the slightest attention to the people of Nebraska's heavily Republican 1st district or heavily Republican 3rd district, because it was a foregone conclusion that McCain would win both of those districts. The issues relevant to voters of the 2nd district (the Omaha area) mattered, while the (very different) issues relevant to the remaining (mostly rural) two-thirds of Nebraska were irrelevant.

Similarly, in Maine (which also awards electoral votes by congressional district), the closely divided 2nd congressional district (in the northern part of the state) re-

---

[222] Walton, Don. Romney will compete for Omaha electoral vote. *Lincoln Journal Star.* July 19, 2012.

[223] Henderson, O. Kay. Obama trip targets seven electoral college votes in Iowa, Nebraska. *Radio Iowa.* August 13, 2012.

ceived campaign events in 2008, whereas Maine's predictably Democratic 1st district was ignored.

When votes matter, presidential candidates vigorously solicit those voters. When votes don't matter, they ignore those areas.

In many cases, small states offer presidential candidates the attraction of considerably lower per-impression media costs (as discussed in section 9.31.7).

Although no one can predict exactly how a presidential campaign would be run under the National Popular Vote plan, we do know how candidates conduct campaigns when running for other offices in elections in which the winner is the candidate who receives the most popular votes in the entire jurisdiction. In campaigns for Governor, U.S. Senator, mayor, and state legislator, candidates pay attention to their entire constituency.

It would be inconceivable for a serious candidate for Governor to ignore four out of five voters in the state.

The 13 small states have approximately the same population as Ohio (about 12 million people). No one would suggest that Ohio would be ignored in a national popular vote for President. Therefore, there is no reason to expect that the 12 million people in the 13 small states would be ignored. Under a national popular vote, a vote in a small state would be equal to a vote in Ohio.

9.4.4. MYTH: The small states oppose a national popular vote for President.

QUICK ANSWER:
- The National Popular Vote bill has been enacted by Hawaii, Vermont, and the District of Columbia. As of 2012, the bill has been approved by a total of nine legislative chambers in small states (i.e., those with three or four electoral votes).
- Public support for a national popular vote for President runs slightly higher than the national average in most of the small states.
- In a 1966 lawsuit, the state of Delaware and a group of 12 predominantly small states argued that the state-by-state winner-take-all rule "debases the national voting rights and political status of Plaintiff's citizens and those of other small states."

MORE DETAILED ANSWER:
The facts speak for themselves. As of 2012, the National Popular Vote bill has been enacted into law by Hawaii, Vermont, and the District of Columbia. In addition, it has passed a total of nine legislative chambers in small states (i.e., those with three or four electoral votes), including the Delaware House, Maine Senate, and both houses in Rhode Island.

The concept of a national popular vote for President has a high level of support in small states.

- Alaska (70%),
- Delaware (75%),
- District of Columbia (76%),
- Idaho (77%),
- Maine (77%),
- Montana (72%),
- New Hampshire (69%),
- Rhode Island (74%),
- South Dakota (75%),
- Vermont (75%), and
- Wyoming (69%).[224]

In fact, public support for a national popular vote runs slightly higher than the national average in most of the small states. The *Washington Post*, Kaiser Family Foundation, and Harvard University poll in 2007 showed 72% support for direct nationwide election of the President. The reason may be that small states are the most disadvantaged group of states under the current system (as discussed in section 9.2).

As discussed in greater detail in section 9.4.1, the state of Delaware and a group of 12 predominantly small states (including North Dakota, South Dakota, Wyoming, Utah, Arkansas, Kansas, Oklahoma, Iowa, Kentucky, Florida, and Pennsylvania) argued in a 1966 lawsuit before the U.S. Supreme Court that the state-by-state winner-take-all rule

"debases the national voting rights and political status of **Plaintiff's citizens and those of other small states**." [Emphasis added]

9.4.5. MYTH: Equal representation of the states in the U.S. Senate is threatened by the National Popular Vote plan.

QUICK ANSWER:

- The equal representation of the states in the U.S. Senate is explicitly established and protected in the U.S. Constitution and cannot be affected by passage of any state law or interstate compact.
- The National Popular Vote plan does not affect the equal representation of the states in the U.S. Senate.

---

[224] These polls (and many others) are available on National Popular Vote's web site at http://www.national-popularvote.com/pages/polls.

MORE DETAILED ANSWER:

Equal representation of the states in the U.S. Senate is explicitly established in the U.S. Constitution. This feature cannot be changed by any state law or an interstate compact.

In fact, equal representation of the states in the U.S. Senate may not even be amended by an ordinary federal constitutional amendment. Article V of the U.S. Constitution provides:

> "No State, without its Consent, shall be deprived of its equal Suffrage in the Senate."

Thus, this feature of the U.S. Constitution may only be changed by a constitutional amendment approved by *unanimous* consent of all 50 states.

In contrast, the U.S. Constitution explicitly assigns the power of selecting the manner of appointing presidential electors to the states. The enactment by a state legislature of the National Popular Vote bill is an exercise of a state legislature's existing powers under the U.S. Constitution.

In short, enactment of the National Popular Vote compact has no bearing on the federal constitutional provisions establishing equal representation of the states in the U.S. Senate.

9.4.6. MYTH: The distribution of political influence envisioned by the Great Compromise would be upset by a national popular vote.

QUICK ANSWER:

- The distribution of political influence among the states in the Electoral College changed dramatically after political parties emerged in 1796 and winner-take-all statutes became widespread (by 1832).
- Political influence in the Electoral College today is not based on the distribution of electoral votes among the states, but instead on whether a state is a closely divided battleground state.

MORE DETAILED ANSWER:

The "Great Compromise" (also known as the "Connecticut Compromise" and "Sherman's Compromise") was adopted by the Constitutional Convention in July 1787. It was one of the most important compromises that permitted the Constitutional Convention to proceed to a successful conclusion.

The Great Compromise established a bicameral national legislature in which the U.S. House of Representatives was apportioned on the basis of population, and the Senate was structured on the basis of equal representation of the states (i.e., two Senators per state).

The National Popular Vote compact deals exclusively with the method of appointing presidential electors. It would, therefore, have no effect on the structure of the nation's national legislature (that is, Congress). Changing the structure of Congress would require a federal constitutional amendment.

The delegates to the Constitutional Convention did not reach a compromise on the method of electing the President until the end of the Convention in September.[225] By that time, all of the other major issues had been settled. In particular, the notion of having a bicameral national legislature was settled at that time.

When the Convention finally agreed that the President would be elected by an Electoral College, each state was allocated as many presidential electors as it had members in the two houses of Congress. That is, the allocation of votes in the Electoral College mirrored the overall allocation of votes in Congress, and the Electoral College became a "shadow" Congress (in which members of Congress are ineligible to serve).

The National Popular Vote bill is state legislation and therefore would have no effect on the formula in the U.S. Constitution for allocating electoral votes among the states. Changing the formula for allocating electoral votes among the states would require a federal constitutional amendment.

A posting to an election blog questioned the constitutionality of the National Popular Vote interstate compact on the basis of the Great Compromise:

> "The NPVIC also undercuts the Great Compromise which was necessary to creation of the Constitution, by in effect **changing the balance of power in choice of the President so that it does not reflect the two electoral votes that each state is to have** as a result of simply being a state."[226] [Emphasis added]

The "balance of power in [the] choice of the President" has been dramatically changed by state legislation in the past—most notably by the widespread adoption of the winner-take-all rule in the 1820s and 1830s by means of state legislation.[227]

Once the winner-take-all rule became widespread, a state's "power in [the] choice of the President" was primarily determined by whether the state was a closely divided battleground state, not its number of electoral votes.

The Great Compromise intended to confer a certain amount of extra influence on the less populous states by giving every state a bonus of two electoral votes corresponding to its two U.S. Senators. The Founders also intended that the Constitution's formula for allocating electoral votes would give the bigger states a larger amount of influence in presidential elections.

---

[225] Edwards, George C. III. 2004. *Why the Electoral College Is Bad for America*. New Haven, CT: Yale University Press.

[226] In order to promote free-flowing debate of speculative ideas, the blog involved does not permit attribution.

[227] The U.S. Supreme Court has ruled the winner-take-all rule is constitutional. *Williams v. Virginia State Board of Elections*, 288 F. Supp. 622 - Dist. Court, ED Virginia 1968. The full opinion may be found in appendix FF. The U.S. Supreme Court affirmed this decision in a *per curiam* decision in 1969. *Williams v. Virginia State Board of Elections*. 393 U.S. 320 (1969) (per curiam).

The Founding Fathers' goals with respect to *both* small states and big states were never achieved because of the widespread adoption by the states of the winner-take-all rule.

Despite the Great Compromise, small states (i.e., those with three and four electoral votes such as Wyoming, Vermont, North Dakota, Alaska, South Dakota, Delaware, Montana, Rhode Island, Hawaii, Maine, and Idaho) have no "power in choice of the President" because they are one-party states that are consistently ignored because of state winner-take-all statutes. The small states still nominally retain the number of electoral votes assigned to them by the Constitution, and they still dutifully cast their full number of electoral votes in the Electoral College in mid-December. However, their political "power in [the] choice of the President" was extinguished in the 1830s as a result of state winner-take-all statutes.

Similarly, numerous big states (e.g., New York, Texas, Illinois, and New Jersey) have had no "power in [the] choice of the President" for decades because of state winner-take-all statutes. These big states still nominally retain the number of electoral votes assigned to them by the Constitution, and they still cast their full number of electoral votes in the Electoral College. However, everyone knows that they don't matter in presidential elections.

The fact that "power in [the] choice of the President" flows from a state's battleground status rather than its number of electoral votes can be seen by comparing two states with an identical number of electoral votes. New York and Florida each have 29 electoral votes. Since 1996, Florida has received considerable attention in presidential campaigns because it has been a closely divided battleground state. Meanwhile, New York (with the same 29 electoral votes as Florida) has been ignored.

One can similarly compare New Hampshire with any small state (say, Rhode Island) possessing the same four electoral votes. For many decades prior to 1992, New Hampshire was consistently ignored in the post-convention general-election campaigns because it was safely Republican. However, since 1992, the issues of concern to New Hampshire voters have been foremost in the minds of the presidential candidates because it has been a closely divided battleground state. Meanwhile, safely democratic Rhode Island was ignored.

The National Popular Vote compact would not change the Constitution's allocation of electoral votes among the states. Nonetheless, like the winner-take-all rule, it would decidedly change "the balance of power in [the] choice of the President." Under the National Popular Vote compact, *every* voter in *every* state would be politically relevant in *every* presidential election.

The Great Compromise still governs a state's relative political influence in terms of the process of activating the National Popular Vote compact. Small states have greater influence than their population would warrant in the process of determining whether the compact has the support of states possessing a majority of the electoral votes.

In short, the Great Compromise relates to the formal structure and numerical allocation of electoral votes among the states—a state's "power in choice of the President."

9.5. MYTHS ABOUT BIG CITIES

9.5.1. MYTH: Big cities, such as Los Angeles, would control a nationwide popular vote for President.

QUICK ANSWER:

* Under a national popular vote, every vote would be equal throughout the United States. A vote cast in a big city would be no more (or less) valuable or controlling than a vote cast anywhere else.
* Los Angeles does not control the outcome of statewide elections in California and therefore is hardly in a position to dominate a nationwide election. The fact that Los Angeles does not control the outcome of statewide elections in its own state is evidenced by the fact that Republicans such as Ronald Reagan, George Deukmejian, Pete Wilson, and Arnold Schwarzenegger were elected Governor in recent years without ever winning Los Angeles.
* The origins of the myth about big cities may stem from the misconceptions that big cities are bigger than they actually are, and that big cities account for a greater fraction of the nation's population than they actually do. In fact, 85% of the population of the United States lives in places with a population of fewer than 365,000 (the population of Arlington, Texas—the nation's 50th biggest city).

MORE DETAILED ANSWER:

In a nationwide vote for President, a vote cast in a big city would be no more (or less) valuable or important than a vote cast in a suburb, an exurb, a small town, or a rural area.

When every vote is equal, candidates know that they need to solicit voters through-out their *entire* constituency in order to win.

A candidate cannot win a statewide election in California by concentrating on Los Angeles. When Ronald Reagan, George Deukmejian, Pete Wilson, and Arnold Schwarzenegger ran for Governor, Los Angeles did not receive all the attention. In fact, none of these four recent Republican Governors ever carried Los Angeles (or San Francisco, San Jose, or Oakland). Los Angeles certainly does not control the outcome of state-wide elections in California. If Los Angeles cannot control statewide elections in its own state, it can hardly control a nationwide election.

It is certainly true that most of the biggest cities in the country vote Democratic. However, the exurbs, small towns, and rural areas usually vote Republican.

If big cities controlled the outcome of elections, every Governor and every U.S. Senator in every state with a significant city would be a Democrat. The facts are that there are examples from every state with a significant city of Republicans who have won races for Governor and U.S. Senator without ever carrying the big cities of their respective states.

Perhaps the best illustration of the fact that big cities do not control elections comes from looking at the way that presidential races are actually run today inside battleground states.

Inside a battleground state in a presidential election *today*, every vote is equal, and the winner is the candidate who receives the most popular votes in that state.

When presidential candidates campaign to win the electoral votes of a closely divided battleground state, they campaign throughout the state. The big cities do not receive all the attention—much less control the outcome. Cleveland and Miami certainly do not receive all the attention when presidential candidates have campaigned in the closely divided battleground states of Ohio and Florida. Moreover, Cleveland and Miami manifestly do not control the statewide outcomes in Ohio and Florida, as evidenced by the outcome of the 2000 and 2004 presidential elections in those states. The Democrats carried both Cleveland and Miami in 2000 and 2004, but the Republicans carried both states. In fact, Senator John Kerry won the five biggest cities in Ohio in 2004, but he did not win the state.

The origins of the myth about big cities may stem from the misconceptions that big cities are bigger than they actually are, and that big cities account for a greater fraction of the nation's population than they actually do.

A look at our country's actual demographics contradicts these misconceptions concerning big cities.

Table 9.37 in section 9.31.6 shows the population of the nation's 50 biggest cities according to the 2010 census.

As can be seen from table 9.37, the population of the nation's five biggest cities (New York, Los Angeles, Chicago, Houston, and Philadelphia) represents only 6% of the nation's population of 308,745,538 (based on the 2010 census).

The population of the nation's 20 biggest cities represents only 10% of the nation's population. To put this group of 20 cities in perspective, Memphis is the nation's 20th biggest city. Memphis had a population of 647,000 in 2010.

The population of the 50 biggest cities together accounts for only 15% of the nation's population. To put this group of 50 cities in perspective, Arlington, Texas is the nation's 50th biggest city (and had a population of 365,438 in 2010).

To put it another way, 85% of the population of the United States lives in places with a population of less than 365,000 (the population of Arlington, Texas).

Moreover, the population of the nation's 50 biggest cities is declining. In 2000, the 50 biggest cities together accounted for 19% of the nation's population (compared to 15% in 2010).

Even if one makes the far-fetched assumption that a candidate could win 100% of the votes in the nation's 50 biggest cities, that candidate would have won only 15% of the national popular vote.

In a nationwide vote for President, a vote cast in a big city would be no more (or less) valuable or controlling than a vote cast in a suburb, an exurb, a small town, or a rural area.

The current state-by-state winner-take-all system does not throttle the political importance of big cities in presidential elections. Big cities, such as Cleveland, Philadelphia, and Miami that are located in closely divided battleground states are critically important in presidential races (as are the suburban, ex-urban, and rural parts of their states). However, big cities such as Houston, Atlanta, and Seattle that are located in spectator states are politically irrelevant (as are all other parts of those states).

The current state-by-state winner-take-all system elevates the political importance of a city such as Milwaukee that is located in the battleground state of Wisconsin, while minimizing the importance of cities such as Minneapolis and Baltimore that are located in spectator states such as Minnesota and Maryland (each of which has the same 10 electoral votes as Wisconsin).

Under the National Popular Vote compact, every vote would be equal throughout the United States. A vote cast in a big state would be no more, or less, valuable or controlling than a vote cast anywhere else.

An additional indication of the way that a nationwide presidential campaign would be run comes from the way that national advertisers conduct nationwide sales campaigns. National advertisers (e.g., Ford, Coca-Cola) seek out customers in small, medium-sized, and large towns as well as rural areas in every state. National advertisers do not advertise exclusively in big cities. Instead, they go after every potential customer, regardless of where the customer is located. In particular, national advertisers do not write off a particular state merely because a competitor already has an 8% lead in sales in that state (whereas presidential candidates routinely do this because of the current state-by-state winner-take-all system). Furthermore, a national advertiser with an 8% edge in a particular state does not stop trying to make additional sales because they are already No. 1 in sales in that state (whereas presidential candidates routinely do this under the current system).

See section 9.31.6 for additional discussion about big cities.

9.5.2. MYTH: A major reason for establishing the Electoral College was to prevent elections from becoming contests where presidential candidates would simply campaign in big cities.

QUICK ANSWER:

- Given the historical fact that 95% of the U.S. population in 1790 lived in places with fewer than 2,500 people, it is unlikely that the Founding Fathers were concerned about presidential candidates campaigning only in big cities.

MORE DETAILED ANSWER:

Hans von Spakovsky has stated that the National Popular Vote compact:

> "would undermine the protections of the Electoral College, elevating the importance of big urban centers like New York and Los Angeles while diminishing the influence of smaller states and rural areas. **That was a major**

reason for establishing the Electoral College in the first place: to prevent elections from becoming contests where presidential candidates would simply campaign in big cities for votes."[228] [Emphasis added]

Table 9.10 shows the only five places in the United States with a population of over 10,000 in 1790. The total population of these five places was 109,835—2.8% of the country's population of 3,929,214, according to the 1790 census.

There were only 24 places with a population over 2,500 in 1790. The total population of those 24 places was 201,655—5% of the country's total population.

Thus, it is implausible that the Founding Fathers were concerned that "presidential candidates would simply campaign in big cities for votes."

Moreover, it is not likely that the Founding Fathers were concerned about "campaigning" *anywhere* because they envisioned that the Electoral College would be a deliberative body.

As John Jay (the presumed author of *Federalist No. 64*) said of presidential electors in 1788:

"As the **select assemblies for choosing the President** . . . will in general be **composed of the most enlightened and respectable citizens**, there is reason to presume that their attention and their votes will be directed to those men only who have become the most distinguished by their abilities and virtues."[229] [Emphasis added]

As Alexander Hamilton (the presumed author of *Federalist No. 68*) wrote in 1788:

"[T]he immediate election should be made by men most capable of analyzing the qualities adapted to the station, and **acting under circumstances favorable to deliberation**, and to a **judicious combination** of all the reasons and inducements which were proper to govern their choice. **A small number of persons**, selected by their fellow-citizens from the general mass, will be most likely to possess **the information and discernment requisite to such complicated investigations**."[230] [Emphasis added]

In any event, the current state-by-state winner-take-all system does not throttle the political importance of big cities in presidential elections. Big cities that are located in closely divided battleground states (such as Cleveland, Philadelphia, and Miami) are important in presidential races, while big cities that are located in spectator states (such as Chicago, Houston, and Seattle) are politically irrelevant.

In any case, the facts today are that rural areas are highly disadvantaged under the current state-by-state winner-take-all system (as discussed in section 9.31.10).

---

[228] von Spakovsky, Hans A. Protecting Electoral College from popular vote. *Washington Times*. October 26, 2011.

[229] The powers of the senate. *Independent Journal*. March 5, 1788. *Federalist No. 64*.

[230] Publius. The mode of electing the President. *Independent Journal*. March 12, 1788. *Federalist No. 68*.

Table 9.10 POPULATION OF THE ONLY
FIVE PLACES IN THE U.S. WITH POPULATION
OVER 10,000 IN 1790

RANK	PLACE	POPULATION
1	New York	33,131
2	Philadelphia	28,522
3	Boston	18,320
4	Charleston	16,359
5	Baltimore	13,503
Total		**109,835**

Moreover, the small states are the most disadvantaged of all under the current state-by-state winner-take-all system (as discussed in section 9.4.1).

Under the National Popular Vote compact, every vote would be equal throughout the United States. A vote cast in a big city would be no more, or less, valuable or controlling than a vote cast anywhere else.

9.5.3. MYTH: Candidates would only campaign in media markets, while ignoring the rest of the country.

QUICK ANSWER:

- Every person in the United States lives in a media market, including the media markets for television, radio, newspapers, magazines, direct mail, billboards, telephone, and the Internet.

MORE DETAILED ANSWER:

This myth appears to be a carry-over from the early days of over-the-air television when political advertising did not reach significant parts of the country.

Today, every person in the United States lives in a media market, including the media markets for television, radio, newspapers, direct mail, billboards, magazines, telephone, and the Internet.

Focusing on television (the largest single component of spending in presidential campaigns), virtually everyone in the United States has access to television. This has been true for decades. No one in the United States will be left out of a presidential campaign because they do not live in a media market, because everyone in the United States lives in some media market.

People are, however, left out of presidential campaigns under the current system because of the state-by-state winner-take-all method of awarding electoral votes. Candidates have no incentive to pay any attention to voters who do not live in closely divided battleground states. Under a national popular vote, every voter would be politically relevant. Every person's vote in every state would matter in every presidential election.

For a comparison of media costs in big cities and other parts of the country, see section 9.31.7.

9.6. MYTH ABOUT STATE IDENTITY

9.6.1. MYTH: The public strongly desires that electoral votes be cast on a state-by-state basis because it provides a sense of "state identity."

QUICK ANSWER:

- A state's political "identity" is based on how *all* its citizens voted—not just how a plurality voted. The National Popular Vote plan would give voice to every voter in every state, as opposed to treating the minority within each state as if it did not exist.
- The choice presented by the National Popular Vote plan is whether it is more important for the winner of the most popular votes in the entire country to become President or for the winner of the popular vote in a particular state to receive that state's electoral votes.
- The most important aspect of a presidential election is to elect someone to serve for four years as the nation's chief executive—not to enable a group of largely unknown party activists to meet for a half hour in mid-December for the ceremonial purpose of casting electoral votes.
- In public opinion polls since the 1940s and in recent state-level polls, the public has strongly favored the idea that the President should be the candidate who receives the most popular votes in the entire country. Support remains strong when people are pointedly asked whether it is more important that a state's electoral votes be cast for the presidential candidate who receives the most popular votes in their own particular state, or whether it is more important to guarantee that the candidate who receives the most popular votes in all 50 states and the District of Columbia becomes President.
- State-level election returns would continue to be published under the National Popular Vote plan, so there would be no lack of information about how the plurality voted in a particular state.

MORE DETAILED ANSWER:

Under the National Popular Vote compact, all the electoral votes from the states belonging to the compact would be awarded to the presidential candidate who receives the most popular votes in all 50 states (and the District of Columbia). The bill would take effect only when enacted by states possessing a majority of the electoral votes—that is, enough electoral votes to elect a President (270 of 538).

The Democrats and Republicans each win the national popular vote in about half of all presidential elections (table 9.25). As a result, in about half of all elections, the presidential electors from a state belonging to the compact will not be from the same political party that received the most votes in that state.

The choice presented by the National Popular Vote plan is whether it is more important for the winner of the most popular votes in the entire country to become President or for the winner in a particular state to receive the state's electoral votes.

It is sometimes asserted that "the voters would rebel" when they discover that, as a result of the National Popular Vote compact, their state's electoral votes were awarded to a candidate who did not carry their own state.

This conjectured voter rebellion is based on the incorrect assumptions that:

- the voters care more about which candidate won their state than who is going to occupy the White House for four years;
- the voters would be surprised and shocked if the National Popular Vote compact resulted in the election of the presidential candidate who receives the most popular votes nationwide; and
- the voters are devoted and attached to the current state-by-state winner-take-all method of electing the President and would be unhappy if it were gone.

First, when voters watch presidential election returns on Election Night, they are primarily interested in finding out which candidate won the Presidency. The question of whether their preferred candidate won their state, county, city, congressional district, or precinct is a secondary concern. When a voter's preferred candidate loses the White House, it is no consolation if the voter's own candidate happened to win a plurality in the voter's own state.

On Election Night in 2008, Senator McCain's supporters in Texas were not celebrating because McCain won the most popular votes in Texas. Barack Obama's supporters in Texas were not disconsolate because McCain won the popular vote in Texas.

Most voters are not concerned about the ceremonial position of presidential elector. The average voter does not derive any satisfaction, on Election Night, from knowing that some little-known person associated with his or her own political party won the honorary position of presidential elector. It is the rare voter who knows the name of any presidential elector. Moreover, most voters are concerned with which candidate won the White House, not which candidate carried their state (or district or county or precinct). Certainly, on Election Night in 2008, McCain's Texas supporters were not celebrating because the Republican Party's 34 nominees for the position of presidential electors would be meeting in Austin, Texas, on December 15, 2008.

Under the National Popular Vote plan, the focus of public attention in the months prior to a presidential election would be on polls of the popular vote from the entire United States—not just on state-level polls from a small handful of closely divided battleground states. In fact, the concept of a battleground state would become obsolete under the National Popular Vote compact, because every voter would matter in every state in every presidential election.

Tellingly, there was no voter rebellion in reaction to the enactment by Maine (in 1969) and Nebraska (in 1992) of state laws that permit the awarding of electoral votes to a candidate who does not carry the state. Similarly, there was no voter rebellion in

Nebraska after Barack Obama carried the 2nd congressional district (the Omaha area) in the 2008 presidential election. The district system was the choice of the people's elected representatives in Nebraska, and it was the law that governed the conduct of the presidential election in Nebraska in 2008. Nebraska's law operated exactly as advertised in that it delivered one of the state's five electoral votes to the winner of the 2nd district (Barack Obama), despite the fact that John McCain won the state as a whole.

Not only was there no voter rebellion in Nebraska in the immediate aftermath of Obama receiving one of the state's electoral votes on December 15, 2008, there was no voter rebellion in 2009, 2010, 2011, or 2012, when the Nebraska legislature had ample opportunity to replace Nebraska's current law for awarding electoral votes on a district-by-district basis with the winner-take-all rule (i.e., awarding all of Nebraska's five electoral votes to the candidate who receives the most popular votes in Nebraska). A bill to switch Nebraska to the winner-take-all rule was introduced in the Nebraska legislature in 2009, 2010, 2011, and 2012. However, the winner-take-all bill never moved out of legislative committee even though Republicans (the party that lost the one electoral vote to Obama in 2008) controlled the legislature by roughly a two-to-one margin during this entire period.[231]

Second, the voters would not be surprised or shocked when the national popular vote winner becomes President under the National Popular Vote plan. The environment of a future presidential election under the National Popular Vote plan would consist of the following elements:

- A nationwide presidential campaign will have been conducted, over a period of many months, with everyone in the United States understanding that the presidential candidate receiving the most votes in all 50 states and the District of Columbia is legally entitled to win the Presidency.
- About 70% of the voters believe that the presidential candidate receiving the most votes in all 50 states and the District of Columbia should win the Presidency.
- The state legislature responded to their voters' wishes and enacted the National Popular Vote law in their state.
- The legislatures and Governors of states possessing a majority of the electoral votes similarly responded to their voters and, as a result, the National Popular Vote compact had sufficient support to take effect nationally.
- The public noticed that presidential candidates were, for the first time, paying attention to voters in every state instead of just the voters in a handful of closely divided battleground states.
- On Election Day in November, the National Popular Vote compact operated

---

[231] The Nebraska legislature is officially non-partisan; however, two-thirds of the legislators are known Republicans.

exactly as advertised and delivered a majority of the electoral votes to the presidential candidate who received the most popular votes in all 50 states and the District of Columbia.

Third, the conjectured voter rebellion would not occur, because most voters are not attached to the current state-by-state winner-take-all method of electing the President. To the contrary—most voters favor a national popular vote for President.

For example, a survey of 800 Utah voters conducted on May 19–20, 2009, showed 70% overall support for the idea that the President of the United States should be the candidate who receives the most popular votes in all 50 states. Voters were asked:

> "How do you think we should elect the President: Should it be the candidate who gets the most votes in all 50 states, or the current Electoral College system?"

By political affiliation, support for a national popular vote on the first question was 82% among Democrats, 66% among Republicans, and 75% among others. By gender, support was 78% among women and 60% among men. By age, support was 70% among 18–29 year-olds, 70% among 30–45 year-olds, 70% among 46–65 year-olds, and 68% for those older than 65.

Then, voters were pointedly asked a "push" question that specifically highlighted the fact that Utah's electoral votes would be awarded to the winner of the national popular vote in all 50 states under the National Popular Vote compact.

> "Do you think it more important that a state's electoral votes be cast for the presidential candidate who receives the most popular votes in that state, or is it more important to guarantee that the candidate who receives the most popular votes in all 50 states becomes President?"

Support for a national popular vote dropped in this "push" question, but only from 70% to 66%.

On this second question, support by political affiliation was as follows: 77% among Democrats, 63% among Republicans, and 62% among others. By gender, support was 72% among women and 58% among men. By age, support was 61% among 18–29 year-olds, 64% among 30–45 year-olds, 68% among 46–65 year-olds, and 66% for those older than 65.[232]

Similarly, a survey of 800 South Dakota voters conducted on May 19–20, 2009, showed 75% overall support for a national popular vote for President for the first question and 67% for the "push" question.

A survey of 800 Connecticut voters conducted on May 14–15, 2009, showed 74% overall support for a national popular vote for President on the first question. The re-

[232] The Utah survey (and the others cited in this section) was conducted by Public Policy Polling and had a margin of error of plus or minus 3 1/2%. See http://www.nationalpopularvote.com/pages/polls.

sults of the first question, by political affiliation, were 80% support among Democrats, 67% among Republicans, and 71% among others.

Then, voters were asked the following "push" question that specifically highlighted the fact that Connecticut's electoral votes would be awarded to the winner of the national popular vote in all 50 states.

> "Do you think it more important that Connecticut's electoral votes be cast for the presidential candidate who receives the most popular votes in Connecticut, or is it more important to guarantee that the candidate who receives the most popular votes in all 50 states becomes President?"

Support for a national popular vote dropped in this "push" question, but only from 74% to 68%.

On the second question, support by political affiliation was 74% among Democrats, 62% among Republicans, and 63% among others.

In Gallup polls since 1944, only about 20% of the public has supported the current system of awarding all of a state's electoral votes to the presidential candidate who receives the most votes in each separate state (with about 70% opposed and about 10% undecided). The 2007 *Washington Post*, Kaiser Family Foundation, and Harvard University poll showed 72% support for direct nationwide election of the President.

For those concerned about "state identity," official election returns showing the popular vote for President would continue to be certified and documented (as required by existing federal and state laws), so the information as to which presidential candidate received a plurality of the votes in a particular state would be known to all.

The concern that a state's electoral votes might be cast, in some elections, in favor of a candidate who did not carry a particular state is a matter of form over substance.

The essence of a nationwide popular vote for President is that the winner would be determined by the nationwide popular vote—not by separate state-by-state outcomes. The National Popular Vote law would be a legally binding agreement among the compacting states to award their electoral votes to the presidential candidate who receives the most popular votes in all 50 states and the District of Columbia. It is a method to reform the Electoral College so that it reflects the nationwide will of the people.

The purpose of the National Popular Vote bill is to replace the state-by-state method of awarding electoral votes with a system based on the national popular vote. State winner-take-all statutes are what enable a second-place candidate to win the White House. It is the current state-by-state winner-take-all system that makes voters unequal in presidential elections. It is the current state-by-state system that makes four out of five states and four out of five Americans politically irrelevant in presidential elections. Under the state-by-state winner-take-all method, candidates have no reason to poll in, conduct campaign events in, advertise in, build a grassroots organization in, or pay attention to the concerns of voters in states where they are comfortably ahead or hopelessly behind. Instead, candidates concentrate their attention on a small handful of closely divided battleground states.

One way to view the National Popular Vote compact is to consider it from the perspective of two states from opposite ends of the political spectrum—say, Alaska and Vermont. Politically, these states are almost mirror images of each other. They have approximately the same population, and they each possess three electoral votes. Alaska is reliably Republican, and Vermont is reliably Democratic in presidential elections. In 2004, Alaska generated a 65,812-vote margin for the Republican presidential nominee, and Vermont generated a 62,911-vote margin for the Democrat.

Under the current state-by-state winner-take-all system of awarding electoral votes, both Alaska and Vermont are totally ignored in presidential elections because neither party has anything to gain by paying any attention to them. Alaska and Vermont are not ignored because they are small. They are ignored because the winner-take-all rule makes them irrelevant in presidential politics.

Consider, for the sake of argument, a hypothetical Alaska–Vermont interstate compact in which both states agree to award their combined six electoral votes to the winner of the combined popular vote in those two states. Such a bi-state compact would create a closely divided political battleground "super-state" that would immediately get the attention of both presidential campaigns. (Note that this hypothetical Alaska–Vermont compact operates differently from the National Popular Vote compact in that Alaska and Vermont would award their six electoral votes based on the total popular vote *inside* those two states, whereas the National Popular Vote compact would award the electoral votes of the enacting states based on the total popular vote in *all* 50 states and the District of Columbia). Under the hypothetical Alaska–Vermont compact, voters in both states would suddenly matter to both parties. Presidential candidates would start thinking about Alaska issues and Vermont issues. We can confidently make this statement about the Alaska–Vermont "super-state" attracting the attention of presidential candidates because the closely divided state of Nevada (which has six electoral votes) received 12 of the 300 post-convention events in 2008. In contrast, neither Alaska nor Vermont received any attention from the presidential campaigns in 2008 (or any other year within memory).

The *benefit* of this hypothetical Alaska–Vermont interstate compact would be that Alaska and Vermont issues would become relevant in presidential campaigns. Presidential candidates would solicit votes in those states.

The *price* of this hypothetical Alaska–Vermont compact would be that Alaska's three presidential electors would be Democrats in about half of all presidential elections and that Vermont's three presidential electors would be Republicans about half of the time.

That is, under this hypothetical Alaska–Vermont compact, the presidential electors who meet in mid-December in Juneau and Montpelier would reflect the outcome of the combined popular vote in the two states—not just the vote in Alaska or just the vote in Vermont.

This hypothetical Alaska–Vermont interstate compact focuses attention on the benefit and cost trade-off inherent in the National Popular Vote compact, namely whether it is more important for the winner in a particular state to receive the state's electoral votes or for the winner of the nationwide vote to receive enough electoral votes to become President. You can't have it both ways.

Currently, the vast majority of states and the vast majority of America's voters are ignored by the presidential candidates because of the state-by-state winner-take-all method of awarding electoral votes. The National Popular Vote compact would put every voter from all 50 states and the District of Columbia into a single pool of votes for purposes of electing the President. For the first time in American history, *every* voter in *every* state would be politically relevant in *every* presidential election. The Electoral College would reflect the choice of the people in all 50 states and the District of Columbia.

9.7. MYTHS ABOUT PROLIFERATION OF CANDIDATES, ABSOLUTE MAJORITIES, AND BREAKDOWN OF THE TWO-PARTY SYSTEM

9.7.1. MYTH: The National Popular Vote plan is defective because it does not require an absolute majority of the popular vote to win.

QUICK ANSWER:
- Under the current system of electing the President, there is no requirement that the winner receive an absolute majority of the national popular vote to win the White House. Fourteen Presidents have been elected with less than a majority of the popular vote.
- An absolute majority of the statewide popular vote is not necessary to win any state's electoral votes under the current system.
- The National Popular Vote plan reflects the nation's consensus that the winner of an election should be the candidate who receives the most popular votes (that is, a plurality of the votes).

MORE DETAILED ANSWER:
Tara Ross, an opponent of the National Popular Vote compact, objects to the compact by saying:

> "The compact contemplated by [the National Popular Vote bill] would give the presidency to the candidate winning the 'largest national popular vote total.' Note that it says the 'largest' total.' It is not looking for a majority winner."[233]

John Samples of the Cato Institute, an opponent of the National Popular Vote compact, has said:

---

[233] Written testimony submitted by Tara Ross to the Delaware Senate in June 2010.

"NPV does not necessarily impose election by a majority. If a plurality suffices for election, **a majority of voters may have chosen someone other than the winner.**"[234] [Emphasis added]

Both of these observations apply equally to the current system.

Nothing in the U.S. Constitution requires that a candidate receive an absolute majority of the national popular vote in order to become President. The following 14 Presidents have been elected with less than a majority of the popular vote:

- James Polk,
- Zachary Taylor,
- James Buchanan,
- Abraham Lincoln (1860),
- Rutherford Hayes,
- James Garfield,
- Grover Cleveland (twice),
- Benjamin Harrison,
- Woodrow Wilson (twice),
- Harry Truman,
- John Kennedy,
- Richard Nixon (1968),
- Bill Clinton (twice), and
- George W. Bush (2000).

Nothing in the law of any state requires that a candidate receive an absolute majority of the state's popular vote in order to win all of that state's electoral votes. In fact, it is common, under existing state laws, for a presidential candidate to win all of a state's electoral votes without receiving an absolute majority of the state's popular vote. In 2008, no candidate received an absolute majority of the popular vote in four states. In 1992, no candidate received an absolute majority of the popular vote in 49 states.[235]

The public seems content with elections that are conducted on the basis that the candidate who receives the most popular votes wins the office. That is how the vast majority of elections are conducted in the United States.

The National Popular Vote plan reflects the nation's consensus that the winner of an election should be the candidate who receives the most popular votes. There was certainly no outcry from the public, the media, Congress, or state legislators when Truman (1948), Kennedy (1960), Nixon (1968), or Clinton (1992 and 1996) were elected with less than an absolute majority of the national popular vote.

---

[234] Samples, John. *A Critique of the National Popular Vote Plan for Electing the President.* Cato Institute Policy Analysis No. 622. October 13, 2008. Page 2.

[235] Bill Clinton received 53% of the popular vote in Arkansas in 1992. He also won 84% of the popular vote in the District of Columbia.

If, at some time in the future, the public demands that an absolute majority be required for election to office, that desire can be accommodated at that time.

9.7.2. MYTH: The National Popular Vote plan is defective because it does not provide for a run-off.

QUICK ANSWER:

- Under the current system, there is no procedure for a run-off. No run-off was conducted when Presidents Lincoln, Wilson, Truman, Kennedy, Nixon, or Clinton failed to receive an absolute majority of the national popular vote.
- Under the current system, there is no requirement for a run-off in a state where no candidate receives an absolute majority of the statewide popular vote.
- The National Popular Vote plan reflects the nation's consensus that the winner of an election should be the candidate who receives the most popular votes. There is no national consensus in favor of run-offs.

MORE DETAILED ANSWER:

Tara Ross complains that the National Popular Vote plan does not require an absolute majority of the national popular vote to win.[236]

Ross' criticism applies equally to the current system. There is no provision in current law for a run-off when no presidential candidate receives an absolute majority of the national popular vote.

Moreover, there is no provision in any state today for a run-off when no presidential candidate receives an absolute majority of the state's popular vote. In fact, it is common, under existing state laws, for a presidential candidate to win all of a state's electoral votes without receiving an absolute majority of the state's popular vote. For example, in 2008, no candidate received an absolute majority of the popular vote in four states.

Tara Ross says:

> "States that have agreed to participate in NPV can't force the other states to take any particular action—including a runoff or other secondary election procedure."[237]

After the 1992 election in which no candidate received an absolute majority of the popular vote in 49 states,[238] we cannot recall any demand from legislators, the public, the media, or anyone else for a run-off presidential election.

---

[236] Written testimony submitted by Tara Ross to the Delaware Senate in June 2010.

[237] Ross, Tara. 2012. *Enlightened Democracy: The Case for the Electoral College.* Los Angeles, CA: World Ahead Publishing Company. Second edition. Page 160.

[238] Bill Clinton received 53% of the popular vote in Arkansas in 1992. He also won 84% of the popular vote in the District of Columbia.

The National Popular Vote compact operates in a manner consistent with the widely held view in the United States that the winner of an election should be the candidate who receives the most popular votes (that is, a plurality).

Note that traditional run-off elections present a number of difficulties. A run-off election would be expensive to administer. It is already difficult to recruit the mass of citizen volunteers needed to operate elections. Given that the President has to be inaugurated on January 20 and that the Electoral College meets in mid-December, it is already difficult to finish the initial counting of votes (and also conduct recounts, litigate disputes, and conduct required audits) in the limited amount of time available after Election Day in November. Turnout in a run-off election could be low. Perhaps most importantly, a run-off election would significantly alter the dynamics of financing of presidential campaigns because it would tilt the playing field in favor of the candidate who is in a position to raise vast amounts of *additional* money on very short notice.[239]

If, at some time in the future, the public demands run-offs, that change can be implemented at that time.

9.7.3. MYTH: A national popular vote will result in a proliferation of candidates, Presidents being elected with as little as 15% of the vote, and a breakdown of the two-party system.

QUICK ANSWER:

- If an Electoral College type of arrangement were essential for avoiding a proliferation of candidates and preventing candidates from winning office with as little as 15% of the vote, we should see evidence of these conjectured problems in elections that do not employ such an arrangement (such as elections for Governor).

- Historical experience in over 5,000 elections for state chief executive shows no evidence of the conjectured proliferation of candidates or the conjectured 15% winners in elections in which the winner is the candidate who receives the most popular votes.

- Duverger's law (which is based on worldwide studies of elections) asserts that plurality-vote elections do not result in a proliferation of candidates or candidates being elected with tiny percentages of the vote.

---

[239] If, at some time in the future, the public decides that it wants the benefits of a run-off election without the problems of a traditional run-off system, instant run-off voting (also called "ranked voting") offers a method for combining a run-off into the original election. In instant run-off voting, voters have the option of indicating their second choice for the office involved (and, in some variations of the system, additional choices). If no candidate receives an absolute majority of the first-place votes, the votes of the candidate receiving the fewest votes are distributed according to the second choices of those voters. This process of redistributing the votes received by the lowest candidate continues until one candidate receives an absolute majority of the voters expressing a choice. Instant run-off voting is currently used in a number of municipalities around the country. It is also used in many elections conducted among delegates at conventions of various organizations. Information about instant run-off voting is available from www.FairVote.org.

- The two-party system is, in fact, sustained by the plurality-vote rule—not the state-by-state winner-take-all rule.

MORE DETAILED ANSWER:

Tara Ross, an opponent of the National Popular Vote plan, predicts that a national popular vote would lead to a proliferation of candidates and a fracturing of the electorate, and that Presidents would be elected with only 15% of the vote:

> "[The National Popular Vote plan] is not even looking for a minimum plurality. Thus, a candidate could win with only 15 percent of votes nationwide."[240]

We do not have to speculate as to whether Ross' prediction is likely to materialize because we can refer to the nation's actual experience in the numerous elections that have been conducted in which the winner was the candidate who received the most popular votes.

If an Electoral College type of arrangement were essential for avoiding Ross' conjectured outcome, we should see evidence of this outcome in elections that did not employ an Electoral College.

When elections are conducted in which the winner is the candidate who receives the most popular votes, candidates do not, in actual practice, win the office with low percentages of the vote (and certainly not percentages such as 15%).

In the 975 general elections for Governor in the United States between 1948 and 2011:[241]

- 90% of the winning candidates received more than 50% of the vote,
- 98% of the winning candidates received more than 45% of the vote,
- 99% of the winning candidates received more than 40% of the vote, and
- 100% of the winning candidates received more than 35% of the vote.

There were only 25 general elections (out of 975) for Governor between 1948 and 2011 in which the winning candidate received less than 45% of the popular vote, as shown in table 9.11.

Over half of the elections in table 9.11 (13 of 25) were in small states (Alaska, Hawaii, Idaho, Maine, New Hampshire, and Vermont).

Elections for U.S. Senate, other statewide offices, Congress, state legislature, and other offices confirm this pattern. In the real world, there are never any 15% winners in general elections in which the winner is the candidate with the most votes. There is no proliferation of candidates. There is no fracturing of the electorate.

Moreover, elections in other countries around the world show a similar pattern.

Duverger's law asserts that a plurality-rule election system tends to favor a two-party system. Maurice Duverger, the French sociologist who observed this tendency

---

[240] Written testimony submitted by Tara Ross to the Delaware Senate in June 2010.
[241] http://www.fairvote.org/plurality-in-gubernatorial-elections/.

Table 9.11 THE 25 GENERAL ELECTIONS FOR GOVERNOR BETWEEN
1948 AND 2011 (OUT OF 975) IN WHICH THE WINNING
CANDIDATE RECEIVED LESS THAN 45% OF THE VOTE

WINNING PERCENTAGE	WINNER	STATE	YEAR
35.4%	Angus King	Maine	1994
36.1%	Lincoln Chafee	Rhode Island	2010
36.2%	John G. Rowland	Connecticut	1994
36.6%	Benjamin J. Cayetano	Hawaii	1994
37.0%	Jesse Ventura	Minnesota	1998
38.1%	John Baldacci	Maine	2006
38.2%	Paul LePage	Maine	2010
38.2%	George D. Clyde	Utah	1956
38.9%	Walter J. Hickel	Alaska	1990
39.0%	Rick Perry	Texas	2006
39.1%	Jay S. Hammond	Alaska	1978
39.1%	James B. Longley	Maine	1974
39.7%	Evan Mecham	Arizona	1986
39.9%	John R. McKernan Jr.	Maine	1986
40.1%	Norman H. Bangerter	Utah	1988
40.4%	Lowell P. Weicker Jr.	Connecticut	1990
41.1%	Tony Knowles	Alaska	1994
41.4%	Meldrim Thomson Jr.	New Hampshire	1972
41.4%	Don Samuelson	Idaho	1966
42.2%	Michael O. Leavitt	Utah	1992
43.3%	Brad Henry	Oklahoma	2002
43.7%	Mark Dayton	Minnesota	2010
44.4%	Tim Pawlenty	Minnesota	2002
44.6%	Nelson A. Rockefeller	New York	1966
44.9%	Jim Douglas	Vermont	2002

in election systems around the world, suggests that plurality voting favors a two-party system because political groups with broadly similar platforms tend to form alliances because it increases their chances of winning office. Voters generally desert weak parties or candidates on the grounds that they have no chance of winning. In practice, ordinary plurality voting discourages the formation of niche parties and candidacies by rewarding the formation of broad coalitions in which various groups and interests join together in order to win the most votes (and thereby win office).

The reason that ordinary plurality voting has this effect is that a vote cast for a splinter candidate frequently produces the politically counter-productive effect of helping the major-party candidate whose views are diametrically opposite of those of the voter. For example, votes cast for Bob Barr (the Libertarian Party candidate for President in 2008) enabled Barack Obama to win the electoral votes of North Carolina,[242]

---

[242] In North Carolina in 2008, Bob Barr (the Libertarian candidate) received considerably more votes than the margin between Barack Obama (the winner of the state) and John McCain (the second-place candidate).

and votes cast for Ralph Nader (the Green Party candidate) in 2000 enabled George W. Bush to win the electoral votes of Florida and New Hampshire.[243]

Ross' criticism of the National Popular Vote plan concerning third-party candidates is an example of a criticism that actually applies more to the current state-by-state winner-take-all system than the National Popular Vote plan.

Under the current system of electing the President, minor-party candidates have significantly affected the outcome in 38% (six out of 17) of the presidential elections since World War II. Specifically, minor-party candidates affected the outcome by either shifting states from one candidate to another or winning electoral votes outright in the 1948, 1968, 1980, 1992, 1996, and 2000 presidential elections.

Segregationists such as Strom Thurmond and George Wallace each won electoral votes in various Southern states. Thurmond won 39 electoral votes in 1948, and George Wallace won 46 electoral votes in 1968. Candidates such as John Anderson (1980), Ross Perot (1992 and 1996), and Ralph Nader (2000) each managed to affect the national outcome by switching electoral votes in numerous states.

None of these third-party candidates had any reasonable expectation of winning the most popular votes nationwide. The reason that the current system has encouraged so many minor-party candidacies is that a third-party candidate has 51 separate opportunities to find particular states that he might win outright or where he might be able to shift electoral votes from one major party to another.

Tara Ross writes:

> "The most likely consequence of a change to a direct popular vote is the breakdown of the two-party system."[244]

Ross' prediction can be tested against actual historical facts.

In 1787, Connecticut, Massachusetts, New Hampshire, and Rhode Island conducted popular elections for the office of Governor.[245]

Today, 100% of the states conduct a direct popular vote for Governor. Yet, after over 5,000 direct popular elections for Governor since 1789, the two-party system has yet to collapse.

The two-party system in the United States (which dominates the electoral landscape for the vast majority of elective offices in the country) is not sustained by the existence of the state-by-state winner-take-all rule for filling the single office of the Presidency.

---

[243] In Florida and New Hampshire in 2000, Ralph Nader received considerably more votes than the margin between George W. Bush (the winner of these two states) and Al Gore (the second-place candidate).

[244] Written testimony submitted by Tara Ross to the Delaware Senate in June 2010.

[245] Dubin, Michael J. 2003. *United States Gubernatorial Elections 1776–1860*. Jefferson, NC: McFarland & Company. Page xx.

About three-quarters of the elections for Governor occur in non-presidential years—that is, they stand entirely apart from the presidential election cycle.

Returning to the history of presidential elections, only three states had winner-take-all statutes in the nation's first presidential election in 1789. Only three states used the winner-take-all rule in 1792 and 1796. Given that political parties first emerged in the 1796 presidential election, it can hardly be argued that the existence of the state-by-state winner-take-all rule in just three states was the force that created the two-party system in the United States.

Instead, the two-party system is the consequence of the plurality voting system in which the candidate who receives the most popular votes wins the office.

There is no reason to expect the emergence of some unique, new political dynamic that would promote multiple candidacies if the President were elected in the same manner as virtually every other elected official in the United States.

What can be said about third-party candidacies in presidential elections is that the current system often perversely discriminates against third-party candidates who have a broad national base of support, while encouraging regional third-party candidates. In 1948, Henry Wallace (a leftist candidate for President) and Strom Thurmond (a pro-segregation candidate for President) each received 1.2 million popular votes. However, Strom Thurmond (whose support was concentrated in the South) won 39 electoral votes in 1948, whereas Henry Wallace (whose support was distributed more evenly throughout the county) received no electoral votes.

Ross Perot's percentage of the national popular vote in 1992 was twice the percentage received in 1968 by George Wallace (a pro-segregation candidate). However, Perot won no electoral votes in 1992, whereas George Wallace won 46 electoral votes in 1968.

Although Ross Perot received eight times Strom Thurmond's percentage of the popular vote in 1948, Perot won no electoral votes in 1992, while Thurmond won 39 electoral votes.[246]

The current state-by-state winner-take-all system certainly does not prevent the proliferation of candidates; however, it does perversely reward regional third-party candidacies while punishing broad-based third-party candidates.

Some argue that third parties are inherently undesirable and that the election system should be skewed so as to strengthen and favor the two-party system. Even if one subscribes to this viewpoint, it is difficult to see what public purpose is served by the current system's perverse discrimination in favor of regionally divisive third parties and against broad-based third parties with nationwide support.

---

[246] A simulation conducted by FairVote suggests that if Ross Perot had doubled his national popular vote from 19% to 38%, he probably would have won a majority of the electoral votes. http://www.fairvote.org/the-perot-simulator. But with 19% of the national popular vote broadly spread out over the entire country, Perot won no electoral votes.

9.7.4. MYTH: The current system requires an absolute majority of the popular vote to win.

QUICK ANSWER:

- Under the current system of electing the President, there is no requirement that the winner receive an absolute majority of the national popular vote to win the Presidency. Presidents Lincoln, Cleveland, Wilson, Truman, Kennedy, Nixon, and Clinton were non-majority Presidents.
- An absolute majority of the statewide popular vote is not necessary to win any state's electoral votes under the current system.

MORE DETAILED ANSWER:

In an article entitled "The Electoral College Is Brilliant, and We Would Be Insane to Abolish It," Walter Hickey writes:

> **"Without the electoral college system, a President could be elected with a plurality rather than an outright majority.**
>
> "Without it—and with a compelling third party—**someone could become president with only 34 percent of the vote**. When 66 percent of the country voted against the President, that doesn't scream stability. How many governments has Italy had in the past fifty years?"[247] [Emphasis added]

Hickey appears to be unaware that nothing in the U.S. Constitution requires that a candidate receive an absolute majority of the national popular vote in order to become President. The following 14 Presidents have been elected with less than a majority of the popular vote: James K. Polk, Zachary Taylor, James Buchanan, Abraham Lincoln (1860), Rutherford B. Hayes, James Garfield, Grover Cleveland (twice), Benjamin Harrison, Woodrow Wilson (twice), Harry Truman, John Kennedy, Richard Nixon (1968), Bill Clinton (twice), and George W. Bush (2000).

Hickey also appears to be unaware that nothing in the law of any state requires that a candidate receive an absolute majority of the state's popular vote in order to win all of that state's electoral votes. In fact, presidential candidates frequently win a state's electoral votes without receiving an absolute majority of the state's popular vote. In 1992, no candidate received an absolute majority of the popular vote in 49 states.[248] In 2008, no candidate received an absolute majority of the popular vote in four states.

Lincoln was elected with 39% of the nationwide popular vote in 1860. There is nothing in the current system to prevent another occurrence of a candidate being elected President with 39% of the nationwide popular vote. A June 1992 nationwide

---

[247] Hickey, Walter. 2012. The Electoral College is brilliant, and we would be insane to abolish it. *Business Insider.* October 3, 2012. http://www.businessinsider.com/the-electoral-college-is-brilliant-2012-10.

[248] In 1992, Bill Clinton received 53% of the popular vote in Arkansas and 84% of the popular vote in the District of Columbia.

poll showed that Ross Perot had 39% support, incumbent President George H.W. Bush had 31%, and Bill Clinton had 25%.[249]

9.8. MYTHS ABOUT EXTREMIST AND REGIONAL CANDIDATES

9.8.1. MYTH: Extremist candidates will proliferate under a national popular vote.

QUICK ANSWER:
- If an Electoral College type of arrangement were essential for avoiding extremist candidates, we would see evidence of extremism in elections (such as gubernatorial elections) that do not employ an Electoral College type of arrangement.
- Actual experience is that extremist candidates are rarely elected in elections in which the winner is the candidate who receives the most votes.

MORE DETAILED ANSWER:
Tara Ross has asserted that if the President were elected by a national popular vote,

"extremist candidates could more easily sway an election."[250]

Hans von Spakovsky has stated that the National Popular Vote plan:

"could also radicalize American politics."[251]

History Professor Daniel J. Singal of Hobart and William Smith Colleges warns:

"Tom Golisano's proposal in his essay 'Make Every State Matter' to elect presidents on the basis of the popular vote rather than the Electoral College may sound appealing at first, but would in fact **wreak havoc on our national political system** in ways that he clearly does not understand.

"Put simply, the Electoral College has turned out to be one of the most brilliant innovations the Founding Fathers devised when writing the Constitution. Its virtue is that **it directs our politics to the center of the political spectrum, helping us to avoid the extremism that might otherwise rule the day**. . . .

"**In states that are up for grabs independent voters in the middle of the political spectrum become crucial**. Since those states are usually decided by a few percentage points, the **candidates must gear their mes-**

---

[249] The 1992 poll was cited in Stanley, Timothy. Why Romney is stronger than he seems. *CNN Election Center.* April 10, 2012.

[250] Written testimony submitted by Tara Ross to the Delaware Senate in June 2010.

[251] Von Spakovsky, Hans. Popular vote scheme. *The Foundry.* October 18, 2011.

sages to appeal to those 'swing voters,' who by definition are not strong partisans and thus open to either side."[252] [Emphasis added]

If an Electoral College type of arrangement were essential for avoiding extremist candidates, we would see evidence of Singal's conjectured "havoc" in elections that do not employ an Electoral College type of arrangement. However, Singal presents no evidence of "havoc" in elections in which the winner is the candidate who receives the most popular votes.

At the time the U.S. Constitution came into effect in 1789, Governors were elected in Rhode Island, Massachusetts, New Hampshire, and Connecticut. The idea of popularly electing the Governor was adopted piecemeal, on a state-by-state basis. Today, Governors are elected in 100% of the states.

After over two centuries of actual experience in over 5,000 statewide elections for state chief executive, the lack of moderation in political discourse predicted by Ross, the radicalization of politics predicted by von Spakovsky, and the "havoc" predicted by Singal have yet to materialize. History indicates that extremist candidates are almost never elected in elections in which the winner is the candidate who receives the most popular votes.

U.S. Senators were elected by state legislatures under the original U.S. Constitution. Since ratification of the 17th Amendment in 1913, U.S. Senators have been elected by the people. After nearly 100 years of actual experience under the 17th Amendment, how many U.S. Senators have been extremists?

Given this historical record, there is no reason to expect the emergence of some new and currently unknown political dynamic if the President were elected in the same manner as virtually every other public official in the United States.

Candidates attempting to win any election have a strong incentive to capture "the middle" of their electorate. Counting the votes on a nationwide basis (instead of a statewide basis) would not change this imperative.

Singal provides no explanation as to why "independent voters in the middle of the political spectrum" would not be similarly "crucial" if the President were elected from a nationwide electorate.

Singal also overlooks the fact that there are millions of "swing voters" in the states that get no attention under the current state-by-state winner-take-all system. What is the justification for making "swing voters" in today's non-battleground states less important than the "swing voters" in battleground states?

Criticism of the National Popular Vote plan on the basis of extremism is yet another example of a criticism that is actually more appropriately applied to the current state-by-state winner-take-all system.

Segregationists such as Strom Thurmond (1948) or George Wallace (1968) won

---

[252] Singal, Daniel J. The genius of the Electoral College. *Democrat and Chronicle*. Rochester, New York. August 23, 2012.

electoral votes in numerous Southern states. Neither Strom Thurmond nor George Wallace had any reasonable expectation of winning the most popular votes nation-wide. Under the current state-by-state winner-take-all system, third-party candidates have 51 separate opportunities to find particular states that they might win outright or where they might be able to shift electoral votes from one major party to another.

The current state-by-state winner-take-all system encourages regional third-party candidates such as Strom Thurmond and George Wallace because it offers them the hope of being able to deny a majority of the Electoral College to the major-party candidates, and thereby throw the election of the President to the U.S. House of Representatives or, alternatively, to bargain with the major-party candidates prior to the meeting of the Electoral College.

9.8.2. MYTH: Regional candidates will proliferate under a national popular vote.

QUICK ANSWER:
- If an Electoral College type of arrangement were essential for avoiding regional candidates, we should see evidence of regional candidates in elections (such as gubernatorial elections) that do not employ an Electoral College type of arrangement.
- There is no evidence of the emergence of regional candidates or regional parties in statewide elections in which the winner is the candidate who receives the most popular votes.

MORE DETAILED ANSWER:
Tara Ross, an opponent of the National Popular Vote plan, raises the following question:

> "What if voters in New York and Massachusetts throw all their weight behind one regional candidate?"[253]

We can easily test Ross' hypothetical scenario about regional candidates against actual historical experience and facts.

If an Electoral College type of arrangement were essential for avoiding Ross' conjectured outcome, we would see evidence of regional parties and regional candidates in elections that do not employ an Electoral College.

When Governors are chosen in elections in which the winner is the candidate who receives the most popular votes, we do not see a Philadelphia Party and a Pittsburgh Party competing for the Governor's office. There is no Eastern Shore Party in Maryland, no Upper Peninsula Party in Michigan, no Northern California Party in California, no Upstate New York Party in New York, and no Panhandle Party in Florida.

---

[253] Oral and written testimony presented by Tara Ross at the Nevada Senate Committee on Legislative Operations and Elections on May 7, 2009.

Similarly, we do not see regional parties nominating regional candidates to run for the U.S. Senate.

In the real world, ordinary plurality voting discourages the formation of niche parties. Instead, ordinary plurality voting rewards the formation of broad coalitions in which various groups and interests join together in order to win the most votes (and thereby win office).

The reason that ordinary plurality voting has this effect is that a vote cast for a splinter candidate generally produces the politically counter-productive effect of helping the major-party candidate whose views are diametrically opposite to those of the voter.

For example, votes cast for Green Party candidate Ralph Nader enabled Republican George W. Bush to win Florida and New Hampshire in 2000.[254] Votes cast for Libertarian Party candidate Bob Barr enabled Democrat Barack Obama to win North Carolina in 2008.[255]

Based on historical evidence, regional candidates are far more common under the state-by-state winner-take-all system of electing the President than in elections in which the winner is the candidate who receives the most popular votes.

Under the current state-by-state winner-take-all system of electing the President, regional segregationist candidates such as Strom Thurmond (1948) and George Wallace (1968) won electoral votes in various Southern states. None of these third-party candidates had any reasonable expectation of winning a plurality of the popular votes nationwide. The current state-by-state winner-take-all system encourages regional candidacies because such candidates can win certain states outright or can affect the national outcome by shifting electoral votes from one major party to another. The current system gives regional candidates the hope of being able to throw the presidential election into the U.S. House of Representatives or to bargain with the major party candidates before the meeting of the Electoral College in mid-December.

9.8.3. MYTH: It is the genius of the Electoral College that Grover Cleveland did not win in 1888 because the Electoral College works as a check against regionalism.

QUICK ANSWER:
- The state-by-state winner-take-all system does not protect against regionalism.
- In 1888, the state-by-state winner-take-all system gave the White House to a *regional* candidate who had fewer popular votes nationwide instead of giving it to the *regional* candidate with more popular votes nationwide.

---

[254] In Florida and New Hampshire in 2000, Ralph Nader received considerably more votes than the margin between George W. Bush (the winner of these two states) and Al Gore (the second-place candidate).

[255] In North Carolina in 2008, Bob Barr (the Libertarian candidate) received considerably more votes than the margin between Barack Obama (the winner of the state) and John McCain (the second-place candidate).

MORE DETAILED ANSWER:

One of the consequences of the state-by-state winner-take-all rule (i.e., awarding all of a state's electoral votes to the presidential candidate who receives the most popular votes in each separate state) is that it is possible for a candidate to win the Presidency without winning the most popular votes nationwide.

Of the 57 presidential elections between 1789 and 2012, there have been four elections in which the candidate with the most popular votes nationwide did not win the Presidency (table 1.22).

The election of 1888 between Democrat Grover Cleveland and Republican Benjamin Harrison was one of four such elections.

Trent England (a lobbyist opposing the National Popular Vote compact and Vice-President of the Evergreen Freedom Foundation of Olympia, Washington) has written:

> "Because of the Electoral College, Cleveland's intense regional popularity—even when it gave him a raw total majority—was not enough to win the presidency.

> "Successful presidential campaigns must assemble broad, national coalitions.

> "It is the genius of the Electoral College that Grover Cleveland did not win in 1888. **The Electoral College works as a check against regionalism** and radicalism.

> "American politics are more inclusive, moderate, stable, and nationally unified because of the Electoral College."[256] [Emphasis added]

Figure 9.2 shows the distribution of electoral votes in the 1888 presidential election. Democrat Grover Cleveland's states are shown in black, and Republican Benjamin Harrison's states are thatched. The white parts of the map represent territories that were not states in 1888.

It is certainly true that figure 9.2 shows that the states (in black) carried by the candidate who received the most popular votes nationwide (Grover Cleveland) were concentrated regionally.

However, as the same figure shows, it is equally true that the states (thatched) carried by the second-place candidate (Benjamin Harrison) were regionally concentrated.

How is "the genius of the Electoral College" illustrated by elevating the *regional* second-place candidate (Benjamin Harrison) to the White House, instead of the *regional* first-place candidate (Grover Cleveland)?

Moreover, given that Grover Cleveland was a conservative (as evidenced by his record as President starting in 1885 and again in 1893), one wonders how the "wrong

---

[256] England, Trent. What Grover learned at (the) Electoral College: American politics are more inclusive, moderate, stable, and nationally unified because of the Electoral College. December 15, 2009. http://www.saveourstates.com/2009/what-grover-learned-at-the-electoral-college/.

winner" outcome of the 1888 election supports Trent England's claim that "the Electoral College works as a check against . . . radicalism?"

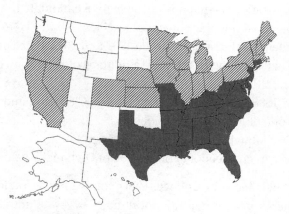

Figure 9.2 Results of 1888 election

As shown in figure 9.3, the regional pattern of the 1880 election was almost identical to that of the Cleveland–Harrison election. In figure 9.3, 1880 Democratic nominee Winfield Hancock's states are shown in black, and Republican nominee James Garfield's states are thatched. Indeed, most of the post-Civil-War elections evidenced a regional pattern similar to that of figures 9.2 and 9.3.

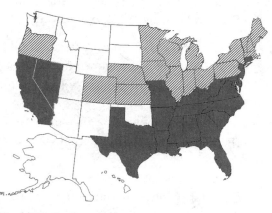

Figure 9.3 Results of 1880 election

How is Trent England's claim that "the Electoral College works as a check against regionalism" illustrated by the election in 1880 of James Garfield, a manifestly regional candidate?

Figure 9.4 shows the results of the 2012 presidential election. Democrat Barack Obama's states are shown in black, and Republican Mitt Romney's states are thatched.

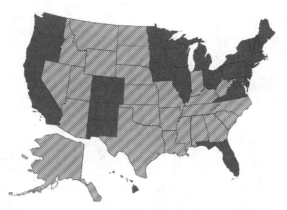

Figure 9.4 Results of 2012 election

A comparison of figure 9.4, figure 9.3, and figure 9.2 shows that regionalism was still quite prominent in the nation's 57th presidential election in 2012—just as it was in 1880 and 1888. After 57 presidential elections, when can we expect Trent England's claim that "the Electoral College works as a check against regionalism" to finally become true?

9.9. MYTHS ABOUT LOGISTICAL NIGHTMARES ARISING FROM DIFFERENCES IN STATE LAWS

9.9.1. MYTH: Logistical nightmares would plague a national popular vote because of differences among the states concerning ballot-access requirements, ex-felon eligibility requirements, poll-closing times, and so forth.

QUICK ANSWER:
- Adding up the number of popular votes that are cast in each state to obtain the nationwide popular vote total for each presidential candidate is not a difficult task, much less a "logistical nightmare."
- There is nothing incompatible between state control over elections and a national popular vote for President.
- Differences in election laws are inherent and inevitable in our federalist system, which gives the states control over elections.
- The National Popular Vote plan is based on the federal constitutional system that exists in the United States and on the political reality that there is widespread public and legislative support for federalism and state control of elections.

MORE DETAILED ANSWER:

Tara Ross, an opponent of the National Popular Vote compact, predicts that the compact would create:

> "logistical nightmares [that] could haunt the country."[257]

Ross also notes:

> "There are . . . inconsistencies among states' ballots that would skew the election results. . . . States differ in their requirements for ballot qualification."[258]

Adding up the popular votes that are cast in each state to obtain the nationwide popular vote total for each presidential candidate is not a difficult task, much less a "logistical nightmare."

Differences in election laws are inherent in our federalist system, which gives the states control over elections.

The Founders gave the states exclusive control over the manner of electing the President so as to provide a check on a sitting President who might try to manipulate the rules for his own re-election in conjunction with a possibly compliant Congress.

There is nothing incompatible between the concept of a national popular vote for President and the inevitable differences in election laws resulting from state control over elections. This was certainly the mainstream view when the U.S. House of Representatives passed a constitutional amendment in 1969 for a national popular vote by a 338–70 margin. That amendment was endorsed by Richard Nixon at the time. That amendment was also endorsed by Gerald Ford, Jimmy Carter, and members of Congress who later became vice-presidential and presidential candidates such as Congressman George H.W. Bush (R–Texas), and Senator Bob Dole (R–Kansas).

The proposed 1969 constitutional amendment provided that the certified popular-vote tallies from each state would be added together to obtain the nationwide total for each candidate. See section 3.4 for more information.

Similarly, the National Popular Vote compact uses the very same process of adding up the popular-vote count from each state.

It is certainly true that some state election laws vary in many ways, including voter-registration policies, poll-closing time, amount of early voting, requirements for absentee voting, ex-felon voting, and so forth.

However, once a vote is cast in accordance with whatever policies are in effect in each state, there is no practical problem in adding up the votes from the 50 states and the District of Columbia.

There is certainly no "logistical nightmare" created by simply adding up the certified popular-vote totals for each candidate from each state just because one state happens to close its polls at a different time than another.

---

[257] Written testimony submitted by Tara Ross to the Delaware Senate in June 2010.
[258] *Id.*

Indeed, *under the current system*, the *electoral-vote* counts from all 50 states are comingled and added together—despite the fact that each of these electoral-vote counts has been significantly impacted by differing state election laws (including laws governing ballot access, poll-closing times, voter registration, ex-felon voting, the extent and nature of early voting, and voter identification requirements).

It is incorrect to argue that the election laws of one state do not matter to citizens of other states.

Under both the *current* system and the National Popular Vote compact, *all* of the people of the United States are impacted by the election practices of *every* state. Everyone in the United States is affected by how electoral votes are awarded by every state. The procedures governing presidential elections in a closely divided battleground state (e.g., Florida and Ohio) can affect—and indeed have affected—the ultimate outcome of national elections.

For example, the 2000 Certificate of Ascertainment (required by federal law) from the state of Florida reported 2,912,790 popular votes for George W. Bush and 2,912,253 popular votes for Al Gore. It also reported 25 electoral votes for George W. Bush and 0 electoral votes for Al Gore. The 25–0 division of the electoral votes from Florida in 2000 was comingled and added together with the count of electoral votes from all the other states. The 25–0 division of the electoral votes from Florida determined the outcome of the national election. In the same manner, a particular division of the popular vote from a particular state might, when added to the popular vote count from other states, decisively affect the national outcome in some future election under the National Popular Vote compact.

Concerning the differences in ballot-access requirements among the states, it is true that it is easier to get on the ballot in some states than others. Nonetheless, serious third-party candidates for President manage to get on the ballot in virtually every state. For example, Ross Perot (who received 19% of the national popular vote in 1992) was on the ballot in all 50 states in 1992 and 1996. John Anderson (who received 7% of the national popular vote in 1980) was on the ballot in all 50 states. The Libertarian Party got its presidential nominee on the ballot in all 50 states in 1980, 1992, and 1996. Lenora Fulani, the nominee of the New Alliance Party, was on the ballot in all 50 states in 1988. Ralph Nader (who received 2.7% of the vote in 2000) got onto the ballot in 48 jurisdictions. In 2012, Gary Johnson (the nominee of the Libertarian Party) was on the ballot in 48 states.[259]

However, even if a particular third-party candidate is not on the ballot in all 50 states, no "logistical nightmare" is created.

The consequence to a candidate of not being on the ballot in a particular state is identical under *both* the current system and the National Popular Vote plan, namely that the candidate is unlikely to receive any substantial number of popular votes from

---

[259] *Ballot Access News.* October 2012.

that particular state (barring the remote possibility of a successful write-in campaign in that state).

In terms of election administration, the absence from the ballot of a particular candidate in a particular state does not create any problem because election officials in each state simply report whatever votes are cast in their state for whichever candidates actually receive votes in their state. Today, each state reports the vote total for each presidential candidate on its Certificate of Ascertainment (required by section 6 of Title 3 of the United States Code).[260]

If a particular candidate does not receive any votes in a particular state, there is no vote total reported for that candidate from the state. If a candidate wins votes in a state where he is on the ballot, his absence from the ballot in another state does not cause him to forfeit his votes from the first state, much less create a "logistical nightmare." All of the votes that the candidate actually receives are added together to arrive at his nationwide total.

In 1860, Abraham Lincoln was the nominee of the newly created Republican Party (which first nominated a candidate for President in 1856). The Republican Party was not on the ballot in 1860 in nine states (Alabama, Arkansas, Florida, Georgia, Louisiana, Mississippi, North Carolina, Tennessee, and Texas). Consequently, Lincoln received no popular votes from those states (and, of course, no electoral votes). No problem of election administration was created by Lincoln's absence from the ballot in nine states. His absence from the ballot in nine states did not cause him to forfeit the votes that he received from other states; it did not prevent him from winning the largest number of popular votes nationwide (39%); it did not prevent him from winning a majority in the Electoral College; it did not prevent him from becoming President; and it did not create a "logistical nightmare" in terms of election administration.

Similarly, Strom Thurmond (1948), George Wallace (1968), and Theodore Roosevelt (1912) were not on the ballot in every state; however, their absence from the ballot in numerous states did not prevent them from receiving the electoral votes from the states that they carried. No "logistical nightmare" was created because of their absence from the ballot in other states.

The National Popular Vote compact provides that the results from each state (and D.C.) would be added together—the very same process of adding up 51 sets of numbers that would have occurred under the constitutional amendment that was approved by the U.S. House of Representatives in 1969.

Tara Ross never specifically says how the adding up of 51 sets of numbers would create a "logistical nightmare"—much less how it "would skew the election results."

It is true that some state election laws vary in many ways.

For example, some states have early poll-closing times (e.g., 6:00 P.M. in Kentucky

---

[260] Figure 9.5 shows North Dakota's 2008 Certificate of Ascertainment.

and Indiana), whereas the polls stay open until 9:00 P.M. in other states. In addition, polls close at different times due to the nation's numerous time zones. Differences in poll-closing times would be handled under the National Popular Vote in the same way they are handled now—that is, the polls would open and close in each state in accordance with prevailing law.[261]

Tara Ross cites the differences among the states concerning the eligibility of ex-felons to vote. Under the National Popular Vote plan, each state would conduct the election under its own laws—the same thing that would have occurred under the constitutional amendment that was approved by the U.S. House of Representatives in 1969. The certified popular vote totals from each state for each candidate would be added up to produce nationwide totals—the same thing that would have occurred under the constitutional amendment that was approved by the U.S. House of Representatives in 1969.

Tara Ross further observes:

> "Inevitably, [a state] would have to abide by national election results derived from policies with which it disagrees."[262]

This is precisely what happens now under the current U.S. Constitution because the Constitution empowers the states to control elections. All of the people of the United States are impacted by the election policies of every other state. No one can dispute that the procedures governing presidential elections in battleground states (e.g., Florida and Ohio) have affected the outcome of national elections and significantly impacted the entire country.

The fact that Oregon conducts its elections 100% by mail and that Minnesota permits voter registration on Election Day arguably contributed to the defeat of two sitting Republican U.S. Senators in November 2008, thereby affecting the course of national legislation because it gave the Democrats 60 votes in the U.S. Senate in 2009. A change in the Massachusetts vacancy-filling law enabled Republican Scott Brown to win the U.S. Senate seat previously occupied by the late Ted Kennedy in 2010 and significantly impacted the course of national legislation (e.g., the Affordable Care Act).

The genius of the federalist approach set forth in the U.S. Constitution is that no single political party is ever in a position to impose politically advantageous voting procedures on the entire country and thereby lock in a self-perpetuating advantage on the national level.

The real question for opponents of state control over elections is whether they would have been comfortable under *all* of the following scenarios:

---

[261] Clause 4 of section 1 of Article II of the U.S. Constitution provides, "The Congress may determine the Time of chusing the Electors." Under existing federal law, Congress has chosen a uniform national day for choosing electors (namely, the Tuesday after the first Monday in November). However, Congress could specify the time of day as well.

[262] Written testimony submitted by Tara Ross to the Delaware Senate in June 2010.

- Suppose that in 2003 (just prior to the 2004 presidential election), the then-Republican-controlled Congress and a then-sitting Republican President enacted uniform national voting procedures, including photo identification; vigorous purging of the voter rolls of those who did not vote in the immediately preceding election; and closing the polls at 6:00 P.M. in every state.
- Suppose that in 2009, the then-Democratic-controlled Congress and the then-sitting Democratic President enacted uniform national voting procedures, including automatic permanent voter registration based on the census; advance voting several weeks before Election Day in every state; and no-excuse absentee voting in every state.
- Suppose that at some future time, one political party controls both houses of Congress and the White House.

There are advantages to uniformity in election laws, and there are advantages to preventing a single political party from adopting uniform national laws that allow it to perpetuate itself in office.

The Founders resolved this dilemma by choosing a federalist approach that gives the states control over elections. Differences in state election laws resulting from our federalist system are not "logistical nightmares [that] could haunt the country" but a strength of our nation's Constitution.

As then-Congressman George H.W. Bush (R-Texas) said on September 18, 1969, in support of direct popular election of the President:

> "This legislation has a great deal to commend it. It will correct the wrongs of the present mechanism . . . by calling for direct election of the President and Vice President. . . . Yet, in spite of these drastic reforms, the bill is **not . . . detrimental to our federal system or one that will change the departmentalized and local nature of voting in this country**.

> "In electing the President and Vice President, the Constitution establishes the principle that votes are cast by States. This legislation does not tamper with that principle. It only changes the manner in which the States vote. Instead of voting by intermediaries, the States will certify their popular vote count to the Congress. **The states will maintain primary responsibility for the ballot and for the qualifications of voters.** In other words, they will still designate the time, place, and manner in which elections will be held. Thus, there is a very good argument to be made that **the basic nature of our federal system has not been disturbed**."[263] [Emphasis added]

Of course, if a national consensus emerges in favor of uniform federal control of elections at some time in the future, the U.S. Constitution can be so amended to eliminate state control over elections at that time.

---

[263] *Congressional Record.* September 18, 1969. Pages 25,990–25,991.

Meanwhile, the National Popular Vote plan is based on the constitutional system that actually exists in the United States and on the reality that there is widespread public and legislative support for state control of elections.

9.9.2. MYTH: A state's electoral votes could be awarded to a candidate not on a state's own ballot.

QUICK ANSWER:

- This hypothesized scenario is politically implausible because a presidential candidate winning the most popular votes throughout the entire United States would, almost certainly, have been on the ballot in all 50 states.

MORE DETAILED ANSWER:

Tara Ross, an opponent of the National Popular Vote compact, has raised the possibility in written testimony to the Delaware Senate that a presidential candidate from Texas (say, Congressman Ron Paul) might not be on the ballot in Delaware but nonetheless could win the national popular vote. She then raises the possibility that:

> "Delaware could be required to cast its electoral votes for a candidate who did not qualify for the ballot in Delaware."[264]

It is most unlikely that a serious candidate for President would run without qualifying for the ballot in all 50 states. Serious candidates for President generally qualify for the ballot in all 50 states.

- Ross Perot was on the ballot in all 50 states in both 1992 and 1996.
- John Anderson was on the ballot in all 50 states in 1980.
- Lenora Fulani, the nominee of the New Alliance Party, was on ballot in all 50 states in 1988.
- The Libertarian Party got its presidential nominee on the ballot in all 50 states in 1980, 1992, and 1996.
- Ralph Nader (who received only 2.7% of the national popular vote in 2000) was on the ballot in 48 jurisdictions.

It would be especially unlikely that Tara Ross' hypothetical Texas regional candidate would have been unable to qualify in Delaware, because a new political party can qualify for the ballot in Delaware with only 650 signatures.

In any event, it would be very unlikely that Ross' hypothesized candidate from Texas would have received the most popular votes in all 50 states and the District of Columbia without being on the ballot in every state (or virtually every state).

But even if Ross' politically implausible scenario were to occur, the National Popular Vote compact would deliver precisely its promised result, namely the election of

---

[264] Written testimony submitted by Tara Ross to the Delaware Senate in June 2010.

the presidential candidate who received the most popular votes in all 50 states and the District of Columbia.

Tara Ross further hypothesized that the presidential candidate from Texas might win the national popular vote and then appoint Texans to represent Delaware in the Electoral College.

> "Delaware probably did not nominate a slate of electors for Paul because he was not on its ballot. NPV's compact offers a solution, but it is doubtful that voters in Delaware will like it. Paul would be entitled to personally appoint the three electors who will represent Delaware in the Electoral College vote. In all likelihood, he would select Texans to represent Delaware in the presidential election. . . ."[265]

First, under the National Popular Vote compact, nominees for the position of presidential elector would be chosen in exactly the same way as they currently are (that is, by local political parties in accordance with existing state law). The provision of the National Popular Vote compact cited in Ross' hypothetical scenario applies *only if* a local political party in a state fails to nominate the exact number of candidates for the position of presidential elector to which the state is entitled. In this unlikely contingency, the compact permits the winning presidential candidate to decisively and quickly untangle any problem that might prevent him or her from receiving the full number of electoral votes to which he or she is entitled. This back-up procedure is designed to ensure that the compact guarantees the election of the presidential candidate who receives the most popular votes in all 50 states and the District of Columbia. Clause 7 of Article III of the compact states:

> **"If, for any reason, the number of presidential electors** nominated in a member state in association with the national popular vote winner **is less than or greater than that state's number of electoral votes**, the presidential candidate on the presidential slate that has been designated as the national popular vote winner shall have the power to nominate the presidential electors for that state and that state's presidential elector certifying official shall certify the appointment of such nominees." [Emphasis added]

Second, there is historical evidence about how real-world politicians would behave in this situation. Under existing law in Pennsylvania, *every* presidential candidate, in *every* election, directly chooses *every* presidential elector in Pennsylvania. Needless to say, no presidential candidate has ever chosen a Texan or any other out-of-state person for the position of presidential elector in Pennsylvania. Indeed, it would be politically preposterous for a presidential candidate to insult Pennsylvania gratuitously by selecting out-of-staters to the ceremonial position of presidential elector. It

---

[265] Written testimony submitted by Tara Ross to the Delaware Senate in June 2010.

would be even more preposterous for someone who had just won the national popular vote (and was about to become President and face the task of unifying the country) to insult a state gratuitously.

Third, it would be extraordinary that Ron Paul (whom Ross hypothesizes just won the most popular votes across the entire United States) would not have three supporters in Delaware.

Fourth, in case any state believes that Ross' hypothetical scenario is politically plausible and potentially harmful, every state has the power, under the U.S. Constitution, to adopt residency qualifications for the position of presidential elector. Indeed, Delaware is an example of a state that has already enacted additional qualifications for the position of presidential elector (albeit not to disqualify non-resident presidential electors).

9.10. MYTHS ABOUT FAITHLESS ELECTORS

9.10.1. MYTH: Faithless presidential electors would be a problem under the National Popular Vote compact.

QUICK ANSWER:

- There is no practical problem with faithless presidential electors. There have been only 17 deviant votes for President out of the 22,991 electoral votes cast in the nation's 57 presidential elections between 1789 and 2012, and only one of them, in 1796, was a true faithless elector.
- To the extent that anyone believes that there is a problem, the states have ample constitutional authority to remedy it, and effective solutions are available (such as the proposed Uniform Faithful Presidential Electors Act).
- One of the collateral benefits of the National Popular Vote plan is that it would virtually eliminate the possibility of faithless electors actually affecting the outcome of a presidential election because it would typically generate an exaggerated margin of victory in the Electoral College of about 75% for the national popular vote winner (namely, an absolute majority of the electoral votes from the compacting states plus about half of the remaining electoral votes of the non-compacting states).

MORE DETAILED ANSWER:

The myth about faithless electors is yet another example of a potential problem that the National Popular Vote plan handles in a manner that is equal to, and arguably superior to, the current system.

The Founding Fathers envisioned that the presidential electors would be outstanding citizens who would meet and debate and exercise independent judgment in choosing the best person to become President. However, that expectation was dashed with the emergence of political parties in the nation's first competitive presidential election in 1796.

Since 1796, presidential electors have been committed party activists who are nominated by their political party to cast their vote in the Electoral College for their party's nominee. That is, presidential electors have simply been willing "rubber-stamps" for their party's nominee for President.

Faithless presidential electors are not a practical problem in the first place. Of the 22,991 electoral votes cast for President in the nation's 57 presidential elections between 1789 and 2012, only 17 were cast in a deviant way.[266] Moreover, among these 17 cases, the unexpected vote of Samuel Miles for Thomas Jefferson in 1796 was the only instance of a true faithless elector (where the elector might have thought, at the time he voted, that his vote might affect the national outcome).

Fifteen of the 17 cases were post-election grand-standing votes cast by publicity-seeking electors who knew, at the time they voted, that their vote would not affect the outcome in the Electoral College.

One electoral vote was accidentally and unintentionally cast by an unidentified Democratic presidential elector in Minnesota who absentmindedly voted for the party's vice-presidential candidate for both President and Vice President.[267]

Nonetheless, the possibility of faithless electors exists under both the current system and the National Popular Vote plan.

For example, in September 2012, three Republican electors (who had favored Ron Paul during the nomination process) publicly raised doubt as to their loyalty to Mitt Romney, the eventual Republican presidential nominee.[268] Defection by multiple presidential electors could potentially throw a close presidential election into the U.S. House of Representatives.[269]

Second, if anyone perceives faithless presidential electors to be a real problem, the states already have ample constitutional authority to remedy the situation by state law.

In most states, each political party nominates candidates for the position of presidential elector (typically at a combination of party conventions at the congressional district level and state level).

---

[266] See section 2.12.

[267] The accidental vote was cast in Minnesota in 2004. After the ballots were counted, all 10 electors said that they intended to vote for John Kerry for President and John Edwards for Vice President. However, one of the 10 accidentally voted for John Edwards for both President and Vice President.

[268] Baker, Mike. Three Electoral College members may pass on GOP ticket. *Associated Press*. September 12, 2012.

[269] As discussed in section 2.12, in 1836, 23 Democratic presidential electors from Virginia did not vote for the Democratic Party's vice-presidential nominee (Richard M. Johnson). The Virginia Democratic Party had announced their vigorous opposition to Johnson at the party's national convention (both before and after Johnson's nomination). Johnson failed to receive an absolute majority of the electoral votes and the vice-presidential election was therefore thrown into the U.S. Senate. The Democratic Party was in control of the Senate, and Johnson won by an overwhelming 33–16 vote.

About half of the states currently have laws involving pledges, penalties, or other procedures to ensure that presidential electors vote for their party's nominees.

In upholding the constitutionality of a pledge guaranteeing faithful voting by presidential electors, U.S. Supreme Court Justice Robert H. Jackson wrote in the 1952 case of *Ray v. Blair*:

> "No one faithful to our history can deny that the plan originally contemplated, what is implicit in its text, that electors would be free agents, to exercise an independent and nonpartisan judgment as to the men best qualified for the Nation's highest offices. . . .

> "This arrangement miscarried. **Electors,** although often personally eminent, independent, and respectable, **officially become voluntary party lackeys and intellectual nonentities** to whose memory we might justly paraphrase a tuneful satire:

>> 'They always voted at their party's call
>> 'And never thought of thinking for themselves at all'"[270] [Emphasis added]

Existing Pennsylvania law is noteworthy in that it empowers each party's presidential candidate to nominate all elector candidates directly. The presidential nominee is, after all, the person whose name actually appears on the ballot on Election Day and who has the greatest immediate interest in faithful voting by presidential electors.

Existing North Carolina law declares vacant the position of any contrary-voting elector, voids that elector's vote, and empowers the state's remaining electors to replace the contrary-voting elector immediately with an elector loyal to the party's nominee.

At its 119th annual meeting in 2010, the Uniform Law Commission (also known as the National Conference of Commissioners on Uniform State Laws) approved a "Uniform Faithful Presidential Electors Act" and submitted this model legislation to the state legislatures for their consideration. The Conference, formed in 1892, is a non-governmental body that has produced more than 200 recommended uniform state laws. The Conference is most widely known for its work on the Uniform Commercial Code.

The Uniform Faithful Presidential Electors Act has many of the features of North Carolina's existing law. The proposed uniform law calls for the election of both electors and alternate electors. The Act has a state-administered pledge of faithfulness. Any attempt by a presidential elector to cast a vote in violation of that pledge effectively constitutes resignation from the office of elector. The Act provides a mechanism for immediately filling a vacancy created for that reason (or any other reason). The National Popular Vote organization has endorsed this proposed uniform law.

Third, in case anyone views faithless presidential electors to be a real problem, the

---

[270] *Ray v. Blair* 343 U.S. 214 at 232. 1952.

National Popular Vote plan is actually superior to the current system in ensuring that a wayward elector would be unlikely to impact the ultimate choice of the President. Under the National Popular Vote compact, the national popular vote winner would generally receive an exaggerated margin (roughly 75%) of the votes in the Electoral College in any given presidential election. The reason is that the National Popular Vote compact guarantees that the presidential candidate receiving the most popular votes in all 50 states and the District of Columbia would receive at least 270 (of the 538) electoral votes from the states belonging to the compact. Then, beyond that guaranteed bloc of at least 270 electoral votes, the national popular vote winner would receive additional electoral votes from whichever non-compacting states he or she happened to carry (presumably under existing winner-take-all statutes in those states). If the non-compacting states divided approximately equally between the candidates, the nationwide winning candidate would generally receive an exaggerated margin (roughly 75%) of the votes in the Electoral College (that is, about 404 out of 538 electoral votes). This cushion would make it highly unlikely that faithless electors could affect the outcome of a presidential election (where 270 electoral votes are required to win the Presidency).

For additional information about faithless electors, see section 2.12.

9.10.2. MYTH: It might be difficult to coerce presidential electors to vote for the national popular vote winner.

QUICK ANSWER:

- No coercion would be required to force presidential electors to vote for the national popular vote winner under the National Popular Vote compact, because the compact (like the current system) would result in the election to the Electoral College of presidential electors who are avid supporters of the national popular vote winner.

MORE DETAILED ANSWER:

No coercion is required to force presidential electors to vote as intended under either the current system or the National Popular Vote system.

Under both systems, each political party nominates opinionated party activists for the ceremonial position of presidential elector under existing state laws. Each party's nominees for the position of presidential elector are selected precisely because they are passionate supporters of their party's candidate and because they can be relied upon to act as willing "rubber-stamps" for their party's nominee.

When voters go to the polls on Election Day in November, they are, in reality, choosing amongst competing slates of presidential electors associated with the Democratic Party, the Republican Party, or some other party. Under the winner-take-all system (currently used in 48 of the 50 states and the District of Columbia), the entire slate of elector candidates associated with the presidential candidate receiving the most popular votes within each separate state is elected as the state's presidential electors.[271]

Under the National Popular Vote compact, the state's presidential electors would be the elector candidates associated with the presidential candidate who won the most popular votes in all 50 states and the District of Columbia. This bloc of 270 (or more) presidential electors would reflect the will of the voters nationwide. All of these 270 or more presidential electors would be loyal and avid supporters of the national popular vote winner. These presidential electors would come from the political party that won the election nationally. Thus, no one in this bloc of 270 (or more) presidential electors would be asked to vote contrary to his or her own political inclinations or conscience. Instead, these electors would vote for their own strongly held personal choice, namely the nominee of their own political party.

Under the National Popular Vote plan, these 270 (or more) presidential electors would operate as willing "rubber-stamps" for the nationwide choice of the voters, just as presidential electors currently act as willing "rubber-stamps" for the statewide choice of the voters (or district-wide choice, in the cases of Maine and Nebraska).

9.10.3. MYTH: Presidential electors might succumb to outside pressure and abandon the national popular vote winner in favor of the winner of the popular vote in their state.

QUICK ANSWER:

- Presidential electors are loyal party activists who are selected precisely because they can be relied upon to act as willing "rubber-stamps" for their party's nominee.
- The low probability of presidential electors succumbing to outside pressure is illustrated by the fact that none of the 271 Republican presidential electors in 2000 voted for Al Gore despite the fact that Gore received the most popular votes nationwide and despite the fact that the American public overwhelmingly believes that the President should be the candidate who receives the most popular votes in all 50 states and the District of Columbia. Instead, all 271 Republican presidential electors dutifully voted for their party's nominee in accordance with the virtually universal view of how the system that was legally in effect at the time was supposed to operate.

[271] In two states (Maine and Nebraska), the elector candidates associated with the presidential candidate who receives the most popular votes in each of the state's congressional districts are elected (along with the two additional at-large elector candidates associated with the presidential candidate who receives the most popular votes in the state as a whole).

MORE DETAILED ANSWER:

Some have suggested that, under the National Popular Vote compact, presidential electors might, after the people vote in November, succumb to outside pressure and abandon the national popular vote in favor of the winner of the popular vote in their state.

This hypothetical scenario is based on the following incorrect assumptions:

- There is any substantial pool of people who would support the notion of changing the rules after the public has voted on Election Day.
- The public favors the current state-by-state winner-take-all approach for electing the President, and hence there would be a vast pool of people to apply such pressure on presidential electors.
- The supporters of the presidential candidate who just won the national popular vote, under laws that were in place on Election Day, would care about—much less actually succumb to—pressure from people representing the losing party.

The reality is that there would be no substantial pressure in the first place. The public simply does not favor the current system of awarding all of a state's electoral votes to the presidential candidate who receives the most popular votes in each separate state (the winner-take-all-rule). In polls since 1944, at least 70% (usually more) of the American people have said that they favored the idea that the presidential candidate receiving the most votes throughout the United States should win the Presidency. A mere 20% of the public supports the current state-by-state winner-take-all system (with 10% undecided). Far from being attached to the state-by-state winner-take-all system of awarding electoral votes, the public strongly opposes it.

The environment in which this hypothetical scenario would arise has the following five elements:

(1) About 70% of the voters of any given state believe that the presidential candidate receiving the most votes in all 50 states and the District of Columbia should win the Presidency;

(2) The state legislature and Governor of the state have responded to the wishes of its own voters and enacted the National Popular Vote law in their state;

(3) States possessing a majority of the electoral votes (essentially more than half the population of the country) have similarly enacted the National Popular Vote law, and the law has taken effect nationally;

(4) A nationwide presidential campaign has been conducted, over a period of many months, with the candidates, the media, and everyone else in the United States knowing that the National Popular Vote plan is the law that will govern the presidential election; and

(5) On Election Day in November, one presidential candidate emerged with the most popular votes in all 50 states and the District of Columbia.

The hypothetical scenario then conjectures that when the time comes for the Electoral College to meet in mid-December, the 270 (or more) presidential electors (who are avid supporters of their own party's presidential candidate who just won the national popular vote) would respond to pressure from supporters of the political party that just lost the election.

In fact, there would be little inclination for party activists to vote against their own strongly held personal preferences, against their own party's presidential nominee, against their own state's law, and against the desires of an overwhelming majority of their state's voters (who favor a national popular vote for President).

The country has actual experience that relates to the hypothesized scenario. In 2000, Al Gore won the national popular vote by a margin of over 537,000 votes. However, under the laws in place at the time, there were 271 Republican presidential electors (just one more than the 270 needed to elect a President) who were nominated for that position by their party on the presumption that they would vote for George W. Bush. About 70% of the American people believed (then and now) that the Presidency should go to the candidate who receives the most popular votes in all 50 states and the District of Columbia. Nevertheless, none of the 271 Republican presidential electors succumbed to public pressure and voted in favor of the winner of the national popular vote.

9.11. MYTHS ABOUT POST-ELECTION CHANGES IN THE RULES OF THE GAME, WITHDRAWAL, AND ENFORCEABILITY

9.11.1. MYTH: A politically motivated state legislature could withdraw from the National Popular Vote compact after the people vote in November, but before the Electoral College meets in December.

QUICK ANSWER:

- There are at least six *separate and independent* reasons why there should be no concern about the hypothetical scenario in which a Governor and legislature attempt—for partisan political reasons—to change a state's method of awarding electoral votes after the people vote in November, but before the Electoral College meets in December.

- The National Popular Vote compact permits a state to withdraw; however, it delays the effective date of a withdrawal until after the inauguration of the new President if the withdrawal occurs during the six-month period between July 20 of a presidential election year and Inauguration Day.

- Any attempt to appoint presidential electors after the people vote in November would be unconstitutional on its face (and subject to summary judgment) because (1) the Constitution gives Congress the power to establish the day for appointing presidential electors, and (2) existing federal law requires that presidential electors be appointed on a *single* specific day in each four-year election cycle (namely, the Tuesday after the first Monday in November). Therefore, no state may appoint presidential electors after the results of an election become known (under either the current state-by-state winner-take-all system or the National Popular Vote compact).

- Any withdrawal that purports to take effect between July 20 of a presidential year and Inauguration Day would be unconstitutional on its face (and subject to summary judgment) because it would violate the Impairments Clause of the U.S. Constitution which states, "No State shall . . . pass any . . . Law impairing the Obligation of Contracts."

- Any attempt to appoint presidential electors after the people vote in November would invalidate the "conclusiveness" of that state's results under existing federal law specifying that presidential electors must be appointed under "laws enacted *prior*" to the single specific date set by federal law for appointing presidential electors (namely, the Tuesday after the first Monday in November).

- The highly partisan maneuver of attempting to appoint presidential electors after the people vote in November could be executed, in practice, in only about four states because of numerous practical political reasons, including (1) high quorum requirements in some state legislatures, (2) lengthy lay-over requirements before a bill may be considered, (3) the fact that many states have politically divided government at any given time, (4) the fact that state constitutions would delay the effective date of the new state law until after the Electoral College met in mid-December, (5) the numerous time-delaying tactics enabling the minority party to delay action in the short period of time between Election Day and the meeting of the Electoral College, and (6) other factors.

- Any attempt to appoint presidential electors after the people vote in November would be politically preposterous in the real world because (1) there would be overwhelming public sentiment against changing the "rules of the game" after the people had voted, (2) the legislature would have to meet in the state capital on Election Day (because this is the only day in the four-year election cycle when presidential electors may legally be appointed), (3) there would be a high level of public support for a national popular vote, and (4) the action would necessarily have to occur in a state where both houses of the legislature and the Governor had already enacted the National Popular Vote compact.

- Any attempt by one state, or even multiple states, to appoint presidential electors after the people vote in November would probably not matter anyway because the national popular vote winner would typically receive an exaggerated margin of victory in the Electoral College (roughly 75%), thereby producing a cushion of about 135 electoral votes above the 270 needed to win the Presidency.

- If the hypothetical scenario of changing the "rules of the game" were legally permissible or politically plausible, it would have occurred in the past *under the current system* on the numerous occasions (including 2000) where a particular presidential candidate was not favored by a particular Governor and legislature.

MORE DETAILED ANSWER:

This section discusses the hypothetical scenario in which a Governor and state legislature might try—for partisan political reasons—to change the "rules of the game" for electing the President by repealing (withdrawing from) the National Popular Vote compact after Election Day in November but before the meeting of the Electoral College in mid-December. Under this scenario, the Governor and legislature would presumably implement some politically advantageous alternative method of appointing presidential electors (say, legislative appointment) after Election Day.

John Samples of the Cato Institute says that the National Popular Vote compact:

> "cannot offer any certainty that states will not withdraw from the compact when the results of an election become known."[272]

There are six *separate and independent* reasons why Sample's hypothetical scenario cannot happen (and a seventh reason applicable if the compact were enacted by the citizen-initiative process in a particular state).

All but two of these independent reasons (the second and sixth) apply to *both* the current system and the National Popular Vote compact. Thus, if John Sample's hypothetical scenario of changing the "rules of the game" were legally permissible or politically plausible, it would have already occurred *under the current system* on the numerous previous occasions when a particular presidential candidate was not favored by a particular Governor and state legislature.

We start with the simplest of the numerous reasons why John Sample's hypothetical scenario is of no concern.

Any attempt to appoint presidential electors after the people vote in November would be unconstitutional on its face because the Constitution gives Congress the power to establish the day for appointing presidential electors and existing federal law allows presidential electors to be appointed on only one specific day in each four-year period (namely, the Tuesday after the first Monday in November).

John Sample's hypothetical scenario in which a politically motivated Governor and legislature try to change their state's law on appointing presidential electors after "the results of an election become known" is legally impossible in the United States.

---

[272] Samples, John. *A Critique of the National Popular Vote Plan for Electing the President.* Cato Institute Policy Analysis No. 622. October 13, 2008. Page 1.

The U.S. Constitution (Article II, section 1, clause 4) specifically grants Congress the power to establish the time for appointing presidential electors:

> **"The Congress may determine the Time of chusing the Electors**, and the Day on which they shall give their Votes; which Day shall be the same throughout the United States." [Spelling as per original] [Emphasis added]

Congress has exercised this power by enacting a federal law (section 1 of Title 3 of the United States Code) that requires presidential electors to be appointed *on one specific day in every four-year period* namely, the Tuesday after the first Monday in November (Election Day).

> **"The electors** of President and Vice President **shall be appointed, in each State, on the Tuesday next after the first Monday in November**, in every fourth year succeeding every election of a President and Vice President." [Emphasis added]

Thus, no state may appoint its presidential electors after "the results of an election become known." This existing federal law is applicable to *both* the National Popular Vote compact and the current system.

Note that the U.S. Constitution does not require a state to permit its own voters to vote directly for President or presidential electors. Under the Constitution, state legislatures have always had the power to appoint presidential electors without consulting the voters.[273] However, if a state legislature decides that it is going to appoint presidential electors itself, it must make the appointments on the specific *single* day established by Congress (the Tuesday next after the first Monday in November). In particular, a state legislature cannot appoint presidential electors *after* Election Day (e.g., after seeing the election results in its own state or other states).

Aside from being illegal, John Sample's hypothetical scenario would be politically implausible. In all but three states, between 50% and 100% of the state legislature is up for re-election on the same day that the President is being elected. That is, on the very day when the legislators are trying to get themselves re-elected, they would have to be sitting in the state capitol attempting to change the "rules of the game" of the ongoing presidential election. In particular, the legislators would not be in their districts campaigning for re-election. Also, in a quarter of the states, the Governor is up for re-election on the same day that the President is being elected.

The role of Article II, section 1, clause 4 of the Constitution in conjunction with

---

[273] The people participated in directly choosing presidential electors in only six states in the nation's first presidential election in 1789. In 1789, state legislatures appointed presidential electors in a number of states. In New Jersey in 1789, the Governor and his Council appointed the state's presidential electors. The last time when the people did not directly choose presidential electors was in 1876, when the Colorado legislature appointed the state's presidential electors.

section 1 of Title 3 of the United States Code in squelching John Sample's hypothetical scenario was illustrated in the 1960 presidential election.

John F. Kennedy won the nationwide popular vote by 114,673 votes. However, Kennedy's majority in the Electoral College (only 34 electoral votes in excess of the majority needed for election) depended on the fact that he had carried Illinois by the slender margin of 4,430 popular votes and carried South Carolina by 4,732 votes. Some members of the South Carolina legislature suggested that the legislature repeal South Carolina's winner-take-all law for awarding the state's electoral votes and appoint non-Kennedy presidential electors themselves.

Nothing came of this suggestion in South Carolina in 1960, because section 1 of Title 3 of the United States Code specifies that Election Day is the single day in the four-year cycle on which presidential electors may be appointed. Election Day had, of course, passed by the time South Carolina leaders realized that Kennedy's margin of victory in the Electoral College depended in large part on South Carolina's electoral votes. If the South Carolina legislature had wanted to appoint presidential electors itself, it could have chosen to do so, but it would have had to have convened in Columbia for this purpose on Election Day (i.e., the Tuesday next after the first Monday in November).[274]

There is only one exception permitted by Congress to section 1's requirement of appointing presidential electors on Election Day, and it does not apply to John Sample's hypothetical scenario. Section 2 of Title 3 of the United States Code provides:

> "Whenever any State has held an election for the purpose of choosing electors, **and has failed to make a choice on the day prescribed by law**, the electors may be appointed on a subsequent day in such a manner as the legislature of such State may direct." [Emphasis added]

This "failure to make a choice" exception covers contingencies such as the occurrence of a tie in a state's popular vote. Accordingly, many states have adopted legislation to deal with ties in a state's popular vote.

The "failure to make a choice" exception offered by section 2 would not be applicable to John Sample's hypothetical scenario involving the National Popular Vote compact, because the voters would have already made a choice on Election Day—simply a choice that a particular Governor and legislature did not like.

The exception in section 2 played a (sometimes misunderstood) role in the debate over the disputed presidential election count in Florida in 2000.[275] Because of section 1 of the United States Code, everyone recognized that there was no possibility that the

---

[274] As explained in a later part of this section, because of section 5 of Title 3 of the United States Code, South Carolina would also have had to repeal its law providing for popular election of presidential electors *prior* to Election Day.

[275] The authors appreciate conversations with former Congressman Tom Feeney, who was Speaker of the Florida House of Representatives in November 2000, for clarifying the nature of the "reaffirming" resolution.

Republican-controlled Florida legislature could meet after Election Day, retroactively decide to ignore the already-cast popular vote, and directly appoint Republican presidential electors favorable to George W. Bush.

However, the argument was advanced that if a recount were ordered by a court, if the court-ordered recount were to vacate the initial count, and if the court-ordered recount were not completed by the "safe harbor" date (i.e., six days prior to the meeting of the Electoral College), then there would have been a "failure to make a choice" in Florida.

Florida could then have been left with no presidential electors by the "safe harbor" day because of its "failure to make a choice." Note that the Constitution does not require an absolute majority of the electoral votes to become President, but only a

"majority of the whole number of electors **appointed**."[276] [Emphasis added].

If Florida had failed to cast its 25 electoral votes in the Electoral College, Al Gore would have been elected President because he would have had a majority of the electors *appointed*.

To forestall that possibility, the Republican-controlled Florida House of Representatives passed a resolution *reaffirming* the initial *already-certified* vote count (in favor of 25 Republican presidential electors pledged to George W. Bush). Nothing came of this "reaffirming" motion in the Republican-controlled state Senate because of subsequent action in the courts (specifically, the U.S. Supreme Court's decision in the case of *Bush v. Gore*).

Finally, it should be noted that if John Sample's hypothetical scenario (of appointing presidential electors after the people voted on Election Day) were legally permissible or politically plausible, it could occur *under the current system*.

The winner-take-all rule is not in the U.S. Constitution. It is simply state law. If post-election changes in the method of appointing presidential electors were legally permissible or politically plausible, it would have been possible for this scenario to have occurred in each of the nation's 57 presidential elections between 1789 and 2012, including the 2000 election.

Of course, we all know that there were no special sessions of legislatures in late November 2000 in Democratic states that George W. Bush carried (North Carolina, West Virginia, Alabama, and Arkansas).[277] None of these four states repealed their

---

[276] The 12th Amendment (ratified in 1804) states, "The person having the greatest number of votes for President, shall be the President, if such number be a majority of the whole number of Electors *appointed*." There have been occasional cases when a state failed to appoint its presidential electors. For example, New York did not in 1789 because the legislature could not agree on how to appoint them. Notably, the Southern states did not appoint presidential electors in 1864.

[277] The Democrats also controlled the Governor's office in North Carolina, West Virginia, and Alabama. In Arkansas (where the governor was Republican at the time), a veto can be overridden by a majority vote in the Legislature, so the Democrats had a veto-proof majority in the legislature.

existing winner-take-all laws and appointed presidential electors who would vote for the candidate who received the most popular votes nationwide. Such an action in *any one* of these four states would have given Al Gore a majority of the Electoral College in 2000—*even after* George W. Bush was awarded all 25 of Florida's electoral votes.

Similarly, the North Carolina Legislature did not switch, after Election Day in 2000, to an allocation of electoral votes based on congressional districts or a proportional allocation of the state's electoral votes. Either of those two actions would have given Al Gore a majority in the Electoral College.

Moreover, the Alabama legislature did not switch, after Election Day, to a proportional allocation of electoral votes—an action that would have given Al Gore a majority in the Electoral College.

Note that these Governors and legislatures could easily have fabricated political "spin" to justify their action based on the widespread public support for the concept that the candidate receiving the most popular votes in all 50 states and the District of Columbia should become President.

Indeed, Gallup polls since 1944 have shown that only about 20% of the public have supported the current system of awarding all of a state's electoral votes to the presidential candidate who receives the most votes in each separate state (with about 70% opposed and about 10% undecided).

The Governors and legislatures of these four states could also have quickly conducted public opinion polls in their own states on the abstract question of whether the winner of the nationwide popular vote should become President. Polls taken later showed that 81% of West Virginia voters, 80% of Arkansas voters, and 74% of North Carolina voters supported the proposition that the winner of the nationwide popular vote should become President.[278]

Of course, as we all know, no state legislatures took any of the above actions after the November 2000 election because everyone recognized that such action would have been unconstitutional on its face under Article II, section 1, clause 4 of the U.S. Constitution and section 1 of Title 3 of the United States Code.[279] If such an action had been attempted, it would have been immediately voided by a state or federal court by summary judgment—with no credance being given to the disingenuous political "spin" offered by the Governor or legislature for their post-election change in the rules of the game.

The American people accepted the ascendancy of the second-place candidate to the White House in 2000 because everyone understood that the election had been conducted under the established "rules of the game" that were known to both candidates,

---

[278] See section 9.35.1 and 7.1 for information about these polls. Detailed reports on these and other polls, including the cross-tabs, are available at the web site of National Popular Vote at http://www.nationalpopularvote.com/pages/polls.php.

[279] As explained in later parts of this section, this hypothetical scenario would also have to overcome potential problems under section 5 of Title 3 of the United States Code.

namely the state-by-state winner-take-all method. This was the case even though a substantial majority of the public disapproved (then and now) of the state-by-state winner-take-all system and favored (then and now) a national popular vote for President.

In summary, Article II, section 1, clause 4 of the U.S. Constitution and section 1 of Title 3 of the United States Code precludes any state from appointing presidential electors after "the results of an election become known"—under either the National Popular Vote compact or the current system.

Any law repealing the compact that purports to take effect between July 20 of a presidential year and Inauguration Day would be unconstitutional on its face, because it would violate the Impairments Clause of the U.S. Constitution.

An interstate compact is a contract. Withdrawal from any contract may only be made in accordance with the contract's own terms.

Like most interstate compacts, the National Popular Vote compact permits states to withdraw from the compact (simply by passing a repeal statute).

And, like most other interstate compacts, the National Popular Vote compact delays the effectiveness of any withdrawal for a certain amount of time appropriate to the subject matter of the compact.

The National Popular Vote compact permits any member state to withdraw, subject to the limitation that a withdrawal cannot take effect during a six-month period between July 20 of a presidential election year and January 20 (Inauguration Day) of the following year. Clause 2 of Article IV of the National Popular Vote compact provides:

> "Any member state may withdraw from this agreement, except that a withdrawal occurring six months or less before the end of a President's term shall not become effective until a President or Vice President shall have been qualified to serve the next term."

This six-month "blackout" period includes six important events relating to presidential elections namely, the:

- national nominating conventions,
- fall general election campaign period,
- Election Day on the Tuesday after the first Monday in November,
- meeting of the Electoral College on the first Monday after the second Wednesday in December,
- counting of the electoral votes by Congress on January 6, and
- inauguration of the President and Vice President for the new term on January 20.

The blackout period in the National Popular Vote compact is aimed at preventing a withdrawal in the midst of the presidential election process and, in particular, during the especially sensitive period (approximately 35 days) between Election Day in early November and the meeting of the Electoral College in mid-December.

The Impairments Clause (sometimes called the "Contracts Clause") of the U.S. Constitution (Article I, section 10, clause 1) provides:

"No State shall . . . pass any . . . Law impairing the Obligation of Contracts."

Because of the Impairments Clause, the courts have never allowed *any* state to withdraw from *any* interstate compact without following the procedure for withdrawal specified by the compact.

The U.S. Supreme Court succinctly dismissed the possibility in *Petty v. Tennessee-Missouri Bridge Commission* in 1952:

"A compact, is after all, a contract."[280]

On numerous occasions, federal and state courts have implemented the U.S. Supreme Court's interpretation of the Impairments Clause and rebuffed the occasional (sometimes creative) attempts by states to evade their obligations under interstate compacts.

The U.S. District Court for the District of Maryland in *Hellmuth and Associates v. Washington Metropolitan Area Transit Authority* stated in 1976:

"Upon entering into an interstate compact, a state effectively surrenders a portion of its sovereignty; **the compact** governs the relations of the parties with respect to the subject matter of the agreement and **is superior to both prior and subsequent law**. Further, when enacted, **a compact constitutes not only law, but a contract which may not be amended, modified, or otherwise altered** without the consent of all parties."[281] [Emphasis added]

The 1999 case of *Aveline v. Pennsylvania Board of Probation and Parole* was concerned with withdrawal from the Interstate Compact for the Supervision of Parolees and Probationers. Section 7 of that compact provides:

"The duties and obligations hereunder of a renouncing state shall continue as to parolees or probationers residing therein at the time of withdrawal until retaken or finally discharged by the sending state. **Renunciation of this compact shall be by the same authority which executed it, by sending six months' notice in writing of its intention to withdraw from the compact to the other states party hereto**."[282] [Emphasis added]

In 1999, the Commonwealth Court of Pennsylvania ruled in *Aveline v. Pennsylvania Board of Probation and Parole*:

---

[280] *Petty v. Tennessee-Missouri Bridge Commission.* 359 U.S. 275 at 285. 79 S.Ct. 785 at 792. 1952.

[281] *Hellmuth and Associates v. Washington Metropolitan Area Transit Authority* (414 F.Supp. 408 at 409). 1976.

[282] Missouri Revised Statutes. Chapter 217. Section 217.810.

"A compact takes precedence over the subsequent statutes of signatory states and, as such, **a state may not unilaterally nullify, revoke, or amend one of its compacts if the compact does not so provide.**"[283] [Emphasis added]

The 1991 case of *McComb v. Wambaugh* was concerned with withdrawal from the Interstate Compact on Placement of Children. The compact permits withdrawal with two-years notice.

"Withdrawal from this compact shall be by the enactment of a statute repealing the same, but **shall not take effect until two years after the effective date of such statute** and until written notice of the withdrawal has been given by the withdrawing state to the Governor of each other party jurisdiction. Withdrawal of a party state shall not affect the rights, duties and obligations under this compact of any sending agency therein with respect to a placement made prior to the effective date of withdrawal." [Emphasis added]

The United States Court of Appeals for the Third Circuit ruled in *McComb v. Wambaugh*:

"Having entered into a contract, a participant state may not unilaterally change its terms. **A Compact also takes precedence over statutory law in member states**."[284] [Emphasis added]

As the Court of Appeal of the State of California said in *The Gillette Company et al. v. Franchise Tax Board* in 2012:

"Interstate compacts are unique in that they empower one state legislature—namely the one that enacted the agreement—to bind all future legislatures to certain principles governing the subject matter of the compact. (Broun on Compacts, supra, § 1.2.2, p. 17.)"[285] [Emphasis added]

The Council of State Governments summarized the nature of interstate compacts as follows:

"Compacts are agreements between two or more states that bind them to the compacts' provisions, just as a contract binds two or more parties in a business deal. As such, compacts are subject to the substantive principles of contract law and are protected by the constitutional prohibition against

---

[283] *Aveline v. Pennsylvania Board of Probation and Parole* (729 A.2d. 1254 at 1257, note 10).

[284] *McComb v. Wambaugh*, 934 F.2d 474 at 479 (3d Cir. 1991).

[285] *The Gillette Company et al. v. Franchise Tax Board. Court of Appeal of the State of California*, First Appellate District, Division Four. July 24, 2012. Page 10. Appendix GG contains the full opinion.

laws that impair the obligations of contracts (U.S. Constitution, Article I, Section 10).

"That means that **compacting states are bound to observe the terms of their agreements, even if those terms are inconsistent with other state laws.** In short, compacts between states are somewhat like treaties between nations. Compacts have the force and effect of statutory law (whether enacted by statute or not) and **they take precedence over conflicting state laws, regardless of when those laws are enacted**.

"However, unlike treaties, compacts are not dependent solely upon the good will of the parties. **Once enacted, compacts may not be unilaterally renounced by a member state, except as provided by the compacts themselves.** Moreover, Congress and the courts can compel compliance with the terms of interstate compacts. That's why **compacts are considered the most effective means of ensuring interstate cooperation**."[286] [Emphasis added]

The occasional attempts by states to evade their obligations under interstate compacts are consistently rejected by the courts.

Both state courts and federal courts have the power to enforce the Impairments Clause.

An example of state-level enforcement of the Impairments Clause is found in the 2012 case of *The Gillette Company et al. v. Franchise Tax Board*. In that case, the California Court of Appeal voided a state law attempting to override a provision of the Multistate Tax Compact (from which California had not withdrawn at the time of the court's decision).[287]

"Some background on the nature of interstate compacts is in order. **These instruments are legislatively enacted, binding and enforceable agreements between two or more states**." [288]

"As we have seen, some interstate compacts require congressional consent, but others, that do not infringe on the federal sphere, do not.[289]

---

[286] The Council of State Governments. 2003. *Interstate Compacts and Agencies 2003*. Lexington, KY: The Council of State Governments. Page 6.

[287] After the California court's decision in *The Gillette Company et al. v. Franchise Tax Board*, the state of California enacted a law (Senate Bill 1015 of 2012) exercising California's right to withdraw from the Multistate Tax Compact. After the effective date of the statute withdrawing from the compact, the state of California became free to change its formula for taxing multi-state businesses. Senate Bill 1015 took effect as a "budget trailer" on July 27, 2012.

[288] *The Gillette Company et al. v. Franchise Tax Board. Court of Appeal of the State of California*, First Appellate District, Division Four. July 24, 2012. Page 8. Appendix GG contains the full opinion.

[289] *Ibid.* Page 9.

"**Where, as here, federal congressional consent was neither given nor required, the Compact must be construed as state law**. (*McComb v. Wambaugh* (3d Cir. 1991) 934 F.2d 474, 479.) Moreover, **since interstate compacts are agreements enacted into state law, they have dual functions as enforceable contracts between member states and as statutes with legal standing within each state**; and thus we interpret them as both. (*Aveline v. Bd. of Probation and Parole* (1999) 729 A.2d 1254, 1257; see Broun et al., *The Evolving Use and the Changing Role of Interstate Com*pacts (ABA 2006) § 1.2.2, pp. 15-24 (Broun on Compacts); 1A Sutherland, Statutory Construction (7th ed. 2009) § 32:5; *In re C.B.* (2010) 188 Cal.App.4th 1024, 1031 [recognizing that Interstate Compact on Placement of Children shares characteristics of both contractual agreements and statutory law].)

"**The contractual nature of a compact is demonstrated by its adoption**: **There is an offer** (a proposal to enact virtually verbatim statutes by each member state), an **acceptance** (enactment of the statutes by the member states), and **consideration** (the settlement of a dispute, creation of an association, or some mechanism to address an issue of mutual interest.)" (Broun on Compacts, supra, § 1.2.2, p. 18.) **As is true of other contracts, the contract clause of the United States Constitution shields compacts from impairment by the states**. (*Aveline v. Bd. of Probation and Parole*, supra, 729 A.2d at p. 1257, fn. 10.) Therefore, upon entering a compact, "it takes precedence over the subsequent statutes of signatory states and, as such, a state may not unilaterally nullify, revoke or amend one of its compacts if the compact does not so provide." (Ibid.; accord, *Intern. Union v. Del. River Joint Toll Bridge* (3d Cir. 2002) 311 F.3d 273, 281.) **Thus interstate compacts are unique in that they empower one state legislature—namely the one that enacted the agreement—to bind all future legislatures to certain principles governing the subject matter of the compact**. (Broun on Compacts, supra, § 1.2.2, p. 17.)

"As explained and summarized in *C.T. Hellmuth v. Washington Metro. Area Trans.* (D.Md. 1976) 414 F.Supp. 408, 409 (*Hellmuth*): '**Upon entering into an interstate compact, a state effectively surrenders a portion of its sovereignty; the compact governs the relations of the parties with respect to the subject matter of the agreement and is superior to both prior and subsequent law. Further, when enacted, a compact constitutes not only law, but a contract which may not be amended, modified, or otherwise altered without the consent of all parties.** It, therefore, appears settled that one party may not enact legislation which would impose burdens upon the compact absent the concurrence of the other signatories.' Cast a little differently, '[i]t is within the competency of a State, which is a party to a compact with another State, to legislate in respect of matters covered by the compact so long as such legislative action is in approbation and not in reprobation of the compact.' (*Henderson v. Delaware River Joint Toll Bridge Com'm* (1949) 66 A.2d 843, 849-450.) Nor may states amend a compact by enacting legislation that is substantially similar, unless the compact itself contains language enabling a state or states to modify it through legislation "'concurred in'" by the other states. (*Intern. Union v. Del. River Joint Toll Bridge*, supra, 311 F.3d at pp. 276-280.)"[290] [Emphasis added]

The court also stated:

"Were this simply a matter of statutory construction involving two statutes—sections 25128 and 38006—we would at least entertain the FTB's argument that section 25128 repealed the section 38006 taxpayer election to apportion under the Compact formula, and now mandates the exclusive use of the double-weighted sales apportionment formula. However, this construct is not sustainable because it completely ignores the dual nature of section 38006. Once one filters in the reality that **section 38006 is not just a statute but is also the codification of the Compact, and that through this enactment California has entered a binding, enforceable agreement with the other signatory states**, the multiple flaws in the FTB's position become apparent. **First, under established compact law, the Compact supersedes subsequent conflicting state law. Second, the federal and state Constitutions prohibit states from passing laws that impair the obligations of contracts.** And finally, the FTB's construction of the effect of the amended section 25128 runs afoul of the reenactment clause of the California Constitution. . . .

"**By its very nature an interstate compact shifts some of a state's authority to another state or states. Thus signatory states cede a level of sovereignty over matters covered in the Compact in favor of pursuing multilateral action to resolve a dispute or regulate an interstate affair.** (Hess v. Port Authority Trans-Hudson Corporation (1994) 513 U.S. 30, 42; Broun on Compacts, supra, § 1.2.2, p. 23.) Because the Compact is both a statute and a binding agreement among sovereign signatory states, having entered into it, California cannot, by subsequent legislation, unilaterally alter or amend its terms. Indeed, as an interstate compact **the Compact is superior to prior and subsequent the statutory law of member states**. (McComb v. Wambaugh, supra, 934 F.2d at

---

[290] *Ibid.* Pages 9–11.

p. 479; Hellmuth, supra, 414 F.Supp. at p. 409.) This means that the Compact trumps section 25128, such that, contrary to the FTB's assertion, section 25128 cannot override the UDITPA election offered to multistate taxpayers in section 38006, article III, subdivision 1. It bears repeating that the Compact requires states to offer this taxpayer option. If a state could unilaterally delete this baseline uniformity provision, it would render the binding nature of the compact illusory and contribute to defeating one of its key purposes, namely to "[p]romote uniformity or compatibility in significant components of tax systems." (§ 38006, art. I, subd. 2.) **Because the Compact takes precedent over subsequent conflicting legislation, these outcomes cannot come to pass.**[291]

The courts have long held that a state belonging to an interstate compact may not unilaterally renounce the agreement. The U.S. Supreme Court addressed this issue in a 1950 case involving the Ohio River Valley Water Sanitation Compact. The parties to this compact included eight states and the federal government. The compact established a commission consisting of representatives from each of the governmental units. It provided that each party state would pay a specified share of the operating expenses of the compact's commission.

> **"The signatory states agree to appropriate for the salaries, office and other administrative expenses**, their proper proportion of the annual budget as determined by the Commission and approved by the Governors of the signatory states, one half of such amount to be prorated among the several states in proportion of their population within the district at the last preceding federal census, the other half to be prorated in proportion to their land area within the district." [Emphasis added]

There was considerable political division in the West Virginia state government over the desirability of the compact. The state legislature ratified the compact and, in 1949, appropriated $12,250 as West Virginia's initial contribution to the expenses of the compact's commission.

The state Auditor, however, refused to make the payment from the state treasury. He argued that the legislature's approval of the compact violated the state constitution in two respects. First, the Auditor argued that the compact was unconstitutional because it delegated the state's police power to an interstate agency involving other states and the federal government. Second, the Auditor argued that the compact was invalid because it bound the West Virginia legislature in advance to make appropriations for the state's share of the commission's operating expenses in violation of a general provision of the state constitution concerning the incurring of "debts."

The West Virginia State Water Commission supported the compact and went to

---

[291] *Ibid.* Pages 15–16.

court requesting a mandamus order (a judicial writ ordering performance of a specific action) to compel the Auditor to make the payment from the state treasury. The Supreme Court of Appeals of West Virginia invalidated the legislature's ratification of the compact on the grounds that the compact violated the state constitution.

In 1950, the U.S. Supreme Court reversed the state ruling and prevented West Virginia from evading its obligations under the compact. The Court wrote in *West Virginia ex rel. Dyer v. Sims*:

> "But a compact is after all a legal document. . . . **It requires no elaborate argument to reject the suggestion that an agreement** solemnly entered into between States by those who alone have political authority to speak for a State **can be unilaterally nullified**, or given final meaning by an organ of one of the contracting States. **A State cannot be its own ultimate judge in a controversy with a sister State.**"[292] [Emphasis added]

The Court continued:

> "That a legislature may delegate to an administrative body the power to make rules and decide particular cases is one of the axioms of modern government. The West Virginia court does not challenge the general proposition but objects to the delegation here involved **because it is to a body outside the State and because its Legislature may not be free, at any time, to withdraw the power delegated**. . . . What is involved is the conventional grant of legislative power. We find nothing in that to indicate that West Virginia may not solve a problem such as the control of river pollution by compact and by the delegation, if such it be, necessary to effectuate such solution by compact. . . . Here, the State has bound itself to control pollution by the more effective means of an agreement with other States. **The Compact involves a reasonable and carefully limited delegation of power to an interstate agency.**"[293] [Emphasis added]

Justice Robert Jackson's concurring opinion set forth an additional justification for the Court's decision. Justice Jackson suggested that the Supreme Court did not need to interpret the West Virginia state constitution in order to conclude that the compact bound West Virginia. Instead, he stated that West Virginia was estopped from changing its position after each of the other governmental entities relied upon, and changed their position because of, the compact.

> "**West Virginia assumed a contractual obligation** with equals by permission of another government that is sovereign in its field (the federal government). After Congress and **sister states had been induced to alter**

---

[292] *West Virginia ex rel. Dyer v. Sims*. 341 U.S. 22 at 28. 1950.
[293] *Id.* at 30–31.

their positions and bind themselves to terms of a covenant, West Virginia should be estopped from repudiating her act. For this reason, I consider that whatever interpretation she put on the generalities of her Constitution, **she is bound by the Compact**."[294] [Emphasis added]

The pre-ratification expectations of states joining a compact are especially important whenever there is a post-ratification dispute among compacting parties concerning voting rights within the compact.

In one case, Nebraska (which was obligated to store radioactive waste under the terms of an interstate compact) sought additional voting power on the compact's commission after the compact had gone into effect. A majority (but not all) of the compact's other members consented to Nebraska's request. Nebraska's request was, however, judicially voided in 1995 in *State of Nebraska v. Central Interstate Low-Level Radioactive Waste Commission*

"because changes in 'voting power' substantially alter the original expectations of the majority of states which comprise the compact."[295]

Amplifying the principle of *West Virginia ex rel. Dyer v. Sims*, the courts have noted that a single state cannot obstruct the workings of a compact. In *Hess v. Port Authority Trans-Hudson Corp.*, the U.S. Supreme Court held in 1994 that a compact is

" . . . not subject to the unilateral control of any one of the States . . . ."[296]

Similarly, in *Lake Country Estates, Inc. v. Tahoe Regional Planning Agency*, the U.S. Supreme Court in 1979 held that a member state may not unilaterally veto the actions of a compact's commission. Instead, the remedy of an aggrieved state consists of withdrawing from the compact in accordance with the compact's terms for withdrawal.[297]

In *Kansas City Area Transportation Authority v. Missouri*, the Eighth Circuit in 1981 held that a member state may not legislatively burden the other member states unless they concur.[298]

Moreover, the courts have prevented a compacting state from undermining the workings of that compact. In the 1993 case of *Alcorn v. Wolfe*, the removal of an appointee to a compact commission, initiated by a Governor to inject his political influence into the operations of the commission, was invalidated because it

"clearly frustrate[d] one of the most important objectives of the compact."[299]

---

[294] *Id.* at 36.

[295] *State of Nebraska v. Central Interstate Low-Level Radioactive Waste Commission.* 902 F.Supp. 1046, 1049 (D.Neb. 1995).

[296] *Hess v. Port Authority Trans-Hudson Corp.* 513 U.S. 30 at 42. 1994.

[297] *Lake Country Estates, Inc. v. Tahoe Regional Planning Agency.* 440 U.S. 391 at 399 and 402. 1979.

[298] *Kansas City Area Transportation Authority v. Missouri.* 640 F.2d 173 at 174 (8th Cir.). 1979.

[299] *Alcorn v. Wolfe.* 827 F.Supp. 47, 53 (D.D.C. 1993).

In *State of Nebraska v. Central Interstate Low-Level Radioactive Waste Commission,* Nebraska was estopped in 1993 from seeking equitable relief to prevent a compact, of which it was a member, from pursuing its central mission.[300] In *New York v. United States,* the U.S. Supreme Court held that the estoppel doctrine was applicable only to the states that have adopted the interstate compact.[301]

In short, a state may be estopped from withdrawing from a compact in any manner not permitted by the terms of the compact.

Recall that most interstate compacts contain obligations that a member state would never have agreed to unless it could rely on the enforceability of the obligations undertaken by its sister states. Consequently, most interstate compacts impose a delay on withdrawal because each member state must be able to rely on each contracting party to fulfill its obligations and must have time (and sometimes compensation) to adjust if another state desires to withdraw.

The six-month blackout period for withdrawing from the proposed "Agreement Among the States to Elect the President by National Popular Vote" is reasonable and appropriate in order to ensure that a politically motivated member state does not change its position after the candidates, the political parties, the voters, and the other compacting states have proceeded through the presidential campaign and presidential election cycle in reliance on each compacting state fulfilling its obligations under the compact.

The enforceability of interstate compacts under the Impairments Clause is precisely the reason why sovereign states enter into interstate compacts. If a state were willing to merely rely on the goodwill and graciousness of other states to undertake certain actions, it could unilaterally enact its own independent law on the subject matter involved (unconnected with the actions of other states), unilaterally enact a uniform state law (and hope that other states did the same), or unilaterally enact a contingent state law (if permitted by the state constitution). However, if a state wants an agreement that is legally binding on other states, it enters into an interstate compact.

Thus, if a Governor and state legislature were to enact legislation purporting to withdraw from the National Popular Vote compact during the six-month period between July 20 of a presidential election year and Inauguration Day (January 20), that legislation would be unconstitutional on its face because of the Impairments Clause.[302]

Professor Norman R. Williams of Willamette University has made the argument that the state legislature's plenary power to choose the manner of appointing presiden-

---

[300] *State of Nebraska v. Central Interstate Low-Level Radioactive Waste Commission.* 834 F.Supp. 1205 at 1215 (D.Neb. 1993).

[301] *New York v. United States.* 505 U.S. 144 at 183. 1992.

[302] Generic contract law (applicable to parties to *any* contact, whether the parties are state governments or not) provides a separate and independent non-constitutional legal basis for preventing a state from attempting to withdraw from a compact except in the manner specified by the compact.

tial electors is not subject to any specific provisions in the Constitution restricting the exercise of legislative power.

> "It is not clear that the NPVC is valid and enforceable against a state that decides to withdraw from it after July 20 in a presidential election year. Article II of the U.S. Constitution entrusts the method of appointment of the presidential electors to the state legislature. For some, that federal constitutional delegation of authority must be read literally, meaning that **the state legislature's power cannot be circumscribed to any extent or in any manner.**"[303] [Emphasis added]

According to Williams' "imperial legislature" theory, specific restrictions in the Constitution, such as the Impairments Clause, cannot restrain the exercise of legislative power.

This argument ignores the reality that the vast majority of interstate compacts involve state plenary powers. States voluntarily enter into interstate compacts precisely because compacts, in conjunction with the Impairments Clause, provide a way to create enforceable restrictions on state action. States mutually agree to these restrictions because each participating state believes that the restrictions are mutually beneficial.

Section 1 of Article II of the U.S. Constitution provides:

> "Each State shall appoint, **in such Manner as the Legislature thereof may direct**, a Number of Electors. . . ."[304] [Emphasis added]

The wording "in such manner as the ___ may direct" is a grant of power permitting each state to exercise a certain power; however, it does not create a power that stands above the rest of the U.S. Constitution or outside the Constitution.

Tellingly, section 1 of Article II does *not* say:

> "**Notwithstanding any other provision of this Constitution**, each State shall appoint, in such Manner as the Legislature thereof may direct, a Number of Electors. . . ."

Section 1 of Article II is neither more nor less than a delegation of a certain power to a certain body (in this case the state legislature). The exercise of that legislative power is subject to all of the other specific restraints in the U.S. Constitution (and state constitution) that may apply to the exercise of legislative power.

Among the specific restrictions on the power of a state under section 1 of Article II are those contained in the 14th Amendment (equal protection), 15th Amendment (prohibiting denial of the vote on account of "race, color, or previous condition of ser-

---

[303] Williams, Norman R. Reforming the Electoral College: Federalism, majoritarianism, and the perils of sub-constitutional change. 100 *Georgetown Law Journal* 173. November 2011. Page 219.

[304] U.S. Constitution. Article II, section 1, clause 2.

vitude"), the 19th Amendment (woman's suffrage), the 24th amendment (prohibiting poll taxes), and the 26th Amendment (18-year-old vote).

Article I, section 10, clause 1 of the U.S. Constitution provides:

> "**No State shall** enter into any Treaty, Alliance, or Confederation; grant Letters of Marque and Reprisal; coin Money; emit Bills of Credit; make any Thing but gold and silver Coin a Tender in Payment of Debts; **pass any** Bill of Attainder, **ex post facto Law, or Law impairing the Obligation of Contracts**, or grant any Title of Nobility." [Emphasis added]

Thus, under section 1 of Article II, a state legislature may, for example, pass a law making it a crime to commit fraud in a presidential election. However, notwithstanding Professor Williams' "imperial legislature" theory, a state legislature may not pass an *ex post facto* (retroactive) law making it a crime to commit fraud in a previous presidential election because the Constitution's explicit prohibition against *ex post facto* laws operates as a restraint on the delegation of power contained in section 1 of Article II.

Similarly, the Constitution's explicit prohibition against a "law impairing the obligation of contract" (appearing adjacent to the prohibition against *ex post facto* laws) operates as a restraint on the delegation of power contained in section 1 of Article II.

It is interesting to note that the wording "in such manner as the ___ may direct" appears in a second place in the Constitution in connection with the specific subject of selecting the manner of appointing presidential electors. The 23rd Amendment to the U.S. Constitution (ratified in 1961) provides:

> "The District constituting the seat of government of the United States shall appoint **in such manner as the Congress may direct** a number of electors of President and Vice President. . . ."

Surely no one would argue that "in such manner as the ___ may direct" (the exact parallel of the wording of section 1 of Article II) means that Congress is not subject to specific provisions of the Constitution restricting the exercise of its plenary legislative power, and that Congress could therefore, for example, exclude women and African-Americans from voting in the selection of presidential electors in the District of Columbia, notwithstanding the specific requirements of the 19th Amendment (ratified in 1920) and the 15th Amendment (ratified in 1870).

The wording "in such manner as the ___ may direct" also appears in the 17th Amendment (ratified in 1913) in connection with temporary appointments to fill U.S. Senate vacancies

> " . . . until the people fill the vacancies by election **as the legislature may direct**." [Emphasis added]

Certainly, no one would argue that the "may direct" wording means that a state legislature is not subject to other specific provisions in the Constitution restricting the exercise of this plenary legislative power such as, say, the 15th Amendment (ratified in 1870) or the Equal Protection clause of the 14th Amendment (ratified in 1868). A state legislature could not, for example, exclude African-American voters in a vacancy-filling election for the U.S. Senate.

In fact, both the U.S. Constitution and state constitutions are replete with plenary powers possessed by their respective legislative bodies. Congress, for example, has plenary power over counterfeiting, the District of Columbia, federal taxation, and numerous other "enumerated" areas, but no one would argue that these plenary powers are not subject to specific provisions of the Constitution restricting the exercise of all legislative power, such as, say, the specific constitutional prohibition against *ex post facto* laws (Article I, section 9, clause 3). For example, Congress may not pass *ex post facto* laws applicable to the District of Columbia under its plenary powers in Article I, section 8, clause 17:

> "The Congress shall have Power . . . to exercise exclusive Legislation in all Cases whatsoever, over such District."

Similarly, state legislatures have plenary power over innumerable matters, but no one would argue that these plenary powers are not subject to specific restrictive provisions of the U.S. Constitution and their state constitutions.

In short, two centuries of settled law concerning the enforceability of interstate compacts under the Impairments Clause would be available to rebuff any attempt to execute the hypothetical scenario concerning withdrawal.

See section 9.11.3 for a detailed discussion of another of Professor Williams' claims that interstate compacts are "toothless."

The Safe Harbor provision of federal law confers conclusiveness only on appointments of presidential electors made under "laws enacted prior to" Election Day.

As already discussed in an earlier part of this section, John Sample's hypothetical scenario about a state withdrawing from the National Popular Vote compact after "the results of an election become known" is legally impossible because of Article II, section 1, clause 4 of the Constitution and section 1 of Title 3 of the United States Code.

Even if a state legislature were to meet on Election Day to appoint presidential electors, that action would not be sufficient.

The "safe harbor" section of federal law (Title 3, section 5) treats a state's appointment of presidential electors as "conclusive" only if the appointment is based on

> **"laws enacted prior to the day** fixed for the appointment of the electors."
> [Emphasis added]

The day fixed by law for appointment of presidential electors is the Tuesday after the first Monday in November (i.e., Election Day).

Thus, the state's pre-existing law specifying the manner of appointing presidential electors (either under the National Popular Vote compact or under the current state-by-state winner-take-all system) would have to have been repealed *prior* to Election Day before the legislature could meet on Election Day to appoint presidential electors.

The hypothetical scenario could only be executed in about three states because of numerous practical political reasons, including high quorum requirements, the fact that many states have politically divided government at any given time, the significant time delay before a new state law may take effect, the numerous time-delaying tactics enabling the minority party to delay action in the short period of time between Election Day and the meeting of the Electoral College, and other factors.

Even if the Impairments Clause of the U.S. Constitution and sections 1 and 5 of Title 3 of the United States Code did not exist, there are practical reasons that would prevent John Sample's hypothetical scenario in which a state legislature and Governor might try, for partisan political advantage, to change the "rules of the game" between Election Day in early November and the meeting of the Electoral College in mid-December.

Changing the way a state chooses its presidential electors requires several distinct steps.

- First, the state legislature and Governor would have to enact a statute repealing (withdrawing from) the National Popular Vote compact.
- Second, after passing the legislature and being signed by the Governor, the repeal statute would have to take effect in the state involved.
- Third, the legislature and Governor would have to enact a statute providing a new way to appoint the state's presidential electors. For example, the legislature and Governor might enact a statute empowering the legislature to appoint the state's presidential electors.
- Fourth, the statute providing a new way to appoint the state's presidential electors would have to take effect in the state involved.
- Fifth, the presidential electors would have to be appointed under the newly enacted procedure.

Because most state legislatures are not in session in November and December, it first would be necessary to call the legislature into special session for this purpose. Governors generally have the power to call their state legislatures into special session. In some states, legislators may have an independent power to convene a special session.

All Governors have the power to veto legislative bills. Thus, the Governor's support would, as a practical matter, be a necessary part of any effort to repeal the compact except in the unusual situation where the legislative leadership possesses the power to convene a special session and controls a veto-proof majority.[305]

An attempt to change the manner of appointing a state's presidential electors after

---

[305] In most states, a super-majority vote of both houses is necessary to override a governor's veto. In Alabama, Arkansas, Indiana, Kentucky, North Carolina, Pennsylvania, Tennessee, and West Virginia, a gubernatorial veto can be overridden by a majority vote of both houses of the legislature.

the state's voters cast their votes on Election Day would be a partisan maneuver of the most extreme and extraordinary nature. It would elicit fierce opposition from the to-be-disadvantaged political party.

Thus, John Sample's hypothetical scenario could not even be contemplated in two-thirds of the states because of

(1) high quorum requirements,

(2) lengthy lay-over requirements before a bill may be considered,

(3) the fact that almost half the states generally have politically divided government at any given time,

(4) the fact that state constitutions in 21 states would delay the effective date of the new state law until after the Electoral College met in mid-December,

(5) numerous time-delaying tactics enabling the minority party to delay action in the short period of time between Election Day and the meeting of the Electoral College, and

(6) other factors.

These practical political difficulties can be appreciated by visualizing what would have happened if John Sample's hypothetical scenario had been contemplated immediately after the November 2008 presidential election.

First, the constitutions of four states (Texas, Oregon, Indiana, and Tennessee) specify a two-thirds quorum requirement for a meeting of the legislature. No political party had two-thirds control of both houses of the legislature in any of these states in November of 2008. Thus, it would be futile to even contemplate executing the hypothetical scenario in these states because the minority party would simply have boycotted the legislative session during the short period of time between Election Day and the meeting of the Electoral College in mid-December. The opposition would simply run out the clock.

Second, in California, there is a constitutional lay-over requirement preventing consideration of any bill for 30 days after its introduction (unless waived by a three-quarters vote). Neither political party had a three-quarters super-majority in the California legislature in 2008. Thus, it would be futile to even contemplate executing the hypothetical scenario in California.

Third, at any given time, the Governor's office and the two houses of state legislatures are not controlled by the same political party in many states. Over half the states had divided political control in the 20-year period starting in 1984. In 2004, 30 states had divided political control.[306, 307] In November of 2008, for example, no politi-

---

[306] The number dropped to 13 after the 2012 elections. See Davey, Monica. One-party control opens states to partisan rush. *New York Times.* November 22, 2012. See chart showing partisan control of state government at http://www.nytimes.com/interactive/2012/11/23/us/state-government-control-since-1938.html?ref =politics.

[307] Dubin, Michael J. 2007. *Party Affiliations in the State Legislatures: A Year by Year Summary 1796–2006.* Jefferson, NC: McFarland & Company Inc.

cal party controlled both houses of the legislature plus the Governor's office (or had a veto-proof legislative majority in both houses) in 18 states *in addition to* the five states mentioned above. These 18 additional states were Alabama, Arizona, Connecticut, Kansas, Kentucky, Michigan, Minnesota, Mississippi, Missouri, Montana, Nevada, New York, Ohio, Oklahoma, Pennsylvania, Vermont, Virginia, and Wisconsin.

Fourth, the constitutions of 21 states significantly delay the effective date of *all* newly enacted state laws. Thus, in 10 states (*in addition to* the above 23 states), a new law changing the method of appointing presidential electors could not even take effect prior to the mid-December meeting of the Electoral College. The 10 additional states are Alaska, Illinois, Louisiana, Maine, Maryland, Nebraska, New Mexico, North Dakota, South Dakota, and Utah.

The shortest such delay in this group of 10 additional states is 60 days after the Governor's signature. There are only about 35 days between Election Day in November and the mid-December meeting of the Electoral College. Thus, the presidential electors from these states would have met and cast their votes under the pre-existing state law long before the politically motivated law repealing the National Popular Vote compact could take effect. In fact, in some of these states, the new President would have been inaugurated before the repeal law could take effect.

Table 9.12 shows the earliest date when a new state law can take effect in a given state.

The only exception to the delays imposed by state constitutions is to give a newly enacted law immediate effect by passing it as an "emergency bill." However, emergency bills require super-majorities (three-fifths, two-thirds, three-quarters, or four-fifths, depending on the state). Column 3 of table 9.12 shows the super-majority needed to give a bill immediate effect. In November 2008, no political party had the super-majorities necessary to pass an emergency bill in the additional group of 10 states. Thus, a statute repealing the compact simply could not take effect prior to the mid-December meeting of the Electoral College. Therefore, it would be pointless to even consider trying to execute John Sample's hypothetical scenario in this group of states.

Note that there are *overlapping* reasons why John Sample's hypothetical scenario could not be executed in most states. For example, two states with a two-thirds quorum (Tennessee and Indiana) also had divided government in November 2008. Moreover, bills passed in a special session in California do not take effect until 91 days after a bill is passed (unless the bill is given immediate effect by a two-thirds vote of each house). Neither party in California in November 2008 had the super-majority necessary to give a bill immediate effect. The state constitutions of many of the states with divided government in November 2008 would delay a new bill's effective date well beyond the mid-December meeting of the Electoral College.

Summarizing the above four points, John Sample's hypothetical scenario could not even be contemplated in 33 states (that is, two-thirds of the states).

Table 9.12 EARLIEST POSSIBLE EFFECTIVE DATE FOR NEW STATE LAWS

STATE	DATE WHEN A BILL ORDINARILY TAKES EFFECT	SUPER-MAJORITY NEEDED TO GIVE BILL IMMEDIATE EFFECT
Alabama	Can be immediate	
Alaska	90 days after enactment	Two-thirds
Arizona	90 days after legislature adjourns	Two-thirds (three-quarters if veto was overridden)
Arkansas	90 days after legislature adjourns	Two-thirds
California	January 1 next following a 90-day period from date of enactment. 91 days after special session adjourns	Two-thirds
Colorado	Can be immediate	
Connecticut	Can be immediate	
Delaware	Can be immediate	
Florida	Can be immediate	
Georgia	Can be immediate	
Hawaii	Can be immediate	
Idaho	Can be immediate	
Illinois	June 1 of the following year (if passed after May 31)	Three-fifths
Indiana	Can be immediate	
Iowa	Can be immediate	
Kansas	Can be immediate	
Kentucky	Can be immediate	
Louisiana	Can be immediate	
Maine	90 days after recess	Two-thirds
Maryland	June 1 after adjournment	Three-fifths
Massachusetts	90 days after enactment	Two-thirds
Michigan	90 days after adjournment	Two-thirds
Minnesota	Can be immediate	
Mississippi	Can be immediate	
Missouri	90 days after adjournment	
Montana	Can be immediate	
North Carolina	Can be immediate	
Nebraska	Three months after adjournment	Two-thirds
Nevada	Can be immediate	
New Hampshire	Can be immediate	
New Jersey	Can be immediate	
New Mexico	90 days after adjournment	Two-thirds
New York	20 days after enactment	
North Dakota	August 1	Two-thirds
Ohio	90 days after enactment	Two-thirds
Oklahoma	90 days after adjournment	Two-thirds
Oregon	Can be immediate	
Pennsylvania	Can be immediate	
Rhode Island	Can be immediate	
South Carolina	Can be immediate	
South Dakota	June 1 after adjournment	Two-thirds
Tennessee	Can be immediate	
Texas	90 days after adjournment	Two-thirds
Utah	60 days after adjournment	Two-thirds
Vermont	Can be immediate	
Virginia	July 1st or first day of 4th month after special session	Four-fifths
West Virginia	90 days after passage	Two-thirds
Washington	Can be immediate	
Wisconsin	Can be immediate	
Wyoming	Can be immediate	

That leaves 17 states where the hypothetical scenario would have been theoretically possible in November 2008. Those 17 states are Arkansas, Colorado, Delaware, Florida, Georgia, Hawaii, Idaho, Iowa, Massachusetts, New Hampshire, New Jersey, North Carolina, Rhode Island, South Carolina, West Virginia, Washington state, and Wyoming. These are states lacking high quorums, lacking significant lay-over requirements, lacking significant delays before new laws take effect, and where one political party was in total control of the law-making process in November 2008 (either by controlling both houses of the legislature and the Governor's office or by enjoying veto-proof majorities in both houses of the legislature).

However, even this small remaining group of 17 states is illusory. This group of 17 states would be immediately winnowed down to about four states because of two independent factors:

(A) A state cannot withdraw from the compact if it is not already a member. John Sample's hypothetical scenario would be irrelevant if the state were not a member of the National Popular Vote compact in the first place. If we make the reasonable assumption that about half of the states will be in the compact when it takes effect, this factor would alone eliminate about half of this group of 17 states.

(B) There would be no reason to withdraw from the compact if the political party controlling a given state is pleased with the outcome of the nationwide popular vote. Thus, the hypothetical scenario would be irrelevant in states where the political party in control of a given state had just won the national popular vote. This factor would independently eliminate about half of the states not eliminated by factor (A). That is, there would only be about four states in which Sample's hypothetical scenario might be possible at any given time.

Even in this winnowed-down group of four states, there are several additional practical reasons why the hypothetical scenario probably could not be executed in the limited amount of time available.

First, a highly motivated minority in most state legislatures can delay the enactment of new legislation for a considerable length of time by invoking various parliamentary tactics. These tactics include offering amendments, filibusters, insisting that no action occur until pending amendments are printed, and, most importantly, "working to rule"—that is, refusing to waive the numerous time-consuming notice, scheduling, and lay-over requirements that are routinely waived in ordinary circumstances. The dilatory tactics available to a legislative minority cannot delay enactment of a particular bill forever; however, in most states, they are more than sufficient to delay a legislative bill in the short time available between Election Day and the mid-November meeting of the Electoral College.

Second, this winnowed-down group of states would probably not possess enough electoral votes to reverse the outcome in the Electoral College. One reason is that the compact might well be enacted by a sufficiently large number of states so that the compacting states would possess significantly more than 270 electoral votes. Another (even more compelling) reason (discussed in greater detail below) is that, in a typical future presidential election under the National Popular Vote compact, the candidate winning the national popular vote would generally receive an exaggerated margin of victory in the Electoral College (roughly 75%).

Third, in several states in this winnowed-down group of 17 (e.g., Colorado, Washington state, and Wyoming), a protest referendum petition could be circulated to suspend the politically motivated action of the state legislature. The filing of a protest referendum petition automatically and unconditionally suspends the effectiveness of any new state law passed by the legislature until a subsequent statewide election. Protest referendum petitions generally require only a modest number of signatures (far smaller than the number of signatures required, say, to initiate a new state law). The aggrieved political party could, almost certainly, quickly acquire the requisite number of signatures. There would, of course, be no time to hold the referendum in the short five-week period between Election Day in early November and the meeting of the Electoral College in mid-December.

Thus, even if the Impairments Clause of the U.S. Constitution and sections 1 and 5 of Title 3 of the United States Code did not exist to prevent John Sample's hypothetical scenario, parliamentary difficulties would make it unlikely that the hypothetical scenario could be successfully implemented in practice.

The next section discusses an additional reason—indeed, the controlling reason—why John Sample's hypothetical scenario could not be executed in the real world, namely public opinion.

Any attempt to appoint presidential electors after the people vote in November would be politically preposterous in the real world.

There would be virtually no public support for John Sample's hypothetical scenario of changing the "rules of the game" after the people voted in November.

John Sample's hypothetical scenario assumes that the public strongly and enthusiastically supports the state-by-state winner-take-all system and would support a high-handed, last-ditch maneuver to restore it (in a state whose Governor and legislature had already enacted the National Popular Vote compact).

Recall that the political context of the hypothetical scenario would be some future time when the National Popular Vote compact is in effect. At that moment, the political environment would be such that

- a nationwide presidential campaign had already been conducted, over a period of many months, in which the candidates and the voters acted in accordance with the expectation that the national popular vote will determine who will become President;
- more than 70% of the American public favors a nationwide vote for President;

- more than 70% of the public in the state involved favors a nationwide vote for President;
- the legislature and Governor of the state involved have enacted the National Popular Vote bill; and
- the National Popular Vote compact has been enacted by (25 or so) states representing a majority of the people of the United States.

In reality, there is no significant public support for the current system at either the national or state level. Over 70% of the American people support the idea that the candidate who receives the most votes in all 50 states and the District of Columbia should win the Presidency (with 20% opposed and 10% undecided). Virtually identical percentages have been registered in state-level polls in big states, small states, spectator states, battleground states, red states, blue states, border states, and Southern states, as detailed in section 7.1.

Given the citizen nature of most state legislatures, it would require an extraordinary degree of control to whip a party's state legislators into line for such an unprecedented and highly partisan maneuver.

To execute John Sample's proposed partisan maneuver, the Governor and both houses of the state legislature would have to convene on Election Day (i.e., the Tuesday after the first Monday in November) because this is the only day in every four-year period when it is legal to choose presidential electors. This is, of course, the very same day when most state legislators would ordinarily be busy campaigning in their own districts (where, in most states, 50% to 100% of them are up for re-election). In addition, about a quarter of the nation's Governors are elected on Election Day in presidential election years. Thus, on the very same day when the voters would be going to the polls to cast their ballots for President in accordance with pre-existing state law (i.e., the National Popular Vote compact), the Governor and his supporters in the legislature would be hunkered down in the state Capitol Building, telling the voters that they intend to ignore the choice the people were in the process of making on Election Day (while simultaneously urging those same voters to re-elect them).

In short, John Sample's hypothetical partisan and illegal maneuver of attempting to withdraw from the National Popular Vote compact is a parlor game with no connection to the real world.

The hypothetical scenario would probably not matter because the national popular vote winner will typically receive about 75% of the electoral votes in the Electoral College, thereby producing a cushion of about 135 electoral votes above the 270 needed to win the Presidency.

Even if the Impairments Clause of the U.S. Constitution and sections 1 and 5 of Title 3 of the United States Code did not exist, John Sample's hypothetical scenario would probably not matter, because the national popular vote winner would typically receive an exaggerated margin in the Electoral College under the National Popular vote compact.

The reason is that the compact guarantees that the presidential candidate receiving the most popular votes in all 50 states and the District of Columbia will receive at least 270 electoral votes (that is, a majority of the 538 electoral votes) from the states belonging to the compact. Then, in addition to this minimum guaranteed bloc of 270 or more electoral votes from the compacting states, the nationwide winning candidate would receive a certain number of additional electoral votes from whichever non-compacting states he or she happened to win under existing (winner-take-all) laws for awarding electoral votes in those states. If the non-compacting states divided approximately equally between the candidates, the nationwide winning candidate would generally receive an exaggerated margin (roughly 75%) of the votes in the Electoral College (that is, about 404 out of 538 electoral votes). Thus, even if it were legally possible to execute John Sample's hypothesized partisan maneuver in one state (or even several states), the maneuver would almost certainly not affect who became President.

State constitutions provide additional constraints on withdrawal from a compact enacted by the citizen-initiative process.

In the case of a compact enacted by the citizen-initiative process, state constitutions would provide an additional constraint on a withdrawal from the National Popular Vote compact during the 35-day period between Election Day in November and the meeting of the Electoral College in mid-December.

In 11 states, there are state constitutional limitations concerning the repeal or amendment of a statute originally enacted by the voters by means of the citizen-initiative process. In seven of these states, the constraint on the legislature runs for a specific period of time. In four of the 11 states, the constraint is permanent—that is, the voters must be consulted in a subsequent referendum about any proposed repeal or amendment.

Table 9.13 briefly describes these constitutional limitations. Appendix R contains the complete constitutional provisions.

Table 9.13 STATE CONSTITUTIONAL LIMITATIONS ON THE REPEAL OR AMENDMENT OF STATUTES ORIGINALLY ENACTED BY THE VOTERS THROUGH THE CITIZEN-INITIATIVE PROCESS

STATE	LIMITATIONS
Alaska	No repeal within two years; amendment by majority vote anytime
Arizona	Three-quarters vote to amend; amending legislation must "further the purpose" of the measure
Arkansas	Two-thirds vote to amend or repeal
California	No amendment or repeal of an initiative statute by the legislature unless the initiative specifically permits it
Michigan	Three-quarters vote to amend or repeal
Nebraska	Two-thirds vote to amend or repeal
Nevada	No amendment or repeal within three years of enactment
North Dakota	Two-thirds vote to amend or repeal within seven years of effective date
Oregon	Two-thirds vote to amend or repeal within two years of enactment
Washington	Two-thirds vote to amend or repeal within two years of enactment
Wyoming	No repeal within two years of effective date; amendment by majority vote any time

In addition to constitutional limitations, public opinion acts as an especially strong inhibition against legislative repeal of a statute that the voters originally enacted by means of the citizen-initiative process. This political inhibition is particularly forceful in Western states where the citizen-initiative process is frequently used.

9.11.2. MYTH: A Secretary of State might change a state's method of awarding electoral votes after the people vote in November, but before the Electoral College meets in December.

QUICK ANSWER:

- No Secretary of State has the power to change a state's method of awarding electoral votes.

MORE DETAILED ANSWER:

The following concern has been raised on an election blog regarding the National Popular Vote bill:

> "In 2004 George Bush won a majority of the votes nationwide, but John Kerry came within something like 60,000 votes in Ohio of winning the Electoral College while losing the popular vote. Say Kerry won those 60,000 votes in Ohio, and the NPV program was in place with California a signer. In that entirely plausible scenario, does anyone think California's (Democratic) Secretary of State, representing a state that Kerry won by a 10% margin (54%–44%), would actually certify George Bush's slate of electors and personally put George Bush over the top for re-election, as the NPV agreement would have required?"[308]

Section 1 of Article II of the U.S. Constitution provides:

> "Each State shall appoint, in such Manner **as the Legislature thereof may direct**, a Number of Electors. . . ."[309] [Emphasis added]

No state legislature has delegated the power to select the manner of appointing the state's presidential electors to the Secretary of State. Instead, the method of awarding electoral votes in each state is controlled by the state's election law—not the personal political preferences of the Secretary of State.

A Secretary of State may not ignore or override the National Popular Vote law any more than he or she may ignore or override the winner-take-all rule that is currently in effect in 48 states.

It does not matter whether the Secretary of State personally thinks that electoral votes should be allocated by congressional district, in a proportional manner, by the

---

[308] In order to promote free-flowing debate of speculative ideas, the blog involved does not permit attribution.
[309] U.S. Constitution. Article II, section 1, clause 2.

winner-take-all rule, or by a national popular vote. The role of the Secretary of State in certifying the winning slate of presidential electors is entirely ministerial. That is, the role of the Secretary of State is to execute existing state law.

In the unlikely and unprecedented event that a Secretary of State were to attempt to certify an election using a method of awarding electoral votes different from the one specified by state law, a state court would immediately prevent the Secretary of State from violating the law's provisions (by injunction) and compel the Secretary of State to execute the provisions of the law (by mandamus).

If this hypothetical scenario were legally permissible or politically plausible, it would have occurred previously *under the current system*.

In 2000, there were 10 states[310] that George W. Bush carried that had a Democratic Secretary of State (or chief elections official).[311]

The electoral votes of *any* of these 10 states would have been sufficient to give Al Gore enough electoral votes to become President (even after Bush received all 25 of Florida's electoral votes).[312] Seventy percent or more of voters in the country supported the proposition that the candidate who receives the most popular votes in all 50 states and the District of Columbia should become President (as discussed in section 7.1).

Nonetheless, it can be safely stated that it did not even occur to any of these 10 Democratic Secretaries of State to attempt to try to override their states' laws by certifying the election of Democratic presidential electors in their states.

Such a post-election change in the rules of the game would not have been supported by the public (even though the public intensely dislikes the winner-take-all system), would immediately have been nullified by a state court, and almost certainly would have led to the subsequent impeachment of any official attempting it.

Moreover, awarding electoral votes proportionally in any of nine states with a Democratic Secretary of State would have been sufficient to give Gore enough electoral votes to become President (even after Bush received all 25 of Florida's electoral votes).[313] A proportional allocation of electoral votes would have, indisputably, represented the will of the people of each of these nine states more accurately than the state-level winner-take-all rule.

In addition, awarding electoral votes by congressional districts in any of three states with a Democratic Secretary of State,[314] would have been sufficient to give Al Gore enough electoral votes to become President (even after Bush received all 25 of Florida's electoral votes). A district allocation of electoral votes arguably would have

---

[310] Al Gore's home state of Tennessee, Alaska, Arkansas, Georgia, Kentucky, Mississippi, Missouri, New Hampshire, North Carolina, and West Virginia.

[311] In Alaska, there is no Secretary of State, and the Lieutenant Governor is the state's chief elections official.

[312] George W. Bush received 271 electoral votes in 2000 (including Florida's 25 electoral votes), and 270 electoral votes are required for election.

[313] All of those previously mentioned except Alaska.

[314] Georgia, Missouri, and North Carolina.

represented the will of the people of each of these three states more closely than the winner-take-all rule.

There has also been speculation that a Secretary of State might be "vilified" by certifying the election of the national popular vote winner. Under the National Popular Vote legislation, a dilemma has been hypothesized as to

> "whether the Secretary of State would really certify the losing panel of electors from the state in question, or find some justification to send the panel actually elected by the voters in the state. That's a very tough call and near-certain political vilification, either way, for the Secretary of State."[315]

This is not a "tough call" at all. In fact, there is no call to make. The Secretary of State is a ministerial official whose actions are directed and controlled by state law.

If 70% of the voters in a state prefer that the President be elected by a national popular vote, and if a state legislature enacts the National Popular Vote bill in response to the strong desires of the state's voters, and if the presidential campaign is then conducted with both voters and candidates knowing that the National Popular Vote compact is going to govern the election in that state, then the voters are not going to complain about a Secretary of State who faithfully executes the state's law.

Aside from the legal issues, the hypothesized scenario presupposes that the people heavily support the currently prevailing winner-take-all rule. In fact, public support for the current system of electing the President is very low (as discussed in section 7.1).

In short, the hypothesized scenario has no basis in law and certainly no basis in political reality.

9.11.3. MYTH: Interstate compacts that do not receive congressional consent are unenforceable and "toothless."

QUICK ANSWER:

- Some interstate compacts require congressional consent; however, those that do not challenge federal supremacy do not require congressional consent.
- Far from being "toothless," all interstate compacts are enforceable contracts (regardless of which combination of political bodies are necessary to approve them).
- In particular, an interstate compact takes precedence over *all* state laws— whether enacted *before* or *after* the state entered the compact. If a state no longer wishes to comply with its obligations under an interstate compact, it must withdraw from the compact in the manner specified by the compact before it adopts a contrary policy.

---

[315] In order to promote free-flowing debate of speculative ideas, the blog involved does not permit attribution. November 13, 2007.

MORE DETAILED ANSWER:

Professor Norman R. Williams of Willamette University discusses a variation on John Sample's hypothetical withdrawal scenario (section 9. 11.1) by saying:

> "In every state where the state legislature is controlled by the party of the national popular vote loser, there will be calls by disaffected constituents to withdraw from the NPVC. . . .

> "In fairness, the NPVC foresees this problem and attempts to address it by forbidding states from withdrawing from the compact after July 20 in a presidential election year. States that are signatories as of July 20 are mandated by the NPVC to adhere to the compact and its rules for appointing electors. Depending on whether Congress ratifies the NPVC, however, that provision is either **toothless** or fraught with difficulties."[316] [Emphasis added]

In support of his claim, Professor Williams has presented the following legally incorrect argument—with some astonishingly inappropriate legal citations—concerning the enforceability of interstate compacts that do not require congressional consent in order to take effect:

> "**Article I, Section 10 of the U.S. Constitution requires Congress to consent to any interstate compact before it can go into operation**. [Williams' footnote 171 appears here]

> "Let's suppose Congress does not consent to the compact, as its supporters urge is unnecessary despite the seemingly categorical command of the Compact Clause.

> "In that case, the compact does not acquire the force of federal law, as congressionally endorsed compacts do, and therefore, **it remains merely the law of the state**.

> "**Its status as state law, however, makes it no different from any other statute enacted by the state legislature**.

> "And, **like any other state statute, a subsequent legislature can amend or repeal the NPVC** consistent with the state's own constitutionally prescribed legislative process. [Williams' footnote 175 appears here]

> "A prior legislature may not bind subsequent legislatures through subconstitutional measures, such as statutes or congressionally unratified interstate compacts.[317] [Williams' footnote 176 appears here] [Emphasis added]

---

[316] Williams, Norman R. Reforming the Electoral College: Federalism, majoritarianism, and the perils of subconstitutional change. 100 *Georgetown Law Journal* 173. November 2011. Pages 215–216.

[317] Williams, Norman R. Reforming the Electoral College: Federalism, majoritarianism, and the perils of subconstitutional change. 100 *Georgetown Law Journal* 173. November 2011. Page 216.

Williams' statement that "the U.S. Constitution requires Congress to consent to any interstate compact before it can go into operation" is supported by his footnote 171 citing the Compacts Clause of the Constitution. However, Williams fails to cite a century and a quarter of settled compact jurisprudence interpreting the Compacts Clause of the Constitution, including rulings of the U.S. Supreme Court such as the 1893 case of *Virginia v. Tennessee*[318] and the 1978 case of *U.S. Steel Corporation v. Multistate Tax Commission*[319] (both quoted at length in section 9.16.5 and contained in full in appendices AA and BB, respectively).

The facts are that numerous interstate compacts that never received congressional consent are in force today based on the U.S. Supreme Court's rulings in *Virginia v. Tennessee* and *U.S. Steel Corporation v. Multistate Tax Commission*. For example, the Supreme Court ruled that the Multistate Tax Compact—the subject of *U.S. Steel Corporation v. Multistate Tax Commission*—did not require congressional consent in order to go into effect.

Williams' characterization of the Compacts Clause as a "categorical command" fails to acknowledge that the U.S. Supreme Court specifically ruled in both *U.S. Steel Corporation v. Multistate Tax Commission* and *Virginia v. Tennessee* that the Compact Clause was not categorical. As the Court said:

> "Read literally, the Compact Clause would require the States to obtain congressional approval before entering into any agreement among themselves, irrespective of form, subject, duration, or interest to the United States.

> "The difficulties with such an interpretation were identified by Mr. Justice Field in his opinion for the Court in [the 1893 case] *Virginia v. Tennessee*.[320] His conclusion [was] that the Clause could not be read literally [and this 1893 conclusion has been] approved in subsequent dicta, but this Court did not have occasion expressly to apply it in a holding until our recent decision in *New Hampshire v. Maine*,[321] supra."

> **"Appellants urge us to abandon *Virginia v. Tennessee* and *New Hampshire v. Maine*, but provide no effective alternative other than a literal reading of the Compact Clause. At this late date, we are reluctant to accept this invitation to circumscribe modes of interstate cooperation that do not enhance state power to the detriment of federal supremacy."[322]** [Emphasis added]

See section 9.16.5 for additional discussion of the U.S. Supreme Court's decisions and criteria for whether a particular interstate compact requires congressional consent.

---

[318] *Virginia v. Tennessee.* 148 U.S. 503. 1893.

[319] *U.S. Steel Corporation v. Multistate Tax Commission.* 434 U.S. 452. 1978.

[320] *Virginia v. Tennessee.* 148 U.S. 503. 1893.

[321] *New Hampshire v. Maine*, 426 U.S. 363. 1976.

[322] *U.S. Steel Corporation v. Multistate Tax Commission.* 434 U.S. 452. at 459–460. 1978.

Williams' statement that a compact's "status as state law . . . makes it no different from any other statute enacted by the state legislature" is legally incorrect.

The fact that a congressionally approved compact acquires the status of federal law is unrelated to the question of whether a compact has gone into effect and is an enforceable contract.

Compacts go into operation in one of two ways.

- First, if the compact requires congressional consent, the compact goes into effect only after (1) being enacted by the requisite combination of states, and (2) Congress confers its consent. A compact that requires congressional consent, but has not received it, simply never goes into effect.

- If the compact does not require congressional consent, the compact goes into effect after being enacted by the requisite combination of states.

The question of whether a particular compact requires congressional consent in order to take effect is a legal question that is answered by whether or not it satisfies the criteria established by rulings of the U.S. Supreme Court.

In practice, there may be litigation to determine whether a particular new compact requires congressional consent.

When Congress consents to an interstate compact, the compact acquires the status of federal law.

Compacts that do not require congressional consent do not acquire the status of federal law.

Once a compact is in effect, it is an enforceable contractual arrangement among participating states. The Impairments Clause of the U.S. Constitution provides:

> "No State shall . . . pass any . . . Law impairing the Obligation of Contracts."[323]

State courts routinely enforce interstate compacts not requiring congressional consent on the basis of the Impairments Clause.

The fact that a compact not requiring congressional consent has not been converted into federal law is unrelated to its enforceability.

A 2012 *state* court ruling involving the Multistate Tax Compact (the same interstate compact that was the subject of the U.S. Supreme Court's decision in *U.S. Steel Corporation v. Multistate Tax Commission*) illustrates this point.

In *The Gillette Company et al. v. Franchise Tax Board*, the California Court of Appeal voided a state law attempting to override a provision of the Multistate Tax Compact (from which California had not withdrawn at the time of the decision).

> "In 1972, a group of multistate corporate taxpayers brought an action on behalf of themselves and all other such taxpayers threatened with audits

---

[323] U.S. Constitution. Article I, section 10, clause 1.

by the Commission. The complaint challenged the constitutionality of the Compact on several grounds, including that it was invalid under the compact clause of the United States Constitution. (*U.S. Steel*, supra, 434 U.S. at p. 458.)

"The high court acknowledged that the compact clause, taken literally, would require the states to obtain congressional approval before entering into any agreement among themselves, 'irrespective of form, subject, duration, or interest to the United States.' (*U.S. Steel*, supra, 434 U.S. at p. 459.) However, it endorsed an interpretation, established by case law, that limited application of the compact clause 'to agreements that are "directed to the formation of any combination tending to the increase of political power in the States, which may encroach upon or interfere with the just supremacy of the United States.' . . . This rule states the proper balance between federal and state power with respect to compacts and agreements among States."' (Id. at p. 471, initial quote from *Virginia v. Tennessee* (1893) 148 U.S. 503, 519.)

"Framing the test as whether the Compact enhances state power with respect to the federal government, the court concluded it did not." [324]

The California court continued:

"Some background on the nature of interstate compacts is in order. **These instruments are legislatively enacted, binding and enforceable agreements between two or more states.**"[325]

"**As we have seen, some interstate compacts require congressional consent, but others, that do not infringe on the federal sphere, do not.**[326]

"**Where, as here, federal congressional consent was neither given nor required, the Compact must be construed as state law**. (*McComb v. Wambaugh* (3d Cir. 1991) 934 F.2d 474, 479.) Moreover, **since interstate compacts are agreements enacted into state law, they have dual functions as enforceable contracts between member states and as statutes with legal standing within each state**; and thus we interpret

---

[324] *The Gillette Company et al. v. Franchise Tax Board. Court of Appeal of the State of California*, First Appellate District, Division Four. July 24, 2012. Page 6. Appendix GG contains the full opinion.

[325] *The Gillette Company et al. v. Franchise Tax Board. Court of Appeal of the State of California*, First Appellate District, Division Four. July 24, 2012. Page 8. Appendix GG contains the full opinion.

[326] *The Gillette Company et al. v. Franchise Tax Board. Court of Appeal of the State of California*, First Appellate District, Division Four. July 24, 2012. Page 9. Appendix GG contains the full opinion.

them as both. (*Aveline v. Bd. of Probation and Parole* (1999) 729 A.2d 1254, 1257; see Broun et al., *The Evolving Use and the Changing Role of Interstate Com*pacts (ABA 2006) § 1.2.2, pp. 15-24 (Broun on Compacts); 1A Sutherland, Statutory Construction (7th ed. 2009) § 32:5; In re C.B. (2010) 188 Cal.App.4th 1024, 1031 [recognizing that Interstate Compact on Placement of Children shares characteristics of both contractual agreements and statutory law].)

"The contractual nature of a compact is demonstrated by its adoption: **"There is an offer** (a proposal to enact virtually verbatim statutes by each member state), an **acceptance** (enactment of the statutes by the member states), and **consideration** (the settlement of a dispute, creation of an association, or some mechanism to address an issue of mutual interest.)" (Broun on Compacts, supra, § 1.2.2, p. 18.) **As is true of other contracts, the contract clause of the United States Constitution shields compacts from impairment by the states**. (*Aveline v. Bd. of Probation and Parole*, supra, 729 A.2d at p. 1257, fn. 10.) Therefore, upon entering a compact, "it takes precedence over the subsequent statutes of signatory states and, as such, a state may not unilaterally nullify, revoke or amend one of its compacts if the compact does not so provide." (Ibid.; accord, *Intern. Union v. Del. River Joint Toll Bridge* (3d Cir. 2002) 311 F.3d 273, 281.) **Thus interstate compacts are unique in that they empower one state legislature—namely the one that enacted the agreement—to bind all future legislatures to certain principles governing the subject matter of the compact**. (Broun on Compacts, supra, § 1.2.2, p. 17.)

"As explained and summarized in *C.T. Hellmuth v. Washington Metro. Area Trans.* (D.Md. 1976) 414 F.Supp. 408, 409 (*Hellmuth*): '**Upon entering into an interstate compact, a state effectively surrenders a portion of its sovereignty; the compact governs the relations of the parties with respect to the subject matter of the agreement and is superior to both prior and subsequent law. Further, when enacted, a compact constitutes not only law, but a contract which may not be amended, modified, or otherwise altered without the consent of all parties**. It, therefore, appears settled that one party may not enact legislation which would impose burdens upon the compact absent the concurrence of the other signatories.' Cast a little differently, '[i]t is within the competency of a State, which is a party to a compact with another State, to legislate in respect of matters covered by the compact so long as such legislative action is in approbation and not in reprobation of the compact.' (*Henderson v. Delaware River Joint Toll Bridge Com'm* (1949) 66 A.2d 843, 849-450.) Nor may states amend a compact by enacting legislation that is substantially similar, unless the compact itself contains language enabling a state or states to modify it through legislation ' "concurred in" ' by the other states. (*Intern. Union v. Del. River Joint Toll Bridge*, supra, 311 F.3d at pp. 276-280.)"[327] [Emphasis added]

The California court thus rejected a California state law overriding the Multistate Tax Compact as unconstitutional.[328]

Although state courts are more than capable of enforcing interstate compacts (and, in particular, voiding state legislation that attempts to evade a particular state's obligations under a compact), interstate compacts may be litigated (and often are litigated) at the U.S. Supreme Court, as explained in *Interstate Disputes: The Supreme Court's Original Jurisdiction*.[329]

The U.S. Constitution states:

> "**In all Cases** affecting Ambassadors, other public Ministers and Consuls, and those **in which a State shall be Party, the Supreme Court shall have original Jurisdiction**."[330]

Williams supports his next legally incorrect statement (that a compact for which congressional consent is unnecessary is "merely" a state law and not an enforceable contract) with a totally inapplicable legal authority. Williams says:

> "A subsequent legislature can amend or repeal the NPVC consistent with the state's own constitutionally prescribed legislative process. [Williams' footnote 175 appears here]"[331]

Williams' authority for this legally incorrect statement (that is, his own footnote 175) is the 1951 U.S. Supreme Court decision in *West Virginia ex rel. Dyer v. Sim.*[332] However, this case is not about a state being allowed to evade its obligations under an interstate compact, but about the U.S. Supreme Court ruling that West Virginia could *not* evade its obligations under the compact. What the U.S. Supreme Court said was:

---

[327] *The Gillette Company et al. v. Franchise Tax Board. Court of Appeal of the State of California*, First Appellate District, Division Four. July 24, 2012. Pages 9–11. Appendix GG contains the full opinion.

[328] After the California court's decision in *The Gillette Company et al. v. Franchise Tax Board*, the state of California enacted a law (Senate Bill 1015 of 2012) exercising California's right to withdraw from the Multistate Tax Compact. After the effective date of the statute withdrawing from the compact, the state of California became free to change its formula for taxing multi-state businesses. Senate Bill 1015 took effect as a "budget trailer" on July 27, 2012.

[329] Zimmerman, Joseph F. 2006. *Interstate Disputes: The Supreme Court's Original Jurisdiction*. Albany, NY: State University of New York Press.

[330] U.S. Constitution. Article III, section 2, clause 2.

[331] Williams, Norman R. Reforming the Electoral College: Federalism, majoritarianism, and the perils of sub-constitutional change. 100 *Georgetown Law Journal* 173. November 2011. Page 216.

[332] *West Virginia ex rel. Dyer v. Sims*, 341 U.S. 22, 33-34 (1951).

"But a compact is after all a legal document. . . . **It requires no elaborate argument to reject the suggestion that an agreement** solemnly entered into between States by those who alone have political authority to speak for a State **can be unilaterally nullified**, or given final meaning by an organ of one of the contracting States. **A State cannot be its own ultimate judge in a controversy with a sister State.**"[333] [Emphasis added]

Williams' final legally incorrect statement and inappropriate footnote are even more astonishing.

"A prior legislature may not bind subsequent legislatures through subconstitutional measures, such as statutes or congressionally unratified interstate compacts. [Williams' footnote 176 appears here]"[334]

Williams cites two authorities for this incorrect statement in his footnote 176:
- the 1996 Nebraska case of *State ex rel. Stenberg v. Moore*,[335] and
- the 1936 Pennsylvania case of *Visor v. Waters*.[336]

In fact, neither case supports Williams' statement, and the ruling in one of them is exactly opposite to what Williams claims.

State ex rel. Stenberg v. Moore was concerned with a 1993 Nebraska state *law* (Legislative Bill 507) that attempted to require future legislatures to provide certain fiscal estimates and provide appropriations at the time when that future legislature took any action that might increase the number of inmates in the state's correctional facilities.

Legislative Bill 507 provided:

"(1) **When any legislation is enacted after June 30, 1993**, which is projected in accordance with this section to increase the total adult inmate population or total juvenile population in state correctional facilities, **the Legislature shall include in the legislation an estimate** of the operating costs resulting from such increased population for the first four fiscal years during which the legislation will be in effect. . . .

(3) **The Legislature shall provide by specific itemized appropriation**, for the fiscal year or years for which it can make valid appropriations, **an amount sufficient to meet the cost indicated in the estimate contained in the legislation for such fiscal year or years**. The appropriation shall be enacted in the same legislative session in which the legislation

---

[333] *West Virginia ex rel. Dyer v. Sims.* 341 U.S. 22 at 28. 1950.

[334] Williams, Norman R. Reforming the Electoral College: Federalism, majoritarianism, and the perils of subconstitutional change. 100 *Georgetown Law Journal* 173. November 2011. Page 216.

[335] *State ex rel. Stenberg v. Moore*, 544 N.W.2d 344, 348 (Neb. 1996).

[336] *Visor v. Waters*, 182 A. 241, 247 (Pa. 1936).

is enacted and shall be contained in a bill which does not contain appropriations for other programs.

"(4) **Any legislation enacted after June 30, 1993, which does not include the estimates required by this section and is not accompanied by the required appropriation shall be null and void.**" [Emphasis added]

In *State ex rel. Stenberg* in 1996, the Nebraska Supreme Court made the unsurprising ruling that it was unconstitutional for the legislature to attempt to bind succeeding legislatures by means of an ordinary state statute.

Significantly, in its ruling, the Nebraska Supreme Court specifically recognized interstate compacts as one of the rare exceptions to the general principle that one legislature cannot bind a future legislature:

> "One legislature cannot bind a succeeding legislature or restrict or limit the power of its successors to enact legislation, **except as to valid contracts entered into by it,** and as to rights which have actually vested under its acts, and no action by one branch of the legislature can bind a subsequent session of the same branch."[337] [Emphasis added]

Thus, the 1996 Nebraska case of *State ex rel. Stenberg v. Moore* cited by Williams is not a legal authority supporting Williams' statement, but a ruling making it clear that Williams is just plain wrong.

Williams' citation of the 1936 Pennsylvania case of *Visor v. Waters* also fails to support Williams' claim. *Visor v. Waters* was concerned with an attempt by one house of the Pennsylvania legislature to nullify a previously enacted state statute by means of a resolution passed only by the one house. *Visor v. Waters* was not even about a state statute (much less an interstate compact). The court's ruling said:

> "It is a settled rule that one Legislature cannot bind another and no action by one House could bind a subsequent session of that same House, but when the constituent bodies are united in a statute, **a single House, by a mere resolution cannot set aside and nullify the positive provisions of a law. . . . A new law can do that, but nothing less than a new law can.**"[338] [Emphasis added]

The fact is that there are no applicable citations in support of Williams' statements about the unenforceability of interstate compacts because Williams is just plain wrong.

---

[337] *State ex rel. Stenberg v. Moore*, 544 N.W.2d 344, 348 (Neb. 1996).

[338] *Visor v. Waters*. 41 *Dauphin County Reports.* Volume 219 at 227. 1935. In 1936, the Pennsylvania Supreme Court upheld the lower court decision by saying, "The judgment in this case is affirmed on the full and comprehensive opinion of the learned President Judge of the lower court, which is printed at length in 41 *Dauphin County Reports* 219. *Visor v. Waters*, 182 A. 241, 247 (Pa. 1936).

Another example of a compact that did not require congressional consent is the Interstate Compact for the Placement of Children. All 50 States and the District of Columbia are parties to this compact.[339]

In the 1991 case of *McComb v. Wambaugh*, the U.S. Court of Appeals for Third Circuit ruled that the compact took precedence over state law.

> **"The Constitution recognizes compacts** in Article I, section 10, clause 3, which reads, 'No state shall, without the Consent of the Congress . . . enter into any Agreement or Compact with another State.' **Despite the broad wording of the clause Congressional approval is necessary only when a Compact is 'directed to the formation of any combination tending to the increase of political power in the States, which may encroach upon or interfere with the just supremacy of the United States.'** *United States Steel Corp. v. Multistate Tax Comm'n*, 434 U.S. 452, 468, 98 S.Ct. 799, 810, 54 L.Ed.2d 682 (1978) (quoting *Virginia v. Tennessee*, 148 U.S. 503, 519, 13 S.Ct. 728, 734, 37 L.Ed. 537 (1893)).

> **"The Interstate Compact on Placement of Children has not received Congressional consent. Rather than altering the balance of power between the states and the federal government, this Compact focuses wholly on adoption and foster care of children—areas of jurisdiction historically retained by the states**. *In re Burrus*, 136 U.S. 586, 593-94, 10 S.Ct. 850, 852-53, 34 L.Ed. 500 (1890); *Lehman v. Lycoming County Children's Services Agency*, 648 F.2d 135, 143 (3d Cir. 1981) (en banc), aff'd, 458 U.S. 502, 102 S.Ct. 3231, 73 L.Ed.2d 928 (1982). **Congressional consent, therefore, was not necessary for the Compact's legitimacy."**

> **"Because Congressional consent was neither given nor required, the Compact does not express federal law.** Cf. *Cuyler v. Adams*, 449 U.S. 433, 440, 101 S.Ct. 703, 707, 66 L.Ed.2d 641 (1981). **Consequently, this Compact must be construed as state law.** See Engdahl, Construction of Interstate Compacts: A Questionable Federal Question, 51 *Va.L.Rev.* 987, 1017 (1965) ('[T]he construction of a compact not requiring consent . . . will not present a federal question. . . .).

---

[339] The Interstate Compact for the Placement of Children was written with the expectation that congressional consent would not be required if its membership were limited to states of the United States, the District of Columbia, and Puerto Rico. However, the compact invites the federal government of Canada and Canadian provincial governments to become members. The compact specifically recognizes that congressional consent would be required if a Canadian entity desired to become a party to the compact by saying, "This compact shall be open to joinder by any state, territory, or possession of the United States, the District of Columbia, the Commonwealth of Puerto Rico, and, with the consent of congress, the government of Canada or any province thereof." At the present time, no Canadian entity has sought membership in the compact.

"Having entered into a contract, a participant state may not unilaterally change its terms. A Compact also takes precedence over
statutory law in member states."[340] [Emphasis added]

9.12. MYTHS ABOUT CAMPAIGN SPENDING AND LENGTH

9.12.1. MYTH: Campaign spending would skyrocket if candidates had to campaign in all 50 states.

QUICK ANSWER:

- The total amount of money that is spent on presidential campaigns is controlled by available money—not by the (virtually unlimited) number of opportunities to spend money. The National Popular Vote compact does not increase the amount of money available from political donors.

- Under both the current state-by-state winner-take-all system and nationwide voting for President, candidates allocate the pool of money available to them from donors in the manner that they believe will maximize their chance of winning. Under the current system, virtually all of the money (and campaign events) are concentrated in a handful of closely divided battleground states, while four out of five states and four out of five voters get virtually no attention. Under a national popular vote, every voter in every state would be politically relevant, and money would therefore be spent differently.

MORE DETAILED ANSWER:

The total amount of money that a presidential campaign can spend is determined by the amount of money that it can raise—not by the virtually unlimited opportunities for spending money.

There are two major steps in campaign budgeting.

First, presidential campaigns and their supporters try to raise as much money as possible from all sources available to them. All serious presidential campaigns raise money nationally, even though they concentrate their campaigning to closely divided battleground states. Table 9.2 shows the contributions to the 2008 presidential campaign from residents of each state.

Second, after an organization ascertains how much money it can raise, it engages in a resource-allocation process in order to decide how to spend the money in the most advantageous way. The controlling factor in allocating resources is the state-by-state winner-take-all method of awarding electoral votes.

Under the current state winner-take-all statutes, campaigns concentrate their

---

[340] *McComb v. Wambaugh*, 934 F.2d 474 at 479 (3d Cir. 1991).

spending on a handful of closely divided battleground states. They do this because they have nothing to lose, and nothing to gain, by trying to win votes in states where they are comfortably ahead or hopelessly behind.

Under the current system, 99% of the money raised in the 2004 presidential campaign was spent in just 16 states. In 2008, candidates concentrated 98% of their campaign events and ad money in just 15 states.[341] In 2012, four out of five states were ignored by the presidential campaigns (section 9.2.1).

Under the current system, a rational resource-allocation process for presidential campaigns involves ignoring all but the closely divided battleground states.

The National Popular Vote compact would not increase the total number of dollars available from donors. Candidates and their supporters would continue to raise as much money as they possibly can on a national basis. The mere existence of several dozen additional states that could not be ignored would not, in itself, generate any additional money.

The resource-allocation process would be different under the National Popular Vote plan than under the current system. The reason is that every voter in every state and the District of Columbia would be politically relevant under a national popular vote. Therefore, it would be suicidal for a presidential campaign to ignore 40 of the 50 states. The available amount of money would be reallocated because every voter in every state would be politically relevant.

Under a national popular vote, it would be impossible to operate a campaign in all 50 states at the same per-capita level of intensity as recent campaigns in a battleground state such as Ohio.

Consider Ohio and Illinois. Both states had 20 electoral votes in the 2008 election. Under the current state-by-state winner-take-all system, Illinois was ignored, while Ohio received an enormous amount of attention in the general-election campaign. In 2008, Ohio received 62 of the 300 post-convention campaign events (table 9.1) and about $17,000,000 in advertising (table 9.2), whereas Illinois received no post-convention campaign events and only $53,896 in advertising.

Although one cannot predict exactly how a future presidential campaign might unfold under the National Popular Vote plan, it would be suicidal, for example, for a presidential campaign to ignore Illinois. Some of the available pool of money would necessarily be reallocated to Illinois because a vote in Illinois would be just as valuable as a vote in Ohio under the National Popular Vote plan. In all likelihood, Ohio and Illinois would receive approximately equal attention (in both campaign events and spending) because they are approximately equal in population.

The role of unpaid volunteers would change under a national popular vote. Under the current system, there is considerable grassroots campaigning for President in the

---

[341] http://fairvote.org/tracker/?page=27&pressmode=showspecific&showarticle=230.

closely divided battleground states because people in those states are aware that their votes and the votes of their neighbors matter. However, in the spectator states, there is no significant grassroots campaigning for President under the current system (except for raising money, making phone calls into battleground states, and traveling to battleground states to campaign). Under a national popular vote, campaigning would become worthwhile in every state. Increased volunteer activity would partially counter-balance the effect of large donations in political campaigns.

9.12.2. MYTH: The length of presidential campaigns would increase if candidates had to travel to all 50 states.

QUICK ANSWER:

- Critics of a national popular vote for President argue that presidential campaigns would lengthen if presidential candidates had to "travel to 50 states to court voters."
- The National Popular Vote compact does not change the amount of time between a candidate's nomination and Election Day.
- There was time to conduct 300 post-convention campaign events in 2008. Under the current state-by-state winner-take-all rule, candidates allocated two-thirds of their time to just six states.
- There was time to conduct 253 post-convention campaign events in 2012. Under the current state-by-state winner-take-all rule, two thirds of the presidential and vice-presidential post-convention campaign events were conducted in just four states (Ohio, Florida, Virginia, and Iowa).
- The effect of the National Popular Vote compact would be that candidates would have to allocate the time available very differently than they do now. Every voter in every state would be politically relevant in every presidential election.
- We view the fact that the National Popular Vote compact would force presidential candidates to "travel to 50 states to court voters" as a highly desirable benefit—not a disadvantage.

MORE DETAILED ANSWER:

In an article entitled "The Electoral College is Brilliant, and We Would Be Insane to Abolish It," Walter Hickey writes:

"Nobody wants to make the presidential election season any longer . . ..

"If you make it so a President has to travel to 50 states to court voters, that's going to take time. . . .

"Dragging it out more months, jet setting from California to New York on weekends, that would make an already annoying election period into a downright intolerable one.

"The best candidate would be the one with either the most frequent flier miles or the strongest immune system."[342] [Emphasis added]

As Hickey correctly points out, the National Popular Vote compact would force presidential candidates to "travel to 50 states to court voters." We view that as a highly desirable benefit of a national popular vote for President.

There was time to conduct 300 post-convention campaign events in 2008. Candidates necessarily must allocate the available amount of time to various activities.

Today, the state-by-state winner-take-all rule determines how presidential candidates allocate their time (and other resources).

Under the current state-by-state winner-take-all rule, candidates allocated two-thirds of their time to just six states.

There was time to conduct 253 post-convention campaign events in 2012. Under the current state-by-state winner-take-all rule, two thirds of the presidential and vice-presidential post-convention campaign events were conducted in just four states in 2012 (Ohio, Florida, Virginia, and Iowa).

The National Popular Vote compact cannot, and does not, change the amount of time between a candidate's nomination and Election Day.

The effect of a national popular vote for President would be that candidates would allocate the time available very differently than they do now. Under a national popular vote, every voter in every state would be politically relevant in every presidential election.

Under the current state-by-state winner-take-all system, New Hampshire received 13 of the 253 campaign events in 2012, while the 12 other smallest states each received none. Under the National Popular Vote plan, it would be inconceivable that presidential candidates would campaign in only one small state, while ignoring the 12 other small states. Most likely, *each* of the 13 smallest states would receive one campaign event under a nationwide vote for President.

Although one cannot predict exactly how a future presidential campaign might unfold under the National Popular Vote plan, a good prediction would be that presidential candidates would probably distribute their limited number of campaign events among the states roughly in proportion to population.

---

[342] Hickey, Walter. 2012. The Electoral College is brilliant, and we would be insane to abolish it. *Business Insider*. October 3, 2012. http://www.businessinsider.com/the-electoral-college-is-brilliant-2012-10.

9.13. MYTHS ABOUT ELECTION ADMINISTRATION

9.13.1. MYTH: Local election officials would be burdened by the National Popular Vote compact.

QUICK ANSWER:

- Local and county elections officials would conduct elections exactly as they do now.

MORE DETAILED ANSWER:

Under the National Popular Vote compact, a presidential election would be administered inside each state in the same way that it is now administered. The compact makes no changes in a state's laws or procedures for preparing ballots, operating polling places, handling absentee ballots or early voting, or counting votes at the precinct, city, town, or county level. Local and county election officials would conduct elections exactly as they do now.

The National Popular Vote compact would make no change in the process of aggregating the vote counts from the local level in order to ascertain the total number of popular votes cast in the state for each presidential slate.

9.13.2. MYTH: The state's chief elections official would be burdened by the National Popular Vote compact.

QUICK ANSWER:

- The state's chief election official would not be burdened by the National Popular Vote compact, because the only difference with respect to the current winner-take-all system is that the chief elections official would add up the popular vote totals for each presidential slate in all 50 states and the District of Columbia to determine the national popular vote winner.

MORE DETAILED ANSWER:

The only change introduced by the National Popular Vote compact occurs *after* a state has finished tallying the statewide total number of popular votes cast for each presidential slate.

At that point, the votes cast for each presidential slate in all 50 states and the District of Columbia would be added together to produce a national grand total for each presidential slate (section 6.3.3). This vote total would be, of course, the official version of the same adding process that the media, the political parties, and various watchdog groups already do on Election Night and in the days immediately following each presidential election.

Under the compact, the presidential slate with the largest national grand total from all 50 states and the District of Columbia would be designated as the "national popular vote winner." The chief election official of each state belonging to the compact would then certify the election of the entire slate of presidential electors that is affiliated with the "national popular vote winner." For example, if the Republican slate is the "national popular vote winner," the state's chief election official in every state belonging to the compact would certify the election of the entire slate of Republican presidential electors.

The effect of the National Popular Vote compact would be that all the presidential electors of all states belonging to the compact would be affiliated with the presidential slate that received the largest total number of popular votes in all 50 states and the District of Columbia. These presidential electors from the states belonging to the compact would collectively represent the nationwide will of the voters.

Under the compact, the presidential electors would meet in their states, as they do now, in mid-December and cast their electoral votes.

Because the compact would only go into effect when it has been enacted by states possessing a majority of the electoral votes, the presidential slate receiving the most popular votes from all 50 states and the District of Columbia would receive a majority of the electoral votes in the Electoral College.

The fiscal analysts associated with virtually every state legislature that has considered the National Popular Vote bill have concluded that there would be no significant additional administrative burden or financial cost associated with implementing the compact.

9.13.3. MYTH: The National Popular Vote compact would burden the state's chief election official with the need to judge the election returns of other states.

QUICK ANSWER:
- The National Popular Vote compact would operate in a manner identical to the current system in that no state election official would have the need or power to judge the presidential election returns of any other state.
- Each candidate's popular vote total in each state would be certified using the same "Certificates of Ascertainment" as are required by existing federal law.

MORE DETAILED ANSWER:
The mechanics for counting and tallying votes at the precinct, city, town, county, and state levels would be the same under the National Popular Vote compact as they are under the current system.

Neither the current system nor the National Popular Vote compact requires—or permits—any state election official to become involved in judging the election returns of other states.

Existing federal law (the "safe harbor" provision in section 5 of Title 3 of the United

States Code) specifies that a state's "final determination" of its presidential election re-turns is "conclusive" in the counting of votes by Congress (if done in a timely manner and in accordance with laws that existed prior to Election Day).

The wording of the National Popular Vote compact is patterned directly after the existing federal "safe harbor" provision. It would require each state to treat as "con-clusive" every other state's "final determination" of its vote for President. Clause 5 of Article III of the National Popular Vote compact provides:

> "The chief election official of each member state shall treat as conclusive an official statement containing the number of popular votes in a state for each presidential slate made by the day established by federal law for mak-ing a state's final determination conclusive as to the counting of electoral votes by Congress."

Accordingly, assuming each state complies with federal law, no state would have any power to examine or judge the presidential election returns of any other state under the National Popular Vote compact.

9.13.4. MYTH: The National Popular Vote compact would be costly.

QUICK ANSWER:

- The National Popular Vote compact would not impose any fiscal burden on any state because voting in presidential elections would be conducted at the precinct, local, and county levels in the same manner as it is today.
- When the National Popular Vote bill has been considered by state legislatures, state fiscal officials have uniformly concluded that it would have no significant fiscal impact.

MORE DETAILED ANSWER:

Under the National Popular Vote compact, the mechanics for counting votes for Presi-dent at the precinct, city, town, county, and state levels would be the same as they are today.

The only administrative difference would be that, after counting all the votes in the state, each state's chief election officer would add up the popular vote totals from all 50 states and the District of Columbia to determine which slate of presidential elec-tors would be called upon to cast the state's electoral votes.

When the National Popular Vote bill has been introduced in state legislatures, state fiscal officials have uniformly concluded that it has no significant fiscal impact on the state. In most states, this determination has been explicitly stated in the finan-cial analysis that is routinely produced by the legislature's professional staff prior to the time that the legislature considers the bill.

9.13.5. MYTH: Post-election audits could not be conducted under a national popular vote.

QUICK ANSWER:

- There is nothing in the National Popular Vote plan that prevents a state from auditing its election results.

MORE DETAILED ANSWER:

The arguments in favor of conducting audits apply to all elections, regardless of the office being filled. The statistical procedures for conducting audits are applicable to all elections.

Audits are conducted in some states today, thanks to statutory audit procedures and administratively established audit procedures.

Federal legislation has been proposed to require audits in all federal elections—including presidential elections. For example, the proposed Voter Confidence and Increased Accessibility Act of 2009 (H.R. 2894 of the 111th Congress introduced by New Jersey Congressman Rush Holt and a considerable number of co-sponsors) would require audits for all federal elections, including presidential elections.

One important difference between presidential elections and elections for the U.S. House and U.S. Senate is that the U.S. Constitution establishes a strict overall national schedule for finalizing the results of a presidential election. The existing constitutional provisions (and existing supporting federal statutes) apply equally to elections conducted under both the National Popular Vote plan and the current system.

Specifically, the U.S. Constitution requires that the Electoral College meet on a uniform nationwide day in every state.[343] Congress has specified the Monday after the second Wednesday in December as the date for the meeting of the Electoral College.[344]

Moreover, the U.S. Supreme Court has made it clear that the states are expected to make their "final determination" six days before the Electoral College meets (the so-called "safe harbor" day established by section 5 of Title 3 of the United States Code).[345]

Thus, under both the current system and the National Popular Vote plan, all counting, recounting, and judicial proceedings must be conducted so as to reach a "final determination" by the "safe harbor" day prior to the uniform nationwide date for the meeting of the Electoral College in mid-December.

Many of the most important reasons for conducting an audit are lost if insuffi-

---

[343] U.S. Constitution. Article II, section 1, clause 4.

[344] United States Code. Title 3, chapter 1, section 7.

[345] For example, in 2008, the election was Tuesday, November 4, and the "safe harbor" day was 33 days later on Monday, December 8. The Electoral College met on the following Monday, December 15 (the Monday after the second Wednesday in December). Congress met to count votes on January 6, 2009. According to the Constitution, the outgoing President's term ended on January 20, 2009.

cient time remains available to conduct a full recount if the audit discovers a problem. Indeed, in the "Principles and Best Practices for Post-Election Audits" endorsed by numerous organizations involved in election-administration issues (including the Brennan Center for Justice, Common Cause, Verified Voting, and numerous state-level groups), one of the best practices is:

> "Post-election audits must be completed prior to finalizing official election results and must either verify the outcome or, through a 100% recount, correct the outcome."

Thus, in the case of presidential elections, a practical and realistic schedule for audits must allow time for a potential full recount (and also time for potential post-recount litigation) prior to the uniform nationwide day for meeting of the Electoral College. Thus, audits in presidential elections must be conducted in an expeditious and timely manner (soon after Election Day) so as to allow time for a potential full recount and potential post-recount litigation.

Fortunately, audits do not take long. Today, audits are routinely conducted within a couple of days by the states that have statutory audit procedures or administratively established audit procedures. There is thus no reason why audits cannot be conducted for presidential elections under either the current system or the National Popular Vote approach.

Proposed legislation such as H.R. 2894 provides for audits of presidential elections. This (generally excellent) proposal could be improved by amending the formula for determining the intensity of auditing that is required in presidential elections so that the level of intensity of the audit is determined by the apparent margin in the nationwide count (as opposed to the apparent statewide count) in case the appointment of presidential electors is based on the national popular vote. Alternatively, the highest level of intensity already provided for in H.R. 2894 for the audit might be *automatically* applied to presidential counts. Note that this suggested improvement concerning the issue of intensity does not relate to whether an audit will be conducted—but merely to the audit's level of intensity.

In short, there is nothing in the National Popular Vote plan that would prevent a post-election audit.

9.13.6. MYTH: Provisional ballots would create problems in a nationwide popular vote because voters in all 50 states (instead of just 10 or so states) would matter in determining the winner.

QUICK ANSWER:

- There is a far greater chance that provisional ballots will create problems in a presidential election under the current state-by-state winner-take-all system than under a system in which there is a single national pool of votes and in which the winner is the candidate receiving the most popular votes nationwide.

- There should be no concern about the delay caused by counting provisional ballots, because the U.S. Constitution establishes a strict overall national schedule for finalizing the results of presidential elections. All counting, recounting, and judicial proceedings must be conducted so as to reach a "final determination" prior to the uniform nationwide date for the meeting of the Electoral College in mid-December. States are expected to make their "final determination" six days before the Electoral College meets (the so-called "safe harbor" date). The nation knows, from experience in 2000, that the outcome of the presidential election must be resolved (one way or the other) in accordance with the schedule specified by the U.S. Constitution.

- We do not view the proper counting of all legitimate votes as an evil. Electing the right person to office is more important than a slight delay in ascertaining the outcome.

MORE DETAILED ANSWER:

The Help America Vote Act of 2002 (HAVA) permits a voter to cast a "provisional ballot" under certain circumstances, including (but not limited to) situations in which:

- the voter does not have the type of identification (if any) that may be required by state law;

- the voter is not listed on the election roll for a particular precinct (perhaps because the voter went to the wrong polling location or because the voter recently moved); and

- the voter arrives at the polling place on Election Day but previously requested an absentee ballot (thus raising the question of whether the voter has already voted).

A provisional ballot is typically inserted into a large envelope whose exterior contains an explanation as to why the ballot was cast on a provisional basis. The outside of the envelope contains the voter's signature and often contains additional identifying information beyond the voter's address (e.g., a driver's license number).

Provisional ballots are usually counted within six to 10 days after the election (depending on state law).

Processing provisional ballots is a tedious administrative process. The specific processing required depends on the reason why the provisional ballot was cast in the first place. For example, if a ballot was cast provisionally because of lack of certain required identification documents, the signature on the outside of the envelope may be compared visually with registration records before the provisional ballot is approved. If a driver's license number is used as part of the identification process, the number provided by the voter on the outside of the envelope may be compared with the state's database of driver's licenses. According to a *Miami Herald* story:

"Each provisional ballot takes about 30 minutes to review and inspect, said Ron Labasky, counsel for the state association of election supervisors."[346]

According to the U.S. Election Assistance Commission (a body established by the Help America Vote Act of 2002), about two-thirds of all provisional ballots are found to have been cast by legitimate voters and, therefore, eventually counted.[347]

Hans von Spakovsky has stated that a nationwide election of the President

"would . . . lead to . . . contentious fights over provisional ballots."[348]

Hans von Spakovsky has also stated:

"Every additional vote found anywhere in the country could make the difference to the losing candidate."[349] [Emphasis added]

We agree with von Spakovsky that any vote "anywhere in the country could make the difference" in a nationwide vote for President. Indeed, the most important reason to adopt the National Popular Vote plan is to make *every* vote in *every* state politically relevant in *every* presidential election. We do not view the fact that every vote "could make the difference" as an evil.

Von Spakovsky continues:

"Provisional ballots may not affect the outcome of the majority vote within a state under the current system because the number of provisional ballots is less than the margin of victory. However, **if the total number of provisional ballots issued in all of the states is greater than the margin of victory**, a national battle over provisional ballots could ensue.

"Losing candidates would then have the incentive to hire lawyers to monitor (and litigate) the decision process of local election officials. . . .

"Lawyers contesting the legitimacy of the decisions made by local election officials on provisional ballots nationwide could significantly delay the outcome of a national election."[350] [Emphasis added]

---

[346] Van Sickler, Michael. Provisional ballots spike, but Florida elections supervisors say they're not needed. *Miami Herald.* December 17, 2012. http://www.miamiherald.com/2012/12/17/3145753/provisional-ballots -spike-but.html.

[347] Langley, Karen and McNulty, Timothy. Verifying provisional ballots may be key to election. *Pittsburgh Post-Gazette.* August 26, 2012.

[348] Von Spakovsky, Hans. Popular vote scheme. *The Foundry.* October 18, 2011.

[349] Von Spakovsky, Hans. Destroying the Electoral College: The Anti-Federalist National Popular Vote Scheme. Legal memo. October 27, 2011. http://www.heritage.org/research/reports/2011/10/destroying-the-electoral -college-the-anti-federalist-national-popular-vote-scheme.

[350] Von Spakovsky, Hans. Destroying the Electoral College: The Anti-Federalist National Popular Vote Scheme. Legal memo. October 27, 2011. http://www.heritage.org/research/reports/2011/10/destroying -the-electoral-college-the-anti-federalist-national-popular-vote-scheme.

Our view is that ballots cast by legitimate voters should be counted. We also believe that a candidate who is slightly behind in a close election has every right to "monitor" the handling of provisional ballots and, if necessary, "litigate" the question of whether a particular voter is legally entitled to have his or her vote counted. A losing candidate is certainly entitled to present his or her case to the courts "if the total number of provisional ballots . . . is greater than the margin of victory" based on the non-provisional ballots.

We do not view the proper counting of all legitimate votes as an evil; however, if anyone entertains this viewpoint, provisional ballots are far more likely to create a problem under the current state-by-state winner-take-all system than under a nationwide vote.

Under the current state-by-state winner-take-all system, the outcome of the national election frequently depends on the outcome of one or more closely divided battleground states. The number of provisional ballots in closely divided states is typically larger than the initial margin of victory based on the non-provisional ballots. Thus, even when there is a clear winner of the national popular vote, the possibility exists, of a dispute involving provisional ballots in a closely divided battleground state that could, under the current system, determine the outcome of the national election.

For example, in 2004, George W. Bush had a nationwide lead of 3,012,171 popular votes—far greater than the number of provisional ballots nationwide. There has been an exceptionally high amount of provisional voting in Ohio in recent elections, including 2004. In 2004, there were more than 150,000 provisional ballots in Ohio, and Bush's margin was 118,601 in Ohio in 2004.[351] The outcome of the 2004 election would have been reversed with a switch of 59,393 votes out of a total of 5,627,903 votes in Ohio. On the Wednesday after Election Day, Senator John Kerry decided that the provisional ballots were unlikely to reverse the apparent outcome in Ohio. If the number of provisional ballots had been somewhat higher or if Bush's margin among the already counted regular ballots had been somewhat lower, the provisional ballots in Ohio would have decided the Presidency in 2004 (despite Bush's already known nationwide lead of three million votes).

There has been about one such "near miss" election each decade under the state-by-state winner-take-all system. Table 1.23 shows there have been six presidential elections since World War II in which a shift of a relatively small number of votes in one or two states would have elected (and, of course, in 2000, did elect) a presidential candidate who lost the popular vote nationwide.

In 1976, for example, Jimmy Carter led Gerald Ford by 1,682,970 votes nationwide; however, a shift of 3,687 votes in Hawaii and 5,559 votes in Ohio would have elected Ford.

---

[351] Langley, Karen and McNulty, Timothy. Verifying provisional ballots may be key to election. *Pittsburgh Post-Gazette.* August 26, 2012.

In 1968, a shift of 10,245 in Missouri and 67,481 in Illinois would have elected Hubert Humphrey as President despite Richard Nixon's nationwide lead of 510,645.

The 2000 presidential election was decided by 537 votes out of a total of 5,963,110 votes in Florida—far greater than the number of provisional ballots that are currently cast in Florida.

Although the 2008 presidential election was not as close as 2000 or 2004, a relatively small number of votes determined the outcome in several states in which the number of provisional ballots exceeded the leading candidate's margin in that state, including Missouri (McCain's 3,903-vote margin out of 2,925,205 votes), North Carolina (Obama's 14,177-vote margin out of 4,310,789 votes), and Indiana (Obama's 28,391-vote margin out of 2,751,054).

There were nine closely divided battleground states in the 2012 election (section 1.3). Thus, there were nine states where provisional ballots could potentially have played a decisive role under the current state-by-state winner-take-all system.

Provisional ballots can be expected to produce disputes in future presidential elections because of the recent enactment of voter-identification laws in some closely divided battleground states. For example, although the voter-identification law enacted in Pennsylvania in 2012 did not take effect in time for the 2012 presidential election, it is expected to take effect in 2013.

The likelihood that provisional ballots might trigger a dispute in a presidential election is higher under the current state-by-state winner-take-all system than under a system in which there is a single national pool of votes.

A November 6, 2012, article in *National Journal* entitled "The Ohio Vote Count Could Be a Mess" stated:

> "The Buckeye State has supplanted its Southern cousin Florida as the marquee battleground of the 2012 presidential election—the state most likely to tip the race to either President Obama or Mitt Romney. . . .

> "Ohio also bears another, more ominous similarity to the 2000 Florida: If a close race demands a recount, conditions are ripe for a repeat of the delays, confusion, and chaos that racked the Sunshine State. And just like 12 years ago, the state's ultimate winner could very well determine who is the next president. . . .

> **"The most obvious flash point involves provisional ballots, those cast if a voter's eligibility is in question. Election officials don't count provisional or absentee ballots until 10 days after Election Day. In case of a narrow margin and with hundreds of thousands of such votes still to be counted, neither candidate could claim victory. (Ohio recorded 200,000 provisional ballots in 2008, a number expected to rise this time.**"[352] [Emphasis added]

---

[352] Roarty, Alex. The Ohio vote count could be a mess. *National Journal.* November 6, 2012.

A similar issue arises in connection with military and overseas absentee ballots. Under the Military and Overseas Voter Empowerment Act (MOVE), each state determines its deadline for receiving absentee ballots from military and overseas voters.

Although the process of properly counting all the legitimate votes may take some time, there should be no concern about the delay. Electing the right person to office is more important than a slight delay in ascertaining the outcome. As discussed in detail in section 9.15.3, the U.S. Constitution establishes a strict overall national schedule for finalizing the results of presidential elections. These existing provisions apply equally to elections conducted under the current state-by-state winner-take-all system as well as elections conducted under the National Popular Vote plan. All counting, recounting, and judicial proceedings must be conducted so as to reach a "final determination" prior to the uniform nationwide date for the meeting of the Electoral College in mid-December. The U.S. Supreme Court has made it clear that the states are expected to make their "final determination" six days before the Electoral College meets (the so-called "safe harbor" date established by section 5 of Title 3 of the United States Code). The nation knows, from experience in 2000, that the outcome of a presidential election must be resolved (one way or the other) in accordance with the schedule specified by the U.S. Constitution.

The possibility of disputes over provisional ballots is an example of a potential problem that is more likely to occur, and more likely to matter, under the current state-by-state winner-take-all system than the National Popular Vote plan.

9.13.7. MYTH: Knowledge of the winner would be delayed under a national popular vote because the votes of all 50 states (instead of just 10 or so battleground states) would matter.

QUICK ANSWER:

- Because of the current state-by-state winner-take-all rule, knowledge about the winner of the Electoral College in 2000 was delayed until 34 days after Election Day despite the fact that the winner of the national popular vote was apparent.
- There is a far greater chance that knowledge of the winner of a presidential election will be delayed under the current state-by-state winner-take-all system than under a system in which there is a single national pool of votes and in which the winner is the candidate receiving the most popular votes nationwide.
- There should be no concern about the delay caused by counting provisional ballots because the U.S. Constitution establishes a strict overall national schedule for finalizing the results of presidential elections. All counting, recounting, and judicial proceedings must be conducted so as to reach a "final determination" prior to the uniform nationwide date for the meeting of the Electoral College in mid-December. States are expected to make their "final

determination" six days before the Electoral College meets (the so-called "safe harbor" date). The nation knows, from experience in 2000, that the outcome of the presidential election must be resolved (one way or the other) in accordance with the schedule specified by the U.S. Constitution.

* Knowing the winner of the presidential election rapidly is not as important as conducting the election for President in the best way.

MORE DETAILED ANSWER:

At about 11:15 PM eastern time on Election Night in 2012 (shortly after the polls closed in California and other western states), the television networks called the 2012 presidential election in favor of President Barack Obama. Shortly thereafter, Governor Mitt Romney addressed the nation to concede that he had not won the election and congratulate the winner.

How is it possible for television networks to "call" elections and why do candidates concede on Election Night when there are:

* millions of votes cast on Election Day that are yet to be counted;
* millions of uncounted mail-in, absentee, and military ballots (which, in some states, need not even arrive at vote-counting centers until several days after the Election Day); and
* millions of uncounted provisional ballots (for which voters, in many cases, are not even required to step forward and provide evidence in support of their right to vote for 6–10 days)?

Both candidates and television networks routinely and confidently make decisions about the ultimate outcome of an election based on a combination of information sources, including:

* exit polls conducted outside polling places on Election Day,
* telephone and other types of polling indicating the likely breakdown of absentee, mail-in, provisional, and military ballots,
* estimates (obtained from both election officials and polling) of the number of uncounted absentee, mail-in, provisional, military, and regular ballots, and
* actual election returns (obtained from elections officials on Election Night).

Using these techniques, knowledge of the winner of the national popular vote for President has *always* been evident on Election Night.

In contrast, knowledge of the winner of the electoral vote has not always been evident on Election Night.

For example, because of the current state-by-state winner-take-all system, knowledge about the winner of the Presidency in 2000 was delayed until 34 days after Election Day (and six days before the meeting of the Electoral College on December 18, 2000). In contrast, the winner of the national popular vote in 2000 was evident shortly after the polls closed.

The 34-day delay in learning the identity of the President was an artificial crisis created by the current state-by-state winner-take-all system. The eventual deciding factor in the 2000 election was George W. Bush's lead of 537 popular votes in Florida rather than Gore's nationwide lead of 537,179 popular votes (1,000 times larger than the disputed 537-vote margin in Florida).

Notwithstanding these facts and history, it has been claimed that if the President were elected by a nationwide popular vote, knowledge of the winner would be delayed because votes from all 50 states (instead of just 10 or so battleground states) would matter in determining the winner.

On November 27, 2012 (three weeks after Election Day), the following complaint concerning the *official* count was posted on an election blog:

> "Apparently only 17 states have completed their count of all ballots. . . .I think the implications for National Popular Vote are pretty obvious—had this been a closer election (say, Bush–Gore or Kennedy–Nixon close) **we'd still not know who the president was**. . . . The Electoral College seems to have provided conclusive clarity rather quickly."[353] [Emphasis added]

Of course, in *the very* election that was "Bush–Gore close"—namely the Bush–Gore election in 2000—knowledge about the winner of the Presidency was delayed for 34 days because of the current state-by-state winner-take-all system.

In 2004, knowledge about the winner of the Electoral College was delayed until Wednesday morning even though it was clear on Election Night that President George W. Bush had won the national popular vote by about three million popular votes. If 59,393 Bush voters in Ohio had shifted to Kerry in 2004, Kerry would have ended up with 272 electoral votes (two more than the 270 necessary for election). The 59,393 voters in Ohio were decisive, whereas Bush's nationwide lead of more than three million votes was irrelevant.[354]

Despite the complaint on the election blog concerning the 2012 election, the 2012 election was not close in terms of the national popular vote. President Obama's multi-million-vote nationwide lead was evident on Election Night. However, the closeness of the race in numerous battleground states (e.g., Ohio, Virginia, Florida, Colorado, Nevada, Iowa, New Hampshire) suggests that if President Obama's nationwide lead had been smaller than his actual nationwide lead of 4,966,945 votes (as discussed in section 9.31.9), knowledge of the winner of the 2012 election would likely have been significantly delayed because of the state-by-state winner-take-all system.

---

[353] November 27, 2012. In order to promote free-flowing debate of speculative ideas, the blog involved does not permit attribution.

[354] Ohio was not the only key state in the Electoral College in 2004. A shift of 6,743 votes in Iowa (with 7 electoral votes), 4,295 in New Mexico (with 5 electoral votes), and 10,784 in Nevada (with 5 electoral votes) would have given George W. Bush and John Kerry each 269 electoral votes. If this shift of 21,822 popular votes had occurred, the presidential election would have been thrown into the House of Representatives (with each state casting one vote, and states with an equal division casting no vote), and the vice-presidential election would have been thrown into the Senate (with each Senator having one vote).

The complaint on this blog fails to distinguish between the two levels of "knowing" the outcome of an election.

The first level of "knowing" typically occurs on Election Night even though there are millions of uncounted ballots—regular, absentee, mail-in, provisional, and military. Nonetheless, sufficient information is available to enable television networks to reliably "call" the election and, more importantly, to compel losing candidates to concede defeat.

The second level of "knowing" the outcome of a presidential election comes later—namely the official count.

The *official* winner of the 10 closely divided battleground states was not known on Election Night. In fact, the official counts from eight of the 10 battleground states did not come in until *after* November 29—the day when the blogger complained that we might not "know who the president was" if the President were elected by a nationwide popular vote.

After Election Day in 2012, David Wasserman of the *Cook Political Report* monitored the official vote counts from each state and immediately posted each new result on the web.[355] Although procedures vary from state to state, the official count typically is certified by the Secretary of State or a board (e.g., Board of Canvassers, Board of Elections). Wasserman announced the completion of the official statewide count for almost all states with a Tweet.

Table 9.14 shows the approximate dates on which the 50 states and District of Columbia announced their official results of the presidential election (based on David Wasserman's Tweets in most cases). The dates for five states are labeled "before"—indicating that the table contains the date on the state's Certificate of Ascertainment. The Certificate of Ascertainment is typically created and signed (by the Governor) several days *after* the completion of certification of the official statewide count. Column 1 of the table indicates the order in which each state completed its official count. Column 5 flags the 10 states that many considered to be battleground states in 2012 (New Hampshire, Florida, Wisconsin, Nevada, Iowa, Ohio, Colorado, North Carolina, Virginia, and Pennsylvania).

As can be seen in table 9.14, eight of the 10 battleground states completed their official presidential count *after* November 29—the day when the blogger complained that we might not "know who the president was" if the President were elected by a nationwide popular vote. These eight states were:

- Wisconsin,
- Nevada,
- Iowa,
- Ohio,
- Colorado,
- North Carolina,
- Virginia, and
- Pennsylvania.

---

[355] Wasserman's counts are at https://docs.google.com/spreadsheet/lv?key=0AjYj9mXElO_QdHpla01oWE1jOF ZRbnhJZkZpVFNKeVE&toomany=true.

Table 9.14 APPROXIMATE DATES WHEN STATES COMPLETED THEIR PRESIDENTIAL VOTE COUNTS IN 2012

	STATE	ELECTORAL VOTES	DATE	BATTLEGROUND STATUS
1	New Hampshire	4	November 13, 2012	Battleground
2	Vermont	3	November 13, 2012	
3	South Dakota	3	Before November 13, 2012	
4	Delaware	3	November 14, 2012	
6	Georgia	16	November 14, 2012	
7	Wyoming	3	November 15, 2012	
8	Louisiana	8	November 16, 2012	
9	North Dakota	3	November 16, 2012	
10	Florida	29	November 19, 2012	Battleground
11	South Carolina	9	November 20, 2012	
12	Oklahoma	7	November 21, 2012	
13	Arkansas	6	November 21, 2012	
14	Idaho	4	November 21, 2012	
15	Michigan	16	November 26, 2012	
16	Hawaii	4	Before November 26, 2012	
17	Maryland	10	November 27, 2012	
18	Rhode Island	4	November 28, 2012	
19	Alaska	3	November 28, 2012	
20	Kentucky	8	November 28, 2012	
20	Connecticut	7	November 28, 2012	
21	D.C.	3	November 29, 2012	
22	Maine	4	November 29, 2012	
23	Wisconsin	10	November 29, 2012	Battleground
24	Kansas	6	November 30, 2012	
25	Indiana	11	November 30, 2012	
26	Massachusetts	11	November 30, 2012	
27	Nevada	6	December 1, 2012	Battleground
28	Utah	6	December 2, 2012	
29	Montana	3	December 2, 2012	
30	Illinois	20	December 3, 2012	
31	Iowa	6	December 3, 2012	Battleground
32	Alabama	9	December 3, 2012	
33	Arizona	11	December 3, 2012	
34	Mississippi	6	December 4, 2012	
35	Minnesota	10	December 4, 2012	
36	Oregon	7	December 5, 2012	
37	Missouri	10	December 5, 2012	
38	Ohio	18	December 5, 2012	Battleground
39	Washington	12	December 6, 2012	
40	Texas	38	December 6, 2012	
41	Colorado	9	December 6, 2012	Battleground
42	North Carolina	15	December 7, 2012	Battleground
43	New Jersey	14	December 7, 2012	
44	Nebraska	5	December 10, 2012	
45	Virginia	13	December 10, 2012	Battleground
46	New Mexico	5	December 10, 2012	
47	New York	29	Before December 10, 2012	
48	Tennessee	11	December 11, 2012	
49	Pennsylvania	20	December 12, 2012	Battleground
50	West Virginia	5	Before December 14, 2012	
51	California	55	Before December 15, 2012	

The blogger's reference to the Kennedy–Nixon election in 1960 was also incorrect.

Kennedy was identified as the clear winner of national popular vote early in the morning after Election Day.

The *New York Times'* front-page headline article on the day after the election (Wednesday, November 9, 1960) was "Kennedy is the Apparent Victor."[356]

On Thursday November 10, 1960, the headline of the *New York Times* was "Kennedy's Victory Won by Close Margin."

> **"Fifty-two additional electoral votes,** including California's thirty-two, **were still in doubt last night. But the popular vote was a different story. . . . Senator Kennedy's lead last night was little more than 300,000** in a total tabulated vote of about 66,000,000 cast in 165,826 precincts."[357] [Emphasis added]

On Friday November 11, 1960, the headline of the *New York Times* was "Kennedy's Margin Is Under 300,000."

Nonetheless, uncertainty about the electoral-vote continued. A front-page article in the *New York Times* on Saturday November 12, 1960, reported:

> "The Republican National Chairman, Senator Thruston B. Morton . . . **asked party officials in eleven states today to begin legal action to get recounts**. The states were Delaware, Illinois, Michigan, Minnesota, Missouri, Nevada, New Mexico, New Jersey, Pennsylvania, South Carolina and Texas."[358] [Emphasis added]

The electoral vote count remained unclear until Thursday November 17, 1960. The headline of a *New York Times* article on that day's front page announced that "California Is Put in Nixon's Column by Absentee Vote."

> "Senator Kennedy led in the tally of regular ballots with a majority of 34,568, but the absentee returns changed the picture. Mr. Nixon's lead rose to 13,160 with about 20,000 absentee ballots still to be counted. Most of these are in Republican areas.

> "The absentee returns gave Mr. Nixon 132,168 to Mr. Kennedy's 84,458. State-wide, absentee and resident, the count was: Mr. Nixon, 3,219,211; Mr. Kennedy, 3,206,051. An official canvass, due by Nov. 28, will give the final result."[359]

---

[356] Kennedy is the apparent victor. *New York Times*. November 9, 1960. Page 1.

[357] Kennedy's victory won by close margin. *New York Times*. November 10, 1960. Page 1.

[358] Nixon shuns move for vote recount. *New York Times*. November 12, 1960. Page 1.

[359] California is put in Nixon's column by absentee vote. *New York Times*. November 17, 1960. Page 1.

The final official count in California in 1960 was 3,259,722 for Nixon and 3,224,099 for Kennedy—a difference of 35,623 out of 6.5 million votes.

Under the current state-by-state winner-take-all system, the outcome of the national election frequently depends on the outcome of one or more closely divided battleground states.

For example, in 2004, George W. Bush had a nationwide lead of 3,012,171 popular votes. There has been an exceptionally high amount of provisional voting in Ohio in recent elections, including 2004. In 2004, there were more than 150,000 provisional ballots in Ohio, while Bush's margin was 118,601 votes.[360] The outcome of the 2004 election would have been reversed with a switch of 59,393 votes out of a total of 5,627,903 votes in Ohio. On the Wednesday after Election Day, Senator John Kerry decided that the provisional ballots were unlikely to reverse the apparent outcome in Ohio. If the number of provisional ballots had been somewhat higher or if Bush's margin among the already counted regular ballots had been somewhat lower, knowledge of the winner of the election in 2004 would have been delayed until the provisional ballots were counted (despite Bush's already known nationwide lead of three million votes).

There is a far greater chance that knowledge of the winner of a presidential election will be delayed under the current state-by-state winner-take-all rule than under a system in which there is a single national pool of votes and in which the winner is the candidate receiving the most popular votes nationwide.

In any event, there should be no concern about the delay introduced by the official counting of ballots, because the U.S. Constitution establishes a strict overall national schedule for finalizing the results of presidential elections. All counting, recounting, and judicial proceedings must be conducted so as to reach a "final determination" prior to the uniform nationwide date for the meeting of the Electoral College in mid-December. States are expected to make their "final determination" six days before the Electoral College meets (the so-called "safe harbor" date). The nation knows, from experience in 2000, that the outcome of the presidential election must be resolved (one way or the other) in accordance with the schedule specified by the U.S. Constitution.

An unusual situation developed in 2012 when Hurricane Sandy disrupted many parts of New York state a week before Election Day. On the day before Election Day, Governor Andrew Cuomo issued Executive Order No. 62, allowing any voter in the federally-declared disaster areas to cast a provisional ballot at *any* polling place in the state. The affected areas consisted of the five counties of New York City (Bronx, Kings, New York, Queens, and Richmond) and the counties of Nassau, Rockland, Suffolk, and Westchester. The Executive Order required every county in the state to transmit the resulting provisional ballots to the Board of Election in the county where the voter was registered.

---

[360] Langley, Karen and McNulty, Timothy. Verifying provisional ballots may be key to election. *Pittsburgh Post-Gazette*. August 26, 2012.

The Executive Order resulted in 400,629 provisional ballots on November 6, 2012—about four times the number of provisional ballots handled in New York in 2008.

Counting provisional ballots is a time-consuming and labor-intensive task even under normal circumstances (see section 9.13.6). One reason that counting the provisional ballots resulting from the Governor's Executive Order was unusually time-consuming is that a provisional ballot given to a voter *outside* his or her normal precinct would, almost always, contain some offices for which the voter was not entitled to vote. The detailed instructions accompanying the Executive Order illustrate the complexity of the situation:

> "For example, a voter staying with family in Orange County who was displaced from Westchester, would be entitled to vote for statewide contests and Supreme Court (because those 2 counties share a judicial district) and possibly a congressional, state senate, or state assembly contest. A voter who sought refuge further upstate might only be eligible to vote in the statewide contests, as they would share no other offices/contests."

Thus, when the provisional ballots resulting from the Executive Order arrived at each voter's own local Board of Election, the receiving county had to determine whether that particular voter was entitled to vote for *each separate office or contest* that appeared on the sending county's provisional ballot. A voter who was temporarily displaced to an adjacent county might, for example, still be in his or her own congressional district and state Senate district, but not his own Assembly district.

Obviously, if New York had been in the position of determining the national outcome of the presidential election (as Florida was in 2000 and as Ohio was in 2004), all of these provisional ballots would have been counted expeditiously—regardless of the cost of the overtime needed to complete the task.

In actual practice, the New York State Board of Elections certified a statewide count for President before the "safe harbor" day without considering the unexpected volume of provisional ballots. The state's first certified count showed that the Obama-Biden slate had received 4,159,441 votes and that the Romney-Ryan slate had received 2,401,799 votes—a margin of 1,757,642 votes.[361]

Then, on December 31, 2012, the Board of Elections certified an amended statewide count showing that the Obama-Biden slate had received 4,471,871 votes and that the Romney-Ryan slate had received 2,485,432 votes—a margin of 1,986,439.

New York was not a closely divided battleground state in 2012, and therefore it was evident that its 400,629 provisional ballots could not have affected the nationwide outcome. Similarly, if the National Popular Vote compact had been in effect in 2012, it would have been evident that New York's 400,629 provisional ballots could not have

---

[361] New York's December 10, 2012, Certificate of Ascertainment showing that the Obama-Biden slate received 4,159,441 votes and that the Romney-Ryan slate had received 2,401,799 votes can be viewed at http://www.archives.gov/federal-register/electoral-college/2012-certificates/pdfs/ascertainment-new-york.pdf.

affected the nationwide outcome. Douglas A. Kellner, Co-Chair of the New York State Board of Elections has stated:

> "If the final New York count had been required to determine the identity of the President, the New York State Board of Elections would have accelerated its official count—regardless of whether the outcome of the election was being determined by the state-level winner-take-all rule or the national popular vote."

9.13.8. MYTH: Elections are so trustworthy in the current battleground states that the country should not risk an election in which other states might affect the outcome of a presidential election.

QUICK ANSWER:

- The trustworthiness of elections is not higher in the closely divided battleground states than the rest of the country. In fact, the trustworthiness of elections is questionable in numerous battleground states, including Ohio, Florida, Colorado, and Pennsylvania.

MORE DETAILED ANSWER:

It is sometimes argued that the quality and trustworthiness of elections is so high in closely divided battleground states that the country should not risk an election in which the 40 or so non-battleground states might affect the outcome of a presidential election.

A small number of questionable votes in a single state is unlikely to change the outcome of a presidential election conducted on the basis of the national popular vote. It is, however, a historical fact that a small number of votes may affect the nationwide outcome of a presidential election under the current state-by-state winner-take-all system. For example, the 2000 presidential election was decided by 537 votes out of a total of 5,963,110 votes in Florida—one of the numerous battleground states that used direct-recording electronic voting machines in 2012.

The trustworthiness of elections has been questioned in numerous closely divided battleground states, including in Ohio, Florida, Colorado, and Pennsylvania.

In each of the states mentioned, proponents of various controversial measures argued that elections were insecure and unreliable.[362] In citing these examples, our purpose is not to agree or disagree with the rationale or propriety of these new measures, but to dispute the claim that elections in today's closely divided battleground states are inherently more trustworthy than the rest of the country.

In Florida, for example, Governor Rick Scott (R) signed into law a controversial

---

[362] Opponents of the proposed controversial measures, in turn, argued that the proposed measures would disenfranchise legitimate voters and discourage voter participation.

measure in 2011 that imposed more than 75 restrictions to combat voter fraud. The changes limited early voting, purged voter rolls of non-citizens, and made it more difficult for third-party organizations to register voters.[363] The article "The Battle over Election Reform in the Swing State of Florida" reviews numerous additional controversies concerning election law in Florida.[364]

In Colorado, Secretary of State Scott Gessler (R) launched efforts to remove certain ineligible registered voters from the voter rolls.[365]

In Pennsylvania, stringent voter identification legislation was enacted. *Politics PA* reported on June 25, 2012:

> "House Majority Leader Mike Turzai (R-Allegheny) suggested that the House's end game in passing the Voter ID law was to benefit the GOP politically.

> "'We are focused on making sure that we meet our obligations that we've talked about for years,' said Turzai in a speech to [Republican State Committee] committee members Saturday. He mentioned the law among a laundry list of accomplishments made by the GOP-run legislature.

> "'Pro-Second Amendment? The Castle Doctrine, it's done. First pro-life legislation—abortion facility regulations—in 22 years, done. **Voter ID, which is gonna allow Governor Romney to win the state of Pennsylvania**, done.'"[366] [Emphasis added]

Ohio was the key battleground state in both the 2004 election and the 2012 election. In 2012, for example, it accounted for 73 of the 253 post-convention campaign events in the 2012 election (table 9.3).

In Ohio, Secretary of State John Husted attempted to eliminate early voting during the weekend before Election Day; however, this change was rejected by federal courts.

A November 6, 2012, article in *National Journal* entitled "The Ohio Vote Count Could Be a Mess" stated:

> "The Buckeye State has supplanted its Southern cousin Florida as the marquee battleground of the 2012 presidential election—the state most likely to tip the race to either President Obama or Mitt Romney. . . .

> "Ohio also bears another, more ominous similarity to the 2000 Florida: If a close race demands a recount, conditions are ripe for a repeat of the de-

---

[363] Florida election laws threaten the vote in a key swing state. *Washington Post*. August 26, 2012.

[364] MacManus, Susan A. The battle over election reform in the swing state of Florida. *New England Journal of Political Science*. Volume VI. Number 2. Pages 237–292.

[365] Election official could be pivotal in battleground Colorado. July 27, 2012. http://nbcpolitics.msnbc.msn.com/_news/2012/07/27/12991424-election-official-could-be-pivotal-in-battleground-colorado#.UBK3Tifzldo.twitter.

[366] Cernetich, Kelly. Turzai: Voter ID Law Means Romney Can Win PA. *PoliticsPA*. June 25, 2012. Video available on YouTube at http://www.youtube.com/watch?v=EuOT1bRYdK8.

lays, confusion, and chaos that racked the Sunshine State. And just like 12 years ago, the state's ultimate winner could very well determine who is the next president. Part of the reason is that swing states such as Ohio haven't adopted some of the reforms that Florida enacted after its infamous recount. . . .

"The most obvious flash point involves provisional ballots, those cast if a voter's eligibility is in question. Election officials don't count provisional or absentee ballots until 10 days after Election Day. In case of a narrow margin and with hundreds of thousands of such votes still to be counted, neither candidate could claim victory. (Ohio recorded 200,000 provisional ballots in 2008, a number expected to rise this time.). . . .

"The possibility of an outright recount further clouds Ohio's outcome. The state will conduct an automatic recount if the difference between Obama's and Romney's tallies is less than one-quarter of 1 percentage point. But officials won't begin that process until the election results are certified, which might not happen until early December. Each county has 21 days to certify its results before submitting them to the secretary of state."[367]

We are not aware of any evidence that the trustworthiness of elections in closely divided battleground states is better than the rest of the country.

9.14. MYTHS ABOUT LACK OF AN OFFICIAL NATIONAL COUNT FOR PRESIDENTIAL ELECTIONS AND SECRET ELECTIONS

9.14.1. MYTH: There is no official count of the national popular vote.

QUICK ANSWER:
- Current federal law provides for an official count of the popular vote for President from each state in the form of a public "Certificate of Ascertainment."

MORE DETAILED ANSWER:
It is sometimes asserted that there is no official national count of the national popular vote for President and, therefore, the National Popular Vote compact would be impossible to implement.

In his testimony on February 19, 2010, to the Alaska Senate Judiciary Committee, Professor Robert Hardaway of the University of Denver Sturm College of Law said:

"Under the Koza scheme, who would be the national official **who would decide what the popular vote is**?" [Emphasis added]

---

[367] Roarty, Alex. The Ohio vote count could be a mess. *National Journal.* November 6, 2012.

The answer is the same under both the current system and under the National Popular Vote compact.

Existing federal law (section 6 of Title 3 of the United States Code) requires that an official count of the *popular vote* for President from each state be certified and sent to various federal officials in the form of a "Certificate of Ascertainment."

> "It shall be the duty of the executive of each State, as soon as practicable after the conclusion of the appointment of the electors in such State by the final ascertainment, under and in pursuance of the laws of such State providing for such ascertainment, to communicate by registered mail under the seal of the State to the Archivist of the United States **a certificate of such ascertainment** of the electors appointed, setting forth the names of such electors and **the canvass or other ascertainment under the laws of such State of the number of votes given or cast for each person for whose appointment any and all votes have been given or cast**. . . ."
> [Emphasis added]

Figure 9.5 shows the Certificate of Ascertainment from Oregon for the 2012 presidential election.

Appendices E, F, G, H, and I show the 2004 Certificate of Ascertainments for Minnesota, Maine, Nebraska, New York, and Mississippi, respectively.

The certificates of ascertainment from all 50 states and the District of Columbia are available on-line for the 2000, 2004, 2008, and 2012 presidential elections.[368]

The national popular vote total for each presidential candidate can be obtained by adding together the popular vote counts from the Certificates of Ascertainment from all 50 states and the District of Columbia.

In fact, the results of this arithmetic process of adding up 51 numbers for each candidate may be viewed on the National Archives and Records Administration's web page entitled "2012 Presidential Election—Popular Vote Totals."[369]

Tara Ross says that supporters of the National Popular Vote

> "**pretend** it is possible to come up with one national vote total." [Emphasis added]

Why does Ross think that the National Archives and Records Administration is "pretending" when it presents a spreadsheet showing the number of popular votes cast for each presidential candidate as certified by each state's Certificate of Ascertainment?

---

[368] For the 2012 presidential election, see http://www.archives.gov/federal-register/electoral-college/2012/certificates_of_ascertainment.html. The web address is the similar for 2000, 2004, and 2008.

[369] For the 2012 presidential election, see http://www.archives.gov/federal-register/electoral-college/2012/popular-vote.html. The web address is the similar for 2000, 2004, and 2008.

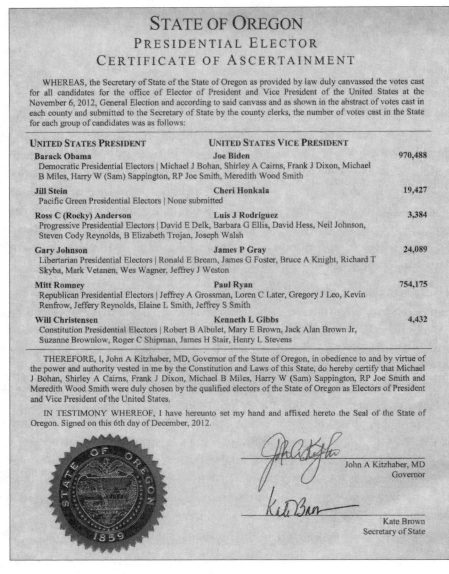

Figure 9.5 Oregon's 2012 Certificate of Ascertainment

In an article entitled "Lawmakers Seek to Change Presidential Elections to Make Them More Risky, Reduce Confidence," Luther Weeks of Connecticut says:

> **"There is no official national popular vote number complied and certified nationally that can be used to officially and accurately determine the winner** in any reasonably close election."[370] [Emphasis added]

---

[370] Weeks, Luther. Lawmakers seek to change presidential elections to make them more risky, reduce confidence. February 3, 2011. http://ctvoterscount.org/lawmakers-seek-to-change-presidential-elections-to-make-them-more-risky-reduce-confidence/.

Of course, the vote counts recorded on the states' Certificates of Ascertainment are used *under the current system* to award electoral votes. Moreover, these vote counts are considered "official" enough and "accurate" enough to elect the President of the United States under the current system.

In particular, the 537-vote lead (out of 5,963,110 votes) recorded on Florida's Certificate of Ascertainment in 2000 was considered "official" enough and "accurate" enough to elect a President. One wonders why Weeks thinks that these state-produced Certificates of Ascertainment (and the legal process behind the "final determinations" reported in these certificates) would suddenly become "more risky" if used to elect a President under the National Popular Vote compact. Why would they suddenly "reduce confidence?"

9.14.2. MYTH: A single state could frustrate the National Popular Vote compact by keeping its election returns secret.

QUICK ANSWER:

- Current federal law provides for an official public count of the popular vote for President in each state.

MORE DETAILED ANSWER:

It has been suggested on an elections blog that a state might pass a law making its election returns secret at the precinct, local, county, and state levels:

> "Couldn't [a state] decide to turn its popular vote totals into a state secret, thereby ruining the pact? What's to stop a state from choosing to count votes behind closed doors?"[371]

Existing federal law (section 6 of Title 3 of the United States Code) requires each state to certify the number of popular votes cast for each presidential elector in a public document, called a "Certificate of Ascertainment," prior to the mid-December meeting of the Electoral College.

> "It shall be the duty of the executive of each State, as soon as practicable after the conclusion of the appointment of the electors in such State by the final ascertainment, under and in pursuance of the laws of such State providing for such ascertainment, to communicate by registered mail under the seal of the State to the Archivist of the United States **a certificate of such ascertainment** of the electors appointed, setting forth the names of such electors and **the canvass or other ascertainment under the laws of such State of the number of votes given or cast for each person for whose appointment any and all votes have been given or cast**; and it

---

[371] In order to promote free-flowing debate of speculative ideas, the blog involved does not permit attribution.

shall also thereupon be the duty of the executive of each State to deliver to the electors of such State, on or before the day on which they are required by section 7 of this title to meet, six duplicate-originals of the same certificate under the seal of the State; and if there shall have been any final determination in a State in the manner provided for by law of a controversy or contest concerning the appointment of all or any of the electors of such State, it shall be the duty of the executive of such State, as soon as practicable after such determination, to communicate under the seal of the State to the Archivist of the United States a certificate of such determination in form and manner as the same shall have been made; and the certificate or certificates so received by the Archivist of the United States shall be preserved by him for one year and shall be a **part of the public records of his office and shall be open to public inspection**; and the Archivist of the United States at the first meeting of Congress thereafter shall transmit to the two Houses of Congress copies in full of each and every such certificate so received at the National Archives and Records Administration." [Emphasis added]

Figure 9.5 shows Oregon's 2012 Certificate of Ascertainment. Appendices E, F, G, H, and I show the Certificates of Ascertainment from Minnesota, Maine, Nebraska, New York, and Mississippi. Figure 6.1 shows Vermont's 2008 Certificate of Ascertainment. The Certificates of Ascertainment from all 50 states and the District of Columbia are available on-line for the 2000, 2004, and 2008 elections.[372]

Professor Norman R. Williams of Willamette University dismisses the federal law by suggesting that presidential elections could nonetheless be conducted in secret.

"States could comply with that requirement without making their actual vote totals public, such as by **releasing the vote totals only to the candidates on the condition that the totals are kept confidential** until after the Electoral College meets. Such **selective release would allow the losing candidate to pursue a judicial election contest, which itself could be kept closed to the public to ensure the vote total's confidentiality**, but it would frustrate the NPVC by keeping other states from knowing the official vote tally."[373] [Emphasis added]

Professor Williams' proposal for secret elections, secret judicial hearings, and non-disclosure agreements assumes that there is a state in which the voters have such a strong attachment to the current winner-take-all rule that they would be willing to abandon the long-standing tradition of having elections closely monitored by the

[372] http://www.archives.gov/federal-register/electoral-college/2004/certificates_of_ascertainment.html.
[373] Williams, Norman R. Reforming the Electoral College: Federalism, majoritarianism, and the perils of sub-constitutional change. 100 *Georgetown Law Journal* 173. November 2011. Page 213.

media, civic groups, and challengers and observers representing the parties, candidates, and ballot propositions that happen to be on the ballot at the same time as the presidential election.[374]

Professor Williams' proposal for conducting secret elections is a parlor game devoid of any connection to real-world political reality.

9.14.3. MYTH: Absentee ballots are not counted in California when the number of absentee ballots is significantly less than the amount by which the Democratic presidential candidate is leading.

QUICK ANSWER:

- It is simply an urban legend that absentee ballots are not counted in California (or any other state) when the number of absentee ballots is significantly less than the amount by which the Democratic presidential candidate is leading.

- A typical ballot in California contains votes for between 50 and 100 individual candidates and ballot propositions. Regardless of whether there is any doubt as to which presidential candidate received the most popular votes in California, 100% of the ballots must be counted in order to determine the outcome of the numerous other offices and propositions on the ballot.

MORE DETAILED ANSWER:

A posting on *Real Clear Politics* stated:

> "One thing worth noting is that **the true popular vote is rarely even tallied**. For example, I remember hearing several times that **California did not count absentee ballots because the number of absentee ballots was significantly less than the amount by which the Democratic candidate was leading.** Since absentee ballots typically include military votes, the gap might have narrowed, even if wasn't even mathematically possible for the ballots to flip the state. In that case, it's possible that, as an example, Al Gore may not have won the actual popular vote. **I believe there were roughly million absentee ballots not counted in California**, and Gore was leading by about 500,000 votes. While that was nowhere near enough to flip the state, it might have changed the popular vote total."[375] [Emphasis added]

---

[374] As for public attachment to the winner-take-all rule, the political reality is that the public is not attached to the winner-take-all rule. Public opinion surveys show high levels of public support for a national popular vote for President in every state for which state-level polls are available, including battleground states, small states, Southern states, border states, and other states (as itemized in section 9.24.1). Numerous polls are available on National Popular Vote's web site at http://www.nationalpopularvote.com/pages/polls.

[375] Blog posting by Southerner01. *Real Clear Politics.* October 12, 2012. http://www.realclearpolitics.com/articles/2012/10/12/how_likely_is_an_electo ral_votepopular_vote_split_115749-comments.html.

Depending on a voter's location, a typical ballot in California contains votes for between 50 and 100 individual candidates and ballot propositions, including:

- members of Congress,
- members of the state legislature,
- county offices,
- judges,
- statewide ballot propositions,
- city offices,
- school boards,
- community college boards,
- public hospital boards, and
- local ballot propositions.

There were 10,965,856 votes cast in California in the November 2000 election.

Although no group of 1,000,000 absentee ballots could have eliminated Al Gore's 1,293,774-vote lead over George W. Bush in the presidential race in California, these same 1,000,000 ballots determined the outcome of numerous other races on the ballot in November 2000.

Regardless of whether there is any doubt as to which presidential candidate received the most popular votes in California, 100% of the ballots must be counted in order to determine the outcome of the numerous other offices and propositions on the ballot.

This urban legend is absurd on its face.

9.15. MYTHS ABOUT RECOUNTS

9.15.1. MYTH: The current system typically produces undisputed outcomes, whereas recounts would be frequent under a national popular vote.

QUICK ANSWER:

- The current state-by-state winner-take-all system of electing the President has repeatedly produced unnecessary artificial crises that would not have arisen if there had been a single large national pool of votes and if the winner had been the candidate who received the most popular votes nationwide.
- There have been five litigated state counts in the nation's 57 presidential elections under the current system. This high frequency contrasts with the mere 22 recounts among the 4,072 statewide general elections in the 13-year period between 2000 and 2012—that is, a probability of 1-in-185. In other words, the probability of a disputed presidential election conducted using the current state-by-state winner-take-all system is dramatically higher than the probability of a recount in an election in which there is a single pool of

votes and in which the winner is the candidate who receives the most popular votes.

- The current state-by-state winner-take-all system repeatedly creates artificial crises because every presidential election generates 51 separate opportunities for a dispute because of an outcome-altering statewide margin. The nation's 57 presidential elections have really been 2,237 separate state-level elections.
- Recounts would be far less likely under the National Popular Vote bill than under the current system because there would be a single large national pool of votes instead of 51 separate pools. Given the 1-in-185 chance of a recount and given that there is a presidential election every four years, one would expect a recount about once in 740 years under a National Popular Vote system. In fact, the probability of a close national election would be even less than 1-in-185 because the 1-in-185 statistic is based on statewide recounts, and recounts become less likely with larger pools of votes. Thus, the probability of a national recount would be even less than 1-in-185 (and even less frequent than once in 740 years).
- Many people do not realize how rare recounts are in actual practice, how few votes are changed by recounts, and how few recounts ever change the outcome of an election.
- The average change in the margin of victory as a result of a statewide recount is a mere 294 votes.
- Only one in seven recounts reverses the original outcome.
- Recounts appear to be becoming rarer. There were no recounts among the 419 statewide elections in November 2012.
- Improved technology can be expected to further reduce the occurrence of recounts in coming years.

MORE DETAILED ANSWER:

Criticism of the National Popular Vote plan in connection with recounts is an example of a criticism that actually applies more to the current state-by-state winner-take-all system than to the National Popular Vote plan. As explained below, recounts in presidential elections would be far less likely to occur under a national popular vote system than under the current state-by-state winner-take-all system.

Indeed, the question of recounts comes to mind in connection with presidential elections only because the current system so frequently creates artificial crises and unnecessary disputes. If we were debating the question of whether to elect state Governors by a popular vote, the issue of recounts would never even come to mind, because everyone knows that recounts rarely occur in elections in which there is a single pool of votes and in which the winner is the candidate who receives the most popular votes.

Tara Ross, an opponent of the National Popular Vote plan, has stated:

"The Electoral College **typically produces** quick and **undisputed outcomes**."[376] [Emphasis added]

Ross has also said:

"The Electoral College encourages stability and certainty in our political system. **Events such as those that occurred in 2000 are rare**."[377] [Emphasis added]

In testimony before the Alaska Senate, Ross stated:

"A direct election system . . . would result in . . . **constant recounts**."[378] [Emphasis added]

Nothing could be further from the truth.

In fact, it is the current state-by-state winner-take-all system (i.e., awarding of all a state's electoral votes to the candidate who receives the most popular votes in the state) that regularly produces artificial crises in the form of unnecessary recounts and disputes.

There have been five litigated state counts in the nation's 57 presidential elections between 1789 and 2012 under the current state-by-state winner-take-all system. This rate is dramatically higher the 1-in-185 chance (documented below) of a recount in which there is a single statewide pool of votes and in which the winner is the candidate who receives the most popular votes.

The current state-by-state winner-take-all system repeatedly creates artificial crises because every presidential election provides 51 separate opportunities for a dispute. This fact is illustrated by examining the five litigated state counts in the nation's 57 presidential elections between 1789 and 2012. All five were artificial crises that would not have arisen if there had been a single large national pool of votes and if the winner had been the candidate who receives the most popular votes.

The 2000 presidential election was an artificial crisis created because of George W. Bush's lead of 537 popular votes in the state of Florida. Gore's nationwide lead was 537,179 popular votes—1,000 times larger than the disputed 537-vote margin in Florida. Given the miniscule number of votes that are changed by the typical statewide recount (about 294 votes), no one would have requested a recount or disputed the results in 2000 if the nationwide margin of 537,179 had controlled the outcome. In the absence of

---

[376] Written testimony submitted by Tara Ross to the Delaware Senate in June 2010.

[377] Oral and written testimony presented by Tara Ross at the Nevada Senate Committee on Legislative Operations and Elections on May 7, 2009.

[378] Oral and written testimony presented by Tara Ross at the hearing of the Alaska Senate State Affairs Committee in February 2011.

the state-level winner-take-all rule, no one (except perhaps almanac writers and trivia buffs) would have noticed that one particular candidate happened to have a 537-vote margin in one particular state.

In 1960, there was a recount and a court case that reversed the original outcome of the presidential race in Hawaii. Kennedy ended up with a 115-vote margin in Hawaii in an election in which his nationwide margin was 118,574.

Samuel Tilden's 3% nationwide lead in 1876 was a solid victory in terms of the national popular vote (equal, for example, to George W. Bush's nationwide percentage lead in the 2004 election). However, an artificial crisis was created because of the razor-thin margins of 889 votes in South Carolina, 922 in Florida, and 4,807 in Louisiana.[379] Few would have cared who received more popular votes in these three closely divided states if the President had been elected by a nationwide popular vote (which Tilden won by 254,694 votes). Again, the state-by-state winner-take-all system created an unnecessary artificial crisis.

Let us start with the facts about how rare recounts are in actual practice, how few votes are actually changed by recounts, and how few recounts actually change the outcome of an election.

FairVote has collected data on every statewide general election in the 13-year period from 2000 to 2012.[380]

There were 22 recounts in 4,072 statewide general elections between 2000 and 2012—that is, one recount for every 185 elections.

Table 9.15 shows, by year, the number of statewide general elections and recounts in the 13-year period from 2000 to 2012.

Table 9.16 shows a breakdown according to the particular elective office or ballot proposition involved in the 4,072 statewide general elections and 22 recounts in the 13-year period between 2000 and 2012.

Table 9.17 provides details about the 22 recounts of statewide general elections in the 13-year period between 2000 and 2012. The recounts in the table are arranged according to the absolute value of number of votes changed by the recount (shown in column 1). Columns 2, 3, and 4 identify the recount. Column 5 shows whether the original count was upheld or reversed. Column 6 shows the original margin, and column 7 shows the margin after the recount. Column 8 shows whether the recount was

---

[379] Although the 1876 dispute focused primarily on the statewide vote counts in Louisiana, South Carolina, and Florida, the vote count was also close in other states, including California (where the margin was 2,798), Oregon (where the margin was 1,050 votes), and Nevada (where the margin was 1,075 votes).

[380] Rob Richie and Mollie Hailey of FairVote updated FairVote's 2010 report covering the 10-year period between 2000 and 2009 by adding data for the three-year period between 2010 and 2012. See Richie, Rob; Talukdar, Monideepa; and Hellman, Emily. 2010. *A Survey and Analysis of Statewide Election Recounts, 2000–2009.* FairVote.

Table 9.15 THE 4,072 STATEWIDE GENERAL ELECTIONS 2000–2012 BY YEAR

YEAR	NUMBER OF ELECTIONS	NUMBER OF RECOUNTS
2000	538	5
2001	52	–
2002	554	–
2003	79	–
2004	448	6
2005	59	1
2006	598	3
2007	70	–
2008	449	2
2009	37	1
2010	708	3
2011	61	–
2012	419	0
Total	4,072	22

Table 9.16 THE 4,072 STATEWIDE GENERAL ELECTIONS 2000–2012 BY TYPE OF ELECTION

OFFICE	NUMBER OF STATEWIDE ELECTIONS	NUMBER OF RECOUNTS
President	200	1
U.S. Senator	240	3
U.S. Representative	49	–
Governor	169	2
Lieutenant Governor	92	–
Secretary of State	116	1
Attorney General	142	1
Treasurer	113	–
Auditor	81	1
Comptroller	27	–
Public Service Commissioner	24	–
Agriculture or Industries Commissioner	38	–
Labor Commissioner	11	–
Insurance Commissioner	33	–
Public Lands Commissioner	17	–
Tax Commissioner	4	–
Corporation Commissioner	20	–
Railroad Commissioner	9	–
Public Utilities Commissioner	7	–
Mine Commissioner	3	–
Supt. of Public Instruction or Education	43	1
Board of Education or Governors	16	1
University Regent	10	–
Trustee	7	–
Judicial positions and retention	941	5
Ballot questions	1,645	6
Other	15	–
Total	4,072	22

Table 9.17 THE 22 RECOUNTS OF STATEWIDE GENERAL ELECTIONS 2000-2012

CHANGE IN VOTE MARGIN	STATE	YEAR	OFFICE OR PROPOSITION	RECOUNT RESULT	ORIGINAL VOTE MARGIN	VOTE MARGIN AFTER RECOUNT	TYPE OF RECOUNT
3	MT	2000	Public Instruction	Upheld	64	61	Requested
4	AL	2004	Amendment 2	Upheld	1,850	1,846	Automatic
−15	GA	2004	Court of Appeals	Upheld	348	363	Automatic
−37	VA	2005	Attorney General	Upheld	323	360	Requested
−50	WY	2004	Amendment C	Upheld	1,282	1,232	Automatic
−50	NC	2006	Court of Appeals	Upheld	3,416	3,466	Requested
−55	WY	2004	Amendment A	Upheld	858	803	Automatic
−66	AZ	2010	Proposition 112	Upheld	128	194	Automatic
86	MN	2010	Governor	Upheld	8,856	8,770	Automatic
−131	OR	2008	Measure 53	Upheld	550	681	Automatic
219	AK	2004	U.S. Senator	Upheld	9,568	9,349	Requested
239	VT	2006	Auditor	Reversed	137	-102	Requested
267	WA	2000	Secretary of State	Upheld	10,489	1,0222	Automatic
−276	WA	2000	U.S. Senator	Upheld	1,953	2,229	Automatic
−281	PA	2009	Superior Court	Upheld	83,693	83,974	Requested
312	WI	2011	Supreme Court	Upheld	7,316	7,004	Requested
390	WA	2004	Governor	Reversed	261	-129	Automatic
440	MN	2008	U.S. Senator	Reversed	215	-225	Automatic
−508	AL	2006	Amendment	Upheld	2,642	3,150	Automatic
−667	NC	2010	Court of Appeals	Upheld	5,988	6,655	Requested
1,121	CO	2000	Education Board	Upheld	1,211	90	Automatic
1,247	FL	2000	President	Upheld	1,784	537	Automatic
294	**Average**						

a candidate-requested or an automatic recount (explained below). Details concerning Wyoming's constitutional amendments A and C of 2004 are explained in a footnote.[381]

The average change in the margin of victory as a result of a statewide recount was a mere 294 votes. This number is obtained by averaging the *absolute* value of the "change in vote" numbers found in column 1 of table 9.17.

As can be seen, the number of votes changed by a statewide recount between 2000 and 2012 ranges from 3 to 1,274.

---

[381] In Wyoming, a constitutional amendment must be approved by a majority of the total number of votes cast on Election Day (rather than a majority of those voting on the amendment). On Election Day in Wyoming in November 2004, 245,789 votes were cast, so the required majority to pass an amendment was 122,896. Thus, the outcome was determined by the difference between the number of "yes" votes and 122,896 (rather than the difference between the number of "yes" and "no" votes). In other words, failure to vote on an amendment counts as a "no" vote. Amendment A received 122,038 "yes" votes (and 96,792 "no" votes) in the initial count and was thus only 858 votes short of the 122,896 votes required for passage. This shortfall (0.3491% of 245,789) triggered an automatic recount of Amendment A. The recount of Amendment A changed 55 votes (0.0223% of 245,789). Amendment C received 124,178 "yes" votes (and 110,169 "no" votes) in the initial count and was thus was only 1,282 over the 122,896 votes required for passage. This overage (0.5216% of 245,789) triggered an automatic recount of Amendment C. The recount of Amendment C changed 50 votes (0.0203% of the 245,789).

All but two of the 22 recounts resulted in only a three-digit change in the original count, and the largest change was a change of 1,247 votes.[382]

As one would expect, half (11 of the 22) of recounts increased the apparent winner's margin, and half decreased it.

The original outcome was reversed in only three of the 22 recounts—that is, about 1-in-7 recounts.

All of the recounts in which the original outcome was reversed had one thing in common, namely a *low-three-digit original margin* (specifically 137, 215, or 261 votes).

The three recounts that reversed the original outcome were:

- the 2004 Governor's race in Washington state (where the original 261-vote lead became a 129-vote loss),
- the 2006 state auditor's race in Vermont (where the original 137-vote lead became a 102-vote loss), and
- the 2008 U.S. Senate election in Minnesota (where the original 215-vote lead became a 225-vote loss).

The probability of a national recount can be estimated from the known probability of statewide recounts.

Using the 1-in-185 chance of a recount, and given that there is one presidential election every four years, one would expect a national recount about once every 740 years under a national popular vote (that is, four times 185).

In fact, the probability of a presidential recount under a national popular vote system would be even less than 1-in-185 (that is, even rarer than once in 740 years) because a close result is less likely to occur as the size of the voting pool increases.

This 1-in-185 frequency of problematic elections is dramatically lower than the five litigated state counts in 57 presidential elections up to 2012 that we have experienced under the current state-by-state winner-take-all system.

The reason there have been so many disputes in the mere 57 presidential elections is that there are 51 separate opportunities for recounts in every presidential election under the current state-by-state winner-take-all system. Our nation's 57 presidential elections between 1789 and 2012 have really been 2,237 separate state-level elections. Thus, the current system repeatedly creates artificial crises in which the vote is extremely close in certain states, but not at all close on a nationwide basis.

One good way to visualize the difference between the two systems is to think of the chance of a recount as being a game of Russian Roulette in which there is one bullet in a 185-chamber gun. Under a national popular vote, the trigger is pulled once every four years. Based on history, we can reasonably expect the gun to fire once every 740 years (185 times 4). In contrast, under the current state-by-state winner-

---

[382] Note that the recount of the presidential vote in Florida in 2000 was the automatic recount that was required by Florida law and that was held shortly after Election Day. This recount did not involve a hand inspection of each ballot. It reduced Bush's initial 1,784-vote lead to a 537-vote lead. The hand recount that was begun later was halted by the U.S. Supreme Court, thus leaving the 537-vote margin as Bush's final margin in Florida.

take-all system, the trigger is pulled 51 times every four years. Thus, we should not be surprised to have had so many litigated state counts in 57 presidential elections between 1789 and 2012. The trigger was pulled 2,237 separate times in 57 presidential elections under the current state-by-state winner-take-all system.

As previously mentioned, one would expect a national recount of a presidential election about once every 740 years under a national popular vote (based on the 1-in-185 chance of a recount and given that there is one presidential election every four years). When that exceedingly rare event occurs, it will also almost certainly be true that the results in one state (and probably several) would also be closely divided. Thus, if the nationwide count were extremely close, the current state-by-state winner-take-all system would very likely also produce a disputed count in one or more closely divided states.

Despite the fact that the average number of votes changed in a recount is very small (a mere 294 votes), it is common on Election Night for disappointed candidates who have lost by thousands of votes to bombastically announce that they are going to demand a recount. However, in the cool light of day, these candidates almost always realize that they have no realistic chance of reversing the outcome.

For example, in a race in North Carolina with a vote gap of 6,658 (0.15% of the 4,368,598 votes cast):

> "The trailing Democratic Party candidate for [North Carolina] lieutenant governor said Monday **she won't seek a statewide recount, admitting that a new tally was unlikely to make up the nearly 6,900 votes she needs**. . . .

> "**'We face the reality that an extended battle would not alter the outcome of this race**,' Linda Coleman said at a news conference after conceding the outcome to Republican Dan Forest. 'It was a hard-fought, spirited campaign and we have stark differences. But in the end, in a tight race, North Carolinians have chosen Mr. Forest as their next lieutenant governor.'

> "Coleman had until Tuesday to demand a recount because her margin with Forest was less than 10,000 votes out of almost 4.4 million cast. . . .

> "'I don't think the money factor was an issue with her in making this decision,' [Coleman spokesman] Beasley spoke said. '**We just were faced with the reality of the numbers and that it's hard to flip 6,000 votes in an extended recount battle**. She [Coleman] doesn't want to put the people of North Carolina and the state board of election employees through that.'"[383] [Emphasis added]

---

[383] Dalesio, Emery P. Democrat concedes in N.C. lieutenant gov. race. Associated Press article in *Pilot On-line*. November 19, 2012. Dalesio, Emery P. Democrat concedes in N.C. lieutenant gov. race. *Pilot OnLine*. November 19, 2012 http://hamptonroads.com/2012/11/democrat-concedes-nc-lieutenant-gov-race.

Similarly, Sandy Welsh decided not to pursue a recount in 2012 of her 2,231-vote loss in her race for Montana Superintendent of Public Instruction (a difference of 0.48% of the 468,563 votes cast).[384]

Not all recounts are conducted because the apparent losing candidate believes that he or she has any realistic probability of changing the result of the initial count. Nineteen states provide for "automatic" recounts of elections that are triggered because the original difference between the candidates is less than some pre-specified statutory percentage or numerical trigger. One reason that states conduct automatic recounts is to maximize public confidence in elections. Another reason is that recounts provide state officials and the public with the periodic opportunities to audit and evaluate the operation of the state's election process. The government pays for automatic recounts. The percentage or numerical trigger for an automatic recount varies considerably among the 19 states. In many of the 19 states, an automatic recount will be conducted if the difference in the initial count between the first-place and second-place candidate (or ballot alternative, in the case of ballot propositions) is less than 0.5% of the votes cast.[385] Several states mandate automatic recounts with even larger differences. In many automatic recounts, no one (including the apparent losing candidate) realistically expects the outcome to change.

About two-thirds of the 22 recounts (14 of 22) in table 9.17 (column 8) were "automatic" recounts (as opposed to candidate-requested recounts).

Table 9.18 presents the percentage change in votes (column 1) that resulted from the 22 recounts of statewide general elections between 2000 and 2012 (table 9.17). Column 6 of the table here shows the total votes cast for the office or ballot proposition. Column 7 shows the percentage lead of the winner of the initial count (that is, the numerical lead shown in column 6 of table 9.17 divided by the total number of votes cast as shown in column 6 of this table). Many of the 19 states that conduct automatic recounts use this percentage as the criterion for deciding whether to conduct an automatic recount. Column 1 shows the percentage change resulting from the recount (that is, the number of votes changed in the recount as shown in column 1 of table 9.17 divided by the total number of votes cast as shown in column 6 of this table). The recounts in this table are arranged according to percentage in column 1.

As can be seen from column 1 of table 9.18, the percentage change that resulted from recounts is very small. Only one of the 22 recounts changed more than 0.1% of the original vote. The percentage change that resulted from 22 recounts ranged between:

- 0.0003%—that is, 3 votes in 1,380,750 (in Alabama) and
- 0.1073%—that is, 137 votes in 222,835 (in Vermont).

Recounts appear to be becoming rarer in recent years.

[384] Associated Press. Welch drops recount after coming up short on $115K. *Independent Record*. Helena, Montana. December 11, 2012. http://helenair.com/news/state-and-regional/welch-drops-recount-after-coming-up-short-on-k/article_8d5e1d2a-efe9-5f59-ba5c-ef91a31e960d.html?comment_form=true.

[385] The National Conference of State Legislatures has summarized the characteristics of the 19 state-level automatic recount laws at http://www.ncsl.org/legislatures-elections/elections/conducting-recounts.aspx.

Table 9.18 PERCENTAGE DIFFERENCES AND CHANGES RESULTING FROM
THE 22 RECOUNTS 2000–2012

PERCENT CHANGE DUE TO RECOUNT	STATE	YEAR	OFFICE OR PROPOSITION	RECOUNT RESULT	TOTAL VOTES IN ORIGINAL COUNT	PERCENT LEAD OF APPARENT WINNER	TYPE OF RECOUNT
0.0003%	AL	2004	Amendment 2	Upheld	1,380,750	0.1340%	Automatic
0.0019%	VA	2005	Attorney General	Upheld	1,941,449	0.0170%	Requested
0.0032%	NC	2006	Court of Appeals	Upheld	1,539,190	0.2220%	Requested
0.0036%	GA	2004	Court of Appeals	Upheld	414,484	0.0840%	Automatic
0.0042%	AZ	2010	Proposition 112	Upheld	1,585,522	0.0080%	Automatic
0.0047%	MN	2010	Governor	Upheld	1,829,620	0.4840%	Automatic
0.0048%	MT	2000	Public Instruction	Upheld	63,080	0.1010%	Requested
0.0115%	WA	2000	U.S. Senator	Upheld	2,396,567	0.0810%	Automatic
0.0125%	WA	2000	Secretary of State	Upheld	2,137,677	0.4910%	Automatic
0.0134%	OR	2008	Measure 53	Upheld	978,634	0.0560%	Automatic
0.0142%	WA	2004	Governor	Reversed	2,742,567	0.0100%	Automatic
0.0154%	PA	2009	Superior Court	Upheld	1,821,869	4.5940%	Requested
0.0182%	MN	2008	U.S. Senator	Reversed	2,422,965	0.0090%	Automatic
0.0203%	WY	2004	Amendment C	Upheld	245,789	0.5216%	Automatic
0.0208%	WI	2011	Supreme Court	Upheld	1,497,330	0.4890%	Requested
0.0214%	FL	2000	President	Upheld	5,816,486	0.0310%	Automatic
0.0223%	WY	2004	Amendment A	Upheld	245,789	0.3491%	Automatic
0.0620%	NC	2010	Court of Appeals	Upheld	1,079,980	0.5540%	Requested
0.0622%	AL	2006	Amendment	Upheld	816,102	0.3240%	Automatic
0.0730%	CO	2000	Education Board	Upheld	1,536,619	0.0790%	Automatic
0.0757%	AK	2004	U.S. Senator	Upheld	289,324	3.3070%	Requested
0.1073%	VT	2006	Auditor	Reversed	222,835	0.0610%	Requested

There were *no* recounts at all among the 419 statewide elections in November 2012.

The frequency of recounts has dropped by about half in recent years. As can be seen in table 9.15, there were twice as many recounts (15 of the 22) between 2000 and 2006 (the top half of the table) than in the six-year period represented by the bottom half of the table (7 of the 22). This apparent decline may be the result of the nationwide efforts made since 2000 to improve election administration and equipment, including enactment of the Help America Vote Act (HAVA) in 2002. One major improvement in election equipment is the drastic reduction since 2000 in the use of punched-card voting (with their hanging chads).

Improved technology can be expected to further reduce the need for recounts in coming years.

For decades, bank tellers, credit-card processors, and state lotteries have routinely and accurately handled and accounted for far more transactions than the mere 130 million votes cast in a presidential election on Election Day. *Every day*, approximately 145 million lottery bets,[386] 300 million bank-teller transactions, and 60 million

---

[386] National Conference of State Legislatures. *Lottery Payouts and State Revenue.* http://www.ncsl.org/issues -research/econ/lottery-payouts-and-state-revenue.aspx.

credit card transactions[387] are accurately handled and accounted for in the United States. In particular, bets in state-administered Lotto games resemble voting in that they require the accurate recording of the player's selection of six (or so) numbers (typically on a paper slip). Unfortunately, the technology for administering elections and handling ballots in the United States is several decades behind that of the banks, credit-card processors, and state lotteries. No doubt, the technology for more accurately handling and accounting for large numbers of votes will catch up with that of these other industries during the next decade or so (and certainly sometime in the next 740 years) so that worries about recounts become a thing of the past.

9.15.2. MYTH: The current state-by-state winner-take-all system acts as a firewall that helpfully isolates recounts to particular states.

QUICK ANSWER:

- Far from acting as a firewall that helpfully isolates recounts to particular states, the current state-by-state winner-take-all system is, instead, the repeated cause of unnecessary fires.
- The current system repeatedly creates artificial crises because every presidential election presents 51 separate opportunities for a dispute.
- There have been five litigated state counts in the nation's 57 presidential elections between 1789 and 2012 under the current state-by-state winner-take-all system. This rate is dramatically higher than the historical 1-in-185 rate for disputed elections in which there is a single pool of votes and in which the winner is the candidate who receives the most popular votes.

MORE DETAILED ANSWER:

Brendan Loomer Loy claims that the current state-by-state winner-take-all system acts as a helpful firewall that

> "isolate[es] post-election disputes to individual close states."[388]

Far from acting as a firewall that helpfully isolates recounts to particular states, the current state-by-state winner-take-all system is, instead, the repeated cause of unnecessary fires.

Under the current system, there are 51 separate statewide vote pools in every presidential election. Thus, our nation's 57 presidential elections between 1789 and 2012 have really been 2,237 separate state-level elections. These 51 separate pools

---

[387] Federal Reserve System. *The 2010 Federal Reserve Payment Study: Noncash Payment Trends in the United States: 2006-2009.* April 5, 2011. Page 54.

[388] Loy, Brendan Loomer, "Count Every Vote—All 538 of Them" *Social Science Research Network.* September 12, 2007. Available at http://ssrn.com/abstract=1014431.

regularly generate 51 separate opportunities for artificial crises in elections in which the vote is not at all close on a nationwide basis (but close in particular states). This is why there have been five litigated state counts in the nation's 57 presidential elections between 1789 and 2012. This rate is dramatically higher than the historical 1-in-185 rate for elections in which there is a single statewide pool of votes and in which the winner is the candidate who receives the most popular votes.

If anyone is genuinely concerned about minimizing the possibility of recounts, then a single national pool of votes provides the way to drastically reduce the likelihood of recounts and eliminate the artificial crises that are regularly produced by the current state-level winner-take-all system.

Trent England (a lobbyist opposing the National Popular Vote compact and Vice-President of the Evergreen Freedom Foundation of Olympia, Washington) has written:

> **"Containing elections within state lines also means containing election problems. The Electoral College turns the states into the equivalent of the watertight compartments on an ocean liner.** Fraud or process failures can be isolated in the state where they occur and need not become national crises.[389] [Emphasis added]

The current system does not contain and isolate problems but instead creates artificial crises.

9.15.3. MYTH: Resolution of a presidential election could be prolonged beyond the inauguration date because of recounts.

QUICK ANSWER:
- The U.S. Constitution establishes a strict overall national schedule for finalizing the results of presidential elections. These existing provisions apply equally to elections conducted under the current system as well as to elections conducted under the National Popular Vote plan.
- Under both the current system and the National Popular Vote plan, all counting, recounting, and judicial proceedings must be conducted so as to reach a "final determination" prior to the uniform nationwide date for the meeting of the Electoral College in mid-December.

MORE DETAILED ANSWER:
Brendan Loomer Loy warns that if we were to have a nationwide popular vote for President:

> "Post-election uncertainty could stretch well into January, raising doubt about whether we would have a clear winner by inauguration day. . . ."

---

[389] England, Trent. Op-Ed: Bypass the Electoral College? *Christian Science Monitor*. August 12, 2010.

"With two centuries of legal precedent tossed aside, courts would have a very difficult time managing it all."[390]

Loy's scenario of a prolonged and unsettled election is based on the incorrect assumption that the existing U.S. Constitution, existing federal statutes, and existing state statutes would somehow be "tossed aside" under the National Popular Vote compact. In fact, the National Popular Vote compact was specifically drafted so as to operate within existing constitutional and statutory provisions in the same way that the current system does.

Finality of presidential elections would be ensured under the National Popular Vote compact by the same machinery that applies to the current system, namely the existing U.S. Constitution, existing federal statutes, and existing state statutes.

The U.S. Constitution establishes a strict overall national schedule for finalizing the results of a presidential election. These existing provisions would apply to elections conducted under the proposed National Popular Vote legislation in the same way that they apply to elections conducted under the current system. No prolonging of a U.S. presidential election until January is possible, thanks to these existing constitutional provisions and existing federal and state statutory provisions.

The U.S. Constitution provides:

> **"The Congress may determine** the Time of chusing the Electors, and **the Day on which they shall give their Votes; which Day shall be the same throughout the United States."**[391] [Spelling as per original] [Emphasis added]

Congress has exercised this constitutional power to set the uniform nationwide date for the meeting of the Electoral College by enacting the following statute:

> "The electors of President and Vice President of each State shall meet and give their votes on the **first Monday after the second Wednesday in December** next following their appointment at such place in each State as the legislature of such State shall direct."[392] [Emphasis added]

Under both the current system and the National Popular Vote approach, all counting, recounting, and judicial proceedings must be conducted so as to reach a "final determination" prior to the uniform nationwide date for the meeting of the Electoral College in mid-December.

The U.S. Supreme Court has made it clear that the states are expected to make

---

[390] Loy, Brendan Loomer. 2007. "Count Every Vote—All 538 of Them. *Social Science Research Network*. September 12, 2007. Available at http://ssrn.com/abstract=1014431.

[391] U.S. Constitution. Article II, section 1, clause 4.

[392] United States Code. Title 3, chapter 1, section 7.

their "final determination" six days before the Electoral College meets (the so-called "safe harbor" date established by section 5 of Title 3 of the United States Code).[393]

In addition, in most states, state statutes already impose independent earlier deadlines for finalizing the count for a presidential election. The U.S. Supreme Court has ruled that state election officials and the state judiciary must conduct counts and recounts in presidential elections within the confines of existing state election laws.

Note that the laws governing the finalization of the count (and completion of any recount) for a presidential election are entirely different from those governing, say, a disputed race for one of the 100 seats in the U.S. Senate (e.g., the 2008 Senate race in Minnesota).

It may be argued that the schedule established by the U.S. Constitution, existing federal statutes, and existing state statutes may sometimes rush the count, prevent recounts, and possibly even create injustice. However, there can be no argument that this schedule exists in the U.S. Constitution, federal statutes, and state statutes or that this existing schedule guarantees "finality" prior to the meeting of the Electoral College in mid-December. The existing constitutional and statutory schedule would govern the National Popular Vote compact in exactly the same way that it governs elections under the current system.

9.15.4. MYTH: Conducting a recount would be a logistical impossibility under a national popular vote.

QUICK ANSWER:

* As a matter of routine and prudent planning, state election officials have contingency plans to conduct a recount for every election.
* The personnel and resources necessary to conduct a recount are indigenous to each state. Thus, a state's ability to conduct a recount inside its own borders is unrelated to whether a recount is being conducted in another state.
* The potential task of recounting the votes cast for President is not a logistical impossibility, as evidenced by the fact that the *original* count is not a logistical impossibility.

MORE DETAILED ANSWER:

A recount is not a logistical impossibility or an unimaginable horror.

The task of recounting the votes cast for President in the nation's 186,000 precincts is not a logistical impossibility, as evidenced by the fact that the *original* count is not a logistical impossibility.

---

[393] For example, in 2008, the election was Tuesday, November 4, and the "safe harbor" date was 33 days later on Monday, December 8. The Electoral College met on the following Monday, December 15 (the Monday after the second Wednesday in December). Congress met to count the votes on January 6, 2009. According to the Constitution, the outgoing President's term ended on January 20, 2009.

A recount is a recognized ever-present contingency whenever a statewide election is conducted. There are about 400 statewide elective offices and statewide propositions on the ballot in a typical November general election in an even-numbered year. There is a probability of about 1-in-185 of a statewide recount (as discussed in section 9.15.1). As a matter of prudent planning, state election officials stand ready with contingency plans to carry out their duty to conduct a recount if one is required.

No state needs the assistance of any personnel or resources from any other state in order to conduct its recount. The personnel and resources necessary to conduct a recount are indigenous to each state. Thus, a state's ability to handle the logistics of a recount within its own borders is unrelated to whether a recount is being conducted in any other state or *all other* states.

Under both the current system and the National Popular Vote approach, all counting, recounting, and judicial proceedings must be conducted so as to reach a "final determination" prior to the uniform nationwide date for the meeting of the Electoral College in mid-December.

The U.S. Supreme Court has made it clear that the states are expected to make their "final determination" six days before the Electoral College meets (the so-called "safe harbor" date established by section 5 of Title 3 of the United States Code).

Because all states must finalize their count (or finish their recount) by the "safe harbor" date in early December, and because the only remaining step required by the National Popular Vote bill is to add up the vote totals from all 50 states and the District of Columbia, the final national vote totals would be available before the Electoral College meets.

Even with a single pool of almost 130,000,000 votes, it is possible that the nationwide popular vote could be extremely close in some future presidential election (say, a few hundred votes or perhaps a few thousand votes). In that event, the initial vote count and the recount would be handled in the same way as they are currently handled—that is, under generally serviceable laws that govern all elections.

Any extremely close election will almost certainly engender controversy, and the eventual loser will often go away unhappy.

The guiding principle in such circumstances should be that all votes should be counted fairly and expeditiously.

Of course, if the popular vote count were extremely close on a nationwide basis, it would be very likely that the vote count would also be close in a number of states.

As U.S. Senator David Durenberger (R–Minnesota) said in the Senate in 1979:

> "There is no reason to doubt the ability of the States and localities to manage a recount, and nothing to suggest that a candidate would frivolously incur the expense of requesting one. And even if this were not the case, the potential danger in selecting a President rejected by a majority of

the voters far outweighs the potential inconvenience in administering a recount."[394]

9.15.5. MYTH: States would be put in the uncomfortable position of judging election returns from other states under a national popular vote.

QUICK ANSWER:

*   No state government has any obligation or power to judge the presidential election returns of any other state under either the current system or the National Popular Vote compact.

MORE DETAILED ANSWER:

No state government has any obligation or power to judge the presidential election returns of any other state under either the current system or the National Popular Vote compact.

Existing federal law specifies that each state's own "final determination" of its presidential election returns is "conclusive" (if done in a timely manner and in accordance with laws in existence prior to Election Day). The existing federal law was originally enacted in substantially the same form that it exists today shortly after the disputed Tilden–Hayes election of 1876.

In particular, the "safe harbor" provision of existing federal law specifies the conditions under which a state's "final determination" is considered "conclusive."

> **"If any State shall have provided**, by laws enacted prior to the day fixed for the appointment of the electors, **for its final determination** of any controversy or contest concerning the appointment of all or any of the electors of such State, by judicial or other methods or procedures, and such determination shall have been made **at least six days before the time fixed for the meeting of the electors, such determination** made pursuant to such law so existing on said day, and made at least six days prior to said time of meeting of the electors, **shall be conclusive, and shall govern in the counting of the electoral votes as provided in the Constitution**, and as hereinafter regulated, so far as the ascertainment of the electors appointed by such State is concerned."[395] [Emphasis added]

The nation's long-standing policy of deferring to the states is echoed in the National Popular Vote compact. In particular, the compact's wording is directly patterned after existing federal law. The compact requires each state to treat as "conclu-

---

[394] *Congressional Record.* July 10, 1979. Pages 17706–17707.

[395] United States Code. Section 5 of Title 3, chapter 1.

sive" each other state's "final determination" of its presidential vote. The fifth clause of Article III of the National Popular Vote compact provides:

> "The chief election official of each member state shall treat as conclusive an official statement containing the number of popular votes in a state for each presidential slate made by the day established by federal law for making a state's final determination conclusive as to the counting of electoral votes by Congress."

Thus, no state government has any obligation or power to judge the presidential election returns of any other state under either the current system or the National Popular Vote compact.

9.15.6. MYTH: A recount might be warranted, but unobtainable, under the National Popular Vote compact.

QUICK ANSWER:

- The reality today, under current laws, is that a timely recount in a presidential race might be warranted, but impossible to obtain in practice in many states (as illustrated by what actually happened in Florida in 2000 and in Hawaii in 1960).

- A recount would be less likely to be needed under the National Popular Vote plan than under the current state-by-state winner-take-all system. There have been five litigated state counts in the nation's 57 presidential elections between 1789 and 2012 under the current state-by-state winner-take-all system. This rate is dramatically higher than the historical 1-in-185 rate for elections in which there is a single statewide pool of votes and in which the winner is the candidate who receives the most popular votes. Given that a recount has occurred only about once in 185 statewide elections and that presidential elections occur once every four years, one would expect a national recount about once every 740 years under the National Popular Vote plan.

- Enactment of the National Popular Vote compact would provide impetus for states to review their imperfect existing laws regarding timely recounts in presidential elections.

- Given that Congress currently has the authority over the count and schedule for presidential elections, federal legislation would be the most expeditious solution to the problem of guaranteeing a timely recount in a presidential election under both the current system and the National Popular Vote plan. Such legislation is, in fact, needed now under the current system because the state-by-state winner-take-all system has resulted in such a high frequency of disputes in presidential elections (five litigated state counts in a mere

57 presidential elections between 1789 and 2012) and because the nation has been in an era of non-landslide presidential elections since 1988. Such a federal law would also be beneficial under the national popular vote approach, even though recounts would be less likely because there would be a single large national pool of votes (instead of 51 separate pools).

MORE DETAILED ANSWER:

Tara Ross criticizes the National Popular Vote plan by saying:

> "States have different criteria for what does (or does not) trigger recounts within their borders. These differences could cause a whole host of problems. What if the national total is close—**close enough to warrant a recount—but a recount can't be conducted** because the margins in individual states were not close?"[396] [Emphasis added]

Of course, the ability to obtain a recount in situations "close enough to warrant a recount" is hardly ensured under the current state-by-state winner-take-all system, as demonstrated by the nation's experience with Florida in 2000.

Moreover, there is no ability under the current system to obtain a recount in situations "close enough to warrant a recount" in the states that do not have recount laws (e.g., Mississippi). If, for the sake of argument, the 537-popular-vote margin that determined the 2000 presidential election had occurred in Mississippi (instead of Florida), there would have been no possibility of a recount. The initial count in Mississippi would have been the first, only, and final count.

In criticizing the National Popular Vote plan, Ross creates an additional misimpression by mentioning only automatic recounts (that is, recounts triggered merely because the original difference between the candidates is less than some fixed legislatively specified threshold). However, automatic recounts are not the only way to obtain a recount (or even the most usual way). In fact, only 19 states have such automatic recount laws.[397] In most states, there are numerous avenues available for obtaining a recount (with some state statutes providing as many as six ways). For example, 42 states allow candidates to petition for a recount. One of the most common forms of state recount laws is to permit a recount if the disgruntled candidate pays for all of the recount's administrative costs in advance (with the candidate typically being reimbursed if he or she is vindicated).

Obtaining a recount under a national popular vote would not be as difficult as Ross suggests (even under the questionable assumption that no changes would be made to existing laws in response to enactment of the National Popular Vote compact).

As will be seen below:

---

[396] Written testimony submitted by Tara Ross to the Delaware Senate in June 2010.

[397] Richie, Rob; Talukdar, Monideepa; and Hellman, Emily. 2010. *A Survey and Analysis of Statewide Election Recounts, 2000–2009.* FairVote.

- Under the current system, a timely recount in a presidential race may be warranted, but impossible to obtain in practice.
- A recount would be less likely to be needed under the National Popular Vote plan than under the current state-by-state winner-take-all system.
- Enactment of the National Popular Vote compact would provide impetus for the states to review and modify their existing laws to ensure timely recounts in presidential elections.
- Federal legislation would be an expeditious solution to the problem of guaranteeing a timely recount in a presidential election under the current system and any future system.

The reality today is that a timely recount in a presidential race under the current system may be warranted, but impossible to obtain in practice, in many states. Presidential elections must be conducted within the constraints of the strict overall national schedule for finalizing the results of a presidential election established by the U.S. Constitution.

In particular, all counting, recounting, and judicial proceedings concerning presidential elections must be conducted so as to reach a "final determination" six days prior to the uniform nationwide date for the meeting of the Electoral College in mid-December. This principle applies equally to both the current state-by-state winner-take-all system of electing the President and the National Popular Vote compact.

The U.S. Constitution (Article II, section 1, clause 4) provides:

> "**The Congress may determine the Time** of chusing the Electors, and **the Day on which they shall give their Votes; which Day shall be the same throughout the United States.**" [Spelling as per original] [Emphasis added]

Congress has exercised its constitutional power to set the uniform nationwide date for the meeting of the Electoral College. Title 3, chapter 1, section 7 of the United States Code states:

> "**The electors** of President and Vice President of each State **shall meet and give their votes on the first Monday after the second Wednesday in December** next following their appointment at such place in each State as the legislature of such State shall direct." [Emphasis added]

This statute was enacted in 1934, just after ratification of the 20th Amendment in 1933. Prior to the 20th Amendment, the President was inaugurated on March 4. The amendment advanced the inauguration to January 20.

Moreover, the U.S. Supreme Court has made it clear that the states are expected to make their "final determination" six days before the Electoral College meets (the so-called "safe harbor" date established by section 5, chapter 1 of Title 3 of the United States Code).

The important point is that there is not much time between Election Day in early November and the "safe harbor" date. For example, in 2008, Election Day was Tuesday, November 4, and the "safe harbor" date was 33 days later on Monday, December 8. In 2008, the Electoral College met on the following Monday, December 15 (the Monday after the second Wednesday in December). Congress met to count votes on January 6, 2009. The outgoing President's term ended on January 20, 2009.

The schedule imposed by the "safe harbor" date was one of the major factors preventing a hand recount of presidential ballots in Florida in 2000.

In 1960, Hawaii conducted a recount under judicial supervision (which reversed Nixon's original lead). However, the recount and judicial proceedings were not completed until after the Electoral College had met. As it happened, Hawaii's three electoral votes did not affect the outcome of the presidential election in 1960. Congress met in joint session in January 1961 to count the electoral votes. The losing presidential candidate, Vice President Richard M. Nixon, presided over the joint session and graciously permitted Hawaii's electoral votes to be counted for John F. Kennedy (while ruling that this action would not constitute a precedent). The reality, however, was that the recount was not timely.

In summary, no full ballot-by-ballot recount has ever been completed in a timely fashion for any U.S. presidential election.

The actual work of a recount does not itself consume a lot of time.

One of the major obstacles to obtaining a timely recount in a presidential race is that there cannot be a recount until there is a count.

Unofficial numbers are, of course, generally available from virtually every precinct and various units of local government on Election Night (or very soon thereafter). Although a candidate may know whether a recount is warranted in a particular election, a candidate's request for a recount under existing laws is generally not legally "ripe" until after the official initial statewide count is complete.

The official initial statewide count typically takes several weeks. The reason for the delay is that official documents certifying the count from each county (or other unit of local government) must be sent to the state's chief election official or state canvassing board. Then, the vote counts contained in these documents are added together to yield the official initial statewide count. The results are often not official until some board meets.

In Ohio in 2004, there were over 200,000 provisional ballots, and Bush's final margin in the state was 118,601.[398] Senator John Kerry decided that the number of

---

[398] Langley, Karen and McNulty, Timothy. Verifying provisional ballots may be key to election. *Pittsburgh Post-Gazette.* August 26, 2012.

provisional ballots in relation to Bush's statewide margin on Election Night (before counting the provisional ballots) did not warrant disputing the results and therefore conceded on the Wednesday after the election. However, had the margins been closer, a recount might have been warranted. A request for a recount is not ripe until the initial count is completed. However, the initial count was not certified in Ohio until the "safe harbor" day! Thus, a recount would have been impossible in the decisive state of the 2004 presidential election had a recount been warranted.

In 2012, eight of the 10 closely divided battleground states did not complete their initial count until November 29; five of the 10 did not complete their initial count until December 5; and two did not complete their initial count until just before the "safe harbor" date.[399]

In many other states, the initial count of a presidential election is generally not completed until a week or so before the "safe harbor" date (six days before the Electoral College meets).

The facts are that, under the *current* system, the possibility of conducting a timely recount of a presidential election is largely an illusion.

In most states, there is no deadline for completing the initial official count in sufficient time to permit the conducting of a recount (and likely post-recount litigation) that is consistent with the federal "safe harbor" date and uniform nationwide date for the meeting of the Electoral College.

Moreover, many state chief election officers can effectively preclude a recount merely by "slow-walking" the initial count so that it is not completed until just before the "safe harbor" date—thus preventing a candidate's request for a recount from being legally "ripe" until it is too late to conduct the recount.

With the rising volume of absentee and mail-in voting in many states, provisional ballots, and military ballots, thousands of ballots are not counted until after Election Day, thereby further delaying completion of the initial count.

Thus, at the present time, a timely recount is impossible to obtain, in practice, under the current system in many states.

A recount would be less likely to be needed under the National Popular Vote plan than under the current state-by-state winner-take-all system.

There have been five litigated state counts in our nation's 57 presidential elections between 1789 and 2012. All five of these disputed state counts were the result of the state-by-state winner-take-all rule in elections where there was a clear nationwide popular vote winner. Far from serving as a firewall that helpfully isolates problems to particular states, the current state-by-state winner-take-all system repeatedly creates artificial crises in situations where no problem existed in the first place.

Five litigated state counts in a mere 57 presidential elections between 1789 and

---

[399] See section 9.13.7 and, in particular, table 9.14.

2012 is a dramatically higher rate than the historical 1-in-185 rate for recounts in state-wide elections in which there is a single pool of votes and in which the winner is the candidate who receives the most popular votes.

Given that a recount has occurred only about once in 185 elections and that presidential elections occur once every four years, one could expect a recount about once in 740 years under the National Popular Vote plan.

The reason why there have been so many disputes in a mere 57 presidential elections between 1789 and 2012 is that each presidential election is really 51 separate state-level elections—with 51 separate opportunities for close results warranting a recount. Our 57 presidential elections between 1789 and 2012 have really been 2,237 separate state-level elections. The current state-by-state winner-take-all system has repeatedly created artificial crises in elections in which the vote was extremely close in certain states—but not close nationwide. This can be seen by reviewing the five litigated state counts in our nation's 57 presidential elections between 1789 and 2012.

The 2000 presidential election was an artificial crisis created because George W. Bush's total of 2,912,790 popular votes in Florida was a mere 537 more than Gore's 2,912,353 votes. Under the statewide winner-take-all rule used in Florida, the 537-vote lead entitled Bush to all 25 of Florida's electoral votes. There was, however, nothing particularly close about the 2000 presidential election on a nationwide basis. Al Gore's nationwide lead was 537,179 popular votes (1,000 times larger) than the 537-vote margin that decided the 2000 presidential election. Given the miniscule number of votes that are changed by a typical recount (averaging only 294 votes), no one would even have considered a recount in 2000 if the nationwide popular vote had controlled the outcome. No one would have cared whether Bush did, or did not, carry Florida by 537 popular votes. There would not have been a dispute in an election where one candidate had a nationwide margin of over a half million votes.

A recount, court case, and reversal of the original outcome occurred in Hawaii in 1960. John F. Kennedy ended up with a 115-vote margin over Richard Nixon in Hawaii in an election in which his nationwide margin was 118,574. There would have been no recount in Hawaii in 1960 if the President had been elected by a nationwide popular vote.

In 1876, Democrat Samuel J. Tilden received 4,288,191 popular votes—254,694 more than the 4,033,497 popular votes received by Republican Rutherford B. Hayes. Tilden's percentage lead of 3.05% was greater than George W. Bush's 2004 lead of 2.8%—a margin generally regarded as "solid." The 1876 election is remembered as having been close because Hayes had extremely narrow popular-vote margins in several states, namely:

- 889 votes in South Carolina,
- 922 votes in Florida,
- 4,807 in Louisiana,
- 1,075 votes in Nevada,

- 1,050 votes in Oregon,[400] and
- 2,798 votes in California.[401,402,403,]

The closeness of the 1876 presidential election in the Electoral College was an artificial crisis created by the state-by-state winner-take-all system. The candidate who received more popular votes in these closely divided states would have been a mere footnote if the President had been elected by a nationwide popular vote (where Tilden had a 254,694-vote margin).

No presidential election since the 19th century has been won with a nationwide margin of fewer than 118,574 votes (Kennedy's margin in 1960).

The closest presidential election since the 19th century (when the number of popular votes cast nationwide never exceeded 14,000,000) was the 1960 election in which John F. Kennedy led Richard M. Nixon by 118,574 popular votes (out of 68,838,219 votes cast nationwide). A margin of 118,574 popular votes is not particularly close on a nationwide basis. A six-digit nationwide margin would be unlikely to be challenged and even less likely to be reversed in a recount.

The 1960 presidential election is remembered as being close because a switch by 4,430 voters in Illinois and a switch by 4,782 voters in South Carolina would have given Nixon a majority of the electoral votes. If Nixon had just barely carried both Illinois and South Carolina, Kennedy still would have been ahead nationwide by almost 110,000 popular votes, but Nixon would have won the Presidency. In any case, the perceived closeness of the 1960 election was an illusion manufactured by the winner-take-all system used in Illinois and South Carolina—not because the nationwide margin of 118,574 was ever likely to be overturned by any recount. Indeed, the average change in the margin of victory as a result of a statewide recount was a mere 294 votes in a 13-year study of 4,072 statewide elections (section 9.15.1).

Table 9.19 shows the popular vote count for the Democratic and Republican presidential candidates in each presidential election between 1900 and 2008. In this two-party table, Theodore Roosevelt's vote is shown in the Republican column for the 1912 election because he polled more votes as the nominee of the Progressive (Bull Moose) Party than did the Republican nominee, William Howard Taft. Column 5 shows the difference between the first- and second-place candidates. None of these elections was particularly close in terms of the nationwide popular vote. The closest election during

---

[400] There was a dispute concerning the 1876 returns from Oregon; however, that dispute did not involve Hayes' relatively small margin in the state (which both parties accepted), but around whether a Republican or Democrat would replace a clearly ineligible Republican presidential elector (a federal appointee). Rehnquist, William H. 2004. *Centennial Crisis: The Disputed Election of 1876*. New York, NY: Alfred A. Knopf. Pages 109–112.

[401] Congressional Quarterly. 2002. *Presidential Elections 1789–2002*. Washington, DC: CQ Press. Page 125.

[402] Morris, Roy B. 2003. *Fraud of the Century: Rutherford B. Hayes, Samuel Tilden, and the Stolen Election of 1876*. Waterville, ME: Thorndike Press.

[403] Robinson, Lloyd. 1996. *The Stolen Election: Hayes versus Tilden—1876*. New York, NY: Tom Doherty Associates Books.

Table 9.19 WINNING MARGINS IN PRESIDENTIAL ELECTIONS 1900–2008

YEAR	TOTAL VOTE	DEMOCRAT	REPUBLICAN	DIFFERENCE
1900	13,576,891	6,357,698	7,219,193	861,495
1904	12,709,100	5,083,501	7,625,599	2,542,098
1908	14,083,472	6,406,874	7,676,598	1,269,724
1912	10,414,533	6,294,326	4,120,207	2,174,119
1916	17,673,102	9,126,063	8,547,039	579,024
1920	25,285,990	9,134,074	16,151,916	7,017,842
1924	24,110,842	8,386,532	15,724,310	7,337,778
1928	36,437,159	15,004,336	21,432,823	6,428,487
1932	38,579,166	22,818,740	15,760,426	7,058,314
1936	44,430,549	27,750,866	16,679,683	11,071,183
1940	49,678,158	27,343,218	22,334,940	5,008,278
1944	47,633,663	25,612,610	22,021,053	3,591,557
1948	46,075,874	24,105,810	21,970,064	2,135,746
1952	61,092,937	27,314,992	33,777,945	6,462,953
1956	61,613,224	26,022,752	35,590,472	9,567,720
1960	68,334,888	34,226,731	34,108,157	118,574
1964	70,307,754	43,129,566	27,178,188	15,951,378
1968	63,060,646	31,275,166	31,785,480	510,314
1972	76,340,294	29,170,383	47,169,911	17,999,528
1976	79,978,556	40,830,763	39,147,793	1,682,970
1980	79,388,036	35,483,883	43,904,153	8,420,270
1984	92,032,260	37,577,185	54,455,075	16,877,890
1988	90,695,171	41,809,074	48,886,097	7,077,023
1992	84,013,208	44,909,326	39,103,882	5,805,444
1996	86,601,112	47,402,357	39,198,755	8,203,602
2000	101,447,491	50,992,335	50,455,156	537,179
2004	121,068,721	59,028,111	62,040,610	3,012,499
2008	129,446,839	69,498,516	59,948,323	9,550,193

this period was in 1960 when the popular-vote difference was 118,574.[404] This is true even though the number of votes cast nationwide in the first few elections of the 20th century was only about 10% of present-day turnouts.

In short, recounts would be far less likely under the National Popular Vote approach than under the current state-by-state winner-take-all system.

Enactment of the National Popular Vote compact would provide impetus for the states to review and modify their laws regarding timely recounts in presidential elections.

The observation that existing state recount laws are not based on national popular vote totals is something of a straw man in that it suggests that existing state recount laws are permanent and unchangeable.

When the U.S. House of Representatives passed a constitutional amendment in

---

[404] The 1960 difference of 118,574 reflects the most commonly used method of accounting for the votes from Alabama as discussed in section 2.11.

1969 to establish a national popular vote for President, by a 338–70 margin, there were no detailed procedures for recounts in the amendment. The House did not pass accompanying recount legislation at the time it passed the amendment. Of course, it was generally understood that implementing legislation would have been enacted if the amendment had been ratified. The ratification of the amendment would have provided the impetus to update existing laws.

Similarly, the enactment of the National Popular Vote compact would provide impetus for the states to review their laws regarding timely recounts in presidential elections.

As Tara Ross says:

> "To be fair, if NPV were implemented, then many state legislatures would probably work to make their recount statutes more lenient. Even if these states otherwise disagree with NPV, they would not want to be caught in a situation where they could not participate in a national recount. Moreover, as alluded to previously, many states already provide 'optional recount' statutes that allow recounts to be requested by candidates or voters even without a close margin."[405]

Given that Congress has authority over the count and schedule for presidential elections, federal legislation is another way to solve the problem of guaranteeing a timely recount in a presidential election under the current system or the National Popular Vote plan.

Another way to remedy the existing practical difficulties of obtaining a timely recount in a presidential election would be for Congress to use its existing authority over the count and schedule for presidential elections to augment state elections with national recount legislation. This approach is discussed in section 9.15.7.

9.15.7. MYTH: There is no mechanism for conducting a national recount.

QUICK ANSWER:
- Congress has authority over the count in presidential elections as well as authority over the schedule of presidential elections.
- Congress should use this authority to enact a federal recount law that would give presidential candidates a right to obtain a recount that would be completed prior to the uniform national date for the meeting of the Electoral College.
- The federal recount law proposed in this section would require states to accelerate their initial count and conduct a full recount upon the request of

---

[405] Ross, Tara. 2012. *Enlightened Democracy: The Case for the Electoral College.* Los Angeles, CA: World Ahead Publishing Company. Second edition. Page 159.

any presidential candidate willing to pay the state, in advance, for the cost of such requests.

- A federal recount law would be highly beneficial to the operation of the current state-by-state winner-take-all method for awarding electoral votes because of the high frequency of disputes in presidential elections under the current system (five litigated state counts in a mere 57 presidential elections). Such a law would also be potentially beneficial under the national popular vote approach, even though the probability of recounts (about 1-in-185) would be much lower under a national popular vote because there would be a single large national pool of votes.

MORE DETAILED ANSWER:

Although Congress does not control the manner of awarding a state's electoral votes, Congress has constitutional authority over both the schedule of presidential elections and the counting of votes in presidential elections under Article II and the 12th Amendment.

One example of the exercise of Congress' authority over the count in presidential elections is the current federal law requiring each state to produce (prior to the meeting of the Electoral College in mid-December) a "Certificate of Ascertainment" containing the state's "final determination" of the number of popular votes cast in the state for each individual presidential candidate. This procedure was first adopted after the disputed 1876 Tilden-Hays election and is now contained in section 6, chapter 1 of Title 3 of the United States Code.

Each state's Certificate of Ascertainment provides the supporting evidence for the state's "Certificate of Election" containing the names of the presidential electors who will cast the state's votes in the Electoral College. In the case of a state using the statewide winner-take-all rule, the supporting evidence consists of the canvass of the statewide popular vote for President.[406] In the case of a state (such as Maine and Nebraska) using the congressional-district approach, the supporting evidence consists of the canvass of the district-wide popular vote for President.[407]

A joint session of Congress in early January reviews each state's Certificate of Ascertainment and Certificate of Election as part of the constitutional process of counting the votes for the presidential election.

One way to solve the problem of guaranteeing a timely recount in a presidential election would be for Congress to pass a law guaranteeing presidential candidates the right to a timely recount.

A federal law would be beneficial to the operation of the current state-by-state winner-take-all method for awarding electoral votes because of the high frequency of

---

[406] See figure 9.5 in section 9.14.1 showing Oregon's 2012 Certificate of Ascertainment.

[407] See appendix F for Maine's 2004 Certificate of Ascertainment and appendix G for Nebraska's 2004 Certificate of Ascertainment.

disputes in presidential elections under the current system (five litigated state counts in the mere 57 presidential elections).

The high frequency of recounts under the current system results from the fact that each presidential election is really 51 separate state-level elections and that the nation's 57 presidential elections have really been 2,237 separate state-level elections. Although the probability of a recount in any single statewide election is low (1-in-185 according to a study of the 4,072 statewide general elections in the 13-year period between 2000 and 2012[408]) and although recounts appear to be becoming rarer (there being no recounts among the 419 statewide elections in November 2012), the fact that each presidential election under the *current* state-by-state winner-take-all system is really 51 separate state-level elections means that there is a significant chance of future disputed presidential elections under the *current* system.

A federal law would also be potentially beneficial under the national popular vote approach, even though the probability of recounts would be much lower under a national popular vote because there would a single large national pool of votes (instead of 51 separate pools). One would expect an election close enough to warrant a recount under the National Popular Vote approach about once in 740 years (185 times four). In fact, the probability of a national recount would be even less than 1-in-185 because that rate is based on the history of statewide recounts, and recounts become less likely with larger pools of votes.

Time is of the essence in conducting a recount in a presidential election. The U.S. Constitution establishes a strict overall national schedule for finalizing the results of a presidential election. In particular, the Constitution requires the Electoral College to meet on the same day throughout the United States (currently the first Monday after the second Wednesday in December).

Because of this firm deadline, all counting, recounting, and judicial proceedings (state or federal) must be conducted so as to reach a "final determination" prior to the uniform nationwide date for the meeting of the Electoral College. The U.S. Supreme Court has made it clear that the states are expected to make their "final determination" six days before the Electoral College meets (the so-called "safe harbor" date established by section 5 of Title 3 of the United States Code).

A key consideration in constructing a practical schedule for recounts in presidential elections is the fact that *there cannot be a recount until there is a count.* That is, a recount cannot be conducted until the official initial count is completed.

Given the actual practices of many states (including many of the closely divided battleground states), there would be no time to conduct a recount under the current system of electing the President.

In Ohio in 2004, there were more than 150,000 provisional ballots. Bush's final

---

[408] See section 9.15.1 for details of the 22 statewide recounts in the 4,072 statewide general elections in the 13-year period between 2000 and 2012.

margin in the state was 118,601.[409] Senator John Kerry decided that the number of provisional ballots in relation to Bush's apparent statewide margin on Election Night (before counting the provisional ballots) did not warrant disputing the results, and he therefore conceded on the Wednesday after the election. However, had the margins been closer, a recount might have been warranted. A request for a recount is not ripe until the initial count is completed. In 2004, the initial count in Ohio was not completed and certified until the "safe harbor" day (thereby precluding a recount).

Professor Danial Tokaji at the Michael E. Moritz College of Law at Ohio State University identifies the difficulties associated with a potential contest or recount in Ohio:

> "There is no specific Ohio statute addressing a contest in a presidential election. Presumably, the generally applicable election contest procedure described above would apply. The Ohio statutory scheme, however, makes no reference to the federal statutes governing presidential election contests. This could prove problematic. **Under the "safe harbor" provision of 3 U.S.C. § 5, Ohio must reach a final determination of election controversies within 35 days of the presidential election.** A quick review of Ohio's election contest procedure illustrates the problem. **A contestor must file the petition within 15 days of the election results being certified** (assuming no automatic or requested recount). R.C. 3515.09. Presumably, a contest concerning presidential electors involves a "statewide office" requiring the petition to be filed with the Chief Justice. See R.C. 3515.08. The court must then set the hearing within the 15-to-30-day window of R.C. 3515.10. Even without considering the time delay from election day to certification of results, **meeting the 35-day safe harbor provision is doubtful**. Add to this mix the uncertainty of the 40-day deposition period of R.C. 3515.16 if the contest is "in the supreme court." Further consider the effect of an appeal—if possible—and the 20-day appellate filing window. **Following the Ohio statutory scheme makes compliance with 3 U.S.C. § 5 unlikely.**"[410] [Emphasis added]

In 2012, eight of the 10 closely divided battleground states did not complete their initial count until November 29; five of the 10 did not complete their initial count until December 5; and two did not complete their initial count until a day before the "safe harbor" date (which was December 11).[411]

In many other states, the initial count of a presidential election is generally not

---

[409] Langley, Karen and McNulty, Timothy. Verifying provisional ballots may be key to election. *Pittsburgh Post-Gazette*. August 26, 2012.

[410] Tokaji, Daniel. 2012. *Election Law@Moritz: Information and Insight on the Laws Governing Federal, State, and Local Elections*. The quotation is from a continuously updated eBook on December 27, 2012. http://moritzlaw.osu.edu/electionlaw/ebook/part5/procedures_recount05.html#_edn9.

[411] See section 9.13.7 and, in particular, table 9.14.

completed until a week or so before the "safe harbor" date (six days before the Electoral College meets).

The facts are that, under the *current* system, the possibility of conducting a timely recount of a presidential election is largely an illusion.

The precondition for conducting a full ballot-by-ballot recount of a presidential election is rapid completion of the initial count. Because there are only a few weeks between Election Day in early November and the meeting of the Electoral College, the initial count must be completed quickly enough to provide time for a full recount *plus* some additional time for post-recount litigation. Thus, an essential element of federal legislation giving presidential candidates the right to a recount must be acceleration of the initial count. Without acceleration of the initial count, there cannot be a timely recount.

Acceleration of the initial count costs money because of the overtime and additional staffing involved. There is, of course, no reason to spend the money necessary to accelerate the initial count unless there is good reason to believe that the presidential result (usually apparent to the candidates themselves on Election Night) is likely to be changed by a recount.

Taking all of the above considerations into account, we believe that an effective federal recount law for presidential elections should have the following features.

First, a federal recount law should move the uniform national day for the meeting of the Electoral College (currently established by federal law as the Monday after the second Wednesday in December) to December 30 (or to the previous Friday, if December 30 falls on a weekend). If there is no controversy over the outcome of a presidential election, the meeting of the Electoral College is ceremonial and irrelevant to implementation of the presidential transition. If there is a controversy, as much time as possible should be available to arrive at the most accurate possible determination of the presidential vote.

Second, a federal recount law should require that each state's chief election official prepare and publish a recount plan 90 days before Election Day. This chief election official's plan would provide for

(1) conducting an accelerated initial count of the presidential vote, if requested, that would be completed by November 30, and

(2) conducting a recount of the presidential vote, if requested, that would be completed by December 14 involving a one-by-one examination of each ballot (to the extent possible given the state's voting equipment and procedures).

In an undisputed presidential election, the only obligation imposed by the proposed federal count law on the state's chief election official would be the preparation of this plan.

Most states would incur substantial incremental costs (notably in the form of overtime and additional staffing) in accelerating their initial count so that it could be completed quickly enough to provide time for a full recount as well as time for post-recount litigation.

States would also incur substantial costs if a full recount had to be conducted.

Thus, the chief election official's plan would include a specification of all reasonable *incremental* costs for accelerating the initial count and all reasonable costs for conducting a recount.

Note that the federal right created by the proposed federal legislation is *not* an unfunded mandate on the states because the requesting candidate would be required to pay, in advance, for all reasonable costs as computed by the state's chief election official.

The chief election official's plan would include standards for determining voter intent for all cases that may be reasonably anticipated, given the state's voting equipment and procedures. Most state-specific problems associated with counting votes are well known to state election officials as a result of their years of experience in conducting elections. However, these standards are, in many states, not clearly delineated. Instead, the standards are a mixture of various state statutes, case law, administrative procedures at the state and local level, and unwritten practices. A clear delineation of the rules for determining voter intent in the form of administrative standards would increase the efficiency of the initial count and recount and effectively reduce the number of issues that could be successfully raised in post-recount litigation.

Third, a federal recount law should give each presidential candidate on the ballot in a state the right to call for acceleration of the initial count of the presidential vote in the state, provided that the requesting candidate pays, in advance, for all reasonable incremental costs of that request.

In addition, a federal recount law should give each presidential candidate on the ballot in a state the right to call for a recount of the presidential vote after completion of the initial count, provided that the requesting candidate pays, in advance, for all reasonable costs of that request.

As a practical matter, a presidential candidate who has a realistic chance of overturning an apparent loss of the White House would have no difficulty in quickly raising the money to pay for the requested actions.

These rights should be extended to the candidate's successor if the candidate dies or resigns.

These rights should be given to the presidential candidates themselves (as opposed to the individual candidates for the position of presidential elector, political parties, or private citizens) because the candidates are in the best position to make a realistic and pragmatic political judgment, based on available information, as to whether the election involved is close enough to warrant a potential recount.

The fact that the candidate would have to pay the costs of a requested acceleration of the initial count and the costs of a requested recount would act as a disincentive against unrealistic requests.

Note that it is not desirable or possible to impose any preconditions on requests by the presidential candidates (e.g., closeness of the results). Such preconditions would necessarily have to be couched in terms of *official* election results which (if the initial count is not yet complete) would not be available at the moment when the candidate's decision is needed.

The request for the acceleration of the initial count would have to be lodged quickly, say within six days after Election Day. In practice, it is usually clear by Election Night whether a particular election is close enough to warrant a dispute.

Television networks regularly make decisions to "call" an election on Election Night. Candidates for President (as well as candidates for Governor, U.S. Senate, and all other offices) regularly concede on Election Night. Both candidates and television networks make such decisions despite the fact that there are large numbers of in-person votes cast earlier in the day that are yet to be counted; large numbers of uncounted mail-in, military, and absentee ballots (which, in some states, need not even arrive at vote-counting centers until several days after the election); and large numbers of uncounted provisional ballots (for which voters have 6–10 days to provide evidence in support of their right to vote).

In practice, a presidential candidate's decision to request an acceleration of the initial count would be made on the basis of the same mixture of political intelligence that candidates use in making their decision to publicly concede an election, namely available actual returns announced by election officials; exit polls; estimates of the number of uncounted absentee ballots, uncounted mail-in ballots, uncounted provisional ballots, and uncounted military ballots; and historical information and current polling indicating the likely breakdown of the absentee, mail-in, provisional, and military ballots.

Candidates make their decision to concede because the information at their disposal makes it clear that they have no realistic possibility of winning.[412]

Note that there is no practical way to refund the cost of accelerating the initial count to a "successful" candidate because no official count exists at the time that the candidate would make the request (and hence no benchmark for "success").

Fourth, a federal recount law should make it clear that it is an option in addition to any procedure available under state law, state administrative procedures, or state case law. Thus, if the candidate fails to act by the deadlines contained in the federal recount law, the candidates would still be able to pursue whatever remedies may be available under existing state law.

Fifth, a federal recount law should clarify that the "safe harbor" date (defined in the existing section 5 of Title 3 of the United States Code) is the deadline for each state to complete its "final determination" of the presidential count in the state.

---

[412] Of course, candidates do not concede on Election Night (or they hastily retract their concession) if available information indicates that the race is close and that they might possibly win.

Sixth, moving the meeting of the Electoral College to December 30 (thus making December 24 the "safe harbor" day) enables a day such as December 14 to be a reasonable deadline for completing both the accelerated initial count and the recount. Such a deadline would leave 10 days for post-recount litigation. Note that five days would remain available for potential litigation after the "safe harbor" date.

Seventh, a federal recount law should give each presidential candidate on the ballot (or his successor) the right to sue to enforce all the provisions of Title 3 of the U.S. Code concerning presidential elections. To avoid forum-shopping within a state, the action should be required to be brought in the federal district court located in the state capital (or the district court located nearest to the state capital if no federal district court is located in the capital).

Note that an additional advantage of a federal right to a recount in presidential elections is that it would preclude state officials from effectively precluding a recount by "slow walking" the state's initial count. Slow-walking of the initial count effectively enables state officials (many elected on a partisan basis) to decide whether their own work product is subject to accountability.

Table 9.20 shows the schedule for 2016 under the proposed legislation.

Table 9.20 SCHEDULE FOR 2016 UNDER PROPOSED FEDERAL RECOUNT LEGISLATION

DATE	EVENT
Tuesday August 9, 2016	90 days prior to Election Day—Each state's chief elections official publishes a plan (1) for conducting an accelerated initial count of the presidential vote that would be completed by November 30 and (2) for conducting a full recount of the presidential vote that would be completed by December 14. Such plan shall specify all reasonable incremental costs for accelerating the initial count and all reasonable costs for conducting the recount. Such plan shall include standards for determining voter intent for all cases that may be reasonably anticipated given the state's voting equipment and procedures.
Tuesday November 8, 2016	Election Day—Tuesday after the first Monday in November
Monday November 14, 2016	Six days after Election Day—Last day for a presidential candidate to request a state to conduct an accelerated initial count that would be completed by November 30. Such request is to be accompanied by full payment by the requesting candidate of all costs specified in the chief elections official's plan.
Wednesday November 30, 2012	Last day for completing the accelerated initial count
Friday December 2, 2016	Last day for any presidential candidate to request state(s) that have completed their initial count to conduct a full recount that would be completed by December 14. Such request is to be accompanied by full payment by the requesting candidate of all costs specified in the chief elections official's plan.
Monday December 14, 2016	Last day for completing the recount—10 days before the "safe harbor" day.
Tuesday December 15, 2016	Beginning of 10-day period for post-recount litigation
Saturday December 24, 2016	"Safe harbor" day—day for the state to make its "final determination" of its count (six days before the meeting of the Electoral College)
Sunday December 25, 2016	Beginning of five-day period for post-Safe-Harbor-Day litigation
Friday December 30, 2016	Meeting of the Electoral College

The proposed federal recount bill (shown below) has the following elements:

- Section 1 of the proposed bill is the bill's title.
- Section 2 of the proposed bill adds a new subsection (b) to section 5 of Title 3 of the United States Code containing five new parts.
    - Part (1) of the new subsection (b) of section 5 of Title 3 makes the "safe harbor" day (defined in the existing portion of section 5—now called subsection (a)) into an actual deadline for each state to complete its "final determination" of the presidential count in the state.
    - Part (2) of the new subsection (b) of section 5 of Title 3 requires the state's chief election official to prepare and publish a plan (1) for conducting an accelerated initial count of the presidential vote that would be completed by November 30 and (2) for conducting a full recount of the presidential vote involving a one-by-one examination (to the extent possible, given the state's voting equipment and procedures) of each ballot that would be completed by December 14—along with all reasonable incremental costs of conducting an accelerated initial count and all reasonable costs of conducting the recount. Such plan shall include standards for determining voter intent for all cases that may be reasonably anticipated given the state's voting equipment and procedures.
    - Part (3) of the new subsection (b) of section 5 of Title 3 gives a presidential candidate on the ballot in the state the opportunity to call for an acceleration of the initial count in a state to be completed by November 30, provided the requesting candidate pays for all reasonable incremental costs of accelerating the initial count. The right to an accelerated initial count created by this subsection must be exercised within six days after Election Day. This right is extended to the presidential candidate's successor if the candidate dies or resigns.
    - Part (4) of the new subsection (b) of section 5 of Title 3 gives a presidential candidate the opportunity to request a recount to be completed by December 14, provided the requesting candidate pays for all reasonable costs of the recount. The right to a recount created by this subsection must be exercised by December 2. This right is extended to the presidential candidate's successor if the candidate dies or resigns.
    - Part (5) of the new subsection (b) of section 5 of Title 3 gives a presidential candidate on the ballot (or his successor) the right to sue to enforce all the requirements of Title 3. To avoid forum-shopping within the state, the action must be brought in the District Court located in the state capital (or the United States District Court located nearest to the state capital if no United States District Court is located in the capital).
    - Part (6) of the new subsection (b) of section 5 of Title 3 explicitly states that the recount made available under part (3) of the new subsection (b) of

section 5 of Title 3 shall be an option available to presidential candidates in addition to any procedure available under state law, administrative procedures, or judicial determinations.

- Section 3 of the proposed bill amends section 6 of Title 3 of the United States Code by requiring that the Certificates of Ascertainment be physically delivered to Washington, D.C., no later than the day after the "safe harbor" day. The current section 6 has an outdated time-consuming process involving registered mail and sets no particular deadline.

- Section 4 of the proposed bill amends section 6 of Title 3 of the United States Code by moving the uniform national day for the meeting of the Electoral College (currently the Monday after the second Wednesday in December) to December 30 (or the previous Friday if December 30 falls on a weekend).

- Section 5 of the proposed bill makes the bill effective for the 2016 elections.

Text of Proposed Federal Recount Bill

To amend title 3, United States Code, to require a State to make available to a presidential candidate a timely initial count and a timely recount of the number of votes cast in the presidential election in the State, to change the date for a State to complete its final canvas or ascertainment of the number of votes cast for each candidate in a presidential election, to change the date of the meeting of presidential electors, and for other purposes.

Be it enacted by the Senate and House of Representatives of the United States of America in Congress assembled,

SECTION 1. SHORT TITLE.

This Act may be cited as the "Presidential Election Recount Act of ___".

SEC. 2. DEADLINE FOR FINAL CANVASS AND ASCERTAINMENT OF NUMBER OF VOTES CAST FOR PRESIDENT AND AVAILABILITY OF RECOUNT.

Section 5 of title 3, United States Code, is amended—

(1) by striking "If any State" and inserting "(a) IN GENERAL.—If any State" and by striking "concerning the appointment" and inserting "concerning the canvass or appointment".

(2) by adding at the end the following new subsection:

"(b) DEADLINE FOR FINAL DETERMINATION OF CANVASS OR ASCERTAINMENT OF VOTES CAST FOR PRESIDENT AND AVAILABILITY OF ACCELERATED INITIAL COUNT AND AVAILABILITY OF RECOUNT—

"(1) DEADLINE FOR FINAL DETERMINATION.—The canvass or ascertainment under the laws of each state of the number of votes given or cast for each candidate for President or presidential elector and the final determination of any controversy or contest concerning such canvass of ascertainment shall be made not later than 6 days before the time fixed for the meeting of the electors under section 7 of this title.

"(2) PREPARATION OF PLAN FOR RECOUNT AND COSTS.—No later than 90 days before the time fixed for appointing electors under section 1 of this title, the state official or body that is authorized to conduct the canvass or ascertainment under the laws of each state of the number of votes given or cast for each candidate for President or presidential elector shall prepare, and make available to the public, a plan for accelerating the initial count of each ballot given or cast for each candidate for President or presidential elector in that state, with such accelerated initial count to be completed by November 30, and a plan for conducting a full recount involving a one-by-one examination (to the extent possible, given the state's voting equipment and procedures) of each ballot given or cast for each candidate for President or presidential elector in that state, with such recount to be completed by December 10. Such plan shall include standards (not inconsistent with state law) for determining voter intent for all cases that may be reasonably anticipated, given the state's voting equipment and procedures. Such plan shall include all reasonable incremental costs to the state associated with accelerating the initial count and all reasonable costs to the state for conducting the recount.

"(3) ACCELERATION OF INITIAL COUNT.—If a candidate for the office of President appearing on the ballot in a given state (or a legal successor nominated in lieu of such candidate) shall, no later than 6 days after the time fixed for appointing electors under section 1 of this title, make a written request, accompanied by payment in full of the costs specified in the plan created under part (2) of this subsection, for accelerating the initial count, the state official or body that is authorized to conduct the canvass or ascertainment under the laws of each state of the number of votes given or cast for each candidate for President or elector shall conduct the initial count of the votes cast for each candidate for President or presidential elector, with such recount to be completed by November 30. If more than one candidate makes a request for accelerating the initial count in the state, the state shall divide the costs among the requesting candidates and refund any excess payments received.

"(4) AVAILABILITY OF RECOUNT.—If a candidate for the office of President appearing on the ballot in a given state (or a legal successor nominated in lieu of such candidate) shall by December 2 make a written request, accompanied by payment in full of the costs specified in the plan created under part (2) of this subsection, for conducting a full recount involving a one-by-one examination (to the extent possible given the State's voting equipment and procedures) of each ballot given or cast for each candidate for President or elector in a given state, the state official or body that is authorized to conduct the canvass or ascertainment under the laws of each state of the number of votes given or cast for each candidate for President or elector shall then conduct a full recount of the votes cast for each candidate for President or presidential elector, with such recount to be completed by December 14. If more than one candidate makes a request for a recount in the state, the state shall divide the costs among the requesting candidates and refund any excess payments received.

"(5) PRIVATE RIGHT OF ACTION.—An individual who is a citizen of the United States who is a resident of the State involved or a candidate for the office of President appearing on the ballot in a given state (or a legal successor nominated in lieu of such candidate) may bring an action against the State in the United States district court located in the capital of the State involved (or the United States district court located nearest to the state capital if no United States district court is located in the capital) for such declaratory or injunctive relief as may be necessary to ensure that the State is in compliance with this title."

"(6) NON-PRE-EMPTION.—The recount made available under part (3) of this subsection shall be an option available to presidential candidates (or a legal successor nominated in lieu of such candidate) in addition to any procedure available under applicable state laws, administrative procedures, or judicial decisions.

SEC. 3. REQUIRING PROMPT TRANSMISSION OF CERTIFICATIONS.

Section 6 of title 3, United States Code, is amended—

(1) by striking "as soon as practicable" each place it appears and inserting "immediately";

(2) by striking "to communicate by registered mail" and inserting "to communicate by overnight courier service"; and

(3) by striking "to communicate under the seal of the State" and inserting "to communicate by overnight courier service under the seal of the State".

SEC. 4. TIME FOR MEETING OF THE ELECTORAL COLLEGE.

Section 7 of title 3, United States Code, is amended by striking "first Monday after the second Wednesday in December next following their appointment" and inserting "30th day of December next following their appointment or the preceding Friday if December 30 is a Saturday or Sunday."

SEC. 5. EFFECTIVE DATE.

The amendments made by this Act shall apply to Presidential elections beginning with the elections held in November 2016.

9.15.8. MYTH: A nationwide vote for President should not be implemented as long as any state uses direct-recording electronic (DRE) voting machines lacking a voter-verifiable paper audit trail.

QUICK ANSWER:
- Today, many direct-recording electronic (DRE) voting machines in many states lack a voter-verifiable paper audit trail (VVPAT), thereby making it impossible to conduct a ballot-by-ballot post-election audit or recount.
- The potential problem that may be created by DRE machines without a VVPAT are not uniquely associated with elections conducted under the current state-by-state winner-take-all system or those conducted under the National Popular Vote plan. Indeed, DRE machines without a VVPAT were used in 2012 in battleground states such as Virginia, Colorado, Pennsylvania, and Florida.
- DRE machines without a VVPAT are more likely to affect an election outcome under the current state-by-state winner-take-all system than an election with a single (much larger) national pool of votes.
- While it would be desirable if all voting machines permitted a ballot-by-ballot recount, the probability of a recount in an election in which there is a single pool of votes (such as a nationwide vote for President) is about 1 in 185 (that is, once in 740 years in the case of presidential elections). Moreover, the probability of a recount (itself a rare event) reversing the outcome of an election is only about one in seven. Thus, the (admittedly undesirable) use of DRE machines without a VVPAT is, as a practical matter, unlikely to affect the outcome of any recount in any presidential election.
- In the second half of the 20th century, about two-thirds of all voting in the United States was done on lever-type voting machines that lacked a voter-verifiable paper audit trail (VVPAT). There were no major adverse consequences to the nation because of the absence of the desirable higher degree of post-election verification, and, in particular, no presidential election was affected by the use of lever-type machines.

MORE DETAILED ANSWER:
A caller to a radio debate on the National Popular Vote plan asked:

"With a lot of voting machines without paper trails, there really isn't a method of doing recounts. So, how would we do an effective recount if we need to?[413]

[413] Question called in by Arthur from Palo Alto, California, on KQED debate on October 26, 2012, involving Dr. John R. Koza (Chair of National Popular Vote), Stanford Professor Jack Rakove, Trent England (a lobbyist

Direct-recording electronic (DRE) voting machines are in widespread use in the United States.

Some DREs produce a voter-verifiable paper audit trail (VVPAT) that permits post-election ballot-by-ballot auditing or recounting of the results; however, others do not.

Computer World reported in October 2012:

> "A total of 16 states use DREs that do not support a paper trail as their standard polling place equipment, according to Verified Voting. Of these, six states—New Jersey, Delaware, Maryland, South Carolina, Georgia, and Louisiana—will be completely paperless. All ballots that are cast in these states will be on DREs that support no paper trail whatsoever.

> "The remaining states, which include Texas, Colorado, Florida, Virginia, and Pennsylvania, will use a mix of paper ballots and DRE voting systems that are paperless. But even here, the states of Virginia, Pennsylvania, and Tennessee will be almost completely reliant on paperless electronic voting systems. In Tennessee, for instance, all but two counties will use paperless DREs, while in Virginia all but seven of 134 countries will use paperless systems. Meanwhile, in a handful of states like Florida, only voters with physical disabilities will use paperless DREs."[414]

The problem of DRE machines without a VVPAT is not uniquely associated with elections conducted under the current state-by-state winner-take-all system or those conducted under the National Popular Vote plan.

The deficiencies of DRE machines without a VVPAT are amplified by the current state-by-state winner-take-all system under which a small number of popular votes in a single battleground state can change the outcome of a national election. In 2000, for example, George W. Bush won Florida by a margin of 537 popular votes out of 5,963,110 votes cast, and those 537 votes determined the outcome of the national election.

Indeed, DRE machines without a VVPAT were used in 2012 in battleground states such as Virginia, Colorado, Pennsylvania, and Florida.

In Virginia, 101 of 134 counties and independent cities in Virginia do not have a paper record of the vote. These places contain over four million voters.[415]

In Pennsylvania, 50 of the 67 counties do not keep a voter-verified paper record of voter choices.[416]

---

opposing the National Popular Vote compact and Vice-President of the Evergreen Freedom Foundation of Olympia, Washington), and Ace Smith (a political consultant headquartered in San Francisco). http://www .kqed.org/a/forum/R201210260900.

[414] Vijayan, Jaikumar. Election watchdogs keep wary eye on paperless e-voting systems. *Computer World.* October 30, 2012.

[415] Norden, Lawrence. Issue Brief: Election 2012 Recounts. New York, NY: Brennan Center for Justice. Page 32.

[416] Norden, Lawrence. Issue Brief: Election 2012 Recounts. New York, NY: Brennan Center for Justice. Page 29.

Jefferson County, Colorado, is the state's fourth most populous county, and it uses iVotronic machines without VVPAT. There are 381,164 registered voters in the county.[417]

Florida uses DRE machines with a VVPAT for handicap-accessible voting.[418]

In terms of actual consequences in the real world, the (admittedly undesirable) use of DRE machines without a VVPAT is unlikely to have any effect on the outcome of any presidential election held under the National Popular Vote plan.

In the first place, the probability of a recount affecting the outcome of a particular presidential election in which there is a single pool of votes (i.e., a national popular vote) is low. As shown in table 9.16, there were 22 recounts in 4,072 statewide general elections in the 13-year period between 2000 and 2012—that is, one recount for every 185 elections. In terms of presidential elections, this probability indicates that there would be a recount in a nationwide popular vote for President only once in 740 years.

Recounts change only a small number of votes (an average of only 294 votes in statewide elections), and the probability of a recount reversing an election outcome is only one in seven.[419] Thus, the (admittedly undesirable) use of DRE machines without a VVPAT is, as a practical matter, unlikely to affect the outcome of any presidential election.

In the second half of the 20th century, about two-thirds of all voting in the United States was done on lever-type voting machines. These machines (like DREs without a VVPAT) recorded the total count for each candidate, but did not keep a record of each individual ballot. Figure 2.13 shows the face of a lever-type voting machine used in 1960 in Alabama. Votes were recorded on mechanical counters on lever-type voting machines. After the polls closed, each voting machine was opened, and the vote count for each office was read from the mechanical counters. During the many decades when lever-type voting machines were in widespread use in the United States, there were no major adverse consequences to the nation because of the absence of the highest desirable degree of post-election verification. In particular, no presidential election was affected by the use of lever-type machines or the absence of a voter-verifiable paper audit trail.

The (unfortunate) inability to conduct a ballot-by-ballot post-election recount of votes cast on DRE machines without a VVPAT does not mean that an election would be thrown into chaos. It would not even mean that a recount could not be conducted. It would simply mean that the quality and thoroughness of the recount on those particular machines would be severely limited to that which lever-type voting machines provided in the second half of the 20th century (e.g., to catching errors such as incorrectly recording the count from a machine, failing to include the count from a machine, or double-counting a machine).

---

[417] Norden, Lawrence. Issue Brief: Election 2012 Recounts. New York, NY: Brennan Center for Justice. Page 3.

[418] See table 9.17 in section 9.15.1..

[419] Richie, Rob; Talukdar, Monideepa; and Hellman, Emily. 2010. *A Survey and Analysis of Statewide Election Recounts, 2000–2009*. FairVote. Moreover, three-quarters of all recounts do not change the outcome.

Election authorities in the states have the ability to replace DRE machines without a VVPAT with machines with a VVPAT. Hopefully, they will exercise their power to do so.

9.16. MYTHS ABOUT INTERSTATE COMPACTS AND CONGRESSIONAL CONSENT

9.16.1. MYTH: Interstate compacts are exotic and fishy.

QUICK ANSWER:
- Interstate compacts are authorized by the U.S. Constitution and are in widespread use by every state.

MORE DETAILED ANSWER:
The U.S. Constitution authorizes states to enter into interstate compacts.

> "No state shall, without the consent of Congress, . . . enter into any agreement or compact with another state or with a foreign power."[420]

Interstate compacts predate the Constitution. One interstate compact approved at the time of the Articles of Confederation remained in force until 1958 (when it was replaced by an updated version).

The subject matter of existing interstate compacts varies widely and has included such topics as agriculture, boundaries, bridges, building construction and safety, child welfare, civil defense, conservation, corrections, crime control, cultural issues, education, emergency management, energy, facilities, flood control, gambling and lotteries, health, insurance, interstate school districts, low-level radioactive waste, metropolitan problems, motor vehicles, national guard, natural resources, navigation, parks and recreation, pest control, planning and development, ports, property, public safety, river basins, taxation, transportation, and water.

Examples of compacts include the
- Colorado River Compact (allocating water among seven western states),
- Port Authority of New York and New Jersey (a two-state compact),
- Multistate Tax Compact (whose membership includes 23 states and the District of Columbia),
- Interstate Oil and Gas Compact,
- Interstate Corrections Compact,
- Mutual Aid Compact,
- Great Lakes Basin Compact (to which the Canadian province of Ontario is a party along with various states), and

---

[420] U.S. Constitution. Article I, section 10, clause 3.

- Multi-State Lottery Compact (which operates the Powerball lotto game in numerous states).

Compacts are often used on a nationwide basis. For example, the Interstate Compact on the Placement of Children and the Interstate Compact on Juveniles are examples of compacts adhered to by all 50 states and the District of Columbia.

Numerous other compacts are listed in appendix M and discussed in chapter 5.

Once a state enters into an interstate compact, the terms of the compact are legally enforceable against the participating states because the Impairments Clause of the U.S. Constitution provides:

"No State shall . . . pass any . . . Law impairing the Obligation of Contracts."[421]

The Council of State Governments summarizes the nature of interstate compacts as follows:

"Compacts are agreements between two or more states that bind them to the compacts' provisions, just as a contract binds two or more parties in a business deal. As such, compacts are subject to the substantive principles of contract law and are protected by the constitutional prohibition against laws that impair the obligations of contracts (U.S. Constitution, Article I, Section 10).

"That means that **compacting states are bound to observe the terms of their agreements, even if those terms are inconsistent with other state laws.** In short, compacts between states are somewhat like treaties between nations. Compacts have the force and effect of statutory law (whether enacted by statute or not) and **they take precedence over conflicting state laws, regardless of when those laws are enacted.**

"However, unlike treaties, compacts are not dependent solely upon the good will of the parties. **Once enacted, compacts may not be unilaterally renounced by a member state, except as provided by the compacts themselves.** Moreover, Congress and the courts can compel compliance with the terms of interstate compacts. That's why **compacts are considered the most effective means of ensuring interstate cooperation.**"[422] [Emphasis added]

The National Popular Vote plan is an interstate compact—a type of state law that is explicitly authorized by the U.S. Constitution to enable otherwise sovereign states to enter into legally enforceable contractual obligations with one another.

---

[421] U.S. Constitution. Article I, section 10, clause 1.

[422] Council of State Governments. 2003. *Interstate Compacts and Agencies 2003.* Lexington, KY: The Council of State Governments. Page 6.

9.16.2. MYTH: The topic of elections addressed by the National Popular Vote compact is not an appropriate subject for an interstate compact.

QUICK ANSWER:

- There are no constitutional restrictions on the subject matter of interstate compacts other than the implicit limitation that a compact's subject matter must be among the powers that the states are permitted to exercise.
- The U.S. Constitution gives each state the "exclusive" and "plenary" power to choose the manner of appointing its presidential electors. Thus, the subject matter of the National Popular Vote compact is among the powers that the states are permitted to exercise.
- The 10th Amendment independently addresses the question of whether the states are prohibited from exercising a particular power when the Constitution contains no specific prohibition against it. It says, "The powers not delegated to the United States by the Constitution, nor prohibited by it to the States, are reserved to the States respectively, or to the people."

MORE DETAILED ANSWER:

The U.S. Constitution places no restriction on the subject matter of an interstate compact other than the implicit limitation that a compact's subject matter must be among the powers that the states are permitted to exercise. That implicit limitation does not apply to the subject matter of the National Popular Vote compact, because the U.S. Supreme Court has ruled that states possess *exclusive* power to choose the method of awarding their electoral votes.

The National Popular Vote compact concerns the method of appointment of a state's presidential electors.

The U.S. Constitution gives each state the power to select the manner of appointing its presidential electors.

> "Each State shall appoint, in such Manner as the Legislature thereof may direct, a Number of Electors. . . ."[423]

The U.S. Supreme Court ruled in *McPherson v. Blacker* in 1892:

> "In short, **the appointment and mode of appointment of electors belong exclusively to the states** under the constitution of the United States. . . . Congress is empowered to determine the time of choosing the electors and the day on which they are to give their votes, which is required to be the same day throughout the United States; but otherwise **the power and jurisdiction of the state is exclusive**, with the exception of the pro-

---

[423] U.S. Constitution. Article II, section 1, clause 2.

visions as to the number of electors and the ineligibility of certain persons, so framed that congressional and federal influence might be excluded."[424] [Emphasis added]

Thus, the subject matter of the National Popular Vote compact is a state power.

The states have used interstate compacts in increasingly creative ways since the 1920s. The judiciary has been repeatedly asked to consider the validity of various novel compacts; however, we are aware of no case in which the courts have invalidated any interstate compact.[425]

Although there is currently no interstate compact concerned with presidential elections, U.S. Supreme Court Justice Potter Stewart noted the possibility of compacts involving elections in his concurring and dissenting opinion in *Oregon v. Mitchell* in 1970. In that case, the U.S. Supreme Court examined the constitutionality of the Voting Rights Act Amendments of 1970 that removed state-imposed durational residency requirements on voters casting ballots in presidential elections. Justice Stewart concurred with the majority that Congress had the power to make durational residency requirements uniform in presidential elections, and observed:

> "Congress could rationally conclude that the imposition of durational residency requirements unreasonably burdens and sanctions the privilege of taking up residence in another State. The objective of § 202 is clearly a legitimate one. Federal action is required if the privilege to change residence is not to be undercut by parochial local sanctions. No State could undertake to guarantee this privilege to its citizens. At most a single State could take steps to resolve that its own laws would not unreasonably discriminate against the newly arrived resident. Even this resolve might not remain firm in the face of discriminations perceived as unfair against those of its own citizens who moved to other States. Thus, the problem could not be wholly solved by a single State, or even by several States, since every State of new residence and every State of prior residence would have a necessary role to play. **In the absence of a unanimous interstate compact, the problem could only be solved by Congress.**"[426] [Emphasis added]

We are not aware of any case in which the courts have invalidated *any* interstate compact.[427] Given the recent tendencies of the courts to accord even greater deference to states' rights and even wider and freer use of interstate compacts by the states, it

---

[424] *McPherson v. Blacker.* 146 U.S. 1 at 35. 1892.

[425] There have been cases where a higher court has invalidated a ruling by a lower court invalidating an interstate compact. See, for example, *West Virginia ex rel. Dyer v. Sims.* 341 U.S. 22. 1950.

[426] *Oregon v. Mitchell.* 400 U.S. 112 at 286–287. 1970.

[427] There have been cases where a higher court corrected a ruling by a lower court invalidating an interstate compact. See, for example, *West Virginia ex rel. Dyer v. Sims.* 341 U.S. 22. 1950.

is unlikely that the courts would invalidate the National Popular Vote compact. The National Popular Vote compact is an example of federalism in action and of states exercising their rightful powers.

The 10th Amendment independently addresses the question of whether the states are prohibited from exercising a particular power when the Constitution contains no specific prohibition against it and, therefore, the question of whether there are unstated implicit restrictions on the allowable methods for appointing presidential electors.

> **"The powers** not delegated to the United States by the Constitution, **nor prohibited by it to the States, are reserved to the States** respectively, or to the people." [Emphasis added]

Section 1 of Article II contains only one restriction on state choices on the manner of appointing their presidential electors, namely that no state may appoint a member of Congress or federal appointees as presidential elector.[428]

The 10th Amendment was ratified in 1791 (that is, after ratification of the original Constitution) and thus takes precedence over the original 1787 Constitution. Even if there were implied restrictions on state choices on the manner of appointing their presidential electors (perhaps from penumbral emanations from section 1 of Article II), such implicit restrictions were extinguished by the 10th Amendment in 1791.

In conclusion, nothing in the U.S. Constitution prevents states from using an interstate compact to specify the manner in which they choose their presidential electors.

9.16.3. MYTH: The National Popular Vote compact is defective because Congress did not consent to it prior to its consideration by state legislatures.

QUICK ANSWER:

- Advance congressional consent is not required, nor is it the norm in the field of interstate compacts.
- If a particular compact requires congressional consent, Congress generally considers the matter only after the compact has been approved by the combination of states required to bring the compact into effect.

---

[428] The original Constitution contains few specific restrictions on state action that bear on the appointment of presidential electors. Thus, under Article II, section 1, clause 1, a state legislature may, for example, pass a law making it a crime to commit fraud in a presidential election. However, a state legislature certainly may not pass an *ex post facto* (retroactive) law making it a crime to commit fraud in a previous presidential election. Similarly, a state legislature may not pass a law imposing criminal penalties on specifically named persons who may have committed fraudulent acts in connection with a presidential election (that is, a bill of attainder). Also, the Constitution's explicit prohibition against a "law impairing the obligation of contract" operates as a restraint on the delegation of power contained in section 1 of Article II. Of course, various later amendments restrict state choices, including the 14th Amendment (equal protection), the 15th Amendment (prohibiting denial of the vote on account of "race, color, or previous condition of servitude"), the 19th Amendment (woman's suffrage), the 24th amendment (prohibiting poll taxes), and the 26th Amendment (18-year-old vote).

MORE DETAILED ANSWER:

Advance congressional consent is not required, nor is it the norm in the field of interstate compacts.

If a particular compact requires congressional consent, Congress generally considers the matter only after the compact has been approved by the combination of states required to bring the compact into effect.[429]

As the U.S. Supreme Court ruled in the 1893 case of *Virginia v. Tennessee*:

> "The constitution does not state when the consent of congress shall be given, **whether it shall precede or may follow the compact made, or whether it shall be express or may be implied.**"[430] [Emphasis added]

9.16.4. MYTH: The National Popular Vote compact is defective because it fails to mention Congress in its text.

QUICK ANSWER:

- Most interstate compacts do not specifically mention congressional consent, regardless of whether the particular compact requires congressional consent.

MORE DETAILED ANSWER:

Most compacts do not specifically mention congressional consent, regardless of whether the states involved intend to seek it.

For example, the Port Authority of New York Compact is silent as to congressional consent. The two states involved did *not* intend to seek congressional consent at the time that they entered into the compact. Later, they decided to seek congressional consent (and received it).

Conversely, the states involved in the Multistate Tax Compact (also silent as to the role of Congress) originally sought congressional consent, but, after realizing that they could not obtain it, the states proceeded to implement the compact without congressional consent. The U.S. Supreme Court ruled in favor of the states (and upheld that sequence of events) in the 1978 case of *U.S. Steel Corporation v. Multistate Tax Commission*[431]—the leading recent case on the issue of congressional consent of interstate compacts (discussed in detail in section 9.16.5).

There is no need for a compact to mention Congress, even if the states involved intend to seek congressional consent.

---

[429] Congress has, on rare occasions, consented to compacts in advance of action by the states. For example, Congress consented in advance to certain interstate crime control compacts in the Crime Control Consent Act of 1934. Other examples include the Weeks Act of 1911 and the Tobacco Control Act of 1936. See section 5.9.

[430] *Virginia v. Tennessee.* 148 U.S. 503 at 521. 1893.

[431] *U.S. Steel Corporation v. Multistate Tax Commission.* 434 U.S. 452. 1978.

9.16.5. MYTH: The National Popular Vote compact requires congressional consent to become effective.

QUICK ANSWER:

- The U.S. Supreme Court has ruled that congressional consent is only necessary for interstate compacts that "encroach upon or interfere with the just supremacy of the United States." Because the choice of method of appointing presidential electors is an "exclusive" and "plenary" state power, there is no encroachment on federal authority.
- Thus, under established compact jurisprudence, congressional consent would not be necessary for the National Popular Vote compact to become effective.
- Nonetheless, National Popular Vote is working to obtain support for the compact in Congress.

MORE DETAILED ANSWER:

The U.S. Constitution provides:

> "No state shall, without the consent of Congress, . . . enter into any agreement or compact with another state. . . ."[432]

The U.S. Supreme Court has ruled, in 1893 and in 1978, that the Compacts Clause can "not be read literally" in deciding the question of whether congressional consent is necessary for a particular interstate compact.

The 1893 case of *Virginia v. Tennessee* involved an interstate compact that had not received congressional consent. The U.S. Supreme Court upheld the constitutionality of the compact, saying:

> "Looking at the clause in which the terms 'compact' or 'agreement' appear, it is evident that **the prohibition is directed to the formation of any combination tending to the increase of political power in the states, which may encroach upon or interfere with the just supremacy of the United States.**"[433] [Emphasis added]

The Court continued:

> "**the test is whether the Compact enhances state power** *quaod* [with regard to] **the National Government**."[434] [Emphasis added]

The 1978 case of *U.S. Steel Corporation v. Multistate Tax Commission* reinforced the Court's 1893 decision as to the criteria for determining whether a particular interstate compact requires congressional consent.

---

[432] U.S. Constitution. Article I, section 10, clause 3.

[433] *Virginia v. Tennessee.* 148 U.S. 503 at 519. 1893.

[434] *Virginia v. Tennessee.* 148 U.S. 503. 1893.

The Multistate Tax Compact was formulated by state tax administrators to stave off federal encroachment on the power of the states to tax multi-state businesses.[435] The compact created a commission empowered to conduct audits of businesses operating in multiple states and gave multistate businesses a choice of formulas for calculating their state taxes.

The Multistate Tax Compact provided that it would come into force when any seven or more states enacted it. By 1967, the requisite number of states had approved the compact.

The Multistate Tax Compact was submitted to Congress for its consent. After encountering fierce political opposition in Congress aroused by various business interests concerned about the more stringent tax audits anticipated under the compact, the compacting states proceeded to implement the compact without congressional consent. U.S. Steel and other companies challenged the states' action.

In upholding the constitutionality of the states' implementation of the compact without congressional consent in 1978, the U.S. Supreme Court ruled in *U.S. Steel Corporation v. Multistate Tax Commission*:

> **"Read literally, the Compact Clause would require the States to obtain congressional approval** before entering into any agreement among themselves, irrespective of form, subject, duration, or interest to the United States.

> **"The difficulties with such an interpretation were identified by Mr. Justice Field in his opinion for the Court in [the 1893 case]** *Virginia v. Tennessee*.[436] **His conclusion [was] that the Clause could not be read literally** [and the Supreme Court's 1893 decision has been] approved in subsequent dicta, but this Court did not have occasion expressly to apply it in a holding until our recent [1976] decision in *New Hampshire v. Maine*,[437] supra."

> "Appellants urge us to abandon *Virginia v. Tennessee* and *New Hampshire v. Maine*, but provide no effective alternative other than a literal reading of the Compact Clause. At this late date, **we are reluctant to accept this invitation to circumscribe modes of interstate cooperation that do not enhance state power to the detriment of federal supremacy.**"[438] [Emphasis added]

---

[435] *The Gillette Company et al. v. Franchise Tax Board. Court of Appeal of the State of California*, First Appellate District, Division Four. July 24, 2012. Page 4. Appendix GG contains the full opinion.

[436] *Virginia v. Tennessee*. 148 U.S. 503. 1893.

[437] *New Hampshire v. Maine*, 426 U.S. 363. 1976.

[438] *U.S. Steel Corporation v. Multistate Tax Commission*. 434 U.S. 452. at 459–460. 1978.

State power over the manner of awarding electoral votes is specified in Article II, section 1, clause 2 of the U.S. Constitution:

> "Each State shall appoint, in such Manner as the Legislature thereof may direct, a Number of Electors. . . ."[439]

In the 1892 case of *McPherson v. Blacker*, the U.S. Supreme Court ruled:

> "The appointment and mode of appointment of electors belong **exclusively** to the states under the constitution of the United States"[440] [Emphasis added]

The National Popular Vote compact would not be a "combination tending to the increase of political power in the states which may encroach upon or interfere with the just supremacy of the United States" because the choice of manner of appointing presidential electors is "exclusively" a state—not federal—power.

The absence of federal power—much less federal supremacy—over the awarding of electoral votes is made especially clear by comparing the constitutional provision (section 1 of Article I) dealing with presidential elections with the constitutional provision (section 4 of Article II) dealing with congressional elections.

Section 4 of Article II states:

> "The Times, Places and Manner of holding Elections for Senators and Representatives, shall be prescribed in each State by the Legislature thereof; **but the Congress may at any time by Law make or alter such Regulations**, except as to the Places of chusing Senators." [Emphasis added]

As can be seen, section 4 of Article II gives states *primary*—but not *exclusive*—control over congressional elections. In contrast, section 1 of Article II gives the states *exclusive* control over the manner of appointing presidential electors.

The National Popular Vote compact would not encroach on the "just supremacy of the United States," because the states have the *exclusive* power to choose the method of appointing their presidential electors.

In upholding the constitutionality of the states' implementation of the Multistate Tax Compact without congressional consent, the U.S. Supreme Court applied the interpretation of the Compact Clause from its 1893 holding in *Virginia v. Tennessee*, writing that:

> "**the test is whether the Compact enhances state power** *quaod* [with regard to] **the National Government.**"[441] [Emphasis added]

The Court also noted that the compact did not

---

[439] U.S. Constitution. Article II, section 1, clause 2.
[440] *McPherson v. Blacker*. 146 U.S. 1 at 29. 1892.
[441] *Virginia v. Tennessee*. 148 U.S. 503. 1893.

"authorize the member states to exercise any powers they could not exercise in its absence."[442]

In discussing whether the National Popular Vote compact requires congressional consent, Tara Ross, an opponent of the National Popular Vote compact, has argued that the federal government has an "interest" in the compact.

> **"The federal government has at least one important interest at stake**. As Professor Judith Best has noted, **the federal government has a vested interest in protecting its constitutional amendment process**. If the NPV compact goes into effect, its proponents will have effectively changed the presidential election procedure described in the Constitution, without the bother of obtaining a constitutional amendment."[443] [Emphasis added]

As discussed at length in section 9.1.1, section 9.1.2, section 9.1.3, section 9.1.4, and section 9.1.6, the National Popular Vote compact would not change "the presidential election procedure described in the Constitution." Indeed, no state law or compact can do that. Instead, the National Popular Vote compact would change *state* winner-take-all statutes. None of these state winner-take-all statutes was originally adopted by means of a federal constitutional amendment. None of these state statutes has constitutional status. The winner-take-all rule was not debated by the Constitutional Convention or mentioned in the *Federalist Papers*. It was used by only three states in the nation's first presidential election in 1789, and all three states (Maryland, New Hampshire, and Pennsylvania) abandoned it by 1800. It was not until the 11th presidential election (1828) that the winner-take-all rule was used by a majority of the states. The winner-take-all rule did not come into widespread use until the Founders had been dead for decades. All of these state statutes may be changed in the same manner as they were adopted, namely by passage of a new state law changing the state's method of appointing its own presidential electors. Thus, the National Popular Vote compact should not arouse federal "interest" in protecting the constitutional amendment process.

In any case, the question of whether the mere existence of a federal "interest" is sufficient to require that a compact obtain congressional consent was specifically addressed by the majority decision in *U.S. Steel Corporation v. Multistate Tax Commission*. The U.S. Supreme Court stated (in footnote 33):

> **"The dissent appears to confuse potential impact on 'federal interests' with threats to 'federal supremacy.'** It dwells at some length

---

[442] *U.S. Steel Corporation v. Multistate Tax Commission*. 434 U.S. 454 at 473. 1978. Justice Powell wrote the opinion of the Court, joined by Chief Justice Burger and Justices Brennan, Stewart, Marshall, Rehnquist, and Stevens.

[443] Ross, Tara. 2010. Federalism & Separation of Powers: Legal and Logistical Ramifications of the National Popular Vote Plan. *Engage*. Volume 11. Number 2. September 2010. Page 40.

on the unsuccessful efforts to obtain express congressional approval of this Compact, relying on the introduction of bills that never reached the floor of either House. This history of congressional inaction is viewed as 'demonstrat[ing] . . . a federal interest in the rules for apportioning multistate and multinational income,' and as showing 'a potential impact on federal concerns.' Post, at 488, 489. **That there is a federal interest no one denies**.

"The dissent's focus on the existence of federal concerns misreads *Virginia v. Tennessee* and *New Hampshire v. Maine*. **The relevant inquiry under those decisions is whether a compact tends to increase the political power of the States in a way that 'may encroach upon or interfere with the just supremacy of the United States.'** *Virginia v. Tennessee*, 148 U.S., at 519. **Absent a threat of encroachment or interference through enhanced state power, the existence of a federal interest is irrelevant. Indeed, every state cooperative action touching interstate or foreign commerce implicates some federal interest. Were that the test under the Compact Clause, virtually all interstate agreements and reciprocal legislation would require congressional approval.**

"In this case, the Multistate Tax Compact is concerned with a number of state activities that affect interstate and foreign commerce. But as we have indicated at some length in this opinion, **the terms of the Compact do not enhance the power of the member States to affect federal supremacy in those areas**.

"**The dissent appears to argue that the political influence of the member States is enhanced by this Compact**, making it more difficult—in terms of the political process—to enact pre-emptive legislation. We may assume that there is strength in numbers and organization. But enhanced capacity to lobby within the federal legislative process falls far short of threatened 'encroach[ment] upon or interfer[ence] with the just supremacy of the United States.' Federal power in the relevant areas remains plenary; no action authorized by the Constitution is 'foreclosed,' see post, at 491, to the Federal Government acting through Congress or the treaty-making power.

"The dissent also offers several aspects of the Compact that are thought to confer 'synergistic' powers upon the member States. Post, at 491-493. **We perceive no threat to federal supremacy in any of those provisions.** See, e.g., *Virginia v. Tennessee*, supra, at 520."[444] [Emphasis added]

An interstate compact may potentially affect non-member states.

In a dissenting opinion in *U.S. Steel Corporation v. Multistate Tax Commission*,

---

[444] *U.S. Steel Corporation v. Multistate Tax Commission*. 434 U.S. 452 at 479. 1978.

U.S. Supreme Court Justices Byron White and Harry Blackmun suggested that courts could consider the possible adverse effects of a compact on non-compacting states in deciding whether congressional consent is necessary for a particular compact.

> "A proper understanding of what would encroach upon federal authority, however, must also incorporate encroachments on the authority and power of non-Compact States."[445]

The U.S. Supreme Court addressed this argument in *U.S. Steel Corp. v. Multistate Tax Commission* by saying:

> "Appellants' final Compact Clause argument charges that the Compact impairs the sovereign rights of nonmember States. Appellants declare, without explanation, that if the use of the unitary business and combination methods continues to spread among the Western States, unfairness in taxation—presumably the risks of multiple taxation—will be avoidable only through the efforts of some coordinating body. Appellants cite the belief of the Commission's Executive Director that the Commission represents the only available vehicle for effective coordination, and conclude that **the Compact exerts undue pressure to join upon nonmember States in violation of their 'sovereign right' to refuse**.

> "We find no support for this conclusion. It has not been shown that any unfair taxation of multistate business resulting from the disparate use of combination and other methods **will redound to the benefit of any particular group of States or to the harm of others. Even if the existence of such a situation were demonstrated, it could not be ascribed to the existence of the Compact. Each member State is free to adopt the auditing procedures it thinks best, just as it could if the Compact did not exist**. Risks of unfairness and double taxation, then, are independent of the Compact.

> "Moreover, it is not explained how any economic pressure that does exist is an affront to the sovereignty of nonmember States. **Any time a State adopts a fiscal or administrative policy that affects the programs of a sister State, pressure to modify those programs may result. Unless that pressure transgresses the bounds of the Commerce Clause or the Privileges and Immunities Clause** of Art. IV, 2, see, e.g., *Austin v. New Hampshire*, 420 U.S. 656 (1975), **it is not clear how our federal structure is implicated**. Appellants do not argue that an individual State's decision to apportion nonbusiness income—or to define business income broadly, as the regulations of the Commission actually do—touches upon constitu-

---

[445] *U.S. Steel Corp. v. Multistate Tax Commission.* 434 U.S. at 494. 1978.

tional strictures. This being so, we are not persuaded that the same decision becomes a threat to the sovereignty of other States if a member State makes this decision upon the Commission's recommendation."[446] [Emphasis added]

In the 1985 case of *Northeast Bancorp, Inc. v. Board of Governors of the Federal Reserve System*, the U.S. Supreme Court again considered (and again rejected) arguments that an interstate compact impaired the sovereign rights of non-member states or enhanced the political power of the member states at the expense of other states. The Court wrote that it

"do[es] not see how the statutes in question . . . enhance the political power of the New England states at the expense of other States . . . ."[447]

Tara Ross has taken note of the dissenting opinion in *U.S. Steel Corporation v. Multistate Tax Commission* and has argued that

"non-compacting states have . . . important interests."[448]

In particular, Ross has identified three potential "interests" of non-compacting states in the National Popular Vote compact.

"NPV deprives these states of their opportunity, under the Constitution's amendment process, to participate in any decision made about changing the nation's presidential election system.

"They are also deprived of the protections provided by the supermajority requirements of Article V. . . .

"The voting power of states relative to other states is changed. NPV is the first to bemoan the fact that 'every vote is not equal' in the presidential election and that the weight of a voters' ballot depends on the state in which he lives. **In equalizing voting power, NPV is by definition increasing the political power of some states and decreasing the political power of other states.**"[449] [Emphasis added]

Concerning Ross' first point, the National Popular Vote bill has been introduced into all 50 state legislatures and the Council of the District of Columbia, thus providing all states with the "opportunity . . . to participate."

Concerning Ross' second point, Article V is the part of the U.S. Constitution that deals with constitutional amendments. The National Popular Vote compact would not

---

[446] *Id.* at 477–478.

[447] *Northeast Bancorp, Inc. v. Board of Governors of the Federal Reserve System.* 472 U.S. 159 at 176. 1985.

[448] Ross, Tara. 2010. Federalism & Separation of Powers: Legal and Logistical Ramifications of the National Popular Vote Plan. *Engage.* Volume 11. Number 2. September 2010. Page 40.

[449] Ross, Tara. 2010. Federalism & Separation of Powers: Legal and Logistical Ramifications of the National Popular Vote Plan. *Engage.* Volume 11. Number 2. September 2010. Page 40.

change the Constitution. It is an exercise of an exclusive power already granted to the states under section 1 of Article II of the Constitution, namely the power of each state to appoint its own presidential electors in the manner it chooses. The compact would change *state* winner-take-all statutes that came into widespread use more than four decades after the Constitution was ratified. None of these state winner-take-all statutes was originally adopted by means of a federal constitutional amendment, and none has constitutional status. All of these state statutes may be changed in the same manner as they were adopted, namely by passage of a new state law changing the state's method of appointing its own presidential electors. See section 9.1.1, section 9.1.2, section 9.1.3, section 9.1.4, and section 9.1.6.

Ross' third point concerns the potential effect on the *political value* of a vote cast by voters in some non-compacting states.

The National Popular Vote compact would treat votes cast in all 50 states and the District of Columbia equally. A vote cast in a compacting state would be, in every way, equal to a vote cast in a non-compacting state. The National Popular Vote compact would not confer any advantage on states belonging to the compact as compared to non-compacting states.

Ross is, in effect, arguing that certain battleground states might have a *constitutional* right to maintain the *excess* political value of votes cast in their states, but that disadvantaged or altruistic states have no right or ability to create equality in the political value of everyone's votes by exercising their *independent* constitutional power over the method of awarding their own electoral votes.

Of course, it has always been the case that one state's choice of the manner of appointing its presidential electors has affected the *political value* of a vote cast in other states. For example, the use of the winner-take-all rule by a closely divided battleground state plainly diminishes the political value of the votes cast by citizens in the non-battleground states.

It is inherent in the grant by the U.S. Constitution, to *each* state, of the power to choose the method of appointing its presidential electors that one state's decision can enhance the political value of its vote and thereby impact (diminish) the political value of the vote in other states. This is a direct consequence of federalism and the fact that the Constitution gave each individual state the power to decide the method of appointing its own presidential electors.

A present-day battleground state could, of course, eliminate the political effect of its winner-take-all rule on other states by changing its method of appointing its presidential electors. For example, if a battleground state were to change its winner-take-all statute to a proportional method for awarding electoral votes, presidential candidates would pay less attention to that state because only one electoral vote would probably be at stake in the state. However, we are not aware of anyone who currently argues that any present-day battleground state has a constitutional obligation to make such a change in order to reduce its impact on the political value of a vote in the non-battleground states.

If the Constitution gives a closely divided battleground state the power to choose a method of awarding its electoral votes that increases the political value of votes cast in its state, it also gives the power to non-battleground states to choose a method for awarding their electoral votes to counter-balance the political effect of the decision made by the battleground state (and, arguably, create a better overall system in the process).

In any case, the electoral votes of the non-compacting states would continue to be cast in the manner specified by the laws of those states. The electoral votes of the non-compacting states would continue to be counted in the Electoral College in the manner provided by the Constitution. In practical terms, that means that the non-compacting states would continue to cast their votes for the winner of the statewide popular vote (or district-wide popular vote in Maine and Nebraska) after the National Popular Vote compact is implemented. No non-compacting state would be compelled to cast its electoral votes for the winner of the national popular vote.

The political impact of the winner-take-all rule on other states has long been recognized as a political reality. It is not California's winner-take-all rule or Wyoming's winner-take-all rule that makes a vote in California and a vote in Wyoming politically irrelevant in presidential elections. Indeed, a vote in California and Wyoming are equal as a result of the widespread use of the state-by-state winner-take-all rule, and both are equally worthless. Instead, it is the use of the winner-take-all rule in closely divided battleground states that diminishes the political value of the votes cast in California and Wyoming.

The Founding Fathers intended, as part of the political compromise that led to the Constitution, to confer a certain amount of extra influence on the less populous states by giving every state a bonus of two electoral votes corresponding to its two U.S. Senators. The Founders also intended that the Constitution's formula for allocating electoral votes would give the bigger states a larger amount of influence in presidential elections. Their goals with respect to *both* small states and big states were never achieved because of the emergence of political parties in the 1796 presidential election and the subsequent widespread adoption by the states of the winner-take-all rule (mostly in the 1820s and 1830s). The winner-take-all rule drastically altered the political value of votes cast in both small and big states throughout the country.

Interstate comparisons of the *political value* of a vote are not, according to past judicial rulings, a legal basis for contesting any state's decision to adopt a certain method of appointing its own presidential electors under Article II, section 1, clause 2 of the Constitution.

In 1966, the U.S. Supreme Court declined to act in response to a complaint concerning the political impact of one state's choice of the manner of appointing its presidential electors on another state. In *State of Delaware v. State of New York*, Delaware led a group of 12 predominantly small states (including North Dakota, South Dakota, Wyoming, Utah, Arkansas, Kansas, Oklahoma, Iowa, Kentucky, Florida, and Pennsylvania) in suing New York in the U.S. Supreme Court. At the time of this lawsuit, New

York was not only a closely divided battleground but also the state possessing the largest number of electoral votes (43). Delaware argued that New York's decision to use the winner-take-all rule effectively disenfranchised voters in the 12 plaintiff states. New York's (defendant) brief is especially pertinent.[450] Despite the fact that the case was brought under the Court's original jurisdiction, the U.S. Supreme Court declined to hear the case (presumably because of the well-established constitutional provision that the manner of awarding electoral votes is exclusively a state decision).[451]

In 1968, the constitutionality of the winner-take-all rule was challenged in *Williams v. Virginia State Board of Elections.*[452] A federal court in Virginia upheld the winner-take-all rule. The full opinion can be found in appendix FF. The U.S. Supreme Court affirmed this decision in a *per curiam* decision in 1969.[453] See section 9.1.18.

Section 9.11.3 discusses the specific claim of Professor Norman Williams of Willamette University that compacts that do not receive congressional consent are "toothless."

There is an additional independent argument that the potential political impact on non-compacting states should not be a consideration in evaluating a compact concerned with how states choose to appoint their presidential electors.

Article II, section 1, clause 2 of the U.S. Constitution provides:

> "**Each State** shall appoint, in such Manner as the Legislature thereof may direct, a Number of Electors. . . ."[454] [Emphasis added]

Article I, section 4, clause 1 provides

> "The Times, Places and Manner of holding Elections for Senators and Representatives, shall be prescribed in each State by the Legislature thereof; but **the Congress may at any time by Law make or alter such Regulations**, except as to the Places of chusing Senators." [Emphasis added]

Article I confers on "each state" the power to choose the manner of electing its members of Congress; however, it subjects those state decisions to being overridden at the national level. Congress has, on occasion, overridden state choices that it deemed to not be in the national interest (e.g., electing members of the U.S. House of Representatives at-large, instead of from single-member districts).

Article II is different in that state decisions are not subjected to such congressional scrutiny. "Each state" is empowered to choose the manner of appointing their presidential electors, irrespective of Congress' opinion of the method.

---

[450] Delaware's brief, New York's brief, and Delaware's argument in its request for a re-hearing in the 1966 case of *State of Delaware v. State of New York* may be found at http://www.nationalpopularvote.com/pages/misc/de_lawsuit.php.

[451] *State of Delaware v. State of New York*, 385 U.S. 895, 87 S.Ct. 198, 17 L.Ed.2d 129 (1966).

[452] *Williams v. Virginia State Board of Elections*, 288 F. Supp. 622 - Dist. Court, ED Virginia 1968.

[453] *Williams v. Virginia State Board of Elections.* 393 U.S. 320 (1969) (per curiam).

[454] U.S. Constitution. Article II, section 1, clause 2.

Of course, there is always the possibility that the U.S. Supreme Court might change the legal standards concerning congressional consent contained in its 1893 and 1978 rulings. Because there could be litigation about congressional consent, National Popular Vote is working to obtain support for the compact in Congress.

Because Congress typically considers a compact only after the compact has been approved by the combination of states required to bring the compact into effect, one would expect that any action in Congress would occur after the compact had been approved by the 25 (or so) states possessing the requisite majority of the electoral votes (i.e., 270 of 538).

Congressional consent can be explicitly conferred by a majority vote in both the U.S. House and Senate and approval of the President (or enactment by a two-thirds majority if the President vetoes the bill).

The question of congressional consent is discussed in greater detail in chapter 5.

The specific additional question of congressional consent in relation to a compact's withdrawal procedure is discussed in section 9.16.6.

9.16.6. MYTH: The National Popular Vote compact requires congressional consent because of its withdrawal procedure.

QUICK ANSWER:

- The test as to whether an interstate compact requires congressional consent is based on whether the compact encroaches on federal supremacy—not on the compact's withdrawal procedure.
- The Interstate Compact for the Placement of Children is an example of a judicially upheld compact that did not require congressional consent to become effective and that imposes a two-year delay on the effectiveness of a state's withdrawal.

MORE DETAILED ANSWER:

In *U.S. Steel Corp. v. Multistate Tax Commission*, the U.S. Supreme Court made three observations about the characteristics of the Multistate Tax Compact, including the fact that states could withdraw from that particular compact without delay.

The Multistate Tax Compact permits withdrawal from the compact, without delay or advance notice to other states.

> "**Any party state may withdraw from this compact by enacting a statute repealing the same**. No withdrawal shall affect any liability already incurred by or chargeable to a party state prior to the time of such withdrawal.

> "No proceeding commenced before an arbitration board prior to the withdrawal of a state and to which the withdrawing state or any subdivision thereof is a party shall be discontinued or terminated by the withdrawal, nor shall the board thereby lose jurisdiction over any of the parties to the

proceeding necessary to make a binding determination therein." [Emphasis added]

Von Spakovsky has incorrectly interpreted the U.S. Supreme Court's observations in *U.S. Steel Corp. v. Multistate Tax Commission* about the characteristics of the Multistate Tax Compact as "prongs" of a legal test as to whether a compact requires congressional consent. Von Spakovsky wrote:

> "In *U.S. Steel Corp. v. Multistate Tax Commission*, the Supreme Court of the United States held that the Compact Clause prohibited compacts that
>
>> 'encroach upon the supremacy of the United States.'
>
> "The Court emphasized that the real test of constitutionality is whether the compact
>
>> 'enhances state power *quoad* the National Government.' . . .
>
> "To determine this qualification, the Court questioned whether:
>
>> (1) The compact authorizes the member states to exercise any powers they could not exercise in its absence;
>> (2) The compact delegates sovereign power to the commission that it created; or
>> (3) The compacting states cannot withdraw from the agreement at any time.
>
> "Unless approved by Congress, **a violation of any one of these three prongs is sufficient to strike down a compact as unconstitutional**. . . .
>
> "**Under the third prong of the test delineated in** *U.S. Steel Corp.*, the compact must allow states to withdraw at any time. The NPV, however, places withdrawal limitations on compacting states. The plan states that
>
>> 'a withdrawal occurring six months or less before the end of a President's term shall not become effective until a President or Vice President shall have been qualified to serve the next term.'
>
> "**This provision is in direct conflict with the** *U.S. Steel Corp.* test."[455] [Emphasis added]

The Supreme Court's three observations about characteristics of the Multistate Tax Compact were not "prongs" of any "test."

The incorrectness of von Spakovsky's interpretation of the Supreme Court's 1978

---

[455] Von Spakovsky, Hans. Destroying the Electoral College: The Anti-Federalist National Popular Vote Scheme. Legal memo. October 27, 2011. http://www.heritage.org/research/reports/2011/10/destroying-the -electoral-college-the-anti-federalist-national-popular-vote-scheme.

decision in *U.S. Steel Corp. v. Multistate Tax Commission* is demonstrated by the 1991 case of *McComb v. Wambaugh* dealing with the enforceability of the Interstate Compact for the Placement of Children.

The Interstate Compact for the Placement of Children did *not require congressional consent* to become effective, and *it delayed withdrawal* for two years.[456]

Article IX of the Interstate Compact for the Placement of Children provides:

> "Withdrawal from this compact shall be by the enactment of a statute repealing the same, **but shall not take effect until two years after the effective date of such statute** and until written notice of the withdrawal has been given by the withdrawing state to the governor of each other party jurisdiction. Withdrawal of a party state shall not affect the rights, duties, and obligations under this compact of any sending agency therein with respect to a placement made prior to the effective date of withdrawal." [Emphasis added]

In *McComb v. Wambaugh*, the U.S. Court of Appeals for the Third Circuit interpreted and applied the test established by the U.S. Supreme Court in *U.S. Steel Corp. v. Multistate Tax Commission* concerning the question of whether congressional consent was necessary for a compact to become effective. The U.S. Court of Appeals wrote:

> "**The Constitution recognizes compacts** in Article I, section 10, clause 3, which reads, 'No state shall, without the Consent of the Congress . . . enter into any Agreement or Compact with another State.' **Despite the broad wording of the clause Congressional approval is necessary only when a Compact is 'directed to the formation of any combination tending to the increase of political power in the States, which may encroach upon or interfere with the just supremacy of the United States.'** *United States Steel Corp. v. Multistate Tax Comm'n*, 434 U.S. 452, 468, 98 S.Ct. 799, 810, 54 L.Ed.2d 682 (1978) (quoting *Virginia v. Tennessee*, 148 U.S. 503, 519, 13 S.Ct. 728, 734, 37 L.Ed. 537 (1893)).

> "**The Interstate Compact on Placement of Children has not received Congressional consent. Rather than altering the balance of power between the states and the federal government, this Compact focuses wholly on adoption and foster care of children—areas of jurisdiction historically retained by the states.** *In re Burrus*, 136 U.S. 586, 593-

---

[456] The Interstate Compact for the Placement of Children was written with the expectation that congressional consent would not be required if its membership were limited to states of the United States, the District of Columbia, and Puerto Rico. However, the compact invites the federal government of Canada and Canadian provincial governments to become members. The compact specifically recognizes that congressional consent would be required if a Canadian entity desired to become a party to the compact by saying, "This compact shall be open to joinder by any state, territory, or possession of the United States, the District of Columbia, the Commonwealth of Puerto Rico, and, with the consent of congress, the government of Canada or any province thereof." As of 1991, no Canadian entity had sought membership in the compact, and the compact was thus put into operation without congressional consent.

94, 10 S.Ct. 850, 852-53, 34 L.Ed. 500 (1890); *Lehman v. Lycoming County Children's Services Agency*, 648 F.2d 135, 143 (3d Cir.1981) (en banc), aff'd, 458 U.S. 502, 102 S.Ct. 3231, 73 L.Ed.2d 928 (1982). **Congressional consent, therefore, was not necessary for the Compact's legitimacy.**"

"**Because Congressional consent was neither given nor required, the Compact does not express federal law.** Cf. *Cuyler v. Adams*, 449 U.S. 433, 440, 101 S.Ct. 703, 707, 66 L.Ed.2d 641 (1981). **Consequently, this Compact must be construed as state law.** See Engdahl, Construction of Interstate Compacts: A Questionable Federal Question, 51 *Va.L.Rev.* 987, 1017 (1965) ('[T]he construction of a compact not requiring consent . . . will not present a federal question....').

"**Having entered into a contract, a participant state may not unilaterally change its terms. A Compact also takes precedence over statutory law in member states.**"[457] [Emphasis added]

As the Third Circuit noted, the test as to whether an interstate compact requires congressional consent is what the U.S. Supreme Court said in the 1978 case of *U.S. Steel Corporation v. Multistate Tax Commission*, namely

"**the test is** whether the Compact enhances state power *quaod* the National Government."[458] [Emphasis added]

Von Spakovsky's "prongs" are not part of any "test" as to whether congressional consent is necessary for an interstate compact to become effective. In particular, the withdrawal provisions of a compact do not determine whether it requires congressional consent to become effective.

9.16.7. MYTH: Adoption of the National Popular Vote compact would establish the precedent that interstate compacts can be used to accomplish something that would otherwise be unconstitutional.

QUICK ANSWER:

- The Compacts Clause of the U.S. Constitution permits states to enter into interstate compacts, but does not expand state powers. All compacts must be consistent with the U.S. Constitution.

MORE DETAILED ANSWER:

Several opponents of the National Popular Vote compact have argued that adoption of the National Popular Vote compact would establish a precedent that interstate compacts can be used to accomplish something that would otherwise be unconstitutional.

---

[457] *McComb v. Wambaugh*, 934 F.2d 474 at 479 (3d Cir. 1991).

[458] *U.S. Steel Corporation v. Multistate Tax Commission.* 434 U.S. 454 at 473. 1978.

Opponents have argued, for example, that adopting the National Popular Vote compact would establish a precedent that could be used to negate a woman's existing constitutional right to an abortion.

The Compacts Clause of the U.S. Constitution permits states to enter into interstate compacts; however, the Compacts Clause does not expand state powers. All compacts must be consistent with the U.S. Constitution. In particular, a compact's subject matter must be among the powers that the states are permitted to exercise (as discussed in section 9.16.2).

This invalid line of argument by opponents is based on the opponents' own invalid argument that a federal constitutional amendment is necessary to change the winner-take-all method of appointing a state's presidential electors. In fact, the National Popular Vote compact does not change anything in the U.S. Constitution, and therefore no federal constitutional amendment is necessary (as discussed at length in section 9.1.1, section 9.1.2, section 9.1.3, section 9.1.4, and section 9.1.6). Instead, the National Popular Vote compact changes *state* winner-take-all statutes that came into widespread use more than four decades after the Constitution was ratified. None of these state winner-take-all statutes was originally adopted by means of a federal constitutional amendment. These state winner-take-all statutes do not have constitutional status. Winner-take-all statutes may be changed in the same manner in which they were adopted, namely by passage of a new state law changing the state's method of appointing its own presidential electors.

9.16.8. MYTH: The National Popular Vote compact is a conspiracy.

QUICK ANSWER:

- An interstate compact is not a "conspiracy" but a mechanism provided by the U.S. Constitution that enables sovereign states to enter voluntarily into binding contractual arrangements with one another.

MORE DETAILED ANSWER:

Professor Robert Hardaway of the University of Denver Sturm College of Law, an opponent of the National Popular Vote compact, presented the following testimony on the National Popular Vote bill on February 19, 2010, to the Alaska Senate Judiciary Committee:

> "And what would happen if, under the Koza scheme, some of the states decided to withdraw from the **conspiracy**? What federal organ would be empowered to enforce the original terms of that **conspiracy**?"[459] [Emphasis added]

Tara Ross, an opponent of the National Popular Vote compact, refers to the states belonging to the compact as

---

[459] See section 9.11 for answers to Professor Hardaway's concern about withdrawal.

"colluding states."[460]

A "conspiracy" is an agreement to commit a crime.

An interstate compact is not a "conspiracy," but, instead, a mechanism provided by the U.S. Constitution that enables sovereign states to enter voluntarily into binding contractual arrangements with one another.

The National Popular Vote compact is based on the exclusive and plenary power of the states to choose the manner of awarding their electoral votes (as provided by section 1 of Article II of the U.S. Constitution):

> "Each State shall appoint, in such Manner **as the Legislature thereof may direct**, a Number of Electors. . . ."[461] [Emphasis added]

Words, such as "conspiracy," "collusion," and "scheme," do not change the fact that the states have the power, under the U.S. Constitution, to award their own electoral votes in the manner that they see fit.

9.17. MYTHS ABOUT MOB RULE, DEMAGOGUES, AND THE ELECTORAL COLLEGE BUFFERING AGAINST POPULAR PASSIONS

9.17.1. MYTH: A national popular vote would be mob rule.

QUICK ANSWER:

- The American people currently cast votes for President in 100% of the states, and they have done so in 100% of the states since the 1880 election. In case anyone thinks it is appropriate to characterize the American electorate as a "mob," it is a long-settled political reality that the "mob" already rules in American presidential elections.
- The issue presented by the National Popular Vote proposal is not whether the "mob" will vote for President, but whether the "mobs" in certain closely divided battleground states should be more important than the "mobs" in the remaining states.

MORE DETAILED ANSWER:

This myth apparently originates from the failure (by some) to realize that the American people cast votes for President in 100% of the states, and that they have done so in 100% of the states since the 1880 election.[462]

In case anyone thinks it is appropriate to characterize the American electorate as

[460] Ross, Tara. 2004. *Enlightened Democracy: The Case for the Electoral College.* Los Angeles, CA: World Ahead Publishing Company. Page 235.

[461] U.S. Constitution. Article II, section 1, clause 2.

[462] State legislatures frequently chose presidential electors in the nation's early years; however, the last time presidential electors were chosen by a state legislature was 1876 in Colorado.

a "mob," it is now long-settled political reality that the "mob" rules in American presidential elections.

The choice presented by the National Popular Vote is not whether the "mob" is going to control presidential elections, but whether the mob's votes are going to be tallied on a state-by-state basis versus a nationwide basis.

The National Popular Vote bill is concerned with the relative political importance of popular votes cast in different states for presidential electors. The currently prevailing winner-take-all method (i.e., awarding all of a state's electoral votes to the candidate who receives the most popular votes in a state) makes votes unequal from state to state. Under the current system, presidential candidates concentrate their attention on voters in a small handful of closely divided battleground states, while ignoring voters in all the other states.

The National Popular Vote plan would address the shortcomings of the current system by making every vote equally important in every state in every presidential election.

Thus, the issue presented by the National Popular Vote proposal is not whether the "mob" will vote for President, but whether the "mobs" in certain closely divided battleground states should be more important than the "mobs" in the remaining states.

9.17.2. MYTH: The Electoral College acts as a buffer against popular passions.

QUICK ANSWER:
- The Electoral College has never operated as a buffer against popular passions.
- There is no reason to think that the Electoral College would ever operate as a buffer against the winner of a presidential election, regardless of whether the winner is determined on the basis of the state-by-state winner-take-all rule or the national popular vote.
- The Electoral College does not operate as a deliberative body.

MORE DETAILED ANSWER:
This myth apparently originates from the failure (by some) to realize that the Electoral College currently does not act as a buffer against popular passions—and indeed never has.

It is true that the Founding Fathers intended that the Electoral College would provide a buffer against the will of the people. They envisioned an Electoral College that would consist of "wise men" who would deliberate on the choice of the President and "judiciously" select the best candidate for the office. As John Jay (the presumed author of *Federalist No. 64*) wrote in 1788:

> "As the **select assemblies for choosing the President** . . . will in general be **composed of the most enlightened and respectable citizens**, there

is reason to presume that their attention and their votes will be directed to those men only who have become the most distinguished by their abilities and virtues."[463] [Emphasis added]

As Alexander Hamilton (the presumed author of *Federalist No. 68*) wrote in 1788:

"[T]he immediate election should be made by men most capable of analyzing the qualities adapted to the station, and **acting under circumstances favorable to deliberation**, and to a **judicious combination** of all the reasons and inducements which were proper to govern their choice. **A small number of persons**, selected by their fellow-citizens from the general mass, will be most likely to possess **the information and discernment requisite to such complicated investigations**."[464] [Emphasis added]

The vision of the Founding Fathers for a deliberative Electoral College was never realized in practice, because the Founders did not anticipate the emergence of political parties (as discussed in section 2.2.2).

In the nation's first two presidential elections (1789 and 1792), the Electoral College *did not* act as a buffer against popular passions but instead, acted in harmony with the virtually unanimous nationwide consensus favoring George Washington as President.

As soon as George Washington announced that he would not run for a third term as President in 1796, political parties emerged. The competition for power was between two opposing groups holding different visions about how the country should be governed.

In 1796, both the Federalist and Anti-Federalist parties nominated their presidential and vice-presidential candidates at caucuses composed of the members of Congress belonging to their respective parties. As soon as there were national nominees, both parties presented the public with candidates for the position of presidential elector, who, in turn, made it known that they intended to act as willing "rubber-stamps" for their party's nominees when the Electoral College met. In 1796, all but one of the presidential electors then dutifully voted as expected when the Electoral College met. Moreover, that election established the expectation that presidential electors should "act" and not "think."[465]

---

[463] The powers of the senate. *Independent Journal.* March 5, 1788. *Federalist No. 64.*

[464] Publius. The mode of electing the President. *Independent Journal.* March 12, 1788. *Federalist No. 68.*

[465] A Federalist supporter famously complained in the December 15, 1796, issue of *United States Gazette* that Samuel Miles, a Federalist presidential elector, had voted for Thomas Jefferson, instead of John Adams, by saying, "What, do I chufe Samuel Miles to determine for me whether John Adams or Thomas Jefferfon is the fittest man to be President of the United States? No, I chufe him to act, not to think." [Spelling per original]. Of the 22,991 electoral votes cast for President in the nation's 57 presidential elections between 1789 and 2012, only 17 were cast in a deviant way. As explained in greater detail in section 2.12, the vote of Federalist elector Samuel Miles for Anti-Federalist Thomas Jefferson in 1796 remains the only instance when the elector might have intended, at the time he cast his unexpected vote, that his vote might affect the national outcome.

The U.S. Supreme Court noted this history in its opinion in the 1892 case of *McPherson v. Blacker*:

> "Doubtless it was supposed that the electors would exercise a reasonable independence and fair judgment in the selection of the chief executive, but experience soon demonstrated that, **whether chosen by the legislatures or by popular suffrage on general ticket or in districts, they were so chosen simply to register the will of the appointing power** in respect of a particular candidate. In relation, then, to the independence of the electors, the original expectation may be said to have been frustrated."[466] [Emphasis added]

The political affiliation of the presidential electors has been determined by "the will of the appointing power"—whether a majority (or plurality) of the voters of a state, a majority (or plurality) of voters of a district, or a majority (or plurality) of state legislators (in cases where the legislature directly appointed the presidential electors).

Since the emergence of political parties in 1796, members of the Electoral College have almost always voted for the nominees determined by the nominating caucus or convention of the elector's own political party.

Thus, the Electoral College has never acted as a buffer against popular passions—either before or after 1796.

There is no reason to think that the Electoral College would ever operate as a buffer against the winner of a presidential election, regardless of whether the winner is determined on the basis of the state-by-state winner-take-all rule or the national popular vote.

Figure 9.6 shows the meeting of the Minnesota Electoral College in St. Paul on December 17, 2012.

Figure 9.6 Meeting of Minnesota Electoral College in St. Paul on December 17, 2012

---

[466] *McPherson v. Blacker.* 146 U.S. 1 at 36. 1892.

9.17.3. MYTH: The current system of electing the President would prevent a Hitler or similar demagogue from coming to power in the United States.

QUICK ANSWER:

* Adolf Hitler did not come to power in Germany as a result of a national popular vote.
* The National Popular Vote compact does not abolish the office of presidential elector or the Electoral College. Thus, there would be no reduction in whatever protection (if any) that the current Electoral College system might provide in terms of preventing a demagogue from coming to power in the United States. However, there is no reason to think that the Electoral College would prevent a demagogue from being elected President of the United States, regardless of whether presidential electors are elected on the basis of the state-by-state winner-take-all rule or the nationwide popular vote.
* It is the responsibility of the voters to ensure that no future President of the United States is a demagogue.

MORE DETAILED ANSWER:

It is sometimes asserted that Adolf Hitler came to power in Germany as a result of a national popular vote and that the current Electoral-College system of electing the President would prevent a similar demagogue from coming to power in the United States.[467]

Adolf Hitler did not come to power in Germany as a result of a national popular vote. In fact, Hitler was rejected by almost a two-to-one nationwide popular-vote margins when he ran for the Presidency of the Weimar Republic.

In the March 13, 1932, election for President, the results were:

* Hindenburg (the incumbent)—49.6%,
* Hitler (National Socialist)—30.1%,
* Thaelmann (Communist)—13.2%, and
* Duesterberg (Nationalist)—6.8%.[468]

Because President Hindenburg did not receive an absolute majority of the votes, a run-off was held on April 10, 1932, among the top three candidates. The results of the run-off were:

* Hindenburg (the incumbent)—53.0%,
* Hitler (National Socialist)—36.8%, and
* Thaelmann (Communist)—10.2%.

---

[467] The issue of a demagogue becoming President comes up with moderate frequency, including at a November 13, 2012, debate on the National Popular Vote compact held at a meeting of the National Policy Council of the American Association of Retired Persons in Washington, DC. The debaters included Vermont State Representative Chris Pearson, Professor Curtis Gans, and Dr. John R. Koza (chair of National Popular Vote).

[468] Shirer, William L. 1960. *The Rise and Fall of the Third Reich.* New York, NY: Simon and Shuster.

On July 31, 1932, parliamentary elections were held in Germany, and Hitler's National Socialist Party won the largest number of seats in the Reichstag (230 out of 608); however, these 230 seats were far from a majority.

On November 6, 1932, another parliamentary election was held, and the strength of Hitler's party was reduced to 196 seats out of 608 in the Reichstag.

On January 30, 1933, a deal was orchestrated by a coalition of parties and power brokers who (mistakenly) thought they could control Hitler. As a result of this deal, President Hindenburg appointed Adolf Hitler as Chancellor of Germany. Once in power as Chancellor, Hitler quickly used his position of Chancellor (and, in particular, the control over the police that his party gained in the deal) to create a one-party dictatorship in Germany.

The National Popular Vote compact would not abolish the office of presidential elector or the Electoral College, so there would be no reduction in whatever protection (if any) that the current structure of the Electoral College might offer in terms of preventing a demagogue from coming to power in the United States.

A demagogue capable of winning the national popular vote in the United States would simultaneously win the popular vote in numerous states, including the closely divided battleground states. There is certainly nothing about the state-by-state winner-take-all method of electing presidential electors that favors or impedes demagogues compared to non-demagogic candidates. The national popular vote winner simultaneously has won a majority of the Electoral College in 53 of the nation's 57 presidential elections from 1789 to 2012, and there is no reason to think that a demagogue would be less likely than a non-demagogic candidate to win a majority of the Electoral College while losing the nationwide popular vote.

Presidential electors are loyal supporters of the nominee of their own political party. There is no reason to think that presidential electors nominated by a demagogue's political party would be any less loyal to their party's nominee than a presidential elector representing a non-demagogic candidate. If anything, presidential electors allied with a demagogue would very likely be more loyal to their candidate.

Thus, it is unlikely that the current Electoral College system could prevent a demagogue from being elected President of the United States, regardless of whether votes for presidential elector are tallied on the basis of the state-by-state winner-take-all rule or on the basis of the total nationwide popular vote.

It is certainly conceivable that a majority of the voters might, at some time in the future, support a demagogue for President of the United States. Indeed, some supporters of the losing presidential candidate entertain this very thought after *every* election. However, if the voters support a demagogue, there is no reason to think that the Electoral College would save the voters from themselves—either under the current state-by-state winner-take-all rule or the National Popular Vote compact.

Ultimately, it is the responsibility of the voters to ensure that no demagogue becomes President of the United States.

9.18. MYTH ABOUT AN INCOMING PRESIDENT'S MANDATE

9.18.1. MYTH: The current state-by-state winner-take-all system gives the incoming President a "mandate" in the form of an exaggerated lead in the Electoral College.

QUICK ANSWER:

- The current system of electing the President does not reliably generate a "mandate" in the form of a larger percentage share of the electoral vote than the candidate's share of the national popular vote.
- In case anyone believes that an exaggerated margin in the Electoral College is desirable in that it enhances a new president's ability to lead, the National Popular Vote plan would do an even better job of creating this illusion than the current system.

MORE DETAILED ANSWER:

UCLA Law Professor Daniel H. Lowenstein has argued:

> "**The Electoral College** turns the many winners who fail to win a majority of the popular vote into majority winners. It also **magnifies small majorities in the popular vote into large majorities.** These effects of the Electoral College enhance Americans' confidence in the outcome of the election and thereby **enhance the new president's ability to lead.**"[469] [Emphasis added]

The historical record shows that the above statement is false about as often as it is true. It is, therefore, not an accurate characterization of what happens in the real world.

The current state-by-state winner-take-all system does not reliably deliver an exaggerated margin to the incoming President. For example, despite winning by almost two million votes nationwide, Jimmy Carter won the Electoral College in 1976 with only 297 electoral votes (27 over the 270 needed for election). Despite winning by over three million votes in 2004, George W. Bush won in the Electoral College with only 286 electoral votes (a mere 16 above the 270 needed).

Moreover, the current state-by-state winner-take-all system does not reliably confer an illusory mandate on an incoming President. As a recent example, Bill Clinton did not receive such deference when he came into office with an eye-catching 370 electoral votes but only 43% of the popular vote in 1992. There is certainly no historical evidence that Congress, the media, the public, or anyone else has been more deferential to an incoming President after an election in which he received a larger percentage of the electoral vote than his percentage of the popular vote.

---

[469] Debate entitled "Should We Dispense with the Electoral College?" sponsored by PENNumbra (University of Pennsylvania Law Review) available at http://www.pennumbra.com/debates/pdfs/electoral_college.pdf.

However, in case anyone believes that an exaggerated margin in the Electoral College "enhance[s] the new president's ability to lead," the National Popular Vote plan would do an even better job of creating this illusion than the current system.

Under the National Popular Vote compact, the nationwide winning candidate would generally receive an exaggerated margin (roughly 75%) of the votes in the Electoral College in any given presidential election. The reason is that the National Popular Vote bill guarantees that the presidential candidate receiving the most popular votes in all 50 states and the District of Columbia would receive at least 270 electoral votes (of 538) from the states belonging to the compact. Then, in addition to this guaranteed minimum bloc of at least 270 electoral votes, the nationwide winning candidate would generally receive some additional electoral votes from whichever non-compacting states he or she happened to carry. If the non-compacting states divided approximately equally between the candidates, the nationwide winning candidate would generally receive an exaggerated margin (roughly 75%) of the votes in the Electoral College (that is, about 404 out of 538 electoral votes).

Of course, the current system often does more than just exaggerate an incoming President's percentage in the Electoral College as compared to his or her percentage in the nationwide popular vote. For example, Samuel Tilden, won the popular vote in 1876 by 3%, but lost the electoral vote. In four of our nation's 57 presidential elections between 1789 and 2012, the current system has actually awarded the Presidency to a candidate who did not receive the most popular votes nationwide.

This is a failure rate of 1 in 14. Moreover, because about half of American presidential elections are popular-vote landslides (i.e., a margin of greater than 10%), the failure rate is actually 1 in 7 among non-landslide elections.

In virtually all other elections in the United States, the winner is the candidate receiving the most popular votes. Tellingly, there are not examples of Governors, U.S. Senators, and other elected officials receiving a modest popular-vote percentage being hobbled in the execution of their office because they did not have the (argued) advantage of an Electoral-College type of arrangement to (sometimes) exaggerate their margin of victory.

9.19. MYTH ABOUT PRESIDENTIAL POWER

9.19.1. MYTH: The President's powers would be changed by a national popular vote.

QUICK ANSWER:
* Because the National Popular Vote compact is state legislation that would not alter the U.S. Constitution, no power that the President possesses under the U.S. Constitution would be enhanced or diminished by it.
* If it were true that electing the President on a nationwide basis would increase presidential authority, then it would necessarily have to be the case

that presidential authority today is hobbled because of the use of the state-by-state winner-take-all rule. We are not aware of any evidence that this is the case today.

MORE DETAILED ANSWER:

The National Popular Vote compact is state legislation. It would not alter the U.S. Constitution. In particular, it would not augment or diminish any power possessed by the President under the U.S. Constitution.

The National Popular Vote compact would, in effect, make a change in the "district" from which presidential electors are elected. Under current state winner-take-all statutes, state boundary lines define the "districts" used to elect presidential electors. Under the National Popular Vote compact, presidential electors would be elected from a single national "district." Changing these "district" boundaries would not diminish or augment any power possessed by the President under the U.S. Constitution.

If it were true that electing the President on a nationwide basis would increase presidential authority, then it would necessarily have to be the case that presidential authority today is hobbled because of the use of the state-by-state winner-take-all rule. We are not aware of any evidence that the power of the Presidency is hobbled by the current system.

9.20. MYTHS ABOUT THE VOTING RIGHTS ACT

9.20.1. MYTH: Section 2 of the Voting Rights Act precludes the National Popular Vote compact.

QUICK ANSWER:

- The National Popular Vote compact would not deny or abridge the right to vote. On the contrary, it would make every person's vote for President equal—consistent with a main goal of the Voting Rights Act.
- The National Popular Vote compact received pre-clearance from the Department of Justice in 2012 under section 5 of the Voting Rights Act.

MORE DETAILED ANSWER:

Dave Gringer has argued that the National Popular Vote compact:

> "may run afoul of sections 2 and 5 of the Voting Rights Act—as either minority vote dilution or retrogression in the ability of minority voters to elect the candidate of their choice."[470,471]

---

[470] Gringer, David. 2008. Why the National Popular Vote plan is the wrong way to abolish the Electoral College. 108 *Columbia Law Review* 182. January 2008.

[471] In fact, Gringer has gone so far as to state (without any knowledge about the operation of the National Popular Vote organization or any attempt to acquire the facts) that the authors of the National Popular

The purpose of the Voting Rights Act is to guarantee voting equality throughout the United States (particularly in relation to racial minorities that historically suffered discrimination in certain states or areas).

Section 2 of the Act prohibits the denial or abridgment of the right to vote.

Section 5 requires certain states (that historically violated the right to vote) to obtain advance approval for proposed changes in their state election laws to ensure that they do not have a discriminatory purpose or effect. The advance approval can be obtained in two ways:

- a favorable declaratory judgment from the U.S. District Court for the District of Columbia, or

- pre-clearance by the U.S. Department of Justice (the more common path).

The National Popular Vote compact manifestly would make every person's vote for President equal throughout the United States in an election to fill that office. It is, therefore, consistent with the goals of the Voting Rights Act.

There have been court cases under the Voting Rights Act concerning contemplated changes in voting methods for various representative legislative bodies (e.g., city councils and county boards). Opponents of the National Popular Vote compact often quote from these cases involving multi-member representative legislative bodies.[472] However, these cases do not bear on elections to fill a *single office* (i.e., the Presidency).

In *Butts v. City of New York Dept. of Housing Preservation and Development*, the United States Court of Appeals for the Second Circuit addressed the question of whether the Voting Rights Act applies to a run-off election for the single office of Mayor, Council President, or City Comptroller in a New York City primary election. The court opined:

> "We cannot . . . take the concept of a class's impaired opportunity for equal representation and uncritically transfer it from the context of elections for multi-member bodies to that of elections for single-member officers."[473]

The court also stated:

> **"There is no such thing as a 'share' of a single member office."** [Emphasis added]

It then added:

Vote compact have "failed to recognize that their plan implicates the Voting Rights Act." The fact that pre-clearance would be required was recognized by the National Popular Vote organization as early as the period when the National Popular Vote legislation was being debated by the California Assembly in 2006.

[472] Gringer, David. 2008. Why the National Popular Vote plan is the wrong way to abolish the Electoral College. 108 *Columbia Law Review* 182. January 2008. Pages 182–230.

[473] *Butts v. City of New York Dept. of Housing Preservation and Development*, 779 F.2d 141 at 148 (1985).

"It suffices to rule in this case that a run-off election requirement in such an election does not deny any class an opportunity for equal representation and therefore cannot violate the Act."

In *Dillard v. Crenshaw County*, the U.S. Court of Appeals for the Eleventh Circuit addressed the question of whether the at-large elected chairperson of the Crenshaw County Commission in Alabama is a single-member office. The office's duties are primarily administrative and executive, but also include presiding over meetings of the commissioners and voting to break a tie. The court stated that it was unsatisfied that

"The chairperson will be sufficiently uninfluential in the activities initiated and in the decisions made by the commission proper to be evaluated as a single-member office."[474]

The case was remanded to the U.S. District Court for either "a reaffirmation of the rotating chairperson system" or approval of an alternative proposal preserving "the elected integrity of the body of associate commissioners."

In 1989, in *Southern Leadership Conference v. Siegelman*,[475] the U.S. District Court for the Middle District of Alabama distinguished between election of a single judge to a one-judge court and the election of multiple judges to a single Alabama circuit court or judicial court. Pre-clearance was required when more than one judge was to be elected, but not when only one judge was to be elected.

Given that every vote would be equal under the National Popular Vote compact, the assertion that the compact would diminish the influence of minorities must be based on the premise that the current state-by-state winner-take-all system of electing the President gives minorities *more than their fair share of influence*. As discussed in section 9.20.2, the facts do not support the notion that minorities receive more than their fair share of influence under current state winner-take-all statutes. The facts do not support Gringer's contention that the National Popular Vote compact would result in:

"minority vote dilution or retrogression in the ability of minority voters to elect the candidate of their choice."[476]

Finally, despite Gringer's arguments, it should be noted that the National Popular Vote compact received pre-clearance from the Department of Justice under section 5 of the Voting Rights Act in January 2012. This pre-clearance was granted shortly after California enacted the National Popular Vote compact in 2011.[477]

---

[474] *Dillard v. Crenshaw County*, 831 F.2d 246 at 253 (11th Cir. 1987).

[475] *Southern Leadership Conference v. Siegelman*, 714 F. Supp. 511 at 518 (M.D. Ala. 1989).

[476] Gringer, David. 2008. Why the National Popular Vote plan is the wrong way to abolish the Electoral College. 108 *Columbia Law Review* 182. January 2008.

[477] Letter dated January 13, 2012, concerning Assembly Bill 459 (the National Popular Vote compact) from T. Christian Herren of the Civil Rights Division of the Department of Justice to Robbie Anderson, Senior Elections Counsel of the state of California.

9.20.2. MYTH: The political influence of racial and ethnic minorities would be diminished by a national popular vote.

QUICK ANSWER:

- Given that every vote would be equal under the National Popular Vote compact, the assertion that the compact would diminish the influence of minorities must be based on the premise that current state winner-take-all statutes give minorities more than their fair share of influence. There is no evidence that this is the case.

MORE DETAILED ANSWER:

Six Colorado professors issued a written statement at a Colorado legislative committee hearing in 2007, arguing that the National Popular Vote plan would

> "diminish the political influence of racial and ethnic minorities in the United States in presidential elections."[478]

Curtis Gans (an opponent of the National Popular Vote plan) made a similar claim in a speech at the National Civic Summit in Minneapolis on July 17, 2009.

Given that every vote would be equal under the National Popular Vote compact, the assertion that the compact would diminish the influence of minorities must be based on the premise that the current state-by-state winner-take-all system of electing the President gives minorities *more than their fair share of influence.*

The facts do not support the notion that minorities receive more than their fair share of influence under current state winner-take-all statutes. As FairVote's *Presidential Election Inequality* report points out:

> "In the 1976 presidential election, 73% of African Americans were in a classic swing voter position; they lived in highly competitive states (where the partisanship is 47.5%–52.5%) in which African Americans made up at least 5% of the population. By 2000, that percentage of potential swing voters declined to 24%. In 2004, it fell to just 17%."[479]

The National Popular Vote bill has been sponsored by 135 minority state legislators and endorsed by organizations such as the National Black Caucus of State Legislators, the National Latino Congreso, and the NAACP.

In endorsing the National Popular Vote bill, the NAACP cited the fact that it supported "the ideal of one person, one vote."

---

[478] Statement signed by Professors Robert D. Loevy, Danial Clayton, Edward Roche, Robert M. Hardaway, Jim L. Riley, and Dennis Steele.

[479] FairVote. 2006. *Presidential Elections Inequality: The Electoral College in the 21st Century.* http://www.fairvote.org/media/perp/presidentialinequality.pdf.

Finally, it should be noted that the National Popular Vote compact received pre-clearance from the U.S. Department of Justice under section 5 of the Voting Rights Act in January 2012. This pre-clearance was granted shortly after California enacted the National Popular Vote compact in 2011.[480]

9.21. MYTH ABOUT A FEDERAL ELECTION BUREAUCRACY

9.21.1. MYTH: A federal election bureaucracy would be created by the National Popular Vote compact.

QUICK ANSWER:
- The National Popular Vote compact would not create any bureaucracy—much less a federal election bureaucracy appointed by the sitting President.
- Implementation of the National Popular Vote compact would not necessitate the creation of any new bureaucracy. It would involve adding up the popular vote totals that are already being routinely tabulated by existing state officials under existing laws and procedures.

MORE DETAILED ANSWER:
A brochure published by the Evergreen Freedom Foundation of Olympia, Washington, suggests that the National Popular Vote plan would result in

> "**nationalizing election administration**, potentially putting presidential appointees in charge of presidential elections."[481] [Emphasis added]

Trent England (a lobbyist opposing the National Popular Vote compact and Vice-President of the Evergreen Freedom Foundation of Olympia, Washington) has written:

> "Because of the Electoral College, **the United States has no national election bureaucracy**—no presidential appointee in charge of presidential elections."[482] [Emphasis added]

Professor Robert Hardaway of the University of Denver Sturm College of Law repeated this theme in his testimony on February 19, 2010, to the Alaska Senate Judiciary Committee:

> "**Under the Koza scheme, who would be the national official who would decide what the popular vote is?** And what would happen if a

---

[480] Letter dated January 13, 2012, concerning Assembly Bill 459 (the National Popular Vote compact) from T. Christian Herren of the Civil Rights Division of the Department of Justice to Robbie Anderson, Senior Elections Counsel of the state of California.

[481] Evergreen Freedom Foundation. Olympia, Washington.

[482] England, Trent. Op-Ed: Bypass the Electoral College? *Christian Science Monitor*. August 12, 2010.

state officer decides that the popular vote tally is one figure, and **someone from the federal government**, like the Congressional Budget Office, the *Congressional Quarterly*,[483] decides that it's something else?"

Gary Gregg II, a strong supporter of the current system of electing the President and editor of a book defending the current system, says:

> "Will we have to create and pay for a new federal agency to verify the accuracy of popular vote totals? Probably."[484]

The National Popular Vote compact provides for the adding up of the vote totals for President from all 50 states and the District of Columbia. These vote totals are election results that are already created by, and certified by, state election officials under existing laws and procedures.

These state-level vote totals would be generated by each state in exactly the same manner as they are today. Each state's vote totals would be officially recorded in a "Certificate of Ascertainment"[485]—just as they are today. Each state's results would then be reported to Congress as required under the 12th Amendment—just as they are today.

The National Popular Vote compact would not create (or necessitate) any bureaucracy—much less a federal bureaucracy.

The states would continue to control elections, as provided by the U.S. Constitution—just as they do today.

The states would continue to reach a "final determination" as to the popular vote count in their state—just as they do today. Section 6 of Title 3 of the United States Code specifies:

> "It shall be the duty of the executive of each State, as soon as practicable after the conclusion of the appointment of the electors in such State by the final ascertainment, under and in pursuance of the laws of such State providing for such ascertainment, to communicate by registered mail under the seal of the State to the Archivist of the United States **a certificate of such ascertainment of the electors appointed, setting forth the names of such electors and the canvass** or other ascertainment under

---

[483] Note that the Congressional Budget Office has nothing to do with elections, and that the Congressional Quarterly is a private publishing corporation.

[484] Gregg, Gary. Keep Electoral College for fair presidential votes. *Politico*. December 5, 2012.

[485] Appendices E, F, G, H, and I show examples of certificates of ascertainment from Minnesota, Maine, Nebraska, New York, and Mississippi. Figure 6.1 shows Vermont's 2008 Certificate of Ascertainment. Figure 9.5 shows Oregon's 2012 Certificate of Ascertainment. The Certificates of Ascertainment from all 50 states and the District of Columbia are available online for the 2000, 2004, and 2008 presidential elections. For the 2004 presidential election, see http://www.archives.gov/federal-register/electoral-college/2004/certificates _of_ascertainment.html.

the laws of such State of **the number of votes** given or cast for each person for whose appointment any and all votes have been given or cast; and it shall also thereupon be the duty of the executive of each State to deliver to the electors of such State, on or before the day on which they are required by section 7 of this title to meet, six duplicate-originals of the same certificate under the seal of the State. . . ." [Emphasis added]

9.22. MYTHS ABOUT THE DISTRICT OF COLUMBIA

9.22.1. MYTH: The National Popular Vote compact would permit the District of Columbia to vote for President, even though it is not a state.

QUICK ANSWER:

- The District of Columbia has had the vote for President since ratification of the 23rd Amendment to the U.S. Constitution in 1961.

MORE DETAILED ANSWER:

This (somewhat widespread) myth stems from a failure to realize that citizens of the District of Columbia already have been able to vote for President and Vice President since ratification of the 23rd Amendment in 1961. The District has three electoral votes.

The 23rd Amendment specifies that presidential electors representing the District of Columbia

"**shall be considered**, for the purposes of the election of President and Vice President, **to be electors appointed by a state**." [Emphasis added]

The National Popular Vote compact is consistent with the 23rd Amendment in that it treats the District of Columbia as a "state" for the purposes of presidential elections. The compact adds up the popular vote from all 50 states and the District of Columbia to determine the national popular vote winner.

9.22.2. MYTH: Because it is not a state, the District of Columbia may not enter into interstate compacts.

QUICK ANSWER:

- The District of Columbia may be a party to interstate compacts, and it indeed belongs to numerous compacts.

MORE DETAILED ANSWER:

The Council of State Governments (CSG) lists 17 major interstate compacts to which the District of Columbia is a party.[486] Examples include the Interstate Com-

---

[486] Council of State Governments. 2003. *Interstate Compacts and Agencies 2003.* Lexington, KY: The Council of State Governments.

pact on Juveniles and the Interstate Compact on the Placement of Children (both of which are compacts to which all 50 states and the District of Columbia belong). The Interstate Compact for Education encompasses 48 states, including the District of Columbia.

The District of Columbia approved the National Popular Vote compact in 2010.

9.22.3. MYTH: Only Congress may enter into interstate compacts on behalf of the District of Columbia.

QUICK ANSWER:

- The Council of the District of Columbia may enter into interstate compacts under Congress' delegation of authority to the Council in the District of Columbia Home Rule Act of 1973.
- The Council has entered into interstate compacts on numerous occasions under the authority of the District of Columbia Home Rule Act of 1973.

MORE DETAILED ANSWER:

Prior to 1973, it was customary for Congress to enact interstate compacts on behalf of the District of Columbia.

However, in the District of Columbia Home Rule Act of 1973, Congress delegated its authority to pass laws concerning the District to the Council of the District of Columbia in all but 10 specifically identified areas listed in section 602(a) of the Act.[487]

None of the 10 specific restrictions in section 602(a) of the Home Rule Act precluded the District of Columbia from entering into interstate compacts.

Accordingly, the District of Columbia Council has entered into numerous interstate compacts since 1973. For example, the Council entered into the Interstate Parole and Probation Compact[488] in 1976 (three years after enactment of the Home Rule Act). In 2000, the Council entered into the Interstate Compact on Adoption and Medical Assistance.[489] In 2002, the Council entered into the Emergency Management Assistance Compact.[490]

In 2010, the District of Columbia approved the National Popular Vote compact.

---

[487] D.C. Code § 1-233.

[488] D.C. Code § 24-452.

[489] Title 4, Chapter 3, D.C. St § 4-326, June 27, 2000, D.C. Law 13-136, § 406, 47 DCR 2850.

[490] Interestingly, the Council originally entered into this compact on an emergency 90-day temporary basis (by D.C. Council Act 14-0081) under the authority of section 412(a) of the Home Rule Act. The Council subsequently entered into this same compact (by D.C. Council Act A14-0317) under the authority of section 602(c)(1) of the Home Rule Act (providing for the usual 30-day congressional review period).

9.22.4. MYTH: Only Congress may change the winner-take-all rule for the District of Columbia.

QUICK ANSWER:

* The District of Columbia Council has authority to change its election laws under Congress' delegation of authority to the Council by the District of Columbia Home Rule Act of 1973.

MORE DETAILED ANSWER:

This question arises because of the appearance of the word "Congress" in the 23rd Amendment to the U.S. Constitution (ratified in 1961):

"Section 1. The District constituting the seat of government of the United States shall appoint **in such manner as the Congress may direct**:

"A number of electors of President and Vice President equal to the whole number of Senators and Representatives in Congress to which the District would be entitled if it were a state, but in no event more than the small state; they shall be in addition to those appointed by the states, but they shall be considered, for the purposes of the election of President and Vice President, to be electors appointed by a state; and they shall meet in the District and perform such duties as provided by the twelfth article of amendment.

"Section 2. The Congress shall have power to enforce this article by appropriate legislation." [Emphasis added]

Of course, the word "Congress" also appears in Article I, section 8, clause 17 of the Constitution concerning the enumerated powers of Congress in connection with the District of Columbia:

"The **Congress shall have Power . . . to exercise exclusive Legislation in all Cases whatsoever, over such District** (not exceeding ten Miles square) as may, by Cession of particular States, and the Acceptance of Congress, become the Seat of the Government of the United States. . . ."

After ratification of the 23rd Amendment to the Constitution in 1961, Congress enacted a law establishing the winner-take-all method of awarding the District of Columbia's electoral votes (which, at the time, was the method used by all 50 states).

The winner-take-all method for awarding the District of Columbia's electoral votes is currently contained in section 1-1001.10(a)(2) of the D.C. Code:

"The electors of President and Vice President of the United States shall be elected on the Tuesday next after the 1st Monday in November in every 4th year succeeding every election of a President and Vice President of the United States. Each vote cast for a candidate for President or Vice President whose name appears on the general election ballot shall be counted as

a vote cast for the candidates for presidential electors of the party supporting such presidential and vice presidential candidate. **Candidates receiving the highest number of votes in such election shall be declared
the winners.**" [Emphasis added]

In the District of Columbia Home Rule Act of 1973, Congress delegated its authority to pass laws concerning the District to the District of Columbia Council in all but
10 specifically identified areas listed in section 602(a) of the Act.[491]

Election law is *not* one of the 10 specifically excluded areas in section 602(a) of
the Home Rule Act.

Moreover, section 752 of the District of Columbia Self-Government and Governmental Reorganization Act passed by Congress in 1973 specifically states:

"Notwithstanding any other provision of this Act [Home Rule Act] or of
any other law, the Council shall have authority to enact **any act or resolution with respect to matters involving or relating to elections in the
District.**"[492] [Emphasis added]

Therefore, the District of Columbia Council may change section 1-1001.10(a)(2)
of the D.C. Code establishing the winner-take-all rule as the method for awarding the
District's electoral votes.

In 2010, the District of Columbia approved the National Popular Vote compact.

9.22.5. MYTH: Because it is not a state, the District of Columbia cannot bind itself by means of an interstate compact.

QUICK ANSWER:

- The District of Columbia Home Rule Act of 1973 specifically applied
  the Impairments Clause of the U.S. Constitution to the District, thereby
  permitting the District to bind itself to an interstate compact in the same
  manner as a state.

MORE DETAILED ANSWER:

Because the District of Columbia is not a state, the question has been raised[493] concerning whether it would be bound by an interstate compact in the same way that a
state is.

Section 302 of the District of Columbia Home Rule Act states:

"Except as provided in sections 601, 602, and 603, the legislative power of
the District shall extend to all rightful subjects of legislation within the

---

[491] D.C. Code § 1-233.

[492] P.L. 93-198 , 87 Stat. 774, (1973), codified at D.C. Statutes section 1-207.52.

[493] In order to promote free-flowing debate of speculative ideas, the blog involved does not permit attribution.
September 23, 2010.

District consistent with the Constitution of the United States and the provisions of this Act **subject to all the restrictions and limitations imposed upon the States by the tenth section of the first article of the Constitution** of the United States." [Emphasis added]

Section 10 of Article I of the U.S. Constitution contains about three dozen restrictions on states. In particular, clause 1 of section 10 contains the Impairments Clause, stating that:

"No State shall . . . pass any . . . Law impairing the Obligation of Contracts."[494]

The Impairments Clause prevents states from violating the terms of an interstate compact.

Section 302 of the Home Rule Act applies the Impairments Clause to the District of Columbia, thereby preventing it from violating the terms of any interstate compact to which it is a party.

The Impairments Clause is discussed in greater detail in section 9.11.1.

9.22.6. MYTH: The enactment of the National Popular Vote compact by the District of Columbia Council is incomplete because Congress has not approved the Council's action.

QUICK ANSWER:

- The process by which Congress approved of the District of Columbia's action on the National Popular Vote compact is specified by the District of Columbia Home Rule Act of 1973. All of the requirements of the process were completed on December 7, 2010.

MORE DETAILED ANSWER:

The enactment of the National Popular Vote compact in the District of Columbia in 2010 was governed by the District of Columbia Home Rule Act of 1973.[495]

Under the Home Rule Act, Congress delegated its plenary authority to pass laws concerning the District regarding certain matters (including elections) to the District of Columbia Council.

Section 102 of the Act states:

"Subject to the retention by Congress of the ultimate legislative authority over the nation's capital granted by article I, 8, of the Constitution, **the intent of Congress is to delegate certain legislative powers to the government of the District of Columbia**. . . ." [Emphasis added]

Section 601 provides:

---

[494] U.S. Constitution. Article I, section 10, clause 3.
[495] D.C. Code § 1-233.

"Notwithstanding any other provision of this Act, the Congress of the United States reserves the right, at any time, to exercise its constitutional authority as legislature for the District, by enacting legislation for the District on any subject, whether within or without the scope of legislative power granted to the Council by this Act, including legislation to amend or repeal any law in force in the District prior to or after enactment of this Act and any act passed by the Council."

The District of Columbia Council gave its final approval to the bill (B18-0769) on September 21, 2010. Bill B18-0769 contained the following provision:

"This act shall take effect following **approval by the Mayor** (or in the event of veto by the Mayor, action by the Council to override the veto), **a 30-day period of Congressional review** as provided in section 602(c)(1) of the District of Columbia Home Rule Act, approved December 21 1973 (87 Stat. 813; D.C. Official Code § 1-206.02(c)(1)), and **publication in the District of Columbia Register.**" [Emphasis added]

On September 22, 2010, Tara Ross, an opponent of the National Popular Vote plan, wrote in the *National Review*:

"And so the dominoes continue to fall. The D.C. Council yesterday approved the National Popular Vote plan that has been pending before several state legislatures. D.C.'s approval comes less than two months after Massachusetts approved the plan. **Two procedural steps remain before NPV is officially enacted in D.C.: The mayor must sign the legislation and Congress has 30 days to review it.** If these two hurdles are overcome, then D.C.'s approval will bring the total number of entities supporting the bill to seven: Hawaii, Illinois, Maryland, Massachusetts, New Jersey, and Washington."[496] [Emphasis added]

Ross then issued a call to action:

"The Council's action gives constitutionalists in both parties an excellent opportunity to highlight their allegiance to the Constitution during this election season. **Constitutionalists in the House and Senate should sponsor resolutions of disapproval** if and when NPV is signed by D.C.'s mayor."[497] [Emphasis added]

Ross' call to action to "Constitutionalists in the House and Senate" to "sponsor resolutions of disapproval" is based on the fact that a *single* member of the U.S. House of Representatives or a *single* member of the U.S. Senate may introduce a joint resolu-

---

[496] Ross, Tara. The electoral college takes another hit. *National Review*. September 22, 2010. http://www.nationalreview.com/corner/247368/electoral-college-takes-another-hit-tara-ross.

[497] *Id.*

tion to disapprove any action of the District of Columbia Council and force a floor vote on the matter.

If the committee to which a disapproval resolution has been referred has not reported it at the end of 20 calendar days after its introduction, it is in order for a *single* member to make a motion on the floor to discharge the committee.

A single member's motion on the floor to discharge the committee is "highly privileged," and debate on the motion to discharge is limited to not more than one hour.

Thus, a motion to discharge the House or Senate committees of a resolution disapproving of an action of the District of Columbia Council is ensured an expeditious vote on the floor of the House or Senate. In particular, a vote on the floor is assured regardless of whether there is majority support in the relevant committee or subcommittee or whether the leadership of the House or Senate wishes the question to come to a vote.

The motion to discharge is *not* subject to a filibuster in the Senate.

The motion to discharge does *not* require the usual discharge petition bearing the signatures of a majority of House members (218 of 435).

After the motion to discharge the committee is agreed to on the floor of the House or Senate, debate on the resolution of disapproval itself is limited to not more than 10 hours. That is, the resolution disapproving of an action of the District of Columbia Council is assured an expeditious vote on the floor of the House or Senate.

The resolution of disapproval is *not* subject to a filibuster in the Senate.

In short, a *single* member of the House or a *single* member of the Senate can, without the support of the subcommittee or committee involved and without the support of the leadership of the chamber, force a vote on the floor of a resolution disapproving of an action of the District of Columbia Council.

The procedure for congressional consideration of an action of the District of Columbia Council is contained in section 604 of the District of Columbia Home Rule Act of 1973.

> "This section is enacted by Congress--
>
> "(1) **as an exercise of the rulemaking power of the Senate and the House of Representatives, respectively, and as such these provisions are deemed a part of the rule of each House**, respectively, but applicable only with respect to the procedure to be followed in that House in the case of resolutions described by this section; and they supersede other rules only to the extent that they are inconsistent therewith; and
>
> "(2) with full recognition of the constitutional right of either House to change the rule (so far as relating to the procedure of that House) at any time, in the same manner and to the same extent as in the case of any other rule of that House.

"(b) For the purpose of this section, **'resolution' means only a joint reso-lution, the matter after the resolving clause of which is as follows: 'That the ___ approves/disapproves of the action of the District of Columbia Council described as follows: ___,** the blank spaces therein being appropriately filled, and either approval or disapproval being appro-priately indicated; but does not include a resolution which specifies more than 1 action.

"(c) A resolution with respect to Council action shall be referred to the Committee on the District of Columbia of the House of Representatives [now the House Committee on Oversight and Government Reform], or the Committee on the District of Columbia of the Senate [now the Senate Committee on Homeland Security and Governmental Affairs], by the President of the Senate or the Speaker of the House of Representatives, as the case may be.

"(d) **If the Committee to which a resolution has been referred has not reported it at the end of 20 calendar days after its introduction, it is in order to move to discharge the Committee** from further con-sideration of any other resolution with respect to the same Council action which has been referred to the Committee.

"(e) **A motion to discharge may be made only by an individual favoring the resolution, is highly privileged** (except that it may not be made after the Committee has reported a resolution with respect to the same action), **and debate thereon shall be limited to not more than 1 hour,** to be divided equally between those favoring and those opposing the resolution. An amendment to the motion is not in order, and it is not in order to move to reconsider the vote by which the motion is agreed to or disagreed to.

"(f) If the motion to discharge is agreed to or disagreed to, the motion may not be renewed, nor may another motion to discharge the Committee be made with respect to any other resolution with respect to the same action.

"(g) **When the Committee has reported, or has been discharged from further consideration of, a resolution, it is at any time thereafter in order** (even though a previous motion to the same effect has been dis-agreed to) **to move to proceed to the consideration of the resolution.** The motion is highly privileged and is not debatable. An amendment to the motion is not in order, and it is not in order to move to reconsider the vote by which the motion is agreed to or disagreed to.

"(h) **Debate on the resolution shall be limited to not more than 10 hours,** which shall be divided equally between those favoring and those opposing the resolution. A motion further to limit debate is not debatable. An amendment to, or motion to recommit, the resolution is not in order, and it is not in order to move to reconsider the vote by which the resolution is agreed to or disagreed to.

"(i) Motions to postpone made with respect to the discharge from Committee or the consideration of a resolution, and motions to proceed to the consideration of other business, shall be decided without debate.

"(j) Appeals from the decisions of the chair relating to the application of the rules of the Senate or the House of Representatives, as the case may be, to the procedure relating to a resolution shall be decided without debate." [Emphasis added]

The National Popular Vote bill was signed by Mayor Adrian Fenty on October 12, 2010.[498]

On October 18, 2010, the bill was transmitted to the Senate Committee on Homeland Security and Governmental Affairs and the House Committee on Oversight and Government Reform. In the Senate, the bill was referred to the Subcommittee on Oversight of Government Management, the Federal Workforce, and the District of Columbia. In the House committee, the bill was referred to the Federal Workforce, Postal Service and the District of Columbia Subcommittee.

On October 22, 2010, the bill was published in the *District of Columbia Register*.[499]

Despite Ross' call to action to "Constitutionalists in the House and Senate" to "sponsor resolutions of disapproval," not a single member of either the U.S, House or Senate introduced a resolution of disapproval or a motion to discharge the committees.

All of the requirements of the District of Columbia Home Rule Act of 1973 concerning congressional consideration were completed on December 7, 2010, and the National Popular Vote compact became District of Columbia law number 18-274.

Representative Chellie Pingree of Maine made the following remarks on the floor of the U.S. House of Representatives in December 2010:

"Madam Speaker, I rise today to recognize and congratulate the District of Columbia for its recent enactment of the National Popular Vote bill, which would guarantee the Presidency to the candidate who receives the most popular votes in all 50 states and the District.

"Just a few weeks ago, Mayor Fenty signed this important legislation, which was passed by unanimous consent by the D.C. Council. National Popular Vote is now law in 7 jurisdictions, and has been passed by 31 legislative chambers in 21 states.

---

[498] The entire legislative history of bill B18-0769 is available at http://www.dccouncil.us/lims/legislation.aspx?LegNo=B18-0769.

[499] District of Columbia Register. Volume 57. Page 9869.

"The shortcomings of the current system stem from the winner-take-all rule. Presidential candidates have no reason to pay attention to the concerns of voters in states where they are comfortably ahead or hopelessly behind. In 2008, candidates concentrated over two-thirds of their campaign visits and ad money in just six closely divided 'battleground' states. A total of 98 percent of their resources went to just 15 states. Voters in two-thirds of the states are essentially just spectators to presidential elections.

"Under the National Popular Vote, all the electoral votes from the enacting states would be awarded to the presidential candidate who receives the most popular votes in all 50 states and D.C.. The bill assures that every vote will matter in every state in every Presidential election.

"I look forward to more states, all across the country passing this important piece of legislation."[500]

9.23. MYTHS ABOUT CONGRESSIONAL OR PROPORTIONAL ALLOCATION OF ELECTORAL VOTES

9.23.1. MYTH: It would be better to allocate electoral votes by congressional district.

QUICK ANSWER:

- Allocating electoral votes by congressional district would make a bad system even worse.
- District allocation would reduce the percentage of Americans living in closely divided battleground areas.
- District allocation would not guarantee the Presidency to the candidate who receives the most popular votes nationwide.
- District allocation would not make every vote equal.
- District allocation would increase the incentive to gerrymander congressional districts and magnify the effects of gerrymandering.

MORE DETAILED ANSWER:

Under the congressional-district approach for allocating electoral votes (as currently used in Maine and Nebraska), the voters elect two presidential electors statewide and one presidential elector for each of a state's congressional districts.[501]

---

[500] *Congressional Record.* December 15, 2010. Page E2143.

[501] There are variations on the district approach. For example, in the nation's first presidential election in 1789, when Virginia had 12 electoral votes, Virginia chose electors from 12 special presidential elector districts. Virginia used this same system in 1789, 1792, and 1796. In 1892, Michigan chose one presidential elector from each of its 12 congressional districts and one additional elector from each of two special districts (each encompassing six congressional districts).

Curtis Gans and Leslie Francis (opponents of direct election of the President) advocate use of the district system.

> "The lack of competition and campaigning in a majority of states owes itself not to the existence of the Electoral College's indirect method of choosing presidents but rather to the winner-take-all method of choosing electors in all but two states. If a party knows either that it can't win a single elector in a state or has an easy road to winning all of them, it sends its resources to where it has a competitive chance.

> "There are alternatives to winner-take-all that do not involve abandoning the positive aspects of the Electoral College. **All states could adopt the system that now exists in Maine and Nebraska**, where all but two electors are chosen by congressional district, and the other two go to the statewide winner. Or states might explore what was recently proposed in Colorado—that electors be allocated in proportion to each candidate's share of the popular vote above a certain threshold. **Either would provide a reason for both parties to compete in most states because there would be electors to win. Either would likely produce an electoral vote count closer to the popular vote.**"[502] [Emphasis added]

In fact, the congressional-district approach fails when evaluated against the criteria of whether it would make presidential elections more competitive, whether it would accurately reflect the nationwide popular vote, and whether it would make every vote equal. In short, allocating electoral votes by congressional district would make a bad system even worse.

As to competitiveness, even fewer Americans live in presidentially competitive congressional districts than live in battleground states. In the 2000 presidential election, there were only 55 congressional districts (out of 435 districts) in which the difference between George W. Bush and Al Gore was 4% or less in the district. Similarly, in 2004, there were only 42 congressional districts nationwide in which the difference between George W. Bush and John Kerry was 4% or less in the district. That is, only about a tenth of the population of the country lives in a congressional district that is closely divided in presidential elections. In contrast, about a fifth of the country's population currently lives in a battleground state.

One reason for this difference is that congressional districts are often gerrymandered in favor of one particular political party in many states. Gerrymandering is most commonly done to give one party an unfair political advantage. If electoral votes were allocated by congressional district, state legislatures would have even greater incentives to gerrymander districts than they do now.

---

[502] Gans, Curtis and Francis, Leslie. Why National Popular Vote is a bad idea. *Huffington Post*. January 6, 2012.

Gerrymandering is also occasionally done as part of a bipartisan agreement to ensure safe seats to incumbents of both parties.

As to accurately reflecting the nationwide popular vote, a second-place candidate could easily win the Presidency under the congressional-district approach. If the congressional-district approach had been applied to the results of the 2000 presidential election, Bush would have received 288 electoral votes (53.3% of the total number of electoral votes), and Gore would have received 250 electoral votes (46.5% of the total). That is, the congressional-district approach would have given Bush a 6.8% lead in electoral votes over Gore in 2000. Under the existing system, Bush received 271 electoral votes in 2000 (50.4% of the total number of electoral votes)—a 0.8% lead in electoral votes over Gore. The congressional district approach would have greatly magnified Bush's lead in electoral votes in an election in which Gore received 50,992,335 popular votes (50.2% of the nationwide two-party popular vote) compared to Bush's 50,455,156 votes. In summary, the congressional-district approach would have been even less accurate than the existing state-by-state winner-take-all system in terms of reflecting the nationwide will of the voters.

In the 2004 presidential election, George W. Bush carried 255 (59%) of the 435 congressional districts, whereas John Kerry carried 180. Bush also carried 31 (61%) of the 51 jurisdictions (the 50 states plus the District of Columbia) entitled to appoint presidential electors. If the congressional-district approach had been used nationwide for the 2004 presidential election, Bush would have won 317 (59%) of the 538 electoral votes in an election in which he received 51.5% of the two-party nationwide popular vote.

As to making every vote equal, there is a wide disparity in the number of votes cast in various congressional districts for a variety of reasons. Inside some states, there is a three-to-one disparity in the number of votes cast in particular districts (due to factors such as population changes since the last federal census and variations in turnout level among districts).

In a 2012 analysis, Thomas, Gelman, King, and Katz concluded that

> "the current electoral college and direct popular vote are both substantially fairer compared to those alternatives where states would have divided their electoral votes by congressional district."[503]

The congressional-district approach could be implemented in two ways.

First, an individual state could decide to allocate its electoral votes by district (as Maine and Nebraska currently do).

Second, a federal constitutional amendment could be adopted to implement the congressional-district approach on a nationwide basis.

Of course, passing a constitutional amendment requires an enormous head of steam at the beginning of the process (i.e., getting a two-thirds vote in both houses of

[503] Thomas, A. C.; Gelman, Andrew; King, Gary; and Katz, Jonathan N. 2012. Estimating partisan bias of the Electoral College under proposed changes in elector apportionment. SSRN-id2136804. August 27, 2012.

Congress). There have been only 17 amendments ratified since the Bill of Rights. The last time Congress successfully launched a federal constitutional amendment (voting by 18-year-olds) was in 1971.

There is a prohibitive political impediment associated with the adoption of the congressional-district approach on a piecemeal basis by individual states. In 1800, Thomas Jefferson argued that Virginia should switch from its then-existing district system of electing presidential electors to the statewide winner-take-all system because of the political disadvantage suffered by states (such as Virginia) that divided their electoral votes by districts in a political environment in which other states used the winner-take-all approach:

> "while 10. states chuse either by their legislatures or by a general ticket [winner-take-all], **it is folly & worse than folly** for the other 6. not to do it."[504] [Spelling and punctuation as per original] [Emphasis added]

Indeed, the now-prevailing statewide winner-take-all system became entrenched in the political landscape in the 1830s precisely because dividing a state's electoral votes diminishes the state's political influence relative to states using the statewide winner-take-all approach.

The "folly" of individual states adopting the congressional-district approach on a piecemeal basis is shown by the fact that there were only 55 congressional districts in which the difference between George W. Bush and Al Gore was 4% or less in the 2000 presidential election. Suppose that as many as 48 or 49 states were to allocate their electoral votes by district, but that just one or two large, closely divided battleground states did not. The one or two state(s) retaining the winner-take-all system would immediately become the only state(s) that would matter in presidential politics. Thus, if states were to start adopting the congressional-district approach on a piecemeal basis, each state adopting the approach would increase the influence of the remaining winner-take-all states and thereby decrease the chance that the remaining states would adopt that approach. A state-by-state process of adopting the congressional-district approach would bring itself to a halt.

For additional information on the congressional-district approach, see sections 3.3 and 4.2.

Congressional-District Proposal in Pennsylvania

In September 2011, Senate Majority Leader Dominic Pileggi (R) introduced a bill in the Pennsylvania legislature to award the state's electoral votes by congressional district.

Pileggi's proposed bill would have replaced Pennsylvania's current winner-take-all statute (allocating all 20 of the state's electoral votes to the candidate who receives

---

[504] The January 12, 1800, letter is discussed in greater detail and quoted in its entirety in section 2.2.3. Ford, Paul Leicester. 1905. *The Works of Thomas Jefferson.* New York, NY: G.P. Putnam's Sons. 9:90.

the most popular votes statewide) with a statute similar to that currently used by Maine and Nebraska. Under Pileggi's proposed bill, the candidate winning each congressional district would receive one electoral vote, and the candidate winning the state would receive a bonus of two at-large electoral votes.

At the time Senator Pileggi introduced his bill in 2011, the Democratic nominee for President had won Pennsylvania in the five elections since 1992. In the fall of 2011, it was widely expected that President Obama would win Pennsylvania again in 2012. In fact, Obama did win Pennsylvania in November 2012.

The Republicans won control of both houses of the Pennsylvania legislature and the Governor's office in November 2010. At the time Senator Pileggi introduced his bill in 2011, it was widely expected that the legislature would adopt a congressional districting plan that would be favorable to the Republican Party. The legislature did, in fact, adopt such a plan in 2012.

The congressional-district approach was criticized on the basis that it would diminish the state's clout in presidential elections by dividing Pennsylvania's 20 electoral votes.

State Senator Daylin Leach (a leading Democratic opponent of the bill) said:

> "Pennsylvania is a battleground state, it gets a ton of attention, a ton of resources. **The day this bill passes we become irrelevant to electoral campaigns**. . . . We become Utah on the day this bill passes."[505] [Emphasis added]

In a September 27, 2011, article entitled "Specter Bluntly Says Electoral Change Will Cut Fed Funding for PA," former U.S. Senator Arlen Specter (who was a Republican until he changed parties in 2009) said:

> "I think it'd be very bad for Pennsylvania because we wouldn't attract attention from Washington on important funding projects for the state."

> **"Under the current electoral system, Obama has good reason to give us the money to carry Pennsylvania. Because Presidents think that way. It affects their decisions."**

> **"In 2004, when I ran with Bush, he was running for re-election and so was I. The President came to Pennsylvania 44 times, and he was looking for items the state needed to help him win the state."**

> "That has been the tradition with the Presidents I served with and it helped us get federal funding throughout the state. It has worked pretty well for us for 30 years, I can tell you."

---

[505] Quinn, Bowman. Pennsylvania Electoral College proposal divides GOP officials, public. *PBS News Hour.* September 27, 2011. http://www.pbs.org/newshour/rundown/2011/09/republican-officials-divided-over-penn sylvania-electoral-college-proposal-slim-majority-of-public-op.html.

"It's undesirable to change the system so Presidents won't be asking us always for what we need, what they can do for us."

"For 30 years, that system has worked pretty well for us, and **it's undesirable to alter a system that is not broken.**"[506] [Emphasis added]

Former Pennsylvania Governor Ed Rendell (D) said on September 17, 2011:

"Why would you pay any attention to Pennsylvania? **Why would you care, day in and day out, about doing things for Pennsylvania?** . . . We're sacrificing tremendous clout that we presently have."[507] [Emphasis added]

On September 13, Rendell said that presidential elections are decided by

"basically Pennsylvania, Michigan, Ohio and Florida . . .."

"That gives us tremendous clout when the governor of Pennsylvania asks the president or Congress for something, such as disaster recovery aid, Rendell said. If the disaster's cost is close to what qualifies the state for federal aid, its electoral votes tip the balance in its favor."[508]

Some Republicans did not support Pileggi's congressional-district proposal in 2011, including Rob Gleason, the Republican State Chairman. Gleason said:

"We would no longer be a battleground state with all the benefits that come with that."[509]

National Republican Congressional Committee Chairman Pete Sessions raised the concern that focusing the presidential campaign on Pennsylvania's closely divided congressional districts might endanger some Republican incumbents (particularly ones elected to Congress for the first time in the November 2010 Republican sweep).[510]

The congressional-district proposal was widely discussed by Republicans in Wisconsin, Michigan, and other states that Obama had carried in 2008 and where the Republican Party controlled both houses of the legislature and the Governor's office.

---

[506] DeCoursey, Peter L. Specter bluntly says electoral change will cut fed funding for PA. *Pennsylvania Capitol Wire*. September 27, 2011. http://www.politicspa.com/927-morning-buzz/28145/.

[507] Chron.com. September 17, 2011.

[508] Wereschagin, Mike and Bumsted, Brad Bumsted. GOP plan could jeopardize Pennsylvania's political clout. *Pittsburgh Tribune-Review*. September 13, 2011. http://triblive.com/x/pittsburghtrib/news/regional/s_756446.html#axzz2FzxzjtKI.

[509] Heidenreich, Sari and Gibson, Keegan. Less hawkish tone from Gleason, Priebus about Electoral College changes. *PoliticsPA*. September 17, 2011. http://www.politicspa.com/less-hawkish-tone-from-gleason-priebus-about-electoral-college-changes/27881/.

[510] Yadron, Danny. Pete Sessions: Pa. Electoral College change would put house races at risk. September 15, 2011. http://blogs.wsj.com/washwire/2011/09/15/pete-sessions-pa-electoral-college-change-would-put-house-races-at-risk/?mod=WSJBlog&utm_source=twitterfeed&utm_medium=twitter.

In the end, the congressional-district proposal was not enacted by Pennsylvania or any other state in 2012.

In a December 2012 article entitled "Electoral College Chaos: How Republicans Could Put a Lock on the Presidency," Rob Richie discussed the political effect of the congressional-district proposal in six states that President Obama won in both 2008 and 2012 and where the Republican party controlled both houses of the legislature and the Governor's office (that is, Pennsylvania, Wisconsin, Michigan, Ohio, Virginia, and Florida).[511]

In November 2012, President Obama won the electoral votes of these six states (Pennsylvania, Wisconsin, Michigan, Ohio, Virginia, and Florida) by a 106–0 margin over Governor Romney. This 106–0 margin helped President Obama win the Electoral College by a 62-vote margin (332–206).

Table 9.21 shows the effect (using data from Richie's article) of applying Senator Pileggi's proposed congressional-district approach to the actual 2012 election returns from six states (Pennsylvania, Wisconsin, Michigan, Ohio, Virginia, and Florida). Columns 2 and 3 show the November 2012 statewide election results. Columns 4 and 5 show the number of congressional districts won by President Obama and Governor Romney in 2012 in each state, respectively. Columns 6 and 7 show the assignment of the bonus of two at-large electoral votes (all of which went to Obama because Obama carried all six states). Columns 8 and 9 show the total Democratic and Republican electoral votes under the congressional-district approach.

Table 9.21 POLITICAL EFFECT OF SENATOR PILEGGI'S CONGRESSIONAL-DISTRICT APPROACH IN SIX STATES THAT OBAMA CARRIED IN 2012

STATE	D	R	D DISTRICTS	R DISTRICTS	D AT-LARGE	R AT-LARGE	D TOTAL	R TOTAL
FL	50%	49%	11	16	2	0	13	16
MI	54%	45%	5	9	2	0	5	9
OH	51%	48%	4	12	2	0	6	12
PA	52%	47%	5	13	2	0	7	13
VA	51%	47%	4	7	2	0	6	7
WI	53%	46%	3	5	2	0	5	5
Total			**32**	**62**	**12**	**0**	**44**	**62**

Under the congressional-district approach (currently used by Maine and Nebraska and proposed by Pennsylvania Senator Pileggi in 2011), President Obama would have received only 44 electoral votes to Governor Romney's 62 electoral votes in the six states in table 9.21, and President Obama would have ended up with a razor-thin 270–268 win in the Electoral College in 2012.

---

[511] Richie, Rob. Electoral College chaos: How Republicans could put a lock on the presidency. December 13, 2012. http://www.fairvote.org/electoral-college-chaos-how-republicans-could-put-a-lock-on-the-presidency.

A *National Journal* article entitled "The GOP's Electoral College Scheme" in December 2012 reported:

> "Republicans alarmed at the apparent challenges they face in winning the White House are preparing an all-out assault on the Electoral College system in critical states, an initiative that would significantly ease the party's path to the Oval Office.
>
> **"Senior Republicans say they will try to leverage their party's majorities in Democratic-leaning states in an effort to end the winner-take-all system of awarding electoral votes. Instead, bills that will be introduced in several Democratic states would award electoral votes on a proportional basis. . . .**
>
> "If more reliably blue states like Michigan, Pennsylvania, and Wisconsin were to award their electoral votes proportionally, Republicans would be able to eat into what has become a deep Democratic advantage.
>
> "All three states have given the Democratic nominee their electoral votes in each of the last six presidential elections. Now, senior Republicans in Washington are overseeing legislation in all three states to end the winner-take-all system. . . .
>
> "The proposals, the senior GOP official said, are likely to come up in each state's legislative session in 2013. Bills have been drafted, and legislators are talking to party bosses to craft strategy. . . .
>
> "In the long run, Republican operatives say they would like to pursue similar Electoral College reform in Florida, Ohio, and Virginia. Obama won all three states, but Romney won a majority of the congressional districts in each state.
>
> **"Rewriting the rules would dramatically shrink or eliminate the Democratic advantage, because of the way House districts are drawn. . . .**
>
> "If Republicans go ahead with their plan, Democrats don't have the option of pushing back. . . . Some consistently blue presidential states have Republican legislatures; the reverse is not true."[512] [Emphasis added]

In December 2012, state Representatives Robert Godshall (R) and Seth Grove (R) announced that they intended to introduce a bill to implement the congressional-district approach in Pennsylvania in 2013.

PoliticsPA pointed out that Pennsylvania lost its battleground status in 2012:

---

[512] Wilson, Reid. The GOP's Electoral College scheme. *National Journal.* December 17, 2012. http://www .nationaljournal.com/columns/on-the-trail/the-gop-s-electoral-college-scheme-20121217.

"Once a reliable battleground state, Pennsylvania spent most of the 2012 presidential campaign on the sidelines."[513]

The memo soliciting colleagues to co-sponsor the congressional-district bill said:

"I believe that the Congressional District Method will increase voter turn-out and **encourage candidates** to **campaign in all states rather than just those that are competitive**. . . . Most importantly, this method of selecting presidential electors will give a stronger voice to voters in **all regions** of our great Commonwealth." [Emphasis added]

For additional information on the congressional-district approach, see sections 3.3 and 4.2.

See section 9.23.2 for a discussion of Senator Pileggi's proposal in December 2012 to divide 18 of Pennsylvania's 20 electoral votes in proportion to each party's state-wide vote for President and to award a bonus of two at-large electoral votes to the candidate winning the state as a whole.

Congressional-District Proposal in Michigan

A December 18, 2012, article entitled "Shake up the Electoral College? GOP Proposal Would Have Helped Mitt Romney Win Michigan" reported that state Representative Pete Lund (R), Chair of the House Redistricting and Elections Committee, announced that he planned to introduce a bill in the legislature in 2012 to enact the congressional-district approach (that is, the approach currently used in Maine and Nebraska and that was proposed by Senator Pileggi in Pennsylvania in 2011).[514]

In another article, Representative Lund stated:

"It's more representative of the people. . . . A person doesn't win a state by 100 percent of the vote, so this is a better, more accurate way. . . . People would feel voting actually matters. It's an idea I've had for several years."[515]

An Associated Press story reported:

"Pete Lund, Michigan's House Republican whip, said next year is an oppor-tune time to renew the push for his bill to award two electoral votes to the statewide winner and allocate the rest based on results in each congres-sional district—the method used by Nebraska and Maine.

[513] Gibson, Keegan. House Republicans resurrect congressional-based Electoral College plan. *PoliticsPA*. December 20, 2012. http://www.politicspa.com/house-rs-resurrect-congressional-based-electoral-college-plan/44960/.

[514] Oosting, Jonathan. Shake up the Electoral College? GOP proposal would have helped Mitt Romney win Michigan. *MLive*. December 18, 2012. http://www.mlive.com/politics/index.ssf/2012/12/shake_up_the_electoral_college.html.

[515] Lund: Divide Electoral College votes by congressional district. *Michigan Information and Research Service*. December 17, 2012. www.mirsnews.com/alert.php?alert_id=1352.

"The 2016 election 'is still a few years away and no one knows who the candidates are going to be,' said Lund."[516]

A December 20, 2012, article in the *Christian Post* entitled "GOP Operatives Eye Reversal of Democrats' Electoral College Edge" reported:

"The current method of calculating electoral college votes in most states gives Democrats an edge in presidential races. Republicans operatives are working to undo that edge, not by supporting a popular vote, though, as most Americans would prefer, but by supporting changes that would give Republicans an edge.

"In all but two states, Maine and Nebraska, the candidate who wins the majority of votes in the state receives all the electors for that state. In Maine and Nebraska, electors are assigned by congressional district. A candidate gets one elector for each congressional district they win and two more electors if they win the popular vote in the state.

"Republican operatives are working to cherry pick a few select states to change the system to one like Maine and Nebraska in order to pick up a few more electors in the next presidential election.

"The states they are looking at are Michigan, Pennsylvania and Wisconsin. Obama won all three of those states in 2008 and 2012. Combined, those states netted 46 electors for President Barack Obama. If those states had assigned electors by congressional district, though, at least 26 electors would have likely gone to Republican presidential candidate Mitt Romney instead of Obama, according to calculations by Reid Wilson for *National Journal*. It would not have been enough for Romney to win, but would at least put future Republican candidates in a better position to win in future elections.

"One aspect that all three of those states have in common is their state governments are controlled by Republicans, making the change possible. It also means that the 2010 redistricting in those states was controlled by the Republicans, thus giving them an advantage in drawing congressional district lines favorable to their party. . . .

"The current plan pursued by some Republicans is not aimed at fixing perceived flaws in the system, though. Rather, it is aimed at simply helping Republicans win. (Notice they are not proposing the same system for states like Texas, which would help Democrats gain a few more electors.)"[517] [Emphasis added]

---

[516] Associated Press. Changes advocated in Pennsylvania electoral vote counting. *PennLive*. December 22, 2012. http://www.pennlive.com/midstate/index.ssf/2012/12/changes_advocated_in_pennsylva.html.

[517] Nazworth, Napp. GOP operatives eye reversal of Democrats' Electoral College edge. *Christian Post*. December 20, 2012. http://www.christianpost.com/news/gop-operatives-eye-reversal-of-democrats-electoral-college-edge-87014/.

Congressional-District Proposal in Virginia

In December 2012, Virginia state Senator Charles Carrico proposed a variation of the congressional-district approach.[518] Under Carrico's proposed legislation, the candidate winning each congressional district would receive one electoral vote, and the candidate winning a majority of Virginia's 13 districts would receive a bonus of two at-large electoral votes.

In November 2012, President Obama won four of Virginia's 11 districts and Governor Romney won seven.

If the congressional-district approach that is currently used in Maine and Nebraska were applied to the 2012 election results in Virginia, President Obama would have won six of the state's 13 electoral votes to Governor Romney's seven (even though Obama carried the state).

If Senator Carrico's proposal were applied to the 2012 election results in Virginia, President Obama would have won four of Virginia's 13 electoral votes to Governor Romney's nine (even though Obama carried the state).

Congressional-District Proposal in Wisconsin

A December 22, 2012, *Milwaukee Journal Sentinel* article entitled "Walker Open to Changing state's Electoral College Allocations" reported that:

> "Gov. Scott Walker is open to having Wisconsin allocate its Electoral College votes based on results from each congressional district—a move that would offer Republicans a chance to score at least a partial victory in a state that has gone Democratic in the last seven presidential elections.

> "The idea is being considered in other battleground states that have tipped toward Democrats as Republicans try to develop a national plan to capture the presidency in future years. . . .

> "In the weeks since Obama won re-election, Republicans are now eyeing splitting up electoral votes in other key battleground states, according to the *National Journal*. If Wisconsin, Michigan and Pennsylvania went to such a system, Republicans would have a chance to edge into the national Electoral College advantage that Democrats now enjoy.

> "While those states lend an advantage to Democrats in presidential years, Republicans control all of state government in those three states after the GOP sweep of 2010. . . .

> "Republicans last year bolstered their chances in congressional races by redrawing district lines. Those boundaries have to be redrawn every decade

---

[518] Lee, Tony. OH, VA Republicans Consider Changes to Electoral Vote System. *Breitbart*. December 10, 2012. http://www.breitbart.com/Big-Government/2012/12/10/OH-VA-Republicans -Float -Idea -Of -Getting -Rid -Of -Winner-Take-All-System-Of-Awarding-Electoral-Votes.

to account for population changes, and Republicans were able to use that opportunity to their advantage since they controlled state government."[519]

A December 27, 2012, *Milwaukee Journal Sentinel* article reported that incoming Assembly Speaker Robin Vos had sponsored a bill (Assembly Bill 589) to divide Wisconsin's electoral votes by congressional district in 2008.[520]

For additional information on the congressional-district approach, see sections 3.3 and 4.2.

9.23.2. MYTH: It would be better to allocate electoral votes proportionally.

QUICK ANSWER:

- Allocating electoral votes proportionally would make a bad system even worse.
- Proportional allocation would not guarantee the Presidency to the candidate who receives the most popular votes nationwide.
- Proportional allocation would not make every vote equal.
- One of the counter-intuitive aspects of the whole-number proportional approach (which retains the Electoral College and the office of presidential elector) would result in most states being ignored in presidential elections.
- The fractional proportional approach (which requires a constitutional amendment to abolish the Electoral College and abolish the office of presidential elector) would make every voter in every state politically relevant to presidential candidates; however, in a close election such as 2000, it would not have given the Presidency to the candidate who received the most popular votes nationwide. Moreover, it would not make every vote equal.

MORE DETAILED ANSWER:

Proportional allocation of electoral votes could be implemented in two ways, and there are significant differences between the two approaches.

First, a federal constitutional amendment could be adopted to implement the system on a nationwide basis. If an amendment were used, the Electoral College and the position of presidential elector would be abolished. It would therefore be possible to divide a state's electoral votes into small decimal *fractions* (say, one-thousandth of an electoral vote). This approach (called the "fractional proportional approach") was advocated in 1950 by Massachusetts Senator Henry Cabot Lodge (R) and Texas Repre-

---

[519] Marley, Patrick. Walker open to changing state's Electoral College allocations. *Milwaukee Journal Sentinel.* December 22, 2012. http://www.jsonline.com/news/statepolitics/walker-open-to-changing-states -electoral-college-allocations-8884ck6-184566961.html.

[520] Marley, Patrick. Vos previously backed changing electoral vote rules. *Milwaukee Journal Sentinel.* December 27, 2012. http://www.jsonline.com/news/statepolitics/vos-previously-backed-changing-electoral-vote -rules-jb865ct-184975431.html.

sentative Ed Gossett (D). The Lodge-Gossett amendment passed the U.S. Senate by a 64–27 margin on February 1, 1950. This "fractional proportional approach" was also advocated by U.S. Senator Howard Cannon in 1969 (as discussed in detail in section 3.2).

Second, an individual state could decide to allocate its own electoral votes proportionally by state legislation. Under this approach (called the "whole-number proportional approach"), the Electoral College and the position of presidential elector would remain in existence. A presidential elector is a person, and a person's vote cannot be divided into fractions. As a result, each state would have to allocate its electoral votes in *whole numbers.* Colorado voters considered a ballot initiative to divide their state's nine electoral votes in this manner in 2004 (but rejected it by a two-to-one margin).

Both forms of the proportional approach fail when evaluated against the criteria of whether they would accurately reflect the nationwide popular vote and whether they would make every vote equal.

As shown in table 4.21, if the whole-number proportional approach had been in use throughout the country in the nation's closest recent presidential election (2000), it would *not* have awarded the most electoral votes to the candidate receiving the most popular votes nationwide. Instead, the result would have been a tie of 269–269 in the Electoral College, even though Al Gore led by 537,179 popular votes across the nation. The presidential election would have been thrown into Congress. Given the composition of the U.S. House of Representatives in January 2001, the whole-number proportional approach would have resulted in the election of the second-place presidential candidate.

If the fractional proportional approach had been used in 2000, it would *not* have awarded the most electoral votes to the candidate receiving the most popular votes nationwide. As shown in table 3.1, Al Gore would have received 259.969 electoral votes; George W. Bush would have received 260.323 electoral votes; and Ralph Nader would have received 17.707 electoral votes. Thus, the election would have been thrown into Congress. Given the composition of the U.S. House of Representatives in January 2001, the fractional proportional approach would have resulted in the election of the second-place presidential candidate.

Concerning the criterion of making every vote equal, every vote would not be equal under the proportional approach. The proportional approach would disadvantage rapidly growing states (e.g., Utah, Nevada) because electoral votes are only redistributed among the states every 10 years (after each federal census). The proportional approach would penalize states with a high degree of civic participation and high voter turnout (e.g., Oregon). The proportional approach would disadvantage certain states in relation to other states. For example, Montana and Wyoming each have one congressman and hence three electoral votes. However, Wyoming had a population of 495,304 in 2010, whereas Montana had a population of 905,316. See section 3.1 for additional details.

If a federal constitutional amendment were adopted along the lines of proposals that have been previously introduced in Congress, the Electoral College and presidential electors would be abolished. Under these proposals, the electoral votes of each state and the District of Columbia would be divided proportionally according to the percentage of votes (carried out to three decimal places) received in that state by each presidential slate.

The fractional proportional approach would succeed in making voters relevant in all 50 states and the District of Columbia because some fraction of an electoral vote would always be at stake in every state.

If, on the other hand, individual states were to adopt the proportional system on a piecemeal basis through state legislation, the proportional system would be constrained to operating with *whole numbers* (not fractions carried out to several decimal places). Each participating state's electoral vote would have to be rounded off to the nearest whole number. This rounding-off has counter-intuitive effects. In particular, there would be fewer battleground states under this system than under the current system.

This counter-intuitive result comes about because of the rounding-off to whole numbers and the relatively small size of the Electoral College. There are only 538 electoral votes in the Electoral College (i.e., one for each U.S. Representative and Senator). The average number of electoral votes per state is, therefore, only about 11. Moreover, about three-quarters (36) of the states have a below-average number of electoral votes. The median number of electoral votes per state is only seven.

Campaigning is rarely capable of shifting more than 8% of the vote during a typical presidential campaign. If one considers an average-sized state (i.e., a state with 11 electoral votes), one electoral vote would correspond to 9% of the popular vote in the state. In smaller states, one electoral vote would correspond to an even larger percentage of the popular vote in the state. In a state of median size (i.e., seven electoral votes), one electoral vote would correspond to 14% of the popular vote in the state. In the case of the seven states with three electoral votes, one electoral vote would correspond to 33% of the popular vote.

As discussed in great detail in section 4.1, the only battleground states under the whole-number proportional approach would be those where popular sentiment in the state fortuitously hovers right at the critical boundary point where one electoral vote might be shifted. The vast majority of the states would not be poised anywhere near that critical boundary point. Presidential campaigns would consequently ignore every state where no electoral votes would be at stake. In the relatively small number of states fortuitously hovering right at the boundary point, the only "battle" in most cases would be for one electoral vote. That is, the whole-number proportional approach would be, in effect, a "winner-take-one" system (that is, the candidate receiving the most popular votes in the state would win an advantage of one electoral vote over the second-place candidate). The only exceptions would be that two or three electoral votes might be in play in California (with 55 electoral votes) and that two electoral votes might occasionally be in play in Texas (38 electoral votes), New York (29 electoral votes), and Florida (29 electoral votes). Texas, New York, and Florida, would be "winner-take-two" or "winner-take-one" states, and California would be a "winner-take-two" or a "winner-take-three" state. Under the whole-number proportional approach, most states would not hover anywhere near the critical boundary point and hence would be ignored by presidential campaigns.[521]

In addition, there is a prohibitive political impediment associated with the adoption of the whole-number proportional approach on a piecemeal basis by individual states. Any state that enacts the proportional approach on its own would reduce its own influence. This was the most telling argument that caused Colorado voters to agree with Republican Governor Bill Owens and to reject, by a two-to-one margin, the ballot measure in November 2004 to award Colorado's electoral votes using the whole-number proportional approach. This inherent defect cannot be remedied unless *all* 50 states and the District of Columbia were to *simultaneously* enact the proportional approach. This inherent defect cannot be remedied if, for example, 10, 20, 30, or even 40 states were to enact the whole-number proportional approach on a piecemeal basis. If as many as 48 or 49 states allocated their electoral votes proportionally, but just one or two large, closely divided battleground winner-take-all states did not, the state(s) continuing to use the winner-take-all system would immediately become the only state(s) that would matter in presidential politics. Thus, if states were to start adopting the proportional approach on a piecemeal basis, each additional state adopting the approach would increase the influence of the remaining winner-take-all states and thereby decrease the chance that the additional winner-take-all states would adopt the approach. A state-by-state process of adopting the proportional approach would bring itself to a halt.

For more details on the fractional proportional approach, see section 3.2.

For more details on the whole-number proportional approach, see section 4.1.

2012 Proportional Proposal in Pennsylvania

In December 2012, Senate Majority Leader Dominic Pileggi (R)[522] announced that he planned to introduce a bill in the Pennsylvania legislature in 2013 to award 18 of Pennsylvania's 20 electoral votes proportionally. Senator Pileggi's proposal called for awarding 18 electoral votes using the whole-number proportional approach, while awarding a bonus of two at-large electoral votes to the candidate winning the state.[523]

Table 9.22 shows how Pennsylvania's 20 electoral votes would be divided under Pileggi's 2012 proportional approach (with a bonus of two at-large electoral votes) in a race with two major-party candidates.[524] In a state with 18 electoral votes, each

---

[521] For more details, see section 3.2 and chapter 4.

[522] As previously discussed in section 9.32.1, Senator Pileggi proposed the congressional-district approach for dividing Pennsylvania's electoral votes in September 2011.

[523] Varghese, Romy. Pennsylvania proposal may help Republicans win electoral votes. *Bloomberg.* December 3, 2012. http://www.bloomberg.com/news/2012-12-03/pennsylvania-proposal-may-help-republicans-win -electoral-votes.html.

[524] The whole-number proportional approach can be implemented in several slightly different ways, depending how third parties, fractions, and round-offs are treated. Senator Pileggi did not release legislative language at the time of announcing his proposal in December 2012. The calculation here assumes use of the whole-number proportional approach as described in section 4.1 of this book and also assumes only two major-party candidates.

Table 9.22 DIVISION OF PENNSYLVANIA'S 20 ELECTORAL VOTES UNDER SENATOR
PILEGGI'S PROPORTIONAL APPROACH (WITH BONUS OF TWO AT-LARGE
ELECTORAL VOTES)

CANDIDATE RECEIVING STATEWIDE POPULAR VOTE OF	WINS THIS NUMBER OF "PROPORTIONAL" ELECTORAL VOTES	WINS THIS NUMBER OF "BONUS" ELECTORAL VOTES	WINS THIS TOTAL NUMBER OF ELECTORAL VOTES
Between 0% and 2.78%	0	0	0
Between 2.78% and 8.33%	1	0	1
Between 8.33% and 13.89%	2	0	2
Between 13.89% and 19.44%	3	0	3
Between 19.44% and 25.00%	4	0	4
Between 25.00% and 30.56%	5	0	5
Between 30.56% and 36.11%	6	0	6
Between 36.11% and 41.67%	7	0	7
Between 41.67% and 47.22%	8	0	8
Between 47.22% and 49.99%	9	0	9
Between 50.01% and 52.78%	9	2	11
Between 52.78% and 58.33%	10	2	12
Between 58.33% and 63.89%	11	2	13
Between 63.89% and 69.44%	12	2	14
Between 69.44% and 75.00%	13	2	15
Between 75.00% and 80.56%	14	2	16
Between 80.56% and 86.11%	15	2	17
Between 86.11% and 91.67%	16	2	18
Between 91.67% and 97.22%	17	2	19
Between 97.22% and 100%	18	2	20

electoral vote represents 5.56% of the statewide vote. Note that a candidate receiving between 47.22% and 49.99% of the statewide vote wins nine electoral votes. However, a candidate receiving between 50.01% and 52.78% of the statewide vote receives 11 electoral votes because of the the bonus of two at-large electoral votes.

In a December 2012 article entitled "Electoral College Chaos: How Republicans Could Put a Lock on the Presidency," Rob Richie discussed the political effect of Senator Pileggi's 2012 proportional proposal (with his proposed bonus of two at-large electoral votes) in six states that President Obama won in both 2008 and 2012 and where the Republican party controlled both houses of the legislature and the Governor's office (that is, Pennsylvania, Wisconsin, Michigan, Ohio, Virginia, and Florida).[525]

In November 2012, President Obama won the electoral votes of these six states (Pennsylvania, Wisconsin, Michigan, Ohio, Virginia, and Florida) by a 106–0 margin over Governor Romney. This 106–0 margin helped President Obama win the Electoral College by a 62-vote margin (332–206).

Table 9.23 shows the effect (using data from Richie's article) of applying Senator Pileggi's 2012 proportional proposal (with his proposed bonus of two at-large electoral

[525] Richie, Rob. Electoral College chaos: How Republicans could put a lock on the presidency. December 13, 2012. http://www.fairvote.org/electoral-college-chaos-how-republicans-could-put-a-lock-on-the-presidency.

Table 9.23 POLITICAL EFFECT OF PILEGGI'S 2012 PROPORTIONAL APPROACH (WITH BONUS OF TWO AT-LARGE ELECTORAL VOTES) IN SIX STATES THAT OBAMA CARRIED IN 2012

STATE	D	R	D PROPORTIONAL	R PROPORTIONAL	D AT-LARGE	R AT-LARGE	D TOTAL	R TOTAL
FL	50%	49%	14	13	2	0	16	13
MI	54%	45%	8	6	2	0	10	6
OH	51%	48%	8	8	2	0	10	8
PA	52%	47%	9	9	2	0	11	9
VA	51%	47%	6	5	2	0	8	5
WI	53%	46%	4	4	2	0	6	4
Total			**49**	**45**	**12**	**0**	**61**	**45**

votes) to the actual 2012 election returns from six states (Pennsylvania, Wisconsin, Michigan, Ohio, Virginia, and Florida).

Under Pileggi's 2012 proportional proposal (with his proposed bonus of two at-large electoral votes), President Obama would have received only 61 electoral votes to Governor Romney's 45 electoral votes in the six states in table 9.23, and President Obama would have ended up with a 287–251 win in the Electoral College (that is, much closer than his actual 332–206 win in 2012).

For comparison, table 9.24 shows the effect of applying the whole-number proportional approach to *all* of a state's electoral votes (as described in section 4.1 of this book) using the actual 2012 election results from the six states (Pennsylvania, Wisconsin, Michigan, Ohio, Virginia, and Florida).[526]

Table 9.24 POLITICAL EFFECT OF WHOLE-NUMBER PROPORTIONAL APPROACH IN SIX STATES THAT OBAMA CARRIED IN 2012

STATE	D	R	D TOTAL	R TOTAL
FL	50%	49%	15	14
MI	54%	45%	9	7
OH	51%	48%	9	9
PA	52%	47%	11	9
VA	51%	47%	7	6
WI	53%	46%	5	5
Total			**56**	**50**

As shown in table 9.24, under the whole-number proportional approach, President Obama would have received only 56 electoral votes to Governor Romney's 50 electoral votes in those six states, and President Obama would have ended up with a 282–256 win in the Electoral College (that is, much closer than his actual 332–206 win in 2012).

---

[526] The whole-number proportional approach can be implemented in several slightly different ways, depending how fractions, round-offs, and third parties are treated. Senator Pileggi did not release legislative language for his 2012 proportional proposal as of the time of this writing. The calculation here assumes use of the whole-number proportional approach as described in chapter 4 of this book.

Clifford B. Levine, a prominent Democrat in Pennsylvania, said the following in a speech to the meeting of the Electoral College in Harrisburg, Pennsylvania, on December 17, 2012:

> **"If Pennsylvania became the third state to split its electors**—lightly populated Maine and Nebraska are the only states that do so now—**it would have little influence in future presidential elections, diminishing the voice of Pennsylvania on the national stage**.
>
> "Worse, seems a more nefarious nationwide scheme is being orchestrated by far-right strategists.
>
> "In 2010, Republicans took control of state legislatures in many battleground states, including Pennsylvania, Ohio, Michigan, Wisconsin, Virginia and Florida, which have voted Democratic in recent presidential elections. Instead of listening to voters, Republican leaders in those states have recently proposed similar drastic changes to the elector-selection process, seeking a pro rata allocation of electors in their states.
>
> "These partisans assert this allocation is fair because the winner-take-all approach deprives the losing party of a voice. What these partisan Republicans do not address—and what every voter and journalist in America should ask—is whether the pro rata systems are being proposed in red states, where Republicans control the state government and which vote Republican in presidential elections. Texas, Georgia, Mississippi, North Carolina and Missouri apparently will retain the winner-take-all selection method. Only in blue states are proposals being made to dilute Democratic strength. **The result would be a country of red states and irrelevant states, with preordained election results.**"[527] [Emphasis added]

9.24. MYTH THAT ONE STATE COULD DERAIL THE NATIONAL POPULAR VOTE COMPACT

9.24.1. MYTH: Abolition of popular voting for President and abolition of the short presidential ballot are "Achilles' heels" that would enable one state to obstruct the National Popular Vote compact.

QUICK ANSWER:

* The National Popular Vote compact was specifically drafted to prevent a single dissident state from derailing the operation of the compact by abolishing popular voting for President or by abolishing the short presidential ballot.

---

[527] Levine, Clifford B. Hands off the Electoral College! *Pittsburgh Post-Gazette.* December 30, 2012. http://www.post-gazette.com/stories/opinion/perspectives/hands-off-the-electoral-college-668327/.

- Proposals to abolish popular voting for President and to deliberately inconvenience and confuse voters are parlor games devoid of any connection to political reality. In fact, the public overwhelmingly supports a nationwide vote for President in every state for which state-level polling data are available.
- Far from representing the "Achilles' heel" of the National Popular Vote compact, these proposals constitute an "Achilles' boot" that would kick out of office any Governor and legislature that attempted to implement them.

MORE DETAILED ANSWER:

All 50 states and the District of Columbia currently permit the people to vote for President.

Professor Norman R. Williams of Willamette University has suggested that a single state could obstruct the operation of the National Popular Vote compact by abolishing popular voting for President.

> "The most dramatic way in which a non-signatory state could obstruct the determination of which candidate was the most popular across the nation is for the state to eliminate its statewide popular elections for President and have its legislature (or somebody other than the state's voters) appoint its Presidential electors."[528]

We certainly acknowledge that Williams' proposal is "dramatic."

We also acknowledge that his proposal would be constitutional. Indeed, in the nation's first presidential election in 1789, presidential electors were chosen by the state legislature in many states. In New Jersey, presidential electors were chosen by the Governor and his Council.

A similarly "dramatic" proposal has been advanced by Professor Alexander S. Belenky, who has suggested that a single state could obstruct the operation of the National Popular Vote compact by abolishing the "short presidential ballot."

All 50 states and the District of Columbia currently use the so-called "short presidential ballot"—that is, they permit their voters to vote for President with a convenient single vote. For example, the "short presidential ballot" permitted a California voter in 2008 to cast a convenient single vote for "McCain" and to have that single vote to be deemed to be a vote for each of the 55 Republican candidates for the position of presidential elector in California. The short presidential ballot eliminates the burden of locating the 55 Republican candidates for presidential elector on the ballot (out of a total of 330 candidates for presidential elector in California in 2008) and then casting 55 separate votes for the Republican candidates.

In the absence of the short presidential ballot, a certain number of voters in Cali-

---

[528] Williams, Norman R. Reforming the Electoral College: Federalism, majoritarianism, and the perils of subconstitutional change. 100 *Georgetown Law Journal* 173. November 2011. Pages 209–210.

fornia, would inevitably get tired or confused by the process of voting separately for 55 candidates from among 330 candidates for the position of presidential elector. Each of the 55 winning elector candidates would thus inevitably receive slightly different numbers of votes. Consequently, there would be no single number of popular votes associated with the candidacy of John McCain or Barack Obama in California.

Professor Belenky claimed in an op-ed:

> "Opposing states can turn the plenary right of every state to choose a manner of appointing its electors . . . into the **NPV's Achilles' heel**.

> "By allowing voters to favor individual electors of their choice from any slate of state electors . . . , **the legislature of each opposing state can make it impossible to tally votes cast there as part of the national popular vote for president**."[529] [Emphasis added]

Belenky's proposed ballot is, of course, constitutional. The short presidential ballot did not come into widespread use until the middle of the 20th century.[530]

Ballots requiring that the voter cast a separate vote for each presidential elector were abolished for the obvious reason that they were inconvenient and confusing and, in a close election in a particular state, frequently resulted in a haphazard division of a state's electoral vote among the political parties.

Figure 2.13 shows the presidential ballot in Alabama in 1960. It illustrates how the presidential ballot would look under Belenky's proposal. In Alabama in 1960, voters cast 10 separate votes for presidential electors (out of a total of 50 candidates on the ballot). Note that the names of the actual candidates (John F. Kennedy and Richard Nixon) did not appear on the ballot when voters voted for individual presidential electors.

Neither Williams' nor Belenky's proposals represent an "Achilles' heel" that would permit a single state to paralyze the operation of the National Popular Vote compact. In fact, the National Popular Vote compact was specifically drafted to prevent a discordant state from derailing the operation of the compact along the lines of Williams' and Belenky's proposals.

Article II of the National Popular Vote compact creates a legally binding obligation to conduct a popular election for President and Vice President in each member state.

> "Each member state shall conduct a **statewide popular election** for President and Vice President of the United States." [Emphasis added]

The term "statewide popular election" is specifically defined in Article V of the compact as

---

[529] Belenky, Alexander S. The Achilles Heel of the popular vote plan. Guest column. *Daily News Tribune.* January 30, 2009. http://www.dailynewstribune.com/opinion/x625264242/Belenky-The-Achilles-Heel-of-the-popular-vote-plan.

[530] The last state to adopt the short presidential ballot was Vermont (in 1980).

"a general election at which **votes are cast for presidential slates** by individual voters and counted on a statewide basis." [Emphasis added]

The term "presidential slate" is defined in Article V of the compact in the following way:

"'Presidential slate' shall mean a slate of two persons, the first of whom has been nominated as a candidate for President of the United States and the second of whom has been nominated as a candidate for Vice President of the United States, or any legal successors to such persons, regardless of whether both names appear on the ballot presented to the voter in a particular state."

That is, the National Popular Vote compact commits each member state to continue to allow its people to vote for President (something the state is not required to do by the U.S. Constitution) and also to vote for "presidential slates" rather than individual candidates for presidential elector (something else that the state is not required to do). These two requirements guarantee that each member state will generate a *single* number representing the popular vote for each presidential-vice-presidential slate as part of a "statewide popular election."

Of course, non-member states are not bound by the National Popular Vote compact. Although all 50 states and the District of Columbia currently (and wisely) permit their voters to vote for President and (wisely) give their voters the convenience of using the "short presidential ballot," a non-member state would not be obligated to continue these policies.

Thus, a non-member state may effectively opt out of participation in the national popular vote either by repealing its current law establishing the "short presidential ballot" or by repealing its current law of permitting its own voters to vote for President.[531]

The National Popular Vote compact addresses both of these unlikely possibilities by specifying that the popular votes that are to be included in the "national popular vote total" are those that are

" . . . cast for each presidential slate in **each State of the United States** and in the District of Columbia **in which votes have been cast in a statewide popular election**." [Emphasis added]

If a state continues to let its people vote for President and continues to employ the convenient "short presidential ballot," it would be conducting a "statewide popular election" (as that term is specifically defined in the compact). That state would, therefore, be automatically included in the "national popular vote total" computed under the National Popular Vote compact.

---

[531] The Colorado Constitution is unique in that it establishes the right of the people to vote for President (starting in 1880). Thus, legislation alone could not deprive the people of the right to vote for President in Colorado. Such a change would require a state constitutional amendment in Colorado.

In the unlikely event that a non-member state were to pass a law abolishing the "short presidential ballot" or abolishing popular voting for President, that state would be effectively choosing to opt out of the national popular vote count. If a state were to opt out of the national popular vote count in either of these two ways, it would, of course, be entitled to appoint its presidential electors in its chosen manner, and its electors would be able to cast their votes for President in the Electoral College. Meanwhile the compact would operate as intended for the remaining 49 states and the District of Columbia.

In short, the National Popular Vote compact automatically includes all 50 states and the District of Columbia for the purpose of determining the national popular vote winner.

Of course, there is no legitimate public policy reason to adopt either Williams' proposal for abolishing popular voting for President or Belenky's proposal to deliberately inconvenience, confuse, and disenfranchise voters other than to attempt to obstruct the operation of the National Popular Vote compact.

Both Williams' and Belenky's proposals assume that there would be a Governor and state legislature that is fanatically opposed to a nationwide vote for President and that public opinion in their state would permit them to disenfranchise their own state's voters in order to protest a national popular vote. However, the political reality is that public opinion surveys show high levels of public support for a national popular vote for President in every state for which state-level polls are available, including battleground states, small states, Southern states, border states, and other states:

- Alaska–70%,
- Arizona–67%,
- Arkansas–80%,
- California–70%,
- Colorado–68%,
- Connecticut–74%,
- Delaware–75%,
- District of Columbia–76%,
- Florida–78%,
- Kentucky–80%,
- Idaho–77%,
- Iowa–75%,
- Maine–77%,
- Massachusetts–73%,
- Michigan–73%,
- Minnesota 75%,
- Mississippi–77%,
- Missouri–70%,
- Montana–72%,
- Nebraska–67%,
- Nevada–72%,
- New Hampshire–69%,
- New Mexico–76%,
- New York–79%,
- North Carolina–74%,
- Ohio–70%,
- Oklahoma–81%,
- Oregon–76%,
- Pennsylvania–78%,
- Rhode Island–74%,
- South Carolina–71%,
- South Dakota–75%,
- Utah–70%,
- Vermont–75%,
- Virginia–74%,
- Washington–77%,
- West Virginia–81%,
- Wisconsin–71%, and
- Wyoming–69%.

In addition, more than 70% of the American people have favored a nationwide election for President since the Gallup poll started asking this question in 1944. The 2007 *Washington Post*, Kaiser Family Foundation, and Harvard University poll showed 72% support for direct nationwide election of the President. Numerous state-level polls confirm this high level of support.[532] Additional polling data are found in section 7.1.

In support of his proposal to abolish popular voting for President, Professor Williams says:

> **"Nonsignatory states that traditionally favor one party in the presidential election could eliminate their popular vote without much outcry**. For example, if Utah's Republican-dominated legislature were to return to legislative appointment of its electors in order to undermine the NPVC, **the state's large majority of Republicans would not likely complain**. The end result—the award of the state's electors to the Republican candidate—would be the same. **Ditto for traditionally Democratic states, such as Vermont.**[533] [Emphasis added]

Professor Williams is apparently unaware that 70% of Utah voters favor a national popular vote for President, including 66% of Utah Republicans. He also is apparently unaware that 75% of Vermont voters favor a national popular vote for President and that Vermont has already enacted the National Popular Vote compact.

Moreover, states such as Utah and Vermont "that traditionally favor one party in the presidential election" are the most disadvantaged under the current state-by-state winner-take-all rule. It has been decades since Utah or Vermont has received any attention from a presidential candidate. In fact, the year 2012 is the 100th anniversary of the last time the popular-vote difference in Utah was less than 6% and the last time that Utah voters were even slightly relevant to the general-election campaign for President.

Before the results of the 2012 presidential election were known, it was generally recognized that Mitt Romney could not be elected President in November 2012 without winning the bulk of the closely divided battleground states that Barack Obama won in 2008. Six of these battleground states (Ohio, Pennsylvania, Virginia, Florida, Michigan, and Wisconsin) had Republican Governors and Republican legislatures in 2012. These six states possessed 95 electoral votes—the exact margin by which Obama won the Electoral College in 2008. State legislatures indisputably have the legal power, *under the current system*, of abolishing popular voting for President in their states and choosing all 95 of these presidential electors themselves. If abolishing the people's vote for President were politically plausible in the 21st century, as Professor Williams claims, the Republican Party could have saved itself the expense, effort, and *risk* of

---

[532] These polls (and many others) are available on National Popular Vote's web site at http://www.national popularvote.com/pages/polls.

[533] Williams, Norman R. Reforming the Electoral College: Federalism, majoritarianism, and the perils of subconstitutional change. 100 *Georgetown Law Journal* 173. November 2011. Pages 214–215.

campaigning for President in these six states and simply appointed 95 Republican presidential electors to represent these states. Those 95 electoral votes would have effectively guaranteed the Presidency to Mitt Romney.

Vikram David Amar commented on Professor Williams' suggestion that popular voting for President could be abolished:

> "Is it really politically plausible to think a state legislature could try, in the twenty-first century, to eliminate the statewide vote for presidential electors? And if it is, **why are we not worried about the equally troubling possibilities for similar subversion under the current regime?** . . .

> "[is it really politically plausible to think] a state legislature could claim the 'plenary' power that Professor Williams discusses to override a state popular vote?

> "The reason these things do not happen is not that the current system lacks loopholes, but rather that the legitimacy of majority rule is so entrenched that **any politician who blatantly tried to subvert the vote would be pilloried**. And given the national polling data in support of a move towards direct national election, it is almost certain that the nonlegal 'democracy norm' would prevent the most blatant of the shenanigans that Professor Williams fears."[534] [Emphasis added]

Professor Williams is probably correct in assuming that only a one-party state (e.g., Utah or Vermont) might consider a proposal as extreme as abolishing popular voting for President.

Utah (one of the states suggested by Professor Williams) generated a margin in 2012 in favor of Governor Romney of 488,787 votes. If Utah were to opt out of the National Popular Vote compact by abolishing popular voting for President, it would cost the Republican nominee for President almost a half million votes—a number approximately equal to Nixon's nationwide popular-vote margin in 1968.

Thus, if the Governor and legislature of a one-party state were to contemplate opting out of the National Popular Vote compact as proposed by Professors Williams, the national committee and prospective presidential candidates of the party that would ordinarily win that state's popular vote would pressure the Governor and legislature not to opt out.

In short, Williams' proposal for abolishing popular voting for President and Belenky's proposal to deliberately inconvenience and confuse voters by abandoning the short presidential ballot are parlor games devoid of any connection to real-world politics.

---

[534] Amar, Vikram David. 2011. Response: The case for reforming presidential elections by sub-constitutional means: The Electoral College, the National Popular Vote compact, and congressional power. 100 *Georgetown Law Journal* 237 at 249.

Far from spotting the "Achilles' heel" of the National Popular Vote compact; Professors Williams and Belenky have actually identified an "Achilles' boot" that would kick out of office any Governor and legislature that attempted to disenfranchise their own voters in the manner proposed by these two opponents of the National Popular Vote plan.

9.25. MYTH ABOUT DECLINE IN VOTER TURNOUT

9.25.1. MYTH: A national popular vote would decrease turnout.

QUICK ANSWER:
- In 2012, voter turnout averaged 11% higher in battleground states than in spectator states. Therefore, one would reasonably expect that voter turnout would rise in the four out of five states that are currently ignored by presidential campaigns if the President were elected on the basis of the national popular vote.

MORE DETAILED ANSWER:
Curtis Gans, in a speech at the National Civic Summit in Minneapolis on July 17, 2009, asserted that a national popular vote would decrease voter turnout in presidential elections.

In 2012, Curtis Gans and Leslie Francis said:

> "By its very size and scope, **a national direct election will lead to nothing more than a national media campaign**, which would propel the parties' media consultants to inflict upon the entire nation what has been heretofore limited to the so-called battleground states: an ever-escalating, distorted arms race of tit-for-tat unanswerable attack advertising polluting the airwaves, denigrating every candidate and eroding citizen faith in their leaders and the political process as a whole."

> "Because a direct election would be, by definition, national and resource allocation would be **overwhelmingly dominated by paid television advertising, there would be little impetus for grass-roots activity. That, in turn, would likely diminish voter turnout**."[535] [Emphasis added]

These criticisms of direct election of the President ignore the political reality that presidential campaigns under the *current* system are "media campaigns" that are "dominated by paid television advertising." Under the current state-by-state winner-take-all system, presidential campaigns cater to the approximately 60,000,000 people living in the closely divided battleground states. The fact that 240,000,000 other Americans are

---

[535] Gans, Curtis and Francis, Leslie. Why National Popular Vote is a bad idea. *Huffington Post.* January 6, 2012.

ignored because they live in spectator states does not change the fact that present-day campaigns are "media campaigns" among the 60,000,000 people who matter.

The claim by Gans and Francis that voter turnout would suffer under a national popular vote is contrary to the evidence about voter turnout from numerous studies over the years.

In 2012, voter turnout was 11% higher in the battleground states than in the remainder of the country.

Professor Michael P. McDonald of George Mason University computed voter turnout for each state and the nation as a whole.[536]

Based on the 130,234,600 ballots that were counted in the November 2012 elections, the national turnout rate was 59.4%.

Voter turnout in the nine battleground states identified by the *Cook Political Report* in its October 18, 2012, electoral scorecard (table 1.18) was as follows:

- 71.1% in Colorado,
- 63.6% in Florida,
- 70.2% in Iowa,
- 57.2% in Nevada,
- 70.9% in New Hampshire,
- 65.2% in North Carolina
- 65.2% in Ohio
- 66.9% in Virginia, and
- 72.5% in Wisconsin.

The average voter turnout in the nine battleground states was 67.0%—11% higher than the 59.4% rate for the nation as a whole.

In *America Goes to the Polls: A Report on Voter Turnout in the 2008 Election*, the Nonprofit Voter Engagement Network found that in 2008

> "Voter turnout in the 15 battleground states averaged **seven points higher** than in the 35 non-battleground states."[537] [Emphasis added]

Concerning the 2004 election, Daniel E. Bergan reported in *Public Opinion Quarterly* that

> "Battleground states had turnout rates that are **five percentage points higher** than those of nonbattleground states."[538] [Emphasis added]

---

[536] The figures are from the web page entitled "2012 General Election Turnout Rates" found at http://elections.gmu.edu/Turnout_2012G.html on December 31, 2012. The voter turnout figures are those for the number of ballots that were counted, except for Wisconsin where the highest office turnout rate was used.

[537] *America Goes to the Polls: A Report on Voter Turnout in the 2008 Election.* Nonprofit Voter Engagement Network. 2008.

[538] Bergan, Daniel E. et al. 2005. Grassroots mobilization and voter turnout in 2004. 69 *Public Opinion Quarterly.* Volume 69. Pages 760 and 772.

USA Today reported the following about the 2012 election:

"Swing-state voters are a bit more enthusiastic about voting this year than those living elsewhere, perhaps reflecting the attention they're given in TV ads and candidate visits. Nearly half of those in battleground states are extremely or very enthusiastic about voting for president this year.[539]

A 2005 Brookings Institution report entitled *Thinking About Political Polarization* pointed out:

"The electoral college can depress voter participation in much of the nation. Overall, the percentage of voters who participated in last fall's election was almost 5 percent higher than the turnout in 2000. Yet, most of the increase was limited to the battleground states. Because the electoral college has effectively narrowed elections like the last one to a quadrennial contest for the votes of a relatively small number of states, people elsewhere are likely to feel that their votes don't matter."[540,541]

If presidential campaigns stopped ignoring 240,000,000 of 300,000,000 Americans, voter turnout would rise in the portion of the country that is currently ignored by presidential campaigns.

Tellingly, the headline of an October 28, 2004, report *issued by Curtis Gans* acknowledged the higher rate of voter participation in closely divided battleground states:

"Registration Rises Moderately—Battleground States Lead the Way."

Curtis Gans' own report goes on to say:

"Registration increases in battleground states were geometrically higher than the increases in non-battleground states."

"Registration increased by 3.9 percentage points in the 12 battleground states which had final figures for this report, while it only increased by 0.1 percentage point in the 14 non-battleground states which reported their final figures." [Emphasis added]

Moreover, *according to Curtis Gans*, the turnout in the 2012 presidential election was higher in the battleground states than spectator states. During a televised panel

---

[539] Page, Susan. Swing states poll: Amid barrage of ads, Obama has edge. *USA Today*. July 8, 2012.

[540] Nivola, Pietro S. 2005. *Thinking About Political Polarization*. Washington, DC: The Brookings Institution. Policy Brief 139. January 2005.

[541] Voter turnout is adversely affected in non-battleground states because voters of both parties in such states realize that their votes do not matter in presidential elections. As reported by the Committee for the Study of the American Electorate, "Turnout in battleground states increased by 6.3 percentage points, while turnout in the other states (and the District of Columbia) increased by only 3.8 percentage points." See Committee for the Study of the American Electorate. President Bush, mobilization drives propel turnout to post-1968 high. November 4, 2004.

discussion on November 9, 2012, at the Bipartisan Policy Center, Curtis Gans said the following:

> **"In the 9 states where we have campaigns**, well I added Pennsylvania, 10 battleground states, **the turnout was 62.8%, In the rest, turnout was 54.8%**."[542] [Emphasis added]

9.26. MYTH THAT OUR NATION'S FREEDOM, SECURITY, AND PROSPERITY ARE PROTECTED BY THE WINNER-TAKE-ALL RULE

9.26.1. MYTH: Our nation's freedom, security, and prosperity are protected by the current winner-take-all method of awarding electoral votes.

QUICK ANSWER:

* The state-by-state winner-take-all method of awarding electoral votes has no connection with our nation's freedom, security, or prosperity.

MORE DETAILED ANSWER:

Tara Ross, an opponent of the National Popular Vote plan, argues:

> "This important aspect of our Constitution [the Electoral College] continues to **protect our freedom**, just as it did when it was created in 1787."[543] [Emphasis added]

A brochure published by the Evergreen Freedom Foundation of Olympia, Washington states:

> "[The Electoral College is] essential to our **security** and **prosperity** and, in the end, to keeping America free."[544] [Emphasis added]

Neither Ross nor the Evergreen Freedom Foundation offers any argument that establishes a cause-and-effect relationship between our nation's prosperity and state winner-take-all statutes (i.e., awarding all of a state's electoral votes to the candidate who receives the most votes in the state).

Similarly, there is no argument as to how the nation's security is enhanced by the winner-take-all rule.

Is there any evidence that our nation's freedom was endangered by the fact that only three states used the winner-take-all rule in our nation's first presidential election in 1789?

---

[542] Bipartisan Policy Center examines voter turnout statistics. C-SPAN. November 9, 2012. Quotation from Curtis Gans appears at time stamp of 36 minutes into program.

[543] Written testimony submitted by Tara Ross to the Delaware Senate in June 2010.

[544] Evergreen Freedom Foundation. 2010. Olympia, Washington.

Was prosperity reduced when Nebraska in 1992, and Maine in 1969, adopted the congressional district system of awarding electoral votes? It should be noted that *all* the states used the winner-take-all rule during the Great Depression.

9.27. MYTH ABOUT THE REPLACEMENT OF A DEAD, DISABLED, OR DISCREDITED PRESIDENTIAL CANDIDATE

9.27.1. MYTH: Use of the winner-take-all rule permits replacement of a dead, disabled, or discredited President-Elect between Election Day and the meeting of the Electoral College, but the National Popular Vote compact does not.

QUICK ANSWER:

* The National Popular Vote compact would not abolish the Electoral College. Therefore, a dead, disabled, or discredited President-Elect could be replaced by the Electoral College in the same manner as is currently the case.

MORE DETAILED ANSWER:

UCLA Law Professor Daniel H. Lowenstein points out that use of the winner-take-all rule permits replacement of a dead, disabled, or discredited President-Elect after the people vote in November, but before the Electoral College meets in December.

Lowenstein says that this feature of the Electoral College is

> "what might someday turn out to be the Electoral College's greatest benefit."

Lowenstein continues:

> "What is needed for such problems is a political solution. And the Electoral College is ideal for the purpose. The decision would be made by people in each state selected for their loyalty to the presidential winner. Therefore, abuse of the system to pull off a *coup d'etat* would be pretty much out of the question. But in a situation in which the death, disability or manifest unsuitability plainly existed, the group would be amenable to a party decision, which seems to me the best solution."

The National Popular Vote compact would not abolish the Electoral College. It would reform the method of choosing the presidential electors so that they reflect the choice of all the people of the United States, instead of the choice of the people on a state-by-state basis using the winner-take-all rule.

Therefore, the National Popular Vote compact does not eliminate the ability of the Electoral College to perform the function envisioned by Professor Lowenstein. Under the National Popular Vote compact, presidential electors associated with the political party that just won the national election would be available to replace a dead, disabled, or discredited President-Elect.

9.28. MYTH THAT THE WINNER-TAKE-ALL RULE PRODUCES GOOD PRESIDENTS

9.28.1. MYTH: The state-by-state winner-take-all method for awarding electoral votes produces good Presidents.

QUICK ANSWER:
* State winner-take-all statutes have nothing to do with producing good Presidents.

MORE DETAILED ANSWER:
UCLA Law Professor Daniel H. Lowenstein has argued that there are "11 good reasons"[545] not to change the current system of electing the President:

> "The Electoral College produces good presidents. . . . The Electoral College has produced Washington, Jefferson, Jackson, Lincoln, Cleveland, Theodore Roosevelt, Wilson, Franklin Roosevelt, Truman, Eisenhower, and Reagan."[546]

Although these 11 Presidents were indeed distinguished, Lowenstein does not offer any argument connecting the ascension of these 11 individuals to the Presidency and the state-by-state winner-take-all rule (i.e., awarding all of a state's electoral votes to the candidate who receives the most votes in the state).

Moreover, Lowenstein does not offer any argument as to why these same talented individuals (or other equally talented individuals) could not have risen to the Presidency without the winner-take-all rule. How, for example, was the winner-take-all rule essential to the emergence of, say, Eisenhower or Reagan?

Moreover, Lowenstein provides no argument as to why a system in which the candidate who receives the most popular votes in all 50 states and the District of Columbia would necessarily not result in good Presidents.

Tellingly, Lowenstein includes two Presidents on his list who were *defeated* in the Electoral College by a candidate who received fewer popular votes nationwide, namely Andrew Jackson in 1824 and Grover Cleveland in 1888. Why does Lowenstein credit the Electoral College with success when it elected "good Presidents" such as Jackson in 1828 and Cleveland in 1892, but not acknowledge the failure of the Electoral College when it rejected "good Presidents" such as Jackson in 1824 and Cleveland in 1888?[547]

Why does Lowenstein credit the Electoral College with success when it elected

---

[545] Panel discussion at the Commonwealth Club in San Francisco on October 24, 2008.

[546] Debate entitled "Should We Dispense with the Electoral College?" sponsored by PENNumbra (University of Pennsylvania Law Review) available at http://www.pennumbra.com/debates/pdfs/electoral_college.pdf.

[547] Lowenstein includes Thomas Jefferson on his list even though the Electoral College defeated Jefferson in 1796.

"good Presidents" such as Thomas Jefferson in 1804, but not acknowledge the failure of the Electoral College when it *defeated* Jefferson in 1796 or handed Jefferson a tie in the Electoral College in 1800 (requiring 36 ballots in the House of Representatives to resolve)?

Moreover, Lowenstein includes two Presidents on his list who were elected *before* the era when the state-by-state winner-take-all rule became widespread. Only three states used the state-by-state winner-take-all rule when George Washington was elected in 1789 and 1792.[548] Only two states used the state-by-state winner-take-all rule when Thomas Jefferson was elected in 1800.[549]

Lowenstein also credits the winner-take-all rule for producing Theodore Roosevelt and Harry Truman, even though they both ascended to the Presidency on the death of their predecessor.

Tellingly, Lowenstein's list of 11 Presidents fails to account for the 33 remaining Presidents produced by the Electoral College, including those who were totally ineffectual when the country was at a moment of crisis (e.g., Pierce, Buchanan, Hoover), those whose administrations were exceedingly corrupt (e.g., Harding, Grant), and those who were thoroughly mediocre and forgettable (but cannot be named here because we have forgotten their names).

9.29. MYTH ABOUT UNEQUAL TREATMENT OF VOTERS IN MEMBER AND NON-MEMBER STATES

9.29.1. MYTH: Voters in states that haven't signed onto the compact will be treated differently than voters in states that have.

QUICK ANSWER:

- The National Popular Vote compact does not treat voters in non-member states differently than voters in member states.

MORE DETAILED ANSWER:

U.S. Senator Mitch McConnell (R–Kentucky) has stated that the National Popular Vote compact

> "violates the equal protection of voters. The Equal Protection Clause of the 14th Amendment, ensures that every voter is treated equally. Yet under NPV, **voters in states that haven't signed onto the compact will be treated differently than voters in states that have.**"[550] [Emphasis added]

---

[548] New Hampshire, Maryland, and Pennsylvania used the winner-take-all rule in the nation's first presidential election (1789) and in the second (1792).

[549] Only Virginia used the winner-take-all rule in the 1800 election. The legislatures of New Hampshire and Pennsylvania directly appointed presidential electors in 1800, and Maryland switched to a district system in 1796.

[550] McConnell, Mitch. The Electoral College and National Popular Vote Plan. December 7, 2011. Washington, DC.

The National Popular Vote compact would not treat voters in non-member states differently than voters in member states.

Voters in all 50 states and the District of Columbia would be treated equally by the National Popular Vote compact—regardless of whether their state belongs to the compact. The first clause of Article III of the compact provides:

> " . . . the chief election official of each member state shall determine the number of votes for each presidential slate **in each State of the United States and in the District of Columbia** in which votes have been cast in a statewide popular election **and shall add such votes together to produce a 'national popular vote total'** for each presidential slate." [Emphasis added]

The popular-vote counts from *all* 50 states and the District of Columbia are included in the "national popular vote total" regardless of whether the jurisdiction is a member of the compact. That is, the compact counts the popular votes from member states on equal footing with those from non-member states. Votes from *all* states and the District of Columbia are treated equally in calculating the "national popular vote total."

Although the National Popular Vote compact would treat all voters equally, it should be noted that the Equal Protection Clause of the 14th Amendment does not apply to interstate matters. The Equal Protection Clause of the 14th Amendment reads:

> "no state shall . . . deny **to any person within its jurisdiction** the equal protection of the laws." [Emphasis added]

As Jennings Wilson observed:

> **"There is no legal precedent for inter-state equal protection claims**. Successful equal protection claims have always been brought by citizens being disadvantaged vis-à-vis other citizens of their own state."[551] [Emphasis added]

The Equal Protection Clause of the 14th Amendment restricts a particular state in the manner in which it treats persons "within its jurisdiction." The Equal Protection Clause imposes no obligation on a given state concerning a "person" in another state who is not "within its [the first state's] jurisdiction."

On the other hand, the current state-by-state winner-take-all system treats voters unequally in several ways:

- Four out of five voters are ignored by presidential campaigns (as discussed in section 1.2.1);

---

[551] Wilson, Jennings Jay. 2006. Bloc voting in the Electoral College: How the ignored states can become relevant and implement popular election along the way. 5 *Election Law Journal* 384 at 387.

- The current system does not reliably reflect the nationwide popular vote (as discussed in section 1.2.2); and
- Every vote is not equal under the current system (as discussed in section 1.2.3).

9.30. MYTH ABOUT VOTERS FROM NON-MEMBER STATES NOT BEING COUNTED BY THE NATIONAL POPULAR VOTE COMPACT

9.30.1. MYTH: The rights of voters from states outside the compact would be diminished because they would not have an equal opportunity to influence the selection of the President.

QUICK ANSWER:

- A quick reading of the National Popular Vote compact will disprove the claim that "For a state outside the compact, voters' rights are diminished because they would not have an equal opportunity to influence the selection of the President in the Electoral College."
- The National Popular Vote compact would count votes from *all* 50 states and the District of Columbia in the "national popular vote total"—regardless of whether the state belongs to the compact.
- All voters in all states would be treated equally under the National Popular Vote compact—regardless of whether their state belongs to the compact.

MORE DETAILED ANSWER:

In a *New York Times* forum on the National Popular Vote compact, Professor Emeritus Martin G. Evans of the Rotman School of Management, University of Toronto, said:

> "For a state outside the compact, voters' rights are diminished because **they would not have an equal opportunity to influence the selection of the president** in the Electoral College." [Emphasis added]

Professor Robert Hardaway of the University of Denver Sturm College of Law said:

> "The idea is as few as 13 states can enter into a conspiracy. **That is an agreement to basically cut out all of the other states.**"[552,553] [Emphasis added]

WND published a "WND Exclusive" subtitled "Plan Would See Majority-Dem States Decide Presidency for All Voters." The article states:

---

[552] Debate at the League of Women Voters of Larimer County, Colorado on June 28, 2012, involving Professor Robert Hardaway of University of Denver Sturm College of Law, Professor Robert Hoffert of Colorado State University, Elena Nuñez of Common Cause of Colorado, and Patrick Rosenstiel of Ainsley-Shea. YouTube video at 31:53. http://www.youtube.com/watch?v=U_yCSqgm_dY.

[553] Our response to Professor Hardaway's claim that the National Popular Vote compact would involve only 13 states is covered in section 9.1.23. Our response to Professor Hardaway's claim that the National Popular Vote compact is a "conspiracy" is covered in section 9.16.8.

"Al Gore's claim that an end to the Electoral College will ensure all voters get equal representation in a popular vote is contradicted by a recently released book that documents how **the 'popular vote' campaign could see only 14 states—those with the largest populations, most of which are majority-Democrat—decide the presidency for voters in all 50 states.**" . . .

"'There is a very interesting movement under way that takes it state by state that may really have a chance of succeeding,' [Gore] said." . . .

"That 'interesting movement' is dissected in the recently released *New York Times* bestselling book, *Fool Me Twice: Obama's Shocking Plans for Four More Years Exposed*, by Aaron Klein and Brenda J. Elliott." . . .

"'**Under the rubric of a National Popular Vote, the plan would allow the 14 most populous American states, mostly majority-Democrat, to determine the outcome of future presidential elections. The voters of the 36 less populous states would then effectively be disenfranchised,**' warn Klein and Elliott."[554] [Emphasis added]

If one simply reads the National Popular Vote compact, it is evident that all of the above statements by Professor Martin G. Evans, Professor Robert Hardaway, and WND are false.

Voters in all 50 states and the District of Columbia would be treated equally by the National Popular Vote compact—regardless of whether their state belongs to the compact.

The popular-vote counts from *all* 50 states and the District of Columbia would be included in the "national popular vote total" regardless of whether or not the jurisdiction happens to be a member of the compact.

The first clause of Article III of the compact provides:

" . . . the chief election official of each member state shall determine the number of votes for each presidential slate **in each State of the United States and in the District of Columbia** in which votes have been cast in a statewide popular election **and shall add such votes together to produce a 'national popular vote total'** for each presidential slate." [Emphasis added]

That is, the compact counts the popular votes from member states on an equal footing with those from non-member states. Votes from *all* 50 states and the District of Columbia are included in calculating the "national popular vote total."

---

[554] WND Exclusive: Gore's 'popular vote' scheme to ensure Democrat rule? Plan would see majority-Dem states decide presidency for all voters. *WND*. August 31, 2012. http://www.wnd.com/2012/08/gores-popular -vote-scheme-to-ensure-democrat-rule/.

All of the above incorrect statements are apparently based on the speaker's incorrect belief that only votes from the member states are added together to determine the awarding of the electoral votes possessed by the member states.

9.31. MYTH THAT A NATIONWIDE VOTE FOR PRESIDENT WOULD FAVOR ONE POLITICAL PARTY OVER THE OTHER

9.31.1. MYTH: The Republican Party would find it difficult to win the most votes nationwide.

QUICK ANSWER:
- Nationwide voting for President would not be advantageous to either political party because, politically, the United States is an evenly divided country.
- The cumulative nationwide presidential vote for the two parties in the 20 presidential elections between 1932 and 2008 has been virtually tied—a grand total of 746,260,766 votes for the Democrats and 745,502,654 for the Republicans.
- The Republican Party has fared well in terms of the national popular vote. Since the formation of the Republican Party, nine Republicans have won more than 53% of the national popular vote, namely Ulysses Grant, Theodore Roosevelt, Warren Harding, Calvin Coolidge, Herbert Hoover, Dwight Eisenhower, Richard Nixon, Ronald Reagan, and George H.W. Bush, whereas only two Democrats have done so (Franklin Roosevelt and Lyndon Johnson).
- The candidate who is best aligned with the views and values of the country's voters generally wins the national popular vote.

MORE DETAILED ANSWER:
If Democrats had an inherent advantage in winning the national popular vote for President, we would see some evidence of this tendency in the historical record.

The United States is, politically, an evenly divided country in which the cumulative nationwide vote for the two parties from the start of the modern political era in 1932 through 2008 (table 9.25) has been virtually tied:
- 746,260,766 total votes for the Democrats and
- 745,502,654 total votes for the Republicans.

Table 9.25 shows the national popular vote for President between 1932 and 2008. Columns 4 and 5 show the Democratic and Republican margin, respectively, in each election.

The Republican Party has fared well in terms of the national popular vote. Since the formation of the Republican Party, nine Republicans have won more than 53% of the national popular vote, namely Ulysses Grant, Theodore Roosevelt, Warren Harding, Calvin Coolidge, Herbert Hoover, Dwight Eisenhower, Richard Nixon, Ronald

Table 9.25 THE NATIONAL POPULAR VOTE FOR PRESIDENT 1932-2008

ELECTION	DEMOCRAT	REPUBLICAN	D MARGIN	R MARGIN
1932	22,818,740	15,760,426	7,058,314	–
1936	27,750,866	16,679,683	11,071,183	–
1940	27,343,218	22,334,940	5,008,278	–
1944	25,612,610	22,021,053	3,591,557	–
1948	24,105,810	21,970,064	2,135,746	–
1952	27,314,992	33,777,945	–	6,462,953
1956	26,022,752	35,590,472	–	9,567,720
1960	34,226,731	34,108,157	118,574	–
1964	43,129,566	27,178,188	15,951,378	–
1968	31,275,166	31,785,480	–	510,314
1972	29,170,383	47,169,911	–	17,999,528
1976	40,830,763	39,147,793	1,682,970	–
1980	35,483,883	43,904,153	–	8,420,270
1984	37,577,185	54,455,075	–	16,877,890
1988	41,809,074	48,886,097	–	7,077,023
1992	44,909,326	39,103,882	5,805,444	–
1996	47,402,357	39,198,755	8,203,602	–
2000	50,992,335	50,455,156	537,179	–
2004	59,028,111	62,040,610	–	3,012,499
2008	69,456,898	59,934,814	9,522,084	–
Total	**746,260,766**	**745,502,654**		

Reagan, and George H.W. Bush, whereas only two Democrats have done so (Franklin Roosevelt and Lyndon Johnson).

Based on past performance, there is nothing to indicate the Republican Party is either advantaged or disadvantaged if presidential elections are decided on the basis of the national popular vote.

The candidate who is best aligned with the views and values of the country's voters generally wins the national popular vote.

Former Congressman and presidential candidate Tom Tancredo (R–Colorado) said in an article entitled "Should Every Vote Count?"

> "There is another reason why I have come to support the concept of the National Popular Vote Initiative. I believe, as do many of my readers, we are a center-right nation."[555]

Those who believe that the United States is inherently a center-right country should expect center-right results from a national popular vote for President. Those who believe that there is no bias in the national popular vote—including the authors of this book—should prefer a level playing field that eliminates the gaming of the system inherent in presidential campaigns that concentrate on only a handful of closely divided battleground states.

---

[555] Tancredo, Tom. Should every vote count? November 11, 2011. http://www.wnd.com/index.php?pageId =366929.

9.31.2. MYTH: Republican voters do not support a national popular vote.

QUICK ANSWER:

- Republican voters support a national popular vote for President by an average of 66% in states where state-level polls are available.

MORE DETAILED ANSWER:

Republican voters support the idea of a national popular vote for President by an average of 66% in states where state-level polls are available.

Table 9.26 shows the results, by party, from these polls.[556]

Table 9.26 RESULTS, BY PARTY, FROM STATE-LEVEL POLLS

STATE	REPUBLICAN	DEMOCRATIC	OTHER	OVERALL
Alaska	66%	78%	69%	70%
Arizona	60%	79%	57%	67%
Arkansas	71%	88%	79%	80%
California	61%	76%	74%	70%
Colorado	56%	79%	70%	68%
Connecticut	67%	80%	71%	74%
Delaware	69%	79%	76%	75%
D.C.	48%	80%	74%	76%
Florida	68%	88%	76%	78%
Idaho	75%	84%	75%	77%
Iowa	63%	82%	77%	75%
Kentucky	71%	88%	70%	80%
Maine	70%	85%	73%	77%
Massachusetts	54%	82%	66%	73%
Michigan	68%	78%	73%	73%
Minnesota	69%	84%	68%	75%
Mississippi	75%	79%	75%	77%
Montana	67%	80%	70%	72%
Nebraska	62%	78%	63%	67%
Nevada	66%	80%	68%	72%
New Hampshire	57%	80%	69%	69%
New Mexico	64%	84%	68%	76%
New York	66%	86%	70%	79%
Ohio	65%	81%	61%	70%
Oklahoma	75%	84%	75%	81%
Oregon	70%	82%	72%	76%
Pennsylvania	68%	87%	76%	78%
South Carolina	64%	81%	68%	71%
South Dakota	67%	84%	75%	75%
Utah	66%	82%	75%	70%
Vermont	61%	86%	74%	75%
Washington	65%	88%	73%	77%
West Virginia	75%	87%	73%	81%
Wisconsin	63%	81%	67%	71%
Wyoming	66%	77%	72%	69%
Average	**66%**	**82%**	**71%**	**74%**

---

[556] Detailed reports on all of these polls (and others), including the cross-tabs, are available at the web site of National Popular Vote at http://www.nationalpopularvote.com/pages/polls.php.

9.31.3. MYTH: The small states give the Republican Party an advantage in presidential elections.

QUICK ANSWER:

- Contrary to political mythology, the Republican Party gains no partisan advantage from the 13 smallest states (i.e., those with three or four electoral votes) under the current state-by-state winner-take-all system. In the six presidential elections between 1992 and 2012, the 13 smallest states have divided 7–6 in favor of the Democrats four times, 8–5 in favor of the Democrats once, and 7–6 in favor of the Republicans once.
- Seven of the 13 smallest states have almost always gone Democratic (Hawaii, Vermont, Maine, Rhode Island, Delaware, the District of Columbia, and New Hampshire), while six others have almost always gone Republican (Alaska, Idaho, Montana, Wyoming, North Dakota, and South Dakota).
- The pattern is similar for the 25 smallest states (i.e., those with seven or fewer electoral votes). The 25 smallest states divided 13–12 in favor of the Republicans in 2008 and 2012. They divided 57–58 in terms of electoral votes in 2008 and 60–56 in 2012. In 2008, the 25 smallest states were approximately tied in popular votes, with the Democrats receiving about 10 million votes, compared to the Republican's 9.8 million votes. In 2012, the Republicans led by 10.1 million to 9.2 million.

MORE DETAILED ANSWER:

The myth that the small states (i.e., those with three or four electoral votes) confer a partisan advantage on the Republican Party is prevalent because *it was once true.* However, this statement is not true today, and it has not been true for two decades.

In the 1960s and 1970s, most of the 13 smallest states usually voted Republican in most presidential elections. During that period, Rhode Island, Hawaii, and the District of Columbia were usually the only small jurisdictions that voted Democratic.

However, in the six presidential elections in the two-decade period between 1992 and 2012, seven of the 13 smallest states have gone Democratic (with only one exception in 2000[557]), namely

- Delaware,
- the District of Columbia,
- Hawaii,
- Maine,
- New Hampshire,
- Rhode Island, and
- Vermont.

---

[557] The exception is that George W. Bush carried New Hampshire in 2000.

During the same two-decade period, six of the 13 smallest states have gone Republican (with only one exception in 1992[558]), namely

- Alaska,
- Idaho,
- Montana,
- North Dakota,
- South Dakota, and
- Wyoming.

Only one of the 13 smallest states (New Hampshire) has been a closely divided battleground state during this two-decade period. Although it has been hotly contested, New Hampshire has ended up supporting the Democratic nominee in five of the six elections between 1992 and 2012.

Curiously, the Democratic presidential candidate has sometimes enjoyed a distinct political advantage among the small states because of the state-by-state winner-take-all system.

In 2004, Senator John Kerry won more electoral votes than President George W. Bush in the 13 smallest states (25 for Kerry to 19 for Bush), despite the fact that Kerry received only about two-thirds as many popular votes as Bush (453,286 for Kerry and 650,421 for Bush).

Table 9.27 BUSH'S 650,421-VOTE LEAD IN THE SIX RELIABLY REPUBLICAN SMALL STATES YIELDED 19 ELECTORAL VOTES.

STATE	BUSH	KERRY	BUSH LEAD	ELECTORAL VOTES
Alaska	151,876	86,064	65,812	3
Idaho	408,254	180,920	227,334	4
Montana	265,473	173,363	92,110	3
North Dakota	195,998	110,662	85,336	3
South Dakota	232,545	149,225	83,320	3
Wyoming	167,129	70,620	96,509	3
Total	**1,421,275**	**770,854**	**650,421**	**19**

Table 9.27 shows the 2004 presidential election results in the six reliably Republican small states. The table shows that George W. Bush's 650,421-vote lead in the six reliably Republican small states yielded him 19 electoral votes.

Table 9.28 shows the 2004 presidential election results in the seven usually-Democratic small states. The table shows that John Kerry's 453,286-vote lead yielded him 25 electoral votes. In other words, Kerry won more electoral votes than Bush with considerably fewer popular votes.

---

[558] The exception is that Bill Clinton carried Montana in 1992 (undoubtedly because of Ross Perot's presence on the ballot).

Table 9.28 KERRY'S 453,286 VOTE LEAD IN THE SEVEN USUALLY DEMOCRATIC SMALL STATES YIELDED 25 ELECTORAL VOTES.

STATE	BUSH	KERRY	KERRY LEAD	ELECTORAL VOTES
Delaware	171,531	199,887	28,356	3
D.C.	19,007	183,876	164,869	3
Hawaii	194,109	231,318	37,209	4
Maine	330,374	395,391	65,017	4
New Hampshire	331,237	340,511	9,274	4
Rhode Island	161,654	247,407	85,753	4
Vermont	120,710	183,621	62,911	3
Total	**997,385**	**1,441,500**	**453,286**	**25**

The reason for this outcome under the current winner-take-all system is that the small red states are redder than the small blue states are blue.

Specifically, the popular-vote percentages in the reliably Republican six small states in 2004 were uniformly overwhelming:

- Alaska–64%,
- Idaho–69%,
- Montana–61%,
- North Dakota–64%,
- South Dakota–61%, and
- Wyoming–70%.

In contrast, the Democrats won three of their small states (Delaware, Hawaii, and Maine) with just 54% of the vote.[559] In addition, the Democrats carried two of their small states (Vermont and Rhode Island) with only 60% of the vote—a percentage smaller than the percentage by which the Republicans carried *any* of their six small states. The District of Columbia (with three electoral votes) is the only small jurisdiction where the Democrats won by an overwhelming margin. The Democrats won the battleground state of New Hampshire by a 2% margin in 2004.

Overall, an enormous number of Republican votes in the small states were wasted because of the overwhelming victory margins in the six reliably Republican small states, compared to the Democrat's modest margins of victory in their states. This can be seen by pairing each of the six Republican states with one of the Democratic states.

- Wyoming's 96,509-vote Republican margin exceeded Vermont's 62,911-vote Democratic margin.
- Alaska's 65,812-vote Republican margin exceeded Delaware's 28,356-vote Democratic margin.

---

[559] A 46%–54% margin is generally viewed as the boundary that places a state out of reach for the opposition during a typical presidential campaign (as discussed in section 1.2.1). Thus, the Democrats secured all the electoral votes from these three states (Delaware, Hawaii, and Maine) without having to devote any effort or money to win them.

- North Dakota's 85,336-vote Republican margin exceeded Hawaii's 37,209-vote Democratic margin.
- Montana's 92,110-vote Republican margin exceeded Rhode Island's 85,753-vote Democratic margin.
- South Dakota's 83,320-vote Republican margin exceeded Maine's 65,017-vote Democratic margin.
- Idaho's 227,334-vote Republican margin exceeded the District of Columbia's 164,869-vote Democratic margin.

To place the magnitude of these wasted Republican votes into perspective, consider the fact that George W. Bush's margin of 227,334 votes in 2004 in Idaho *alone* was almost twice his margin of 118,599 votes in the crucial and decisive state of Ohio. Presidential candidates of both parties vigorously solicited votes in Ohio on the basis of Ohio issues and values because Ohio voters were important, while they ignored Idaho issues and values.

Even if one expands the discussion from the nation's 13 smallest states (i.e., those with three or four electoral votes) to the 25 smallest states (i.e., those with seven or fewer electoral votes), the Republican Party receives no partisan advantage under the state-by-state winner-take-all system.

In the 2008 election, the 25 smallest states
- divided 12–13 by party,
- divided 57–58 in electoral votes, and
- the Democrats led with 9,965,724 votes (compared to the Republicans' 9,821,558 votes).

Table 9.29 shows that the 25 smallest states divided almost equally in 2008 in terms of number of states won, electoral votes, and the popular vote. Column 1 shows each state's number of electoral votes (EV). Columns 3 and 4 show the number of popular votes won by the Democrats (D) and the Republicans (R), respectively. Columns 5 and 6 show the number of electoral votes won by the Democrats and the Republicans, respectively.[560] Columns 7 and 8 show the Democratic and Republican margins, respectively, for each state that the party carried. Column 9 shows the number of campaign events (a total of 43) out of 300 post-convention events in these states in 2008.

In the 2012 election, the 25 smallest states
- divided 12–13 by party (exactly the same states and numbers),
- divided 60–56 in electoral votes, and
- the Republicans led with 10,098,119 votes (compared to the Democrats' 9,221,230 votes).

---

[560] Nebraska awards three of its five electoral votes by congressional district. In 2008, Barack Obama won one electoral vote by carrying the 2nd congressional district of Nebraska (the Omaha area). Thus, Nebraska's electoral votes in 2008 were divided 4–1 in favor of McCain. In 2012, Governor Romney won all three of Nebraska's congressional districts.

Table 9.29 THE 25 SMALLEST STATES DIVIDED ALMOST EQUALLY IN 2008.

EV	STATE	D VOTES	R VOTES	D EV	R EV	D MARGIN	R MARGIN	EVENTS
3	Wyoming	82,868	164,958	–	3	–	82,090	–
3	North Dakota	141,278	168,601	–	3	–	27,323	–
3	Alaska	123,594	193,841	–	3	–	70,247	–
3	South Dakota	170,924	203,054	–	3	–	32,130	–
3	Montana	231,667	242,763	–	3	–	11,096	–
3	Vermont	219,262	98,974	3	–	120,288	–	–
3	D. C.	245,800	17,367	3	–	228,433	–	1
3	Delaware	255,459	152,374	3	–	103,085	–	–
4	Hawaii	325,871	120,566	4	–	205,305	–	–
4	Rhode Island	296,571	165,391	4	–	131,180	–	–
4	Maine	421,923	295,273	4	–	126,650	–	2
4	New Hampshire	384,826	316,534	4	–	68,292	–	12
4	Idaho	236,440	403,012	–	4	–	166,572	–
5	Nebraska	333,319	452,979	1	4	–	119,660	–
5	West Virginia	303,857	397,466	–	5	–	93,609	1
5	Utah	327,670	596,030	–	5	–	268,360	–
5	New Mexico	472,422	346,832	5	–	125,590	–	8
5	Nevada	533,736	412,827	5	–	120,909	–	12
6	Arkansas	422,310	638,017	–	6	–	215,707	–
6	Kansas	514,765	699,655	–	6	–	184,890	–
6	Mississippi	554,662	724,597	–	6	–	169,935	–
7	Oklahoma	502,496	960,165	–	7	–	457,669	–
7	Iowa	828,940	682,379	7	–	146,561	–	7
7	Connecticut	997,773	629,428	7	–	368,345	–	–
7	Oregon	1,037,291	738,475	7	–	298,816	–	–
115	**Total**	**9,965,724**	**9,821,558**	**57**	**58**			**43**

Table 9.30 shows that the 25 smallest states divided almost equally in 2012 in terms of number of states won, electoral votes, and the popular vote. Column 9 shows the number of campaign events (a total of 53) out of 253 post-convention events in these states in 2012.

Appendices CC, DD, and EE show the popular vote for President for 2000, 2004, and 2008, respectively. Appendix HH shows the 2012 results.

Former Congressman and presidential candidate Tom Tancredo (R–Colorado) wrote the following in an article entitled "Should Every Vote Count?"

> "Today the chase for electoral votes is a force for corruption and special-interest payoffs. I will never forget the torture of sitting in the House and watching as our 'leadership' went about threatening, bribing and breaking arms of my colleagues until they got the requisite number of votes to pass Bush's trillion-dollar Medicare prescription drug plan. A bigger piece of garbage I have never seen—especially one being pushed by the Republican Party.

> "One could rationally ask **why, in heaven's name, the party of smaller government would push so hard for what was, at the time, the big-**

Table 9.30 THE 25 SMALLEST STATES DIVIDED ALMOST EQUALLY IN 2012.

EV	STATE	D VOTES	R VOTES	D EV	R EV	D MARGIN	R MARGIN	EVENTS
3	Alaska	122,640	164,676	–	3	–	42,036	–
3	Delaware	242,584	165,484	3	–	77,100	–	–
3	D.C.	267,070	21,381	3	–	245,689	–	–
3	Montana	201,839	267,928	–	3	–	66,089	–
3	North Dakota	124,966	188,320	–	3	–	63,354	–
3	South Dakota	145,039	210,610	–	3	–	65,571	–
3	Vermont	199,239	92,698	3	–	106,541	–	–
3	Wyoming	69,286	170,962	–	3	–	101,676	–
4	Hawaii	306,658	121,015	4	–	185,643	–	–
4	Idaho	212,787	420,911	–	4	–	208,124	–
4	Maine	401,306	292,276	4	–	109,030	–	–
4	New Hampshire	369,561	329,918	4	–	39,643	–	13
4	Rhode Island	279,677	157,204	4	–	122,473	–	–
5	Nebraska	302,081	475,064	–	5	–	172,983	–
5	New Mexico	415,335	335,788	5	–	79,547	–	–
5	West Virginia	238,230	417,584	–	5	–	179,354	–
6	Arkansas	394,409	647,744	–	6	–	253,335	–
6	Iowa	822,544	730,617	6	–	91,927	–	27
6	Kansas	440,726	692,634	–	6	–	251,908	–
6	Mississippi	562,949	710,746	–	6	–	147,797	–
6	Nevada	531,373	463,567	6	–	67,806	–	13
6	Utah	251,813	740,600	–	6	–	488,787	–
7	Connecticut	905,083	634,892	7	–	270,191	–	–
7	Oklahoma	443,547	891,325	–	7	–	447,778	–
7	Oregon	970,488	754,175	7	–	216,313	–	–
116	**Total**	**9,221,230**	**10,098,119**	**56**	**60**			**53**

gest increase in government since the creation of Medicare. Alas the reason was crystal clear: Bush needed Florida for his re-election.

"I wish I could say that was the only time something like that happened, but, of course, it's not. It is part of the routine practice of buying electoral votes. I am sick of it. **Whether it's buying Pennsylvania's electoral votes with steel tariffs or Ohio's with 'No Child Left Behind,' it all stinks to high heaven. . . .**

"Some argue that the present system protects the interests of small states, especially those that hold conservative values. However, today 12 of the 13 smallest states are ignored after party conventions and are derisively referred to as 'flyover' country. . . .

"Under the [National Popular Vote] plan, an evangelical voter in rural Wyoming would count the same as the union steward in Cleveland."[561] [Emphasis added]

---

[561] Tancredo, Tom. Should every vote count? November 11, 2011. http://www.wnd.com/index.php?pageId =366929.

9.31.4. MYTH: The National Popular Vote effort is funded by left-wingers.

QUICK ANSWER:

- Over 90% of the contributions supporting the National Popular Vote effort have come—in about equal total amounts—from a pro-life, anti-Buffett-rule, registered Republican businessman and a pro-choice, pro-Buffett-rule, registered Democratic businessman.

MORE DETAILED ANSWER:

Hans von Spakovsky has stated:

> "National Popular Vote Inc. is one of California's lesser-known advocacy organizations. Its chairman, John Koza, is best known as the co-founder of Scientific Games Inc., the company that invented the instant lottery ticket.

> "Now Mr. Koza **and his fellow liberal activists** want to 'scratch off' the Electoral College."[562] [Emphasis added]

The facts are that over 90% of the contributions supporting the National Popular Vote effort have come—in about equal total amounts—from

- Tom Golisano (a pro-life, anti-Buffett-rule, registered Republican businessman residing in Florida) and
- John R. Koza (l a pro-choice, pro-Buffett-rule, registered Democratic businessman residing in California).

John R. Koza's contributions have largely been spent by National Popular Vote, a 501(c)4 non-profit corporation.

Tom Golisano's contributions have largely been spent by Support Popular Vote, a 501(c)4 non-profit corporation (originally called "National Popular Vote Initiative").

Support for a nationwide popular vote for President has been bipartisan for some time. Appendix S shows, state by state, members of Congress who have sponsored proposed constitutional amendments for nationwide popular election of the President in recent years or who voted in favor of constitutional amendments in the 338–70 roll call in the House of Representatives in 1969 or the 1979 roll call in the Senate. As shown in appendix S, there has been at least one supporter in Congress from each of the 50 states. As of 2012, over 250 Republican state legislators have either sponsored or cast a recorded vote in favor of the National Popular Vote bill. See section 9.31.2 for recent state-level polling results showing that Republican voters support a nationwide vote for President.

---

[562] von Spakovsky, Hans A. Protecting Electoral College from popular vote. *Washington Times*. October 26, 2011.

9.31.5. MYTH: The long-term trend in the Electoral College favors the Republicans because Republican-leaning states have gained electoral votes with each recent census.

QUICK ANSWER:

- The fact that Republican-leaning states have gained population with each recent census is not necessarily helpful to the Republican cause. Population growth may upset a state's political complexion depending on the relative number of newcomers and leavers and the (usually very significant) difference in political outlook between newcomers and leavers.

- Recent rapid population growth in Virginia, North Carolina, Colorado, Nevada, and Florida was not helpful to the Republican cause because it converted states that had voted Republican for decades in presidential elections into battleground states (all won by Obama in 2008).

- Arizona's recent rapid population growth (largely due to an influx of Hispanics and, to a lesser extent, former California residents) has the potential of changing Arizona from a reliably Republican state into a battleground state (perhaps as soon as 2016 or 2020).

- Texas's recent rapid population growth (largely due to Hispanics) has the potential of changing Texas from a reliably Republican state in presidential elections into a battleground state (perhaps as soon as 2020).

MORE DETAILED ANSWER:

As a result of each recent census, Republican-leaning states have gained population (and hence electoral votes) at the expense of Democratic-leaning states. Some have argued that this fact should be interpreted as a long-term trend favoring the Republican Party in the Electoral College. In fact, this trend is not necessarily helpful to the Republican cause.

Consider the 2010 census. The Republican Party would have received 12 more electoral votes in the 2008 presidential election if the allocation of electoral votes based on the 2010 census had been in effect for the 2008 election. Five states that voted Republican in the 2008 presidential election gained electoral votes as a result of the 2010 census, namely Arizona (+1), Georgia (+1), South Carolina (+1), Utah (+1), and Texas (+4), but only two states that voted Republican in 2008 lost electoral votes, namely Louisiana (–1) and Missouri (–1). In addition, eight states that voted Democratic in the 2008 presidential election lost electoral votes as a result of the 2010 census, namely Illinois (–1), Iowa (–1), Massachusetts (–1), Michigan (–1), New Jersey (–1), New York (–2), Ohio (–2), and Pennsylvania (–1), but only three states that voted Democratic in 2008 gained electoral votes, namely Florida (+2), Nevada (+1), and Washington state (+1).[563]

---

[563] See table 2.1 for the distribution of electoral votes for the elections between 1992 and 2020.

The above facts about the census do not, however, constitute a long-term trend favoring the Republicans in the Electoral College because population growth does not necessarily reinforce a state's pre-existing political complexion. In fact, population growth frequently upsets a state's political complexion.

Population growth occurs as the result of a net difference in the number of newcomers versus the number of leavers.

There is usually a considerable difference in the political outlook of

* newcomers to a state,
* leavers, and
* those staying in a state.

People come to a state, leave a state, and stay in a state because of numerous economic, demographic, and psychological factors. As a result, population growth is not necessarily advantageous to the currently dominant political party in a given state.

For example, Florida, Virginia, Colorado, Nevada, and North Carolina were reliably Republican for decades in presidential elections until recently. Virginia, Colorado, Nevada, and North Carolina were not even considered battleground states as recently as 2004. Rapid population growth converted Florida into a battleground state in 1996 (when Clinton carried the state after several decades of Republican victories at the presidential level). However, population growth upset the political equilibrium of these states with the result that Obama swept *all* of these states in 2008. Population growth not only contributed to the Republican's loss of all these states in 2008, but also increased the electoral-vote prize when the Democratic Party won them.

Arizona's recent rapid population growth (largely due to an influx of Hispanics and, to a lesser extent, newcomers from California) appears to be transforming it from a reliably Republican state in presidential elections into a battleground state (perhaps as early as 2016).[564]

Rapid population growth (largely due to Hispanics) in Texas (with 38 electoral votes) creates the possibility of destabilizing Republican control of the nation's second largest state (perhaps as early as 2020). As Charles Mahtesian wrote in a *Politico* article entitled "Obama's Texas Battleground Prediction":

> "When **Barack Obama asserted Tuesday that Texas will be a battleground state 'soon,'** he was echoing the belief, commonly held among

---

[564] Arizona has voted Republican in every presidential election since 1952, except for Johnson's win in 1964 and Clinton's win in 1996, Obama lost Arizona in 2008 by only 8%, despite Arizona being John McCain's home state. The Obama campaign tested the waters in Arizona in 2012 to determine whether it might become a battleground state. The growth of the state's Hispanic population has suggested that Arizona might soon become a battleground state. As a result, the Obama campaign opened numerous campaign offices in Arizona in early 2012. However, Arizona did not become a battleground state in 2012. The 2012 Obama campaign made similar explorations in Georgia.

Democrats, that the state's changing demographics make the transition from red to blue inevitable."[565],[566] [Emphasis added]

Meanwhile, there does not appear to be any Democratic-leaning big state (even among the numerous Democratic-leaning states that lost electoral votes as a result of the 2010 census) moving in the Republican direction to counter-balance possible future changes in the political environment in states such as Arizona and Texas.

9.31.6. MYTH: Nationwide voting for President would give voters of as few as 11 or 12 states a controlling majority of the Electoral College, enabling them to decide presidential elections.

QUICK ANSWER:
* Under a national popular vote, every vote in every state would be equal throughout the United States. The votes cast in the 12 biggest states would be no more, or less, valuable or controlling than votes cast anywhere else.
* Many criticisms of nationwide popular voting for President are based on a hypothetical scenario in which a candidate wins the White House by receiving 100% of the popular vote in the 12 biggest states and 0% in the remaining 39 smaller jurisdictions. Such scenarios are politically implausible because the popular vote is relatively close in the 12 biggest states (e.g., it split 54%–46% in 2012 and split 50.2%–49.8% in 2004). Moreover, *no* big state delivered more than 63% of its popular vote (that is, five out of eight votes) to *any* candidate in the 2000, 2004, 2008, or 2012 presidential elections.
* Opponents of a nationwide vote for President complain that if 100% of the voters of the 11 biggest states were to vote for one candidate, they alone could elect a President—while ignoring the fact that 50.01% of the voters of these same 11 states could elect a President *today* under the *current* state-by-state winner-take-all system.

MORE DETAILED ANSWER:
The 12 biggest states contain more than half the population of the United States and possess 53% of the electoral votes (283 of 538). In fact, the 11 biggest states contain a bare majority of the electoral votes (270 of 538).

Critics of a nationwide popular vote for President sometimes argue that only the 12 biggest states would matter under such a system.

Under the critics' hypothetical scenario, candidates would win the White House

[565] Mahtesian, Charles. Obama's Texas battleground prediction. *Politico*. July 18, 2012.
[566] Hallman, Tristan. Obama: Texas will be a battleground state "soon." *Dallas Morning News*. July 17, 2012. The quote from Obama was "You're not considered one of the battleground states, although that's going to be changing soon."

by winning 100% of the popular vote in the 12 biggest states and 0% in the 39 remaining jurisdictions (i.e., 38 states and the District of Columbia).

Referring to the National Popular Vote compact, Hans A. von Spakovsky stated in 2011:

> "This would give the most populous states **a controlling majority** of the Electoral College, **letting the voters of as few as 11 states control the outcome of presidential elections.**"[567] [Emphasis added]

Senator Mitch McConnell said in 2011:

> **"This would mean that from now on, just 12 states could decide our presidential elections.** A few of the most populous and most liberal states determine who actually wins."[568] [Emphasis added]

Ed Gillespie stated in 2011:

> "With 11 of the most populous states accounting for 56 percent[569] of the population, **the presidential election will essentially become a race for a dozen states with big cities.**"[570] [Emphasis added]

A 2011 letter signed by House Speaker John Boehner (R–Ohio), Senator Mitch McConnell (R–Kentucky), and Governor Rick Perry (R–Texas) stated:

> "The goal of this effort is clear: to put the fate of every presidential election in the hands of the voters in as few as 11 states and thus to **give a handful of populous states a controlling majority of the Electoral College.**"[571] [Emphasis added]

None of the above quotations about 11 or 12 states "controlling" the national popular vote reflects political reality.

It is the *current* state-by-state winner-take-all system—*not* the national popular vote approach—that would theoretically permit the 11 most populous states to control the outcome of presidential elections.

Under the *current* winner-take-all system, a candidate could win the Presidency by winning only 50.01% of the popular vote in the 11 biggest states. That is, under the *current* system, a President could be elected with about a quarter of the nationwide popular vote.

---

[567] Von Spakovsky, Hans A. Protecting Electoral College from popular vote. *Washington Times*, October 26, 2011.

[568] McConnell, Mitch. The Electoral College and National Popular Vote Plan. December 7, 2011. Washington, DC.

[569] Note that Gillespie's statement that the 11 biggest states possessed 56% of the nation's population was correct according to the 2000 census, but not according to the 2010 census. Hence, criticisms of this genre are couched in terms of both 11 and 12 states.

[570] Gillespie, Ed. National Popular Vote compact won't be popular, or democratic. *Washington Examiner*. January 30, 2012.

[571] Letter dated June 29, 2011.

Opponents of a nationwide vote for President complain that if 100% of the voters of the 11 biggest states were to vote for one candidate, they could elect a President— while ignoring the fact that 50.01% of the voters of these same 11 states could elect a President *today* under the *current* state-by-state winner-take-all system.

That is, 26% of the nation's voters could elect a President under the *current system.*

Moreover, getting 50.01% in 11 states is a far more likely scenario than getting 100% of the vote from these 11 states.

Curiously, the current system permits even fewer than 26% of the voters to elect a President. According to calculations (shown in table 9.31) made by MIT Professor Alexander S. Belenky using actual voter turnout data, an Electoral-College majority theoretically could have been won, under the *current* winner-take-all system, with between 16% and 22% of the national popular vote in the 15 elections between 1948 and 2004.[572]

Table 9.31 SMALLEST PERCENTAGE OF VOTERS WHO THEORETICALLY COULD HAVE ELECTED A PRESIDENT UNDER THE CURRENT SYSTEM

YEAR	PERCENTAGE
1948	16.072%
1952	17.547%
1956	17.455%
1960	17.544%
1964	18.875%
1968	19.97%
1972	20.101%
1976	21.202%
1980	21.348%
1984	21.53%
1988	21.506%
1992	21.944%
1996	22.103%
2000	21.107%
2004	21.666%

The implausibility of the hypothetical scenario in which one candidate receives 100% of the popular vote from the 12 biggest states is demonstrated by the fact that *no* big state delivered more than 63% of its popular vote (that is, five out of eight votes) to *any* candidate in the 2000, 2004, 2008, or 2012 presidential elections.

Table 9.32 shows the percentage of the popular vote won by the winner of the 12 biggest states between 2000 and 2012.

In fact, many of the winning percentages in table 9.32 are *near 50%* because many of the 12 biggest states (e.g., Ohio, Florida, Virginia, Pennsylvania, Michigan, and North Carolina) were battleground states in one or more elections shown in the table.

The 12 biggest states are not, of course, all Democratic bastions. In both 2000 and 2004, for example, the 12 biggest states divided 6–6 between the political parties (with

---

[572] Belenky, Alexander S. 2008. A 0-1 knapsack model for evaluating the possible Electoral College performance in two-party U.S. presidential elections. *Mathematical and Computer Modelling.* Volume 48. Pages 665–676.

Table 9.32 POPULAR-VOTE PERCENTAGE WON BY THE
WINNER OF THE 12 BIGGEST STATES 2000–2012

STATE	2000	2004	2008	2012
California	53%	54%	61%	60%
Texas	59%	61%	56%	57%
New York	60%	58%	63%	63%
Florida	49%	52%	51%	50%
Illinois	55%	55%	62%	57%
Pennsylvania	51%	51%	55%	52%
Ohio	50%	51%	52%	51%
Michigan	51%	51%	57%	54%
Georgia	55%	58%	52%	53%
New Jersey	56%	53%	57%	58%
North Carolina	56%	56%	49%	50%
Virginia	52%	54%	53%	51%

Texas, Florida, Ohio, North Carolina, Georgia, and Virginia voting for George W. Bush in both years).

The popular vote in the 12 biggest states split 54%–46% in 2012 and split 50.2%–49.8% in 2004.

In short, no candidate could win 100% of the popular vote in the 12 biggest states (or, indeed, any percentage close to 100%).

The relatively close campaigns of 2004 and 2012 convey a far more realistic picture of presidential politics than any contrived scenario.

The winner's two-party popular-vote percentage was almost identical in these two re-election campaigns:

- 51.2% for Bush in 2004,[573] and
- 51.96% for Obama in 2012.[574]

The two elections were mirror images of one another in terms of the popular-vote margin generated by the 12 biggest states and the 39 smallest jurisdictions:

- In 2004, Bush fought Kerry to a near-tie in the popular vote in the 12 biggest states (50.2% to 49.8%), and Bush's margin from the 39 smallest jurisdictions was roughly equal to his nationwide margin (3,012,171 votes).
- In 2012, Obama fought Romney to a near-tie in the popular vote in the 39 smallest jurisdictions (51% to 49%), and Obama's margin from the 12 biggest states was roughly equal to his nationwide margin (4,966,945).

In 2004, the voters in the 39 smallest jurisdictions did not "control the outcome of the presidential election" in terms of the national popular vote. Every vote from every state—not just those 39 states—contributed to producing Bush's nationwide popular

---

[573] In 2004, Bush received 62,040,610 votes nationwide and Kerry received 59,028,439 votes. Bush's nationwide margin of victory was 3,012,171 votes. Bush received 51.2% of these 121,069,049 votes.

[574] In 2012, Obama received 65,897,727 votes nationwide and Romney received 60,930,782 votes. Obama's nationwide margin of victory was 4,966,945 votes. Obama received 51.96% of these 126,828,509 votes.

vote total. The voters in the 39 smallest jurisdictions were not any more important or "controlling" than the voters of the 12 biggest states.

Similarly, in 2012, the voters in the 12 biggest states did not "control the outcome of the presidential election" in terms of the national popular vote. Every vote from every state contributed to producing Obama's nationwide popular vote total. The voters in the 12 biggest states were not any more important or "controlling" than the voters of the 39 smallest jurisdictions.

2004—Bush Ties in the 12 Biggest States

In 2004, the 69,323,699 votes cast in the 12 biggest states divided almost equally:

- 34,784,178 votes were for Kerry, and
- 34,539,521 votes were for Bush.

Kerry's slender 244,657-vote margin of victory in the 12 biggest states was about *one-third of one percent* of the 69,323,699 votes cast in those states (and about one-fifth of one percent of the votes cast nationwide).

Kerry received 50.2% of the popular vote from the 12 biggest states, and Bush received 49.8%.

Having fought Kerry to a near-tie in the 12 biggest states, Bush then won the 39 smallest jurisdictions by a margin of 3.256.828 votes (out of 51,745,350 votes cast in those states), thereby ending up with a margin of victory of 3,012,171 in the national popular vote.

Table 9.33 shows the popular vote for Senator John Kerry and President George W. Bush in the 2004 election in the 12 biggest states. Column 4 shows Bush's percentage of the two-party vote. Columns 5 and 6 show the Republican and Democratic margins, respectively, for each state. Columns 7 and 8 show the Republican and Democratic electoral votes, respectively, for each state.

Table 9.33 RESULTS OF THE 2004 ELECTION IN THE 12 BIGGEST STATES

STATE	BUSH	KERRY	R PERCENT	R MARGIN	D MARGIN	R EV	D EV
California	5,509,826	6,745,485	45.0%	–	1,235,659	–	55
Texas	4,526,917	2,832,704	61.5%	1,694,213	–	34	–
New York	2,962,567	4,314,280	40.7%	–	1,351,713	–	31
Florida	3,964,522	3,583,544	52.5%	380,978	–	27	–
Illinois	2,345,946	2,891,550	44.8%	–	545,604	–	21
Pennsylvania	2,793,847	2,938,095	48.7%	–	144,248	–	21
Ohio	2,859,768	2,741,167	51.1%	118,601	–	20	–
Michigan	2,313,746	2,479,183	48.3%	–	165,437	–	17
Georgia	1,914,254	1,366,149	58.4%	548,105	–	15	–
New Jersey	1,670,003	1,911,430	46.6%	–	241,427	–	15
North Carolina	1,961,166	1,525,849	56.2%	435,317	–	15	–
Virginia	1,716,959	1,454,742	58.4%	262,217	–	13	–
Totals	**34,539,521**	**34,784,178**	**49.8%**	**3,439,431**	**3,684,088**	**124**	**160**

Table 9.34 shows the popular vote for President George W. Bush and Senator John Kerry in the 2004 election in the 39 smallest jurisdictions.

Table 9.34 RESULTS OF THE 2004 ELECTION IN THE 39 SMALLEST JURISDICTIONS

STATE	BUSH	KERRY	R PERCENT	R MARGIN	D MARGIN	R EV	D EV
Massachusetts	1,071,109	1,803,800	37.3%	–	732,691	–	12
Indiana	1,479,438	969,011	60.4%	510,427	–	11	–
Missouri	1,455,713	1,259,171	53.6%	196,542	–	11	–
Tennessee	1,384,375	1,036,477	57.2%	347,898	–	11	–
Washington	1,304,894	1,510,201	46.4%	–	205,307	–	11
Arizona	1,104,294	893,524	55.3%	210,770	–	10	–
Maryland	1,024,703	1,334,493	43.4%	–	309,790	–	10
Minnesota	1,346,695	1,445,014	48.2%	–	98,319	–	10
Wisconsin	1,478,120	1,489,504	49.8%	–	11,384	–	10
Alabama	1,176,394	693,933	62.9%	482,461	–	9	–
Colorado	1,101,255	1,001,732	52.4%	99,523	–	9	–
Louisiana	1,102,169	820,299	57.3%	281,870	–	9	–
Kentucky	1,069,439	712,733	60.0%	356,706	–	8	–
South Carolina	937,974	661,699	58.6%	276,275	–	8	–
Connecticut	693,826	857,488	44.7%	–	163,662	–	7
Iowa	751,957	741,898	50.3%	10,059	–	7	–
Oklahoma	959,792	503,966	65.6%	455,826	–	7	–
Oregon	866,831	943,163	47.9%	–	76,332	–	7
Arkansas	572,898	469,953	54.9%	102,945	–	6	–
Kansas	736,456	434,993	62.9%	301,463	–	6	–
Mississippi	684,981	458,094	59.9%	226,887	–	6	–
Nebraska	512,814	254,328	66.8%	258,486	–	5	–
Nevada	418,690	397,190	51.3%	21,500	–	5	–
New Mexico	376,930	370,942	50.4%	5,988	–	5	–
Utah	663,742	241,199	73.3%	422,543	–	5	–
West Virginia	423,778	326,541	56.5%	97,237	–	5	–
Hawaii	194,191	231,708	45.6%	–	37,517	–	4
Idaho	409,235	181,098	69.3%	228,137	–	4	–
Maine	330,201	396,842	45.4%	–	66,641	–	4
New Hampshire	331,237	340,511	49.3%	–	9,274	–	4
Rhode Island	169,046	259,760	39.4%	–	90,714	–	4
Alaska	190,889	111,025	63.2%	79,864	–	3	–
Delaware	171,660	200,152	46.2%	–	28,492	–	3
D. C.	21,256	202,970	9.5%	–	181,714	–	3
Montana	266,063	173,710	60.5%	92,353	–	3	–
North Dakota	196,651	111,052	63.9%	85,599	–	3	–
South Dakota	232,584	149,244	60.9%	83,340	–	3	–
Vermont	121,180	184,067	39.7%	–	62,887	–	3
Wyoming	167,629	70,776	70.3%	96,853	–	3	–
Total	**27,501,089**	**24,244,261**	**53.1%**			**162**	**92**

2012—Obama Ties in the 39 Smallest Jurisdictions

In 2012, the 54,209,884 votes cast in the 39 smallest jurisdictions divided almost equally:

- 26,578,682 votes were for Obama, and
- 27,631,202 were for Romney.

Romney's 1,052,520-vote margin in the 39 smallest jurisdictions give him a slender 51%–49% win from the 54,209,884 votes cast in those states.

Having fought Romney to a near-tie in the 39 smallest jurisdictions, Obama then

Table 9.35 RESULTS OF THE 2012 ELECTION IN THE 39 SMALLEST JURISDICTIONS.

STATE	ROMNEY	OBAMA	R PERCENT	R MARGIN	D MARGIN	R EV	D EV
Washington	1,290,670	1,755,396	42.4%	–	464,726	–	12
Arizona	1,233,654	1,025,232	54.6%	208,422	–	11	–
Indiana	1,420,543	1,152,887	55.2%	267,656	–	11	–
Massachusetts	1,188,314	1,921,290	38.2%	–	732,976	–	11
Tennessee	1,462,330	960,709	60.4%	501,621	–	11	–
Maryland	971,869	1,677,844	36.7%	–	705,975	–	10
Minnesota	1,320,225	1,546,167	46.1%	–	225,942	–	10
Missouri	1,482,440	1,223,796	54.8%	258,644	–	10	–
Wisconsin	1,410,966	1,620,985	46.5%	–	210,019	–	10
Alabama	1,255,925	795,696	61.2%	460,229	–	9	–
Colorado	1,185,050	1,322,998	47.2%	–	137,948	–	9
South Carolina	1,071,645	865,941	55.3%	205,704	–	9	–
Kentucky	1,087,190	679,370	61.5%	407,820	–	8	–
Louisiana	1,152,262	809,141	58.7%	343,121	–	8	–
Connecticut	634,892	905,083	41.2%	–	270,191	–	7
Oklahoma	891,325	443,547	66.8%	447,778	–	7	–
Oregon	754,175	970,488	43.7%	–	216,313	–	7
Arkansas	647,744	394,409	62.2%	253,335	–	6	–
Iowa	730,617	822,544	47.0%	–	91,927	–	6
Kansas	692,634	440,726	61.1%	251,908	–	6	–
Mississippi	710,746	562,949	55.8%	147,797	–	6	–
Nevada	463,567	531,373	46.6%	–	67,806	–	6
Utah	740,600	251,813	74.6%	488,787	–	6	–
Nebraska	475,064	302,081	61.1%	172,983	–	5	–
New Mexico	335,788	415,335	44.7%	–	79,547	–	5
West Virginia	417,584	238,230	63.7%	179,354	–	5	–
Hawaii	121,015	306,658	28.3%	–	185,643	–	4
Idaho	420,911	212,787	66.4%	208,124	–	4	–
Maine	292,276	401,306	42.1%	–	109,030	–	4
New Hampshire	329,918	369,561	47.2%	–	39,643	–	4
Rhode Island	157,204	279,677	36.0%	–	122,473	–	4
Alaska	164,676	122,640	57.3%	42,036	–	3	–
Delaware	165,484	242,584	40.6%	–	77,100	–	3
D.C.	21,381	267,070	7.4%	–	245,689	–	3
Montana	267,928	201,839	57.0%	66,089	–	3	–
North Dakota	188,320	124,966	60.1%	63,354	–	3	–
South Dakota	210,610	145,039	59.2%	65,571	–	3	–
Vermont	92,698	199,239	31.8%	–	106,541	–	3
Wyoming	170,962	69,286	71.2%	101,676	–	3	–
Total	**27,631,202**	**26,578,682**	**51.0%**			**137**	**118**

won the 12 biggest states by a margin of 6,019,465 votes (out of 72,618,625 votes cast in those states), thereby ending up with a margin of victory of 4,966,945 in the national popular vote.

Table 9.35 shows the popular vote for Governor Mitt Romney and President Barack Obama in the 2012 election in the 39 smallest jurisdictions.

Table 9.36 shows the popular vote for Governor Mitt Romney and President Barack Obama in the 2012 election in the 12 biggest states.

Table 9.36 RESULTS OF THE 2012 ELECTION IN THE 12 BIGGEST STATES

STATE	ROMNEY	OBAMA	R PERCENT	R MARGIN	D MARGIN	R EV	D EV
Virginia	1,822,522	1,971,820	48.0%	–	149,298	–	13
New Jersey	1,478,088	2,122,786	41.0%	–	644,698	–	14
North Carolina	2,270,395	2,178,391	51.0%	92,004	–	15	–
Georgia	2,078,688	1,773,827	54.0%	304,861	–	16	–
Michigan	2,115,256	2,564,569	45.2%	–	449,313	–	16
Ohio	2,661,407	2,827,621	48.5%	–	166,214	–	18
Illinois	2,135,216	3,019,512	41.4%	–	884,296	–	20
Pennsylvania	2,680,434	2,990,274	47.3%	–	309,840	–	20
Florida	4,162,341	4,235,965	49.6%	–	73,624	–	29
New York	2,485,432	4,471,871	35.7%	–	1,986,439	–	29
Texas	4,569,843	3,308,124	58.0%	1,261,719	–	38	–
California	4,839,958	7,854,285	38.1%	–	3,014,327	–	55
Total	**33,299,580**	**39,319,045**	**45.9%**			**69**	**214**

Appendix HH presents the 2012 two-party presidential vote for all 50 states and the District of Columbia in alphabetical order.[575] See table 9.45 for the presidential vote for Barack Obama (D), Mitt Romney (R), Gary Johnson (Libertarian), Jill Stein (Green), and the other 22 minor-party and independent candidates who were on the ballot in 2012 in at least one state.

Erroneous Statements about Big States May Possibly Be the Result of Misunderstanding the Way that the National Popular Vote Compact Operates

The four statements quoted at the beginning of this section are so far removed from what actually happens in the real world that we should mention the following possibility. *It is possible that all four statements quoted at the beginning of this section are based on a total misunderstanding of how the National Popular Vote compact would operate.*

---

[575] The 2012 election returns shown in table 9.35, table 9.36, table 9.45, and appendix HH were obtained from the National Archives and Record Administration (NARA) web site at http://www.archives.gov/federal -register/electoral-college/2012/popular-vote.html. The NARA web site presents the number of votes shown on each state's Certificate of Ascertainment. There are two differences between our tables and that on the NARA web site. First, the NARA web site presents votes *by party*, whereas our table is based on votes *by candidate*. This difference in treatment creates a difference in the case of New York (which uses fusion voting). The NARA web site (as of January 4, 2013) showed the 141,056 votes that the Obama-Biden slate received on the Working Families Party line (and contained in New York's Certificate of Ascertainment) as minor-party votes in column 6 of their table, instead of showing these votes as Obama-Biden votes in column 2 of their table. Similarly, the web site shows the 256,171 votes that the Romney-Ryan slate received on the Conservative Party line as minor-party votes in column 6, instead of showing these votes as Romney-Ryan votes in column 3. Our table puts these Obama-Biden votes and Romney-Ryan votes in columns 2 and 3, respectively, in conformity with the practice of the New York State Board of Elections. Thus, our table shows (in column 6) only 8,652 votes for minor-party candidates in New York. See section 2.10 for additional details on fusion in New York and figure 2.11 for an example of a presidential ballot in New York. Secondly, our table reflects the adjustment (certified on December 31, 2012) to New York state's vote totals resulting from the fact that an executive order issued on the evening before Election Day allowed voters in counties affected by Hurricane Sandy to cast a provisional ballot at *any* polling place in the state. A total of 400,629 additional ballots (over 300,000 in New York City alone) were counted as a result of this executive order.

The National Popular Vote compact would take effect when enacted by states possessing a majority of the electoral votes (270 of 538).

The assertion that the National Popular Vote compact would

> "give a handful of populous states a controlling majority of the Electoral College"

could conceivably be true *if* the National Popular Vote compact were written so that it counted *only* the popular votes of the states belonging to the compact. *If* that were the case (and it is not) *and if* one makes the additional implausible assumption that the compact consisted only of the 12 biggest states, the four statements would be true. However, the National Popular Vote compact would not operate that way even if only the 12 biggest states belonged to the compact.

The National Popular Vote compact would add up the votes cast in *all* 50 states and the District of Columbia to determine the national popular-vote winner *regardless of whether a state is a member of the compact*. Under the National Popular Vote compact, every vote in *all* 50 states would be counted in arriving at the national popular vote total for each candidate. Under the National Popular Vote compact, there would be nothing special about a vote cast in the member states (or in the 12 biggest states) in comparison to votes cast anywhere else. Every vote would be equal throughout the United States under the National Popular Vote compact.

Note also that the National Popular Vote compact has not been enacted primarily by big states. As of 2012, the compact has been enacted by nine jurisdictions, including three small jurisdictions (Hawaii, Vermont, and the District of Columbia), three medium-sized states (Maryland, Massachusetts, and Washington state), and three of the 12 biggest states (California, Illinois, and New Jersey).

Role of Big Cities

Many of the critics of a nationwide popular vote for President who argue that the 12 biggest states would control a nationwide election for President also claim that big cities, such as Los Angeles, would control a nationwide election.

Big cities, such as Los Angeles, do not even control California elections, as evidenced by the historical fact that Republicans Ronald Reagan, George Deukmejian, Pete Wilson, and Arnold Schwarzenegger were all elected Governor without ever carrying Los Angeles (or San Francisco, San Jose, Oakland, or most of the other big cities in the state). If Los Angeles cannot control statewide elections in its own state, it can hardly control a nationwide election.

While is certainly true that most of the biggest cities in the country vote Democratic, smaller cities and towns, exurbs, rural areas, and many suburbs usually vote Republican.

If big cities controlled the outcome of elections, every Governor and every U.S. Senator would be a Democrat in every state with a significant city. There are, of course, examples from every state with a significant city, of Republicans winning races for Governor and U.S. Senator without ever carrying the state's biggest city.

Table 9.37 POPULATION OF THE 50 BIGGEST U.S. CITIES

RANK	CITY	2010 POPULATION	RANK	CITY	2010 POPULATION
1	New York	8,175,133	26	Nashville	601,222
2	Los Angeles	3,792,621	27	Louisville	597,337
3	Chicago	2,695,598	28	Milwaukee	594,833
4	Houston	2,099,451	29	Portland	583,776
5	Philadelphia	1,526,006	30	Oklahoma City	579,999
6	Phoenix	1,445,632	31	Las Vegas	583,756
7	San Antonio	1,327,407	32	Albuquerque	545,852
8	San Diego	1,307,402	33	Tucson	520,116
9	Dallas	1,197,816	34	Fresno	494,665
10	San Jose	945,942	35	Sacramento	466,488
11	Jacksonville	821,784	36	Long Beach	462,257
12	Indianapolis	820,445	37	Kansas City	459,787
13	Austin	790,390	38	Mesa	439,041
14	San Francisco	805,235	39	Virginia Beach	437,994
15	Columbus	787,033	40	Atlanta	420,003
16	Fort Worth	741,206	41	Colorado Springs	416,427
17	Charlotte	731,424	42	Raleigh	403,892
18	Detroit	713,777	43	Omaha	408,958
19	El Paso	649,121	44	Miami	399,457
20	Memphis	646,889	45	Tulsa	391,906
21	Boston	617,594	46	Oakland	390,724
22	Seattle	608,660	47	Cleveland	396,815
23	Denver	600,158	48	Minneapolis	382,578
24	Baltimore	620,961	49	Wichita	382,368
25	Washington	601,723	50	Arlington, Texas	365,438
			Total		**46,795,097**

The origins of the myth about big cities may stem from the incorrect belief that big cities are bigger than they actually are, and that big cities account for a greater fraction of the nation's population than they actually do.

A look at our country's actual demographics contradicts these misconceptions concerning big cities.

Table 9.37 shows the population of the nation's 50 biggest cities according to the 2010 census.

The combined population of the nation's five biggest cities (New York, Los Angeles, Chicago, Houston, and Philadelphia) constitutes only 6% of the nation's population of 308,745,538 (based on the 2010 census).

The combined population of the 20 biggest cities constitutes only 10% of the nation's population. To put this group of 20 cities in perspective, Memphis is the nation's 20th biggest city. Memphis had a population of 646,889 in 2010.

The combined population of the 50 biggest cities constitutes only 15% of the nation's population. To put this group of 50 cities in perspective, Arlington, Texas, is the nation's 50th biggest city (and had a population of 365,438 in 2010).

To put it another way, 85% of the population of the United States lives in places with a population of less than 365,000 (the population of Arlington, Texas).

Moreover, the population of the nation's 50 biggest cities is declining. In 2000, the 50 biggest cities together accounted for 19% of the nation's population (compared to 15% in 2010).

Even if one makes the far-fetched assumption that a candidate could win 100% of the votes in the nation's 50 biggest cities, that candidate would win only 15% of the national popular vote.

In a nationwide vote for President, a vote cast in a big city would be no more (or less) valuable or controlling than a vote cast in a suburb, an exurb, a small town, or a rural area.

When every vote is equal and the winner is the candidate who receives the most popular votes, candidates know that they need to solicit voters throughout their entire constituency in order to win.

Perhaps the most convincing evidence for the fact that big cities do not control elections comes from looking at the way that presidential races are actually run today.

Inside a battleground state in a presidential election *today*, every vote is equal, and the winner is the candidate who receives the most popular votes.

When presidential candidates campaign to win the electoral votes of a closely divided battleground state, they campaign throughout the state. The big cities do not receive all the attention—much less control the outcome. Cleveland and Miami have certainly not received all the attention when presidential candidates have campaigned in the closely divided battleground states of Ohio and Florida. Moreover, Cleveland and Miami manifestly do not control the statewide outcomes in Ohio and Florida, as evidenced by the outcome of the 2000 and 2004 presidential elections in those states. The Democrats carried both Cleveland and Miami in 2000 and 2004, but the Republicans carried both states. In fact, Senator John Kerry won the five biggest cities in Ohio in 2004, but he did not win the state.

In summary, under the National Popular Vote compact, every vote would be equal throughout the United States. Votes cast in all 50 states and the District of Columbia would be added together to determine the national popular vote winner. A vote cast in a big city or state would be no more, or less, valuable or "controlling" than a vote cast anywhere else.

9.31.7. MYTH: Candidates would concentrate on Democratic-leaning metropolitan markets because of lower advertising costs.

QUICK ANSWER:

- The cost per impression of television advertising (by far the costliest component of presidential campaigns) is generally higher—not lower—in major metropolitan media markets.

MORE DETAILED ANSWER:

John Samples of the Cato Institute has stated:

> "NPV will encourage presidential campaigns to focus their efforts in **dense media markets where costs per vote are lowest**. . . .

> "In general, because of the relative costs of attracting votes, the NPV proposal seems likely at the margin to **attract candidate attention to populous states**."[576] [Emphasis added]

Claremont College Professor Michael Uhlmann stated in a January 20, 2012, debate at the Sutherland Institute in Salt Lake City:

> "Under the National Popular Vote system, necessarily, there's going to be tilting toward where the greater masses of votes are contained—in the larger cities and the immediate suburbs. That's where the votes are. **That's where they can be reached the most cheaply. That's where the maximum bang for the media buck gets paid**. I think that's the likely tendency."[577] [Emphasis added]

The arguments made by both Samples and Uhlmann are contrary to the facts.

Television advertising (by far the costliest component of presidential campaigns) is generally *higher* on a per-impression basis in the larger media markets than in smaller markets.

Based on 488 quotations from television stations in media markets of various sizes for 30-second prime-time television ads for the weeks of October 15 and 22, 2012, compiled by Ainsley-Shea (a Minneapolis public relations firm) in July 2012, the average cost per impression was:

- 4.235 cents for the 1st–5th markets,
- 4.099 cents for the 26th–30th markets, and
- 3.892 cents for the 101st–105th markets.

The details of television advertising costs in the 1st, 26th, and 101st largest media markets further illustrate the conclusion that television advertising is generally more expensive in the larger media markets than in smaller markets.

Table 9.38 shows the cost of a 30-second prime-time television slot in New York City—the nation's No. 1 media market. Columns 1, 2, and 3 show the station, the time of day (all P.M.), and the program name, respectively. Columns 4, 5, and 6 show the

---

[576] Samples, John. *A Critique of the National Popular Vote Plan for Electing the President.* Cato Institute Policy Analysis No. 622. October 13, 2008.

[577] The debate at the Sutherland Institute on January 20, 2012, in Salt Lake City involved Dr. John R. Koza, Chair of National Popular Vote, Claremont College Professor Michael Uhlmann, and Trent England (a lobbyist opposing the National Popular Vote compact and Vice-President of the Evergreen Freedom Foundation of Olympia, Washington). The event was moderated by Sutherland President Paul T. Mero.

Table 9.38 TELEVISION ADS IN NEW YORK CITY—THE NATION'S NO. 1 MEDIA MARKET—AVERAGED 5.190 CENTS PER IMPRESSION.

STATION	TIME	PROGRAM	RATING	SHARE	GROSS RATING POINTS	COST	COST PER 1000
WABC	M 10–11	Castle	4.2	13.0%	8.4	$60,027	$46.58
WABC	Tu 9–10	Happy Endings	7.4	16.0%	14.8	$70,032	$31.06
WABC	W 10–11	Nashville	4.4	10.2%	8.8	$70,032	$51.55
WABC	Th 9–10	Grey's Anatomy	5.1	11.1%	10.2	$100,045	$63.94
WABC	F 8–9	Shark Tank	1.4	4.0%	2.8	$36,016	$81.45
WABC	Sa 8–11	ABC College Football	1	3.8%	2	$24,011	$74.53
WABC	Su 7–8	America's Funniest Home Videos	1.3	4.4%	2.6	$20,009	$49.26
WNBC	M 8–10	The Voice	1.3	3.6%	2.6	$80,036	$203.05
WNBC	Tu 10–11	Parenthood	2.8	6.4%	5.6	$45,020	$52.45
WNBC	W 9–10	Law & Order SVU	3.4	7.5%	6.8	$60,027	$57.14
WNBC	Th 10–11	Rock Center	2.6	6.1%	5.2	$30,014	$37.50
WNBC	F 10–11	Dateline FR–NBC	2	5.0%	4	$25,011	$41.67
WNBC	Sa 9–10	Dateline	1	3.6%	2	$15,007	$49.02
WNBC	Su 8:15–11:30	NFL Regular Season Football	6.8	20.1%	13.6	$100,045	$47.98
WCBS	M 8–9	How I met your mother/Partners	4.1	12.0%	8.2	$60,027	$47.85
WCBS	Tu 10–11	Vegas	4.9	11.1%	9.8	$50,023	$33.47
WCBS	W 8–9	Survivors	3.6	8.8%	7.2	$50,023	$45.37
WCBS	Th 8–9	BIG BANG–CBS/RLS–ENGMNT–CBS	5.6	13.3%	11.2	$80,036	$46.78
WCBS	F 8–9	CSI:NY	3.3	9.2%	6.6	$30,014	$29.41
WCBS	Sa 9–10	Average	2.2	7.9%	4.4	$13,006	$19.40
WCBS	Su 10–11	The Mentalist	3.2	9.7%	6.4	$60,027	$61.60
WPIX	M 8–10	90210/Gossip Girl	0.8	2.2%	1.6	$28,013	$115.70
WPIX	Tu 8–10	Hart of Dixie/Emily Owens	1.1	2.5%	2.2	$28,013	$81.87
WPIX	W 8–10	Arrow/Supernatural	0.7	1.7%	1.4	$28,013	$127.27
WPIX	Th 8–10	Vampire Diaries/Beauty	2.4	5.4%	4.8	$28,013	$38.25
WPIX	F 8–10	Top Model/Nikita	0.8	2.2%	1.6	$17,008	$66.93
WPIX	Sa 8–10	Friends	0.2	0.9%	0.4	$17,008	$223.68
WPIX	Su 8–10	Seinfeld	0.3	0.9%	0.6	$17,008	$173.47
		Total			**155.8**	**$1,241,558**	**$51.90**

rating,[578] share, and gross rating points (GRP), respectively, for adults age 18 and older. Column 7 shows the cost of the slot. Column 8 shows the cost per 1,000 impressions (that is, the cost in column 7 divided by the media market's population of 15,334,000). The average cost for New York City was $51.90 per 1,000 impressions—5.190 cents per impression.

The similarly computed cost of a 30-second prime-time television slot in Los Angeles—the nation's No. 2 media market—averaged $56.53 per 1,000 impressions—5.653 cents per impression.

---

[578] The Nielsen "Live+3" ratings track both live airings and DVR playback (through 3:00 a.m.). Based on November 2011 DMA.

Table 9.39 TELEVISION ADS IN INDIANAPOLIS—THE NATION'S NO. 26 MEDIA MARKET—
AVERAGED 3.980 CENTS PER IMPRESSION.

STATION	TIME	PROGRAM	RATING	SHARE	GROSS RATING POINTS	COST	COST PER 1000
WRTV	M 8-10	Dancing with the Stars	8.5	15.6%	17	$16,007	$44.94
WRTV	Tu 10-11	Private Practice	6	12.6%	12	$16,007	$63.49
WRTV	W 10-11	Nashville	5.5	12.6%	11	$16,007	$69.57
WRTV	Th 9-10	Grey's Anatomy	6.8	12.4%	13.6	$20,009	$70.42
WRTV	F 9-10	Primetime	2	4.4%	4	$10,005	$119.05
WRTV	Sa 8-11	Saturday Movie	2.7	7.1%	5.4	$4,802	$42.86
WRTV	Su 7-8	America's Funniest Home Videos	2.2	4.8%	4.4	$12,005	$130.43
WTHR	M 10-11	Revolution	3.2	7.1%	6.4	$6,003	$44.78
WTHR	Tu 10-11	Parenthood-NBC	4	8.4%	8	$8,004	$47.62
WTHR	W 9-10	Law & Order	6	12.1%	12	$7,003	$27.78
WTHR	Th 9-10	Office/Parks & Recreation	4.4	8.1%	8.8	$8,004	$43.48
WTHR	F 10-11	Dateline FR-NBC	2.9	7.2%	5.8	$4,002	$33.33
WTHR	Sa 8-9	NBC Encores	2.3	6.4%	4.6	$2,401	$25.00
WISH	M 10-11	Hawaii 5-0-CBS	6.2	13.9%	12.4	$5,002	$19.08
WISH	Tu 9-10	NCIS:LA-CBS	9	17.7%	18	$8,004	421.28
WISH	W 10-11	CSI	5.8	13.1%	11.6	$6,003	$25.00
WISH	Th 9-10	PERSON-INT-CBS	6	11.0%	12	$10,005	$39.68
WISH	F 8-9	CSI:NY	4.2	10.9%	8.4	$3,201	$18.18
WISH	Sa 10-11	48 Hours	4.5	12.0%	9	$2,001	$10.64
WISH	Su 9-10	The Good Wife	7	11.7%	14	$7,003	$23.81
WTTV+S2	M-Su 8-11	Average	1.2	2.6%	16.8	$7,003	$19.23
		Total			**215.2**	**$178,480**	**39.80**

Table 9.39 shows the cost of a 30-second prime-time television slot in Indianapolis—the nation's No. 26 media market. Column 8 shows the cost per 1,000 impressions (that is, the cost in column 7 divided by the market's population of 2,094,000). The average cost for Indianapolis was $39.80 per 1,000 impressions—3.980 cents per impression.

Table 9.40 shows the cost of a 30-second prime-time television slot in the nation's No. 101 media market—Fort Smith, Fayetteville, Springdale, and Rogers, Arkansas. Column 8 shows the cost per 1,000 impressions (that is, the cost in column 7 divided by the market's population of 573,000). The average cost for this market was $30.84 per 1,000 impressions—3.084 cents per impression.

An NPR story entitled "Ads Slice Up Swing States With Growing Precision" reported on presidential campaigning in Colorado's small media markets:

"Republicans outnumber Democrats in El Paso County more than 2 to 1. Barack Obama lost this part of Colorado to John McCain by 19 points in 2008.

"'It's not a matter of just winning; it's winning by how much,' says Rich Beeson, a fifth-generation Coloradan and political director for the Romney campaign.

Table 9.40 TELEVISION ADS IN THE FORT SMITH, FAYETTEVILLE, SPRINGDALE, AND
ROGERS, ARKANSAS MARKET—THE NATION'S NO. 101 MEDIA MARKET—
AVERAGED 3.084 CENTS PER IMPRESSION.

STATION	TIME	PROGRAM	RATING	SHARE	GROSS RATING POINTS	COST	COST PER 1000
KHBS+S2	M 9-10	Castle	8.7	19.7%	17.4	$2,401	$24.00
KHBS+S2	Tu 9-10	Private Practice	6.4	14.9%	12.8	$2,401	$32.43
KHBS+S2	W 9-10	Nashville	5.7	15.2%	11.4	$2,601	$39.39
KHBS+S2	Th 8-9	Grey's Anatomy	5.6	12.0%	11.2	$3,602	$56.25
KHBS+S2	F 8-9	Shark Tank	2.3	6.1%	4.6	$700	$26.92
	Su 6-7	America's Funniest Home Videos	3.8	10.7%	7.6	$1,201	$27.27
KNWA	M 9-10	ROCK-WLLMS-NBC	1.4	3.2%	2.8	$1,921	$120.00
KNWA	Tu 9-10	Parenthood-NBC	2.5	5.8%	5	$3,602	$128.57
KNWA	W 9-10	AVG. ALL WKS	1.5	4.1%	3	$1,501	$83.33
KNWA	Th 9-10	PRIME SUSP-NBC	1.2	2.9%	2.4	$1,201	$85.71
KNWA	F 8-9	GRIMM-NBC	3.9	10.1%	7.8	$1,501	$34.09
KFSM	M 7-8	HW I-MOTHR-CBS/2BROKE GRL-CBS	8.4	18.3%	16.8	$1,601	$16.67
KFSM	Tu 7-8	NCIS-CBS	14	31.6%	28	$2,401	$15.00
KFSM	W 8-9	Criminal Minds	5.5	14.2%	11	$1,801	$28.13
KFSM	Th 8-9	PERSON-INT-CBS	9.5	20.4%	19	$1,901	$17.59
KFSM	F 7-8	CSI	5.5	17.1%	11	$1,201	$18.75
KFSM	Sa 9-10	48 Hour Mystery	4.5	12.7%	9	$1,000	$19.23
KFSM	Su 9-10	The Mentalist	6.5	15.8%	13	$1,901	$25.68
		Total			**193.8**	**$34,435**	**$30.84**

"Presidential campaigns know exactly the margin of victory or defeat that they have to hit in each town in order to carry an entire state. Democratic media strategist Tad Devine says campaigns set extremely specific goals based on hard data. . . .

"Although no one suggests that President Obama will win Colorado Springs, whether he loses it by 15 or 25 points could determine whether he carries Colorado.

"Beeson of the Romney campaign says smaller cities are vital to this chess game, especially since they're cheaper to advertise in.

"'A lot of secondary markets are very key to the overall map, whether it's a Charlottesville in Virginia or a Colorado Springs in Colorado,' he says. 'You can't ever cede the ground to anyone.'"[579] [Emphasis added]

Soliciting every available vote is a strategic necessity when the winner of an election is the candidate who receives the most popular votes.

---

[579] Shapiro, Ari. Ads slice up swing states with growing precision. *NPR.* September 24, 2012. http://www.npr.org/2012/09/24/161616073/ads-slice-up-swing-states-with-growing-precision.

9.31.8. MYTH: Only citizens impact the allocation of electoral votes under the current system.

QUICK ANSWER:

- Even though they cannot vote for President, non-citizens impact the allocation of electoral votes. The U.S. Constitution requires that the census count all "persons"—including non-citizens—for the purpose of apportioning electoral votes among the states.

- Under the current method of electing the President, *legal* voters in states that acquired additional electoral votes (because of the disproportionate presence of non-citizens in their states) deliver additional electoral votes to their candidate. Voters in states that lost electoral votes have correspondingly less influence.

- Five states with disproportionally large numbers of non-citizens (relative to other states) acquired additional electoral votes as a result of the 2010 census, while 10 states each lost one electoral vote.

- Overall, the Democrats have a net 10 electoral-vote advantage in the 2012, 2016, and 2020 elections from the 15 states whose representation was affected by the counting of non-citizens in allocating electoral votes among the states.

- The National Popular Vote compact would eliminate the distortion in presidential elections caused by the disproportionate presence of non-citizens in certain states.

MORE DETAILED ANSWER:

Under federal law, non-citizens cannot vote in presidential elections. Nonetheless, non-citizens significantly impact presidential elections because they affect the allocation of electoral votes among the states.

As Professor George C. Edwards III has pointed out:

> "Representation in the House is based on the decennial census, which counts all residents—whether citizens or not. . . . States . . . where non-citizens compose a larger percentage of the population receive more electoral votes than they would if electoral votes were allocated on the basis of the number of a state's citizens."[580]

The U.S. Constitution requires that the census be used to determine each state's number of seats in the U.S. House of Representatives. Each state receives a number of electoral votes equal to the state's number of U.S. Representatives plus two (representing the state's two U.S. Senators).

---

[580] Edwards, George C., III. 2011. *Why the Electoral College Is Bad for America*. New Haven, CT: Yale University Press. Second edition. Page 46.

The Constitution specifies that the census count all "persons," thereby including non-citizens living in the United States in the count:

> "Representatives . . . shall be apportioned among the several States which may be included within this Union, according to their respective Numbers, which shall be determined by adding to the whole Number of free **Persons**, including those bound to Service for a Term of Years, and excluding Indians not taxed, three fifths of all other Persons."[581,582] [Emphasis added]

The Census Bureau uses a mathematical formula (specified by a federal statute adopted in 1941) known as the "method of equal proportions" to apportion seats in the U.S. House of Representatives automatically among the states.[583]

A state having a disproportionally large number of non-citizens (relative to other states) acquires additional U.S. House seats and, hence, additional electoral votes.

Because of the winner-take-all rule, *legal* voters in a state that acquired additional electoral votes by virtue of the disproportionate presence of non-citizens deliver an enlarged bloc of electoral votes to the candidate receiving the most popular votes in their state. That is, the influence of the *legal* voters is increased because of the presence of non-citizens.

Similarly, legal voters in a state that lost electoral votes deliver a diminished bloc of electoral votes.

The apportionment of the U.S. House and Electoral College resulting from the 2010 census governs the 2012, 2016, and 2020 elections.

Professor Leonard Steinhorn of American University has computed the effect of non-citizens on presidential elections. He plugged American Community Survey data on the number of citizens and non-citizens in each state in 2010 into the statutory formula to apportion U.S. House seat among the states.[584]

In an article entitled "Without Voting, Noncitizens Could Swing the Election for Obama," Steinhorn found that non-citizens affected the number of electoral votes possessed by 15 states.

Five states gained between one and five electoral votes, and 10 states each lost one electoral vote because of non-citizens.

---

[581] U.S. Constitution. Article I, section 2, clause 3. The provisions concerning indentured servants, "Indians not taxed," and slaves ("other persons") are not applicable today.

[582] No doubt, the reason why the Constitution specified that the census would count "persons," instead of trying to count eligible voters, was that the states had complicated and widely varying criteria for voter eligibility in 1787. In most states, eligibility depended on property, wealth, or income. Moreover, the requirements for voting often differed for the lower versus upper house of the state legislature.

[583] The mathematical formula is presented at https://www.census.gov/population/apportionment/about/computing.html. The history of methods used to apportion seats in the U.S. House of Representatives is discussed at https://www.census.gov/population/apportionment/about/history.html. The U.S. Supreme Court upheld the constitutionality of the "method of equal proportions" in 1992 in *Department of Commerce v. Montana* (112 S.Ct. 1415) and *Franklin v. Massachusetts* (112 S.Ct. 2767).

[584] Steinhorn, Leonard. Without voting, noncitizens could swing the election for Obama. *Washington Post.* October 5, 2012.

Overall, the Democrats have a net 10 electoral-vote advantage in the 2012, 2016, and 2020 elections from the 15 states whose representation was affected by the counting of non-citizens in allocating electoral votes among the states.

Democratic non-battleground states gained 7 electoral votes:

- +5 for California
- +1 for New York
- +1 for Washington state.

Republican non-battleground states lost 3 electoral votes:

- +2 for Texas.
- –1 for Indiana
- –1 for Missouri
- –1 for Louisiana
- –1 for Montana
- –1 for Oklahoma.

Six Battleground states were affected:

- +1 Florida
- –1 for Iowa
- –1 for Michigan
- –1 for North Carolina
- –1 for Ohio
- –1 for Pennsylvania.

Battleground states can, by definition, go either way, and therefore do not constitute a built-in advantage to either party.

Excluding non-citizens from the calculation used to apportion seats in the U.S. House of Representatives would require a federal constitutional amendment.

The National Popular Vote compact would eliminate the distortion in presidential elections caused by the disproportionate presence of non-citizens in certain states. Nationwide voting for President would equalize the vote of every legal voter in the country by guaranteeing the Presidency to the candidate who receives the most popular votes in all 50 states and the District of Columbia.

9.31.9. MYTH: The Republican Party has a lock on the Electoral College.

QUICK ANSWER:

- An argument became prevalent during the 1980s that the Republican Party had a permanent "lock" on the Electoral College because numerous states had repeatedly voted Republican for President between 1968 and 1988.
- Current political data do not support the notion of the existence of an "electoral lock" today in favor of the Republican Party.

- Neither party has a lock on the Electoral College because the United States is, politically, an evenly divided country in which the cumulative nationwide vote for the two parties from the start of the modern political era in 1932 through 2008 has been virtually tied.

- To the extent that this kind of "electoral lock" argument has a small element of validity, if the Electoral College map of 2012 were to persist, the electoral map would, if anything, be slightly unfavorable to the Republican Party. Of the 32 states that voted for the same party in all six presidential elections between 1992 and 2012, 19 states (possessing 242 electoral votes) voted Democratic in all six presidential elections, and 13 states (possessing 102 electoral votes) voted Republican in all six presidential elections. If the 2016 presidential election is conducted under the state-by-state winner-take-all rule and is reasonably close, it is likely that all (or almost all) of the 32 states that have voted for the same party in the past six presidential elections will continue to support that same party.

MORE DETAILED ANSWER:

An argument became prevalent during the 1980s that the Republican Party had a permanent "lock" on the Electoral College because a large number of states had repeatedly voted Republican for President between 1968 and 1988.

The notion of a "lock" arose from the fact that Republicans won five of the six presidential elections during this period, and that Republicans won landslide victories in 1972 and 1984.

In fact, neither party has a lock on the Electoral College because the United States is, politically, an evenly divided country in which the cumulative nationwide vote for the two parties from the start of the modern political era in 1932 through 2008 (table 9.25) has been virtually tied:

- 746,260,766 total votes for the Democrats and
- 745,502,654 total votes for the Republicans.

The Republican Party won five of the six presidential elections between 1972 and 1984. The reason for this result was that more voters (often in landslide numbers) voted for the Republican nominee during that period—not because of the mechanics of the Electoral College.

In any event, the Republican Party does not have any such "electoral lock" today.

To the extent that this kind of "electoral lock" argument has a small element of validity, if the Electoral College map of 2012 were to persist, the electoral map would, if anything, be slightly unfavorable to the Republican Party.

Table 9.41 shows that 32 states that voted for the same party in all six presidential elections between 1992 and 2012. These 32 states possess about two-thirds (64%) of the 538 votes in the Electoral College. Of these 32 states, 19 states (possessing 242 electoral votes after the 2010 census) voted Democratic in all six presidential elec-

Table 9.41 THE 32 STATES THAT VOTED FOR THE SAME PARTY IN THE SIX PRESIDENTIAL ELECTIONS BETWEEN 1992 AND 2012

DEM 6 TIMES	DEM 5 TIMES	DEM 4 TIMES	DEM 3 TIMES	DEM 2 TIMES	DEM 1 TIME	DEM 0 TIMES
CA (55)	IA (6)	NV (6)	CO (9)	AR (6)	AZ (11)	AL (9)
CT (7)	NH (4)	OH (18)	FL (29)	KY (8)	GA (16)	AK (3)
DE (3)	NM (5)			LA (8)	IN (11)	ID (4)
D.C. (3)				MO (10)	MT (3)	KS (6)
HI (4)				TN (11)	NC (15)	MS (6)
IL (20)				VA (13)		NE (5)
MA (11)				WV (5)		ND (3)
ME (4)						OK (7)
MD (10)						SC (9)
MI (16)						SD (3)
MN (10)						TX (38)
NJ (14)						UT (6)
NY (29)						WY (3)
OR (7)						
PA (20)						
RI (4)						
VT (3)						
WA (12)						
WI (10)						
242 EV	**15 EV**	**24 EV**	**38EV**	**61 EV**	**56 EV**	**102 EV**

tions between 1992 and 2012, and 13 states (possessing 102 electoral votes after the 2010 census) voted Republican in the six elections. The table is organized in terms of number of elections (from zero to six) in which a state voted Democratic. The number of electoral votes shown in the table are those applicable to the 2012 election.

Table 9.41 reflects one aspect of the current polarization of American politics. One possible cause of this polarization may be the tendency, discussed in Bill Bishop's book *The Big Sort,* of like-minded Americans to cluster together geographically.[585]

Regardless of the causes behind the behavior shown in table 9.41, if the 2016 presidential election is conducted under the state-by-state winner-take-all rule and is reasonably close, it is likely that most of the 32 states that have voted consistently for the same party in the past six presidential elections would continue to support that same party.[586]

In any event, table 9.41 certainly does not support the notion of the existence today of an "electoral lock" in favor of the Republican Party.

Table 9.42 shows a simulation of the 2012 presidential election produced by applying a tie-producing uniform shift to actual election returns (as shown in table 9.35, table 9.36, table 9.45, and appendix HH). In 2012, Governor Romney received

---

[585] Bishop, Bill. 2008. *The Big Sort: Why the Clustering of Like-Minded America Is Tearing Us Apart.* Boston, MA: Houghton Mifflin Harcourt.

[586] Nine of the states in table 9.41 that voted Democratic once or twice between 1992 and 2012 did so during the Clinton years. Since then, these nine states have voted Republican in presidential elections consistently between 2000 and 2012. These nine states are Arkansas, Kentucky, Louisiana, Missouri, Tennessee, West Virginia, Arizona, Georgia, and Montana. Thus, there are 41 states that have voted for the same party between 2000 and 2012.

Table 9.42 SIMULATED TIE-PRODUCING UNIFORM SHIFT OF 2012 ELECTION DATA

STATE	ROMNEY	OBAMA	R-PERCENT	R- MARGIN	D-MARGIN	R-EV	D-EV
D.C.	27,029	261,422	9.37%	–	234,392	–	3
HI	129,389	298,284	30.25%	–	168,894	–	4
VT	98,415	193,522	33.71%	–	95,108	–	3
NY	2,621,665	4,335,638	37.68%	–	1,713,972	–	29
RI	165,759	271,122	37.94%	–	105,364	–	4
MD	1,023,754	1,625,959	38.64%	–	602,205	–	10
CA	5,088,528	7,605,715	40.09%	–	2,517,186	–	55
MA	1,249,204	1,860,400	40.17%	–	611,196	–	11
DE	173,475	234,593	42.51%	–	61,119	–	3
NJ	1,548,598	2,052,276	43.01%	–	503,678	–	14
CT	665,047	874,928	43.19%	–	209,881	–	7
IL	2,236,152	2,918,576	43.38%	–	682,423	–	20
ME	305,857	387,725	44.10%	–	81,867	–	4
WA	1,350,316	1,695,750	44.33%	–	345,434	–	12
OR	787,946	936,717	45.69%	–	148,771	–	7
NM	350,496	400,627	46.66%	–	50,131	–	5
MI	2,206,893	2,472,932	47.16%	–	266,038	–	16
MN	1,376,353	1,490,039	48.02%	–	113,686	–	10
WI	1,470,336	1,561,615	48.49%	–	91,280	–	10
NV	483,049	511,891	48.55%	–	28,841	–	6
IA	761,030	792,131	49.00%	–	31,101	–	6
NH	343,615	355,864	49.12%	–	12,250	–	4
CO	1,234,161	1,273,887	49.21%	–	39,726	–	9
PA	2,791,474	2,879,234	49.23%	–	87,760	–	20
VA	1,896,820	1,897,522	49.99%	–	701	–	13
OH	2,768,890	2,720,138	50.44%	48,751	–	18	–
FL	4,326,791	4,071,515	51.52%	255,276	–	29	–
NC	2,357,508	2,091,278	52.99%	266,230	–	15	–
GA	2,154,125	1,698,390	55.91%	455,736	–	16	–
AZ	1,277,886	981,000	56.57%	296,886	–	11	–
MO	1,535,432	1,170,804	56.74%	364,627	–	10	–
IN	1,470,934	1,102,496	57.16%	368,438	–	11	–
SC	1,109,586	828,000	57.27%	281,585	–	9	–
MS	735,687	538,008	57.76%	197,678	–	6	–
MT	277,127	192,640	58.99%	84,486	–	3	–
AK	170,302	117,014	59.27%	53,288	–	3	–
TX	4,724,104	3,153,863	59.97%	1,570,241	–	38	–
LA	1,190,669	770,734	60.70%	419,935	–	8	–
SD	217,574	138,075	61.18%	79,499	–	3	–
ND	194,455	118,831	62.07%	75,623	–	3	–
TN	1,509,776	913,263	62.31%	596,514	–	11	–
KS	714,827	418,533	63.07%	296,293	–	6	–
NE	490,282	286,863	63.09%	203,418	–	5	–
AL	1,296,098	755,523	63.17%	540,576	–	9	–
KY	1,121,782	644,778	63.50%	477,003	–	8	–
AR	668,151	374,002	64.11%	294,149	–	6	–
WV	430,426	225,388	65.63%	205,037	–	5	–
ID	433,320	200,378	68.38%	232,941	–	4	–
OK	917,464	417,408	68.73%	500,055	–	7	–
WY	175,666	64,582	73.12%	111,085	–	3	–
UT	760,033	232,380	76.58%	527,653	–	6	–
Total	**63,414,254**	**63,414,255**				**253**	**285**

48.0418657% of the two-party national popular vote—a shortfall of 1.9581343%. Column 2 shows the simulated figures for Romney obtained by applying a uniform upward adjustment of 1.9581343% to Romney's actual vote in each state (and a corresponding downward adjustment to Obama's actual vote in each state), thereby producing a virtual tie in the national popular vote (63,414,254 to 63,414,255). Column 4 shows Romney's percentage of the two-party vote using this method of simulation. Columns 5 and 6 show the Republican and Democratic margins, respectively, for each state using this method of simulation. Columns 7 and 8 show the Republican and Democratic electoral votes, respectively, for each state using this method of simulation. The table is sorted according to the simulated Republican percentage in column 4.

The result of the tie-producing uniform shift shown in table 9.42 is that President Obama loses Florida (29 electoral votes) and Ohio (18 electoral votes), but still ends up with a 285–253 lead in the Electoral College. Thus, even if Romney had received enough additional voter support to create a tie in the national popular vote (preserving each candidate's relative profile in each state), Obama would still have ended up with a lead of 28 electoral votes using this method of simulation.

Table 9.42 also shows that Obama's lead in Virginia (13 electoral votes) shrinks to an eminently recountable 701 votes (1,897,522 to 1,896,820) using this method of simulation. Even if Romney had won Virginia, Obama would still have had a 272–266 lead in the Electoral College.

In a second simulation (shown in table 9.43), Romney's actual results are adjusted uniformly upward by 2.732% in each state (with Obama's vote receiving a corresponding downward adjustment in each state). This adjustment would give Romney a lead of 1,962,965 votes nationwide (64,395,737 to 62,432,772). This adjustment is just sufficient to move both Virginia and Pennsylvania (by 8 votes) into Romney's column, thus giving Romney a winning 286–252 margin in the Electoral College. The table is sorted according to the simulated Republican percentage in column 4.

In other words, it takes a national popular vote lead of almost two million votes to yield a simulated win for Romney in the Electoral College using this method of simulation.

If Romney's simulated lead were to be increased slightly beyond the 1,962,965-vote nationwide lead shown in table 9.43, Colorado (nine electoral votes), New Hampshire (four electoral votes), Iowa (six electoral votes), and Nevada (six electoral votes) would move into the Republican column.

Of course, no future election will exactly replicate the state-by-state percentage contour of the two major parties in 2012. President Obama cannot run for another term, and Governor Romney will almost certainly not be a candidate in 2016. Candidates with different personalities and records will compete on the basis of different issues in a political environment consisting of a different history of immediate past events and changed demographics.

Nonetheless, the simulations in table 9.42 and table 9.43 certainly do not support the notion of the existence today of an "electoral lock" in favor of the Republican Party.

Table 9.43 SIMULATED UNIFORM SHIFT PRODUCING A 1,962,965-VOTE NATIONWIDE LEAD FOR ROMNEY

STATE	ROMNEY	OBAMA	R-PERCENT	R- MARGIN	D-MARGIN	R-EV	D-EV
D.C.	29,261	259,190	10.14%	—	229,928	—	3
HI	132,699	294,974	31.03%	—	162,275	—	4
VT	100,674	191,263	34.48%	—	90,590	—	3
NY	2,675,506	4,281,797	38.46%	—	1,606,292	—	29
RI	169,140	267,741	38.72%	—	98,602	—	4
MD	1,044,259	1,605,454	39.41%	—	561,195	—	10
CA	5,186,765	7,507,478	40.86%	—	2,320,714	—	55
MA	1,273,268	1,836,336	40.95%	—	563,067	—	11
DE	176,632	231,436	43.29%	—	54,803	—	3
NJ	1,576,464	2,024,410	43.78%	—	447,946	—	14
CT	676,964	863,011	43.96%	—	186,047	—	7
IL	2,276,043	2,878,685	44.15%	—	602,642	—	20
ME	311,225	382,357	44.87%	—	71,133	—	4
WA	1,373,889	1,672,177	45.10%	—	298,289	—	12
OR	801,293	923,370	46.46%	—	122,077	—	7
NM	356,309	394,814	47.44%	—	38,506	—	5
MI	2,243,109	2,436,716	47.93%	—	193,607	—	16
MN	1,398,535	1,467,857	48.79%	—	69,322	—	10
WI	1,493,799	1,538,152	49.27%	—	44,353	—	10
NV	490,749	504,191	49.32%	—	13,442	—	6
IA	773,049	780,112	49.77%	—	7,062	—	6
NH	349,028	350,451	49.90%	—	1,423	—	4
CO	1,253,570	1,254,478	49.98%	—	908	—	9
PA	2,835,358	2,835,350	50.00%	7	—	20	—
VA	1,926,183	1,868,159	50.76%	58,025	—	13	—
OH	2,811,367	2,677,661	51.22%	133,706	—	18	—
FL	4,391,783	4,006,523	52.29%	385,259	—	29	—
NC	2,391,936	2,056,850	53.77%	335,086	—	15	—
GA	2,183,939	1,668,576	56.69%	515,362	—	16	—
AZ	1,295,367	963,519	57.35%	331,848	—	11	—
MO	1,556,374	1,149,862	57.51%	406,513	—	10	—
IN	1,490,849	1,082,581	57.93%	408,268	—	11	—
SC	1,124,580	813,006	58.04%	311,574	—	9	—
MS	745,543	528,152	58.53%	217,392	—	6	—
MT	280,762	189,005	59.77%	91,757	—	3	—
AK	172,525	114,791	60.05%	57,735	—	3	—
TX	4,785,069	3,092,898	60.74%	1,692,171	—	38	—
LA	1,205,848	755,555	61.48%	450,292	—	8	—
SD	220,326	135,323	61.95%	85,004	—	3	—
ND	196,879	116,407	62.84%	80,472	—	3	—
TN	1,528,527	894,512	63.08%	634,016	—	11	—
KS	723,597	409,763	63.85%	313,835	—	6	—
NE	496,296	280,849	63.86%	215,446	—	5	—
AL	1,311,975	739,646	63.95%	572,330	—	9	—
KY	1,135,452	631,108	64.27%	504,345	—	8	—
AR	676,216	365,937	64.89%	310,278	—	6	—
WV	435,501	220,313	66.41%	215,188	—	5	—
ID	438,224	195,474	69.15%	242,749	—	4	—
OK	927,794	407,078	69.50%	520,715	—	7	—
WY	177,526	62,722	73.89%	114,803	—	3	—
UT	767,713	224,700	77.36%	543,012	—	6	—
Total	**64,395,737**	**62,432,772**				**286**	**252**

9.31.10. MYTH: The rural states would lose their advantage in the Electoral College under a national popular vote.

QUICK ANSWER:

- The facts are that the current state-by-state winner-take-all method of awarding electoral votes diminishes the influence of rural states because rural states are generally not battleground states.

MORE DETAILED ANSWER:

The mythology that the current state-by-state winner-take-all method of awarding electoral votes is advantageous to rural states is not supported by the facts.

Tara Ross, an opponent of the National Popular Vote plan, writes:

> **"NPV will lessen the need of presidential candidates to obtain the support of voters in rural areas** and in small states."[587] [Emphasis added]

Hans von Spakovsky has stated:

> "The NPV scheme would . . . diminish the influence of smaller states and rural areas of the country."[588]

The opposite is the case.

Political influence in the Electoral College is based on whether the state is a closely divided battleground state. The current state-by-state winner-take-all method of awarding electoral votes does not enhance the influence of rural states, because most rural states are not battleground states.

Table 9.44 shows, for each state, the rural population (column 2 using the 2000 definition found in the *Statistical Abstract of the United States*), the state's total population (column 3), the rural percentage (column 2 divided by column 3), and the rural index (obtained by dividing the state's rural percentage by the overall national rural percentage of 20.11%). An index above 100 indicates that the state is more rural than the nation as a whole, whereas an index below 100 indicates that the state is less rural. Thirty-three states have an index above 100 (meaning that more than 20.11% of their population is rural), whereas 18 have an index below 100 (that is, they are less rural than the nation as a whole).

As can be seen from table 9.44, the 10 most rural states are:

- Vermont (60.61% rural),
- Maine (57.86% rural),
- West Virginia (53.75% rural),

[587] Written testimony submitted by Tara Ross to the Delaware Senate in June 2010.

[588] Von Spakovsky, Hans. Destroying the Electoral College: The Anti-Federalist National Popular Vote Scheme. Legal memo. October 27, 2011. http://www.heritage.org/research/reports/2011/10/destroying-the-electoral-college-the-anti-federalist-national-popular-vote-scheme.

Table 9.44 RURAL POPULATION OF THE UNITED STATES

STATE	RURAL POPULATION	TOTAL POPULATION	RURAL PERCENT	RURAL INDEX
Vermont	376,379	621,000	60.61%	301
Maine	762,045	1,317,000	57.86%	288
West Virginia	975,564	1,815,000	53.75%	267
Mississippi	1,457,307	2,903,000	50.20%	250
South Dakota	363,417	771,000	47.14%	234
Arkansas	1,269,221	2,753,000	46.10%	229
Montana	414,317	927,000	44.69%	222
North Dakota	283,242	634,000	44.68%	222
Alabama	1,981,427	4,530,000	43.74%	218
Kentucky	1,787,969	4,146,000	43.13%	214
New Hampshire	503,451	1,300,000	38.73%	193
Iowa	1,138,892	2,954,000	38.55%	192
South Carolina	1,584,888	4,198,000	37.75%	188
North Carolina	3,199,831	8,541,000	37.46%	186
Tennessee	2,069,265	5,901,000	35.07%	174
Wyoming	172,438	507,000	34.01%	169
Oklahoma	1,196,091	3,524,000	33.94%	169
Alaska	215,675	655,000	32.93%	164
Idaho	434,456	1,393,000	31.19%	155
Wisconsin	1,700,032	5,509,000	30.86%	153
Missouri	1,711,769	5,755,000	29.74%	148
Nebraska	517,538	1,747,000	29.62%	147
Indiana	1,776,474	6,238,000	28.48%	142
Kansas	767,749	2,736,000	28.06%	140
Minnesota	1,429,420	5,101,000	28.02%	139
Louisiana	1,223,311	4,516,000	27.09%	135
Georgia	2,322,290	8,829,000	26.30%	131
Virginia	1,908,560	7,460,000	25.58%	127
Michigan	2,518,987	10,113,000	24.91%	124
New Mexico	455,545	1,903,000	23.94%	119
Pennsylvania	2,816,953	12,406,000	22.71%	113
Ohio	2,570,811	11,459,000	22.43%	112
Oregon	727,255	3,595,000	20.23%	101
Delaware	155,842	830,000	18.78%	93
Washington	1,063,015	6,204,000	17.13%	85
Texas	3,647,539	22,490,000	16.22%	81
Colorado	668,076	4,601,000	14.52%	72
Maryland	737,818	5,558,000	13.27%	66
New York	2,373,875	19,227,000	12.35%	61
Connecticut	417,506	3,504,000	11.92%	59
Illinois	1,509,773	12,714,000	11.87%	59
Utah	262,825	2,389,000	11.00%	55
Arizona	607,097	5,744,000	10.57%	53
Florida	1,712,358	17,397,000	9.84%	49
Rhode Island	95,173	1,081,000	8.80%	44
Massachusetts	547,730	6,417,000	8.54%	42
Hawaii	103,312	1,263,000	8.18%	41
Nevada	169,611	2,335,000	7.26%	36
New Jersey	475,263	8,699,000	5.46%	27
California	1,881,985	35,894,000	5.24%	26
D.C.	0	554,000	0.00%	0
Total	**59,061,367**	**293,658,000**	**20.11%**	**100**

- Mississippi (50.20% rural),
- South Dakota (47.14% rural),
- Arkansas (46.10% rural),
- Montana (44.69% rural),
- North Dakota (44.68% rural),
- Alabama (43.74% rural), and
- Kentucky (43.13% rural).

None of the 10 most rural states is a closely divided battleground state. The battleground states that receive attention in presidential campaigns are generally not rural states.

In contrast, under the National Popular Vote compact, votes cast in rural states would all become politically relevant.

9.31.11. MYTH: A national popular vote would be a guarantee of corruption because every ballot box in every state would become a chance to steal the Presidency.

QUICK ANSWER:
- Under the *current* system of electing the President, every vote in every precinct matters *inside every* battleground state. If it were true that an election in which the winner is the candidate who receives the most popular votes is "a guarantee of corruption," then we should see today a wealth of evidence of rampant fraud in presidential elections *inside* every battleground state. Similarly, we should see evidence of rampant fraud today in every gubernatorial election in every state.
- Executing electoral fraud without detection requires a situation in which a very small number of people can have a very large impact.
- Under the current state-by-state winner-take-all system, there are huge incentives for fraud and mischief, because a small number of people in a battleground state can affect enough popular votes to swing all of that state's electoral votes.
- In 2004, President George W. Bush had a nationwide lead of 3,012,171 popular votes. However, if 59,393 Bush voters in Ohio had shifted to Senator John Kerry, Kerry would have carried Ohio and thus become President. It would be far easier for potential fraudsters to manufacture 59,393 votes in Ohio than to manufacture 3,012,171 million votes (51 times more votes) nationwide. Moreover, it would be far more difficult to conceal fraud involving three million votes.
- In 2012, a shift of 214,390 popular votes in four states (Florida, Ohio, Virginia, and New Hampshire) would have elected Governor Romney as President,

despite President Obama's nationwide lead of almost five million votes. It would be far easier for potential fraudsters to manufacture 214,390 votes in four states than to manufacture five million votes nationwide (23 times more votes). Moreover, it would be far more difficult to conceal fraud involving five million votes.

- There were seven closely divided battleground states possessing 102 electoral votes that President Obama carried and that had Republican Attorneys General in November 2008. President Obama received 95 more electoral votes than the 270 electoral votes necessary for election. Where were the prosecutions for election fraud in these states in the period immediately following the November 2008 election?

MORE DETAILED ANSWER:

The 2012 Republican National Platform states that electing the President by a national popular vote would be

> "a guarantee of corruption as every ballot box in every state would become a chance to steal the Presidency."[589]

Under the *current* system of electing the President, *every* vote in *every* ballot box matters inside *every* closely divided battleground state and therefore today represents "a chance to steal the Presidency."

If an election in which the winner is the candidate who receives the most popular votes is "a guarantee of corruption," then we should see voluminous evidence today of rampant corruption *inside* every battleground state in every presidential election and, in particular, the elections of 2000, 2004, 2008, and 2012.

Similarly, every vote in every precinct matters in gubernatorial elections today in all 50 states. If conducting a popular-vote election is "a guarantee of corruption," then we should see evidence today of rampant fraud in every gubernatorial election in *all* 50 states.

Executing electoral fraud without detection requires a situation in which a very small number of people can have a very large impact. Under the current state-by-state winner-take-all system, there is a huge payoff for fraud and mischief in the closely divided battleground states, because a small number of people in a battleground state can use a small number of popular votes to flip 100% of that state's electoral votes.

Under the current state-by-state winner-take-all system, those who wish to cheat know exactly where they need to go in order to potentially sway the national outcome (namely the battleground states).

In 2012, a shift of 214,390 popular votes in four states (Florida, Ohio, Virginia, and

---

[589] 2012 Republican National Platform adopted in Tampa, Florida, on August 28, 2012.

New Hampshire) would have elected Governor Romney as President, despite President Obama's nationwide lead of 4,966,945 votes.[590] It would be far easier for potential fraudsters to manufacture 214,390 votes in four states than to manufacture five million votes nationwide (23 times more votes). Moreover, it would be far more difficult to conceal fraud involving five million votes.

In 2004, President George W. Bush had a nationwide lead of 3,012,171 popular votes. However, if 59,393 Bush voters in Ohio had shifted to Senator John Kerry, Kerry would have carried Ohio and thus become President. It would be far easier for potential fraudsters to manufacture 59,393 votes in Ohio than to manufacture 3,012,171 million votes (51 times more votes) nationwide. Moreover, it would be far more difficult to conceal fraud involving three million votes.

In 2000, a significant number of electoral votes were determined by a relatively small number of popular votes:

- Florida—537 votes,
- Iowa—4,144 votes,
- New Hampshire—7,211 votes,
- New Mexico—366 votes,
- Oregon—6,765 votes, and
- Wisconsin—5,708 votes.

None of these blocks of votes was large in comparison to the nationwide margin of 537,179 in the national popular vote in 2000.

In the 1950s and 1960s, accusations of voter fraud by both political parties were commonplace in numerous states. In the 1960 presidential election, a switch of 4,430 votes in Illinois and a simultaneous switch of 4,782 votes in South Carolina would have denied Kennedy a majority of the electoral votes. Four thousand votes in two states would not have been decisive in 1960 in terms of changing the outcome if the outcome had been based on the national popular vote. John F. Kennedy led Richard M. Nixon by 118,574 popular votes nationwide. The potential switch of 4,430 or 4,782 votes was only relevant in 1960 because of the state-by-state winner-take-all rule.

In short, the outcome of a presidential election is less likely to be affected by fraud with a single large nationwide pool of votes than under the current state-by-state winner-take-all system.

As former Congressman and presidential candidate Tom Tancredo (R–Colorado) wrote in an article entitled "Should Every Vote Count?"

---

[590] The four states involved are Florida (29 electoral votes), Ohio (18), New Hampshire (4), and Virginia (13). They cumulatively possess 64 electoral votes. A shift of 64 electoral votes would have given Mitt Romney the 270 electoral votes needed for election. See appendix HH for the two-party results of the 2012 election. Table 9.45 presents the presidential vote for Barack Obama (Democrat), Mitt Romney (Republican), Gary Johnson (Libertarian), Jill Stein (Green), and the other 22 minor-party and independent candidates who were on the ballot in 2012 in at least one state.

"The issue of voter fraud . . . won't entirely go away with the National Popular Vote plan, but it is harder to mobilize massive voter fraud on the national level without getting caught, than it is to do so in a few key states. Voter fraud is already a problem. The National Popular Vote makes it a smaller one."[591]

U.S. Senator Birch Bayh (D–Indiana) summed up the concerns about possible fraud in a 1979 Senate speech by saying:

"Fraud is an ever present possibility in the electoral college system, even if it rarely has become a proven reality. With the electoral college, relatively few irregular votes can reap a healthy reward in the form of a bloc of electoral votes, because of the unit rule or winner take all rule. Under the present system, fraudulent popular votes are much more likely to have a great impact by swinging enough blocs of electoral votes to reverse the election. A like number of fraudulent popular votes under direct election would likely have little effect on the national vote totals.

"I have said repeatedly in previous debates that there is no way in which anyone would want to excuse fraud. We have to do everything we can to find it, to punish those who participate in it; but **one of the things we can do to limit fraud is to limit the benefits to be gained by fraud.**

"**Under a direct popular vote system, one fraudulent vote wins one vote in the return. In the electoral college system, one fraudulent vote could mean 45 electoral votes, 28 electoral votes.**

"So the incentive to participate in 'a little bit of fraud,' if I may use that phrase advisedly, can have the impact of turning a whole electoral block, a whole State operating under the unit rule. Therefore, so the incentive to participate in fraud is significantly greater than it would be under the direct popular vote system."[592] [Emphasis added]

At any given time, there are about two dozen Republican and about two dozen Democratic state Attorneys General. Specifically, there were 26 Republican state Attorneys General and 24 Democratic Attorneys General in November 2012. There are also, at any given time, roughly two thousand Republican county prosecuting attorneys and roughly a thousand Democratic county prosecuting attorneys.

If conducting an election in which the winner is the candidate receiving the most popular votes is "a guarantee of corruption," then we should have seen a voluminous

---

[591] Tancredo, Tom. Should every vote count? November 11, 2011. http://www.wnd.com/index.php?pageId =366929.

[592] *Congressional Record*. March 14, 1979. Page 5000.

number of prosecutions for election fraud in presidential elections in battleground states (and in gubernatorial elections in all 50 states).

Where are the prosecutions?

In November 2008, there were Republican Attorneys General in seven closely divided battleground states that Barack Obama carried. These states possessed more electoral votes (102) than Obama's 95-vote margin of victory in the Electoral College in 2008:

- Colorado (9 electoral votes),
- Florida (27),
- Michigan (18),
- New Hampshire (4),
- Pennsylvania (21),
- Virginia (13), and
- Wisconsin (10).

Were these seven Republican Attorneys General derelict in the period immediately following the November 2008 election in fulfilling their legal duty to prosecute crime in their own states?

Are these seven Republican Attorneys General also guilty of not promoting the interests of their own political party in attempting to prosecute cases of election fraud that would, at the minimum, embarrass (if not convict) members of the Democratic Party?

If it were actually true that an election in which the winner is the candidate receiving the most popular votes is

"a guarantee of corruption as every ballot box in every state would become a chance to steal the Presidency,"[593]

then we should surely have seen a voluminous number of prosecutions involving the tens of thousands of ballot boxes in these seven outcome-determining states in the period immediately following the 2008 election.

In November 2012, there were Republican Attorneys General in most of the battleground states that determined the outcome of the 2012 presidential election:

- Florida—29 electoral votes,[594]
- Ohio—18 electoral votes,
- Virginia—13 electoral votes,
- Wisconsin—10 electoral votes,
- Colorado—9 electoral votes,
- Pennsylvania—20 electoral votes, and
- Michigan—16 electoral votes.

---

[593] 2012 Republican National Platform adopted in Tampa, Florida, on August 28, 2012.

[594] The number of electoral votes shown here are those applicable to the 2012 presidential election.

These seven battleground states with Republican Attorneys General together possessed 115 electoral Votes. President Obama won each of these battleground states by *low-single-digit* margins. In 2012, President Obama received only 64 more than the 270 electoral votes necessary for election.

As of the time of this writing, there have been no reports of prosecutions involving the tens of thousands of ballot boxes in these seven outcome-determining states in the 2012 presidential election.

If it is conceded that fraud is not rampant today in presidential elections in the battleground states (or gubernatorial elections in all 50 states), then why would one suddenly expect a massive outbreak of criminal activity in the 40 or so states that are currently politically irrelevant in the presidential election if the National Popular Vote compact were to become operative?

9.31.12. MYTH: Fraud is minimized under the current system because it is hard to predict where stolen votes will matter.

QUICK ANSWER:

* It is *not* hard to predict where stolen votes will matter under the current state-by-state winner-take-all system of electing the President. Stolen votes matter in the closely divided battleground states.

MORE DETAILED ANSWER:

Tara Ross, an opponent of the National Popular Vote plan, made the following comment about fraud under the current state-by-state winner-take-all system of electing the President:

> "Fraud is minimized because it is hard to predict where stolen votes will matter."[595]

Contrary to what Ross asserts, there is no difficulty in determining where stolen votes will matter—they matter in the closely divided battleground states.

The battleground states are well-known to anyone who follows politics. For example, in a July 2012 article describing his "3-2-1 strategy," Karl Rove identified six states that he believed would probably decide the 2012 election.[596] Most political observers agreed with Rove's list of states.

Five and a half months before Election Day in 2012, Mitt Romney acknowledged the small number of battleground states during a fund-raising dinner in Boca Raton, Florida. In the May 17, 2012, *Mother Jones* video, Romney said:

> "All the money will be spent in 10 states."

---

[595] Written testimony submitted by Tara Ross to the Delaware Senate in June 2010.

[596] Rove, Karl. Romney's roads to the White House: A 3-2-1 strategy can get him to the magic 270 electoral votes. *Wall Street Journal.* May 23, 2012.

The 2012 Obama campaign, of course, operated on a similar basis.

In October 2000, the *New York Times* reported:

> **"The parties and the presidential candidates are concentrating their campaigns in Florida in these last, tense days before the election on the cities and towns along Interstate 4**.

> "The nearly three million voters who live more or less along the maddeningly overcrowded, 100-mile-long highway that bisects the state from Daytona Beach on the Atlantic Coast to the Tampa Bay on the Gulf of Mexico are the swing voters in this, the largest of the swing states.

> "They may be getting more attention these days than any other voters in the country as the candidates compete for Florida's 25 electoral votes.

> **"'This state is the key to this election,' Vice President Al Gore declared** at a rally in Orlando earlier this month, 'and Central Florida is the key to this state.'"[597] [Emphasis added]

Under the current state-by-state winner-take-all system, those who wish to cheat know exactly where they need to go in order to potentially sway the national outcome. In 2000, for example, a significant number of electoral votes were determined by a small handful of popular votes:

- Florida—537 votes,
- Iowa—4,144 votes,
- New Hampshire—7,211 votes,
- New Mexico—366 votes,
- Oregon—6,765 votes, and
- Wisconsin—5,708 votes.

Under a National Popular Vote, the amount of fraud that would have to be perpetrated to impact the outcome of an election would be so massive that it could not go unnoticed.

9.31.13. MYTH: The 2000 election illustrates the Republican Party's structural advantage under the current state-by-state winner-take-all system.

QUICK ANSWER:

- The Republicans won the 2000 presidential election because of George W. Bush's 537-vote margin in Florida—not because of any built-in Republican structural advantage conferred by the state-by-state winner-take-all rule.

---

[597] Rosenbaum, David E. The 2000 campaign: The Battlegrounds: Florida interstate's heavy campaign traffic. *New York Times*. October 25, 2000.

- It is impossible to say whether Al Gore would have been elected President in 2000 under the National Popular Vote system, because the campaign would have been conducted very differently.

MORE DETAILED ANSWER:

It is sometimes argued that the Republican victory in the 2000 election is evidence that the Republican Party has a built-in *structural* advantage under the current state-by-state winner-take-all system.

George W. Bush won Florida by a margin of 537 popular votes out of 5,963,110 votes cast.

When an election is decided by a margin of 537 votes out of 5,963,110, numerous factors (large and small) necessarily affected the outcome.

We select two relatively minor and *politically neutral* factors to make the point that Bush's 537-vote margin in Florida can be explained by entirely accidental factors operating locally in Florida—not any built-in Republican structural advantage conferred by the state-by-state winner-take-all rule.

A 2007 study in *The Journal of Politics* analyzed the effect of the weather on election outcomes:

> "Using GIS interpolations, we employ meteorological data drawn from over 22,000 U.S. weather stations to provide election day estimates of rain and snow for each U.S. county. We find that, when compared to normal conditions, rain significantly reduces voter participation by a rate of just less than 1% per inch, while an inch of snowfall decreases turnout by almost .5%. Poor weather is also shown to benefit the Republican party's vote share. . . .

> "The results of the zero precipitation scenarios reveal only two instances in which a perfectly dry election day would have changed an Electoral College outcome. **Dry elections would have led Bill Clinton to win North Carolina in 1992 and Al Gore to win Florida in 2000.** This latter change in the allocation of Florida's electors would have swung the incredibly close 2000 election in Gore's favor. Of course, the converse is that a rainier day would have increased George W. Bush's margin and may have reduced the importance of issues with the butterfly ballot, overvotes, etc."[598] [Emphasis added]

A *Democratic* election administrator in one county designed a ballot that presented the candidates' names in a confusing arrangement (the so-called "butterfly

---

[598] Brad T. Gomez, Brad T.; Hansford, Thomas G.; and Krause, George A. 2007. The Republicans should pray for rain: weather, turnout, and voting in U.S. Presidential Elections. *The Journal of Politics.* Volume 69, number 3. August 2007. Pages 649–663.

ballot"). The ballot's confusing arrangement resulted in third-party candidate Pat Buchanan receiving thousands of votes that were, as Buchanan acknowledged, almost certainly intended for Al Gore. A paper in the *American Political Science Review* agreed with Buchanan's assessment and concluded that this action by a *Democratic* election administrator was alone sufficient to cause Gore to lose Florida.

> "The butterfly ballot used in Palm Beach County, Florida, in the 2000 presidential election caused more than 2,000 Democratic voters to vote by mistake for Reform candidate Pat Buchanan, a number larger than George W. Bush's certified margin of victory in Florida. . . .

> "Multiple methods and several kinds of data [were used] to rule out alternative explanations for the votes Buchanan received in Palm Beach County. . . .

> "In Palm Beach County, Buchanan's proportion of the vote on election-day ballots is four times larger than his proportion on absentee (non-butterfly) ballots, but Buchanan's proportion does not differ significantly between election-day and absentee ballots in any other Florida county.

> "Unlike other Reform candidates in Palm Beach County, Buchanan tended to receive election-day votes in Democratic precincts and from individuals who voted for the Democratic U.S. Senate candidate."

> "Among 3,053 U.S. counties where Buchanan was on the ballot, Palm Beach County has the most anomalous excess of votes for him."[599]

Immediately prior to Election Day in 2000, neither Republicans nor anyone else thought that there was any structural advantage working in favor of the Republican Party because of the state-by-state winner-take-all rule. In the week before Election Day in 2000, most polls indicated that George W. Bush was poised to win the national popular vote—but not necessarily the electoral vote. Indeed, the Bush campaign was planning for just that eventuality. As the *New York Daily News* reported on Wednesday November 2, 2000, "Bush [is] set to fight an Electoral College loss."

> "Quietly, some of George W. Bush's advisers are preparing for the ultimate 'what if' scenario: What happens if Bush wins the popular vote for President, but loses the White House because Al Gore won the majority of electoral votes? . . ."

> "'The one thing we don't do is roll over,' says a Bush aide. 'We fight.'

---

[599] Wand, Jonathan N.; Shotts, Kenneth W.; Sekhon, Jasjeet S.; Mebane, Walter R.; Herron, Michael C.; and Brady, Henry E. The butterfly did it: The aberrant vote for Buchanan in Palm Beach County, Florida. *American Political Science Review.* Volume 95. Number 1. December 2001. sekhon.berkeley.edu/elections/election2000/butterfly.review.pdf.

"How? The core of the emerging Bush strategy assumes a popular uprising, stoked by the Bushies themselves, of course.

"In league with the campaign—which is preparing talking points about the Electoral College's essential unfairness—a massive talk-radio operation would be encouraged. 'We'd have ads, too,' says a Bush aide, 'and I think you can count on the media to fuel the thing big-time. Even papers that supported Gore might turn against him because the will of the people will have been thwarted.'

"Local business leaders will be urged to lobby their customers, the clergy will be asked to speak up for the popular will and Team Bush will enlist as many Democrats as possible to scream as loud as they can. 'You think 'Democrats for Democracy' would be a catchy term for them?' asks a Bush adviser.

"The universe of people who would be targeted by this insurrection is small—the 538 currently anonymous folks called electors, people chosen by the campaigns and their state party organizations as a reward for their service over the years. . . .

"Enough of the electors could theoretically switch to Bush if they wanted to—if there was sufficient pressure on them to ratify the popular verdict."[600]

9.31.14. MYTH: Al Gore would have been elected President under a national popular vote in 2000.

QUICK ANSWER:

- It is impossible to say whether Al Gore would have been elected President in 2000 under the National Popular Vote system, because the campaign would have been conducted very differently.
- Soliciting every available vote is a strategic necessity when the winner of an election is the candidate who receives the most popular votes.

MORE DETAILED ANSWER:

There is no way to say whether Al Gore would have become President had the 2000 campaign been conducted under the National Popular Vote plan.

The 2000 campaign would have been conducted very differently if the candidates had gone into the election under a different electoral system.

---

[600] Kramer, Michael. Bush set to fight an electoral college loss: They're not only thinking the unthinkable, They're planning for it. *New York Daily News.* November 1, 2000. http://articles.nydailynews.com/2000-11-01/news/18145743_1_electoral-votes-popular-vote-bush-aide.

The pattern of candidate travel and advertising would have been entirely different under a national popular vote because candidates would have solicited votes in every state—not just 15.

Candidates certainly would not have ignored 35 or so states during the campaign. Candidates would not have concentrated their efforts so heavily on Florida. Candidates would certainly not have ignored Ohio (as they did in the 2000 campaign).

The issues discussed in the 2000 campaign would have been different because the candidates would have had to appeal to more than just the battleground-state voters.

9.32. MYTH THAT MAJOR PARTIES WILL BE TAKEN OFF THE BALLOT BECAUSE OF NATIONAL POPULAR VOTE

9.32.1. MYTH: Major parties will be taken off the ballot because of National Popular Vote.

QUICK ANSWER:
- The fact that the *major* political parties are usually unable to keep *minor* parties off the ballot in presidential elections indicates that it would be very difficult for one major party to keep the other major party off the ballot in any state.
- The public would not tolerate having only one presidential candidate on the ballot even in states where one political party is dominant.
- The Equal Protection Clause and the Guarantee Clause of the Constitution provide a strong legal basis for thwarting any attempt to create a one-party state.

MORE DETAILED ANSWER:

On September 13, 2012, the Kansas State Objections Board (consisting of Republican Secretary of State Kris Kobach and two other Republican statewide officeholders) considered a motion to keep Democrat Barack Obama off the presidential ballot in Kansas.

The *New York Times* reported that the motion was abandoned a day later as a result of "a wave of angry backlash."[601]

The Board's short-lived effort to turn Kansas into a one-party state immediately generated speculation on an elections blog that the National Popular Vote plan would result in major political parties being thrown off the ballot in states dominated by the other political party, thereby preventing the removed party from getting any substantial number of votes in the state.

On one blog, Valarauko said:

---

[601] Eligon, John. Kansas ballot challenge over Obama's birth is ended. *New York Times*. September 14, 2012.

"A state dominated by one party could try to use NPV to rig a presidential election, by setting ballot qualification requirements that would be very tough for the other party to meet (e.g., Massachusetts could grant general election Presidential ballot status automatically only to parties that have >20% of the registered voters, and impose a huge signature-gathering requirement for ballot status on any that don't), thus knocking the other party's votes in that state to 0."[602]

Creation of a one-party state as a result of the National Popular Vote plan should not be a realistic concern for several reasons.

First, *major* political parties frequently use sharp-elbowed tactics to try to keep *minor* parties off the ballot; however, these efforts generally fail. For example, in October 2012, the Pennsylvania Republican Party tried to keep Libertarian presidential nominee Gary Johnson (a former Republican governor of New Mexico) off the presidential ballot in Pennsylvania.

"The Pennsylvania Republican Party chairman . . . said he was not about to give Mr. Johnson an easy opening to play a Nader to Mr. Romney's Gore in Pennsylvania this year."[603]

Despite Pennsylvania Republican Party efforts, Johnson appeared on the 2012 ballot in Pennsylvania (and in a total of 48 states).

Similarly, despite vigorous opposition from the Democratic Party, Ralph Nader (who received 2.7% of the vote in 2000) got onto the ballot in 47 states and the District of Columbia in his race for President.

John Anderson (who received 7% of the national popular vote in 1980) was on the ballot in all 50 states.

Ross Perot (who received 19% of the national popular vote in 1992) was on the ballot in all 50 states in both 1992 and 1996.

In summary, third-party presidential candidates who had substantial support (such as John Anderson in 1980 and Ross Perot in 1992 and 1996) got on the ballot in all 50 states, and third-party candidates with low-single-digit support succeeded in getting onto the ballot in almost every state (e.g., 47 or 48).

The lack of success by *major* political parties in keeping *minor* parties off the ballot indicates that it would be even less likely that a major party could be taken off the ballot in any state.

Second, the immediate and harsh public reaction to the Republican challenge to Obama in Kansas in 2012 is a reminder of the fact that the public (even in a state that

---

[602] Valarauko. October 20, 2012. http://www.volokh.com/2012/10/30/the-popular-vote-and-presidential-legitimacy/

[603] Rutenberg, Jim. Spoiler alert! G.O.P. fighting Libertarian's spot on the ballot. *New York Times*. October 15, 2012.

votes heavily Republican) would not tolerate the creation of a one-party state in the United States.

Despite the impression created by the bloggers, there is political diversity and competition in both Kansas and Massachusetts. Kansas had Democratic governors from 2003–2011 (Kathleen Sibelius from 2003–2009 and Mark Parkinson from 2009–2011), and Massachusetts had Republican governors from 1991–2007 (most recently Mitt Romney from 2003–2007).

Third, the Equal Protection Clause of the 14th Amendment to the U.S. Constitution provides a strong legal basis for challenging any attempt to create a one-party state.

> "No state shall . . . deny to any person within its jurisdiction the equal protection of the laws."

Fourth, the Guarantee Clause of the U.S. Constitution provides an additional legal basis for challenging any attempt to create a one-party state.

> "The United States shall guarantee to every State in this Union a Republican Form of Government."[604]

In summary, speculation that the National Popular Vote would create one-party enclaves is a parlor game having no connection to real-world political reality, the legal environment in which American elections are conducted, or the sense of fairness demanded by the American people.

9.33. MYTH ABOUT TYRANNY OF THE MAJORITY

9.33.1. MYTH: The state-by-state winner-take-all rule prevents tyranny of the majority

QUICK ANSWER:
- Winner-take-all statutes enable a mere *plurality* of voters in each state to control 100% of a state's electoral vote, thereby extinguishing the voice of the remainder of the state's voters. The state-by-state winner-take-all rule does not prevent a "tyranny of the majority" but instead *is an example of it*. As Missouri Senator Thomas Hart Benton said in 1824, "This is . . . a case . . . of votes taken away, added to those of the majority, and given to a person to whom the minority is opposed."
- It is impossible to discern any specific threat of "tyranny of the majority" that was posed by the first-place candidates in the four elections in which the Electoral College elected the second-place candidate to the Presidency (1824, 1876, 1888, and 2000).

---

[604] U.S. Constitution. Article IV, section 4, clause 1.

- Under the American system of government, protection against a "tyranny of the majority" comes from specific protections of individual rights contained in the original Constitution and the Bill of Rights; the "checks and balances" provided by dividing government into three branches (legislative, executive, and judicial); the existence of an independent judiciary; and the fact that the United States is a "compound republic" in which governmental power is divided between two distinct levels of government—state and national.

MORE DETAILED ANSWER:

Hans von Spakovsky has written:

> "The U.S. election system addresses the Founders' fears of a 'tyranny of the majority,' a topic frequently discussed in the Federalist Papers. In the eyes of the Founders, this tyranny was as dangerous as the risks posed by despots like King George." [605]

State winner-take-all statutes enable a mere *plurality* of voters in each state to control 100% of a state's electoral vote, thereby extinguishing the voice of all the other voters in a state.

Suppressing the voice of a state's minority is, by definition, an example of "tyranny of the majority." The state-by-state winner-take-all rule does not prevent a "tyranny of the majority" but instead *is an example of it.*

In 1824, Missouri Senator Thomas Hart Benton said the following about the winner-take-all rule in a Senate speech:

> "The general ticket system, now existing in 10 States was the offspring of policy, and not of any disposition to give fair play to the will of the people. It was adopted by the leading men of those States, to enable them to consolidate the vote of the State. . . .**The rights of minorities are violated** because a majority of one will carry the vote of the whole State. . . . **This is . . . a case . . . of votes taken away, added to those of the majority, and given to a person to whom the minority is opposed.**"[606] [Emphasis added]

The winner-take-all rule treats all the voters who did not vote for the first-place candidate *as if* they had voted for the first-place candidate.

In 2012, 56,256,178 (44%) of the 128,954,498 voters had their vote diverted by the winner-take-all rule to a candidate they opposed (namely, their state's first-place candidate).

---

[605] Von Spakovsky, Hans. Destroying the Electoral College: The Anti-Federalist National Popular Vote Scheme. Legal memo. October 27, 2011. http://www.heritage.org/research/reports/2011/10/destroying-the -electoral-college-the-anti-federalist-national-popular-vote-scheme.

[606] 41 *Annals of Congress* 169–170. 1824.

Table 9.45 shows the number of voters who opposed the candidate who received the most votes in each separate state in 2012.[607] Columns 2 through 5 show the number of votes cast in each state in 2012 for Barack Obama (Democrat), Mitt Romney (Republican), Gary Johnson (Libertarian), and Jill Stein (Green). Column 6 presents the number of votes received by the other 22 minor-party and independent candidates that were on the ballot in 2012 in at least one state (and write-in candidates). Column 7 shows the total vote for each state.

Column 8 of table 9.45 shows the number of voters who did not vote for the candidate who received the most votes in each state. Taking Alabama as an example, former Massachusetts Governor Romney received the most popular votes in the state (1,255,925 out of a total of 2,074,338 votes). However, a total of 818,413 other voters in Alabama did not favor Romney, but instead voted for President Obama, former New Mexico Governor Gary Johnson, Dr. Jill Stein, or one of the other minor-party candidates. Nonetheless, the winner-take-all rule diverted the 818,413 votes cast for Obama, Johnson, Stein, and other minor-party candidates and treated them as if they had been cast for Mitt Romney.

The candidate receiving the most popular votes nationwide did not win the Presidency in four of our nation's 57 presidential elections.

If the winner-take-all rule protects the nation against a "tyranny of the majority," it is appropriate to inquire as to what specific threat of "tyranny" was posed by the first-place candidate in the four elections in which the Electoral College elected the second-place candidate (1824, 1876, 1888, and 2000)?

What "tyranny" did the winner-take-all rule prevent by not giving the White House to the candidate receiving the most popular votes nationwide in 1888 (Grover Cleveland) and instead installing the second-place candidate (Benjamin Harrison)?[608]

If Andrew Jackson presented the threat of "tyranny" in 1824 (when the Electoral

---

[607] The 2012 election returns shown in table 9.35, table 9.36, table 9.45, and appendix HH were obtained from the National Archives and Record Administration (NARA) web site at http://www.archives.gov/federal-register/electoral-college/2012/popular-vote.html. The NARA web site presents the number of votes shown on each state's Certificate of Ascertainment. There are two differences between our tables and that on the NARA web site. First, the NARA web site presents votes *by party*, whereas our table is based on votes *by candidate*. This difference in treatment creates a difference in the case of New York (which uses fusion voting). The NARA web site (as of January 4, 2013) showed the 141,056 votes that the Obama-Biden slate received on the Working Families Party line (and contained in New York's Certificate of Ascertainment) as minor-party votes in column 6 of their table, instead of showing these votes as Obama-Biden votes in column 2 of their table. Similarly, the web site shows the 256,171 votes that the Romney-Ryan slate received on the Conservative Party line as minor-party votes in column 6, instead of showing these votes as Romney-Ryan votes in column 3. Our table puts these Obama-Biden votes and Romney-Ryan votes in columns 2 and 3, respectively, in conformity with the practice of the New York State Board of Elections. Thus, our table shows (in column 6) only 8,652 votes for minor-party candidates in New York. See section 2.10 for additional details on fusion in New York and figure 2.11 for an example of a presidential ballot in New York. Secondly, our table reflects the adjustment (certified on December 31, 2012) to New York state's vote totals resulting from the fact that an executive order issued on the evening before Election Day allowed voters in counties affected by Hurricane Sandy to cast a provisional ballot at *any* polling place in the state. A total of 400,629 additional ballots (over 300,000 in New York City alone) were counted as a result of this executive order.

[608] See the discussion of the 1888 election in section 9.8.3.

Table 9.45 VOTES DIVERTED BY THE WINNER-TAKE-ALL RULE IN 2012.

STATE	OBAMA	ROMNEY	JOHNSON	STEIN	OTHERS	TOTAL	DIVERTED
AL	795,696	1,255,925	12,328	3,397	6,992	2,074,338	818,413
AK	122,640	164,676	7,392	2,917	–	297,625	132,949
AZ	1,025,232	1,233,654	32,100	7,816	452	2,299,254	1,065,600
AR	394,409	647,744	16,276	9,305	1,734	1,069,468	421,724
CA	7,854,285	4,839,958	143,221	85,638	115,455	13,038,557	5,184,272
CO	1,322,998	1,185,050	35,540	7,508	18,121	2,569,217	1,246,219
CT	905,083	634,892	12,580	863	5,542	1,558,960	653,877
DE	242,584	165,484	3,882	1,940	31	413,921	171,337
D.C.	267,070	21,381	2,083	2,458	772	293,764	26,694
FL	4,235,965	4,162,341	44,681	8,933	19,281	8,471,201	4,235,236
GA	1,773,827	2,078,688	45,324	–	–	3,897,839	1,819,151
HI	306,658	121,015	3,840	3,184	–	434,697	128,039
ID	212,787	420,911	9,453	4,402	4,721	652,274	231,363
IL	3,019,512	2,135,216	56,229	30,222	–	5,241,179	2,221,667
IN	1,152,887	1,420,543	50,111	625	368	2,624,534	1,203,991
IA	822,544	730,617	12,926	3,769	4,882	1,574,738	752,194
KS	440,726	692,634	20,456	–	5,017	1,158,833	466,199
KY	679,370	1,087,190	17,063	6,337	7,252	1,797,212	710,022
LA	809,141	1,152,262	18,157	6,978	7,527	1,994,065	841,803
ME	401,306	292,276	9,352	8,119	–	711,053	309,747
MD	1,677,844	971,869	30,195	17,110	1,521	2,698,539	1,020,695
MA	1,921,290	1,188,314	30,920	20,691	–	3,161,215	1,239,925
MI	2,564,569	2,115,256	7,774	21,897	21,465	4,730,961	2,166,392
MN	1,546,167	1,320,225	35,098	13,023	11,515	2,926,028	1,379,861
MS	562,949	710,746	6,676	1,588	3,625	1,285,584	574,838
MO	1,223,796	1,482,440	43,151	–	7,936	2,757,323	1,274,883
MT	201,839	267,928	14,165	–	–	483,932	216,004
NE	302,081	475,064	11,109	–	2,408	790,662	315,598
NV	531,373	463,567	10,968	–	3,240	1,009,148	477,775
NH	369,561	329,918	8,212	–	708	708,399	338,838
NJ	2,122,786	1,478,088	21,035	9,886	6,704	3,638,499	1,515,713
NM	415,335	335,788	27,787	2,691	2,156	783,757	368,422
NY	4,471,871	2,485,432	47,092	39,856	8,652	7,052,903	2,581,032
NC	2,178,391	2,270,395	44,515	–	619	4,493,920	2,223,525
ND	124,966	188,320	5,238	1,362	3,046	322,932	134,612
OH	2,827,621	2,661,407	49,493	18,574	23,736	5,580,831	2,753,210
OK	443,547	891,325	–	–	–	1,334,872	443,547
OR	970,488	754,175	24,089	19,427	7,816	1,775,995	805,507
PA	2,990,274	2,680,434	49,441	21,341	–	5,741,490	2,751,216
RI	279,677	157,204	4,388	2,421	2,359	446,049	166,372
SC	865,941	1,071,645	16,321	5,446	4,765	1,964,118	892,473
SD	145,039	210,610	5,795	–	2,371	363,815	153,205
TN	960,709	1,462,330	18,623	6,515	8,661	2,456,838	994,508
TX	3,308,124	4,569,843	88,580	24,657	2,647	7,993,851	3,424,008
UT	251,813	740,600	12,572	3,817	8,206	1,017,008	276,408
VT	199,239	92,698	3,487	–	3,866	299,290	100,051
VA	1,971,820	1,822,522	31,216	8,627	13,058	3,847,243	1,875,423
WA	1,755,396	1,290,670	42,202	20,928	16,320	3,125,516	1,370,120
WV	238,230	417,584	6,114	4,593	4,035	670,556	252,972
WI	1,620,985	1,410,966	20,439	7,665	11,379	3,071,434	1,450,449
WY	69,286	170,962	5,326	–	3,487	249,061	78,099
Total	**65,897,727**	**60,930,782**	**1,275,015**	**466,526**	**384,448**	**128,954,498**	**56,256,178**

College denied him the Presidency), why did Jackson not present an equal threat in 1828 and 1832 (when he *was* elected by the Electoral College)?

Under the American system of government, protection against a "tyranny of the majority" primarily comes from the numerous protections of individual rights contained in the Bill of Rights as well as numerous specific clauses of the original constitution, including, but not limited to, the prohibition of *ex post facto* laws, prohibition of bills of attainder (i.e., legislative acts that impose criminal penalties on named individuals), and prohibition on religious tests for office.

The "checks and balances" provided by dividing government into three branches (legislative, executive, and judicial) provides additional protection against a "tyranny of the majority." In particular, the existence of an independent judiciary provides significant protection against "tyranny of the majority."

Additional protection comes from the fact that the United States is a "compound republic" in which governmental power is divided between two distinct levels of government—state and national. James Madison explains the concept of a "compound republic" in *Federalist No. 51*.

> **"In the compound republic of America, the power surrendered by the people is first divided between two distinct governments**, and then the portion allotted to each subdivided among distinct and separate departments. **Hence a double security arises to the rights of the people. The different governments will control each other**, at the same time that each will be controlled by itself."[609] [Emphasis added]

9.34. MYTH ABOUT POLITICALLY-MOTIVATED MID-YEAR ENACTMENT

9.34.1. MYTH: The Texas legislature might enact the National Popular Vote compact based on a mid-year poll indicating that its favored candidate is poised to win the popular vote in November—but not the electoral vote.

QUICK ANSWER:

- The National Popular Vote compact governs the conduct of a particular presidential election only if it has been enacted (and in effect) in states possessing 270 electoral votes on July 20 of a presidential election year.
- It is virtually impossible to predict whether a candidate is going to win the national popular vote—but not the electoral vote—immediately before Election Day, much less as early as July 20 of a presidential election year.
- Elections in which the candidate winning the electoral vote did not win the nationwide popular vote have occurred when the winning margin is small (e.g., the ½% margin in 2000). These small winning margins are well *inside*

---

[609] Publius. The structure of the government must furnish the proper checks and balances between the different departments. *Independent Journal.* February 6, 1788. *Federalist No. 51.*

the margin of error of most political polls (which is typically plus or minus 3% or 4%).

- A decision to enact the National Popular Vote compact would have to be made considerably earlier in the year than July 20. Winning approval of a new state law in a given state is a multi-step process in which each step is subject to numerous time-consuming delays. Moreover, most state constitutions provide for a significant delay between the time of the Governor's signature and the effective date of a newly enacted law.

MORE DETAILED ANSWER:

David Gringer has propounded a hypothetical scenario in which the Texas legislature might "perniciously" gain partisan advantage by enacting the National Popular Vote compact on the basis of a mid-year poll indicating that its favored presidential candidate is poised to win the popular vote—but not the electoral vote—in an upcoming presidential election.

"Until now, this Note has assumed that states are not acting perniciously in considering the NPV. . . . This Note [now] poses a hypothetical scenario in which a state moves to the NPV to achieve partisan advantage, not to remove the inequities of the electoral college or to increase its influence in the presidential election process.

"As the 2020 elections approach, the Republicans who control the Texas Legislature are getting nervous. The Latino population has grown from 28.6% of the overall state population in 2006 to 37.6%. This growth has led the state's politics to trend Democratic. Republicans need not worry about losing their majority in the state legislature, however, because that legislature enacted an extreme partisan gerrymander during the 2010 redistricting.

"Unfortunately for the Republicans, early polling shows likely Democratic nominee New York Governor Eliot Spitzer with a substantial lead in Texas over the soon-to-be Republican nominee South Dakota Senator John Thune. If the Democratic nominee carries Texas in the general election, he will have a 'lock' on the electoral college, as Democrats still dominate the Eastern seaboard, California, and Illinois.

"At the behest of Republican Party leaders, the state legislature passes a bill awarding its electoral votes to the winner of the national popular vote. The Republican Governor of Texas signs the bill into law."

"With the addition of Texas, enough states now participate for the NPV to take effect."[610]

---

[610] Gringer, David. 2008. Why the National Popular Vote plan is the wrong way to abolish the Electoral College. 108 *Columbia Law Review* 182. January 2008. Pages 219–220.

Gringer certainly makes a plausible case that demographic changes might cause Texas (with its 38 electoral votes) to become Democratic by 2020. He also makes a plausible case that a future Republican presidential candidate would probably find it difficult to assemble a majority in the Electoral College if the Republicans could not rely on Texas' formidable bloc of 38 electoral votes.

Gringer's hypothetical scenario about a state activating the National Popular Vote compact in mid-July for partisan advantage is, however, implausible for several reasons.

First, the National Popular Vote compact cannot be brought into effect at the spur of the moment. The compact governs the conduct of a particular presidential election only if it has been enacted (and, importantly, has taken effect) in states possessing 270 electoral votes on July 20 of the presidential election year.

Second, Gringer's hypothetical scenario is based on the existence of mid-year polling that is sufficiently persuasive to cause a state legislature and Governor to make a significant political decision before July 20 of the presidential election year.

It is virtually impossible to predict whether a particular presidential candidate is going to win the national popular vote—but not the electoral vote—immediately before Election Day, much less as early as July 20 of a presidential election year.

This point was illustrated in the week before Election Day in 2000, when most polls indicated that George W. Bush was poised to win the national popular vote—but not the electoral vote. Indeed, the Bush campaign was planning for just that eventuality.

As the *New York Daily News* reported on Wednesday November 2, 2000, in an article entitled "Bush [is] set to fight an Electoral College loss:"

> "Quietly, some of George W. Bush's advisers are preparing for the ultimate 'what if' scenario: What happens if Bush wins the popular vote for President, but loses the White House because Al Gore won the majority of electoral votes? . . ."

> "'The one thing we don't do is roll over,' says a Bush aide. 'We fight.'

> "How? The core of the emerging Bush strategy assumes a popular uprising, stoked by the Bushies themselves, of course.

> "In league with the campaign—which is preparing talking points about the Electoral College's essential unfairness—a massive talk-radio operation would be encouraged. 'We'd have ads, too,' says a Bush aide, 'and I think you can count on the media to fuel the thing big-time. Even papers that supported Gore might turn against him because the will of the people will have been thwarted.'

> "Local business leaders will be urged to lobby their customers, the clergy will be asked to speak up for the popular will and Team Bush will enlist as many Democrats as possible to scream as loud as they can. 'You think

'Democrats for Democracy' would be a catchy term for them?' asks a Bush adviser.

"The universe of people who would be targeted by this insurrection is small—the 538 currently anonymous folks called electors, people chosen by the campaigns and their state party organizations as a reward for their service over the years. . . .

"Enough of the electors could theoretically switch to Bush if they wanted to—if there was sufficient pressure on them to ratify the popular verdict."[611]

Nate Cohn wrote in 2012:

"There is a high evidentiary burden for demonstrating that any candidate holds a structural advantage in the Electoral College. The Electoral College almost always follows the popular vote, and **even when the popular vote winner fails to secure the necessary electoral votes, it isn't necessarily apparent in advance**. Heading into Election Night 2000, the fear was Gore winning the Electoral College and Bush winning the popular vote. The exact opposite happened only a few hours later. In an extremely close national election, deviations of only a few percentage points in the closest few states can complicate even the best gamed electoral scenarios."[612] [Emphasis added]

Third, presidential elections in which one candidate wins the popular vote—but not the electoral vote—are necessarily *close elections*. Tilden's 3% margin in 1876 was the largest difference in the national popular vote among the nation's four "wrong winner" elections (table 1.22). In 2000, the difference in the national popular vote between the two candidates was ½% (about a half million votes nationwide). Modest winning margins such as 3% are *inside* the margin of error of political polls.

An article on July 24, 2012 (four days after July 20), by Nate Silver in the *New York Times*, entitled "State and National Polls Tell Different Tales About State of Campaign"[613] reinforces the point. Silver pointed out that the *Real Clear Politics* average of national polls at the time gave President Obama a nationwide lead of 1.3%. However, at the same moment, Obama led by a mean of 3.5% in the *Real Clear Politics* averages for 10 battleground states (Ohio, Virginia, Florida, Pennsylvania, Colorado, Iowa, Nevada, Michigan, New Hampshire, and Wisconsin) that were considered (at the

---

[611] Kramer, Michael. Bush set to fight an electoral college loss: They're not only thinking the unthinkable, They're planning for it. *New York Daily News*. November 1, 2000. http://articles.nydailynews.com/2000-11-01/news/18145743_1_electoral-votes-popular-vote-bush-aide.

[612] Cohn, Nate. 2012. No, we don't have evidence of an Obama advantage in the Electoral College. *The New Republic*. June 27, 2012.

[613] Silver, Nate. State and national polls tell different tales about state of campaign. FiveThirtyEight column in *New York Times*. July 24, 2012.

time) to be most likely to determine the outcome of the 2012 election. Both the 1.3% margin and the 3.5% margin were *inside* the margin of error for most political polls (typically plus or minus 3% or 4%). It seems implausible that mid-year polls in 2020 showing 1.3% and 3.5% margins similar to the just-mentioned July 2012 polling would be sufficiently persuasive to cause Texas Republicans to "perniciously" enact the National Popular Vote compact.

Fourth, even if political polls had *no* margin of error, they merely reflect public opinion at the time they are taken. Many things can happen between July 20 and Election Day in November.

July 20 is three and a half months before the November presidential election. That date is well before the national nominating conventions of the major political parties, and it is well before the date when a party's (non-incumbent) vice-presidential choice is typically announced. The impression created by a party's national convention (particularly the keynote speech, nominating speeches, acceptance speeches, and the absence of divisive intra-party fighting), the choice of the vice-presidential candidate, the debates, the day-to-day conduct of the campaign are examples of the numerous post-July-20 events can significantly impact the eventual outcome in November.

In August 1988, Michael Dukakis led George H.W. Bush by 18% in national polls; however, Bush won on Election Day by an 8% national margin.

A June 1992 nationwide poll taken immediately before the Democratic National Convention showed that Bill Clinton had 25% support (with Perot having 39% support and incumbent President George H.W. Bush having 31%).[614] However, Bill Clinton took the lead immediately after his convention and retained the lead all the way to Election Day.

Fifth, as a practical matter of state legislative scheduling, a decision to enact the National Popular Vote compact would have to be made considerably earlier in the year than July 20. Winning approval of a new state law in a given state is a multi-step process in which each step is subject to numerous time-consuming delays.

The ninth clause of Article III of the compact provides:

> "This article shall govern the appointment of presidential electors in each member state in any year in which this agreement is, on July 20, **in effect** in states cumulatively possessing a majority of the electoral votes." [Emphasis added]

A new state law can be "in effect" by July 20 only if it has previously been
- approved by both houses of the state legislature,
- acquired the Governor's signature (or been passed by overriding the Governor's veto), and
- taken effect in accordance with the state's constitution schedule specifying when state laws take effect.

---

[614] The 1992 poll was cited in Stanley, Timothy. *Why Romney is stronger than he seems. CNN Election Center.* April 10, 2012.

Although procedures exist in each state legislature to accelerate the progress of a bill, these exceptional procedures can generally only be invoked by super-majorities. Given that the premise of Gringer's hypothetical scenario is that partisan advantage is a "pernicious" partisan motivation for the enactment of the National Popular Vote compact, the minority party in the legislature would oppose such efforts. In fact, the minority party would vigorously employ the numerous tools at its disposal to slow or block the bill. Taking the specific case of Texas mentioned in Gringer's article, Texas is one of four states with a two-thirds quorum in the legislature. Texas Republicans did not have a two-thirds majority in either chamber of the Texas legislature as of November 2012. Section 9.11.1 provides additional details on the difficulties associated with trying to pass legislation over the determined opposition of a legislature's minority.

Moreover, even if a new state law could be *instantly* enacted, most state constitutions provide for a significant delay between the time of the Governor's signature and the effective date of the newly enacted law (e.g., 60, 90, 120 days, in many cases, longer). The information in table 9.12 and the accompanying discussion in section 9.11.1 indicate that Gringer's hypothesized partisan maneuver would have to be executed *many months before* July 20 in most states.

In Texas, for example, new laws take effect 90 days after enactment. Thus, the National Popular Vote compact would have to be enacted by April 20, 2020, in order to be "in effect" by July 20, 2020. This 90-day delay can only be waived by a two-thirds vote of both houses of the legislature.

Sixth, there is an additional reason why Gringer's hypothetical scenario could not be executed in Texas even by a date as early as April 20, 2020. The Texas legislature only meets for a few months in *odd-numbered* years for passing general bills. Gringer's hypothetical scenario could be executed in Texas during the spring of 2019—that is, 18 months before the November 2020 presidential election. However, if the bill were not passed in the regular session in the odd-numbered year (2019), a special session would have to be called to consider the bill. If a special session were called in the even-numbered year (that is, 2020) for the purpose of passing an elections bill that is perceived to be of immediate partisan advantage to the Republican Party, Texas Democrats would fiercely oppose that bill. Given the two-thirds quorum in the Texas legislature, it would be impossible to pass the bill in the spring of 2020 or, indeed, any time after the legislature's regular session in the odd-numbered year (2019).

If this partisan maneuver were contemplated in a state possessing fewer electoral votes than Texas, the question would arise as to whether that state could alone make the difference.

Others have suggested an even less plausible hypothetical scenario, namely that a politically motivated state legislature might repeal the compact before July 20 of a presidential-election year based on mid-year polls indicating that its favored presidential candidate is poised to win the electoral vote—but not the popular vote. This hypothetical scenario is implausible for all the same reasons mentioned in connection with Gringer's hypothetical scenario involving Texas.

9.35. MYTH THAT NATIONAL POPULAR VOTE IS UNPOPULAR

9.35.1. MYTH: National Popular Vote is being imposed without the consent of the majority of Americans.

QUICK ANSWER:

- The National Popular Vote compact would go into effect when enacted by states possessing a majority of the votes in the Electoral College.
- The compact thus represents a majority of Americans using the metric established in the Constitution for representing the people in presidential elections, namely the Electoral College.
- Numerous polls conducted by different polling organizations over a number of years, using a variety of different wordings of questions, all report high levels of support for a national popular vote.

MORE DETAILED ANSWER:

Hans von Spakovsky has stated:

> "National Popular Vote Inc., . . . one of California's lesser-known advocacy organizations, want[s] to 'scratch off' the Electoral College—**without getting the consent of the majority of Americans.**"[615] [Emphasis added]

The National Popular Vote compact would go into effect when enacted by states possessing a majority of the votes in the Electoral College.

The compact would thus represent a majority of Americans using the very metric established in the Constitution for representing the people in presidential elections, namely the Electoral College.

Public opinion has supported nationwide popular election of the President for over six decades by overwhelming margins. Section 7.1 presents numerous polls conducted over a number of years by many different polling organizations, using a variety of different wordings of questions, and all of them report high levels of support for a national popular vote.

Recent state-level polls show a high level of public support for a national popular vote in battleground states, small states, Southern states, border states, and elsewhere.[616]

---

[615] Von Spakovsky, Hans A. Protecting Electoral College from popular vote. *Washington Times*. October 26, 2011.

[616] Detailed reports on the polls, including the cross-tabs, are available on the web site of National Popular Vote at http://www.nationalpopularvote.com/pages/polls.php.

- Alaska–70%,
- Arizona–67%,
- Arkansas–80%,
- California–70%,
- Colorado–68%,
- Connecticut–74%,
- Delaware–75%,
- District of Columbia–76%,
- Florida–78%,
- Kentucky–80%,
- Idaho–77%,
- Iowa–75%,
- Maine–77%,
- Massachusetts–73%,
- Michigan–73%,
- Minnesota 75%,
- Mississippi–77%,
- Missouri–70%,
- Montana–72%,
- Nebraska–67%,

- Nevada–72%,
- New Hampshire–69%,
- New Mexico–76%,
- New York–79%,
- North Carolina–74%,
- Ohio–70%,
- Oklahoma–81%,
- Oregon–76%,
- Pennsylvania–78%,
- Rhode Island–74%,
- South Carolina–71%,
- South Dakota–75%,
- Tennessee–83%,
- Utah–70%,
- Vermont–75%,
- Virginia–74%,
- Washington–77%,
- West Virginia–81%,
- Wisconsin–71%, and
- Wyoming–69%.

9.36. MYTH ABOUT THE WEATHER

9.36.1. MYTH: The state-by-state winner-take-all rule minimizes the effects of hurricanes and bad weather.

QUICK ANSWER:
- Under the current state-by-state winner-take-all rule, a small difference in turnout (caused by bad weather or any other factor) in one part of a closely divided battleground state can potentially switch the electoral-vote outcome in that state (and hence the national outcome of the presidential election). In contrast, a localized reduction in turnout is unlikely to materially affect the outcome of a nationwide vote for President.
- Bad weather regularly affects the outcome of elections—both state and federal. A study of past weather conditions indicates that bad weather reversed the statewide outcome for President in Florida in 2000 (and hence the national outcome).
- Neither the National Popular Vote compact nor the winner-take-all rule can do anything about the weather; however, a national popular vote for President

would reduce the likelihood that bad weather could reverse the outcome of a presidential election.

MORE DETAILED ANSWER:

It is often said that everybody talks about the weather, but nobody does anything about it. Neither the National Popular Vote compact nor the winner-take-all rule can do anything about the weather. However, a national popular vote would reduce the likelihood that bad weather could actually change the overall outcome of a presidential election.

Thaddeus Dobracki has stated that the current state-by-state winner-take-all method of electing the President:

> "negates the effect of exceptionally high or low turn-out in a state by giving the state a fix[ed] number of electors. For example, if bad weather, such as a hurricane, were to hit North Carolina, then instead of losing influence because of a low turnout, that state would still get its normal allocation of Electoral College votes."[617]

The state-by-state winner-take-all rule does indeed ensure that a state affected by turnout-depressing weather (such as a hurricane) will nonetheless cast its *full number* of electoral votes in the Electoral College. However, the winner-take-all rule can result in those electoral votes being cast in a way that is unrepresentative of normal voter sentiment in the state.

Under the current state-by-state winner-take-all rule, a small difference in turnout (caused by bad weather or any other factor) in one part of a closely divided battleground state can potentially reverse the electoral-vote outcome in that state (and hence the national outcome of the presidential election). In contrast, a localized reduction in turnout is unlikely to materially affect the outcome of a nationwide vote for President.

Bad weather regularly affects the outcome of both state and federal elections.

John F. Kennedy might have received a far larger majority of the popular vote in the then-battleground states of Illinois and Michigan had the weather been better in Detroit and Chicago on Election Day in 1960. Theodore White wrote in *The Making of the President 1968*:

> "The weather was clear all across Massachusetts and New England, perfect for voting as far as the crest of the Alleghenies. But from Michigan through Illinois and the Northern Plains states it was cloudy: **rain in Detroit and Chicago**, light snow falling in some states on the approaches of the Rockies."[618] [Emphasis added]

---

[617] Dobracki, Thaddeus. *The Morning Call*. September 21, 2012. http://discussions.mcall.com/20/allnews/mc-electoral-college-madonna-young-yv–20120920/10?page=2.

[618] White, Theodore H. 1969. *The Making of the President 1968*. New York, NY: Atheneum Publishers. Page 7.

Table 9.46. VOTE OF NORTH CAROLINA IN 17 COASTAL COUNTIES IN 2008

COASTAL COUNTY	MCCAIN	OBAMA	REPUBLICAN MARGIN	DEMOCRATIC MARGIN
Currituck	7,234	3,737	3,497	–
Camden	3,140	1,597	1,543	–
Pasquotank	7,778	10,272	–	2,494
Perquimans	3,678	2,772	906	–
Chowan	3,773	3,688	85	–
Bertie	3,376	6,365	–	2,989
Washington	2,670	3,748	–	1,078
Tyrrell	960	933	27	–
Dare	9,745	8,074	1,671	–
Hyde	1,212	1,241	–	29
Beaufort	13,460	9,454	4,006	–
Pamlico	3,823	2,838	985	–
Carteret	23,131	11,130	12,001	–
Onslow	30,278	19,499	10,779	–
Pender	13,618	9,907	3,711	–
New Hanover	50,544	49,145	1,399	–
Brunswick	30,753	21,331	9,422	–
Total	**209,173**	**165,731**	**50,032**	**6,590**

Similarly, bad weather in upstate New York, downstate Illinois, western Michigan, and southern Ohio frequently affects which candidate carries the state in a federal or state election.

A turnout-depressing weather event on North Carolina's hurricane-prone coast would adversely affect the Republican Party under the winner-take-all rule if it occurred on Election Day. North Carolina was a closely divided battleground state in 2008 and 2012. The disposition of all of North Carolina's electoral votes was decided in 2008 by President Obama's statewide plurality of only 14,177.

Table 9.46 shows that 14 of the 17 counties on North Carolina's Atlantic coast voted heavily Republican in the 2008 presidential election. As can been seen from the table, John McCain built up a net 43,433-vote margin from the state's 17 coastal counties. Thus, a hurricane hitting North Carolina's coast (causing disruption and evacuations) could easily shift the state's potentially critical 15 electoral votes from one party to the other (potentially resulting in the state's electoral votes being cast in a way that is unrepresentative of voter sentiment in the state).

There was considerable speculation that Hurricane Sandy (which made landfall in Pennsylvania a week before the November 6, 2012, presidential election) might reduce voter turnout in the heavily Democratic city of Philadelphia (in the eastern part of the state). In contrast, the Republican central part of the state (often called the "T" area) is much farther from the Atlantic Ocean. Lower turnout in Philadelphia had the potential of flipping the statewide plurality from Democrat Barack Obama to Republican Mitt Romney (and thereby flipping the state's 20 potentially critical electoral votes).

Such an outcome would not have been reflective of normal voter sentiment in Pennsylvania as indicated by virtually every statewide poll before Election Day in 2012[619] and the fact that the Democrats have carried Pennsylvania in every presidential election since 1992.

In a state such as Florida, the political effect of a hurricane would depend on the location of the hurricane's landfall.

Tampa is in Hillsborough County on the state's west coast. Tampa was the site of the 2012 Republican National Convention. That convention was, in fact, disrupted by a hurricane (Issac) that only minimally impacted Florida's southeastern coast. In the November 2000 presidential election, George W. Bush received 180,794 votes in Hillsborough County to Al Gore's 169,576 votes—giving Bush a county-wide margin of 11,218 votes. In 2000, Bush won Florida by 537 votes out of 5,963,110 votes. If a hurricane had even slightly depressed turnout in Hillsborough County on Election Day in November 2000, 100% of Florida's electoral votes would have gone to Al Gore (giving Al Gore all of Florida's 25 electoral votes and making him President).

Conversely, if bad weather were to depress turnout in heavily Democratic counties (such as Miami-Dade, Broward, and Palm Beach) in southeastern Florida, the Republicans would benefit.

There is evidence that the weather has affected the outcome of presidential elections under the current state-by-state winner-take-all system. For example, an article entitled "The Weather and the Election" from the Oklahoma Weather Lab at the University of Oklahoma commented on a 2007 county-by-county study of the weather in the *Journal of Politics*:

> "Gomez et al. collected meteorological data recorded at weather stations across the lower 48 United States for presidential election days between 1948 and 2000, and interpolated these data to get rain and snowfall totals for each election day for each county in the entire nation. They then compared the rain and snowfall data with voter turnout for each county, and performed statistical regressions to determine whether or not rain and snow (bad weather) had a negative impact on voter turnout.

> "What they found was that **each inch of rain experienced on election day drove down voter turnout by an average of just under 1%**, while each inch of snow knocked 0.5% off turnout. Though the effect of snow is less on a 'per inch' basis, since multiple-inch snowfall totals are far more common than multiple-inch rainfall events, we can conclude that **snow is likely to have a bigger negative impact on voter turnout**.

---

[619] See the tabulation of statewide polls found at the web site using the Gott-Colley median method of analyzing poll statistics at http://www.colleyrankings.com/election2012/.

"Furthermore, Gomez et al. noted that when bad weather did suppress voter turnout, it tended to do so in favor of the Republican candidate, to the tune of around 2.5% for each inch of rainfall above normal. In fact, when they simulated the 14 presidential elections between 1948 and 2000 with sunny conditions nationwide, they found two instances in which **bad weather likely changed the electoral college outcome—once in North Carolina in 1992, and once in Florida in 2000. The latter change is particularly notable, as it would have resulted in Al Gore rather than George Bush winning the presidential election that year.**"[620],[621] [Emphasis added]

Fortunately, hurricane Sandy did not hit the northeast on Election Day. Instead, it arrived a week before Election Day. This is a reminder that a convergence of unlikely events would be needed to materially affect a presidential election, namely the unlikely event of a major hurricane combined with the unlikely event of a major hurricane on Election Day.

What can be said about hurricane Sandy is that it probably impacted the 2012 presidential election in terms of its effect on political discourse in the week prior to Election Day. As former Mississippi Governor Haley Barbour (R) said:

"The hurricane is what broke Romney's momentum. I don't think there's any question about it. Any day that the news media is not talking about jobs and the economy, taxes and spending, deficit and debt, 'ObamaCare' and energy, is a good day for Barack Obama."[622]

Note that the potential effects of bad weather on elections are decreasing from year to year because of the increasing use of mail-in voting, absentee voting, and early voting. In 2012, 100% of the voting was done by mail in Washington state and Oregon. In numerous states, a substantial fraction of a state's vote now comes from absentee voting and early voting. In California, for example, 51% of the vote in the November 2012 presidential election was cast by mail.

Nonetheless, the fact that a hurricane (such as Sandy) could hit on Election Day is a reminder that weather can, and does, affect the outcome of elections.

---

[620] The weather and the election. 2008. Oklahoma Weather Lab at the University of Oklahoma. http://hoot. metr.ou.edu/archive/story&docId=21. See also http://www.thorntonweather.com/blog/local-news/will-the-weather-determine-the-next-president/. See section 9.31.13 for a quotation from the Gomez article from the August 2007 issue of *Journal of Politics*.

[621] Brad T. Gomez, Brad T.; Hansford, Thomas G.; and Krause, George A. 2007. The Republicans should pray for rain: weather, turnout, and voting in U.S. Presidential Elections. *The Journal of Politics*. Volume 69, number 3. August 2007. Pages 649–663.

[622] Herb, Jeremy. Former Gov. Barbour: Hurricane Sandy broke Romney's momentum. *The Hill*. November 4, 2012.

9.37. MYTH ABOUT OUT-OF-STATE PRESIDENTIAL ELECTORS

9.37.1. MYTH: The National Popular Vote compact will result in out-of-state presidential electors.

QUICK ANSWER:

- The possibility of out-of-staters serving as presidential electors is based on the unlikely scenario that a third-party candidate wins the most popular votes nationwide without being on the ballot in all 50 states combined with the politically preposterous prediction that a third-party President-Elect would gratuitously offend people in some state by appointing non-resident presidential electors.
- If anyone considers the hypothesized scenario to be a significant potential problem, the states have ample constitutional authority to prevent it by simply establishing residency requirements for their presidential electors.
- Even if the hypothesized scenario were to occur, the National Popular Vote compact would nonetheless have delivered precisely its advertised result namely, the election of the presidential candidate who received the most popular votes in all 50 states and the District of Columbia.

MORE DETAILED ANSWER:

Tara Ross discussed a hypothetical third-party candidacy of Texas Congressman Ron Paul when the Vermont legislature was debating the National Popular Vote bill:

> "Vermont probably did not nominate a slate of electors for Paul because he was not on its ballot. NPV's compact offers a solution, but it is doubtful that voters in Vermont will like it. Paul would be entitled to personally appoint the three electors who will represent Vermont in the Electoral College vote. In all likelihood, he would select Texans to represent Vermont."[623]

Ross is referring to a back-up provision in the National Popular Vote compact that provides a procedure to fill a vacancy in the unlikely situation that a particular political party in a particular state fails to nominate the exact number of presidential electors to which it is entitled in a particular state.

The seventh clause of Article III of the compact provides:

> "If, for any reason, the number of presidential electors nominated in a member state in association with the national popular vote winner is less than or greater than that state's number of electoral votes, the presidential candidate on the presidential slate that has been designated as the national popular vote winner shall have the power to nominate the presidential

---

[623] Written testimony submitted by Tara Ross to the Vermont Committee on Government Operations. February 9, 2011.

electors for that state and that state's presidential elector certifying official shall certify the appointment of such nominees."

This back-up procedure is modeled after the method of nominating presidential electors that is routinely used today in Pennsylvania in all elections. Under Section 2878 of the Pennsylvania election code, each presidential nominee directly nominates the presidential electors who will run in association with the nominee's presidential slate in Pennsylvania. Section 6.3.2 contains a more detailed discussion of this provision.

It is, of course, unlikely that a third-party presidential candidate (such as Ron Paul) could win the national popular vote without being on the ballot in all 50 states. Serious candidates for President qualify for the ballot in all 50 states. Ross Perot was on the ballot in all 50 states in both 1992 and 1996. John Anderson was on the ballot in all 50 states in 1980. The Libertarian Party got its presidential nominee on the ballot in all 50 states in 1980, 1992, and 1996. Lenora Fulani, the nominee of the New Alliance Party, was on ballot in all 50 states in 1988. Ralph Nader (who received only about ½% of the national popular vote in 2008) was on the ballot in 45 states.

It is especially unlikely that a third-party candidate would fail to get the 1,000 signatures required to get on the ballot in Vermont (which, like most small states, has especially low requirements for ballot access).

In the unlikely event that a third-party candidate wins the Presidency without being on the ballot in all 50 states, that President-Elect would not want to begin his Presidency by gratuitously offending Vermont by appointing Texans as his choices for the position of presidential elector in Vermont. President-Elect Ron Paul could—and certainly would—find three supporters in Vermont to serve as his presidential electors in Vermont.

There is historical evidence about how real-world politicians would behave in this situation. Under existing law in Pennsylvania, *every* presidential candidate, in *every* election, directly chooses *every* presidential elector in Pennsylvania. Needless to say, no presidential candidate has ever chosen a Texan or any other out-of-state person for the position of presidential elector in Pennsylvania. Indeed, it would be politically preposterous for a presidential candidate to insult Pennsylvania gratuitously by naming out-of-staters for the ceremonial position of presidential elector. It would be even more preposterous for someone who had just won the national popular vote (and was about to become President and face the task of unifying the country) to insult a state gratuitously.

Moreover, if a state were to become concerned about the possibility of out-of-state presidential electors, it could simply enact legislation providing residency requirements for its presidential electors.

Finally, it should be noted that the sole job of a presidential elector—under both the current system and the National Popular Vote compact—is to appear in the state capital in mid-December and spend about 15 minutes casting his vote for the candidate for whom everyone expects him or her to vote. Even in the unlikely event that a third-party candidate were to win the national popular vote, were to do so without being on the ballot in every state, and then were to make politically offensive appointments to the ceremonial position of presidential elector, the practical result would still be that the National Popular Vote compact would have delivered precisely its advertised result, namely the election of the presidential candidate who received the most popular votes in all 50 states and the District of Columbia.

9.38. MYTH ABOUT THE FRENCH PRESIDENTIAL ELECTION SYSTEM

9.38.1. MYTH: National Popular Vote seeks to import the flawed French presidential election system into the United States.

QUICK ANSWER:

* The National Popular Vote compact would not import France's presidential election system into the United States.
* The 2002 French presidential election forced voters to choose between two right-wing candidates in the general election because the left-wing candidates were eliminated in France's "top two" multi-party primary.
* The existing American system for nominating presidential candidates does not have the flaws of the French system, and, in any case, the National Popular Vote compact would not affect the nominating process.

MORE DETAILED ANSWER:

Professor Norman R. Williams of Willamette University incorrectly equates the National Popular Vote compact with France's flawed "top two" multi-party primary system for nominating presidential candidates.

> "The French President is elected on a nationwide popular vote of the sort that the NPVC seeks to introduce in the U.S."[624]

Williams goes on to criticize the 2002 French presidential election.

The French presidential election system starts with a *multi-party* primary in which candidates *from different parties* are forced to compete directly against each other for a spot in the final general election. The "top two" candidates from the primary then compete against each other in the general election.

In 2002, the primary in France included two prominent right-wing candidates, namely the conservative Gaullist Mayor of Paris Jacques Chirac and the ultra-conservative Jean-Marie Le Pen. The primary also included a multiplicity of prominent left-wing candidates of whom the most popular was Prime Minister Lionel Jospin.

---

[624] Williams, Norman R. Reforming the Electoral College: Federalism, majoritarianism, and the perils of sub-constitutional change. 100 *Georgetown Law Journal* 173. November 2011. Page 204.

In previous French presidential elections conducted under the Fifth Republic's constitution (adopted in 1958), one right-wing candidate and one left-wing candidate had always emerged from this multi-party "top two" primary system. Accordingly, it was widely expected that the conservative Chirac and leftist Jospin would run against one another in the 2002 general election.

However, because an unusually large number of left-wing candidates entered the primary (including a Green, an independent socialist, a Trotskyist, and others), the left-wing vote in the primary was fragmented while the conservative vote was divided only two ways. In the primary, the conservative Chirac received 5.6 million votes; the ultra-conservative Le Pen received 4.8 million votes; and leftist Jospin trailed with 4.6 million votes. That is, the "top two" candidates were both conservatives.

The result was a general election in which voters were forced to choose between conservative Chirac and an ultra-conservative Le Pen. Left-wing voters (who would certainly have enthusiastically voted for Jospin over Chirac) were forced to vote for one of the two conservatives. Chirac won with 82% of the vote in the general election.

Williams (and virtually every other observer) has justifiably criticized the French presidential election system for denying the voters any real choice in the 2002 general election.

However, contrary to the impression created by Williams, the National Popular Vote compact would not import the egregiously flawed features of the French multi-party primary system into the United States.

First, the existing American system of nominating presidential candidates is not a "top two" *multi-party* primary such as used in France.

Second, the National Popular Vote compact would not affect the existing American system of nominating presidential candidates.

Under the existing system for nominating presidential candidates in the United States, one Democratic nominee emerges after competing with other Democrats in primaries (and caucuses), and one Republican candidate emerges after competing with fellow Republicans. Third-party nominees are similarly nominated in competitive processes in which they compete with other members of their own party for their own party's nomination.

Then, after the nominating process is over, the eventual Democratic nominee competes in the November general election against the eventual Republican nominee (and any third-party nominees). Under the existing system for nominating presidential candidates in the United States, there is no possibility that the voters would face a choice such as that faced by French voters in 2002 (namely two Republicans but no Democrat or no third-party alternatives in the November general election).

Note that Louisiana has long used a "top two" multi-party system that is virtually identical to the French system (the so-called "jungle" primary). Washington state and California recently adopted the "top two" approach for their state elections. The "top two" multi-party primary system regularly produces situations similar to the

2002 French presidential elections. For example, the June 2012 primary in California's newly created 31st congressional district included two prominent Republicans (Congressman Gary G. Miller and outgoing State Senate Republican leader Bob Dutton) and multiple Democrats (including San Bernardino Council member Pete Aguilar). Because of the fragmentation of the Democratic vote, the two Republicans emerged from the "top two" primary as the district's candidates for the November 2012 general election (with Aguilar running third with 23% of the vote). Even though the district is heavily Democratic, the district's voters were forced to choose between two Republicans (but no Democrats and no third-party candidates) in the November general election.

Also note that the multiplicity of political parties in France existed before the 1958 Constitution (as opposed to being created by it). Prior to 1958, France had a parliamentary system in which the Prime Minister was selected by parliament. The 1958 Constitution created a President elected in a nationwide popular election. The 1958 Constitution attempted to accommodate the country's pre-existing multiplicity of parties by adopting the "top two" multi-party primary.

In summary, the National Popular Vote compact would not import France's presidential election system into the United States. Instead, it applies the method long used to fill almost every other public office in the United States to the election of the President.

9.39. MYTHS ABOUT UNINTENDED CONSEQUENCES

9.39.1. MYTH: There could be unintended consequences of a nationwide vote for President.

QUICK ANSWER:

- Change can have unintended and unexpected *desirable* consequences just as easily as it can have undesirable consequences.
- The consequences of inaction are known and *undesirable* in the case of the current system of electing the President.
- When the states switched to direct popular election of Governors in the late 18th and early 19th centuries, there were no significant unintended or unexpected undesirable consequences.
- If some undesirable unexpected consequence materializes, or some adjustment becomes advisable in the National Popular Vote compact, state legislation may be repealed or amended more easily than a federal constitutional amendment.

MORE DETAILED ANSWER:

One of the generic arguments against *any* proposed change is that there might be unintended or unexpected consequences.

The attractiveness of this generic argument is that opponents need not identify any specific consequence, and therefore no thoughtful discussion is possible.

Nonetheless, there are several responses to this generic argument:

(1) Change can have unintended and unexpected *desirable* consequences just as easily as it can have undesirable consequences.

(2) No significant unexpected undesirable consequences surfaced when an analogous action was taken in a closely related situation.

(3) Reversing the proposed action would be relatively easy if there were significant unexpected undesirable consequences.

(4) The consequence of inaction is that the known shortcomings of the existing system will not be corrected.

Concerning item (1), opponents do not specify what the consequences might be. Hence, we cannot ascertain whether these consequences are desirable or undesirable.

Concerning item (2), there certainly were no significant unexpected undesirable consequences when the states switched to direct popular election of their chief executives. In 1787, only Connecticut, Massachusetts, New Hampshire, Rhode Island, and Vermont conducted popular elections for the office of Governor.[625] During the late 18th and early 19th centuries, the states switched, one-by-one, to direct popular election of Governors. Today, 100% of the states elect their Governors by direct popular vote. After over 5,000 direct popular elections for Governor in over two centuries, no state has ever decided to eliminate its direct popular election for Governor, and there is virtually no editorial, academic, legislative, or public criticism of direct election of Governors.

Concerning item (3), the National Popular Vote compact is state legislation. If some undesirable unexpected consequence materializes or some adjustment becomes advisable, an interstate compact may be repealed or amended more easily than a federal constitutional amendment.

Concerning item (4), the consequences of inaction are known and undesirable.

- **Four out of five states and four out of five voters are ignored in Presidential Elections**. One of the consequences of the current winner-take-all rule (i.e., awarding all of a state's electoral votes to the presidential candidate who receives the most popular votes in each separate state) is that presidential candidates do not expend significant time, effort, or money in states in which they are comfortably ahead or hopelessly behind. Presidential candidates ignore such states because they do not receive additional or fewer electoral votes based on the size of the margin by which they win or lose a state (as discussed in section 1.2.1).

- **The Current System Does Not Reliably Reflect the Nationwide Popular Vote**. The state-by-state winner-take-all rule makes it possible for a candidate

---

[625] Dubin, Michael J. 2003. *United States Gubernatorial Elections 1776–1860*. Jefferson, NC: McFarland & Company. Page xx.

to win the Presidency without winning the most popular votes nationwide. This has occurred in four of the nation's 57 presidential elections between 1789 and 2012—1 in 14 (as detailed in section 1.2.2). In the past six decades, there have been six presidential elections in which a shift of a relatively small number of votes in one or two states would have elected (and, of course, in 2000, did elect) a presidential candidate who lost the popular vote nationwide (as discussed in section 1.2.2).

- **Not Every Vote Is Equal.** The state-by-state winner-take-all rule creates variations of 1000-to-1 and more in the weight of a vote (as detailed in section 1.2.3).

9.40. MYTH ABOUT PERFECTION

9.40.1. MYTH: The National Popular Vote compact is not perfect.

QUICK ANSWER:
- The test of whether the National Popular Vote compact should be adopted is whether it is an improvement over the current system of electing the President—not whether it is perfect.

MORE DETAILED ANSWER:

The authors believe that their responses in this book to the numerous myths about the National Popular Vote compact establish that the compact would address the short-comings of the current state-by-state winner-take-all method of awarding electoral votes, while handling conjectured adverse scenarios in a manner that is equal to, or superior to, the current system.

There is, however, no need to address the philosophical question as to whether the National Popular Vote compact is perfect. The test of whether the National Popular Vote compact should be adopted is whether it is a significant improvement over the current system of electing the President—not whether it is perfect. The authors of this book believe that they have made the case that the National Popular Vote compact is a significant improvement over the current system because it would remedy the current system's three major shortcomings, namely

- Four out of five states and four out of five voters are ignored in presidential campaigns under the current system (as discussed in section 1.2.1);
- The current system does not reliably reflect the nationwide popular vote (as discussed in section 1.2.2); and
- Every vote is not equal under the current system (as discussed in section 1.2.3).

10 | Epilogue

The epilogue to this book will be written by the people, the state legislatures, and the Congress as they consider the proposed "Agreement Among the States to Elect the President by National Popular Vote" described in this book.

APPENDIX A: U.S. CONSTITUTIONAL PROVISIONS ON PRESIDENTIAL ELECTIONS

Article II, Section 1, Clause 1

The executive Power shall be vested in a President of the United States of America. He shall hold his Office during the Term of four Years, and, together with the Vice President, chosen for the same Term, be elected, as follows

Article II, Section 1, Clause 2

Each State shall appoint, in such Manner as the Legislature thereof may direct, a Number of Electors, equal to the whole Number of Senators and Representatives to which the State may be entitled in the Congress: but no Senator or Representative, or Person holding an Office of Trust or Profit under the United States, shall be appointed an Elector.

Article II, Section 1, Clause 3

The Electors shall meet in their respective States, and vote by Ballot for two Persons, of whom one at least shall not be an Inhabitant of the same State with themselves. And they shall make a List of all the Persons voted for, and of the Number of Votes for each; which List they shall sign and certify, and transmit sealed to the Seat of the Government of the United States, directed to the President of the Senate. The President of the Senate shall, in the Presence of the Senate and House of Representatives, open all the Certificates, and the Votes shall then be counted. The Person having the greatest Number of Votes shall be the President, if such Number be a Majority of the whole Number of Electors appointed; and if there be more than one who have such Majority, and have an equal Number of Votes, then the House of Representatives shall immediately chuse by Ballot one of them for President; and if no Person have a Majority, then from the five highest on the List the said House shall in like Manner chuse the President. But in chusing the President, the Votes shall be taken by States, the Representation from each State having one Vote; A quorum for this Purpose shall consist of a Member or Members from two thirds of the States, and a Majority of all the States shall be necessary to a Choice. In every Case, after the Choice of the President, the Person having the greatest Number of Votes of the Electors shall be the Vice President. But if there should remain two or more who have equal Votes, the Senate shall chuse from them by Ballot the Vice President.

Article II, Section 1, Clause 4

The Congress may determine the Time of chusing the Electors, and the Day on which they shall give their Votes; which Day shall be the same throughout the United States.

12th Amendment

The Electors shall meet in their respective states, and vote by ballot for President and Vice-President, one of whom, at least, shall not be an inhabitant of the same state with themselves; they shall name in their ballots the person voted for as President, and in distinct ballots the person voted for as Vice-President, and they shall make distinct lists of all persons voted for as President, and of all persons voted for as Vice-President, and of the number of votes for each, which lists they shall sign and certify, and transmit sealed to the seat of the government of the United States, directed to the President of the Senate;--The President of the Senate shall, in the presence of the Senate and House of Representatives, open all the certificates and the votes shall then be counted;--The person having the greatest number of votes for President, shall be the President, if such number be a majority of the whole number of Electors appointed; and if no person have such majority, then from the persons having the highest numbers not exceeding three on the list of those voted for as President, the House of Representatives shall choose immediately, by ballot, the President. But in choosing the President, the votes shall be taken by states, the representation from each state having one vote; a quorum for this purpose shall consist of a member or members from two-thirds of the states, and a majority of all the states shall be necessary to a choice. And if the House of Representatives shall not choose a President whenever the right of choice shall devolve upon them, before the fourth day of March next following, then the Vice-President shall act as President, as in the case of the death or other constitutional disability of the President. The person having the greatest number of votes as Vice-President, shall be the Vice-President, if such number be a majority of the whole number of Electors appointed, and if no person have a majority, then from the two highest numbers on the list, the Senate shall choose the Vice-President; a quorum for the purpose shall consist of two-thirds of the whole number of Senators, and a majority of the whole number shall be necessary to a choice. But no person constitutionally ineligible to the office of President shall be eligible to that of Vice-President of the United States.

14th Amendment—Sections 2 and 3

Section 2. Representatives shall be apportioned among the several States according to their respective numbers, counting the whole number of persons in each State, excluding Indians not taxed. But when the right to vote at any election for the choice of electors for President and Vice President of the United States, Representatives in Congress, the Executive and Judicial officers of a State, or the members of the Legislature thereof, is denied to any of the male inhabitants of such State, being twenty-one years of age, and citizens of the United States, or in any way abridged, except for participation in rebellion, or other crime, the basis of representation therein shall be reduced in the proportion which the number of such male citizens shall bear to the whole number of male citizens twenty-one years of age in such State.

Section 3. No person shall be a Senator or Representative in Congress, or elector of President and Vice President, or hold any office, civil or military, under the United States, or under any State, who, having previously taken an oath, as a member of Congress, or as an officer of the United States, or as a member of any State legislature, or as an executive or judicial officer of any State, to support the Constitution of the United States, shall have engaged in insurrection or rebellion against the same, or given aid or comfort to the enemies thereof. But Congress may by a vote of two-thirds of each House, remove such disability.

15th Amendment—Section 1

Section 1. The right of citizens of the United States to vote shall not be denied or abridged by the United States or by any State on account of race, color, or previous condition of servitude.

19th Amendment

The right of citizens of the United States to vote shall not be denied or abridged by the United States or by any State on account of sex.

Congress shall have power to enforce this article by appropriate legislation.

20th Amendment—Sections 1–5

Section 1. The terms of the President and Vice President shall end at noon on the 20th day of January, and the terms of Senators and Representatives at noon on the 3d day of January, of the years in which such terms would have ended if this article had not been ratified; and the terms of their successors shall then begin.

Section 2. The Congress shall assemble at least once in every year, and such meeting shall begin at noon on the 3d day of January, unless they shall by law appoint a different day.

Section 3. If, at the time fixed for the beginning of the term of the President, the President elect shall have died, the Vice President elect shall become President. If a President shall not have been chosen before the time fixed for the beginning of his term, or if the President elect shall have failed to qualify, then the Vice President elect shall act as President until a President shall have qualified; and the Congress may by law provide for the case wherein neither a President elect nor a Vice President elect shall have qualified, declaring who shall then act as President, or the manner in which one who is to act shall be selected, and such person shall act accordingly until a President or Vice President shall have qualified.

Section 4. The Congress may by law provide for the case of the death of any of the persons from whom the House of Representatives may choose a President whenever the right of choice shall have devolved upon them, and for the case of the death of any of the persons from whom the Senate may choose a Vice President whenever the right of choice shall have devolved upon them.

Section 5. Sections 1 and 2 shall take effect on the 15th day of October following the ratification of this article.

22nd Amendment—Section 1

Section 1. No person shall be elected to the office of the President more than twice, and no person who has held the office of President, or acted as President, for more than two years of a term to which some other person was elected President shall be elected to the office of the President more than once. But this Article shall not apply to any person holding the office of President when this Article was proposed by the Congress, and shall not prevent any person who may be holding the office of President, or acting as President, during the term within which this Article becomes operative from holding the office of President or acting as President during the remainder of such term.

23rd Amendment

Section 1. The District constituting the seat of government of the United States shall appoint in such manner as the Congress may direct:

A number of electors of President and Vice President equal to the whole number of Senators and Representatives in Congress to which the District would be entitled if it were a state, but in no event more than the least populous state; they shall be in addition to those appointed by the states, but they shall be considered, for the purposes of the election of President and Vice President, to be electors appointed by a state; and they shall meet in the District and perform such duties as provided by the twelfth article of amendment.

Section 2. The Congress shall have power to enforce this article by appropriate legislation.

24th Amendment

Section 1. The right of citizens of the United States to vote in any primary or other election for President or Vice President, for electors for President or Vice President, or for Senator or Representative in Congress, shall not be denied or abridged by the United States or any state by reason of failure to pay any poll tax or other tax.

Section 2. The Congress shall have power to enforce this article by appropriate legislation.

25th Amendment

Section 1. In case of the removal of the President from office or of his death or resignation, the Vice President shall become President.

Section 2. Whenever there is a vacancy in the office of the Vice President, the President shall nominate a Vice President who shall take office upon confirmation by a majority vote of both Houses of Congress.

Section 3. Whenever the President transmits to the President pro tempore of the Senate and the Speaker of the House of Representatives his written declaration that he is unable to discharge the powers and duties of his office, and until he transmits to them a written declaration to the contrary, such powers and duties shall be discharged by the Vice President as Acting President.

Section 4. Whenever the Vice President and a majority of either the principal officers of the executive departments or of such other body as Congress may by law provide, transmit to the President pro tempore of the Senate and the Speaker of the

House of Representatives their written declaration that the President is unable to discharge the powers and duties of his office, the Vice President shall immediately assume the powers and duties of the office as Acting President.

Thereafter, when the President transmits to the President pro tempore of the Senate and the Speaker of the House of Representatives his written declaration that no inability exists, he shall resume the powers and duties of his office unless the Vice President and a majority of either the principal officers of the executive department or of such other body as Congress may by law provide, transmit within four days to the President pro tempore of the Senate and the Speaker of the House of Representatives their written declaration that the President is unable to discharge the powers and duties of his office. Thereupon Congress shall decide the issue, assembling within forty-eight hours for that purpose if not in session. If the Congress, within twenty-one days after receipt of the latter written declaration, or, if Congress is not in session, within twenty-one days after Congress is required to assemble, determines by two-thirds vote of both Houses that the President is unable to discharge the powers and duties of his office, the Vice President shall continue to discharge the same as Acting President; otherwise, the President shall resume the powers and duties of his office.

26th Amendment

Section 1. The right of citizens of the United States, who are eighteen years of age or older, to vote shall not be denied or abridged by the United States or by any State on account of age.

Section 2. The Congress shall have the power to enforce this article by appropriate legislation.

APPENDIX B: FEDERAL LAW ON PRESIDENTIAL ELECTIONS

UNITED STATES CODE
TITLE 3, CHAPTER 1. PRESIDENTIAL ELECTIONS AND VACANCIES

Time of appointing electors

§1. The electors of President and Vice President shall be appointed, in each State, on the Tuesday next after the first Monday in November, in every fourth year succeeding every election of a President and Vice President.

Failure to make choice on prescribed day

§2. Whenever any State has held an election for the purpose of choosing electors, and has failed to make a choice on the day prescribed by law, the electors may be appointed on a subsequent day in such a manner as the legislature of such State may direct.

Number of electors

§3. The number of electors shall be equal to the number of Senators and Representatives to which the several States are by law entitled at the time when the President and Vice President to be chosen come into office; except, that where no apportionment of Representatives has been made after any enumeration, at the time of choosing electors, the number of electors shall be according to the then existing apportionment of Senators and Representatives.

Vacancies in electoral college

§4. Each State may, by law, provide for the filling of any vacancies which may occur in its college of electors when such college meets to give its electoral vote.

Determination of controversy as to appointment of electors

§5. If any State shall have provided, by laws enacted prior to the day fixed for the appointment of the electors, for its final determination of any controversy or contest concerning the appointment of all or any of the electors of such State, by judicial or other methods or procedures, and such determination shall have been made at least six days before the time fixed for the meeting of the electors, such determination made pursuant to such law so existing on said day, and made at least six days prior to said time of meeting of the electors, shall be conclusive, and shall govern in the counting of the electoral votes as provided in the Constitution, and as hereinafter regulated, so far as the ascertainment of the electors appointed by such State is concerned.

Credentials of electors; transmission to archivist of the United States and to Congress; public inspection

§6. It shall be the duty of the executive of each State, as soon as practicable after the conclusion of the appointment of the electors in such State by the final ascertainment, under and in pursuance of the laws of such State providing for such ascertainment, to communicate by registered mail under the seal of the State to the Archivist of the United States a certificate of such ascertainment of the electors appointed, setting forth the names of such electors and the canvass or other ascertainment under the laws of such State of the number of votes given or cast for each person for whose appointment any and all votes have been given or cast; and it shall also thereupon be the duty of the executive of each State to deliver to the electors of such State, on or before the day on which they are required by section 7 of this title to meet, six duplicate-originals of the same certificate under the seal of the State; and if there shall have been any final determination in a State in the manner provided for by law of a controversy or contest concerning the appointment of all or any of the electors of such State, it shall be the duty of the executive of such State, as soon as practicable after such determination, to communicate under the seal of the State to the Archivist of the United States a certificate of such determination in form and manner as the same shall have been made; and the certificate or certificates so received by the Archivist of the United States shall be preserved by him for one year and shall be a part of the public records of his office and shall be open to public inspection; and the Archivist of the United States at the first meeting of Congress thereafter shall transmit to the two Houses of Congress copies in full of each and every such certificate so received at the National Archives and Records Administration.

Meeting and vote of electors

§7. The electors of President and Vice President of each State shall meet and give their votes on the first Monday after the second Wednesday in December next following their appointment at such place in each State as the legislature of such State shall direct.

Manner of voting

§8. The electors shall vote for President and Vice President, respectively, in the manner directed by the Constitution.

Certificates of votes for President and Vice President

§9. The electors shall make and sign six certificates of all the votes given by them, each of which certificates shall contain two distinct lists, one of the votes for President and the other of the votes for Vice President, and shall annex to each of the certificates one of the lists of the electors which shall have been furnished to them by direction of the executive of the State.

Sealing and endorsing certificates

§10. The electors shall seal up the certificates so made by them, and certify upon each that the lists of all the votes of such State given for President, and of all the votes given for Vice President, are contained therein.

Disposition of certificates

§11. The electors shall dispose of the certificates so made by them and the lists attached thereto in the following manner:

First. They shall forthwith forward by registered mail one of the same to the President of the Senate at the seat of government.

Second. Two of the same shall be delivered to the secretary of state of the State, one of which shall be held subject to the order of the President of the Senate, the other to be preserved by him for one year and shall be a part of the public records of his office and shall be open to public inspection.

Third. On the day thereafter they shall forward by registered mail two of such certificates and lists to the Archivist of the United States at the seat of government, one of which shall be held subject to the order of the President of the Senate. The other shall be preserved by the Archivist of the United States for one year and shall be a part of the public records of his office and shall be open to public inspection.

Fourth. They shall forthwith cause the other of the certificates and lists to be delivered to the judge of the district in which the electors shall have assembled.

Failure of certificates of electors to reach President of the Senate or archivist of the United States; demand on state for certificate

§12. When no certificate of vote and list mentioned in sections 9 and 11 and of this title from any State shall have been received by the President of the Senate or by the Archivist of the United States by the fourth Wednesday in December, after the meeting of the electors shall have been held, the President of the Senate or, if he be absent from the seat of government, the Archivist of the United States shall request, by the most expeditious method available, the secretary of state of the State to send up the certificate and list lodged with him by the electors of such State; and it shall be his duty upon receipt of such request immediately to transmit same by registered mail to the President of the Senate at the seat of government.

Same; demand on district judge for certificate

§13. When no certificates of votes from any State shall have been received at the seat of government on the fourth Wednesday in December, after the meeting of the electors shall have been held, the President of the Senate or, if he be absent from the seat of government, the Archivist of the United States shall send a special messenger to the district judge in whose custody one certificate of votes from that State has been lodged, and such judge shall forthwith transmit that list by the hand of such messenger to the seat of government.

Forfeiture for messenger's neglect of duty

§14. Every person who, having been appointed, pursuant to section 13 of this title, to deliver the certificates of the votes of the electors to the President of the Senate, and having accepted such appointment, shall neglect to perform the services required from him, shall forfeit the sum of $1,000.

Counting electoral votes in Congress

§15. Congress shall be in session on the sixth day of January succeeding every meeting of the electors. The Senate and House of Representatives shall meet in the Hall of the House of Representatives at the hour of 1 o'clock in the afternoon on that day, and the President of the Senate shall be their presiding officer. Two tellers shall be previously appointed on the part of the Senate and two on the part of the House of Representatives, to whom shall be handed, as they are opened by the President of the Senate, all the certificates and papers purporting to be certificates of the electoral votes, which certificates and papers shall be opened, presented, and acted upon in the alphabetical order of the States, beginning with the letter A; and said tellers, having then read the same in the presence and hearing of the two Houses, shall make a list of the votes as they shall appear from the said certificates; and the votes having been ascertained and counted according to the rules in this subchapter provided, the result of the same shall be delivered to the President of the Senate, who shall thereupon announce the state of the vote, which announcement shall be deemed a sufficient declaration of the persons, if any, elected President and Vice President of the United States, and, together with a list of the votes, be entered on the Journals of the two Houses. Upon such reading of any such certificate or paper, the President of the Senate shall call for objections, if any. Every objection shall be made in writing, and shall state clearly and concisely, and without argument, the ground thereof, and shall be signed by at least one Senator and one Member of the House of Representatives before the same shall be received. When all objections so made to any vote or paper from a State shall have been received and read, the Senate shall thereupon withdraw, and such objections shall be submitted to the Senate for its decision; and the Speaker of the House of Representatives shall, in like manner, submit such objections to the House of Representatives for its decision; and no electoral vote or votes from any State which shall have been regularly given by electors whose appointment has been lawfully certified to according to section 6 of this title from which but one return has been received shall be rejected, but the two Houses concurrently may reject the vote or votes when they agree that such vote or votes have not been so regularly given by electors whose appointment has been so certified. If more than one return or paper purporting to be a return from a State shall have been received by the President of the Senate, those votes, and those only, shall be counted which shall have been regularly given by the electors who are shown by the determination mentioned in section 5 of this title to have been appointed, if the determination in said section provided for shall have been made, or by such successors or substitutes, in case of a vacancy in the board of electors so ascertained, as have been appointed to fill such vacancy in the mode provided by the laws of the State; but in case there shall arise the question which of two or more of such State authorities determining what electors have been appointed, as mentioned in section 5 of this title, is the lawful tribunal of such State, the votes regularly given of those electors, and those only, of such State shall be counted whose title as electors the two Houses, acting separately, shall concurrently decide is supported by the decision of such State so authorized by its law; and in such case of more than one return or paper purporting to be a return from a State, if there shall have been no such determination of the question in the State aforesaid, then those votes, and those only, shall be counted which the two Houses shall concurrently decide were cast by lawful electors appointed in accordance with the laws of the State, unless the two Houses, acting separately, shall concurrently decide such votes not to be the lawful votes of the legally appointed electors of such State. But if the two Houses shall disagree in respect of the counting of such votes, then, and in that case, the votes of the electors whose appointment shall have been certified by the executive of the State, under the seal thereof, shall be counted. When the two Houses have voted, they shall immediately again meet, and the presiding officer shall then announce the decision of the questions submitted. No votes or papers from any other State shall be acted upon until the objections previously made to the votes or papers from any State shall have been finally disposed of.

Same; seats for officers and members of two houses in joint meeting

§16. At such joint meeting of the two Houses seats shall be provided as follows: For the President of the Senate, the Speaker's chair; for the Speaker, immediately upon his left; the Senators, in the body of the Hall upon the right of the presiding officer; for the Representatives, in the body of the Hall not provided for the Senators; for the tellers, Secretary of the Senate, and Clerk of the House of Representatives, at the Clerk's desk; for the other officers of the two Houses, in front of the Clerk's desk and upon each side of the Speaker's platform. Such joint meeting shall not be dissolved until the count of electoral votes shall be completed and the result declared; and no recess shall be taken unless a question shall have arisen in regard to counting any such votes, or otherwise under this subchapter, in which case it shall be competent for either House, acting separately, in the manner hereinbefore provided, to direct a recess of such House not beyond the next calendar day, Sunday excepted, at the hour of 10 o'clock in the forenoon. But if the counting of the electoral votes and the declaration of the result shall not have been completed before the fifth calendar day next after such first meeting of the two Houses, no further or other recess shall be taken by either House.

Same; limit of debate in each house

§17. When the two Houses separate to decide upon an objection that may have been made to the counting of any electoral vote or votes from any State, or other question arising in the matter, each Senator and Representative may speak to such objection or question five minutes, and not more than once; but after such debate shall have lasted two hours it shall be the duty of the presiding officer of each House to put the main question without further debate.

Same; parliamentary procedure at joint meeting

§18. While the two Houses shall be in meeting as provided in this chapter, the President of the Senate shall have power to preserve order; and no debate shall be allowed and no question shall be put by the presiding officer except to either House on a motion to withdraw.

Vacancy in offices of both President and Vice President; officers eligible to act

§19. (a)

(1) If, by reason of death, resignation, removal from office, inability, or failure to qualify, there is neither a President nor Vice President to discharge the powers and duties of the office of President, then the Speaker of the House of Representatives shall, upon his resignation as Speaker and as Representative in Congress, act as President.

(2) The same rule shall apply in the case of the death, resignation, removal from office, or inability of an individual acting as President under this subsection.

(b) If, at the time when under subsection (a) of this section a Speaker is to begin the discharge of the powers and duties of the office of President, there is no Speaker, or the Speaker fails to qualify as Acting President, then the President pro tempore of the Senate shall, upon his resignation as President pro tempore and as Senator, act as President.

(c) An individual acting as President under subsection (a) or subsection (b) of this section shall continue to act until the expiration of the then current Presidential term, except that

(1) if his discharge of the powers and duties of the office is founded in whole or in part on the failure of both the President-elect and the Vice-President-elect to qualify, then he shall act only until a President or Vice President qualifies; and

(2) if his discharge of the powers and duties of the office is founded in whole or in part on the inability of the President or Vice President, then he shall act only until the removal of the disability of one of such individuals.

(d)

(1) If, by reason of death, resignation, removal from office, inability, or failure to qualify, there is no President pro tempore to act as President under subsection (b) of this section, then the officer of the United States who is highest on the following list, and who is not

under disability to discharge the powers and duties of the office of President shall act as President: Secretary of State, Secretary of the Treasury, Secretary of Defense, Attorney General, Secretary of the Interior, Secretary of Agriculture, Secretary of Commerce, Secretary of Labor, Secretary of Health and Human Services, Secretary of Housing and Urban Development, Secretary of Transportation, Secretary of Energy, Secretary of Education, Secretary of Veterans Affairs.

(2) An individual acting as President under this subsection shall continue so to do until the expiration of the then current Presidential term, but not after a qualified and prior-entitled individual is able to act, except that the removal of the disability of an individual higher on the list contained in paragraph (1) of this subsection or the ability to qualify on the part of an individual higher on such list shall not terminate his service.

(3) The taking of the oath of office by an individual specified in the list in paragraph (1) of this subsection shall be held to constitute his resignation from the office by virtue of the holding of which he qualifies to act as President.

(e) Subsections (a), (b), and (d) of this section shall apply only to such officers as are eligible to the office of President under the Constitution. Subsection (d) of this section shall apply only to officers appointed, by and with the advice and consent of the Senate, prior to the time of the death, resignation, removal from office, inability, or failure to qualify, of the President pro tempore, and only to officers not under impeachment by the House of Representatives at the time the powers and duties of the office of President devolve upon them.

(f) During the period that any individual acts as President under this section, his compensation shall be at the rate then provided by law in the case of the President.

Resignation or refusal of office

§20. The only evidence of a refusal to accept, or of a resignation of the office of President or Vice President, shall be an instrument in writing, declaring the same, and subscribed by the person refusing to accept or resigning, as the case may be, and delivered into the office of the Secretary of State.

Definitions

§21. As used in this chapter the term—

(a) "State" includes the District of Columbia.

(b) "executives of each State" includes the Board of Commissioners of the District of Columbia.

APPENDIX C: U.S. CONSTITUTION ON INTERSTATE COMPACTS AND CONTRACTS

Article I, Section 10, Clause 1

No State shall enter into any Treaty, Alliance, or Confederation; grant Letters of Marque and Reprisal; coin Money; emit Bills of Credit; make any Thing but gold and silver Coin a Tender in Payment of Debts; pass any Bill of Attainder, ex post facto Law, or Law impairing the Obligation of Contracts, or grant any Title of Nobility.

Article I, Section 10, Clause 3

No State shall, without the Consent of Congress, lay any Duty of Tonnage, keep Troops, or Ships of War in time of Peace, enter into any Agreement or Compact with another State, or with a foreign Power, or engage in War, unless actually invaded, or in such imminent Danger as will not admit of delay.

APPENDIX D: MINNESOTA LAWS ON PRESIDENTIAL ELECTIONS

208.02. Election of presidential electors

Presidential electors shall be chosen at the state general election held in the year preceding the expiration of the term of the president of the United States.

208.03. Nomination of presidential electors

Presidential electors for the major political parties of this state shall be nominated by delegate conventions called and held under the supervision of the respective state central committees of the parties of this state. On or before primary election day the chair of the major political party shall certify to the secretary of state the names of the persons nominated as Presidential electors and the names of the party candidates for president and vice-president.

208.04. Preparation of ballots

Subdivision 1. When Presidential electors are to be voted for, a vote cast for the party candidates for president and vice-president shall be deemed a vote for that party's electors as filed with the secretary of state. The secretary of state shall certify the names of all duly nominated Presidential and vice-Presidential candidates to the county auditors of the counties of the state. Each county auditor, subject to the rules of the secretary of state, shall cause the names of the candidates of each major political party and the candidates nominated by petition to be printed in capital letters, set in type of the same size and style as for candidates on the state white ballot, before the party designation. To the left of, and on the same line with the names of the candidates for president and vice-president, near the margin, shall be placed a square or box, in which the voters may indicate their choice by marking an "X."

The form for the Presidential ballot and the relative position of the several candidates shall be determined by the rules applicable to other state officers. The state ballot, with the required heading, shall be printed on the same piece of paper and shall be below the Presidential ballot with a blank space between one inch in width.

Subdivision 2. The rules for preparation, state contribution to the cost of printing, and delivery of Presidential ballots are the same as the rules for white ballots under section 204D.11, subdivision 1.

208.05. State canvassing board

The state canvassing board at its meeting on the second Tuesday after each state general election shall open and canvass the returns made to the secretary of state for Presidential electors, prepare a statement of the number of votes cast for the persons receiving votes for these offices, and declare the person or persons receiving the highest number of votes for each office duly elected. When it appears that more than the number of persons to be elected as Presidential electors have the highest and an equal number of votes, the secretary of state, in the presence of the board shall decide by lot which of the persons shall be declared elected. The governor shall transmit to each person declared elected a certificate of election, signed by the governor, sealed with the state seal, and countersigned by the secretary of state.

208.06. Electors to meet at capitol; filling of vacancies

The Presidential electors, before 12:00 M. on the day before that fixed by congress for the electors to vote for president and vice-president of the United States, shall notify the governor that they are at the state capitol and ready at the proper time to fulfill their duties as electors. The governor shall deliver to the electors present a certificate of the names of all the electors. If any elector named therein fails to appear before 9:00 a.m. on the day, and at the place, fixed for voting for president and vice-president of the United States, the electors present shall, in the presence of the governor, immediately elect by ballot a person to fill the vacancy. If more than the number of persons required have the highest and an equal number of votes, the governor, in the presence of the electors attending, shall decide by lot which of those persons shall be elected.

208.07. Certificate of electors

Immediately after the vacancies have been filled, the original electors present shall certify to the governor the names of the persons elected to complete their number, and the governor shall at once cause written notice to be given to each person elected to fill a vacancy. The persons so chosen shall be Presidential electors and shall meet and act with the other electors.

208.08. Electors to meet at state capitol

The original and substituted Presidential electors, at 12:00 M., shall meet in the executive chamber at the state capitol and shall perform all the duties imposed upon them as electors by the constitution and laws of the United States and this state.

204B.07. Nominating petitions

Subdivision 1. Form of petition. A nominating petition may consist of one or more separate pages each of which shall state:

(a) The office sought;

(b) The candidate's name and residence address, including street and number if any; and

(c) The candidate's political party or political principle expressed in not more than three words. No candidate who files for a partisan office by nominating petition shall use the term "nonpartisan" as a statement of political principle or the name of the candidate's political party. No part of the name of a major political party may be used to designate the political party or principle of a candidate who files for a partisan office by nominating petition, except that the word "independent" may be used to designate the party or principle. A candidate who files by nominating petition to fill a vacancy in nomination for a nonpartisan office pursuant to section 204B.13, shall not state any political principle or the name of any political party on the petition.

Subdivision 2. Petitions for presidential electors. This subdivision does not apply to candidates for Presidential elector nominated by major political parties. Major party candidates for Presidential elector are certified under section 208.03. Other Presidential electors are nominated by petition pursuant to this section. On petitions nominating Presidential electors, the names of the candidates for president and vice-president shall be added to the political party or political principle stated on the petition. One petition may be filed to nominate a slate of Presidential electors equal in number to the number of electors to which the state is entitled.

Subdivision 3. Number of candidates nominated. No nominating petition shall contain the name of more than one candidate except a petition jointly nominating individuals for governor and lieutenant governor or nominating a slate of Presidential electors.

Subdivision 4. Oath and address of signer. Following the information required by subdivisions 1 and 2 and before the space for signing, each separate page that is part of the petition shall include an oath in the following form:

> "I solemnly swear (or affirm) that I know the contents and purpose of this petition, that I do not intend to vote at the primary election for the office for which this nominating petition is made, and that I signed this petition of my own free will."

Notarization or certification of the signatures on a nominating petition is not required. Immediately after the signature, the signer shall write on the petition the signer's residence address including street and number, if any, and mailing address if different from residence address.

Subdivision 5. Sample forms. An official with whom petitions are filed shall make sample forms for nominating petitions available upon request.

Subdivision 6. Penalty. An individual who, in signing a nominating petition, makes a false oath is guilty of perjury.

204B.09. Time and place of filing affidavits and petitions

Subdivision 1. Candidates in state and county general elections.

(a) Except as otherwise provided by this subdivision, affidavits of candidacy and nominating petitions for county, state, and federal offices filled at the state general election shall be filed not more than 70 days nor less than 56 days before the state primary. The affidavit may be prepared and signed at any time between 60 days before the filing period opens and the last day of the filing period.

(b) Notwithstanding other law to the contrary, the affidavit of candidacy must be signed in the presence of a notarial officer or an individual authorized to administer oaths under section 358.10.

(c) This provision does not apply to candidates for Presidential elector nominated by major political parties. Major party candidates for Presidential elector are certified under section 208.03. Other candidates for Presidential electors may file petitions on or before the state primary day pursuant to section 204B.07. Nominating petitions to fill vacancies in nominations shall be filed as provided in section 204B.13. No affidavit or petition shall be accepted later than 5:00 p.m. on the last day for filing.

(d) Affidavits and petitions for offices to be voted on in only one county shall be filed with the county auditor of that county. Affidavits and petitions for offices to be voted on in more than one county shall be filed with the secretary of state.

Subdivision 1a. Absent candidates. A candidate for special district, county, state, or federal office who will be absent from the state during the filing period may submit a properly executed affidavit of candidacy, the appropriate filing fee, and any necessary petitions in person to the filing officer. The candidate shall state in writing the reason for being unable to submit the affidavit during the filing period. The affidavit, filing fee, and petitions must be submitted to the filing officer during the seven days immediately preceding the candidate's absence from the state. Nominating petitions may be signed during the 14 days immediately preceding the date when the affidavit of candidacy is filed.

Subdivision 2. Other elections. Affidavits of candidacy and nominating petitions for city, town or other elective offices shall be filed during the time and with the official specified in chapter 205 or other applicable law or charter, except as provided for a special district candidate under subdivision 1a. Affidavits of candidacy and applications filed on behalf of eligible voters for school board office shall be filed during the time and with the official specified in chapter 205A or other applicable law.

Subdivision 3. Write-in candidates.

(a) A candidate for state or federal office who wants write-in votes for the candidate to be counted must file a written request with the filing office for the office sought no later than the fifth day before the general election. The filing officer shall provide copies of the form to make the request.

(b) A candidate for president of the United States who files a request under this subdivision must include the name of a candidate for vice-president of the United States. The request must also include the name of at least one candidate for Presidential elector. The total number of names of candidates for Presidential elector on the request may not exceed the total number of electoral votes to be cast by Minnesota in the presidential election.

(c) A candidate for governor who files a request under this subdivision must include the name of a candidate for lieutenant governor.

State of Minnesota
Certificate of Ascertainment, 2004, Page 2 of 8

Minnesota Democratic-Farmer-Labor Party
Electors pledged to John F. Kerry for President of the United States
and John Edwards for Vice President of the United States.
These candidates for presidential elector each received 1,445,014
votes:

> Sonja Berg, of St. Cloud
> Vi Grooms-Alban, of Cohasset
> Matthew Little, of Maplewood
> Michael Meuers, of Bemidji
> Tim O'Brien, of Edina
> Lil Ortendahl, of Osakis
> Everett Pettiford, of Minneapolis
> Jean Schiebel, of Brooklyn Center
> Frank Simon, of Chaska
> Chandler Harrison Stevens, of Austin

I further certify that the returns of the votes cast for Presidential Electors at the
General Election were canvassed and certified by the State Canvassing Board
on the 16th day of November, 2004 in accordance with the laws of the State of
Minnesota, and that the number of votes cast for each candidate for Presidential
Elector at the General Election is as follows:

Green Party of Minnesota
Electors pledged to David Cobb for President of the United States
and Pat LaMarche for Vice President of the United States.
These candidates for presidential elector each received 4,408 votes:

> Scott Bol
> Kellie Burriss
> Michael Cavlan
> Amber Garlan
> Jenny Heiser
> Molly Nutting
> Douglas Root
> Mark Wahl
> Annie Young
> Dean Zimmermann

State of Minnesota
Certificate of Ascertainment 2004, Page 3 of 8

Republican Party of Minnesota
Electors pledged to George W. Bush for President of the United States
and Dick Cheney for Vice President of the United States.
Each elector received 1,346,695 votes:

George Cable
Jeff Cames
Ronald Eibensteiner
Angie Erhard
Eileen Fiore
Walter Klaus
Michelle Rifenberg
Julie Rosendahl
Lyall Schwarzkopf
Armin Tesch

Socialist Equality Party
Electors pledged to Bill Van Auken for President of the United States
and Jim Lawrence for Vice President of the United States.
These candidates for presidential elector each received 539 votes:

Nathan Andrew
Dan W. Blais
William J. Campbell-Bezat
Christopher M. Isett
Cory R. Johnson
Cynthia B. Moore
Thomas G. Moore
Stephen M. Paulson
Emanuele Saccarelli
James Strouf

State of Minnesota
Certificate of Ascertainment 2004, Page 4 of 8

Socialist Workers Party
Electors pledged to Roger Calero for President of the United States
and Arrin Hawkins for Vice President of the United States.
These candidates for presidential elector each received 416 votes:

Dennis Drake
Rebecca L. Ellis
Catherine S. Fowlkes
Allan J. Grady
Bryce J. Grady
Louise M. Halverson
Bernadette Kuhn
Thomas O'Brien
Michael Pennock
Sandra M. Sherman

Christian Freedom Party
Electors pledged to Thomas J. Harens for President of the United States
and Jennifer A. Ryan for Vice President of the United States.
These candidates for presidential elector each received 2,387 votes:

Gail Froncek
Brian Harens
Kaja R. King
Wayne Kruekeberg
Sally Paulsen
Janine Quaile
Susan Smith
Nadine Snyder
Susan M. Style
John Vinje

State of Minnesota
Certificate of Ascertainment 2004, Page 5 of 8

Better Life Party
Electors pledged to Ralph Nader for President of the United States
and Peter Miguel Camejo for Vice President of the United States.
These candidates for presidential elector each received 18,683 votes:

Cassandra Lynn Carlson
Enrique Pedro Gentzsch
Rhoda Jean Gilman
Kari Elizabeth Kyle
Linda Shannon Mann
Corey Scott Mattson
Lois Minna Piper
Preston George Piper
Matthew Alan Ryg
Suzanne Shelley Skorich

Constitution Party
Electors pledged to Michael Peroutka for President of the United States
and Chuck Baldwin for Vice President of the United States.
These candidates for presidential elector each received 3,074 votes:

Arthur Becker
Patricia Becker
Kent Berdahl
Bill Dodge
Rev. Dr. Tom Jestus Sr.
Lars Johnson
Don Koehler
Marilyn Nibbe
John Robillard
Wayne Zimmerscheid

State of Minnesota
Certificate of Ascertainment 2004, Page 6 of 8

Libertarian Party
Electors pledged to Michael Badnarik for President of the United States
and Richard Campagna for Vice President of the United States.
These candidates for presidential elector each received 4,639 votes:

    Stephen Baker
    Kathy Helwig
    Beatrice Kurk
    Jeremy Mackinney
    Mary O'Connor
    Corey Stern
    Shelby Thorsted
    David Wiester
    Colin Wilkinson
    Jill Wilkinson

Elector Pledged to Declared Write-In Candidates
Debra Joyce Renderos for President of the United States
and Oscar Renderos Castillo for Vice President of the United States.
This candidate for presidential elector received 2 votes:

    Henry Ford

Elector Pledged to Declared Write-In Candidates
Martin Wishnatsky for President of the United States
and Andrew Vanyo for Vice President of the United States.
This candidate for presidential elector received 2 votes:

    Chris Welle

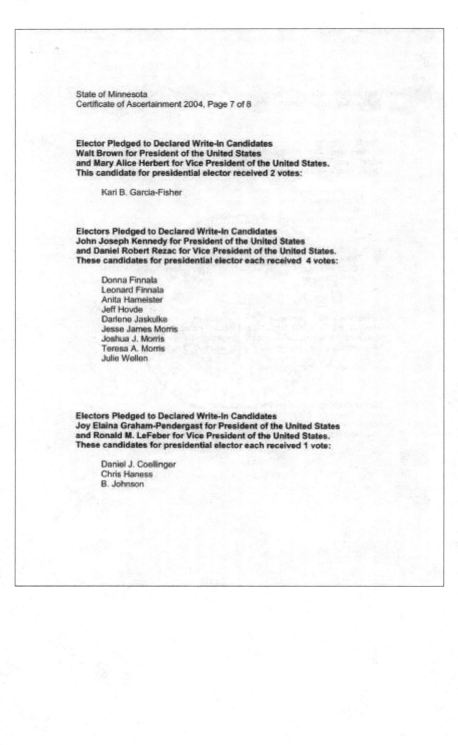

State of Minnesota
Certificate of Ascertainment 2004, Page 7 of 8

Elector Pledged to Declared Write-In Candidates
Walt Brown for President of the United States
and Mary Alice Herbert for Vice President of the United States.
This candidate for presidential elector received 2 votes:

    Kari B. Garcia-Fisher

Electors Pledged to Declared Write-In Candidates
John Joseph Kennedy for President of the United States
and Daniel Robert Rezac for Vice President of the United States.
These candidates for presidential elector each received 4 votes:

    Donna Finnala
    Leonard Finnala
    Anita Hameister
    Jeff Hovde
    Darlene Jaskulke
    Jesse James Morris
    Joshua J. Morris
    Teresa A. Morris
    Julie Wellen

Electors Pledged to Declared Write-In Candidates
Joy Elaina Graham-Pendergast for President of the United States
and Ronald M. LeFeber for Vice President of the United States.
These candidates for presidential elector each received 1 vote:

    Daniel J. Coellinger
    Chris Haness
    B. Johnson

State of Minnesota
Certificate of Ascertainment 2004, Page 8 of 8

IN WITNESS WHEREOF,
I have set my hand and the Great Seal
of the State of Minnesota at the Capitol
in Saint Paul this 8th day of December,
2004, being the 228th year of
Independence, and the 146th year of
Statehood.

TIM PAWLENTY
Governor

ATTEST:

MARY KIFFMEYER
Secretary of State

APPENDIX F: MAINE 2004 CERTIFICATE OF ASCERTAINMENT

STATE OF MAINE

Certificate of Ascertainment of Electors

I, John Elias Baldacci, Governor of the State of Maine, *do hereby certify that Jill Duson of Portland; Samuel Shapiro of Waterville; Lu Bauer of Standish and David Garrity of Portland have been duly chosen and appointed*

ELECTORS OF PRESIDENT AND VICE PRESIDENT
OF THE UNITED STATES

for the State of Maine, at an election for that purpose which was held on the Tuesday following the first Monday in November, in the year two thousand and four, in accordance with the provisions of the laws of the State of Maine and in conformity with the Constitution and laws of the United States, for the purpose of giving their votes for President and Vice President of the United States for the respective terms commencing on the twentieth day of January, in the year two thousand and five; and

I further certify, that, *the votes given at said election for Electors of President and Vice President of the United States as appears by the returns from the several cities, towns and plantations in the State, which were duly received and examined by me in accordance with the laws, were as follows:*

The LIBERTARIAN PARTY Electors supporting the candidacy of Michael Badnarik for President and Richard Campagna for Vice President received the following votes:

First Congressional District
Mark Cenci, Portland — 1,047

Second Congressional District
Dana Snowman, Alton — 918

At-Large
Richard W. Eaton, Westbrook — 1,965

At-Large
Geoffrey H. Keller, Dayton — 1,965

The REPUBLICAN PARTY Electors supporting the candidacy of George W. Bush for President and Dick Cheney for Vice President received the following votes:

First Congressional District
Kenneth M. Cole, III, Falmouth — 165,824

Second Congressional District
Katherine L. Watson, Pittsfield — 164,377

At-Large
Peter E. Cianchette, South Portland — 330,201

At-Large
James D. Tobin, Bangor — 330,201

The GREEN INDEPENDENT PARTY Electors supporting the candidacy of David Cobb for President and Patricia LaMarche for Vice President received the following votes:

First Congressional District
Larry Dean Lofton-McGee, Augusta — 1,468

Second Congressional District
Heather E. Garrold, Brooks — 1,468

At-Large
Charlene Decker, Machias — 2,936

At-Large
Ruth Z. Gabey, West Gardiner — 2,936

The DEMOCRATIC PARTY Electors supporting the candidacy of John F. Kerry for President and John Edwards for Vice President received the following votes:

First Congressional District
Jill Duson, Portland   211,703

Second Congressional District
Samuel Shapiro, Waterville   185,139

At-Large
Lu Bauer, Standish   396,842

At-Large
David Garrity, Portland   396,842

The BETTER LIFE PARTY Electors supporting the candidacy of Ralph Nader for President and Peter Miguel Camejo for Vice President received the following votes:

First Congressional District
Rosemary L. Whittaker, South Portland   4,004

Second Congressional District
Christopher M. Droznick, Auburn   4,065

At-Large
Nancy Oden, Jonesboro   8,069

At-Large
J. Noble Snowdeal, Jonesboro   8,069

The CONSTITUTION PARTY Electors supporting the candidacy of Michael Anthony Peroutka for President and Chuck Baldwin for Vice President received the following votes:

First Congressional District
Stanley Jones, Hallowell   346

Second Congressional District
Harvey R. Lord, Paris   389

At-Large
Mary-Ann Greiner, St. George   735

At-Large
Patricia Truman, Hallowell   735

In Testimony Whereof, I have caused the Great Seal of the State of Maine to be hereunto affixed, given under my hand, this twenty-third day of November in the year two thousand and four.

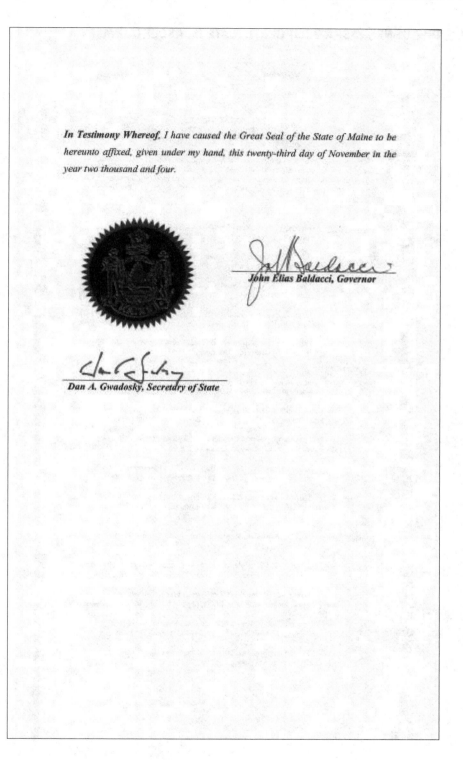

John Elias Baldacci, Governor

Dan A. Gwadosky, Secretary of State

APPENDIX G: NEBRASKA 2004 CERTIFICATE OF ASCERTAINMENT

STATE OF NEBRASKA
ELECTORAL COLLEGE
CERTIFICATE OF ASCERTAINMENT

We, Mike Johanns, Governor of the State of Nebraska, and John A. Gale, Secretary of State of the State of Nebraska, do hereby certify the following is a certified list of the five Presidential Electors in and for the State of Nebraska, including the names of the Presidential and Vice Presidential candidates and the votes received by each as duly canvassed by the State Canvassing Board on November 29, 2004.

Republican Party George W. Bush, President/Dick Cheney, Vice President
Statewide Total Votes Received: 512,814

Electors: Ms. Kay Orr 1610 Brent Blvd. Lincoln, NE 68506 (At Large)
Mr. Ken Stinson 14349 Hamilton St. Omaha, NE 68154 (At Large)

First Congressional District Total Votes Received: 169,888
The Honorable Curt Bromm 1448 N Pine St. Wahoo, NE 68066 (1st District)

Second Congressional District Total Votes Received: 153,041
Mr. Michael John Hogan 16212 Wakely St. Omaha, NE 68118 (2nd District)

Third Congressional District Total Votes Received: 189,885
Mr. Bill Barrett P.O. Box 366 Lexington, NE 68850 (3rd District)

Democratic Party John F. Kerry, President/John Edwards, Vice President
Statewide Total Votes Received: 254,328

Electors: Ms. Carol Yoakum 1145 Rose St., #117 Lincoln, NE 68502-2268 (At Large)
Mr. Frank Johannsen HC 86, Box 149 Bayard, NE 69334 (At Large)

First Congressional District Total Votes Received: 96,314
The Honorable Diana Schimek 2321 Camelot Ct. Lincoln, NE 68512 (1st District)

Second Congressional District Total Votes Received: 97,858
Ms. Sandi Skorniak 6324 Blondo St. Omaha, NE 68104 (2nd District)

Third Congressional District Total Votes Received: 60,156
Deb Hardin Quirk P.O. Box 1142 Hastings, NE 68902 (3rd District)

Libertarian Party Michael Badnarik, President/Richard V. Campagna, Vice President
Statewide Total Votes Received: 2,041

Electors: Mr. Paul Tripp 12216 Poppleton Plz., #238 Omaha, NE 68144 (At Large)
Ms. Nydra Smart 310 Fawn Ct. Bellevue, NE 68005-2006 (At Large)

First Congressional District Total Votes Received: 656
Mr. Gerald F. Kosch 775 N 11th St, #4 David City, NE 68632 (1st District)

Second Congressional District Total Votes Received: 813
Mr. Jack Graziano 1513 N 112th Ct., #5413 Omaha, NE 68154

Third Congressional District Total Votes Received: 572
Mr. Jerry Hickman Rt. 2 Box 91 Loup City, NE 68853-9632

Nebraska Party — Michael Anthony Peroutka, President/Chuck Baldwin, Vice President
Statewide Total Votes Received: 1,314

Electors:
Mr. Duane Dufek Box 555 Creighton, NE 68729 (At Large)
Mr. Gene Dobias 510 Washington Ave. Creighton, NE 68729 (At Large)

First Congressional District Total Votes Received: 405
Mr. Peter Rosberg 83626 557 Ave. Norfolk NE 68701 (1st District)

Second Congressional District Total Votes Received: 305
Mr. Tim Larson 15709 O Cir. Omaha, NE 68135 (2nd District)

Third Congressional District Total Votes Received: 604
Mr. Joseph Rosberg 54288 874 Rd. Wausa, NE 68786

Green Party — David Cobb, President/Patricia LaMarche, Vice President
Statewide Total Votes Received: 978

Electors:
Mr. Tim Jensen 307 W. Charleston, #1232 Lincoln, NE 68528 (At Large)
Ms. Elaine Santore 609 N 17th St. Lincoln, NE 68508 (At Large)

First Congressional District Total Votes Received: 453
Ms. Ginny Crisco 1601 F St. Lincoln, NE 68508 (1st District)

Second Congressional District Total Votes Received: 261
Mr. Charles Ostdiek 3808 Harney St., #4 Omaha, NE 68131 (2nd District)

Third Congressional District Total Votes Received: 264
Mr. Josh Skufca 3058 S. 41 Omaha, NE 68105 (3rd District)

By Petition — Roger Calero, President/Arrin Hawkins, Vice President
Statewide Total Votes Received: 82

Electors:
Mr. Nelson F. González 4731 S 24th St., Apt. 209 Omaha, NE 68107 (At Large)
Mr. David Z. Rosenfeld 4841 S 24th St. Omaha, NE 68107 (At Large)

First Congressional District Total Votes Received: 30
Ms. Lisa J. Krueger 5951 Oakridge Dr. Lincoln, NE 68516 (1st District)

Second Congressional District Total Votes Received: 23
Ms. Lisa M. Rottach 4841 S 24th St. Omaha, NE 68107 (2nd District)

Third Congressional District Total Votes Received: 29
Mr. Wayne Honsermeier 1206 Nebraska Hwy 2 Phillips, NE 68865 (3rd District)

By Petition — Ralph Nader, President, Peter Miguel Camejo, Vice President
Statewide Total Votes Received: 5,698

Electors:
Ms. Diana McIntyre-Wright 5621 Dogwood Dr. Lincoln, NE 68516 (At Large)
Ms. Irma Sarata 2000 SW 47th St. Lincoln, NE 68522 (At Large)

First Congressional District Total Votes Received: 2,025
Ms. Amber McIntyre 5621 Dogwood Dr. Lincoln, NE 68516 (1st District)

Second Congressional District Total Votes Received: 1,731
Ms. Susan Robinson 9815 Pasadena Ave. Omaha, NE 68124 (2nd District)

Third Congressional District Total Votes Received: 1,942
Mr. Lee R. Heerten HC 81 PO Box 121 Springview, NE 68778

We hereby certify the names of the Republican Party Electors associated with the Bush-Cheney ticket have been duly appointed and notified by certified mail by the Governor and will appear at the State Capitol, Lincoln, Nebraska on the 13th day of December 2004, for the purpose of casting Nebraska's five Electoral College votes.

We hereunto affix our signatures this 13th day of December, 2004, at Lincoln, Nebraska.

Mike Johanns
Governor

John A. Gale
Secretary of State

STATE OF NEW YORK

BY

George E. Pataki

GOVERNOR

I, **GEORGE E. PATAKI**, Governor of the State of New York, do hereby certify, that the statement containing the Canvass and Certificate of Determination by the State Board of Canvassers of the State of New York, as to **ELECTORS of PRESIDENT and VICE-PRESIDENT** hereto annexed, and certified by the Chairperson of the State Board of Elections of said State, under her seal of office, contains a true and correct list setting forth the names of Electors of President and Vice-President, elected in said State, at the General Election held in said State on the Tuesday after the First Monday in November (November second), in the year two thousand four, pursuant to the Constitution and Laws of the United States and of the State of New York, to wit:

Joseph Ashton	Bertha Lewis
Bill De Blasio	Alan Lubin
Molly Clifford	Thomas Manton
Lorraine Cortes-Vazquez	Dennis Mehiel
Inez Dickens	June O'Neill
Danny Donahue	David Paterson
Herman D. Farrell	Jose Rivera
Virginia Fields	Rich Schaffer
Emily Giske	Chung Seto
Bea Gonzalez	Sheldon Silver
Alan Hevesi	Eliot Spitzer
Frank Hoare	Antoine Thompson
Virginia Kee	Paul Tokasz
Peggy Kerry	Bill Wood
Denise King	Robert Zimmerman
Len Lenihan	

And further that the Statement of Canvass and Certificate of Determination certified by the Chairperson of the State Board of Elections of said State, as aforesaid, correctly sets forth the Canvass of Determination under the Laws of said State of New York, of the number of votes given or cast for each person for whose elections any and all votes have been given or cast at said election as aforesaid.

In Testimony Whereof, The Great Seal of the State is hereunto affixed.

Witness my hand at the City of Albany, the tenth day of December, in the year two thousand four.

Attested by

Secretary of State

We, the State Board of Elections, constituting the State Board of Canvassers, having canvassed the whole number of votes given for the office of ELECTOR of PRESIDENT and VICE-PRESIDENT at the general election held in said State, on the Second day of November, 2004, according to the certified statement of canvass received by the State Board of Elections, in the manner directed by law, do hereby determine, declare and certify that

Joseph Ashton	Bertha Lewis
Bill De Blasio	Alan Lubin
Molly Clifford	Thomas Manton
Lorraine Cortes-Vazquez	Dennis Mehiel
Inez Dickens	June O'Neill
Danny Donahue	David Paterson
Herman D. Farrell	Jose Rivera
Virginia Fields	Rich Schaffer
Emily Giske	Chung Seto
Bea Gonzalez	Sheldon Silver
Alan Hevesi	Eliot Spitzer
Frank Hoare	Antoine Thompson
Virginia Kee	Paul Tokasz
Peggy Kerry	Bill Wood
Denise King	Robert Zimmerman
Len Lenihan	

were, by the greatest number of votes given at said election duly elected ELECTOR of PRESIDENT and VICE-PRESIDENT of the United States.

GIVEN under our hands in Sloatsburg, New York, the 6th day of December in the year two thousand four.

Carol Berman	Commissioner
Neil W. Kelleher	Commissioner
Evelyn J. Aquila	Commissioner
Helena Moses Donohue	Commissioner

STATE OF NEW YORK ;
                : ss:
STATE BOARD OF ELECTIONS :

I certify that I have compared the foregoing with the original certificate filed in this office, and that the same is a correct transcript therefrom and of the whole of such original.

GIVEN under my hand and official seal of office of the State Board of Elections, in Sloatsburg, New York, this 6th day of December in the year two thousand four.

Carol Berman

Carol Berman   Chairperson

STATE OF NEW YORK, ss:

Statement of the whole number of votes cast for all the candidates for the office of ELECTOR OF PRESIDENT and VICE-PRESIDENT at a General Election held in said State on the Second day of November, 2004.

The whole number of votes given for the office of ELECTOR OF PRESIDENT and VICE-PRESIDENT was **7,448,266** of which

		REPUBLICAN	CONSERVATIVE	TOTAL
George E. Pataki	received	2,806,993	155,574	2,962,567
Alexander F. Treadwell	received	2,806,993	155,574	2,962,567
Joseph Bruno	received	2,806,993	155,574	2,962,567
Charles Nesbitt	received	2,806,993	155,574	2,962,567
Mary Donohue	received	2,806,993	155,574	2,962,567
Rudolph Giuliani	received	2,806,993	155,574	2,962,567
Charles Gargano	received	2,806,993	155,574	2,962,567
Joseph Mondello	received	2,806,993	155,574	2,962,567
J. Patrick Barrett	received	2,806,993	155,574	2,962,567
John F. Nolan	received	2,806,993	155,574	2,962,567
Robert Davis	received	2,806,993	155,574	2,962,567
Peter J. Savago	received	2,806,993	155,574	2,962,567
Maggie Brooks	received	2,806,993	155,574	2,962,567
Catherine Blaney	received	2,806,993	155,574	2,962,567
Howard Mills	received	2,806,993	155,574	2,962,567
John Cahill	received	2,806,993	155,574	2,962,567
Rita DiMartino	received	2,806,993	155,574	2,962,567
Libby Pataki	received	2,806,993	155,574	2,962,567
Stephen Minarik	received	2,806,993	155,574	2,962,567
Raymond Meier	received	2,806,993	155,574	2,962,567
Thomas M. Reynolds	received	2,806,993	155,574	2,962,567
Adam Stoll	received	2,806,993	155,574	2,962,567
Herman Badillo	received	2,806,993	155,574	2,962,567
Jane Forbes Clark	received	2,806,993	155,574	2,962,567
James Garner	received	2,806,993	155,574	2,962,567
Shawn Marie Levine	received	2,806,993	155,574	2,962,567
Viola J. Hunter	received	2,806,993	155,574	2,962,567
Laura Schreiner	received	2,806,993	155,574	2,962,567
Carmen Gomez Goldberg	received	2,806,993	155,574	2,962,567
Bernadette Castro	received	2,806,993	155,574	2,962,567
Cathy Jimino	received	2,806,993	155,574	2,962,567

		DEMOCRATIC	WORKING FAM.	TOTAL
Joseph Ashton	received	4,180,755	133,525	4,314,280
Bill De Blasio	received	4,180,755	133,525	4,314,280
Molly Clifford	received	4,180,755	133,525	4,314,280
Lorraine Cortes-Vazquez	received	4,180,755	133,525	4,314,280
Inez Dickens	received	4,180,755	133,525	4,314,280
Danny Donahue	received	4,180,755	133,525	4,314,280
Herman D. Farrell	received	4,180,755	133,525	4,314,280
Virginia Fields	received	4,180,755	133,525	4,314,280
Emily Giske	received	4,180,755	133,525	4,314,280
Bea Gonzalez	received	4,180,755	133,525	4,314,280
Alan Hevesi	received	4,180,755	133,525	4,314,280
Frank Hoare	received	4,180,755	133,525	4,314,280
Virginia Kee	received	4,180,755	133,525	4,314,280
Peggy Kerry	received	4,180,755	133,525	4,314,280
Denise King	received	4,180,755	133,525	4,314,280
Len Lenihan	received	4,180,755	133,525	4,314,280
Bertha Lewis	received	4,180,755	133,525	4,314,280
Alan Lubin	received	4,180,755	133,525	4,314,280
Thomas Manton	received	4,180,755	133,525	4,314,280
Dennis Mehiel	received	4,180,755	133,525	4,314,280
June O'Neill	received	4,180,755	133,525	4,314,280
David Paterson	received	4,180,755	133,525	4,314,280
Jose Rivera	received	4,180,755	133,525	4,314,280
Rich Schaffer	received	4,180,755	133,525	4,314,280
Chung Seto	received	4,180,755	133,525	4,314,280
Sheldon Silver	received	4,180,755	133,525	4,314,280
Eliot Spitzer	received	4,180,755	133,525	4,314,280
Antoine Thompson	received	4,180,755	133,525	4,314,280
Paul Tokasz	received	4,180,755	133,525	4,314,280
Bill Wood	received	4,180,755	133,525	4,314,280
Robert Zimmerman	received	4,180,755	133,525	4,314,280

		INDEPENDENCE	TOTAL
Fran Siems	received	84,247	84,247
Barbara Smith	received	84,247	84,247
Theresa Smith	received	84,247	84,247
Joseph Beruth	received	84,247	84,247
Howard Edelbaum	received	84,247	84,247
Bryan Puertas	received	84,247	84,247
Barbara Pershay	received	84,247	84,247
Elizabeth Allen	received	84,247	84,247
Paul Gouldin	received	84,247	84,247
Joan Fleischman	received	84,247	84,247
Ken Gallashaw	received	84,247	84,247
Robert Conroy	received	84,247	84,247
Bobby Soto	received	84,247	84,247
Lenora Fulani	received	84,247	84,247
Harry Kresky	received	84,247	84,247
Amy Jo Butler	received	84,247	84,247
Rebecca Seward	received	84,247	84,247
Lili Vega	received	84,247	84,247
Jeff Graham	received	84,247	84,247
Patricia Anken	received	84,247	84,247
Judith Resen	received	84,247	84,247
Paul Caputo	received	84,247	84,247
Jessie Field	received	84,247	84,247
Sarah Lyons	received	84,247	84,247
Judith A. Orsini	received	84,247	84,247
Lee Kolesnikoff	received	84,247	84,247
Ben Curtis	received	84,247	84,247
Lorraine Stevens	received	84,247	84,247
Frank Mackay	received	84,247	84,247
Eileen Trace	received	84,247	84,247
Richard Schulman	received	84,247	84,247

		PEACE & JUSTICE	TOTAL
Sally J. Cass	received	15,626	15,626
Mitchel Cohen	received	15,626	15,626
Millicent Y. Collins	received	15,626	15,626
Edward T. Dodge	received	15,626	15,626
Mark A. Dunlea	received	15,626	15,626
J. David Edelstein	received	15,626	15,626
James Farney	received	15,626	15,626
Leslie Farney	received	15,626	15,626
Anthony Gronowicz	received	15,626	15,626
Howie Hawkins	received	15,626	15,626
Gerald F. Kann	received	15,626	15,626
Alan B. Kendrick-Bowser	received	15,626	15,626
James C. Lane	received	15,626	15,626
Peter LaVenia	received	15,626	15,626
Daniella Liebling	received	15,626	15,626
Joseph Lombardo	received	15,626	15,626
Ronald J. MacKinnon	received	15,626	15,626
Jessica L. Maxwell	received	15,626	15,626
Robin L. Miller	received	15,626	15,626
Steven Penn	received	15,626	15,626
Stephen H. Reynolds	received	15,626	15,626
Rebecca Rotzler	received	15,626	15,626
Leigh C. Safford	received	15,626	15,626
Eric Salzman	received	15,626	15,626
Lorna Salzman	received	15,626	15,626
Rachel Treichler	received	15,626	15,626
Jason West	received	15,626	15,626
Betty K. Wood	received	15,626	15,626
Paul H. Zulkowitz	received	15,626	15,626

		SOCIALIST WORKERS	TOTAL
Michael J. Fitzsimmons	received	2,405	2,405
Olga L. Rodriguez	received	2,405	2,405

		LIBERTARIAN	TOTAL
Richard A. Cooper	received	11,607	11,607
Dawn Davis	received	11,607	11,607
Donald H. Davis	received	11,607	11,607
Robert S. Flanzer	received	11,607	11,607
Christopher B. Garvey	received	11,607	11,607
David A. Harnett	received	11,607	11,607
James E. Harris	received	11,607	11,607
Loretta K. Hetzner	received	11,607	11,607
Werner Hetzner	received	11,607	11,607
David J. Hopwood	received	11,607	11,607
Nicolas Leobold	received	11,607	11,607
Jim Lesczynski	received	11,607	11,607
Adam Martin	received	11,607	11,607
Bruce A. Martin	received	11,607	11,607
Crystal Martin	received	11,607	11,607
William P. McMillen	received	11,607	11,607
Ronald G. Moore	received	11,607	11,607
John C. Mounteer	received	11,607	11,607
Christian Padgett	received	11,607	11,607
Audrey M. Pappaeliou	received	11,607	11,607
Gary S. Popkin	received	11,607	11,607
Louise Popkin	received	11,607	11,607
Eleanor Rosenblatt	received	11,607	11,607
Catherine Ruks	received	11,607	11,607
Thomas Ruks	received	11,607	11,607
Norma Segal	received	11,607	11,607
Donald Silberger	received	11,607	11,607
Sam Sloan	received	11,607	11,607
Thomas Robert Stevens	received	11,607	11,607
Michael L. Trombetta	received	11,607	11,607
Alexander E. Ullmann, III	received	11,607	11,607

GIVEN under our hands in Sloatsburg, New York, the 6th day of December in the year two thousand four.

Carol Berman	Commissioner
Neil W. Kelleher	Commissioner
Evelyn J. Aquila	Commissioner
Helena Moses Donohue	Commissioner

STATE OF NEW YORK   :
                                   : ss:

STATE BOARD OF ELECTIONS   :

I certify that I have compared the foregoing with the original certificate filed in this office, and that the same is a correct transcript therefrom and of the whole of such original.

GIVEN under my hand and official seal of office of the State Board of Elections, in the City of Albany, this 6th day of December, 2004.

_____

Peter S. Kosinski   Deputy Executive Director

CERTIFICATE OF ASCERTAINMENT

TO: THE HONORABLE JOHN W. CARLIN
ARCHIVIST OF THE UNITED STATES
NATIONAL ARCHIVES AND RECORDS ADMINISTRATION

I, HALEY BARBOUR, Governor of the State of Mississippi, in accordance with Chapter 1, Section 6 of Title 3, United States Code, do hereby certify as follows:

At the General Election held on Tuesday, November 2, 2004, the qualified electors of the state at large elected and appointed six (6) Presidential and Vice Presidential Electors for the State of Mississippi; and

There was no controversy or contest concerning the election of all or of any of such Electors; and

Pursuant to the applicable laws of this state, final ascertainment has now been made of the results of the November 2, 2004, General Election, and the following named persons have been elected and appointed to serve as, and to discharge the duties of, Presidential and Vice Presidential Electors for the State of Mississippi:

ELECTORS FOR GEORGE W. BUSH FOR PRESIDENT AND DICK CHENEY FOR VICE PRESIDENT (REPUBLICAN PARTY)

Mr. James H. "Jimmy" Creekmore	672,660
Mr. Victor Mavar	672,660
Mr. W.D. "Billy" Mounger	672,660
Mr. Wayne Parker	672,660
Mr. John F. Phillips	672,660
Dr. Kelly S. Segars	672,660.

I do further certify that the number of votes cast at the November 2, 2004, General Election for the other candidates for election as Presidential and Vice Presidential Electors has been finally ascertained to be:

ELECTORS FOR JOHN F. KERRY FOR PRESIDENT AND JOHN EDWARDS FOR VICE PRESIDENT (DEMOCRATIC PARTY)

Mr. Gary Bailey	457,766
Ms. Janice Carr	457,766
Mr. Robert Hooks	457,766
Ms. Tamara Longmire	457,766
Mrs. Tyna Stewart	457,766
Mr. Al Tate	457,766

ELECTORS FOR MICHAEL BADNARIK FOR PRESIDENT AND RICHARD V. CAMPAGNA FOR VICE PRESIDENT (LIBERTARIAN PARTY)

Mr. Mark G. Bushman	1,793
Mr. Victor G. Dostrow	1,793
Ms. Lana Renee Ethridge	1,793
Mr. Lewis W. Napper	1,793
Mr. Harold M. Taylor	1,793
Ms. Leighanne A. Taylor	1,793

ELECTORS FOR DAVID COBB FOR PRESIDENT AND PATRICIA LAMARCHE FOR VICE PRESIDENT (GREEN PARTY)

Mr. Sherman Lee Dillon	1,073
Mr. Ray Gebhart	1,073
Ms. Jan Hillegas	1,073
Mr. Greg Johnson	1,073
Mr. Claude Evan Peacock	1,073
Ms. Gwendolyn M. Wages	1,073

ELECTORS FOR JAMES HARRIS FOR PRESIDENT AND MARGARET TROWE FOR VICE PRESIDENT (INDEPENDENT)

Ms. Barbara Bell	1,268
Mr. Roy Bell	1,268
Ms. Joann Hogan	1,268
Ms. Penny Hogan	1,268
Mr. R.C. Howard	1,268
Ms. Linda Miles	1,268

ELECTORS FOR RALPH NADER FOR PRESIDENT AND PETER MIGUEL CAMEJO FOR VICE PRESIDENT (REFORM PARTY)

Mr. Rodney (Billy) Fulgham	3,177
Ms. Carroll Gunilham	3,177
Mr. John A. Hailey	3,177
Ms. Lunyonica L. Magee	3,177
Mr. Billy Minshew	3,177
Mr. Christopher Minshew	3,177

ELECTORS FOR MICHAEL A. PEROUTKA FOR PRESIDENT AND CHUCK BALDWIN FOR VICE PRESIDENT (CONSTITUTION PARTY)

Mr. John C. Bethea	1,759
Mr. Jim Bourland	1,759
Mr. Tim Delrie	1,759
Mr. Thomas R. Floyd	1,759
Mr. Leslie Riley	1,759
Mr. Steve C. Thornton	1,759

IN WITNESS WHEREOF, I have hereunto set my hand and caused the Great Seal of the State of Mississippi to be affixed.

DONE at the Capitol, in the City of Jackson, this the 22nd day of March, in the year of our Lord, Two thousand and five, and of the Independence of the United States of America, the two hundred and twenty ninth.

GOVERNOR

BY THE GOVERNOR

SECRETARY OF STATE

APPENDIX J: DATES APPEARING ON CERTIFICATES OF ASCERTAINMENT FOR 2000–2008 PRESIDENTIAL ELECTIONS

This appendix contains a table (table J.1) showing the key dates in the presidential election process for 2000–2008 and a table (table J.2) showing the dates appearing on the Certificates of Ascertainment from each state and the District of Columbia for the 2000–2008 elections.

Table J.1 Key Dates in Presidential Election Process for 2000–2008

	DATE FOR 2000	DATE FOR 2004	DATE FOR 2008
Election day	November 7, 2000	November 2, 2004	November 4, 2008
Safe harbor day	December 12, 2000	December 7, 2004	December 9, 2008
Electoral college meeting day	December 18, 2000	December 13, 2004	December 15, 2008

Table J.2 Dates Appearing on 2000–2008 Certificates of Ascertainment

JURISDICTION	DATE FOR 2000	DATE FOR 2004	DATE FOR 2008
Alabama	December 8, 2000	November 29, 2004	December 10, 2008
Alaska	December 5, 2000	December 7, 2004	December 8, 2008
Arizona	December 4, 2000	November 22, 2004	December 1, 2008
Arkansas	November 30, 2000	November 23, 2004	December 4, 2008
California	December 14, 2000	December 13, 2004	December 15, 2008
Colorado	December 4, 2000	December 13, 2004	December 11, 2008
Connecticut	November 29, 2000	November 24, 2004	November 26, 2008
Delaware	December 4, 2000	November 30, 2004	November 29, 2008
District of Columbia	December 6, 2000	December 7, 2004	December 10, 2008
Florida	November 26, 2000	November 18, 2004	November 24, 2008
Georgia	December 1, 2000	November 23, 2004	December 9, 2008
Hawaii	November 27, 2000	November 22, 2004	November 24, 2008
Idaho	November 22, 2000	November 17, 2004	November 19, 2008
Illinois	November 27, 2000	December 3, 2004	November 30, 2008
Indiana	December 5, 2000	December 7, 2004	December 8, 2008
Iowa	December 14, 2000	December 13, 2004	December 9, 2008
Kansas	December 6, 2000	December 8, 2004	December 3, 2008
Kentucky	December 4, 2000	December 1, 2004	December 3, 2008
Louisiana	November 21, 2000	November 16, 2004	November 17, 2008
Maine	November 27, 2000	November 23, 2004	November 25, 2008
Maryland	December 18, 2000	December 13, 2004	December 15, 2008
Massachusetts	December 6, 2000	December 13, 2004	December 9, 2008
Michigan	November 30, 2000	November 30, 2004	December 1, 2008
Minnesota	December 5, 2000	November 30, 2004	December 9, 2008
Mississippi	December 7, 2000	December 13, 2004	December 3, 2008
Missouri	December 11, 2000	December 13, 2004	December 5, 2008
Montana	December 6, 2000	December 8, 2004	December 9, 2008
Nebraska	December 18, 2000	December 13, 2004	December 15, 2008
Nevada	December 4, 2000	December 7, 2004	December 8, 2008
New Hampshire	December 6, 2000	December 1, 2004	December 3, 2008
New Jersey	December 8, 2000	December 13, 2004	December 4, 2008
New Mexico	December 5, 2000	December 3, 2004	December 7, 2008
New York	December 12, 2000	December 6, 2004	December 11, 2008
North Carolina	December 8, 2000	December 1, 2004	December 8, 2008
North Dakota	November 27, 2000	December 3, 2004	November 28, 2008
Ohio	December 11, 2000	December 6, 2004	December 11, 2008
Oklahoma	December 8, 2000	December 13, 2004	December 15, 2008
Oregon	No date	No date	No date
Pennsylvania	December 14, 2000	December 10, 2004	December 8, 2008
Rhode Island	November 22, 2000	November 23, 2004	November 24, 2008
South Carolina	November 28, 2000	December 3, 2004	November 20, 2008
South Dakota	November 28, 2000	December 13, 2004	November 13, 2008
Tennessee	November 28, 2000	December 7, 2004	December 8, 2008
Texas	November 27, 2000	November 18, 2004	November 19, 2008
Utah	December 1, 2000	December 13, 2004	November 24, 2008
Vermont	December 9, 2000	December 3, 2004	December 3, 2008
Virginia	November 29, 2000	December 13, 2004	November 25, 2008
Washington	December 7, 2000	December 9, 2004	December 4, 2008
West Virginia	December 11, 2000	December 13, 2004	December 16, 2008
Wisconsin	December 11, 2000	December 6, 2004	December 6, 2008
Wyoming	November 22, 2000	December 2, 2004	November 12, 2008

SECTION 6161.01 (EFFECTIVE ON OCTOBER 9, 1963)

The "great lakes basin compact" is hereby ratified, enacted into law, and entered into by this state as a party thereto with any other state or province which, pursuant to Article II of said compact, has legally joined in the compact as follows:

GREAT LAKES BASIN COMPACT

The party states solemnly agree:

Article I

The purposes of this compact are, through means of joint or co-operative action:

(A) To promote the orderly, integrated, and comprehensive development, use, and conservation of the water sources of the great lakes basin (hereinafter called the basin);

(B) To plan for the welfare and development of the water resources of the basin as a whole, as well as for those portions of the basin which may have problems of special concern;

(C) To make it possible for the states of the basin and their people to derive the maximum benefit from utilization of public works, in the form of navigational aids or otherwise, which may exist or which may be constructed from time to time;

(D) To advise in securing and maintaining a proper balance among industrial, commercial, agricultural, water supply, residential, recreational, and other legitimate uses of the water resources of the basin;

(E) To establish and maintain an intergovernmental agency to the end that the purposes of this compact may be accomplished more effectively.

Article II

(A) This compact shall enter into force and become effective and binding when it has been enacted by the legislatures of any four of the states of Illinois, Indiana, Michigan, Minnesota, New York, Ohio, Pennsylvania, and Wisconsin and thereafter shall enter into force and become effective and binding as to any other of said states when enacted by the legislature thereof.

(B) The province of Ontario and the province of Quebec, or either of them, may become states party to this compact by taking such action as their laws and the laws of the government of Canada may prescribe for adherence thereto. For the purpose of this compact the word "state" shall be construed in include a province of Canada.

Article III

The great lakes commission created by Article IV of this compact shall exercise its powers and perform its functions in respect to the basin which, for the purposes of this compact, shall consist of so much of the following as may be within the party states:

(A) Lakes Erie, Huron, Michigan, Ontario, St. Clair, Superior, and the St. Lawrence River, together with any and all natural or man-made water interconnections between or among them;

(B) All rivers, ponds, lakes, streams, and other watercourses which, in their natural state or in their prevailing condition, are tributary to Lakes Erie, Huron, Michigan, Ontario, St. Clair, and Superior, or any of them, or which comprise part of any watershed draining into any of said lakes.

Article IV

(A) There is hereby created an agency of the party states to be known as the great lakes commission (hereinafter called the commission). In that name the commission may sue and be sued, acquire, hold and convey real and personal property, and any interest therein. The commission shall have a seal with the words "the great lakes commission" and such other design as it may prescribe engraved thereon by which it shall authenticate its proceedings. Transactions involving real or personal property shall conform to the laws of the state in which the property is located, and the commission may by bylaws provide for the execution and acknowledgment of all instruments in its behalf.

(B) The commission shall be composed of not less than three commissioners nor more than five commissioners from each party state designated or appointed in accordance with the law of the state which they represent and serving and subject to removal in accordance with such law.

(C) Each state delegation shall be entitled to three votes in the commission. The presence of commissioners from a majority of the party states shall constitute a quorum for the transaction of business at any meeting of the commission. Actions of the commission shall be by a majority of the votes cast except that any recommendations made pursuant to Article VI of this compact shall require an affirmative vote of not less than a majority of the votes cast from each of a majority of the states present and voting.

(D) The commissioners of any two or more party states may meet separately to consider problems of particular interest to their states but no action taken at any such meeting shall be deemed an action of the commission unless and until the commission shall specifically approve the same.

(E) In the absence of any commissioner, his vote may be cast by another representative or commissioner of his state provided that said commissioner or other representative casting said vote shall have a written proxy in proper form as may be required by the commission.

(F) The commission shall elect annually from among its members a chairman and vice-chairman. The commission shall appoint an executive director who shall also act as secretary-treasurer, and who shall be bonded in such amount as the commission may require. The executive director shall serve at the pleasure of the commission and at such compensation and under such terms and conditions as may be fixed by it. The executive director shall be custodian of the records of the commission with authority to affix the commission's official seal and to attest and certify such records or copies thereof.

(G) The executive director, subject to the approval of the commission in such cases as its bylaws may provide, shall appoint and remove or discharge such personnel as may be necessary for the performance of the commission's functions. Subject to the aforesaid approval, the executive director may fix their compensation, define their duties, and require bonds of such of them as the commission may designate.

(H) The executive director, on behalf of, as trustee for, and with the approval of the commission, may borrow, accept, or contract for the services of personnel from any state or government or any subdivision or agency thereof, from any intergovernmental agency, or from any institution, person, firm, or corporation; and may accept for any of the commission's purposes and functions under this compact any and all donations, gifts, and grants of money, equipment, supplies, materials, and services from any state or government or any subdivision or agency thereof or intergovernmental agency or from any institution, person, firm, or corporation and may receive and utilize the same.

(I) The commission may establish and maintain one or more offices for the transacting of its business and for such purposes the executive director, on behalf of, as trustee for, and with the approval of the commission, may acquire, hold, and dispose of real and personal property necessary to the performance of its functions.

(J) No tax levied or imposed by any party state or any political subdivision thereof shall be deemed to apply to property, transactions, or income of the commission.

(K) The commission may adopt, amend, and rescind bylaws, rules, and regulations for the conduct of its business.

(L) The organization meeting of the commission shall be held within six months from the effective date of this compact.

(M) The commission and its executive director shall make available to the party states any information within its possession and shall always provide free access to its records by duly authorized representatives of such party states.

(N) The commission shall keep a written record of its meetings and proceedings and shall annually make a report thereof to be submitted to the duly designated official of each party state.

(O) The commission shall make and transmit annually to the legislature and governor of each party state a report covering the activities of the commission for the preceding year and embodying such recommendations as may have been adopted by the commission. The commission may issue such additional reports as it may deem desirable.

Article V

(A) The members of the commission shall serve without compensation, but the expenses of each commissioner shall be met by the state which he represents in accordance with the law of that state. All other expenses incurred by the commission in the course of exercising the powers conferred upon it by this compact, unless met in some other manner specifically provided by this compact, shall be paid by the commission out of its own funds.

(B) The commission shall submit to the executive head or designated officer of each party state a budget of its estimated expenditures for such period as may be required by the laws of the state for presentation to the legislature thereof.

(C) Each of the commission's budgets of estimated expenditures shall contain specific recommendations of the amount or amounts to be appropriated by each of the party states. Detailed commission budgets shall be recommended by a majority of the votes cast, and the costs shall be allocated equitably among the party states in accordance with their respective interests.

(D) The commission shall not pledge the credit of any party state. The commission may meet any of its obligations in whole or in part with funds available to it under Article IV (H) of this compact, provided that the commission takes specific action setting aside such funds prior to the incurring of any obligations to be met in whole or in part in this manner. Except where the commission makes use of funds available to it under Article IV (H) hereof, the commission shall not incur any obligations prior to the allotment of funds by the party states adequate to meet the same.

(E) The commission shall keep accurate accounts of all receipts and disbursements. The receipts and disbursements of the commission shall be subject to the audit and accounting procedures established under the bylaws. However, all receipts and disbursements of funds handled by the commission shall be audited yearly by a qualified public accountant and the report of the audit shall be included in and become a part of the annual report of the commission.

(F) The accounts of the commission shall be open at any reasonable time for inspection by such agency, representative, or representatives of the party states as may be duly constituted for that purpose and by others who may be authorized by the commission.

Article VI

The commission shall have power to:

(A) Collect, correlate, interpret, and report on data relating to the water resources and the use thereof in the basin or any portion thereof;

(B) Recommend methods for the orderly, efficient, and balanced development, use, and conservation of the water resources of the basin or any portion thereof to the party states and to any other governments or agencies having interests in or jurisdiction over the basin or any portion thereof;

(C) Consider the need for and desirability of public works and improvements relating to the water resources in the basin or any portion thereof;

(D) Consider means of improving navigation and port facilities in the basin or any portion thereof;

(E) Consider means of improving and maintaining the fisheries of the basin or any portion thereof;

(F) Recommend policies relating to water resources including the institution and alteration of flood plain and other zoning laws, ordinances, and regulations;

(G) Recommend uniform or other laws, ordinances, or regulations relating to the development, use, and conservation of the basin's water resources to the party states or any of them and to other governments, political subdivisions, agencies, or intergovernmental bodies having interests in or jurisdiction sufficient to affect conditions in the basin or any portion thereof;

(H) Consider and recommend amendments or agreements supplementary to this compact to the party states or any of them, and assist in the formulation and drafting of such amendments or supplementary agreements;

(I) Prepare and publish reports, bulletins, and publications appropriate to this work and fix reasonable sale prices therefor;

(J) With respect to the water resources of the basin or any portion thereof, recommend agreements between the governments of the United States and Canada;

(K) Recommend mutual arrangements expressed by concurrent or reciprocal legislation on the part of congress and the parliament of Canada including but not limited to such agreements and mutual arrangement as are provided for by Article XIII of the Treaty of 1909 Relating to Boundary Waters and Questions Arising Between the United States and Canada. (Treaty Series, No. 548);

(L) Co-operate with the governments of the United States and of Canada, the party states and any public or private agencies or bodies having interests in or jurisdiction sufficient to affect the basin or any portion thereof;

(M) At the request of the United States, or in the event that a province shall be a party state, at the request of the government of Canada, assist in the negotiation and formulation of any treaty or other mutual arrangement or agreement between the United States and Canada with reference to the basin or any portion thereof;

(N) Make any recommendation and do all things necessary and proper to carry out the powers conferred upon the commission by this compact, provided that no action of the commission shall have the force of law in, or be binding upon, any party state.

Article VII

Each party state agrees to consider the action the commission recommends in respect to:

(A) Stabilization of lake levels;

(B) Measures for combating pollution, beach erosion, floods, and shore inundation;

(C) Uniformity in navigation regulations within the constitutional powers of the states;

(D) Proposed navigation aids and improvements;

(E) Uniformity or effective co-ordinating action in fishing laws and regulations and co-operative action to eradicate destructive and parasitical forces endangering the fisheries, wild life, and other water resources;

(F) Suitable hydroelectric power developments;

(G) Co-operative programs for control of soil and bank erosion for the general improvement of the basin;

(H) Diversion of waters from and into the basin;

(I) Other measures the commission may recommend to the states pursuant to Article VI of this compact.

Article VIII

This compact shall continue in force and remain binding upon each party state until renounced by act of the legislature of such state, in such form and manner as it may choose and as may be valid and effective to repeal a statute of said state, provided that such renunciation shall not become effective until six months after notice of such action shall have been officially communicated in writing to the executive head of the other party states.

Article IX

It is intended that the provisions of this compact shall be reasonably and liberally construed to effectuate the purposes thereof. The provisions of this compact shall be severable and if any phrase, clause, sentence, or provision of this compact is declared to be contrary to the constitution of any party state or of the United States, or in the case of a province, to the British North America Act of 1867 as amended, or the applicability thereof to any state, agency, person, or circumstance is held invalid, the constitutionality of the remainder of this compact and the applicability thereof to any state, agency, person, or circumstance shall not be affected thereby, provided further that if this compact shall be held contrary to the constitution of the United States, or in the case of a province, to the British North America Act of 1867 as amended, or of any party state, the compact shall remain in full force and effect as to the remaining states and in full force and effect as to the state affected as to all severable matters.

APPENDIX L: CONGRESSIONAL CONSENT TO THE INTERSTATE AGREEMENT ON DETAINERS

PUBLIC LAW 91-538 OF 1970

AN ACT
To enact the Interstate Agreement on Detainers into law

Be it enacted by the Senate and House of Representatives of the United States of America in congress assembled, That this Act may be cited as the "Interstate Agreement on Detainers Act."

Sec. 2. The Interstate Agreement on Detainers is hereby enacted into law and entered into by the United States on its own behalf and on behalf of the District of Columbia with all jurisdictions legally joining in substantially the following form:

"The contracting States solemnly agree that:

"Article I
"The party States find that charges outstanding against a prisoner, detainers based on untried indictments, informations, or complaints and difficulties in securing speedy trial of persons already incarcerated in other jurisdictions, produce uncertainties which obstruct programs of prisoner treatment and rehabilitation. Accordingly, it is the policy of the party States and the purpose of this agreement to encourage the expeditious and orderly disposition of such charges and determination of the proper status of any and all detainers based on untried indictments, informations, or complaints. The party States also find that proceedings with reference to such charges and detainers, when emanating from another jurisdiction, cannot properly be had in the absence of cooperative procedures. It is the further purpose of this agreement to provide such cooperative procedures.

"Article II
"As used in this agreement:
"(a) 'State' shall mean a State of the United States; the United States of America; a territory or possession of the United States; the District of Columbia; the Commonwealth of Puerto Rico.
"(b) 'Sending State' shall mean a State in which a prisoner is incarcerated at the time that he initiates a request for final disposition pursuant to article III hereof or at the time that a request for custody or availability is initiated pursuant to article IV hereof.

"(c) 'Receiving State' shall mean the State in which trial is to be had on an indictment, information, or complaint pursuant to article III or article IV hereof.

"Article III

"(a) Whenever a person has entered upon a term of imprisonment in a penal or correctional institution of a party State, and whenever during the continuance of the term of imprisonment there is pending in any other party State any untried indictment, information, or complaint on the basis of which a detainer has been lodged against the prisoner, he shall be brought to trial within one hundred and eighty days after he shall have caused to be delivered to the prosecuting officer and the appropriate court of the prosecuting officer's jurisdiction written notice of the place of his imprisonment and his request for a final disposition to be made of the indictment, information, or complaint: Provided, That, for good cause shown in open court, the prisoner or his counsel being present, the court having jurisdiction of the matter may grant any necessary or reasonable continuance. The request of the prisoner shall be accompanied by a certificate of the appropriate official having custody of the prisoner, stating the term of commitment under which the prisoner is being held, the time already served, the time remaining to be served on the sentence, the amount of good time earned, the time of parole eligibility of the prisoner, and any decision of the State parole agency relating to the prisoner.

"(b) The written notice and request for final disposition referred to in paragraph (a) hereof shall be given or sent by the prisoner to the warden, commissioner of corrections, or other official having custody of him, who shall promptly forward it together with the certificate to the appropriate prosecuting official and court by registered or certified mail, return receipt requested.

"(c) The warden, commissioner of corrections, or other official having custody of the prisoner shall promptly inform him of the source and contents of any detainer lodged against him and shall also inform him of his right to make a request for final disposition of the indictment, information, or complaint on which the detainer is based.

"(d) Any request for final disposition made by a prisoner pursuant to paragraph (a) hereof shall operate as a request for final disposition of all untried indictments, informations, or complaints on the basis of which detainers have been lodged against the prisoner from the State to whose prosecuting official the request for final disposition is specifically directed. The warden, commissioner of corrections, or other official having custody of the prisoner shall forthwith notify all appropriate prosecuting officers and courts in the several jurisdictions within the State to which the prisoner's request for final disposition is being sent of the proceeding being initiated by the prisoner. Any notification sent pursuant to this paragraph shall be accompanied by copies of the prisoner's written notice, request, and the certificate. If trial is not had on any indictment, information, or complaint contemplated hereby prior to the return of the prisoner to the original place of imprisonment, such indictment, information, or complaint shall not be of any further force or effect, and the court shall enter an order dismissing the same with prejudice.

"(e) Any request for final disposition made by a prisoner pursuant to paragraph (a) hereof shall also be deemed to be a waiver of extradition with respect to any charge or proceeding contemplated thereby or included therein by reason of paragraph (d) hereof, and a waiver of extradition to the receiving State to serve any sentence there imposed upon him after completion of his term of imprisonment in the sending State. The request for final disposition shall also constitute a consent by the prisoner to the production of his body in any court where his presence may be required in order to effectuate the purposes of this agreement and a further consent voluntarily to be returned to the original place of imprisonment in accordance with the provisions of this agreement. Nothing in this paragraph shall prevent the imposition of a concurrent sentence if otherwise permitted by law.

"(f) Escape from custody by the prisoner subsequent to his execution of the request for final disposition referred to in paragraph (a) hereof shall void the request.

"Article IV

"(a) The appropriate officer of the jurisdiction in which an untried indictment, information, or complaint is pending shall be entitled to have a prisoner against whom he has lodged a detainer and who is serving a term of imprisonment in any party State made available in accordance with article V(a) hereof upon presentation of a written request for temporary custody or availability to the appropriate authorities of the State in which the prisoner is incarcerated: Provided, That the court having jurisdiction of such indictment, information, or complaint shall have duly approved recorded, and transmitted the request: And provided further, That there shall be a period of thirty days after receipt by the appropriate authorities before the request be honored, within which period the Governor of the sending State may disapprove the request for temporary custody or availability, either upon his own motion or upon motion of the prisoner.

"(b) Upon request of the officer's written request as provided in paragraph (a) hereof, the appropriate authorities having the prisoner in custody shall furnish the officer with a certificate stating the term of commitment under which the prisoner is being held, the time already served, the time remaining to be served on the sentence, the amount of good time earned, the time of parole eligibility of the prisoner, and any decisions of the State parole agency relating to the prisoner. Said authorities simultaneously shall furnish all other officers and appropriate courts in the receiving State who has lodged detainers against the prisoner with similar certificates and with notices informing them of the request for custody or availability and of the reasons therefor.

"(c) In respect of any proceeding made possible by this article, trial shall be commenced within one hundred and twenty days of the arrival of the prisoner in the receiving State but for good cause shown in open court, the prisoner or his counsel being present, the court having jurisdiction of the matter may grant any necessary or reasonable continuance.

"(d) Nothing contained in this article shall be construed to deprive any prisoner of any right which he may have to contest the legality of his delivery as provided in paragraph (a) hereof, but such delivery may not be opposed or denied on the ground that the executive authority of the sending State has not affirmatively consented to or ordered such delivery.

"(e) If trial is not had on any indictment, information, or complaint contemplated hereby prior to the prisoner's being returned to the original place of imprisonment pursuant to article V(e) hereof, such indictment, information, or complaint shall not be of any further fore or effect, and the court shall enter an order dismissing the same with prejudice.

"Article V

"(a) In response to a request made under article III or article IV hereof, the appropriate authority in the sending State shall offer to deliver temporary custody of such prisoner to the appropriate authority in the State where such indictment, information, or complaint is pending against such person in order that speedy and efficient prosecution may be had. If the request for final disposition is made by the prisoner, the offer of temporary custody shall accompany the written notice provided for in article III of this agreement. In the case of a Federal prisoner, the appropriate authority in the receiving State shall be entitled to temporary custody as provided by this agreement or to the prisoner's presence in Federal custody at the place of trial, whichever custodial arrangement may be approved by the custodian.

"(b) The officer or other representative of a State accepting an offer of temporary custody shall present the following upon demand:

"(1) Proper identification and evidence of his authority to act for the State into whose temporary custody this prisoner is to be given.

"(2) A duly certified copy of the indictment, information, or complaint on the basis of which the detainer has been lodged and on the basis of which the request for temporary custody of the prisoner has been made.

"(c) If the appropriate authority shall refuse or fail to accept temporary custody of said person, or in the event that an action on the indictment, information, or complaint on the basis of which the detainer has been lodged is not brought to trial within the period provided in article III or article IV hereof, the appropriate court of the jurisdiction where the indictment, information, or complaint has been pending shall enter an order dismissing the same with prejudice, and any detainer based thereon shall cease to be of any force or effect.

"(d) The temporary custody referred to in this agreement shall be only for the purpose of permitting prosecution on the charge or charges contained in one or more untried indictments, informations, or complaints which form the basis of the detainer or detainers or for prosecution on any other charge or charges arising out of the same transaction. Except for his attendance at court and while being transported to or from any place at which his presence may be required, the prisoner shall be held in a suitable jail or other facility regularly used for persons awaiting prosecution.

"(e) At the earliest practicable time consonant with the purposes of this agreement, the prisoner shall be returned to the sending State.

"(f) During the continuance of temporary custody or while the prisoner is otherwise being made available for trial as required by this agreement, time being served on the sentence shall continue to run but good time shall be earned by the prisoner only if, and to the extent that, the law and practice of the jurisdiction which imposed the sentence may allow.

"(g) For all purposes other than that for which temporary custody as provided in this agreement is exercised, the prisoner shall be deemed to remain in the custody of and subject to the jurisdiction of the sending State and any escape from temporary custody may be dealt with in the same manner as an escape from the original place of imprisonment or in any other manner permitted by law.

"(h) From the time that a party State receives custody of a prisoner pursuant to this agreement until such prisoner is returned to the territory and custody of the sending State, the State in which the one or more untried indictments, informations, or complaints are pending or in which trial is being had shall be responsible for the prisoner and shall also pay all costs of transporting, caring for, keeping, and returning the prisoner. The provisions of this paragraph shall govern unless the States concerned shall have entered into a supplementary agreement providing for a different allocation of costs and responsibilities as between or among themselves. Nothing herein contained shall be construed to alter or affect any internal relationship among the departments, agencies, and officers of and in the government of a party State, or between a party State and its subdivisions, as to the payment of costs, or responsibilities therefor.

"Article VI
"(a) In determining the duration and expiration dates of the time periods provided in articles III and IV of this agreement, the running of said time periods shall be tolled whenever and for as long as the prisoner is unable to stand trial, as determined by the court having jurisdiction of the matter.
"(b) No provision of this agreement, and no remedy made available by this agreement shall apply to any person who is adjudged to be mentally ill.

"Article VII

"Each State party to this agreement shall designate an officer who, acting jointly with like officers of other party States shall promulgate rules and regulations to carry out more effectively the terms and provisions of this agreement, and who shall provide, within and without the State, information necessary to the effective operation of this agreement.

"Article VIII

"This agreement shall enter into full force and effect as to a party State when such State has enacted the same into law. A State party to this agreement may withdraw herefrom by enacting a statute repealing the same. However, the withdrawal of any State shall not affect the status of any proceedings already initiated by inmates or by State officers at the time such withdrawal takes effect, nor shall it affect their rights in respect thereof.

"Article IX
"This agreement shall be liberally construed so as to effectuate its purposes. The provisions of this agreement shall be severable and if any phrase, clause, sentence, or provision of this agreement is declared to be contrary to the constitution of any party State or of the United States or the applicability thereof to any government, agency, person, or circumstance is held invalid, the validity of the remainder of this agreement and the applicability thereof to any government, agency, person or circumstance shall not be affected thereby. If this agreement shall be held contrary to the constitution of any State party hereto, the agreement shall remain in full force and effect as to the remaining States and in full force and effect as to the State affected as to all severable matters."

Sec. 3. The term "Governor" as used in the agreement on detainers shall mean with respect to the United States, the Attorney General, and with respect to the District of Columbia, the Commissioner of the District of Columbia.

Sec. 4. The term "appropriate court" as used in the agreement on detainers shall mean with respect to the United States, the courts of the United States, and with respect to the District of Columbia, the courts of the District of Columbia, in which indictments, informations, or complaints, for which disposition is sought, are pending.

Sec. 5. All courts, departments, agencies officers, and employees of the United States and of the District of Columbia are hereby directed to enforce the agreement on detainers and to cooperate with one another and with all party States in enforcing the agreement and effectuating its purpose.

Sec. 6. For the United States, the Attorney General, and for the District of Columbia, the Commissioner of the District of Columbia, shall establish such regulations, prescribe such forms, issue such instructions, and perform such other acts as he deems necessary for carrying out the provisions of this Act.

Sec. 7. The right to alter, amend, or repeal this Act is expressly reserved.

Sec. 8. This Act shall take effect on the ninetieth day after the date of its enactment.

APPENDIX M: LIST OF INTERSTATE COMPACTS

The National Center for Interstate Compacts of the Council of State Governments has compiled the following list of 196 interstate compacts believed to be currently in force as of 2006.

The National Center for Interstate Compacts (NCIC) is designed to be an information clearinghouse, a provider of training and technical assistance, and a primary facilitator in assisting states in their review, revision, and creation of new interstate compacts to solve multi-state problems or to provide alternatives to federal preemption. As such, the NCIC combines policy research and best practices, and functions as a membership association, serving the needs of compact administrators, compact commissions, and state agencies where interstate compacts are in effect.

For additional information on the National Center for Interstate Compacts (NCIC), visit http://www.csg.org/ncic/.

List of Interstate Compacts

- Apalachicola-Chattahoochee-Flint River Basin Compact,
- Alabama-Coosa-Tallapossa River Basin Compact,
- Animas–La Plata Project Compact,
- Appalachian States Low-Level Radioactive Waste Compact,
- Arkansas-Mississippi Great River Bridge Construction Compact Arkansas,
- Arkansas River Basin Compact of 1970,
- Arkansas River Compact of 1949,
- Arkansas River Compact of 1965 (Arkansas River Basin Compact, Kansas, Oklahoma),
- Atlantic States Marine Fisheries Compact Delaware,
- Bay State–Ocean State Compact,
- Bear River Compact,
- Belle Fourche River Compact,
- Chesapeake Bay Commission Agreement (Bi/Tri-State Agreement on the Chesapeake Bay)—Chesapeake Bay Commission,
- Bi-State Criminal Justice Center Compact Arkansas,
- Bi-State Development Agency Compact Missouri (Bi-State Metropolitan District),
- Boating Offense Compact,
- Breaks Interstate Park Compact,
- Buffalo and Fort Erie Bridge Compact New York,
- Bus Taxation Proration and Reciprocity Agreement,
- California-Nevada Compact for Jurisdiction on Interstate Waters,

- Canadian River Compact—Canadian River Compact Commission,
- Central Interstate Low-Level Radioactive Waste Compact—Central Interstate Low-Level Radioactive Waste Commission,
- Central Midwest Low-Level Radioactive Waste Compact,
- Chesapeake Regional Olympic Games Authority,
- Chickasaw Trail Economic Development Compact,
- Colorado River Compact,
- Colorado River Crime Enforcement Compact (Interstate Compact for Jurisdiction on the Colorado River),
- Columbia River Compact (Oregon-Washington Columbia River Fish Compact),
- (Columbia River Gorge Compact)—Columbia River Gorge Commission,
- Compact for Pension Portability for Educators,
- (Connecticut–New York) Railroad Passenger Transportation Compact,
- Connecticut River Atlantic Salmon Compact—Connecticut River Atlantic Salmon Compact Commission,
- Connecticut River Valley Flood Control Compact,
- Costilla Creek Compact Colorado,
- Cumberland Gap National Park Compact Virginia,
- Cumbres and Toltec Scenic Railroad Compact,
- Delaware River and Bay Authority Compact (Delaware–New Jersey Compact),
- Delaware River Basin Compact—Delaware River Basin Commission,
- Delaware River Joint Toll Bridge Compact,
- Delaware River and Port Authority Compact—Delaware River Port Authority,
- Delaware Valley Urban Area Compact—Delaware Valley Regional Planning Commission,
- Delmarva Advisory Council Agreement Virginia,
- Desert Pacific Economic Region Compact,
- Drivers' License Compact—American Association of Motor Vehicle Administrators,
- Emergency Management Assistance Compact,
- Great Lakes Basin Compact Indiana—Great Lakes Basin Commission,
- Great Lakes Forest Fire Compact—Great Lakes Forest Fire Compact Board,
- Gulf States Marine Fisheries Compact,
- Historic Chattahoochee Compact,
- International Registration Plan,
- International Fuel Tax Agreement (Motor Carriers),
- Interpleader Compact,

- Interstate Adoption Assistance Compact,
- (Interstate) Agreement on Qualification of Educational Personnel,
- (Interstate) Civil Defense (and Disaster Compact),
- (Interstate) Compact for (on) Adoption and Medical Assistance,
- Interstate Compact for Adult offender Supervision,
- (Interstate) Compact for Education (Compact)—Education Commission of the States,
- (Interstate) Compact(s) on Parole and Probation (the Supervision of Parolees and Probationers) (for the Supervision of) (Interstate Compact for Supervision of Parolees and Probationers),
- (Interstate) Civil Defense (and Disaster) Compact,
- Interstate Compact on Energy (Midwest Energy Compact),
- Interstate Compact on Industrialized/Modular Buildings,
- Interstate Compact on Juveniles—Association of Juvenile Compact Administrators,
- Interstate Compact on Licensure of Participants in Live Racing with Parimutuel Wagering,
- Interstate (Compact on) Pest Control Compact—Interstate Pest Control Governing Board,
- (Interstate) Compact on (the) Placement of Children,
- Interstate (Compact to Conserve) Oil and Gas Compact Illinois—Interstate Oil and Gas Compact Commission,
- Interstate Corrections Compact,
- Interstate Dealer Licensing Compact,
- Interstate Earthquake Emergency Compact,
- Interstate Forest Fire Suppression Compact,
- Interstate Furlough Compact Utah,
- Interstate High Speed Intercity Rail Passenger Network Compact/Interstate High Speed Rail Compact,
- Interstate Insurance Receivership Compact,
- Interstate Jobs Protection Compact,
- Interstate Library Compact,
- Interstate Mining Compact—Interstate Mining Compact Commission,
- (Interstate) Mutual Aid (Agreements) Compact,
- Interstate Rail Passenger Network Compact,
- Interstate Solid Waste Compact,
- (Interstate) (Uniform) Agreement on Detainers (Interstate Compact on),
- Interstate Water Supply Compact (Vermont–New Hampshire),

- (Interstate) Wildlife Violator Compact,
- Jennings Randolph Lake Project Compact,
- Kansas City Area Transportation District and Authority Compact,
- Kansas-Missouri Flood Prevention and Control Compact Missouri,
- (Kansas-Nebraska) Big Blue River Compact,
- Klamath River Compact,
- La Plata River Compact,
- Low-Level Radioactive Waste Disposal,
- Live Horseracing Compact (the Interstate Compact on Licensure of Participants in Horse Racing with Pari-Mutuel Wagering),
- Maine–New Hampshire School District Compact,
- Mentally Disordered Offender Compact,
- Middle Atlantic (Interstate) Forest Fire Protection Compact,
- Midwestern Higher Education Compact—Midwestern Higher Education Commission,
- Midwest Interstate Passenger Rail Compact,
- Midwest Interstate Low-Level Radioactive Waste Compact,
- Minnesota-Wisconsin Boundary (Area) Compact,
- Mississippi River Interstate Pollution Phase Out Compact,
- Missouri and Kansas Metropolitan Culture District Compact,
- Missouri River Toll Bridge Compact,
- Motor Vehicle Safety Equipment Compact,
- Multistate Highway Transportation Agreement,
- Multistate Lottery Agreement,
- Multistate Tax Compact—The Multistate Tax Commission,
- Mutual Interstate Aid Agreements and Compacts,
- Mutual/Military Aid Compact,
- National Crime Prevention and Privacy Compact,
- National Guard Mutual Assistance Compact,
- National Guard Mutual Assistance Counter-Drug Activities Compact,
- New England Compact on Radiological Health Protection,
- New England Compact on Involuntary Detention for Tuberculosis Control,
- New England (Interstate) Corrections Compact,
- New England Higher Education Compact—New England Board of Higher Education,
- New England Interstate Water Pollution Control Compact—New England Interstate Water Pollution Control Commission,
- New England States Emergency Military Aid Compact,

- New England (State) Police Compact Massachusetts,
- New England Truckers Compact,
- New England Truck Permit Agreement for Oversize, Non-Divisible, Interstate Loads,
- New Hampshire–Massachusetts Interstate Sewage and Waste Disposal Facilities Compact,
- New Hampshire–Vermont Interstate School Compact (Hanover-Norwich District),
- New Hampshire–Vermont Interstate Sewage and Waste Disposal Facilities Compact,
- New Jersey–Pennsylvania Turnpike Bridge Compact,
- New York–New Jersey Port Authority Compact—The Port Authority of New York and New Jersey,
- New York–Vermont Interstate School Compact,
- Nonresident Violator Compact—American Association of Motor Vehicle Administrators,
- Northern New England Low-Level Radioactive Waste Compact,
- Northeast Interstate Dairy Compact,
- Northeast Interstate Low-Level Radioactive Waste Management Compact,
- Northeast Mississippi–Northwest Alabama Railroad Authority Compact,
- Northeastern (Interstate) Forest Fire Protection Compact—Northeastern Forest Fire Protection Commission,
- Northeast Interstate Dairy Compact—Northeast Interstate Dairy Compact Committee,
- Northeast Interstate Low-Level Radioactive Waste Management Compact,
- Northwest (Interstate) Compact on Low-Level Radioactive Waste Management,
- Nurse Licensure Compact,
- Ogdensburg Bridge and Port Authority,
- Ohio River Valley Water Sanitation Compact—Ohio River Valley Sanitation Commission,
- Out-of-State Parollee Supervision,
- Pacific Marine Fisheries Compact—Pacific States Marine Fisheries Commission,
- Pacific Ocean Resources Compact,
- Pacific States Agreement on Radioactive Materials Transportation,
- Palisades Interstate Park Compact New Jersey—Palisades Interstate Park Commission,
- Pecos River Compact Texas—Pecos River Compact Commission,

- Portsmouth-Kittery Bridge Compact,
- Potomac Highlands Airport Authority,
- Potomac River Bridges Towing Compact,
- Potomac River Compact of 1958,
- Potomac Valley Compact (Conservancy District) (Potomac River Basin Interstate Compact of 1940),
- Pymatuning Lake Compact,
- Quad Cities Interstate Metropolitan Authority Compact,
- Red River Compact—Red River Compact Commission,
- Republican River Compact,
- Rio Grande Interstate Compact—Rio Grande Compact Commission,
- Rocky Mountain Low-Level Radioactive Waste Compact,
- Sabine River Compact,
- Snake River Compact,
- South Central (Interstate) Forest Fire Protection Compact,
- South Platte River Compact,
- Southern Dairy Compact,
- Southern Growth Policies (Agreements) (Board) (Compact)—Southern Growth Policies Board,
- Southern (Interstate) (Energy) (Nuclear) Compact (Southern States Energy Compact),
- Southeastern (Interstate) Forest Fire Protection Compact,
- Southeast Interstate Low-Level Radioactive Waste (Management) Compact—Southeast Interstate Low-Level Radioactive Waste Commission,
- (Southern) Rapid Rail Transit Compact (Mississippi-Louisiana-Alabama-Georgia Rapid Rail Transit Compact),
- Southern Regional Education Compact—Southern Regional Education Board,
- Southwestern Low-Level Radioactive Waste Disposal Compact,
- Susquehanna River Basin Compact—Susquehanna River Basin Commission,
- Tahoe Regional Planning Compact,
- Tangipahoa River Waterway Compact,
- Taxation of Motor Fuels Consumed by Interstate Buses,
- Tennessee-Tombigbee Waterway Development Compact—Tombigbee Waterway Development Authority,
- Tennessee Interstate Furlough Compact,
- (Texas) Low-Level Radioactive Waste Disposal Compact,
- (The) Interstate Compact on Agricultural Grain Marketing,
- (The) (Interstate) Compact on Mental Health,

- Thames River Flood Control Compact,
- Tri-State Agreement on the Chesapeake Bay,
- Tri-State Delta Economic Compact,
- Tri-State Lotto Compact,
- Tri-State Sanitation Compact (Interstate Environmental Commission, Tri-State Compact),
- Tuberculosis Control Compact,
- Unclaimed (Abandoned or Uniform) Property Compact (Act) (Uniform Disposition of Unclaimed Property Act),
- Upper Colorado River Basin Compact,
- Upper Niobrara River Compact,
- Vehicle Equipment Safety Compact—American Association of Motor Vehicle Administrators,
- Wabash Valley Compact,
- Washington Metropolitan Area Transit Authority—Washington Metropolitan Area Transit Authority,
- Washington Metropolitan Area Transit District,
- Waterfront Commission Compact,
- Western (Interstate) Corrections Compact,
- Western Interstate Nuclear (Energy) (Cooperation) Compact,
- Western Regional (Higher) Education Compact—Western Interstate Commission for Higher Education,
- Wheeling Creek Watershed Protection and Flood Prevention Compact,
- Woodrow Wilson Bridge and Tunnel Compact, and
- Yellowstone River Compact.

The above information is reprinted here with the kind permission of the National Center for Interstate Compacts.

APPENDIX N: CONGRESSIONAL CONSENT TO THE EMERGENCY MANAGEMENT ASSISTANCE COMPACT

PUBLIC LAW 104–321 OF 1996

JOINT RESOLUTION
Granting the consent of Congress to
the Emergency Management Assistance Compact

Resolved by the Senate and House of Representatives of the United States of America in Congress assembled,

SECTION 1. CONGRESSIONAL CONSENT.

The Congress consents to the Emergency Management Assistance Compact entered into by Delaware, Florida, Georgia, Louisiana, Maryland, Mississippi, Missouri, Oklahoma, South Carolina, South Dakota, Tennessee, Virginia, and West Virginia. The compact reads substantially as follows:

"Emergency Management Assistance Compact

"ARTICLE I.
"PURPOSE AND AUTHORITIES.
"This compact is made and entered into by and between the participating member states which enact this compact, hereinafter called party states. For the purposes of this compact, the term 'states' is taken to mean the several states, the Commonwealth of Puerto Rico, the District of Columbia, and all U.S. territorial possessions.

"The purpose of this compact is to provide for mutual assistance between the states entering into this compact in managing any emergency disaster that is duly declared by the Governor of the affected state, whether arising from natural disaster, technological hazard, man-made disaster, civil emergency aspects of resources shortages, community disorders, insurgency, or enemy attack.

"This compact shall also provide for mutual cooperation in emergency-related exercises, testing, or other training activities using equipment and personnel simulating performance of any aspect of the giving and receiving of aid by party states or subdivisions of party states during emergencies, such actions occurring outside actual declared emergency periods. Mutual assistance in this compact may include the use of the states' National Guard forces, either in accordance with the National Guard Mutual Assistance Compact or by mutual agreement between states.

"ARTICLE II.

"GENERAL IMPLEMENTATION.

"Each party state entering into this compact recognizes that many emergencies transcend political jurisdictional boundaries and that intergovernmental coordination is essential in managing these and other emergencies under this compact. Each state further recognizes that there will be emergencies which require immediate access and present procedures to apply outside resources to make a prompt and effective response to such an emergency. This is because few, if any, individual states have all the resources they may need in all types of emergencies or the capability of delivering resources to areas where emergencies exist.

"The prompt, full, and effective utilization of resources of the participating states, including any resources on hand or available from the federal government or any other source, that are essential to the safety, care, and welfare of the people in the event of any emergency or disaster declared by a party state, shall be the underlying principle on which all articles of this compact shall be understood.

"On behalf of the Governor of each state participating in the compact, the legally designated state official who is assigned responsibility for emergency management will be responsible for formulation of the appropriate interstate mutual aid plans and procedures necessary to implement this compact.

"ARTICLE III.

"PARTY STATE RESPONSIBILITIES.

"A. It shall be the responsibility of each party state to formulate procedural plans and programs for interstate cooperation in the performance of the responsibilities listed in this article. In formulating such plans, and in carrying them out, the party states, insofar as practical, shall:

"1. Review individual state hazards analyses and, to the extent reasonably possible, determine all those potential emergencies the party states might jointly suffer, whether due to natural disaster, technological hazard, man-made disaster, emergency aspects of resources shortages, civil disorders, insurgency, or enemy attack;

"2. Review party states' individual emergency plans and develop a plan which will determine the mechanism for the interstate management and provision of assistance concerning any potential emergency;

"3. Develop interstate procedures to fill any identified gaps and to resolve any identified inconsistencies or overlaps in existing or developed plans;

"4. Assist in warning communities adjacent to or crossing the state boundaries;

"5. Protect and assure uninterrupted delivery of services, medicines, water, food, energy and fuel, search and rescue, and critical lifeline equipment, services, and resources, both human and material;

"6. Inventory and set procedures for the interstate loan and delivery of human and material resources, together with procedures for reimbursement or forgiveness; and

"7. Provide, to the extent authorized by law, for temporary suspension of any statutes or ordinances that restrict the implementation of the above responsibilities.

"B. The authorized representative of a party state may request assistance to another party state by contacting the authorized representative of that state. The provisions of this compact shall only apply to requests for assistance made by and to authorized representatives. Requests may be verbal or in writing. If verbal, the request shall be confirmed in writing within thirty days of the verbal request. Requests shall provide the following information:

"1. A description of the emergency service function for which assistance is needed, including, but not limited to, fire services, law enforcement, emergency medical, transportation, communications, public works and engineering, building, inspection, planning and information assistance, mass care, resource support, health and medical services, and search and rescue;

"2. The amount and type of personnel, equipment, materials and supplies needed, and a reasonable estimate of the length of time they will be needed; and

"3. The specific place and time for staging of the assisting party's response and a point of contact at that location.

"C. There shall be frequent consultation between state officials who have assigned emergency management responsibilities and other appropriate representatives of the party states with affected jurisdictions and the United States Government, with free exchange of information, plans, and resource records relating to emergency capabilities.

"ARTICLE IV.
"LIMITATIONS.
"Any party state requested to render mutual aid or conduct exercises and training for mutual aid shall take such action as is necessary to provide and make available the resources covered by this compact in accordance with the terms hereof; provided that it is understood that the state rendering aid may withhold resources to the extent necessary to provide reasonable protection for such state.

"Each party state shall afford to the emergency forces of any party state, while operating within its state limits under the terms and conditions of this compact, the same powers, except that of arrest unless specifically authorized by the receiving state, duties, rights, and privileges as are afforded forces of the state in which they are performing emergency services. Emergency forces will continue under the command and control of their regular leaders, but the organizational units will come under the operational control of the emergency services authorities of the state receiving assistance. These conditions may be activated, as needed, only subsequent to a declaration of a state emergency or disaster by the governor of the party state that is to receive assistance or upon commencement of exercises or training for mutual aid and shall continue so long as the exercises or training for mutual aid are in progress, the state of emergency or disaster remains in effect, or loaned resources remain in the receiving state, whichever is longer.

"ARTICLE V.
"LICENSES AND PERMITS.
"Whenever any person holds a license, certificate, or other permit issued by any state party to the compact evidencing the meeting of qualifications for professional, mechanical, or other skills, and when such assistance is requested by the receiving party state, such person shall be deemed licensed, certified, or permitted by the state requesting assistance to render aid involving such skill to meet a declared emergency or disaster, subject to such limitations and conditions as the Governor of the requesting state may prescribe by executive order or otherwise.

"ARTICLE VI.
"LIABILITY.
"Officers or employees of a party state rendering aid in another state pursuant to this compact shall be considered agents of the requesting state for tort liability and immunity purposes. No party state or its officers or employees rendering aid in another state pursuant to this compact shall be liable on account of any act or omission in good faith on the part of such forces while so engaged or on account of the maintenance or use of any equipment or supplies in connection therewith. Good faith in this article shall not include willful misconduct, gross negligence, or recklessness.

"ARTICLE VII.
"SUPPLEMENTARY AGREEMENTS.
"Inasmuch as it is probable that the pattern and detail of the machinery for mutual aid among two or more states may differ from that among the states that are party hereto, this compact contains elements of a broad base

common to all states, and nothing herein shall preclude any state entering into supplementary agreements with another state or affect any other agreements already in force between states. Supplementary agreements may comprehend, but shall not be limited to, provisions for evacuation and reception of injured and other persons and the exchange of medical, fire, police, public utility, reconnaissance, welfare, transportation and communications personnel, and equipment and supplies.

"ARTICLE VIII.

"COMPENSATION.

"Each party state shall provide for the payment of compensation and death benefits to injured members of the emergency forces of that state and representatives of deceased members of such forces in case such members sustain injuries or are killed while rendering aid pursuant to this compact, in the same manner and on the same terms as if the injury or death were sustained within their own state.

"ARTICLE IX.

"REIMBURSEMENT.

"Any party state rendering aid in another state pursuant to this compact shall be reimbursed by the party state receiving such aid for any loss or damage to or expense incurred in the operation of any equipment and the provision of any service in answering a request for aid and for the costs incurred in connection with such requests; provided, that any aiding party state may assume in whole or in part such loss, damage, expense, or other cost, or may loan such equipment or donate such services to the receiving party state without charge or cost; and provided further, that any two or more party states may enter into supplementary agreements establishing a different allocation of costs among those states. Article VIII expenses shall not be reimbursable under this article.

"ARTICLE X.

"EVACUATION.

"Plans for the orderly evacuation and interstate reception of portions of the civilian population as the result of any emergency or disaster of sufficient proportions to so warrant, shall be worked out and maintained between the party states and the emergency management/services directors of the various jurisdictions where any type of incident requiring evacuations might occur. Such plans shall be put into effect by request of the state from which evacuees come and shall include the manner of transporting such evacuees, the number of evacuees to be received in different areas, the manner in which food, clothing, housing, and medical care will be provided, the registration of the evacuees, the providing of facilities for the notification of relatives or friends, and the forwarding of such evacuees to other areas or the bringing in of additional materials, supplies, and all other relevant factors. Such plans shall provide that the party state receiving evacuees and the party state from which the evacuees come shall mutually agree as to reimbursement of out-of-pocket expenses incurred in receiving and caring for such evacuees, for expenditures for transportation, food, clothing, medicines, and medical care, and like items. Such expenditures shall be reimbursed as agreed by the party state from which the evacuees come. After the termination of the emergency or disaster, the party state from which the evacuees come shall assume the responsibility for the ultimate support of repatriation of such evacuees.

"ARTICLE XI.
"IMPLEMENTATION.
"A. This compact shall become effective immediately upon its enactment into law by any two states. Thereafter, this compact shall become effective as to any other state upon enactment by such state.
"B. Any party state may withdraw from this compact by enacting a statute repealing the same, but no such withdrawal shall take effect until thirty days after the Governor of the withdrawing state has given notice in writing of such withdrawal to the Governors of all other party states. Such action shall not relieve the withdrawing state from obligations assumed hereunder prior to the effective date of withdrawal.
"C. Duly authenticated copies of this compact and of such supplementary agreements as may be entered into shall, at the time of their approval, be deposited with each of the party states and with the Federal Emergency Management Agency and other appropriate agencies of the United States Government.

"ARTICLE XII.
"VALIDITY.
"This compact shall be construed to effectuate the purposes stated in Article I. If any provision of this compact is declared unconstitutional, or the applicability thereof to any person or circumstances is held invalid, the constitutionality of the remainder of this compact and the applicability thereof to other persons and circumstances shall not be affected.

"ARTICLE XIII.
"ADDITIONAL PROVISIONS.
"Nothing in this compact shall authorize or permit the use of military force by the National Guard of a state at any place outside that state in any emer-

gency for which the President is authorized by law to call into federal service the militia, or for any purpose for which the use of the Army or the Air Force would in the absence of express statutory authorization be prohibited under § 1385 of Title 18 of the United States Code."

SEC. 2. RIGHT TO ALTER, AMEND, OR REPEAL.

The right to alter, amend, or repeal this joint resolution is hereby expressly reserved. The consent granted by this joint resolution shall—

(1) not be construed as impairing or in any manner affecting any right or jurisdiction of the United States in and over the subject of the compact;

(2) not be construed as consent to the National Guard Mutual Assistance Compact;

(3) be construed as understanding that the first paragraph of Article II of the compact provides that emergencies will require procedures to provide immediate access to existing resources to make a prompt and effective response;

(4) not be construed as providing authority in Article III A. 7. that does not otherwise exist for the suspension of statutes or ordinances;

(5) be construed as understanding that Article III C. does not impose any affirmative obligation to exchange information, plans, and resource records on the United States or any party which has not entered into the compact; and

(6) be construed as understanding that Article XIII does not affect the authority of the President over the National Guard provided by article I of the Constitution and title 10 of the United States Code.

SEC. 3. CONSTRUCTION AND SEVERABILITY.

It is intended that the provisions of this compact shall be reasonably and liberally construed to effectuate the purposes thereof. If any part or application of this compact, or legislation enabling the compact, is held invalid, the remainder of the compact or its application to other situations or persons shall not be affected.

SEC. 4. INCONSISTENCY OF LANGUAGE.

The validity of this compact shall not be affected by any insubstantial difference in its form or language as adopted by the States.

U.S. Supreme Court
146 U.S. 1
McPherson et al. v. Blacker, Secretary of State
No. 1,170
October 17, 1892

Statement by Mr. Chief Justice FULLER:

William McPherson, Jr., Jay A. Hubbell, J. Henry Carstens, Charles E. Hiscock, Otto Ihling, Philip T. Colgrove, Conrad G. Swensburg, Henry A. Haigh, James H. White, Fred. Slocum, Justus S. Stearns, John Millen, Julius T. Hannah, and J. H. Comstock filed their petition and affidavits in the supreme court of the state of Michigan on May 2, 1892, as nominees for presidential electors, against Robert R. Blacker, secretary of state of Michigan, praying that the court declare the act of the legislature, approved May 1, 1891, (Act No. 50, Pub. Acts Mich. 1891,) entitled "An act to provide for the election of electors of president and vice president of the United States, and to repeal all other acts and parts of acts in conflict herewith," void and of no effect, and that a writ of mandamus be directed to be issued to the said secretary of state, commanding him to cause to be delivered to the sheriff of each county in the state, between the 1st of July and the 1st of September, 1892, "a notice in writing that at the next general election in this state, to be held on Tuesday, the 8th day of November, 1892, there will be chosen (among other officers to be named in said notice) as many electors of president and vice president of the United States as this state may be entitled to elect senators and representatives in the congress."

The statute of Michigan (1 How. Ann. St. Mich. 147, c. 9, p. 133) provided: "The secretary of the state shall, between the 1st day of July and the 1st day of September preceding a general election, direct and cause to be delivered to the sheriff of each county in this state a notice in writing that, at the next general election, there will be chosen as many of the following officers as are to be elected at such general election, viz.: A governor, lieutenant governor, secretary of state, state treasurer, auditor general, attorney general, superintendent of public instruction, commissioner of state land office, members of the state board of education, electors of president and vice president of the United States, and a representative in congress for the district to which each of such counties shall belong."

A rule to show cause having been issued, the respondent, as secretary of state, answered the petition, and denied that he had refused to give the notice thus required, but he said "that it has always been the custom in the office of the secretary of state, in giving notices under said section 147, to state in the notice the number of electors that should be printed on the ticket in each voting precinct in each county in this state, and following such custom with reference to such notice, it is the intention of this respondent in giving notice under section 147 to state in said notice that there will be elected one presidential elector at large and one district presidential elector and two alternate presidential electors, one for the elector at large and one for the district presidential elector, in each voting precinct, so that the election may be held under and in accordance with the provisions of Act No. 50 of the Public Acts of the state of Michigan of 1891."

By an amended answer the respondent claimed the same benefit as if he had demurred.

Relators relied in their petition upon various grounds as invalidating Act No. 50 of the Public Acts of Michigan of 1891, and, among them, that the act was void because in conflict with clause 2 of section 1 of article 2 of the constitution of the United States, and with the fourteenth amendment to that instrument, and also in some of its provisions in conflict with the act of congress of February 3, 1887, entitled "An act to fix the day for the meeting of the electors of president and vice president, and to provide for and regulate the counting of the votes for president and vice president, and the decision of questions arising thereon." The supreme court of Michigan unanimously held that none of the objections urged against the validity of the act were tenable; that it did not conflict with clause 2, 1, art. 2, of the constitution, or with the fourteenth amendment thereof; and that the law was only inoperative so far as in conflict with the law of congress in a matter in reference to which congress had the right to legislate. The opinion of the court will be found reported, in advance of the official series, in 52 N. W. Rep. 469.

Judgment was given, June 17, 1892, denying the writ of mandamus, whereupon a writ of error was allowed to this court.

The October term, 1892, commenced on Monday, October 10th, and on Tuesday, October 11th, the first day upon which the application could be made, a motion to advance the case was submitted by counsel, granted at once in view of the exigency disclosed upon the face of the papers, and the cause heard that day. The attention of the court having been called to other provisions of the election laws of Michigan than those supposed to be immediately involved, (Act No. 190, Pub. Acts Mich. 1891, pp. 258, 263,) the chief justice, on Monday, October 17th, announced the conclusions of the court, and directed the entry of judgment affirming the judgment of the supreme court of Michigan, and ordering the mandate to issue at once, it being stated that this was done because immediate action under the state statutes was apparently required and might be affected by delay, but it was added that the court would thereafter file an opinion stating fully the grounds of the decision.

Act No. 50 of the Public Acts of 1891 of Michigan is as follows:

"An act to provide for the election of electors of president and vice president of the United States, and to repeal all other acts and parts of acts in conflict herewith.

"*Section 1.* The people of the state of Michigan enact that, at the general election next preceding the choice of president and vice president of the United States, there shall be elected as many electors of president and vice president as this state may be entitled to elect of senators and representatives in congress in the following manner, that is to say: There shall be elected by the electors of the districts hereinafter defined one elector of president and vice president of the United States in each district, who shall be known and designated on the ballot, respectively, as 'eastern district elector of president and vice president of the United States at large,' and 'western district elector of president and vice president of the United States at large.' There shall also be elected, in like manner, two alternate electors of president and vice president, who shall be known and designated on the ballot as 'eastern district alternate elector of president and vice president of the United States at large,' and 'western district alternate elector of president and vice president of the United States at large;' for which purpose the first, second, sixth, seventh, eighth, and tenth congressional districts shall compose one district, to be known as the 'Eastern Electoral District,' and the third, fourth, fifth, ninth, eleventh, and twelfth congressional districts shall compose the other district, to be known as the 'Western Electoral District.' There shall also be elected, by the electors in each congressional district into which the state is or shall be divided, one elector of president and vice president, and one alternate elector of president and vice president, the ballots for which shall designate the number of the congressional district and the persons to be voted for therein, as 'district elector' and 'alternate district elector' of president and vice president of the United States, respectively.

"*Sec. 2.* The counting, canvassing, and certifying of the votes cast for said electors at large and their alternates, and said district electors and their alternates, shall be done as near as may be in the same manner as is now provided by law for the election of electors of president and vice president of the United States.

"*Sec. 3.* The secretary of state shall prepare three lists of the names of the electors and the alternate electors, procure thereto the signature of the governor, affix the seal of the state to the same, and deliver such certificates thus signed and sealed to one of the electors, on or before the first Wednesday of December next following said general election. In case of death, disability, refusal to act, or neglect to attend, by the hour of twelve o'clock at noon of said day, of either of said electors at large, the duties of the office shall be performed by the alternate electors at large, that is to say: The eastern district alternate elector at large shall supply the place of the eastern district elector at large, and the western district alternate elector at large shall supply the place of the western district elector at large. In like case, the alternate congressional district elector shall supply the place of the congressional district elector. In case two or more persons have an equal and the highest number of votes for any office created by this act as canvassed by the board of state canvassers, the legislature in joint convention shall choose one of said persons to fill such office, and it shall be the duty of the governor to convene the legislature in special session for such purpose immediately upon such determination by said board of state canvassers.

"*Sec. 4.* The said electors of president and vice president shall convene in the senate chamber at the capital of the state at the hour of twelve o'clock at noon, on the first Wednesday of December immediately following their election, and shall proceed to perform the duties of such electors as required by the constitution and the laws of the United States. The alternate electors shall also be in attendance, but shall take no part in the proceedings, except as herein provided.

"*Sec. 5.* Each of said electors and alternate electors shall receive the sum of five dollars for each day's attendance at the meetings of the electors as above provided, and five cents per mile for the actual and necessary distance traveled each way in going to and returning from said place of meeting, the same to be paid by the state treasurer upon the allowance of the board of state auditors.

"*Sec. 6.* All acts and parts of acts in conflict with the provisions of this act are hereby repealed." Pub. Acts Mich. 1891, pp. 50, 51.

Section 211 of Howell's Annotated Statutes of Michigan (volume 1, c. 9, p. 145) reads:

"For the purpose of canvassing and ascertaining the votes given for electors of president and vice president of the United States, the board of state canvassers shall meet on the Wednesday next after the third Monday of November, or on such other day before that time as the secretary of state shall appoint; and the powers, duties, and proceedings of said board, and of the secretary of state, in sending for, examining, ascertaining, determining, certifying, and recording the votes and results of the election of such electors, shall be in all respects, as near as may be, as hereinbefore provided in relation to sending for, examining, ascertaining, determining, certifying, and recording the votes and results of the election of state officers."

Section 240 of Howell's Statutes, in force prior to May 1, 1891, provided: "At the general election next preceding the choice of president and vice president of the United States, there shall be elected by general ticket as many electors of president and vice president as this state may be entitled to elect of senators and representatives in congress."

The following are sections of article 8 of the constitution of Michigan:

"*Sec. 4.* The secretary of state, state treasurer, and commissioner of the state land office shall constitute a board of state auditors, to examine and adjust all claims against the state, not otherwise provided for by general law. They shall constitute a board of state canvassers, to determine the result of all elections for governor, lieutenant governor, and state officers, and of such other officers as shall by law be referred to them.

"*Sec. 5.* In case two or more persons have an equal and the highest number of votes for any office, as canvassed by the board of state canvassers, the legislature in joint convention shall choose one of said persons to fill such office. When the determination of the board of state canvassers is contested, the legislature in joint convention shall decide which person is elected." 1 How. Ann. St. Mich. p. 57.

Reference was also made in argument to the act of congress of February 3, 1887, to fix the day for the meeting of the electors of president and vice president, and to provide for and regulate and counting of the votes. 24 St. p. 373.

Henry M. Duffield, W. H. H. Miller, and Fred A. Baker, for plaintiff in error.

Otto Kirchner, A. A. Ellis, and John W. Champlin, for defendant in error.

Mr. Chief Justice FULLER, after stating the facts in the foregoing language, delivered the opinion of the court. The supreme court of Michigan held, in effect, that if the act in question were invalid, the proper remedy had been sought. In other words, if the court had been of opinion that the act was void, the writ of mandamus would have been awarded.

And having ruled all objections to the validity of the act urged as arising under the state constitution and laws adversely to the plaintiffs in error, the court was compelled to, and did, consider and dispose of the contention that the act was invalid because repugnant to the constitution and laws of the United States.

We are not authorized to revise the conclusions of the state court on these matters of local law, and, those conclusions being accepted, it follows that the decision of the federal questions is to be regarded as necessary to the determination of the cause. *De Saussure v. Gaillard*, 127 U.S. 216, 8 Sup. Ct. Rep. 1053.

Inasmuch as, under section 709 of the Revised Statutes of the United States, we have jurisdiction by writ of error to re-examine and reverse or affirm the final judgment in any suit in the highest court of a state in which a decision could be had, where the validity of a statute of the state is drawn in question on the ground that it is repugnant to the constitution and laws of the United States, and the decision is in favor of its validity, we perceive no reason for holding that this writ was improvidently brought.

It is argued that the subject-matter of the controversy is not of judicial cognizance, because it is said that all questions connected with the election of a presidential elector are political in their nature; that the court has no power finally to dispose of them; and that its decision would be subject to review by political officers and agencies, as the state board of canvassers, the legislature in joint convention, and the governor, or, finally, the congress.

But the judicial power of the United States extends to all cases in law or equity arising under the constitution and laws of the United States, and this is a case so arising, since the validity of the state law was drawn in question as repugnant to such constitution and laws, and its validity was sustained. *Boyd v. State*, 143 U.S. 135, 12 Sup. Ct. Rep. 375. And it matters not that the judgment to be reviewed may be rendered in a proceeding for mandamus. *Hartman v. Greenhow*, 102 U.S. 672.

As we concur with the state court, its judgment has been affirmed; if we had not, its judgment would have been reversed. In either event, the questions submitted are finally and definitely disposed of by the judgment which we pronounce, and that judgment is carried into effect by the transmission of our mandate to the state court.

The question of the validity of this act, as presented to us by this record, is a judicial question, and we cannot decline the exercise of our jurisdiction upon the inadmissible suggestion that action might be taken by political agencies in disregard of the judgment of the highest tribunal of the state, as revised by our own.

On behalf of plaintiffs in error it is contended that the act is void because in conflict with (1) clause 2, 1, art. 2, of the constitution of the United States; (2) the fourteenth and fifteenth amendments to the constitution; and (3) the act of congress, of February 3, 1887.

The second clause of section 1 of article 2 of the constitution is in these words: "Each state shall appoint, in such manner as the legislature thereof may direct, a number of electors, equal to the whole number of senators and representatives to which the state may be entitled in the congress; but no senator or representative, or person holding an office of trust or profit under the United States, shall be appointed an elector."

The manner of the appointment of electors directed by the act of Michigan is the election of an elector and an alternate elector in each of the twelve congressional districts into which the state of Michigan is divided, and of an elector and an alternate elector at large in each of two districts defined by the act. It is insisted that it was not competent for the legislature to direct this manner of appointment, because the state is to appoint as a body politic and corporate, and so must act as a unit, and cannot delegate the authority to subdivisions created for the purpose; and it is argued that the appointment of electors by districts is not an appointment by the state, because all its citizens otherwise qualified are not permitted to vote for all the presidential electors.

"A state, in the ordinary sense of the constitution," said Chief Justice Chase, (*Texas v. White*, 7 Wall. 700, 731,) "is a political community of free citizens, occupying a territory of defined boundaries, and organized under a government sanctioned and limited by a written constitution, and established by the consent of the governed." The state does not act by its people in their collective capacity, but through such political agencies as are duly constituted and established. The legislative power is the supreme authority, except as limited by the constitution of the state, and the sovereignty of the people is exercised through their representatives in the legislature, unless by the fundamental law power is elsewhere reposed. The constitution of the United States frequently refers to the state as a political community, and also in terms to the people of the several states and the citizens of each state. What is forbidden or required to be done by a state is forbidden or required of the legislative power under state constitutions as they exist. The clause under consideration does not read that the people or the citizens shall appoint, but that "each state shall;" and if the words, "in such manner as the legislature thereof may direct," had been omitted, it would seem that the legislative power of appointment could not have been successfully questioned in the absence of any provision in the state constitution in that regard. Hence the insertion of those words, while operating as a limitation upon the state in respect of any attempt to circumscribe the legislative power, cannot be held to operate as a limitation on that power itself.

If the legislature possesses plenary authority to direct the manner of appointment, and might itself exercise the appointing power by joint ballot or concurrence of the two houses, or according to such mode as designated, it is difficult to perceive why, if the legislature prescribes as a method of appointment choice by vote, it must necessarily be by general ticket, and not by districts. In other words, the act of appointment is none the less the act of the state in its entirety because arrived at by districts, for the act is the act of political agencies duly authorized to speak for the state, and the combined result is the expression of the voice of the state, a result reached by direction of the legislature, to whom the whole subject is committed.

By the first paragraph of section 2, art. 1, it is provided: "The house of representatives shall be composed of members chosen every second year by the people of the several states, and the electors in each state shall have the qualifications requisite for electors of the most numerous branch of the state legislature;" and by the third paragraph, "when vacancies happen in the representation from any state, the executive authority thereof shall issue writs of election to fill such vacancies." Section 4 reads: "The times, places, and manner of holding elections for senators and representatives shall be prescribed in each state by the legislature thereof; but the congress may at any time by law make or alter such regulations, except as to the places of choosing senators."

Although it is thus declared that the people of the several states shall choose the members of congress, (language which induced the state of New York to insert a salvo as to the power to divide into districts, in its resolutions of ratification,) the state legislatures, prior to 1842, in prescribing the times, places, and manner of holding elections for representatives, had usually apportioned the state into districts, and assigned to each a representative; and by act of congress of June 25, 1842, (carried forward as section 23 of the Revised Statutes,) it was provided that, where a state was entitled to more than one representative, the election should be by districts. It has never been doubted that representatives in congress thus chosen represented the entire people of the state acting in their sovereign capacity.

By original clause 3, 1, art. 2, and by the twelfth amendment, which superseded that clause in case of a failure in the election of president by the people the house of representatives is to choose the president; and "the vote shall be taken by states, the representation from each state having one vote." The state acts as a unit, and its vote is given as a unit, but that vote is arrived at through the votes of its representatives in congress elected by districts.

The state also acts individually through its electoral college, although, by reason of the power of its legislature over the manner of appointment, the vote of its electors may be divided.

The constitution does not provide that the appointment of electors shall be by popular vote, nor that the electors shall be voted for upon a general ticket, nor that the majority of those who exercise the elective franchise can alone choose the electors. It recognizes that the people act through their representatives in the legislature, and leaves it to the legislature exclusively to define the method of effecting the object.

The framers of the constitution employed words in their natural sense; and, where they are plain and clear, resort to collateral aids to interpretation is unnecessary, and cannot be indulged in to narrow or enlarge the text; but where there is ambiguity or doubt, or where two views may well be entertained, contemporaneous and subsequent practical construction is entitled to the greatest weight. Certainly, plaintiffs in error cannot reasonably assert that the clause of the constitution under consideration so plainly sustains their position as to entitle them to object that contemporaneous history and practical construction are not to be allowed their legitimate force, and, conceding that their argument inspires a doubt sufficient to justify resort to the aids of interpretation thus afforded, we are of opinion that such doubt is thereby resolved against them, the contemporaneous practical exposition of the constitution being too strong and obstinate to be shaken or controlled. *Stuart v. Laird*, 1 Cranch, 299, 309.

It has been said that the word "appoint" is not the most appropriate word to describe the result of a popular election. Perhaps not; but it is sufficiently comprehensive to cover that mode, and was manifestly used as conveying the broadest power of determination. It was used in article 5 of the articles of confederation, which provided that "delegates shall be annually appointed in such manner as the legislature of each state shall direct;" and in the resolution of congress of February 21, 1787, which declared it expedient that "a convention of delegates who shall have been appointed by the several states" should be held. The appointment of delegates was, in fact, made by the legislatures directly, but that involved no denial of authority to direct some other mode. The constitutional convention, by resolution of September 17, 1787, expressed the opinion that the congress should fix a day "on which electors should be appointed by the states which shall have ratified the same," etc., and that, "after such publication, the electors should be appointed, and the senators and representatives elected."

The journal of the convention discloses that propositions that the president should be elected by "the citizens of the United States," or by the "people," or "by electors to be chosen by the people of the several states," instead of by the congress, were voted down, (Jour. Conv. 286, 288; 1 Elliot, Deb. 208, 262,) as was the proposition that the president should be "chosen by electors appointed for that purpose by the legislatures of the states," though at one time adopted, (Jour. Conv. 190; 1 Elliot, Deb. 208, 211, 217;) and a motion to postpone the consideration of the choice "by the national legislature," in order to take up a resolution providing for electors to be elected by the qualified voters in districts, was negatived in committee of the whole, (Jour. Conv. 92; 1 Elliot, Deb. 156.) Gerry proposed that the choice should be made by the state executives; Hamilton, that the election be by electors chosen by electors chosen by the people; James Wilson and Gouverneur Morris were strongly in favor of popular vote; Ellsworth and Luther Martin preferred the choice by electors elected by the legislatures; and Roger Sherman, appointment by congress. The final result seems to have reconciled contrariety of views by leaving it to the state legislatures to appoint directly by joint ballot or concurrent separate action, or through popular election by districts or by general ticket, or as otherwise might be directed.

Therefore, on reference to contemporaneous and subsequent action under the clause, we should expect to find, as we do, that various modes of choosing the electors were pursued, as, by the legislature itself on joint ballot; by the legislature through a concurrent vote of the two houses; by vote of the people for a general ticket; by vote of the people in districts; by choice partly by the people voting in districts and partly by the people voting in districts and partly by the candidates voted for by the people in districts; and in other ways, as, notably, by North Carolina in 1792, and Tennessee in 1796 and 1800. No question was raised as to the power of the state to appoint in any mode its legislature saw fit to adopt, and none that a single method, applicable without exception, must be pursued in the absence of an amendment to the constitution. The district system was largely considered the most equitable, and Madison wrote that it was that system which was contemplated by the framers of the constitution, although it was soon seen that its adoption by some states might place them at a disadvantage by a division of their strength, and that a uniform rule was preferable.

At the first presidential election, the appointment of electors was made by the legislatures of Connecticut, Delaware, Georgia, New Jersey, and South Carolina. Pennsylvania, by act of October 4, 1788, (Acts Pa. 1787–88, p. 513,) provided for the election of electors on a general ticket. Virginia, by act of November 17, 1788, was divided into 12 separate districts, and an elector elected in each district, while for the election of congressmen the state was divided into 10 other districts. Laws Va. Oct.

Sess. 1788, pp. 1, 2. In Massachusetts, the general court, by resolve of November 17, 1788, divided the state into districts for the election of representatives in congress, and provided for their election, December 18, 1788, and that at the same time the qualified inhabitants of each district should give their votes for two persons as candidates for an elector of president and vice president of the United States, and, from the two persons in each district having the greatest number of votes, the two houses of the general court by joint ballot should elect one as elector, and in the same way should elect two electors at large. Mass. Resolves 1788, p. 53. In Maryland, under elected on general ticket, five being residents elected on general ticket, five being residents of the Western Shore, and three of the Eastern Shore. Laws Md. 1788, c. 10. In New Hampshire an act was passed November 12, 1788, (Laws N. H. 1789, p. 169,) providing for the election of five electors by majority popular vote, and in case of no choice that the legislature should appoint out of so many of the candidates as equaled double the number of electors elected. There being no choice, the appointment was made by the legislature. The senate would not agree to a joint ballot, and the house was compelled, that the vote of the state might not be lost, to concur in the electors chosen by the senate. The state of New York lost its vote through a similar contest. The assembly was willing to elect by joint ballot of the two branches or to divide the electors with the senate, but the senate would assent to nothing short of a complete negative upon the action of the assembly, and the time for election passed without an appointment. North Carolina and Rhode Island had not then ratified the constitution.

Fifteen states participated in the second presidential election, in nine of which electors were chosen by the legislatures. Maryland, Laws Md. 1790, c. 16; Laws 1791, c. 62,) New Hampshire, (Laws N. H. 1792, pp. 398, 401,) and Pennsylvania, (Laws Pa. 1792, p. 240,) elected their electors on a general ticket, and Virginia by districts, (Laws Va. 1792, p. 87.) In Massachusetts the general court, by resolution of June 30, 1792, divided the state into four districts, in each of two of which five electors were elected, and in each of the other two three electors. Mass. Resolves, June, 1792, p. 25. Under the apportionment of April 13, 1792, North Carolina was entitled to ten members of the house of representatives. The legislature was not in session, and did not meet until November 15th, while under the act of congress of March 1, 1792, (1 St. p. 239,) the electors were to assemble on December 5th. The legislature passed an act dividing the state into four districts, and directing the members of the legislature residing in each district to meet on the 25th of November, and choose three electors. 2 Ired. N. C. Laws, 1715–1800, c. 15 of 1792. At the same session an act was passed dividing the state into districts for the election of electors in 1796, and every four years thereafter. *Id.* c. 16.

Sixteen states took part in the third presidential election, Tennessee having been admitted June 1, 1796. In nine states the electors were appointed by the legislatures, and in Pennsylvania and New Hampshire by popular vote for a general ticket. Virginia, North Carolina, and Maryland elected by districts. The Maryland law of December 24, 1795, was entitled "An act to alter the mode of electing electors," and provided for dividing the state into ten districts, each of which districts should "elect and appoint one person, being a resident of the said district, as an elector." Laws Md. 1795, c. 73. Massachusetts adhered to the district system, electing one elector in each congressional district by a majority vote. It was provided that, if no one had a majority, the legislature should make the appointment on joint ballot, and the legislature also appointed two electors at large in the same manner. Mass. Resolves, June, 1796, p. 12. In Tennessee an act was passed August 8, 1796, which provided for the election of three electors, "one in the district of Washington, one in the district of Hamilton, and one in the district of Mero," and, "that the said electors may be elected with as little trouble to the citizens as possible," certain persons of the counties of Washington, Sullivan, Green, and Hawkins were named in the act and appointed electors to elect an elector for the district of Washington; certain other persons of the counties of Knox, Jefferson, Sevier, and Blount were by name appointed to elect an elector for the district of Hamilton; and certain others of the counties of Davidson, Sumner, and Tennessee to elect an elector for the district of Mero. Laws Tenn. 1794, 1803, p. 209; Acts 2d Sess. 1st Gen. Assem. Tenn. c. 4. Electors were chosen by the persons thus designated.

In the fourth presidential election, Virginia, under the advice of Mr. Jefferson, adopted the general ticket, at least "until some uniform mode of choosing a president and vice president of the United States shall be prescribed by an amendment to the constitution." Laws Va. 1799–1800, p. 3. Massachusetts passed a resolution providing that the electors of that state should be appointed by joint ballot of the senate and house. Mass. Resolves, June, 1800, p. 13. Pennsylvania appointed by the legislature, and, upon a contest between the senate and house, the latter was forced to yield to the senate in agreeing to an arrangement which resulted in dividing the vote of the electors. 26 Niles' Reg. 17. Six states, however, chose electors by popular vote, Rhode Island supplying the place of Pennsylvania, which had theretofore followed that course. Tennessee, by act October 26, 1799, designated persons by name to choose its three electors, as under the act of 1796. Laws Tenn, 1794–1803, p. 211; Acts 2d Sess. 2d Gen. Assem, Tenn. c. 46.

Without pursuing the subject further, it is sufficient to observe that, while most of the states adopted the general ticket system, the district method obtained in Kentucky until 1824; in Tennessee and Maryland until 1832; in Indiana in 1824 and 1828; in Illinois in 1820 and 1824; and in Maine in 1820, 1824, and 1828. Massachusetts used the general ticket system in 1804, (Mass. Resolves, June, 1804, p. 19;) chose electors by joint ballot of the legislature in 1808 and in 1816, (Mass. Resolves 1808, pp. 205, 207, 209; Mass. Resolves 1816, p. 233;) used the district system again in 1812 and 1820, (Mass. Resolves 1812, p. 94; Mass. Resolves 1820, p. 245;) and returned to the general ticket system in 1824, (Mass. Resolves 1824, p. 40.) In New York the electors were elected in 1828 by districts, the district electors choosing the electors at large. Rev. St. N. Y. 1827, tit. 6, p. 24. The appointment of electors by the legislature, instead of by popular vote, was made use of by North Carolina, Vermont, and New Jersey in 1812.

In 1824 the electors were chosen by popular vote, by districts, and by general ticket, in all the states excepting Delaware, Georgia, Louisiana, New York, South Carolina, and Vermont, where they were still chosen by the legislature. After 1832 electors were chosen by general ticket in all the states excepting South Carolina, where the legislature chose them up to and including 1860. Journals 1860, Senate, pp. 12, 13; House, 11, 15, 17. And this was the mode adopted by Florida in 1868, (Laws 1868, p. 166,) and by Colorado in 1876, as prescribed by section 19 of the schedule to the constitution of the state, which was admitted into the Union, August 1, 1876, (Gen. Laws Colo. 1877, pp. 79, 990.)[1]

Mr. Justice Story, in considering the subject in his Commentaries on the Constitution, and writing nearly 50 years after the adoption of that instrument, after stating that "in some states the legislatures have directly chosen the electors by themselves; in others, they have been chosen by the people by a general ticket throughout the whole state; and in others, by the people by electoral districts, fixed by the legislature, a certain number of electors being apportioned to each district,"—adds: "No question has ever arisen as to the constitutionality of either mode, except that by a direct choice by the legislature. But this, though often doubted by able and ingenious minds, (3 Elliot, Deb. 100, 101,) has been firmly established in practice ever since the adoption of the constitution, and does not now seem to admit of controversy, even if a suitable tribunal existed to adjudicate upon it." And he remarks that "it has been thought desirable by many statesmen to have the constitution amended so as to provide for a uniform mode of choice by the people." Story, Const. (1st Ed.) 1466.

Such an amendment was urged at the time of the adoption of the twelfth amendment, the suggestion being that all electors should be chosen by popular vote, the states to be divided for that purpose into districts. It was brought up again in congress in December, 1813, but the resolution for submitting the amendment failed to be carried. The amendment was renewed in the house of representatives in December, 1816, and a provision for the division of the states into single districts for the choice of electors received a majority vote, but not two thirds. Like amendments were offered in the senate by Messrs. Sanford of New York, Dickerson of New Jersey, and Macon of North Carolina. December 11, 1823, Senator Benton introduced an amendment providing that each legislature should divide its state into electoral districts, and that the voters of each district "should vote, in their own proper persons," for president and vice president, but it was not acted upon. December 16 and December 24, 1823, amendments were introduced in the senate by Messrs. Dickerson, of New Jersey, and Van

---

[1] See Stanwood, Presidential Elections, (3d Ed.) and Appleton, Presidential Counts, passim; 2 Lalor, Enc. Pol. Science, 68; 4 Hild. Hist. U. S. (Rev. Ed.) 39, 382, 689; 5 Hild. Hist. U. S. 389, 531; 1 Schouler, Hist. U. S. 72, 334; 2 Schouler, Hist. U. S. 184; 3 Schouler, Hist. U. S. 313, 439; 2 Adams, Hist. U. S. 201; 4 Adams, Hist. U. S. 285; 6 Adams, Hist. U. S. 409, 413; 9 Adams, Hist. U. S. 139; 1 McMaster, Hist. Peopel U. S. 525; 2 McMaster, Hist. People U. S. 85, 509; 3 McMaster, Hist. People U. S. 188, 189, 194, 317; 2 Scharf, Hist. Md. 547; 2 Bradf. Mass. 335; Life of Plumer, 104; 3 Niles' Reg. 160; 5 Niles' Reg. 372; 9 Niles' Reg. 319, 349; 10 Niles' Reg. 45, 177, 409; 11 Niles' Reg.

Buren, of New York, requiring the choice of electors to be by districts; but these and others failed of adoption, although there was favorable action in that direction by the senate in 1818, 1819, and 1822. December 22, 1823, an amendment was introduced in the house by Mr. McDuffie, of South Carolina, providing that electors should be chosen by districts assigned by the legislatures, but action was not taken[2]. The subject was again brought forward in 1835, 1844, and subsequently, but need not be further dwelt upon, except that it may be added that, on the 28th of May, 1874, a report was made by Senator Morton, chairman of the senate committee on privileges and elections, recommending an amendment dividing the states into electoral districts, and that the majority of the popular vote of each district should give the candidate one presidential vote, but this also failed to obtain action. In this report it was said: "The appointment of these electors is thus placed absolutely and wholly with the legislatures of the several states. They may be chosen by the legislature, or the legislature may provide that they shall be elected by the people of the state at large, or in districts, as are members of congress, which was the case formerly in many states; and it is no doubt competent for the legislature to authorize the governor, or the supreme court of the state, or any other agent of its will, to appoint these electors. This power is conferred upon the legislatures of the states by the constitution of the United States, and cannot be taken from them or modified by their state constitutions any more than can their power to elect senators of the United States. Whatever provisions may be made by statute, or by the state constitution, to choose electors by the people, there is no doubt of the right of the legislature to resume the power at any time, for it can neither be taken away nor abdicated." Senate Rep. 1st Sess. 43d Cong. No. 395.

From this review, in which we have been assisted by the laborious research of counsel, and which might have been greatly expanded, it is seen that from the formation of the government until now the practical construction of the clause has conceded plenary power to the state legislatures in the matter of the appointment of electors.

Even in the heated controversy of 1876–77 the electoral vote of Colorado cast by electors chosen by the legislature passed unchallenged, and our attention has not been drawn to any previous attempt to submit to the courts the determination of the constitutionality of state action.

In short, the appointment and mode of appointment of electors belong exclusively to the states under the constitution of the United States. They are, as remarked by Mr. Justice Gray *in Re Green*, 134 U.S. 377, 379, 10 S. Sup. Ct. Rep. 586, "no more officers or agents of the United States than are the members of the state legislatures when acting as electors of federal senators, or the people of the states when acting as the electors of representatives in congress." Congress is empowered to determine the

---

[2] 1 Benton, Thirty Years' View, 37; 5 Benton, Cong. Deb. 110, 677; 7 Benton, Cong. Deb. 472–474, 600; 3 Niles' Reg. 240, 334; 11 Niles' Reg. 258, 274, 293, 349; Annals Cong. (1812–13,) 847.

time of choosing the electors and the day on which they are to give their votes, which is required to be the same day throughout the United States; but otherwise the power and jurisdiction of the state is exclusive, with the exception of the provisions as to the number of electors and the ineligibility of certain persons, so framed that congressional and federal influence might be excluded.

The question before us is not one of policy, but of power; and, while public opinion had gradually brought all the states as matter of fact to the pursuit of a uniform system of popular election by general ticket, that fact does not tend to weaken the force of contemporaneous and long-continued previous practice when and as different views of expediency prevailed. The prescription of the written law cannot be overthrown because the states have laterally exercised, in a particular way, a power which they might have exercised in some other way. The construction to which we have referred has prevailed too long and been too uniform to justify us in interpreting the language of the constitution as conveying any other meaning than that heretofore ascribed, and it must be treated as decisive.

It is argued that the district mode of choosing electors, while not obnoxious to constitutional objection, if the operation of the electoral system had conformed to its original object and purpose, had become so in view of the practical working of that system. Doubtless it was supposed that the electors would exercise a reasonable independence and fair judgment in the selection of the chief executive, but experience soon demonstrated that, whether chosen by the legislatures or by popular suffrage on general ticket or in districts, they were so chosen simply to register the will of the appointing power in respect of a particular candidate. In relation, then, to the independence of the electors, the original expectation may be said to have been frustrated. Miller, Const. Law, 149; Rawle, Const. 55; Story, Const. 1473; Federalist, No. 68. But we can perceive no reason for holding that the power confided to the states by the constitution has ceased to exist because the operation of the system has not fully realized the hopes of those by whom it was created. Still less can we recognize the doctrine that because the constitution has been found in the march of time sufficiently comprehensive to be applicable to conditions not within the minds of its framers, and not arising in their time, it may therefore be wrenched from the subjects expressly embraced within it, and amended by judicial decision without action by the designated organs in the mode by which alone amendments can be made. Nor are we able to discover any conflict between this act and the fourteenth and fifteenth amendments to the constitution. The fourteenth amendment provides:

> "*Section 1.* All persons born or naturalized in the United States, and subject to the jurisdiction thereof, are citizens of the United States and of the state wherein they reside. No state shall make or enforce any law which shall abridge the privileges or immunities of citizens of the United States; nor shall any state deprive any person of life, liberty, or property without

due process of law, nor deny to any person within its jurisdiction the equal protection of the laws.

"*Sec. 2.* Representatives shall be apportioned among the several states according to their respective numbers, counting the whole number of persons in each state, excluding Indians not taxed. But when the right to vote at any election for the choice of electors for president and vice president of the United States, representatives in congress, the executive and judicial officers of a state, or the members of the legislature thereof, is denied to any of the male inhabitants of such state, being twenty-one years of age, and citizens of the United States, or in any way abridged, except for participation in rebellion or other crime, the basis of representation therein shall be reduced in the proportion which the number of such male citizens shall bear to the whole number of male citizens twenty-one years of age in such state."

The first section of the fifteenth amendment reads: "The right of citizens of the United States to vote shall not be denied or abridged by the United States or by any state on account of race, color, or previous condition of servitude."

In the Slaughterhouse Cases, 16 Wall. 36, this court held that the first clause of the fourteenth amendment was primarily intended to confer citizenship on the negro race; and, secondly, to give definitions of citizenship of the United States, and citizenship of the states; and it recognized the distinction between citizenship of a state and citizenship of the United States by those definitions; that the privileges and immunities of citizens of the states embrace generally those fundamental civil rights for the security and establishment of which organized society was instituted, and which remain, with certain exceptions mentioned in the federal constitution, under the care of the state governments; while the privileges and immunities of citizens of the United States are those which arise out of the nature and essential character of the national government, the provisions of its constitution, or its laws and treaties made in pursuance thereof; and that it is the latter which are placed under the protection of congress by the second clause of the fourteenth amendment.

We decided in *Minor v. Happersett,* 21 Wall. 162, that the right of suffrage was not necessarily one of the privileges or immunities of citizenship before the adoption of the fourteenth amendment, and that that amendment does not add to these privileges and immunities, but simply furnishes an additional guaranty for the protection of such as the citizen already has; that, at the time of the adoption of that amendment, suffrage was not coextensive with the citizenship of the state, nor was it at the time of the adoption of the constitution; and that neither the constitution nor the fourteenth amendment made all citizens voters.

The fifteenth amendment exempted citizens of the United States from discrimination in the exercise of the elective franchise on account of race, color, or previous condition of servitude. The right to vote in the states comes from the states, but the right of exemption from the prohibited discrimination comes from the United States. The first has not been granted or secured by the constitution of the United States, but the last has been. *U.S. v. Cruikshank*, 92 U.S. 542; *U.S. v. Reese, Id.* 214.

If, because it happened, at the time of the adoption of the fourteenth amendment, that those who exercised the elective franchise in the state of Michigan were entitled to vote for all the presidential electors, this right was rendered permanent by that amendment, then the second clause of article 2 has been so amended that the states can no longer appoint in such manner as the legislatures thereof may direct; and yet no such result is indicated by the language used, nor are the amendments necessarily inconsistent with that clause. The first section of the fourteenth amendment does not refer to the exercise of the elective franchise, though the second provides that if the right to vote is denied or abridged to any male inhabitant of the state having attained majority, and being a citizen of the United States, then the basis of representation to which each state is entitled in the congress shall be proportionately reduced. Whenever presidential electors are appointed by popular election, then the right to vote cannot be denied or abridged without invoking the penalty; and so of the right to vote for representatives in congress, the executive and judicial officers of a state, or the members of the legislature thereof. The right to vote intended to be protected refers to the right to vote as established by the laws and constitution of the state. There is no color for the contention that under the amendments every male inhabitant of the state, being a citizen of the United States, has from the time of his majority a right to vote for presidential electors.

The object of the fourteenth amendment in respect of citizenship was to preserve equality of rights and to prevent discrimination as between citizens, but not to radically change the whole theory of the relations of the state and federal governments to each other, and of both governments to the people. *In re Kemmler*, 136 U.S. 436, 10 Sup. Ct. Rep. 930.

The inhibition that no state shall deprive any person within its jurisdiction of the equal protection of the laws was designed to prevent any person or class of persons from being singled out as a special subject for discriminating and hostile legislation. *Milling Co. v. Pennsylvania*, 125 U.S. 181, 188, Sup. Ct. Rep. 737.

In *Hayes v. Missouri*, 120 U.S. 68, 71, 7 S. Sup. Ct. Rep. 350, Mr. Justice Field, speaking for the court, said: "The fourteenth amendment to the constitution of the United States does not prohibit legislation which is limited either in the objects to which it is directed or by the territory within which it is to operate. It merely requires that all persons subjected to such legislation shall be treated alike, under like circumstances and conditions, both in the privileges and in the liabilities imposed. As we said in *Barbier v. Connolly*, speaking of the fourteenth amendment: 'Class legislation, discriminating against some and favoring others, is prohibited; but legislation which, in carrying out a public purpose, is limited in its application, if within the sphere of its operation it affects alike all persons similarly situated, is not within the amendment' 113 U.S. 27, 32, 5 S. Sup. Ct. Rep. 357."

If presidential electors are appointed by the legislatures, no discrimination is made; if they are elected in districts where each citizen has an equal right to vote, the same as any other citizen has, no discrimination is made. Unless the authority vested in the legislatures by the second clause of section 1 of article 2 has been divested, and the state has lost its power of appointment, except in one manner, the position taken on behalf of relators is untenable, and it is apparent that neither of these amendments can be given such effect.

The third clause of section 1 of article 2 of the constitution is: "The congress may determine the time of choosing the electors, and the day on which they shall give their votes; which day shall be the same throughout the United States."

Under the act of congress of March 1, 1792, (1 St. p. 239, c. 8,) it was provided that the electors should meet and give their votes on the first Wednesday in December at such place in each state as should be directed by the legislature thereof, and by act of congress of January 23, 1845, (5 St. p. 721,) that the electors should be appointed in each state on the Tuesday next after the first Monday in the month of November in the year in which they were to be appointed: provided, that each state might by law provide for the filling of any vacancies in its college of electors when such college meets to give its electoral vote: and provided that when any state shall have held an election for the purpose of choosing electors, and has failed to make a choice on the day prescribed, then the electors may be appointed on a subsequent day, in such manner as the state may by law provide. These provisions were carried forward into sections 131, 133, 134, and 135 of the Revised Statutes, (Rev. St. tit. 3, c. 1, p. 22.)

By the act of congress of February 3, 1887, entitled "An act to fix the day for the meeting of the electors of president and vice president," etc., (24 St. p. 373.) it was provided that the electors of each state should meet and give their votes on the second Monday in January next following their appointment. The state law in question here fixes the first Wednesday of December as the day for the meeting of the electors, as originally designated by congress. In this respect it is in conflict with the act of congress, and must necessarily give way. But this part of the act is not so inseparably connected, in substance, with the other parts as to work the destruction of the whole act. Striking out the day for the meeting, which had already been otherwise determined by the act of congress, the act remains complete in itself, and capable of being carried out in accordance with the legislative intent. The state law yields only to the extent of the collision. *Cooley, Const. Lim.* 178; *Com. v. Kimball,* 24 Pick. 359; *Houston v. Moore,* 5 Wheat. 1, 49. The construction to this effect by the state court is of persuasive force, if not of controlling weight.

We do not think this result affected by the provision in Act No. 50 in relation to a tie vote. Under the constitution of the state of Michigan, in case two or more persons have an equal and the highest number of votes for any office, as canvassed by the board of state canvassers, the legislature in joint convention chooses one of these persons to fill the office. This rule is recognized in this act, which also makes it the duty of the governor in such case to convene the legislature in special session for the purpose of its application, immediately upon the determination by the board of state canvassers.

We entirely agree with the supreme court of Michigan that it cannot be held, as matter of law, that the legislature would not have provided for being convened in special session but for the provision relating to the time of the meeting of the electors contained in the act, and are of opinion that that date may be rejected, and the act be held to remain otherwise complete and valid.

And as the state is fully empowered to fill any vacancy which may occur in its electoral college, when it meets to give its electoral vote, we find nothing in the mode provided for anticipating such an exigency which operates to invalidate the law. We repeat that the main question arising for consideration is one of power, and not of policy, and we are unable to arrive at any other conclusion than that the act of the legislature of Michigan of May 1, 1891, is not void as in contravention of the constitution of the United States, for want of power in its enactment.

The judgment of the supreme court of Michigan must be affirmed.

U.S. Supreme Court

241 U.S. 565

STATE OF OHIO ON RELATION OF DAVID DAVIS, Plff. in Err.,

v.

CHARLES Q. HILDEBRANT, Secretary of State of Ohio, State Supervisor and Inspector of Elections, and State Supervisor of Elections, et al.

No. 987

Submitted May 22, 1916

Decided June 12, 1916

Messrs. Sherman T. McPherson and J. Warren Keifer for plaintiff in error.

Mr. Edward C. Turner, Attorney General of Ohio, and Messrs. Edmond H. Moore and Timothy S. Hogan for defendants in error.

Mr. Chief Justice White delivered the opinion of the court:

By an amendment to the Constitution of Ohio, adopted September 3d, 1912, the legislative power was expressly declared to be vested not only in the senate and house of representatives of the state, constituting the general assembly, but in the people, in whom a right was reserved by way of referendum to approve or disapprove by popular vote any law enacted by the general assembly. And by other constitutional provisions the machinery to carry out the referendum was created. Briefly they were this: Within a certain time after the enactment of a law by the senate and house of representatives, and its approval by the governor, upon petition of 6 per centum of the voters, the question of whether the law should become operative was to be submitted to a vote of the people, and, if approved, the law should be operative; and, if not approved, it should have no effect whatever.

In May, 1915, the general assembly of Ohio passed an act redistricting the state for the purpose of congressional elections, by which act twenty-two congressional districts were created, in some respects differing from the previously established districts, and this act, after approval by the governor, was filed in the office of the secretary of state. The requisite number of electors under the referendum provision having petitioned for a submission of the law to a popular vote, such vote was taken and the law was disapproved. Thereupon, in the supreme court of the state, the suit before us was begun against state election officers for the purpose of procuring a mandamus, directing them to disregard the vote of the people on the referendum, disapproving the law, and to proceed to discharge their duties as such officers in the next congressional election, upon the assumption that the action by way of referendum was void, and that the law which was disapproved was subsisting and valid. The right to this relief was based upon the charge that the referendum vote was not and could not be a part of the legislative authority of the state, and therefore could have no influence on the subject of the law creating congressional districts for the purpose of representation in Congress. Indeed, it was in substance charged that both from the point of view of the state Constitution and laws and from that of the Constitution of the United States, especially 4 of article 1, providing that 'the times, places and manner of holding elections for Senators and Representatives, shall be prescribed in each state by the legislature thereof; but the Congress may at any time by law, make or alter such regulations, except as to the places of choosing Senators;' and also from that of the provisions of the controlling act of Congress of August 8, 1911 (chap. 5, 37 Stat. at L. 13, Comp. Stat. 1913, 15), apportioning representation among the states, the attempt to make the referendum a component part of the legislative authority empowered to deal with the election of members of Congress was absolutely void. The court below adversely disposed of these contentions, and held that the provisions as to referendum were a part of the legislative power of the state, made so by the Constitution, and that nothing in the act of Congress of 1911, or in the constitutional provision, operated to the contrary, and that therefore the disapproved law had no existence and was not entitled to be enforced by mandamus.

Without going into the many irrelevant points which are pressed in the argument, and the various inapposite authorities cited, although we have considered them all, we think it is apparent that the whole case and every real question in it will be disposed of by looking at it from three points of view,—the state power, the power of Congress, and the operation of the provision of the Constitution of the United States, referred to.

1. As to the state power, we pass from its consideration, since it is obvious that the decision below is conclusive on that subject, and makes it clear that, so far as the state had the power to do it, the referendum constituted a part of the state Constitution and laws, and was contained within the legislative power; and therefore the claim that the law which was disapproved and was no law under the Constitution and laws of the state was yet valid and operative is conclusively established to be wanting in merit.

2. So far as the subject may be influenced by the power of Congress, that is, to the extent that the will of Congress has been expressed on the subject, we think the case is equally without merit. We say this because we think it is clear that Congress, in 1911, in enacting the controlling law concerning the duties of the states, through their legislative authority, to deal with the subject of the creation of congressional districts, expressly modified the phraseology of the previous acts relating to that subject by inserting a clause plainly intended to provide that where, by the state Constitution and laws, the referendum was treated as part of the legislative power, the power as thus constituted should be held and treated to be the state legislative power for the purpose of

creating congressional districts by law. This is the case since, under the act of Congress dealing with apportionment, which preceded the act of 1911, by 4 it was commanded that the existing districts in a state should continue in force 'until the legislature of such state, in the manner herein prescribed, shall redistrict such state' (act of February 7, 1891, chap. 116, 26 Stat. at L. 735); while in the act of 1911 there was substituted a provision that the redistricting should be made by a state 'in the manner provided by the laws thereof.' And the legislative history of this last act leaves no room for doubt that the prior words were stricken out and the new words inserted for the express purpose, in so far as Congress had power to do it, of excluding the possibility of making the contention as to referendum which is now urged. Cong. Rec. vol. 47, pp. 3436, 3437, 3507.

3. To the extent that the contention urges that to include the referendum within state legislative power for the purpose of apportionment is repugnant to 4 of article 1 of the Constitution and hence void, even if sanctioned by Congress, because beyond the constitutional authority of that body, and hence that it is the duty of the judicial power so to declare, we again think the contention is plainly without substance, for the following reasons: It must rest upon the assumption that to include the referendum in the scope of the legislative power is to introduce a virus which destroys that power, which in effect annihilates representative government, and causes a state where such condition exists to be not republican in form, in violation of the guaranty of the Constitution. Const. 4, art. 4. But the proposition and the argument disregard the settled rule that the question of whether that guaranty of the Constitution has been disregarded presents no justiciable controversy, but involves the exercise by Congress of the authority vested in it by the Constitution. *Pacific States Teleph. & Teleg. Co. v. Oregon*, 223 U.S. 118, 56 L. ed. 377, 32 Sup. Ct. Rep. 224. In so far as the proposition challenges the power of Congress, as manifested by the clause in the act of 1911, treating the referendum as a part of the legislative power for the purpose of apportionment, where so ordained by the state Constitutions and laws, the argument but asserts, on the one hand, that Congress had no power to do that which, from the point of view of 4 of article 1, previously considered, the Constitution expressly gave the right to do. In so far as the proposition may be considered as asserting, on the other hand, that any attempt by Congress to recognize the referendum as a part of the legislative authority of a state is obnoxious to a republican form of government as provided by 4 of article 4, the contention necessarily but reasserts the proposition on that subject previously adversely disposed of. And that this is the inevitable result of the contention is plainly manifest, since at best the proposition comes to the assertion that because Congress, upon whom the

Constitution has conferred the exclusive authority to uphold the guaranty of a republican form of government, has done something which it is deemed is repugnant to that guaranty, therefore there was automatically created judicial authority to go beyond the limits of judicial power, and, in doing so, to usurp congressional power, on the ground that Congress had mistakenly dealt with a subject which was within its exclusive control, free from judicial interference.

It is apparent from these reasons that there must either be a dismissal for want of jurisdiction, because there is no power to re-examine the state questions foreclosed by the decision below, and because of the want of merit in the Federal questions relied upon, or a judgment of affirmance, it being absolutely indifferent, as to the result, which of the two be applied. In view, however, of the subject-matter of the controversy and the Federal characteristics which inhere in it, we are of opinion, applying the rule laid down in *Swafford v. Templeton*, 185 U.S. 487, 46 L. ed. 1005, 22 Sup. Ct. Rep. 783, the decree proper to be rendered is one of affirmance, and such a decree is therefore ordered.

Affirmed.

Maine Supreme Court
107 A. 705
In re Opinion of the Justices
August 28, 1919

Answer to question propounded to the Justices of the Supreme Judicial Court by the Governor.

To the Honorable Carl E. Milliken, Governor of Maine:

The undersigned Justices of the Supreme Judicial Court, having considered the question propounded by you under date of July 9, 1919, concerning the necessity of submitting by referendum to the qualified voters of the state a certain act of the Legislature of Maine, entitled "An act granting to women the right to vote for presidential electors," respectfully submit the following answer:

The request contains certain recitals of fact, the substance of which is that the above statute was passed by the concurrent action of both branches of the Legislature and was duly approved by the Governor; that the Legislature adjourned without day on April 4, 1919, and within 90 days thereafter petitions, apparently bearing the requisite number of signatures, were filed with the secretary of state, requesting that this act be referred to the people under Amendment 31 of article 4 of the Constitution of Maine, known as the initiative and referendum amendment.

QUESTION.

"Is the effect of the act of the Legislature of Maine of 1919, entitled 'An act granting to women the right to vote for presidential electors,' approved by the Governor on March 28, 1919, suspended by valid written petitions of not less than 10,000 electors, addressed to the Governor and filed in the office of the secretary of state within 90 days after the recess of the Legislature, requesting that it be referred to the people, and should the act be referred to the people as provided in article 4 of the Constitution of Maine, as amended by Amendment 31, adopted September 14, 1908?"

ANSWER.

This question we answer in the affirmative. In our opinion this legislative act comes within the provisions of the initiative and referendum amendment, and should be referred to the people for adoption or rejection by them.

To solve this problem it is necessary to pursue the same general course as in deciding the question concerning the prohibitory amendment to the federal Constitution, by an examination, first, of the provisions and requirements of the Constitution of the United States relating to this subject-matter, and, second, of the provisions and requirements of the Constitution of Maine.

The first question that naturally arises is this: Where, under the federal Constitution, is lodged the power of determining in what manner presidential electors shall be chosen and of prescribing the qualifications of the voters therefor?

It was competent for the people of the United States, in creating the compact known as the federal Constitution, to lodge this power wherever they saw fit. It was a matter wholly within their discretion. It is a well-known historical fact that there was a long and spirited debate in the constitutional convention over this very question; that is, the method to be adopted in electing the chief magistrate of the nation. Many plans were submitted, such as election by Congress, by the people at large, by the chief executives of the several states, and by electors appointed by the Legislatures. 1 Elliot, Deb. 208, 211, 217, 262.

Finally the following provisions, which were presented by Gouveneur Morris for the special committee, were adopted by the convention after much discussion, and were incorporated in article 11 of the perfected instrument, where they stand unchanged today, viz.:

> "Each state shall appoint, in such manner as the Legislature thereof may direct, a number of electors equal to the whole number of Senators and Representatives to which the state may be entitled in the Congress," etc. Article 2, § 1, subd. 2.

> "The Congress may determine the time of choosing the electors, and the day on which they shall give their votes, which day shall be the same throughout the United States." Article 2, § 1, subd. 4.

These two subdivisions comprise all the provisions of the federal Constitution applicable to the point in issue here. Under section 1, subd. 4, Congress is given the power to determine the date of holding presidential elections and of the meeting of the electors, but that marks the limit of its constitutional power. *In re Green*, 134 U.S. 377, 10 Sup. Ct. 586, 33 L. Ed. 951. All other powers in connection with this subject are expressly reserved to the states. *McPherson v. Blacker*, 146 U.S. 1, 13 Sup. Ct. 3, 36 L. Ed. 869; *Pope v. Williams*, 193 U.S. 621, 24 Sup. Ct. 573, 48 L. Ed. 817.

In the case last cited the Supreme Court of the United States say:

> "The privilege to vote in a state is within the jurisdiction of the state itself, to be exercised as the state may direct, and upon such terms as to it may seem proper, provided, of course, no discrimination is made between individuals in violation of the federal Constitution."

The word "appoint" as employed in subdivision 2 has been interpreted to be sufficiently comprehensive to include the result of a popular election and to convey the broadest powers of determination. *McPherson v. Blacker*, 146 U.S. 1, 27, 13 Sup. Ct. 3, 36 L. Ed. 869.

The language of section 1, subd. 2, is clear and unambiguous. It admits of no doubt as to where the constitutional power of appointment is vested, namely, in the several states. "Each state shall appoint in such manner as the Legislature thereof may direct" are the significant words of the section, and their plain meaning is that each state is thereby clothed with the absolute power to appoint electors in such manner as it may see fit, without any interference or control on the part of the federal government, except, of course, in case of attempted discrimination as to race, color, or previous condition of servitude under the fifteenth amendment. The clause, "in such manner as the Legislature thereof may direct," means, simply that the state shall give expression to its will, as it must, of necessity, through its law-making body, the Legislature. The will of the state in this respect must be voiced in legislative acts or resolves, which shall prescribe in detail the manner of choosing electors, the qualifications of voters therefor, and the proceedings on the part of the electors when chosen.

But these acts and resolves must be passed and become effective in accordance with and in subjection to the Constitution of the state, like all other acts and resolves having the force of law. The Legislature was not given in this respect any superiority over or independence from the organic law of the state in force at the time when a given law is passed. Nor was it designated by the federal Constitution as a mere agency or representative of the people to perform a certain act, as it was under article 5 in ratifying a federal amendment, a point more fully discussed in the answer to the question concerning the federal prohibitory amendment. 107 Atl. 673. It is simply the ordinary instrumentality of the state, the legislative branch of the government, the law-making power, to put into words the will of the state in connection with the choice of presidential electors. The distinction between the function and power of the Legislature in the case under consideration and its function and power as a particular body designated by the federal Constitution to ratify or reject a federal amendment is sharp and clear and must be borne in mind.

It follows, therefore, that under the provisions of the federal Constitution the state by its legislative direction may establish such a method of choosing its presidential electors as it may see fit, and may change that method from time to time as it may deem advisable; but the legislative acts both of establishment and of change must always be subject to the provisions of the Constitution of the state in force at the time such acts are passed and can be valid and effective only when enacted in compliance therewith.

In the exercise of the power thus conferred by the federal Constitution, various methods of electing presidential electors were adopted in the early days by the several states, as set forth in detail in *McPherson v. Blacker*, 146 U.S. at pages 29 to 35, 13 Sup. Ct. 3, 36 L. Ed. 869.

In our own state the same holds true to a certain extent. Prior to 1847 the legislative direction expressed itself in the form of a joint resolution, passed every fourth year, at the session immediately preceding a presidential election. These resolves had the force of law, and with the exception of those of 1820 and 1824 they were uniformly presented to and were approved by the Governor.

Prior to 1840 the district prevailed in whole or in part. Res. 1820, c. 19; 1824, c. 76; 1828, c. 23; 1832, c. 65; 1836, c. 9. In 1840 (Res. c. 55) 10 electors at large were provided for, and since that time the electors have been chosen at large upon a single ballot. This method was followed in 1844. Res. 1844, c. 295.

Under the resolves of 1820, 1824, and 1828, the qualifications of voters for representatives and senators to the Legislature were made the qualifications of voters for presidential electors. By the resolves of 1832 and 1836, the qualifications of voters for representatives alone were made the test, and by the resolve of 1840 this was changed to qualifications of voters for senators alone.

The Legislature of 1847 directed for the first time by a general act, instead of by a quadrennial resolve, the manner in which the voters should proceed in the election of presidential electors (Pub. L. 1847, c. 26), and, following the resolves of 1840 and 1844, prescribed the qualified voters therefor to be "the people of this state qualified to vote for senators in its Legislature." This qualification established by the act of 1847 has been preserved in all the subsequent revisions. R. S. 1857, c. 4, § 79; R. S. 1871, c. 4, § 78; R. S. 1883, c. 4, § 86; R. S. 1903, c. 6, § 123; R. S. 1916, c. 7, § 57. And such was the law of this state when the act in question (chapter 120 of the Public Laws of 1919) was passed. The qualification of voters for senators, as well as for representatives, is fixed by the Constitution of Maine as "every male citizen of the United States of the age of twenty-one years and upwards," etc. Article 2, § 1. Therefore, prior to the act of 1919, only male citizens could vote for presidential electors. It is clear that this act, extending this privilege to women, constitutes a change in the method of electing presidential electors, and is a virtual amendment of R. S. 1916, c. 7, § 57, not in express terms, but by necessary implication.

In other words, this state during the century of its existence prior to 1919, had by appropriate legislative act or resolve directed that only male citizens were qualified to vote for presidential electors. By the act of 1919 it has attempted to change that direction, by extending the privilege of suffrage, so far as presidential electors are concerned, to women. Had this act been passed prior to the adoption of the initiative and referendum amendment in 1908, it would have become effective, so far as legal enactment is concerned, without being referred to the people; but now under Amendment 31 such reference must be had, if the necessary steps therefor are taken.

The language of that amendment is as follows:

"No act or joint resolution of the Legislature, except such orders or resolutions as pertain solely to facilitating the performance of the business of the Legislature, of either branch, or of any committee or officer thereof, or appropriate money therefor or for the payment of salaries fixed by law, shall take effect until ninety days after the recess of the Legislature passing it, unless in case of emergency," etc.

None of the exceptions applies here. Section 17 provides that upon written petition of not less than 10,000 electors, filed in the office of the Secretary of State within 90 days after the recess of the Legislature, requesting that—

"one or more acts, bills, resolves or resolutions, or part or parts thereof passed by the Legislature, not then in effect by reason of the provisions of the preceding section be referred to the people, such acts, bills, resolves or resolutions shall not take effect until thirty days after the Governor shall have announced by public proclamation that the same have been ratified by a majority of the electors voting thereon at a general or special election."

It is evident that the act in question falls within the terms and scope of this amendment. This is an ordinary legislative act, a bill in the form prescribed by Amendment 31. It is entitled "An act granting," etc. The enacting clause is, "Be it enacted by the people of the state of Maine." It was presented to the Governor for his approval, and was signed by him, as required by section 2 of part third of article 4 of the Constitution of Maine, viz.:

"Every bill or resolution having the force of law, to which the concurrence of both houses may be necessary, . . . which shall have passed both houses, shall be presented to the Governor, and if he approves, he shall sign it," etc.

It has been published as chapter 120 of Public Laws of 1919.

This is not a mere joint resolution, addressed to the Governor, asking for the removal of a public official, as in *Moulton v. Scully*, 111 Me. 428, 89 Atl. 944, nor is it a joint resolution ratifying an amendment to the federal Constitution, as in the other question propounded to us herewith, in neither of which cases did the referendum attach, because neither resolution had the force of law. This is the public statute of a law-making body, and is as fully within the control of the referendum amendment as is any other of the 239 public acts passed at the last session of the Legislature, excepting, of course, emergency acts. It is shielded from the jurisdiction of that referendum neither by the state nor by the federal Constitution. In short, the state, through its Legislature, has taken merely the first step toward effecting a change in the appointment of presidential electors; but, because of the petitions filed, it must await the second step which is the vote of the people. The legislative attempt in this case cannot be fully effective until "thirty days after the Governor shall have announced by public proclamation that the same has been ratified by a majority of the electors voting thereon at a general or special election."

It follows that, for the reasons already stated, this question is answered in the affirmative.

Very respectfully,

LESLIE C. CORNISH
ALBERT M. SPEAR
GEORGE M. HANSON
WARREN C. PHILBROOK
CHARLES J. DUNN
JOHN A. MORRILL
SCOTT WILSON
LUERE B. DEASY

APPENDIX R: STATE CONSTITUTIONAL PROVISIONS RELATING TO REPEALING OR AMENDING VOTER INITIATIVES

ALASKA CONSTITUTION—ARTICLE XI

SECTION 6. ENACTMENT. If a majority of the votes cast on the proposition favor its adoption, the initiated measure is enacted. If a majority of the votes cast on the proposition favor the rejection of an act referred, it is rejected. The lieutenant governor shall certify the election returns. An initiated law becomes effective ninety days after certification, is not subject to veto, and may not be repealed by the legislature within two years of its effective date. It may be amended at any time. An act rejected by referendum is void thirty days after certification. Additional procedures for the initiative and referendum may be prescribed by law.

ARIZONA CONSTITUTION—ARTICLE 4, PART 1(6)

(A) Veto of initiative or referendum. The veto power of the governor shall not extend to an initiative measure approved by a majority of the votes cast thereon or to a referendum measure decided by a majority of the votes cast thereon.

(B) Legislature's power to repeal initiative or referendum. The legislature shall not have the power to repeal an initiative measure approved by a majority of the votes cast thereon or to repeal a referendum measure decided by a majority of the votes cast thereon.

(C) Legislature's power to amend initiative or referendum. The legislature shall not have the power to amend an initiative measure approved by a majority of the votes cast thereon, or to amend a referendum measure decided by a majority of the votes cast thereon, unless the amending legislation furthers the purposes of such measure and at least three-fourths of the members of each house of the legislature, by a roll call of ayes and nays, vote to amend such measure.

ARKANSAS CONSTITUTION—AMENDMENT

No Veto: The veto power of the Governor or Mayor shall not extend to measures initiated by or referred to the people.

Amendment and Repeal: No measure approved by a vote of the people shall be amended or repealed by the General Assembly or by any City Council, except upon a yea and nay vote on roll call of two-thirds of all the members elected to each house of the General Assembly, or of the City Council, as the case may be.

CALIFORNIA CONSTITUTION—ARTICLE 2, SECTION 10(C)

The Legislature may amend or repeal referendum statutes. It may amend or repeal an initiative statute by another statute that becomes effective only when approved by the electors unless the initiative statute permits amendment or repeal without their approval.

MASSACHUSETTS CONSTITUTION—AMENDMENT ARTICLE 4

Section 3. Amendment of Proposed Amendments. —A proposal for an amendment to the constitution introduced by initiative petition shall be voted upon in the form in which it was introduced, unless such amendment is amended by vote of three-fourths of the members voting thereon in joint session, which vote shall be taken by call of the yeas and nays if called for by any member.

MICHIGAN CONSTITUTION—ARTICLE 2, SECTION 9

Initiative; duty of legislature, referendum. Any law proposed by initiative petition shall be either enacted or rejected by the legislature without change or amendment within 40 session days from the time such petition is received by the legislature. If any law proposed by such petition shall be enacted by the legislature it shall be subject to referendum, as hereinafter provided.

Legislative rejection of initiated measure; different measure; submission to people. If the law so proposed is not enacted by the legislature within the 40 days, the state officer authorized by law shall submit such proposed law to the people for approval or rejection at the next general election. The legislature may reject any measure so proposed by initiative petition and propose a different measure upon the same subject by a yea and nay vote upon separate roll calls, and in such event both measures shall be submitted by such state officer to the electors for approval or rejection at the next general election.

Initiative or referendum law; effective date, veto, amendment and repeal. Any law submitted to the people by either initiative or referendum petition and approved by a majority of the votes cast thereon at any election shall take effect 10 days after the date of the official declaration of the vote. No law initiated or adopted by the people shall be subject to the veto power of the governor, and no law adopted by the people at the polls under the initiative provisions of this section shall be amended or repealed, except by a vote of the electors unless otherwise provided in the initiative measure or by three-fourths of the members elected to and serving in each house of the legislature. Laws approved by the people under the referendum provision of this section may be amended by the legislature at any subsequent session thereof. If two or more measures approved by the electors at the same election conflict, that receiving the highest affirmative vote shall prevail.

NEBRASKA CONSTITUTION—ARTICLE III, SECTION 2

. . . The Legislature shall not amend, repeal, modify, or impair a law enacted by the people by initiative, contemporaneously with the adoption of this initiative measure or at any time thereafter, except upon a vote of at least two-thirds of all the members of the Legislature.

NEVADA CONSTITUTION—ARTICLE 19, SECTION 2

3. . . . An initiative measure so approved by the voters shall not be amended, annulled, repealed, set aside or suspended by the legislature within 3 years from the date it takes effect. . . .

NORTH DAKOTA CONSTITUTION—ARTICLE 3, SECTION 8

. . . A measure approved by the electors may not be repealed or amended by the legislative assembly for seven years from its effective date, except by a two-thirds vote of the members elected to each house . . .

WASHINGTON CONSTITUTION, ARTICLE 2, SECTION 41

. . . No act, law or bill approved by a majority of the electors voting thereon shall be amended or repealed by the legislature within a period of two years following such enactment: Provided, That any such act, law or bill may be amended within two years after such enactment at any regular or special session of the legislature by a vote of two-thirds of all the members elected to each house with full compliance with section 12, Article III, of the Washington Constitution, and no amendatory law adopted in accordance with this provision shall be subject to referendum. But such enactment may be amended or repealed at any general regular or special election by direct vote of the people thereon. These provisions supersede the provisions of subsection (c) of section 1 of this article as amended by the seventh amendment to the Constitution of this state.

WYOMING CONSTITUTION—ARTICLE 3, SECTION 52

(f) If votes in an amount in excess of fifty percent (50%) of those voting in the general election are cast in favor of adoption of an initiated measure, the measure is enacted. If votes in an amount in excess of fifty percent (50%) of those voted in the general election are cast in favor of rejection of an act referred, it is rejected. The secretary of state shall certify the election returns. An initiated law becomes effective ninety (90) days after certification, is not subject to veto, and may not be repealed by the legislature within two (2) years of its effective date. It may be amended at any time. An act rejected by referendum is void thirty (30) days after certification. Additional procedures for the initiative and referendum may be prescribed by law.

APPENDIX S: SUPPORTERS IN CONGRESS OF NATIONWIDE POPULAR ELECTION OF THE PRESIDENT IN ROLL CALLS AND SPONSORS OF CONSTITUTIONAL AMENDMENTS

S.1 ALABAMA

SPONSOR OF A CONSTITUTIONAL AMENDMENT	VOTED FOR SJR 28 IN 1979 ROLL CALL	VOTED FOR HJR 681 IN 1969 ROLL CALL
Rep. John H. Buchanan (R) · HJR 228 - 95th Congress · HJR 288 - 96th Congress		Rep. John H. Buchanan (R)
		Rep. William Dickinson (R)
Rep. William Edwards (R) · HJR 138 - 95th Congress · HJR 189 - 96th Congress · HJR 195 - 97th Congress		Rep. William Edwards (R)
	Sen. Donald Stewart (D)	

S.2 ALASKA

SPONSOR OF A CONSTITUTIONAL AMENDMENT	VOTED FOR SJR 28 IN 1979 ROLL CALL	VOTED FOR HJR 681 IN 1969 ROLL CALL
Sen. Maurice Gravel (D) · SJR 1 - 94th Congress · SJR 1 - 95th Congress · SJR 1 - 96th Congress · SJR 28 - 96th Congress	Sen. Maurice Gravel (D)	

S.3 ARIZONA

SPONSOR OF A CONSTITUTIONAL AMENDMENT	VOTED FOR SJR 28 IN 1979 ROLL CALL	VOTED FOR HJR 681 IN 1969 ROLL CALL
		Rep. John Rhodes (R)
		Rep. Sam Steiger (R)
Rep. Morris K. Udall (D) · HJR 168 - 95th Congress		Rep. Morris K. Udall (D)
Sen. Dennis DeConcini (D) · SJR 1 - 95th Congress · SJR 1 - 96th Congress · SJR 28 - 96th Congress · SJR 3 - 97th Congress · SJR 17 - 98th Congress · SJR 297 - 102nd Congress	Sen. Dennis DeConcini (D)	

S.4 ARKANSAS

SPONSOR OF A CONSTITUTIONAL AMENDMENT	VOTED FOR SJR 28 IN 1979 ROLL CALL	VOTED FOR HJR 681 IN 1969 ROLL CALL
Rep. William Vollie Alexander, Jr. (D) · HJR 137 - 93rd Congress		Rep. William Vollie Alexander, Jr. (D)
		Rep. John Hammerschmidt (R)
		Rep. Wilbur Mills (D)
Sen. David H. Pryor (D) · SJR 1 - 96th Congress · SJR 28 - 96th Congress · SJR 3 - 97th Congress · SJR 17 - 98th Congress · SJR 163 - 101st Congress · SJR 297 - 102nd Congress	Sen. David H. Pryor (D)	Rep. David H. Pryor (D)

S.5 CALIFORNIA

SPONSOR OF A CONSTITUTIONAL AMENDMENT	VOTED FOR SJR 28 IN 1979 ROLL CALL	VOTED FOR HJR 681 IN 1969 ROLL CALL
		Rep. Glenn Anderson (D)
Rep. Jim Bates (D) · HJR 137 - 101st Congress		
Rep. Anthony Beilenson (D) · HJR 9 - 102nd Congress		
Rep. Alphonza Bell (R) · HJR 237 - 93rd Congress		Rep. Alphonza Bell (R)
Sen. Barbara Boxer (D) · HJR 5 - 100th Congress		
Rep. George Brown (D) · HJR 228 - 95th Congress · HJR 254 - 96th Congress		Rep. George Brown (D)
Rep. Clair Burgener (R) · HJR 228 - 95th Congress		
		Rep. Phillip Burton (D)
Rep. Tom Campbell (R) · HJR 180 - 104th Congress · HJR 43 - 105th Congress		
		Rep. Donald Clausen (R)
		Rep. Delwin Clawson (R)
Rep. Anthony Coelho (D) · HJR 254 - 96th Congress		
		Rep. Jeffery Cohelan (D)
		Rep. James Corman (D)
Sen. Alan Cranston (D) · SJR 1 - 94th Congress · SJR 1 - 95th Congress · SJR 1 - 96th Congress · SJR 28 - 96th Congress · SJR 3 - 97th Congress · SJR 297 - 102nd Congress	Sen. Alan Cranston (D)	

S.5 CALIFORNIA *(continued)*

SPONSOR OF A CONSTITUTIONAL AMENDMENT	VOTED FOR SJR 28 IN 1979 ROLL CALL	VOTED FOR HJR 681 IN 1969 ROLL CALL
Rep. George Danielson (D) · HJR 207 - 93rd Congress · HJR 149 - 95th Congress · HJR 7 - 96th Congress		
Rep. Ronald Dellums (D) · HJR 117 - 104th Congress		
Rep. Calvin Dooley (D) · HJR 28 - 103rd Congress		
		Rep. William Edwards (D)
Rep. Vic Fazio (D) · HJR 254 - 96th Congress		
Sen. Diane Feinstein (D) · SJR 11 - 109th Congress		
Rep. Bob Filner (D) · HJR 103 - 108th Congress		
		Rep. Charles Gubser (R)
		Rep. Richard Hanna (D)
Rep. Mark W. Hannaford (D) · HJR 229 - 95th Congress		
Rep. Augustus Hawkins (D) · HJR 384 - 95th Congress		Rep. Augustus Hawkins (D)
Rep. Andrew Hinshaw (R) · HJR 207 - 93rd Congress		
Rep. Chester Holifield (D) · HJR 207 - 93rd Congress		Rep. Chester Holifield (D)
		Rep. Craig Hosmer (R)
		Rep. Harold Johnson (D)
Rep. William M. Ketchum (R) · HJR 168 - 95th Congress · HJR 230 - 95th Congress · HJR 384 - 95th Congress		
Rep. Jay Kim (R) · HJR 28 - 103rd Congress		
Rep. John H. Krebs (D) · HJR 228 - 95th Congress		
Rep. Robert L. Leggett (D) · HJR 207 - 93rd Congress · HJR 231 - 95th Congress		Rep. Robert L. Leggett (D)
Rep. James Fredrick Lloyd (D) · HJR 168 - 95th Congress		
Rep. Zoe Lofgren (D) · HJR 112 - 108th Congress · HJR 50 - 109th Congress		
		Rep. William Mailliard (R)
Rep. Matthew Martinez (D) · HJR 137 - 101st Congress		

(continued)

S.5 CALIFORNIA *(continued)*

SPONSOR OF A CONSTITUTIONAL AMENDMENT	VOTED FOR SJR 28 IN 1979 ROLL CALL	VOTED FOR HJR 681 IN 1969 ROLL CALL
		Rep. Robert Mathias (R)
Rep. Alfred McCandless (R) · HJR 28 - 103rd Congress		
		Rep. Paul McCloskey (R)
		Rep. John McFall (D)
		Rep. George Miller (D)
Rep. John Moss (D) · HJR 70 - 95th Congress · HJR 168 - 95th Congress		Rep. John Moss (D)
Rep. Jerry M. Patterson (D) · HJR 231 - 95th Congress · HJR 397 - 95th Congress · HJR 254 - 96th Congress		
Rep. Nancy Pelosi (D) · HJR 137 - 101st Congress		
		Rep. Jerry Pettis (R)
Rep. Shirley N. Pettis (R) · HJR 228 - 95th Congress		
		Rep. Thomas Rees (D)
Rep. Edward R. Roybal (D) · HJR 228 - 95th Congress		
Rep. Bernice Sisk (D) · HJR 207 - 93rd Congress		
		Rep. Allen Smith (R)
Rep. Fortney Stark (D) · HJR 228 - 95th Congress · HJR 299 - 96th Congress · HJR 36 - 109th Congress · HJR 50 - 109th Congress		
		Rep. Burt Talcott (R)
Rep. Walter R. Tucker III (D) · HJR 65 - 103rd Congress		
Sen. John Tunney (D) · SJR 1 - 94th Congress		Sen. John Tunney (D)
Rep. Lionel Van Deerlin (D) · HJR 254 - 96th Congress		Rep. Lionel Van Deerlin (D)
		Rep. Jerome Waldie (D)
		Rep. Charles Wiggins (R)
Rep. Charles H. Wilson (D) · HJR 231 - 95th Congress		Rep. Charles H. Wilson (D)
		Rep. Robert Wilson (R)
Rep. Lynn Woolsey · HJR 50 - 109th Congress		

S.6 COLORADO

SPONSOR OF A CONSTITUTIONAL AMENDMENT	VOTED FOR SJR 28 IN 1979 ROLL CALL	VOTED FOR HJR 681 IN 1969 ROLL CALL
	Sen. William Armstrong (R)	
		Rep. Wayne Aspinall (D)
		Rep. Donald Brotzman (R)
Sen. Ben Campbell (R) · HJR 9 - 102nd Congress		
Rep. Frank Evans (D) · HJR 137 - 93rd Congress		Rep. Frank Evans (D)
Sen. Gary W. Hart (D) · SJR 1 - 94th Congress · SJR 1 - 95th Congress	Sen. Gary W. Hart (D)	
Sen. Floyd Haskell (D) · SJR 1 - 95th Congress · SJR 1 - 99th Congress		
		Rep. Byron Rogers (D)

S.7 CONNECTICUT

SPONSOR OF A CONSTITUTIONAL AMENDMENT	VOTED FOR SJR 28 IN 1979 ROLL CALL	VOTED FOR HJR 681 IN 1969 ROLL CALL
		Rep. Emilio Daddario (D)
Rep. Robert Giaimo (D) · HJR 137 - 93rd Congress		Rep. Robert Giaimo (D)
Rep. Stewart McKinney (R) · HJR 197 - 95th Congress		
		Rep. Thomas Meskill (R)
		Rep. John Monagan (D)
Rep. Bill Ratchford (D) · HJR 254 - 96th Congress		
Sen. Abaraham A. Ribicoff (D) · SJR 1 - 94th Congress · SJR 1 - 95th Congress · SJR 1 - 96th Congress · SJR 28 - 96th Congress	Sen. Abaraham A. Ribicoff (D)	
Rep. Ronald A. Sarasin (R) · HJR 300 - 93rd Congress · HJR 230 - 95th Congress		
		Rep. William St. Onge (D)
		Rep. Lowell Palmer Weicker (R)

S.8 DELAWARE

SPONSOR OF A CONSTITUTIONAL AMENDMENT	VOTED FOR SJR 28 IN 1979 ROLL CALL	VOTED FOR HJR 681 IN 1969 ROLL CALL
		Rep. William Victor Roth (R)
Sen. Thomas Carper (D) · HJR 137 - 101st Congress		

S.9 FLORIDA

SPONSOR OF A CONSTITUTIONAL AMENDMENT	VOTED FOR SJR 28 IN 1979 ROLL CALL	VOTED FOR HJR 681 IN 1969 ROLL CALL
Rep. Jim Bacchus (D) · HJR 506 - 102nd Congress · HJR 28 - 103rd Congress		
Rep. Charles E. Bennett (D) · HJR 13 - 93rd Congress · HJR 3 - 94th Congress · HJR 33 - 95th Congress · HJR 24 - 96th Congress · HJR 20 - 97th Congress · HJR 11 - 98th Congress · HJR 19 - 99th Congress · HJR 12 - 100th Congress · HJR 11 - 101st Congress · HJR 9 - 102nd Congress		Rep. Charles E. Bennett (D)
		Rep. Herbert Burke (R)
		Rep. William Cramer (R)
Rep. Dante Fascell (D) · HJR 207 - 93rd Congress		Rep. Dante Fascell (D)
		Rep. Louis Frey (R)
Rep. Don Fuqua (D) · HJR 31 - 93rd Congress		
Rep. Sam Gibbons (D) · HJR 228 - 95th Congress · HJR 261 - 96th Congress		Rep. Sam Gibbons (D)
Rep. Alcee Hastings (D) · HJR 28 - 103rd Congress · HJR 17 - 109th Congress		
Rep. Claude Pepper (D) · HJR 207 - 93rd Congress · HJR 228 - 95th Congress · HJR 288 - 96th Congress		Rep. Claude Pepper (D)
		Rep. Paul Rogers (D)

S.10 GEORGIA

SPONSOR OF A CONSTITUTIONAL AMENDMENT	VOTED FOR SJR 28 IN 1979 ROLL CALL	VOTED FOR HJR 681 IN 1969 ROLL CALL
		Rep. John Davis (D)
		Rep. Phillip Landrum (D)
Rep. John Lewis (D) · HJR 137 - 101st Congress · HJR 9 - 102nd Congress		
		Rep. Robert G. Stephens, Jr. (D)
		Rep. Standish Thompson (R)

S.11 HAWAII

SPONSOR OF A CONSTITUTIONAL AMENDMENT	VOTED FOR SJR 28 IN 1979 ROLL CALL	VOTED FOR HJR 681 IN 1969 ROLL CALL
Rep. Cecil Heftel (D) · HJR 168 - 95th Congress		
Sen. Daniel K. Inouye (D) · SJR 1 - 94th Congress · SJR 1 - 95th Congress · SJR 1 - 96th Congress · SJR 28 - 96th Congress · SJR 3 - 97th Congress · SJR 362 - 100th Congress	Sen. Daniel K. Inouye (D)	
Sen. Spark M. Matsunaga (D) · SJR 1 - 95th Congress · SJR 1 - 96th Congress · SJR 28 - 96th Congress · SJR 3 - 97th Congress · SJR 17 - 98th Congress	Sen. Spark M. Matsunaga (D)	Rep. Spark M. Matsunaga (D)
		Rep. Patsy Mink (D)

S.12 IDAHO

SPONSOR OF A CONSTITUTIONAL AMENDMENT	VOTED FOR SJR 28 IN 1979 ROLL CALL	VOTED FOR HJR 681 IN 1969 ROLL CALL
Sen. Frank F. Church (D) · SJR 1 - 94th Congress · SJR 1 - 95th Congress	Sen. Frank F. Church (D)	
		Rep. Orval Hansen (R)
Rep. George Hansen (R) · HJR 207 - 93rd Congress		

S.13 ILLINOIS

SPONSOR OF A CONSTITUTIONAL AMENDMENT	VOTED FOR SJR 28 IN 1979 ROLL CALL	VOTED FOR HJR 681 IN 1969 ROLL CALL
Rep. John Anderson (R) · HJR 228 - 95th Congress · HJR 288 - 96th Congress		Rep. John Anderson (R)
Rep. Frank Annunzio (D) · HJR 137 - 93rd Congress		Rep. Frank Annunzio (D)
		Rep. Leslie Arends (R)
Rep. Rod Blagojevich (D) · HJR 23 - 106th Congress		
Rep. Harold Collier (R) · HJR 137 - 93rd Congress · HJR 462 - 93rd Congress		Rep. Harold Collier (R)
		Rep. George Collins (D)[1]
Rep. Cardiss Collins (D) · HJR 229 - 95th Congress · HJR 137 - 101st Congress · HJR 28 - 103rd Congress · HJR 117 - 104th Congress		
Rep. Philip Crane (R) · HJR 28 - 105th Congress		
Sen. Richard Durbin (D) · HJR 60 - 103rd Congress · SJR 56 - 106th Congress		
		Rep. John Erlenborn (R)
Rep. Lane Evans (D) · HJR 506 - 102nd Congress · HJR 28 - 103rd Congress · HJR 23 - 106th Congress · HJR 17 - 109th Congress		
		Rep. Paul Findley (R)
		Rep. Kenneth Gray (D)
Rep. Robert Hanrahan (R) · HJR 207 - 93rd Congress		
Rep. Jesse Jackson, Jr. (D) · HJR 109 - 108th Congress · HJR 36 - 109th Congress		
		Rep. John Kluczynski (D)
Rep. Ray LaHood (R) · HJR 28 - 105th Congress · HJR 23 - 106th Congress		
Rep. William O. Lipinski (D) · HJR 9 - 102nd Congress · HJR 28 - 105th Congress		
Rep. Robert McClory (R) · HJR 118 - 95th Congress · HJR 197 - 95th Congress · HJR 240 - 96th Congress		Rep. Robert McClory (R)

[1] The roll call does not make clear whether this Representative Collins or the one from Texas voted for HJR 681 in 1969.

S.13 ILLINOIS *(continued)*

SPONSOR OF A CONSTITUTIONAL AMENDMENT	VOTED FOR SJR 28 IN 1979 ROLL CALL	VOTED FOR HJR 681 IN 1969 ROLL CALL
		Rep. Robert Michel (R)
		Rep. Abner Mikva (D)
		Rep. William Murphy (D)
Rep. Charles Price (D) · HJR 228 - 95th Congress · HJR 261 - 96th Congress		Rep. Charles Price (D)
		Rep. Roman Pucinski (D)
		Rep. Thomas Railsback (R)
		Rep. Charlotte Reid (R)
		Rep. Daniel Rostenkowski (D)
Rep. Martin A. Russo (D) · HJR 288 - 96th Congress · HJR 384 - 96th Congress		
Rep. Janice Schakowsky (D) · HJR 109 - 108th Congress		
		Rep. George Shipley (D)
		Rep. William Springer (R)
Sen. Aldai Stevenson III (D) · SJR 1 - 94th Congress · SJR 1 - 95th Congress · SJR 1 - 96th Congress · SJR 28 - 96th Congress	Sen. Aldai Stevenson III (D)	
		Rep. Sidney Yates (D)

S.14 INDIANA

SPONSOR OF A CONSTITUTIONAL AMENDMENT	VOTED FOR SJR 28 IN 1979 ROLL CALL	VOTED FOR HJR 681 IN 1969 ROLL CALL
		Rep. Edwin Adair (R)
Sen. Birch E. Bayh (D) · SJR 1 - 94th Congress · SJR 1 - 95th Congress · SJR 123 - 95th Congress · SJR 1 - 96th Congress · SJR 28 - 96th Congress	Sen. Birch E. Bayh (D)	
Rep. Adam Benjamin, Jr. (D) · HJR 384 - 95th Congress		
		Rep. John Brademas (D)
Rep. William Bray (R) · HJR 137 - 93rd Congress		Rep. William Bray (R)
Rep. Floyd Fithian (D) · HJR 521 - 94th Congress · HJR 350 - 95th Congress · HJR 208 - 96th Congress · HJR 254 - 96th Congress		

(continued)

S.14 INDIANA *(continued)*

SPONSOR OF A CONSTITUTIONAL AMENDMENT	VOTED FOR SJR 28 IN 1979 ROLL CALL	VOTED FOR HJR 681 IN 1969 ROLL CALL
Rep. Lee Hamilton (D) · HJR 137 - 93rd Congress · HJR 207 - 95th Congress · HJR 137 - 101st Congress · HJR 9 - 102nd Congress · HJR 28 - 103rd Congress · HJR 28 - 105th Congress		Rep. Lee Hamilton (D)
Rep. Andrew Jacobs, Jr. (D) · HJR 28 - 103rd Congress · HJR 33 - 103rd Congress · HJR 117 - 104th Congress · HJR 180 - 104th Congress		Rep. Andrew Jacobs, Jr. (D)
		Rep. Ray Madden (D)
		Rep. John Myers (R)
Rep. Tim Roemer (D) · HJR 506 - 102nd Congress		
		Rep. Richard Roudebush (R)
Rep. John Roush (D) · HJR 106 - 93rd Congress		
		Rep. Roger Zion (R)

S.15 IOWA

SPONSOR OF A CONSTITUTIONAL AMENDMENT	VOTED FOR SJR 28 IN 1979 ROLL CALL	VOTED FOR HJR 681 IN 1969 ROLL CALL
Rep. Berkley W. Bedell (D) · HJR 229 - 95th Congress · HJR 230 - 95th Congress · HJR 254 - 96th Congress		
Rep. Michael T. Blouin (D) · HJR 1100 - 94th Congress · HJR 676 - 95th Congress		
Sen. Richard Clark (D) · SJR 1 - 94th Congress · SJR 1 - 95th Congress		
	Sen. John Culver (D)	Rep. John Culver (D)
Rep. James Leach (R) · HJR 585 - 96th Congress · HJR 516 - 102nd Congress · HJR 113 - 106th Congress		
		Rep. Frederick Schwengel (R)

S.16 KANSAS

SPONSOR OF A CONSTITUTIONAL AMENDMENT	VOTED FOR SJR 28 IN 1979 ROLL CALL	VOTED FOR HJR 681 IN 1969 ROLL CALL
Sen. Robert J. Dole (R) · SJR 1 - 94th Congress · SJR 1 - 95th Congress · SJR 1 - 96th Congress · SJR 28 - 96th Congress · SJR 3 - 97th Congress · SJR 17 - 98th Congress	Sen. Robert J. Dole (R)	
Rep. Dan Glickman (D) · HJR 673 - 100th Congress · HJR 137 - 101st Congress · HJR 516 - 102nd Congress · HJR 28 - 103rd Congress		
Sen. James Pearson (R) · SJR 1 - 94th Congress		
Rep. William Roy (D) · HJR 207 - 93rd Congress		
		Rep. Garner Shriver (R)
		Rep. Joe Skubitz (R)
Rep. James Slattery (D) · HJR 137 - 101st Congress		
Rep. Edward Winn (R) · HJR 231 - 95th Congress		Rep. Edward Winn (R)

S.17 KENTUCKY

SPONSOR OF A CONSTITUTIONAL AMENDMENT	VOTED FOR SJR 28 IN 1979 ROLL CALL	VOTED FOR HJR 681 IN 1969 ROLL CALL
Rep. Scotty Baesler (D) · HJR 28 - 103rd Congress		
Rep. John Breckinridge (D) · HJR 384 - 95th Congress		
		Rep. Tim Carter (R)
		Rep. William Cowger (R)
Sen. Wendell H. Ford (D) · SJR 1 - 94th Congress · SJR 1 - 95th Congress · SJR 1 - 96th Congress · SJR 28 - 96th Congress · SJR 3 - 97th Congress · SJR 17 - 98th Congress	Sen. Wendell H. Ford (D)	

(continued)

S.17 KENTUCKY *(continued)*

SPONSOR OF A CONSTITUTIONAL AMENDMENT	VOTED FOR SJR 28 IN 1979 ROLL CALL	VOTED FOR HJR 681 IN 1969 ROLL CALL
Sen. Walter Huddleston (D) · SJR 1 - 94th Congress · SJR 1 - 95th Congress · SJR 1 - 96th Congress · SJR 28 - 96th Congress · SJR 3 - 97th Congress · SJR 17 - 98th Congress	Sen. Walter Huddleston (D)	
		Rep. William Natcher (D)
Rep. Carl D. Perkins (D) · HJR 228 - 95th Congress		Rep. Carl D. Perkins (D)
		Rep. Marion Snyder (R)
		Rep. Frank Stubblefield (D)
		Rep. John Watts (D)

S.18 LOUISIANA

SPONSOR OF A CONSTITUTIONAL AMENDMENT	VOTED FOR SJR 28 IN 1979 ROLL CALL	VOTED FOR HJR 681 IN 1969 ROLL CALL
		Rep. Thomas Hale Boggs (D)
Sen. John Breaux (D) · HJR 229 - 95th Congress		
		Rep. Edwin Edwards (D)
Rep. Thomas J. Huckaby (D) · HJR 516 - 102nd Congress · HJR 526 - 102nd Congress		
Sen. John B. Johnston, Jr. (D) · SJR 1 - 96th Congress · SJR 28 - 96th Congress	Sen. John B. Johnston, Jr. (D)	
Rep. Richard A. Tonry (D) · HJR 228 - 95th Congress		

S.19 MAINE

SPONSOR OF A CONSTITUTIONAL AMENDMENT	VOTED FOR SJR 28 IN 1979 ROLL CALL	VOTED FOR HJR 681 IN 1969 ROLL CALL
Rep. Thomas Andrews (D) · HJR 28 - 103rd Congress		
Rep. David Emery (R) · HJR 228 - 95th Congress		
Sen. William Hathaway (D) · SJR 1 - 94th Congress		Rep. William Hathaway (D)
		Rep. Peter Kyros (D)

S.20 MARYLAND

SPONSOR OF A CONSTITUTIONAL AMENDMENT	VOTED FOR SJR 28 IN 1979 ROLL CALL	VOTED FOR HJR 681 IN 1969 ROLL CALL
		Rep. John Glenn Beall (R)
Rep. Elijah E. Cummings (D) · HJR 109 - 108th Congress		
		Rep. George Fallon (D)
		Rep. Samuel Friedel (D)
		Rep. Edward Garmatz (D)
		Rep. Gilbert Gude (R)
		Rep. Lawrence Hogan (R)
		Rep. Clarence Long (D)
Sen. Charles McCurdy Mathias, Jr. (R) · SJR 1 - 94th Congress · SJR 1 - 95th Congress · SJR 1 - 96th Congress · SJR 28 - 96th Congress · SJR 8 - 97th Congress · SJR 17 - 98th Congress	Sen. Charles McCurdy Mathias, Jr. (R)	
Rep. Kweisi Mfume (D) · HJR 117 - 104th Congress		
Rep. Parren Mitchell (D) · HJR 229 - 95th Congress · HJR 261 - 96th Congress		
		Rep. Rogers Morton (R)
Rep. Gladys Spellman (D) · HJR 384 - 95th Congress		
Rep. Albert Wynn (D) · HJR 103 - 108th Congress		

S.21 MASSACHUSETTS

SPONSOR OF A CONSTITUTIONAL AMENDMENT	VOTED FOR SJR 28 IN 1979 ROLL CALL	VOTED FOR HJR 681 IN 1969 ROLL CALL
Rep. Chester Atkins (D) · HJR 137 - 101st Congress		
Rep. Edward Boland (D) · HJR 137 - 93rd Congress		Rep. Edward Boland (D)
Sen. Edward W. Brooke (R) · SJR 1 - 94th Congress · SJR 1 - 95th Congress		
		Rep. James Burke (D)

(continued)

2.21 MASSACHUSETTS *(continued)*

SPONSOR OF A CONSTITUTIONAL AMENDMENT	VOTED FOR SJR 28 IN 1979 ROLL CALL	VOTED FOR HJR 681 IN 1969 ROLL CALL
Rep. Silvio Conte (R) · HJR 300 - 93rd Congress · HJR 38 - 94th Congress · HJR 45 - 95th Congress · HJR 230 - 95th Congress · HJR 231 - 95th Congress · HJR 373 - 95th Congress · HJR 150 - 96th Congress		Rep. Silvio Conte (R)
Rep. William D. Delahunt (D) · HJR 5 - 107th Congress · HJR 103 - 108th Congress · HJR 8 - 109th Congress		
Rep. Brian Donnelly (D) · HJR 288 - 96th Congress		
		Rep. Harold Donohue (D)
Rep. Barney Frank (D) · HJR 137 - 101st Congress · HJR 9 - 102nd Congress · HJR 28 - 103rd Congress · HJR 117 - 104th Congress · HJR 28 - 105th Congress · HJR 17 - 109th Congress · HJR 36 - 109th Congress		
		Rep. Margaret Heckler (R)
		Rep. Hastings Keith (R)
Sen. Ted Kennedy (D) · SJR 1 - 94th Congress · SJR 1 - 95th Congress · SJR 1 - 96th Congress · SJR 28 - 96th Congress	Sen. Ted Kennedy (D)	
Rep. Torbert MacDonald (D) · HJR 336 - 94th Congress		Rep. Torbert MacDonald (D)
Rep. Edward Markey (D) · HJR 373 - 95th Congress		
		Rep. Frank Morse (R)
		Rep. David Obey (D)
		Rep. Thomas O'Neill (D)
		Rep. Philip Philbin (D)
Rep. Gerry Studds (D) · HJR 208 - 93rd Congress · HJR 384 - 95th Congress · HJR 261 - 96th Congress · HJR 591 - 96th Congress · HJR 70 - 97th Congress · HJR 124 - 98th Congress · HJR 137 - 101st Congress · HJR 117 - 104th Congress		
Sen. Paul Tsongas (D) · SJR 1 - 96th Congress · SJR 28 - 96th Congress	Sen. Paul Tsongas (D)	

S.22 MICHIGAN

SPONSOR OF A CONSTITUTIONAL AMENDMENT	VOTED FOR SJR 28 IN 1979 ROLL CALL	VOTED FOR HJR 681 IN 1969 ROLL CALL
Rep. James A. Barcia (D) · HJR 117 - 104th Congress		
Rep. James J. Blanchard (D) · HJR 168 - 95th Congress		
Rep. David Bonior (D) · HJR 230 - 95th Congress · HJR 145 - 102nd Congress · HJR 28 - 103rd Congress		
Rep. William Broomfield (R) · HJR 137 - 93rd Congress · HJR 288 - 94th Congress		Rep. William Broomfield (R)
		Rep. Garry Brown (R)
Rep. Milton R. Carr (D) · HJR 397 - 95th Congress · HJR 261 - 96th Congress		
Rep. Elford Cederberg (R) · HJR 168 - 95th Congress		Rep. Elford Cederberg (R)
Rep. Charles Chamberlain (R) · HJR 202 - 93rd Congress		Rep. Charles Chamberlain (R)
Rep. John Conyers, Jr. (D) · HJR 137 - 93rd Congress · HJR 109 - 108th Congress		Rep. John Conyers, Jr. (D)
Rep. George Crockett (D) · HJR 137 - 101st Congress		
Rep. John David Dingell, Jr. (D) · HJR 137 - 93rd Congress		Rep. John David Dingell, Jr. (D)
Rep. Marvin Esch (R) · HJR 137 - 93rd Congress		Rep. Marvin Esch (R)
		Rep. Gerald Ford (R)
Rep. W. D. Ford (D) · HJR 137 - 93rd Congress · HJR 229 - 95th Congress · HJR 288 - 96th Congress		Rep. W. D. Ford (D)
Sen. Robert Griffin (R) · SJR 1 - 94th Congress		
Sen. Philip Hart (D) · SJR 1 - 94th Congress		
Sen. Rupert Hartke (D) · SJR 1 - 94th Congress		
Rep. James Harvey (R) · HJR 207 - 93rd Congress		Rep. James Harvey (R)
Rep. Dale E. Kildee (D) · HJR 229 - 95th Congress · HJR 254 - 96th Congress · HJR 261 - 96th Congress		

(continued)

S.22 MICHIGAN *(continued)*

SPONSOR OF A CONSTITUTIONAL AMENDMENT	VOTED FOR SJR 28 IN 1979 ROLL CALL	VOTED FOR HJR 681 IN 1969 ROLL CALL
Sen. Carl Levin (D) · SJR 1 - 96th Congress · SJR 28 - 96th Congress · SJR 3 - 97th Congress · SJR 17 - 98th Congress · SJR 362 - 100th Congress · SJR 163 - 101st Congress	Sen. Carl Levin (D)	
		Rep. Jack McDonald (R)
Rep. Lucien Nedzi (D) · HJR 168 - 95th Congress · HJR 231 - 95th Congress · HJR 384 - 95th Congress		Rep. Lucien Nedzi (D)
Rep. James O'Hara (D) · HJR 137 - 93rd Congress · HJR 139 - 93rd Congress · HJR 207 - 93rd Congress · HJR 208 - 93rd Congress		Rep. James O'Hara (D)
Rep. Carl D. Pursell (R) · HJR 168 - 95th Congress · HJR 230 - 95th Congress		
Sen. Donald Riegle (D) · SJR 1 - 95th Congress · SJR 1 - 96th Congress · SJR 28 - 96th Congress	Sen. Donald Riegle (D)	Rep. Donald Riegle (D)
		Rep. Philip Ruppe (R)
Rep. Harold Sawyer (R) · HJR 384 - 95th Congress		
Rep. Bart Stupak (D) · HJR 28 - 103rd Congress		
		Rep. Guy Vander Jagt (R)
Rep. Howard Wolpe (D) · HJR 288 - 96th Congress		

S.23 MINNESOTA

SPONSOR OF A CONSTITUTIONAL AMENDMENT	VOTED FOR SJR 28 IN 1979 ROLL CALL	VOTED FOR HJR 681 IN 1969 ROLL CALL
Sen. Wendell Anderson (D) · SJR 1 - 95th Congress		
		Rep. John Blatnik (D)
Sen. Dave Durenberger (R) · SJR 1 - 96th Congress · SJR 28 - 96th Congress · SJR 3 - 97th Congress	Sen. Dave Durenberger (R)	
Rep. Donald Fraser (D) · HJR 207 - 93rd Congress · HJR 384 - 95th Congress		Rep. Donald Fraser (D)
Rep. William Frenzel (R) · HJR 300 - 93rd Congress · HJR 253 - 95th Congress		
Sen. Hubert Humphrey (D) · SJR 1 - 94th Congress · SJR 1 - 95th Congress		
Rep. Joseph Karth (D) · HJR 204 - 94th Congress		Rep. Joseph Karth (D)
		Rep. Odin Langen (R)
Rep. Bill Luther (D) · HJR 117 - 104th Congress · HJR 28 - 105th Congress		
		Rep. Clark MacGregor (R)
Rep. Betty McCollum (D) · HJR 103 - 108th Congress		
Rep. David Minge (D) · HJR 28 - 103rd Congress · HJR 23 - 106th Congress		
Sen. Walter Mondale (D) · SJR 1 - 94th Congress		
		Rep. Ancher Nelsen (R)
Rep. Richard M. Nolan (D) · HJR 229 - 95th Congress · HJR 308 - 96th Congress		
Rep. Collin Peterson (D) · HJR 28 - 103rd Congress		
Rep. Albert H. Quie (R) · HJR 151 - 94th Congress · HJR 434 - 95th Congress		Rep. Albert H. Quie (R)
Rep. Bruce F. Vento (D) · HJR 288 - 96th Congress · HJR 137 - 101st Congress		
		Rep. John Zwach (R)

S.24 MISSISSIPPI

SPONSOR OF A CONSTITUTIONAL AMENDMENT	VOTED FOR SJR 28 IN 1979 ROLL CALL	VOTED FOR HJR 681 IN 1969 ROLL CALL
Rep. Gene Taylor (D) · HJR 506 - 102nd Congress		

S.25 MISSOURI

SPONSOR OF A CONSTITUTIONAL AMENDMENT	VOTED FOR SJR 28 IN 1979 ROLL CALL	VOTED FOR HJR 681 IN 1969 ROLL CALL
Rep. Richard Bolling (D) · HJR 207 - 93rd Congress		
Rep. William D. Burlison (D) · HJR 137 - 93rd Congress · HJR 786 - 94th Congress · HJR 39 - 95th Congress · HJR 228 - 95th Congress · HJR 229 - 95th Congress · HJR 281 - 95th Congress · HJR 384 - 95th Congress · HJR 397 - 95th Congress · HJR 254 - 96th Congress · HJR 261 - 96th Congress · HJR 288 - 96th Congress · HJR 299 - 96th Congress · HJR 308 - 96th Congress · HJR 332 - 96th Congress		Rep. William D. Burlison (D)
Sen. John C. Danforth (R) · SJR 1 - 95th Congress · SJR 1 - 96th Congress · SJR 28 - 96th Congress	Sen. John C. Danforth (R)	
Rep. Pat Danner (D) · HJR 117 - 104th Congress · HJR 28 - 105th Congress		
Rep. Richard Gephardt (D) · HJR 228 - 95th Congress		
		Rep. William Raleigh Hull (D)
		Rep. William Hungate (D)
		Rep. Richard Ichord (D)
		Rep. William Randall (D)
Sen. William Symington (D) · SJR 1 - 94th Congress		
Rep. James Symington (D) · HJR 300 - 93rd Congress		Rep. James Symington (D)
Rep. Alan Wheat (D) · HJR 137 - 101st Congress · HJR 145 - 102nd Congress · HJR 65 - 103rd Congress		
Rep. Robert Young (D) · HJR 261 - 96th Congress		

S.26 MONTANA

SPONSOR OF A CONSTITUTIONAL AMENDMENT	VOTED FOR SJR 28 IN 1979 ROLL CALL	VOTED FOR HJR 681 IN 1969 ROLL CALL
Sen. Max Baucus (D) · HJR 197 - 95th Congress · HJR 229 - 95th Congress · HJR 230 - 95th Congress · SJR 3 - 97th Congress · SJR 17 - 98th Congress	Sen. Max Baucus (D)	
Sen. Michael Mansfield (D) · SJR 1 - 94th Congress		
		Rep. Arnold Olsen (D)

S.27 NEBRASKA

SPONSOR OF A CONSTITUTIONAL AMENDMENT	VOTED FOR SJR 28 IN 1979 ROLL CALL	VOTED FOR HJR 681 IN 1969 ROLL CALL
Rep. John J. Cavanaugh (D) · HJR 228 - 95th Congress · HJR 332 - 96th Congress		
		Rep. Glenn Cunningham (R)
		Rep. Robert Denney (R)
Sen. J. James Exon (D) · SJR 3 - 97th Congress · SJR 362 - 100th Congress · SJR 163 - 101st Congress · SJR 302 - 102nd Congress · SJR 173 - 103rd Congress	Sen. J. James Exon (D)	
		Rep. David Martin (R)
Sen. Edward Zorinsky (D) · SJR 1 - 95th Congress · SJR 1 - 96th Congress · SJR 28 - 96th Congress	Sen. Edward Zorinsky (D)	

S.28 NEVADA

SPONSOR OF A CONSTITUTIONAL AMENDMENT	VOTED FOR SJR 28 IN 1979 ROLL CALL	VOTED FOR HJR 681 IN 1969 ROLL CALL
Sen. Harry M. Reid (D) · SJR 297 - 102nd Congress		

S.29 NEW HAMPSHIRE

SPONSOR OF A CONSTITUTIONAL AMENDMENT	VOTED FOR SJR 28 IN 1979 ROLL CALL	VOTED FOR HJR 681 IN 1969 ROLL CALL
Sen. Thomas J. McIntyre (D) · SJR 1 - 94th Congress · SJR 1 - 95th Congress		
		Rep. Louis Wyman (R)

S.30 NEW JERSEY

SPONSOR OF A CONSTITUTIONAL AMENDMENT	VOTED FOR SJR 28 IN 1979 ROLL CALL	VOTED FOR HJR 681 IN 1969 ROLL CALL
		Rep. William Cahill (R)
Rep. Dominick Daniels (D) · HJR 137 - 93rd Congress		Rep. Dominick Daniels (D)
		Rep. Florence Dwyer (R)
Rep. Edwin Forsythe (R) · HJR 207 - 93rd Congress		
		Rep. Peter Frelinghuysen (R)
		Rep. Cornelius Gallagher (D)
		Rep. Henry Helstoski (D)
Rep. James J. Howard (D) · HJR 228 - 95th Congress · HJR 288 - 96th Congress · HJR 130 - 97th Congress		Rep. James J. Howard (D)
Rep. William J. Hughes (D) · HJR 114 - 95th Congress		
		Rep. John Hunt (R)
Rep. Joseph G. Minish (D) · HJR 231 - 95th Congress		Rep. Joseph G. Minish (D)
Rep. Edward Patten (D) · HJR 820 - 93rd Congress		Rep. Edward Patten (D)
Rep. Matthew Rinaldo (R) · HJR 300 - 93rd Congress		
Rep. Peter Rodino (D) · HJR 144 - 95th Congress		Rep. Peter Rodino (D)
		Rep. Charles Sandman (R)
		Rep. Frank Thompson (D)
Rep. William Widnall (R) · HJR 208 - 93rd Congress		Rep. William Widnall (R)
Sen. Harrison Williams (D) · SJR 1 - 94th Congress · SJR 1 - 95th Congress · SJR 1 - 96th Congress · SJR 28 - 96th Congress	Sen. Harrison Williams (D)	

S.31 NEW MEXICO

SPONSOR OF A CONSTITUTIONAL AMENDMENT	VOTED FOR SJR 28 IN 1979 ROLL CALL	VOTED FOR HJR 681 IN 1969 ROLL CALL
		Rep. Manuel Lujan (R)
Sen. Joseph Montoya (D) · SJR 1 - 94th Congress		

S.32 NEW YORK

SPONSOR OF A CONSTITUTIONAL AMENDMENT	VOTED FOR SJR 28 IN 1979 ROLL CALL	VOTED FOR HJR 681 IN 1969 ROLL CALL
Rep. Joseph P. Addabbo (D) · HJR 207 - 93rd Congress · HJR 168 - 95th Congress		Rep. Joseph P. Addabbo (D)
Rep. Herman Badillo (D) · HJR 207 - 93rd Congress		
		Rep. Mario Biaggi (D)
Rep. Jonathan Bingham (D) · HJR 352 - 95th Congress · HJR 384 - 95th Congress		Rep. Jonathan Bingham (D)
Rep. Frank James Brasco (D) · HJR 137 - 93rd Congress		Rep. Frank James Brasco (D)
		Rep. Daniel Button (R)
		Rep. Hugh Carey (D)
		Rep. Emanuel Celler (D)
Rep. Shirley A. Chisholm (D) · HJR 197 - 93rd Congress · HJR 300 - 93rd Congress · HJR 254 - 96th Congress		Rep. Shirley A. Chisholm (D)
		Rep. Barber Conable (R)
		Rep. James Delaney (D)
Rep. Thomas J. Downey (D) · HJR 229 - 95th Congress · HJR 288 - 96th Congress		
		Rep. Thaddeus Dulski (D)
Rep. Eliot L. Engel (D) · HJR 17 - 109th Congress		
		Rep. Leonard Farbstein (D)
Rep. Hamilton Fish, Jr. (R) · HJR 137 - 93rd Congress · HJR 50 - 94th Congress		Rep. Hamilton Fish, Jr. (R)
		Rep. Jacob Gilbert (D)
Rep. James Russell Grover, Jr. (R) · HJR 137 - 93rd Congress		Rep. James Russell Grover, Jr. (R)
		Rep. Seymour Halpern (R)
Rep. James Hanley (D) · HJR 228 - 95th Congress · HJR 261 - 96th Congress		Rep. James Hanley (D)
Rep. James Hastings (R) · HJR 207 - 93rd Congress		Rep. James Hastings (R)
		Rep. Frank Horton (R)
Sen. Jacob Javits (R) · SJR 1 - 94th Congress · SJR 1 - 95th Congress · SJR 1 - 96th Congress · SJR 28 - 96th Congress	Sen. Jacob Javits (R)	

(continued)

S.32 NEW YORK *(continued)*

SPONSOR OF A CONSTITUTIONAL AMENDMENT	VOTED FOR SJR 28 IN 1979 ROLL CALL	VOTED FOR HJR 681 IN 1969 ROLL CALL
		Rep. Carleton King (R)
		Rep. Edward Koch (D)
		Rep. Allard Lowenstein (D)
		Rep. Richard McCarthy (D)
		Rep. Robert McEwen (R)
		Rep. Martin McKneally (R)
Rep. Michael McNulty (D) · HJR 28 - 103rd Congress · HJR 60 - 103rd Congress · HJR 28 - 105th Congress · HJR 23 - 106th Congress · HJR 103 - 108th Congress · HJR 17 - 109th Congress		
Rep. Donald Mitchell (R) · HJR 750 - 94th Congress · HJR 168 - 95th Congress · HJR 228 - 95th Congress · HJR 288 - 96th Congress		
Rep. Susan Molinari (R) · HJR 28 - 103rd Congress		
		Rep. John Murphy (D)
Rep. Jerrold Nadler (D) · HJR 109 - 108th Congress		
Rep. Richard L. Ottinger (D) · HJR 231 - 95th Congress · HJR 384 - 95th Congress · HJR 288 - 96th Congress		Rep. Richard L. Ottinger (D)
Rep. Major Owens (D) · HJR 117 - 104th Congress · HJR 109 - 108th Congress		
		Rep. Otis Pike (D)
		Rep. Alexander Pirnie (R)
Rep. Bertram Podell (D) · HJR 207 - 93rd Congress		Rep. Bertram Podell (D)
Rep. Charles B. Rangel (D) · HJR 300 - 95th Congress		
		Rep. Ogden Reid (D)
Rep. Frederick Richmond (D) · HJR 229 - 95th Congress · HJR 254 - 96th Congress		
		Rep. Howard Robison (R)
		Rep. John Rooney (D)
Rep. Benjamin Rosenthal (D) · HJR 207 - 93rd Congress		Rep. Benjamin Rosenthal (D)

S.32 NEW YORK *(continued)*

SPONSOR OF A CONSTITUTIONAL AMENDMENT	VOTED FOR SJR 28 IN 1979 ROLL CALL	VOTED FOR HJR 681 IN 1969 ROLL CALL
		Rep. William Ryan (D)
		Rep. James Scheuer (D)
Rep. Jose E. Serrano (D) · HJR 103 - 108th Congress · HJR 50 - 109th Congress		
		Rep. Henry Smith (R)
		Rep. Samuel Stratton (D)
Rep. Anthony Weiner (D) · HJR 103 - 108th Congress		
Rep. Theodore S. Weiss (D) · HJR 228 - 95th Congress		
Rep. Lester L. Wolff (D) · HJR 208 - 93rd Congress · HJR 228 - 95th Congress		Rep. Lester L. Wolff (D)
		Rep. John Wydler (R)

S.33 NORTH CAROLINA

SPONSOR OF A CONSTITUTIONAL AMENDMENT	VOTED FOR SJR 28 IN 1979 ROLL CALL	VOTED FOR HJR 681 IN 1969 ROLL CALL
		Rep. James Broyhill (R)
		Rep. Lawrence Fountain (D)
		Rep. Nick Galifianakis (D)
		Rep. David Henderson (D)
		Rep. Charles Jonas (R)
Rep. Walter Beaman Jones, Sr. (D) · HJR 207 - 93rd Congress		Rep. Walter Beaman Jones, Sr. (D)
		Rep. Wilmer Mizell (R)
		Rep. Lunsford Preyer (D)
		Rep. Earl Ruth (R)
		Rep. Roy Taylor (D)

S.34 NORTH DAKOTA

SPONSOR OF A CONSTITUTIONAL AMENDMENT	VOTED FOR SJR 28 IN 1979 ROLL CALL	VOTED FOR HJR 681 IN 1969 ROLL CALL
		Rep. Mark Andrews (R)
Sen. Quentin N. Burdick (D) · SJR 1 - 94th Congress · SJR 1 - 96th Congress · SJR 28 - 96th Congress · SJR 17 - 98th Congress	Sen. Quentin N. Burdick (D)	

S.35 OHIO

SPONSOR OF A CONSTITUTIONAL AMENDMENT	VOTED FOR SJR 28 IN 1979 ROLL CALL	VOTED FOR HJR 681 IN 1969 ROLL CALL
Rep. Thomas Ashley (D) · HJR 137 - 93rd Congress		Rep. Thomas Ashley (D)
		Rep. William Ayers (R)
		Rep. Jackson Betts (R)
		Rep. Frank Bow (R)
		Rep. Clarence J. Brown (R)
Rep. Charles J. Carney (D) · HJR 35 - 94th Congress · HJR 40 - 95th Congress · HJR 384 - 95th Congress		
		Rep. Donald Clancy (R)
Rep. Dennis Eckart (D) · HJR 9 - 102nd Congress		
		Rep. Michael Feighan (D)
Sen. John H. Glenn, Jr. (D) · SJR 1 - 94th Congress · SJR 1 - 95th Congress · SJR 1 - 96th Congress · SJR 3 - 97th Congress · SJR 17 - 98th Congress	Sen. John H. Glenn, Jr. (D)	
		Rep. William Harsha (R)
		Rep. Wayne Hays (D)
Rep. Dennis J. Kucinich (D) · HJR 109 - 108th Congress		
		Rep. Delbert Latta (R)
Rep. Thomas Luken (D) · HJR 228 - 95th Congress		
		Rep. William McCulloch (R)
Sen. Howard M. Metzenbaum (D) · SJR 1 - 95th Congress · SJR 1 - 96th Congress · SJR 3 - 97th Congress · SJR 17 - 98th Congress	Sen. Howard M. Metzenbaum (D)	
		Rep. Clarence Miller (R)
		Rep. William Minshall (R)
		Rep. Charles Mosher (R)
Rep. Ronald Mottl (D) · HJR 168 - 95th Congress		
Rep. Donald J. Pease (D) · HJR 168 - 95th Congress · HJR 229 - 95th Congress · HJR 288 - 96th Congress		

(continued)

S.35 OHIO *(continued)*

SPONSOR OF A CONSTITUTIONAL AMENDMENT	VOTED FOR SJR 28 IN 1979 ROLL CALL	VOTED FOR HJR 681 IN 1969 ROLL CALL
Rep. John F. Seiberling (D) · HJR 229 - 95th Congress		
		Rep. John Stanton (R)
Rep. Louis Stokes (D) · HJR 254 - 96th Congress		Rep. Louis Stokes (D)
Sen. Robert Taft, Jr. (R) · SJR 1 - 94th Congress		Rep. Robert Taft, Jr. (R)
Rep. James A. Traficant, Jr. (D) · HJR 511 - 102nd Congress · HJR 117 - 104th Congress		
Rep. Charles Vanik (D) · HJR 139 - 93rd Congress		Rep. Charles Vanik (D)
Rep. Charles Whalen (R) · HJR 300 - 93rd Congress · HJR 345 - 94th Congress · HJR 238 - 95th Congress		Rep. Charles Whalen (R)
		Rep. Chalmers Wylie (R)

S.36 OKLAHOMA

SPONSOR OF A CONSTITUTIONAL AMENDMENT	VOTED FOR SJR 28 IN 1979 ROLL CALL	VOTED FOR HJR 681 IN 1969 ROLL CALL
		Rep. Carl Albert (D)
Sen. Dewey F. Bartlett (R) · SJR 1 - 95th Congress		
		Rep. Page Belcher (R)
Sen. Henry Bellmon (R) · SJR 101 - 93rd Congress · SJR 1 - 94th Congress · SJR 1 - 95th Congress · SJR 1 - 96th Congress · SJR 28 - 96th Congress	Sen. Henry Bellmon (R)	
Sen. David L. Boren (D) · SJR 3 - 97th Congress · SJR 17 - 98th Congress · SJR 297 - 102nd Congress · SJR 302 - 102nd Congress	Sen. David L. Boren (D)	
		Rep. John Camp (R)
		Rep. Edmond Edmondson (D)
		Rep. John Jarman (D)
		Rep. Thomas Steed (D)

S.37 OREGON

SPONSOR OF A CONSTITUTIONAL AMENDMENT	VOTED FOR SJR 28 IN 1979 ROLL CALL	VOTED FOR HJR 681 IN 1969 ROLL CALL
Rep. John Dellenback (R) · HJR 78 - 93rd Congress · HJR 137 - 93rd Congress		Rep. John Dellenback (R)
Rep. Robert B. Duncan (D) · HJR 229 - 95th Congress · HJR 230 - 95th Congress		
		Rep. Edith Green (D)
Sen. Mark O. Hatfield (R) · SJR 1 - 94th Congress · SJR 1 - 95th Congress · SJR 1 - 96th Congress · SJR 28 - 96th Congress · SJR 8 - 97th Congress · SJR 17 - 98th Congress	Sen. Mark O. Hatfield (R)	
Sen. Robert W. Packwood (R) · SJR 1 - 94th Congress · SJR 1 - 95th Congress · SJR 1 - 96th Congress · SJR 28 - 96th Congress	Sen. Robert W. Packwood (R)[2]	
Rep. Albert Ullman (D) · HJR 384 - 95th Congress		Rep. Albert Ullman (D)
		Rep. Wendell Wyatt (R)

[2]Senator Packwood was announced in favor of SJR 28, but did not cast a vote in the roll call.

S.38 PENNSYLVANIA

SPONSOR OF A CONSTITUTIONAL AMENDMENT	VOTED FOR SJR 28 IN 1979 ROLL CALL	VOTED FOR HJR 681 IN 1969 ROLL CALL
Rep. Joseph Ammerman (D) · HJR 384 - 95th Congress		
		Rep. William Barrett (D)
Rep. Edward George Biester, Jr. (R) · HJR 207 - 93rd Congress		Rep. Edward George Biester, Jr. (R)
		Rep. James Byrne (D)
Rep. Frank Clark (D) · HJR 137 - 93rd Congress		Rep. Frank Clark (D)
		Rep. Robert Corbett (R)
		Rep. Robert Coughlin (R)
		Rep. John Dent (D)
Rep. Robert Edgar (D) · HJR 230 - 95th Congress · HJR 384 - 95th Congress		
Rep. Joshua Eilberg (D) · HJR 127 - 95th Congress		Rep. Joshua Eilberg (D)

S.38 PENNSYLVANIA *(continued)*

SPONSOR OF A CONSTITUTIONAL AMENDMENT	VOTED FOR SJR 28 IN 1979 ROLL CALL	VOTED FOR HJR 681 IN 1969 ROLL CALL
Rep. Allen E. Ertel (D) · HJR 384 - 95th Congress · HJR 288 - 96th Congress		
		Rep. Edwin Eshleman (R)
Rep. Daniel J. Flood (D) · HJR 137 - 93rd Congress · HJR 288 - 96th Congress		Rep. Daniel J. Flood (D)
		Rep. James Fulton (R)
Rep. Joseph Gaydos (D) · HR 2063 - 95th Congress		Rep. Joseph Gaydos (D)
Rep. William F. Goodling (R) · HJR 150 - 96th Congress		Rep. George Goodling (R)
		Rep. William Green (D)
Rep. James Greenwood (R) · HJR 28 - 103rd Congress		
		Rep. Albert Johnson (R)
Rep. Joseph P. Kolter (D) · HJR 506 - 102nd Congress		
Rep. Peter H. Kostmayer (D) · HJR 506 - 102nd Congress		
Rep. Joseph McDade (R) · HJR 207 - 93rd Congress		Rep. Joseph McDade (R)
Rep. Paul McHale (D) · HJR 28 - 103rd Congress		
		Rep. William Moorhead (D)
		Rep. Thomas Morgan (D)
Rep. Austin Murphy (D) · HJR 228 - 95th Congress · HJR 288 - 96th Congress		
		Rep. Robert Nix (D)
		Rep. Frederick Rooney (D)
		Rep. John Saylor (R)
		Rep. Herman Schneebeli (R)
Sen. Richard Schweiker (R) · SJR 1 - 94th Congress · SJR 1 - 95th Congress		
		Rep. Joseph Vigorito (D)
		Rep. George Watkins (R)
		Rep. Lawrence Williams (R)
Rep. Gus Yatron (D) · HJR 139 - 93rd Congress · HJR 168 - 95th Congress · HJR 231 - 95th Congress · HJR 261 - 96th Congress		Rep. Gus Yatron (D)

S.39 RHODE ISLAND

SPONSOR OF A CONSTITUTIONAL AMENDMENT	VOTED FOR SJR 28 IN 1979 ROLL CALL	VOTED FOR HJR 681 IN 1969 ROLL CALL
Rep. Edward P. Beard (D) · HJR 168 - 95th Congress		
Sen. John H. Chafee (R) · SJR 1 - 95th Congress · SJR 1 - 96th Congress · SJR 28 - 96th Congress · SJR 3 - 97th Congress · SJR 17 - 98th Congress	Sen. John H. Chafee (R)	
Sen. John Pastore (D) · SJR 1 - 94th Congress		
Sen. Claiborne Pell (D) · SJR 1 - 94th Congress · SJR 1 - 95th Congress · SJR 1 - 96th Congress · SJR 28 - 96th Congress · SJR 3 - 97th Congress · SJR 17 - 98th Congress	Sen. Claiborne Pell (D)	
		Rep. Fernand St. Germain (D)
Rep. Robert Tiernan (D) · HJR 208 - 93rd Congress		Rep. Robert Tiernan (D)

S.40 SOUTH CAROLINA

SPONSOR OF A CONSTITUTIONAL AMENDMENT	VOTED FOR SJR 28 IN 1979 ROLL CALL	VOTED FOR HJR 681 IN 1969 ROLL CALL
Rep. John Wilson Jenrette, Jr. (D) · HJR 384 - 95th Congress		

S.41 SOUTH DAKOTA

SPONSOR OF A CONSTITUTIONAL AMENDMENT	VOTED FOR SJR 28 IN 1979 ROLL CALL	VOTED FOR HJR 681 IN 1969 ROLL CALL
Sen. James G. Abourezk (D) · SJR 1 - 94th Congress · SJR 1 - 95th Congress		
Sen. Thomas A. Daschle (D) · SJR 297 - 102nd Congress		
Sen. Tim Johnson (D) · HJR 145 - 102nd Congress · HJR 28 - 103rd Congress · SJR 56 - 106th Congress		
Sen. George McGovern (D) · SJR 1 - 94th Congress	Sen. George McGovern (D)	

S.42 TENNESSEE

SPONSOR OF A CONSTITUTIONAL AMENDMENT	VOTED FOR SJR 28 IN 1979 ROLL CALL	VOTED FOR HJR 681 IN 1969 ROLL CALL
		Rep. William Anderson (D)
Sen. Howard H. Baker, Jr. (R) · SJR 1 - 94th Congress · SJR 1 - 95th Congress · SJR 1 - 96th Congress · SJR 28 - 96th Congress · SJR 3 - 97th Congress	Sen. Howard H. Baker, Jr. (R)	
		Rep. Leonard Blanton (D)
Rep. William Boner (D) · HJR 252 - 96th Congress		
Rep. Bob Clement (D) · HJR 28 - 103rd Congress		
		Rep. Richard Fulton (D)
		Rep. John Kyl (R)
	Sen. James Sasser (D)	

S.43 TEXAS

SPONSOR OF A CONSTITUTIONAL AMENDMENT	VOTED FOR SJR 28 IN 1979 ROLL CALL	VOTED FOR HJR 681 IN 1969 ROLL CALL
	Sen. Lloyd Millard Bentsen, Jr. (D)	
Rep. Jack Bascom Brooks (D) · HJR 137 - 93rd Congress · HJR 80 - 97th Congress · HJR 5 - 98th Congress · HJR 5 - 99th Congress · HJR 5 - 100th Congress · HJR 2 - 101st Congress		Rep. Jack Bascom Brooks (D)
		Rep. George H.W. Bush (R)
		Rep. Earle Cabell (D)
		Rep. Robert Casey (D)
		Rep. James Collins (R)[3]
Rep. Lloyd Doggett (D) · HJR 36 - 109th Congress		
Rep. Henry Gonzalez (D) · HJR 167 - 93rd Congress		Rep. Henry Gonzalez (D)
Rep. Gene Green (D) · HJR 28 - 103rd Congress · HJR 117 - 104th Congress · HJR 180 - 104th Congress · HJR 28 - 105th Congress · HJR 132 - 106th Congress · HJR 3 - 107th Congress · HJR 103 - 108th Congress · HJR 8 - 109th Congress		

(continued)

S.43 TEXAS *(continued)*

SPONSOR OF A CONSTITUTIONAL AMENDMENT	VOTED FOR SJR 28 IN 1979 ROLL CALL	VOTED FOR HJR 681 IN 1969 ROLL CALL
Rep. Sam Blakeley Hall (D) · HJR 384 - 95th Congress		
		Rep. Abraham Kazen (D)
Rep. Dale Milford (D) · HJR 239 - 93rd Congress · HJR 230 - 95th Congress		
		Rep. Herbert Roberts (D)
Rep. Bill Sarpalius (D) · HJR 28 - 103rd Congress		
		Rep. Olin Teague (D)
		Rep. Richard White (D)
		Rep. James Claude Wright (D)
		Rep. John Young (D)

[3] The roll call does not make clear whether this Representative Collins or the one from Illinois voted for HJR 681 in 1969.

S.44 UTAH

SPONSOR OF A CONSTITUTIONAL AMENDMENT	VOTED FOR SJR 28 IN 1979 ROLL CALL	VOTED FOR HJR 681 IN 1969 ROLL CALL
Sen. E. J. Garn (R) · SJR 1 - 95th Congress · SJR 1 - 96th Congress · SJR 28 - 96th Congress · SJR 3 - 97th Congress	Sen. E. J. Garn (R)	
Rep. James Hansen (R) · HJR 28 - 103rd Congress		
		Rep. Sherman Lloyd (R)
Sen. Frank Moss (D) · SJR 1 - 94th Congress		
Rep. Bill Orton (D) · HJR 506 - 102nd Congress · HJR 169 - 103rd Congress · HJR 36 - 104th Congress		
Rep. Douglas Owens (D) · HJR 347 - 93rd Congress		
Rep. Karen Shepherd (D) · HJR 28 - 103rd Congress		

S.45 VERMONT

SPONSOR OF A CONSTITUTIONAL AMENDMENT	VOTED FOR SJR 28 IN 1979 ROLL CALL	VOTED FOR HJR 681 IN 1969 ROLL CALL
Sen. Patrick J. Leahy (D) · SJR 1 - 95th Congress · SJR 1 - 96th Congress · SJR 28 - 96th Congress · SJR 3 - 97th Congress	Sen. Patrick J. Leahy (D)	
Rep. Bernard Sanders (I) · HJR 28 - 103rd Congress		
Sen. Robert T. Stafford (R) · SJR 1 - 94th Congress · SJR 1 - 95th Congress · SJR 1 - 96th Congress · SJR 28 - 96th Congress · SJR 17 - 98th Congress	Sen. Robert T. Stafford (R)	Rep. Robert T. Stafford (R)

S.46 VIRGINIA

SPONSOR OF A CONSTITUTIONAL AMENDMENT	VOTED FOR SJR 28 IN 1979 ROLL CALL	VOTED FOR HJR 681 IN 1969 ROLL CALL
Rep. Rick Boucher (D) · HJR 28 - 105th Congress · HJR 23 - 106th Congress		
		Rep. Joel Broyhill (R)
Rep. Leslie Byrne (D) · HJR 28 - 103rd Congress		
Rep. Thomas Downing (D) · HJR 207 - 93rd Congress · HJR 43 - 94th Congress		Rep. Thomas Downing (D)
		Rep. John Marsh (D)
		Rep. Richard Poff (R)
		Rep. William Scott (R)
		Rep. William Wampler (R)
		Rep. George Whitehurst (R)

S.47 WASHINGTON

SPONSOR OF A CONSTITUTIONAL AMENDMENT	VOTED FOR SJR 28 IN 1979 ROLL CALL	VOTED FOR HJR 681 IN 1969 ROLL CALL
		Rep. Brockman Adams (D)
Rep. Brian Baird (D) · HJR 103 - 108th Congress · HJR 8 - 109th Congress		
Rep. Norman Dicks (D) · HJR 384 - 95th Congress		
		Rep. Thomas Foley (D)

(continued)

S.47 WASHINGTON *(continued)*

SPONSOR OF A CONSTITUTIONAL AMENDMENT	VOTED FOR SJR 28 IN 1979 ROLL CALL	VOTED FOR HJR 681 IN 1969 ROLL CALL
		Rep. Julia Hansen (D)
Rep. Floyd Hicks (D) · HJR 300 - 93rd Congress		Rep. Floyd Hicks (D)
Sen. Henry M. Jackson (D) · SJR 1 - 94th Congress · SJR 1 - 95th Congress · SJR 1 - 96th Congress · SJR 28 - 96th Congress · SJR 3 - 97th Congress · SJR 17 - 98th Congress	Sen. Henry M. Jackson (D)	
Sen. Warren G. Magnuson (D) · SJR 1 - 94th Congress · SJR 1 - 95th Congress · SJR 1 - 96th Congress · SJR 28 - 96th Congress	Sen. Warren G. Magnuson (D)	
		Rep. Catherine May (R)
Rep. Mike McCormack (D) · HJR 281 - 95th Congress		
Rep. Jim McDermott (D) · HJR 117 - 104th Congress · HJR 50 - 109th Congress		
Rep. Lloyd Meeds (D) · HJR 66 - 94th Congress · HJR 228 - 95th Congress		Rep. Lloyd Meeds (D)
		Rep. Thomas Pelly (R)
Rep. Joel Pritchard (R) · HJR 384 - 95th Congress		

S.48 WEST VIRGINIA

SPONSOR OF A CONSTITUTIONAL AMENDMENT	VOTED FOR SJR 28 IN 1979 ROLL CALL	VOTED FOR HJR 681 IN 1969 ROLL CALL
	Sen. Robert Byrd (D)	
		Rep. Kenneth Hechler (D)
		Rep. James Kee (D)
Rep. Robert H. Mollohan (D) · HJR 197 - 95th Congress · HJR 308 - 96th Congress		Rep. Robert H. Mollohan (D)
Sen. Jennings Randolph (D) · SJR 1 - 94th Congress · SJR 1 - 95th Congress · SJR 1 - 96th Congress · SJR 28 - 96th Congress · SJR 3 - 97th Congress · SJR 17 - 98th Congress	Sen. Jennings Randolph (D)	
		Rep. John Mark Slack (D)

S.48 WEST VIRGINIA *(continued)*

SPONSOR OF A CONSTITUTIONAL AMENDMENT	VOTED FOR SJR 28 IN 1979 ROLL CALL	VOTED FOR HJR 681 IN 1969 ROLL CALL
		Rep. Harley Staggers (D)
Rep. Robert E. Wise, Jr. (D) · HJR 137 - 101st Congress · HJR 28 - 103rd Congress · HJR 117 - 104th Congress · HJR 28 - 105th Congress		

S.49 WISCONSIN

SPONSOR OF A CONSTITUTIONAL AMENDMENT	VOTED FOR SJR 28 IN 1979 ROLL CALL	VOTED FOR HJR 681 IN 1969 ROLL CALL
Rep. Alvin J. Baldus (D) · HJR 231 - 95th Congress		
		Rep. John Byrnes (R)
Rep. Robert J. Cornell (D) · HJR 229 - 95th Congress		
		Rep. Glenn Davis (R)
Rep. Robert Kastenmeier (D) · HJR 62 - 94th Congress · HJR 70 - 95th Congress · HJR 57 - 96th Congress		Rep. Robert Kastenmeier (D)
Rep. Gerald D. Kleczka (D) · HJR 145 - 102nd Congress · HJR 60 - 103rd Congress		
Sen. Gaylord Nelson (D) · SJR 1 - 94th Congress	Sen. Gaylord Nelson (D)	
Sen. William Proxmire (D) · SJR 1 - 94th Congress · SJR 1 - 95th Congress · SJR 1 - 96th Congress · SJR 28 - 96th Congress · SJR 3 - 97th Congress · SJR 17 - 98th Congress	Sen. William Proxmire (D)	
		Rep. Henry Reuss (D)
		Rep. Henry Schadeberg (R)
Rep. William Steiger (R) · HJR 207 - 93rd Congress		Rep. William Steiger (R)
		Rep. Vernon Thomson (R)
		Rep. Clement Zablocki (D)

S.50 WYOMING

SPONSOR OF A CONSTITUTIONAL AMENDMENT	VOTED FOR SJR 28 IN 1979 ROLL CALL	VOTED FOR HJR 681 IN 1969 ROLL CALL
		Rep. John Wold (R)

APPENDIX T: STATE STATUTORY DEADLINES FOR CERTIFICATION OF ELECTIONS

Table T.1 State statutory deadlines for certification of elections for the 50 states and District of Columbia

JURISDICTION	CERTIFIER	CERTIFICATION DEADLINE
Alabama	Governor	Within 22 days after the election
Alaska	Director	No date specified
Arizona	Secretary of State	On the third Monday following a general election
Arkansas	Governor	Within 20 days after the election
California	Secretary of State	On the first Monday in the month following the election
Colorado	Secretary of State	No later than the fifteenth day after any election
Connecticut	Secretary of State / Superior Court	Last Wednesday in the month in which votes were cast
Delaware	Board of Elections	No date specified
District of Columbia	Superior Court	No date specified
Florida	Canvassing Commission	No date specified
Georgia	Secretary of State	No later than 5:00 p.m. on the fourteenth day following the date on which such election was conducted
Hawaii	Governor	No later than 4:30 p.m. on the last day in the month of the election or as soon as returns received from all counties
Idaho	Secretary of State	On or before the second Wednesday in December next after such election
Illinois	Governor	Within 31 days after holding the election
Indiana	Secretary of State	Not later than noon on the last Tuesday in November
Iowa	Governor	At the expiration of 10 days after the completed canvass
Kansas	Governor	Before the first Wednesday in December next after such election
Kentucky	State Board	State Board shall meet to count when all the returns are in or no later than the third Monday after the election
Louisiana	Governor	On or before the 12th day after the general election
Maine	Governor	Within 20 days after the election
Maryland	Board of Canvassers	Within 35 days of the election
Massachusetts	Governor	Within 10 days after they have been transmitted to the Secretary of State
Michigan	Secretary of State	On or before the 20th day after the election and no later than the 40th day
Minnesota	Governor	On the second Tuesday after each state general election the state canvassing board shall open and canvass the returns
Mississippi	Secretary of State	Within 30 days after the date of the election
Missouri	Governor	Within two days after the election, the clerks shall, within eight days after they receive the returns, certify and transmit them to the Governor

Table T.1 *(continued)*

JURISDICTION	CERTIFIER	CERTIFICATION DEADLINE
Montana	Secretary of State	No date specified
Nebraska	Secretary of State	Within 40 days
Nevada	Governor	On the fourth Tuesday of November canvass the vote, must be completed within 20 days
New Hampshire	Governor	No date specified
New Jersey	Secretary of State	No later than the 28th day after the election
New Mexico	Secretary of State	On the third Tuesday after each election board will meet to canvass and declare the results of the election
New York	State Board of Elections	No date specified
North Carolina	Governor	Board of elections shall meet at 11:00 a.m. on the seventh day after every election or a reasonable time thereafter if the counting of the votes has not been completed
North Dakota	Secretary of State	Within ten days and before 4 p.m. on the tenth day following any general election
Ohio	Board of Elections	No date specified
Oklahoma	Secretary of State	Election board shall convene on the day of and remaining session until all returns are delivered
Oregon	Secretary of State	No later than the 30th day after any election
Pennsylvania	Governor	No date specified
Rhode Island	State Board	State board shall commence the canvass at 9:00 p.m. on election day and shall continue and complete the tabulation with all reasonable expedition
South Carolina	State Board	State board shall meet within 10 days after any general election
South Dakota	Governor	Within seven days after the day of election
Tennessee	Secretary of State	No date specified
Texas	Secretary of State	No date specified
Utah	Lieutenant Governor	Fourth Monday of November at noon
Vermont	Canvassing Committee	Canvassing committee shall meet at 10:00 a.m. one week after the day of the election
Virginia	State Board	Fourth Monday in November, if the Board is unable to ascertain results on that day, the meeting shall stand adjourned for not more than three days
Washington	Secretary of State	Not later than 30 days after the election
West Virginia	Board of Canvassers	Fifth day after every election
Wisconsin	Elections Board	The first day of December following a general election
Wyoming	Canvassing Board	No later than the second Wednesday following the election

APPENDIX U: U.S. SUPREME COURT DECISION IN *HAWKE V. SMITH* (1920)

U.S. Supreme Court
253 U.S. 221
Hawke v. Smith, Secretary of State of Ohio. No. 582.
Argued April 23, 1920
Decided June 1, 1920

Mr. J. Frank Hanly, of Indianapolis, Ind., for plaintiff in error.

Mr. Lawrence Maxwell, of Cincinnati, Ohio, for defendant in error.

Mr. Justice DAY delivered the opinion of the Court.

Plaintiff in error (plaintiff below) filed a petition for an injunction in the court of common pleas of Franklin county, Ohio, seeking to enjoin the secretary of state of Ohio from spending the public money in preparing and printing forms of ballot for submission of a referendum to the electors of that state on the question of the ratification which the General Assembly had made of the proposed Eighteenth Amendment to the federal Constitution. A demurrer to the petition was sustained in the court of common pleas. Its judgment was affirmed by the Court of Appeals of Franklin County, which judgment was affirmed by the Supreme Court of Ohio, and the case was brought here.

A joint resolution proposing to the states this amendment to the Constitution of the United States was adopted on the 3d day of December, 1917. 40 Stat. 1050. The amendment prohibits the manufacture, sale or transportation of intoxicating liquors within, the importation thereof into, or the exportation thereof from, the United States and all territory subject to the jurisdiction thereof for beverage purposes. The several states were given concurrent power to enforce the amendment by appropriate legislation. The resolution provided that the amendment should be inoperative unless ratified as an amendment of the Constitution by the Legislatures of the several states, as provide in the Constitution, within seven years from the date of the submission thereof to the states. The Senate and House of Representatives of the state of Ohio adopted a resolution ratifying the proposed amendment by the General Assembly of the state of Ohio, and ordered that certified copies of the joint resolution of ratification be forwarded by the Governor to the Secretary of State at Washington and to the presiding officer of each House of Congress. This resolution was adopted on January 7, 1919; on January 27, 1919, the Governor of Ohio complied with the resolution. On January 29, 1919, the Secretary of State of the United States proclaimed the ratification of the amendment, naming 36 states as having ratified the same, among them the state of Ohio.

The question for our consideration is: Whether the provision of the Ohio Constitution, adopted at the general election, November, 1918, extending the referendum to the ratification by the General Assembly of proposed amendments to the federal Constitution is in conflict with article 5 of the Constitution of the United States. The amendment of 1918 provides:

> "The people also reserve to themselves the legislative power of the referendum on the action of the General Assembly ratifying any proposed amendment to the Constitution of the United States."

Article 5 of the federal Constitution provides:

> "The Congress, whenever two-thirds of both houses shall deem it necessary, shall propose amendments to this Constitution, or, on the application of the Legislatures of two-thirds of the several states, shall call a convention for proposing amendments, which, in either case, shall be valid to all intents and purposes, as part of this Constitution, when ratified by the Legislatures of three-fourths of the several states, or by conventions in three-fourths thereof, as the one or the other mode of ratification may be proposed by the Congress: Provided that no amendment which may be made prior to the year one thousand eight hundred and eight shall in any manner affect the first and fourth clauses in the ninth section of the first article; and that no state, without its consent, shall be deprived of its equal suffrage in the Senate."

The Constitution of the United States was ordained by the people, and, when duly ratified, it became the Constitution of the people of the United States. *McCulloch v. Maryland*, 4 Wheat. 316, 402. The states surrendered to the general government the powers specifically conferred upon the nation, and the Constitution and the laws of the United States are the supreme law of the land.

The framers of the Constitution realized that it might in the progress of time and the development of new conditions require changes, and they intended to provide an orderly manner in which these could be accomplished; to that end they adopted the fifth article.

This article makes provision for the proposal of amendments either by two-thirds of both houses of Congress, or on application of the Legislatures of two-thirds of the states; thus securing deliberation and consideration before any change can be proposed. The proposed change can only become effective by the ratification of the Legislatures of three-fourths of the states, or by conventions in a like number of states. The method of ratification is left to the choice of Congress. Both methods of ratification, by Legislatures or conventions, call for action by deliberative assemblages representative of the people, which it was assumed would voice the will of the people.

The fifth article is a grant of authority by the people to Congress. The determination of the method of ratification is the exercise of a national power specifically granted by the Constitution; that power is conferred upon Congress, and is limited to two methods, by action of the Legislatures of three-fourths of the states, or conventions in a like number of states. *Dodge v. Woolsey*, 18 How. 331, 348. The framers of the Constitution might have adopted a different method. Ratification might have been left to a vote of the people, or to some authority of government other than that selected. The language of the article is plain, and admits of no doubt in its interpretation. It is not the function of courts or legislative bodies, national or state, to alter the method which the Constitution has fixed.

All of the amendments to the Constitution have been submitted with a requirement for legislative ratification; by this method all of them have been adopted.

The only question really for determination is: What did the framers of the Constitution mean in requiring ratification by "legislatures"? That was not a term of uncertain meaning when incorporated into the Constitution. What it meant when adopted it still means for the purpose of interpretation. A Legislature was then the representative body which made the laws of the people. The term is often used in the Constitution with this evident meaning. Article 1, section 2, prescribes the qualifications of electors of Congressmen as those "requisite for electors of the most numerous branch of the state Legislature." Article 1, section 3, provided that Senators shall be chosen in each state by the Legislature thereof, and this was the method of choosing senators until the adoption of the Seventeenth Amendment, which made provision for the election of Senators by vote of the people, the electors to have the qualifications requisite for electors of the most numerous branch of the state Legislature. That Congress and the states understood that this election by the people was entirely distinct from legislative action is shown by the provision of the amendment giving the Legislature of any state the power to authorize the executive to make temporary appointments until the people shall fill the vacancies by election. It was never suggested, so far as we are aware, that the purpose of making the office of Senator elective by the people could be accomplished by a referendum vote. The necessity of the amendment to accomplish the purpose of popular election is shown in the adoption of the amendment. In article 4 the United States is required to protect every state against domestic violence upon application of the Legislature, or of the executive when the Legislature cannot be convened. Article 6 requires the members of the several Legislatures to be bound by oath, or affirmation, to support the Constitution of the United States. By article 1, section 8, Congress is given exclusive jurisdiction over all places purchased by the consent of the Legislature of the state in which the same shall be. Article 4, section 3, provides that no new states shall be carved out of old states without the consent of the Legislatures of the states concerned.

There can be no question that the framers of the Constitution clearly understood and carefully used the terms in which that instrument referred to the action of the Legislatures of the states. When they intended that direct action by the people should be had they were no less accurate in the use of apt phraseology to carry out such purpose. The members of the House of Representatives were required to be chosen by the people of the several states. Article 1, section 2.

The Constitution of Ohio in its present form, although making provision for a referendum, vests the legislative power primarily in a General Assembly, consisting of a Senate and House of Representatives. Article 2, section 1, provides:

> "The legislative power of the state shall be vested in a General Assembly consisting of a Senate and House of Representatives, but the people reserve to themselves the power to propose to the General Assembly laws and amendments to the Constitution, and to adopt or reject the same at the polls on a referendum vote as hereinafter provided."

The argument to support the power of the state to require the approval by the people of the state of the ratification of amendments to the federal Constitution through the medium of a referendum rests upon the proposition that the federal Constitution requires ratification by the legislative action of the states through the medium provided at the time of the proposed approval of an amendment. This argument is fallacious in this—ratification by a state of a constitutional amendment is not an act of legislation within the proper sense of the word. It is but the expression of the assent of the state to a proposed amendment.

At an early day this court settled that the submission of a constitutional amendment did not require the action of the President. The question arose over the adoption of the Eleventh Amendment. *Hollingsworth et al. v. Virginia*, 3 Dall. 378. In that case is was contended that the amendment had not been proposed in the manner provided in the Constitution as an inspection of the original roll showed that it had never been submitted to the President for his approval in accordance with article 1, section 7, of the Constitution. The Attorney General answered that the case of amendments is a substantive act, unconnected with the ordinary business of legislation, and not within the policy or terms of the Constitution investing the President with a qualified negative on the acts and resolutions of Congress. In a footnote to this argument of the Attorney General, Justice Chase said:

> "There can, surely, be no necessity to answer that argument. The negative of the President applies only to the ordinary cases of legislation. He has nothing to do with the proposition, or adoption, of amendments to the Constitution."

The court by a unanimous judgment held that the amendment was constitutionally adopted.

It is true that the power to legislate in the enactment of the laws of a state is derived from the people of the state. But the power to ratify a proposed amendment to the federal Constitution has its source in the federal Constitution. The act of ratification by the state derives its authority from the federal Constitution to which the state and its people have alike assented.

This view of the amendment is confirmed in the history of its adoption found in

2 Watson on the Constitution, 1301 et seq. Any other view might lead to endless confusion in the manner of ratification of federal amendments. The choice of means of ratification was wisely withheld from conflicting action in the several states.

But it is said this view runs counter to the decision of this court in *Davis v. Hildebrant*, 241 U.S. 565, 36 S. Ct. 708. But that case is inapposite. It dealt with article 1 section 4, of the Constitution, which provides that the times, places, and manners of holding elections for Senators and Representatives in each state shall be determined by the respective Legislatures thereof, but that Congress may at any time make or alter such regulations, except as to the place for choosing Senators. As shown in the opinion in that case, Congress had itself recognized the referendum as part of the legislative authority of the state for the purpose stated. It was held, affirming the judgment of the Supreme Court of Ohio, that the referendum provision of the state Constitution, when applied to a law redistricting the state with a view to representation in Congress, was not unconstitutional. Article 1, section 4, plainly gives authority to the state to legislate within the limitations therein named. Such legislative action is entirely different from the requirement of the Constitution as to the expression of assent or dissent to a proposed amendment to the Constitution. In such expression no legislative action is authorized or required.

It follows that the court erred in holding that the state had authority to require the submission of the ratification to a referendum under the state Constitution, and its judgment is reversed and the cause remanded for further proceedings not inconsistent with this opinion.

Reversed.

APPENDIX V: U.S. SUPREME COURT DECISION IN *SMILEY V. HOLM* (1932)

U.S. Supreme Court

***Smiley v. Holm*, 285 U.S. 355 (1932)**

285 U.S. 355

Smiley v. Holm, as Secretary of State of Minnesota

No. 617.

Argued March 16, 17, 1932

Decided April 11, 1932

Messrs. George T. Simpson, Alfred W. Bowen, W. Yale Smiley, John A. Weeks, and F. J. Donahue, all of Minneapolis, Minn., for petitioner.

Messrs. Henry N. Benson, Atty. Gen., and William H. Gurnee, Asst. Atty. Gen., both of St. Paul, Minn., for respondent.

Mr. Chief Justice HUGHES delivered the opinion of the Court.

Under the reapportionment following the fifteenth decennial census, as provided by the Act of Congress of June 18, 1929 (c. 28, 22, 46 Stat. 21, 26 (2 USCA 2a)), Minnesota is entitled to nine Representatives in Congress, being one less than the number previously allotted. In April, 1931, the bill known as House File No. 1456 (Laws Minn. 1931, p. 640), dividing the state into nine congressional districts and specifying the counties of which they should be composed, was passed by the House of Representatives and the Senate of the state, and was transmitted to the Governor, who returned it without his approval. Thereupon, without further action upon the measure by the House of Representatives and the Senate, and in compliance with a resolution of the House of Representatives, House File No. 1456 was deposited with the secretary of state of Minnesota. This suit was brought by the petitioner as a "citizen, elector and taxpayer" of the state to obtain a judgment declaring invalid all fillings for nomination for the office of Representative in Congress, which should designate a subdivision of the state as a congressional district, and to enjoin the secretary of state from giving notice of the holding of elections for that office in such subdivisions. The petition alleged that House File No. 1456 was a nullity, in that, after the Governor's veto, it was not repassed by the Legislature as required by law, and also in that the proposed congressional districts were not "compact" and did not "contain an equal number of inhabitants as nearly as practicable" in accordance with the Act of Congress of August 8, 1911.[1]

The respondent, secretary of state, demurred to the petition upon the ground that

---

[1] The Act of August 8, 1911, c. 5, 37 Stat. 13 (2 USCA 2 and note, 3-5), provided for the apportionment of Representatives in Congress among the several states under the thirteenth census. After fixing the total number of Representatives and their apportionment, in sections 1 and 2, the act provided as follows:

"Sec. 3. That in each State entitled under this apportionment to more than one Representative, the Representatives to the Sixty-third and each subsequent Congress shall be elected by districts composed of a contiguous and compact territory, and containing as nearly as practicable an equal

it did not state facts sufficient to constitute a cause of action. He maintained the validity of House File No. 1456 by virtue of the authority conferred upon the Legislature by article 1, 4, of the Federal Constitution, and he insisted that the act of Congress of August 8, 1911, was no longer in force, and that the asserted inequalities in redistricting presented a political and not a judicial question. The trial court sustained the demurrer, and its order was affirmed by the Supreme Court of the state. 238 N. W. 494. The action was then dismissed upon the merits, and the Supreme Court affirmed the judgment upon its previous opinion. 238 N. W. 792. This Court granted a writ of certiorari. 284 U.S. 616, 52 S. Ct. 266, 76 L. Ed.

Article 1, 4, of the Constitution of the United States, provides:

> "The times, places and manner of holding elections for senators and representatives, shall be prescribed in each state by the legislature thereof; but the Congress may at any time by law make or alter such regulations, except as to the places of choosing senators."

Under the Constitution of Minnesota, the "legislature" consists "of the senate and house of representatives." Const. Minn. art. 4, 1. Before any bill passed by the Senate and House of Representatives "becomes a law," it must "be presented to the governor of the state," and if he returns it, within the time stated, without his approval, the bill may become a law provided it is reconsidered and thereupon passed by each house by a two-thirds vote. *Id.* art. 4, 11. The state Constitution also provides that, after each Federal census, "the legislature shall have the power to prescribe the bounds of congressional . . . districts." *Id.* art. 4, 23. We do not understand that the Supreme Court of the state has held that, under these provisions, a measure redistricting the state for congressional elections could be put in force by the Legislature without participation by the Governor, as required in the case of legislative bills, if such action were regarded as a performance of the function of the Legislature as a lawmaking body. No decision to that effect has been cited. It appears that "on seven occasions" prior to the measure now under consideration the Legislature of Minnesota had "made state and federal reapportionments in the form of a bill for an act which was approved by

---

number of inhabitants. The said districts shall be equal to the number of Representatives to which such State may be entitled in Congress, no district electing more than one Representative.

"Sec. 4. That in case of an increase in the number of Representatives in any State under this apportionment such additional Representative or Representatives shall be elected by the State at large and the other Representatives by the districts now prescribed by law until such State shall be redistricted in the manner provided by the laws thereof and in accordance with the rules enumerated in section three of this Act; and if there be no change in the number of Representatives from a State, the Representatives thereof shall be elected from the districts now prescribed by law until such State shall be redistricted as herein prescribed.

"Sec. 5. That candidates for Representative or Representatives to be elected at large in any State shall be nominated in the same manner as candidates for governor, unless otherwise provided by the laws of such State.'"

the Governor."[2] While, in the instant case, the Supreme Court regarded that procedure as insufficient to support the petitioner's contention as to practical construction, that question was dismissed from consideration because of the controlling effect which the court ascribed to the federal provision. 238 N. W. page 500. The court expressed the opinion that "the various provisions of our state Constitution cited in the briefs are of little importance in relation to the matter now in controversy"; that "the power of the state Legislature to prescribe congressional districts rests exclusively and solely in the language of article 1, 4, of the United States Constitution." *Id.* 238 N. W. page 497. Construing that provision, the court reached the conclusion that the Legislature in redistricting the state was not acting strictly in the exercise of the lawmaking power, but merely as an agency, discharging a particular duty in the manner which the Federal Constitution required. Upon this point the court said (*Id.* 238 N. W. page 499):

> "The Legislature in districting the state is not strictly in the discharge of legislative duties as a lawmaking body, acting in its sovereign capacity, but is acting as representative of the people of the state under the power granted by said article 1, 4. It merely gives expression as to district lines in aid of the election of certain federal officials; prescribing one of the essential details serving primarily the federal government and secondly the people of the state. The Legislature is designated as a mere agency to discharge the particular duty. The Governor's veto has no relation to such matters; that power pertains, under the state Constitution, exclusively to state affairs. The word 'legislature' has reference to the well-recognized branch of the state government—created by the state as one of its three branches for a specific purpose—and when the framers of the Federal Constitution employed this term, we believe they made use of it in the ordinary sense with reference to the official body invested with the functions of making laws, the legislative body of the state; and that they did not intend to include the state's chief executive as a part thereof. We would not be justified in construing the term as being used in its enlarged sense as meaning the state or as meaning the lawmaking power of the state."

The question then is whether the provision of the Federal Constitution, thus regarded as determinative, invests the Legislature with a particular authority, and imposes upon it a corresponding duty, the definition of which imports a function different from that of lawgiver, and thus renders inapplicable the conditions which attach to the making of state laws. Much that is urged in argument with regard to the meaning of the term "Legislature" is beside the point. As this Court said in *Hawke v. Smith*, No. 1, 253 U.S. 221, 227, 40 S. Ct. 495, 497, 10 A. L. R. 1504, the term was not one "of uncertain meaning when incorporated into the Constitution. What it meant when adopted

---

[2] See Laws of Minnesota 1858, c. 83; 1872, c. 21; 1881, c. 128; 1891, c. 3; 1901, c. 92; 1913, c. 513; 1929, c. 64.

it still means for the purpose of interpretation. A Legislature was then the representative body which made the laws of the people." The question here is not with respect to the "body" as thus described but as to the function to be performed. The use in the Federal Constitution of the same term in different relations does not always imply the performance of the same function. The Legislature may act as an electoral body, as in the choice of United States Senators under article 1, 3, prior to the adoption of the Seventeenth Amendment. It may act as a ratifying body, as in the case of proposed amendments to the Constitution under article 5. *Hawke v. Smith*, No. 1, supra; *Hawke v. Smith*, No. 2, 253 U.S. 231, 40 S. Ct. 498; *Leser v. Garnett*, 258 U.S. 130, 137, 42 S. Ct. 217. It may act as a consenting body, as in relation to the acquisition of lands by the United States under article 1, 8, par. 17. Wherever the term "legislature" is used in the Constitution, it is necessary to consider the nature of the particular action in view. The primary question now before the Court is whether the function contemplated by article 1, 4, is that of making laws.

Consideration of the subject-matter and of the terms of the provision requires affirmative answer. The subject-matter is the "times, places and manner of holding elections for senators and representatives." It cannot be doubted that these comprehensive words embrace authority to provide a complete code for congressional elections, not only as to times and places, but in relation to notices, registration, supervision of voting, protection of voters, prevention of fraud and corrupt practices, counting of votes, duties of inspectors and canvassers, and making and publication of election returns; in short, to enact the numerous requirements as to procedure and safeguards which experience shows are necessary in order to enforce the fundamental right involved. And these requirements would be nugatory if they did not have appropriate sanctions in the definition of offenses and punishments. All this is comprised in the subject of "times, places and manner of holding elections," and involves lawmaking in its essential features and most important aspect.

This view is confirmed by the second clause of article 1, 4, which provides that "the Congress may at any time by law make or alter such regulations," with the single exception stated. The phrase "such regulations" plainly refers to regulations of the same general character that the legislature of the State is authorized to prescribe with respect to congressional elections. In exercising this power, the Congress may supplement these state regulations or may substitute its own. It may impose additional penalties for the violation of the state laws or provide independent sanctions. It "has a general supervisory power over the whole subject." *Ex parte Siebold*, 100 U.S. 371, 387; *Ex parte Yarbrough*, 110 U.S. 651, 661, 4 S. Ct. 152; *Ex parte Clarke*, 100 U.S. 399; *United States v. Mosley*, 238 U.S. 383, 386, 35 S. Ct. 904; *Newberry v. United States*, 256 U.S. 232, 255, 41 S. Ct. 469. But this broad authority is conferred by the constitutional provision now under consideration, and is exercised by the Congress in making "such regulations"; that is, regulations of the sort which, if there be no overruling action by the Congress, may be provided by the Legislature of the state upon the same subject.

The term defining the method of action, equally with the nature of the subject matter, aptly points to the making of laws. The state Legislature is authorized to "prescribe" the times, places, and manner of holding elections. Respondent urges that the fact that the words "by law" are found in the clause relating to the action of the Congress, and not in the clause giving authority to the state Legislature, supports the contention that the latter was not to act in the exercise of the lawmaking power. We think that the inference is strongly to the contrary. It is the nature of the function that makes the phrase "by law" apposite. That is the same whether it is performed by state or national Legislature, and the use of the phrase places the intent of the whole provision in a strong light. Prescribing regulations to govern the conduct of the citizen, under the first clause, and making and altering such rules by law, under the second clause, involve action of the same inherent character.

As the authority is conferred for the purpose of making laws for the state, it follows, in the absence of an indication of a contrary intent, that the exercise of the authority must be in accordance with the method which the state has prescribed for legislative enactments. We find no suggestion in the federal constitutional provision of an attempt to endow the Legislature of the state with power to enact laws in any manner other than that in which the Constitution of the state has provided that laws shall be enacted. Whether the Governor of the state, through the veto power, shall have a part in the making of state laws, is a matter of state polity. Article 1, 4, of the Federal Constitution, neither requires nor excludes such participation. And provision for it, as a check in the legislative process, cannot be regarded as repugnant to the grant of legislative authority. At the time of the adoption of the Federal Constitution, it appears that only two states had provided for a veto upon the passage of legislative bills; Massachusetts, through the Governor, and New York, through a council of revision.[3] But the restriction which existed in the case of these states was well known. That the state Legislature might be subject to such a limitation, either then or thereafter imposed as the several states might think wise, was no more incongruous with the grant of legislative authority to regulate congressional elections than the fact that the Congress in making its regulations under the same provision would be subject to the veto power of the President, as provided in article 1, 7. The latter consequence was not expressed, but there is no question that it was necessarily implied, as the Congress was to act by law; and there is no intimation, either in the debates in the Federal Convention or in contemporaneous exposition, of a purpose to exclude a similar re-

---

[3] The Constitution of Massachusetts of 1780 provided for the Governor's veto of "bills" or "resolves." Part Second, ch. 1, 1, art. 2; 3 Thorpe, *American Charters, Constitutions and Organic Laws*, 1893, 1894. The council of revision in New York, which had the veto power under the first Constitution of 1777 (art. 3), was composed of the Governor, the chancellor, and the judges of the Supreme Court, "or any two of them, together with the Governor." The veto power was given to the Governor alone by the Constitution of 1821. Article 1, 12, 3 Thorpe, op. cit. 2628, 2641, 2642. In South Carolina, the veto power had been given by the Constitution of 1776 to the "president" (article 7), but under the Constitution of 1778 the Governor had no veto power; see article 14, 6 Thorpe, op. cit., 3244, 3252.

striction imposed by state Constitutions upon state Legislatures when exercising the lawmaking power.

The practical construction of article 1, 4, is impressive. General acquiescence cannot justify departure from the law, but long and continuous interpretation in the course of official action under the law may aid in removing doubts as to its meaning. This is especially true in the case of constitutional provisions governing the exercise of political rights, and hence subject to constant and careful scrutiny. Certainly, the terms of the constitutional provision furnish no such clear and definite support for a contrary construction as to justify disregard of the established practice in the states. *McPherson v. Blacker*, 146 U.S. 1, 36, 13 S. Ct. 3; *Missouri Pacific Railway Co. v. Kansas*, 248 U.S. 276, 284, 39 S. Ct. 93, 2 A. L. R. 1589; *Myers v. United States*, 272 U.S. 52, 119, 136 S., 47 S. Ct. 21; *The Pocket Veto Case*, 279 U.S. 655, 688-690, 49 S. Ct. 463, 64 A. L. R. 1434. That practice is eloquent of the conviction of the people of the states, and of their representatives in state Legislatures and executive office, that in providing for congressional elections, and for the districts in which they were to be held, these Legislatures were exercising the lawmaking power and thus subject, where the state Constitution so provided, to the veto of the Governor as a part of the legislative process. The early action in Massachusetts under this authority was by "resolves," and these, under the Constitution of 1780, were required to be submitted to the Governor, and it appears that they were so submitted and approved by him.[4] In New York, from the outset, provision for congressional districts was made by statute,[5] and this method was followed until 1931. The argument based on the disposition, during the early period, to curtail executive authority in the states, and on the long time which elapsed in a number of states before the veto power was granted to the Governor, is of slight weight in the light of the fact that this power was given in four states shortly after the adoption of the Federal Constitution,[6] that the use of this check has gradually been extended, and that the uniform practice (prior to the questions raised in relation to the present reapportionment) has been to provide for congressional districts by the enactment of statutes with the participation of the Governor wherever the state Constitution provided for such participation as part of the process of making laws. See *Moran v. Bowley*, 347 Ill. 148, 179 N. E. 526, 527; *Koening v. Flynn*, 258 N. Y. 292, 300, 179 N. E. 705; *Carroll v. Becker* (Mo. Sup.) 45 S.W.(2d) 533; *State ex rel. Schrader v. Polley*, 26 S. D. 5, 7, 127 N. W. 848. The Attorney General of Minnesota, in his argument in the

---

[4] Const. Mass. 1780; 3 Thorpe, op. cit. 1893, 1894, Mass. Resolves, Oct.–Nov., 1788, c. XLIX, p. 52; May–June, 1792, c. LXIX, p. 23.

[5] New York, *Laws of 1789*, c. 11; 1797, c. 62; 1802, c. 72. See *Koenig v. Flynn*, 258 N. Y. 292.

[6] Georgia, Const. 1789, art. 2, 10, 2 Thorpe, op. cit. 788; Pennsylvania, Const. 1790, art. 1, 22, 5 Thorpe, op. cit., 3094; New Hampshire, Const. 1792; Part Second, 44, 4 Thorpe, op. cit., 2482; Kentucky, Const. 1792, art. 1, 28, 3 Thorpe, op. cit., 1267. In Vermont, the Constitution of 1793 (chapter 2, 16) gave the Governor and council a power of suspension similar to that for which provision had been made in the Constitution of 1786 (chapter 2, 14) before the admission of Vermont to the Union. See, also, Constitution of 1777 (chapter 2, 14), 6 Thorpe, op. cit., 3744, 3757, 3767.

instant case, states: "It is conceded that until 1931 whenever the State of Minnesota was divided into districts for the purpose of congressional elections such action was taken by the legislature in the form of a bill and presented to and approved by the governor." That the constitutional provision contemplates the exercise of the lawmaking power was definitely recognized by the Congress in the Act of August 8, 1911,[7] which expressly provided in section 4 for the election of Representatives in Congress, as stated, "by the districts now prescribed by law until such State shall be redistricted in the manner provided by the laws thereof, and in accordance with the rules enumerated in section three of this Act." The significance of the clause "in the manner provided by the laws thereof" is manifest from its occasion and purpose. It was to recognize the propriety of the referendum in establishing congressional districts where the state had made it a part of the legislative process. "It is clear," said this Court in *Davis v. Hildebrant,* 241 U.S. 565, 568, 36 S. Ct. 708, 710, "that Congress, in 1911, in enacting the controlling law concerning the duties of the states, through their legislative authority, to deal with the subject of the creation of congressional districts, expressly modified the phraseology of the previous acts relating to that subject by inserting a clause plainly intended to provide that where, by the state Constitution and laws, the referendum was treated as part of the legislative power, the power as thus constituted should be held and treated to be the state legislative power for the purpose of creating congressional districts by law."

The case of *Davis v. Hildebrant,* supra, arose under the amendment of 1912 to the Constitution of Ohio reserving the right "by way of referendum to approve or disapprove by popular vote any law enacted by the general assembly." *Id.,* 241 U.S. page 566, 36 S. Ct. 708, 709. The act passed by the General Assembly of Ohio in 1915, redistricting the state for the purpose of congressional elections, was disapproved under the referendum provision, and the validity of that action was challenged under article 1, 4, of the Federal Constitution. The Supreme Court of the state, denying a mandamus to enforce the disapproved act, "held that the provisions as to referendum were a part of the legislative power of the state, made so by the Constitution, and that nothing in the act of Congress of 1911, or in the constitutional provision, operated to the contrary, and that therefore the disapproved law had no existence." *Id.* 241 U.S. page 567, 36 S. Ct. 708, 709. This Court affirmed the judgment of the state court. It is manifest that the Congress had no power to alter article 1, 4, and that the act of 1911, in its reference to state laws, could but operate as a legislative recognition of the nature of the authority deemed to have been conferred by the constitutional provision. And it was because of the authority of the state to determine what should constitute its legislative process that the validity of the requirement of the state Constitution of Ohio, in its application to congressional elections, was sustained. This was explicitly stated by this Court as the ground of the distinction which was made in *Hawke v. Smith No.*

---

[7] See note 1.

1, supra, where, referring to the Davis Case, the Court said: "As shown in the opinion in that case, Congress had itself recognized the referendum as part of the legislative authority of the state for the purpose stated. It was held, affirming the judgment of the Supreme Court of Ohio, that the referendum provision of the state Constitution, when applied to a law redistricting the state with a view to representation in Congress, was not unconstitutional. Article 1, section 4, plainly gives authority to the state to legislate within the limitations therein named. Such legislative action is entirely different from the requirement of the Constitution as to the expression of assent or dissent to a proposed amendment to the Constitution. In such expression no legislative action is authorized or required."

It clearly follows that there is nothing in article 1, 4, which precludes a state from providing that legislative action in districting the state for congressional elections shall be subject to the veto power of the Governor as in other cases of the exercise of the lawmaking power. Accordingly, in this instance, the validity of House File No. 1456 cannot be sustained by virtue of any authority conferred by the Federal Constitution upon the Legislature of Minnesota to create congressional districts independently of the participation of the Governor as required by the state Constitution with respect to the enactment of laws.

The further question has been presented whether the Act of Congress of August 8, 1911,[8] is still in force. The state court held that it was not, that it had been wholly replaced by the Act of June 18, 1929. Sections 1 and 2 of the former act, making specific provision for the apportionment under the thirteenth census, are, of course, superseded; the present question relates to the other sections. These have not been expressly repealed. The act of 1929 repeals "all other laws and parts of laws" that are inconsistent with its provisions (section 21 (46 Stat. 26, 13 USCA 1 note)). The petitioner urges that this act contains nothing inconsistent with sections 3, 4, and 58 of the act of 1911, and the only question is whether these sections by their very terms have ceased to be effective. It is pointed out that the provisions of the act of 1911 were carried into the United States Code. U.S. C., tit. 2, 2–5 (2 USCA 2 and note 3–5). Inclusion in the Code does not operate as a re-enactment; it establishes "prima facie the laws of the United States, general and permanent in their nature, in force on the 7th day of December, 1925." Act of June 30, 1926, c. 712, 44 Stat. 777. While sections 3 and 4 of the act of 1911 expressly referred to "this apportionment" (the one made by that Act), the argument is pressed that they contain provisions setting forth a general policy which was intended to apply to the future creation of congressional districts, and the election of Representatives, until Congress should provide otherwise.

There are three classes of states with respect to the number of Representatives under the present apportionment pursuant to the act of 1929, (1) where the number remains the same, (2) where it is increased, and (3) where it is decreased. In states where

---

[8] See note 1.

the number of Representatives remains the same, and the districts are unchanged, no question is presented; there is nothing inconsistent with any of the requirements of the Congress in proceeding with the election of Representatives in such states in the same manner as heretofore. Section 4 of the act of 1911 (2 USCA 4) provided that, in case of an increase in the number of Representatives in any state, "such additional Representative or Representatives shall be elected by the State at large and the other Representatives by the districts now prescribed by law" until such state shall be redistricted. The Constitution itself provides in article 1, 2, that "The house of representatives shall be composed of members chosen every second year by the people of the several states," and we are of the opinion that under this provision, in the absence of the creation of new districts, additional Representatives allotted to a state under the present reapportionment would appropriately be elected by the state at large. Such a course, with the election of the other Representatives in the existing districts until a redistricting act was passed, would present no inconsistency with any policy declared in the act of 1911

Where, as in the case of Minnesota, the number of Representatives has been decreased, there is a different situation, as existing districts are not at all adapted to the new apportionment. It follows that in such a case, unless and until new districts are created, all Representatives allotted to the state must be elected by the state at large. That would be required, in the absence of a redistricting act, in order to afford the representation to which the state is constitutionally entitled, and the general provisions of the act of 1911 cannot be regarded as intended to have a different import.

This conclusion disposes of all the questions properly before the Court. Questions in relation to the application of the standards defined in section 3 of the act of 1911 to a redistricting statute, if such a statute should hereafter be enacted, are wholly abstract. The judgment is reversed, and the cause is remanded for further proceedings not inconsistent with this opinion.

It is so ordered.

Mr. Justice CARDOZO took no part in the consideration and decision of this case.

APPENDIX W: SPEECH OF SENATOR BIRCH BAYH (D-INDIANA) ON MARCH 14, 1979

Mr. President, today we begin debate on a constitutional amendment to abolish the Electoral College and establish direct popular election of the President and Vice President. This proposal has been studied intensively in the Senate for well over a decade, but has only once reached the Senate floor and has never reached a vote. In 1970 it was approved in the House by a vote of 339 to 70, but the Senate was denied its opportunity to vote due to a filibuster, which occurred during the closing days of the session when many of the Senators were running for election and there was the problem of getting them back, so we took it off the calendar and it was never voted on by the Senate.

I am confident that the 96th Congress will pass this joint resolution by the necessary two-thirds vote and the State Legislatures will ratify this amendment, thereby finally providing our political system with a safe and fair means of electing the President and Vice President.

John Roche once described the Electoral College as "merely a jerry-rigged improvisation which has subsequently been endowed with a high theoretical content. The future was left to cope with the problem of what to do with this Rube Goldberg mechanism."

That two-sentence quote from John Roche carries a lot of meaning for anyone who has had a chance to really study the way in which the electoral college actually works.

Despite its eccentricities the electoral college is not a lovable old mechanism to be kept and treasured. Mr. President, the electoral college is not harmless. If, as its defenders like to say, it has worked it has worked oftentimes in strange ways. It carries with it always the risk that it may not work at all. As the Presidential election of 1980 approaches, I hope that the Congress will take heed of the ominous rumblings we have had from this cumbersome counting machine in the past, and begin the amendment process that would provide the country with political protection from a breakdown which could occur anytime in the future. To finally replace the electoral college with direct election is simply to give us insurance before it is needed.

I have read with a great deal of interest certain editorials of very distinguished columnists, the essence of which was, "If it ain't broke, Birch, don't fix it."

That is almost like saying, "If your house is not on fire, don't take out fire insurance. If you don't have heart trouble or if you don't have cancer or if you haven't had an accident on the way to the Senate that broke both legs and put you in the hospital at $150 a day, don't take out health insurance."

What we are trying to do in this effort is not to revolutionize the electoral process or dramatically change the constitutional structure of this country; what we are trying to do is put a little grease on a very squeaky wheel, which has come very close to having consequences which could prove unacceptable to the people of this country.

The electoral college has given problems since it was first created. Speaking in Federalist 67 of the manner of electing a President which had been chosen by the 1787 convention, Alexander Hamilton said:

> "There is hardly any part of the system which could have been attended with greater difficulty in the arrangements of it than this. . . ."

That was Alexander Hamilton speaking, yet we are going to be told here by some of the opponents of this effort that the Founding Fathers had infinite wisdom and all believed they had come forth with a majestic solution to electing the President. Not so, Mr. President.

The manner of electing the President was debated extensively during the summer of 1787. Debate centered mainly between those who believed in a direct popular vote and those who wanted election by the National Legislature. However, John Feerick, chairman of the American Bar Association Committee on Election Reform, an outstanding scholar of the workings and mechanism of the electoral college, reports from the historical records, that on July 25 the following proposals were all debated but none adopted:

> "Among the proposals made, but not adopted were that he be chosen by: Congress and, when running for re-election, by electors appointed by the state legislatures; the chief executives of the states, with the advice of their councils, or, if not councils, with the advice of electors chosen by their legislatures, with the votes of all states equal; the people; and the people of each state choosing its best citizen and Congress, or electors chosen by it, selecting the President from those citizens."

A committee of 11 finally was appointed to break the deadlock over how votes for President would be apportioned in the National Legislature. The committee discarded the legislative election method, and in the final days of the convention recommended a system of intermediate electors. Their recommendation was accepted.

I will say, Mr. President, that this was after the great compromise which put the union together. The Federal system had already been formulated; the compromise between the large and small States, the large States being represented in the House and the small being represented in the Senate.

The electoral college was not considered to be an indispensable part of that compromise. It was not even considered at that time.

Clearly, the electoral college system was neither the most obvious, the most popular nor the most inspired of the Founding Fathers' great works in framing the Constitution. What is more, the Founders did not envision political parties, the unit rule, or popular election of electors. These aspects of the present system of electing a President evolved quickly and changed the system dramatically, but not by design of the delegates to the 1787 Convention.

James Madison, one of the original Founding Fathers, wrote some 36 years later, as he looked back on his offspring:

> "The difficulty of finding an unexceptionable process for appointing the Executive Organ of a Government such as that of the U.S., was deeply felt by the Convention; and as the final arrangement took place in the latter stages of the session, it was not exempt from a degree of the hurrying influence produced by fatigue and impatience in all such bodies, tho' the degree was much less than usually prevails in them."

For its time, however, the electoral college made some sense.

I think it would be wrong for me to stand here and criticize this as a solution, but this was done 200 years ago by our Founding Fathers. We were living in a different age. The Founding Fathers were dealing with a much different society and the electoral college was a device for that society. The land mass of the country was huge; communication was primitive; and education was limited at best. Lack of information about possible Presidential candidates was in fact a very real consideration. Direct election would have been a difficult proposition, a reality which James Madison, one of its strong proponents, acknowledged reluctantly. Added to this were the problems involving suffrage. Out of a total population of 4,000,000, almost 700,000 were slaves, almost 90 percent of the South. It was not possible to count the slaves along the lines of a 3 to 5 compromise type of solution in a direct popular vote system. This would have led to northern-dominated elections and would have been wholly unacceptable unless the slaves were permitted to vote which was equally unacceptable.

James Madison spoke to this problem on July 19, 1787:

> "There was one difficulty however of a serious nature attending an immediate choice by the people. The right of suffrage was much more diffusive in the Northern than the Southern States; and the latter could have no influence in the election on the score of the Negroes. The substitution of electors obviated this difficulty."

From the beginning the electoral college did not work as intended. Those who feel this has been a perfect mechanism should harken back to 1800. By 1800, the first crisis occurred when Burr and Jefferson tied in the electoral vote for President. Thus, the election was put to the House of Representatives. After 36 ballots and 6 days, Jefferson finally won, but it was clear that an amendment was needed. In 1804 the 12th amendment was ratified, solving only the immediate problem of the 1800 election, but leaving the already outmoded electoral college in place.

As has been often said, the system has backfired three times. In the elections of 1824, 1876 and 1888 the candidate who received the most votes did not win. That is three election out of the 39 which have recorded popular votes, or a failure rate of

8 percent. Each of these elections has shown some peculiar flaw of the electoral college system.

Mr. President, as I pointed out just a moment ago, those who say, "If it ain't broke, don't fix it," are poor readers of history.

A failure rate of 8 percent, and some very near misses that increase the almost failure rate to an unacceptable level, hardly support the notion that "it ain't broke."

I will deal with these near misses of more recent vintage in the memory of most of us in just a moment.

The election of 1824 ended up in the House of Representatives. It taught us a lesson to be carried to this day. What happened then was remembered 144 years later and hovered behind the fears about George Wallace's third party candidacy in 1968. Despite a popular vote plurality of 40,000 votes out of almost 400,000 votes cast—a 10 percent popular vote plurality—Andrew Jackson did not receive sufficient electoral votes to win. During the period between the election and House action, the Nation was subjected to the spectacle of the asking and the suspected granting of every manner of favor as Jackson and Adams vied for the votes of House Members. Charges of a corrupt deal followed Adams through his presidency and as a result of his anger over the election, Andrew Jackson formed our modern Democratic Party.

With direct election, no such deal-making or charges of deal-making ever would be possible. In the unlikely event that the leading candidate does not receive 40 percent of the popular vote, an event which has occurred only once in our history, the people themselves will get to choose the candidate they prefer in a runoff election.

The decision will not be made in a smoke-filled room where the vote of representatives could likely go to the highest bidder.

The election of 1876 was the result of a system steeped in corruption before the election, a nation not yet recovered from the bitterness and division of a Civil War and a system that permitted fraud in a handful of States to decide an election. Even President Rutherford Hayes, in his diary, admits that Samuel Tilden, in fact, won the Presidency. Fraud is an ever-present possibility in the electoral college system, even if it rarely has become a proven reality. With the electoral college, relatively few irregular votes can reap a healthy reward in the form of a bloc of electoral votes, because of the unit rule or winner take all rule. Under the present system, fraudulent popular votes are much more likely to have a great impact by swinging enough blocs of electoral votes to reverse the election. A like number of fraudulent popular votes under direct election would likely have little effect on the national vote totals.

I have said repeatedly in previous debates that there is no way in which anyone would want to excuse fraud. We have to do everything we can to find it, to punish those who participate in it; but one of the things we can do to limit fraud is to limit the benefits to be gained by fraud.

Under a direct popular vote system, one fraudulent vote wins one vote in the return. In the electoral college system, one fraudulent vote could mean 45 electoral votes, 28 electoral votes.

So the incentive to participate in "a little bit of fraud," if I may use that phrase advisedly, can have the impact of turning a whole electoral block, a whole State operating under the unit rule. Therefore, so the incentive to participate in fraud is significantly greater than it would be under the direct popular vote system.

In addition, there is one other incentive, it seems to me, which does not exist today, to guard against fraud under the direct popular vote. In a direct popular vote, each vote counts. It does not make any difference whether you are going to win or lose by 1 vote or a million. Each vote adds to the national total. So each precinct committeeman and committeewoman standing at that polling place, representing his or her party, has an incentive to police each of those votes to see that it is a legitimate vote.

On the other hand, in the electoral college system, in which, if you are going to lose by 100,000, you might as well lose by 200,000, because either way you lose all the electors, there is no benefit given to the party that comes close. There is no incentive to either the winner or the loser at the precinct level to get out more votes; because once you have lost a State by one vote, you have lost everything you had to lose—namely, all the electoral votes. In a direct popular election each vote would count on the national scale, committeewoman would know in advance that that was going to be the case. You would have a much more severe policing of the precincts as the votes were counted, and you would have a self-policing mechanism the likes of which is not present in many precincts today.

We may cite New York in 1976 as an example. Cries of voting irregularities arose on election night. At stake were 41 electoral votes—more than enough to elect Ford over Carter in the electoral college. Carter's popular margin was 290,000. The calls for recount were eventually dropped, but if fraud had been present in New York, Carter's plurality of 290,000 would have been enough to determine the outcome of the entire national election. Under direct election, Carter's entire national margin of 1.7 million votes would have had to have been irregular to affect the outcome.

Fraud was also involved in the election of 1888, but there is no question that Grover Cleveland won the popular vote by a 23,000 plurality and lost the electoral vote 219 to 182, simply because the electoral system allowed it to happen. Had Cleveland not been so willing to return to public life; had he, like Jackson, gone home and created a great storm of controversy, we have no way of knowing how the people would have reacted.

What happened in 1888 represents the greatest danger presented to us by the electoral college. Of course, no one can foretell with accuracy what would be the reaction in the United States in the second half of the twentieth century if the duly elected President were not the popular vote winner. But we should be thinking about it. There have been three near misses in the last five elections.

Let us think of that. There have been three near misses in the last five elections. It may be broken; it sure is rumbling and sputtering, if in three of the last five Presidential elections we almost had a miscarriage of what we traditionally would call electoral justice.

When we consider our present day increased suffrage, widespread education, ever-present communications systems, and, perhaps most important, popular dissatisfaction with and distrust in the political process, it is reasonable to predict that there would be a political crisis if a President were elected and tried to govern after receiving fewer votes than the candidate against whom he was running. Surely, there is nothing speculative in the view that the mandate of the President to lead would be severely, perhaps irreparably, weakened.

This morning, about 12:30 or 1 o'clock, I stood at Andrews Air Force base with my son and others of my countrymen, with my heart in my throat, as Air Force I came wheeling to a stop and the Marine Corps Band played "Hail to the Chief." As the President of the United States left the plane, to the cheers of the multitude, I could not help thinking how difficult a burden that man carries. It has become almost impossible to be a good President of the United States because of the complex society in which we live today.

It would increase the difficulty of governing for any President if he knew in the back of his mind, if Congress knew, if the people knew, that the man sitting down there, calling orders in the White House, was not the choice of most of the people, but was defeated by the popular vote in the last election.

Mr. President, that is what concerns me—not that the President who has fewer votes might not be an outstanding President. He or she might be a great American, but how could such a President lead our people effectively if more voters chose his opponent. We are living in a time when the people are looking with great dissatisfaction, distrust, and disenchantment at the political process, and I do not know how the public would respond to the leadership of a President who is not the choice of the people of this country.

Mr. President, I emphasize that the danger that the electoral college will produce a President who is not the choice of the voters is not remote—it is not a speculative danger. On several occasions in this century, a shift of less than 1 percent of the popular vote would have produced an electoral majority for the candidate who received fewer popular votes. I repeat: A change of 1 percent would have produced this electoral majority for the candidate who received fewer popular votes.

To reflect on recent years 1960, 1968, and 1976, most of us remember those years. We should remember the dangers that have been all too close.

To this day we cannot be absolutely certain whether John Kennedy in fact won the popular vote or not in 1960.

If you look at the record, in the States of Alabama and Mississippi, States where unpledged Democratic electors were run and some of them won positions as Presidential electors, many did not vote for President Kennedy when the electoral college met; yet the popular votes for these electors was included in the Kennedy tally by the television networks and by the newspapers and most of those who did the counting.

So we really do not know what the national tally was. We do know it was frighteningly close to a backfire, though we do know if there had been a change of a few thousand votes in the State of Illinois we would have had a much different situation.

Most frightening in this election was an attempt by a Republican elector from Oklahoma to combine with other conservative electors, to disregard the popular vote and vote a Byrd-Goldwater ticket out of the electoral college.

My distinguished colleague, the Senator from Virginia, should be assured that we mean no disrespect for his distinguished father who was highly considered by many people throughout the country and performed a great service in this body. I use this as an example to show what actually has, in fact, happened under the system. Persons not even on the ballot have been urged in the electoral college—and in recent years.

Henry Irwin sent the following telegram in 1960 to his fellow electors:

> "I am an Oklahoma Republican elector. The Republican Electors cannot deny election to Kennedy. Sufficient conservative Democratic electors available to deny labor socialist nominee. Would you consider Byrd President, Goldwater Vice President, or wire any acceptable substitute. All replies strict confidence."

That is a fact. That is not some cheap TV-only novel that we have to watch interspersed with commercials.

In 1968, which concerned me, very frankly, much more, we entered an election and built a strategy based on the notion George Wallace could deadlock the electoral college and broker the Presidency there.

Here are the questions and answers by candidate Wallace in a press conference:

> "Question. If none of the three candidates get a majority, is the election going to be decided in the Electoral College or in the House of Representatives?
>
> "Wallace. I think it would be settled in the electoral college.
>
> "Question. Two of the candidates get together or their electors get together and determine who is to be President?
>
> "Wallace. That is right."

In other words, the Constitution requires that, when the votes are cast by the electors in December, if a majority is not received by one candidate then the matter goes to the House of Representatives. But what Governor Wallace was saying plainly, openly, for everyone to see, was that he intended to broker his support to one of the other candidates in the electoral college, and it was perfectly legal under the Constitution.

We are not accusing him of being devious—quite the contrary, he was quite open and flagrant—what he was trying to do he nearly accomplished. His purpose was to get electors, and he got 36. If there had been a change of a handful of votes, neither Nixon nor Humphrey would have had a majority of electoral votes, and Wallace would have prevented the matter from going to the House of Representatives. He would first sit down with Mr. Nixon, and then Mr. Humphrey, or vice versa, and cut a deal.

But I am here to say, without any irreverence to either one of these men, practical politics being what it is, one of those would have literally purchased, and I use the term advisedly, purchased the Wallace electors and the decision would have been made then in the Electoral College. There the independent Wallace electors would have joined with the electors of the other candidates and there would have been a majority without the matter having to go to the House of Representatives.

Wallace managed to get his name on the ballot in all 50 States and came within 54,000 votes of accomplishing this goal. We can only speculate how the American people at the height of the controversy over the Vietnam War would have reacted to the kind of deals that might well have taken place between election day and the meeting of the electors.

We might even ask ourselves more significantly how the voters would react today where their faith and confidence in the political processes and the political leaders of our country has gone even lower than it was at the height of the Vietnam War.

In the last election, in 1976, a change of less than 9,500 votes combined, in Ohio and Hawaii would have made Ford the President while Carter had an almost 1.7 million vote plurality. Such a misfiring of the system in our present climate could have grave consequences for our system and for the person charged with carrying out the duties of the Presidency.

One of the things that I have really appreciated about the particular effort that many of us have been involved in over the years is that it is a really bipartisan, multi-philosophy effort. We cannot say everyone who is for direct election belongs to one party or one part of either party. It has been a conglomeration of Senators, House Members, and individual citizens who are concerned about the problem.

One of our distinguished allies from the moment he had the opportunity to serve on the American Bar Association panel back in the late 1960s, was our distinguished colleague, the senior Senator from Oklahoma, Senator Bellmon. He will have his say on this and so I will not relate his experience as he sat there and watched how this system really works and determined that he was not going to support the electoral college system which prior to that time he had thought benefited his relatively sparsely populated State.

The reason I bring this up right now is that I recall after that spectacle of election night, with Carter with almost a 2 million vote plurality, and Ford with a change of less than 10,000 votes having the opportunity to get an electoral college majority. I called Henry Bellmon and I said:

"Henry, what do you think? Do you think we ought to give it another try?"

He said:

"Well, I have been intending to call you. If that had backfired and Ford had been elected it would have been good for the Republicans but it would have been bad for the Republic."

That takes a pretty big man to say something like that, but that is the truth.

I would have said the same thing about the 1968 election. As most of you know, I am not one of Richard Nixon's most avid supporters. But if Nixon had a plurality of that popular vote he ought to be elected President, and we should not have some jerry rigged kind of situation to end up with throwing out the popular vote winner.

In a runaway election—like that of 1972—any system will produce an electoral victory for the popular vote winner. But the real test of a system is whether it really will stand the test in close elections and in elections as close as that of 1960 the present system offered only a 50-50 chance that the electoral results would agree with the popular vote. For an election as close as 1968, where some 500,000 popular votes separated the candidates, there was one chance in three that the electoral vote winner would not be the popular vote winner as well. Even in the 1976 election, where Mr. Carter's plurality was 1.7 million, our statistical experts who run this through their computers tell us the chance of misfiring was one out of every four. According to the evidence, the danger of an electoral backfire is clear and present.

It is easy for us to forget, when a near miss is past, that we should prepare for the future. Not enough of us remember the flood of magazine and newspaper articles speculating on disaster when the possibility of an electoral college backfire was imminent in 1968.

And I think it is important that we remember that in the days just prior to the 1976 election the cry began again only to subside when all turned out to be safe. I would hope that we would not allow ourselves to wait until the electoral college actually does backfire again before we rouse ourselves to act. Insurance cannot be bought after the house has burned down.

Forgive me for reminiscing just a moment at this hour of the evening, but I cannot help but remark to my very sincere colleague and some who study and write about this outside of this Chamber: We talk about: "Well it never has backfired. It ain't broke. Don't fix it." This is not all that important.

It was that similar kind of cry that some of us faced when we tried to amend the Constitution with the 25th amendment. "Two hundred years of history had never presented us with a sequence of circumstances that would be met by filling a Vice-Presidential vacancy, so you do not really need to act." Or, "Put it aside. Wait for another day. Other things are more important."

As a matter of fact, the ink was hardly dry on the 25th Amendment when we were confronted with a crisis, a dual crisis, where it was necessary to appoint two Vice Presidents.

My judgment is that if it had not been for the 25th Amendment, this Congress and the country would have been subjected to tortuous and divisive impeachment trials the like of which would have done severe damage to this country. But the Congress in its wisdom then did not put it off. It acted and, hopefully, Congress will take out the same kind of insurance policy so far as our electoral process is concerned.

Mr. President, the history of the electoral college is not significant simply because it has carried the threat of misfiring. Its very nature is contrary to the political ideals which we as a nation have come to realize over the years. In a very basic way, the electoral college is inimical to our political life. Unlike any other election in the United States from county commissioner to U.S. Senator, in a Presidential election all votes do not count the same.

What we want to do is to see that we return the election of the President and the Vice President to the same basis which has held up and held up very well in the election of every other official in the country. Under the electoral college, one American's vote is not equal to another's, simply on the basis of where he happens to live. Only with the direct election systems would all votes be equal. The electoral college's strange alchemy of apportioning electoral votes plus its "winner-take-all" rule produces the anomalous result that, for example, a citizen from Iowa's vote is actually worth less that his neighbor's in Illinois, but more than his neighbor's in Nebraska. This effect is contrary to our experience in all other elections and the principles behind our form of government. I am sometimes told that with direct election I am trying to make a major change in our political system. Far from it. With direct election, I think, we would simply be bringing our method of Presidential choice in line with all the rest of our voting process.

We worry a great deal nowadays about the "empty voting booth" in America. We speculate on why so few of us choose to take advantage of our right to vote.

The fact of the matter is I think a lot of people are smart enough to know that in that electoral college their votes do not count in some circumstances, and in others they count for the candidate they actually voted against. The time has come to put this aside so that I, in Indiana, when I vote for Carter, do not have my vote cast for Ford; and when a colleague of mine in Ohio, who voted for Ford, just as surely had that vote counted for Carter.

The time has come to convince people that if they come to the polls, their vote is going to count no matter whether the state goes big for the candidate they want or big against their candidate, or get out and vote, and see that those votes are counted.

Mr. President, in my opinion, the inequities inherent in the electoral college are also inimical to voter participation. The electoral college system provides a disincentive to voter turnout, and this is reflected in the way Presidential campaigns are conducted. It makes no difference to a Presidential candidate how many people show up on election day in any state so long as he receives a plurality of one, for that one extra vote determines the outcome of the State's bloc of electoral votes. The votes constituting the plurality over the winner's vote of one are actually worthless. Conversely, all the votes for the loser are not simply lost; they are in effect recast for the winner along with the State's bloc of electoral votes.

These iniquities are of great consequence to the way campaigns are run and thus on the degree of encouragement by candidates for voter participation. With the electoral college, some States are inherently more influential than others, helping a candidate to decide where he will spend his time and effort. Therefore he will, in all likelihood, ignore much of the plains and mountain states and the South. If he reasonably expects to either win or lose a state, however, he will probably write it off as well. Thus, few Democratic candidates go to Massachusetts or Rhode Island, or Republicans to Wyoming. The Electoral College gives neither the candidate nor the national party any motivation to either work to turn out the votes in those States, or widen the margin of victory if he expects to win, or narrow it if he expects to lose.

There is no advantage in building significant margins of victory. As an example of what I mean, in 1976 Mr. Ford picked up 45 electoral votes in California with a 127,000 plurality; Mr. Carter earned 45 electoral votes in five Southern States with a 1,044,000 plurality. The difference in popular votes made no difference in the electoral votes.

Winning under direct election, however, depends precisely on a party's ability to get out the vote and to build sizable pluralities in every community simply because every vote counts and, therefore, no State nor population can easily be ignored.

Mr. President, there is little doubt that American citizens are ready to abolish the electoral college and establish direct election in its place. For over 10 years, polls have shown that support of direct election is over 75 percent, and that support comes from every region of the country, every political ideology, both parties and independents, all races and religions, all professions and economic strata, consistently across the board. The amendment is endorsed by an array of national organizations including the America Bar Association, the U.S. Chamber of Commerce, AFL-CIO, UAW, League of Women Voters, Common Cause, National Federation of Independent Businesses, the ACLU, National Small Business Association, the ADA, the American Federation of Teachers, and the National Farmer's Union.

You name it, the list is long. This is another example of why we have frustrations in our society, where the people are out ahead of our leaders.

When I ask a question why should we have the direct election for President, most people look back at me and say, "Why shouldn't we?" Most people think it already exists.

All the more reason to fear the consequences when they awaken on election night or the morning after and find out that although candidate A has scored a smashing popular vote victory, because of the nuances of the electoral college system, his opponent, who may have garnered, perhaps, only 40 percent of the popular vote still, because of his concentrated effort in the large metropolitan areas, where we can elect a President of the United States by carrying 10 states, plus the District of Columbia, has turned out to be a loser who becomes the winner. The people of this country will scratch their heads and say, "It can't happen here." Let us act now so that it will not happen here.

In the 95th Congress it was cosponsored by 45 Senators, including 28 Senators from small States. It has broad support in the House where it passed by an 83-percent vote in 1969.

The direct election amendment should have been before this body years ago, but despite 43 days of hearings, including 9 in the last congress, for one reason or another, direct election has consistently been delayed in committee until floor action was virtually impossible. Now we have an opportunity to take advantage of all this study and to come to grips with the issue on the merits. I am sure that my 36 colleagues who have chosen to cosponsor the direct election amendment in the beginning of this 96th Congress join me in urging that in 1979 the time has come to replace the strange mode of Presidential election which was left to us in the last harried hours of the constitutional convention. It is time, Mr. President that we in Congress take the action that a great majority of our constituents long have supported and for which many of our colleagues have labored, and pass the direct election amendment. It is long overdue.

I invite any of my colleagues who remain yet uncertain, and who have heard varying arguments about why it is not in their interest, their State's interest, the country's interest, perhaps even the world's interest, to change the electoral process for President, to look at that strange amalgam of U.S. Senators who have joined in supporting this measure.

It is impossible to find one philosophical strain, one political strain, or one geographical strain. It is hard to convince a CLAIBORNE PELL or a JOHN CHAFEE, or a FRANK CHURCH or a JAKE GARN that the small States are going to be disadvantaged by the change. It is hard to convince JAKE JAVITS, JOHN GLENN, HOWARD METZENBAUM, CARL LEVIN that the large States are going to be disadvantaged. The fact of the matter is going to be disadvantaged if this process backfires, and the country will be served if we are successful in our efforts.[1]

---

[1] *Congressional Record.* March 14, 1979. Pages 4999–5003.

APPENDIX X: SOURCES OF INFORMATION ON THE WEB

Interstate Compacts
The National Center for Interstate Compacts (NCIC) of the Council for State Governments (CSG) maintains a web site on interstate compacts at

    http://www.csg.org/ncic/

The NCIC web site contains links to the texts of numerous interstate compacts currently in force.

Electoral College Certificates of Ascertainment
The National Archives and Records Administration (NARA) maintains a web site on the Electoral College, including the Certificates of Ascertainment from 2000, 2004, and 2008 presidential elections, at

    http://www.archives.gov/federal_register/electoral_college/
    index.html

Electoral College Maps and Political Campaign Trackers
Various newspapers and political publications have Electoral College maps and trackers of candidate travels, including:

New York Times Interactive Electoral Map

    http://elections.nytimes.com/2012/electoral-map?smid=
    tw-nytimes

New York Times Campaign Tracker

    http://politics.nytimes.com/election-guide/2008/schedules/
    pastevents/index.html#candidate1

Los Angeles Times Interactive Electoral Map

    http://www.latimes.com/news/politics/la-pn-electoral-college
    -10-states-matter-20120525,0,90732.story

Politico Campaign Tracker

    http://www.politico.com/2012-election/candidate-map/

Uniform State Laws
The National Conference of Commissioners on Uniform State Laws (NCCUSL) maintains a web site on uniform state laws at

    http://www.nccusl.org

NCCUSL is an advocate for a proposal for a uniform state law concerning faithful presidential electors.

Federal Election Commission
The web site of the Federal Election Commission (FEC) on the Electoral College is at

    http://www.fec.gov/pages/ecmenu2.htm

FairVote (formerly The Center for Voting and Democracy)

www.FairVote.org

National Popular Vote

www.NationalPopularVote.com

Every Vote Equal Web Site for This Book

www.every-vote-equal.com

APPENDIX Y: NATIONAL POPULAR VOTE BILL IN VERMONT

1   H.103

2   Introduced by Representatives Jerman of Essex, Aswad of Burlington, Atkins

3   of Winooski, Bartholomew of Hartland, Bissonnette of

4   Winooski, Bohi of Hartford, Branagan of Georgia, Burke of

5   Brattleboro, Cheney of Norwich, Consejo of Sheldon, Courcelle

6   of Rutland City, Dakin of Chester, Davis of Washington, Deen

7   of Westminster, Donahue of Northfield, Donovan of

8   Burlington, Edwards of Brattleboro, Emmons of Springfield,

9   Evans of Essex, Fisher of Lincoln, Font-Russell of Rutland

10   City, Frank of Underhill, French of Shrewsbury, French of

11   Randolph, Gilbert of Fairfax, Grad of Moretown, Haas of

12   Rochester, Head of South Burlington, Heath of Westford,

13   Hooper of Montpelier, Howrigan of Fairfield, Kitzmiller of

14   Montpelier, Klein of East Montpelier, Krebs of South Hero,

15   Kupersmith of South Burlington, Lanpher of Vergennes, Larson

16   of Burlington, Lenes of Shelburne, Lippert of Hinesburg,

17   Lorber of Burlington, Macaig of Williston, Malcolm of Pawlet,

18   Marek of Newfane, Martin of Springfield, Martin of Wolcott,

19   Masland of Thetford, McCullough of Williston, Miller of

20   Shaftsbury, Minter of Waterbury, Mitchell of Barnard, Moran

21   of Wardsboro, Mrowicki of Putney, Munger of South

VT LEG 262198.1

1   Burlington, Nease of Johnson, Nuovo of Middlebury, O'Brien

2   of Richmond, Obuchowski of Rockingham, Partridge of

3   Windham, Peltz of Woodbury, Poirier of Barre City, Potter of

4   Clarendon, Pugh of South Burlington, Ram of Burlington,

5   Shand of Weathersfield, Sharpe of Bristol, South of St.

6   Johnsbury, Spengler of Colchester, Stevens of Waterbury,

7   Stevens of Shoreham, Taylor of Barre City, Till of Jericho, Toll

8   of Danville, Waite-Simpson of Essex, Webb of Shelburne,

9   Weston of Burlington, Wilson of Manchester, Wizowaty of

10   Burlington, Wright of Burlington, Yantachka of Charlotte and

11   Young of Albany

12   Referred to Committee on

13   Date:

14   Subject: Elections; president; national popular vote; agreement among the

15   states

16   Statement of purpose: This bill proposes to adopt the Agreement Among the

17   States to Elect the President by National Popular Vote.

18   An act relating to the Agreement Among the States to Elect the President by
19   National Popular Vote

20   It is hereby enacted by the General Assembly of the State of Vermont:

VT LEG 262198.1

1   Sec. 1. 17 V.S.A. chapter 58 is added to read:

2   CHAPTER 58. AGREEMENT AMONG THE STATES TO ELECT THE

3   PRESIDENT BY NATIONAL POPULAR VOTE

4   § 2751. ARTICLE I–MEMBERSHIP

5   Any state of the United States and the District of Columbia may become a

6   member of this agreement by enacting this agreement.

7   § 2752. ARTICLE II–RIGHT OF THE PEOPLE IN MEMBER STATES TO

8   VOTE FOR PRESIDENT AND VICE PRESIDENT

9   Each member state shall conduct a statewide popular election for President

10   and Vice President of the United States.

11   § 2753. ARTICLE III–MANNER OF APPOINTING PRESIDENTIAL

12   ELECTORS IN MEMBER STATES

13   (a) Prior to the time set by law for the meeting and voting by the

14   presidential electors, the chief election official of each member state shall

15   determine the number of votes for each presidential slate in each State of the

16   United States and in the District of Columbia in which votes have been cast in

17   a statewide popular election and shall add such votes together to produce a

18   "national popular vote total" for each presidential slate.

19   (b) The chief election official of each member state shall designate the

20   presidential slate with the largest national popular vote total as the "national

21   popular vote winner."

1 (c) The presidential elector certifying official of each member state shall

2 certify the appointment in that official's own state of the elector slate

3 nominated in that state in association with the national popular vote winner.

4 (d) At least six days before the day fixed by law for the meeting and voting

5 by the presidential electors, each member state shall make a final

6 determination of the number of popular votes cast in the state for each

7 presidential slate and shall communicate an official statement of such

8 determination within 24 hours to the chief election official of each other

9 member state.

10 (e) The chief election official of each member state shall treat as conclusive

11 an official statement containing the number of popular votes in a state for each

12 presidential slate made by the day established by federal law for making a

13 state's final determination conclusive as to the counting of electoral votes by

14 Congress.

15 (f) In event of a tie for the national popular vote winner, the presidential

16 elector-certifying official of each member state shall certify the appointment of

17 the elector slate nominated in association with the presidential slate receiving

18 the largest number of popular votes within that official's own state.

19 (g) If, for any reason, the number of presidential electors nominated in a

20 member state in association with the national popular vote winner is less than

21 or greater than that state's number of electoral votes, the presidential candidate

1 on the presidential slate that has been designated as the national popular vote

2 winner shall have the power to nominate the presidential electors for that state

3 and that state's presidential elector certifying official shall certify the

4 appointment of such nominees.

5 (h) The chief election official of each member state shall immediately

6 release to the public all vote counts or statements of votes as they are

7 determined or obtained.

8 (i) This article shall govern the appointment of presidential electors in each

9 member state in any year in which this agreement is, on July 20, in effect in

10 states cumulatively possessing a majority of the electoral votes.

11 § 2754. ARTICLE IV–OTHER PROVISIONS

12 (a) This agreement shall take effect when states cumulatively possessing a

13 majority of the electoral votes have enacted this agreement in substantially the

14 same form and the enactments by such states have taken effect in each state.

15 (b) Any member state may withdraw from this agreement, except that a

16 withdrawal occurring six months or less before the end of a President's term

17 shall not become effective until a President or Vice President shall have been

18 qualified to serve the next term.

19 (c) The chief executive of each member state shall promptly notify the

20 chief executive of all other states of when this agreement has been enacted and

1   has taken effect in that official's state, when the state has withdrawn from this

2   agreement, and when this agreement takes effect generally.

3   (d) This agreement shall terminate if the electoral college is abolished.

4   (e) If any provision of this agreement is held invalid, the remaining

5   provisions shall not be affected.

6   § 2755. ARTICLE V–DEFINITIONS

7   For purposes of this agreement:

8   (1) "Chief election official" shall mean the state official or body that is

9   authorized to certify the total number of popular votes for each presidential

10   slate.

11   (2) "Chief executive" shall mean the governor of a state of the United

12   States or the mayor of the District of Columbia.

13   (3) "Elector slate" shall mean a slate of candidates who have been

14   nominated in a state for the position of presidential elector in association with a

15   presidential slate.

16   (4) "Presidential elector" shall mean an elector for President and Vice

17   President of the United States.

18   (5) "Presidential elector certifying official" shall mean the state official

19   or body that is authorized to certify the appointment of the state's presidential

20   electors.

1   (6) "Presidential slate" shall mean a slate of two persons, the first of

2   whom has been nominated as a candidate for President of the United States and

3   the second of whom has been nominated as a candidate for Vice President of

4   the United States, or any legal successors to such persons, regardless of

5   whether both names appear on the ballot presented to the voter in a particular

6   state.

7   (7) "State" shall mean a state of the United States and the District of

8   Columbia; and

9   (8) "Statewide popular election" shall mean a general election in which

10   votes are cast for presidential slates by individual voters and counted on a

11   statewide basis.

APPENDIX Z: HISTORY OF THE NATIONAL POPULAR VOTE BILL

August 8, 2011	California Governor Jerry Brown signed the National Popular Vote bill, making California the ninth jurisdiction to enact the bill, and giving the bill 49% of the electoral votes (132 out of 270) needed to bring it into effect.
June 7, 2011	The Republican-controlled New York Senate passed the National Popular Vote bill by a 47–13 margin.
April 22, 2011	Vermont Governor Peter Schumlin signed the National Popular Vote bill, making Vermont the eighth jurisdiction to enact the bill.
October 12, 2010	Mayor Adrian Fenty of the District of Columbia signed the National Popular Vote bill, making the District of Columbia the seventh jurisdiction to enact the bill.
August 4, 2010	Massachusetts Governor Deval Patrick signed the National Popular Vote bill, making Massachusetts the sixth state to enact the bill.
June 7, 2010	The Democratic-controlled New York Senate passed the National Popular Vote bill in a 52–7 roll call.
June 24, 2009	The Delaware House of Representatives passed the National Popular Vote bill.
May 12, 2009	The Connecticut House of Representatives passed the National Popular Vote bill.
April 28, 2009	Washington State Governor Chris Gregoire signed the National Popular Vote bill, making Washington the fifth state to enact the bill.
April 21, 2009	The Nevada Assembly passed the National Popular Vote bill.
March 17, 2009	The Colorado House of Representatives passed the National Popular Vote bill.
March 12, 2009	The Oregon House of Representatives passed the National Popular Vote bill.
February 20, 2009	The New Mexico House of Representatives passed the National Popular Vote bill.
December 11, 2008	The Michigan House of Representatives passed the National Popular Vote bill.
June 20, 2008	The Rhode Island House passed the National Popular Vote bill.
May 27, 2008	The Rhode Island Senate passed the National Popular Vote bill.

May 1, 2008	The National Popular Vote bill was enacted into law in Hawaii, making Washington State the fourth state to enact the bill.
April 7, 2008	Illinois Governor Rod R. Blagojevich signed the National Popular Vote bill, making Illinois the third state to enact the legislation.
April 2, 2008	The Maine Senate passed the National Popular Vote bill.
January 13, 2008	New Jersey Governor Jon Corzine signed the National Popular Vote Bill into law. New Jersey thus became the second state to enact the legislation.
May 14, 2007	The North Carolina Senate passed the National Popular Vote bill.
April 10, 2007	Maryland Governor Martin O'Malley signed the National Popular Vote bill, making Maryland the first state to enact the interstate compact entitled the "Agreement Among the States to Elect the President by National Popular Vote" proposed by National Popular Vote.
March 21, 2007	The Arkansas House passed the National Popular Vote bill.
January 24, 2007	National Popular Vote announced that its bill had sponsors in 45 states for the 2007 state legislative sessions.
April 2006	The Colorado State Senate passed the National Popular Vote bill, becoming the first legislative chamber in the country to pass the bill.
March 2006	The National Popular Vote bill was endorsed in editorials by *Chicago Sun Times*, *New York Times*, and *Minneapolis Star-Tribune*.
February 23, 2006	National Popular Vote held its initial press conference in Washington, D.C. and released the first edition of its book *Every Vote Equal: A State-Based Plan for Electing the President by National Popular Vote*. The press conference featured former Congressmen John Anderson (R-Illinois and Independent presidential candidate) and John Buchanan (R-Alabama), former Senator Birch Bayh (D-Indiana), Common Cause President Chellie Pingree, FairVote Executive Director Rob Richie, National Popular Vote President Barry Fadem, and Dr. John R. Koza, originator of the plan.

APPENDIX AA: U.S. SUPREME COURT DECISION IN *VIRGINIA V. TENNESSEE* (1893)

U.S. Supreme Court

148 U.S. 503

State of Virginia v. State of Tennessee

April 3, 1893

R. Taylor Scott, R. W. Ayers, and W. F. Rhea, for complainant.

G. W. Pickle, N. M. Taylor, Thos. Curtin, C. J. St. John, A. L. Demoss, and A. S. Colyer, for defendant.

Mr. Justice FIELD delivered the opinion of the court.

This is a suit to establish by judicial decree the true boundary line between the states of Virginia and Tennessee. It embraces a controversy of which this court has original jurisdiction, and in this respect the judicial department of our government is distinguished from the judicial department of any other country, drawing to itself by the ordinary modes of peaceful procedure the settlement of questions as to boundaries and consequent rights of soil and jurisdiction between states, possessed, for purposes of internal government, of the powers of independent communities, which otherwise might be the fruitful cause of prolonged and harassing conflicts.

The state of Virginia, as the complainant, summoning her sister state, Tennessee, to the bar of this court,—a jurisdiction to which the latter promptly yields,—sets forth in her bill the sources of her title to the territory embraced within her limits, and also of the title to the territory embraced by Tennessee.

The claim of Virginia is that by the charters of the English sovereigns, under which the colonies of Virginia and North Carolina were formed, the boundary line between them was intended and declared to be a line running due west from a point on the Atlantic ocean on the parallel of latitude 36 deg. and 30 min. N., and that the state of Tennessee, having been created out of the territory formerly constituting a part of North Carolina, the same boundary line continued between her and Virginia; and the contention of Virginia is that the boundary line claimed by Tennessee does not follow this parallel of latitude, but varies from it by running too far north, so as to unjustly include a strip of land about 113 miles in length, and varying from 2 to 8 miles in width, over which she asserts and unlawfully exercises sovereign jurisdiction.

On the other hand, the claim of Tennessee is that the boundary line, as declared in the English charters, between the colonies of Virginia and North Carolina, was run and established by commissioners appointed by Virginia and Tennessee after they became states of the Union, by Virginia in 1800, and by Tennessee in 1801, and that the line they established was subsequently approved in 1803 by the legislative action of both states, and has been recognized and acted upon as the true and real boundary between them ever since, until the commencement of this suit, a period of over 85 years; and the contention of Tennessee is that the line thus established and acted upon is not open to contestation as to its correctness at this day, but is to be held and adjudged to be the real and true boundary line between the states, even though some deviations from the line of the parallel of latitude 36 deg. and 30 min. N. may have been made by the commissioners in the measurement and demarcation of the line.

In order to clearly understand and appreciate the force and effect to be accorded to the respective claims and contentions of the parties, a brief history of preceding measures should be given, with reference to the charters and legislation under which they were taken.

On the 23d of May, 1609, James the First of England, by letters patent, reciting previous letters, gave to Robert, Earl of Salisbury, Thomas, Earl of Suffolk, and divers other persons associated with them, a charter which organized them into a corporation by the name of the 'Treasurer & Company of Adventurers & Planters of the City of London,' for the first colony of Virginia, and granted to them all those lands and territories lying 'in that part of America called 'Virginia,' from the point of land called 'Cape or Point Comfort,' along the seacoast to the northward 200 miles, and from the said point of Cape Comfort along the seacoast to the southward 200 miles, and all that space and circuit of land lying from the seacoast of the precinct aforesaid up into the land throughout, from sea to sea, west and northwest;' and 'also all the islands lying within 100 miles along the coast of both seas of the precinct aforesaid.' On the 24th of March, 1663, Charles the Second of England granted to Edward, Earl of Clarendon, and others of his subjects, all that territory within his dominion of America 'extending from the north end of the island called 'Lucke Island,' which lieth in the Southern Virginia seas, and within six and thirty degrees of the northern latitude, and to the west as far as the South seas, and so southerly as far as the river Mathias, which bordereth upon the coast of Florida, and within one and thirty degrees of northern latitude, and so west in a direct line as far as the South seas aforesaid,' and gave them full authority to organize and govern the territory granted under the name of the 'Province of Carolina.'

On the 30th of May, 1665, Charles the Second granted to the above proprietors of Carolina a charter, confirming the previous grant, and enlarging the same so as to include the following described territory: All that province and territory within America 'extending north and eastward as far as the north end of Currituck river or inlet, upon a straight westerly line to Wyonoke creek, which lies within or about the degrees of thirty-six and thirty minutes northern latitude; and so west in a direct line as far as the South seas; and south and westward so far as the degrees of twenty-nine inclusive of northern latitude; and so west in a direct line as far as the South seas.'

The northern and southern settlements of Carolina were separated from each other by nearly 300 miles, and numerous Indians resided upon the intervening territory; and, though the whole province belonged to the same proprietors, the legislation of the settlements was by different assemblies, acting at times under different governors. Early in 1700 the northern part of the province was sometimes called the 'Colony of North Carolina,' although the province was not divided by the crown into North and South Carolina until 1732. Story, Const. 137. Previously to this division the settlements on the borders of Virginia, and of what was called the 'Colony of North Carolina,' had largely increased, and disputes and altercations frequently occurred between the settlers, growing out of the unlocated boundary between the provinces. Virginians were charged with taking up lands, under titles of the crown, south of the proper limits of their province, and Carolinians were charged with taking up lands which belonged to the crown with warrants from the proprietors. The troubles arising from this source were the occasion of much disturbance to the communities, and various attempts were made by parties in authority in the two provinces to remove the cause of them. Previously to January, 1711, commissioners were appointed on the part of Virginia and North Carolina to run the boundary line between them, and proclamations were made forbidding surveys of the grounds until that line within the disputed limits should be marked. But these efforts for the settlement of the difficulties were unavailing.

In January, 1711, commissioners were again appointed, but failed, for want of the requisite means to accomplish their intended object.

In 1728 an attempt to settle the difficulties was renewed, but, as on previous occasions, it failed. The commissioners of the colonies met, but they could not agree at what place to fix the latitude 36 deg. 30 min. N., nor upon the place called 'Wyonoke,' and they broke up without doing anything. The governors of North Carolina and Virginia then entered into a convention upon the subject of the boundary between the two provinces, and transmitted it to England for approval. The king and council approved of it, and so did the lords and proprietors, and returned it to the governors to be executed. The agreement was as follows:

> 'That from the mouth of Currituck river, setting the compass on the north shore thereof, a due west line shall be run and fairly marked; and, if it happen to cut Chowan river between the mouth of Nottaway river and Wiccacon creek, then the same direct course shall be continued towards the mountains, and be ever deemed the dividing line between Virginia and Carolina; but, if the said west line cuts Chowan river to the southward of Wiccacon creek, then from that point of intersection the bounds shall be allowed to continue up the middle of Chowan river to the middle of the entrance into said Wiccacon creek, and from thence a due west line shall divide the two governments. That, if said west line cuts Blackwater river to the northward of Nottaway river, then from the point of intersection the bounds shall be allowed to be continued down the middle of said Blackwater to the middle of the entrance into said Nottaway river, and from thence a due west line shall divide the two governments.
>
> 'That, if a due west line shall be found to pass through islands, or cut out small slips of land, which might much more conveniently be included in

one province or other, by natural water bounds, in such case the persons appointed for running the line shall have the power to settle the natural bounds, provided the commissioners on both sides agree thereto, and that all variations from the west line be punctually noted on the premises or plats, which they shall return to be put upon the record of both governments.'

Commissioners were appointed by Virginia and North Carolina to carry this agreement into effect. They met at Currituck inlet in March, 1728. The variation of the compass was then found to be 3 deg. 1 min. and 2 sec. W. nearly, and the latitude 36 deg. 31 min. The dividing line between the provinces struck Blackwater 176 poles above the mouth of Nottaway. The variation of the compass at the mouth of Nottaway was 2 deg. 30 min. The line was afterwards extended to Steep Rock creek, 320 miles from the coast, by Commissioners Joshua Fry and Peter Jefferson, on the part of Virginia, and Daniel Weldon and William Churton, on the part of North Carolina.

In 1778 and 1779, Virginia and North Carolina, having become, by their separation in 1776 from the British crown, independent states, again took up the question of the boundary between them, and appointed commissioners to extend and complete the line from the point at which the previous commissioners, Fry and Jefferson and others, had ended their work, on Steep Rock creek, to Tennessee river. The commissioners undertook the work with which they were charged, but they could not find the line on Steep Rock creek, owing, as they supposed, to the large amount of timber which had decayed since it was marked. The report of their labors was signed only by the Virginia commissioners. Their report was, in substance, that after running the line as far as Carter's valley, 45 miles west of Steep Rock creek, the commissioners of Carolina conceived the idea that the line was further south than it ought to be, and, on trial, it appeared that there was a slight variation of the needle, which the Virginia commissioners thought arose from their proximity to some iron ore, that various expedients to harmonize the action of the commissioners were unavailing, and the Carolina commissioners, agreeing that they were more than two miles too far south of the proper latitude, measured off that distance directly north, and ran the line eastwardly from that place, superintended by two of the Carolina and one of the Virginia commissioners, while from the same place it was continued westwardly, superintended by the others, for the sake of expediting the business. The Virginia commissioners subsequently became satisfied that the first line run by them was correct, and they therefore continued it from Carter's valley, where it had been left, westward to Tennessee river. The North Carolina commissioners carried their line as far as Cumberland mountains, protesting against the line run by the Virginia commissioners.

This was in 1779 and 1780. The line adopted by the Virginia commissioners was known as the 'Walker Line,' and the line adopted by the commissioners of North Carolina was known as the 'Henderson Line.' Walker's line was approved by the legislature of Virginia in 1791, but it never received the approval of the legislature of Tennessee. Previously to the appointment of these commissioners, and on the 6th of May, 1776, the state of Virginia, in a general convention, with that generous public spirit which on all occasions since has characterized her conduct in the disposition of her claims to territory under different charters from the English government, had declared that the territories within the charters erecting the colonies of Maryland, Pennsylvania, North Carolina, and South Carolina were thereby ceded and forever confirmed to the people of those colonies, respectively. On the 25th of February, 1790, North Carolina ceded to the United States the territory which afterwards became the state of Tennessee, and which was admitted into the Union on the 1st of June, 1796. Subsequently the states of Virginia and Tennessee both took steps for the final settlement of the controversy as to the boundary between them. On the 10th of January, 1800, the house of delegates of the general assembly of Virginia adopted the following resolution:

> 'Whereas, it is represented to the present general assembly that the people living between what are called 'Walker's' and 'Henderson's' lines, so far as the same run between the state of Tennessee and this state, do not consider themselves under either the jurisdiction of that or this state, and therefore refuse the payment of any taxes to either of said states, or to the collectors of either for the general government, because the state of North Carolina, on the 25th of February, 1790, ceded the said state of Tennessee, then called the 'Southwestern Territory,' to the government of the United States; and therefore the act entitled 'An act concerning the southern boundary of this state,' passed on the 7th of December, 1791, in this legislature, to establish the line commonly called 'Walker's Line' as the boundary between North Carolina and this state, could only bind the state of North Carolina as far as her territorial limits extended on the line of this state, and could not bind the said Southwestern Territory, which had previously been conveyed, as aforesaid; and

> 'Whereas, since the said cession, the general government hath erected the said Southwestern Territory into an independent state, by their act, June 1st, 1796, whereby it has become the duty of the said state of Tennessee and of this state to settle all differences between them with respect to the said boundary line:

> 'Resolved, therefore, that the executive be authorized and requested to appoint three commissioners, whose duty it shall be to meet commissioners to be appointed by the state of Tennessee, to settle and adjust all differences concerning the said boundary line, and to establish the one or the other of the said lines, as the case may be, or to run any other line which may be agreed on, for settling the same; and that the executive be also re-

quested to transmit a copy of this resolution to the executive authority of the state of Tennessee.'

On the 13th of January, 1800, this resolution was agreed to by the senate.

On the 13th day of November, 1801, the general assembly of Tennessee passed an act on the same subject, the first section of which is these words:

'Be it enacted by the general assembly of the state of Tennessee, that the governor, for the time being, is hereby authorized and required, as soon as may be convenient after the passing of this act, to appoint three commissioners on the part of this state, one of whom shall be a mathematician capable of taking latitude, who, when so appointed, are hereby authorized and empowered, or a majority of them, to act in conjunction with such commissioners as are or may be appointed by the state of Virginia to settle and designate a true line between the aforesaid states.'

The second section is as follows:

'And whereas, it may be difficult for this legislature to ascertain with precision what powers ought of right to be delegated to the said commissioners: Therefore,

'Be it enacted, that the governor is hereby authorized and required, from time to time, to issue such power to the commissioners as he may deem proper for the purpose of carrying into effect the object intended by this act, consistent with the true interest of the state.'

On the 22d day of January, 1803, a report having been made by the commissioners, which is copied into the act, the legislature of Virginia ratified what had been done in the following act:

'Whereas, the commissioners appointed to ascertain and adjust the boundary line between this state and the state of Tennessee, in conformity to the resolution passed by the legislature of this state for that purpose, have proceeded to the execution of that business, and made a report thereof in the words following, to wit: "The commissioners for ascertaining and adjusting the boundary line between the states of Virginia and Tennessee appointed pursuant to public authority on the part of each, namely, General Joseph Martin, Creed Taylor, and Peter Johnson, for the former, and Moses Fisk, General John Sevier, and General George Rutledge, for the latter, having met at the place previously appointed for that purpose, and not uniting, from the general result of their astronomical observations, to establish either of the former lines called 'Walker's' and 'Henderson's,' unanimously agreed, in order to end all controversy respecting the subject, to run a due west line equally distant from both, beginning on the summit of the mountain generally known by the name of 'White Top Mountain,' where the northeastern corner of Tennessee terminates, to the top of Cumberland mountain, where the southwestern corner of Virginia terminates, which is hereby declared to be the true boundary line between the said states, and has been accordingly run by Brice Martin and Nathan B. Markland, the surveyors duly appointed for that purpose, and marked under the directions of the said commissioners, as will more at large appear by the report of the said surveyors, hereto annexed, and bearing equal date herewith.

"(2) And the said commissioners do further unanimously agree to recommend to their respective states that individuals having claims or titles to lands on either side of the said line, as now fixed and agreed on, and between the lines aforesaid, shall not, in consequence thereof, in anywise be prejudiced or affected thereby; and that the legislatures of their respective states should pass mutual laws to render all such claims or titles secure to the owners thereof.

"(3) And the said commissioners do further agree unanimously to recommend to their states, respectively, that reciprocal laws should be passed confirming the acts of all public officers, whether magistrates, sheriffs, coroners, surveyors, or constables, between the said lines, which would have been legal in either of the said states had no difference of opinion existed about the true boundary line.

"(4) This agreement shall be of no effect until ratified by the legislatures of the states aforesaid. Given under our hands and seals, at William Robertson's, near Cumberland Gap, December the eighth, eighteen hundred and two. (Dec. 8th, 1802.)

"Jos. Martin. [L. S.]
"Creed Taylor. [L. S.]
"Peter Johnson. [L. S.]
"John Sevier. [L. S.]
"Moses Fisk. [L. S.]
"George Rutledge. [L. S.]'

'(5) And whereas, Brice Martin and Nathan B. Markland, the surveyors duly appointed to run and mark the said line, have granted their certificate of the execution of their duties, which certificate is in the words following, to wit: 'The undersigned surveyors, having been fully appointed to run the boundary line between the states of Virginia and Tennessee, as directed by the commissioners for that purpose, have agreeably to their orders run the same, beginning on the summit of the White Top mountain, at the termination of the northeastern corner of the state of Tennessee, a due west course to the top of the Cumberland mountains, where the southwestern corner of Virginia terminates, keeping at an equal distance from the lines called 'Walker's' and 'Henderson's,' and have had the new line run as aforesaid marked with five chops, in the form of a diamond, as directed by the said commissioners. Given under our hands and seals, this eighth day of December, eighteen hundred and two. (8th December, 1802.)

"B. Martin. [L. S.]
"Nat. B. Markland. [L. S.]

'And it is deemed proper and expedient that the said boundary line, so fixed and ascertained as aforesaid, should be established and confirmed on the part of this commonwealth:

'(6) Be it therefore enacted by the general assembly of the commonwealth of Virginia, that said boundary line between this state and the state of Tennessee, as laid down, fixed, and ascertained by the said commissioners above named in their said report above recited, shall be, and is hereby, fully and absolutely, to all intents and purposes whatsoever, ratified, established, and confirmed on the part of this commonwealth as the true, certain, and real boundary line between the said states.

'(7) All claims or titles derived from the government of North Carolina or Tennessee which said lands, by the adjustment and establishment of the line aforesaid, have fallen into this state, shall remain as secure to the owners thereof as if derived from the government of Virginia, and shall not be in any wise prejudiced or affected in consequence of the establishment of the said line.

'(8) The acts of all public officers, whether magistrates, sheriffs, coroners, surveyors, or constables, heretofore done or performed in that portion of the territory between the lines called 'Walker's' and 'Henderson's' lines which has fallen into this state by the adjustment of the present line, and which would have been legal if done or performed in the states of North Carolina or Tennessee, are hereby recognized and confirmed.

'(9) This act shall commence and be in force from and after the passing of a like law on the part of the state of Tennessee.'

And on the 3d of November, 1803, Tennessee passed the following ratifying act:

'Whereas, the commissioners appointed to settle and designate the true boundary between this state and the state of Virginia, in conformity to the act passed by the legislature of this state for the purpose, on the thirteenth day of November, one thousand eight hundred and one, have proceeded to the execution of said business, and made a report thereof in the words following, to wit:

'[Here follows the report named in the Virginia act.]

'And it is deemed proper and expedient that the said boundary line, so fixed and ascertained as aforesaid, should be established and confirmed on the part of this state:

'(1) Be it enacted by the general assembly of the state of Tennessee, that the said boundary line between this state and the state of Virginia, as laid down, fixed, and ascertained by the said commissioners above named in their said report above recited, shall be, and is hereby, fully and absolutely, to all intents and purposes whatsoever, ratified, established, and confirmed on the part of this state as the true, certain, and real boundary line between the said states.

'(2) Be it enacted, that all claims or titles to lands derived from the government of Virginia, which said lands, by the adjustment and establishment of the line aforesaid have fallen into this state, shall remain as secure to the owners thereof as if derived from the government of North Carolina or Tennessee, and shall not be in anywise prejudiced or affected in consequence of the establishment of the said line.

'(3) Be it enacted, that the acts of all officers, whether magistrates, sheriffs, coroners, surveyors, or constables, heretofore done or performed in that portion of territory between the lines called 'Walker's' and 'Henderson's' lines which has fallen into this state by the adjustment of the present line, and which would have been legal if done or performed in the state of Virginia, are hereby recognized and confirmed.'

This line thus run was accepted by both states as a satisfactory settlement of a controversy which had, under their governments and that of the colonies which preceded them, lasted for nearly a century. As seen from the acts recited, both states, through their legislatures, declared in the most solemn and authoritative manner that it was fully and absolutely ratified, established, and confirmed as the true, certain, and real boundary line between them; and this declaration could not have been more significant had it added, in express terms, what was plainly implied, that it should never be departed from by the government of either, but be respected, maintained, and enforced by the governments of both. All modes of legislative action which followed it indicated its approval. Each state asserted jurisdiction on its side up to the line designated, and recognized the lawful jurisdiction of the adjoining state up to the line on the opposite side. Both states levied taxes on the lands on their respective sides, and granted franchises to the people resident thereon. The people on the south side voted at state and municipal elections for representatives and officers of Tennessee, and the people on the north side at such state and municipal elections voted for representatives and officers of Virginia. The courts of the two states exercised jurisdiction, civil and criminal, on their respective side, and enforced their process up to that line; and the legislation of congress, in the designation of districts for the jurisdiction of courts, and in prescribing limits for collection districts and for purposes of election, made no exception to the boundary as thus established. 12 St. pp. 432, 433.

The line was marked with great care by the commissioners of the states, with five chops on the trees, in the form of a diamond, at such intervals between them as they deemed sufficient to identify and trace the line. Not a whisper of fraud or misconduct is made by either side against the commissioners for the conclusions they reached and the line they established. It is true that in the year 1856 (54 years after the line was thus settled) Virginia, reciting that the line as marked by the commissioners in 1802 had, by lapse of time, the improvement of the country, natural waste and destruction, and other causes, become indistinct, uncertain, and to some extent unknown, so that many inconveniences and difficulties occurred between the citizens of the respective states, and in the administration of their governments, passed an act for the appointment of commissioners, to meet commissioners to be appointed by Tennessee, to again run and mark said line, not to run and mark a new line; and provided that where there was no growing timber on any part of the line by which it might be plainly marked, if the old marks were gone, the commissioners should cause monuments of stone to be permanently planted on the line, at least one at every five miles or less, where it might seem best to the commissioners to do so, that the line might be readily identified for its entire length. The whole purpose of the act, as is evident on its face, was not to change the old boundary line, but only to more perfectly identify it. Tennessee responded to that invitation, and appointed commissioners to act with those from Virginia. The commissioners together re-ran and re-marked the line as it was established in 1802, and planted such additional monuments as were deemed necessary; and they reported to their respective legislatures that they had 'accurately run, re-marked, and measured the old line of 1802, with all its offsets and irregularities as shown in the surveyor's report' therein incorporated, and on the accompanying map therewith submitted. The legislature of Tennessee approved of the action of the commissioners, but Virginia withheld her approval and called for a new appointment of commissioners to re-run and re-mark the line, which was refused by Tennessee as unnecessary. No complaint as to the correctness of the line run and established in 1802 was made by Virginia until within a recent period. She now by her bill asks that the compact entered into between her and the state of Tennessee, as set forth in the act of the general assembly of Virginia of January 22, 1803, and which became operative by similar action of the legislature of Tennessee on the 3d of November following, be declared null and void, as having been entered into between the states without the consent of congress; and prays that this court will establish the true boundary line between those states due east and west, in latitude 36 deg. and 30 min. N., in accordance with what it alleges to be the ancient chartered rights of that commonwealth, and the laws creating the state of Tennessee and admitting it into the Union.

The constitution provides that 'no state shall, without the consent of congress, lay any duty of tonnage, keep troops or ships of war in time of peace, enter into any agreement or compact with another state or with a foreign power, or engage in war, unless actually invaded, or in such imminent danger as will not admit of delay.'

Is the agreement, made without the consent of congress, between Virginia and Tennessee, to appoint commissioners to run and mark the boundary line between them, within the prohibition of this clause? The terms 'agreement' or 'compact,' taken by themselves, are sufficiently comprehensive to embrace all forms of stipulation, written or verbal, and relating to all kinds of subjects; to those to which the United States can have no possible objection or have any interest in interfering with, as well as to those which may tend to increase and build up the political influence of the contracting states, so as to encroach upon or impair the supremacy of the United States, or interfere with their rightful management of particular subjects placed under their entire control.

There are many matters upon which different states may agree that can in no respect concern the United States. If, for instance, Virginia should come into possession and ownership of a small parcel of land in New York, which the latter state might desire to acquire as a site for a public building, it would hardly be deemed essential for the latter state to obtain the consent of congress before it could make a valid agreement with Virginia for the purchase of the land. If Massachusetts, in forwarding its exhibits to the World's Fair at Chicago, should desire to transport them a part of the distance over the Erie canal, it would hardly be deemed essential for that state to obtain the consent of congress before it could contract with New York for the transportation of the exhibits through that state in that way. If the bordering line of two states should cross some malarious and disease-producing district, there could be no possible reason, on any conceivable public grounds, to obtain the consent of congress for the bordering states to agree to unite in draining the district, and thus removing the cause of disease. So, in case of threatened invasion of cholera, plague, or other causes of sickness and death, it would be the height of absurdity to hold that the threatened states could not unite in providing means to prevent and repel the invasion of the pestilence without obtaining the consent of congress, which might not be at the time in session. If, then, the terms 'compact' or 'agreement' in the constitution do not apply to every possible compact or agreement between one state and another, for the validity of which the consent of congress must be obtained, to what compacts or agreements does the constitution apply? We can only reply by looking at the object of the constitutional provision, and construing the terms 'agreement' and 'compact' by reference to it. It is a familiar rule in the construction of terms to apply to them the meaning naturally attaching to them from their context. 'Noscitur a sociis' is a rule of construction applicable to all written instruments. Where any particular word is obscure or of doubtful meaning, taken by itself, its obscurity or doubt may be removed by reference to associated words; and the meaning of a term may be enlarged or restrained by reference to the object of the whole clause in which it is used.

Looking at the clause in which the terms 'compact' or 'agreement' appear, it is evident that the prohibition is directed to the formation of any combination tending to the increase of political power in the states, which may encroach upon or interfere with the just supremacy of the United States. Story, in his Commentaries, (section 1403,) referring to a previous part of the same section of the constitution in which the clause in question appears, observes that its language 'may be more plausibly interpreted from the terms used, 'treaty, alliance, or confederation,' and upon the ground that the sense of each is best known by its association ('noscitur a sociis') to apply to treaties of a political character; such as treaties of alliance for purposes of peace and war, and treaties of confederation, in which the parties are leagued for mutual government, political co-operation, and the exercise of political sovereignty, and treaties of cession of sovereignty, or conferring internal political jurisdiction, or external political dependence, or general commercial privileges;' and that 'the latter clause, 'compacts and agreement,' might then very properly apply to such as regarded what might be deemed mere private rights of sovereignty; such as questions of boundary, interests in land situate in the territory of each other, and other internal regulations for the mutual comfort and convenience of states bordering on each other.' And he adds: 'In such cases the consent of congress may be properly required, in order to check any infringement of the rights of the national government; and, at the same time, a total prohibition to enter any compact or agreement might be attended with permanent inconvenience or public mischief.

Compacts or agreements—and we do not perceive any difference in the meaning, except that the word 'compact' is generally used with reference to more formal and serious engagements than is usually implied in the term 'agreement'—cover all stipulations affecting the conduct or claims of the parties. The mere selection of parties to run and designate the boundary line between two states, or to designate what line should be run, of itself imports no agreement to accept the line run by them, and such action of itself does not come within the prohibition. Nor does a legislative declaration, following such line, that is correct, and shall thereafter be deemed the true and established line, import by itself a contract or agreement with the adjoining state. It is a legislative declaration which the state and individuals affected by the recognized boundary line may invoke against the state as an admission, but not as a compact or agreement. The legislative declaration will take the form of an agreement or compact when it recites some consideration for it from the other party affected by it; for example, as made upon a similar declaration of the border or contracting state. The mutual declarations may then be reasonably treated as made upon mutual considerations. The compact or agreement will then be within the prohibition of the constitution, or without it, according as the establishment of the boundary line may lead or not to the increase of the political power or influence of the states affected, and thus encroach or not upon the full and free exercise of federal authority. If the boundary established is so run as to cut off an important and valuable portion of a state, the political power of the state enlarged would be affected by the settlement of the boundary; and to an agreement for the running of such a boundary, or rather for its adoption afterwards, the consent of congress may well be required. But the running of a boundary may have no effect upon the political influence of either state; it may simply serve to mark and define that which actually existed before, but was undefined and unmarked. In that case the agreement for the running of the line, or its actual survey, would in no respect displace the relation of either of the states to the general government. There was, therefore, no compact or agreement between the states in this case which required, for its validity, the consent of congress, within the meaning of the constitution, until they had passed upon the report of the commissioners, ratified their action, and mutually declared the boundary established by them to be the true and real boundary between the states. Such ratification was mutually made by each state in consideration of the ratification of the other.

The constitution does not state when the consent of congress shall be given, whether it shall precede or may follow the compact made, or whether it shall be express or may be implied. In many cases the consent will usually precede the compact or agreement, as where it is to lay a duty of tonnage, to keep troops or ships of war in time of peace, or to engage in war. But where the agreement relates to a matter which could not well be considered until its nature is fully developed, it is not perceived why the consent may not be subsequently given. Story says that the consent may be implied, and is always to be implied when congress adopts the particular act by sanctioning its objects and aiding in enforcing them; and observes that where a state is admitted into the Union, notoriously upon a compact made between it and the state of which it previously composed a part, there the act of congress admitting such state into the Union is an implied consent to the terms of the compact. Knowledge by congress of the boundaries of a state and of its political subdivisions may reasonably be presumed, as much of its legislation is affected by them, such as relate to the territorial jurisdiction of the courts of the United States, the extent of their collection districts, and of districts in which process, civil and criminal, of their courts may be served and enforced.

In the present case the consent of congress could not have preceded the execution of the compact, for until the line was run it could not be known where it would lie, and whether or not it would receive the approval of the states. The preliminary agreement was not to accept a line run, whatever it might be, but to receive from the commissioners designated a report as to the line which might be run and established by them. After its consideration each state was free to take such action as it might judge expedient upon their report. The approval by congress of the compact entered into between the states upon their ratification of the action of their commissioners is fairly implied from its subsequent legislation and proceedings. The line established was treated by that body as the true boundary between the states in the assignment of territory north of it as a portion of districts set apart for judicial and revenue purposes in Virginia, and as included in territory in which federal elections were to be held, and for which appointments were to be made by federal authority in that state, and in the assignment of territory south of it as a portion of districts set apart for judicial and revenue purposes in Tennessee, and as included in territory in which federal elections were to be held, and for which federal appointments were to be made for that state. Such use of the territory on different sides of the boundary designated in a single instance would not, perhaps, be considered as absolute proof of the assent or approval of congress to the boundary line; but the exercise of jurisdiction by congress over the country as a part of Tennessee on one side, and as a part of Virginia on the other, for a long succession of years, without question or dispute from any quarter, furnishes as conclusive proof of assent to it by that body as can usually be obtained from its most formal proceedings.

Independently of any effect due to the compact as such, a boundary line between the states or provinces, as between private persons, which has been run out, located, and marked upon the earth, and afterwards recognized and acquiesced in by the parties for a long course of years, is conclusive, even if it be ascertained that it varies somewhat from the courses given in the original grant; and the line so established takes effect, not as an alienation of territory, but as a definition of the true and ancient boundary. Lord Hardwicke, in *Penn v. Lord Baltimore*, 1 Ves. Sr. 444, 448; *Boyd v. Graves*, 4 Wheat. 513; *Rhode Island v. Massachusetts*, 12 Pet. 657, 734; *U.S. v. Stone*, 2 Wall. 525, 537; *Kellogg v. Smith*, 7 Cush. 375, 382; *Chenery v. Waltham*, 8 Cush. 327; Hunt, Bound. (3d Ed.) 306.

As said by this court in the recent case of the *State of Indiana v. Kentucky*, 136 U.S. 479, 516, 10 S. Sup. Ct. Rep. 1051, it is a principle of public law, universally recognized, that long acquiescence in the possession of territory, and in the exercise of dominion and sovereignty over it, is conclusive of the nation's title and rightful authority. In the case of *Rhode Island v. Massachusetts*, 4 How. 591, 639, this court, speaking of the long possession of Massachusetts, and the delays in alleging any mistake in the action of the commissioners of the colonies, said: 'Surely this, connected with the lapse of time, must remove all doubts as to the right of the respondent under the agreements of 1711 and 1718. No human transactions are unaffected by time. Its influence is seen on all things subject to change; and this is peculiarly the case in regard to matters which rest in memory, and which consequently fade with the lapse of time, and fall with the lives of individuals. For the security of rights, whether of states or individuals, long possession under a claim of title is protected; and there is no controversy in which this great principle may be invoked with greater justice and propriety than in a case of disputed boundary.'

Vattel, in his Law of Nations, speaking on this subject, says: 'The tranquility of the people, the safety of states, the happiness of the human race, do not allow that the possessions, empire, and other rights of nations should remain uncertain, subject to dispute and ever ready to occasion bloody wars. Between nations, therefore, it becomes necessary to admit prescription founded on length of time as a valid and incontestable title.' Book 2, c. 11, 149. And Wheaton, in his International Law, says: 'The writers on natural law have questioned how far that peculiar species of presumption, arising from the lapse of time, which is called 'prescription,' is justly applicable as between nation and nation; but the constant and approved practice of nations shows that, by whatever name it be called, the uninterrupted possession of territory or other property for a certain length of time by one state excludes the claim of every other in the same manner as, by the law of nature and the municipal code of every civilized nation, a similar possession by an individual excludes the claim of every other person to the article of property in question.' Part 2, c. 4, 164.

There are also moral considerations which should prevent any disturbance of long recognized boundary lines,—considerations springing from regard to the natural sentiments and affections which grow up for places on which persons have long resided; the attachments to country, to home, and to family, on which is based all that is dearest and most valuable in life.

Notwithstanding the legislative declaration of Virginia in 1803 that the line marked by the joint commissioners of the two states was ratified as the true and real boundary between them, and the repeated reaffirmation of the same declaration in her laws since that date, notably in the Code of 1858, in the Code of 1860, and in the Code of 1887; notwithstanding that the state has in various modes attested to the correctness of the boundary, by solemn affirmations in terms, by legislation, in the administration of its government, in the levy of taxes and the election of officers, and in its acquiescence for over 85 years, embracing nearly the lives of three generations,—she now, by her bill, seeks to throw aside the obligation from her legislative declaration, because, as alleged, not made upon the express consent in terms of congress, although such consent has been indicated by long acquiescence in the assumption of the validity of the proceedings resulting in the establishment of the boundary, and to have a new boundary line between Virginia and Tennessee established running due east and west on latitude 36 deg. 30 min. N. But to this position there is, in addition to what has already been said, a conclusive answer in the language of this court in *Poole v. Fleeger*, 11 Pet. 185, 209. In that case Mr. Justice Story, after observing that 'it is a part of the general right of sovereignty belonging to independent nations to establish and fix the disputed boundaries between their respective territories, and the boundaries so established and fixed by compact between nations become conclusive upon all the subjects and citizens thereof, and bind their rights, and are to be treated, to all intents and purposes, as the true and real boundary,' adds: 'This is a doctrine universally recognized in the law and practice of nations. It is a right equally belonging to the states of this Union, unless it has been surrendered under the constitution of the United States. So far from there being any pretense of such a general surrender of the right, it is expressly recognized by the constitution, and guarded in its exercise by a single limitation or restriction, requiring the consent of congress.' The constitution in imposing this limitation plainly admits that with such consent a compact as to boundaries may be made between two states; and it follows that when thus made it has full validity, and all the terms and conditions of it are equally obligatory upon the citizens of both states.

The compact in this case, having received the consent of congress, though not in express terms, yet impliedly, subsequently, which is equally effective, became obligatory and binding upon all the citizens of both Virginia and Tennessee. Nor is it any objection that there may have been errors in the demarcation of the line which the states thus by their compact sanctioned. After such compacts have been adhered to from years, neither party can be absolved from them upon showing errors, mistakes, or misapprehension of their terms, or in the line established; and this is a complete and perfect answer to complainant's position in this case.

It may also be stated that if the work of the joint commissioners, under the laws of 1800 and 1801, approved by the legislative action of both states in 1803, could be left out of consideration, and a new line run, it would not follow that the parallel of latitude 36 deg. 30 min. N. would be strictly followed. The charter of Charles the Second designates the northern boundary line of the province of North Carolina as extending from Currituck river or inlet upon a straight westerly line to Wyonoke creek, which lies within or about 36 deg. 30 min. N. latitude, from which it is evident that that parallel was only to be the general direction of the line, not one to be strictly and always followed without any variations from it. The purpose of the declaration in the charter of Charles the Second was only that the northern boundary line was to be run in the neighborhood of that parallel. The condition of the country at the time the charter was granted (1665) would have made the running of a boundary line strictly on that parallel a matter of great difficulty, if not impossible. Nor did the needs of grantor or chartered proprietors call for any such strict adherence to the parallel of latitude designated. That neither party expected it is evident from the agreement made between the governors of Virginia and North Carolina as to running the boundary line between them, and sent to England for approval by the king and council. That agreement provided that, if the west line run should be found to pass through islands or to cut small slips of land, which might much more conveniently be included in one province than the other by natural water bounds, in such case the persons appointed to run the line should have power to settle natural water bounds, provided the commissioners on both sides agreed, and that all variations from the west line should be noted on the premises, or on plats which they should return, to be put on record by both governors. A possible—indeed, a probable—variation from the line of the parallel of latitude, or the straight line, designated, was contemplated by both Virginia and Tennessee. With full knowledge of the line actually designated, and of the ancient charter to Carolina, and of the description in the constitution of Tennessee, in appointing the joint commissioners, they provided that they should settle and adjust all differences concerning the boundary line, and establish either the Walker or Henderson line, or run any other line which might be agreed on for settling the same; and that means any line run and measured with or without deviations from time to time from a straight line, or the line of latitude mentioned as might in their judgment be most convenient as the proper boundary for both states. It was made with numerous variations from a straight line, and from the line of the designated parallel of latitude for the convenience of the two states, and, with the full knowledge of both, was ratified, established, and confirmed as the true, certain, and real boundary line between them. And when, 56 years afterwards, in consequence of the line thus marked becoming indistinct, it was re-run and re-marked, by new commissioners under the directions of the statutes of 1800 and 1801, in strict conformity with the old line. The compact of the two states establishing the line adopted by their commissioners, and to which congress impliedly assented after its execution, is binding upon both states and their citizens. Neither can be heard at this date to say that it was entered into upon any misapprehension of facts. No treaty, as said by this court, has been held void on the ground of misapprehension of facts, by either or both of the parties. *Rhode Island v. Massachusetts*, 4 How. 635.

The general testimony, with hardly a dissent, is that the old line of 1802 can be readily traced throughout its whole length; and, moreover, that line has been recognized by all the residents near it, except those in the triangle at Denton's valley and in another district of small dimensions, in which it is stated that the people have voted as citizens of Virginia, and have recognized themselves as citizens of that state. That fact, however, cannot affect the potency and conclusiveness of the compact between the states by which the line was established in 1803. The small number of citizens whose expectations will be disappointed by being included in Tennessee are secured in all their rights of property by provisions of the compact passed especially for the protection of their claims.

Some observations were made upon the argument of the case upon the propriety and necessity, if the line established in 1803 be sustained, of having it re-run and re-marked, so as hereafter to be more readily identified and traced. But a careful examination of the testimony of the numerous witnesses in the case (most of them residing in the neighborhood of the boundary line) as to the marks and identification of the line originally established in 1802, and re-run and re-marked in 1859, satisfy us that no new marking of the line is required for its ready identification. The commissioners appointed under the act of Virginia of 1856, and under the act of Tennessee of 1858, found all the old marks upon the trees in the forest through which the line established ran, in the form of a diamond; and whenever they were indistinct, or, in the judgment of the commissioners, too far removed from each other, new marks were made upon the trees, or, if no trees were found at particular places to be marked, monuments in stone were planted. Besides this, the state of Virginia does not ask that the line agreed upon in 1803 shall be re-run or re-marked, but prays that a new boundary line be run on the line of 36 deg. 30 min. Tennessee does not ask that the line of 1803 be re-run or re-marked. Nevertheless, under the prayer of Virginia for general relief, there can be no objection to the restoration of any marks which may be found to have been obliterated or become indistinct upon the line as herein defined.

Our judgment, therefore, is that the boundary line established by the states of Virginia and Tennessee by the compact of 1803 is the true boundary between them, and that, on a proper application, based upon a showing that any marks for the identification of that line have been obliterated or have become indistinct, an order may be made at any time during the present term for the restoration of such marks without any change of the line. A decree will therefore be entered declaring and adjudging that the boundary line established between the states of Virginia and Tennessee by the compact of 1803 is the real, certain, and true boundary between the said states, and that the prayer of the complainant to have the said compact set aside and annulled, and to have a new boundary line run between them on the parallel of 36 deg. 30 min. N. latitude should be and is denied, at the cost of the complainant.

And it is so ordered.

U.S. Supreme Court
434 U.S. 452
U.S. Steel v. Multistate Tax Commission
February 21, 1978

The Multistate Tax Compact was entered into by a number of States for the stated purposes of (1) facilitating proper determination of state and local tax liability of multistate taxpayers; (2) promoting uniformity and compatibility in state tax systems; (3) facilitating taxpayer convenience and compliance in the filing of tax returns and in other phases of tax administration; and (4) avoiding duplicative taxation. To these ends, the Compact created the appellee Multistate Tax Commission. Each member State is authorized to request that the Commission perform an audit on its behalf, and the Commission may seek compulsory process in aid of its auditing power in the courts of any State specifically permitting such procedure. Individual States retain complete control over all legislative and administrative action affecting tax rates, the composition of the tax base, and the means and methods of determining tax liability and collecting any taxes due. Each member State is free to adopt or reject the Commission's rules and regulations, and to withdraw from the Compact at any time. Appellants, on behalf of themselves and all other multistate taxpayers threatened with Commission audits, brought this action in District Court against appellees (the Commission, its members, and its Executive Director) challenging the constitutionality of the Compact on the grounds, *inter alia*, that (1) it is invalid under the Compact Clause of the Constitution (which provides: "No State shall, without the Consent of Congress, . . . enter into any Agreement or Compact with another State"); (2) it unreasonably burdens interstate commerce; and (3) it violates the rights of multistate taxpayers under the Fourteenth Amendment. A three-judge court granted summary judgment for appellees. Held:

"1. The Multistate Tax Compact is not invalid under the rule of *Virginia v. Tennessee*, 148 U.S. 503, 519, that the application of the Compact Clause is limited to agreements that are 'directed to the formation of any combination tending to the increase of political power in the States, which may encroach upon or interfere with the just supremacy of the United States.' Pp. 459–478.

"(a) The Compact's multilateral nature and its establishment of an ongoing administrative body do not, standing alone, present significant potential for conflict with the principles underlying the Compact Clause. The number of parties to an agreement is irrelevant if it does not impermissibly enhance state power at the expense of federal supremacy, and the powers delegated to the administrative body must also be judged in terms of such enhancement. P. 472.

"(b) Under the test of whether the particular compact enhances state power *quoad* the Federal Government, this Compact does not purport to authorize member States to exercise any powers they could not exercise in its absence, nor is there any delegation of sovereign power to the Commission, each State being free to adopt or reject the Commission's rules and regulations and to withdraw from the Compact at any time. Pp. 472–473.

"(c) Appellants' various contentions that certain procedures and requirements of the Commission encroach upon federal supremacy with respect to interstate commerce and foreign relations and impair the sovereign rights of nonmember States, are without merit, primarily because each member State could adopt similar procedures and requirements individually without regard to the Compact. Even if state power is enhanced to some degree, it is not at the expense of federal supremacy. Pp. 473–478.

"2. Appellants' allegations that the Commission has abused its powers by harassing members of the plaintiff class in that it induced several States to issue burdensome requests for production of documents and to deviate from state law by issuing arbitrary assessments against taxpayers who refuse to comply with such orders, do not establish that the Compact violates the Commerce Clause or the Fourteenth Amendment. But even if such allegations were supported by the record, they are irrelevant to the facial validity of the Compact, it being only the individual State, not the Commission, that has the power to issue an assessment, whether arbitrary or not. Pp. 478–479.

"417 F. Supp. 795, affirmed."

POWELL, J., delivered the opinion of the Court, in which BURGER, C. J., and BRENNAN, STEWART, MARSHALL, REHNQUIST, and STEVENS, J., joined. WHITE, J., filed a dissenting opinion, in which BLACKMUN, J., joined, post, p. 479.

Erwin N. Griswold argued the cause for appellants. With him on the briefs were Thomas McGanney, Richard A. Hoppe, and Todd B. Sollis.

William D. Dexter argued the cause for appellees. With him on the brief was Samuel N. Greenspoon.*

MR. JUSTICE POWELL delivered the opinion of the Court.

---

* A brief of amici curiae urging affirmance was filed for their respective States by William J. Baxley, Attorney General of Alabama; Bruce E. Babbitt, Attorney General of Arizona; Carl R. Ajello, Attorney General of Connecticut; Robert L. Shevin, Attorney General of Florida; Arthur K. Bolton, Attorney General of Georgia; William J. Scott, Attorney General of Illinois; Francis B. Burch, Attorney General of Maryland; Francis X. Bellotti, Attorney General of Massachusetts; Rufus L. Edmisten, Attorney General of North Carolina; Warren R. Spannaus, Attorney General of Minnesota; Brooks McLemore, Attorney General of Tennessee; Chauncey H. Browning, Jr., Attorney General of West Virginia; and for the State of Louisiana by David Dawson.

John H. Larson filed a brief for the County of Los Angeles as amicus curiae.

The Compact Clause of Art. I, 10, cl. 3, of the Constitution provides: "No State shall, without the Consent of Congress, . . . enter into any Agreement or Compact with another State, or with a foreign Power. . . ." The Multistate Tax Compact, which established the Multistate Tax Commission, has not received congressional approval. This appeal requires us to decide whether the Compact is invalid for that reason. We also are required to decide whether it impermissibly encroaches on congressional power under the Commerce Clause and whether it operates in violation of the Fourteenth Amendment.

I

The Multistate Tax Compact was drafted in 1966 and became effective, according to its own terms, on August 4, 1967, after seven States had adopted it. By the inception of this litigation in 1972, 21 States had become members.[1] Its formation was a response to this Court's decision in *Northwestern States Portland Cement Co. v. Minnesota,* 358 U.S. 450 (1959), and the congressional activity that followed in its wake.

In *Northwestern States,* this Court held that net income from the interstate operations of a foreign corporation may be subjected to state taxation, provided that the levy is nondiscriminatory and is fairly apportioned to local activities that form a sufficient nexus to support the exercise of the taxing power. This prompted Congress to enact a statute, Act of Sept. 14, 1959, Pub. L. 86-272, 73 Stat. 555, which sets forth certain minimum standards for the exercise of that power.[2] It also authorized a study for the purpose of recommending legislation establishing uniform standards to be observed by the States in taxing income of interstate businesses. Although the results of the study were published in 1964 and 1965,[3] Congress has not enacted any legislation dealing with the subject.[4]

---

[1] Those States were: Alaska, Alaska Stat. Ann. 43.19.010 (1977); Arkansas, Ark. Stat. Ann. 84-4101 (Supp. 1977); Colorado, Colo. Rev. Stat. 24-60-1301 (1973); Florida, Fla. Stat. 213.15 (1971); Haw. Rev. Stat. 255-1 (Supp. 1976); Idaho, Idaho Code 63-3701 (1976); Illinois, Ill. Rev. Stat., ch. 120, 871 (1973); Indiana, Ind. Code 6-8-9-101 (1972); Kansas, Kan. Stat. Ann. 79-4301 (1969); Michigan, Mich. Comp. Laws 205.581 (1970); Missouri, Mo. Rev. Stat. 32.200 (1969); Montana, Mont. Rev. Codes Ann. 84-6701 (Supp. 1977); Nebraska, Neb. Rev. Stat. 77-2901 (1943); Nevada, Nev. Rev. Stat. 376.010 (1973); New Mexico, N. M. Stat. Ann. 72-15A-37 (Supp. 1975); North Dakota, N. D. Cent. Code 57-59-01 (1972); Oregon, Ore. Rev. Stat. 305.655 (1977); Texas, Tex. Rev. Civ. Stat. Ann., Art. 7359a (Vernon Supp. 1977); Utah, Utah Code Ann. 59-22-1 (1953 and Supp. 1977); Washington, Wash. Rev. Code 82.56.010 (1974); Wyoming, Wyo. Stat. 39-376 (Supp. 1975).

Since the suit began, four States—Florida, Illinois, Indiana, and Wyoming—have withdrawn from the Compact, see 1976 Fla. Laws, ch. 76-149, 1; 1975 Ill. Laws, No. 79-639, 1; 1977 Ind. Acts, No. 90; 1977 Wyo. Sess. Laws, ch. 44, 1. Two others—California and South Dakota—have joined it, see Cal. Rev. & Tax. Code Ann. 38001 (West Supp. 1977); S. D. Comp. Laws Ann. 10-54-1 (Supp. 1977), for a current total of 19 members.

[2] Title I of Pub. L. 86-272, codified as 15 U.S.C. 381-384, essentially forbids the imposition of a tax on a foreign corporation's net income derived from activities within a State, if those activities are limited to the solicitation of orders that are approved, filled, and shipped from a point outside the State.

[3] H. R. Rep. No. 1480, 88th Cong., 2d Sess. (1964); H. R. Rep. No. 565, 89th Cong., 1st Sess. (1965); H. R. Rep. No. 952, 89th Cong., 1st Sess. (1965).

[4] There have been several unsuccessful attempts. H. R. 11798, 89th Cong., 1st Sess. (1965); H. R. 16491, 89th Cong., 2d Sess. (1966); S. 317, 92d Cong., 1st Sess. (1971); H. R. 1538, 92d Cong., 1st Sess. (1971); S. 1245, 93d Cong., 1st Sess. (1973); H. R. 977, 93d Cong., 1st Sess. (1973); S. 2080, 94th Cong., 1st Sess. (1975); H. R. 9, 94th Cong., 1st Sess. (1975).

While Congress was wrestling with the problem, the Multistate Tax Compact was drafted.[5] It symbolized the recognition that, as applied to multistate businesses, traditional state tax administration was inefficient and costly to both State and taxpayer. In accord with that recognition, Art. I of the Compact states four purposes: (1) facilitating proper determination of state and local tax liability of multistate taxpayers, including the equitable apportionment of tax bases and settlement of apportionment disputes; (2) promoting uniformity and compatibility in state tax systems; (3) facilitating taxpayer convenience and compliance in the filing of tax returns and in other phases of tax administration; and (4) avoiding duplicative taxation.

To these ends, Art. VI creates the Multistate Tax Commission, composed of the tax administrators from all the member States. Section 3 of Art. VI authorizes the Commission (i) to study state and local tax systems; (ii) to develop and recommend proposals for an increase in uniformity and compatibility of state and local tax laws in order to encourage simplicity and improvement in state and local tax law and administration; (iii) to compile and publish information that may assist member States in implementing the Compact and taxpayers in complying with the tax laws; and (iv) to do all things necessary and incidental to the administration of its functions pursuant to the Compact.

Articles VII and VIII detail more specific powers of the Commission. Under Art. VII, the Commission may adopt uniform administrative regulations in the event that two or more States have uniform provisions relating to specified types of taxes. These regulations are advisory only. Each member State has the power to reject, disregard, amend, or modify any rules or regulations promulgated by the Commission. They have no force in any member State until adopted by that State in accordance with its own law.

Article VIII applies only in those States that specifically adopt it by statute. It authorizes any member State or its subdivision to request that the Commission perform an audit on its behalf. The Commission, as the State's auditing agent, may seek compulsory process in aid of its auditing power in the courts of any State that has adopted Art. VIII. Information obtained by the audit may be disclosed only in accordance with the laws of the requesting State. Moreover, individual member States retain complete control over all legislation and administrative action affecting the rate of tax, the composition of the tax base (including the determination of the components of taxable income), and the means and methods of determining tax liability and collecting any taxes determined to be due.

Article X permits any party to withdraw from the Compact by enacting a repealing statute. The Compact's other provisions are of less relevance to the matter before us.[6]

---

[5] The model Act proposed as the Multistate Tax Compact, with minor exceptions, has been adopted by each member State.

[6] Article II consists of definitions. Article III permits small taxpayers—those whose only activities within the jurisdiction consist of sales totaling less than $100,000—to elect to pay a tax on gross sales in lieu of a levy

In 1972, appellants brought this action on behalf of themselves[7] and all other multistate taxpayers threatened with audits by the Commission. They named the Commission, its individual Commissioners, and its Executive Director as defendants. Their complaint challenged the constitutionality of the Compact on four grounds: (1) the Compact, never having received the consent of Congress,[8] is invalid under the Compact Clause; (2) it unreasonably burdens interstate commerce; (3) it violates the rights of multistate taxpayers under the Fourteenth Amendment; and (4) its audit provisions violate the Fourth and Fourteenth Amendments. Appellants sought a declaratory judgment that the Compact is invalid and a permanent injunction barring its operation.

The complaint survived a motion to dismiss. 367 F. Supp. 107 (SDNY 1973). After extensive discovery, appellees moved for summary judgment. A three-judge District Court, convened pursuant to 28 U.S.C. 2281, rejected appellants' claim that the record would not support summary judgment. 417 F. Supp. 795, 798 (SDNY 1976). Turning to the merits, the District Court first rejected the contention that the Compact Clause requires congressional consent to every agreement between two or more States. The court cited *Virginia v. Tennessee*, 148 U.S. 503 (1893), and *New Hampshire v. Maine*, 426 U.S. 363 (1976), in support of its holding that consent is necessary only in the case of a compact that enhances the political power of the member States in relation to the Federal Government. The District Court found neither enhancement of state political power nor encroachment upon federal supremacy. Concluding that appellants' Commerce Clause, Fourth Amendment, and Fourteenth Amendment claims also lacked merit, the District Court granted summary judgment for appellees.

Before this Court, appellants have abandoned their search-and-seizure claim. Although they preserved their claim relating to the propriety of summary judgment, we find no reason to disturb the conclusion of the court below on that point. We have before

---

[7] on net income. The Uniform Division of Income for Tax Purposes Act, contained in Art. IV, allows multistate taxpayers to apportion and allocate their income under formulae and rules set forth in the Compact or by any other method available under state law. It was approved by the National Conference of Commissioners on Uniform State Laws and the American Bar Association in 1957. Article V deals with sales and use taxes. Article IX provides for arbitration of disputes, but is not in effect. Article XI disclaims any attempt to affect the power of member States to fix rates of taxation or limit the jurisdiction of any court. Finally, Art. XII provides for liberal construction and severability.

[7] The action was filed by United States Steel Corp., Standard Brands Inc., General Mills, Inc., and the Procter & Gamble Distributing Co. On February 5, 1974, the court below permitted Bethlehem Steel Corp., Bristol Myers Co., Eltra Corp., Goodyear Tire & Rubber Co., Green Giant Co., International Business Machines Corp., International Harvester Co., International Paper Co., International Telephone & Telegraph Corp., McGraw-Hill, Inc., NL Industries, Inc., Union Carbide Corp., and Xerox Corp. to intervene as plaintiffs. The court below ordered that the suit proceed as a class action. International Business Machines and Xerox withdrew as intervenor plaintiffs before decision.

[8] Congressional consent has been sought, but never obtained. See S. 3892, 89th Cong., 2d Sess. (1966); S. 883, 90th Cong., 1st Sess. (1967); S. 1551, 90th Cong., 1st Sess. (1967); H. R. 9476, 90th Cong., 1st Sess. (1967); H. R. 13682, 90th Cong., 1st Sess. (1967); S. 1198, 91st Cong., 1st Sess. (1969); H. R. 6246, 91st Cong., 1st Sess. (1969); H. R. 9873, 91st Cong., 1st Sess. (1969); S. 1883, 92d Cong., 1st Sess. (1971); H. R. 6160, 92d Cong., 1st Sess. (1971); S. 3333, 92d Cong., 2d Sess. (1972); S. 2092, 93d Cong., 1st Sess. (1973).

us, therefore, appellant's contentions under the Compact Clause, the Commerce Clause, and the Fourteenth Amendment. We consider first the Compact Clause contention.

II

Read literally, the Compact Clause would require the States to obtain congressional approval before entering into any agreement among themselves, irrespective of form, subject, duration, or interest to the United States. The difficulties with such an interpretation were identified by Mr. Justice Field in his opinion for the Court in *Virginia v. Tennessee*, supra. His conclusion that the Clause could not be read literally was approved in subsequent dicta,[9] but this Court did not have occasion expressly to apply it in a holding until our recent decision in *New Hampshire v. Maine*, supra.

Appellants urge us to abandon *Virginia v. Tennessee* and *New Hampshire v. Maine*, but provide no effective alternative other than a literal reading of the Compact Clause. At this late date, we are reluctant to accept this invitation to circumscribe modes of interstate cooperation that do not enhance state power to the detriment of federal supremacy. We have examined, nevertheless, the origin and development of the Clause, to determine whether history lends controlling support to appellants' position.

Article I, 10, cl. 1, of the Constitution—the Treaty Clause—declares: "No State, shall enter into Any Treaty, Alliance or Confederation. . . ." Yet Art. I, 10, cl. 3—the Compact Clause—permits the States to enter into "agreements" or "compacts," so long as congressional consent is obtained. The Framers clearly perceived compacts and agreements as differing from treaties.[10] The records of the Constitutional Convention, however, are barren of any clue as to the precise contours of the agreements and com-

---

[9] E. g., *Wharton v. Wise*, 153 U.S. 155, 168–170 (1894); *North Carolina v. Tennessee*, 235 U.S. 1, 16 (1914).

[10] The history of interstate agreements under the Articles of Confederation suggests the same distinction between "treaties, alliances, and confederations" on the one hand, and "agreements and compacts" on the other. Article VI provided in part as follows:

> "No State without the consent of the United States, in Congress assembled, shall send any embassy to, or receive any embassy from, or enter into any confe[r]ence, agreement, alliance or treaty, with any king, prince or state. . . .

> "No two or more States shall enter into any treaty, confederation, or alliance whatever, between them, without the consent of the United States, in Congress assembled, specifying accurately the purposes for which the same is to be entered into, and how long it shall continue."

Congressional consent clearly was required before a State could enter into an "agreement" with a foreign state or power or before two or more States could enter into "treaties, alliances, or confederations." Apparently, however, consent was not required for mere "agreements" between States. "The articles inhibiting any treaty, confederation, or alliance between the States without the consent of Congress . . . were not designed to prevent arrangements between adjoining States to facilitate the free intercourse of their citizens, or remove barriers to their peace and prosperity. . . ." *Wharton v. Wise*, *supra*, at 167.

For example, the Virginia-Maryland Compact of 1785, which governed navigation and fishing rights in the Potomac River, the Pocomoke River, and the Chesapeake Bay, did not receive congressional approval, yet no question concerning its validity under Art. VI ever arose. As the Court noted in *Wharton v. Wise*, in reference to the 1785 Compact, "looking at the object evidently intended by the prohibition of the Articles of Confederation, we are clear they were not directed against agreements of the character expressed by the compact under consideration. Its execution could in no respect encroach upon or weaken the general authority of Congress under those articles. Various compacts were entered into between Pennsylvania and New Jersey and between Pennsylvania and Virginia, during the Confederation, in reference to boundaries between them,

pacts governed by the Compact Clause.[11] This suggests that the Framers used the words "treaty," "compact," and "agreement" as terms of art, for which no explanation was required[12] and with which we are unfamiliar. Further evidence that the Framers ascribed precise meanings to these words appears in contemporary commentary.[13]

---

and to rights of fishery in their waters, and to titles to land in their respective States, without the consent of Congress, which indicated that such consent was not deemed essential to their validity." 153 U.S., at 170–171.

[11] On July 25, 1787, the Convention created a Committee of Detail composed of John Rutledge, James Wilson, Edmund Randolph, Nathaniel Gorham, and Oliver Elsworth. The Convention then adjourned until August 6 to allow the Committee to prepare a draft. 2 M. Farrand, Records of the Federal Convention of 1787, pp. 97, 128 (1911). Section 10 of the Committee's first draft provided in part: "No State shall enter into any Treaty, Alliance or Confederation with any foreign Power nor witht. Const. of U.S. into any agreemt. or compact wh another State or Power. . . ." *Id.*, at 169 (abbreviations in original). On August 6, the Committee submitted a draft to the Convention containing the following articles:

"XII No State shall . . . enter into any treaty, alliance, or confederation. . . .

"XIII No State, without the consent of the Legislature of the United States, shall . . . enter into any agreement or compact with another State, or with any foreign power. . . ." *Id.*, at 187.

The Committee of Style, created to revise the draft, reported on September 12, id., at 590, but nothing appears to have been said about Art. I, 10, which contained the treaty and compact language incorporated into the Constitution as approved on September 17. The records of the state ratification conventions also shed no light. Publius declared only that the prohibition against treaties, alliances, and confederation, "for reasons which need no explanation, is copied into the new Constitution," while the portion of Art. I, 10, containing the Compact Clause fell "within reasonings which are either so obvious, or have been so fully developed, that they may be passed over without remark." The *Federalist*, No. 44, pp. 299, 302 (J. Cooke ed. 1961) (J. Madison).

[12] Some commentators have theorized that the Framers understood those terms in relation to the precisely defined categories, fashionable in the contemporary literature of international law, of accords between sovereigns. See, e. g., Engdahl, Characterization of Interstate Arrangements: When Is a Compact Not a Compact?, 64 Mich. L. Rev. 63 (1965); Weinfeld, What Did the Framers of the Federal Constitution Mean by "Agreements or Compacts"?, 3 U. Chi. L. Rev. 453 (1936). The international jurist most widely cited in the first 50 years after the Revolution was Emmerich de Vattel. 1 J. Kent, Commentaries on American Law 18 (1826). In 1775, Benjamin Franklin acknowledged receipt of three copies of a new edition, in French, of Vattel's Law of Nations and remarked that the book "has been continually in the hands of the members of our Congress now sitting. . . ." 2 F. Wharton, United States Revolutionary Diplomatic Correspondence 64 (1889), cited in Weinfeld, supra, at 458.

Vattel differentiated between "treaties," which were made either for perpetuity or for a considerable period, and "agreements, conventions, and pactions," which "are perfected in their execution once for all." E. Vattel, Law of Nations 192 (J. Chitty ed. 1883). Unlike a "treaty" or "alliance," an "agreement" or "paction" was perfected upon execution:

"[T]hose compacts, which are accomplished once for all, and not by successive acts,—are no sooner executed then they are completed and perfected. If they are valid, they have in their own nature a perpetual and irrevocable effect. . . ." *Id.*, at 208.

This distinction between supposedly ongoing accords, such as military alliances, and instantaneously executed, though perpetually effective, agreements, such as boundary settlements, may have informed the drafting in Art. I, 10. The Framers clearly recognized the necessity for amicable resolution of boundary disputes and related grievances. See *Virginia v. West Virginia*, 246 U.S. 565, 597–600 (1918); Frankfurter & Landis, The Compact Clause of the Constitution—A Study in Interstate Adjustments, 34 *Yale L. J.* 685, 692–695 (1925). Interstate agreements were a method with which they were familiar. *Id.*, at 694, 732–734. Although these dispositive compacts affected the interests of the States involved, they did not represent the continuing threat to the other States embodied in a "treaty of alliance," to use Vattel's words. E. Vattel, supra, at 192.

[13] St. George Tucker, who along with Madison and Edmund Randolph was a Virginia commissioner to the Annapolis Convention of 1786, drew a distinction between "treaties, alliances, and confederations" on the one hand, and "agreements or compacts" on the other:

"The former relate ordinarily to subjects of great national magnitude and importance, and are often perpetual, or made for a considerable period of time; the power of making these is altogether

Whatever distinct meanings the Framers attributed to the terms in Art. I, 10, those meanings were soon lost. In 1833, Mr. Justice Story perceived no clear distinction among any of the terms.[14] Lacking any clue as to the categorical definitions the Framers has ascribed to them, Mr. Justice Story developed his own theory. Treaties, alliances, and confederations, he wrote, generally connote military and political accords and are forbidden to the States. Compacts and agreements, on the other hand, embrace "mere private rights of sovereignty; such as questions of boundary; interests in land situate in the territory of each other; and other internal regulations for the mutual comfort and convenience of States bordering on each other." 2 J. Story, *Commentaries on the Constitution of the United States* 1403, p. 264 (T. Cooley ed. 1873). In the latter situations, congressional consent was required, Story felt, "in order to check any infringement of the rights of the national government." *Ibid.*

The Court's first opportunity to comment on the scope of the Compact Clause, *Holmes v. Jennison*, 14 *Pet.* 540 (1840), proved inconclusive. Holmes had been arrested in Vermont on a warrant issued by Jennison, the Governor. The warrant apparently reflected an informal agreement by Jennison to deliver Holmes to authorities in Canada, where he had been indicted for murder. On a petition for habeas corpus, the Supreme Court of Vermont held Holmes' detention lawful. Although this Court divided evenly on the question of its jurisdiction to review the decision, Mr. Chief Justice Taney, in an opinion joined by Mr. Justice Story and two others, addressed the merits of Holmes' claim that Jennison's informal agreement to surrender him fell within the scope of the Compact Clause. Mr. Chief Justice Taney focused on the fact that the agreement in question was between a State and a foreign government. Since

---

prohibited to the individual states; but agreements, or compacts, concerning transitory or local affairs, or such as cannot possibly affect any other interest but that of the parties, may still be entered into by the respective states, with the consent of congress." 1 W. Blackstone, Commentaries, Appendix 310 (S. Tucker ed. 1803) (footnotes omitted).

Tucker cited Vattel as authority for his interpretation of Art. I, 10.

[14] Mr. Justice Story found Tucker's view, see n. 13, supra, unilluminating:

"What precise distinction is here intended to be taken between treaties, and agreements, and compacts, is nowhere explained, and has never as yet been subjected to any exact judicial or other examination. A learned commentator, however, supposes, that the former ordinarily relate to subjects of great national magnitude and importance, and are often perpetual, or for a great length of time; but that the latter relate to transitory or local concerns, or such as cannot possibly affect any other interests but those of the parties [citing Tucker]. But this is at best a very loose and unsatisfactory exposition, leaving the whole matter open to the most latitudinarian construction. What are subjects of great national magnitude and importance? Why may not a compact or agreement between States be perpetual? If it may not, what shall be its duration? Are not treaties often made for short periods, and upon questions of local interest, and for temporary objects?" 2 J. Story, *Commentaries on the Constitution of the United States* 1402, p. 263 (T. Cooley ed. 1873) (footnotes omitted).

In *Green v. Biddle*, 8 *Wheat.* 1 (1823), the Court, including Mr. Justice Story, had been presented with a question of the validity of the Virginia-Kentucky Compact of 1789, to which Congress had never expressly assented. Henry Clay argued to the Court that the Compact Clause extended "to all agreements or compacts, no matter what is the subject of them. It is immaterial, therefore, whether that subject be harmless or dangerous to the Union." *Id.*, at 39. The Court did not address that issue, however, for it held that Congress' consent could be implied. *Id.*, at 87.

the clear intention of the Framers had been to cut off all communication between the States and foreign powers, *id.*, at 568–579, he concluded that the Compact Clause would permit an arrangement such as the one at issue only if "made under the supervision of the United States . . . ," *id.*, at 578. In his separate opinion, Mr. Justice Catron expressed disquiet over what he viewed as Mr. Chief Justice Taney's literal reading of the Compact Clause, noting that it might threaten agreements between States theretofore considered lawful.[15]

Despite Mr. Justice Catron's fears, courts faced with the task of applying the Compact Clause appeared reluctant to strike down newly emerging forms of interstate cooperation.[16] For example, in *Union Branch R. Co. v. East Tennessee & G. R. Co.*, 14 Ga. 327 (1853), the Supreme Court of Georgia rejected a Compact Clause challenge to an agreement between Tennessee and Georgia concerning the construction of an interstate railroad. Omitting any mention of *Holmes v. Jennison*, the Georgia court seized upon Story's observation that the words "treaty, alliance, and confederation" generally were known to apply to treaties of a political character. Without explanation, the court transferred this description of the Treaty Clause to the Compact Clause, which it perceived as restraining the power of the States only with respect to agreements "which might limit, or infringe upon a full and complete execution by the General Government, of the powers intended to be delegated by the Federal Constitution. . . ." 14 Ga., at 339.[17] A broader prohibition could not have been intended, since it was unnecessary to protect the Federal Government.[18] Unless this view was taken, said the court:

---

[15] Notwithstanding Mr. Justice Catron's unease, Mr. Chief Justice Taney's opinion in *Jennison* is not inconsistent with the rule of *Virginia v. Tennessee*. At some length, Taney emphasized that the State was exercising the power to extradite persons sought for crimes in other countries, which was part of the exclusive foreign relations power expressly reserved to the Federal Government. He concluded, therefore, that the State's agreement would be constitutional only if made under the supervision of the United States.

After the *Jennison* case had been disposed of by the Court, the Vermont court discharged Holmes. It concluded from an examination of the five separate opinions in the case that a majority of this Court believed the Governor had no power to deliver Holmes to Canadian authorities. *Holmes v. Jennison*, 14 Pet. 540, 597 (1840) (Reporter's Note).

[16] See generally Abel, Interstate Cooperation as a Child, 32 *Iowa L. Rev.* 203 (1947); Engdahl, supra, n. 12, at 86.

[17] The court failed to mention that Story described the terms of the Treaty Clause, not the Compact Clause, as political. It was the political character of treaties, in his view, that led to their absolute prohibition. Story theorized that the Compact Clause dealt with "private rights of sovereignty," see supra, at 464, but that congressional consent was required to prevent possible abuses.

[18] Taking a similar view of the Compact Clause, and also ignoring *Holmes v. Jennison*, were *Dover v. Portsmouth Bridge*, 17 N. H. 200 (1845), and *Fisher v. Steele*, 39 La. Ann. 447, 1 So. 882 (1887). *Holmes v. Jennison* apparently was not cited in a case relating to the Compact Clause until 1917, 14 years after Mr. Justice Field formulated the rule of *Virginia v. Tennessee*. See *McHenry County v. Brady*, 37 N. D. 59, 70, 163 N. W. 540, 544 (1917).

Mr. Chief Justice Taney may have shared the Georgia court's view of compacts which, unlike the "agreement" in *Holmes v. Jennison*, did not implicate the foreign relations power of the United States. A year after *Union Branch R. Co.* was decided, he suggested in dictum that the Compact Clause is aimed at an accord that is "in its nature, a political question, to be settled by compact made by the political departments of the government." *Florida v. Georgia*, 17 How. 478, 494 (1855). The purpose of the Clause, he declared, is "to

> "We must hold that a State, without the consent of Congress, can make
> no sort of contract, whatever, with another State. That it cannot sell to
> another state, any portion of public property, . . . though it may so sell to
> individuals. . . .
> "We can see no advantage to be gained by, or benefit in such a provision;
> and hence, we think it was not intended." *Id.*, at 340.

It was precisely this approach that formed the basis in 1893 for Mr. Justice Field's
interpretation of the Compact Clause in *Virginia v. Tennessee.* In that case, the Court
held that Congress tacitly had assented to the running of a boundary between the two
States. In an extended dictum, however, Mr. Justice Field took the Court's first opportunity to comment upon the Compact Clause since the neglected essay in *Holmes
v. Jennison.* Mr. Justice Field, echoing the puzzlement expressed by Story 60 years
earlier, observed:

> "The terms 'agreement' or 'compact' taken by themselves are sufficiently
> comprehensive to embrace all forms of stipulation, written or verbal, and
> relating to all kinds of subjects; to those to which the United States can
> have no possible objection or have any interest in interfering with, as well
> as to those which may tend to increase and build up the political influence
> of the contracting States, so as to encroach upon or impair the supremacy
> of the United States or interfere with their rightful management of particu-
> lar subjects placed under their entire control." 148 U.S., at 517–518.

Mr. Justice Field followed with four examples of interstate agreements that could in
"no respect concern the United States": (1) an agreement by one State to purchase land
within its borders owned by another State; (2) an agreement by one State to ship mer-
chandise over a canal owned by another; (3) an agreement to drain a malarial district
on the border between two States; and (4) an agreement to combat an immediate threat,
such as invasion or epidemic. As the Compact Clause could not have been intended to
reach every possible interstate agreement, it was necessary to construe the terms of the
Compact Clause by reference to the object of the entire section in which it appears:[19]

---

guard the rights and interests of the other States, and to prevent any compact or agreement between any
two States, which might affect injuriously the interest of the others." A similar concern with agreements of
a political nature may be found in a dictum of Mr. Chief Justice Marshall:

> "It is worthy of remark, too, that these inhibitions [of Art. I, 10] generally restrain state legislation
> on subjects entrusted to the general government, or in which the people of all the states feel an
> interest.
> "A state is forbidden to enter into any treaty, alliance or confederation. If these compacts are with
> foreign nations, they interfere with the treaty making power which is conferred entirely on the
> general government; if with each other, for political purposes, they can scarcely fail to interfere
> with the general purpose and intent of the constitution." *Barron v. Baltimore*, 7 Pet. 243, 249 (1833).

[19] In support of this conclusion, Mr. Justice Field misread Story's Commentaries in precisely the same way as
the Georgia court did in *Union Branch R. Co.* See n. 17, supra.

"Looking at the clause in which the terms 'compact' or 'agreement' appear, it is evident that the prohibition is directed to the formation of any combination tending to the increase of political power in the States, which may encroach upon or interfere with the just supremacy of the United States." *Id.*, at 519.

Mr. Justice Field reiterated this functional view of the Compact Clause a year later in *Wharton v. Wise*, 153 U.S. 155, 168–170 (1894).

Although this Court did not have occasion to apply Mr. Justice Field's test for many years, it has been cited with approval on several occasions. *Louisiana v. Texas*, 176 U.S. 1, 17 (1900); *Stearns v. Minnesota*, 179 U.S. 223, 246–248 (1900); *North Carolina v. Tennessee*, 235 U.S. 1, 16 (1914).[20] Moreover, several decisions of this Court have upheld a variety of interstate agreements effected through reciprocal legislation without congressional consent. E.g., *St. Louis & S. F. R. Co. v. James*, 161 U.S. 545 (1896); *Hendrick v. Maryland*, 235 U.S. 610 (1915); *Bode v. Barrett*, 344 U.S. 583 (1953); *New York v. O'Neill*, 359 U.S. 1 (1959). While none of these cases explicitly applied the *Virginia v. Tennessee* test, they reaffirmed its underlying assumption: not all agreements between States are subject to the strictures of the Compact Clause.[21] In *O'Neill*, for example, this Court upheld the Uniform Law to Secure the Attendance of Witnesses from Within or Without the State in Criminal Proceedings, which had been enacted in 41 States and Puerto Rico. That statute permitted the judge of a court of any enacting State to invoke the process of the courts of a sister State for the purpose of compelling the attendance of witnesses at criminal proceedings in the requesting State. Although

---

[20] State courts repeatedly have applied the test in confirming the validity of a variety of interstate agreements. E.g., *McHenry Country v. Brady*, supra; *Dixie Wholesale Grocery, Inc. v. Martin*, 278 Ky. 705, 129 S. W. 2d 181, cert. denied, 308 U.S. 609 (1939); *Ham v. Maine-New Hampshire Interstate Bridge Authority*, 92 N. H. 268, 30 A. 2d 1 (1943); *Roberts Tobacco Co. v. Department of Revenue*, 322 Mich. 519, 34 N. W 2d 54 (1948); *Bode v. Barrett*, 412 Ill. 204, 106 N. E. 2d 521 (1952), aff'd, 344 U.S. 583 (1953); *Landes v. Landes*, 1 N. Y. 2d 358, 135 N. E. 2d 562, appeal dismissed, 352 U.S. 948 (1956); *Ivey v. Ayers*, 301 S. W. 2d 790 (Mo. 1957); *State v. Doe*, 149 Conn. 216, 178 A. 2d 271 (1962); *General Expressways, Inc. v. Iowa Reciprocity Board*, 163 N. W. 2d 413 (Iowa, 1968); *Kinnear v. Hertz Corp.*, 86 Wash. 2d 407, 545 P. 2d 1186 (1976). See also *Henderson v. Delaware River Joint Toll Bridge Comm'n*, 362 Pa. 475, 66 A. 2d 843 (1949); *Opinion of the Justices*, 344 Mass. 770, 184 N. E. 2d 353 (1962); *State v. Ford*, 213 Tenn. 582, 376 S. W. 2d 486 (1964); *Dresden School Dist. v. Hanover School Dist.*, 105 N. H. 286, 198 A. 2d 656 (1964); *Colgate-Palmolive Co. v. Dorgan*, 225 N. W. 2d 278 (N. D. 1974).

[21] One commentator has noted the relevance of reciprocal-legislation cases, particularly those involving reciprocal tax statutes, to Compact Clause adjudication:

"Compact clause adjudication focuses on a federalism formula suggested in an 1893 Supreme Court case [*Virginia v. Tennessee*]: congressional consent is required to validate only those compacts infringing upon 'the political power or influence' of particular states and 'encroaching . . . upon the full and free exercise of Federal authority.' Reciprocal tax statutes, which provide the paradigm instance of arrangements not deemed to require the consent of Congress, illustrate this principle in that they neither project a new presence onto the federal system nor alter any state's basic sphere of authority." Tribe, Intergovernmental Immunities in Litigation, Taxation, and Regulation: Separation of Powers Issues in Controversies about Federalism, 89 *Harv. L. Rev.* 682, 712 (1976) (footnotes omitted).

no Compact Clause question was directly presented, the Court's opinion touched upon similar concerns:

> "The Constitution did not purport to exhaust imagination and resourcefulness in devising fruitful interstate relationships. It is not to be constructed to limit the variety of arrangements which are possible through the voluntary and cooperative actions of individual States with a view to increasing harmony within the federalism created by the Constitution. Far from being divisive, this legislation is a catalyst of cohesion. It is within the unrestricted area of action left to the States by the Constitution." 359 U.S., at 6.

The reciprocal-legislation cases support the soundness of the *Virginia v. Tennessee* rule, since the mere form of the interstate agreement cannot be dispositive. Agreements effected through reciprocal legislation[22] may present opportunities for enhancement of state power at the expense of the federal supremacy similar to the threats inherent in a more formalized "compact." Mr. Chief Justice Taney considered this point in *Holmes v. Jennison*, 14 Pet., at 573:

> "Can it be supposed, that the constitutionality of the act depends on the mere form of the agreement? We think not. The Constitution looked to the essence and substance of things, and not to mere form. It would be but an evasion of the constitution to place the question upon the formality with which the agreement is made."

The Clause reaches both "agreements" and "compacts," the formal as well as the informal.[23] The relevant inquiry must be one of impact on our federal structure.

This was the status of the *Virginia v. Tennessee* test until two Terms ago, when we decided *New Hampshire v. Maine*, 426 U.S. 363 (1976). In that case we specifically applied the test and held that an interstate agreement locating an ancient boundary did not require congressional consent. We reaffirmed Mr. Justice Field's view that the "application of the Compact Clause is limited to agreements that are 'directed to the formation of any combination tending to the increase of political power in the States, which may encroach upon or interfere with the just supremacy of the United States.'" *Id.*, at 369, quoting *Virginia v. Tennessee*, 148 U.S., at 519. This rule states the proper balance between federal and state power with respect to compacts and agreements among States.

Appellants maintain that history constrains us to limit application of this rule to

[22] See also Frankfurter & Landis, supra, n. 12, at 690–691.

[23] Although there is language in *West Virginia ex rel. Dyer v. Sims*, 341 U.S. 22, 27 (1951), that could be read to suggest that the formal nature of a "compact" distinguishes it from reciprocal legislation, that language, properly understood, does not undercut our analysis. Referring in dictum to the compact at issue in Dyer, Mr. Justice Frankfurter observed that congressional consent had been required, "as for all compacts." The word "compact" in that phrase must be understood as a term of art, meaning those agreements falling within the scope of the Compact Clause. Cf. Frankfurter & Landis, supra n. 12, at 690, and n. 22a. Otherwise, the word "agreement" is read out of Art. I, 10, cl. 3, entirely.

bilateral agreements involving no independent administrative body. They argue that this Court never has upheld a multilateral agreement creating an active administrative body with extensive powers delegated to it by the States, but lacking congressional consent. It is true that most multilateral compacts have been submitted for congressional approval. But this historical practice, which may simply reflect considerations of caution and convenience on the part of the submitting States, is not controlling.[24] It is also true that the precise interstate mechanism involved in this case has not been presented to this Court before. *New York v. O'Neill*, supra, however, involving analogous multilateral arrangements, stands as an implicit rejection of appellants' proposed limitation of the *Virginia v. Tennessee* rule.

Appellants further urge that the pertinent inquiry is one of potential, rather than actual, impact upon federal supremacy. We agree. But the multilateral nature of the agreement and its establishment of an ongoing administrative body do not, standing alone, present significant potential for conflict with the principles underlying the Compact Clause. The number of parties to an agreement is irrelevant if it does not impermissibly enhance state power at the expense of federal supremacy. As to the powers delegated to the administrative body, we think these also must be judged in terms of enhancement of state power in relation to the Federal Government. See *Virginia v. Tennessee*, supra, at 520 (establishment of commission to run boundary not a "compact"). We turn, therefore, to the application of the *Virginia v. Tennessee* rule to the Compact before us.

III

On its face the Multistate Tax Compact contains no provisions that would enhance the political power of the member States in a way that encroaches upon the supremacy of the United States. There well may be some incremental increase in the bargaining power of the member States *quoad* the corporations subject to their respective taxing jurisdictions. Group action in itself may be more influential than independent actions by the States. But the test is whether the Compact enhances state power *quoad* the National Government. This pact does not purport to authorize the member States to exercise any powers they could not exercise in its absence. Nor is there any delegation of sovereign power to the Commission; each State retains complete freedom to adopt or reject the rules and regulations of the Commission. Moreover, as noted above, each State is free to withdraw at any time. Despite this apparent compatibility of the

---

[24] Appellants describe various Compacts, including the Interstate Compact to Conserve Oil and Gas Act of 1935, 49 Stat. 939, and the Interstate Compact to Conserve Oil and Gas (Extension) of 1976, 90 Stat. 2365, and attempt to show that they are similar to the Compact before us. They then point out that the Compacts they describe received the consent of Congress and argue from this fact that the Multistate Tax Compact also must receive congressional consent in order to be valid. These other Compacts are not before us. We have no occasion to decide whether congressional consent was necessary to their constitutional operation, nor have we any reason to compare those Compacts to the one before us. It suffices to test the Multistate Tax Compact under the rule of *Virginia v. Tennessee*.

Compact with the interpretation of the Clause established by our cases, appellants argue that the Compact's effect is to threaten federal supremacy.

A

Appellants contend initially that the Compact encroaches upon federal supremacy with respect to interstate commerce. This argument, as we understand it, has four principal components. It is claimed, first, that the Commission's use in its audits of "unitary business" and "combination of income" methods[25] for determining a corporate taxpayer's income creates a risk of multiple taxation for multistate businesses. Whether or not this risk is a real one, it cannot be attributed to the existence of the Multistate Tax Commission. When the Commission conducts an audit at the request of a member State, it uses the methods adopted by that State. Since appellants do not contest the right of each State to adopt these procedures if it conducted the audits separately,[26] they cannot be heard to complain that a threat to federal supremacy arises from the Commission's adoption of the unitary-business standard in accord with the wishes of the member States. Indeed, to the extent that the Commission succeeds in promoting uniformity in the application of state taxing principles, the risks of multiple taxation should be diminished.

Appellants' second contention as to enhancement of state power over interstate commerce is that the Commission's regulations provide for apportionment of nonbusiness income. This allegedly creates a substantial risk of multiple taxation, since other States are said to allocate this income to the place of commercial domicile.[27] We note first that the regulations of the Commission do not require the apportionment of nonbusiness income. They do define business income, which is apportionable under the regulations, to include elements that might be regarded as nonbusiness income

---

[25] The "unitary business" technique involves calculating a corporate tax-payer's net income on the basis of all phases of the operation of a single enterprise (e.g., production of components, assembly, packing, distribution, sales), even if located outside the jurisdiction. The portion of that income attributable to activities within the taxing State is then determined by means of an apportionment formula. See, e.g., *Underwood Typewriter Co. v. Chamberlain*, 254 U.S. 113 (1920). "Combination of income" involves applying the unitary business concept to separately incorporated entities engaged in a single enterprise. See *Edison California Stores, Inc. v. McColgan*, 30 Cal. 2d 472, 183 P. 2d 16 (1947).

[26] Individual States are free to employ the unitary-business standard. *Underwood Typewriter Co. v. Chamberlain*, supra; accord, *Bass, Ratcliff & Gretton, Ltd. v. State Tax Comm'n*, 266 U.S. 271 (1924). Nor do appellants claim that individual States could not employ the combination method of determining taxpayer income. Cf. *Edison California Stores*, supra.

[27] Taxable income deemed apportionable is that which is not considered to have its source totally within one State. It is distributed by means of an apportionment formula among the States in which the multistate business operates. Taxable income deemed allocable is that which is considered as having its source within one State and is assigned entirely to that State for tax purposes. See generally Sharpe, State Taxation of Interstate Business and the Multistate Tax Compact: The Search for a Delicate Uniformity, 11 *Colum. J. Law & Soc. Prob.* 231, 233–239 (1975). "Business income" is defined generally as income arising from activities in the regular course of the taxpayer's business. See, e.g., Uniform Division of Income for Tax Purposes Act 1 (a). Definitions of income arising in the regular course of business vary from one State to another. For example, rents and royalties may be considered business income in one State, but not in another. See generally *Sharpe*, supra, at 233–239.

in some States. *P-H State & Local Tax Serv.* 6100–6286 (1973). But again there is no claim that the member States could not adopt similar definitions in the absence of the Compact. Any State's ability to exact additional tax revenues from multistate businesses cannot be attributed to the Compact; it is the result of the State's freedom to select, within constitutional limits, the method it prefers.

The third aspect of the Compact's operation said to encroach upon federal commerce power involves the Commission's requirement that multistate business under audit file data concerning affiliated corporations. Appellants argue that the costs of compiling financial data of related corporations burden the conduct of interstate commerce for the benefit of the taxing States. Since each State presumably could impose similar filing requirements individually, however, appellants again do not show that the Commission's practices, as auditing agent for member States, aggrandize their power or threaten federal control of commerce. Moreover, to the extent that the Commission is engaged in joint audits, appellants' filing burdens well may be reduced.

Appellants' final claim of enhanced state power with respect to commerce is that the "enforcement powers" conferred upon the Commission enable that body to exercise authority over interstate business to a greater extent than the sum of the States' authority acting individually. This claim also falls short of meeting the standard of *Virginia v. Tennessee.* Article VIII of the Compact authorizes the Commission to require the attendance of persons and the production of documents in connection with its audits. The Commission, however, has no power to punish failures to comply. It must resort to the courts for compulsory process, as would any auditing agent employed by the individual States. The only novel feature of the Commission's "enforcement powers" is the provision in Art. VIII permitting the Commission to resort to the courts of any State adopting that Article. Adoption of the Article, then, amounts to nothing more than reciprocal legislation for providing mutual assistance to the auditors of the member States. Reciprocal legislation making the courts of one State available for the better administration of justice in another has been upheld by this Court as a method "to accomplish fruitful and unprohibited ends." *New York v. O'Neill*, 359 U.S., at 11. Appellees make no showing that increased effectiveness in the administration of state tax laws, promoted by such legislation,[28] threatens federal supremacy. See n. 21, supra.

B

Appellants further argue that the Compact encroaches upon the power of the United States with respect to foreign relations. They contend that the Commission

---

[28] For example, appellants raise no challenge to the many reciprocal statutes providing for recovery of taxes owing to one State in the courts of another. A typical statute is Tennessee's: "Any state of the United States or the political subdivisions thereof shall have the right to sue in the courts of Tennessee to recover any tax which may be owing to it when the like right is accorded to the state of Tennessee and its political subdivisions by such state." Tenn. Code Ann. 20-1709 (1955). See generally Leflar, Out-of-State Collection of State and Local Taxes, 29 *Vand. L. Rev.* 443 (1976).

has conducted multinational audits in which it applied the unitary business method to foreign corporate taxpayers, in conflict with federal policy concerning the taxation of foreign corporations.[29]

This contention was not presented to the court below and in any event lacks substance. The existence of the Compact simply has no bearing on an individual State's ability to utilize the unitary business method in determining the income of a particular multinational taxpayer. *Bass, Ratcliff & Gretton, Ltd. v. State Tax Comm'n*, 266 U.S. 271 (1924). The Commission, as auditing agent, adopts the method only at the behest of a State requesting an audit. To the extent that its use contravenes any foreign policy of the United States, the facial validity of the Compact is not implicated.

C

Appellants' final Compact Clause argument charges that the Compact impairs the sovereign rights of nonmember States. Appellants declare, without explanation, that if the use of the unitary business and combination methods continues to spread among the Western States, unfairness in taxation—presumably the risks of multiple taxation—will be avoidable only through the efforts of some coordinating body. Appellants cite the belief of the Commission's Executive Director that the Commission represents the only available vehicle for effective coordination,[30] and conclude that the Compact exerts undue pressure to join upon nonmember States in violation of their "sovereign right" to refuse.

We find no support for this conclusion. It has not been shown that any unfair taxation of multistate business resulting from the disparate use of combination and other methods will redound to the benefit of any particular group of States or to the harm of others. Even if the existence of such a situation were demonstrated, it could not be ascribed to the existence of the Compact. Each member State is free to adopt the auditing procedures it thinks best, just as it could if the Compact did not exist. Risks of unfairness and double taxation, then, are independent of the Compact.

Moreover, it is not explained how any economic pressure that does exist is an affront to the sovereignty of nonmember States. Any time a State adopts a fiscal or administrative policy that affects the programs of a sister State, pressure to modify those programs may result. Unless that pressure transgresses the bounds of the Commerce Clause or the Privileges and Immunities Clause of Art. IV, 2, see, e.g., *Austin v. New*

---

[29] Tax Convention with the United Kingdom of Great Britain and Northern Ireland, 94th Cong., 2d Sess. (1976) (as published in Message from President submitting Convention); Protocol to the 1975 Tax Convention with the United Kingdom of Great Britain and Northern Ireland, 94th Cong., 2d Sess. (1976) (as published in Message from President submitting Protocol); Second Protocol to the 1975 Tax Convention with the United Kingdom of Great Britain and Northern Ireland, 95th Cong., 1st Sess. (1977) (as published in Message from President submitting Second Protocol). Article 9, 4, of the treaty, which is currently pending before the Senate, would prohibit the combination of the income of any enterprise doing business in the United States with the income of related enterprises located in the United Kingdom.

[30] Corrigan, Interstate Corporate Income Taxation—Recent Revolutions and a Modern Response, 29 *Vand. L. Rev.* 423, 441–442 (1976).

Hampshire, 420 U.S. 656 (1975), it is not clear how our federal structure is implicated. Appellants do not argue that an individual State's decision to apportion nonbusiness income—or to define business income broadly, as the regulations of the Commission actually do—touches upon constitutional strictures. This being so, we are not persuaded that the same decision becomes a threat to the sovereignty of other States if a member State makes this decision upon the Commission's recommendation.

IV

Appellants further challenge, on relatively narrow grounds, the validity of the Multistate Tax Compact under the Commerce Clause and the Fourteenth Amendment.[31] They allege that the Commission has abused its powers by conducting a campaign of harassment against members of the plaintiff class. Specifically, they claim that the Commission induced eight States to issue burdensome requests for production of documents and to deviate from the provisions of state law by issuing arbitrary assessments against taxpayers who refuse to comply with these harassing production orders.

These allegations do not establish that the Compact is in violation either of the Commerce Clause or the Fourteenth Amendment. We observe first that this contention was not presented to the court below. The only evidence of record relating to the allegations are statements in the affidavit of appellants' counsel and an ambiguous excerpt from a letter of the Commission to the Director of Taxation of the State of Hawaii, quoted therein. App. 51–53. On this fragile basis, we hardly would be justified in making an initial finding of fact that appellees engaged in the campaign sketched in the affidavit.

Even if appellants' factual allegations were supported by the record, they would be irrelevant to the facial validity of the Compact. As we have noted above, it is only the individual State, not the Commission, that has the power to issue an assessment—whether arbitrary or not. If the assessment violates state law, we must assume that state remedies are available.[32] E.g., *Colgate-Palmolive Co. v. Dorgan*, 225 N. W. 2d 278 (N. D. 1974).

V

We conclude that appellants' constitutional challenge to the Multistate Tax Compact fails.[33] We affirm the judgment of the District Court.

Affirmed.

---

[31] Appellants do not specify in their brief which Clause of the Fourteenth Amendment is violated. Our conclusion makes it unnecessary to consider each one.

[32] Appellants conceded this point in the hearing before the three-judge court. Tr. of Hearing, Feb. 3, 1976, pp. 16–18. Cf. *State Tax Comm'n v. Union Carbide Corp.*, 386 F. Supp. 250 (Idaho 1974).

[33] The dissent appears to confuse potential impact on "federal interests" with threats to "federal supremacy." It dwells at some length on the unsuccessful efforts to obtain express congressional approval of this Compact, relying on the introduction of bills that never reached the floor of either House. This history of congressional inaction is viewed as "demonstrat[ing] . . . a federal interest in the rules for apportioning

MR. JUSTICE WHITE, with whom MR. JUSTICE BLACKMUN joins, dissenting.

The majority opinion appears to concede, as I think it should, that the Compact Clause reaches interstate agreements presenting even potential encroachments on federal supremacy. In applying its Compact Clause theory to the circumstances of the Multistate Tax Compact, however, the majority is not true to this view. For if the Compact Clause has any independent protective force at all, it must require the consent of Congress to an interstate scheme of such complexity and detail as this. The majority states it will watch for the mere potential of harm to federal interests, but then approves the Compact here for lack of actual proved harm.

I

The Constitution incorporates many restrictions on the powers of individual States. Some of these are explicit, some are inferred from positive delegations of power to the Federal Government. In the latter category falls the federal authority over interstate commerce.[1] The individual States have long been permitted to legislate, in a nondiscriminatory manner, over matters affecting interstate commerce, where Congress has not exerted its authority, and where the federal interest does not require a uniform rule. *Cooley v. Board of Wardens*, 12 How. 299 (1852); *Southern Pacific Co. v. Arizona ex rel. Sullivan*, 325 U.S. 761 (1945).

It is not denied by any party to this case that the apportionment of revenues, sales, and income of multistate and multinational corporations for taxation purposes is an area over which the Congress could exert authority, ousting the efforts of any States

---

multistate and multinational income," and as showing "a potential impact on federal concerns." Post, at 488, 489. That there is a federal interest no one denies.

The dissent's focus on the existence of federal concerns misreads *Virginia v. Tennessee* and *New Hampshire v. Maine*. The relevant inquiry under those decisions is whether a compact tends to increase the political power of the States in a way that "may encroach upon or interfere with the just supremacy of the United States." *Virginia v. Tennessee*, 148 U.S., at 519. Absent a threat of encroachment or interference through enhanced state power, the existence of a federal interest is irrelevant. Indeed, every state cooperative action touching interstate or foreign commerce implicates some federal interest. Were that the test under the Compact Clause, virtually all interstate agreements and reciprocal legislation would require congressional approval.

In this case, the Multistate Tax Compact is concerned with a number of state activities that affect interstate and foreign commerce. But as we have indicated at some length in this opinion, the terms of the Compact do not enhance the power of the member States to affect federal supremacy in those areas.

The dissent appears to argue that the political influence of the member States is enhanced by this Compact, making it more difficult—in terms of the political process—to enact pre-emptive legislation. We may assume that there is strength in numbers and organization. But enhanced capacity to lobby within the federal legislative process falls far short of threatened "encroach[ment] upon or interfer[ence] with the just supremacy of the United States." Federal power in the relevant areas remains plenary; no action authorized by the Constitution is "foreclosed," see post, at 491, to the Federal Government acting through Congress or the treaty-making power.

The dissent also offers several aspects of the Compact that are thought to confer "synergistic" powers upon the member States. Post, at 491–493. We perceive no threat to federal supremacy in any of those provisions. See, e.g., *Virginia v. Tennessee*, supra, at 520.

[1] The Congress shall have Power . . . To regulate Commerce with foreign Nations, and among the several States. . . ." U.S. Const., Art. I, 8.

in the field. To date, however, the Federal Government has taken only limited steps in this context.[2] No federal legislation has been enacted, nor tax treaties ratified, that would interfere with any State's efforts to apply uniform apportionment rules, unitary business concepts, or single multistate audits of corporations. Hence, leaving to one side appellants' contentions that these matters inherently require uniform federal treatment, there is obstacle in the Commerce Clause to such action by an individual State.

The Compact Clause, however, is directed to joint action by more than one State. If its only purpose in the present context were to require the consent of Congress to agreements between States that would otherwise violate the Commerce Clause, it would have no independent meaning. The Clause must mean that some actions which would be permissible for individual States to undertake are not permissible for a group of States to agree to undertake.

There is much history from the Articles of Confederation to support that conclusion.[3] In framing the Constitution the new Republic was at pains to correct the divisive

---

[2] Title 15 U.S.C. 381–384, passed in 1959 as Pub. L. No. 86–272, 73 Stat. 555, limits the jurisdictional bases open to States whereby taxation authority may be exerted. More comprehensive federal regulation of this area has often been proposed; see ante, at 456 n. 4.

[3] Under the Articles of Confederation, dealings of the States with foreign governments and among themselves were separately treated. Article VI of the Articles of Confederation provided:

> "1. No State, without the Consent of the United States, in Congress assembled, shall send any embassy to, or receive any embassy from, or enter into any confe[r]ence, agreement, alliance, or treaty, with any king, prince or State. . . ."

Thereafter, in that same Article, it was provided:

> "2. No two or more States shall enter into any treaty, confederation, or alliance whatever, between them, without the consent of the United States, in Congress assembled, specifying accurately the purposes for which the same is to be entered into, and how long it shall continue."

There was thus no requirement that mere "agreements" between States be subjected to the approval of Congress. That the framers of the Articles recognized a distinction between treaties, alliances, and confederations on the one hand and agreements on the other is demonstrated by the differing language in the two paragraphs above quoted, taken from the same Article.

David Engdahl, in Characterization of Interstate Arrangements: When is a Compact not a Compact?, 64 *Mich. L. Rev.* 63, 81 (1965), has suggested a perceptive rationale for this difference in treatment. Article IX, 2, of the Articles of Confederation provided:

> "The United States, in Congress assembled, shall also be the last resort on appeal in all disputes and differences now subsisting, or that hereafter may arise between two or more States concerning boundary, jurisdiction, or any other cause whatever. . . ."

And it specified an elaborate system by which the Congress would constitute a court for the resolution of interstate disputes. Hence, if there were a disagreement over a compact that had been reached between two or more States, it could be adjudicated amicably before the Congress without risk of disrupting the Union. Treaties with foreign states, on the other hand, were much more dangerous and could embroil a State in serious obligations and even war. Of almost the same level of seriousness were alliances between the States, of potential long duration and obliging one State to treat two sister States in different fashion. For these reasons, prior approval by the Congress was required.

As Madison's commentary quoted in the text indicates, there was dissatisfaction with the way in which the Articles of Confederation provided for interstate compacts. The Constitution adopted an absolute prohibition against treaties, alliances, or confederations by the States; and imposed the requirement of congressional approval for "any Agreement or Compact with another State, or with a foreign Power." U.S. Const., Art. I, 10.

factors of the Government under the Articles; and among the most important of these were "compacts with. the consent of Congs. as between Pena. and N. Jersey, and between Virga. & Maryd." James Madison, "Preface to Debates in the Convention of 1787," 3 M. Farrand, *Records of the Federal Convention of 1787*, p. 548 (1937). A compact between two States necessarily achieved some object unattainable, or attainable less conveniently, by separate States acting alone. Such effects were jealously guarded against, lest "the Fedl authy [be] violated." Ibid. It was the Federal Government's province to oversee conduct of a greater effect than a single State could accomplish, to protect both its own prerogative and that of the excluded States.[4]

Compacts and agreements between States were put in a separate constitutional category, and purposefully so. Nor is the form used by the agreeing States important; as the majority correctly observes:

> "Agreements effected through reciprocal legislation may present opportunities for enhancement of state power at the expense of the federal supremacy similar to the threats inherent in a more formalized 'compact.' . . . The Clause reaches both 'agreements' and 'compacts,' the formal as well as the informal. The relevant inquiry must be one of impact on our federal structure." Ante, at 470–471 (footnotes omitted).
> "Appellants further urge that the pertinent inquiry is one of potential, rather than actual, impact upon federal supremacy. We agree." Ante, at 472.

This is an apt recognition of the important distinction between the Compact Clause and the Commerce Clause. States may legislate in interstate commerce until an actual impact upon federal supremacy occurs. For individual States, the harm of potential impact is insufficiently upsetting to require prior congressional approval. For States acting in concert, however, whether through informal agreement, reciprocal legislation, or formal compact, "potential . . . impact upon federal supremacy" is enough to invoke the requirement of congressional approval.[5]

To this point, my views do not diverge from those of the majority as I understand them. But we do differ markedly in the application of those views to the Multistate Tax Compact.

II

Congressional consent to an interstate compact may be expressed in several ways. In the leading case of *Virginia v. Tennessee*, 148 U.S. 503 (1893), congressional consent to a compact setting a boundary was inferred from years of acquiescence to

---

[4] See infra, at 493–496.

[5] The frequent circumstance of potential impact would make that standard unworkable in the Commerce Clause context since the result is pre-emption of state effort; but where the result is merely the requirement that Congress be consulted about the State's effort, as is the case with the Compact Clause, the application of that standard is not nearly so obstructive.

that line by the Congress in delimiting federal judicial and electoral districts. *Id.*, at 522. Congressional consent may also be given in advance of the adoption of any specific compacts, by general consent resolutions, as was the case for the highway safety compacts, 72 Stat. 635, and the Crime Control Compact Consent Act of 1934, ch. 406, 48 Stat. 909.

Congress does not pass upon a submitted compact in the manner of a court of law deciding a question of constitutionality. Rather, the requirement that Congress approve a compact is to obtain its political judgment:[6] Is the agreement likely to interfere with federal activity in the area, is it likely to disadvantage other States to an important extent, is it a matter that would better be left untouched by state and federal regulation?[7] It comports with the purpose of seeking the political consent Congress affords that such consent may be expressed in ways as informal as tacit recognition[8] or prior approval, that Congress be permitted to attach conditions upon its consent,[9] and that congressional approval be a continuing requirement.[10]

In the present case, it would not be possible to infer approval from the congressional reaction to the Multistate Tax Compact. Indeed, the history of the Congress and the Compact is a chronicle of jealous attempts of one to close out the efforts of the other.[11]

On the congressional side of this long-lived battle, bills to approve the Compact

---

[6] See n. 3, *supra*.

[7] The pioneer article in the compact literature, Frankfurter & Landis, The Compact Clause of the Constitution—A Study in Interstate Adjustments, 34 *Yale L. J.* 685 (1925), recognized the preferability of compacts to litigation in light of the political factors that could be balanced in the process of submitting and approving a compact. See *id.*, at 696, 706–707. This Court has also observed the peculiar amenability of some problems to settlement by compact rather than litigation. See *Colorado v. Kansas*, 320 U.S. 383, 392 (1943). See also F. Zimmermann & M. Wendell, *The Interstate Compact Since 1925*, pp. 102–103 (1951).

[8] A statute-of-limitations type of approach to the necessary duration of congressional silence before consent may be inferred has been suggested by one commentator. Note, The Constitutionality of the Multistate Tax Compact, 29 *Vand. L. Rev.* 453, 460 (1976). The National Association of Attorneys General has also declared its support for the use of informal procedures. F. Zimmermann & M. Wendell, *The Law and Use of Interstate Compacts* 25 (1961).

[9] In *West Virginia ex rel. Dyer v. Sims*, 341 U.S. 22, 27 (1951), this Court commented favorably on the provisions of the Compact involved which allowed continuing participation by the Federal Government through the President's power to designate members of the supervisory commission. The Port of New York Authority Compacts of 1921 and 1922 were among the first to provide for direct continuing supervisory authority by Congress. See Celler, Congress, Compacts, and Interstate Authorities, 26 *Law & Contemp. Prob.* 682, 688 (1961) (hereinafter Celler). It has been suggested that the imposition of conditions and the continuing nature of Congress' supervision are perceived as drawbacks by compacting States, and have led to a hesitancy to submit interstate agreements to Congress. See Note, supra, n. 8, at 461.

[10] This Court has held that Congress must possess the continuing power to reconsider terms approved in compacts, lest "[C]ongress and two States . . . possess the power to modify and alter the [C]onstitution itself." *Pennsylvania v. Wheeling & Belmont Bridge Co.*, 18 How. 421, 433 (1856). See also Celler 685, and authorities cited therein.

[11] An excellent summary of the several battles in this war is recounted in Hellerstein, State Taxation Under the Commerce Clause: An Historical Perspective, 29 *Vand. L. Rev.* 335, 339–342 (1976). See also Sharpe, State Taxation of Interstate Businesses and the Multistate Tax Compact: The Search for a Delicate Uniformity, 11 *Colum. J. L. & Soc. Prob.* 231, 240–244 (1975) (hereinafter Sharpe).

have been introduced 12 separate times,[12] but all have faltered before arriving at a vote. Congress took the first step in the field of interstate tax apportionment with Pub. L. No. 86-272, 73 Stat. 555, passed the same year that this Court's opinion in *Northwestern States Portland Cement Co. v. Minnesota*, 358 U.S. 450 (1959), approved state taxation of reasonably identified multistate corporate income. A special subcommittee (the Willis Committee) was established which reported five years later with specific recommendations for federal statutory solution to the interstate allocation problem. In the Multistate Tax Commission's own words:

> "The origin and history of the Multistate Tax Compact are intimately related and bound up with the history of the states' struggle to save their fiscal and political independence from encroachments of certain federal legislation introduced in [C]ongress during the past three years. These were the Interstate Taxation Acts, better known as the Willis Bills."[13]

A special meeting of the National Association of Tax Administrators was called in January 1966; that gathering was the genesis of the Multistate Tax Compact. Over the course of 11 years, numerous bills have been introduced in the Congress as successors to the original Willis Bills, but none has ever become law.[14]

For its part, the Multistate Tax Commission has made no attempt to disguise its purpose. In its First Annual Report, the Commission spoke proudly of "bottling up the Willis Bill [alternative federal legislation] for an extended period," but warned that "it cannot be said that the threat of coercive, restrictive federal legislation is gone." 1 Multistate Tax Commission Ann. Rep. 10 (1968). In the most recent annual report, the tone has not changed. The Commission lists as one of its "major goals" the desire to "guard against restrictive federal legislation and other federal action which impinges upon the ability of state tax administrators to carry out the laws of their states effectively." 9 Multistate Tax Commission Ann. Rep. 1 (1976). The same report pledged continued opposition to specific bills introduced in Congress restricting the States' utilization of the unitary-business concept and providing alternatives to the Compact's recommended method of apportioning multistate corporate earnings to the various States.[15] Even more importantly, the Commission denounced the tax treaty already signed with Great Britain (though not yet ratified),[16] for its prohibition of the unitary-business concept, the practice whereby a State combines for tax purposes the incomes from several related companies belonging to a single parent, even when the business carried on in a particular State is conducted by only one of the related companies. The President has negotiated this treaty in the diplomatic interest of the United States;

---

[12] See ante, at 458 n. 8.
[13] 1 Multistate Tax Commission Ann. Rep. 1 (1968).
[14] See ante, at 456 n. 4.
[15] See also 7 Multistate Tax Commission Ann. Rep. 3 (1974).
[16] See ante, at 476 n. 29.

but acting together through their joint agency, the Multistate Tax Commission, the Compact States are opposing its ratification. Of course, the Compact States have every right, in their own interest, to petition the branches of the Federal Government. Still, it cannot be disputed that the action of over 20 States, speaking through a single, established authority, carries an influence far stronger than would 20 separate voices.

A hostile stalemate characterizes the present position of the parties: the Multistate Tax Compact States opposing the Federal Congress and, since the proposed new tax treaty, the Federal Executive as well. No one could view this history and conclude that the Congress has acquiesced in the Multistate Tax Compact.

But more is demonstrated by this long dispute underlying the present case: Not only has Congress failed to acquiesce in the Multistate Tax Compact, but both Congress and the Executive have clearly demonstrated that there is a federal interest in the rules for apportioning multistate and multinational income. The Executive cannot constitutionally express his federal sovereign interest in the matter any more unambiguously. He has negotiated a treaty with a foreign power and submitted that treaty to the Senate. As for the Congress, its federal sovereign interest in the topic was early established in Pub. L. No. 86-272. While the following years have produced no new legislation, the activity over the Willis Report, the Willis Bills, the successor bills, and the dozen shelvings of compact ratification bills establish at the very least that the Congress believes a federal interest is involved.[17] That a potential impact on federal concerns is at stake is indisputable.

It might be argued that Congress could more clearly have expressed its federal interest by passing a statute pre-empting the field, possibly in the form of an alternative apportionment formula. To hold Congress to the necessity of such action, however, accords no force to the Compact Clause independent of the Commerce Clause, as explained above. If the way to show a "potential federal interest" requires an exercise of the actual federal commerce power, then the purposes of the Compact Clause, and the Framers' deep-seated and special fear of agreements between States, would be accorded absolutely no respect.

III

Virginia v. Tennessee[18] quite clearly holds that not all agreements and compacts must be submitted to the Congress. The majority's phraseology of the test as "potential impact upon federal supremacy" incorporates the *Virginia v. Tennessee* standard. Nor do I disagree that many interstate agreements are legally effective without congressional consent. "Potential impact upon federal supremacy" requires some demonstration of a federal interest in the matter under consideration, and a threat to that interest. In very few cases, short of a direct conflict, will the record of congressional and executive action demonstrate as clearly as the record in the present case that

---

[17] For contrasting examples, where Congress perceived no federal interest, see Zimmermann & Wendell, supra, n. 8, at 21.

[18] See also *Wharton v. Wise*, 153 U.S. 155 (1894), applying the *Virginia v. Tennessee* dicta.

the Federal Government considers itself to have a valid interest in the subject matter. Examples of compacts over which no federal concern was inferable have already been suggested.[19]

It seems to me, however, that even if a realistic potential impact on federal supremacy failed to materialize at one historic moment, that should not mean that an interstate compact or agreement is forever immune from congressional disapproval on an absolute or conditional basis. Yet the majority's approach appears to be that, because the instant agreement is, in the majority's view, initially without the Clause, it will never require congressional approval. The majority would approve this Compact without congressional ratification purely on the basis of its form: that no power is conferred upon the Multistate Tax Commission that could not be independently exercised by a member State. Such a view pretermits the possibility of requiring congressional approval in the future should circumstances later present even more clearly a potential federal interest, so long as the form of the Compact has not changed. That consequence fails to provide the ongoing congressional oversight that is part of the Compact Clause's protections.[20]

IV

For appellants' many suggestions of extraordinary authority wielded by the Multistate Tax Commission, the majority has but one repeated answer: that each member State is free to adopt the procedures in question just as it could as if the Compact did not exist.

This cannot be an adequate answer even for the majority, which holds that "[a]greements effected through reciprocal legislation may present opportunities for enhancement of state power at the expense of the federal supremacy similar to the threats inherent in a more formalized 'compact.'" Ante, at 470 (footnote omitted). Reciprocal legislation is adopted by each State independently, yet derives its force from the knowledge that other States are acting in identical fashion. In recognizing Compact Clause concerns even in reciprocal legislation, the majority correctly lays the premise that the absence of an autonomous authority would not be controlling.

So here, that the Compact States act in concerted fashion to foreclose federal law and treaties on apportionment of income, multistate audits, and unitary-business concepts[21] tells us at the least that a potential impact on federal supremacy exists.

---

[19] See ante, at 471–472, n. 24 (discussion of Interstate Compact to Conserve Oil and Gas).

[20] See n. 10, supra. Frankfurter and Landis found great value in interstate compacts because of their "[c]ontinuous and creative administration." See Frankfurter & Landis, supra, n. 7, at 707. By excluding Congress from the administration of the Multistate Tax Compact, the majority opinion restricts this facet of the Compact's attractiveness.

[21] For a detailed analysis of the complex taxation issues underlying each of these terms, see Carlson, State Taxation of Corporate Income from Foreign Sources, Department of Treasury Tax Policy Research Study Number Three, *Essays in International Taxation*: 1976, pp. 231, 235–252. For a thorough treatment of the income-allocation problem in the multinational setting, see Note. Multinational Corporations and Income Allocation Under Section 482 of the Internal Revenue Code, 89 *Harv. L. Rev.* 1202 (1976).

No realistic view of that impact could maintain that it is no greater than if individual States, acting purely spontaneously and without concert, had taken the same steps. It is pure fantasy to suggest that 21 States could conceivably have arrived independently at identical regulations for apportioning income, reciprocal subpoena powers, and identical interstate audits of multinational corporations, in the absence of some agreement among them.

Further, it is not clear upon reading the majority's opinion that appellants' suggestions of actual synergistic powers in the Multistate Tax Commission have been adequately answered. The Commission does have some life of its own. Under Art. VIII, providing for interstate audits, the Commission is given authority to offer to conduct audits even if no State has made a request.

> "If the Commission, on the basis of its experience, has reason to believe that an audit of a particular taxpayer, either at a particular time or on a particular schedule, would be of interest to a number of party States or their subdivisions, it may offer to make the audit or audits, the offer to be contingent on sufficient participation therein as determined by the Commission."
> Multistate Tax Compact, Art. VIII, 5.

If not for the Commission's acting on its own, in the absence of a suggestion from any State, the audit would not come about, even if the States subsequently approve. That implies some effects can be achieved beyond what the individual States themselves would have achieved, since, by hypothesis, no State would have proposed the audit on its own.

Other troubling provisions are Art. III, 1, requiring that all member States must allow taxpayers to apportion their income in accord with Art. IV (the substance of which is similar to the Uniform Division of Income for Tax Purposes Act); and Art. III, 2, requiring that all member States must offer a short-form option for small-business income tax.[22] If Compact States have no choice in the matter, these sections unquestionably go beyond the mere advisory role in which the majority would cast the Multistate Commission.

On its face, the Compact also provides in Art. IX for compulsory arbitration of allocation disputes among the member States at the option of any taxpayer electing to apportion his income in accord with Art. IV. Although Art. IX is not now operative (it requires passage of a regulation by the Commission to revive the arbitration mechanism), it was in effect for two and a half years. This provision binds the member States' participation, even against their will in any particular case. In two final respects, the Compact also differs significantly from reciprocal legislation. The subpoena power which the Compact makes possible (auditors can obtain subpoenas in any one of the

---

[22] There is some question as to whether this Article is as mandatory as its language suggests. Several States in the Compact do not provide the option, and several others have not adopted the requisite rates to accompany the option. See Sharpe 245 n. 55. However, most of the member States have complied.

States which have adopted Art. VIII of the Compact) is far different from what would be accomplished through reciprocal laws, in that it places an unusual "all-or-nothing" pressure on the non-Compact States. The usual form of reciprocal law is a statute passed by State Y, saying that any other State which accords Y access to its courts for the enforcement of tax obligations likewise will have access to the courts of Y. This Compact says that an outsider State will obtain reciprocal subpoena powers only as part of a package of Art. VIII Compact States—its own courts must be opened to all these States, and in return it will obtain Compact-wide access for judicial process needed in its own tax enforcement.

Lastly, the very creation of the Compact sets it apart from separate state action. The Compact did not become effective in any of the ratifying States until at least seven States had adopted it. Thus, unlike reciprocal legislation, the Compact provided a means by which a State could assure itself that a certain number of other States would go along before committing itself to an apportionment formula.

V

One aspect of the *Virginia v. Tennessee* test for congressional approval of inter-state compacts requires specific emphasis. The *Virginia v. Tennessee* opinion speaks of whether a combination tends "to the increase of political power in the States, which may encroach upon or interfere with the just supremacy of the United States," 148 U.S., at 519, and later, whether a compact or agreement would "encroach or not upon the full and free exercise of Federal authority." *Id.*, at 520.

The majority properly notes that any agreement among the States will increase their power, and focuses on the critical question of whether such an increase will enhance "state power *quoad* the National Government." Ante, at 473. A proper under-standing of what would encroach upon federal authority, however, must also incorpo-rate encroachments on the authority and power of non-Compact States.

In *Rhode Island v. Massachusetts*, 12 *Pet.* 657, 726 (1838), this Court held that the purpose of requiring the submission to Congress of a compact (in that case, regard-ing a boundary) between two States was "to guard against the derangement of their federal relations with the other states of the Union, and the federal government; which might be injuriously affected, if the contracting states might act upon their boundar-ies at their pleasure." See also *Florida v. Georgia*, 17 *How.* 478, 494 (1855). There is no want of authority for the conclusion that encroachments upon non-compact States are as seriously to be guarded against as encroachments upon the federal authority,[23]

---

[23] See, e.g., *United States v. Tobin*, 195 F. Supp. 588, 606 (DC 1961); Tribe, Intergovernmental Immunities in Litigation, Taxation, and Regulation: Separation of Powers Issues in Controversies About Federalism, 89 Harv. L. Rev. 682, 712 (1976); Sharp 265–272 (specifically observing state complaints about the Multistate Tax Compact); Zimmermann & Wendell, supra, n. 8, at 23; Celler 684 (purpose of Compact Clause "'to pre-vent undue injury to the interests of noncompacting states,'" quoting *United States v. Tobin*, supra); and Frankfurter & Landis, supra, n. 7, at 694–695. The Frankfurter and Landis treatment is perhaps the clearest

nor is that surprising in view of the federal Government's pre-eminent purpose to protect the rights of one State against another. If the effect of a compact were to put non-compact States at a serious disadvantage, the federal interest would thereby be affected as well.

The majority appears to recognize that allegations of harmful impact on other States is a cognizable challenge to a compact. See ante, at 477–478, 462–463, n. 12. The response the majority opinion provides is by now a familiar one: "Each member State is free to adopt the auditing procedures it thinks best, just as it could if the Compact did not exist." Ante, at 477–478. The criticism of this reasoning offered above, in the context of encroachment on federal power, is applicable here as well. Judging by effect, not form, it is obvious that non-Compact States can be placed at a competitive disadvantage by the Multistate Tax Compact.

One example is in the attraction of multistate corporations to locate within a certain State's borders. Before the Multistate Tax Compact, "nonbusiness" dividend income was most commonly allocated to the State where a corporation was domiciled.[24] Under the Compact's "advisory" regulations, this type of income is apportioned among the several States where the company conducts its business. Hence, a non-Compact State will run the risk of taxing a domiciliary multistate corporation on more than 100% of its nonbusiness income, unless, of course, the State agrees to follow the rule of the Compact. Another way to view the impact on a nonmember State is that if it wished to attract a multistate corporation to become a domiciliary, it might offer not to tax nonbusiness income. But with such income being apportioned by several other States anyway, the lure of the domicile State's exemption is effectively dissipated.

None of these results is necessarily "bad." The only conclusion urged here is that the effect on non-Compact States be recognized as sufficiently serious that Congress should be consulted. As the constitutional arbiter of political differences between States, the Congress is the proper body to evaluate the extent of harm being imposed on non-Compact States, and to impose ameliorative restrictions as might be necessary.

The Compact Clause is an important, intended safeguard within our constitutional structure. It is functionally a conciliatory rather than a prohibitive clause. All it requires is that Congress review interstate agreements that are capable of affecting

---

expression of how the protection of federal and noncompact state interests blend in the rationale for the Compact Clause:

> "But the Constitution plainly had two very practical objectives in view in conditioning agreement by States upon consent of Congress. For only Congress is the appropriate organ for determining what arrangements between States might fall within the prohibited class of 'Treaty, Alliance, or Confederation,' and what arrangements come within the permissive class of 'Agreement or Compact.' But even the permissive agreements may affect the interests of State other than those parties to the agreement: the national, and not merely a regional, interest may be involved. Therefore, Congress must exercise national supervision through its power to grant or withhold consent, or to grant it under appropriate conditions." Ibid.

[24] See Sharpe 269.

federal or other States' rights. In the Court's decision today, a highly complex multi-state compact, detailed in structure and pervasive in its effect on the important area of interstate and international business taxation, has been legitimized without the consent of Congress. If the Multi-state Tax Compact is not a compact within the meaning of Art. I, 10, then I fear there is very little life remaining in that section of our Constitution.

I respectfully dissent.

APPENDIX CC: RESULTS OF 2000 PRESIDENTIAL ELECTION

STATE	BUSH	GORE	BUSH MARGIN	GORE MARGIN	BUSH EV	GORE EV
Alabama	944,409	695,602	248,807		9	
Alaska	167,398	79,004	88,394		3	
Arizona	781,652	685,341	96,311		8	
Arkansas	472,940	422,768	50,172		6	
California	4,567,429	5,861,203		1,293,774		54
Colorado	883,745	738,227	145,518		8	
Connecticut	561,094	816,015		254,921		8
D.C.	137,288	180,068		42,780		3
Delaware	18,073	171,923		153,850		3
Florida	2,912,790	2,912,253	537		25	
Georgia	1,419,720	1,116,230	303,490		13	
Hawaii	137,845	205,286		67,441		4
Idaho	336,937	138,637	198,300		4	
Illinois	2,019,421	2,589,026		569,605		22
Indiana	1,245,836	901,980	343,856		12	
Iowa	634,373	638,517		4,144		7
Kansas	622,332	399,276	223,056		6	
Kentucky	872,492	638,898	233,594		8	
Louisiana	927,871	792,344	135,527		9	
Maine	286,616	319,951		33,335		4
Maryland	813,797	1,145,782		331,985		10
Massachusetts	878,502	1,616,487		737,985		12
Michigan	1,953,139	2,170,418		217,279		18
Minnesota	1,109,659	1,168,266		58,607		10
Mississippi	573,230	404,964	168,266		7	
Missouri	1,189,924	1,111,138	78,786		11	
Montana	240,178	137,126	103,052		3	
Nebraska	433,862	231,780	202,082		5	
Nevada	301,575	279,978	21,597		4	
New Hampshire	273,559	266,348	7,211		4	
New Jersey	1,284,173	1,788,850		504,677		15
New Mexico	286,417	286,783		366		5
New York	2,403,374	4,107,907		1,704,533		33
North Carolina	1,631,163	1,257,692	373,471		14	
North Dakota	174,852	95,284	79,568		3	
Ohio	2,351,209	2,186,190	165,019		21	
Oklahoma	744,337	474,276	270,061		8	
Oregon	713,577	720,342		6,765		7
Pennsylvania	2,281,127	2,485,967		204,840		23
Rhode Island	130,555	249,508		118,953		4
South Carolina	786,426	566,039	220,387		8	
South Dakota	190,700	118,804	71,896		3	
Tennessee	1,061,949	981,720	80,229		11	
Texas	3,799,639	2,433,746	1,365,893		32	
Utah	515,096	203,053	312,043		5	
Vermont	119,775	149,022		29,247		3
Virginia	1,437,490	1,217,290	220,200		13	
Washington	1,108,864	1,247,652		138,788		11
West Virginia	336,475	295,497	40,978		5	
Wisconsin	1,237,279	1,242,987		5,708		11
Wyoming	147,947	60,481	87,466		3	
Total	**50,460,110**	**51,003,926**			**271**	**267**

APPENDIX DD: RESULTS OF 2004 PRESIDENTIAL ELECTION

STATE	BUSH	KERRY	BUSH MARGIN	KERRY MARGIN	BUSH EV	KERRY EV
Alabama	1,176,394	693,933	482,461		9	
Alaska	190,889	111,025	79,864		3	
Arizona	1,104,294	893,524	210,770		10	
Arkansas	572,898	469,953	102,945		6	
California	5,509,826	6,745,485		1,235,659		55
Colorado	1,101,255	1,001,732	99,523		9	
Connecticut	693,826	857,488		163,662		7
D. C.	21,256	202,970		181,714		3
Delaware	171,660	200,152		28,492		3
Florida	3,964,522	3,583,544	380,978		27	
Georgia	1,914,254	1,366,149	548,105		15	
Hawaii	194,191	231,708		37,517		4
Idaho	409,235	181,098	228,137		4	
Illinois	2,345,946	2,891,550		545,604		21
Indiana	1,479,438	969,011	510,427		11	
Iowa	751,957	741,898	10,059		7	
Kansas	736,456	434,993	301,463		6	
Kentucky	1,069,439	712,733	356,706		8	
Louisiana	1,102,169	820,299	281,870		9	
Maine	330,201	396,842		66,641		4
Maryland	1,024,703	1,334,493		309,790		10
Massachusetts	1,071,109	1,803,800		732,691		12
Michigan	2,313,746	2,479,183		165,437		17
Minnesota	1,346,695	1,445,014		98,319		10
Mississippi	684,981	458,094	226,887		6	
Missouri	1,455,713	1,259,171	196,542		11	
Montana	266,063	173,710	92,353		3	
Nebraska	512,814	254,328	258,486		5	
Nevada	418,690	397,190	21,500		5	
New Hampshire	331,237	340,511		9,274		4
New Jersey	1,670,003	1,911,430		241,427		15
New Mexico	376,930	370,942	5,988		5	
New York	2,962,567	4,314,280		1,351,713		31
North Carolina	1,961,166	1,525,849	435,317		15	
North Dakota	196,651	111,052	85,599		3	
Ohio	2,859,768	2,741,167	118,601		20	
Oklahoma	959,792	503,966	455,826		7	
Oregon	866,831	943,163		76,332		7
Pennsylvania	2,793,847	2,938,095		144,248		21
Rhode Island	169,046	259,760		90,714		4
South Carolina	937,974	661,699	276,275		8	
South Dakota	232,584	149,244	83,340		3	
Tennessee	1,384,375	1,036,477	347,898		11	
Texas	4,526,917	2,832,704	1,694,213		34	
Utah	663,742	241,199	422,543		5	
Vermont	121,180	184,067		62,887		3
Virginia	1,716,959	1,454,742	262,217		13	
Washington	1,304,894	1,510,201		205,307		11
West Virginia	423,778	326,541	97,237		5	
Wisconsin	1,478,120	1,489,504		11,384		10
Wyoming	167,629	70,776	96,853		3	
Total	**62,040,610**	**59,028,439**			**286**	**252**

APPENDIX EE: RESULTS OF 2008 PRESIDENTIAL ELECTION

STATE	MCCAIN	OBAMA	MCCAIN MARGIN	OBAMA MARGIN	MCCAIN EV	OBAMA EV
Alabama	1,266,546	813,479	453,067		9	
Alaska	193,841	123,594	70,247		3	
Arizona	1,230,111	1,034,707	195,404		10	
Arkansas	638,017	422,310	215,707		6	
California	5,011,781	8,274,473		3,262,692		55
Colorado	1,073,589	1,288,576		214,987		9
Connecticut	629,428	997,773		368,345		7
Delaware	152,374	255,459		103,085		3
D.C.	17,367	245,800		228,433		3
Florida	4,045,624	4,282,074		236,450		27
Georgia	2,048,759	1,844,123	204,636		15	
Hawaii	120,566	325,871		205,305		4
Idaho	403,012	236,440	166,572		4	
Illinois	2,031,179	3,419,348		1,388,169		21
Indiana	1,345,648	1,374,039		28,391		11
Iowa	682,379	828,940		146,561		7
Kansas	699,655	514,765	184,890		6	
Kentucky	1,048,462	751,985	296,477		8	
Louisiana	1,148,275	782,989	365,286		9	
Maine	295,273	421,923		126,650		4
Maryland	959,862	1,629,467		669,605		10
Massachusetts	1,108,854	1,904,097		795,243		12
Michigan	2,048,639	2,872,579		823,940		17
Minnesota	1,275,409	1,573,354		297,945		10
Mississippi	724,597	554,662	169,935		6	
Missouri	1,445,814	1,441,911	3,903		11	
Montana	242,763	231,667	11,096		3	
Nebraska	452,979	333,319	119,660		4	1[1]
Nevada	412,827	533,736		120,909		5
New Hampshire	316,534	384,826		68,292		4
New Jersey	1,613,207	2,215,422		602,215		15
New Mexico	346,832	472,422		125,590		5
New York	2,752,728	4,804,701		2,051,973		31
North Carolina	2,128,474	2,142,651		14,177		15
North Dakota	168,601	141,278	27,323		3	
Ohio	2,677,820	2,940,044		262,224		20
Oklahoma	960,165	502,496	457,669		7	
Oregon	738,475	1,037,291		298,816		7
Pennsylvania	2,655,885	3,276,363		620,478		21
Rhode Island	165,391	296,571		131,180		4
South Carolina	1,034,896	862,449	172,447		8	
South Dakota	203,054	170,924	32,130		3	
Tennessee	1,479,178	1,087,437	391,741		11	
Texas	4,479,328	3,528,633	950,695		34	
Utah	596,030	327,670	268,360		5	
Vermont	98,974	219,262		120,288		3
Virginia	1,725,005	1,959,532		234,527		13
Washington	1,229,216	1,750,848		521,632		11
West Virginia	397,466	303,857	93,609		5	
Wisconsin	1,262,393	1,677,211		414,818		10
Wyoming	164,958	82,868	82,090		3	
Total	**59,948,240**	**69,498,216**			**173**	**365**

Source: David Leip's *Atlas of U.S. Presidential Elections*
[1] Nebraska awards electoral votes by congressional district.

APPENDIX FF: THREE-JUDGE FEDERAL COURT DECISION IN *WILLIAMS V. VIRGINIA STATE BOARD OF ELECTIONS* (1968)

This decision was affirmed by U.S. Supreme Court at 393 U.S. 320 (1969) (per curiam).

United States District Court—Eastern District at Alexandria

J. Harvie Williams et al., Plaintiffs,

v.

Virginia State Board of Elections, etc., et al., Defendants

Civ. A. No. 4768-A.

288 F.Supp. 622 (1968)

United States District Court E. D. Virginia, at Alexandria.

July 16, 1968.

Howard S. Spering, Washington, D.C., Robert L. Montague, III, Alexandria, Va., for plaintiffs.

Robert Y. Button, Atty. Gen. of Virginia, Richmond, Va., Robert D. McIlwaine, III, Richard N. Harris, Asst. Attys. Gen. of Virginia, Richmond, Va., for defendants.

Before BRYAN, Circuit Judge, and LEWIS and MERHIGE, District Judges.

ALBERT V. BRYAN, Circuit Judge:

Presidential electors provided for in Article II of the Constitution of the United States cannot be selected, plaintiffs charge, by a statewide general election as directed by the Virginia statute.[1] Under it *all* of the State's electors are collectively chosen in the Presidential election by the greatest number of votes cast throughout the entire State, instead of choosing them by Congressional districts, *one* elector for each, exclusively by the votes cast in that district.

Unfairness is imputed to the plan because it gives the choice of *all* of the electors to the statewide plurality of those voting in the election—"winner take all"—and accords no representation among the electors to the minority of the voters. An additional prejudice is found in the result of the system as between voters in different States. We must reject these contentions.

The Constitution provides for the election of the President and Vice President by electors in these words:

> Article II
>
> "Section 1. . . . He [the President] shall . . . together with the Vice President . . . be elected, as follows:
>
> "Each State shall appoint, in such Manner as the Legislature thereof may direct, a Number of Electors, equal to the whole Number of Senators and Representatives to which the State may be entitled in the Congress. . . ."

---

[1] *Code of Va.*, 1950, Section 24-7, quoted infra. The same general plan now prevails in every State.

Article XII [Twelfth Amendment]

"The Electors shall meet in their respective states, and vote by ballot for President and Vice-President, one of whom, at least, shall not be an inhabitant of the same state with themselves; they shall name in their ballots the person voted for as President, and in distinct ballots the person voted for as Vice-President, and they shall make distinct lists of all persons voted for as President, and of all persons voted for as Vice-President, and of the number of votes for each, which lists they shall sign and certify, and transmit sealed to the seat of the government of the United States, directed to the President of the Senate. . . . "

Plaintiffs' proposition is advanced on three counts: (1) the intendment of Article II, Section 1, providing for the appointment of electors is that they be chosen in the same manner as Senators and Representatives, that is two at large and the remainder by Congressional or other equal districts; (2) the general ticket method violates the "one-person, one-vote" principle of the Equal Protection Clause of the Fourteenth Amendment, i.e., the weight of each citizen's vote must be substantially equal to that of every other citizen. *Gray v. Sanders*, 372 U.S. 368, 381, 83 S.Ct. 801, 9 L.Ed. 2d 821 (1963); *Wesberry v. Sanders*, 376 U.S. 1, 18, 84 S.Ct. 526, 11 L.Ed.2d 481 (1964); and (3) the general ticket system gives a citizen in a State having a larger number of electors than Virginia the opportunity to effectuate by his vote the selection of more electors than can the Virginian. On these bases the plaintiffs pray for a declaration that the Virginia statute is invalid and for an injunction against its use by the defendant State election officials.

The Code of Virginia, 1950, Section 24-7 directs:

"§ 24-7. Electors for President and Vice President.—There shall be chosen by the qualified voters of the Commonwealth, . . . at elections to be held on the Tuesday after the first Monday in November in each fourth year [after 1948], so many electors for President and Vice President of the United States as this State shall be entitled to at the time of such election under the Constitution and laws of the United States. Each voter may vote for one elector from each congressional district of the State, as the same shall be constituted and apportioned for the election of representatives in the Congress of the United States from this State at the time when such election shall be held, and for two electors from the State at large; . . . "

Congress has prescribed that henceforth the Representatives from each State, when more than one, be chosen by districts, 2 U.S.C. §§ 2a, 2c. Similar provision is made by Article IV, Section 55 of the Constitution of Virginia as well as by statute, *Code of Va.*, Section 24-4. Virginia has ten Representatives besides two Senators. Save to analogize the selection of electors with the selection of Senators and Representatives the plaintiffs make no point, of course, against the election statewide of the two electors corresponding to the Senators. Our discussion, therefore, will refer solely to those electors who are the counterparts of Representatives in Congress.

Throughout, it must be kept constantly in mind that the wisdom of the continued use of the electoral college for choosing the President and Vice President is not at issue here. As here posed the question recognizes the predominance of that Constitutional design. The inquiry is whether Article II, Section 1 considered alone or with Constitutional safeguards, permits the selection of the electors by a general election in which the entire electorate of the State may collectively vote at one time upon all of the electors.

Plaintiffs are ten in number, one from each of the Congressional districts of Virginia, and all of them qualified to vote in their respective districts in the coming fall election. Their brief describes their purpose:

> "This action is brought to protect and restore the full benefit of plaintiffs' right to vote. Plaintiffs seek to elect one presidential elector in, and solely by a plurality of the votes cast in, their own respective Congressional districts. They seek thereby to prevent the dilution of their own votes, and the denial of any possibility of their having any electoral representation when not part of the state-wide plurality, that now result from counting the votes of all voters throughout the state in determining the plurality of votes for the election of the one presidential elector that has been apportioned to the people resident in their respective Congressional district by virtue of their numbers. Thus, they seek to prevent the votes of residents in other Congressional districts of Virginia from being counted in determining the plurality of votes for the election of one presidential elector in, by, and from their own respective Congressional district."

We think they have the requisite standing to maintain the suit they plead; that it is an acceptable class action; that the defendants, save the Governor of Virginia, are proper parties, as the officials entrusted with the conduct of the election of presidential electors; and that this court has jurisdiction of the complaint. *Flast et al. v. Cohen, Secretary of Health, et al.*, 392 U.S. 83, 88 S.Ct. 1942, 20 L.Ed.2d 947 (June 10, 1968); 28 U.S.C. § 1343; 42 U.S.C. § 1983; 42 U.S.C. § 1988; *Baker v. Carr*, 369 U.S. 186, 82 S.Ct. 691, 7 L. Ed.2d 663 (1962); *Gray v. Sanders*, 372 U.S. 368, 83 S.Ct. 801, 9 L.Ed.2d 821 (1963); *Wesberry v. Sanders*, 376 U.S. 1, 84 S.Ct. 526, 11 L.Ed.2d 481 (1964); *Reynolds v. Sims*, 377 U.S. 533, 84 S.Ct. 1362, 12 L.Ed.2d 506 (1964); F.R.Civ.P. 23. Because of its special circumstances, we do not think *Penton v. Humphrey*, 264 F.Supp. 250 (S.D.Miss.1967 —3-judge court) dictates rejection of the present action; nor do we believe on reading of the pleadings in *State of Delaware v. State of New York*, 385 U.S. 895, 87 S.Ct. 198, 17 L.Ed.2d 129 (1966), cited by the defendants, that it forecloses entertainment of plaintiffs' plaint.

I.

The first argument of the plaintiffs is that the college of electors was envisaged by the Constitution as delegates of the people—although to exercise their own judgment—in naming the President and Vice President, thus according the people a truer representation in the choosing of these officers. The electors, they aver, were to be as directly and immediately representative of the people as the college method permitted.

To this extent and to this end, a voice in selection of the President and Vice President, the argument is, was avouched the people in the same measure as is assured them in picking members of the legislative branch of the Federal government. If, continue plaintiffs, Representatives in Congress are—in fairness to the people—chosen by districts, so should be electors.

Primary citation for this position is the parallelism drawn by the Constitution in the numerical correspondence of electors with the State's total of Senators and Representatives. This conformity is marked also by the requirement of varying the number of electors as the number of Representatives change.

Admittedly, the designation of all presidential electors by the ballot of all who voted throughout the State does not produce a group as representative of the people as would an election of one elector by each district alone. For instance, as the plaintiffs demonstrate, while in 1960 the popular vote in Virginia for the Republican nominee was only 52.4%, and the Democratic nominee received 47%, of the vote cast, the Republican was credited with 100% of Virginia's electoral votes and the Democrat with none. With the popular count reversed, the candidates in 1964 were favored and unfavored in electoral votes by the same formula. If plaintiffs' contention for single-elector district voting had prevailed, it would have been possible for the Democratic and Republican parties to have had proportionate representation among Virginia's electors in the same degree as they shared in the statewide tally.

Many of the Brahmins of the Constitutional Convention, such as Thomas Jefferson, James Madison and James Wilson, held the district plan more advisable. Indeed, Virginia and several of the other States for some years chose electors by district. However, it was Jefferson who advised Virginia to switch to the general ticket. His advice sprang from a desire to protect his State against the use of the general ticket by other States. He found that when chosen by districts, Virginia's representation among the electors was divided, while other States made their votes mean more in the college by adoption of the general ticket scheme of selection. This contention is no less true today.[2]

Thus, it cannot be safely said that the draftsmen of Article II, Section 1 believed that the electors must be chosen by congressional or other districts, as plaintiffs here contend. The clause literally leaves to the State legislature the appointment of elec-

---

[2] For a comprehensive and thoughtful disquisition upon the election of electors, consult Peirce, *The People's President* (1968), and the Memorandum of the Subcommittee on Constitutional Amendments of the Committee on the Judiciary, United States Senate, October 10, 1961.

tors "in such manner" as it may direct. Bestowal of this discretion is emphasized in *McPherson v. Blacker*, 146 U.S. 1, 13 S.Ct. 3, 36 L.Ed. 869 (1892). There the history of Article II is so fully traced that repetition of it may well be omitted. Nevertheless, that decision did no more than hold permissible and valid Michigan's determination to select electors by districts. Anything in the opinion appearing to rule on the acceptableness of some other plan is obiter; it is not authority for the assertion that the manner a State legislature adopts to appoint electors is beyond judicial review.

II.

On the contrary, in our opinion the authorization of each State by Article II to "appoint, in such manner as the Legislature thereof may direct," is "subject to possible constitutional limitations." *Ray v. Blair*, 343 U.S. 214, 227, 72 S.Ct. 654, 96 L.Ed. 894 (1952). In short, the manner of appointment must itself be free of Constitutional infirmity.

It is on this premise that plaintiffs, in their second argument, ask us to declare the general ticket system invalid as "debasing, abridging or misrepresenting the weight of the votes of citizens of the United States in presidential elections unconstitutionally." Principal reliance for this argument is the "one-person, one-vote" doctrine announced in *Gray v. Sanders*, supra, 372 U.S. 368, 381, 83 S.Ct. 801 (1953) and reaffirmed in *Wesberry v. Sanders*, supra, 376 U.S. 1, 18, 84 S.Ct. 526 (1964). Clearly, these decisions do condemn any such trespass. *Reynolds v. Sims*, 377 U.S. 533, 555, 84 S.Ct. 1362, 12 L.Ed.2d 506 (1964).

However, in our judgment the general ticket does not come within the brand of these decisions. Actually, the system is but another form of the unit rule. A familiar application is in the casting of a constituency's single vote by its several delegates in a convention. It also appears in Article II (Twelfth Amendment) making provision for the election of the President by the House of Representatives when no majority is obtained in the electoral college. Representatives cast the vote of their State according as the greater number of them vote.

We see nothing in the unit rule offensive to the Constitution. Concededly, its effect is exceptionable in many aspects. Some are enumerated in the Memorandum of the Subcommittee on Constitutional Amendments of the Committee on the Judiciary, United States Senate, at p. 22, supra footnote 2. Among possible objectionable results it listed disfranchisement of voters and the possibility of "minority presidents," that is one having a majority of electoral votes but not having a larger count in the popular vote than one of his opponents. Added to these detractions is the greater opportunity for the creation of "splinter" parties.

Discussing the disfranchisement defect, the Memorandum continues, p. 23, in this language:

> "Above the minimum of three, additional electoral votes to which a State is entitled are based upon population. Nevertheless as much as 49 percent of a

State's voters may see the portion of its electoral votes attributable to them cast for a candidate whom they oppose. It is not merely that their votes are wasted in the sense that they were cast for a loser, the unit rule not only extinguishes the voice of State minorities, but it allows State majorities to speak for them. . . .

. . .

"Some defenders of the unit-rule system dispute the logic of this argument. They answer that no votes are lost when validly cast in an election; that they are actually counted toward the final decision and if, insufficient for victory, they have simply exhausted their power as votes.

"However, the effect of the unit rule is to exhaust the power of millions of individual votes at the State level before the election is actually determined at the national level. They lose their effect on the outcome at a preliminary stage in the counting. These voters are disfranchised in the sense that their votes have no bearing on the national electoral vote totals which determine the winner.

"It is sometimes said that the thousands or millions of voters in a State whose candidate was defeated in its popular election might as well not have voted at all because the State's electoral vote would have gone the same way if they had stayed at home. This is not totally realistic. If they had not voted at all, one vote would have been sufficient to deliver the State's electoral vote for the opposing candidate. By voting, the minority party voters have set a figure which must be matched and exceeded by opposing voters before the State's electoral vote bloc is awarded to the opponent."

Many other reputable authorities have inveighed against the system when applied to the selection of electors. Their strictures include excoriation of the electoral college both as an original and current institution.

Notwithstanding, it is difficult to equate the deprivations imposed by the unit rule with the denial of privileges outlawed by the one-person, one-vote doctrine or banned by Constitutional mandates of protection. In the selection of electors the rule does not in any way denigrate the power of one citizen's ballot and heighten the influence of another's vote. Admittedly, once the electoral slate is chosen, it speaks only for the element with the largest number of votes. This in a sense is discrimination against the minority voters, but in a democratic society the majority must rule, unless the discrimination is invidious. No such evil has been made manifest here. Every citizen is offered equal suffrage and no deprivation of the franchise is suffered by anyone.

Furthermore, adoption of the general election system in Virginia is grounded on what has historically been deemed to her best interests in the workings of the electoral college. The legislature of the Commonwealth had the choice of appointing electors in a manner which will fairly reflect the popular vote but thereby weaken the potential impact of Virginia as a State in the nationwide counting of electoral ballots, or to allow the majority to rule and thereby maximize the impact of Virginia's 12 electoral votes in the electoral college tally. The latter course was taken, and we cannot say unwisely.

Reverting to the unit rule, it has never been rejected as unfair in the election of members of the United States House of Representatives when two or more or all are running at large, that is statewide. In the midst of the one-person, one-vote decisions, this practice was noticed without any question of its validity. In *Wesberry v. Sanders*, supra, 376 U.S. 1, 7, 84 S.Ct. 526, 530, the Court said:

> "We hold that, construed in its historical context, the command of Art. I, § 2, that Representatives be chosen 'by the People of the several States' means that as nearly as is practicable one man's vote in a congressional election is to be worth as much as another's. This rule is followed automatically, of course, when Representatives are chosen as a group on a statewide basis, as was a widespread practice in the first 50 years of our Nation's history." (Footnotes omitted.)

In this consideration it is notable that Congress in its amendments of the statute relating to the election of Representatives by districts, has expressly countenanced the election of them from the "State at large." 2 U.S.C. §§ 2a and 2c, supra. Presumably Congress would not have done so if it meant a breach of the one-person, one-vote principle, by then securely established. If the plan is legally permissible in the selection of Congressmen, it may hardly be stigmatized as unlawful in choosing electors.

III.

Further instances of inequality in the ballot's worth between them as Virginia citizens, plaintiffs continue, and citizens of other States, exists as a result of the assignment of electors among the States. To illustrate, New York is apportioned 43 electors and the citizen there, in the general system plan, participates in the selection of 43 electors while his Virginia compatriot has a part in choosing only 12. His ballot, if creating a plurality for his preference, wins the whole number of 43 electors while the Virginian in the same circumstances could acquire only 12. Again, party-wise, it is alleged that on a national basis, the State unit system's cancellation of States' minority votes causes inequities and distortions of voting rights among citizens of the several States, by arbitrarily isolating the effects of votes cast by persons of a particular political persuasion or party in one State, from those cast by voters of the same persuasion or party in other States.

Disparities of this sort are to be found throughout the United States wherever there is a State numerical difference in electors. But plainly this unevenness is directly traceable to the Constitution's presidential electoral scheme and to the permissible unit system.

For these reasons the injustice cannot be corrected by suit, especially one in which but a single State is impleaded. Litigation of the common national problem by a joinder of all the States was evidently unacceptable to the Supreme Court. *State of Delaware v. State of New York*, supra, 385 U.S. 895, 87 S.Ct. 198. Readily recognizing these impediments, plaintiffs point to the district selection of electors as a solution, or at least an amelioration, of this interstate inequality of voters. However, to repeat, this method cannot be forced upon the State legislatures, for the Constitution gives them the choice, and use of the unit method of tallying is not unlawful.

Adverting to certain procedural points made by the parties, the Governor of Virginia, in view of his detachment from the election machinery in the State, we find is neither a necessary nor a proper defendant here, and should be dropped as a party; we overrule all objections which have been reserved in the admission of evidence on the hearing of this cause.

The merits and advantages of the plaintiffs' thesis are readily recognizable. We do not discount or deride their motives, but we are of the opinion that a compulsory compliance with their demand or any other proposed limitation on the selection by the State of its presidential electors would require a Constitutional amendment. Also, we observe, that the change to a district system would not, for the reasons expressed by Jefferson, warrant Virginia or any other State to adopt an individual plan. Whatever the pattern, to succeed it must be nationwide. As was aptly stated by Professor Robert G. Dixon, " . . . any modification of the electoral college system should be on a uniform national basis in order to avoid creating additional inequities on an interstate basis."[3]

As Virginia's design for selecting presidential electors does not disserve the Constitution, we decline to place an injunction upon its effectuation. Plaintiffs' complaint will be dismissed.

ORDER ON OPINION

Upon consideration of the pleadings, the stipulations of counsel, the exhibits and the entire record in this action, as well as the arguments thereon of counsel orally and on brief, the court for the reasons stated in its opinion filed herewith finds, adjudges and orders as follows:

1. That the Governor of Virginia be, and he is hereby, dropped as a party defendant herein;

2. That the prayers of the complaint be, and they are hereby denied, and that the complaint herein be, and it is hereby, dismissed; and

3. That the defendants recover of the plaintiffs the costs of this action, and nothing further remaining to be done in the cause, it be stricken from the docket.

---

[3] Remarks before the Subcommittee on Constitutional Amendments of the Senate Committee on the Judiciary, July 14, 1967, regarding proposed amendments to the Constitution relating to nomination and election of the President and Vice President.

Filed 7/24/12

CERTIFIED FOR PUBLICATION

IN THE COURT OF APPEAL OF THE STATE OF CALIFORNIA

FIRST APPELLATE DISTRICT

DIVISION FOUR

THE GILLETTE COMPANY et al.,
 	
    Plaintiffs and Appellants,
 	
v.
 	
FRANCHISE TAX BOARD,
 	
    Defendant and Respondent.
	A130803
	
	(San Francisco City & County
	Super. Ct. Nos. CGC-10-495911,
	CGC-10-495912, CGC-10-495916,
	CGC-10-496437, CGC-10-496438,
	CGC-10-499083)

   California is a signatory to the Multistate Tax Compact (Compact). (Rev. & Tax. Code,[1] § 38001, California's enactment of the Compact.) This binding, multistate agreement obligates member states to offer its multistate taxpayers the option of using either the Compact's three-factor formula to apportion and allocate income for state income tax purposes, or the state's own alternative apportionment formula. (§ 38006, art. III, subd. 1.) This is one of the Compact's key mandatory provisions designed to secure a baseline level of uniformity in state income tax systems, a central purpose of the agreement.

   Prior to 1993, California subscribed to a single method of apportioning and allocating income, the Compact formula, which ascribed equal weight to three factors: property, payroll and sales. (Former § 25128, as added by Stats. 1966, ch. 2, § 7, p. 179.) Then, in 1993 the Legislature amended section 25128 to give double weight to the sales factor for most business activity, specifying that "[n]otwithstanding Section 38006, all

---

  [1] Unless noted otherwise, all statutory references are to the Revenue and Taxation Code.

1

business income shall be apportioned to this state by multiplying the [business] income by a fraction, the numerator of which is the property factor plus the payroll factor *plus twice the sales factor*, and the denominator of which is four . . . ." (Former § 25128, subd. (a), italics added, as amended by Stats. 1993, ch. 946, § 1, p. 5441.)[2]

These consolidated appeals brought by appellants the Gillette Company and its subsidiaries, and other corporate entities (Taxpayers),[3] present the issue of whether, for the tax years at issue since 1993, Taxpayers were entitled to elect the Compact formula, or, as respondent Franchise Tax Board (FTB) asserts, did the 1993 amendment to section 25128 repeal and supersede that formula, thereby making the state formula mandatory? We conclude that the Compact is a valid multistate compact, and California is bound by it and its apportionment election provision unless and until California withdraws from the Compact by enacting a statute that repeals section 38006. Accordingly, since California has not repealed section 38006 and withdrawn from the Compact, we reverse the trial court's order sustaining the FTB's demurrer without leave to amend.[4]

I. BACKGROUND

A. *Historical Context Leading to Enactment of the Compact*

Recognizing the need for uniformity in the apportionment of corporate income for tax purposes among the various taxing states, in 1957 the National Conference of Commissioners on Uniform State Laws promulgated the Uniform Division of Income for

---

[2] For purposes of this appeal, the current version of section 25128, subdivision (a) is similar in all material respects to the 1993 amendment, reading as follows: "Notwithstanding Section 38006, all business income shall be apportioned to this state by multiplying the business income by a fraction, the numerator of which is the property factor plus the payroll factor plus twice the sales factor, and the denominator of which is four . . . ."

[3] Other appellants are Procter & Gamble Manufacturing Company; Kimberly-Clark Worldwide, Inc., and its subsidiaries; Sigma-Aldrich, Inc.; RB Holdings (USA) Inc., and Jones Apparel Group, Inc.

[4] Despite the absence of a judgment of dismissal, we deem the order to incorporate such judgment because the trial court sustained a demurrer to all causes of action, and all that remains to render the order appealable is the formality of entering a judgment of dismissal. (*Melton v. Boustred* (2010) 183 Cal.App.4th 521, 527-528, fn. 1.)

2

Tax Purposes Act (UDITPA). (7A pt. 1 West's U. Laws Ann. (2002) pp. 141-142 & § 9.) To apportion a multistate corporation's business income among the various taxing states, UDITPA uses a three-factor, equally weighted formula consisting of property, payroll and sales receipts. (*Id.*, § 9.) California adopted the UDITPA in 1966. (§ 25120 et seq.; Stats. 1966, ch. 2, § 7, pp. 177-181.)

By 1959, only a few states had adopted the UDITPA. (7A pt. I, West's U. Laws Ann., *supra*, p. 141.) That year, the United States Supreme Court delivered its decision in *Northwestern Cement Co. v. Minn.* (1959) 358 U.S. 450, 452 (*Northwestern Cement*), holding that "net income from the interstate operations of a foreign corporation may be subjected to state taxation provided the levy is not discriminatory and is properly apportioned to local activities within the taxing State forming sufficient nexus to support the same." *Northwestern Cement* raised concerns in the business community and within weeks of the decision, Congress commenced hearings, culminating in the passage of Public Law No. 86-272 as an emergency, temporary measure some six months later. This law was intended to restrict the application of *Northwestern Cement* and created a subcommittee to study state business taxes and recommend legislation establishing uniform standards which states would observe in taxing income of interstate companies. (Fatale, Federalism and State Business Activity Tax Nexus; Revisiting Public Law No. 86-272 (Spring 2002) 21 Va. Tax Review, 435, 475-476; *U.S. Steel Corp. v. Multistate Tax Comm'n* (1978) 434 U.S. 452, 455 (*U.S. Steel*).) The subsequent study, commonly referred to as the "Willis Report" after Congressman Edwin E. Willis who chaired the subcommittee,[5] called for federal legislation that would have limited state authority to tax interstate business operations and imposed a uniform apportionment regime on the states. (State Taxation of Interstate Commerce, Rep. of the Special Subcommittee on State Taxation of Interstate Commerce of the Com. on the Judiciary, House of Representatives (Sept. 2, 1965) vol. 4, chs. 38, 39, pp. 1135-1136, 1143, 1161.)

---

[5] Fatale, *supra*, at page 477.

3

In the wake of the Willis Report, Congress introduced a number of bills incorporating its recommendations. (*U.S. Steel, supra,* 434 U.S. at p. 456, fn. 4; Sharpe, *State Taxation of Interstate Businesses and the Multistate Tax Compact: The Search for a Delicate Uniformity* (1974) 11 Colum. J. of Law and Social Problems, 231, 242 & n. 43.) To stave off federal encroachment on their taxing powers and devise workable alternatives that would eliminate the need for congressional action, state tax administrators and other state leaders drafted the Compact; by June 1967, nine states had enacted the Compact, which by its terms became effective after seven states had adopted it. (Multistate Tax Com., First Ann. Rep. (1968) pp. 1-2; § 38006, art. X, subd. 1.)

B. *Compact Provisions*

California enacted the Compact in 1974. (§ 38001, Stats. 1974, ch. 93, § 3, p. 193.) Its purposes are to "1. Facilitate proper determination of State and local tax liability of multistate taxpayers, including the equitable apportionment of tax bases and settlement of apportionment disputes. [¶] 2. Promote uniformity or compatibility in significant components of tax systems. [¶] 3. Facilitate taxpayer convenience and compliance in the filing of tax returns . . . . [¶] 4. Avoid duplicative taxation." (§ 38006, art. I.)

Article IV adopts the UDITPA and its equally weighted, three-factor apportionment formula, stating in part: "All business income shall be apportioned to this State by multiplying the income by a fraction, the numerator of which is the property factor plus the payroll factor plus the sales factor, and the denominator of which is three." (§ 38006, art. IV, subd. 9.) However, article III allows taxpayers the option of apportioning and allocating income pursuant to the UDITPA formula *or* pursuant to a given state's alternative apportionment provisions: "Any taxpayer subject to an income tax whose income is subject to apportionment and allocation for tax purposes pursuant to the laws of a party State . . . may elect to apportion and allocate his income in the manner provided by the laws of such State . . . without reference to this compact, or may elect to apportion and allocate in accordance with Article IV." (§ 38006, art. III, subd. 1.) As noted in the Multistate Tax Commission's Third Annual Report (1969-1970),[6] "The Multistate Tax Compact makes UDITPA available to each taxpayer on an optional basis, thereby preserving for him the substantial advantages with which lack of uniformity provides him in some states. Thus a corporation which is selling into a state in which it has little property or payroll will want to insist upon the use of the three-factor formula (sales, property and payroll) which is included in UDITPA because that will substantially reduce his tax liability to that state below what it would be if a single sales factor formula were applied to him[;] on the other hand, he will look with favor upon the application of the single sales factor formula to him by a state from which he is selling into other states, since that will reduce his tax liability to that state. The Multistate Tax Compact thus preserves the right of the states to make such alternative formulas available to taxpayers even though it makes uniformity available to taxpayers where and when desired." (*Id.* at p. 3.)

Article V sets out the rules for sales and use tax credits and exemptions, therein obligating each party state to provide a full credit to taxpayers who previously paid sales or use tax to another state with respect to the same property, and to honor sales and use tax exemption certificates from other states. (§ 38006, art. V, subd. 1.)

The Compact leaves other matters entirely to state control. For example, it reserves to the states control over the rate of tax (§ 38006, art. XI, subd. (a)), and simply does not address the composition of a corporation's tax base.

As well, the Compact creates the Multistate Tax Commission (Commission) with powers to study state and local tax systems, develop and recommend proposals for greater uniformity of state and local tax laws, and compile and publish information helpful to the states. (§ 38006, art. VI, subds. 1, 3.) Each party state appoints a member to the Commission and pays its share of expenses. (*Id.*, art. VI, subds. 1(a), 4(b).) The Commission may adopt uniform regulations in cases where two or more states have uniform or similar provisions relating to specific types of taxes. (*Id.*, art. VII.) However,

---

[6] Hereafter, Third Commission Report.

such regulations are advisory only—each state makes its own decision whether to adopt the regulation in accordance with its own law. (*Id.*, art. VII, subd. 3.) Additionally, the Commission may perform interstate audits, if requested by a party state; the governing article applies only in states that specifically adopt it by statute. (*Id.*, art. VIII, subds. 1, 2.)

Finally, under the Compact, states are free to withdraw from the Compact at any time "by enacting a statute repealing the same." (§ 38006, art. X, subd. 2.)

C. *U.S. Steel*

In 1972, a group of multistate corporate taxpayers brought an action on behalf of themselves and all other such taxpayers threatened with audits by the Commission. The complaint challenged the constitutionality of the Compact on several grounds, including that it was invalid under the compact clause of the United States Constitution.[7] (*U.S. Steel, supra*, 434 U.S. at p. 458.)

The high court acknowledged that the compact clause, taken literally, would require the states to obtain congressional approval before entering into any agreement among themselves, "irrespective of form, subject, duration, or interest to the United States." (*U.S. Steel, supra,* 434 U.S. at p. 459.) However, it endorsed an interpretation, established by case law, that limited application of the compact clause " 'to agreements that are "directed to the formation of any combination tending to the increase of political power in the States, which may encroach upon or interfere with the just supremacy of the United States." [Citations.]' This rule states the proper balance between federal and state power with respect to compacts and agreements among States." (*Id.* at p. 471, initial quote from *Virginia v. Tennessee* (1893) 148 U.S. 503, 519.)

Framing the test as whether the Compact enhances state power with respect to the federal government, the court concluded it did not: "This pact does not purport to authorize the member States to exercise any powers they could not exercise in its

---

[7] The compact clause of article I, section 10, clause 3 of the United States Constitution states: "No state shall, without the consent of Congress, . . . enter into any agreement or compact with another state, or with a foreign power . . . ."

absence. Nor is there any delegation of sovereign power to the Commission; each State retains complete freedom to adopt or reject the rules and regulations of the Commission. Moreover . . . , each State is free to withdraw at any time." (*U.S. Steel, supra,* 434 U.S. at p. 473.) In the end the court rejected all of the plaintiffs' challenges to the constitutional validity of the Compact. (*Id.* at p. 479.)

D. *Amendment of Section 25128; Litigation*

Prior to 1993, California required corporations to apportion their business income to California using the standard UDITPA, equally weighted three-factor apportionment formula. (§ 25128, as adopted in 1966; see also § 38006, art. IV, subd. 9.) In 1993, the Legislature amended this formula to give double weight to the sales factor and specified that the new formula was mandatory, providing in relevant part: "*Notwithstanding Section 38006* [the Compact], all business income shall be apportioned to this state by multiplying the [business] income by a fraction, the numerator of which is the property factor plus the payroll factor *plus twice the sales factor*, and the denominator of which is four . . . ." (§ 25128, subd. (a), italics added; Stats. 1993, ch. 946, § 1, p. 5441.)

In January 2010, the Taxpayers lodged six complaints for the refund of taxes which the court thereafter consolidated. Therein, they argued that the amended section 25128 did not override or repeal the UDITPA formula set forth in section 38006, and sought a refund of approximately $34 million. The Taxpayers alleged that they began filing claims for refund in 2006,[8] based on their election to compute their California apportionable income "using the three-factor apportionment formula (property, payroll, and single-weighted sales) set forth in . . . § 38006." The FTB denied the refund claims for the years at issue.

The FTB demurred on grounds that the amended section 25128 mandated the exclusive use of the double-weighted sales factor, and according to its plain and unambiguous language, negated the Taxpayers' claim of entitlement to elect the UDITPA formula. The trial court agreed that section 25128 "clearly express[ed] an intention to

---

[8] Sigma-Aldrich, Inc., began filing refund claims in 2003; RB Holdings (USA), Inc., began filing refund claims in 2007.

take away the alternative under [section] 38006," and additionally the court in *U.S. Steel* determined that this alternative statutory scheme "could be obviated in the manner that the Legislature did." Therefore, it sustained the FTB's demurrer to the complaints without leave to amend and entered judgment accordingly.

II. DISCUSSION

A. *Introduction*

The Taxpayers are adamant that the Compact is a valid, binding compact and as such, the Legislature cannot override and eliminate the section 38006 option for taxpayers to elect the Compact's apportionment formula. The FTB maintains as a threshold matter that the Taxpayers lack standing to complain of any purported violation of the Compact. On the substantive front the FTB contends that the plain language of section 25128 mandates the exclusive use of the double-weighted sales apportionment formula, thereby eliminating use of the equally weighted three-factor apportionment formula set forth as a taxpayer option in section 38006. Further, it urges that under California statutory and contract law, the Legislature had the power, and properly enacted legislation, to repeal section 38006 to the extent necessary to impose this mandatory apportionment formula on taxpayers.

B. *Nature of Interstate Compacts*

Some background on the nature of interstate compacts is in order. These instruments are legislatively enacted, binding and enforceable agreements between two or more states. (Litwak, *Interstate Compact Law: Cases and Materials* (Semaphore Press 2011) pp. 5, 12.) Initially used to resolve boundary disputes, today interstate compacts are a staple of interstate cooperation and, in addition to taxes, span a wide range of subject matter and issues including forest firefighting; water allocation; mining regulation; storage of low level radioactive waste; transportation; environmental preservation and resource conservation; regulation of electric energy; higher education and regional cultural development. (Davis, *Interstate Compacts in Commerce and Industry* (1998) 23 Vt. L.Rev. 133, 139-143.)

8

As we have seen, some interstate compacts require congressional consent, but others, that do not infringe on the federal sphere, do not. Questioning whether similar statutes in two states constituted a compact, the Supreme Court has outlined what it deemed "classic indicia" of such instruments: "We have some doubt as to whether there is an agreement amounting to a compact. The two statutes are similar in that they both require reciprocity and impose a regional limitation, both legislatures favor the establishment of regional banking in New England, and there is evidence of cooperation among legislators, officials, bankers, and others in the two States in studying the idea and lobbying for the statutes. But several of the classic indicia of a compact are missing. No joint organization or body has been established to regulate regional banking or for any other purpose. Neither statute is conditioned on action by the other State, and each State is free to modify or repeal its law unilaterally. Most importantly, neither statute requires a reciprocation of the regional limitation." (*Northeast Bancorp v. Board of Governors, FRS* (1985) 472 U.S. 159, 175 (*Bancorp*).) The Ninth Circuit Court of Appeals has aptly summarized *Bancorp* as setting forth three primary indicia: "These are establishment of a joint organization for regulatory purposes; conditional consent by member states in which each state is not free to modify or repeal its participation unilaterally; and state enactments which require reciprocal action for their effectiveness." (*Seattle Master Builders v. Pacific N.W. Elec. Power* (9th Cir. 1986) 786 F.2d 1359, 1363.)

Where, as here, federal congressional consent was neither given nor required, the Compact must be construed as state law. (*McComb v. Wambaugh* (3d Cir. 1991) 934 F.2d 474, 479.) Moreover, since interstate compacts are agreements enacted into state law, they have dual functions as enforceable contracts between member states and as statutes with legal standing within each state; and thus we interpret them as both. (*Aveline v. Bd. of Probation and Parole* (1999) 729 A.2d 1254, 1257; see Broun et al., *The Evolving Use and the Changing Role of Interstate Compacts* (ABA 2006) § 1.2.2, pp. 15-24 (Broun on Compacts); 1A Sutherland, Statutory Construction (7th ed. 2009) § 32:5; *In re C.B.* (2010) 188 Cal.App.4th 1024, 1031 [recognizing that Interstate

9

Compact on Placement of Children shares characteristics of both contractual agreements and statutory law].)

The contractual nature of a compact is demonstrated by its adoption: "There is an offer (a proposal to enact virtually verbatim statutes by each member state), an acceptance (enactment of the statutes by the member states), and consideration (the settlement of a dispute, creation of an association, or some mechanism to address an issue of mutual interest.)" (Broun on Compacts, *supra,* § 1.2.2, p. 18.) As is true of other contracts, the contract clause of the United States Constitution shields compacts from impairment by the states. (*Aveline v. Bd. of Probation and Parole, supra,* 729 A.2d at p. 1257, fn. 10.) Therefore, upon entering a compact, "it takes precedence over the subsequent statutes of signatory states and, as such, a state may not unilaterally nullify, revoke or amend one of its compacts if the compact does not so provide." (*Ibid.*; accord, *Intern. Union v. Del. River Joint Toll Bridge* (3d Cir. 2002) 311 F.3d 273, 281.) Thus interstate compacts are unique in that they empower one state legislature—namely the one that enacted the agreement—to bind all future legislatures to certain principles governing the subject matter of the compact. (Broun on Compacts, *supra,* § 1.2.2, p. 17.)

As explained and summarized in *C.T. Hellmuth v. Washington Metro. Area Trans.* (D.Md. 1976) 414 F.Supp. 408, 409 (*Hellmuth*): "Upon entering into an interstate compact, a state effectively surrenders a portion of its sovereignty; the compact governs the relations of the parties with respect to the subject matter of the agreement and is superior to both prior and subsequent law. Further, when enacted, a compact constitutes not only law, but a contract which may not be amended, modified, or otherwise altered without the consent of all parties. It, therefore, appears settled that one party may not enact legislation which would impose burdens upon the compact absent the concurrence of the other signatories." Cast a little differently, "[i]t is within the competency of a State, which is a party to a compact with another State, to legislate in respect of matters covered by the compact so long as such legislative action is in approbation and not in reprobation of the compact." (*Henderson v. Delaware River Joint Toll Bridge Com'm* (1949) 66 A.2d 843, 849-450.) Nor may states amend a compact by enacting legislation

10

that is substantially similar, unless the compact itself contains language enabling a state or states to modify it through legislation " 'concurred in' " by the other states. (*Intern. Union v. Del. River Joint Toll Bridge, supra,* 311 F.3d at pp. 276-280.)

C. *Taxpayers Have Standing to Pursue These Actions*

The FTB asserts that even if California breached its obligations under the Compact, the Taxpayers have no judicial remedy, are not parties to the agreement and have no enforceable rights under it.

First, this is an action for the refund of corporate taxes paid to the state pursuant to section 19382, and without question the Taxpayers have standing in such an action to claim "that the tax computed and assessed is void in whole or in part . . . ." (*Ibid.*)

Furthermore, the Compact, at section 38006, article III, subdivision 1 explicitly gives taxpayers whose income is subject to apportionment and allocation under the laws of a party state the option to elect to apportion its taxes under UDITPA, the Compact formula. This is a right specifically extended not to the party states but to taxpayers as third parties regulated under the Compact, and as such Taxpayers may seek to enforce this right as part of its tax refund suit. Moreover, the stated purposes of the Compact explicitly embrace taxpayer interests. These purposes include facilitating (1) "proper determination of State and local tax liability of multistate taxpayers, including the equitable apportionment of tax bases" and (2) "taxpayer convenience." (§ 38006, art. I, subds. 1, 3.)

Alabama v. North Carolina (2010) ___ U.S. ___ [130 S.Ct. 2295], characterized as "particularly instructive" by the FTB, is not. There, the Supreme Court ruled that the agency created by the Compact could not bring claims for breach of compact by a party state *in a stand-alone action under the Supreme Court's original jurisdiction* because it had "neither a contractual right to performance by the party States nor enforceable statutory rights under [the compact]." (*Id.* at p. 2315.) Our case has nothing to do with the unique features of federal original jurisdiction. (U.S. Const., art. III, § 2, cl. 2.)

In any event, in contrast, here the codified compact extends the right to election to appropriate taxpayers. We find the decision in *Borough of Morrisville v. Delaware Riv.*

11

Bas. Com'n (E.D.Pa. 1975) 399 F.Supp. 469, 472-473, footnote 3 persuasive. There, the plaintiff municipalities who used water from the Delaware River claimed that the compact commission in question exceeded its authority and violated the compact and federal law by imposing certain water charges. Resolving the standing issue in favor of the plaintiffs, the district court further stated that " '[t]o hold that the Compact is an agreement between the political signatories imputing only to those signatories standing to challenge actions pursuant to it would be unduly narrow in view of the direct impact on plaintiffs and other taxpayers.' " (*Id.* at p. 473.) This view is reinforced by commentators: "For the most part, interstate compacts have not created any privately assertable rights . . . . However, this is not invariably the case. For example, water allocation compacts, while they apportion water among states, may affect the rights of individual water users in such a way as to make them proper parties to suits. In such situations, the governing fact is that compacts are statutory law. Consequently, the assertion of private rights created or otherwise affected by a compact is procedurally similar to the assertion of such rights conferred by other statutes of the jurisdiction dealing with similar subject matter." (Zimmerman & Wendell, *The Law and Use of Interstate Compact*s (The Council of State Governments 1976) Compact Law, ch. 1, pp. 14-15.)

D. *The Compact Is a Valid, Enforceable Interstate Compact*

To reiterate, the high court in *U.S. Steel* upheld the facial validity of the Compact against various constitutional challenges. (*U.S. Steel, supra,* 434 U.S. at pp. 473-479.) Our own Attorney General has acknowledged the binding force of the Compact. (80 Ops.Cal.Atty.Gen. 213, 214 (1997): by virtue of enacting the Compact as part of the law of this state, the Compact makes California a member of the Commission and the only way to withdraw from commission membership is by enacting repealing legislation.)

Moreover, the Compact satisfies indicia of a compact. (See *Seattle Master Builders v. Pacific N.W. Elec. Power, supra,* 786 F.2d at p. 1363.) The Commission is an operational body charged with duties and powers in furtherance of the Compact's purposes. It oversees the Compact, is composed of tax administrators from all member

12

states, and is financed through a process of allocation and apportionment. (§ 38006, art. VI.) Meeting on at least an annual basis, and with representation from each signatory state, the Commission is a vehicle for continuing cooperative action among those states.

Additionally, the Compact builds in binding reciprocal obligations that advance uniformity. First, as we have discussed, it secures an election for multistate taxpayers to opt for apportioning their business income under UDITPA, the Compact formula, or in accordance with the state's own apportionment formula. (§ 38006, art. III, subd. 1.) The election provision is not optional for party states. Because any multistate taxpayer "may elect" either approach, the party states must make the election available. As set forth above, the Commission has explained that the mandate to make UDITPA available on an optional basis to taxpayers preserves "the substantial advantages with which lack of uniformity provides [the taxpayer] in some states." (Third Commission Report, *supra*, at p. 3.) Thus the Compact reserves to the states the right to provide taxpayers with alternative formulas, while at the same time making uniformity available when and where desired. (*Ibid.*)

As well, the Compact commits each state to provide sales and use tax credits and exemptions. (§ 38006, art. V.) Again, the sales and use tax provisions are mandatory on signatory states.

Finally, the Compact provides for a state's orderly withdrawal, namely by enacting a statute repealing the Compact. However, any repealing legislation must be prospective in nature, because it cannot "affect any liability already incurred by or chargeable to a party State prior to the time of such withdrawal." (§ 38006, art. X, subd. 2.) Although notice to sister states is not specifically required, by requiring repealing state legislation, the process itself calls for a measured, deliberative decision prior to withdrawal. Moreover, advance notice could easily be accomplished through the work of the Commission.

Nevertheless, the right to withdraw is unilateral. Citing *Bancorp*, the FTB suggests that the withdrawal provision renders the Compact something less than a binding agreement. However, this type of withdrawal provision is common in other

13

interstate compacts and has not been the death knell rendering them nonbinding and invalid. California is a party to a number of interstate compacts containing virtually identical withdrawal provisions, coupled with some type of notice requirement. (See Gov. Code, § 66801 (art. X, subd. (c)) [delineating withdrawal provision for Tahoe Regional Planning Compact]; Veh. Code, § 15027 [same for Driver License Compact]; Welf. & Inst. Code, § 1400, art. XI, subd. (a) [same for Interstate Compact on Juveniles]; Pen. Code, § 11180, art. XII, § A [Interstate Compact for Adult Offender Supervision]; Ed. Code, § 12510, art. VIII [Compact for Education].)

Furthermore, the situation in *Bancorp*, cited by the FTB, differs dramatically from the case at hand. There, Massachusetts and Connecticut enacted similar statutes allowing regional interstate banking acquisitions. However, unlike section 38006, these statutes were not jointly entered into as a binding agreement; they did not create an administrative body nor did they require reciprocation in key respects; and they could be changed as well as repealed at will. (*Bancorp, supra*, 472 U.S. at p. 175.)

The FTB also points to a recent Commission document that refers to the Compact as a "model law" and "not truly a compact."[9] The Commission's statements do not alter the reality that the Compact is binding on California. Indeed, the Compact operates as a model law as to those states that choose to be associate members, rather than signatory members. Pursuant to the Commission bylaws, the Commission may grant associate membership to states which have not enacted the Compact but which have, for example, enacted legislation that makes effective adoption of the Compact dependent on a subsequent condition. (Third Commission Report, *supra*, at p. 96.) Before the Legislature enacted the Compact, California was an associate member. Now it is a full Compact member, having enacted the Compact "into law and entered into [it] with all

---

[9] Multistate Tax Compact, Suggested State Legislation and Enabling Act, accessed on the Web site of the Multistate Tax Commission on July 23, 2012. <http://www.mtc.gov/uploadedFiles/Multistate_Tax_Commission/About_MTC/MTC_C ompact/COMPACT(1).pdf>

14

jurisdictions legally joining therein . . . ." (§ 38001.) That the Compact did not "enter into force" until enacted into law by seven states also distinguishes it from a model law.

The FTB also intimates that the Compact is invalid under article 13, clause 31 of our state Constitution, which states: "The power to tax may not be surrendered or suspended by grant or contract." But of course by entering the Compact, California has neither surrendered nor suspended its taxing powers. California retains full control of its tax base, tax rate and tax revenues; it simply has obligated itself to provide taxpayers with an option to use UDITPA or the state formula and can rescind that obligation by withdrawing from the Compact.

E. *California Cannot Unilaterally Repeal Compact Terms*

The thrust of the FTB on appeal is this: Confirming the Legislature's authority to amend, repeal or supersede existing statutes, it proceeds to urge as a matter of statutory construction that the Legislature's choice of the "[n]otwithstanding Section 38006" language in the 1993 amended section 25128 overrides section 38006, thus excising the taxpayer option to use UDITPA, the Compact apportionment formula. Indeed, it goes so far as to say that this language "constitutes a repeal of section 38006 to the extent necessary to impose a mandatory double-weighted sales apportionment formula upon taxpayers."

Were this simply a matter of statutory construction involving two statutes— sections 25128 and 38006—we would at least entertain the FTB's argument that section 25128 repealed the section 38006 taxpayer election to apportion under the Compact formula, and now mandates the exclusive use of the double-weighted sales apportionment formula. However, this construct is not sustainable because it completely ignores the dual nature of section 38006. Once one filters in the reality that section 38006 is not just a statute but is also the codification of the Compact, and that through this enactment California has entered a binding, enforceable agreement with the other signatory states, the multiple flaws in the FTB's position become apparent. First, under established compact law, the Compact supersedes subsequent conflicting state law. Second, the federal and state Constitutions prohibit states from passing laws that impair the obligations of contracts. And finally, the FTB's construction of the effect of the amended section 25128 runs afoul of the reenactment clause of the California Constitution.

1. *The Compact Supersedes Section 25128*

By its very nature an interstate compact shifts some of a state's authority to another state or states. Thus signatory states cede a level of sovereignty over matters covered in the Compact in favor of pursuing multilateral action to resolve a dispute or regulate an interstate affair. (*Hess v. Port Authority Trans-Hudson Corporation* (1994) 513 U.S. 30, 42; Broun on Compacts, *supra*, § 1.2.2, p. 23.) Because the Compact is both a statute and a binding agreement among sovereign signatory states, *having entered into it, California cannot, by subsequent legislation, unilaterally alter or amend its terms.* Indeed, as an interstate compact the Compact *is superior to prior and subsequent the statutory law of member states.* (*McComb v. Wambaugh, supra*, 934 F.2d at p. 479; *Hellmuth, supra*, 414 F.Supp. at p. 409.)

This means that the Compact trumps section 25128, such that, contrary to the FTB's assertion, section 25128 *cannot override* the UDITPA election offered to multistate taxpayers in section 38006, article III, subdivision 1. It bears repeating that the Compact *requires* states to offer this taxpayer option. If a state could unilaterally delete this baseline uniformity provision, it would render the binding nature of the compact illusory and contribute to defeating one of its key purposes, namely to "[p]romote uniformity or compatibility in significant components of tax systems." (§ 38006, art. I, subd. 2.) Because the Compact takes precedent over subsequent conflicting legislation, these outcomes cannot come to pass.

The FTB offers an alternative argument, namely that the UDITPA election can be superseded and repealed pursuant to the Compact's own withdrawal provision. Specifically, it casts the withdrawal clause as a flexible tool giving member states the "means of overriding any and all of its provisions, including the election and apportionment provisions. Member states can simply utilize the unrestricted withdrawal provision . . . to repeal and withdraw from the Multistate Tax Compact, in whole or in part."

16

As a matter of compact law, this cannot be. Having established that the Compact is a binding, valid compact, we construe and apply it according to its terms. (*Texas v. New Mexico* (1983) 462 U.S. 554, 564.) In part because compacts are agreements among sovereign states, we will not read absent terms into them or dictate relief inconsistent with their express terms. (*Alabama v. North Carolina, supra*, 130 S.Ct at p. 2313.)

With these concepts in mind, it is obvious that the plain language of the withdrawal provision, enabling a party state to withdraw from the Compact "by enacting a statute repealing the same," allows only for complete withdrawal from the Compact. California has *not* withdrawn from the Compact. After withdrawal, a state remains liable for any obligations incurred prior to withdrawal. Faced with the desire to escape an obligation under the Compact, a state's only option is to withdraw completely by enacting a repealing statute. That is what the plain language says, and we will not read into that language an inconsistent term allowing for piecemeal amendment or elimination of compact provisions.

The FTB refers us to *Alabama v. North Carolina, supra,* involving the same compact withdrawal provision, to support its position that we should not restrictively interpret the withdrawal provisions of the Compact. The FTB focuses on the following passage: "The Compact imposes no limitation on North Carolina's exercise of its statutory right to withdraw. . . . There is no restriction upon a party State's enactment of such a law . . . ." (*Alabama v. North Carolina, supra*, 130 S.Ct. at p. 2313, italics omitted.) However, the FTB omits the context, which is crucial. North Carolina withdrew from the compact in question by enacting a law repealing its status as a member state, *as required by the compact.* (*Id.* at p. 2304.) The plaintiffs alleged that North Carolina withdrew *in bad faith* to avoid monetary sanctions. Holding that there was no limitation on North Carolina's exercise of its withdrawal right, the Supreme Court explained that there was nothing in the compact suggesting that there were certain purposes for which the conferred withdrawal power could not be employed. (*Id.* at p. 2313.) In context, it is apparent that the case does not support the principle of partial

17

withdrawal or piecemeal alteration or amendment. Rather, the withdrawal provision calls for withdrawal from the Compact by passing a law repealing the Compact, period.

In further support of its position that the withdrawal provision should be construed to permit partial repeal or unilateral amendment, the FTB interprets the severability clause as providing for liberal construction of Compact provisions. This standard clause says that if any provision is declared invalid, the remaining provisions will not be affected. In other words, if a court declares any provision unconstitutional or invalid, it will be severed to avoid invalidation of the entire Compact. (§ 38006, art. XII.) How this clause advances the FTB's cause is not apparent to this court. It has nothing to do with liberal construction or the validity of state action to alter or amend existing Compact provisions.

Taking a slightly different tact, the FTB points out that a number of parties to the Compact have adopted statutes over the years that deviate from the Compact's taxing provisions. According to materials furnished in the FTB's request for judicial notice and summarized in its brief, 14 of 20 member states have passed some variation of a *mandatory*, state-specific apportionment formula that departs from the Compact provisions. The states have accomplished this in a variety of ways.

The FTB recommends that we consider the extrinsic evidence of this "course of conduct" in ascertaining whether the Compact is reasonably susceptible to an interpretation that renders its taxing provisions nonbinding and capable of being amended, superseded and repealed, in whole or part, by member states. Both parties concur that the key is whether the Compact is reasonably susceptible to the interpretation offered. (*Cedars-Sinai Medical Center v. Shewry* (2006) 137 Cal.App.4th 964, 980.)[10] It

---

[10] The FTB adds that "[i]n interpreting a compact, 'the parties' course of performance under the Compact is highly significant,' " quoting *Alabama v. North Carolina, supra*, 130 S.Ct. at page 2309. As a general statement this is highly misleading. The court's reference to the course of performance pertained to "whether, in terminating its efforts to obtain a license, North Carolina failed to take what the parties considered 'appropriate' steps . . . ." (*Alabama v. North Carolina, supra*, 130 S.Ct. at p. 2309.) The compact in question obligated the defendant to take appropriate steps to

is not. As we have demonstrated, the Compact's express, unambiguous terms require extending taxpayers the option of electing UDITPA, and set forth reciprocal repeal terms allowing a member state to cease its participation and reclaim its sovereignty.

As important, the proffered interpretation runs counter to the express purposes of the Compact, which include facilitating "equitable apportionment of tax bases" and promoting "uniformity or compatibility in significant components of tax systems." (§ 38006, art. I, subds. 1, 2.) The FTB's interpretation, that the Compact does not require states to provide multistate taxpayers with the election to use the UDITPA formula, would eviscerate the availability of a common formula for all taxpayers to use as an alternative, thereby diluting a potent uniformity provision of the Compact. Moreover, the course of performance of a contract is only relevant to ascertaining the parties' intention *at the time of contracting.* (Civ. Code, § 1636; *Cedars-Sinai Medical Center v. Shewry, supra,* 137 Cal.App. 4th at p. 983.) The express, stated purposes of the Compact are a much truer measure of that intent than the subsequent statutory changes to state apportionment formulae.

Similarly, the purpose of admitting course of performance evidence is grounded in common sense: "[W]hen the parties perform under a contract, without objection or dispute, they are fulfilling their understanding of the terms of the contract." (*Employers Reinsurance Co. v. Superior Court* (2008) 161 Cal.App.4th 906, 922.) The course of performance doctrine is thus premised on the assumption that one party's response to another party's action is probative of their understanding of the contract terms. But in the context of the Compact, the member states do not perform or deliver their obligations to one another, unlike a typical contract in which a party provides services or goods to the other party, who in turns monitors the first party's compliance with contract terms. Thus the foundation for finding course of performance evidence relevant and reliable is faulty.

---

ensure that an application to construct and operate the facility in question was filed and issued by the proper authority. (*Id.* at p. 2303.) The issue was what constituted "appropriate steps" under the compact. Of course, in this particular context, the parties' course of performance would help flesh out that concept.

19

For example, in *Cedars-Sinai*, the reviewing court concluded that course of conduct performance was *not* relevant to interpret a disputed provision because the conduct in question had nothing to do with providing incentives to monitor or enforce contract compliance. (*Cedars-Sinai Medical Center v. Shewry, supra*, 137 Cal.App.4th at p. 983.)

F. *The FTB's Construction Violates the Federal and State Constitutional Prohibition Against Impairment of Contracts*

Our federal and state Constitutions forbid enactment of state laws that impair contractual obligations. "No state shall . . . pass any . . . law impairing the obligation of contracts . . . ." (U.S. Const., art. I, § 10, cl. 1.) "A . . . law impairing the obligation of contracts may not be passed." (Cal. Const., art. I, § 9.) This constitutional prohibition extends to interstate compacts. (*Green v. Biddle* (1823) 21 U.S. 1, 12-13, 17 [Kentucky law that narrowed rights and diminished interests of landowners under compact between Kentucky and Virginia violated compact and was unconstitutional]; (*Doe v. Ward* (W.D.Pa. 2000) 124 F.Supp.2d 900, 915, fn. 20.) A construction of section 25128 that overrides and disables California's obligation under the Compact to afford taxpayers the option of apportioning income under the UDITPA formula would be unconstitutional, violative of the prohibition against impairing contracts.

G. *The FTB's Construction Runs Afoul of the Constitutional Reenactment Rule*

The FTB is adamant that the intent of the "[n]otwithstanding Section 38006" language in section 25128 is to repeal and supersede the taxpayer election to apportion under the Compact formula. At a minimum this outcome would eliminate or rewrite article III, subdivision 1 and eliminate article IV, subdivision 9 of section 38006. However, this result flies in the face of the California Constitution, article IV, section 9, stating in part: "A statute may not be amended by reference to its title. A section of a statute may not be amended unless the section is re-enacted as amended."

Long ago our Supreme Court expressed the purpose of the reenactment rule as avoiding " 'the enactment of statutes in terms so blind that legislators themselves [are] sometimes deceived in regard to their effect, and the public, from the difficulty of making the necessary examination and comparison, fail[s] to become appraised [*sic*] of the changes made in the laws.' " (*Hellman v. Shoulters* (1896) 114 Cal. 136, 152; accord *American Lung Assn. v. Wilson* (1996) 51 Cal.App.4th 743, 748.) Clearly the reenactment rule applies to acts " 'which are in terms . . . amendatory of some former act.' [Citation.]" (*American Lung Assn. v. Wilson, supra,* 51 Cal.App.4th at p. 749.) Its applicability does not depend on the method of amendment, but rather "on whether legislators and the public have been reasonably notified of direct changes in the law." (*Ibid.*)

The FTB's construct would trigger the reenactment statute because it posits that the newly amended section 25128 repealed and superseded the UDITPA apportionment formula. Nonetheless, the purportedly deleted UDITPA election remains in section 38006, causing confusion such that neither the public nor legislators would have adequate notice that section 38006 had been eviscerated by the later enactment.

III. DISPOSITION

The judgment of dismissal is reversed. FTB to bear costs on appeal.

_____
Reardon, J.

We concur:

_____
Ruvolo, P.J.

_____
Sepulveda, J.*

_____
 * Retired Associate Justice of the Court of Appeal, First Appellate District, assigned by the Chief Justice pursuant to article VI, section 6 of the California Constitution.

22

Trial Court:	San Francisco Superior Court
Trial Judge:	Hon. Richard A. Kramer
Counsel for Appellants:	Silverstein & Pomerantz, Amy L. Silverstein, Edwin P. Antolin, Johanna W. Roberts and Charles E. Olson
Counsel for Amici Curiae on Behalf of Appellants:	BraunHagey & Borden and Matthew Borden
	Jeffrey B. Litwak
	Wm. Gregory Turner
	Law Offices of Miriam Hiser and Miriam Hiser
	Masters, Mullins & Arrington and Richard L. Masters
Counsel for Respondent:	Kamala D. Harris, Attorney General Paul D. Gifford, Senior Assistant Attorney General Joyce E. Hee, Supervising Deputy Attorney General Lucy F. Wang, Deputy Attorney General
Counsel for Amicus Curiae on Behalf of Respondent:	Joe Huddleston, Shirley Sicilian and Sheldon Laskin

APPENDIX HH: RESULTS OF 2012 PRESIDENTIAL ELECTION

STATE	MCCAIN	OBAMA	REP MARGIN	DEM MARGIN	REP EV	DEM EV
Alabama	1,255,925	795,696	460,229		9	
Alaska	164,676	122,640	42,036		3	
Arizona	1,233,654	1,025,232	208,422		11	
Arkansas	647,744	394,409	253,335		6	
California	4,839,958	7,854,285		3,014,327		55
Colorado	1,185,050	1,322,998		137,948		9
Connecticut	634,892	905,083		270,191		7
Delaware	165,484	242,584		77,100		3
DC	21,381	267,070		245,689		3
Florida	4,162,341	4,235,965		73,624		29
Georgia	2,078,688	1,773,827	304,861		16	
Hawaii	121,015	306,658		185,643		4
Idaho	420,911	212,787	208,124		4	
Illinois	2,135,216	3,019,512		884,296		20
Indiana	1,420,543	1,152,887	267,656		11	
Iowa	730,617	822,544		91,927		6
Kansas	692,634	440,726	251,908		6	
Kentucky	1,087,190	679,370	407,820		8	
Louisiana	1,152,262	809,141	343,121		8	
Maine	292,276	401,306		109,030		4
Maryland	971,869	1,677,844		705,975		10
Massachusetts	1,188,314	1,921,290		732,976		11
Michigan	2,115,256	2,564,569		449,313		16
Minnesota	1,320,225	1,546,167		225,942		10
Mississippi	710,746	562,949	147,797		6	
Missouri	1,482,440	1,223,796	258,644		10	
Montana	267,928	201,839	66,089		3	
Nebraska	475,064	302,081	172,983		5	
Nevada	463,567	531,373		67,806		6
New Hampshire	329,918	369,561		39,643		4
New Jersey	1,478,088	2,122,786		644,698		14
New Mexico	335,788	415,335		79,547		5
New York	2,485,432	4,471,871		1,986,439		29
North Carolina	2,270,395	2,178,391	92,004		15	
North Dakota	188,320	124,966	63,354		3	
Ohio	2,661,407	2,827,621		166,214		18
Oklahoma	891,325	443,547	447,778		7	
Oregon	754,175	970,488		216,313		7
Pennsylvania	2,680,434	2,990,274		309,840		20
Rhode Island	157,204	279,677		122,473		4
South Carolina	1,071,645	865,941	205,704		9	
South Dakota	210,610	145,039	65,571		3	
Tennessee	1,462,330	960,709	501,621		11	
Texas	4,569,843	3,308,124	1,261,719		38	
Utah	740,600	251,813	488,787		6	
Vermont	92,698	199,239		106,541		3
Virginia	1,822,522	1,971,820		149,298		13
Washington	1,290,670	1,755,396		464,726		12
West Virginia	417,584	238,230	179,354		5	
Wisconsin	1,410,966	1,620,985		210,019		10
Wyoming	170,962	69,286	101,676		3	
Total	**60,930,782**	**65,897,727**			**206**	**332**

BIBLIOGRAPHY

Abbott, David W. and Levine, James P. 1991. *Wrong Winner: The Coming Debacle in the Electoral College*. Westport, CT: Praeger.

Amar, Akhil Reed and Amar, Vikram David Amar. 2001. How to achieve direct national election of the president without amending the constitution: Part three of a three-part series on the 2000 election and the electoral college. *Findlaw's Writ*. December 28, 2001. http://writ.news.findlaw.com/amar/20011228.html

Amar, Akhil Reed and Amar, Vikram David. 2001. Rethinking the electoral college debate: The Framers, federalism, and one person, one vote. 114 *Harvard Law Review* 2526.

Amar, Vikram David. 2011. Response: The case for reforming presidential elections by subconstitutional means: The Electoral College, the National Popular Vote compact, and congressional power. 100 *Georgetown Law Journal* 237.

American Bar Association Commission on Electoral College Reform. 1967. *Electing the President: A Report of the Commission on Electoral College Reform*. Chicago, IL: American Bar Association.

American Enterprise Institute for Public Policy Research. 1969. *Proposals for Revision of the Electoral College System: Legislative Analysis*. Washington, D.C.: AEI.

Barone, Michael; Cohen, Michael; and Ujifusa, Grant. 2003. *The 2004 Almanac of American Politics*. Washington, D.C.: National Journal Group.

Barton, Weldon V. 1967. *Interstate Compacts in the Political Process*. Chapel Hill, NC: University of North Carolina Press.

Bayh, Birch. 1969. Electing a president: The case for direct election. 6 *Harvard Journal on Legislation* 1.

Bennett, Robert W. 2001. Popular election of the president without a constitutional amendment. 4 *Green Bag*. Spring 2001. Posted on April 19, 2001.

Bennett, Robert W. 2002. Popular election of the president without a constitutional amendment. In Jacobson, Arthur J. and Rosenfeld, Michel (editors). *The Longest Night: Polemics and Perspectives on Election 2000*. Berkeley, CA: University of California Press. Pages 391-396.

Bennett, Robert W. 2002. Popular election of the president II: State coordination in popular election of the president without a constitutional amendment. *Green Bag*. Winter 2002.

Bennett, Robert W. 2006. *Taming the Electoral College*. Stanford, CA: Stanford University Press.

Berns, Walter (editor). 1992. *After the People Vote: A Guide to the Electoral College*. Washington, D.C.: The AEI Press.

Best, Judith A. 1996. *Choice of the People? Debating the Electoral College*. Lanham, MD: Rowman & Littlefield.

Best, Judith Vairo. 1975. *The Case Against Direct Election of the President: A Defense of the Electoral College*. Ithaca, NY: Cornell University Press.

Bishop, Bill. 2008. *The Big Sort: Why the Clustering of Like-Minded America is Tearing Us Apart*. Boston, MA: Houghton Mifflin Harcourt.

Bowman, Ann O'M. 2004. Trends and issues in interstate cooperation. In *The Book of the States 2004 Edition*. Chicago, IL: The Council of State Governments.

Brams, Steven J. 1978. *The Presidential Election Game*. New Haven, CT: Yale University Press.

Brown, Everett Sumerville. 1938. *Ratification of the Twenty-First Amendment to the Constitution of the United States*. Ann Arbor, MI: The University of Michigan Press.

Bugh, Gary (editor). 2010. *Electoral College Reform: Challenges and Possibilities*. Burlington, VT: Ashgate.

Busch, Andrew E. 2001. The development and democratization of the electoral college. In Gregg, Gary L. II (editor). *Securing Democracy: Why We Have an Electoral College*. Wilmington, DE: ISI Books.

Chace, James. 2004. *1912: Wilson, Roosevelt, Taft & Debs-The Election that Changed the Country*. New York, NY: Simon and Schuster.

Chang, Stanley. 2007 Recent development: Updating the Electoral College: The National Popular Vote legislation. 44 *Harvard Journal on Legislation* 205.

Committee for the Study of the American Electorate (2004). "President Bush, Mobilization Drives Propel Turnout to Post-1968 High." November 4, 2004.

Congressional Quarterly. 1979. *Presidential Elections Since 1789*. Second Edition. Washington, D.C.: CQ Press.

Congressional Quarterly. 2002. *Presidential Elections 1789-2002*. Washington, D.C.: CQ Press.

Cook, Charlie. 2004. Convention dispatches-As the nation goes, so do swing states. *Charlie Cook's Political Report*. August 31, 2004.

Cook, Charlie. 2005. Off to the races: 435 ways to parse the presidential election results. *Charlie Cook's Political Report*. March 29, 2005.

Council of State Governments. 2003. *Interstate Compacts and Agencies 2003*. Lexington, KY: The Council of State Governments.

Council of State Governments. 2005. *The Book of the States*. Lexington, KY: The Council of State Governments. 2005 Edition. Volume 37.

DenBoer, Gordon; Brown, Lucy Trumbull; and Hagermann, Charles D. (editors). 1984. *The Documentary History of the First Federal Elections 1788-1790*. Madison, WI: University of Wisconsin Press. Volume II.

DenBoer, Gordon; Brown, Lucy Trumbull; and Hagermann, Charles D. (editors). 1986. *The Documentary History of the First Federal Elections 1788-1790*. Madison, WI: University of Wisconsin Press. Volume III.

DenBoer, Gordon; Brown, Lucy Trumbull; Skerpan, Alfred Lindsay; and Hagermann, Charles D. (editors). 1989. *The Documentary History of the First Federal Elections 1788-1790*. Madison, WI: University of Wisconsin Press. Volume IV.

Doherty, Brendan J. 2012. *The Rise of the President's Permanent Campaign*. Lawrence, KS: University Press of Kansas.

Dover, Edwin D. 2003. *The Disputed Presidential Election of 2000: A History and Reference Guide*. Westport, CT: Greenwood Press.

Dubin, Michael J. 2007. *Party Affiliations in the State Legislatures: A Year by Year Summary 1796-2006*. Jefferson, NC: McFarland& Company Inc.

Dunn, Susan. 2004. Jefferson's Second Revolution: *The Elections Crisis of 1800 and the Triumph of Republicanism*. Boston, MA: Houghton Mifflin.

Edwards, George C., III. 2004. *Why the Electoral College Is Bad for America*. New Haven, CT: Yale University Press. First edition.

Edwards, George C., III. 2011. *Why the Electoral College Is Bad for America*. New Haven, CT: Yale University Press. Second edition.

FairVote. 2005. *The Shrinking Battleground: The 2008 Presidential Election and Beyond*. Takoma Park, MD: The Center for Voting and Democracy. http://archive.fairvote. org/?page=1555.

FairVote. 2005. *Who Picks the President?* Takoma Park, MD: The Center for Voting and Democracy. www.fairvote.org/whopicks.

Feeley, Kristin. 2009. Guaranteeing a federally elected president. 103 *Northwestern University Law Review* 1427-1460.

Ferling, John. 2004. *Adams vs. Jefferson: The Tumultuous Election of 1800*. Oxford, UK: Oxford University Press.

Ford, Paul Leicester. 1905. *The Works of Thomas Jefferson*. New York, NY: G.P. Putnam's Sons. 9:90.

Fortier, John C. and Ornstein, Norman. 2004. If Terrorists Attack Our Presidential Elections. 3 *Election Law Journal* 4, 597-612.

Frankfurter, Felix and Landis, James. 1925. The compact clause of the constitution-A study in interstate adjustments. 34 *Yale Law Journal* 692-693 and 730-732. May 1925.

Gallup News Service. 2000. Americans have Historically Favored Changing Way Presidents Are Elected. November 10, 2000.

Gettleman, Marvin E. 1973. *The Dorr Rebellion: A Study in American Radicalism 1833-1849*. New York, NY: Random House.

Goldfeder, Jerry H. 2005. Could Terrorists Derail a Presidential Election. 32 *Fordham Urban Law Journal* 3, 523-566. May 2005.

Gordon, James D. and Magleby, David B. 1989. Pre-Election Judicial Review of Initiatives and Referendums. 64 *Notre Dame Law Review* 298-320.

Grace, Adam S. 2005. *Federal-State "Negotiations" over Federal Enclaves in the Early Republic: Finding Solutions to Constitutional Problems at the Birth of the Lighthouse System*. Berkeley, CA: Berkeley Electronic Press. Working Paper 509. http://law.bepress.com/expresso/eps/509.

Grant, George. 2004. *The Importance of the Electoral College*. San Antonio, TX: Vision Forum Ministries.

Gregg, Gary L. II. (editor). 2001. *Securing Democracy: Why We Have an Electoral College*. Wilmington, DE: ISI Books.

Gringer, David. 2008. Why the National Popular Vote plan is the wrong way to abolish the Electoral College. 108 *Columbia Law Review* 182.

Hardaway, Robert M. 1994. *The Electoral College and the Constitution: The Case for Preserving Federalism*. Westport, CT: Praeger.

Hardy, Paul T. 1982. *Interstate Compacts: The Ties That Bind*. Athens, GA: Institute of Government, University of Georgia.

Hendricks, Jennifer S. 2008. Popular election of the president: Using or abusing the Electoral College? 7 *Election Law Journal* 218.

Hume, R.D., with R.E. Weber, J.A. Palmer, R.S. Montjoy, E.D. Feigenbaum, H.A. Sanders. 1978 *An Analysis of Laws and Procedures Governing Contested Elections and Recounts* (three volumes). National Clearinghouse on Election Administration, Federal Election Commission: Washington, D.C. FEC-CH-78-010, 011, 012.

Jacobson, Arthur J. and Rosenfeld, Michel (editors). 2002. *The Longest Night: Polemics and Perspectives on Election 2000*. Berkeley, CA: University of California Press.

Jensen, Merrill and Becker, Robert A. (editors). 1976. *The Documentary History of the First Federal Elections 1788-1790*. Madison, WI: University of Wisconsin Press. Volume I.

Keyssar, Alexander. 2000. *The Right to Vote: The Contested history of Democracy in the United States*. New York, NY: Basic Books.

Kirby, J. 1962. Limitations on the powers of the state legislatures over presidential elections. 27 *Law and Contemporary Problems* 495.

Kole, Edward A. 1999. *The First 13 Constitutions of the First American States*. Haverford, PA: Infinity Publishing.

Kole, Edward A. 1999. *The True Intent of the First American Constitutions of 1776-1791*. Haverford, PA: Infinity Publishing.

Kramer, Michael. 2000. Bush set to fight an electoral college loss: They're not only thinking the unthinkable, They're planning for it. *New York Daily News*. November 1, 2000.

Kuroda, Tadahisa. 1994. *The Origins of the Twelfth Amendment: The Electoral College in the Early Republic, 1787-1804*. Westport, CT: Greenwood Press.

Leach, Richard H. and Sugg, Redding S. Jr. 1959. *The Administration of Interstate Compacts*. Louisiana State University Press.

LeVert, Suzanne. 2004. *The Electoral College*. New York, NY: Franklin Watts.

Longley, Lawrence D. and Braun, Alan G. 1972. *The Politics of Electoral College Reform*. New Haven, CT: Yale University Press.

Longley, Lawrence D. and Peirce, Neal R. 1999. *The Electoral College Primer 2000*. New Haven, CT: Yale University Press.

Loy, Brendan Loomer, "Count Every Vote-All 538 of Them" *Social Science Research Network*. September 12, 2007. Available at http://ssrn.com/abstract=1014431.

Morris, Roy B. 2003. *Fraud of the Century: Rutherford B. Hayes, Samuel Tilden, and the Stolen Election of 1876*. Waterville, ME: Thorndike Press.

Muller, Derek T. 2012. Invisible Federalism and the Electoral College http://papers.ssrn.com/sol3/papers.cfm?abstract_id=2049630.

Muller, Derek T. 2007. The compact clause and the National Popular Vote Interstate Compact. 6 *Election Law Journal* 372.

Nelson, Suzanne. Three-month period imperils presidency. *Roll Call*. November 2, 2004.

Nivola, Pietro S. 2005. *Thinking About Political Polarization*. Washington, D.C.: The Brookings Institution. Policy Brief 139. January 2005.

Orfield, Lester Bernhardt. 1942. *The Amending of the Federal Constitution*. Ann Arbor, MI: The University of Michigan Press.

Ornstein, Norman. 2004. *Roll Call*. October 21, 2004.

Patel, Ronak, Chapter 188: Forget College, You're Popular! A Review of the National Popular Vote Interstate Compact (July 12, 2012). *McGeorge Law Review*, Vol. 43, No. 3, 2012. Available at SSRN: http://ssrn.com/abstract=2104340.

Peirce, Neal R. 1968. *The People's President: The Electoral College in American History and Direct-Vote Alternative*. New York, NY: Simon and Schuster.

Peirce, Neal R. and Longley, Lawrence D. 1981. *The People's President: The Electoral College in American History and the Direct-Vote Alternative, Revised Edition*. New Haven, CT: Yale University Press.

Peterson, Svend. 1981. *A Statistical History of the American Presidential Elections : With Supplementary Tables Covering 1968-1980*. Westport, CT: Greenwood Press Reprint.

Posner, Richard A. 2001. *Breaking the Deadlock: The 2000 Election, the Constitution, and the Courts*. Princeton, NJ: Princeton University Press.

Raskin, Jamin B. 2008. Neither the red states nor the blue states but the United States: The National Popular Vote and American political democracy. 7 *Election Law Journal*. 188.

Rehnquist, William H. 2004. *Centennial Crisis: The Disputed Election of 1876*. New York, NY: Alfred A. Knopf.

Ridgeway, Marian E. 1971. *Interstate Compacts: A Question of Federalism*. Carbondale, IL: Southern Illinois University Press.

Robinson, Lloyd. 1996. *The Stolen Election: Hayes versus Tilden-1876*. New York, NY: Tom Doherty Associates Books.

Ross, Tara. 2004. *Enlightened Democracy: The Case for the Electoral College*. Los Angeles, CA: World Ahead Publishing Company.

Ross, Tara. 2010. Federalism & Separation of Powers: Legal and Logistical Ramifications of the National Popular Vote Plan. *Engage*. Volume 11. Number 2. September 2010.

Ross, Tara. 2012. *Enlightened Democracy: The Case for the Electoral College*. Los Angeles, CA: World Ahead Publishing Company. Second edition.

Schleifer, Adam. Interstate agreement for electoral reform. 40 *Akron Law Review*. Page 717.

Schumaker, Paul D. and Loomis, Burdett A. (editors). 2002. *Choosing a President*. New York, NY: Chatham House Publishers.

Schlesinger, Arthur M., Jr. and Israel, Fred L. (editors). 2002. *History of American Presidential Elections 1878-2001*. Philadelphia, PA: Chelsea House Publishers. (11 volumes).

Shambon, Leonard M. 2004. Electoral-College reform requires change of timing. *Roll Call*. June 15, 2004.

Smith, Hayward H. 2001. *Symposium, Law of Presidential Elections: Issues in the Wake of Florida 2000*. History of the Article II Independent State legislature Doctrine. 29 *Florida State University Law Review* 731-785. Issue 2.

Stanwood, Edward. 1912. *A History of the Presidency from 1897 to 1909*. Boston, MA: Houghton Mifflin Company.

Stanwood, Edward. 1916. *A History of the Presidency from 1897 to 1916*. Boston, MA: Houghton Mifflin Company.

Stanwood, Edward. 1924. *A History of the Presidency from 1788 to 1897*. Boston, MA: Houghton Mifflin Company.

Stock, Margaret. 2012. Practical problems with attempts to change the Fourteenth Amendment through an interstate birth certificate compact. *Bender's Immigration Bulletin*. May 1, 2012. Pages 1057-1067.

Tribe, Laurence H. 2000. *American Constitutional Law*. Third Edition. Volume 1. New York, NY: Foundation Press.

Turflinger, Bradley T. 2011. Fifty republics and the national popular vote: How the guarantee clause should protect states striving for equal protection in presidential elections. 45 *Valparaiso University Law Review* 793.

U.S. House of Representatives Committee on the Judiciary. 1969. *Electoral College Reform: Hearings on H.J. Res. 179, H.J. Res. 181, and Similar Proposals to Amend the Constitution Relating to Electoral College Reform*. 91st Congress, 1st Session. February 5, 6, 19, 20, 26, and 27; March 5, 6, 12, and 13, 1969. Washington, D.C.: U.S. Government Printing Office.

U.S. House of Representatives Committee on the Judiciary. 1999. *Proposals for Electoral College Reform: Hearing on H.J. Res. 28 and H.J. Res. 43*. 105th Congress, 1st Session. September 4, 1997. Washington, D.C.: U.S. Government Printing Office.

U.S. Senate Committee on the Judiciary. 1967. *Election of the President: Hearings on S.J. Res. 4, 7, 11, 12, 28, 58, 62, 138, and 139, 89th Congress; and S.J. Res. 2, 3, 6, 7, 12, 15, 21, 25, 55, 84, and 86*. 89th Congress, 2nd Session and 90th Congress, 1st Session. February 28-August 23, 1967. Washington, D.C.: U.S. Government Printing Office.

U.S. Senate Committee on the Judiciary. 1969. *Electing the President: Hearings on S.J. Res. 1, S.J. Res. 2, S.J. Res. 4, S.J. Res. 12, S.J. Res. 18, S.J. Res. 20, S.J. Res. 25, S.J. Res. 30, S.J. Res. 31, S.J. Res. 33, S.J. Res. 71, and S.J. Res. 72 to Amend the Constitution Relating to Electoral College Reform*. 91st Congress, 1st Session. January 23 and 24; March 10, 11, 12, 13, 20, and 21; April 30; May 1 and 2, 1969. Washington, D.C.: U.S. Government Printing Office.

U.S. Senate Committee on the Judiciary. 1969. *Direct Popular Election of the President: Report, with Additional Minority, Individual, and Separate Views on H.J. Res. 681, Proposing an Amendment to the Constitution of the United States Relating to the Election of the President and Vice President*. 91st Congress, 1st Session. Washington, D.C.: U.S. Government Printing Office.

U.S. Senate Committee on the Judiciary. 1975. *Direct Popular Election of the President: Report (to Accompany S.J. Res. 1)*. 94th Congress, 1st Session. Washington, D.C.: U.S. Government Printing Office.

U.S. Senate Committee on the Judiciary. 1977. *The Electoral College and Direct Election: Hearings on the Electoral College and Direct Election of the President and Vice President (S.J. Res. 1, 8, and 18): Supplement*. 95th Congress, 1st Session. July 20, 22, and 28; and August 2, 1977. Washington, D.C.: U.S. Government Printing Office.

U.S. Senate Committee on the Judiciary. 1979. *Direct Popular Election of the President and Vice President of the United States: Hearings on S.J. Res. 28, Joint Resolution Propos-*

ing an Amendment to the Constitution to Provide for the Direct Popular Election of the President and Vice President of the United States. 96th Congress, 1st Session. March 27 and 30; April 3 and 9, 1979. Washington, D.C.: U.S. Government Printing Office.

U.S. Senate Committee on the Judiciary. 1993. *The Electoral College and Direct Election of the President: Hearing on S.J. Res. 297, S.J. Res. 302, and S.J. Res. 312, Measures Proposing Amendments to the Constitution Relating to the Direct Election of the President and Vice President of the United States.* 102nd Congress, 2nd Session. July 22, 1992. Washington, D.C.: U.S. Government Printing Office.

Weisberger, Bernard A. 2001. *America Afire: Jefferson, Adams, and the First Contested Election.* William Morrow.

White, Theodore H. 1969. *The Making of the President 1968.* New York, NY: Atheneum Publishers.

Wiecek, William M. 1972. *The Guarantee Clause of the U.S. Constitution.* Ithaca, NY: Cornell University Press.

Williams, Norman R. 2011. Reforming the Electoral College: Federalism, majoritarianism, and the perils of sub-constitutional change. 100 Georgetown Law Journal 173.

Wilmerding, Lucius Jr. 1958. *The Electoral College.* Boston, MA: Beacon Press.

Wilson, Jennings "Jay". 2006. Bloc voting in the Electoral College: How the ignored states can become relevant and implement popular election along the way. 5 *Election Law Journal* 384.

Zimmermann, Frederick L. and Wendell, Mitchell. 1976. *The Law and Use of Interstate Compacts.* Lexington, KY: Council of State Governments.

Zimmerman, Joseph F. 1992. *Contemporary American Federalism.* Westport, CT: Praeger.

Zimmerman, Joseph F. *Contemporary American Federalism: The Growth of National Power.* Leicester: Leicester University Press, 1992.

Zimmerman, Joseph F. 1996. *Interstate Relations: The Neglected Dimension of Federalism.* Westport, CT: Praeger.

Zimmerman, Joseph F. 1997. *The Recall: Tribunal of the People.* Westport, CT: Praeger.

Zimmerman, Joseph F. 1997. *The Referendum: The People Decide Public Policy.* Westport, CT: Praeger.

Zimmerman, Joseph F. 1999. *The Initiative: Citizen Law-Making.* Westport, CT: Praeger.

Zimmerman, Joseph F. 2002. *Interstate Cooperation: Compacts and Administrative Agreements.* Westport, CT: Praeger Publishers.

Zimmerman, Joseph F. 2004. *Interstate Economic Relations.* Albany, NY: State University of New York Press.

Zimmerman, Joseph F. 2005. *Congressional Preemption: Regulatory Federalism* Albany, NY: State University of New York Press.

Zimmerman, Joseph F. 2004. Regulation of professions by interstate compact. *The CPA Journal.* May 2004. http://www.nysscpa.org/cpajournal/2004/504/infocus/p22.htm

Zimmerman, Joseph F. 2006. *Interstate Disputes: The Supreme Court's Original Jurisdiction.* Albany, NY: State University of New York Press.

Zimmerman, Joseph F. 2008. Contemporary American Federalism: The Growth of National Power. Albany, NY: State University of New York Press. Second edition.

Zimmerman, Joseph F. 2010 The interstate agreement for the popular election of the president of the United States. *National Civic Review.* Volume 99. Number 1. Pages 48-54.

Zimmerman, Joseph F. 2011. *Horizontal Federalism: Interstate Relations.* Albany, NY: State University of New York Press.

Zimmerman, Joseph F. 2012. *Interstate Cooperation: Compacts and Administrative Agreements.* Albany, NY: State University of New York Press. Second edition.

Zimmerman, Joseph F. 2012. *Interstate Water Compacts: Intergovernmental Efforts to Manage America's Water Resources.* Albany, NY: State University of New York Press.

INDEX